Retailing Management

9e

ISBN-13: 9781308147055

ISBN-10: 1308147058

Contents

PREFACE

Our primary objective in the ninth edition of *Retailing Management* is to inform students about the exciting new developments in the retail industry. Retailing has evolved into a high-tech, global growth industry. Retailers like Walmart, Home Depot, Amazon, Starbucks, and Kroger are some of the most admired and sophisticated businesses in the world. The developments in the industry are providing challenging and rewarding opportunities for students interested in retailing careers and companies supporting the retail industry such as IBM, Procter & Gamble, and Google.

We are pleased to announce the addition of Professor Dhruv Grewal, The Toyota Chair of Commerce and Electronic Business and Professor of Marketing at Babson College, to the *Retailing Management* author team. Dhruv brings years of academic experience to the project, as evidenced by dozens of retailing-related articles that he has coauthored. He also co-edited the *Journal of Retailing* from 2001 to 2007 with Michael Levy, a close colleague and collaborator for more than 20 years.

ABOUT THE COVER

The cover of this textbook illustrates just one example of how retailers are utilizing technological innovation to provide consumers with a rewarding shopping experience. Homeplus, owned by UK-based supermarket giant, Tesco, is utilizing "virtual" stores at South Korean bus stops and underground subways. Shoppers order products to be delivered to their homes by scanning QR codes using their smartphones.

NEW FEATURES IN THE NINTH EDITION OF *RETAILING MANAGEMENT*

In preparing this edition, we focused on five important developments: (1) the use of big data and analytical methods for decision making, (2) the application of social media and smartphones for communicating with customers and enhancing their shopping experience, (3) the issues involved in utilizing a mobile channel and providing a seamless multichannel experience for customers, (4) the engagement in corporate social responsibility activities, that is, the consideration of society when making business decisions; and (5) the impact of globalization on the retail industry.

Big Data and the Use of Analytical Methods in Retailing   *Big data* refers to the collection and analysis of data sets so large and complex that they cannot be handled using traditional data-processing techniques. Retailers are at the forefront of the big data phenomenon. For example, Walmart processes more than 100 million transactions per hour through its point-of-sale terminals in stores around the world. Its customer database contains more than 2.5 petabytes of data, which is equal to nearly 170 times the data in all of the books in the Library of Congress. In Chapter 11 (Customer Relationship Management) of the ninth edition, we extend the discussion of how retailers use frequent-shopper programs to collect customer data by including a new section on the analysis of big data to improve decision making. Some examples of the use of analytical methods discussed in the new edition are:

- Improving store design and promotion planning using market basket analysis (Chapters 11, 15, and 17).
- Two approaches for SKU rationalization (Chapters 11, 12).
- Optimizing the timing and depth of markdown decisions (Chapter 14).
- Targeting promotions to increase effectiveness (Chapters 11, 15).
- Dynamic pricing (Chapter 14).

- Determining where merchandise categories should be placed in a store and on a website (Chapter 17).
- Scheduling store employees to make sure there is an appropriate number of sales associates at different times of the day and days in the week (Chapter 15).

We have also added a number of new illustrations (Retailing Views) of how retailers such as CVS and Kroger are using these retail analytics to gain a competitive advantage. The executive profile for Chapter 11 outlines how an entrepreneur built a successful consulting business by developing and implementing the use of retail analytics on big data.

Social Media   Over the past five years, there has been an explosion in the use of social media. Facebook, Twitter, Pinterest, and Instagram are now part of everyone's vocabulary. The revision to Chapter 15 (Retail Communications) focuses on how retailers are using social media to provide more information about their offerings and to build relationships with their customers. Examples of other applications of social media, illustrated with an icon in the margin, that are new in this edition are:

- The impact of social media and a multichannel offering on the consumer buying process (Chapters 3, 4).
- Discussion on how to build a retail community using social media (Chapter 5).
- Executive briefing on a young social media manager working for a fashion apparel retail chain discussing how she develops relationships with fashion bloggers (Chapter 15).
- The use of social media in developing an integrated marketing communication program (Chapter 15).
- Illustrations of how REI (Chapter 15), Build-A-Bear (Chapter 3), and American Girl (Chapter 11) use social media to build a sense of community and loyalty among their customers.
- New Retailing View highlighting the social media elements of "Pinning" and "Likes" (Chapter 4).

Mobile Channel as Part of a Multichannel Offering   Our textbook has always included a cutting-edge treatment of the role of the Internet in retailing. Most retailers are now multichannel because they have added an Internet channel to their store and/or catalog offering. In the past, we have had a chapter that specifically discussed the opportunities and issues facing multichannel retailers. In this edition, we have expanded our discussion of the mobile channel in Chapter 3 and throughout the textbook. For example, we have:

- Reviewed the benefits and limitations of the mobile channel compared with other channels (Chapter 3).
- Outlined the impact of mobile on shopping behaviors such as showrooming and how retailers are dealing with the increased ease of getting price information (Chapters 3, 14).
- Discussed the role of the mobile channel in providing a seamless, omnichannel interface for customers (Chapter 3).
- Described the use of mobile channels in delivering coupons and in-store promotions (Chapter 15).
- Added a new Retailing View on Staples' mobile strategy and how it reaches out to its customers through their smartphones (Chapter 15).

Social Responsibility of Retailers   The retail industry has a major impact on important social issues such as global warming, immigration, health care, and working conditions in less-developed economies. Our illustrations of the role retailers play in addressing social welfare issues are highlighted with legal/ethical icons in the margins. Some new examples examined in this edition are:

- New Retailing View on Walmart's greener supply chain (Chapter 10).
- Consumer interest in green and local products (Chapter 4).

- New Retailing View of buying green on an Amazon-owned site—Vine.com (Chapter 10).
- New Retailing View on Amazon's price check apps and showrooming.
- Expanded discussion of privacy issues arising from collecting customer data (Chapter 11).
- Ethical issues in sourcing merchandise globally (Chapter 13).
- New Retailing View on how Grupo Elektra is improving the lifestyle of Latin America's working poor (Chapter 1).
- New Retailing View on TOMS Shoes' social objectives (Chapter 6).
- Sustainability issues in store operations (Chapter 16) and design (Chapter 17).
- Role of retailing in advancing the welfare of people at the bottom of the pyramid (Chapter 1).

Globalization of the Retail Industry   Retailing is a global industry. With a greater emphasis being placed on private-label merchandise, retailers are working with manufacturers throughout the world to acquire merchandise. In addition, retailers are increasingly looking to international markets for growth opportunities. For instance, Carrefour, France's hypermarket chain and the second-largest retailer in the world, is focusing its growth investments in 25 countries—but not in France where its headquarters are located. Some examples of the global retailing issues, identified with icons in the margins, examined in this edition are:

- New Retailing View on wet markets in Shanghai (Chapter 1).
- New Retailing View discussing how China has developed a special relationship with its high-end fashion consumers (Chapter 7).
- New Executive Briefing describes how the CEO of Outback Steakhouse International deals with international expansion (Chapter 5).
- New Retailing View of 7-Eleven in Indonesia (Chapter 5).
- Retail efficiencies in different economies (Chapter 1).
- Two Executive Briefings from senior managers in retail companies headquartered outside the United States (Chapters 2, 17).
- Five of the new cases at the end of the text are based on retailers operating outside of the United States.

Improvements in Pedagogy   We have made some changes in the format of the textbook to facilitate students' learning experience. First, in each chapter, we have identified four to six Learning Objectives and organized the chapter around these objectives. Each chapter has three to six Retailing Views that describe how a retailer deals with the issues raised in the chapter. We have added a discussion question to each of these Retailing Views to motivate students to develop a better understanding of the application of the concepts presented in the text. More than 50 percent of the Retailing Views are new, and the rest have been updated. Some examples of the Retailing Views in the ninth edition are:

- Avon's direct selling channel in Brazil (Chapter 3).
- Gender issues in consumer behavior (Chapter 4).
- Private-equity firms investing in retailers (Chapter 6).
- Stage Stores' big payoff from locating in small towns (Chapter 8).
- Macy's use of employment branding to attract talent (Chapter 9).
- Costco's mastery of assortment planning (Chapter 12).
- IKEA's unique store design (Chapter 17).
- Zappos' excellent customer service through speaking with one voice (Chapter 18).

Eleven New Cases   There are 11 brand new cases in the ninth edition, including Blue Tomato: Internationalization of a Multichannel Retailer (Austria); Staples

Inc.; Parisian Patisserie "Maison Ladurée": The Conquest of the U.S. Market (France); Starbucks' Expansion into China; Walmart: Pioneer in Supply Chain Management; Tiffany & Co. and TJX: Comparing Financial Performance; Sephora Loyalty Programs: A Comparison between France and the United States; Mel's Department Store under New Management; Kroger and Fred Meyer: Sourcing Products in a Global Marketplace; Target and Its New Generation of Partnerships; and Zipcar: Delivering Only as Much Driving as You Want. Five of these cases are about global issues. All 38 cases in the textbook are either new or updated with current information.

Eighteen New Videos   There are 18 new videos, many of which are coordinated with discussion questions on Connect Marketing for *Retailing Management*. The new videos are Panera Bread's Commitment to Excellence; Zappos.com; Working for the Best: The Container Store; Walmart's Public Image Campaign; McDonald's Taps Ethnic Subcultures for Ongoing Growth; Bass Pro Shops: Maximizing the In-Store Experience; Inside One of Amazon's Busiest Days; Customer Service at Ritz Carlton and Apple; Future of Retail; The Mobile Factor [The Connected Consumer]; Tesco Virtual Stores in Korea; RFID Network Retail; Starbucks Human Resource Management; and Lord & Taylor Shoe Department.

BASIC PHILOSOPHY

The ninth edition of *Retailing Management* builds on the basic philosophy reflected in the previous eight editions. We continue to focus on key strategic issues with an emphasis on financial considerations and implementation through merchandise and store management. These strategic and more tactical issues are examined for a broad spectrum of retailers, both large and small, domestic and international, selling merchandise and services.

Strategic Focus   The entire textbook is organized around a model of strategic decision making outlined in Exhibit 1–6 in Chapter 1. Each section and chapter relates back to this overarching strategic framework. In addition, the second section of the book focuses exclusively on critical strategic decisions, such as selecting target markets, developing a sustainable competitive advantage, building an organizational structure and information and distribution systems to support the strategic direction, building customer loyalty, and managing customer relationships. The text explores in depth the resources that retailers use to develop sustainable competitive advantage, such as

- Selecting store location (Chapters 7, 8).
- Developing and maintaining human resources (Chapter 9).
- Managing information systems and supply chains (Chapter 10).
- Managing customer relationship management, and collecting and analyzing big data to make better decisions (Chapter 11).
- Developing unique private-label merchandise (Chapter 13).
- Providing outstanding customer service (Chapter 18).

Financial Analysis   The success of any retailer, like any other business, depends on its ability to make a profit, provide an adequate return to its owners, and be financially stable. The financial problems experienced by some well-known retail firms—like Circuit City, Sharper Image, and K-B Toys—highlight the need for a thorough understanding of the financial implications of strategic retail decisions. Financial analysis is emphasized in selected chapters, such as Chapter 6 on the overall strategy of the firm using the strategic profit model and the financial strength of retailers using cash flow and ratio analysis, Chapter 11 on the evaluation of customer lifetime value, and Chapter 12 on retail buying systems. Financial issues are also raised in the sections on negotiating leases, bargaining with suppliers, pricing merchandise, developing a communication budget, and compensating salespeople.

Implementing a Retail Strategy Although developing a retail strategy is critical to long-term financial performance, the execution of strategies is as important as the development of the strategy. Traditionally, retailers have exalted the merchant prince—the buyer who knew what the hot trends were going to be. While we provide a thorough review of merchandise management issues, the emphasis in retailing is shifting from merchandise management to the block-and-tackle activities of getting merchandise to the stores and customers and providing excellent customer service and an exciting shopping experience. Due to this shift toward store management, most students embarking on retail careers go into distribution and store management rather than merchandise buying. Thus, this text devotes an entire chapter to information systems and supply chain management and an entire section to store management.

Up-to-Date Information Retailing is a very dynamic industry, with new ideas and formats developing and traditional retailers constantly adapting to the changing environment or suffering financially. Most of the examples provided in the text have taken place in the last two years.

Balanced Approach The ninth edition continues to offer a balanced approach for teaching an introductory retailing course by including descriptive, how-to, and conceptual information in a highly readable format.

Descriptive Information Students can learn about the vocabulary and practice of retailing from the descriptive information throughout the text. Examples of this material are:
- Leading U.S. and international retailers (Chapter 1).
- Management decisions made by retailers (Chapter 1).
- Types of store-based and nonstore retailers (Chapters 2 and 3).
- Approaches for entering international markets (Chapter 5).
- Location options (Chapter 7).
- Lease terms (Chapter 8).
- Organization structure of typical retailers (Chapter 9).
- Flow of information and merchandise (Chapter 10).
- Branding strategies (Chapter 13).
- Methods for communicating with customers (Chapter 15).
- Store layout options and merchandise display techniques (Chapter 17).
- Career opportunities (Appendix 1A to Chapter 1).

How-to Information *Retailing Management* goes beyond this descriptive information to illustrate how and why retailers, large and small, make decisions. Procedures with examples are provided for making the following decisions:
- Managing a multichannel operation (Chapter 3).
- Scanning the environment and developing a retail strategy (Chapter 5).
- Analyzing the financial implications of retail strategy (Chapter 6).
- Evaluating location decisions (Chapter 8).
- Developing a merchandise assortment and budget plan (Chapter 12).
- Negotiating with vendors (Chapter 13).
- Pricing merchandise (Chapter 14).
- Recruiting, selecting, training, evaluating, and compensating sales associates (Chapter 16).
- Designing the layout for a store (Chapter 17).
- Providing superior customer service (Chapter 18).

Conceptual Information   *Retailing Management* also includes conceptual information that enables students to understand why decisions are made, as outlined in the text. As Mark Twain said, "There is nothing as practical as a good theory." Students need to know these basic concepts so they can make effective decisions in new situations. Examples of this conceptual information in the ninth edition are:

- Customers' decision-making process (Chapter 4).
- The strategic profit model and approach for evaluating financial performance (Chapter 6).
- Price theory and marginal analysis (Chapters 14 and 15).
- Motivation of employees (Chapter 16).
- In-store shopping behaviors (Chapter 17).
- The Service Gaps model for service quality management (Chapter 18).

Student-Friendly Textbook   This ninth edition creates interest and involves students in the course and the industry by making the textbook a "good read" for students. We use Refacts (retailing factoids), Retailing Views, and retail manager profiles at the beginning of each chapter to engage students.

Refacts   We have updated and added more interesting facts about retailing, called Refacts, in the margins of each chapter. Did you know that the first use of an Internet retail channel was on August 11, 1994, when a CD by Sting was sold by NetMarket over the Internet? Or that the teabag was developed by a Macy's buyer and pantyhose was developed by a JCPenney buyer? Or that Chipotle is by far the largest purchaser of natural meat in the United States?

Retailing Views   Each chapter contains either new or updated vignettes, called Retailing Views, to relate concepts to activities and decisions made by retailers. In the ninth edition, more than 50 percent of Retailing Views are new, and the remaining have been updated. The vignettes look at major retailers, like Walmart, Walgreens, Target, Kohl's, Neiman Marcus, and Macy's, that interview students on campus for management training positions. They also discuss innovative retailers like REI, Starbucks, Zara, Mango, Amazon, The Container Store, Sephora, Forever 21, Chico's, and Bass Pro Shops. Finally, a number of Retailing Views focus on entrepreneurial retailers competing effectively against national chains.

Profiles of Retail Managers   To illustrate the challenges and opportunities in retailing, each chapter in the ninth edition begins with a brief profile, in their own words, of a manager or industry expert whose job or expertise is related to the material in the chapter. These profiles range from Debbie Harvey, president of Ron Jon Surf Shop, and Ken Hicks, CEO of Foot Locker, and include people who have extensive experience in a specific aspect of retailing, like Tim Hourigan, human resource vice president at Home Depot and Moussa Coulibaly, senior vice president of planning at Dick's Sporting Goods. The profiles illustrate how senior executives view the industry and suggest career opportunities for college students. They also provide students with firsthand information about what people in retailing do and the rewards and challenges of their jobs and careers.

SUPPLEMENTAL MATERIALS

To enhance the student learning experience, the ninth edition includes new cases and videos illustrating state-of-the-art retail practices, a web-based computer exercise package for students, and a comprehensive online instructor's manual with additional cases and teaching suggestions.

    Get Out and Do It! exercises are found at the end of each chapter. These exercises suggest projects that students can undertake by visiting local retail stores, surfing the Internet, or using the student website. A continuing assignment exercise is included so that students can engage in an exercise involving the same retailer throughout the course. The exercises are designed to provide a hands-on learning experience for students.

Monthly Newsletters with Short Cases are based on recent retailing articles appearing in the business and trade press. Instructors can use these short cases to stimulate class discussions about current issues confronting retailers. The newsletter is e-mailed to instructors and archived on the text's web page.

Chapter	Key Changes
Broad Changes	• 90 percent new Executive Briefings
	• Expanded treatment of the role of social and mobile marketing by retailers (e.g., Macy's, Staples)
	• Increased discussion of going green (e.g., Walmart), CSR, and bottom of the pyramid marketing by retailers
	• Greater content on franchising and franchisers' expansion efforts, global retailers (e.g., Ikea, H&M, ICA, Grupo Electra—major vehicle for international expansion) and multi-channel retailing and how technology is changing how consumers search and buy
	• Numerous new Retailing Views focusing on innovative strategy elements by very visible retailers
	• All Retailing Views new or updated
	• Content has been updated in each chapter to reflect latest insights from research and practice
	• New list of additional readings
1	• New Executive Briefing on HSN and Mindy Grossman
	• New Retail Quiz to motivate study of retailing
	• Greater Global Focus—examples of retailing in China
	• Greater focus on CSR and bottom of pyramid retailing
	• New Retailing View on Grupo Elektra improving the lifestyle of Latin America's working poor
	• Updated exhibit highlighting the 20 largest retailers
	• Highlighted entrepreneurs—Howard Shultz (Starbucks) and Do Wan and Jin-Sook Chang (Forever 21).
	• New Retailing View on Whole Foods—the birth of the organic supermarket
2	• New Executive Briefing on Debbie Ferree, DSW's head of merchandise
	• New Retailing View on Amazon
	• Updated trends in supermarket retailing
	• New Retailing View on convenience stores in Japan
	• Coverage of social media (also identified by social media icons)
	• New Retailing View on Nordstrom
	• Greater coverage of franchising
3	• New Executive Briefing on Luiza Helena Trajano, president, Magazine Luiza
	• Chapter reorganized to highlight the evolution of multi-channel retailing and non-store channel options
	• Expanded discussion of mobile retailing
	• New Retailing View on Avon in Brazil
	• Expanded discussions of challenges facing retailers in providing a multi-channel offering
	• Updated illustration of shopping in the future
4	• Increased discussion about the role of the economy in the buying process
	• New Retailing View highlighting the social media element of "Pinning" and "Likes"
	• New Retailing View on gender differences
5	• New Executive Briefing on David Berg, Outback Steakhouse, CEO International
	• Discussion on how to build a retail community using social media
	• New Retailing View of wet markets in Shanghai
	• New Retailing View of 7-Eleven in Indonesia
6	• New Executive Briefing on Ken Hicks, Foot Locker CEO
	• New Retailing view on TOMS Shoes' social objectives
	• Discussion of venture capital interest in retailing industry
	• New Retailing View on Macy's and Costco—successful retailers using different financial models
	• Comparison of Macy's vs. Costco financial performance carried throughout the chapter
7	• New Retailing View on Simon Properties—the largest shopping center management company in the world
	• New Retailing View—For China's high-end fashion consumers, 'Italy' now just a bullet train away
	• Numerous updates throughout chapter

The World of Retailing

The World of Retailing

The chapters in Section I provide background information about the types of retailers, the different channels they use, their customers, and competitors: information that is used to effectively develop and implement a retail strategy.

Chapter 1 describes the importance of retail industry to the U.S. economy and, more generally, to society as a whole, as well as the organization of this book around the decisions retailers make to satisfy their customers' needs.

Chapter 2 describes different types of food, merchandise, and services retailers and their ownership structures.

Chapter 3 examines the channels retailers use to satisfy the needs of their customers and the challenges they face in coordinating these multiple channels—stores, the Internet, catalogs, and mobile—when interacting with their customers.

Chapter 4 discusses the process that consumers go through when choosing retail outlets and channels to buy merchandise and how retailers can affect this buying process.

The chapters in Section II focus on the decisions retailers make to develop strategic assets—assets that enable retailers to build sustainable competitive advantages.

The chapters in Sections III and IV explore the more tactical execution decisions involving merchandise and store management.

Introduction to the World of Retailing

EXECUTIVE BRIEFING

Mindy Grossman,
Chief Executive Officer, HSN Inc.

When I was a senior in college, I had a revelation about my life and the direction in which I was heading. I immediately called my parents and told them that I was not going to marry my high school boyfriend and go to law school like I had planned. I was going to follow my passion and head to New York to work in the fashion industry. Needless to say, they were surprised.

When I received my first VP position at 26, my parents finally stopped asking when I was going to go back and get my law degree. I've been on an exciting ride since then and have been fortunate enough to hold esteemed positions at great companies, such as the SVP of menswear at Warnaco, VP of new business development at Polo Ralph Lauren, president of Chaps Ralph Lauren, president and CEO of Polo Jeans Company, and global VP for Nike.

Then I received a call one day to meet with Barry Diller, who was the president of IAC, which owned HSN at the time. After discussing my ideas with him, I discovered I had the ability to make an impact on this company and transform HSN into a lifestyle network. My friends and colleagues were shocked when I announced that I was leaving Nike and going to HSN. They had gone through eight CEOs in 10 years and I would be the first female CEO of the company. I saw the company's potential and was excited to take on the challenge.

Over the last seven years, we have transformed HSN into a dynamic, interactive, multichannel retailer that offers a curated assortment of exclusive products from top lifestyle brands and engages our customers wherever and whenever they would like to shop. As a matter fact, close to 40 percent of our HSN sales come from our digital platform—online, tablet, mobile, and social media.

Our product offering is diverse with 79,000 unique products, 70 percent of which are proprietary to HSN. Widely respected celebrities and designers, such as Queen Latifah, India Hicks, Badgley Mischka, Naeem Khan, and New York fashion icon, Iris Apfel, have come to our campus in St. Petersburg, Florida to promote their products. We also have had Mary J. Blige, Mariah Carey, and P. Diddy sell their fragrances on HSN.

CHAPTER 1

LEARNING OBJECTIVES

LO1 Identify retailing activities.

LO2 Realize the importance of retailing in the U.S. and world economies.

LO3 Analyze the changing retail industry.

LO4 Recognize the opportunities in retailing for you.

LO5 Understand the strategic retail management decision process.

Our ability to entertain and inspire versus just selling a product is really how retail is evolving. We bring content, community, and commerce to life through our strategic partnerships with the entertainment community across film, music, and live events. We were Universal's partner for the launch of *Snow White and the Huntsman* and our 24-hour event featured 25 designers and brands that created over 220 unique products inspired by the film, including the launch of Oscar-winning costume designer Colleen Atwood's first consumer collection. Our HSN Live concert series provides our customers with a live music experience featuring some of the music industry's biggest stars. Lionel Richie held a concert at HSN's studios to kick off the release of *Tuskegee,* his first best-selling album in more than 25 years. The power of appearing on HSN is unparalleled.

When I met with Lady Gaga about potentially developing a line for HSN, she said, "You have the coolest job." Think of all the amazing things she has done in her career, and here she was telling me I had a cool job. And you know what? She's absolutely right.

Retailing is such a common part of our everyday lives that we often take it for granted. For most people, retailers simply are places to buy things. At a very young age, children know what stores have the things they want, and they expect to find the products they want when they visit a store or website. Sometimes consumers talk to a sales associate when they visit a store, and other times the only retail employees they interact with are cashiers collecting the money for purchases. Some college students work part-time or over the holidays for retailers and have a somewhat deeper insight into what retailers do. But these limited exposures to retailing are just the tip of the iceberg. Behind the stores, website, sales associates, and cashiers are an army of managers responsible for making sure that the products and services that people want are available when

EXHIBIT 1–1
Quiz on What You
Know about Retailing

1. Which of the following companies is *not* a retailer:
   (a) McDonald's
   (b) Holiday Inn
   (c) Macy's
   (d) eBay
   (e) All are retailers

2. What is the annual compensation (salary plus bonus) of a typical Walmart Supercenter 30-something store manager?
   (a) Under $49,999
   (b) $50,000 to $89,999
   (c) $90,000 to $149,999
   (d) over $150,000

3. Which of the following products/concepts was initiated or developed by retailer buyers?
   (a) tea bags
   (b) panty hose
   (c) Rudolph the Red-Nosed Reindeer
   (d) establishing Thanksgiving on the third Thursday of November
   (e) All of these products/concepts were developed/initiated by retailers.

4. What is the largest company in the world in terms of number of employees?
   (a) Walmart
   (b) General Electric
   (c) IBM
   (d) ExxonMobil
   (e) Mitsubishi

5. Which of the following retailers is owned by a company headquartered outside the United States?
   (a) Food Lion
   (b) Ben & Jerry's Ice Cream
   (c) 7-Eleven
   (d) A&P supermarkets
   (e) All of these are owned by foreign companies.

6. What country has the most efficient retail structure (lowest cost to move merchandise from a manufacturer's factory to a retail stores)?
   (a) Japan
   (b) United States
   (c) South Korea
   (d) France
   (e) Germany

7. What percentage of total retailer sales in the United States are made over the Internet?
   (a) 30 percent
   (b) 20 percent
   (c) 14 percent
   (d) 8 percent
   (e) 3 percent

8. What percent of the U.S. workforce is employed by retailers or firms selling products or providing services to retailers?
   (a) 10 percent
   (b) 17 percent
   (c) 25 percent
   (d) 43 percent
   (e) 62 percent

they want them, where they want them, and at a fair price. Take the quiz in Exhibit 1–1 to check out the accuracy of your views about the retail industry and career opportunities the industry offers. The answers are at the end of the chapter.

To illustrate what is below the tip of the iceberg, consider Macy's. Macy's stocks and sells more than 100,000 different sizes, colors, and brands of products. Managers at Macy's need to determine what subset of these 100,000 items they are going to offer from the millions of potential products Macy's could sell. Then managers negotiate with more than 3,000 suppliers the price they will pay the supplier for the products and the prices they will charge their customers. Managers decide which of the 100,000 products will be sold at each of Macy's 840 stores and how they will be displayed. Managers select, train, and motivate the 150,000 store employees to make sure the merchandise is attractively displayed and customers get the service they expect. And, perhaps most importantly, Macy's managers develop strategies to guide these decisions and provide a good return to its stock-holders while facing intense competition.[1]

Working in this highly competitive, rapidly changing retail environment is both challenging and exciting, and it offers significant financial rewards. This book describes the world of retailing and offers key principles for effectively managing retail businesses. Knowledge of retailing principles and practices will help you develop management skills for many business contexts. For example, retailers are the customers for most business-to-consumer (B-to-C) companies such as Procter & Gamble and Hewlett-Packard. Thus, brand managers in B-to-C companies need to have a thorough understanding of how retailers operate and make money so that they can encourage retailers to offer and promote their products. Financial and health care institutions use retail principles to develop their offerings; improve customer service; and provide convenient, easy access to their customers. Thus, any student interested in professional B-to-C selling, marketing management, or finance should find this book useful.

WHAT IS RETAILING?

Retailing is the set of business activities that adds value to products and services sold to consumers for their personal or family use. Often, people think of retailing only as the sale of products in stores, but retailing also involves the sale of services such as overnight lodging in a motel, a doctor's exam, a haircut, or a home-delivered pizza. Not all retailing is done in stores. Examples of nonstore retailing include ordering a T-shirt on your mobile phone app, buying cosmetics from an Avon salesperson, ordering hiking boots from an L.L. Bean catalog, and renting a Blu-Ray from a Redbox kiosk.

LO1

Identify retailing activities.

REFACT

The word *retail* is derived from the French word *retailer,* meaning to cut a piece off or break bulk.[2]

The Retailer's Role in a Supply Chain

A **retailer** is a business that sells products and/or services to consumers for their personal or family use. Retailers are a key component in a supply chain that links manufacturers to consumers. A **supply chain** is a set of firms that make and deliver goods and services to consumers. Exhibit 1–2 shows the retailer's position within a supply chain.

Retailers typically buy products from wholesalers and/or manufacturers and resell them to consumers. Why are retailers needed? Wouldn't it be easier and cheaper for consumers to cut out the middlemen, the wholesalers and retailers, and buy directly from manufacturers? The answer, generally, is no, because retailers add value and are more efficient at adding this value than manufacturers or wholesalers.

Retailers Create Value

The value-creating activities undertaken by retailers include (1) providing an assortment of products and services, (2) breaking bulk, (3) holding inventory, and (4) providing services.

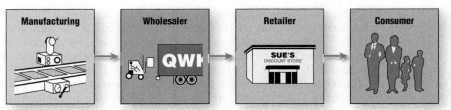

EXHIBIT 1–2
Example of a Supply Chain

Retailers add value by providing an assortment of products that customers can buy at one location when they want them.

Providing Assortments Conventional supermarkets typically carry about 30,000 different items made by more than 500 companies. Offering an assortment enables their customers to choose from a wide selection of products, brands, sizes, and prices at one location. Manufacturers specialize in producing specific types of products. For example, Frito-Lay makes snacks, Yoplait makes yogurt, Skippy makes peanut butter, and Heinz makes ketchup. If each of these manufacturers had its own stores that sold only its own products, consumers would have to go to many different stores to buy the groceries needed to prepare a single meal.

Breaking Bulk To reduce transportation costs, manufacturers and wholesalers typically ship cases of frozen dinners or cartons of blouses to retailers. Retailers then offer the products in smaller quantities tailored to individual consumers' and households' consumption patterns—an activity called **breaking bulk**. Breaking bulk is important to both manufacturers and consumers. It allows manufacturers to efficiently make and ship merchandise in larger quantities at one time and enables consumers to purchase merchandise in smaller, more useful quantities.

Holding Inventory A major value-providing activity performed by retailers is **holding inventory** so that products will be available when consumers want them. Thus, consumers can keep a smaller inventory of products at home because they know local retailers will have the products available when they need more. This activity is particularly important to consumers with limited storage space, such as families living in small apartments.

Providing Services Retailers provide services that make it easier for customers to buy and use products. For example, retailers offer credit so that consumers can have a product now and pay for it later. They display products so that consumers can see and test them before buying. Some retailers employ salespeople in stores or maintain Web sites to answer questions and provide additional information about the products they sell.

Costs of Channel Activities

While the value-creating activities undertaken by channel members provide benefits to customers, they also increase the cost of products and services. Exhibit 1–3 illustrates the supply chain costs of getting a T-shirt from the manufacturer to the consumer. In this example, it costs the T-shirt manufacturer $10.00 to make and market the T-shirt. These costs include the design, raw materials, labor, production equipment, transportation to the wholesaler, and so on. The manufacturer sells the T-shirt to the wholesaler for $11.00 and makes $1.00 profit. The wholesaler incurs $2.00 to handle and store the T-shirt and transport it to the retailers. The wholesaler sells the T-shirt to the retailers for $14.00, making a $1.00 profit.

Channel Member			Profit as a Percentage of Sales
Manufacturer	Cost	$10.00	
	Profit	$1.00	9.10%
	Selling price to wholesaler	$11.00	
Wholesaler	Price paid to manufacturer	$11.00	
	Cost to add value	$2.00	
	Profit	$1.00	8.00%
	Selling price to retailer	$14.00	
Retailer	Price paid to distributor	$14.00	
	Cost to add value	$4.00	
	Profit	$1.95	
	Selling price to customer	$19.95	9.77%

EXHIBIT 1–3
Costs Incurred to Undertake Value-Added Activities in the Distribution Channel for a T-Shirt

The retailer then incurs costs to fold the shirt, put price tags on it, store it, employ sales associates, light and air condition the store, and so on. The retailer sells the shirt to a customer for $19.95, making a profit of $1.95.

Note that the costs in the supply chain, $8.95 ($19.95 − $11.00), are almost as much as the cost to make the product. These costs are justified by the considerable value added by the wholesaler and retailers to the product. By providing assortments, breaking bulk, holding inventory, and providing services, retailers increase the benefits that consumers receive from their products and services.

Consider a T-shirt in a shipping crate in an Iowa manufacturer's warehouse. The T-shirt will not satisfy the needs of a student who wants to have something to wear at the basketball game tonight. The student finds the T-shirt more valuable and will pay more for it if it is available from a nearby department store that also sells pants, belts, and other items complementing the T-shirt and provides sales associates who can help the student find what he likes. If retailers did not provide these benefits, wholesalers or manufacturers would have to provide them, and they would typically not be as efficient as retailers in providing these benefits.

Retailers Perform Wholesaling and Production Activities

Wholesalers buy and store merchandise in large quantities from manufacturers and then resell the merchandise (usually in smaller quantities) to retailers. When manufacturers like Apple and Nike sell directly to consumers, they are performing the production, wholesaling, and retail business activities. Some large retailers, like Costco and Home Depot, function as both retailers and wholesalers: They perform retailing activities when they sell to consumers, but they engage in wholesaling activities when they sell to other businesses, such as restaurants or building contractors.

In some supply chains, the manufacturing, wholesaling, and retailing activities are performed by independent firms, but most supply chains feature some vertical integration. **Vertical integration** means that a firm performs more than one set of activities in the channel, as occurs when a retailer engages in wholesaling activities by operating its own distribution centers to supply its stores. **Backward integration** arises when a retailer performs some wholesaling and manufacturing activities, such as operating warehouses or designing private-label merchandise. **Forward integration** occurs when a manufacturer undertakes retailing and wholesaling activities, such as Apple operating its own retail stores.

Most large retailers such as Safeway, Walmart, and Lowe's manage their own distribution centers and perform activities undertaken by wholesalers. They buy directly from manufacturers, have merchandise shipped to their warehouses, and then distribute the merchandise to their stores. Other retailers, such as J. Crew and Victoria's Secret, are even more vertically integrated. They design the merchandise they sell and then contract with manufacturers to produce it exclusively for them.

Apple is a vertically integrated company because it performs the manufacturing, distribution, and retailing activities in its supply chain.

Differences in Distribution Channels around the World

Some critical differences among the retailing and distribution systems in the United States, European Union, China, and India are summarized in Exhibit 1–4. As this exhibit suggests, the U.S. retail industry has the greatest retail density (retail stores per person) and concentration of large retail firms. Real estate in the United States is relatively inexpensive, and most consumers own automobiles. Thus, retailers often operate large stores in lightly populated areas. Many U.S. retailers have stores with more than 20,000 square feet. Due to their size, they have the scale economies to operate their own warehouses, eliminating the need for wholesalers. This combination of large stores and large firms in the United States results in a very efficient distribution system.

In contrast, the Indian distribution system is characterized by small stores operated by relatively small firms and a large independent wholesale industry. To make the daily deliveries to these small retailers efficiently, the merchandise often passes through several different wholesalers. In addition, the infrastructure to support modern retailing, especially the transportation and communication systems, is not as well developed in India as it is in more developed economies. These efficiency

EXHIBIT 1–4   Comparison of Retailing and Distribution across the World

	United States	Northern Europe	India	China
Concentration (percent of sales made by large retailers)	Highest	High	Lowest	Low
Retail density (square feet of retail space per person)	Highest	Modest	Lowest	Low
Average store size	Highest	Modest	Lowest	Modest
Role of wholesalers	Minimal	Modest	Extensive	Extensive
Infrastructure supporting efficient supply chain	Best	Good	Weakest	Weak
Restrictions on retail locations, store size, and ownership	Minimal	Extensive	Extensive	Modest

The retail industry in India is dominated by small, local retailers with few modern national chains.

differences mean that a much larger percentage of the Indian labor force is employed in distribution and retailing than is the case in the United States, and the supply chain costs in India are higher.[3]

China's retail industry is highly fragmented like the retail industry in India. It is composed of many small and medium-sized firms. The number of national and even regional chains is limited. However, China's retail distribution system is going through a period of rapid development. This development is spurred by the government's shifting interest from focusing on exports and satisfying basic consumer needs that provide a higher quality of life. In China, the government removed most restrictions on direct foreign investments, and global retailers flocked to this huge and growing market. Now, Walmart operates 370 stores in China, and Carrefour, the second largest retailer in the world, operates 204. However, there is great disparity between the distribution system in the first-tier, eastern coastal cities—Beijing, Shanghai, and Guangdong—and the smaller western cities. The retail offering in the first-tier cities is very similar to the urban retail environment in U.S. cities such as New York and Chicago. In contrast, retailing in the smaller western cities is more similar to retailing in India.[4]

The European distribution system falls between the American and Indian systems on this continuum of efficiency and scale. In northern Europe, retailing is similar to that in the United States, with high concentration levels in some national markets. For example, 80 percent or more of sales in sectors such as food and home improvements are made by five or fewer firms. Southern European retailing is more fragmented across all sectors. For example, traditional farmers' market retailing remains important in some sectors, operating alongside large "big-box" formats.[5]

Social and political objectives have created some of these differences in distribution systems in countries. An important priority of the Indian and European economic policies is to reduce unemployment by protecting small businesses such as independent neighborhood retailers.[6] Some countries have passed laws prohibiting large stores, as well as strict zoning laws to preserve green spaces, protect town centers, and inhibit the development of large-scale retailing in the suburbs.

Finally, retail productivity is reduced when countries restrict the hours that stores can operate. For example, in France, many stores close at 7 p.m. on weeknights. Labor unions in France and elsewhere in Europe are opposed to U.S.-style 24/7 shopping because of the strains it could put on store employees.[7]

SOCIAL AND ECONOMIC SIGNIFICANCE OF RETAILING

Role in Developed Economies

LO2

Realize the importance of retailing in the U.S. and world economies.

Retail sales (excluding automobile and automotive parts sales) in 2011 were $4.3 trillion. More than 8 percent of the total U.S. gross domestic product comes from retailing, almost as much as the contribution of the entire U.S. manufacturing industry sector.[8] But this sales level underestimates the impact of retailing on the U.S. economy because it does not include the sales and employment of many firms providing consumer services such as entertainment, home repairs, and health care.

Consumer spending plays a critical role in the economies of the United States and other developed countries. When consumers spend more money buying goods and services from retailers, a country's economy flourishes. Merchandise flies off the shelves, and retailers place orders for replacement merchandise. Manufacturers hire more employees, place orders for raw materials, and make more products. However, if consumers feel uncertain about their financial future and decide to refrain from buying new refrigerators or blue jeans, the economy slows down.

The retail sector plays a key role in developed economies, not only because consumer demand is an indication of a vibrant financial system, but also because retailers are large employers. More than 14 million people were employed in retailing in 2012—approximately 11 percent of the U.S. workforce—and an additional 15 percent work for companies that either provide services to and/or sell products through retailers.[9]

Corporate Social Responsibility

In addition to providing the benefit to their customers outlined in the previous section and a fair return for their stockholders, most retailers engage in socially responsible activities. **Corporate social responsibility (CSR)** involves an organization voluntarily engaging in business practices that meet or exceed the ethical and legal expectations of its stakeholders—its employees, customers, community, and society in general.

Many retailers now go the extra mile to support their communities, environment, and social causes. Examples include reducing their use of energy, supporting local schools, and working with national organizations such as the American Red Cross and Habitat for Humanity. These corporate social responsibility activities promote a positive image to customers, build employee morale, and save money—a win–win scenario for both the companies and their stakeholders.[10]

For example, community philanthropy is the cornerstone of Target's CSR activities. Store managers have a budget for donations they can make to local events. Since 1946, Target has given 5 percent of its income to support local activities in the communities in which it has stores, such as company-sponsored youth leagues or a special exhibit at the local zoo. Target has been innovative in using social media to support its CSR program. Target's "Bullseye Gives" program asked its million Facebook fans to vote on how the company should allocate $3 million among 10 nonprofits.[11]

Many retailers are building LEED-certified stores. The Leadership in Energy and Environmental Design (LEED) certification is based on an assessment of the store's impact on human and environmental health, sustainable site development, water savings, energy efficiency, materials selection, and indoor environmental

REFACT

Shoppers in the United Kingdom are more likely to buy goods on the basis of environmental, animal welfare, or fair trade claims than their counterparts in continental Europe. About 41 percent of British consumers have bought ethically produced products, compared with 34 percent in Germany, 31 percent in France, and 12 percent in Spain.[12]

Home Depot employees' involvement with Habitat for Humanity helps the local community and builds company morale.

quality. Some features in a prototype LEED-certified McDonald's restaurant are its permeable pavement that cleans rainwater; a cistern buried behind the restaurant that collects rainwater, which is used to water the landscaping; a roof garden that insulates the restaurant; the use of less-toxic cleaners and of paints and resins that do not emit chemical odors; and the installation of low-flow toilets and urinals that use less water than standard low-flow toilets. Walmart's new stores have fuel cells that supply half of the electricity. Holes are punched in the roof for skylights that provide 70 percent of the store's lighting needs during the day. To help keep the scorching sun at bay and cool the building naturally, roofs are painted white.[13]

The production of apparel has adverse effects on the environment because it involves the use of dyes, solvents, and huge amounts of water and petroleum for transportation. An industry group called the Sustainable Apparel Coalition has developed an index to rate the relative sustainability of apparel. Some members of the coalition are Walmart, Target, Kohl's, Nordstrom, and Patagonia. Environmentalists anticipate that the index will be used by consumers when selecting products and by retail buyers when they select the assortments of products to offer. The index considers the entire life of a product—from raw materials to disposal. Brands can get higher scores by asking consumers to wash items in cold, rather than hot, water. Some buyers are rewarded for the design of products with high index levels. A new Nike "Flyknit" running shoe worn by U.S., Kenyan, and other marathoners at the London Olympics was designed based on the index. The shoe is knit from polyester, eliminating the waste of shoes sewn from cut textiles.[14]

Companies typically go through several stages before they fully integrate CSR into their strategy. Companies in the first stage engage only in CSR activities required by law. In this stage, companies are not actually convinced of the importance of CSR actions. In the second stage, companies go beyond activities required by law to engage in CSR activities that also provide a short-term financial benefit to the

The Nike Flyknit receives a high Sustainable Apparel Coalition index because its construction reduces waste by an average of 80 percent when compared to typical Nike running footwear.

company. For example, a retailer might reduce the energy consumption of its stores just because doing so reduces its costs. In the third stage, companies operate responsibly because they believe this is the "right thing" to do. Companies in the fourth and final stage engage in socially and environmentally responsible actions because they believe these activities must be done for the "well-being" of everyone. These companies have truly incorporated the concept of CSR into their business strategy.[15]

Role in Developing Economies— The Bottom of the Pyramid

Retailers need to also focus on opportunities available by serving the needs of the 4 billion people (25 percent of the world's population) at the lowest end of the income distribution. Serving these customers also provides an important social benefit: reducing worldwide poverty.[16] Consumers in this low income consumer segment, referred to as the **base of the pyramid** or **bottom of the pyramid (BoP)**, have a potential spending power of more than $5 trillion. The sheer size and growth of the BoP markets, especially in the countries with emerging economies such as China, India, and Brazil, and maturation of consumer goods and retail markets in developed economies is motivating firms to enter the BoP market.

Undertaking retailing activities to the BoP market is challenging. It is difficult to communicate and complete transactions with people in the BoP market because they are more likely to lack access to mass media, the Internet, mobile phones, or credit cards than more affluent markets. Most people in BoP markets live in rural areas—remote villages that are not connected to the outside world through adequate roads. Limited local demand combined with the high cost of transporting goods to and from remote villages results in higher costs and prices for consumer goods. Thus, engagement at the BoP markets requires innovative approaches for doing business. Retrofitting business models used in the more developed markets will not work.[17] Retailing View 1.1 describes how Grupo Elektra has improved the lifestyle of Latin America's working poor.

THE GROWING IMPORTANCE OF RETAILING AND RETAILERS

Evolution of the Retail Industry

LO3

Analyze the changing retail industry.

REFACT

James Cash Penney opened the first JCPenney store, called Golden Rule, in Kemmerer, Wyoming, in 1902.[18]

From a consumer's perspective, retailers are local businesses. Even though many consumers collect information and make purchases using the Internet or a mobile device, more than 90 percent of all retail sales are made in stores—usually stores that are less than a 15-minute drive from the consumer's home or workplace. Thus, retail stores predominately compete against other stores that are located nearby.

There has been a dramatic change in the structure of the retail industry over the past 50 years. Fifty years ago, Sears and JCPenney were the only retail firms that had chains of stores across the United States. The retail industry consisted of the small, independent, local retailers competing against other small, independent retailers in the same community. Walmart, Home Depot, Staples, and Best Buy did not exist or were small companies with a few stores. Now, the retail industry is dominated by large, national, and even international retail firms. While there are more than 1 million retailers in the United States, over 40 percent of U.S. retail sales are made by companies with more than 10,000 employees. Home improvement centers are the most concentrated sector in the retail industry, with the four largest firms accounting for 92.7 percent of U.S. annual sales in the sector. The top four department store chains account for 73.2 percent of annual U.S. sales in that sector, and the top four drug store chains account for 63.0 percent in that sector. On the other hand, the least concentrated sectors are food service and drinking, where only 5.8 percent of sales are represented by the top four firms in the sector, and furniture stores where only 13.9 percent of sales are represented by the top four firms in the sector.[19]

The largest retailers in the world are shown in Exhibit 1–5. Nine of the top 20 retailers are headquartered in the United States; while Germany has five. Of these top 20 retailers, the U.S. retailers have fewer global operations than the non-U.S. based retailers. The average number of countries that these U.S.-based retailers operate in is five, compared to the non-U.S.-headquartered retailers, who operate in an average of 16 countries. Five of the largest U.S.-based retailers operate in only one or two countries. Only four of the 11 non-U.S-based retailers operate stores in the United States, the largest retail market in the world.

The development of information systems is one the forces facilitating the growth of large retail firms—the shift from an industry dominated by small, local retailers to large multinational chains. Prior to the development of these systems, it was difficult for someone other than the local store manager to track

REFACT

Walmart's annual sales are five times greater than the sales of Procter & Gamble, the largest consumer product producer.[20]

RETAILING VIEW   Grupo Elektra Improves the Lifestyle of Latin America's Working Poor

1.1

Grupo Elektra, with headquarters in Mexico City, owns and operates more than 2,600 specialty stores in Mexico, Brazil, Argentina, Guatemala, El Salvador, Honduras, Panama, and Peru. Its stores sell consumer electronics and appliances to Latin America's working poor. It is quite a challenge to sell consumer durable goods to families earning less than $400 per month and spend 90 percent of their income on basic necessities, such as food and housing. In addition, these BoP consumers often do not have formal jobs or bank accounts. But Grupo Elektra, and its banking affiliate, Banco Azteca, have been increasing sales and profits during one of the worst economic recessions in decades by servicing these low-income consumers. For the past five years, revenues and operating profits have grown at a double-digit rate.

Rather than wait for low-income consumers to open their own bank accounts so they can afford to buy its products, Elektra launched its own banks inside its network of specialty retail shops. These banks make small "micro-loans" to Elektra's customers so they can afford to buy its appliances. It determines how much money its new customers can really afford to borrow—and then pay back. Within 24 hours, the bank approves or denies a client's loan application using the information gathered by the credit officer at the branch. The officer visits the customers' houses to determine their income and expenses. The bank then establishes weekly installment payments that match the borrowing capacity of each customer. More than 5,000 loan officers travel by motorcycles to the applicants' homes to assess their creditworthiness and, when necessary, to collect payments from customers. Usually, however, cash payments are made once a week at an Electra store.

This approach has enabled thousands of low-income consumers to acquire durables that have long been inaccessible to them because they lacked the opportunity to use credit. Traditionally, these low-income people—the taxi drivers, mango vendors, and cleaning ladies of Latin

Grupo Elektra has developed a successful strategy for selling products and providing micro-loans to its customers at the base of the pyramid.

America—put their money in a cookie jar or below their mattresses. Now, they can establish a bank account for a minimum of only US $5 and have access to a debit card.

Sources: Erin Carlyle, "Billionaire Ricardo Salinas: Mexico's Credit Card," *Forbes*, May 7, 2012, p.100; Erin Carlyle, "Mexican Billionaire Buys Advance America, Largest Payday Lender In U.S.," *Forbes*, April 23, 2012, p. 102; and "Grupo Elektra: Will Selling in Brazil Prove to Be the Retailer's Next 'Growth Moment?" *Knowledge @ Wharton,* April 07, 2010.

DISCUSSION QUESTION

The typical interest rate charged by Grupo Elektra is 50 percent, a rate that would be illegal in most U.S. states. Is Elektra providing a benefit to its customers or taking advantage of its customers' lack of knowledge about these financial contracts?

EXHIBIT 1–5   The 20 Largest Retailers in the World

Rank	Name	Headquarters Location	Number of Countries	Stores in U.S.	Sales ($ millions)	Primary Format
1	Walmart	U.S.	16	Yes	418,993	Supercenter
2	Carrefour	France	33	No	119,652	Supercenter
3	Tesco	UK	13	Yes	92,171	Supercenter
4	Metro	Germany	33	No	86,931	Warehouse club
5	Kroger	U.S.	1	Yes	82,189	Supermarket
6	Schwarz Untematmens Trauhard	Germany	26	No	79,119	Discount store
7	Costco	U.S.	9	Yes	76,225	Warehouse club
8	Home Depot	U.S.	5	Yes	67,997	Home improvement
9	Walgreens	U.S.	2	Yes	67,420	Drug store
10	Aldi Einkauf	Germany	18	Yes	67,112	Discount store
11	Target	U.S.	1	Yes	65,786	Discount store
12	Rewe	Germany	13	No	61,134	Supermarket
13	CVS	U.S.	2	Yes	57,345	Drug store
14	Seven & Holding	Japan	18	Yes	57,055	Convenience store
15	Groupe Auchan	France	13	No	55,212	Supercenter
16	Edeka Zentrale	Germany	1	No	54,074	Supermarket
17	Aeon	Japan	8	No	53,458	Supercenter
18	Woolworth	Australia	2	No	51,171	Supermarket
19	Best Buy	U.S.	15	Yes	50,272	Electronics category specialist
20	Lowe's	U.S.	3	Yes	48,815	Home improvement

Source: "2011 Global 250 Retailers," *Stores Magazine,* January 2012.

REFACT

Walmart processes more than 100 million transactions per hour through its POS terminals in stores around the world.[21]

REFACT

Walmart has a data warehouse with more than 2.5 petabytes (2,500 terrabytes) of information—the equivalent of 167 times more than all of the books in America's Library of Congress.[22]

how the merchandise in the store was selling—whether it was selling above plan and needed to be reordered or was selling below plan and needed to have its price reduced. It was also difficult to collect and consolidate the plans from a number of different stores so that a buyer could place large orders with vendors to get price discounts. Thus, before the availability of modern information systems, it was difficult for retailers to lower costs through scale economies, and larger retailers had limited advantages over small local or regional retailers.

Most consumers shopping in their local stores don't realize the sophisticated information systems used by retailers today to manage these large, complex supply chain systems. To illustrate the complexity of these systems, consider the following example. You go to Best Buy and find a tablet you are going to buy. When you decide to buy a tablet in a store, the point-of-sale (POS) terminal transmits data about the transaction to the retailer's distribution center and then on to the manufacturer. Data about your purchase are incorporated into a sophisticated inventory management system. When the in-store inventory level drops below a prespecified level, an electronic notice is automatically transmitted, authorizing the shipment of more units to the retailer's distribution center and then to the store. The retail buyer or a computer program analyzes the sales data to determine how many and which tablet models will be stocked in the retailer's stores and what price will be charged.

To add even another layer of complexity, most large retailers contract with factories around the world to have merchandise made for them. Thus, for example, nearly 1,500 employees, working in both quality-control and full-service buying centers, help Target ensure that any factory worldwide that produces products with the Target name meet Target's own standards for product quality, without violating ethical labor standards.[23]

Role of Information Systems

Now, retailers are inundated with data about the thousands of transactions that take place each day. The challenge for retailers is to convert this raw data into information that managers can use to make better decisions. Many retailers now use the data they have on their customers to identify their best customers and target customized promotions to them, place products close to each other when they find that many customers are buying the same products at the same time, and tailor the assortment of products in each store to better match the needs of the store's local market.

In addition to playing an important role in society in general, retailing provides personal opportunities to work for a company in an exciting, challenging environment or to start an entrepreneurial venture. These opportunities are discussed in the next section.

Sophisticated supply chains have facilitated the economies of scale that large retailers have been able to achieve.

MANAGEMENT AND ENTREPRENEURIAL OPPORTUNITIES

Management Opportunities

To exploit these new technologies and systems and gain advantage in a highly competitive and challenging environment, retailers need to hire and promote the best and brightest. Sherry Hollack, a former vice president of talent development at Macy's, emphasized this point: "One of the biggest challenges facing Macy's, and most other retail chains, is hiring and retaining managers to lead our company in the coming years. The changing demographics are working against us. Over the next ten years, a lot of our senior managers, members of the Baby Boomer generation, will be retiring. So we are going to be competing with other retailers and firms in other industries for a smaller pool of available managers in the generations behind the Boomers. In addition, retailing is becoming a much more sophisticated business. Our managers need to be comfortable with new technologies, information and supply chain management systems, and international business as well as managing a diverse workforce and buying merchandise."[24]

Students often view retailing as part of marketing because managing distribution (place) is one of the 4 Ps of marketing. But retailers are businesses and, like manufacturers, undertake all the traditional business activities. Retailers raise capital from financial institutions; purchase goods and services; use accounting and

LO4

Recognize the opportunities in retailing for you.

management information systems to control their operations; manage warehouses and distribution systems; design and develop new products; and undertake marketing activities such as advertising, promotion, sales force management, and market research. Thus, retailers employ people with expertise and interests in finance, accounting, human resource management, supply chain management, and computer systems, as well as management and marketing.

Retail managers are often given considerable responsibility early in their careers. Retail management is also financially rewarding. Starting salaries are typically between $35,000 and $65,000 for college graduates entering management trainee positions. After completing a management training program, retail managers can

1.2   RETAILING VIEW   Sam Walton, Founder of Walmart (1918–1992)

Like Henry Ford with his Model T, Sam Walton revolutionized the retail industry. After graduating from the University of Missouri in 1940, Walton began working at a JCPenney store in Des Moines, Iowa. He served in the army during World War II and then purchased a Ben Franklin variety store franchise in Newport, Arkansas. He boosted sales by finding suppliers that would sell him merchandise at lower prices than his cost to buy from Ben Franklin.

REFACT

With 2.2 million employees, Walmart is the largest company in the world in terms of number of employees.[25]

Walton lost his store, however, in 1950 when the landlord refused to renew his lease. He then moved to Bentonville, Arkansas, where he and a younger brother franchised another Ben Franklin store. Walton employed a new self-service system that he had discovered at two Ben Franklin stores in Minnesota. He placed the checkout registers and clerks at the front of the store rather than scattering them throughout. By 1960, Walton had 15 stores in Arkansas and Missouri that laid the foundation for Walmart.

By the early 1960s, some retailers in large, urban, eastern cities had developed the discount store concept, incorporating self-service, shallow but broad assortments, low overhead costs, and large parking lots. In 1962, Walton brought this format to small southern towns, opening his first Walmart Discount City in Rogers, Arkansas.

Walton often visited his stores, dropping in unannounced to check the merchandise presentation or financial performance and talk to his "associates." He prided himself on a profit-sharing program and a friendly, open, supportive atmosphere—business practices he had learned when working for JCPenney. He often led his workers in the Walmart cheer: "Give me a W! Give me an A! Give me an L! Give me a Squiggly! (Here, everybody sort of does the twist. As part of Walmart's campaign to modernize its image, in 1998, it dropped the squiggly from its trademark.) Give me an M! Give me an A! Give me an R! Give me a T! What's that spell? Walmart! What's that spell? Walmart! Who's number one? THE CUSTOMER!"

He offered his own formula for how a large company should operate: "Think one store at a time. That sounds easy enough, but it's something we've constantly had to

Sam Walton believed in "management by walking around."

stay on top of. Communicate, communicate, communicate: What good is figuring out a better way to sell beach towels if you aren't going to tell everybody in your company about it? Keep your ear to the ground: A computer is not—and will never be—a substitute for getting out in your stores and learning what's going on."

In 1991, due to the success of his concept and management practices, Walton became America's wealthiest person; however, he maintained his simple, unassuming lifestyle. Whenever he traveled on business, he rented the same compact economy cars and stayed in the same inexpensive hotels as his employees did. He died of leukemia in 1992. Walmart is now the world's largest corporation.

Sources: Michael Bergdahl, *The Retail Revolution: How Wal-Mart Created a Brave New World of Business* (New York: Metropolitan Books, 2009); and Michael Bergdahl, *The 10 Rules of Sam Walton: Success Secrets for Remarkable Results* (Hoboken, NJ: Wiley, 2006).

DISCUSSION QUESTION

What were the key factors that led to Walmart's phenomenal growth and dominance of the retail industry?

double their starting salary in three to five years if they perform well. Senior buyers and others in higher managerial positions and store managers make between $120,000 and $300,000. (See Appendix 1A at the end of this chapter.)

Entrepreneurial Opportunities

Retailing also provides opportunities for people who wish to start their own business. Some of the world's most successful people are retailing entrepreneurs. Many are well known because their names appear over stores' doors; others you may not recognize. Retailing View 1.2 examines the life of one of the world's greatest entrepreneurs, Sam Walton. Some other innovative retail entrepreneurs include Jeff Bezos, Do Won and Jin Sook Chang, Ingvar Kamprad, and Howard Schultz. These entrepreneurs came from humble backgrounds and changed the way retailing is done.

Jeff Bezos (Amazon.com)   After his research uncovered that Internet usage was growing at a 2,300 percent annual rate in 1994, Jeffrey Bezos, the 30-year-old son of a Cuban refugee, quit his job on Wall Street and left behind a hefty bonus to start an Internet business. While his wife MacKenzie was driving their car across country, Jeff pecked out his business plan on a laptop computer. By the time they reached Seattle, he had rounded up the investment capital to launch the first Internet book retailer. The company, Amazon.com, is named after the river that carries the greatest amount of water, symbolizing Bezos's objective of achieving the greatest volume of Internet sales. Under his leadership, Amazon developed technologies to make shopping on the Internet faster, easier, and more personal than shopping in stores by offering personalized recommendations and home pages. Amazon.com has become more than a bookstore. It is now the largest on-line retailer, with annual sales greater than $48 billion. Amazon also provides virtual stores and fulfillment services for many other retailers.[26]

Do Won and Jin Sook Chang (Forever 21)   Do Won and Jin Sook Chang are self-made billionaires. In 1984, they cofounded the "fast fashion" retail chain Forever 21. The pair emigrated from South Korea in 1981 and became naturalized

Forever 21 founder Do Won and his daughter Linda Chang (senior marketing manager) visiting their flagship store in Times Square.

American citizens. The couple opened their first store in 1984, focused on trendy, exciting clothing options. That year, sales grew from $35,000 to $700,000. Forever 21 has continued to experience explosive growth, as evidenced by recent store openings, like a flagship Las Vegas attraction with 127,000 square feet, a massive 45,000-square-foot store in Los Angeles, and two new megastores in New York of 86,000 and 91,000 square feet. Today, it operates more than 500 stores worldwide with more than 35,000 employees and projected sales of greater than $3.5 billion. Forever 21 is a family operation with Do Won at the helm, Jin Sook in charge of merchandising, eldest daughter Linda running marketing, and daughter Esther managing visuals.[27]

Ingvar Kamprad (IKEA)   Ingvar Kamprad, the founder of the Swedish-based home furnishing retailer chain IKEA, was always an entrepreneur. His first business was selling matches to neighbors from his bicycle. He discovered he could make a good profit by buying matches in bulk and selling them individually at a low price. He then expanded to selling fish, Christmas tree decorations, seeds, ballpoint pens, and pencils. By the time he was 17 years of age, he had earned a reward for succeeding in school. His father gave him the money to establish what is now IKEA. Like Sam Walton, the founder of Walmart, Kamprad is known for his frugality. He drives an old Volvo, flies economy class, and encourages IKEA employees to write on both sides of a sheet of paper. This thriftiness has translated into a corporate philosophy of cost cutting throughout IKEA so that the chain can offer quality furniture with innovative designs at low prices. According to *Forbes* magazine, Kamprad is the richest person in Europe and the fourth-richest person in the world, with an estimated net worth of around $33 billion.[29]

Howard Schulz (Starbucks)   In 1982, Howard Schultz, a salesperson for a plastic manufacturer, was hired as the new head of marketing for Starbucks, a coffee roaster with six cafés. Shortly after he was hired, he went Verona, Italy, to attend an international housewares show. He had his first latte in Verona, but he saw something more important than the coffee. The café patrons were enjoying themselves while sipping their coffees in the elegant surroundings. He had a vision of recreating the Old World magic and romance behind the Italian coffee bar. The owner wanted to focus on his plan to sell roasted whole beans, and eventually Schultz acquired Starbucks and began the company's march across the world. Schultz's father struggled at low-paying jobs with little to show for it when he died. "He was beaten down, he wasn't respected," Schultz said. "He had no health insurance, and he had no workers' compensation when he got hurt on the job." So with Starbucks, Schultz "wanted to build the kind of company that my father never got a chance to work for, in which people were respected." Due to this childhood experience, Schultz initiated practices at Starbucks that are still uncommon in retailing, such as providing comprehensive health care for all employees working at least 20 hours a week, including coverage for unmarried spouses, and offering an employee stock-option plan. In 2012, Starbucks' sales were greater than $11 billion from the 17,000 stores it operates in 40 countries.[31]

In the next section, we discuss the decisions that retailers make to design and implement their retail strategy. This book is organized around this strategic decision-making process.

REFACT

The acronym IKEA is made up of the initials of the founder's name (Ingvar Kamprad) plus those of Elmtaryd, his family farm, and the nearby village Agunnaryd.[28]

REFACT

At $300 million, Starbucks spends more on health care insurance for its employees than on coffee beans.[30]

THE RETAIL MANAGEMENT DECISION PROCESS

LO5

Understand the strategic retail management decision process.

This book is organized around the management decisions that retailers make to provide value to their customers and develop an advantage over their competitors. Exhibit 1–6 identifies the chapters in this book associated with each type of decision.

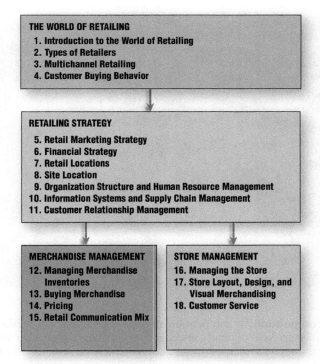

EXHIBIT 1–6
Retail Management
Decision Process

Understanding the World of Retailing—Section I

The first step in the retail management decision process, as Exhibit 1–6 shows, is understanding the world of retailing. Retail managers need to know the environment in which they operate before they can develop and implement effective strategies. The first section of this book therefore provides a general overview of the retailing industry and its customers.

The critical environmental factors in the world of retailing are (1) the macroenvironment and (2) the microenvironment. The impacts of the macroenvironment—including technological, social, and ethical/legal/political factors—on retailing are discussed throughout this book. For example, the influence of technology on the rise of multichannel retailing is reviewed in Chapter 3, the use of new information and supply chain technologies are examined in Chapter 10, customer relationship management systems are reviewed in Chapter 11, and new communication technologies are discussed in Chapter 15.

Competitors   The retailer's microenvironment focuses specifically on its competitors and customers. At first glance, identifying competitors appears easy: A retailer's primary competitors are other retailers that use the same retail approach. Thus, department stores compete against other department stores, and supermarkets compete with other supermarkets. This competition between the same type of retailers is called **intratype competition**.

Yet to appeal to a broader group of consumers, many retailers are increasing the variety of merchandise they offer. By offering greater variety, retailers satisfy the needs of customers seeking a one-stop shopping experience. For example, Walgreens has added jewelry, accessories, and apparel to its already extensive health and beauty categories to meet the lifestyle needs of its customers. Amazon seems to offer any product you might ever want to buy or rent. When retailers offer merchandise not typically associated with their type of store, such as clothing in a drugstore, the result is **scrambled merchandising**. Scrambled merchandising increases

Scrambled merchandise increases the level of intertype competition.

intertype competition, or competition among retailers that sell similar merchandise using different types of retail outlets, such as drug and department stores.

Increasing intertype competition makes it harder for retailers to identify and monitor their competition. In one sense, all retailers compete against one another for the dollars that consumers spend on goods and services. But the intensity of competition is greatest among retailers whose offerings are viewed as very similar.

Management's view of competition also may differ depending on the manager's position within the retail firm. For example, the manager of the Saks Fifth Avenue women's sportswear department in Bergen County, New Jersey, views the other women's sportswear specialty stores in the Riverside Square mall as her major competitors. But the Saks store manager views the Bloomingdale's store in a nearby mall as her strongest competitor. These differences in perspective arise because the department sales manager is primarily concerned with customers for a specific category of merchandise, whereas the store manager is concerned with customers seeking the entire selection of all merchandise and services offered by a department store. The chief executive officer (CEO) of a retail chain, in contrast, views competition from a much broader perspective. For example, Nordstrom might identify its strongest competitor as Saks, Neiman Marcus, Bloomingdale's, and even Bluefly.com.

Chapter 2 discusses various types of retailers and their competitive strategies, and Chapter 3 concentrates on different types of channels that retailers use to complete transactions with their customers.

Customers The second factor in the microenvironment is customers. Retailers must respond to broad demographic and lifestyle trends in our society, such as the growth in the senior and minority segments of the U.S. population or the importance of shopping convenience to the increasing number of two-income families. To develop and implement an effective strategy, retailers must understand why customers shop, how they select a store, and how they select among that store's merchandise—the information found in Chapter 4.

Developing a Retail Strategy—Section II

The next stages in the retail management decision-making process, formulating and implementing a retail strategy, are based on an understanding of the macro- and microenvironments developed in the first section of this book. Section II

Toys R Us focuses on toys and apparel for children, while Walmart's strategic focus is much broader.

focuses on decisions related to developing a retail strategy, whereas Sections III and IV pertain to decisions surrounding the implementation of the strategy and building a long-term competitive advantage. The decisions discussed in Sections III and IV are more tactical.

Retail Strategy   The **retail strategy** identifies (1) the target market, or markets, toward which the retailer will direct its efforts; (2) the nature of the merchandise and services the retailer will offer to satisfy the needs of the target market; and (3) how the retailer will develop unique assets that enable it to achieve long-term advantage over its competitors.

The nature of a retail strategy can be illustrated by comparing the strategies of Walmart and Toys R Us. Initially, Walmart identified its target market as small towns (fewer than 35,000 in population) in Arkansas, Texas, and Oklahoma. It offered name-brand merchandise at low prices in a broad array of categories, ranging from laundry detergent to girls' dresses, but offerings in each category were limited. Today, even as Walmart stores have expanded across the world, the selection in each category remains limited. A Walmart store might have only 3 models of flat-screen television sets, while an electronic category specialist like Best Buy might carry 30 models.

In contrast to Walmart, Toys R Us defines its primary target as consumers living in suburban areas of large cities. Rather than carrying many merchandise categories, Toys R Us stores specialize in toys and children's apparel and carry most types and brands currently available in the market. Walmart emphasizes self-service: Customers select their merchandise, bring it to the checkout line, and then carry it to their cars. But Toys R Us provides more customer service. It has salespeople to assist customers with certain types of merchandise.

Because Walmart and Toys R Us both emphasize competitive prices, they have made strategic decisions to sustain their low prices by developing a cost advantage over their competitors. Both firms have sophisticated distribution and management information systems to manage inventory. Their strong relationships with their suppliers enable them to buy merchandise at low prices.

Strategic Decision Areas   The key strategic decisions a retailer makes are defining its target market and its financial objectives. Chapter 5 discusses how the selection of a retail market strategy requires analyzing the environment and the firm's strengths and weaknesses. When major environmental changes occur, the current strategy and the reasoning behind it must be reexamined. The retailer then decides what, if any, strategy changes are needed to take advantage of new opportunities or avoid new threats in the environment. The retailer's market strategy must be consistent with the firm's financial objectives. Chapter 6 reviews how financial variables, such as return on investment, inventory turnover, and profit margin, can be used to evaluate the market strategy and its implementation.

The next set of strategic decisions involves the development of critical assets that enable retailers to build strategic advantages. These strategic assets are location, human resource, information and supply chain systems, supply chain organization, and customer loyalty.

Decisions regarding location (reviewed in Chapters 7 and 8) are important because location is typically consumers' top consideration when selecting a store. Generally, consumers buy gas at the closest service station and patronize the shopping mall that's most convenient to their home or office. In addition, location offers an opportunity to gain a long-term advantage over the competition. When a retailer has the best location, a competing retailer must settle for the second-best location.

Retailing is a very labor-intensive industry. Employees play a critical role in providing the services customers seek when patronizing a retailer. Chapter 9 outlines how retailers coordinate the activities of buyers, store managers, and sales associates in the implementation of the retailing strategy.

Retail information and supply chain management systems also offer a significant opportunity for retailers to gain strategic advantage. Chapter 10 reviews how retailers are developing sophisticated computer and distribution technologies to monitor flows of information and merchandise from vendors to retail distribution centers to retail stores. These technologies are part of an overall inventory management system that enables retailers to (1) make sure desired merchandise is available when customers want it and (2) minimize the retailer's inventory investment.

Retailers, like most businesses, want to develop repeat purchases and loyalty in their best customers. Chapter 11 examines the process that retailers use to identify, design programs for, increase the share of wallet of, provide more value to, and build loyalty among their best customers. The implementation decisions are discussed in the next two sections.

Implementing the Retail Strategy—Sections III and IV

To implement a retail strategy, retailers develop a retail mix that satisfies the needs of its target market better than that of its competitors. The **retail mix** is a set of decisions retailers make to satisfy customer needs and influence their purchase decisions. Elements in the retail mix (Exhibit 1–7) include the types of merchandise and services offered, merchandise pricing, advertising and promotional

EXHIBIT 1–7
The Retail Mix

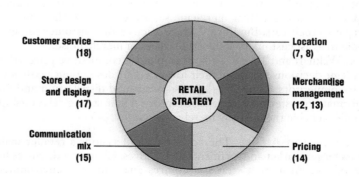

programs, store design, merchandise display, assistance to customers provided by salespeople, and convenience of the store's location. Section III reviews the implementation decisions made by buyers, and Section IV focuses on decisions made by store managers.

Managers in the merchandise management area decide how much and what types of merchandise to buy (Chapter 12), what vendors to use and how to interact with them (Chapter 13), the retail prices to set (Chapter 14), and how to advertise and promote merchandise (Chapter 15). Store managers must determine how to recruit, select, and motivate sales associates (Chapter 16); where and how merchandise will be displayed (Chapter 17); and the nature of services to provide for customers (Chapter 18). Whole Foods Market is one of the fastest growing and most profitable supermarket chains. In the next section, we illustrate the strategic and more tactical decisions Whole Foods has made and continues to make to achieve and sustain its success. The background of its founder and CEO, John Mackey, is described in Retailing View 1.3.

Whole Foods Market: An Organic and Natural Food Supermarket Chain

Retail Strategy   In the 1960s, natural, organic foods were available only in farmers' markets or small specialty stores catering to counterculture consumers. Consumers who patronized these health food stores felt that eating organic food would liberate them from the grasp of big agribusiness and food processors that were destroying the land with chemical pesticides, mistreating migrant farmworkers, and encouraging people to consume unhealthy processed foods. Whole Foods' strategy is to target health-conscious, environmentally conscious, middle-class consumers by using a modern supermarket format, rather than small, specialty health food stores. Its mission is to promote the vitality and well-being of all individuals by supplying the highest quality, most wholesome foods available.

Strategic Advantages   Some of the strategic assets Whole Foods has developed over the years to provide long-term advantages are a strong brand image that builds customer loyalty; committed employees who provide excellent customer service; good relationships with organic food suppliers that ensures a supply of organic food, even as demand for organic food grows faster than supply; an efficient supply chain connecting local growers to a national store network; and extensive information about its customers that it uses to develop assortments and target promotions.

Merchandise Management   In terms of merchandise, Whole Foods stores offer the array of food categories typically found in a supermarket. However, the assortment emphasizes organic and natural products that are fresh, nutritious, and safe to eat. Products are free of artificial preservatives, colors, flavors, and sweeteners, as well as hydrogenated fats and other unacceptable ingredients. In addition, Whole Foods seeks out and supports local producers whose fruits and vegetables meet its standards, particularly those who farm organically and are dedicated to environmentally friendly, sustainable agriculture.

Whole Foods offers seven lines of private-label products. Buyers work with artisan food producers and organic farmers to attain products sold under the super-premium Authentic Food Artisan brand. Its core private brands are called Whole Brands (department-specific products), Whole Foods (premium products), and Whole Kids Organic (organic products for children). The 365 Day Everyday Value and 365 Day Organic Everyday Value line provide natural products at value prices.

Whole Foods communicates the benefits of its offering through its website and social media. Its website has extensive information about natural and organic

1.3 RETAILING VIEW Whole Foods: The Birth of the Organic Supermarket

John Mackey had a relatively conventional, middle-class, suburban upbringing. But it was the 1970s, so Mackey quit college and embraced an alternative lifestyle (e.g., long beard, wild hair). After having worked for a time in a vegetarian collective, he solicited money from family and friends so that he could open a new sort of co-op in 1978: organic food store on the first floor, restaurant on the second floor, and living quarters on the top of the old Victorian house he had found.

REFACT

Whole Foods has a rule that no employee can have a salary greater than 19 times the average salary of store employees. On average, a U.S. CEO makes 319 times the compensation of a production worker in their companies.[32]

A couple of years later, Mackey went further and opened the first Whole Foods store in a 10,000-square-foot space that had once been a nightclub. In keeping with its history, Mackey made sure his natural food store was no stodgy, boring site with just granola. He stocked beer, meat, and wine, and he "loved it. I loved retail. I loved being around food. I loved natural foods. I loved organic foods. I loved the whole idea of it. And a thought entered into my mind that maybe this is what I could do."

But being a grocer was not a particularly popular aspiration with his family. His mother, a former teacher, strongly discouraged his interest in Whole Foods. According to Mackey's account, on her deathbed in 1987, she asked him to promise to return to school to get his college degree; when he demurred, she complained, "I wish you'd just give up that stupid health-food store. Your father and I gave you a fine mind, and you're wasting it being a grocer."

He never did give up on his "stupid" store, though. Instead, as the concept spread across the United States, Mackey adopted and adapted his ideas to fit local tastes. Through decentralized decision-making units, Whole Foods stores could choose to stock items specific to the preferences of the local markets, like live lobsters in Portland, Maine, or a kombucha bar in Venice, California. Through acquisitions, Whole Foods gained additional knowledge, too. In buying Wellspring Grocery, it learned about private-label options. The purchase of Mrs. Gooch's provided Whole Foods with insights into diet supplements. When it purchased

Whole Foods founder and CEO, John Mackey

Bread & Circus, it gained access to the Boston chain's famed seafood procurement expertise.

Sources: www.wholefoodsmarket.com/company-info/whole-foods-market-history; and Nick Paumgarten, "Food Fighter," *New Yorker*, January 4, 2010.

DISCUSSION QUESTION

What factors in Whole Foods' macro- and microenvironment contributed to its success?

Employees at Whole Foods participate in decision making through self-managed teams.

foods. Its iPhone app provides not just the location information about the nearest Whole Foods store (by zip code) but also approximately 2,000 recipes, searchable by various criteria, including diet restrictions, ingredients, budgets, or family appeal. The "On Hand" option allows users to input the items on their pantry shelves and receive recommendations for some meal options. Moreover, the app offers special deals for each store, right next to a map that shows customers how to get there.[33]

Whole Foods also uses social media extensively. A global manager and community manager assigned at every store are responsible for customer engagement. A single Global Online Community Manager runs the company's central Twitter link, @Whole Foods. Most of the tweets in this realm come from individual customers with questions, complaints, or suggestions. The manager makes sure to respond almost immediately, to ensure that no customers get the sense Whole Foods is uninterested or ignoring their concerns. Then, in each community, another manager attends to local needs, including special deal postings, charity opportunities, and upcoming events. A Los Angeles store located on Third Street owns the Twitter handle @WholeFoods3rdSt; a Mount Washington location, near Baltimore, tweets from the @WholeFoodsMTW account.[34]

Store Management   All Whole Foods employees are organized into self-managed teams that meet regularly to discuss issues and solve problems. Almost all team members have stock options in the firm. They also receive a 20 percent discount in stores. Their personal wellness accounts help them cover health care expenses, both for themselves and their domestic partners. To select the benefits package, the entire company takes a vote every three years. Whole Foods thus has been on *Fortune* magazine's "100 Best Companies to Work For" list for 13 consecutive years.[35]

Whole Foods' decisions on visual merchandising and store design reinforce its strategy.[36] Its stores are designed to make grocery shopping fun—to transform a supermarket into an interactive theater with corporate staff serving as the producer and store management as the director. Sections of its newer stores are designed with self-contained architecture that curves inward, creating a feeling of intimacy that encourages shoppers to linger. The warm feeling of the store is enhanced by signs made of an eco-friendly, woodlike material rather than plastic. Art gallery–type lighting focuses attention on produce.

Finally, Whole Foods' store management provides excellent customer service. Curious about the life of a chicken in the display case? It comes with a 16-page booklet and an invitation to visit the live chickens at the company's Pennsylvania farm. Want to know the name of the farmer who grew those organic tomatoes? That information, along with some personal details, is readily available. Curious about the fish you're getting dressed at the free filleting station? The employee can offer not just ideas for cooking it but also the identity of the Whole Foods boat and the captain who caught it for you.[37]

Ethical and Legal Considerations

 When making the decisions discussed previously, managers need to consider the ethical and legal implications of their decisions, in addition to the effects that those decisions have on the profitability of their firms and the satisfaction of their customers. **Ethics** are the principles governing individuals and companies that establish appropriate behavior and indicate what is right and wrong. Defining the term is easy, but determining what the principles are is difficult. What one person thinks is ethical, another may consider unethical.

What is ethical can vary from country to country and from industry to industry. For example, offering bribes to overcome bureaucratic roadblocks is an accepted practice in Middle Eastern countries but is considered unethical, and even illegal, in the United States. Ethical principles also can change over time. For example, some years ago, doctors and lawyers who advertised their services were considered unethical. Today, such advertising is accepted as common practice.

Examples of difficult situations that retail managers face include the following:

- Should a retailer sell merchandise that it suspects was made using child labor?
- Should a retailer advertise that its prices are the lowest available in the market, even though some are not?
- Should a retail buyer accept an expensive gift from a vendor?
- Should a retailer charge a supplier a fee for getting a new item in its store?
- Should retail salespeople use a high-pressure sales approach when they know the product is not the best for the customer's needs?
- Should a retailer disclose product information that may affect whether or not it is purchased?
- Should a retailer promote a product as being "on sale" if it never sold at a higher, nonsale price?
- Should a retailer offer credit at a higher interest rate or sell products at higher prices in stores patronized mostly by low-income customers?

Laws dictate which activities society has deemed to be clearly wrong, those activities for which retailers and their employees will be punished through the federal or state legal systems. However, most business decisions are not regulated by laws. Often retail managers have to rely on their firms' and industries' codes of ethics and/or their own codes of ethics to determine the right thing to do.

Many companies have codes of ethics to provide guidelines for their employees in making their ethical decisions. These ethical policies provide a clear sense of right and wrong so that companies and their customers can depend on their employees when questionable situations arise. However, in many situations, retail managers need to rely on their personal code of ethics—their personal sense of what is right or wrong.

Exhibit 1–8 lists some questions you can ask yourself to determine whether a behavior or activity is unethical. The questions emphasize that ethical behavior is determined by widely accepted views of what is right and wrong. Thus, you should engage only in activities about which you would be proud to tell your family, friends, employer, and customers. If the answer to any of these questions is yes, the behavior or activity is probably unethical, and you should not do it.

| 1. Would I be embarrassed if a customer found out about this behavior? |
| 2. Would my supervisor disapprove of this behavior? |
| 3. Would most coworkers feel that this behavior is unusual? |
| 4. Am I about to do this because I think I can get away with it? |
| 5. Would I be upset if a company did this to me? |
| 6. Would my family or friends think less of me if I told them about engaging in this activity? |
| 7. Am I concerned about the possible consequences of this behavior? |
| 8. Would I be upset if this behavior or activity was publicized in a newspaper article? |
| 9. Would society be worse off if everyone engaged in this behavior or activity? |

EXHIBIT 1–8
Checklist for Making
Ethical Decisions

Your firm can strongly affect the ethical choices you will have to make. When you view your firm's policies or requests as improper, you have three choices:

1. *Ignore your personal values, and do what your company asks you to do.* Self-respect suffers when you have to compromise your principles to please an employer. If you take this path, you will probably feel guilty and be dissatisfied with your job in the long run.

2. *Take a stand, and tell your employer what you think.* Try to influence the decisions and policies of your company and supervisors.

3. *Refuse to compromise your principles.* Taking this path may mean you will get fired or be forced to quit.

You should not take a job with a company whose products, policies, and conduct conflict with your standards. Before taking a job, investigate the company's procedures and selling approach to see whether they conflict with your personal ethical standards. Throughout this text, we will highlight the legal and ethical issues associated with the retail decisions made by managers.

SUMMARY

LO1 **Identify retailing activities.**

Retailing is defined as a set of business activities that add value to the products and services sold to consumers for their personal or family use. These value-added activities include providing assortments, breaking bulk, holding inventory, and providing services.

LO2 **Realize the importance of retailing in the U.S. and world economies.**

Retailing plays an important role in the U.S. economy. One out of four workers in the United States works for a retailer or for a company selling products to a retailer, and the U.S. retail sector accounts for about the same percentage of the U.S. GDP as the entire manufacturing sector. Retailing also plays an important role in developing economies. Some business scholars feel that there is need for modern retail methods to be used to serve consumers at the bottom of the pyramid.

LO3 **Analyze the changing retail industry.**

The retail industry has changed dramatically over the last 50 years. Many well-known national and international retailers were small startup companies 50 years ago. Now the industry is dominated by large firms. The development of information systems is one the forces facilitating the growth of large retailers.

Before the availability of modern information systems, it was difficult for retailers to lower costs through economies of scale, and larger retailers had limited advantages over small local or regional retailers. With these information systems, retailers are able to efficiently and effectively manage millions of customer transactions with thousands of stores and suppliers across the globe.

LO4 **Recognize the opportunities in retailing for you.**

Retailing offers opportunities for exciting, challenging careers, either by working for a retail firm or starting your own business. Aspects of retail careers are discussed in Appendix 1A. Suggestions about starting your own business appear in Appendix A at the end of the book.

LO5 **Understand the strategic retail management decision process.**

The retail management decision process involves developing a strategy for creating a competitive advantage in the marketplace and then developing a retail mix to implement that strategy. The strategic decisions, discussed in the first section of this textbook, involve selecting a target market; defining the nature of the retailer's offering; and building a competitive advantage through locations, human resource management, information and supply chain management systems, and customer relationship management programs.

The merchandise and store management decisions for implementing the strategy, discussed in the second half of this textbook, involve selecting a merchandise assortment, buying merchandise, setting prices, communicating with customers, managing the store, presenting merchandise in stores, and providing customer service. Large retail chains use sophisticated information systems to analyze business opportunities and make these decisions about how to operate their businesses in multiple countries.

Answers to the Quiz in Exhibit 1–1

1. (d)   **3.** (e)   **5.** (e)   **7.** (d)
2. (d)   **4.** (a)   **6.** (b)   **8.** (b)

KEY TERMS

backward integration, *9*
base of the pyramid, *14*
bottom of the pyramid (BoP), *14*
breaking bulk, *8*
corporate social responsibility (CSR), *12*
ethics, *28*

forward integration, *9*
holding inventory, *8*
intertype competition, *22*
intratype competition, *21*
retailer, *7*
retailing, *7*

retail mix, *24*
retail strategy, *23*
scrambled merchandising, *21*
supply chain, *7*
vertical integration, *9*
wholesalers, *9*

GET OUT AND DO IT!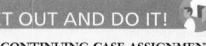

1. **CONTINUING CASE ASSIGNMENT** In most chapters of this textbook, there will be a GET OUT AND DO IT! assignment that will give you an opportunity to examine the strategy and tactics of one retailer. Your first assignment is to select a retailer and prepare a report on the retailer's history, including when it was founded and how it has evolved over time. To ensure that you can get information about the retailer for subsequent Continuing Case Assignments, the retailer you select should:

   • *Be a publicly held company so that you can access its financial statements and annual reports.* Do not select a retailer that is owned by another company. For example, Bath & Body Works is owned by Limited Brands, so you can get financial information about only the holding company and not the individual companies it owns, such as Victoria's Secret and White Barn Candle.

   • *Focus on one type of retailing.* For example, Abercrombie & Fitch operates just one type of specialty store and thus would be a good choice. However, Walmart operates discount stores, warehouse club stores, and supercenters and thus would not be a good choice.

   • *Be easy to visit and collect information about.* Some retailers and store managers may not allow you to interview them about the store, take pictures of the store, talk with sales associates, or analyze the merchandise assortment in the store. Try to pick a retailer with a local store manager who can help you complete the assignments.

   Some examples of retailers that meet the first two criteria are Whole Foods Market, Dress Barn, Burlington Coat Factory, Ross Stores, Ann Taylor, Cato, Finish Line, Foot Locker, Brookstone, Claire's, Walgreens, Staples, Office Depot, American Eagle Outfitter, Pacific Sunwear, Abercrombie & Fitch, Tiffany & Co., Zales, Autozone, Pep Boys, Hot Topic, Wet Seal, Best Buy, Family Dollar, Dollar General, Michaels, PetSmart, Dillard's, Pier 1 Imports, Home Depot, Lowe's, Bed Bath & Beyond, Men's Wearhouse, Kroger, Kohl's, Radio Shack, Safeway, and Target.

2. **GO SHOPPING** Visit a local retail store, and describe each of the elements in its retail mix.

3. **INTERNET EXERCISE** Data on U.S. retail sales are available at the U.S. Bureau of the Census Internet site at www.census.gov/retail/#ecommerce. Look at "Estimates of Monthly Retail and Food Services Sales by Kind of Business" for the most recent year. In which months are sales the highest? Which kinds of businesses experience the greatest fluctuations in monthly sales? List reasons that help explain your findings.

4. **INTERNET EXERCISE** Go to the home pages of Macy's, Target, Walmart, Toys R Us, and the National Retail Federation Retail Careers Center (www.nrf.com/RetailCareers/) to find information about retail careers with these organizations. Review the information about the different positions described. In which positions would you be interested? Which positions are not of interest to you? Which employer would interest you? Why?

5. **INTERNET EXERCISE** Choose one of the top 20 retailers (Exhibit 1–5). Go to the company's website, and find out how the company started and how it has changed over time.

6. **INTERNET EXERCISE** Go online and find an example of a retailer involved in corporate social responsibility. In a brief paragraph, describe how this retailer is taking steps to contribute to a social or ethical cause.

DISCUSSION QUESTIONS AND PROBLEMS

1. How do retailers add value to the products bought by consumers?

2. What is your favorite retailer? Why do you like this retailer? What would a competitive retailer have to do to get your patronage?

3. What are the benefits and limitations of purchasing a home entertainment system directly from a number of component manufacturers rather than from a retailer?

4. What retailers would be considered intratype competitors for a convenience store chain such as 7-Eleven? What firms would be intertype competitors?

5. How does Walmart contribute and/or detract from the communities in which it operates stores?

6. The same brand and style of men's suits are sold at different prices at a department store like Macy's and at a specialty store like Men's Wearhouse. Why would a customer choose to buy the suit from one store rather than the other?

7. Compare and contrast the retail mixes of department stores and full-line discount stores. Use bullet points or a table to list the similarities and differences.

8. An entrepreneur approaches you about how to sell her new writing pens to consumers. The pens have a unique benefit—they are more comfortable to use than traditional pens. The entrepreneur is concerned the retailers she has approached want to buy the pens from her at $10.00 a piece and then sell the pens in their stores at $18.00 to consumers. The entrepreneur is dismayed at the extra $8.00 the retailers are getting and has decided to sell the product directly to consumers for $10.00. She wants to know your opinion. What do you think? Why?

9. From a personal perspective, how does retailing rate as a potential career compared with others you are considering? Why?

10. In this chapter, some socially responsible activities engaged in by retailers are described. Take the perspective of a stockholder in one of these companies. What effect will these activities have on the value of its stock? Why might they have a positive or negative effect?

SUGGESTED READINGS

"2012 Global Retail Industry Trends." *Stores Magazine*, January 2012.

Ferrell, O.C., John Fraedrich, and Linda Ferrell. *Business Ethics: Ethical Decision Making & Cases*, 9th ed., Impendence, KY: Southwestern, 2012.

Fisher, Marshall L., and Ananth Raman. *The New Science of Retailing: How Analytics Are Improving Performance*. Boston: Harvard Business Press, 2010.

"Global Powers of Retailing Top 250." *Stores Magazine*, January 2012.

Lee, Min-young, Ann Fairhurst, and Scarlett Wesley. "Corporate Social Responsibility: A Review of the Top 100 US Retailers." *Corporate Reputation Review* (London) 12 (Summer 2009), pp. 140–159.

Mantrala, Murali K., and Manfred Krafft (Eds). *Retailing in the 21st Century: Current and Future Trends*, 2nd ed. Berlin: Springer, 2010.

Ortinau, David J., Barry J. Babin, and Jean-Charles Chebat, "Retailing Evolution Research: Introduction to the Special Section on Retailing Research," *Journal of Business Research*, 64, no. 6 (June 2011), pp. 541–542.

Plunkett, Jack (Ed). *Plunkett's Retail Industry Almanac 2012*. Houston: Plunkett Research, 2012.

Roberts, Bryan. *Walmart: Key Insights and Practical Lessons from the World's Largest Retailer*. Philadelphia: Kogan Page, 2012.

APPENDIX 1A　Careers in Retailing

Retailing offers exciting and challenging career opportunities. Few other industries grant as many responsibilities to young managers. When students asked Dave Fuente, former CEO of Office Depot, what they needed to become a CEO someday, he responded, "You need to have profit and loss responsibility and the experience of managing people early in your career." Entry-level retail jobs for college graduates offer both these opportunities. Most college graduates begin their retail careers as assistant buyers, merchandise planners, or department managers in stores. In these positions, they are responsible for the profitability of a line of merchandise or an area of the store, and they manage people who work for them.

Even if you work for a large company, retailing provides an opportunity for you to do your own thing and be rewarded. You can come with an idea, execute it almost immediately, and see how well it is doing by reviewing the sales data at the end of the day.

Retailing offers a variety of career paths, such as buying, store management, sales promotion and advertising, personnel, operations/distribution, real estate, loss prevention, and finance. In addition, retailing offers almost immediate accountability for talented people, so they can reach key management positions fairly quickly. Starting salaries are competitive, and the compensation of top management ranks among the highest in any industry.

CAREER OPPORTUNITIES

In retail firms, career opportunities are in merchandising/buying, store management, and corporate staff functions. Corporate positions are in accounting, finance, real estate, promotions and advertising, computer and distribution systems, and human resources.

The primary entry-level opportunities for a retailing career are in the areas of buying and store management. Buying positions are more numbers-oriented, whereas store management positions are more people-oriented. Entry-level positions on the corporate staff are limited. Retailers typically want all of their employees to understand their customers and their merchandise. Therefore, most executives and corporate staff managers begin their careers in merchandise or store management.

Store Management

Successful store managers must have the ability to lead and motivate employees. They also need to be sensitive to customers' needs by making sure that merchandise is available and neatly displayed.

Store management involves all the discipline necessary to run a successful business: sales planning and goal setting, overall store image and merchandise presentation, budgets and expense control, customer service and sales supervision, personnel administration and development, and community relations.

Because store managers work in stores, they are often at quite a distance from the home office, which means they have limited direct supervision. Their hours generally mirror those of their store and can therefore include some weekends and evenings. In addition, they spend time during nonoperating hours tending to administrative responsibilities.

The typical entry-level store management position is a department manager with responsibility for merchandise presentation, customer service, and inventory control for an area of the store. The next level is an area or group manager with responsibility for executing merchandising plans and achieving sales goals for several areas, as well as supervising, training, and developing department managers. Beyond these positions, you might be promoted to store manager, then to district manager responsible for a group of stores, and then to regional manager responsible for a group of districts.

Merchandise Management

Merchandise management attracts people with strong analytical capabilities, an ability to predict what merchandise will appeal to their target markets, and a skill for negotiating with vendors as well as store management to get things done. Many retailers have broken the merchandising management activities into two different yet parallel career paths: buying and merchandise planning.

Retail merchandise buyers are similar to financial portfolio managers. They invest in a portfolio of merchandise; monitor the performance (sales) of the merchandise; and on the basis of the sales, either decide to buy more merchandise that is selling well or get rid of (discount) merchandise that is selling poorly. Buyers are responsible for selecting the type and amount of merchandise to buy, negotiating the wholesale price and payment terms with suppliers, setting the initial retail price for the merchandise, monitoring merchandise sales, and making appropriate retail price adjustments. Thus buyers need to have good financial planning skills, knowledge of their customers' needs and wants and competitive activities, and the ability to develop good working relationships with vendors. To develop a better understanding of their customers, buyers typically stay in contact with their stores by visiting them, talking to sales associates and managers, and monitoring the sales data available through their merchandise management systems.

Planners have an even more analytical role than buyers. Their primary responsibility is to determine the assortment of merchandise sent to each store—how many styles, colors, sizes, and individual items. Once the merchandise is in the stores, planners closely monitor sales and work with buyers on decisions such as how much additional merchandise to purchase if the merchandise is doing well or when to mark down the merchandise if sales are below expectations.

The typical entry-level position of college graduates interested in merchandise management is either assistant buyer or assistant planner in a merchandise category such as men's athletic shoes or consumer electronics. In these positions, you will do the sales analysis needed to support the decisions eventually made by the planner or buyer for whom you work. From this entry-level position, you could be promoted to buyer and then divisional merchandise manager, responsible for a number of merchandise categories. Most retailers believe that merchandise management skills are not category-specific. Thus, as you are promoted in the buying organization, you will probably work in various merchandise categories.

Corporate Staff

The corporate staff positions in retail firms involve activities and require knowledge, skills, and abilities similar to those in comparable positions in nonretail firms. Thus, many managers in these positions identify with their profession rather than the retail industry. For example, accountants in retail firms view themselves as accountant, not retailers.

Management Information Systems (MISs) Employees in this area are involved with applications for capturing data and developing and maintaining inventory, as well as the design of store systems such as POS terminals, self-checkout systems, and in-store kiosks.

Operations/Distribution Operations employees are responsible for operating and maintaining the store's physical plant; providing various customer services; overseeing the receipt, ticketing, warehousing, and distribution of a store's inventory; and buying and maintaining store supplies and operating equipment. Students in operations and MIS typically major in production, operations, or computer information systems.

Promotions/Advertising Promotion's many aspects include public relations, advertising, visual merchandising, and special events. This department attempts to build the retail firm's brand image and encourage customers to visit the retailer's stores and/or website. Managers in this area typically major in marketing or mass communications.

Loss Prevention Loss prevention employees are responsible for protecting the retailer's assets. They develop systems and procedures to minimize employee theft and shoplifting. Managers in this area often major in sociology or criminology, although, as we discuss in Chapters 9 and 16, loss prevention is beginning to be viewed as a human resource management issue.

Finance/Accounting Many retailers are large businesses involved in complicated corporate structures. Most retailers also operate with a tight net profit margin. With such a fine line between success and failure, retailers continue to require financial experts. The finance/accounting division is responsible for the financial health of the company. Employees in this division prepare financial reports for all aspects of the business, including long-range forecasting and planning, economic trend analysis and budgeting, shortage control and internal audits, gross and net profit, accounts payable to vendors, and accounts receivable from charge customers. In addition, they manage the retailer's relationship with the financial community. Students interested in this area often major in finance or accounting.

Real Estate Employees in the real estate division are responsible for selecting locations for stores, negotiating leases and land purchases, and managing the leasehold costs. Students entering this area typically major in real estate or finance.

Store Design Employees working in this area are responsible for designing the store and presenting merchandise and fixtures in the store. Talented, creative students in business, architecture, art, and other related fields will have innumerable opportunities for growth in the area of retail store design.

Human Resource Management Human resource management is responsible for the effective selection, training, placement, advancement, and welfare of employees. Because there are seasonal peaks in retailing (such as Christmas, when many extra people must be hired), human resource personnel must be flexible and highly efficient.

ATTRACTIVENESS OF RETAILING CAREERS

Immediate Responsibility
Management trainees in retailing are given more responsibility more quickly than their counterparts in other industries. Buyers are responsible for choosing, promoting, pricing, distributing, and selling millions of dollars' worth of merchandise each season. The department manager, generally the first position after a training program, is often responsible for merchandising one or more departments, as well as managing 20 or more full- and part-time sales associates.

Many students and their parents think that people working in retailing have jobs as sales clerks and cashiers. They hold this view because, as customers in retail stores, they typically interact only with sales associates, not their managers. But as we have discussed in this chapter, retail firms are large, sophisticated corporations that employ managers with a wide variety of knowledge, skills, and abilities. Entry-level positions for college are typically management trainees in the buying or store organization, not sales associates.

While some employees are promoted on the basis of their retail experience, a college degree is needed for most retail management positions, ranging from store manager to CEO. More than 150 colleges and universities in the United States offer programs of study and degrees or majors in retailing.

Financial Rewards
Starting salaries for management trainees with a college degree range from $30,000 to $60,000 a year, and the compensation of top management ranks with the highest in any industry. For example, store managers with only a few years of experience can earn up to $100,000 or more, depending on their performance bonuses. A senior buyer for a department store earns from $50,000 to $90,000 or more. A big-box store manager can earn from $50,000 to $150,000; a discount store manager makes from $70,000 to $100,000 or more; and a specialty store manager earns from $35,000 to $60,000 or more.

Compensation varies according to the amount of responsibility. Specialty store managers are generally paid less than department store managers because their annual sales volume is lower. But advancements in this area can be faster. Aggressive specialty store managers often are promoted to district managers and run 8 to 15 units after a few years, so they quickly move into higher pay brackets.

Because information systems enable retailers to assess the sales and profit performance of each manager, and even each sales associate, the compensation of retail managers is closely linked to objective measures of their performance. As a result, in addition to their salaries, retail managers are generally given strong monetary incentives based on the sales they create.

A compensation package consists of more than salary alone. In retailing, the benefits package is often substantial and may include a profit-sharing plan, savings plan, stock options, medical and dental insurance, life insurance, long-term disability protection and income protection plans, and paid vacations and holidays. Two additional benefits of retailing careers are that most retailers offer employees valuable discounts on the merchandise they sell, and some buying positions include extensive foreign travel.

Opportunities for Advancement
While the growth rate of retail parallels the growth rate of the overall economy, many opportunities for rapid advancement exist simply because of the sheer size of the retail industry. With so many retail firms, there is always a large number of firms that are experiencing a high growth rate, opening many new stores, and needing store managers and support staff positions.

Types of Retailers

EXECUTIVE BRIEFING
Debbie Ferree, Vice Chairman and
Chief Merchant, DSW Inc.

Math was always my favorite subject in school and came quite naturally to me, so it was no surprise that I entered college with the goal to become a college math professor, but my passion for fashion and love for business and retail caused me to change my career aspirations and transfer to the college of business.

Before joining DSW (Designer Shoe Warehouse), I worked in senior management positions for a variety of retailers, which gave me broad experience in different channels of distribution and business models: May Company and Burdines/Federated Department Stores—department stores; Ross Dress for Less—discount stores; and Harris Company—specialty retail.

In 1997, I joined DSW, a true off-price retailer, offering customers an assortment of end-of-season, closeout merchandise at deeply discounted prices. The department store landscape was changing rapidly and dramatically, where point-of-service discounting was the norm and customers were confused about the price they paid for a product. This created an opportunity in DSW to architect a new "hybrid" business model that would provide a very different shopping experience for the customer: an assortment of current, on-trend, in-season, fashion merchandise from well-known national brands at fair, everyday value (EDV) in an open-sell, attractive environment. This would define a new direction for the future in

retail. In 2004, I was promoted to president and chief merchandising officer of DSW and we took the company public in 2005.

To implement this new concept, we developed strategic partnerships with the leading designer brands in footwear. These vendors were focused on selling their brands through the department store channel and were initially skeptical about the new business model. The new model had many advantages and financial benefits: when they sold to DSW, there would be no extra charges such as advertising allowances or vendor chargebacks, and no renegotiations on prices at the end of the season or merchandise returns. Through collaboration and the development of financial and strategic plans that would support mutually profitable growth for both parties, we aligned on a plan that today generates over $2 billion in sales revenue in over 375 stores, an e-commerce business, and provides a long-term plan for continued growth.

The pillars of our success are a breathtaking assortment of on-trend merchandise, simple convenience, and irresistible value. We are using social media to create a community of shoe lovers who are loyal to our offerings, and regularly inform their friends about the new additions to our assortment and about their shopping experience in our stores

CHAPTER 2

LEARNING OBJECTIVES

LO1 List the different characteristics that define retailers.

LO2 Categorize the various types of food retailers.

LO3 Identify the various types of general merchandise retailers.

LO4 Explain the differences between service and merchandise retailers.

LO5 Illustrate the types of ownership for retail firms.

and on our website. Our fan page is a place where shoe lovers can hang out and talk about shoes. We stimulate interaction between our over two million followers by presenting what our followers think of new styles, thanking them for their suggestions, answering their questions promptly, and running fun trivia contests with free pairs of shoes as prizes.

DSW's aspiration is to become "America's Favorite Place for Shoes" and "America's Favorite Place to Work." We have a strong culture that incorporates our core values—humility, accountability, collaboration, and passion—into a fun environment that stretches talent, supports individual development, and provides a rewarding career experience!

Y ou want to have a good cup of coffee in the morning, not instant, but you don't want to bother with grinding coffee beans, boiling water, pouring it through ground coffee in a filter, and waiting. Think of all the different retailers that could help you satisfy this need. You could get your cup of brewed coffee from the drive-through window at the local Starbucks, or you could decide to buy an automatic coffeemaker with a timer so that your coffee will be ready when you wake up. You could purchase the coffeemaker at a discount store like Walmart or Target, a department store such as Macy's, a drugstore like CVS, or a category specialist such as Best Buy. If you want to buy the coffeemaker without taking the time to visit a store, you could visit www.thefind.com, search for "coffee and espresso maker," and review the details about 83,392 products sold by 5,485 retailers, ranging from Bed Bath & Beyond to Sur La Table to Newegg.

All these retailers are competing against one another to satisfy your need for a hassle-free, good cup of coffee. Many are selling the same brands, but they offer different services, prices, environments, and convenience. For example, if you want to buy a low-priced, basic coffeemaker, you can go to a discount store. But if you are interested in a coffeemaker with more features and want to have someone explain the different features, you can visit a department store or a category specialist.

To develop and implement a retail strategy, retailers need to understand the nature of competition in the retail marketplace. This chapter describes the different types of retailers and how they compete against one another by offering different benefits to consumers. These benefits are reflected in the nature of the retail mixes used by the retailers to satisfy customer needs: the types of merchandise and services offered, the degree to which their offerings emphasize services versus merchandise, and the prices charged.

RETAILER CHARACTERISTICS

LO1

List the different characteristics that define retailers.

The 1.1 million[1] retailers in the United States range from individual street vendors selling hot dogs to multichannel retailers that offer thousands of products in their stores and through catalog and Internet channels. The different types of retailers offer unique benefits. The type of retailer a consumer chooses to patronize depends on the benefits the consumer is seeking. For example, if you are shopping for a gift, you might value the convenience of buying a shirt from a retailer's Internet channel so the retailer will ship it to a friend in another city. Alternatively, you might prefer to buy a shirt from a local store when making a purchase for yourself so that you can try it on. You might go to a discount store to buy an inexpensive shirt for a camping trip or a sporting goods specialty store to buy a shirt with the insignia of your favorite football team.

All these retailers survive and prosper because they satisfy a group of consumers' needs more effectively than their competitors, and thus consumers patronize different retail types when they have different needs. As consumer needs and competition change, new retail formats are created and existing formats evolve.

Many retailers also are broadening their assortments, which means that their offerings overlap and competition increases. At eBay Motors, for example, consumers can buy cars and motorcycles from thousands of individual sellers and established dealers. The eBay sellers compete with traditional automobile dealers that sell cars and motorcycles through conventional dealerships. In another example, office supply stores compete with warehouse clubs, supercenters, supermarkets, and convenience stores because they sell many of the same products.

The most basic characteristic used to describe the different types of retailers is their retail mix, or the elements retailers use to satisfy their customers' needs. Four elements of the retail mix are particularly useful for classifying retailers: the type of merchandise and/or services offered, the variety and assortment of merchandise offered, the level of customer service, and the price of the merchandise.

Type of Merchandise

The United States, Canada, and Mexico have developed a classification scheme, called the **North American Industry Classification System (NAICS),** to collect data on business activity in each country. Every business is assigned a hierarchical, six-digit code based on the type of products and services it sells. The first two digits identify the firm's business sector, and the remaining four digits identify various subsectors.

The classifications for retailers selling merchandise, based largely on the type of merchandise sold, are illustrated in Exhibit 2–1. Merchandise retailers are in sectors 44 and 45. The next three digits provide a finer classification of merchandise retailers. For example, retailers selling clothing and clothing accessories are classified as 448, clothing stores as 4481, and men's clothing stores as 44811. The sixth digit, not illustrated in Exhibit 2–1, captures differences between the North American countries using the classification scheme.

NAICS Codes for Retailers   **EXHIBIT 2–1**

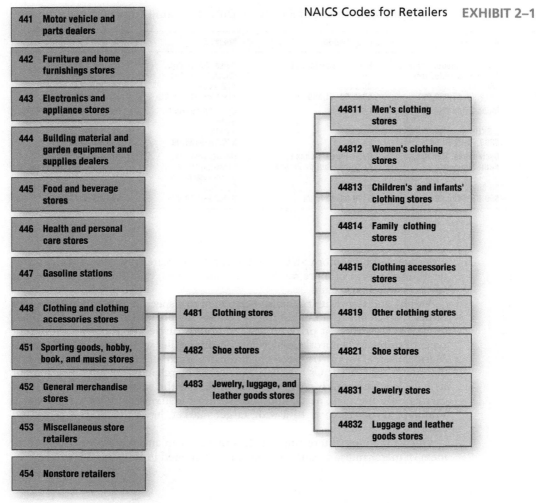

SOURCE: "North American Industry Classification System (NAICS)," U.S. Census Bureau, www.census.gov/epcd/www/naics.html.

Most services retailers are classified in sectors 71 (arts, entertainment, and recreation) and 72 (accommodation and food services). For example, food services and drinking places are in category 722, which is subdivided into full-service restaurants (7221) and limited-service eating places like fast-food restaurants (7222).

Variety and Assortment

Retailers can offer the same merchandise but differ in the variety and assortment of merchandise offered. **Variety** is the number of merchandise categories a retailer offers. **Assortment** is the number of different items offered in a merchandise category. Variety is often referred to as the **breadth of merchandise,** and assortment is referred to as the **depth of merchandise.** Each different item of merchandise is called a **stock-keeping unit (SKU).** Some examples of SKUs include an original scent, 33-ounce box of Tide laundry detergent with bleach or a blue, long-sleeve, button-down-collar Ralph Lauren shirt, size medium.

Warehouse clubs, discount stores, and toy stores all sell toys, but warehouse clubs and full-line discount stores sell many other categories of merchandise in addition to toys (i.e., they have greater variety). Stores specializing in toys stock

EXHIBIT 2-2   Variety and Assortment of Bicycles in Different Retail Outlets

	Adult Road	Adult Hybrid	Mountain	Child
Wheelworks	Bianci, Colnago, Peter Mooney, Serotta, Trek 150 SKUs $419.99–$7,999.99	Bianchi, Specialized, Trek 96 SKUs $349.99–$1,899.99	Salsa, Santa Cruz, Specialized, Trek 122 SKUs $299.99–$1,899.99	Electra, Gary Fisher, Haro, Kettler, Trek 56 SKUs $159.99–$429.99
Toys R Us	Mobo Triton Pro 3 SKUs $299.99–$359.99	—	Cycle Force, Huffy, Schwinn 4 SKUs $79.98–$135.99	Avigo, Cycle Force, Huffy, Mongoose, Pacific Cycle 228 SKUs $45.99–$499.99
Walmart	Cycle Force, Genesis, Kent, Mongoose 26 SKUs $99.97–$499.00	Cycle Force, Genesis, Schwinn, Tour de France 9 SKUs $179.00–$349.00	Havoc, Genesis, Schwinn, NEXT, Roadmaster 63 SKUs $88.00–$379.00	Huffy, Koxx, Micargi, Schwinn, Tour De France 195 SKUs $28.13–$675.00

more types of toys (more SKUs) and thus offer a greater assortment (i.e., greater depth in the form of more models, sizes, and brands) than the full-line discount stores or warehouse clubs.

Variety and assortment can also be applied to a specific merchandise category rather than an entire store. Exhibit 2–2 shows the breadth and depth of bicycles, as well as the different price points and brands carried by three very different types of stores: Wheelworks, a bicycle specialty retailer with one store in Belmont, Massachusetts; Toys R Us, a toy big-box category killer; and Walmart, a full-line discount store. Toys R Us has a large variety of merchandise besides bicycles, but its bicycle assortment is narrow. Wheelworks has the smallest variety because it carries only bicycles, parts, and accessories; but its assortment is very deep. Walmart, trying to cater to a wide target market, has a moderate variety and assortment.

One of the most interesting retailers that sells an amazing variety and assortment of merchandise is Amazon, which is highlighted in Retailing View 2.1.

How does Wheelworks' variety and assortment compare with Toys R Us and Walmart?

Why do the three retailers' assortments differ from each other?

Services Offered

Retailers also differ in the services they offer customers. Customers expect almost all retailers to provide certain services: displaying merchandise, accepting credit cards, providing parking, and being open at convenient hours. Some retailers charge customers for other services, such as home delivery and gift wrapping. However, retailers may differ on other services. For example, Wheelworks offers assistance in selecting the appropriate bicycle, as well as repairs. Walmart does not provide these services.

Prices and the Cost of Offering Breadth and Depth of Merchandise and Services

Stocking a deep and broad assortment, like the one Wheelworks offers in bicycles, is appealing to customers but costly for retailers. When a retailer offers many SKUs, its inventory investment increases because the retailer must have backup stock for each and every SKU.

Similarly, services attract customers to the retailer, but they also are costly. More staff must be paid to provide information and assist customers, alter products to meet customers' needs, and demonstrate merchandise. Child care facilities, restrooms, dressing rooms, and coat check rooms take up valuable store space that could be used to stock and display merchandise. Offering delayed billing, credit, or installment payments requires a financial investment that could be otherwise used to buy more merchandise.

To make a profit, retailers that offer broader variety, deeper assortments, and/or additional services need to charge higher prices. For example, department stores have higher prices than discount stores partially because of their higher costs. Department stores stock more fashionable merchandise and have to reduce prices when they make a mistake in guessing what the popular styles will be. They also provide more personal sales service and have more expensive mall locations. In contrast, discount stores appeal to customers who are looking for lower prices. These consumers are less interested in the costly services provided by department stores. Thus, a critical retail decision involves the trade-off between the costs and benefits of maintaining additional inventory or providing additional services. Chapters 6 and 12 address the considerations required in making this trade-off. In the next sections, we discuss the different types of food and general merchandise retailers.

2.1 RETAILING VIEW   Amazon: The Jack of All (Retail) Trades and Master of Many

When it started out in 1994, Amazon simply promised more books than anyone else. It took a few years for the online retailer to grow large enough to threaten the big names—Borders, Barnes & Noble, and so on. But today, its competitive threat spreads far beyond bookstores to take on virtually any type of retailer you might find.

Consider, for example, evidence showing that Walmart is losing sales to Amazon. Now that Amazon stocks items such as baby formula, clothing, and electronic goods,

Rate this packaging: www.amazon
amazon.c

Amazon offers the largest variety and assortment of any retailer in the world.

often at lower prices than even the low-price master, people see little reason to fight with traffic or search for parking at the world's largest retailer. Instead, they sit at home and wait for the items to arrive. Won't be home during the day to receive your delivery? No problem—Amazon is testing an option to ship deliveries to local 7-Eleven convenience stores, then e-mail customers with bar codes that identify them, and their package, to the convenience store clerks.

As we know though, retail isn't simply about physical goods. It also includes services, and on that front, Amazon is also taking on a wide spread of competitors. It offers textbook rentals through its Kindle products to college students. The Kindle Lending Library allows Amazon Prime members to receive free books each month. It provides authors an easy route to self-publishing their work. Its cloud computing services are free for the first year— and its cloud offers enough storage for every person on the planet to store 82 books. With the Amazon Flow Powered app, shoppers in stores also can scan barcodes and find Amazon's (usually competitive) price immediately. And of course, for Prime customers, Amazon always offers free shipping.

But its influence is not all threat. For small-business owners, the opportunity to sell through Amazon provides unparalleled exposure. Amazon actively seeks small retailers with interesting products but insufficient resources to distribute those offerings widely. To them, Amazon is less a threat and more a golden opportunity.

Sources: Chantal Tode, "Amazon Makes Play for Greater Influence Over In-Store Shoppers," *Mobile Commerce Daily*, July 3, 2012; Brad Tuttle, "Today's Value Shopper Heads to Amazon, Not Walmart," *Time*, April 10, 2012; Greg Bensinger, "Amazon's Tough Call," *The Wall Street Journal*, July 11, 2012; Molly McHugh, "Saving Cash on College Textbooks," *Digital Trends*, July 18, 2011; Maggie Shader, "Amazon Tests After-Hours Package Pickup at 7-Eleven Locations," *Consumer Reports*, September 8, 2011; James Kendrick, "Amazon Debits Kindle Owner Lending Library," *ZDNet*, November 3, 2011; Vanchi Govind, "Amazon.com Offers Cloud Computing Services for Free," *InfoTech*, November 3, 2010; Jeffrey A. Trachtenberg, "Secret of Self-Publishing: Success," *The Wall Street Journal*, October 31, 2011; and Zoe Fox, "How Amazon Became the World's Largest Retailer," *Mashable*, November 17, 2011.

DISCUSSION QUESTIONS

What categories is Amazon competing in? Which retailers are they competing against?

FOOD RETAILERS

LO2

Categorize the various types of food retailers.

The food retailing landscape is changing dramatically. Twenty years ago, consumers purchased food primarily at conventional supermarkets. Now conventional supermarkets only account for slightly more than 60 percent of food sales (not including restaurants).[3] Not only do full-line discount stores like Walmart and Target now offer a full assortment of grocery items in their superstores, but traditional supermarkets also are carrying more nonfood items. Many supermarkets

	Estimated Sales, 2013 ($ millions)	Estimated Sales Growth 2008–2013 (%)
Food Retailers		
Conventional supermarkets	$622,896	3.3
Supercenters	354,905	7.1
Warehouse clubs	159,075	6.7
Convenience stores	748,186	3.0
General Merchandise Retailers		
Department stores	73,291	−0.9
Apparel and accessory specialty stores	210,236	4.5
Jewelry stores	36,848	3.4
Shoe stores	29,606	1.8
Furniture stores	66,262	2.2
Home furnishing stores	59,465	2.8
Office supply stores	26,404	2.2
Sporting goods stores	49,717	5.3
Bookstores	19,101	2.1
Building material, hardware, and garden supply stores	393,254	3.6
Consumer electronics and appliance stores	141,800	4.4
Drugstores	250,172	4.2
Full-line discount stores	126,385	0.0
Extreme-value stores	52,454	3.1
Nonstore Retailers		
Nonstore retailing	340,421	9.0
E-commerce	282,055	15.0

EXHIBIT 2–3
Sales and Growth Rate for Retail Sectors

Sources: *Economic Forecast: Outlook to 2013 Food, Drug, Mass* (Columbus, OH: Retail Forward, November 2008); *Economic Forecast: Outlook to 2013 Homegoods* (Columbus, OH.: Retail Forward, November 2008); *Economic Forecast: Outlook to 2013 Softgoods* (Columbus, OH: Retail Forward, November 2008).

offer pharmacies, health care clinics, banks, and cafés. Exhibit 2–3 contains information about the size and growth rates for each of these retail sectors.

The world's largest food retailer, Walmart, attains more than $443 billion in sales of supermarket-type merchandise. On this measure, it is followed by Carrefour (France), Tesco (United Kingdom), Metro Group (Germany), Schwartz Group (Germany), and Kroger (United States).[4] In North America specifically, the largest supermarket chains in order are Walmart, Kroger, Costco, Target, Safeway, Supervalu, Loblaw, Publix, and Ahold US.[5]

Kroger is the largest supermarket chain in the United States.

EXHIBIT 2–4
Characteristics of Food
Retailers

	Conventional Supermarket	Limited-Assortment Supermarket	Supercenter	Warehouse Club	Convenience Store
Percentage food	70–80	80–90	30–40	60	90
Size (000 sq. ft.)	35–40	7–10	160–200	100–150	3–5
SKUs (000)	30–40	1–1.5	100–150	20	2–3
Variety	Average	Narrow	Broad	Broad	Narrow
Assortment	Average	Shallow	Deep	Shallow	Shallow
Ambience	Pleasant	Minimal	Average	Minimal	Average
Service	Modest	Limited	Limited	Limited	Limited
Prices	Average	Lowest	Low	Low	High
Gross margin (%)	20–22	10–12	15–18	12–15	25–30

Despite their similarly large sizes, most of Walmart's food sales are generated from its supercenter format, whereas Carrefour garners most of its sales using the hypermarket format that it developed. The remaining larger food retailers primarily sell through conventional supermarkets. Exhibit 2–4 shows the retail mixes for different types of food retailers.

Supermarkets

A **conventional supermarket** is a large, self-service retail food store offering groceries, meat, and produce, as well as some nonfood items, such as health and beauty aids and general merchandise.[7] Perishables, including meat, produce, baked goods, and dairy products, account for 30 percent of supermarket sales and typically have higher margins than packaged goods.[8]

Whereas conventional supermarkets carry about 30,000 SKUs, **limited-assortment supermarkets,** or **extreme-value food retailers,** only stock about 1,500 SKUs.[10] The two largest limited-assortment supermarket chains in the United States are Save-A-Lot and ALDI.

Rather than carrying 20 brands of laundry detergent, limited-assortment supermarkets offer one or two brands and sizes, one of which is a store brand. Stores are designed to maximize efficiency and reduce costs. For example, merchandise is shipped in cartons on crates that can serve as displays so that no unloading is needed. Some costly services that consumers take for granted, such as free bags and paying with credit cards, are not provided. Stores are typically located in second- or third-tier shopping centers with low rents. By trimming costs, limited-assortment supermarkets can offer merchandise at prices 40 percent lower than those at conventional supermarkets.[11] These features have supported the substantial growth of such retailers, which appeal strongly to customers who are not loyal to national brands and more willing to try a store brand, especially if it means they pay lower prices.[12]

Trends in Supermarket Retailing   Although conventional supermarkets still sell the majority of food merchandise, they are under substantial competitive pressure on multiple sides: from supercenters, warehouse clubs, extreme-value retailers, convenience stores, and even drug stores.[13] All these types of retailers have increased the amount of space they devote to consumables. Family Dollar, which previously offered only discounted store brands, has expanded its assortment by about 20 percent, to include national brands such as Pepsi.[14]

Because consumers typically make three trips a week to buy food, but less than one trip a week to buy nonfood items, these competing retailers typically offer food merchandise to build the traffic in their stores and increase the sales of more profitable nonfood merchandise. They also have superior operating efficiencies and bargaining power with vendors that enable them to achieve low costs and offer low prices. These competing retailers have invested heavily in state-of-the-art supply chains, assortment planning, and pricing systems that reduce their inventories while increasing their sales and margins. These activities are discussed in more detail in Chapters 10 and 12.

To compete successfully against intrusions by other food retailing formats, conventional supermarkets are differentiating their offerings by (1) emphasizing fresh perishables, (2) targeting green and ethnic consumers, (3) providing better value with private-label merchandise, and (4) providing a better shopping experience.

Fresh Merchandise   Fresh-merchandise categories are located in the areas around the outer walls of a supermarket, known as the **"power perimeter,"** and include the dairy, bakery, meat, florist, produce, deli, and coffee bar. These departments attract consumers and are very profitable. Conventional supermarkets are building on their strength in these categories and devoting more space and attention to them. They are promoting fresh merchandise with cooking exhibitions and "action" stations, such as store-made sushi and freshly grilled meat. In response to this consumer desire for more and better fresh merchandise, food retailers such as Fresh Fare (Kroger) and Fresh Market are opening food stores focusing on the power perimeter merchandise.

Another example of the emphasis on "fresh" is the meal solutions offered to time-pressured consumers. A recent survey found that 64 percent of adult consumers have purchased ready-to-eat or heat-and-eat food from a grocery in the past month.[16] The choices in the stores are as varied as the stores themselves. Market District offers smoothies; Buehler's Fresh Food sells crab cakes and beef burgundy on a rotating "Dinner for 2" menu; Safeway's Lifestyle stores have sandwich and sushi stations. The ready-to-eat meals at a Publix store in Florida take up 4,500 square feet of space and include more than 80 entrees, such as cedar-plank salmon and Kung Pao scallops.[17]

Green Merchandise   Conventional supermarkets are offering more fair trade, natural, organic, and locally sourced foods for the growing segment of consumers who are health- and environmentally conscious. **Fair trade** is the practice of purchasing from factories that pay workers a living wage, considerably more than the prevailing minimum wage, and offer other benefits such as onsite medical treatment. Organic food purchases have jumped in recent years, with sales increasing by nearly 20 percent annually. Consumers also are buying a wider range of organic products, including staple items such as milk, eggs, and vegetables, as well as more fun options, such as ice cream and hair care products.[19]

Traditional supermarket chains also are opening smaller-format stores such as GreenWise Market (Publix) targeting health-conscious consumers who patronize Whole Foods. In a related food retailing trend, they offer locally grown products, a trend brought about in response to environmental concerns and the increasing financial costs (e.g., fuel) of transporting food long distances. The **locavore movement** focuses on reducing the carbon footprint caused by the

Health-conscious and environmentally conscious consumers are demanding organic and locally produced foods from food retailers.

transportation of food throughout the world. Food miles are calculated using the distance that foods travel from the farm to the plate. Many Americans appreciate the idea of supporting local businesses, but they also want the variety of products they can find everyday in their grocery store. It is difficult to maintain a balance between buying locally and maintaining such variety.

Ethnic Merchandise   Hispanics, who now constitute 15 percent of the U.S. population, have significantly different shopping and eating patterns from those of the general population.[20] They are more likely to prepare meals from scratch, spend more on groceries, prefer stores with bilingual staff and signage, and place importance on fresh food. In addition to adding more ethnic merchandise in conventional supermarkets, retailers are opening supermarkets targeting Hispanic consumers.

For example, Northgate markets in California cater to just Hispanic consumers. Their 36 stores, each approximately 50,000 square feet, feature both domestic and imported Latin American grocery items. Furthermore, they contain a dedicated tortilleria, prepared foods, and a well-stocked and staffed meat department.[21]

Supercenters offer a vast assortments under one roof.

Private-Label Merchandise   Conventional supermarket chains are leveraging their quality reputation to offer more private-label merchandise. Private-label brands (discussed in Chapter 13) benefit both customers and retailers. The benefits to customers include having more choices and finding the same ingredients and quality as in national brands at a lower price or higher quality at a similar price to the national brands. The benefits of private-label brands to retailers include increased store loyalty, the ability to differentiate themselves from the competition, lower promotional costs, and higher gross margins compared with national brands.

Improving the Shopping Experience   Creating an enjoyable shopping experience through better store ambience and customer service is another approach that supermarket chains use to differentiate themselves from low-cost, low-price competitors. Supermarkets are increasingly incorporating "food as theater" concepts, such as in-store restaurants, open-air market designs, cooking and nutrition classes, demonstrations, baby-sitting services, and food and wine tasting. To appeal to on-the-go consumers, other supermarkets are offering self-service kiosks that are both fun and convenient. Among the offerings, in place at both conventional supermarkets and limited-assortment stores, are Coinstar, a change counting machine; Redbox, a movie rental kiosk; and Starbucks kiosks selling freshly ground and brewed cups of its subbranded Seattle's Best Coffee.[22]

Supercenters

Supercenters are large stores (160,000 to 200,000 square feet) that combine a supermarket with a full-line discount store. Walmart operates more than 3,000 supercenters in the United States. Its leading competitors include Meijer, SuperTarget (Target),

Fred Meyer (Kroger), and Super Kmart Center (Sears Holding). By offering broad assortments of grocery and general merchandise products under one roof, supercenters provide a one-stop shopping experience.

General merchandise (nonfood) items are often purchased on impulse when customers' primary reason for coming to the supercenter is to buy groceries. General merchandise has higher margins, enabling the supercenters to price food items more aggressively. However, supercenters are very large, so some customers find them inconvenient because it can take a long time to find the items they want.

Hypermarkets are also large (160,000 to 200,000 square feet), combination food (60 to 70 percent) and general merchandise (30 to 40 percent) stores. The world's second-largest retailer, Carrefour, operates hypermarkets. Hypermarkets typically stock fewer SKUs than do supercenters—between 40,000 and 60,000 items, ranging from groceries, hardware, and sports equipment to furniture and appliances to computers and electronics.

Hypermarkets were created in France after World War II. By building large stores on the outskirts of metropolitan areas, French retailers could attract customers and not violate strict land-use laws. They have spread throughout Europe and become popular in some South American countries such as Argentina and Brazil.

Hypermarkets are not common in the United States, though they are similar to supercenters. Both hypermarkets and supercenters are large, carry grocery and general merchandise categories, offer self-service, and are located in warehouse-type structures with large parking facilities. However, hypermarkets carry a larger proportion of food items than do supercenters and have a greater emphasis on perishables—produce, meat, fish, and bakery items. Supercenters, in contrast, have a larger percentage of nonfood items and focus more on dry groceries, such as breakfast cereal and canned goods, instead of fresh items.

Both supercenters and hypermarkets face challenges in finding locations for new **big-box** (large, limited-service) **stores.** Although Brazil and China are promising emerging markets, many others are shrinking.[23] In Europe and Japan, land for building large stores is limited and expensive. New supercenters and hypermarkets in these areas often have to be multistory, which increases operating costs and reduces shopper convenience. Furthermore, some countries place restrictions on the size of new retail outlets. In the United States, there has been a backlash against large retail stores, particularly Walmart outlets. These opposing sentiments are based on local views that big-box stores drive local retailers out of business, offer low wages, provide nonunion jobs, have unfair labor practices, threaten U.S. workers through their purchase of imported merchandise, and cause excessive automobile and delivery truck traffic.

Warehouse Clubs

Warehouse clubs are retailers that offer a limited and irregular assortment of food and general merchandise with little service at low prices for ultimate consumers and small businesses. The largest warehouse club chains are Costco, Sam's Club (Walmart), and BJ's Wholesale Club (operating only on the East Coast of the United States). Customers are attracted to these stores because they

People go to warehouse clubs such as Costco to search for treasures like computers at prices lower than those of competitors.

can stock up on large packs of basics like paper towels, large-size packaged groceries like a quart of ketchup, best-selling books and CDs, fresh meat and produce, and an unpredictable assortment of upscale merchandise and services at low prices. For example, at Costco you can buy a 5-carat diamond ring for $99,999.99 with an appraised value of $153,450. Heavy food sampling adds to the shopping experience. Sam's Club focuses more on small businesses, providing services such as group health insurance as well as products. BJ's has beefed up its assortment of fresh meat and produce in recent years. Although package sizes are large compared to those in conventional grocery stores, BJ's provides convenient individual packaging—an attribute that is particularly appealing to its more upscale customers.

Warehouse clubs are large (100,000 to 150,000 square feet) and typically located in low-rent districts. They have simple interiors and concrete floors. Aisles are wide so that forklifts can pick up pallets of merchandise and arrange them on the selling floor. Little service is offered. Warehouse clubs can offer low prices because they use low-cost locations, have inexpensive store designs, and offer little customer service; they further keep inventory holding costs low by carrying a limited assortment of fast-selling items. In addition, they buy merchandise opportunistically. For example, if Hewlett-Packard is introducing new models of its printers, warehouse clubs will buy the inventory of the older models at a significant discount and then offer them for sale until the inventory is depleted.

Most warehouse clubs have two types of members: wholesale members who own small businesses and individual members who purchase for their own use. For example, many small restaurants are wholesale customers that buy their supplies, food ingredients, and desserts from a warehouse club rather than from food distributors. To cater to their business customers, warehouse clubs sell food items in very large containers and packages—sizes that also appeal to larger families. Typically, members pay an annual fee of around $50, which amounts to significant additional income for the chains.

REFACT

Food service sales account for 30 percent of in-store profits for convenience stores while accounting for only 17.3 percent of sales.[24]

Convenience Stores

Convenience stores provide a limited variety and assortment of merchandise at a convenient location in 3,000- to 5,000-square-foot stores with speedy checkout. Convenience stores enable consumers to make purchases quickly, without having to search through a large store and wait in a long checkout line. More than half the items bought are consumed within 30 minutes of purchase.

Convenience stores generally charge higher prices than supermarkets for similar products like milk, eggs, and bread. These products once represented the majority of their sales, but now the majority of sales come from lower profit products, such as gasoline and cigarettes, putting a strain on their profits.

Convenience stores also face increased competition from other formats. Supercenter and supermarket chains are attempting to appeal to customers by offering gasoline and tying gasoline sales to their frequent shopper programs. For example, shoppers who spend at least $50 and swipe their Giant Eagle Advantage Card at any

At convenience stores you can jump out of your car and pick up a Coke and some chewing gum while getting gas.

GetGo, Market District, Giant Eagle, or Giant Eagle Express location receive a 10-cent discount per gallon on their next fill-up.[25] Drugstores and full-line discount stores also have easily accessible areas of their stores filled with convenience store merchandise.

In response to these competitive pressures, convenience stores are taking steps to decrease their dependency on gasoline sales, tailor assortments to local markets, offer more fresh options, and make their stores even more convenient to shop. For example, to get gasoline customers to spend more on other merchandise and services, convenience stores are offering more food options that appeal to on-the-go consumers, especially women and young adults.[26] Finally, convenience stores are adding new services, such as financial service kiosks that give customers the opportunity to cash checks, pay bills, and buy prepaid telephone minutes, theater tickets, and gift cards.

To increase convenience, convenience stores are opening smaller stores close to where consumers shop and work. For example, 7-Eleven has stores in airports, office buildings, and schools. Easy access, storefront parking, and quick in-and-out access are key benefits offered by convenience stores. They also are exploring the use of technology to increase shopping convenience. Sheetz, a Pennsylvania-based convenience store chain, has touch-screen "Made-to-Order" kiosks at which customers can order customized deli sandwiches, wraps, salads, subs, and nachos while pumping gasoline.[28] Retailing View 2.2 describes the difference between convenience stores in the United States and Japan.

REFACT

Gasoline sales at combination gas station–convenience stores contribute 71 percent of the store's sales. Cigarette and tobacco products contribute 38 percent of in-store merchandise sales.[27]

RETAILING VIEW   Convenience Stores in Japan Are Different   2.2

Japanese corporations might own several U.S. convenience store chains (e.g., 7-Eleven, Circle K), but convenience stores (*konbinis*) in Japan and in the United States have little in common. Whereas shoppers in the United States depend heavily on their cars, most Japanese consumers commute using public transportation and work very long hours. To be convenient, the convenience stores thus locate in central business districts and train and subway stations. Rather than gasoline, *konbinis* sell a broad assortment of services, in addition to their extensive food options, including concert and amusement park tickets. Shoppers can pay their bills or make copies, as well as pick up some fashionable clothing. In turn, Japanese consumers visit convenience stores for approximately 30 percent of their food purchases, whereas in the United States, convenience stores only account for 5 to 10 percent of this market.

Part of the reason for this greater share is the quality of food available in *konbinis*. Whereas late night U.S. snackers might embrace microwaveable burritos, *konbinis* often offer pasta dishes, fresh vegetables, fruit, and prepared meals of restaurant quality. Although they traditionally catered to male customers, more Japanese women in the workforce have led the *konbinis* to adjust their assortments accordingly. A traditional bento box might contain rice with grilled fish or fatty meat—a meal not particularly appealing to female customers. Instead, today's chains prepare healthier food in nicer looking packages, such as *pho* Vietnamese-style noodles; soup in bowls; and elaborate, high-quality desserts.

With their relatively small sizes—around 300 to 600 square feet—and limited storage space, Japanese convenience stores need stellar information and supply chain management capabilities to succeed. That is, they must precisely match store-specific demand with just-in-time supply provisions. The most successful store operators gather customer information during every checkout: automatically, with a system that specifies the time of purchase, product barcode, and price, and manually, when the cashier notes the customer's approximate age and gender. An efficient data analysis system then determines when, how, and what to send to restock each *konbini*. Some stores even might receive up to seven restocking deliveries per day.

Sources: Kazuaki Nagata, "Convenience Store Chains Go With Flow, Grow," *The Japan Times,* May 8, 2012; and Stephanie Strom, "7-Eleven Shifts Focus to Healthier Food Options," *The New York Times,* December, 2012, p. B.1.

REFACT

Convenience store operator 7-Eleven has replaced McDonald's as the world's largest chain in terms of number of outlets. As of July 2012, 7-Eleven had a total of 46,000 stores in 16 countries, compared with 33,510 McDonald's outlets.[29]

DISCUSSION QUESTION

Would Japanese-style convenience stores be successful in the United States? Why or why not?

GENERAL MERCHANDISE RETAILERS

LO3

Identify the various types of general merchandise retailers.

The major types of general merchandise retailers are department stores, full-line discount stores, specialty stores, drugstores, category specialists, extreme-value retailers, off-price retailers, and outlet stores. Exhibit 2–5 summarizes the characteristics of general merchandise retailers that sell through stores.

Department Stores

REFACT

T. Stewart was the first U.S. department store, opening in 1847 in New York.[31]

Department stores are retailers that carry a broad variety and deep assortment, offer customer services, and organize their stores into distinct departments for displaying merchandise. The largest department store chains in the United States are Sears, Macy's, Kohl's, JCPenney, Nordstrom, and Dillards.[30]

Traditionally, department stores attracted customers by offering a pleasing ambience, attentive service, and a wide variety of merchandise under one roof. They sold both **soft goods** (nondurable or consumable goods), which have a shorter lifespan such as cosmetics, clothing, and bedding) and **hard goods,** also known as **durable goods,** which are manufactured items that are expected to last several years, such as appliances, furniture, and consumer electronics. But now, most department stores focus almost exclusively on soft goods. The major departments are women's, men's, and children's apparel; home furnishings; cosmetics; kitchenware; and small appliances. Each department within the store has a specific selling space allocated to it, as well as salespeople to assist customers. The department store often resembles a collection of specialty shops.

Department store chains can be categorized into three tiers. The first tier includes upscale, high-fashion chains with exclusive designer merchandise and excellent customer service, such as Neiman Marcus, Bloomingdale's (part of Macy's Inc.), Nordstrom, and Saks Fifth Avenue (part of Saks Inc.). Macy's and Dillards are in the second tier of traditional department stores, in which retailers sell more modestly priced merchandise with less customer service. The value-oriented third tier—Sears, JCPenney, and Kohl's—caters to more price-conscious consumers.

Department stores account for some of retailing's most cherished traditions—special events and parades (Macy's Thanksgiving parade in New York City), Santa Claus lands, and holiday decorations. But many consumers question the benefits and costs of shopping at department stores. Department stores are not

EXHIBIT 2–5   Characteristics of General Merchandise Retailers

Type	Variety	Assortment	Service	Prices	Size (000 sq. ft.)	SKUs (000)	Location
Department stores	Broad	Deep to average	Average to high	Average to high	100–200	100	Regional malls
Discount stores	Broad	Average to shallow	Low	Low	60–80	30	Stand alone, power strip centers
Category specialists	Narrow	Very deep	Low to high	Low	50–100	20–40	Stand alone, power strip centers
Specialty stores	Narrow	Deep	High	High	4–12	5	Regional malls
Home improvement centers	Narrow	Very deep	Low to high	Low	80–120	20–40	Stand alone, power strip centers
Drugstores	Narrow	Very deep	Average	Average to high	3–15	10–20	Stand alone, strip centers
Off-price stores	Average	Deep but varying	Low	Low	20–30	50	Outlet malls
Extreme-value retailers	Average	Average and varying	Low	Low	7–15	3–4	Urban, strip

Macy's is a very popular department store known for great sales.

as convenient as discount stores, such as Target, because they are located in large regional malls rather than local neighborhoods. JCPenney and Sears thus are following Kohl's by opening stores in nonmall locations. Customer service has diminished in the second- and third-tier stores because of the retailers' desire to increase profits by reducing labor costs.[32]

To deal with their eroding market share, department stores are (1) increasing the amount of exclusive merchandise they sell, (2) increasing their use of private-label merchandise, (3) expanding their multichannel presence.

- *Increase exclusive merchandise.* To differentiate their merchandise offerings and strengthen their image, department stores are aggressively seeking **exclusive brands** in which national brand vendors sell them merchandise that is not available elsewhere. Jennifer Lopez has a clothing line at Kohl's. Ralph Lauren designed a line of casual apparel exclusively for JCPenney called American Living. Furthermore, clothing is not the only category with exclusive lines: Customers looking for exclusive dinnerware collections can go to Macy's and get the Rachel Bilson line or else find the Kardashian Kollection at Sears.[33]

- *Increase private-label merchandise.* Department stores are placing more emphasis on developing their own **private-label brands,** or **store brands.** These items are developed and marketed by the retailer, available only in its stores. Macy's has been very successful in developing a strong image for its brands, including Alfani (women's fashion), Hotel Collection (luxury fabrics), and Tools of the Trade (housewares).[35]

- *Expand multichannel and social media presence.* Finally, like most retailers, most department stores have become active participants in multichannel retailing. At Macy's and Nordstrom, customers can buy or reserve products online and then pick them up at the store. Customers can also return online purchases to stores. At Macy's and JCPenney, sales associates can order out-of-stock merchandise online via their point-of-sale (POS) terminals and have it delivered directly to the customer. As Retailing View 2.3 describes, Nordstrom may be one of the most connected companies in the world.

REFACT

Almost 50 percent of JCPenney sales involve exclusive lines. Kohl's sells approximately 48 percent, and Macy's level is 40 percent of total sales.[34]

50   SECTION I   The World of Retailing

2.3   RETAILING VIEW   Going Where the Customers Are

For Nordstrom, electronic offerings, such as a Facebook site or allowing customers to order online and pick up their purchases in stores, are old news. Its forward-looking, aggressive approach to social and mobile retailing has earned Nordstrom widespread recognition as a leader in terms of its connectivity—as well as a strong competitive advantage as retail continues to go virtual.

Back in 2010, Nordstrom introduced free wi-fi availability in its stores. This move exemplifies its superior recognition of how modern customers shop. Nearly all its in-store merchandise is available on its website. Furthermore, sales personnel are equipped with iPod Touch and iPad devices so that they can help a customer check out immediately, track inventory levels, and get suggestions for various departments. Staff members also are encouraged to interact with customers through social media, following Nordstrom's detailed guidelines. Such efforts reflect its goal to achieve seamless integration in its customer engagement, whether online, through mobile devices, or in stores.

Continuing its cutting-edge approach, social media for Nordstrom goes far beyond the basics of Facebook, Twitter, and YouTube. It also makes it presence felt on Pinterest, the online bulletin board; Instagram, Facebook's photo-sharing site; and the fashionista meeting place Polyvore. As a Nordstrom representative asserted, "Some people look at it as, 'If you have a Facebook site,

then you've got a social media strategy.' I think that's shortsighted."

To expand its online reach, Nordstrom has turned to an acquisitions strategy, purchasing shares in the flash sale site HauteLook, the children's clothing retailer Peek, the Sole Society shoe club, and the rapidly growing Bonobos menswear site. It also purchased advertising space in places with widespread reach, like in the massively popular Words with Friends game application.

Its efforts have paid off, not only in its image as a connected retailer, but also in the bottom line. It has attracted more than 1 million followers on Twitter. And the retailer's Internet sales grew by 30 percent in 2011. This result has prompted it to invest even more in its e-commerce efforts, up to $140 million in 2012.

Sources: David Hatch, "Nordstrom in Fashion with Social Media, Mobile Tech," *U.S. News and World Report*, May 15, 2012; Rimma Kats, "Nordstrom Put Focus on Social with New Media Initiative," *Mobile Marketer*, June 11, 2012; Sherilynn Macale, "This Retailer's Social-Powered Santa Claus Puts the Christmas Spirit Back in Gift Giving," *The Next Web*, November 25, 2011; and "Social Networking Guidelines," http://shop.nordstrom.com/c/social-networking-guidelines.

DISCUSSION QUESTION

How is social media helping Nordstrom stay connected with its customer base?

Full-Line Discount Stores

Full-line discount stores are retailers that offer a broad variety of merchandise, limited service, and low prices. Discount stores offer both private labels and national brands. The largest full-line discount store chains are Walmart, Target, and Kmart (Sears Holding). However, these full-line discount stores confront intense competition from category specialists that focus on a single category of merchandise, such as Staples, Best Buy, Bed Bath & Beyond, Sports Authority, and Lowe's.

In response, Walmart has taken a couple of routes. First, it has converted many of its discount stores into supercenters,[36] which are more efficient than traditional discount stores because of the economies of scale that result from the high traffic generated by the food offering. Second, it is expanding into more urban locations, using smaller storefronts that can be located in existing buildings, and appealing to price-oriented markets.[37]

Target has experienced considerable growth in the last decade because its stores offer fashionable merchandise at low prices in a pleasant shopping environment. It has developed an image of "cheap chic," continuously offering limited-edition exclusive apparel and cosmetic lines. In its GO International campaign, the retailer has teamed with such well-known designers as Missoni, Stefani, Harajuku Mini, Albertus Swanepoel, and Josie Natori.[38]

In contrast, Sears—and its Kmart brand—has struggled a bit in recent years and therefore is attempting an innovative and unusual solution. It will lease retail space in its stores to independent merchants. For example, in a huge Sears store in California, Western Athletic has leased approximately one-quarter of the space to insert a health club.[40]

REFACT

Hudson's Bay Company, the oldest retailer in North America, conquered the Canadian wilderness by trading furs more than 300 years ago. Today, it is one of the largest retailers in Canada, operating chains of discount, department, and home stores.[39]

Apparel/Shoe/ Accessories	Furniture	Sporting Goods	Office Supply
Mens Wearhouse	IKEA	Bass Pro Shops Outdoor World	Office Depot
DSW	Pier 1	Cabela's	Staples
Books	Sofa Express	Dick's Sporting Goods	Office Max
Barnes & Noble	**Home**	L.L. Bean	**Pet Supplies**
Consumer Electronics	Bed Bath & Beyond	Golfsmith	PetSmart
Best Buy	The Container Store	REI	PETCO
Crafts	World Market	Sports Authority	**Musical Instruments**
Michaels	**Home Improvement**	**Toys**	Guitar Center
	Home Depot	Toys "R" Us	
	Lowe's		

EXHIBIT 2–6
Category Specialists

Category Specialists

Category specialists are big-box stores that offer a narrow but deep assortment of merchandise. Exhibit 2–6 lists some of the largest category specialists in the United States.

Most category specialists predominantly use a self-service approach, but they offer assistance to customers in some areas of the stores. For example, Staples stores have a warehouse atmosphere, with cartons of copy paper stacked on pallets, plus equipment in boxes on shelves. But in some departments, such as computers and other high-tech products, it provides salespeople in the display area to answer questions and make suggestions. Bass Pro Shops Outdoor World is a category specialist offering merchandise for outdoor recreational activities. The stores offer everything a person needs for hunting and fishing—from 27-cent plastic bait to boats and recreational vehicles costing $45,000. Sales associates are knowledgeable outdoors people. Each is hired for a particular department that matches that person's expertise. All private-branded products are field-tested by Bass Pro Shops' professional teams: the Redhead Pro Hunting Team and Tracker Pro Fishing Team.

By offering a complete assortment in a category, category specialists can "kill" a category of merchandise for other retailers and thus are frequently called **category killers.** Using their category dominance and buying power, they buy products at low prices and are ensured of supply when items are scarce. Department stores and full-line discount stores located near category specialists often have to reduce their offerings in the category because consumers are drawn to the deep assortment and competitive prices at the category killer.

Although category specialists compete with other types of retailers, competition between them is intense. Competing category specialists such as Lowe's and Home Depot, or Staples and Office Depot, have difficulty differentiating themselves on most of the elements of their retail mixes. They all provide similar assortments because they have similar access to national brands, and they all provide a similar level of service. Primarily then, they compete on price and location. Some category specialists are also experiencing intense competition from warehouse clubs like Sam's Club and Costco.[42]

REFACT

The three office superstore chains—Staples, Office Depot, and Office Max—dominate the business with a combined $41.6 billion in annual sales, out of an estimated $100 billion market. They generally have margins of 25 to 28 percent of sales, higher than their warehouse club competition, Sam's Club and Costco.[41]

Category specialists, like Staples, offer a deep assortment of merchandise at low prices.

Therefore, many of them are attempting to differentiate themselves with customer service. For example, Home Depot and Lowe's hire experienced builders as sales associates to help customers with electrical and plumbing repairs. They also provide classes to train home owners in tiling, painting, and other tasks to give shoppers the confidence to tackle their do-it-yourself (DIY) projects on their own. Home Depot offers an integrated line of Martha Stewart brand products, with different themes marked by unique icons, such that a customer can create a professional-looking decorated space simply by choosing products with matching icons.[44] Besides beefing up its sales associates' training to help customers purchase high-tech products like computers and printers, Staples has implemented "Easy Tech" in its stores to help people with computer and related problems and has installed Staples Copy and Print shops to compete with FedEx Office.

Specialty Stores

Specialty stores concentrate on a limited number of complementary merchandise categories and provide a high level of service. Exhibit 2–7 lists some of the largest specialty store chains.

Specialty stores tailor their retail strategy toward very specific market segments by offering deep but narrow assortments and sales associate expertise. Victoria's Secret is the leading specialty retailer of lingerie and beauty products in the United States. Using a multipronged location strategy that includes malls, lifestyle centers, and central business districts, the company conveys its message using supermodels and world-famous runway shows.[45]

Sephora, France's leading perfume and cosmetic chain—a division of luxury-goods conglomerate LVMH (Louis Vuitton-Moet Hennessy)—is another example of an innovative specialty store concept. Sephora provides a cosmetic and perfume specialty store offering a deep assortment in a self-service format. It also maintains separate stores-within-stores at JCPenney. The approximately 15,000 SKUs and 200 brands, including its own private-label brand, are grouped by product category instead of by brand like in department stores, with brands displayed alphabetically so customers can locate them easily. Customers are free to shop and experiment on their own. Sampling is encouraged. Knowledgeable salespeople are available to assist customers. The low-key environment results in customers' spending more time shopping.

Specialty retailers have such great appeal that they rank among the most profitable and fastest growing firms in the world. Apple stores sell a remarkable

EXHIBIT 2–7
Specialty Store
Retailers

Apparel	Electronics/Software	Jewelry	GNC
Abercrombie & Fitch	Ascend Acoustics	Blue Nile	Kiehl's
Brooks Brothers	Apple	Tiffany & Co.	M.A.C.
The Buckle	Brookstone	Zales	MakeupMania.com
Forever 21	Crutchfield		
The Gap	GameStop	**Optical**	Sephora
H&M	Newegg	1-800 Contacts	**Shoes**
Indochino.com	Radio Shack	LensCrafters	ALDO
Ralph Lauren	Tiger Direct	Pearle Vision	Allen Edmonds
J. Crew		Sunglass Hut	FootLocker
Threadless	**Housewares**		Nine West
Urban Outfitters	Crate & Barrel	**Health/Beauty**	Steve Madden
Victoria's Secret	Pottery Barn	Aveda	The Walking Company
Zara	Sur la Table	Bath & Body Works	
	Williams Sonoma	The Body Shop	Zappos

$5,647 per square foot on average, and its stock price jumped more than 25 percent in 2011. Lululemon's specialty is far less technical, involving yoga-inspired apparel and accessories, but it keeps opening its specialty stores at a remarkable rate of several per month. These stores earn an average of $1,800 per square foot.[46]

Charming Charlie stores are not quite as well known as the preceding brands, but the small company's success confirms the appeal of specialty retailers. In just seven years, the accessories and jewelry chain has grown to 178 stores, spread over 33 states. Its rapid growth is well matched by its influence: It was one of the first retailers to group merchandise by color instead of category. Furthermore, it works to maintain affordable prices ranging from less than $5 to no more than $50. That is, this specialty store specializes in helping customers update their wardrobes with new pieces, rather than forcing them to start all over again.[47]

In addition, many manufacturers have opened their own specialty stores. Consider, for instance, Levi's (jeans and casual apparel), Godiva (chocolate), Cole Haan (shoes and accessories), Lacoste (apparel), Coach (purses and leather accessories), Tumi (luggage), Wolford (intimate apparel), Lucky brand (jeans and casual apparel), Samsonite (luggage), and Polo/Ralph Lauren (apparel and home). Tired of being at the mercy of retailers to purchase and merchandise their products, these manufacturers and specialty retailers can control their own destiny by operating their own stores.

Another growing specialty store sector is the resale store. Resale stores are retailers that sell secondhand or used merchandise. A special type of resale store is the **thrift store,** where merchandise is donated and proceeds go to charity. Another type of resale store is the **consignment shop,** a store that accepts used merchandise from people and pays them after it is sold. Resale stores earn national revenues of more than $13 billion. They also have enjoyed double-digit growth rates in the past few years.[49] Although the ambiance of resale stores traditionally was less appealing than that of other clothing or housewares retailers, the remarkable prices for used merchandise drew in customers.

Today, many resale stores also have increased their value by making their shopping space more pleasant and increasing levels of service.[50] With their lower expenses (in that they pay a discounted price to people selling their used apparel), resale stores are moving into storefronts in higher-end locations that have been abandoned by traditional retailers.[51]

Perhaps the best known and most widely expanded thrift shop is Goodwill Industries. In addition to its retail outlets, Goodwill runs an extensive job training and placement division, such that customers shopping at these outlets get a warm glow from knowing that their purchases help others. Unlike most other resale stores, Goodwill accepts all goods. The old stereotype of a cluttered, dark, odd-smelling Goodwill store has changed. The company has revamped and updated stores nationwide. Local stores seek to meet local needs, such that the New England–area Goodwill stores host annual bridal dress sales, and the Suncoast division in Florida maintains a catering department.[52]

Sephora is an innovative specialty store selling perfume and cosmetics.

REFACT

Approximately 16 to 18 percent of Americans shop at thrift resale stores.[48]

Drugstores

Drugstores are specialty stores that concentrate on health and beauty care (HBC) products. Many drug stores have steadily increased the space devoted to cosmetics. Prescription pharmaceuticals often represent almost 65 percent of drugstore sales.[53]

The largest drugstore chains in the United States are Walgreens, CVS, and Rite Aid, which together run more than 36,000 stores, or 60 percent of the drug stores in the United States.[54] Much of this increased concentration has occurred through mergers and acquisitions. For instance, CVS acquired Longs, Sav-On, and Osco (as well as Caremark, which manages the prescription drug aspect for many insurance plans); Rite Aid acquired Brooks and Eckerd.

Drugstores face competition from pharmacies in discount stores and from pressure to reduce health care costs. In response, the major drugstore chains are offering a wider assortment of merchandise, including more frequently purchased food items, as well as new services, such as the convenience of drive-through windows for picking up prescriptions, in-store medical clinics, and even makeovers and spa treatments.[55]

In the Duane Reade store on Wall Street, near the New York Stock Exchange, customers find a vast array of offerings, such as $10 manicures, a hair salon staffed by a dedicated beauty consultant, a juice bar, and sushi chefs, next to typical drugstore products. Medical questions can be answered by the doctor who works there. In this store, the top sellers are now sushi, fresh juice, and bananas—though customers have not changed completely, so rounding out the top five sellers are coffee and Marlboro cigarettes.[56]

Walgreens hosts a café in its Chicago flagship store, where customers waiting to pick up a prescription can enjoy fresh coffee, breads, and pastries; munch on sushi or sandwiches; or visit the juice bar for a healthy smoothie or a nostalgic chocolate malted milkshake. But if they stop by later in the day, shoppers might prefer to browse the store's stock of 700 fine wines, artisanal cheeses, and gourmet chocolates.[57]

Although drugstores thus offer major advantages, especially in terms of convenience, they suffer from a price comparison when it comes to their grocery merchandise. A recent study indicated that the same selection of goods that cost $75.60 at a supermarket would run customers $102.94 at a nearby drug store.[58]

REFACT

Walgreens' merger/acquisition of Alliance Boots has resulted in the largest pharmaceutical distribution network with more than 11,000 stores in 12 countries.[59]

Extreme-Value Retailers

Extreme-value retailers, also called **dollar stores,** are small discount stores that offer a broad variety but shallow assortment of household goods, health and beauty care (HBC) products, and groceries. The largest extreme-value retailers are Dollar General and Family Dollar.[60] As noted in the discussion of trends in food retailing, these stores have been expanding their assortments to include more private-label options, food, tobacco, and impulse buys such as candy, magazines, and gift cards.[61] Some extreme-value retailers, such as Dollar General, are adding refrigerated coolers and expanding their food offerings so that they can be known as the best destination store for a greater variety of household necessities. As a result, this retail model continues to attract significantly increasing numbers of shopper visits.[62]

Extreme-value retailers primarily target low-income consumers. These customers want well-known brands but cannot afford to buy the large-size packages offered by full-line discount stores or warehouse clubs. Vendors such as Procter & Gamble often create special, smaller packages for extreme-value retailers. Because these stores appeal to low-income consumers, are located where they live, and have expanded their assortments while keeping their unit prices low, they have cut into other retailers' businesses, including Walmart. Always ready for a good competitive battle, Walmart is opening smaller stores called Walmart Express in urban locations and creating smaller and less expensive packages to better compete.[63]

What you can still get for a dollar?

Despite some of these chains' names, few just sell merchandise for a dollar. The two largest—Dollar General and Family Dollar—do not employ a strict dollar limit and sell merchandise for up to $20. The names imply a good value but do not limit customers to the arbitrary dollar price point. Dollar Tree experimented with selling merchandise for more than a dollar, but it is back to being a dollar purist.[65]

Off-Price Retailers

Off-price retailers offer an inconsistent assortment of brand-name merchandise at a significant discount off the manufacturers' suggested retail price (MSRP). America's largest off-price retail chains are TJX Companies (which operates TJ Maxx, Marshalls, Winners, HomeGoods, TKMaxx, AJWright, and HomeSense), Ross Stores, Burlington Coat Factory, and Big Lots. Overstock.com and Bluefly.com are the largest Internet off-price retailers.

Off-price retailers are able to sell brand-name and even designer-label merchandise at 20 to 60 percent lower than the manufacturer's suggested retail price because of their unique buying and merchandising practices. Much of the merchandise is bought opportunistically from manufacturers that have overruns, canceled orders, forecasting mistakes causing excess inventory, closeouts, and irregulars. They also buy excess inventory from other retailers. **Closeouts** are end-of-season merchandise that will not be used in following seasons. **Irregulars** are merchandise with minor mistakes in construction. Off-price retailers can buy at low prices because they do not ask suppliers for advertising allowances, return privileges, markdown adjustments, or delayed payments. (These terms and conditions for buying merchandise are detailed in Chapter 13.)

Due to this opportunistic buying, customers cannot be confident that the same type of merchandise will be in stock each time they visit the store. Different bargains will be available on each visit. For many off-price shoppers, inconsistency is exactly why they like to go there. They enjoy hunting for hidden treasures. To improve their offerings' consistency, some off-price retailers complement their opportunistically bought merchandise with merchandise purchased at regular wholesale prices. Although not well known because few vendors to off-price retailers want to advertise their presence, the CEO of TJX asserts that the vast majority

Luxury merchandise at great prices.

of merchandise in its stores is same-season items, purchased directly from manufacturers.[66] She also claims less than 5 percent of TJX merchandise is irregular.

An online twist to off-price retailing are flash-sale sights such as Gilt Groupe, Rue La La, and HauteLook. They are called **flash sales** because each day at the same time, members receive an e-mail that announces the deals available. Each deal lasts for a specific and limited time, and the sales are first-come, first-served. A shopper who misses out on a great deal is far more likely to buy the next time around. These sites often require members to register.

A special type of off-price retailer is the outlet store. **Outlet stores** are off-price retailers owned by manufacturers or retailers. Those owned by manufacturers are also referred to as **factory outlets.** Manufacturers view outlet stores as an opportunity to improve their revenues from irregulars, production overruns, and merchandise returned by retailers. Others view it as simply another channel in which to sell their merchandise. Retailers with strong brand names such as Saks Fifth Avenue (Saks Fifth Avenue's Off 5th) and Williams-Sonoma operate outlet stores too. By selling excess merchandise in outlet stores rather than at markdown prices in their primary stores, these department and specialty store chains can maintain an image of offering desirable merchandise at full price.[67] For some retailers, their outlet stores are the wave of the future. Nordstrom expects that sometime soon, it will have more Nordstrom Rack stores than regular Nordstrom department stores.[68]

Outlet stores can have an adverse effect on profits, however, because they shift sales from full-price retailers to the lower-priced outlets. Additionally, outlet stores are becoming more promotional to compete with increased activity at other outlet stores within the same mall and with traditional off-price stores.[69]

SERVICE RETAILING

LO4

Explain the differences between service and merchandise retailers.

The retail firms discussed in the previous sections sell products to consumers. However, **service retailers,** or firms that primarily sell services rather than merchandise, are a large and growing part of the retail industry. Consider a typical Saturday: After a bagel and cup of coffee at a nearby Einstein Bros. Bagels, you go to the laundromat to wash and dry your clothes, drop a suit off at a dry cleaner, leave your computer to be serviced by the Geek Squad at Best Buy, and make your way to Jiffy Lube to have your car's oil changed. In a hurry, you drive through a Taco Bell so that you can eat lunch quickly and not be late for your 1:00 p.m. haircut. By midafternoon, you're ready for a workout at your health club. After stopping at home for a change of clothes, you're off to dinner, a movie, and finally clubbing with a friend. You end your day having interacted with 10 different services retailers throughout the day.

Several trends suggest considerable future growth in service retailing. For example, the aging population will increase demand for health care services. Younger people are also spending more time and money on health and fitness. Busy parents in two-income families are willing to pay to have their homes cleaned, lawns maintained, clothes washed and pressed, and meals prepared so that they can spend more time with their families.

Exhibit 2–8 shows the wide variety of services, along with some national companies that provide these services. These companies are retailers because they sell

Type of Service	Service Retail Firms
Airlines	American, Southwest, British Airways, JetBlue
Automobile maintenance and repair	Jiffy Lube, Midas, AAMCO
Automobile rental	Hertz, Avis, Budget, Enterprise
Banks	Citi, Wachovia, Bank of America
Child care centers	Kindercare, Gymboree
Dry cleaners	Zoots
Education	Babson College, University of Florida, Princeton Review
Entertainment	Disney World, Six Flags, Chuck E. Cheese, Dave & Busters
Express package delivery	FedEx, UPS, U.S. Postal Service
Fast food	Wendy's, McDonald's, Starbucks
Financial services	Merrill Lynch, Morgan Stanley, American Express, VISA
Fitness	Jazzercise, Bally's, Gold's Gym
Health care	Humana, HCA, Kaiser
Home maintenance	Chemlawn, Mini Maid, Roto-Rooter
Hotels and motels	Hyatt, Sheraton, Marriott, Days Inn
Income tax preparation	H&R Block
Insurance	Allstate, State Farm, Geico
Internet access/electronic information	Google, Internet Explorer, Mozilla Firefox, Safari
Movie theaters	AMC, Odeon/Cineplex
QSR	Panera Bread, Red Mango, Pinkberry
Real estate	Century 21, Coldwell Banker
Restaurants	Applebees's, Cheesecake Factory
Truck rentals	U-Haul, Ryder
Weight loss	Weight Watchers, Jenny Craig, Curves
Video rental	Blockbuster
Vision centers	LensCrafters, Pearle

EXHIBIT 2–8
Services Retailers

goods and services to consumers. However, some are not just retailers. For example, airlines, banks, hotels, and insurance and express mail companies sell their services to businesses as well as consumers.

Organizations such as banks, hospitals, health spas, legal clinics, entertainment firms, and universities that offer services to consumers traditionally have not considered themselves retailers. Yet due to increased competition, these organizations are adopting retailing principles to attract customers and satisfy their needs. For example, Zoots is a dry-cleaning chain in the Boston area.[70] Founded by a former Staples executive, Zoots has adopted many retailing best practices: It has convenient locations, and it offers pickup and delivery service. Zoots stores also provide extended hours, are open on weekends, and offer a drop-off option for those who cannot get to the store during operating hours. The stores are bright and clean. Customers can check their order status, schedule a pickup, and provide special instructions using the online MY ZOOTS service. Clerks are taught to welcome customers and acknowledge their presence, especially if there is a line.

Most retailers provide both merchandise and services for their customers. However, the emphasis placed on the merchandise versus the service differs across retail formats, as Exhibit 2–9 shows. On the left side of the exhibit

Going to Zoots to pick up laundry and dry cleaning is as easy as going to an ATM machine.

EXHIBIT 2–9   Continuum of Merchandise and Services Retailers

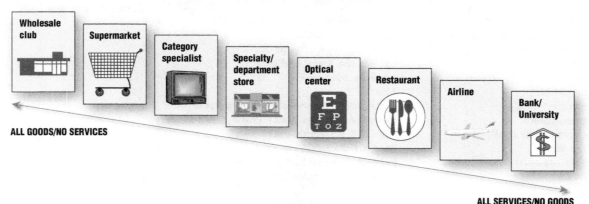

are supermarkets and warehouse clubs. These retail formats consist of self-service stores that offer very few services, except perhaps cashing checks and assisting customers at checkout.

Moving along the continuum from left to right, department and specialty stores provide higher levels of service. In addition to providing assistance from sales associates, they offer services such as gift wrapping, bridal registries, and alterations. Optical centers and restaurants lie somewhere in the middle of the merchandise-service continuum. In addition to selling frames, eyeglasses, and contact lenses, optical centers provide important services like eye examinations and eyeglass fittings. Similarly, restaurants offer food plus a place to eat, music in the background, a pleasant ambience, and table service.

As we move to the right end of the continuum, we encounter retailers whose offerings are primarily services. However, even these retailers have some products associated with the services offered, such as a meal on an airplane or a checkbook at a bank.

Differences between Service and Merchandise Retailers

Four important differences in the nature of the offerings provided by services and merchandise retailers are (1) intangibility, (2) simultaneous production and consumption, (3) perishability, and (4) inconsistency of the offering to customers.

Intangibility   Services are less tangible than products—customers cannot see or touch them. They are performances or actions rather than objects. For example, health care services cannot be seen or touched by a patient. Intangibility introduces several challenges for services retailers. Because customers cannot touch and feel services, it is difficult for them to evaluate services before they buy them or even after they buy and consume them. Due to the intangibility of their offerings, services retailers often use tangible symbols to inform customers about the quality of their services. For example, lawyers frequently have elegant, carpeted offices with expensive antique furniture. Services retailers also have difficulty evaluating the quality of services they are providing. For example, it can be hard for a law firm to evaluate how well its lawyers are performing their jobs. To determine the quality of their offerings, services retailers often solicit customer evaluations and scrutinize complaints. In addition, online evaluation systems such as Angie's List and Yelp compile reviews from other consumers. The summary reviews give a sense of how well the service provider performs, according to people who have already purchased the service.

Simultaneous Production and Consumption   Products are typically made in a factory, stored and sold by a retailer, and then used by consumers in their homes. Service providers, however, create and deliver the service as the customer is consuming it. For example, when you eat at a restaurant, the meal is prepared and consumed almost at the same time. The simultaneity of production and consumption also creates some special problems for services retailers. First, the customers are present when the service is produced, may even have an opportunity to see it produced, and in some cases may be part of the production process. For example, customers at Build-A-Bear Workshop make their own teddy bears. Second, other customers consuming the service at the same time can affect the quality of the service provided. For example, an obnoxious passenger next to you on an airplane can make the flight very unpleasant. Third, services retailers often do not get a second chance to satisfy the needs of their customers. Whereas customers can return damaged merchandise to a store, customers who are dissatisfied with services have limited recourse. Thus, it is critical for services retailers to get it right the first time.

Because services are produced and consumed at the same time, it is difficult to reduce costs through mass production. For this reason, most services retailers are small, local firms. Some national services retailers are able to reduce costs by "industrializing" the services they offer. They make substantial investments in equipment and training to provide a uniform service.

Perishability   Services are perishable. They cannot be saved, stored, or resold. Once an airplane takes off with an empty seat, the sale is lost forever. In contrast, merchandise can be held in inventory until a customer is ready to buy it. Due to the perishability of services, services retailing must match supply and demand. Most services retailers have a capacity constraint, and their capacity cannot be changed easily. There are a fixed number of tables in a restaurant, seats in a classroom, beds in a hospital, and electricity that can be generated by a power plant. To increase capacity, services retailers need to make major investments, such as buying more airplanes or building an addition to increase the size of the hospital or restaurant. In addition, demand for service varies considerably over time. Consumers are most likely to fly on airplanes during holidays and the summer, eat in restaurants at lunch- and dinnertime, and use electricity in the evening rather than earlier in the day.

Services retailers use a variety of programs to match demand and supply. For example, airlines and hotels set lower prices on weekends, when they have excess capacity because businesspeople are not traveling. To achieve more capacity flexibility, health clinics stay open longer during flu season and tax preparation services are open on weekends during March and April. Restaurants increase staffing on weekends, may not open until dinnertime, and use a reservation system to guarantee service delivery at a specific time. Finally, services retailers attempt to make customers' waiting time more enjoyable. For example, videos and park employees entertain customers while they wait in line at Disney theme parks.

Inconsistency   Products can be produced by machines with very tight quality control, so customers are reasonably assured that all boxes of Cheerios will be identical. But because services are performances produced by people (employees and customers), no two services will be identical. For example, tax accountants can have different knowledge and skills for preparing tax returns. The waiter at the Olive Garden can be in a bad mood and make your dining experience a disaster. Thus, an important challenge for services retailers is to provide consistent high-quality services. Many factors that determine service quality are beyond the control of retailers; however, services retailers expend considerable time and effort selecting, training, managing, and motivating their service providers.

TYPES OF OWNERSHIP

LO5

Explain the types of ownership for retail firms.

Previous sections of this chapter discussed how retailers may be classified in terms of their retail mix and the merchandise and services they sell. Another way to classify retailers is by their ownership. The major classifications of retail ownership are (1) independent, single-store establishments; (2) corporate chains; and (3) franchises.

Independent, Single-Store Establishments

Retailing is one of the few sectors in most countries in which entrepreneurial activity is extensive. Many retail start-ups are owner-managed, which means management has direct contact with customers and can respond quickly to their needs. Small retailers are also very flexible and can react quickly to market changes and customer needs. They are not bound by the bureaucracies inherent in large retail organizations.[71]

For example, after more than a decade working for other UK fashion firms, Deryane Todd decided to open her own shop and, since then has expanded multiple times. The secret to the success of The Dressing Room is Todd's strong attention to determining and then providing exactly what her customers want. Despite the long hours and seven-day workweek, Todd expresses her love for her job because of the options it provides her. Todd hires her staff, trains them in her own way, determines the layout of the store, and designs the website.[72]

Whereas single-store retailers can tailor their offerings to their customers' needs, corporate chains can more effectively negotiate lower prices for merchandise and advertising because of their larger size. Corporate chains can and do invest in sophisticated analytical systems to help them buy and price merchandise. In addition, corporate chains have a broader management base, with people who specialize in specific retail activities. Single-store retailers typically must rely on their owner-managers' capabilities to make the broad range of necessary retail decisions.

To compete against corporate chains, some independent retailers join a **wholesale-sponsored voluntary cooperative group,** which is an organization operated by a wholesaler offering a merchandising program to small, independent

The secret of success to The Dressing Room in the United Kingdom is the owner's attention to understanding what her customers want.

retailers on a voluntary basis. The Independent Grocers Alliance (IGA), Tru Serv (supplier to True Value Hardware), and Ace Hardware are wholesale-sponsored voluntary cooperative groups. In addition to engaging in buying, warehousing, and distribution, these groups offer members services such as advice on store design and layout, site selection, bookkeeping and inventory management systems, and employee training programs.

Corporate Retail Chains

A **retail chain** is a company that operates multiple retail units under common ownership and usually has centralized decision making for defining and implementing its strategy. Retail chains can range in size from a drugstore with two stores to retailers with thousands of stores, such as Kroger, Walmart, Best Buy, and Macy's. Some retail chains are divisions of larger corporations or holding companies. For example, the Williams Sonoma corporation actually consists of four brands, Williams Sonoma, Pottery Barn, west elm, and Rejuvenation. Furthermore, its Pottery Barn branch features the PB teen and pottery barn kids lines. Royal Ahold owns 14 retail chains, including Stop and Shop, Giant, and Peapod in the United States and ICA and Albert Heijh in Europe.

Franchising[73]

Franchising is a contractual agreement in which the franchisor (the company) sells the rights to use its business trademark, service mark, or trade name, or another commercial symbol of the company, to the franchisee for a one-time franchise fee and an ongoing royalty fee, typically expressed as a percentage of gross monthly sales. More than 40 percent of all U.S. retail sales are made by franchisees,[74] and this type of retail ownership is growing around the world.[75]

When considering the franchise option, potential franchisees must understand the attractions and drawbacks of buying a franchise versus starting a retail business from scratch. There are many reasons to consider franchise ownership, including the success rate, which results partially from the proven business model that the franchisor offers. Success also results from the unique relationship between the franchisor and the franchisee, in which both parties benefit from the success of the franchisee. To get franchisees off to a good start, most franchisors provide off- and onsite training, location analysis assistance, advertising, and sometimes a protected territory (i.e., no other franchise may open a store within a certain radius of the first store). Some franchisors even provide financing or offer third-party financing opportunities.

There are also several drawbacks to franchise ownership. In addition to having to pay money to the franchisor, the franchisee needs financing for start-up costs, including rent or purchase price of office/retail space; modification of the space according to the guidelines of the franchisor (e.g., paint colors, flooring, lighting, layout); signage; opening inventory; and equipment. In addition to incurring the capital costs, the franchisee must adhere to the franchisor's rules and operating guidelines. In many

McDonald's franchises are growing all over the world.

2.4   RETAILING VIEW   Tart Frozen Yogurt—The Sweet Franchise

Frozen yogurt franchise operations Pinkberry and Red Mango both opened in the mid-2000s; they compete with old standby TCBY and some smaller regional chains. The appeal of Pinkberry and Red Mango to customers is not just the low fat of frozen yogurt but also its ability to boost people's immune system and improve calcium absorption. The tart frozen yogurt is dense with active cultures and probiotics. These health benefits, along with the great taste, has changed the way consumers think about frozen yogurt. Consumers are making multiple yogurt purchases each week, instead of buying it as an occasional nonroutine indulgence.

In addition to a limited number of exotic flavors—coconut, lychee and mango, many of which are seasonal—both Pinkberry and Red Mango offer a wide array of high-end toppings. The minimalism in the flavor choices is part of both companies' brand image, as reflected in the stark, bright store layouts. That is, these popular new chains offer consistency across their products and store images, even as it promises that customers can eat healthy, low-fat, hormone-free milk products, and still indulge in unusual yogurt flavors and interesting toppings.

Howard Schultz, the chair of Starbucks, invested $27.5 million in Pinkberry through his venture capital firm and appears to be trying to make it the Starbucks of frozen yogurt chains. Expectations are high, including a growth plan to have one Pinkberry for every 10 Starbucks in the country. Red Mango would like to have 500 units in the United States but is controlling its growth by carefully selecting its franchisees and monitoring their performance. Many franchises become very popular and ultimately fail within five years as a result of growing too large, too fast. An interesting incentive to attract franchisees by reducing their risk is Red Mango's Store Buy Back

New franchises like Red Mango appeal to customers because its frozen yogurt is low-fat, boosts people's immune systems, and improves calcium absorption.

program, in which the corporate franchise will buy back a store in the first six months if the franchisee is not satisfied.

If the frozen yogurt market becomes as competitive as the premium coffee market, then TCBY may become the Dunkin' Donuts of yogurt franchises, while Red Mango and Pinkberry will be the Starbucks.

Sources: Jaime Levy Pessin, "Yogurt Chains Give Power to the People," *The Wall Street Journal*, August 22, 2011; Yolanda Santosa, "The Making of Pinkberry," *Brand Packaging*, November 2, 2011; Blair Chancey, "Red Mango Revolution," *QSR Magazine*, October 1, 2009; and Kelly Bayliss, "Free Fro-Yo Today," *NBC Philadelphia*, September 23, 2009.

cases, the franchisee is required to purchase operating materials from the franchisor, especially in fast-food franchises that rely on standardized products across franchises for the success of the brand. The franchisor also might require the franchisee to purchase the equipment needed to offer a new product, such as fryers at a McDonald's or beds at a Holiday Inn. The hours of operation and days of the year that the business is allowed to close also may be dictated by the franchisor.

Retailing View 2.4 describes the sweet and tart world of frozen-yogurt franchises.

SUMMARY

LO1 **List the different characteristics that define retailers.**

To collect statistics about retailing, the federal government classifies retailers by the type of merchandise and services they sell. But this classification method may not be useful to determine a retailer's

major competitors. A more useful approach for understanding the retail marketplace is to classify retailers on the basis of the retail mix, merchandise variety and assortment, services, location, pricing, and promotion decisions they make to attract customers.

LO2 **Categorize the various types of food retailers.**

Food retailing has undergone substantial expansion. Whereas once supermarkets were nearly the only source for food shoppers, today they can choose among traditional supermarkets, hypermarkets or superstores, limited-assortment markets, warehouse clubs, and convenience stores, to name a few.

LO3 **Identify the various types of general merchandise retailers.**

General merchandise retailers come in various forms, each with its own offerings, benefits, and limitations. These formats include department stores, full-line discount stores, specialty stores, drugstores, category specialists, extreme-value retailers, off-price retailers, and outlet stores.

LO4 **Explain the differences between service and merchandise retailers.**

The inherent differences between services and merchandise result in services retailers' emphasizing training of employees, whereas merchandise retailers emphasize inventory management issues. Retail institutions have changed in response to a changing marketplace, such that there is significant crossover between these types of retailers.

LO5 **Illustrate the types of ownership for retail firms.**

Small, independent retailers are usually owned and managed by a single founder. In contrast, corporate retail chains involve vast organizations and operate multiple stores. Another option that allows individual entrepreneurs to enjoy the security of corporate chains is franchising, a growing type of retail organization.

KEY TERMS

assortment, *37*
big-box store, *45*
breadth of merchandise, *37*
category killer, *51*
category specialist, *51*
closeouts, *55*
consignment shop, *53*
convenience store, *46*
conventional supermarket, *42*
department store, *48*
depth of merchandise, *37*
dollar store, *54*
drugstore, *54*
durable goods, *48*
exclusive brand, *49*
extreme-value food retailer, *42*

extreme-value retailer, *54*
factory outlet, *56*
fair trade, *43*
flash sale, *56*
franchising, *61*
full-line discount store, *50*
hard goods, *48*
hypermarket, *45*
irregulars, *55*
limited-assortment
  supermarket, *42*
locavore movement, *43*
**North American Industry
  Classification System
  (NAICS)**, *36*
off-price retailer, *55*

outlet store, *56*
power perimeter, *43*
private-label brand, *49*
retail chain, *61*
services retailer, *56*
soft goods, *48*
specialty store, *52*
stock-keeping unit (SKU), *37*
store brand, *49*
supercenter, *44*
thrift store, *53*
variety, *37*
warehouse club, *45*
**wholesale-sponsored voluntary
  cooperative group**, *60*

GET OUT AND DO IT!

1. **CONTINUING CASE ASSIGNMENT: GO SHOPPING** The objective of this assignment is to have you take the retailer's, rather than the consumer's, perspective and think about the different strategies that the retailer you selected and another retailer might have, as well as how these strategies result in different retail mixes. The assignment is to conduct a comparison of the retail offerings for a specific merchandise category, such as tablets, men's suits, country/western CDs, women's athletic shoes, or house paint, for two different retailers. The other retailer selected might be a direct competitor using the same format or a retailer selling similar merchandise to a different target market with a different format.

Your comparison should include the following:
- The strategy pursued by the two retailers—each retailer's target market(s) and general approach to satisfying the needs of that target market.
- The retail mixes (store location, merchandise, pricing, advertising and promotion, location of merchandise category in store, store design, customer service) used by each of the retailers.
- With respect to the merchandise category, a detailed comparison of the variety and depth of assortment. In comparing the merchandise offerings, use a table similar to that in Exhibit 2–2.

To prepare this comparison, you need to visit the stores, observe the retail mixes in the stores, and play the role of a customer to observe the service.

2. **GO SHOPPING** Go to an athletic footwear specialty store such as Foot Locker, a department store, and a discount store. Analyze their variety and assortment of athletic footwear by creating a table similar to that in Exhibit 2–2.

3. **GO SHOPPING** Keep a diary for two weeks of where you shop, what you buy, and how much you spend. Get your parents to do the same thing. Tabulate your results by type of retailer. Are your shopping habits significantly different from or are they similar to those of your parents? Do your and your parents' shopping habits coincide with the trends discussed in this chapter? Why or why not?

4. **GO SHOPPING** Describe how the supermarket where you shop is implementing organic, locally grown, ethnic, and private-label merchandise. If any of these categories of merchandise are missing, explain whether you believe it could be a potential opportunity for growth for this supermarket. Then describe any strategies or activities that you believe are providing a better shopping experience than its competition. If you believe that competing stores are providing a better shopping experience than your store, explain what they are doing, and evaluate whether or not these activities would benefit your supermarket.

5. **INTERNET EXERCISE** Data on U.S. retail sales are available from the U.S. Bureau of the Census Internet site at www.census.gov/retail/. Look at the unadjusted monthly sales by NAICS (found in the Monthly Retail Trade Report section). Which categories of retailers have the largest percentage of sales in November and December (the holiday season)? Do your findings make sense to you? Why or why not?

6. **INTERNET EXERCISE** Three large associations of retailers are the National Retail Federation (www.nrf.com), the Food Marketing Institute (www.fmi.org), and the National Association of Convenience and Petroleum Stores (www.nacsonline.com). Visit these sites, and report on the latest retail developments and issues confronting the industry.

7. **INTERNET EXERCISE** Go to Entrepreneur Magazine's Franchise Zone web page at www.entrepreneur.com/franchise500, and view the top 500 franchises for the past year. How many of the retailers in the top 10 have you patronized as a customer? Did you know that they were operated as a franchise? Look at the lists from previous years to see changes in the rankings. Finally, what is the nature of the businesses that seem to lend themselves to franchising?

8. Bed Bath & Beyond is a category specialist with about 1,000 stores throughout the United States and Ontario, Canada. It sells domestics (bed linens, bathroom and kitchen items) and home furnishings (cookware and cutlery, small household appliances, picture frames, and organizing supplies). What are the SIC and NAICS codes used by this retailer? What other retailers compete against Bed Bath & Beyond, and which store format is implemented by each competitor?

DISCUSSION QUESTIONS AND PROBLEMS

1. Distinguish between variety and assortment. Why are these important elements of the retail market structure?

2. What sorts of competitive pressures are confronting traditional grocery stores? What options do these stores have to ease the pressure?

3. What do off-price retailers need to do to compete against other formats in the future?

4. Compare and contrast the retail mixes of convenience stores, traditional supermarkets, supercenters, and warehouse stores. Can all of these food retail institutions be successful over the long run? How? Why?

5. Why is Walmart, the largest retailer in the world, facing slower growth than in the past? What can it do to accelerate its growth?

6. Why are retailers in the limited-assortment supermarket and extreme-value discount store sectors growing so rapidly? From which retailers are they getting these additional sales?

7. The same brand and model of tablet is sold by specialty computer stores, discount stores, category specialists, online retailers, and warehouse stores. Why would a customer choose one retail format over the others?

8. Choose a product category that both you and your parents purchase (e.g., business clothing, casual clothing, music, electronic equipment, shampoo). In which type of store do you typically purchase this merchandise? What about your parents? Explain why there is, or is not, a difference in your store choices.

9. At many optical stores, you can get your eyes checked *and* purchase glasses or contact lenses. How is the shopping experience different for the service as compared to the product? Design a strategy to get customers to purchase both the service and the product. In so doing, delineate specific actions that should be taken to acquire and retain optical customers.

10. There are services and products involved when buying or renting a car, and in both cases, the customer drives away in a car. But buying a car focuses more on the product, whereas renting involves the service. Explain four ways in which marketing for a rental car company differs from marketing for an automobile dealership.

SUGGESTED READINGS

Borghini, Stefania, Nina Diamond, Roberts Kozinets, Mary Ann McGrath, Albert M. Muñiz Jr., and John F. Sherry Jr. "Why Are Themed Brandstores So Powerful? Retail Brand Ideology at *American Girl Place*." *Journal of Retailing* 85, no. 3 (2009).

Cuthbertson, Christine. *Retail Strategy: The View From the Bridge*, Oxford: Elsevier, 2012.

Enrique, Badia. *Zara and Her Sisters: The Story of the World's Largest Clothing Retailer*. New York: Palgrave Macmillan, 2009.

Fishman, Charles. *The Wal-Mart Effect*. New York: Penguin, 2007.

Grewal, Dhruv, Gopalkrishnan Iyer, Rajshekhar G. Javalgi, and Lori Radulovich. "Franchise Partnership and International Expansion: A Conceptual Framework and Research Propositions." *Entrepreneurial Theory & Practice*, May 2011, pp. 533–557.

Hammond, Richard. *Smart Retail: Practical Winning Ideas and Strategies from the Most Successful Retailers in the World*, New Jersey: FT Press, 2012.

Mitchell, Stacy. *Big-Box Swindle: The True Cost of Mega-Retailers and the Fight for America's Independent Businesses*. Boston: Beacon Press, 2006.

Roberts, Bryan, and Natalie Berg. *Walmart: Key Insights and Practical Lessons from the World's Largest Retailer*. Philadelphia: Koran Page, 2012.

Spector, Robert, and Patrick McCarthy. *The Nordstrom Way to Customer Service Excellence: The Handbook For Becoming the "Nordstrom" of Your Industry*. New Jersey: John Wiley & Sons, 2012.

Spector, Robert. *The Mom & Pop Store: True Stories from the Heart of America*. New York: Walker & Company, 2009.

Thain, Greg, and John Bradley. *Store Wars: The Worldwide Battle for Mindspace and Shelfspace, Online and In-Store*. West Sussex, UK: John Wiley & Sons, 2012.

Whitaker, Jan. *Service and Style: How the American Department Store Fashioned the Middle Class*. New York: St. Martin's Press, 2006.

Multichannel Retailing

EXECUTIVE BRIEFING
Luiza Helena Trajano
President, Magazine Luiza

I am from Franca, a small city in the state of São Paulo, Brazil. As a child, I loved to give presents to friends and relatives. When I was 12 years old, my mother told me that I would have to earn money to continue my "hobby" of giving presents. So I started working during vacations at a store owned by my Uncle Pelegrino and Aunt Luiza and have been working there ever since. I went to college in Franca during the evenings, and worked during the day at the store. In 1991, I was selected as the CEO of the company.

The company's early growth came from acquisitions of small town retailers in the state of São Paulo. We catered to the needs of consumers of all social classes. While the lower-income consumers had limited incomes, they sought the same respect shown to upper-income consumers. Our stores offered them respect and credit. With annual sales of about US$ 4 billion in 2012, our company now has more than 800 stores in Brazil selling furniture, appliances, consumer electronics, and home products. Although we are now in the major metro areas of Brazil, we have tried hard to preserve our company culture characterized by respect for our customers and employees and continuous innovation. These elements are in our DNA. Our transparent management system is designed to make associates feel part of the company, and we share the profits of the company with all employees.

In 1992, almost 10 years before e-commerce was introduced in Brazil, we used a multichannel approach. Our sales associates assisted customers placing orders on the stores' computers and having products delivered to their homes.

In 2012, we were invited to present at the National Retail Federation convention, in New York, our creative and very successful "Magazine Voce" (or Your Luiza Store) system. This system allowed our "agents" to create their own virtual Luiza store on Facebook with 20 products and sell these products to their friends. We now have more than 10,000 agents affiliated with our company.

Three years ago, we hired a new CEO, and I no longer am involved in the day-to-day operations. But I maintain our Luiza company culture by holding meetings with the staff of new stores. I also maintain direct supervision of the customer relations

CHAPTER 3

LEARNING OBJECTIVES

LO1 Understand the nonstore channels offered by retailers.

LO2 Compare the benefits offered by the four major retail channels: stores, Internet, mobile, and catalogs.

LO3 Analyze the challenges facing multichannel retailers.

LO4 Consider the multichannel shopping experience in the future.

department. This gives me the opportunity to pass along our values to the new associates, demonstrate the respect we have for them and our customers, and also highlight to all in the company our passion to serve our customers. And I still like to give presents.

A **retail channel** is the way a retailer sells and delivers merchandise and services to its customers. The most common channel used by retailers is a store. Retailers also use a variety of nonstore channels, including the Internet, mobile, catalogs and direct mail, direct selling, television home shopping, direct-response TV, and automated retailing (vending machines) to make sales to customers. This definition makes a distinction between a channel and a medium such as TV advertising. A *channel* involves the opportunity to complete a transaction—to sell and deliver merchandise—while a *medium* is primarily used to communicate information to consumers. Retailers communicate information through channels as well as complete transactions; however, the primary objective of the channel is to complete transactions.

Multichannel retailing involves using more than one channel to sell and deliver merchandise and services to consumers.[1] Note the term **omniretailing** is frequently used when discussing multichannel retailing; it refers to a coordinated multichannel retail offering that provides a seamless customer experience when using all of the retailer's shopping channels.

The birth of multichannel retailing can be traced back to when Sears opened its first store in 1925, 33 years after it launched its catalog that offered merchandise previously unavailable to the American masses.[2] Now, almost all large retailers

Even small, single-store retailers like Trealy Farm interact with their customers through multiple channels.

that operate stores are multichannel retailers. Most have added an Internet channel that offers customers an opportunity to buy merchandise or services by accessing their website, as well as patronizing their stores.[3]

Many small, store-based retailers also use multiple channels. For example, in its 8,000-square-foot retail store near Miami's Little River district, Capt. Harry's Fishing Supply's offers more than 20,000 products, including rods and reels, as well as at least 1,000 lures and teasers in every color, designed to tempt fish onto an angler's line. The biggest lure is nearly two feet long and the smallest less than an inch. There are scented lures, mirrored lures, lures with holographic features, and ones designed to move like a frightened fish. In the early 1980s, Harry Vernon, Jr., the company president, noticed that about 40 percent of the foot traffic was from foreign customers. So, he launched a catalog and eventually Internet channels. Now, from a second-floor warehouse, pickers fill orders from nearly every U.S. state and 120 countries.[4]

In this chapter, we take a strategic perspective to examine the four primary channels through which retailers sell merchandise and services to their customers. We first briefly describe all of the nonstore retail channels; retailers typically evolve to multichannel retailers by adding a nonstore channel to their store channel. We then review the unique benefits that each of the four major channels offer to consumers and outline the retailers' benefits from providing a multichannel offering. Next, we describe the challenges multichannel retailers face when using these channels synergistically and how they provide a seamless offering for their customers. At the end of the chapter, we illustrate how integrating these channels and using new technologies will create a compelling shopping experience in the future.

Nonstore Retail Channels

LO1
Understand the nonstore channels offered by retailers.

The estimated percentage of annual retail sales (excluding motor vehicles and food services annual sales) made through each channel is shown in Exhibit 3–1. The vast majority of sales are made through the store channel, but the Internet and catalog channels also account for significant sales, while the mobile channel has the highest growth rate.

Internet Retailing Channels—Electronic and Mobile Retailing

Internet retailing is the fastest growing channel. It involves retailers interacting with consumers via the Internet, whether they use a traditional computer or a laptop, a variety of sizes of tablets or a smartphone. We refer to the channel that

Multichannel Retailing   CHAPTER 3   69

EXHIBIT 3–1
U.S. Retail Sales by
Channel

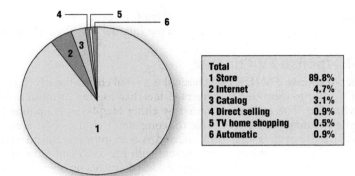

Total	
1 Store	89.8%
2 Internet	4.7%
3 Catalog	3.1%
4 Direct selling	0.9%
5 TV home shopping	0.5%
6 Automatic	0.9%

SOURCES: U.S. Census Bureau, "Estimates of Monthly Retail and Food Services Sales by Kind of Business: 2009," www.census.gov/retail/mrts/www/data/excel/mrtssales92-09.xls; personal communication with the Direct Selling Association, Direct Marketing Association, and National Automatic Merchandising Association.

*Excluding sales of motor vehicles, food services, and travel.

involves accessing the Internet through a traditional computer as the electronic channel. The mobile channel (also called **mobile retailing,** mobile commerce, or m-commerce), involves accessing the Internet using a smartphone. From a retailing perspective, smartphones differ from traditional computers in that they are more portable, have a smaller display, are location-aware, use different touch screen technology to access the Internet, and as a result of these factors produce a different interface experience with the user. Tablets retain some of the advantages and disadvantages of using a traditional computer with some of the mobility benefits and problems associated with shopping with a mobile phone.

Two decades ago, experts thought by now everyone would be doing their shopping over the Internet. These experts predicted that a new breed of high-tech, web-savvy entrepreneurs would dominate the retail industry. Stores would close due to lack of traffic, and paper catalogs would become obsolete. However, these predictions of Internet retailing transforming the retail industry have not occurred. Even though U.S. sales through Internet channels are forecasted to grow at about 10 percent annually, more than three times faster than sales growth through store channels, Internet sales are expected to only account for 11 percent of retail sales (excluding automotive and food services) by 2015, with the mobile channel accounting for 9 percent of Internet retail sales.[6]

The Internet is, therefore, a facilitating, rather than transformational, technology with respect to most sectors of the retail industry. Almost all of the traditional store-based retailers utilize Internet channels to provide a better shopping experience for their customers and now dominate these channels. Almost 75 percent of U.S. consumers use the Internet to search for information about clothes, shoes, toys, and health and beauty aids before they go to a store to buy the items. Eighty-three percent go online before buying electronics, computers, books, music, and movies in stores.[7] Just over half of all adults who own mobile phones use them to get either product reviews or pricing information while in a physical store, a process known as showrooming.[8]

Catalog Channel

The **catalog channel** is a nonstore retail channel in which the retail offering is communicated to customers through a catalog mailed to customers. About half of U.S. consumers shop through catalogs each year. The merchandise categories with the greatest catalog sales are drugs, beauty aids, computers, software, clothing, accessories, furniture, and housewares.[9] The use of catalogs has come under attack from consumer groups that believe that catalogs are an unnecessary waste of natural resources. In the United States, catalogs account for 3 percent of the roughly 80 million tons of paper products used annually. That is more than either magazines or books.[10] Further, catalogs' share of sales is declining relative to the Internet. But

REFACT

The first use of an Internet retail channel was on August 11, 1994, when a CD by Sting was sold by NetMarket over the Internet.[5]

catalogs are not going away. Their role is shifting from primarily generating sales to building a brand image and driving traffic to the Internet and physical stores.[11]

Direct-Response TV Channel

The **direct-response TV (DRTV) channel** is a retail channel in which customers watch a TV advertisement that demonstrates merchandise and then place orders for that merchandise. The orders are placed by either telephoning a phone bank of operators or accessing the Internet to use the company's website. There are two types of DRTV advertisements: a long form, referred to as an **infomercial** and typically 30 to 60 minutes long, that mixes entertainment with product demonstrations, and a short form consisting of one- to two-minute advertisements on television. Approximately $150 million in annual retail sales is made through the DRTV channel.

Unlike most TV advertising, the impact of a DRTV advertisement is precisely measureable. Within 24 hours, retailers using this channel can determine how many customers responded to each exposure to an ad. The results can be analyzed to determine the effects of location, time of week, time of day, and different scripts and creative responses.

Television Home Shopping Channel

Television home shopping is a retail channel in which customers watch a TV network with programs that demonstrate merchandise and then place orders for that merchandise, usually by telephone or via the Internet. Annual U.S. sales through TV shopping networks are approximately $20 billion. The two largest retailers using this channel are HSN and QVC, followed by ShopNBC and Jewelry Television. Although most consumers with cable or satellite television access can patronize a television shopping channel, relatively few watch on a regular basis. Furthermore, most of the purchases are made by a relatively small percentage of viewers. Like catalogs, TV home shopping networks have embraced the Internet for taking customer orders, although it is still possible to place an order by telephone and mail.

The major advantage of TV home shopping is that customers can see the merchandise demonstrated either on their television screens or through streaming videos on the Internet. In response to the increase in cooking, decorating, do-it-yourself, and other lifestyle programming, home shopping retailers have incorporated more demonstrations into their programming in an attempt to educate their potential customers.

TV home shopping retailers are also embracing social media. Today's consumer is interacting with TV home shopping channels on multiple screens. They have a smartphone, laptop computer, or tablet next to them as they view the program. The tweets that these media-savvy customers send to the network appear on live scrolls, adding user comments about various products and guests to the broadcast. At the same time, on HSN's Facebook page, they can ask questions and chat about the program as it happens; the really interesting comments and questions then get read on the air by the customers' favorite hosts.[13]

Direct Selling Channel

Direct selling is a retail channel in which salespeople interact with customers face-to-face in a convenient location, either at the customer's home or at work. Direct salespeople demonstrate merchandise benefits and/or

HSN's sales have more than doubled after it started selling more well-known brands.

explain a service, take an order, and deliver the merchandise. Direct selling is a highly interactive retail channel in which considerable information is conveyed to customers through face-to-face discussions and demonstrations. However, providing this high level of personalized information, including extensive demonstrations, is costly.

Annual U.S. sales through direct selling are about $30 billion; worldwide, sales are more than $100 billion. More than 60 percent of the products sold through the direct selling channel are home/family care/home durables (cleaning products, cookware, cutlery, etc.), wellness (weight loss products, vitamins, etc.) and personal care (cosmetics, jewelry, skin care, etc.)[15]

Almost all the 15 million salespeople in the United States who work in direct sales are independent agents.[16] They are not employed by the direct sales firm but, rather, act as independent distributors, buying merchandise from the firms and then reselling it to consumers. In most cases, direct salespeople may sell their merchandise to anyone, but some companies, such as Avon, assign territories to salespeople who regularly contact households in their territory. Retailing View 3.1 describes how the direct selling channel is particularly effective in less developed countries.

RETAILING VIEW   Avon's Direct Selling Channel in Brazil   3.1

Baixada Fluminense might be one of the toughest neighborhoods in Rio de Janeiro, but that doesn't mean its residents don't worry about lipstick colors. It might even mean they worry more. Thus, Heloisa Almada Contreira visits her 80 or so customers regularly in their homes, earning weekly sales of about $930 by selling Avon products. Spending 50 reais ($27) on cosmetics might seem like a lot for many low-income consumers, but, according to Almada Contreira, "For them, it's a necessity. Brazilian women can't go without their makeup."

Her impression might be anecdotal, but the statistics back up this claim, in that Brazil constitutes the world's third largest market for beauty care products, behind only the United States and Japan. With its expansive coastline and warm climate, Brazil invites residents to visit beaches all year, though the approach of summer often finds millions of women initiating a diet and beauty regime that will enable them to live *verão sem kanga*—that is, as part of a robe-free summer on the beach. Such hot weather may be great for a beach day, but it also means that people often need at least a couple of showers. Thus, Brazilians use twice the shampoo, conditioner, and soap compared with residents of other countries. And then women need to apply their makeup a second time each day!

The constant demand for cosmetics and beauty products is no problem for Almada Contreira and her 1.1 million sales colleagues. Avon's Brazilian sales force sells door-to-door, whether their customers live in city slums, the Amazonian rainforest, or remote towns. These sorts of direct sales have long been a staple of American life, but companies such as Avon, as well as Herbalife and Amway, increasingly turn to this channel to sell to consumers in less developed countries. In these areas, direct sales can be particularly effective, because the channel does not require a sophisticated or expensive infrastructure. Instead, salespeople handle distribution on their own. These independent agents not only sell and distribute the

Avon's direct selling channel is particularly effective in developing economies such as Brazil.

products to their customers, but they also take responsibility for ordering merchandise to restock their inventory. To reach customers in the Amazon, Avon salespeople might need to hire a small boat or plane, and the product delivery might be delayed for a week or more. But for those waiting for just the right color to apply to their cheeks, a week is not too long to wait.

Sources: Christina Passariello and Emily Glazer, "Coty Knocks on Brazil's Door; Part of Avon's Allure to Fragrance Maker Is Its Sales Network in South America," *The Wall Street Journal (Online)*, April 5, 2012; Jenney Barchfield, "In Beauty-Obsessed Brazil, Clinics Offer Free Plastic Surgery to Poor," *Los Angeles Times*, March 25 2012, A.4; and Jonathan Wheatley, "Beauty Business Turns Heads in Brazil," *Investor's Choice*, January 19, 2010.

DISCUSSION QUESTION

Why is the direct sales channel so much more popular and effective in Brazil than in the United States?

Two special types of direct selling are the party plan and multilevel systems. About one-quarter of all direct sales are made using a **party plan system.** Salespeople encourage customers to act as hosts and invite friends or coworkers to a "party." The host or hostess receives a gift or commission for arranging the party. At the party, the merchandise is demonstrated and attendees place orders.

In a **multilevel system,** independent businesspeople serve as master distributors, recruiting other people to become distributors in their network. The master distributors either buy merchandise from the firm and resell it to their distributors or receive a commission on all merchandise purchased by the distributors in their network. In addition to selling merchandise themselves, the master distributors are involved in recruiting and training other distributors.

Some multilevel direct selling firms are illegal pyramid schemes. A **pyramid scheme** develops when the firm and its program are designed to sell merchandise and services to other distributors, rather than to end-users. The founders and initial distributors in pyramid schemes profit from the inventory bought by later participants, but little merchandise is sold to consumers who use it.

Automated Retailing (Vending Machines) Channel

Automated retailing is a retail channel in which merchandise or services are stored in a machine and dispensed to customers when they deposit cash or use a credit card. Automated retailing machines, also known as **vending machines,** are typically placed at convenient, high-traffic locations. About 80 percent of the automated retailing channel sales are from cold beverages, prepared food service, candy, and snacks. Annual U.S. sales in the channel were $40 billion, but between 2007 and 2010, sales declined by more than 11 percent.[17]

As a result of this decline, vending machines also are disappearing from stores and sidewalks. Unwilling to give up on this channel, some entrepreneurs are reimagining the uses of vending machines. Many of them are going high-tech, with sophisticated service offerings. Machines maintained by Minnesota-based InstyMeds Corp. appear in health clinics and dispense prescription medicines. To prevent fraud, the machines maintain an electronic link to the doctor's computer system, which allows them to confirm each patient's identity and prescription, using a unique code assigned by the doctor to each patient.[19]

Another interesting automated retailing application is taking the DVD rental business by storm. Redbox rents DVDs for $1 a day in more than 22,000 locations, including McDonald's, Walmart, Walgreens, Albertsons, and 7-Eleven Circle-K. The retailer rents more than 7.5 million movies weekly, close to the sales reported by its mail-order rival Netflix. Redbox's success, as well as its challenge, is keeping its inventory of DVDs fresh and available when customers want to rent them. Customers can check the inventory of a particular machine and reserve a copy of any title at Redbox's Internet site.[20]

REFACT

The Greek mathematician Hero invented the first vending machine in 215 B.C., selling holy water to worshippers in Egyptian temples. In the early 1880s, the first coin-operated vending machines allowed customers in London, England, to purchase postcards.[18]

RELATIVE BENEFITS OF RETAIL CHANNELS

LO2

Compare the benefits offered by the four major retail channels: stores, Internet, mobile, and catalogs.

In this section, we discuss the relative benefits and limitations of the four major retail channels: stores, catalogs, electronic, and mobile. Exhibit 3–2 summarizes these unique benefits. In the following section, we discuss how retailers provide a better customer shopping experience by integrating these channels into a true multichannel experience.

Store Channel

Stores offer several benefits to customers that they cannot get when they shop through nonstore channels such as mobile, electronic, or catalogs.

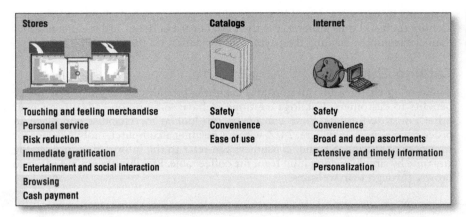

Stores	Catalogs	Internet
Touching and feeling merchandise	Safety	Safety
Personal service	Convenience	Convenience
Risk reduction	Ease of use	Broad and deep assortments
Immediate gratification		Extensive and timely information
Entertainment and social interaction		Personalization
Browsing		
Cash payment		

EXHIBIT 3–2
Benefits Provided by
Different Channels

Touching and Feeling Products   Perhaps the greatest benefit offered by stores is the opportunity for customers to use all five senses—touching, smelling, tasting, seeing, and hearing—when examining and evaluating products. Although new technologies such as three-dimensional and 360-degree projections can enhance representations of products on a computer or mobile phone screen, these visual improvements do not provide the same level of information customers get when they actually try on a swimsuit or smell the fragrance of a candle.

Personal Service   Although consumers are often critical of the personal service they get in stores, sales associates still have the unique ability to provide meaningful, personalized information. They can tell customers if a suit looks good on them, suggest a tie to go with a dress shirt, or answer questions customers might have about what is appropriate to wear at a business-casual event.

Risk Reduction   The physical presence of the store reduces perceived risk and increases customers' confidence that any problems with a purchase will be corrected. Customers can easily access people in the store to resolve issues concerning defective or unsuitable merchandise or get additional information on how to use a product.

Immediate Gratification   Customers can use merchandise immediately after they buy it in stores. Thus, when customers have a fever or need a last-minute gift, for example, they do not have to wait a day or two for the delivery of a prescription from Drugstore.com or of a gift from Amazon.com.

Entertainment and Social Experience   In-store shopping can be a stimulating experience for some people, providing a break in their daily routine and enabling them to interact with friends. All nonstore retail formats are limited in the degree to which they can satisfy these entertainment and social needs. Retailing View 3.2 describes how Bass Pro Shops offer an exciting and rewarding shopping experience for their customers.

Browsing   Shoppers often have only a general sense of what they want (e.g., a sweater, something for dinner, a gift) but don't know the specific item they want, so they go to a store to see what is available before they decide what to buy. Although consumers can surf the web or look through catalogs for ideas, most consumers still find it easier to browse in stores.

Cash Payment   Stores are the only channel through which consumers can make cash payments. Some customers prefer to pay with cash because it is quicker, resolves the transaction immediately, and does not result in potential interest payments or excessive debt. Other customers are concerned about security and identity theft and thus prefer to use their credit card or debit card in person rather than electronically sending the payment information via the Internet.

Catalog Channel

The catalog channel, like all nonstore channels, provides safety and convenience benefits to customers. Catalogs continue to have some unique advantages over other nonstore formats. First, consumers can look at merchandise and place an order from almost anywhere, 24/7, without needing a computer, mobile device, or Internet connection. Second, consumers can refer to the information in a catalog any time by simply picking it up from the coffee table. Finally, catalogs are easier to browse through than websites.

3.2   RETAILING VIEW   Bass Pro Shops Makes Shopping Fun

How would you like to spend your vacation? Playing in a laser arcade, rock climbing, practicing your aim in a pistol shooting range, or trying out your archery skills? If that sounds great, you're probably among the millions of people who drive for hours just to visit one of Bass Pro Shops' stores. Made to look something like hunting lodges, the stores also feature massive product displays, aided by a professional sales staff who use all the products in their own, outdoorsy lifestyles. Behind the deep product assortment, the stores' decor is enhanced by massive indoor waterfalls, aquariums, and mounted wildlife.

But a cool look isn't all there is to Bass Pro Shops. Shoppers can enjoy free activities, like making their way up the rock climbing wall or challenging their friends to a round of laser tag in the attached arcade. In soundproof rooms, surrounded by shatter-resistant glass, they can pretend to be Dirty Harry—or Katniss Everdeen, if they prefer bows and arrows. For those not quite as practiced, on-hand experts offer advice about how to sight a gun or draw a bow.

It might not be a surprise to learn that customers of Bass Pro Shops tend to be men, who otherwise proclaim just how much they hate shopping. Even a man whose wife claims that in their 35-year marriage, he'd joined her only twice on shopping trips, gets in the spirit at Bass Pro Shops, calling himself, "a kid in a candy store here."

Although these customers might drive hundreds of miles to get to them, the stores reflect their environment. In north-central Alabama, the Leeds store spreads across 120 acres, including a mile-long entryway that moves slowly through the surrounding nature park, including three bridges and a four-acre lake. But one lake isn't enough in this fish-loving area,

More than 100 million people annually visit Bass Pro Shops, compared with 60 million visitors to Disney World in Orlando. The excitement generated in a Bass Pro Shops' store cannot be equaled by other channels.

so an 18,500-gallon aquarium inside the store features fish native to Alabama, and a 3,500-gallon trout pond allows shoppers to test out the fishing equipment available in the store. Fishing too tame for you? Then how about the NASCAR ride simulator that mimics nearby Talladega Speedway? It's waiting outside the store, too.

Sources: www.bassproshop.com; Tom Bailey Jr., "Bass Pro to Open 'Newest Generation' Megastore in Little Rock," *McClatchy–Tribune Business News*, June, 15, 2012; "Outdoors Lovers Find Their 'Disneyland' in Stores Such as Bass Pro Shops," *Sacramento Bee*, September 23, 2009; "Retailer Scores by Luring Men Who Hate to Shop," *The Wall Street Journal*, December 17, 2002.

DISCUSSION QUESTION

What are the pros and cons of Bass Pro Shops' exciting store environment from the perspective of consumers? From the perspective of Bass Pro Shops?

REFACT

Bass Pro Shops' first store in Springfield, Missouri, attracts 4 million visitors a year and is the most visited tourist attraction in Missouri.

IKEA's 2013 catalog illustrates the use of a retailer's website to augment its catalog channel. IKEA dramatically improved the content and user experience with its widely distributed housewares catalog by including augmented reality. In the 2013 catalog, shoppers can place their smartphones over selected pages to get additional content from the retailer's website, such as image galleries and videos. After downloading an app, customers can interact with a series of icons in the catalog to see more information about selected products. The information ranges from how-to videos to "X-ray" photographs of the inside of storage systems. Rooms with and without textiles are shown, allowing users to build up decorative elements and explore color options.[21]

The Internet Channel

In the previous section, we detailed the relative benefits of stores from the consumers' perspective. In this section, we examine how the addition of Internet channels to traditional store-based retailers and catalogers has improved their ability to serve their customers and build a competitive advantage in several ways:

1. The addition of the Internet channels has the potential to offer a greater selection of products.

2. They allow retailers to provide more information.

3. They enable retailers to provide customers with more personalized information about products and services.

4. They offer sellers the unique opportunity to collect information about consumer shopping.

5. Internet channels provide an opportunity for retailers to enter new markets economically.

6. They provide information that they can use to improve the shopping experience across all channels.

While Internet channels offer many benefits to consumers, they also increase consumers' risks, discussed at the end of the section.

Deeper and Broader Selection   One benefit of adding the Internet channels is the vast number of alternatives retailers can make available to consumers without crowding their aisles or increasing their square footage. Stores and catalogs are limited by their size. By shopping on the Internet, consumers can easily "visit" and select merchandise from a broader array of retailers. Individual retailers' websites typically offer deeper assortments of merchandise (more colors, brands, and sizes) than are available in stores or catalogs. This expanded offering enables them to satisfy consumer demand for less popular styles, colors, or sizes. Many retailers also offer a broader assortment (more categories) on their websites. Staples.com, for instance, offers soft drinks and cleaning supplies, which are not available in stores, so that its business customers will view it as a one-stop shop.

More Information for Evaluating Merchandise   An important service offered by retailers is providing information that helps consumers make better buying decisions. Retail channels differ in terms of how much information customers can access. The amount of information available through the store channel is limited by the number and training of sales associates and the space allocated to informative signage. Similarly, the information available through a catalog channel is limited by the number of pages in the catalog. In contrast, the information provided through the Internet channels is unlimited.

The vast amount of information available through these channels enables customers using this channel to solve problems, rather than just get information about specific products. Retailing View 3.3 describes an Internet site that offers products plus information, some of which is generated by customers, that can help couples solve the problems associated with planning their wedding.

Personalization   Due to the Internet's interactive nature, the most significant potential benefit of Internet channels is their ability to economically personalize merchandise offerings and information for each customer. Customers control

3.3   RETAILING VIEW   Helping Couples Get Ready for the Big Day

Not only does the typical engagement and wedding today last seemingly forever (14 months) and cost a lot ($25,000), it also demands that brides, grooms, and their families make often difficult, usually emotionally charged decisions. Who gets invited? What should the invitations look like, and should they be preceded by save-the-date cards? What kind of music should be played at the reception? Wait, where should the reception be held? And just how much can a couple register for before they look greedy?

Although, at one time, the bride and her family were responsible for most of the wedding planning, modern trends—including couples who delay marriage until later, dual-income households, and transient populations who live far from their parents—mean that many of the traditional norms have gone out the window. To help these couples plan, including figuring out how to spend, Internet wedding sites such as The Knot (www.theknot.com) and WeddingChannel (www.weddingchannel.com) provide a budgeting tool. Brides enter the dollar amount they want to spend (e.g., $9,000) and the number of guests (e.g., 30). Using national averages, the website calculates how much they should spend on each feature: $540 for the bride's dress and $68 for her bouquet, in this example. As the plans progress, users enter their spending, and the tool recalculates the amounts available to be expended elsewhere.

Moving beyond the financial questions, visitors to the sites can interact with other couples, as well as etiquette experts, to get advice on how to deal with a meddling mother-in-law or where to seat divorced parents during the reception. Recommendations from other consumers seem less biased and thus more appealing than information provided by a retailer or manufacturer. Thus, shoppers turn to posted reviews of products or services.

Another planning tool sends reminders of key dates, such as the date the band needs to be reconfirmed or when the reception hall deposit is due. The sites also gather registries from various retailers, available for guests to seek out, all in one place. Bands even upload audio clips of their performances, helping bridal couples choose which one will play during their first dance. Once the reception hall and all hotels have been chosen, the website provides maps showing the best routes between

Planning Tools
from *the knot*

From keeping track of your wedding budget to managing all your to-dos, we've got the best online wedding planning tools -- and they're all free! Keep your RSVPs organized with our wedding guest list tool, spread the word with your own wedding website, and plan on the go with our iPhone wedding apps.

planning checklist
Don't miss a step with our week-by-week to-do list

wedding budgeter
Track your wedding expenses with our easy budget tool!

guest list manager
Stay on top of your guest list, RSVPs, and more

save-the-date
Give your guests a heads up with an email save-the-date

wedding websites
Share the details! Choose from 40+ stylish designs

registry central
Get our top registry picks, plus the ultimate registry checklist

my real wedding
Get inspired by other Knotties or upload your own photos

inspiration boards
Show off your wedding style with 1,000s of photos

the knot notebook
See something you like? Save gowns, articles, and more

The Knot offers information and merchandise to help couples plan their wedding.

locations, as well as online booking services for hotel reservations. And then when all is said and done, the married couple can maintain a personal site for recollections and posting wedding pictures.

Sources: www.weddingchannel.com and www.theknot.com.

DISCUSSION QUESTION

Would you use these websites to plan your wedding? Why or why not?

some of this personalization by drilling down through web pages until they have enough information to make a purchase decision. In addition, when using Internet channels, customers can format the information so that it can be effectively used when they are comparing alternatives. For example, Office Depot provides information about alternatives selected by the customer in a side-by-side comparison format. In contrast, customers in stores usually have to inspect each brand, one item at a time, and then remember the different attributes to make a comparison.

The retailer can play a more proactive role in personalizing merchandise and information through the Internet channels. For example, many retailers offer **live chats:** Customers can click a button at any time and have an instant messaging e-mail or voice conversation with a customer service representative. This technology also enables retailers to send a proactive chat invitation automatically to customers on the site. The timing of these invitations can be based on the time the visitor has spent on the site, the specific page the customer is viewing, or a product on which the customer has clicked. For example, Bluefly.com has learned that reviewing several items in a short period implies the visitor has more than a passing interest in its offerings. Therefore, the site displays a pop-up window with a friendly face offering help.[22]

The interactive nature of the Internet also provides an opportunity for retailers to personalize their offerings for each of their customers. For example, Amazon.com serves customers a personalized landing page with information about books and other products of interest based on the customer's past purchases and search behavior on the website. Amazon also sends interested customers customized e-mail messages that notify them that their favorite author or recording artist has published a new book or released a new CD. Amazon further personalizes customers' shopping experience by recommending complementary merchandise.

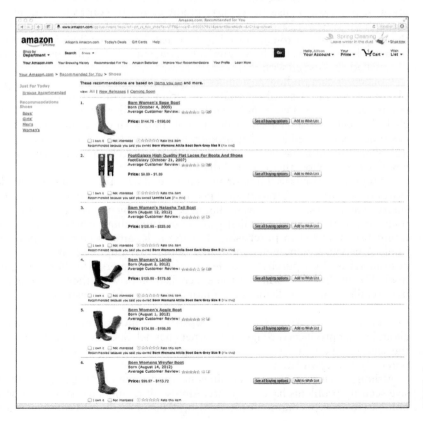

The Internet channels are particularly effective at making personalized recommendations.

Just as a well-trained salesperson would make recommendations to customers before checkout, an interactive web page can make suggestions to shoppers about additional items that they might like to consider.

Some multichannel retailers are able to personalize promotions and Internet homepages on the basis of several attributes tied to the shopper's current or previous web sessions, such as the time of day, time zone as determined by a computer's Internet address, and assumed gender.[23] However, some consumers worry about this ability to collect information about purchase histories, personal information, and search behavior on the Internet. How will this information be used in the future? Will it be sold to other firms, or will the consumer receive unwanted promotional materials online or in the mail?

Expand Market Presence   The market for customers who shop in stores is typically limited to consumers living in proximity those stores. The market for catalogs is limited by the high cost of printing and mailing them and increasing consumer interest in environmentally friendly practices. By adding the Internet channel, retailers can expand their market without having to build new stores or incur the high cost of additional catalogs. Adding an Internet channel is particularly attractive to retailers with strong brand names but limited locations and distribution. For example, retailers such as Neiman Marcus, REI, IKEA, and L.L. Bean are widely known for offering unique, high-quality merchandise. If these retailers only had a store, customers would have to travel vast distances to buy the merchandise they carry.

Provide Information to Improve Shopping Experience Across Channels
It is difficult for most store-based retailers to develop extensive purchase histories of their customers because the retailers are unable to link transactions to customers who pay cash or use third-party credit cards. In contrast, all transactions through the Internet have the customer identification information needed to send the product to the customer as well as their search behavior. This information can be used to provide valuable insights into how and why customers shop and are dissatisfied or satisfied with their experiences.[24]

Collecting data on how customers navigate through a website is quite easy. By placing a cookie (a small computer program that collects information about computer usage) on a customer's hard drive, the retailer can monitor each mouse click. The click-stream data provides insights into what characteristics of products customers considered and what products customers looked at but did not buy.[25] To collect this information from store shoppers would be quite difficult; someone would have to follow them around the store.

This information is useful to retailers in several ways. First, it helps them design stores or websites. By knowing how people shop, a retailer can determine, for instance, whether a store or website should be laid out by brands, size, color, or price point. It can also help the retailer give suggestions about what items a customer might be interested in purchasing. For example, after a customer purchases a book, Amazon recommends additional books that might be of interest to the customer based on purchases made by other customers who have bought that book. Finally, based on what customers clicked on or what they purchased in the past, retailers can provide unique promotions to individual customers.

Perceived Risks in Internet Shopping   Some consumers are concerned about buying products through an Internet channel. Specifically, some believe that the security of credit card transactions is greater than in stores and that there are potential privacy violations.

Although many consumers remain concerned about credit card security, extensive security problems have been rare. Almost all retailers use sophisticated technologies to encrypt communications. Also, all major credit card companies provide some consumer protection for retail transactions. Typically, customers are not liable for more than $50 as long as they report the unauthorized use in a timely manner. The consequences of security breaches can be far worse for the retailer from which the card number was stolen. Security breaches can ruin a retailer's reputation and possibly expose it to legal liability.[26]

Consumers also are concerned about the ability of retailers to collect information about their purchase history, personal information, and search behavior on the Internet without their knowledge.[27] They are worried about how this information will be used in the future. Will it be sold to other retailers, or will the consumer receive unwanted promotional materials online or in the mail? Issues related to privacy are discussed in more detail in Chapters 11 and 15.

Comparison of Electronic and Mobile Phone Internet Channels

Due to the rapid growth of domestic and international broadband access through handheld devices, such as tablets and mobile phones, retailers are very interested in developing this channel's potential. While the mobile Internet channel retains the same benefits over stores as the computer-based electronic Internet channel, it has its own unique benefits and limitations. In particular, customers can easily carry the device in their purses or pockets, and access the retailer's website from any place they are, as long as there is a mobile phone connection available.

Another advantage of a mobile channel is that customer–retailer interactions can be location-sensitive. For example, a retailer can determine where a customer is located and send location-relevant information to the customer, such as promotions, to encourage customers to buy other products nearby the store or go to another area of the store.

The major disadvantage of a mobile channel, compared to a computer-based Internet channel, is the mobile device's smaller screen and slower download speeds. To accommodate the smaller screen size, the software interface for interacting with mobile devices and computers is different. When using mobile channels, customers typically navigate using a touch screen with side scrolling, while a mouse is used with an electronic channel. The smaller screen size and touch screen navigation means that consumers using a mobile channel have to go through many more screens when browsing or trying to locate information.[29]

Apps   To provide their customers with a better shopping experience when using their mobile channels, many retailers have developed mobile shopping apps. **Apps** are software applications designed to improve the consumers' shopping experiences when using smartphones and tablets. Apps developed by retailers are typically used to easily perform some specific functions available on the retailer's website but do not provide access to all of the functions available on the website. The Amazon Mobile app offers product price comparisons with thousands of retailers. Its Snap It feature lets consumers take a photo of a product to search for it, and access to Amazon's one-click purchasing is available. Target's Shop Target makes it easy for consumers to scan barcodes and find daily and weekly deals. Users can also check product availability, search for nearby stores, and set up text alerts for discounts.

The use of tablets may provide the best trade-off between the portability of mobile phones and the navigation ease of websites accessed by computers. Most retailers serve the firm's website, rather a specially designed mobile website when a customer accesses an Internet channel. But now, some retailers are designing websites and apps for tablets. On Anthropologie's app, for example, consumers can not only browse items but also clip pictures of the most appealing options to add to their social networks, as well as check out detailed, thumbnail views of the offerings. The collage option allows them to put together outfits, including accessories

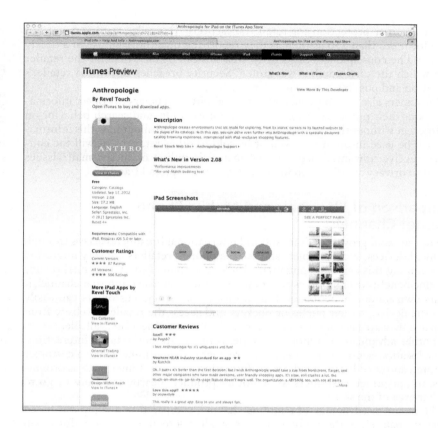

Anthropologie's app improves the usability of mobile devices.

and jewelry, to buy as a set. The percentage of shoppers accessing Anthropologie's website through tablets has tripled, to 6 percent, since the introduction of the app; the retailer expects that number to jump to 20 percent within about a year.[32]

CHALLENGES FACING MULTICHANNEL RETAILERS

LO3

Analyze the challenges facing multichannel retailers.

In the previous section, we outlined the benefits offered by the different retail channels. In this section, we describe how retailers are using multiple channels to improve their offerings to their customers and build a competitive advantage. The typical examples of the evolution toward multichannel retailing are when store-based retailers and catalogers add Internet channels. But retailers that focus on direct selling and TV home shopping network channels have also added Internet channels. Amazon, a retailer using only Internet channels, is even considering establishing a physical presence by having lockers in which customers can access merchandise they purchased online and/or actual stores to overcome some of the limitations of their Internet channel.[33]

Regardless of how they come to find a multichannel retailer, consumers want a seamless experience: Whether they solicit a sales associate for help, seek out an in-store kiosk, call in to the call center, or log on to the website, they also like to be recognized. Once recognized, they also need the retailer to facilitate their ability to find and pick up their purchases, even if they want to buy online and then pick up in the store, or vice versa. In addition, the various channels need to be consistent in the information they provide.

Retailers also benefit by using multiple channels synergistically. Multichannel retailers can use one channel to promote the services offered by other channels. For example, the URL of a store's website can be advertised on in-store signs, shopping bags, credit card billing statements, point-of-sale (POS) receipts, and the print or broadcast advertising used to promote the store. The physical stores and catalogs are also advertisements for a retailer's other channels. The retailer's channels can be used to stimulate store visits by announcing special store events and promotions.

Multichannel retailers can leverage their stores to lower the cost of fulfilling orders and processing returned merchandise. They can use their stores as "warehouses" for gathering merchandise for delivery to customers. Customers also can be offered the opportunity to pick up and return merchandise at the retailer's stores rather than pay shipping charges. Many retailers will waive shipping charges when orders are placed online or through the catalog if the customer physically comes into the store.

Offering customers the opportunity to buy online and pick up merchandise in a store is an example of the seamless interface customers are seeking.

However, as illustrated in Exhibit 3–3, most multichannel retailers have yet to provide these seamless customer-facing processes. This apparent lack of progress should not be interpreted as a lack of interest. The results of a recent survey indicate that cross-channel coordination is extremely important to retailers, even if they have yet to reach their full potential.[34]

In the next section, several challenges and trade-off decisions confronting multichannel retailers are discussed, including multichannel supply chain and information system issues, centralized versus decentralized multichannel retailing, maintaining a consistent brand image across channels, merchandise assortment trade-offs, pricing issues, and the challenge surrounding channel migration and showrooming.

Multichannel Supply Chains and Information Systems

Multichannel retailers still struggle to provide an integrated shopping experience because the various channels demand various skills, as well as unique resources.[35] When retail distribution centers (DCs) support a store channel, they move merchandise, packed in cartons, off the suppliers' trucks, into the DC inventory, and then onto new trucks heading to retail stores. When retailers get efficient enough, merchandise sits in the DC only briefly, often for less than a day. But DCs that supply catalog and Internet channels have other roles to fulfill as well: receive merchandise packed in cartons, then separate out the individual items to be repacked and shipped to individual end-customers. Handling individual items, rather than cartons, and shipping them to individual consumers, instead of retailers, requires unique packaging, different transportation systems, and new intermediaries.

Cross-Channel Fulfillment Activities	High-Performance Retailers	Others
Buy online, return in store	70%	59%
Buy in store, fulfill through online	70	41
Buy online, pick up in store	50	52
Buy via mobile	35	48
Buy via social media source	30	11
Buy online, fulfill through any stop	30	30

EXHIBIT 3–3
Percentage of Multichannel Retailers Offering Cross-Channel Fulfillment

Source: *Omni-Channel 2012: Cross-Channel Comes of Age, 2012 Benchmark*, RSR, June 2012.

Due to these operational differences, many store-based retailers have a separate organization to manage their Internet and catalog operations. But as the multi-channel operation matures, retailers tend to integrate all operations under one organization. Both Walmart and JCPenney initially had separate organizations for their Internet channel but subsequently integrated them with stores and catalogs.

Centralized versus Decentralized Multichannel Retailing

Because each of the channels offer a unique set of benefits, the profiles of a retailer's customers who use the different channels are not the same. Thus, a critical decision facing multichannel retailers is the degree to which they should integrate the operations of the channels or have different organizations for each channel. At one extreme of this continuum is complete integration—selling the same products at the same prices through the same distribution system for all channels. At the other extreme is having different organizations manage each channel so that the channels are tailored to different target markets. However, few retailers actually take the extreme route to pursue a strategy at one end of the continuum or the other.

Consistent Brand Image across Channels

Retailers need to provide a consistent brand image of themselves and their private-label merchandise across all channels. For example, Patagonia reinforces its image of selling high-quality, environmentally friendly sports equipment in its stores, catalogs, and website. Each of these channels emphasizes function, not fashion, in the descriptions of Patagonia's products. Patagonia's concerns about the environment are communicated by carefully lighting its stores and using re-cycled polyester in many of its clothes, as well as only organic, rather than pesti-cide-intensive, cotton. Its weblog, www.thecleanestline.com, is dedicated to essays and other features on environmental activism, innovative design, and sports. Retailing View 3.4 describes how Build-A-Bear Workshop uses multiple channels to build and reinforce its image.

Merchandise Assortment

Typically, different assortments are often appropriate for each of the channels. For example, multichannel retailers offer a broader and deeper merchandise assort-ment through their Internet channel than through their store channel. Because the Internet channel can have a much larger assortment, it can satisfy the needs of a larger variety of customer groups. For instance, multichannel apparel retailers can carry fringe sizes on their Internet channel, but it would be too expensive and space constricting to do so in their store channel.

The channels also differ in terms of their effectiveness in generating sales for different types of merchandise. For example, the store channel is better suited for selling products with important "touch-and-feel" attributes such as the fit of a shirt, the taste of an ice cream flavor, or the smell of a perfume. On the other hand, an Internet channel might be just as effective as a store channel for selling products with important "look-and-see" attributes such as price, color, and grams of fat. Evaluating these products does not require senses beyond sight. Because of the problems of providing touch-and-feel information, apparel retailers experi-ence return rates of more than 20 percent on purchases made through Internet channels, but only 5 percent on purchases made in stores.

Pricing

Pricing represents another difficult decision for a multichannel retailer. Many customers expect prices to be the same across channels (excluding shipping charges). However, in some cases, retailers need to adjust their pricing strategy because of the competition they face in different channels. For example, BarnesandNoble.com offers lower prices through its Internet channels than through its stores to compete effectively against Amazon.com.

Retailers with stores in multiple markets often set different prices for the same merchandise to deal with differences in local competition. They can do so because most customers don't know about these price differences because they are exposed only to the prices in their local markets. However, multichannel retailers may have difficulties sustaining regional price differences when customers can easily check prices on the Internet.

Reduction of Channel Migration

An Internet channel helps customers search for information about products and prices. The most common multichannel usage involves an initial search online, followed by a purchase in stores. Whereas approximately 78 percent of U.S. consumers adopt this pattern of consumption, only 8 percent browse through

 RETAILING VIEW   The Build-A-Bear Workshop Uses Multiple Channels to Enhance Its Image   **3.4**

The Build-A-Bear Workshop website reinforces the brand image generated by its stores.

On Bearville.com, stuffed animal fans of all ages and backgounds can enjoy the entertaining content provided by Build-A-Bear Workshop. The content includes online games, access to fun merit "certificates" and thank-you cards, and options for organizing a party. The site thus is closely integrated with the Build-A-Bear Workshop stores, as well as the company's mobile app—and of course, the cuddly products.

Just as youthful customers can name their furry friends, players of the online Bearville game can personalize their characters and purchase virtual outfits for them, then play with other global customers. These visitors spend approximately 25 million hours on the site, playing its free online games. With this Internet channel, Build-A-Bear thus hopes not only to improve its brand image, but also to keep children interested and interacting with the retailer, leading them to beg to make yet another visit to the local store.

Build-A-Bear also promises a safe and useful site. The Find-A-Bear identification program helps users find lost bears. As soon as children register, the company sends an e-mail to their parents, with a link that allows them to determine the level of communications the company will initiate, depending on their children's age, maturity, and comfort level. Furthermore, Build-A-Bear monitors the site to ensure all socialization is appropriate; as the founder of the company notes, "We're conscious of the issues of cyber-bullying, for example."

Sources: www.bearville.com, accessed September 1, 2012; "Build-a-Bear Workshop: The Bear Necessities," *Retail Week,* January 13, 2012; and "Build-A-Bear Workshop Creates Entertainment Destination," *Internet Wire,* February 9, 2011.

DISCUSSION QUESTION

Are these Internet channel activities consistent with its in-store brand?

stores first, then make their purchases via the Internet.[36] As long as the store and the Internet channel represent the same retailer, the firm is happy. But if customers gather information from one of its channels, then buy from a channel hosted by a competitor, the retailer suffers from the frustrating problem of **channel migration**.[37] Modern technologies, including those that allow customers to gather information and buy online or through their mobile devices, also make channel migration really easy. Thus, retaining customers remains a constant challenge for multichannel retailers.

As mentioned earlier in the chapter, a particularly concerning form of channel migration is called showrooming. **Showrooming** occurs when a consumer goes into a store to learn about different brands and products and then searches the Internet for the same product sold at a lower price. Three approaches that multichannel retailers can use to reduce showrooming are (1) providing better customer service, (2) offering uniquely relevant information based on proprietary data the retailer has collected about the customers, and (3) promoting private-label merchandise that can be purchased only from the retailer. These approaches are discussed in more detail in Chapter 5.[38]

MULTICHANNEL SHOPPING IN THE FUTURE

LO4

Consider the multichannel shopping experience in the future.

The following hypothetical scenario illustrates the technologies and seamless interface across channels that customers in the future may experience.

Shopping Experience Scenario

It's Tuesday morning, and Judy Jamison is eating breakfast thinking about buying a new dress for the party she'll be attending this Friday night at the new club downtown. She sends a tweet to her friends about her plans to go shopping after work today and asks for suggestions of retailers she might visit. She gets some suggestions from friends and then decides to do some research on the Internet. She logs on to her tablet, accesses her personal shopper program called FRED, and has the following interactive dialog:

> **FRED:** Do you wish to browse, go to a specific store, or buy a specific item?
>
> **Judy:** Specific item.
>
> **FRED:** What is the item? [Menu appears and Judy selects.]
>
> **Judy:** Dress.
>
> **FRED:** Occasion? [Menu appears and Judy selects.]
>
> **Judy:** Cocktail.
>
> **FRED:** Price range? [Menu appears.]
>
> **Judy:** $175–$200.
>
> [Now FRED goes out and literally shops the world electronically, visiting the servers for companies selling cocktail dresses in Europe, Asia, Africa, Australia, and North and South America.]
>
> **FRED:** 1,231 items have been identified. How many do you want to review? [Menu appears.]
>
> **Judy:** Just 7
>
> [FRED selects the seven best alternatives on the basis of information it has about Judy's style preferences. The seven cocktail dresses appear on the screen with the price, brand name, and retailer listed beneath each one. Judy clicks on each dress to get more information about it. With another click, she sees a full-motion video of a woman who looks similar to Judy modeling the dress. She selects several dresses she finds most appealing.]

However, Judy decides not to buy the dress because she is not sure the dress will fit right when it arrives, and she will not have time to return it and get another size. She likes the Robert Rodriguez styles FRED found, so she goes to Brand-Habit.com, types in the designer's name and her zip code, and finds the closest store that carries his designs and has her size in stock. The site directs her to the store's website to look at more dresses. She decides to visit the store after work.

Shortly after Judy walks into the store, a chip in her credit card signals her presence and status as a frequent shopper to a mobile device held by the store sales associate responsible for preferred clients. Information about items in which Judy might be interested, including the items she viewed on the website through FRED, is downloaded from the store server to Judy's and the sales associate's devices.

A sales associate approaches Judy and says, "Hello, Ms. Jamison. My name is Joan Bradford. How can I help you?" Judy tells the associate she needs to buy a dress for a party. She has seen some dresses on the store's website and would like to look at them in the store. The sales associate takes Judy to a virtual dressing room.

In the dressing room, Judy sits in a comfortable chair and views the dresses displayed on her image, which has been drawn from a body scan stored in Judy's customer file. Information about Judy's recent visit to the retailer's website and her past purchases is used to select the dresses displayed.

Using her mobile phone, Judy shares this personalized viewing with her friend, who is still at work in California. They discuss which dress looks best on Judy. Then, using her mobile phone again, Judy drills down to find more information about the dress—the fabric, cleaning instructions, and so forth. Finally, she selects a dress that is of most interest to her and tries it on. When she tries is on, the video cameras in the room enable her to see what she looks like from all angles. She notices that from some angles the dress does not have a flattering fit. The sales associate suggests that this problem can be overcome with a minor alteration and shows Judy how she will look in the altered dress. Using information displayed on her mobile device, the sales associate Joan suggests a handbag and scarf that would complement the dress. These accessories are added to the image of Judy in the dress. Judy decides to buy the scarf but not the handbag. Judy is informed that she will get a message on her mobile when the alterations are completed, and then she can indicate whether she wants the dress delivered to her home or she will pick it up at the store.

As Judy passes through the cosmetics department on her way to her car, she sees an appealing new lipstick shade. She decides to purchase the lipstick and a 3-ounce bottle of her favorite perfume and walks out of the store. The store systems sense her departure, and the merchandise she has selected is automatically charged to her account through signals from radio-frequency identification (RFID) chips.

Supporting the Shopping Experience

This scenario illustrates the advantages of having a customer database shared by all channels and integrated across all systems. The sales associate and the store systems are able to offer superior customer service based on this database, which contains information about Judy's body scan image, her interaction with the retailer's website, and her past purchases and preferences. The technology also supports the retailer's business model, which determines how to offer customers the products and services that will provide the best shopping experience.

Before Judy went into the store, she interacted with a search engine to find where the particular brand and product she was looking for could be found. She then interacted with the retailer's website to review the available merchandise before she went to the store, check the status of her alterations, and decide about having the merchandise delivered to her home. The scenario also includes some new technologies that will exist in the store of the future, such as RFID, self-checkout, and personalized virtual reality displays.

SUMMARY

LO1 **Understand the nonstore channels offered by retailers.**

A *retail channel* is the way a retailer sells *and* delivers merchandise and services to its customers. The most common channel used by retailers is a store. Retailers also use a variety of nonstore channels including the Internet, mobile, catalogs, direct mail, direct selling, television home shopping, direct response TV, and automated retailing (vending machines) to make sales to customers. *Multichannel retailing* involves using more than one channel to enhance the customer satisfaction experience and exploit the synergies between channels. Some of the challenges facing multichannel retailers are due to the operational and organizational differences inherent in managing multiple information and supply chain systems, channel operations, pricing, branding, and assortments.

LO2 **Compare the benefits offered by the four major retail channels: stores, Internet, and catalogs**

Stores offer several benefits to customers that they cannot get when they shop through non-store channels such as Internet, or catalogs. These benefits include touching and feeling products, personal service, increased customer service, risk reduction, immediate gratification, cash payments, and entertainment and social experiences.

The catalog channel, like all non-store channels, provides safety and convenience benefits to customers. Using the catalog channel, consumers can look at merchandise and place an order from almost anywhere 24/7 without needing a computer, mobile device, or Internet connection. Second, consumers can refer to the information in a catalog anytime by simply picking it up from the coffee table. Finally, catalogs are easier to browse through than Web sites.

There are five advantages of the Internet channels. First, the addition of the Internet channels has

the potential to offer a greater selection of products. Second, they allow retailers to provide more information. Third, they enable retailers to provide customers with more personalized information about products and services. Fourth, they offer sellers the unique opportunity to collect information about consumer shopping. Fifth, the Internet channels provide an opportunity for retailers to enter new markets economically. Finally, they provide information that they can use to improve the shopping experience across all channels. Some consumers are concerned about buying products through an Internet channel.

LO3 **Understand the issues facing multichannel retailers**

Multichannel retailers are still struggling to provide an integrated shopping experience across all their channels because unique skills and resources are needed to manage each channel. A critical decision facing multichannel retailers is the degree to which they should integrate the operations of the channels or have different organizations for each channel. Since each of the channels offers a unique set of benefits, the profiles of a retailer's customers who use the different channels are not the same. Retailers need to provide a consistent brand image of themselves and their private-label merchandise across all channels. Pricing represents another difficult decision for a multichannel retailer. Finally, the availability of an Internet channel enables customers to easily search for information about products and their prices during a shopping episode.

LO4 **Consider the multichannel shopping experience in the future**

This scenario illustrates shopping in the future from an integrated multi-channel retailer.

KEY TERMS

GET OUT AND DO IT!

1. **CONTINUING CASE ASSIGNMENT: GO SHOPPING** Assume that you are shopping on the Internet for an item in the same merchandise category

you analyzed for the Comparison Shopping exercise in Chapter 2. Go to the retailer's website, and compare the merchandise assortment offered, the prices, and the shopping experience in the store and on the store's website. How easy was it to locate what you were looking for? What were the assortment and pricing like? What was the checkout like? What are the categories and/or sub-categories? How many SKUs were in each category and subcategory? What features of the sites did you like and dislike, such as the look and feel of the site, navigation, and special features?

2. **INTERNET EXERCISE** Go to the websites of J. Crew (www.jcrew.com), JCPenney (www.jcpenney.com), and American Eagle Outfitters (www.ae.com), and shop for a pair of khaki pants. Evaluate your shopping experience at each site. Compare and contrast the sites and your experiences on the basis of characteristics you think are important to consumers.

3. **INTERNET EXERCISE** Assume that you are getting married and planning your wedding. Compare and contrast the usefulness of www.theknot.com and www.weddingchannel.com for planning your wedding. What features of the sites do you like and dislike? Indicate the specific services offered by these sites that you would use.

4. **INTERNET AND SHOPPING EXERCISE** Pick a merchandise category like microwave ovens, power drills, digital cameras, blenders, or coffee makers. Compare a retailer's offering in its local store and on its Internet site. What are the differences in the assortments offered through its store and Internet channel? Are the prices the same or different? What has the retailer done to exploit the synergies between the channels?

5. **INTERNET AND SHOPPING EXERCISE** Access the websites of Home Depot and Macy's using your mobile phone and computer. What are the differences in the ease of navigation when looking at the presentation of merchandise using the two methods of accessing the websites?

DISCUSSION QUESTIONS AND PROBLEMS

1. Why are store-based retailers aggressively pursuing sales through Internet channels?

2. From a customer's perspective, what are the benefits and limitations of stores? Catalogs? Retailer websites?

3. Would you buy clothes on the basis of the way they look on a customized virtual model? Why or why not?

4. Why are the Internet and catalog channels so popular for gift giving?

5. Should a multichannel retailer offer the same assortment of merchandise for sale, at the same price, on its website and in its stores? Why or why not?

6. Which of the following categories of merchandise do you think could be sold most successfully through an Internet channel: jewelry; TV sets; computer software; high-fashion apparel; pharmaceuticals; health care products such as toothpaste, shampoo, and cold remedies? Why?

7. Assume you are interested in investing in a startup Internet retailer that targets people who enjoy active outdoor recreation, such as hiking, rock climbing, and kayaking. What merchandise and information would you offer on the site? What type of entity do you think would be most effective in running the site: a well-known outdoors person, a magazine targeting outdoor activity, or a retailer selling outdoor merchandise, such as Patagonia or REI? Why?

8. What are the advantages to customers of accessing the Internet through a mobile device or a computer when browsing a website? When learning special promotions?

9. When you shop online for merchandise, how much time do you spend browsing versus buying? When you shop in a store for merchandise, how much time do you spend browsing versus buying?

SUGGESTED READINGS

Avery, Jill, Thomas J. Steenburgh, John Deighton, and Mary Caravella, "Adding Bricks to Clicks: Predicting the Patterns of Cross-Channel Elasticities Over Time," *Journal of Marketing* 76(May 2012), 7, pp. 96–111.

Brynjolfsson, Erik, Hu, Yu (Jeffrey), Rahmanand Mohammad S., "Battle of the Retail Channels: How Product Selection and Geography Drive Cross-Channel Competition," *Management Science*, November 2009, Vol. 55 Issue 11, pp. 1755–1765.

Hsiao, Cheng-Chieh; Yen, Ju Rebecca Hsiu, and Eldon Y. Li, "Exploring Consumer Value of Multi-Channel Shopping: A Perspective of Means-End Theory," *Internet Research*, 22: 3, 2012, pp. 318–339.

Lee, Hyun-Hwa and Jihyun Kim (2010), "Investigating Dimensionality of Multichannel Retailer's Cross-Channel Integration Practices and Effectiveness: Shopping Orientation and Loyalty Intention," *Journal of Marketing Channels*, 17:4, 2010, pp. 281–312.

Neslin, S.A. and V. Shankar (2009), "Keys Issues in Multichannel Customer Management: Current Knowledge and Future Directions," *Journal of Interactive Marketing*, 23: 1, pp. 70–81.

Poloian, Lynda Gamans. *Retailing Principles: Global, Multichannel, and Management Viewpoints, 2nd Ed.* Fairchild Publication: New York, 2012.

Schramm-Klein, Hanna, Gerhard Wagner, Sascha Steinmann and Dirk Morschett, "Cross-Channel Integration—Is It Valued By Customers?," *The International Review of Retail, Distribution and Consumer Research*, 21: 5, 2011, pp. 501–511.

Weitz, Barton A. "Electronic Retailing," in Retailing in the 21st Century—Current and Future Trends, 2nd ed., eds. Manfred Kraft and Murali Mantrala. Berlin: Springer, 2010, pp. 309–323.

Zhang, Jie, Paul W. Farris, John W. Irvin, Tarun Kushwaha, Thomas J. Steenburgh, Barton A. Weitz, Crafting Integrated Multichannel Retailing Strategies," *Journal of Interactive Marketing*, Volume 24, Issue 2, May 2010, pp. 168–180.

Customer Buying Behavior

EXECUTIVE BRIEFING

Don Unser, Group President, Retail Business Group, The NPD Group, Inc.

The NPD Group provides information about consumer buying behavior that helps our clients, both retailers and vendors, make better, fact-based decisions. The reports provided by our system are derived from two sources: point-of-sale (POS) data and consumer panel data.

The POS data are supplied by over 900 retail clients around the world, detailing sales in over 150,000 stores. The database provides sales for products and their prices across general merchandise categories offered by a broad cross-section of retailers including department, discount, and specialty stores. Retailers share this sales data in exchange for the knowledge we provide from our analyses.

The online consumer panel consists of over 2 million people who have agreed to participate in surveys and provide information on their purchase behavior. In addition to sales by product and retailer, the database includes demographic and other information about the panel members including customer satisfaction evaluations following specific purchase occasions. This database allows sales tracking across all channels, by demographic segments. Our technology ensures survey samples are representative of the total population or a client's particular target audience.

Our systems are designed to make it easy for retailers to get the data that help them analyze market performance and make fact-based decisions. A variety of reports are available drawing on both databases. For example, an automotive parts retailer reviewed a fair-share report that compared its market share in each merchandise category to its overall market share and discovered some areas in which it was not getting its fair share—it had a market share of 8 percent in the category compared to its overall market share of 11 percent. By drilling down into the data, the buyer for the category adjusted the assortment plan, changing the emphasis placed on specific brands and SKUs. The result was an increase in annual sales of $3 million and a promotion for the buyer.

Due to the breadth and depth of data we collect and analyze, we are able to identify key consumer trends and business opportunities. The choice of food and meals by consumers in their 20s, referred to as Gen Y or millennials, differs from other generations. We find that this segment of consumers has a high degree of confidence in their judgments, heed cravings quickly, and place high value on minimal preparation time. They are more likely than consumers in other age groups to use frozen entrées

CHAPTER 4

LEARNING OBJECTIVES

LO1 Describe the process that consumers go through when making retail patronage and buying decisions.

LO2 Identify the different types of buying processes.

LO3 Summarize how the economy and social factors affect customer purchase decisions.

LO4 Determine why and how retailers group customers into market segments.

and other quick-prep items. These young adults have been among the hardest-hit by the recession and are heavy patrons of low-priced retailers. One-third of millennials shop at Walmart and other mass merchants. For food retailers and restaurants, a major opportunity—and challenge—exists in learning how to communicate effectively with this "connected" generation, as well as offering products and meal/snack solutions that fit their spontaneous, budget-conscious lifestyles.

As discussed in Chapter 1, an effective retail strategy satisfies customer needs better than do competitors' strategies. Successful retailers are customer-centric—their strategic and tactical decisions revolve around their present and potential customers. Thus, understanding customer needs and buying behavior is critical to formulating and implementing an effective retail strategy.

This chapter focuses on how customers process information and make decisions about what stores to patronize, what channels to use, and what products and services to buy.[1] It describes the stages customers go through when making purchase decisions and the factors that influence their buying process. Because typically it is not cost-efficient for retailers to develop unique offerings for individual customers, retailers target their offerings to groups of customers (market segments) with similar needs and buying processes. Thus, this chapter continues with a discussion of how market segments are formed. We use information about the buying process to discuss how retailers can identify the market segments that will be the target of their retail strategy. The appendix to this chapter examines special aspects of consumer behavior that are of concern to retailers selling fashion merchandise.

THE BUYING PROCESS

LO1

Describe the process that consumers go through when making retail patronage and buying decisions.

The following scenario illustrates the steps consumers go through when purchasing merchandise. Eva Mendoza, a student at the University of Washington, is beginning to interview for jobs. Eva planned to wear the blue suit her parents gave her several years ago to the interviews. But looking at her suit, she realizes that it's not very stylish and that the jacket is beginning to show signs of wear. Wanting to make a good first impression during her interviews, she decides to buy a new suit.

Eva surfs the Internet for tips on dressing for interviews and looks through some catalogs to see the styles and prices being offered. Eva surfs fashion blogs such as Nubry and checks what her friends are wearing on Facebook and then checks what they "Like" and what they have "pinned" on Pinterest. She goes to retailers' websites to examine and compare all their suits. She then decides to go to a store so that she can try on a suit and have it altered if necessary. She likes to shop at American Eagle Outfitters and Banana Republic, but neither sells business suits. Before going to the Northgate Mall in Seattle, she issues a status update on her Facebook page, announcing her intentions to go to the mall and inviting friends to join her. Britt responds to her Facebook posting, and they decide to meet at the mall entrance. Betsy also responds, but she has a cold and wants to rest.

Eva and Britt first go to Macy's and are approached by a salesperson in the career women's department. After asking Eva what type of suit she wants and her size, the salesperson shows her three suits. Eva talks with Britt about the suits, and they decide to get Betsy's opinion. So Eva takes photos of the suits with her mobile phone and sends them to Betsy at her apartment. Betsy likes all three, so Eva tries them on.

When Eva comes out of the dressing room, she is unsure which suit to select, but after sending Betsy some more photos, she, Britt, and the salesperson decide the second suit is the most attractive and appropriate for interviewing. Eva is happy with the color, fit, fabric, and length of the suit, but she is concerned that it will require dry cleaning. It also costs more than she had planned to spend. Eva decides to buy the suit after another customer in the store, seeing her wearing the suit, tells her she looks very professional.

As Britt and Eva are walking toward the door, they pass the shoe department. Britt tells Eva, "You need to buy shoes that go with your suit." Eva finds a pair of Steve Madden pumps that are perfect. She tries on a few pairs to get

Consumers are increasingly turning to fashionista blogs to read reviews and pick up the latest fashion tips.

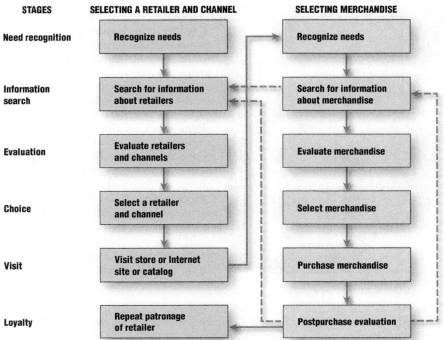

EXHIBIT 4–1
Stages in the Buying Process

the right size. Then Britt tells her that she thinks the shoes are overpriced. Eva scans the UPC code for the shoes using her mobile phone's shopping app and finds that Zappos is selling the shoes for $20 less and with no sales tax. So she orders the shoes from Zappos for delivery to her apartment the next day.

Consider Eva's shopping trip as we describe the customer buying process. The **buying process**—the steps consumers go through when buying a product or service—begins when customers recognize an unsatisfied need. Then they seek information about how to satisfy the need—what retailers, channels, and products or services might satisfy the need. Customers then evaluate the alternatives and choose a store or Internet site to visit or a catalog to review. Their encounter with a retailer provides more information and may alert customers to additional needs. After evaluating the retailer's offering, customers may make a purchase or go to another retailer to collect more information. Eventually, customers purchase a product, use the product, and then decide whether the retailer, channel, and product satisfy their needs during the postpurchase evaluation stage of the customer buying process.

Exhibit 4–1 outlines the buying process—the stages consumers go through to select a retailer and channel and to buy a specific item. The exhibit suggests that the buying process is linear, as shown by the solid lines. First, the channel and retailer are selected and then the specific items. For each of these decisions, customers go through five stages, beginning with need recognition and ending with loyalty. As we discuss the stages in the buying process, you should recognize that customers might not go through all the stages and/or might not go through the stages in the order shown in Exhibit 4–1. For example, Eva might have decided on the brand of suit she wanted before selecting a store, or she might have collected information about suits sold at Macy's and, on the basis of this information, decided to go to another store or to use another channel, such as the Internet, to buy the suit.

Retailers attempt to influence consumers as they go through the buying process to encourage consumers to buy merchandise and services from them. Each stage in the buying process is examined in the following sections.

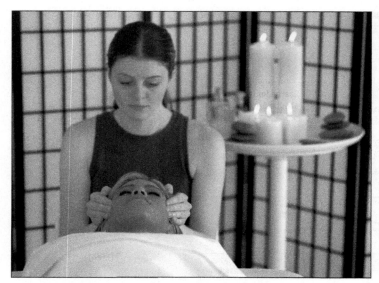

Spas make guests the center of attention and satisfy hedonic needs.

Need Recognition

The buying process is triggered when consumers recognize they have an unsatisfied need. An **unsatisfied need** arises when customers' desired level of satisfaction differs from their present level of satisfaction. For example, Eva recognized that she had a need when she was faced with the prospect of interviewing for jobs in her blue suit. She needed a suit that would make a good impression and realized her worn, outdated blue suit would not satisfy this need. Need recognition can be as straightforward as realizing you need a haircut, feeling the need for an uplifting experience after a final exam, or receiving a message about something a friend bought.

Types of Needs   The needs that motivate customers to go shopping can be classified as utilitarian or hedonic. When consumers go shopping to accomplish a specific task, such as Eva buying a suit for job interviews, they are seeking to satisfy **utilitarian needs.** When consumers go shopping for pleasure, they are seeking to satisfy their **hedonic needs**—their needs for entertaining, emotional, and recreational experiences. Thus, from the consumer's perspective, utilitarian needs are associated with work, whereas hedonic needs are associated with pleasure.[2]

Successful retailers attempt to satisfy both the utilitarian and the hedonic needs of their customers. Consumers motivated by utilitarian needs typically shop in a more deliberate and efficient manner. Thus, retailers need to provide adequate information and an effortless shopping experience for utilitarian shoppers. On the other hand, shoppers with hedonic needs desire excitement, stimulation, status and power, recreation, and adventure.[3] Examples of how retailers satisfy hedonic needs are listed next:

1. *Stimulation.* Retailers and mall managers use background music, visual displays, scents, and demonstrations in stores and malls to create a carnival-like, stimulating experience for their customers. (See Chapter 17.) Such environments encourage consumers to take a break from their everyday lives and visit stores. Retailers also attempt to stimulate customers with exciting graphics and photography in their catalogs and on their websites.

2. *Status and power.* Some people choose retailers based on the attention and respect they receive. For example, Canyon Ranch offers upscale health resorts in Tucson, Arizona, and Lenox, Massachusetts, as well as spa clubs in Las Vegas, Nevada, and on cruises, such as Oceania, Regent Seven Seas, and the Queen Mary 2. All Canyon Ranch resorts and spas make the customer the center of attention, offering spa services, medical and nutritional consultations, workshops, spiritual pursuits, and healthy gourmet cuisine.

3. *Adventure.* Often, consumers go shopping because they enjoy finding bargains, looking for sales, and finding discounts or low prices. They treat shopping as a game to be "won." Off-price retailers like Marshalls and Trader Joe's, warehouse clubs like Costco, and fast-fashion specialty retailers like Zara cater to this need by constantly changing their assortment so that customers never know what kind of treasure they will find.

Saks Fifth Avenue uses its exciting window displays to stimulate need recognition.

Conflicting Needs   Most customers have multiple needs. Moreover, these needs often conflict. For example, Eva Mendoza would like to wear a DKNY suit, which would enhance her self-image and earn her the admiration of her college friends. But satisfying these hedonic needs might conflict with her utilitarian needs—the need to stay within her budget and the need to get a job. Employers might feel that she's not responsible if she wears a suit that is too expensive for an interview for an entry-level position. Later in this chapter, we discuss a model of how customers make trade-offs between conflicting needs.

The needs and decision-making processes may differ depending on the specific situation. For example, a skier may purchase expensive Spyder goggles but wear an inexpensive snowsuit from Target. A grocery shopper might buy an inexpensive store brand of paper towels and a premium national brand of orange juice. This pattern of buying both premium and low-priced merchandise or patronizing both expensive, status-oriented retailers and price-oriented retailers is called **cross-shopping**.[4]

Stimulating Need Recognition   Customers must first recognize unsatisfied needs before they are motivated to visit a store or go online to buy merchandise. Sometimes these needs are stimulated by an event in a person's life, like Eva's impending interviews. But retailers use a variety of approaches to stimulate unmet needs. Advertising, e-mails, direct mail, publicity, and special events communicate the availability of new merchandise or special prices. Visits to SeenOn (www.SeenOn.com) can stimulate need recognition by showing products that celebrities or television characters have worn. In a social media campaign, Melrose Jewelers encouraged visitors to its Facebook page to consider a watch purchase by giving them a personality quiz that claimed to reveal which watch style best suited them.[5] Within a store, visual merchandising and salespeople can stimulate need recognition. For example, the display of shoes stimulated Eva's need for shoes to complement her new suit.

Information Search

Once customers identify a need, they typically seek information about retailers, channels, or products to help them satisfy that need. Eva's search started on the Internet and then narrowed to the three suits shown to her by the salesperson at Macy's and the opinions of her friends.[6] In other situations, Eva might have

94   SECTION I   The World of Retailing

collected a lot more information by visiting several retailers and/or spending more time on the Internet getting information from fashion blogs like College Fashion, Refinery29, and FabSugar.[7]

Sources of Information   Customers have two sources of information: internal and external. **Internal sources** are information in a customer's memory, such as names, images, and past experiences with different stores. The major source of internal information is the customer's past shopping experience. Even if they remember only a small fraction of the information to which they are exposed, customers have an extensive internal information bank to draw on when deciding where to shop and what to buy.

External sources consist of information provided by a host of sources. People search for products and information using search engines such as Google, visit the websites maintained by manufacturers and retailers, acquire information from traditional media (e.g., advertising), read blogs, watch product demonstrations on YouTube, and ask friends, in person and through social media.

When customers believe that they are not well enough informed or that their internal information is inadequate, they turn to external information sources. For example, Eva asked her friends, Betsy and Britt, to help her make the purchase decision. To find out if the price of the shoes she liked was reasonable, she turned to an online shoe seller. Such external sources of information play a major role in the acceptance of fashions, as discussed in the appendix to this chapter.

Amount of Information Searched   In general, the amount of **information search** undertaken depends on the value customers believe they can gain from searching versus the cost of searching.[9] The value of the search stems from the degree to which the additional information improves the customer's purchase decision. Will the search help the customer find a lower-priced product or one that will give superior performance? The costs of the search include the customer's time and money. Traveling from store to store can cost money for gas and parking, but the major cost incurred is the customer's time.

Technology has dramatically reduced the cost of information search. For example, vast information about merchandise sold across the world is just a smartphone search away. Retailing View 4.1 describes how readily available information on the Web affects the automobile buying process.

The amount of information search is affected by (1) characteristics of the individual customer and (2) aspects of the market and buying situation in which the purchase is made.[10] Some people search more than others. Shoppers seeking hedonic benefits typically spend more time collecting information and shopping because they enjoy the process. Customers who have prior experience purchasing and using the product or service tend to search less.

Two marketplace and situational factors affecting information search are (1) the number of competing brands and retail outlets and (2) the time pressure under which the purchase must be made.[11] When competition is greater and there are more alternatives to consider, the amount of information search increases. However, the amount decreases with greater time pressures.

Reducing Information Search   The retailer's objective for customers in the information search stage is to limit the customer's search to its store or website. One measure of a retailer's performance on this objective is the **conversion rate**— the percentage of customers who enter a store or access a website and then buy a product from that same store or website.

Each element of the retailing mix can be used to increase a retailer's conversion rate. Category specialists such as Best Buy provide a very deep assortment of merchandise, everything a customer might want to consider, so that the customer can collect all the information and make the necessary comparisons between products in their stores or on their websites.

At Old Navy, the remodeled layout features a racetrack format that reduces information search by giving customers a better sense of the vast options available. It also displays more items around the checkout area.[12]

Services provided by retailers can also limit the search once at the retailer's location. By offering credit and having informed salespeople, a retailer can convince consumers that they don't need to collect additional information from other retailers. Lowe's has equipped its floor staff with iPhones to enable them to check

RETAILING VIEW   The Internet Has Changed the Car-Buying Process

4.1

Ten years ago, if consumers wanted to buy a car, they would visit several dealers, look at different models, test drive the cars sold by each dealer, and then negotiate price and financing with a dealer. Many consumers viewed this traditional process of buying a car as about as pleasurable as a visit to the dentist. But now the Internet has changed this experience, as well as the nature of automobile retailing.

The Internet has given consumers more control over the car-buying process. Consumers can visit websites such as www.autobytel.com, www.cars.com, or www.edmunds.com; access a wealth of information, including the dealer's costs for cars and options; compare vehicles in a side-by-side chart that lists their price, features, horsepower, mileage, legroom, and options; read multiple reviews for most models; and even take a 360-degree photo tour of car interiors that gives them an idea of what the view looks like from the driver's seat.

Through the sites' relationships with car dealers, consumers can request prices from dealers in their area. A handy calculator tells customers how much the monthly payment would be if they were to buy a car on credit. The sites also have calculators to help car buyers figure out how much they can afford to spend on a car, whether they should buy a new or used car, and whether they should lease or buy. This information enables consumers to walk into a dealership knowing as much as or more than the dealer's salespeople.

On the TrueCar website, consumers find information about recent purchases in their area. Thus, for a specific car make and model, they see a bell curve that shows them what represents a great price, what is a reasonable price, and what is simply too much to pay. The site also identifies the local dealership that will offer the lowest price, so car buyers know where to start their search.

CarFax (www.carfax.com) enables customers to access a vehicle's history report by typing in its vehicle identification number (VIN). This history describes any accidents the vehicle was in, its past ownership, odometer fraud, and any other events that might be related to the vehicle. Services such as CarFax make it much easier for customers to purchase used cars with confidence.

REFACT

Nearly three-quarters of new-vehicle buyers use the Internet during the shopping process, and 54 percent watch online videos.[13]

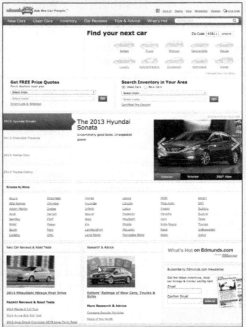

The Internet has dramatically reduced the time and effort needed to collect information and increased the quality of information acquired to make a decision when buying an automobile.

Sources: Edward Niedermeyer, "TrueCar Versus Honda: Online Car Buying Challenges Hit Home," *The Truth About Cars*, December 21, 2011; Geoffrey A. Fowler, John D. Stoll, and Scott Morrison, "GM, eBay Will Let Car Buyers Dicker Online," *The Wall Street Journal*, August 11, 2009, p. B1; Thomas Pack, "Kicking the Virtual Tires: Car Research on the Web," *Information Today*, January 2009, pp. 44–45; www.cars.com; and www.carfax.com.

DISCUSSION QUESTIONS

How did you use the Internet to purchase your last car? Was your method of searching for information different than that of your parents?

Lowe's uses iPhones to help customers with their shopping.

inventory levels for customers on the spot. Similarly, Pacific Sunwear gives salespeople iPads that help them create virtual outfits to show customers. Foot Locker is relying on old-fashioned training, such that employees have a better sense of how to engage customers and encourage them to buy in the store.[14]

Walmart utilizes an **everyday low pricing (EDLP) strategy** that stresses continuity of retail prices at a level somewhere between the regular nonsale price and the deep-discount sale price of its competitors. This strategy helps assure customers that they won't find a lower price for these products at a different store the next time they go shopping. In addition, many stores with everyday low prices offer money-back guarantees if a competitor offers the same merchandise at a lower price. These pricing policies tend to limit the customer information search to the retailer's offering.

Internet, Mobile, Information Search, and Price Competition   The Internet and smartphones have had a profound impact on consumers' ability to gather external information. In addition to placing their own information on their websites and smartphone apps, retailers encourage their customers to post information such as product reviews, ratings, and, in some cases, photos and videos. Consumer reviews are emerging as a prime information source for shoppers as they collect information during the buying process.[16] The Internet and new mobile apps that encourage showrooming—a practice in which consumers visit stores to gather information about the product, then buy online—enable consumers to find the best prices for any product quickly.

Retailers and manufacturers are concerned that the ease of collecting price information through the Internet increases price competition. Traditionally, store-based retailers, offering the same merchandise, experienced limited price competition because of their geographic separation. The Internet means that consumers' ability to compare prices no longer is limited by physical distance. In addition, the ease of searching for price information is facilitated by shopping sites such as mysimon.com. Or consumers can use one of the many mobile phone apps to learn about prices and availability of products at stores near where they are located.[18]

The Internet not only helps online consumers collect price information, but also gives them information about the quality and performance of products, all at a low search cost. With more information about product quality, customers might be willing to pay more for high-quality products, which would mitigate the importance of price.[20] Finally, retailers that use an Internet channel can clearly differentiate their offerings by providing better services and information.

Evaluation of Alternatives: The Multiattribute Model

The multiattribute attitude model provides a useful way to summarize how customers use the information they have collected to evaluate and select retailers, channels, and products. We discuss this model in detail because it offers a framework for developing a retailing strategy.[21]

The **multiattribute attitude model** is based on the notion that customers see a retailer, a product, or a channel as a collection of attributes or characteristics. The model is designed to predict a customer's evaluation of a product, retailer, or channel on the basis of (1) its performance on relevant attributes and (2) the importance of those attributes to the customer.

Beliefs about Performance   To illustrate this model, consider the store choice decision confronting a young, single, professional Milwaukee woman who needs groceries. She considers three alternatives: (1) a supercenter store in the next suburb, (2) her local supermarket store, or (3) a grocer that operates only an Internet channel, such as Fresh Direct. Her perception of the offerings provided by these retailers is shown in Exhibit 4–2.

The customer mentally processes the "objective" information about each grocery retailer in part A of Exhibit 4–2 and forms an impression of the benefits each one provides. Part B of Exhibit 4–2 shows her beliefs about these benefits. Notice that some benefits combine several objective characteristics. For example, the convenience benefit combines travel time, checkout time, and ease of finding products. Grocery prices and delivery cost affect her beliefs about the economy of shopping at the various retail outlets.

The degree to which each retailer provides each benefit is represented on a 10-point scale: 10 means the retailer performs very well in providing the benefit; 1 means it performs very poorly. In this example, no retailer has superior performance on all benefits. The supercenter performs well on economy and assortment

A. INFORMATION ABOUT STORES SELLING GROCERIES			
Store Characteristics	Supercenter	Supermarket	Internet Grocer
Grocery prices	20% below average	Average	10% above average
Delivery cost ($)	0	0	10
Total travel time (minutes)	30	15	0
Typical checkout time (minutes)	10	5	2
Number of products, brands, and sizes	40,000	30,000	40,000
Fresh produce	Yes	Yes	Yes
Fresh fish	Yes	Yes	No
Ease of finding products	Difficult	Easy	Easy
Ease of collecting nutritional information about products	Difficult	Difficult	Easy

B. BELIEFS ABOUT STORES' PERFORMANCE BENEFITS*			
Performance Benefits	Supercenter	Supermarket	Internet Grocer
Economy	10	8	6
Convenience	3	5	10
Assortment	9	7	5
Availability of product Information	4	4	8

*10 = excellent, 1 = poor.

EXHIBIT 4–2
Characteristics of Food Retailers

but is low on convenience. The Internet grocer offers the best convenience but is weak on economy and assortment.

Importance Weights   The young woman in the preceding example forms an overall evaluation of each alternative on the basis of the importance she places on each benefit the retailers provide. The importance she places on a benefit can also be represented using a 10-point rating scale, with 10 indicating the benefit is very important to her and 1 indicating it's very unimportant. Using this rating scale, the importance of the retailers' benefits for the young woman and for a parent with four children is shown in Exhibit 4–3, along with the performance beliefs previously discussed. Notice that the single woman values convenience and the availability of product information much more than economy and assortment. But to the parent, economy is very important and assortment is moderately important, whereas convenience and product information aren't very important.

The importance of a retailer's benefits differs for each customer and also may differ for each shopping trip. For example, the parent with four children may stress economy for major shopping trips but place more importance on convenience for a fill-in trip.

In Exhibit 4–3, the single woman and parent have the same beliefs about each retailer's performance, but they differ in the importance they place on the benefits the retailers offer. In general, customers can differ in their beliefs about retailers' performances as well as in their importance weights.

Evaluating Retailers   Research has shown that a customer's overall evaluation of an alternative (in this situation, three retailers) is related to the sum of the performance beliefs multiplied by the importance weights. Thus, we calculate the young, single woman's overall evaluation or score for the supercenter as follows:

$$
\begin{array}{rcl}
4 \times 10 & = & 40 \\
10 \times 3 & = & 30 \\
5 \times 9 & = & 45 \\
9 \times 4 & = & \underline{36} \\
& & 151
\end{array}
$$

Exhibit 4–3 shows the overall evaluations of the three retailers using the importance weights of the single woman and the parent. For the single woman, the Internet grocer has the highest score, 221, and thus has the most favorable evaluation. She would probably select this retailer for most of her grocery shopping. On the other hand, the supercenter has the highest score, 192, for the parent, who'd probably buy the family's weekly groceries there.

When customers are about to select a retailer, they don't actually go through the process of listing store characteristics, evaluating retailers' performances on these

EXHIBIT 4–3
Evaluation of Retailers

Characteristic	IMPORTANCE WEIGHTS*		PERFORMANCE BELIEFS		
	Young Single Woman	Parent with Four Children	Supercenter	Supermarket	Internet Grocer
Economy	4	10	10	8	6
Convenience	10	4	3	5	10
Assortment	5	8	9	7	5
Availability of product information	9	2	4	4	8
OVERALL EVALUATION					
Young single woman			151	153	221
Parent with four children			192	164	156

*10 = very important, 1 = very unimportant.

characteristics, determining each characteristic's importance, calculating each store's overall score, and then patronizing the retailer with the highest score. The multiattribute attitude model does not reflect customers' actual decision process, but it does predict their evaluation of alternatives and their choice. In addition, the model provides useful information for designing a retail offering. For example, if the supermarket could increase its performance rating on assortment from 7 to 10 (perhaps by adding a bakery and a wide selection of prepared meals), customers like the parent might shop at the supermarket more often than at the supercenter.

The application of the multiattribute attitude model in Exhibit 4–3 deals with a customer who is evaluating and selecting a retailer. The same model can also be used to describe how a customer evaluates and selects which channel to use (store, Internet, or catalog) or what merchandise to buy from a retailer. For example, the model could be used to describe Eva Mendoza's choice among the three suits she was considering.

Implications for Retailers   In this section, we describe how a retailer can use the multiattribute attitude model to encourage customers to shop at the retailer more frequently. First, the model indicates what information customers use to decide which retailer to patronize or which channel to use. Second, it suggests tactics that retailers can undertake to influence customers' store, channel, and merchandise choices.

To develop a program for attracting customers, retailers need to do market research to collect the following information:

1. Alternative retailers that customers consider.
2. Characteristics or benefits that customers consider when evaluating and choosing a retailer.
3. Customers' ratings of each retailer's performance on the characteristics.
4. The importance weights that customers attach to the characteristics.

Armed with this information, the retailer can use several approaches to influence customers to patronize its store or Internet site.

Getting into the Consideration Set   Retailers need to be included in the customer's **consideration set,** or the set of alternatives the customer evaluates when making a choice of a retailer to patronize. To be included in the consideration set, retailers develop programs to increase the likelihood that customers will remember them when they're about to go shopping. Retailers can increase customer awareness through communication and location decisions. For example, retailers can buy placement at the top of the screen when consumers are using a search engine term for products they sell. They can develop communication programs that link categories they sell with their name. Starbucks locates several stores in the same area so that customers are exposed more frequently to the store name as they drive through the area.

After ensuring that it is in consumers' consideration set, a retailer can use three methods to increase the chances that customers will select it for a visit:

1. Increase beliefs about the store's performance.
2. Change customers' importance weights.
3. Add a new benefit.

Changing Performance Beliefs   The first approach involves altering customers' beliefs about the retailer's performance by increasing the retailer's performance rating on a characteristic. For example, the supermarket in Exhibit 4–3 would want to increase its overall rating by improving its rating on all four benefits. The supermarket could improve its rating on economy by lowering prices and its assortment rating by stocking more gourmet and ethnic foods. Retailing View 4.2 illustrates how Lowe's altered the performance beliefs of women about its stores.

Because it can get costly for a retailer to improve its performance on all benefits, retailers must focus on improving their performance on those benefits that are important to customers in their target market. For example, Best Buy knows that an important benefit for its customers is not to be without their computers for lengthy amounts of time when repairs are needed. So it maintains a 240,000-square-foot "Geek Squad City" warehouse, with more than 1,200 employees, dedicated to reducing the time it takes to repair and return a computer. Geek Squad "agents" fix more than 4,000 laptops per day.[22]

Changing Importance Weights   Altering customers' importance weights is another approach to influencing store choice. A retailer wants to increase the importance customers place on benefits for which its performance is superior and decrease the importance of benefits for which it has inferior performance.

For example, if the supermarket in Exhibit 4–3 tried to attract families who shop at supercenters, it could increase the importance of convenience for them. Typically, changing importance weights is harder than changing performance beliefs because importance weights reflect customers' personal values.

Adding a New Benefit   Finally, retailers might try to add a new benefit to the set of benefits customers consider when selecting a retailer. Senda (www.sendaathletics.com) does not just offer the typical assortment of athletic

---

4.2   RETAILING VIEW   Do It Herself at Lowe's

You might think that home improvement centers are a retail recreation destination mostly for men. Men visit the stores on the weekends to check out the new tools and buy material for do-it-yourself (DIY) projects. But more than 50 percent of the sales at home improvement centers actually are made to women—who make decisions about what materials to use in home improvement projects and often do much of the work themselves.

Lowe's was early to recognize the importance of female customers—though it is not the only traditionally male-oriented retailer to do so. It redesigned its stores to be brighter, lose the warehouse look, and feature departments more appealing to women. With wider aisles, shoppers can avoid uncomfortable, unintended contact with items on shelves—otherwise known as "butt brush." The shelves also are a bit shorter, to make it easy to reach the easy-to-find products that are well marked by aisle markers and maps.

But these changes need to be restrained, to avoid causing male customers to reject the stores as overly feminine. Moreover, women express negative views of offerings that seem condescending in their "girlie" appeals. To balance its recent findings with its long-standing performance tactics, Lowe's offers workshops to teach women about tools, rather than carrying tools specifically designed for women. One section of its website, www.lowes.com/howto, provides online clinics

REFACT

Women make more than 85 percent of all consumer purchases and purchase 50 percent or more in categories typically considered male—banking and financial services, electronics, automobiles, PCs, and many other big-ticket items. Their purchases represent more than half of the U.S. GDP.[23]

Lowe's changed its store design to change women's beliefs about the pleasantness of its store environment.

and videos to help customers successfully implement their own DIY projects at home.

Sources: Tony Bingham and Pat Galagan, "Training at Lowe's: Let's Learn Something Together," *T + D*, November 2009, pp. 35–41; Amanda Junk, "Women Wield the Tools: Lowe's, Habitat for Humanity Teaches Them How," *McClatchy-Tribune Business News*, July 18, 2009; Cecile B. Corral, "Lowe's Outlines Expansion Plans," *Home Textiles Today*, October 5, 2009, p. 6; and Fara Warner, "Yes, Women Spend (And Saw and Sand)," *The New York Times*, February 29, 2004.

DISCUSSION QUESTION

Does feminizing a Lowe's make it less attractive to men?

gear; it sells unusual items such as customizable soccer balls and training vests. It believes that by providing a wider variety than its competition, its customers will find it more attractive. Other retailers attempt to add new benefits by emphasizing that their merchandise is **fair trade**—made by workers who are paid a fair wage, not just a minimum wage.[24] A fair wage means that workers are able to live relatively comfortably within the context of their local area. Offering fair trade merchandise is a benefit that is important to consumers who are concerned about the welfare of people in less developed countries.

Purchasing the Merchandise or Service

Customers don't always patronize a store or purchase a brand or item of merchandise with the highest overall evaluation. The product or service offering the greatest benefits (having the highest evaluation) may not be available from the retailer, or the customer may feel that its risks outweigh the potential benefits. Other consumers make purchase choices based on a single attribute, regardless of how well the offering performs on other characteristics. For example, Eva visited Macy's because the local store is convenient to her apartment, even though other department stores might have a wider selection of women's suits. One measure of retailers' success at converting positive evaluations to purchases is a reduction in the number of real or virtual abandoned carts in the retailer's store or website.

Retailers use various tactics to increase the chances that customers will convert their positive evaluations into purchases. First, they attempt to make it easy to purchase merchandise. More and more retailers are ensuring that their websites are mobile friendly. In their stores, they can reduce the actual wait time for buying merchandise by having more checkout lanes open and placing them conveniently in the store. In addition to reducing actual waiting time, they can reduce perceived wait times by installing digital displays to entertain customers waiting in line.[25] Many Internet retailers send reminder e-mails to visitors about items in carts they have abandoned.[26]

REFACT

A recent study found that one in five smartphone shoppers made a purchase via his or her smartphone in April 2012. A third of the purchases were for clothing or accessories.[27]

Second, retailers' ability to turn a positive purchase intention into a sale can also be increased by providing sufficient information that reinforces the customer's positive evaluation. For example, Eva's friend Britt, the salesperson, and another potential customer also provided Eva with positive feedback to support her purchase decision.

Third, retailers can increase the chances of making a sale by reducing the risk of making a purchase mistake. For instance, retailers can offer liberal return policies, money-back guarantees, and refunds if customers find the same merchandise available at lower prices from another retailer.

Finally, retailers often create a sense of urgency or scarcity to encourage customers to make a purchase decision. Zappos.com and Overstock.com alert customers if an item in their shopping carts is about to sell out. Flash-sale sites offer items for a specified time period; Neiman Marcus hosts two-hour online sales. The limited assortments offered by fast-fashion retailers like Zara and off-price retailers like TJX Corporation (TJ Maxx and Marshalls) have conditioned customers to buy it when they see it. Otherwise, it may be gone the next time they visit the store.

Postpurchase Evaluation

The buying process doesn't end when a customer purchases a product. After making a purchase, the customer uses the product and then evaluates the experience to determine whether it was satisfactory or unsatisfactory. **Satisfaction** is a postconsumption evaluation of how well a store or product meets or exceeds customer expectations. This **postpurchase evaluation** then becomes part of the customer's internal information and affects store and product evaluations and purchase decisions. Unsatisfactory experiences can motivate customers to complain to the retailer, patronize other stores, and select different brands in the future. Consistently high levels of satisfaction build store and brand loyalty, important sources of competitive advantage for retailers.[28]

To improve postpurchase assessments and satisfaction, retailers can take several steps. First, they must make sure to build realistic customer expectations, so they never let those shoppers down with their performance. Second, they should provide information about proper use and care of the items purchased. Third, as mentioned previously, guarantees and warranties reduce a negative feeling of risk, both before and after the purchase. Fourth, the best retailers make contact periodically with their customers to make sure they are satisfied, correct any problems, and remind customers of their availability. This last effort also can improve the chances that a customer puts the retailer in his or her consideration set for the next purchase occasion.

TYPES OF BUYING DECISIONS

LO2

Identify the different types of buying processes.

In some situations, customers like Eva Mendoza spend considerable time and effort selecting a retailer and evaluating alternative products—going through all the steps in the buying process described in the preceding section. In other situations, buying decisions are made automatically with little thought. This section examines three types of customer decision-making processes: extended problem solving, limited problem solving, and habitual decision making.

Extended Problem Solving

Extended problem solving is a purchase decision process in which customers devote considerable time and effort to analyze their alternatives. Customers typically engage in extended problem solving when the purchase decision involves a lot of risk and uncertainty. **Financial risks** arise when customers purchase an expensive product or service. **Physical risks** are important when customers feel that a product or service may affect their health or safety. **Social risks** arise when customers believe a product will affect how others view them. Lasik eye surgery, for instance, involves all three types of risks: It can be expensive, potentially damage the eyes, and change a person's appearance.

Consumers engage in extended problem solving when they are making a buying decision to satisfy an important need or when they have little knowledge about the product or service, as we described with car buyers in Retailing View 4.1. Due to the high risk in such situations, customers go beyond their internal knowledge to consult with friends, family members, or experts. They might also peruse online blogs; examine online reviews, both retailer-sponsored and independent review sites; and read *Consumer Reports*. They may also visit several retailers before making a purchase decision.

Retailers stimulate sales from customers engaged in extended problem solving by providing the necessary information in a readily available and easily understood manner and by offering money-back guarantees. For example, retailers that sell merchandise involving extended problem solving provide information on their websites describing the merchandise and its specifications, have informational displays in their stores (such as a sofa cut in half to show its construction), and use salespeople to demonstrate features and answer questions.

Limited Problem Solving

Limited problem solving is a purchase decision process involving a moderate amount of effort and time. Customers engage in this type of buying process when they have had some prior experience with the product or service and their risk is moderate. In such situations, customers tend to rely more on personal knowledge than on external information. They usually choose a retailer they have shopped at before and select merchandise they have bought in the past. The majority of customer purchase decisions involve limited problem solving.

Retailers attempt to reinforce this buying pattern and make it habitual when customers are buying merchandise from them. If customers are shopping elsewhere, however, retailers need to break this buying pattern by introducing new information or offering different merchandise or services. A common way to adjust the pattern is through coupons. Companies such as CVS and Walgreens often offer deep coupon discounts on commonly purchased products to get customers into their stores. Retailers are willing to give such steep discounts for two reasons. First, it breaks the established habit a customer may have of shopping elsewhere, and second, they know customers often buy many other, undiscounted items once they are in the store. After customers make these purchases, the retailers analyze their spending patterns and offer targeted coupons to encourage repatronage.[29]

Eva Mendoza's buying process illustrates both limited and extended problem solving. Her store choice decision was based on her knowledge of the merchandise in various stores she had shopped in and her search on Nubry.com. Considering this information, she felt the store choice decision was not very risky; thus, she engaged in limited problem solving when deciding to visit Macy's. But her buying process for the suit was extended. This decision was important to her; thus, she spent time acquiring information from a friend, the salesperson, and another shopper to evaluate and select a suit.

One common type of limited problem solving is **impulse buying,** or **unplanned purchasing,** which is a buying decision made by customers on the spot after seeing the merchandise.[30] Retailers encourage impulse-buying behavior by using prominent point-of-purchase (POP) or point-of-sale (POS) displays to attract customers' attention. Retailers have long recognized that the most valuable real estate in the store is at the point of purchase. An increasing number of non-food retailers (such as Old Navy, as mentioned previously) are looking to increase impulse buys from customers by offering candy, gum, mints, and other fun, hedonic items at their cash registers. Electronic shoppers are also stimulated to purchase impulsively when Internet retailers put special merchandise on their home pages and suggest complementary merchandise just before checkout.

Habitual Decision Making

Habitual decision making is a purchase decision process involving little or no conscious effort. Today's customers have many demands on their time. One way they cope with these time pressures is by simplifying their decision-making process. When a need arises, customers may automatically respond with, "I'll buy the same thing I bought last time from the same store." Typically, this habitual decision-making process occurs when decisions aren't very important to customers and involve familiar merchandise they have bought in the past. When customers are loyal to a brand or a store, they engage in habitual decision making.

Brand loyalty means that customers like and consistently buy a specific brand in a product category. They are reluctant to switch to other brands if their favorite brand isn't available. For example, loyal Coca-Cola drinkers won't buy Pepsi, no matter what. Thus, retailers can satisfy these customers' needs only if they offer the specific brands desired.

Brand loyalty creates both opportunities and problems for retailers.[31] Customers are attracted to stores that carry popular brands, but because retailers must carry these high-loyalty brands, they may not be able to negotiate favorable terms with the suppliers of the popular national brands. If, however, the high-loyalty brands are private-label brands (i.e., brands owned by the retailer), retailer loyalty is heightened.

Retailer loyalty means that customers like and habitually visit the same retailer to purchase a type of merchandise. All retailers would like to increase their customers' loyalty, and they can do so by selecting a convenient location (see Chapters 7 and 8), offering complete assortments of national and private-label brands (Chapter 13), reducing the number of stockouts (Chapter 13), rewarding customers for frequent purchases (Chapter 11), or providing good customer service (Chapter 18).

SOCIAL FACTORS INFLUENCING THE BUYING PROCESS

LO3

Summarize how the economy and social factors affect customer purchase decisions.

Exhibit 4–4 illustrates how customer buying decisions are influenced by four influential social factors: the economy, family, reference groups, and culture.

The Economy

The state of the national and global economy has significant effects on the way people buy. In terms of the most recent global recession, the effects have lingered because consumers continue to feel a sense of uncertainty and risk.[32] At the same time, many shoppers have discovered that shopping for bargains is fun. Even if their incomes have stabilized, they see little reason to switch back to name brands when the private-label offerings they have been buying work just fine.[33]

The outcomes in terms of consumers' buying processes have been both expected and unexpected. Predictably, people have reduced their spending on luxury brands, leading retailers to revamp their offerings. For example, Neiman Marcus broadened its jewelry lines to include more funky, less expensive designs and fewer precious metals.[34] In addition, consumers make fewer shopping trips and appreciate the convenience of one-stop shopping (which also lowers gasoline expenditures) at hypermarkets or supercenters.

More surprising are the trends that suggest some buyers actually are spending a little more on higher-quality products in an effort to gain more value and make purchases last. When they do spend more lavishly, consumers tend to feel guilty. Thus, the Ritz-Carlton began avoiding its "silver tray" image in its advertising and instead encouraged visitors to consider their hotel stay a time to reconnect with family. Consumers want to splurge a little when they can; retailers have to find ways to enable them to do so without guilt.[35]

Family

Many purchase decisions involve products that the entire family will consume or use. The previous discussion of the buying process focused on how one person makes a decision. When families make purchase decisions, they often consider the needs of all family members.[36]

EXHIBIT 4–4
Social Factors
Affecting Buying
Decisions

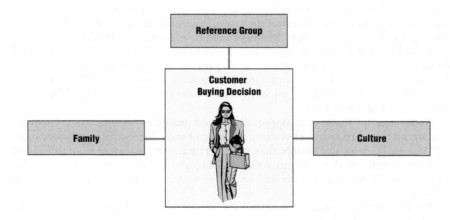

When choosing a vacation site, for example, all family members may participate in the decision making. In other situations, one member of the family may assume the decision-making role. For example, the husband might buy the groceries, which the wife then uses to prepare their child's lunch, which the child consumes in school. In this situation, the store choice decision might be made by the husband, but the brand choice decision might be made by the wife, though it likely is greatly influenced by the child.

Children play an important role in family buying decisions. Resort hotels now realize they must satisfy children's needs as well as those of adults. The Hyatt hotel chain thus cooperates with a mail-order baby supply company, Babies Travel Lite. After parents book a room, they can order all the diapers, formula, and organic baby food they will need for the trip. The items will be ready for them when they check in, which reduces the amount of baggage and increases convenience. For older children, Hyatt offers toys, available to be checked out from the front desk. In addition, working with the famous chef Alice Waters, it has revamped the children's menus in its hotel restaurants to offer nutritious, but also fun meal options.[37]

Retailers also can attract consumers who shop with other family members by satisfying the needs of all those family members. For example, Anthropologie has enlarged its dressing rooms so families (and friends) can provide advice and try on clothes together. Macy's has added comfortable seating and televisions outside dressing rooms to keep other family members entertained.[38]

Reference Groups

A **reference group** includes one or more people whom a person uses as a basis of comparison for beliefs, feelings, and behaviors. A consumer might have a number of different reference groups, such as family, friends, celebrities, and opinion leaders. These reference groups affect buying decisions by (1) offering information, (2) providing rewards for specific purchasing behaviors, and (3) enhancing a consumer's self-image.

Reference groups provide information to consumers directly through conversation, either face-to-face or electronically, or indirectly through observation. For example, Eva received valuable information from her friend about the suits she was considering. On other occasions, Eva might look to women like soccer player Hope Solo and tennis player Caroline Wozniacki to guide her selection of athletic apparel or Demi Lovato and Katy

Shoppers look to celebrities like Katy Perry for fashion tips.

REFACT

Amazon has the most loyal customers of any brand. It has more than 5 million customers signed up for its loyalty program *Amazon Prime*.[39]

Perry for casual fashion advice. The role of reference groups in creating fashion is discussed in the appendix to this chapter.

By identifying and affiliating with reference groups, consumers create, enhance, and maintain their self-image. Customers who want to be seen as members of an elite social class may shop at prestige retailers, whereas others who want to create the image of an outdoor enthusiast might buy merchandise from the L.L. Bean website.

Retailers are particularly interested in identifying and reaching out to those in a reference group who act as store advocates and actively influence others in the group. **Store advocates** are customers who like a store so much that they actively share their positive experiences with friends and family. Retailing View 4.3 details how social media sites such as Pinterest and Facebook make sharing ideas, reviews, and "likes" even easier. Consumers see so much advertising that they have become suspicious of the claims being made. Thus, they are relying more on their own social networks for information about stores to patronize and merchandise to buy.

Culture

Culture is the meaning, beliefs, morals, and values shared by most members of a society. As the basis of the social factors that influence people's buying decisions, the culture or cultures in which each consumer participates often align with his or her reference groups. For example, Eva's cultural groups include her Latino heritage and the Pacific Northwest culture in which she lives. These cultural influences affect her consumer behavior. Because the culture at Eva's college is rather

---

4.3   RETAILING VIEW   Pinning Consumption Choices on Online Reference Groups

With a simple logo—a thumb pointing up and the word "Like"—Facebook revamped the way people share recommendations and interests. Users can show their approval of other users' posts and pictures. But they also can click the nearly ubiquitous Like button on retailers' sites to show their Facebook friends which retailer, merchandise item, or service they consider worthy of their approval.

The "Like" generation relies heavily on such social media recommendations. A recent study indicated that 62 percent of social media users read their friends' "social sharing" about items to purchase. Of these, 75 percent click on the link. And of the people who click, 53 percent of them actually buy the shared product. Of course, after they buy, they also share their purchase with their social network, starting the virtuous cycle (for retailers) all over again.

But purchasing is not the only promising outcome of social sharing. On Pinterest, a sort of online scrapbook for users' interests, the predominantly female (68 percent) members create pin boards that reflect their interests in their favorite retailers and the merchandise they carry. Then they post pictures to reflect those interests, which others can check to find their own inspiration. Retailers are using pin boards to enhance brand awareness among consumers who might buy later. American Eagle Outfitters (http://pinterest.com/americaneagle/) has 51 pin boards with 2,020 pins, listing images such as "Fall Shoes from AE" or "Best Gifts to Give." Saks Fifth Avenue has 52 pin boards focusing on topics like decorative fabrics, printed pants, and saturated lip colors.[40]

The increasing popularity of Pinterest seems to reflect the old adage that a picture is worth a thousand words. It also represents a new trend: Everyone is a voyeur. That is, consumers today feel as if they must know what their reference groups are doing, wearing, or buying. Retailers embrace the notion. When a retailer gets Liked or Pinned, the virtuous cycle of social sharing is likely to enhance its sales, profits, and chances of success.

Sources: Andy Kessler, "The Button That Made Facebook Billions," *The Wall Street Journal*, February 2, 2012; Social Labs, "Social Impact Study 2012 Infographic on Social Sharing," March 20, 2012; Tanzina Vega, "Marketers Find a Friend in Pinterest," *The New York Times*, April 17, 2012; and Sarah E. Needleman and Pui-Wing Tam, "Pinterest's Rite of Web Passage—Huge Traffic, No Revenues," *The Wall Street Journal*, February 16, 2012.

DISCUSSION QUESTION

Do you like the "like" button? If yes, why? If no, why not?

fashion conscious, she was immediately aware that her old suit was out of date and considered buying fashionable shoes a reasonable addition.

Many retailers and shopping center managers have recognized the importance of appealing to different cultures and subcultures.[41] For instance, the U.S. Hispanic population is growing faster than any other market segment, and Hispanics' purchasing power is rising faster than that of the general population. Many retailers, particularly supermarkets in areas with large Hispanic populations, have dedicated significant space to products that are indigenous to particular Spanish-speaking countries. The product mix will, however, differ depending on the region of the country. Merchandise should reflect that, for instance, Miami has a large Cuban and Latin American population, whereas Los Angeles and Texas have more people from Mexico. Bilingual employees are a critical success factor for stores catering to the Hispanic population. Some retailers with a long history of serving Hispanic customers even found that they needed to start adding more English to their products and marketing materials to better target their customers' children. Thus, Pizza Patrón, a Dallas-based pizza chain, has begun shifting its menu boards from purely Spanish to a combination of Spanish and English, and Curacao, a big box store in California serving Hispanics, has shifted from Spanish-only speaking employees and advertising to a similar mixed format.[42]

Many retailers and shopping center managers have adjusted their strategies to appeal to different cultures and subcultures.

MARKET SEGMENTATION

The preceding discussion focused on (1) how individual customers evaluate and select stores, channels, and merchandise and (2) the factors affecting their decision making. To be cost-effective, retailers identify groups of these customers (market segments) and target their offerings to meet the needs of typical customers in a segment rather than the needs of a specific customer. At one time, Walmart used a "one-size-fits-all" strategy. The merchandise selection was very similar across the United States, without much regard to geographic or demographic variations. This approach worked well when most of its stores were located in rural areas in the Southeast. But as it opened stores in more diverse locations, it realized it had to develop different retail mixes for different market segments. For example, in urban locations, it has begun opening smaller Walmart Express and Market stores, in already-built storefronts, which feature more grocery items and a small selection of lawn furniture.[43]

A **retail market segment** is a group of customers who are attracted to the same retail mix because they have similar needs. For example, young, hip 20-somethings have different needs than executives on business trips. Thus, Marriott offers hotel chains with different retail mixes for each of these segments—AC Hotels by

LO4
Determine why and how retailers group customers into market segments.

Marriott for the young and hip and Marriott Hotels and Conference Centers for business executives and conferences.

The Internet enables retailers to target individual customers efficiently and market products to them on a one-to-one basis. This one-to-one marketing concept is discussed in Chapter 11 as it pertains to customer relationship management.

Criteria for Evaluating Market Segments

Customers can be grouped into segments in many different ways. Exhibit 4–5 shows some different methods of segmenting retail markets. There's no simple way to determine which method is best, though four criteria useful for evaluating whether a retail segment is a viable target market are as follows: actionable, identifiable, substantial, and reachable.

Actionable The fundamental criteria for evaluating a retail market segment are that (1) customers in the segment must have similar needs, seek similar benefits, and be satisfied by a similar retail offering and (2) those customers' needs must differ from the needs of customers in other segments. **Actionable** means that the retailer should know what to do to satisfy needs for the consumers in the

EXHIBIT 4–5
Methods for
Segmenting Retail
Markets

Segmentation Descriptor	Example of Categories
GEOGRAPHIC	
Region	Pacific, Mountain, Central, South, Mid-Atlantic, Northeast
Population density	Rural, suburban, urban
Climate	Cold, warm
DEMOGRAPHIC	
Age	Under 6, 6–12, 13–19, 20–29, 30–49, 50–65, over 65
Gender	Male, female
Family life cycle	Single, married with no children, married with youngest child under 6, married with youngest child over 6, married with children no longer living at home, widowed
Family income	Under $19,999; $20,000–29,999; $30,000–49,999; $50,000–$74,999; over $75,000
Occupation	Professional, clerical, sales, craftsperson, retired, student, homemaker
Education	Some high school, high school graduate, some college, college graduate, graduate degree
Religion	Catholic, Protestant, Jewish, Muslim
Race	Caucasian, African-American, Hispanic, Asian
Nationality	American, Japanese, British, French, German, Italian, Chinese
PSYCHOSOCIAL	
Social class	Lower, middle, upper
Lifestyle	Striver, driver, devoted, intimate, altruist, fun seeker, creative
Personality	Aggressive, shy, emotional
FEELINGS AND BEHAVIORS	
Attitudes	Positive, neutral, negative
Benefit sought	Convenience, economy, prestige
Stage in decision process	Unaware, aware, informed, interested, intend to buy, bought previously
Perceived risk	High, medium, low
Innovativeness	Innovator, early adopter, early majority, late majority, laggard
Loyalty	None, some, completely
Usage rate	None, light, medium, heavy
Usage situation	Home, work, vacation, leisure
User status	Nonuser, ex-user, potential user, current user

segment. According to this criterion, it makes sense for Banana Republic to segment the apparel market on the basis of the demographic characteristic of physical size. Customers who wear petite sizes have different needs than those who wear regular or large sizes, so they are attracted to a store offering a unique merchandise mix. In the context of the multiattribute attitude model discussed previously, people who wear small sizes place more importance on fit and customer service because it is generally more difficult for them to get the appropriate fit and because they need knowledgeable sales associates who know and can cater to their specific needs.

In contrast, it wouldn't make sense for a supermarket to segment its market on the basis of customer size. Large and small men and women probably have the same needs, seek the same benefits, and go through the same buying process for groceries. This segmentation approach wouldn't be actionable for a supermarket retailer because the retailer couldn't develop unique mixes for large and small customers. However, a segmentation scheme based on geography or demographics such as household income and ethnicity would be actionable.

Identifiable   **Identifiable** means that the retailer is able to determine which customers are in the market segment. When customers are identifiable, the retailer can determine (1) the segment's size and (2) the consumers to whom the retailer needs to target its communications and promotions. For example, supermarket retailers use customer demographics to identify where they should put their stores and the merchandise that they should carry. More prepared and gourmet foods, fancy produce, and expensive cuts of meat would go into stores in neighborhoods with higher average incomes. Snack foods likely predominate in stores located near a college campus. It is equally important to ensure that the segments are distinct from one another because too much overlap between segments means that distinct marketing strategies aren't needed. If, for example, a regional grocery store chain had stores located in neighborhoods containing people with similar demographics, there would be no need to vary its merchandise selection.

Substantial   If a market is too small or its buying power insignificant (i.e., not **substantial**), it cannot generate sufficient profits to support the retailing mix activities. For example, the market for pet pharmaceuticals is probably not large enough in one local area to serve as a target market segment, but a national market could be served through the Internet channel.

Reachable   **Reachable** means that the retailer can target promotions and other elements of the retail mix to consumers in the segment. For example, AutoZone targets men who repair their automobiles themselves. Potential customers in this segment are reachable because they read car magazines, watch NASCAR on TV, and have distinct television viewing habits.

Approaches for Segmenting Markets

Exhibit 4–5 illustrates the wide variety of approaches for segmenting retail markets. No one approach is best for all retailers. Instead, they must explore various factors that affect customer buying behavior and determine which factors are most important for them.

Geographic Segmentation   **Geographic segmentation** groups customers according to where they live. A retail market can be segmented by countries (Japan, Mexico) or by areas within a country, such as states, cities, and neighborhoods.[44] Because customers typically shop at stores convenient to where they live and work, individual retail outlets usually focus on the customer segment reasonably close to the outlet.

4.4   RETAILING VIEW   Where Gender Matters—and Where It Doesn't

In the past, the demographic patterns seemed clear: Women bought personal care products, fragrances, women's clothing, and groceries. Men bought stereo equipment, video games, tires, and men's clothing—if they had to. But in modern-day retail environments, virtually all of these easy classifications are being challenged by shoppers who have little time to waste with gender stereotypes. And retailers are quickly catching on.

For example, when Urban Outfitters was redesigning its website, it stumbled on what the web designers thought was a brilliant and simple change. They would personalize the site so that female visitors immediately were directed to dresses and blouses, while male visitors saw work shirts and tough-guy jeans. The response was quick—and negative. Female visitors complained that they were the ones buying most of the clothing for the men in their lives. And on top of that, they found the gender-biased marketing offensive.

At the same time, more and more men are in the market for grooming and personal care products. The suggested reasons are many. Maybe the modern generation simply is more accustomed to shopping for themselves. Or perhaps job seekers in a tight economy need any edge they can get, and feeling confident about their personal grooming as they head to interviews might tip the scales in their favor. But regardless of the reason, the conventional wisdom that personal care and fragrance sellers could market just to women has gone out the window.

Overall, it appears that men and women actually have approximately equal influences on households' spending. In a recent survey, 85 percent of women and 84 percent of men agreed that they shared responsibility for shopping decisions.

Such equality of influence is not to say that women and men shop the same way, though. As men take on more grocery shopping tasks—a role traditionally assigned to women—some grocery retailers are experimenting with ways to appeal to them. For example, men appear to hate to ask for help, so the stores need to be efficient and clearly laid out with good signage, rather than providing an abundance of customer service.

Best Buy similarly recognized that women are a massive market for electronics, smartphones, and mobile devices. But its stores tended to attract very few female shoppers. Therefore, its recent store design revisions aim to appeal to women with household appliance sections that look more like kitchens than like industrial shipyards and hand sanitizer dispensers placed next to the video game test consoles.

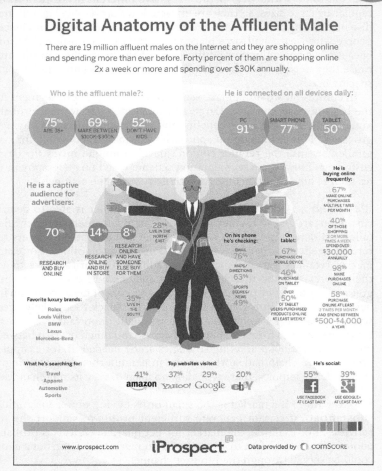

Who is the affluent male? How connected is he to his devices?
Source: www.iprospect.com/digital-affluent-male

REFACT

19 million "affluent males" shop on the Internet. They tend to be over 35 years old and make between $100,000 and $300,000 a year. They generally search for travel, apparel, automotive, and sports. Their favorite brands are Rolex, Louis Vuitton, BMW, Lexus, and Mercedes-Benz.[45]

Sources: Natasha Singer, "E-Tailer Customization: Convenient or Creepy?" *The New York Times*, June 23, 2012; "Who Makes the Call at the Mall, Men or Women?" *The Wall Street Journal*, April 23, 2011; Tom Ryan, "'His' and 'Her' Grocery Aisles," *Retail Wire*, June 6, 2011; Susan Reda, "Guess What? Men Shop, Too!" *Stores*, April 2010; and Miguel Bustillo and Mary Ellen Lloyd, "Best Buy Tests New Appeals to Women," *The Wall Street Journal*, June 16, 2010.

DISCUSSION QUESTION

How are your shopping habits different from someone you are close to of the opposite sex?

Segments based on geography can be identifiable, substantial, and reachable. It's easy to determine who lives in a geographic segment, such as the Paris metropolitan area, and then determine how many potential customers are in that area. It is also relatively simple to target communications and locate retail outlets for customers in Paris and then determine if customers are being responsive to those communications. However, when customers in different geographic segments have similar needs, it is inefficient to develop unique retail offerings by geographic markets. For example, a fast-food customer in Detroit probably seeks the same benefits as a fast-food customer in Los Angeles. Thus, it wouldn't be useful to segment the U.S. fast-food market geographically.

Demographic Segmentation   **Demographic segmentation** groups consumers on the basis of easily measured, objective characteristics such as age, gender, income, and education. Demographic variables are the most common means of defining segments, because consumers in these segments can be easily identified, their size can be determined, and the degree to which they can be reached by and are responsive to media can be easily assessed.

However, demographics may not be useful for defining segments for some retailers because the motivations for purchasing transcend simple demographics. For example, demographics are poor predictors of users of activewear, such as jogging suits and running shoes. At one time, retailers assumed that activewear would be purchased exclusively by young athletic people, but the health and fitness trend has led people of all ages to buy this merchandise. Relatively inactive consumers also find activewear to be comfortable. Several other long-held assumptions about who buys what also are being challenged in today's retail environment, as Retailing View 4.4 describes.

Geodemographic Segmentation   **Geodemographic segmentation** uses both geographic and demographic characteristics to classify consumers. This segmentation scheme is based on the principle that "birds of a feather flock together." Consumers in the same neighborhoods tend to buy the same types of cars, appliances, and apparel and shop at the same types of retailers.[46]

One widely used tool for geodemographic market segmentation is the Tapestry Segmentation system developed and marketed by Esri.[47] Tapestry Segmentation classifies all U.S. residential neighborhoods into 65 distinctive segments based on socioeconomic and demographic characteristics.[48] The information in Exhibit 4–6 describes three Tapestry segments. These neighborhoods, with their similar demographics and buying behaviors, can be any place in the United States.

Geodemographic segmentation is particularly appealing for managing the store channel because customers typically patronize stores close to their neighborhoods. Thus, retailers can use geodemographic segmentation to select locations for their stores and tailor the assortment in the stores to the preferences of the local community. In Chapter 8, we illustrate how geodemographic segmentation is used to make store location decisions.

Lifestyle Segmentation   Of the various methods of segmenting, lifestyle is the one that delves the most into how consumers describe themselves. **Lifestyle,** or **psychographics,** refers to how people live, how they spend their time and money, what activities they pursue, and their attitudes and opinions about the world in which they live. For example, a person may have a strong need for conservation. This need then motivates the person to buy products compatible with that lifestyle. Shoppers at the Austin, Texas–based, environmentally sustainable, zero-waste grocery chain in.gredients bring their own containers and purchase the organic food products they need from bulk bins.[49]

EXHIBIT 4–6
Examples of Tapestry

	Segment 01 - *Top Rung*	Segment 18 - *Cozy and Comfortable*	Segment 52 - *Inner City Tenants*
LifeMode Summary Group	L1 *High Society*	L2 *Upscale Avenues*	L8 *Global Roots*
Urbanization Summary Group	U3 *Metro Cities I*	U8 *Suburban Periphery II*	U4 *Metro Cities II*
Household Type	Married-Couple Families	Married-Couple Families	Mixed
Median Age	44.6	41.7	28.8
Income	High	Upper Middle	Lower Middle
Employment	Prof/Mgmt	Prof/Mgmt	Srvc/Prof/Mgmt/Skilled
Education	Bach/Grad Degree	Some College	No HS Diploma; HS; Some Coll
Residential	Single Family	Single Family	Multiunit Rentals
Activity	Participate in public/civic activities	Dine out often at family restaurants	Play football, basketball
Financial	Own stock worth $75,000+	Have personal line of credit	Have personal education loan
Activity	Vacation overseas	Shop at Kohl's	Go dancing
Media	Listen to classical, all-news radio	Listen to sporting events on radio	Read music, baby, fashion magazines
Vehicle	Own/Lease luxury car	Own/Lease minivan	Own/Lease Honda

SOURCE: Esri, "Tapestry Segmentation: The Fabric of America's Neighborhoods."
(Left and middle): ©appleuzr/DigitalVision Vectors/Getty Images; (right): ©macrovector/iStock/Getty Images

Lifestyle segments can be identified through consumer surveys that ask respondents to indicate whether they agree or disagree with statements such as, "My idea of fun in a national park would be to stay in an expensive lodge and dress up for dinner," "I often crave excitement," or "I could not stand to skin a dead animal." Retailers today are placing more emphasis on lifestyles than on demographics to define a target segment.

One of the most widely used tools for **lifestyle segmentation** is **VALS**, by Strategic Business Insights. On the basis of responses to the VALS survey (www.strategicbusinessinsights.com/vals/presurvey.shtml), consumers are classified into the eight segments shown in Exhibit 4–7. On the horizontal dimension, the segments reflect people's primary motivation for buying, which stem from their self-image. There are three primary motivations of U.S. consumers: ideals, achievement, and self-expression. People who are primarily motivated by ideals are guided by knowledge and principles. Those who are motivated by achievement look for products and services that demonstrate success to their peers. Consumers who are primarily motivated by self-expression desire social or physical activity, variety, and risk. On the vertical dimension, the descriptions refer instead to consumers' resources, including their income, education, health, and energy level, as well as their degree of innovativeness. The segments on top have more resources and are more innovative; those on the bottom have fewer resources and are less innovative. The demographics of each group are provided in the figure.

EXHIBIT 4–7
VALS American
Lifestyle

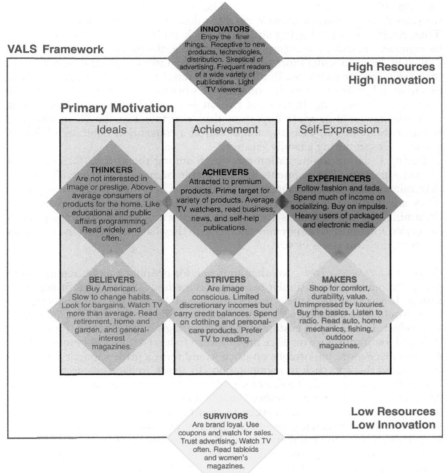

SOURCE: **Strategic** Business Insights (SBI) (www.strategicbusinessinsights.com/).

Firms are finding that lifestyles are often more useful for predicting consumer behavior than are demographics. In particular, VALS enables firms to identify target segments and their underlying motivations. It also reveals correlations between psychology and lifestyle choices. People who share demographics actually tend to have varying psychological traits. Two shoppers with similar demographic appearances still might have different levels of risk-taking propensity, social consciousness, or preferred benefits. College students and day laborers might earn similar incomes, but they spend that income quite differently because of their very different values and lifestyles.

There are limitations to using lifestyle segmentation, however. Lifestyles are not as objective as demographics, and it is harder to identify potential customers. With demographics, a firm like Nike can easily identify its customers as men or women and its marketing strategies to each group differently. For these reasons, lifestyle segmentation is often used in conjunction with other segmentation methods. In addition, psychographics are more expensive as a means to identify potential customers. To identify VALS segments, companies use the VALS questionnaire in surveys or focus groups. Then VALS provides segment description linkages with consumer product and media data, communication styles, and zip code location.

Buying Situation Segmentation   The buying behavior of customers with the same demographics or lifestyle can differ depending on their buying situation. Thus, retailers may use **buying situations,** such as fill-in versus weekly shopping, to segment a market. For example, in Exhibit 4–3, the parent with four children evaluated the supercenter more positively than the Internet grocer or supermarket for weekly grocery purchases. But if the parent ran out of milk during the week, he or she would probably go to the convenience store rather than the wholesale club for this fill-in shopping. In terms of Exhibit 4–3's multiattribute attitude model, convenience would be more important than assortment in the fill-in shopping situation. Similarly, an executive might stay at a convention hotel on a business trip and a resort during a family vacation.

Buying situation segmentation rates high among the criteria for evaluating market segments. The segments are actionable because it is relatively easy to determine what a marketer should do to satisfy the needs of a particular segment. They are identifiable and accessible because retailers or service providers can determine who the customers are on the basis of who has purchased the product or service and under what circumstances. Once they have identified the customer segment, they can assess its size.

Benefit Segmentation   Another approach for defining a target segment is to group customers seeking similar benefits; this method is called **benefit segmentation.** In the multiattribute attitude model, customers in the same benefit segment would have a similar set of importance weights for the attributes of a store or product. For example, customers who place high importance on fashion and style and low importance on price might form a fashion segment, whereas customers who place more importance on price would form a price segment. Hershey's has adopted this approach to segmentation: To appeal to hand-to-mouth munchers, it offers packages of bite-size candy versions of its popular candy bars, such as Almond Joys, Reese's Peanut Butter Cups, and Hershey's Chocolate. It also tailors its packaging in international markets to offer the key benefits demanded by consumers. When its research showed that Chinese consumers prefer gold over silver, Hershey's changed the foil that wraps its Kisses candies in China.[50]

Benefit segments are very actionable. The benefits sought by customers in the target segment clearly indicate how retailers should design their offerings to appeal to those customers. But customers in benefit segments aren't easily identified or accessed; it's hard to look at a person and determine what benefits he or she is seeking. Typically, the audience for the media used by retailers is described by demographics rather than by the benefits they seek.

Composite Segmentation Approaches

No segmentation approach meets all the criteria. For example, segmenting by demographics and geography is ideal for identifying and accessing customers, but these characteristics often are unrelated to customers' needs. Thus, these approaches may not indicate the actions necessary to attract customers in these segments. In contrast, knowing what benefits customers are seeking is useful for designing an effective retail offering; the problem is identifying which customers are seeking these benefits. For these reasons, **composite segmentation** uses multiple variables to identify customers in the target segment according to their benefits sought, lifestyles, and demographics.

CVS uses what it calls the "CVS personalities" to target three composite segments. Each of these segments, referred to by a first name, is used to develop a retail strategy for the market segment.[51] "**Caroline,**" is a segment composed of 18- to 24-year-old single or new moms who have a lower income but have the highest number of items purchased per trip. "**Vanessa**" targets a segment of 35- to 54-year-old women with children, at the peak of their income and generating the highest spending, frequency of purchases, and overall basket size. Finally, "**S**ophie" is a 55-plus empty nester woman with a median income and a health focus. These segments are useful in developing positioning messages that can be used in their ads, flyers, and displays. This information is also useful for manufacturers who sell their products through CVS. For example, for "Caroline," Dove could be positioned as a convenient reenergizer. For "Vanessa," it could be positioned as an escape. Finally, for "Sophie," it could be touted as beneficial to health.

SUMMARY

LO1 **Describe the process that consumers go through when making retail patronage and buying decisions.**

Consumers go through several stages when making a purchase decision: need recognition, information search, evaluation of alternatives, choice of alternatives, purchase, and postpurchase evaluation. It is important for retailers to understand how they can nudge their customers closer to a buying decision at each step of their buying process

LO2 **Identify the different types of buying processes.**

The importance of the stages depends on the nature of the customer's decision. When decisions are important and risky, the buying process is longer because customers spend more time and effort on the information search and evaluation of alternatives. When buying decisions are less important to customers, they spend little time in the buying process, and their buying behavior may become habitual.

LO3 **Summarize how the economy and social factors affect customer purchase decisions.**

The buying process of consumers is influenced by their personal beliefs, attitudes, and values, as well as by their social environment. The primary social influences are provided by the economy, consumers' families, their reference groups, and culture.

LO4 **Determine why and how retailers group customers into market segments.**

To develop cost-effective retail programs, retailers group customers into segments. Some approaches for segmenting markets are based on geography, demographics, geodemographics, lifestyle, usage situations, and benefits sought. Because each approach has its advantages and disadvantages, retailers typically define their target segment by several characteristics.

KEY TERMS

actionable, *108*
benefit segmentation, *114*
brand loyalty, *103*
buying process, *91*
buying situation, *114*
compatibility, *119*
complexity, *119*
composite segmentation, *114*
consideration set, *99*
conversion rate, *94*
cross-shopping, *93*
culture, *106*
demographic segmentation, *111*
everyday low pricing (**EDLP**) strategy, *96*
extended problem solving, *102*
external sources, *94*
fair trade, *101*
fashion, *117*

fashion leader, *118*
financial risks, *102*
geodemographic segmentation, *111*
geographic segmentation, *109*
habitual decision making, *103*
hedonic needs, *92*
identifiable, *109*
impulse buying, *103*
information search, *94*
innovator, *118*
internal sources, *94*
knockoff, *118*
lifestyle, *111*
lifestyle segmentation, *112*
limited problem solving, *102*
mass-market theory, *119*
multiattribute attitude model, *97*
observability, *119*
physical risks, *102*

postpurchase evaluation, *101*
psychographics, *111*
reachable, *109*
reference group, *105*
retailer loyalty, *103*
retail market segment, *107*
satisfaction, *101*
social risks, *102*
store advocate, *106*
subculture theory, *119*
substantial, *109*
trend setter, *118*
trialability, *119*
trickle-down theory, *118*
unplanned purchasing, *103*
unsatisfied need, *92*
utilitarian needs, *92*
VALS, *112*

GET OUT AND DO IT!

1. **CONTINUING CASE ASSIGNMENT: GO SHOPPING** Visit the retail store operated by the target firm for your continuing assignment. Determine all the things that the store does to try to stimulate customers to buy merchandise at each stage of the buying process. In which types of buying decisions are most customers involved? Based on your observations and what you know about the target firm, what type(s) of market segmentation strategies are they involved in? Do you believe these are the best strategies for this firm?

2. **GO SHOPPING** Go to a supermarket, and watch people selecting products to put in their shopping carts. How much time do they spend selecting products? Do some people spend more time than others? Why is this the case? Does consumer behavior vary in the store perimeter versus in the aisles? Explain your observations.

3. **OLC EXERCISE** Go to the student side of the book's website to develop a multiattribute attitude model describing your evaluation of and decision about some relatively expensive product you bought recently, such as a car or a consumer electronics product. Open the multiattribute model exercise. List the attributes you considered in the left-hand column. List the alternatives you considered in the top row. Fill in the importance weights for each attribute in the second column (10 = very important, 1 = very unimportant); then fill in your evaluation of each product on each attribute (10 = excellent performance, 1 = poor performance). Based on your importance weights and performance beliefs, the evaluation of each product appears in the bottom row. Did you buy the product with the highest evaluation?

4. **INTERNET EXERCISE** To better understand the segmentation classification of consumers, Strategic Business Insights has developed the VALS tool, which uses psychology to segment people according to their distinct personality traits. Go to the firm's home page at www.strategicbusinessinsights.com/vals/presurvey.shtml, and take the survey to identify your VALS profile according to your values, attitudes, and lifestyle. According to the results, what is your VALS profile type? Do you agree with your consumer profile? Why or why not? How can retailers effectively use the results of this survey when planning and implementing their business strategies?

5. **INTERNET EXERCISE** Retailers want to segment the market on the basis of the geographic classification of customers to select the best sites for their businesses. Go to the Esri Business Information Solutions home page at www.esri.com/data/esri_data/tapestry, type in the zip code for your hometown or your campus, and read the results. How would a retailer, such as a local restaurant, use the information in this report when making a decision about whether to open a location in this zip code?

6. **INTERNET EXERCISE** Go to the following Internet sites offering information about the latest fashions: *New York Magazine's* The Cut at http://nymag.com/thecut/, *New York Times'* Fashion & Style at www.nytimes.com/pages/fashion/index.html, and the U.K. *Telegraph* at fashion.telegraph.co.uk, Write a brief report describing the latest apparel fashions that are being shown by designers. Which of these fashion trends do you think will be popular with college students? Why?

DISCUSSION QUESTIONS AND PROBLEMS

1. Does the customer buying process end when a customer buys some merchandise? Explain your answer.

2. Describe how service retailers, such as hotels, provide information to potential customers to answer questions about rates, services offered, and other amenities.

3. Considering the steps in the consumer buying process (Exhibit 4–1), describe how you (and your family) used this process to select your college or university. How many schools did you consider? How much time did you invest in this purchase decision? When you were deciding on which college to attend, what objective and subjective criteria did you use in the alternative evaluation portion of the consumer buying process?

4. In Exhibit 4–6, The Inner City Tenant is described. How should banks, restaurants, drugstores, and car dealers alter their retail mixes to meet the needs of this segment compared to the Top Rung segment?

5. Any retailer's goal is to get customers in its store so that they can find the merchandise that they are looking for and make a purchase at this location. How could a sporting goods retailer ensure that the customer buys athletic equipment at its outlet?

6. A family-owned used-book store across the street from a major university campus wants to identify the various segments in its market. What approaches might the store owner use to segment this market? List two potential target market segments based on this segmentation approach. Then contrast the retail mix that would be most appropriate for the two potential target segments.

7. How does the buying decision process differ when consumers are shopping on the Internet or mobile device compared with shopping in a store in terms of locations or sites visited, time spent, and brands examined?

8. Using the multiattribute attitude model, identify the probable choice of a local car dealer for a young, single woman and for a retired couple with limited income (see the accompanying table). What can the national retail chain do to increase the chances of the retired couple patronizing its dealership? You can use the multiattribute model template on the student side of the book's website to analyze this information.

	IMPORTANCE WEIGHTS		PERFORMANCE BELIEFS		
Performance Attributes	Young, Single Woman	Retired Couple	Local Gas Station	National Service Chain	Local Car Dealer
Price	2	10	9	10	3
Time to complete repair	8	5	5	9	7
Reliability	2	9	2	7	10
Convenience	8	3	3	6	5

9. Think of a recent purchase that you made, and describe how economic and social environmental factors (e.g., reference group, family, and culture) influenced your buying decision. How are retailers using social media to affect your buying decisions?

10. Think about the merchandise sold at Office Depot, Staples, and Office Max, and list three to four types of merchandise that fall into extended problem solving, limited problem solving, and habitual decision making for college students. Explain how the categories of merchandise would change for each type of buying decision if the customer was the owner of a medium-size business.

SUGGESTED READINGS

Arnold, Mark J., and Kristy E. Reynolds. "Approach and Avoidance Motivation: Investigating Hedonic Consumption in a Retail Setting." *Journal of Retailing* 88, no. 3 (September 2012), pp. 399–411.

Dahl, Darren W., Jennifer J. Argo, and Andrea C. Morales. "Social Information in the Retail Environment: The Importance of Consumption Alignment, Referent Identity, and Self-Esteem." *Journal of Consumer Research*, February 2012, pp. 860–71.

Gauri, Kulkarni, Brian Ratchford, and P. K. Kannan. "The Impact of Online and Offline Information Sources on Automobile Choice Behavior." *Journal of Interactive Marketing* 26, no. 3 (2012), pp. 167–75.

Hawkins, Delbert, David L. Mothersbaugh, and Roger J. Best. *Consumer Behavior: Building Marketing Strategy*, 12th ed. New York: McGraw-Hill/Irwin, 2012.

Iverson, Annemarie. *In Fashion: From Retail to the Runway, Everything You Need to Know to Break into the Fashion Industry*. New York: Clarkson Potter, 2010.

Ma, Yu, Kusum L Ailawadi, Dinesh K Gauri, and Dhruv Grewal, "An Empirical Investigation of the Impact of Gasoline Prices on Grocery Shopping Behavior." *Journal of Marketing* 75, no. 2 (2011), pp. 18–35.

Solomon, Michael. *Consumer Behavior: Buying, Having, and Being*, 10th ed. Englewood Cliffs, NJ: Prentice Hall, 2012.

Sorensen, Herb. *Inside the Mind of the Shopper*. Philadelphia: Wharton School, 2009.

Underhill, Paco. *Why We Buy: The Science of Shopping*, updated and revised. New York: Simon & Schuster, 2008.

APPENDIX 4A   Customer Buying Behavior and Fashion

Many retailers sell fashionable merchandise. To sell this type of merchandise profitably, retailers need to (1) understand how fashions develop and diffuse throughout the marketplace and (2) use operating systems that enable them to match supply and demand for this seasonal merchandise. This appendix reviews the consumer behavior aspects of fashion; the operating systems for matching supply of and demand for fashion merchandise are discussed in Chapter 12.

Fashion is a type of product or a way of behaving that is temporarily adopted by a large number of consumers because the product, service, or behavior is considered socially appropriate for the time and place.[52] For example, in some social groups, it is or has been fashionable to have brightly colored hair or tattoos, wear a coat made from animal fur, or have a beard. Even though a wide range of activities and products go in and out of fashion, in many retail environments the term *fashion* is associated with apparel and accessories.

CUSTOMER NEEDS SATISFIED BY FASHION

Fashion gives people an opportunity to satisfy many emotional and practical needs. Through fashions, people develop their own identity. They also can use fashions to manage their appearance, express their self-image and feelings, enhance their egos, and make an impression on others. Through the years, fashions have become associated with specific lifestyles or the roles people play. You wear different clothing styles when you are attending class, going out on a date, or interviewing for a job.

People use fashions to both develop their own identity and gain acceptance from others. These two benefits of fashion can be opposing forces. If you choose to wear something radically different, you will achieve recognition for your individuality but might not be accepted by your peers. To satisfy these conflicting needs, manufacturers and retailers offer customers designs that are fashionable but that still enable consumers to express their individuality.

Consumers also adopt fashions to overcome boredom. People get tired of wearing the same clothing and seeing the same furniture in their living rooms. They seek changes in their lifestyles by buying new clothes or redecorating their houses to meet their changing tastes, preferences, and income.

HOW DO FASHIONS DEVELOP AND SPREAD?

Fashions are not universal. A fashion might be accepted in one geographic region, country, or age group and not in another. Consider how your idea of "fashionable" differs from that of your parents. Many of you might have a hard time imagining them dressed in distressed, hip-hugging jeans and a tight T-shirt. Well, they might have just as much trouble picturing you in a double-breasted business suit. One interesting sports fashion trend has been the uniforms for college and NBA basketball players. Forty years ago, they sported long hair and wore tight, short shorts and Converse shoes. Now they have short hair and wear baggy shorts and Nike shoes (see www.nba.com/photostore/).

The stages in the fashion life cycle are shown in Exhibit 4–8. The cycle begins with the creation of a new design or style. Then some consumers recognized as fashion leaders or innovators adopt the fashion and start a trend in their social group. The fashion spreads from the leaders to others and is accepted widely as a fashion. Eventually, the fashion is accepted by most people in the social group and can become overused. Saturation and overuse

set the stage for that fashion's decline in popularity and the creation of new fashions. The time span of a fashion life cycle varies depending on the type of product and the market. The cycle for apparel fashions for young teenagers is measured in months or even weeks, whereas the fashion cycle for home furnishings may last several years.

Creation

New fashions arise from a number of sources. Fashion designers are one source of creative inspirations, but fashions are also developed by creative consumers, celebrities, and even retailers. When high-profile actors, performers, and athletes wear the latest styles in television shows and movies, on stage, or on the red carpet, consumers interested in fashion often adopt and follow these trends.

Adoption by Fashion Leaders

The fashion life cycle really starts when the fashion is adopted by leading consumers. These initial adopters of a new fashion are called **fashion leaders, innovators,** or **trendsetters,** and they are the first people to display the new fashion in their social group or write about them in social media, like fashion blogs. If the fashion is too innovative or very different from currently accepted fashion, it might not be accepted by the social group, thereby prematurely ending its life cycle.

Three theories have been proposed to explain how fashion spreads within a society. The **trickle-down theory** suggests that fashion leaders are consumers with the highest social status—wealthy, well-educated consumers. After they adopt a fashion, the fashion trickles down to consumers in lower social classes. When the fashion is accepted in the lowest social class, it is no longer acceptable to the fashion leaders in the highest social class.

Manufacturers and retailers stimulate this trickle-down process by copying the latest styles displayed at designer fashion shows and sold in exclusive specialty stores. These copies, referred to as **knockoffs,** are sold at lower prices through retailers targeting a broader market. For example, designers at retailers like Forever 21 view fashion shows and interpret the designs for their market.[53] If the designers in Paris and Milan are showing turtlenecks, the

REFACT

The bikini was designed by a former civil engineer, Louis Reard, in 1947.[54]

EXHIBIT 4–8
Stages in the Fashion Life Cycle

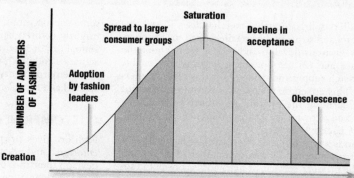

Forever 21 designers determine what aspects of that fashion will appeal to their broader market and then have their designs manufactured in Asia. It is likely that the knockoff turtlenecks will be on the shelves at Forever 21 well before the higher-priced originals get to the high-end specialty and department stores.

The second theory, the **mass-market theory,** suggests that fashions spread across different peer groups. Each group has its own fashion leaders who play key roles in their own social networks. Fashion information trickles across groups rather than down from the upper classes to the lower classes. Spain-based fast-fashion retailer Zara solicits new fashion advice from its store management all over the world. These managers funnel information to the corporate offices in Spain about fashion requests from its customers, what they are wearing, and how they are interpreting and changing off-the-rack apparel to adapt to their unique fashion senses. Zara's fashion designers synthesize the information and reinterpret this information into their own new fashions.

The third theory, the **subculture theory,** is based on the development of recent fashions. Subcultures of mostly young and less affluent consumers, such as urban youth, started fashions for such things as colorful fabrics, T-shirts, sneakers, jeans, black leather jackets, and surplus military clothing. Many times, fashions are started unintentionally by people in lower-income consumer groups and trickle up to mainstream consumer classes. For example, workers wear blue jeans that have holes in them and are distressed from manual labor, their T-shirts are faded from working in the sun, and people who paint houses are covered in splashes of paint. These looks have been adapted by manufacturers and sold to many different consumer groups. The more distress, the more people are willing to pay.

These theories of fashion development indicate that fashion leaders can come from many different places and social groups. In our diverse society, many types of consumers have the opportunity to be the leaders in setting fashion trends.

Spread to Large Consumer Groups

During this stage, the fashion is accepted by a wider group of consumers referred to as early adopters. The fashion becomes increasingly visible, receives greater publicity and media attention, and is readily available in retail stores. The relative advantage, compatibility, complexity, trialability, and observability of a fashion affect the time it takes for that fashion to spread through a social group. New fashions that provide more benefits have a higher relative advantage compared with existing fashions, and these new fashions spread faster. Fashions are often adopted by consumers because they make people feel special. Thus, more exclusive fashions like expensive clothing are adopted more quickly in an affluent target market. On a more utilitarian level, clothing that is easy to maintain, such as wrinkle-free pants, will diffuse quickly in the general population.

Compatibility is the degree to which the fashion is consistent with existing norms, values, and behaviors. When new fashions aren't consistent with existing norms, the number of adopters and the speed of adoption are lower. Head-to-toe leather apparel is only compatible with a relatively small percentage of the public. Although this look may be moderately successful for a season or two, it will never achieve widespread acceptance.

Complexity refers to how easy it is to understand and use the new fashion. Consumers have to learn how to incorporate a new fashion into their lifestyles. For example, a platform, 6-inch, stiletto-heeled pump is difficult to walk in unless you are only taking a quick strut down the runway.

Trialability refers to the costs and commitment required to adopt the fashion initially. For example, consumers buying fashions through Internet channels or catalogs cannot examine the garments or try them on before making a purchase commitment—the trialability is low compared to shopping in stores. New size-matching machines are being used in several shopping centers around the United States. The machines take consumers' measurements and match them with specifications provided by clothing manufacturers, thus providing a proper fit and increasing trialability by reducing the risk associated with buying apparel that has not been tried on.[55]

Observability is the degree to which the new fashion is visible and easily communicated to others in the social group. Clothing fashions are very observable compared with fashions for the home, such as sheets and towels. It is, therefore, likely that a fashion in clothing will spread more quickly than a new color scheme or style for the bedroom.

Fashion retailers engage in many activities to increase the adoption and spread of a new fashion throughout their target market. Compatibility is increased and complexity is decreased by showing consumers how to coordinate a new article of fashion clothing with other items the consumer already owns. Trialability is increased by providing actual or virtual dressing rooms so that customers can try on clothing and see how it looks on them. Providing opportunities for customers to return merchandise also increases trialability because it reduces purchase risk. Retailers increase observability by displaying fashion merchandise in their stores, advertising it in the media, and facilitating coverage through social media like YouTube and fashion blogs.

Saturation

In this stage, the fashion achieves its highest level of social acceptance. Almost all consumers in the target market are aware of the fashion and have decided to either accept or reject it. At this point, the fashion has become old and boring to many people.

Decline in Acceptance and Obsolescence

When fashions reach saturation, they have become less appealing to consumers. Because most people have already adopted the fashion, it no longer provides an opportunity for people to express their individuality. Fashion creators and leaders thus are beginning to experiment with new fashions. The introduction of a new fashion speeds the decline of the preceding fashion.

Retailing Strategy

Retailing Strategy

Section I described the decisions retail managers make in formulating and implementing their strategy; the different types of retailers; the multiple channels—stores, the Internet, and catalogs—that retailers use to interact with and sell merchandise to their customers; and factors that affect consumers' choices of retailers, channels, and merchandise. This broad overview of retailing provides the background information needed to develop and implement an effective retail strategy.

The chapters in Section II discuss specific strategic decisions made by retailers:

Chapter 5 describes the development of a retail market strategy.

Chapter 6 examines the financial strategy associated with the market strategy.

Chapters 7 and 8 discuss the location strategy for retail outlets.

Chapter 9 looks at the firm's organization and human resource strategies.

Chapter 10 examines systems used to control the flow of information and merchandise.

Chapter 11 details approaches that retailers take to manage relationships with their customers.

As outlined in Chapter 1, the decisions discussed in Section II are more strategic than tactical because they involve committing significant resources to developing long-term advantages over the competition in a target market segment.

Sections III and IV review the more tactical decisions regarding merchandise and store management that are involved in implementing the retail strategy. These implementation decisions affect a retailer's efficiency, but their impact is shorter-term than that of the strategic decisions reviewed in Section II.

Retail Market Strategy

My career path in retailing is somewhat unusual. After graduating from Emory University with a degree in economics, I went to law school at the University of Florida. During law school, I was attracted to corporate law, which was a good fit with my undergraduate training in economics. I took a position in the corporate counsel's office at Nordic-Track. At the time, NordicTrack was best known for its cross-country ski simulator, which dominated the home fitness market in the late 1980s.

As the U.S. market for the NordicTrack's simulator matured, the company became interested in expanding internationally. I volunteered to set up a network of international distributors. While I did not have a lot of retail experience, in law school, I had learned how to be an effective negotiator and how to logically analyze situations—skills that were very valuable in developing a worldwide distribution network.

After NordicTrack, I went to work for Best Buy and eventually was promoted to COO of Best Buy International, responsible for the operations of all of Best Buy's brands and businesses outside of the United States. I was deeply involved in the sale of Best Buy's Musicland subsidiary; its acquisition of a majority interest in Jiangsu Five Star Appliance in China; its

expansion into Mexico and Turkey; and the creation of its joint venture with The Carphone Warehouse, which provided an opportunity to introduce the Best Buy brand in Europe.

My present position is challenging and exciting. Our corporation owns and operates more than 400 restaurants under the brands names of Outback Steakhouse, Carrabba's Italian Grill, Bonefish Grill, Roy's, and Fleming's Prime Steakhouse & Wine Bar. While we have more than 200 Outback Steakhouses in 19 countries, our potential for international expansion is tremendous.

The dining experience for our international customers is similar to our domestic experience. Our international restaurants tend to follow U.S. design guidelines with some modifications to account for local needs and customs. Most restaurants are in shopping centers or office buildings; very few are free standing. In Asian cities, where space is at a particular premium, many restaurants are located above the ground floor and sometimes split in two separate floors.

The international menu is also similar to the U.S. menu, with some changes made to meet local taste preferences. For example, we feature local beef cuts

CHAPTER 5

LEARNING OBJECTIVES

LO1 Define the retail strategy.

LO2 Illustrate how retailers build a sustainable competitive advantage.

LO3 Classify the different strategic growth opportunities retailers pursue.

LO4 Identify issues that arise as domestic retailers become global retailers.

LO5 Know the steps retailers go through to develop a strategic plan.

such as Picanha in Brazil or Neobiani in Korea, in addition to the traditional Outback Special sirloin. Product and ingredient availability in a region also drive specific menu offerings. For example, our iconic Bloomin' Onion is replaced by the Typhoon Bloom in Southeast Asia because the exact onion needed for the Bloomin' Onion is not readily available there.

Going global with retail services, particularly restaurants, is more challenging than the international expansion of product-focused retailing. Tastes in food vary significantly from country to country and even within countries, but preferences for products is pretty homogenous across the globe—shopping for flat-panel TVs is pretty universal. While we need a great deal of local input as we expand internationally, we have found that direct foreign investment is more than three times more profitable than franchising.

Retailers need to focus on long-term strategic planning to cope effectively with the growing intensity of retail competition as well as the emergence of new channels, technologies, and globalization. The retail strategy indicates how a retailer will deal effectively with its environment, customers, and competitors.[1] As the retail management decision-making process (discussed in Chapter 1) indicates, the retail strategy (Section II) is the bridge between understanding the world of retailing (Section I) and the more tactical merchandise management and store operations activities (Sections III and IV) undertaken to implement the retail strategy.

The first part of this chapter defines the term *retail strategy* and discusses three important elements of retail strategy: (1) the target market segment, (2) the retail format, and (3) the retailer's bases of sustainable competitive advantage. Then we outline approaches retailers use to build a sustainable competitive advantage. After reviewing the various growth opportunities, specifically international expansion, that retailers can pursue, the chapter concludes with a discussion of the strategic retail planning process.

WHAT IS A RETAIL STRATEGY?

LO1

Define the retail strategy.

REFACT

The word *strategy* comes from the Greek word meaning the "art of the general."[2]

The term *strategy* is frequently used in retailing. For example, retailers talk about their merchandise strategy, promotion strategy, location strategy, channel strategy, or branding strategy. The term is used so commonly that it might appear that all retailing decisions are strategic decisions, but retail strategy isn't just another expression for retail management.

Definition of Retail Market Strategy

A **retail strategy** is a statement identifying (1) the retailer's target market, (2) the format and resources the retailer plans to use to satisfy the target market's needs, and (3) the bases on which the retailer plans to build a sustainable competitive advantage.[3] The **target market** is the market segment(s) toward which the retailer plans to focus its resources and retail mix. A **retail format** describes the nature of the retailer's operations—its retail mix (type of merchandise and services offered, pricing policy, advertising and promotion programs, store design and visual merchandising, typical locations, and customer services)—that it will use to satisfy the needs of its target market. A **sustainable competitive advantage** is an advantage the retailer has over its competition that is not easily copied by competitors and thus can be maintained over a long period of time. The following are Founder's name is Ells. a few examples of retail strategies:

REFACT

Chipotle is by far the largest purchaser of natural meat in the United States.[5]

- *Chipotle Mexican Grill.* Steve Ells, founder and co-chair of Chipotle Mexican Grill, is changing the way America eats, one burrito at a time. The first store of this fast, casual restaurant chain was opened in Denver in 1993 and has grown to 1,200 locations with annual sales of more than $2 billion. Its menu consists of only four items: burritos, burrito bowls, tacos, and salads. When asked about expanding the menu, Steve Ells said, "[I]t's important to keep the menu focused, because if you just do a few things, you can ensure that you do them better than anybody else." Its mission statement, Food With Integrity, highlights its efforts to increase the use of naturally raised meat, organic produce, and dairy without added hormones. This philosophy goes beyond using fresh ingredients to understanding how the animals are raised. The majority of food is prepared in each restaurant. None of the restaurants have freezers, microwave ovens, or can openers.[4]

- *Lululemon Athletica.* Lululemon is a Canadian specialty store chain selling apparel and accessories that support the practice of yoga. The products it sells include headbands, bamboo

Lululemon's retail strategy is selling merchandise that appeals to consumers seeking spiritual enrichment through yoga.

blocks, and yoga mats printed with encouraging healthy-living slogans like "Drink fresh water." The signature Lulu item is the Groove Pant, cut with special gussets and flat seams to create a feeling of a drop of water free from gravity. Lululemon's apparel is made with special materials, Silverescent and Luon, enabling customers to engage in vigorous yoga exercises and still look attractive. Lululemon stores are a community hub where people can learn about and discuss the physical aspects of healthy living, from yoga and diet to running and cycling, as well as the spiritual aspects of life. To create this community, the company recruits local ambassadors before opening a store. These ambassadors, usually popular yoga teachers, are featured on Lululemon's website and on bulletin boards in the store.[6]

- *Chico's.* Chico's is a specialty apparel chain serving the lifestyle needs of fashion-savvy women over 30 years old with a household income of $50,000 to $100,000. Its apparel uses easy-to-care-for fabrics; distinctive, fashionable designs; and a comfortable, relaxed fit. Accessories, such as handbags, belts, scarves, earrings, necklaces, and bracelets, are designed to coordinate with the assortment of clothing, allowing customers to easily personalize their wardrobes. All of the merchandise offered is private label, so Chico's designers and buyers specify the patterns, prints, construction, designs, fabrics, finishes, and colors. The distinctive nature of Chico's clothing is carried through to its sizing. Chico's uses sizes of 0, 1, 2, 3, rather than the more commonly used sizes of 1 to 16 so women are less sensitive to large sizes. The relaxed styles of the clothing allow Chico's to utilize a reduced number of sizes and still offer a wide selection of clothing without having to invest in a large number of different sizes within a single style.[7]

- *Save-A-Lot.* From a single store in 1977, Save-A-Lot, a wholly owned subsidiary of SuperValu, has grown to more than 1,300 stores, making it the nation's 13th-largest U.S. supermarket chain. Save-A-Lot stores offer a limited assortment of 1,250 SKUs compared to 20,000 to 30,000 SKUs in a conventional supermarket. By offering only the most popular items in each category, most of which are private-label merchandise, Save-A-Lot reduces its costs and is able to price its merchandise 40 percent lower than prices at conventional supermarkets. Due to its buying power, Save-A-Lot is able to develop customized product specifications that provide high-quality, private-label merchandise at low prices. Because the stores generally do not feature grocery store–style shelving, items instead are available in specially printed, cut-out shipping containers. Finally, most customers bring their own bags; the stores charge those customers who forget their own and need to obtain bags from the retailer.[8]

CENTRAL CONCEPTS IN A RETAIL MARKET STRATEGY

Each of these retail strategies described in the preceding section involves (1) the selection of target market segment(s), (2) the selection of a retail format (the elements in the retailer's retail mix), and (3) the development of a sustainable competitive advantage that enables the retailer to reduce the level of competition it faces. Now let's examine these central concepts of a retail strategy.

LO2

Illustrate how retailers build a sustainable competitive advantage.

Target Market and Retail Format

A **retail market** is a group of consumers with similar needs and a group of retailers that satisfy those needs using a similar retail channels and format.[9] Exhibit 5–1 illustrates a set of retail market segments for women's clothing. It lists various retail formats in the left-hand column. Each format offers a different retail mix to its customers. Market segments are listed in the exhibit's top row. As mentioned in Chapter 4, these segments could be defined in terms of the customers' geographic location, demographics, lifestyle, buying situation, or benefits sought. In this exhibit, we divide the market into three fashion-related

EXHIBIT 5–1   Retail Market Segments for Apparel

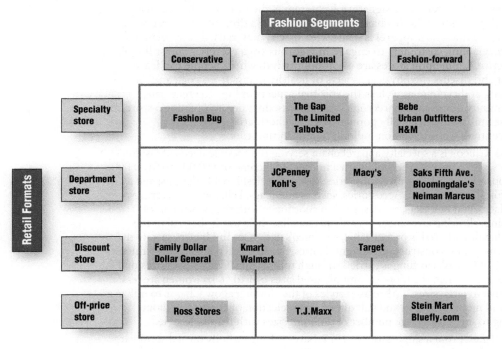

segments: (1) conservative—consumers who place little importance on fashion; (2) traditional—those who want classic styles; and (3) fashion-forward—those who want the latest fashions.

Each square of the matrix in Exhibit 5–1 describes a potential retail market in which retailers compete for consumers with similar needs. For example, Walmart and Kmart stores in the same geographic area compete with each other using a full-line discount store format to target conservative customers. Bloomingdale's and Neiman Marcus compete against each other using a department store format targeting the fashion-forward segment.

Exhibit 5–1's matrix describes the battlefields on which women's apparel retailers compete. The position in each battlefield (cell in the matrix) indicates the first two elements of a retailer's strategy: the fashion segment (the x-axis) and the retail format (the y-axis).

Consider the situation confronting Target as it refines its retail strategy for the women's clothing market. Should Target compete in all 15 retail markets shown in Exhibit 5–1, or should it focus on a limited set of markets? If Target decides to focus on a limited set of markets, which should it pursue? Target's answers to these questions define its retail strategy and indicate how it will focus its resources.

The women's clothing market in Exhibit 5–1 is just one of several representations that we could have used. Retail formats might be expanded to include off-price stores and category specialists. Although Exhibit 5–1 isn't the only way to describe the women's retail apparel market segments, it does illustrate how retail market segments can be defined in terms of retail format and customer market segments.

Building a Sustainable Competitive Advantage

After selecting a target market and a retail mix, the final element in a retail strategy is the retailer's approach to building a sustainable competitive advantage.[10] Establishing a competitive advantage means that the retailer, in effect, builds a wall around its position in a retail market, that is, around its present and potential

EXHIBIT 5–2
Approaches for
Developing a
Sustainable
Competitive
Advantage

Sources of Advantage	SUSTAINABILITY OF ADVANTAGE	
	Less Sustainable	More Sustainable
Customer loyalty (Chapters 11 and 16)	Habitual repeat purchasing because of limited competition in the local area	Building a brand image with an emotional connection with customers; using databases to develop and utilize a deeper understanding of customers
Location (Chapters 7 and 8)		Convenient locations
Human resource management (Chapter 9)	More employees	Committed, knowledgeable employees
Distribution and information systems (Chapter 10)	Bigger warehouses; automated warehouses	Shared systems with vendors
Unique merchandise (Chapters 12 and 13)	More merchandise; greater assortment; lower price; higher advertising budgets; more sales promotions	Exclusive merchandise
Vendor relations (Chapter 13)	Repeat purchases from vendor due to limited alternatives	Coordination of procurement efforts; ability to get scarce merchandise
Customer service (Chapter 18)	Hours of operation	Knowledgeable and helpful salespeople

EXHIBIT 5–2 Approaches for Developing a Sustainable Competitive Advantage

customers and its competitors. When the wall is high, it will be hard for competitors outside the wall (i.e., retailers operating in other markets or entrepreneurs) to enter the market and compete for the retailer's target customers.

Any business activity that a retailer engages in can be the basis for a competitive advantage. But some advantages are sustainable over a long period of time, while others can be duplicated by competitors almost immediately. For example, it would be hard for Peets Coffee & Tea to establish a long-term advantage over Starbucks by simply offering the same coffee specialties at lower prices. If Peets' lower prices were successful in attracting a significant number of customers, Starbucks would soon realize that Peets had lowered its prices and would quickly match the price reduction. This might lead to a price war that Starbucks is likely to win because it has lower costs due to its larger size. Similarly, it's hard for retailers to develop a long-term advantage by offering broader or deeper assortments of national brands. If the broader and deeper assortment attracts a lot of customers, competitors will simply go out and buy the same branded merchandise. Exhibit 5–2 indicates which aspects of these potential sources of advantage are more and less sustainable.

Over time, all advantages erode due to competitive forces, but by building high walls, retailers can sustain their advantage for a longer time. Thus, establishing a sustainable competitive advantage is the key to long-term financial performance.

Three approaches for developing a sustainable competitive advantage are (1) building strong relationships with customers, (2) building strong relationships with suppliers, and (3) achieving efficient internal operations. Each of these approaches involves developing an asset—loyal customers, strong vendor relationships, committed effective human resources, efficient systems, and attractive locations—that is not easily duplicated by competitors. Let's look at each of these approaches.

Relationships with Customers—Customer Loyalty

Customer loyalty means that customers are committed to buying merchandise and services from a particular retailer. Loyalty is more than simply liking one retailer over another. Loyalty means that customers will be reluctant to switch and patronize a competitive retailer. For example, loyal customers will continue to have their car serviced at Jiffy Lube, even if a competitor opens a store nearby and charges

REFACT

Approximately half of food and beverage shoppers and nearly 60 percent of consumers of health/ beauty and household goods would purchase their preferred brands, even if a less expensive alternative were to become available.[11]

McDonald's has developed a competitive advantage by projecting an image of fast service, consistent quality, and clean restrooms.

slightly lower prices. Approaches for developing loyalty discussed in this section are building a strong brand image, creating a unique positioning in the target market, offering unique merchandise, providing excellent customer service, implementing a customer relationship management program, and building a retail community.

Brand Image   Retailers build customer loyalty by developing a well-known, attractive image of their brands and of the name over their doors. For example, when most consumers think about fast food or hamburgers or French fries, they immediately think of McDonald's. Their image of McDonald's includes many favorable beliefs such as fast service, consistent quality, and clean restrooms.

Strong brand images facilitate customer loyalty because they reduce the customers' risks associated with purchases. They assure customers that they will receive a consistent level of quality and satisfaction from the retailer. The retailer's image can also create an emotional tie with a customer that leads the customer to trust the retailer. The steps retailers take to develop a strong brand image are discussed in Chapter 15.

Positioning   A retailer's brand image reflects its positioning strategy. **Positioning** is the design and implementation of a retail mix to create an image of the retailer in the customer's mind relative to its competitors. A **perceptual map** is frequently used to represent the customer's image and preferences for retailers.

Exhibit 5–3 offers a hypothetical perceptual map of retailers selling women's clothing. The two dimensions in this map, fashion and service, represent two important characteristics that consumers in this example use in forming their images of retailers.

Perceptual maps are developed in a way so that the distance between two retailers' positions on the map indicates how similar the stores appear to consumers. For example, Neiman Marcus and Saks Fifth Avenue are very close to each other on the map because consumers in this illustration see them as offering similar services and fashion. In contrast, Nordstrom and Marshalls are far apart, indicating consumers think they're quite different. Note that stores close to each other compete vigorously because consumers feel they provide similar benefits and have similar images.

REFACT

Brooks Brothers, a men's specialty store chain, sold the rights to the Polo brand name to Ralph Lauren.[12]

REFACT

Because brands build loyalty, they are very valuable. The five most valuable U.S. retail brands are Walmart (worth $142 billion), Target ($32 billion), Home Depot ($20 billion), Best Buy ($19 billion), and CVS ($17 billion).[13]

Hypothetical Perceptual Map of Women's Apparel Market   **EXHIBIT 5–3**

In this example, Macy's has an image of offering moderately priced, fashionable women's clothing with good service. TJ Maxx offers slightly less fashionable clothing with considerably less service. Sears is viewed as a retailer offering women's clothing that is not very fashionable with moderate customer service.

The ideal points (marked by red dots on the map) indicate the characteristics of an ideal retailer for consumers in different market segments. For example, consumers in segment 3 prefer a retailer that offers high-fashion merchandise with low service, while consumers in segment 1 want more traditional apparel and aren't concerned about service. The ideal points are located so that the distance between the needs of customers in the segment (marked with a blue "x"), and the perception of the retailer's offering (marked with a red dot) indicates the consumer's probability the consumers in the segment with patronize the retailer.

Retailers that are closer to an ideal point are evaluated more favorably by the consumers in the segment than are retailers located farther away. Thus, consumers in segment 6 prefer Forever 21 and Bebe to Neiman Marcus because these retailers are more fashion-forward and their target customers do not require such high service levels. Retailers strive to develop an image desired by customers in their target segment and thus develop loyalty with those customers.

Unique Merchandise   It is difficult for a retailer to develop customer loyalty through its merchandise offerings because most competitors can purchase and sell the same popular national brands. But many retailers build customer loyalty by developing **private-label brands** (also called **store brands** or **own brands**)—products developed and marketed by a retailer and available only from that retailer.[14] For example, Costco's highly regarded private-label brand, Kirkland Signature, engenders strong brand loyalty and consequently generates considerable loyalty toward Costco. The quality image of its private-label products makes a significant contribution to the image of Costco. Retailing View 5.1 describes how IKEA builds customer loyalty through its unique merchandise. Issues pertaining to the development of store-brand merchandise are discussed in Chapter 13.

REFACT

The Ritz-Carlton is the only hotel chain and the first service company to win the annual Malcolm Baldrige National Quality Award. It has won the award twice.[16]

Customer Service   Retailers also can develop customer loyalty by offering excellent customer service.[15] Consistently offering good service is difficult because customer service is provided by retail employees who are less consistent than machines. Machines can be programmed to make every box of Cheerios identical, but employees do not provide a consistent level of service because they vary in their training, motivation, and mood.

5.1 RETAILING VIEW   The IKEA Way

IKEA, a global retailer headquartered in Sweden, offers a wide range of well-designed, functional home furnishing products at low prices. It's easy to make high-quality products and sell them at a high price or make low-quality products to sell at a low price. But IKEA has to be cost-effective and innovative to sell quality products at low prices.

Creating IKEA's unique merchandise starts on the factory floor. IKEA product developers and designers work closely with suppliers to efficiently use production equipment and raw materials and keep waste to a minimum. For example, an IKEA product developer learned about board-on-frame construction touring a door factory. This technique is cost-effective and environmentally friendly because sheets of wood are layered over a honeycomb core to provide a strong, lightweight structure with a minimal wood content. This type of construction is used in many IKEA products, such as its LACK tables.

Many items IKEA sells are shipped and sold disassembled in flat packs to reduce transportation costs and make it easier for customers to take them home. However, some products like lamps take up a lot of space even when disassembled. The LAMPAN illustrates the IKEA way of offering extremely low price with beautiful design and high quality. This was achieved by developing a new packing method in which the lamp shade could be used as a bucket for the lamp base.

IKEA reduces labor costs in its stores by providing signage with extensive information about its products and their quality, presenting its products in room settings, and prominently displaying price tags. These features enable customers to serve themselves and reduce IKEA's labor costs.

REFACT

Annually 600 million customers visit IKEA's stores, eat two billion of those meatballs, and carry off 168 million catalogues.[17]

The LACK table and LAMPAN are classic IKEA designs only available at IKEA's stores and website.

Sources: www.IKEA.com; Deniz Caglar, Marco Kesteloo, and Artt Kleiner, "How Ikea Reassembled Its Growth Strategy," *Strategy+Business*, May 2012; "The Man Who Named the Furniture," *Financial Times*, January 16, 2010, p. 30; and Yongquan Hu and Huifang Jiang, "Innovation Strategy of Retailers: From the View of Global Value Chains," *6th International Conference on Service Systems and Service Management*, 2009, pp. 340–345.

DISCUSSION QUESTION

Why does IKEA's private-label furniture create a sustainable competitive advantage?

It takes considerable time and effort to build a tradition and reputation for customer service. But once a retailer has earned a service reputation, it can sustain this advantage for a long time because it's hard for a competitor to develop a comparable reputation. For example, Ritz-Carlton hotels are world-renowned for providing outstanding customer service. Employees gather daily for a 15-minute staff meeting, during which they share accounts of how they or their peers have gone above and beyond the call for conventional customer service, also known as "WOW stories." A great example involved a chef in a Balinese Ritz-Carlton who learned that a guest had extensive food allergies and responded by having special eggs and milk flown in from a small grocery store, located in another country. Such WOW stories help maintain employees' focus on customer service and gives them recognitions for the efforts they make.[18] Chapter 18 discusses how retailers develop a customer service advantage.

Ritz Carlton's outstanding service builds customer loyalty.

Customer Relationship Management Programs

Customer relationship management (CRM) programs, also called **loyalty** or **frequent shopper programs,** are activities that focus on identifying and building loyalty with a retailer's most valued customers.[19] These programs typically involve offering customers rewards based on the amount of services or merchandise they purchase. For example, airlines offer free tickets to travelers who have flown a prescribed number of miles, and Subway gives customers a free sandwich for each 10 they purchase.

The discounts offered by these programs may not create loyalty. Customers may join loyalty programs of competing retailers and continue to patronize multiple retailers. However, the data collected about customer shopping behavior by these programs can provide insights that enable retailers to build and maintain loyalty. For instance, CVS Caremark's CRM program enables the retailer to collect extensive information about each of its customers and use this information to increase sales. For example, if customers shop relatively infrequently, e.g., once a month for prescriptions, CVS Caremark may provide incentives that expire in a week to encourage more frequent visits. Alternatively, if customers buy frequently, but buy less than $20 per visit, CVS Caremark offers incentives to increase each visit's purchases to, say, $25. It may provide incentives to get customers who are purchasing only national brands to purchase more private-label merchandise. CVS also uses the loyalty data to determine if a household is purchasing less of a category than it should based on usage in similar households, and therefore provide it with a "buy one, get one free" coupon. Thus, the data developed through the loyalty program enable a retailer to develop a personal relationship with customers that builds loyalty. CRM programs are discussed in detail in Chapter 11.

Building a Retail Community Using Social Media

Retailers are beginning to use their websites and social media to develop retail communities. A **retail community** is a group of consumers who have a shared involvement with a retailer. The members of the community share information with respect to the retailer's activities. The involvement in the community can range from simply becoming a fan of a retailer's Facebook page to meeting face-to-face with community members to share experiences. Increased involvement in the community by its members leads to a greater emotional feeling and loyalty toward the retailer.[20]

REFACT

Starbucks, with 29 million fans, ranks second after Coca-Cola on Facebook and ranks third after Facebook and Whole-Foods on Twitter.[21]

Starbucks builds customer loyalty by developing a community of customers who offer suggestions for improving Starbucks' offering.

Starbucks started building a community in 2008 when it launched My Starbucks Ideas (http://mystarbucksidea.force.com). The website was initially a hub for Starbucks customers to share their ideas, suggestions, and even frustrations on this mini social network. As Starbucks customers started enjoying their time interacting with other customers, the website evolved into a community. Now, the online community gives customers the ability to see what others are suggesting, vote on ideas, and check out the results. Starbucks actually implements the most popular ideas, resulting in customers feeling that they have a say on what their favorite coffee does.[22] Starbucks has extended its online efforts into the social media space. Its Facebook page (www.facebook.com/Starbucks) has more than 32 million likes.

Relationships with Suppliers

A second approach for developing a competitive advantage is to develop strong relationships with companies that provide merchandise and services to the retailer, such as real estate developers, advertising agencies, and transportation companies. Of these relationships with suppliers, the most important are relationships with vendors. For example, the relationship between Walmart and Procter & Gamble initially focused on improving supply chain efficiencies. Today, the partners in this relationship share sensitive information with each other so that Walmart is better able to plan for the introduction of new P&G products and even develop some unique packaging for P&G's national brands exclusively available at Walmart. Walmart shares its sales data with P&G so that P&G can better plan its production and use a just-in-time inventory management system to reduce the level of inventory in the system. By strengthening relationships with each other, both retailers and vendors can develop mutually beneficial assets and programs that give the retailer–vendor pair an advantage over competing pairs.[23]

Relationships with vendors, like relationships with customers, are developed over a long time and may not be easily offset by a competitor.[25] Chapter 13 examines how retailers work with their vendors to build mutually beneficial, long-term relationships.

Efficiency of Internal Operations

In addition to strong relationships with external parties, customers, and suppliers, retailers can develop competitive advantages by having more efficient internal operations. Efficient internal operations enable retailers to have a cost advantage over competitors or offer customers more benefits than competitors at the same cost.

Larger companies typically have greater internal operations efficiency. Larger retailers can invest in developing sophisticated systems and spread the fixed cost of these systems over more sales. In addition to size, other approaches for improving internal operating efficiencies are human resource management and information and supply chain management systems.

Human Resource Management
Retailing is a labor-intensive business, in which employees play a major role providing services to customers and building customer loyalty.[26] Some retailers view employees as an expense that needs to be reduced over the long run. But research has found that highly successful retail chains such as Costco invest heavily in store employees, but still have low prices, solid financial performance, and better customer service than their competitors. They recognize that under-investing in their employees makes their operations more inefficient and, therefore, much less profitable. Knowledgeable and skilled employees committed to the retailer's objectives are critical assets that support the success of these retailers. The retail landscape is increasingly dominated by retailers such as Wegman's and Costco that have adapted to this new reality.[27]

Chapter 9 examines how retailers build their human resource assets by developing programs to motivate and coordinate employee efforts, provide appropriate incentives, foster a strong and positive organizational culture and environment, and manage diversity. In Chapter 16, additional information is presented on increasing employee productivity and retention through recruiting, training, and leadership.

Distribution and Information Systems
The use of sophisticated distribution and information systems offers an opportunity for retailers to reduce operating costs—the costs associated with running the business—and make sure that the right merchandise is available at the right time and place.[28] Information flows seamlessly from Walmart to its vendors to facilitate quick and efficient merchandise replenishment and reduce stockouts. Walmart's distribution and information systems have enabled it to have a cost advantage that its competitors cannot overcome. This component of competitive advantage is discussed in Chapter 10.

In addition to using information systems to improve supply chain efficiency, the customers' purchase data collected by information systems provide an opportunity for retailers to tailor store merchandise assortments to the market served by each of its stores and to tailor promotion to the specific needs of individual customers. These data about its customers' buying behavior are a valuable asset offering an advantage that is not easily duplicated by competitors. These applications of information systems are discussed in more detail in Chapter 11.

Location

While committed relationships with customers and vendors and efficient internal operations are important sources of advantage, location is a pervasive source of advantage in retailing. The classic response to the question, "What are the three most important things in retailing?" is "Location, location, location." Location is a critical opportunity for developing competitive advantage for two reasons: (1) Location is the most important factor determining which store a consumer patronizes. For example, most people shop at the supermarket closest to where they live. (2) Location is a sustainable competitive advantage because it is not easily duplicated. Once Walgreens has put a store at the best location at an

Starbucks creates a competitive advantage by saturating an area with stores, which makes it difficult for competitors to find good locations.

intersection, CVS is relegated to the second-best location.

Starbucks has developed a strong competitive advantage with its locations. As it expanded across the United States, it saturated each market before entering a new market. For example, there were more than 100 Starbucks outlets in the Seattle area before the company expanded to a new region. Starbucks frequently opens several stores close to one another. It has two stores on two corners of the intersection of Robson and Thurlow in Vancouver. By having such a high density of stores, Starbucks makes it very difficult for a competitor to enter a market and find good locations. Approaches for evaluating and selecting locations are discussed in Chapters 7 and 8.

Multiple Sources of Advantage

To build an advantage that is sustainable for a long period of time, retailers typically cannot rely on a single approach, such as good locations or excellent customer service. Instead, they use multiple approaches to build as high a wall around their position as possible.[30] For example, McDonald's long-term success is based on providing customers with a good value that meets their expectations, having efficient customer service, possessing a strong brand name, and offering convenient locations. By building strategic assets in all of these areas, McDonald's has developed a strong competitive position in the quick-service restaurant market.[31]

In addition to its unique products and associated customer loyalty, IKEA has a large group of loyal customers due to its strong brand image and the stimulating shopping experience it provides its customers. Walmart complements its size advantage with strong vendor relationships and the clear positioning of a retailer that offers superior value. Starbucks combines its location advantage with unique products, committed employees, a strong brand name, and strong relationships with coffee growers to build an overall advantage that is very difficult for competitors to erode. Retailing View 5.2 describes The Container Store, a retailer that has also built multiple bases of sustainable competitive advantages through unique merchandise, excellent customer service, and strong customer and vendor relationships.

GROWTH STRATEGIES

LO3

Classify the different strategic growth opportunities retailers pursue.

In the preceding sections, we have focused on a retailer's strategy, its target market and retail format, and the approaches that retailers take to build a sustainable competitive advantage and defend their position from competitive attacks. When retailers develop these competitive advantages, they have valuable assets. In this section, we discuss how retailers leverage these assets to expand their businesses.

Growth Opportunities

Four types of growth opportunities that retailers may pursue—market penetration, market expansion, retail format development, and diversification—are shown in Exhibit 5–4.[32] The vertical axis indicates the synergies between the retailer's present markets and the growth opportunity—whether the opportunity involves markets the retailer is presently pursuing or new markets. The horizontal axis indicates the synergies between the retailer's present retail mix and the retail mix of the growth opportunity—whether the opportunity exploits the retailer's skills and knowledge in operating its present format or requires new capabilities to operate a new format.

Market Penetration   A **market penetration growth opportunity** is a growth opportunity directed toward existing customers using the retailer's present retailing format. Such opportunities involve either attracting new consumers from the retailer's current target market who don't patronize the retailer currently or devising approaches that get current customers to visit the retailer more often and/or buy more merchandise on each visit.

Market penetration approaches include opening more stores in the target market and/or keeping existing stores open for longer hours. Other approaches involve displaying merchandise to increase impulse purchases and training salespeople to

RETAILING VIEW   The Container Store—Building a Competitive Advantage by Selling Products That Make Life Simpler

5.2

The Container Store sells products to help customers solve problems, or challenges, as the company likes to call them, in organizing their lives. It offers more than 10,000 innovative products, including multipurpose shelving and garment bags to organize closets; portable file cabinets and magazine holders to create order in home offices; backpacks, modular shelving, and DVD holders to make dorm rooms less cluttered; and recipe holders, bottles, jars, and recycling bins to bring harmony to kitchens. More than 1,500 new products are added to its assortment every year.

Over the years, the company has developed strong vendor relationships. Most of its vendors' primary focus was to manufacture products for industrial use. Yet, over time, the company has worked closely with its vendors to develop products that are appropriate for the home.

The Container Store's sales associates provide outstanding customer service. The company actively recruits customers who are intrigued with helping people organize. It spends considerable time educating sales associates about the merchandise (240 hours versus the typical 12 hours for new retail employees) and then empowering them to use their own intuition and creativity to solve customer challenges.

Employees are very committed to the company; as a result, its turnover rate is among the lowest in the retail industry. The Container Store also has appeared on *Fortune*'s list of the "100 Best Companies to Work For" in each of the last 11 years.

The Container Store has multiple sources of competitive advantage, including unique merchandise, excellent customer service, strong vendor relationships, and committed employees.

and Angela Ellis, "Inside the Container Store: Secrets of America's Favorite Stores," *ABC News*, March 30, 2010; and "Three Good Hires? He'll Pay More for One Who's Great," *The New York Times*, March 14, 2010.

DISCUSSION QUESTION

How does the Container Store maintain its competitive advantage?

Sources: Steven R. Thompson, "Container Store Uses Personal Approach in New Strategy," *Dallas Business Journal*, April 27, 2012; Bianna Golodryga

EXHIBIT 5–4
Growth Opportunities

TARGET MARKETS

	Existing	New
Existing	Market Penetration	Market Expansion
New	Format Development	Diversification (unrelated/related)

RETAIL FORMAT

cross-sell. **Cross-selling** means that sales associates in one department attempt to sell complementary merchandise from other departments to their customers. For example, a sales associate who has just sold a Blu-Ray player to a customer will take the customer to the accessories department to sell special cables to improve the performance of the player.

Market Expansion A **market expansion growth opportunity** involves using the retailer's existing retail format in new market segments. For example, Dunkin' Donuts has been opening new stores outside its traditional target market in the northeastern United States.[33] When Chico's acquired White House Black Market, it engaged in a market expansion growth opportunity. Chico's and White House Black Market have similar retail formats. They are both mall-based specialty apparel stores. But Chico's targets women over 30 years old, while White House Black Market targets a younger age segment. In contrast, Chico's acquisition of Soma, a mall-based specialty store chain offering lingerie for women between 35 and 55, was a market penetration opportunity—same market and similar operations; however, Chico's and Soma offer different products.

Retail Format Development A **retail format development growth opportunity** is an opportunity in which a retailer develops a new retail format—a format with a different retail mix—for the same target market. The U.K.-based retailer Tesco has employed a retail format development growth strategy by operating several different food store formats that all cater to essentially the same target market. The smallest is Tesco Express, up to 3,000 square feet. These stores are located close to where customers live and work. Tesco Metro stores are 7,000 to 15,000 square feet, bring convenience to city center locations, and specialize in offering a wide range of ready-to-eat meals. Tesco Superstores, up to 50,000 square feet, are the oldest format. In recent years, the company has added nonfood products, such as Blu-Rays and books, to improve customer satisfaction. Finally, Tesco Extra stores, more than 60,000 square feet, are designed to be a one-stop destination, with the widest range of food and nonfood products, from housewares and clothing to garden furniture.[34]

Diversification A **diversification growth opportunity** is one in which a retailer introduces a new retail format directed toward a market segment that's not currently served by the retailer. Diversification opportunities are either related or unrelated.

Related versus Unrelated Diversification   In a **related diversification growth opportunity,** the retailer's present target market and retail format shares something in common with the new opportunity. This commonality might entail purchasing from the same vendors, operating in similar locations, using the same distribution or management information system, or advertising in the same newspapers to similar target markets. In contrast, an **unrelated diversification growth opportunity** has little commonality between the retailer's present business and the new growth opportunity.

Through acquisition, Home Depot built a wholesale building supply business, called HD Supply, which had generated more than $3 billion in annual sales. Management felt that this growth opportunity would be synergistic with the firm's retail business, because its stores were already selling similar merchandise to contractors. Thus, Home Depot viewed this growth opportunity as a related diversification, because the targeted customers (i.e., contractors) would be similar, and the new large contractor market could be served using a retail mix similar to Home Depot's present retail mix. In addition, Home Depot would realize cost savings by placing larger orders with vendors because it would be selling to both retail and wholesale large and small customers.

In hindsight, though, the HD Supply actually was an unrelated diversification. The large contractor market served by HD Supply sold primarily pipes, lumber, and concrete—products with limited sales in Home Depot's retail stores. Selling these supplies to large contractors involved competitive bidding and transporting large, bulky orders to job sites—skills that Home Depot lacked. So Home Depot sold this unrelated diversification to concentrate on its core retail, small-contractor business.[35]

Vertical Integration   **Vertical integration** describes diversification by retailers into wholesaling or manufacturing. For example, some retailers go beyond designing their private-label merchandise to owning factories that manufacture the merchandise. When retailers integrate backward and manufacture products, they are making risky investments because the requisite skills to make products are different from those associated with retailing them. In addition, retailers and manufacturers have different customers. The immediate customers for a manufacturer's products are retailers, while a retailer's customers are consumers. Thus, a manufacturer's marketing activities are very different from those of a retailer. Note that designing private-label merchandise is a related diversification because it builds on the retailer's knowledge of its customers, whereas actually making the merchandise is an unrelated diversification.

Growth Opportunities and Competitive Advantage

Typically, retailers have the greatest competitive advantage and most success when they engage in opportunities that are similar to their present retail operations and markets. Thus, market penetration growth opportunities have the greatest chances of succeeding because they build on the retailer's present bases of advantage and don't involve entering new, unfamiliar markets or operating new, unfamiliar retail formats.

When retailers pursue market expansion opportunities, they build on their advantages in operating a retail format and apply this competitive advantage in a new market. A retail format development opportunity builds on the retailer's relationships and loyalty of present customers. Even if a retailer doesn't have experience and skills in operating the new format, it hopes to attract its loyal customers to it. Retailers have the least opportunity to exploit a competitive advantage when they pursue diversification opportunities.

GLOBAL GROWTH OPPORTUNITIES

LO4

Identify issues that arise as domestic retailers become global retailers.

In this section, we provide a more detailed discussion of one type of growth opportunity—expanding operations to international markets. This growth opportunity is becoming particularly attractive to large retailers as they begin to saturate their domestic market. Of the 20 largest retailers in the world, only 3 operate in one country.[36] By expanding internationally, retailers can increase their sales, leverage their knowledge and systems across a greater sales base, and gain more bargaining power with vendors. But international expansion is risky because retailers must deal with different government regulations, cultural traditions, consumer preferences, supply chains, and languages. Retailing View 5.3 describes the substantial differences in grocery shopping in Shanghai.

We first discuss the attractiveness of different opportunities for global expansion and then the keys to success for expanding globally. Finally, we review the approaches that retailers can take to enter international markets.

Attractiveness of International Markets

Three factors that are often used to determine the attractiveness of international opportunities are (1) the potential size of the retail market in the country, (2) the degree to which the country does and can support the entry of foreign retailers engaged in modern retail practices, and (3) the risks or uncertainties in sales and profits.[37] Some indicators of these factors are shown in Exhibit 5–5. The (+) or (−) indicates whether the indicator is positively or negatively related to the factor.

Note that the importance of some country characteristics depends on the type of retailer evaluating the country for entry. For example, a retailer of video games, such as Gamestop, would find a country with a large percentage of people under 19 to be more attractive than a country with a large percentage of people over 65. High-fashion retailers that sell expensive merchandise, such as Neiman Marcus and Cartier, would find a country that has a significant percentage of the population with high incomes to be more attractive than a country that has a large percentage of people in poverty.

Most retailers considering entry into foreign markets are successful multinational retailers that use sophisticated management practices. Thus, they would find countries that have modern retailing, more advanced infrastructures, and significant urban populations to be more supportive. In addition, countries lacking strong domestic retailers but having a stable economy and political environment would be more supportive.

The factors outlined in Exhibit 5–5 are weighted to develop an index scoring each country on the attractiveness dimensions. One index ranking the 20 most

EXHIBIT 5–5   Indicators of the Potential, Support, and Risk in International Markets

Country Potential	Country Support	Country Risk
Population (+)	Market share of modern retailing (+)	Political stability (+)
Population growth rate (+)	Quality of infrastructure (roads, trains, etc.) (+)	Business-friendly laws and regulations (+)
GDP (+)	Urban population (+)	Access to bank financing (+)
GDP growth rate (+)	Market share of domestic retailers (+)	National debt (−)
GDP per capita (+)	Market share of international retailers (+)	Crime (−)
Retail sales (+)	Market share of largest retailers (+)	Violence (−)
Retail sales growth rate (+)		Corruption (−)
Retail sales per capita (+)		
Population (+)		
Income distribution (+ or −)		
Age (+ or −)		

attractive international retail markets on market potential (country potential and support) and risk is shown in Exhibit 5–6. Of the top 20 counties in this ranking, 10 are emerging economies. The emerging international markets that receive the most attention from global retailers are India, China, Russia, and Brazil, collectively referred to as "the BRIC" (Brazil, Russia, India, China) countries. However, in this analysis, Russia is not in the top 20 because of its high risk.

RETAILING VIEW   Wet Markets in Shanghai   5.3

Shanghai, with more than 23 million inhabitants, is the largest city by population in the world. It is a sophisticated international city, like New York, London, and Tokyo, with substantial influence in global commerce, culture, finance, media, fashion, technology, and transportation. It is a major financial center and the busiest container port in the world. The major international food retailers (Walmart, Carrefour, Metro, and Tesco) have now opened more than 200 Western-style hypermarkets in Shanghai. In addition, there are more than 2,000 modern supermarkets operated mostly by Chinese firms. But the majority of perishable goods (fish, meat, chicken, pork, vegetables, and fruit) sales still are made in traditional wet markets.

Wet markets are buildings divided into small stalls lined along narrow corridors with small, independent retailers selling perishables in the stalls. The retailers lease the stalls from market operators. They buy the perishables from various sources, including wholesale markets, rural merchants, and farmers' cooperatives, and then sort, clean, and package the perishables for sale to their customers. These markets are called "wet markets" because the concrete floor is constantly wet from the spraying of perishables and cleaning of live meat and fish. There are more than 900 wet markets in Shanghai.

The Chinese government would like to close all wet markets because they do not reflect the modern China and because they pose health risks due to poor hygiene. But Chinese urban consumers cross-format shop for groceries: They buy manufactured goods in supermarkets and hypermarkets but perishables in wet markets. Two factors contribute to this preference for wet markets.

First, Chinese consumers place great importance on freshness. Perishables sold at supermarkets and hypermarkets usually get to the store around eight o'clock the night before and have been shelved for at least half a day before reaching consumers. At wet markets, vendors buy their perishables around four o'clock in the morning and constantly trim, spray, clean, and sort the perishables to keep them fresh. Also, wet-market vendors do not have or use refrigerators for storage; thus, they have to replenish their inventory with fresh supplies every day. The modern-format retailers simply cannot win the freshness contest.

Even though there are many modern supermarkets and hypermarkets in Shanghai, the majority of perishable groceries are still bought at traditional wet markets.

Second, for logistical reasons, most Chinese consumers shop for groceries every day and buy just enough to prepare for that day's meals. In their small homes, the average kitchen size is about 60 square feet, leaving little room to store any items for extended periods, especially perishable foods that require refrigeration. Furthermore, though the automotive market is growing in China, many families still travel by other means. In Shanghai for example, bicycles (20 percent), buses (30 percent), and walking (40 percent) are more common means of transport for shopping trips. In these locations, the small wet markets provide far more convenient locations than larger super- or hypermarkets.

Sources: "Buying the Store," *China Economic Review*, June 14, 2012; Louise Herring, Daniel Hui, Paul Morgan, and Caroline Tufft, *Inside China's Hypermarkets: Past and Prospects* (Hong Kong: McKinsey By McKinsey, 2012); and Qian Forrest Zhang and Zi Pan, *The Transformation of Urban Vegetable Retail in China: Wet Markets, Supermarkets, and Informal Markets in Shanghai*, Research Collection School of Social Sciences, 2012.

DISCUSSION QUESTION

Given the Chinese government's disdain for wet markets, do you think they will endure?

EXHIBIT 5–6   Country Attractiveness

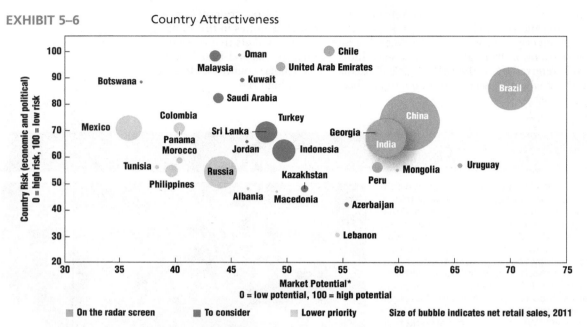

On the radar screen ■   To consider ■   Lower priority ■   Size of bubble indicates net retail sales, 2011

*Based on weighted score of market attractiveness, market saturation, and time pressure of top 30 countries

SOURCE: Hana Ben-Shabat, Helen Rhim, Mike Moriarity, and Fabiola Salman, *Global Retail Expansion Keeps Moving—2012* (New York: ATKearney, 2012).

 India and China are by far the largest and most attractive retail markets. However, these two countries offer different opportunities and challenges for retailers contemplating entry.[38]

India   In India and most emerging economies, the retail industry is divided into organized and unorganized sectors. The **unorganized retailing** includes the small independent retailers—the local *kirana* shops, owner-operated general stores, *paan/beedi* shops, convenience stores, and handcart and street vendors. Most Indians shop in open markets and millions of independent grocery shops called *kirana*. However, India's growing, well-educated, aspirational middle class wants a more sophisticated retail environment and global brands.

REFACT

Less than 5 percent of India's retail sales are through organized retail channels.[39]

While the demand for modern (organized) retailing exists in India, entering the Indian market is challenging. As the world's largest pluralistic democracy, with myriad cultures and 22 official languages, India actually is a conglomeration of discrete markets. In addition, government regulations impede foreign investment in retailing. Retailers must comply with a myriad of regulations before opening stores and shipping merchandise. For example, there are taxes for moving goods to different states and even within states. Initially, Walmart's entry into India is a partnership with Bharti Enterprises to open wholesale outlets called Best Price Modern Wholesale. The outlets initially were allowed to

In India, most consumers shop at small, independent retail outlets.

sell only to firms that register by showing tax documents that prove they own retail outlets. The development of organized retailing is being undertaken by industrial conglomerates that have limited expertise in running retail chains.[40]

China   Government regulations of retailing are much less onerous in China than in India, and direct foreign investment is encouraged. Since the lifting of most operational restrictions on international retailers, six global food retailers (Auchan, Carrefour, Ito-Yokado, Metro, Tesco, and Walmart) have entered China, although much of this retail development has been in the large eastern coastal cities of Shanghai, Beijing, Guangzhou, and Shenzhen.[41]

China is rapidly developing the infrastructure to support modern retailing. Highway density in China is already approaching similar levels as the United States. China has a number of high-quality airports and a rapidly developing sophisticated railroad network.

However, doing business in China is still challenging. Operating costs are increasing, managerial talent is becoming more difficult to find and retain, and an underdeveloped and inefficient supply chain predominates.

Brazil   Brazil has the largest population and strongest economy in Latin America. It is a country of many poor people and a few very wealthy families. Brazilian retailers have developed some very innovative practices for retailing to low-income families, including offering credit and installment purchases. The very wealthy Brazilians provide a significant market for luxury goods and retailers. Even though they are approximately 1 percent of the population, this equates to approximately 19 million people, a market just a little smaller than all of Australia.

Russia   In Russia, the impediments to market entry are less visible but more problematic. Corruption is rampant, with various administrative authorities capable of impeding operations if payments are not made. Retailers encounter severe logistical challenges in supporting operations in Russia. There are long delays at borders and ports and a scarcity of containers. More than 70 percent of international container shipments come through the St. Petersburg port, which is very congested. Retailers often cannot rely on domestic products because the quality of products made in Russia is poor. Most major retailers offer their own credit card facility, with "signing up" booths at the entrances to their stores. Many low-income customers go from week to week paying their credit card commitments. Finally, much of the purchasing power is concentrated in Moscow, where salaries are about double those in other regions. But Moscow is already saturated with shopping centers.

REFACT

The anticorruption group Transparency International ranks Russia 143th out of 183 countries on its most recent index of the most corrupt countries.[42]

Keys to Success in Global Retailing

Four characteristics of retailers that have successfully exploited international growth opportunities are (1) a globally sustainable competitive advantage, (2) adaptability, (3) a global culture, and (4) financial resources.

Globally Sustainable Competitive Advantage   Entry into nondomestic markets is most successful when the expansion opportunity builds on the retailer's core bases of competitive advantage. For example, Walmart and ALDI have a significant cost advantage that facilitates success in international markets in which price plays an important role in consumer decision making and a distribution infrastructure is available to enable these firms to exploit their logistical capabilities. In contrast, H&M and Zara are more successful in international markets that value lower-priced, fashionable merchandise.

Some U.S. retailers have a competitive advantage in global markets because American culture is emulated in many countries, particularly by young people. Due to rising prosperity, the rapidly increasing access to broadband Internet, social media like Facebook and networks such as MTV that feature American programming, fashion trends in the United States have spread to young people in emerging countries. The global MTV generation prefers Coke to tea, Nikes to sandals, Chicken McNuggets to rice, and credit cards to cash. China's major cities have American stores and restaurants, including KFC, Pizza Hut, and McDonald's. Shanghai and Beijing have more than 100 Starbucks stores even though coffee had never been the drink of choice before Starbucks came to town. But Chinese urban dwellers go to Starbucks to impress a friend or because it's a symbol of a new kind of lifestyle. Although Western products and stores have gained a reputation for high quality and good service in China, in some ways it is the American culture that many Chinese consumers want.

Adaptability   Although successful global retailers build on their core competencies, they also recognize cultural differences and adapt their core strategy to the needs of local markets. Retailing View 5.4 illustrates how 7-Eleven changed its retail offering to be more appealing in Indonesia.

Carrefour is an expert at understanding and integrating itself into local regions. For example, it realized early on that the merchandising of fish differs for each local market. In San Francisco, fish is sold dead and filleted; in France, fish is sold

---

5.4   RETAILING VIEW   7-Eleven Is Trendy Hangout in Indonesia

In a local hangout in Jakarta, hipsters gather to drink iced coffee, gossip, eat nachos, listen to a live band, and text their friends. This sort of hanging out is so popular and common among young Indonesians that their language includes a word to describe sitting around, chatting, and generally doing nothing productive: *nongkrong*. For years, the most popular gathering spots were food stalls, located along the sides of roads, known as *warung*. But the *warung* are giving way to another popular *nongkrong* location: local 7-Eleven stores.

This shift is exactly the response that 7-Eleven hoped to achieve when it instituted a new strategy in Indonesia: adding seating to its existing small supermarkets and offering inexpensive, ready-to-eat meals, such as fried rice and pillow bread (i.e., small cheese- or chocolate-filled sandwiches). Jakarta is notably lacking in outdoor recreation space, so the little hangouts effectively attract social customers. And Indonesia has plenty of those, as evidenced by its massive social networking rates. In Indonesia alone, 7-Eleven has attracted nearly 60,000 Twitter followers and almost as many Facebook fans.

The strategy also means that the franchise mainly targets young customers, who constitute 65 percent of its market. These Millennials make use of the 24/7 access that 7-Eleven offers, surfing the Internet at all hours, before or after gathering with their friends. In Indonesia, one of the most electronically connected nations in the world, customers constantly update their social networks to alert them about when a band is about to start playing at the local 7-Eleven, for example. Among this generational cohort, the store appeals to a wide range of economic classes, such that the parking lots fill with Mercedes-Benzes interspersed with rusted-out motor bikes.

Despite these unique offerings, 7-Elevens are still 7-Elevens: They sell Big Gulps, flavored Slurpees, doughnuts,

7-Eleven is a trendy place for young Indonesians to hang out with their friends.

and hot coffee. But in locations in the world's most populous Muslim country, 7-Eleven only sells alcohol after conducting neighborhood surveys to obtain community approval.

Sources: Sara Schonhardt, "7-Eleven Finds a Niche by Adapting to Indonesian Ways," *The New York Times*, May 28, 2012; and Anthony Deutsch, "7-Eleven Becomes Indonesia's Trendy Hangout," *Financial Times*, September 13, 2011.

DISCUSSION QUESTION

Could 7-Eleven adapt what it has learned in Indonesia to the United States to attract young urban customers? Would it want to?

dead but whole on ice with the head still intact; and in China, fish is sold live. However, consumers in the middle and western parts of China have more confidence in frozen fish, because they are so far from the ocean.[43] Carrefour and Tesco make sure that more than 90 percent of the merchandise they sell is produced in the country in which it is sold.[44]

Peak selling seasons also vary across countries. In the United States, many stores experience a sales increase in August, when families stock up on back-to-school supplies and apparel. However, this month is one of the slowest sales periods in Europe because most people are on vacation. Back-to-school season in Japan occurs in April.

Store designs and layouts often need to be adjusted in different parts of the world. In the United States, for instance, supercenters are usually quite large and on one level, except in a few urban areas. In other parts of the world, such as Europe and parts of Asia, where space is at a premium, stores must be designed to fit smaller footprints and are often housed in multiple levels. In some cultures, social norms dictate that men's and women's clothing cannot be displayed next to each other.

Government regulations and cultural values can also affect store operations. Some differences, such as holidays, hours of operation, and regulations governing part-time employees and terminations, are easy to identify. Other factors require a deeper understanding. For example, Latin American culture is very family oriented, so traditional U.S. work schedules would need to be adjusted so that Latin American employees could have more time with their families during family meals. Boots, a U.K. drugstore chain owned by Walgreens, has the checkout clerks in its Japanese stores stand up because it discovered that Japanese shoppers found it offensive to pay money to a seated clerk, but retailers have to provide seating for checkout clerks in Germany. Retailers in Germany also must recycle packaging materials sold in their stores. Also in Germany, seasonal sales can be held only during specific weeks and apply only to specific product categories, and the amount of the discounts are limited. Spanish and French retailers work under government-controlled operating hours and must mind policies prohibiting midseason sales.

Global Culture   To be global, retailers must think globally. It is not sufficient to transplant a home-country culture and infrastructure to another country. In this regard, Carrefour is truly global. In the early years of its international expansion, it started in each country slowly, an approach that reduced the company's ethnocentrism. Further enriching its global perspective, Carrefour has always encouraged the rapid development of local management and retains few expatriates in its overseas operations. Carrefour's management ranks are truly international. One is just as likely to run across a Portuguese regional manager in Hong Kong as a French or Chinese one. Finally, Carrefour discourages the classic overseas "tour of duty" mentality often found in U.S. firms. International assignments are important in themselves, not just as stepping stones to ultimate career advancement back in France. The globalization of Carrefour's culture is perhaps most evident in the speed with which ideas flow throughout the organization. A global management structure of regional committees, which meet regularly, advances the awareness and implementation of global best practices. The proof of Carrefour's global commitment lies in the numbers: It has had more than 30 years of international experience in 30 countries, both developed and developing.[45]

Financial Resources   Expansion into international markets requires a long-term commitment and considerable up-front planning. Retailers find it very difficult to generate short-term profits when they make the transition to global retailing. Although firms such as Walmart, Carrefour, Office Depot, and Costco often initially have difficulty achieving success in new global markets, these large firms generally are in a strong financial position and therefore have the ability to keep investing in projects long enough to become successful.

Entry Strategies

Four approaches that retailers can take when entering nondomestic markets are direct investment, joint venture, strategic alliance, and franchising.[46]

Direct Investment   **Direct investment** occurs when a retail firm invests in and owns a retail operation in a foreign country. This entry strategy requires the highest level of investment and exposes the retailer to the greatest risks, but it also has the highest potential returns. A key advantage of direct investment is that the retailer has complete control of the operations. For example, McDonald's chose this entry strategy for the U.K. market, building a plant to produce buns when local suppliers could not meet its specifications.

Joint Venture   A **joint venture** is formed when the entering retailer pools its resources with a local retailer to form a new company in which ownership, control, and profits are shared. A joint-venture entry strategy reduces the entrant's risks. In addition to sharing the financial burden, the local partner provides an understanding of the market and has access to local resources, such as vendors and real estate. Many foreign countries require that foreign entrants partner with domestic firms. Problems with this entry approach can arise if the partners disagree or the government places restrictions on the repatriation of profits.

Strategic Alliance   A **strategic alliance** is a collaborative relationship between independent firms. For example, a retailer might enter an international market through direct investment but use independent firms to facilitate its local logistical and warehousing activities.

Franchising   **Franchising** offers the lowest risk and requires the least investment, but also has the lowest potential return on investment. The retailer has limited control over the retail operations in the foreign country, its potential profit is reduced, and the risk of assisting in the creation of a local domestic competitor increases. The U.K.-based Marks & Spencer, for example, has franchised stores in 30 countries.[47]

THE STRATEGIC RETAIL PLANNING PROCESS

LO5

Know the steps retailers go through to develop a strategic plan.

In the previous sections, we reviewed the elements in a strategy statement, the approaches for building a sustainable competitive advantage, the growth opportunities that retailers consider, and the factors they consider when evaluating and pursuing a global growth opportunity. In this section, we outline the process retailers use to review their present situation and decide on a strategy to pursue.

The **strategic retail planning process** is the set of steps a retailer goes through to develop a strategy and plan[48] (see Exhibit 5–7). It describes how retailers select target market segments, determine the appropriate retail format, and build sustainable competitive advantages. As indicated in Exhibit 5–7, it is not always necessary to go through the entire process each time a strategy and plan are developed (step 7). For instance, a retailer could evaluate its performance and go directly to step 2 to conduct a SWOT analysis.

The planning process can be used to formulate strategic plans at different levels within a retail corporation. For example, the corporate strategic plan of Tesco indicates how to allocate resources across the corporation's various divisions, such as Tesco, Tesco Extra, Tesco Express, Tesco Metro, Tesco Homeplus, and One Stop. Each division, in turn, develops its own strategic plan.

As we discuss the steps in the retail planning process, we will apply each step to the planning process for a hypothetical retailer owned by Kelly Bradford. Kelly owns Gifts To Go, a small, two-store chain in the Chicago area. One of her 1,000-square-foot stores is located in the downtown area; the other is in an upscale suburban mall. The target market for Gifts To Go is upper-income men and women looking for gifts in the $50 to $500 price range. The stores have an eclectic

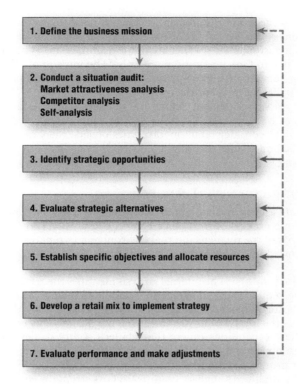

EXHIBIT 5–7
Stages in the Strategic
Planning Process

selection of merchandise, including handmade jewelry and crafts, fine china and glassware, perfume, watches, writing instruments, and a variety of one-of-a-kind items. Gifts To Go also has developed a number of loyal customers who are contacted by sales associates when family anniversaries and birthdays come up. In many cases, customers have a close relationship with a sales associate and enough confidence in the associate's judgment that they tell the associate to pick out an appropriate gift. The turnover of Gifts To Go sales associates is low for the industry because Kelly treats associates as part of the family. The company pays for health insurance for all associates, and the associates share in the profits of the firm.

Step 1: Define the Business Mission

The first step in the strategic retail planning process is to define the business mission. The **mission statement** is a broad description of a retailer's objectives and the scope of activities it plans to undertake.[49] While the principle objective of a publicly held firm is to maximize its stockholders' wealth, firms also are concerned about their impact on society.

For example, Maxine Clark, founder and chief executive bear at Build-A-Bear Workshop, in discussing her goals for the company, says, "We also believe strongly that we need to give back to the communities in which we have stores. For example, as part of our on-going commitment to children's health and wellness, we introduced a series of Nicki Bears to honor Nicki Giampolo, a young girl who lost her life to cancer. A portion of the sales of each Nicki is donated to support programs that help children maintain normal lives while they struggle with difficult health issues."[50] Owners of small, privately held firms frequently have other objectives, such as achieving a specific level of income and avoiding uncertainty rather than maximizing income.

The mission statement defines the general nature of the target segments and retail formats on which the firm will focus. For example, the mission statement "Serve the customer, build value for shareholders, and create opportunities for associates," is too broad. It fails to provide a sense of strategic direction.

In developing the mission statement, managers need to answer five questions: (1) What business are we in? (2) What should our business be in the future? (3) Who are our customers? (4) What are our capabilities? (5) What do we want to accomplish? Gifts To Go's mission statement is "The mission of Gifts To Go is to be the leading retailer of higher-priced gifts in Chicago and provide a stable income of $100,000 per year for the owner."

Because the mission statement defines the retailer's objectives and the scope of activities it plans to undertake, Gifts To Go's mission statement clarifies that its management won't consider retail opportunities outside the Chicago area, selling low-priced gifts, or activities that might jeopardize its ability to generate $100,000 in annual income.

Step 2: Conduct a SWOT Analysis

After developing a mission statement and setting objectives, the next step in the strategic planning process is to conduct a **SWOT analysis.** A SWOT analysis involves an analysis of the retailer's internal environment (strengths and weaknesses) and external environment (opportunities and threats).

Internal Environment   The internal analysis identifies the retailer's *strengths and weaknesses*—the retailer's unique strategic capabilities relative to its competition. These unique capabilities are the assets, knowledge, and skills that the retailer possesses such as the loyalty of its customers and the quality of its relationships with its vendor. These capabilities reflect the retailer's ability to develop a strategic advantage as an opportunity it is considering. Exhibit 5–8 outlines some issues to consider in performing a **strengths and weaknesses analysis.**

Here is Kelly Bradford's analysis of Gifts To Go's strengths and weaknesses:

Capabilities	Gifts To Go Strength and Weaknesses
Financial resources	Good—Gifts To Go had no debt and a good relationship with a bank. Kelly has saved $255,000 that she has in liquid securities.
Customer loyalty	Good—While Gifts To Go did not achieve the sales volume in gifts done in department stores, the company has a loyal base of customers.
Locations	Excellent—Both of Gifts To Go's locations are excellent. The downtown location is convenient for office workers. The suburban mall location is at a heavily trafficked juncture.
HUMAN RESOURCES	
Merchandise management	Limited—Kelly has a flair for selecting unique gifts but has no systems to support her.
Store management	Excellent—The store managers and sales associates are excellent. They are very attentive to customers and loyal to the firm. Employee and customer theft is kept to a minimum.
Other staff and systems	Limited—An accounting firm keeps the financial records for the business.
Vendor relationships	Kelly has excellent relationships with vendors providing one-of-a-kind merchandise.
Supply chain management and information systems	Poor—While Kelly feels Gifts To Go has relatively low overhead, the company does not have a computer-based inventory control system or management and customer information systems. Her competitors (local department stores, catalog, and Internet retailers) certainly have superior systems. No skills in developing and utilizing customer databases.

EXHIBIT 5–8
Elements in a
Strengths and
Weaknesses Analysis

Financial resources	**Human resources**
Customer loyalty	Top managers
Strength of brand image	Store manager
Development of unique merchandise	Merchandise managers
Quality of customer service	Operation managers
Information about customers	Vendor relationships
Size and involvement of community	Supply chain management systems
Locations	Information systems

Market Factors	Competitive Factors	Environmental Dynamics
Market size	Barriers to entry	New technology
Market growth	Bargaining power of vendors	Economic conditions
Cyclicality of sales	Competitive rivalry	Changes in governmental regulations
Seasonality		Social changes

EXHIBIT 5–9
Opportunities and
Threats

External Environment   The external analysis identifies the retailer's opportunities and threats—the aspect of the environment that might positively or negatively affect the retailer's performance. These factors associated with the market, competition, and environment dynamics are typically beyond the retailer's control. Exhibit 5–9 outlines some issues to consider when doing an **opportunities and threats analysis.**

Market Factors   The attractiveness of a target market in which a retailer is involved or considering is affected by the size of the market, market growth, cyclicality of sales, and seasonality. Market size is important because it indicates a retailer's opportunity to generate revenues to cover its investment.

Growing markets are typically more attractive than mature or declining markets. For example, retail markets for limited-assortment, extreme-value retailers are growing faster than are those for department stores. Typically, the return on investment may be higher in growing markets because competition is less intense than in mature markets. Because new customers are just beginning to patronize stores in growing markets, they may not have developed strong store loyalties and thus might be easier to attract to new retail offerings.

Firms are often interested in minimizing the business cycle's impact on their sales. Thus, retail markets for merchandise that is affected by economic conditions (such as cars and major appliances) are less attractive than retail markets that are less affected by economic conditions (such as food). In general, markets with highly seasonal sales are unattractive because a lot of resources are needed to accommodate the peak season and then the resources go underutilized the rest of the year. Retailers can take steps to reduce seasonality; for instance, ski resorts can promote summer vacations.

To conduct an analysis of the market factors for Gifts To Go, Kelly Bradford went on the Internet to get information about the size, growth, and cyclical and seasonal nature of the gift market in general and, more specifically, in Chicago. On the basis of her analysis, she concluded that the market factors were attractive. The market for more expensive gifts was large, growing, and not vulnerable to business cycles. The only negative aspect was the high seasonality of gifts, with peaks at Valentine's Day, June (due to weddings), Christmas, and other holidays.

Competitive Factors   The nature of the competition in retail markets is affected by barriers to entry, the bargaining power of vendors, and competitive rivalry.[51] Retail markets are more attractive when competitive entry is costly. **Barriers to entry** are conditions in a retail market that make it difficult for other firms to enter the market. Some of these conditions are (1) scale economies, (2) customer loyalty, and (3) the availability of great locations.

Scale economies are cost advantages due to a retailer's size. Markets dominated by large competitors with scale economies are typically unattractive because the dominant firms have sustainable cost advantages. For example, an entrepreneur would view the drugstore market as unattractive because it is dominated by three large firms: Walgreens, CVS, and Rite Aid. These firms have considerable cost advantages over an entrepreneur because they have significant bargaining power over suppliers and can buy merchandise at lower prices. They have the resources to invest in the latest technology and can spread the fixed costs of such investments across more outlets.

Retail markets dominated by a well-established retailer that has developed a loyal group of customers also are unattractive. For example, Home Depot's high customer loyalty in Atlanta, where it has its corporate offices, makes it hard for a competing home improvement center like Lowe's to compete effectively in the Atlanta market.

The availability of locations may impede competitive entry. Staples, for instance, attributes part of its success over its rivals in the northeastern United States to its first-mover advantage. The Northeast has a preponderance of mature but stable retail markets, so finding new locations is more difficult there than it is in most of the rest of the United States. Because Staples started in the Northeast, it was able to open stores in the best available locations.

Entry barriers are a double-edged sword. A retail market with high entry barriers is very attractive for retailers presently competing in that market, because those barriers limit competition. However, markets with high entry barriers are unattractive for retailers not already in the market.

Another competitive factor is the **bargaining power of vendors.** Markets are less attractive when only a few vendors control the merchandise sold in the market. In such situations, vendors have the opportunity to dictate prices and other terms (like delivery dates), reducing the retailer's profits. For example, the market for retailing fashionable cosmetics is less attractive because two suppliers, Estée Lauder (Estée Lauder, Clinique, Prescriptives, Aveda, Jo Malone, Bumble and Bumble, Tommy Hilfiger, MAC, and Origins) and L'Oréal (Maybelline, Giorgio Armani, Redken, Lancôme, Garnier, and Ralph Lauren) provide most of the desirable premium brands. Because department stores need these brands to support a fashion image, the vendors have the power to sell their products to retailers at high prices.

The final competitive factor is the level of competitive rivalry in the retail market. **Competitive rivalry** is the frequency and intensity of reactions to actions undertaken by competitors. When rivalry is high, price wars erupt, retailers attempt to "steal" employees from one another, advertising and promotion expenses increase, and profit potential falls. Conditions that may lead to intense rivalry include (1) a large number of competitors that are all about the same size, (2) slow growth, (3) high fixed costs, and (4) a lack of perceived differences between competing retailers. For example, Home Depot and Lowe's have an intense rivalry in many markets.

When Kelly Bradford started to analyze the competitive factors for Gifts To Go, she realized that identifying her competitors wasn't easy. Although there were no gift stores carrying similar merchandise at the same price points in the Chicago area, there were various other retailers from which a customer could buy gifts. She identified her primary competitors as department stores, craft galleries, catalogs, and Internet retailers. Kelly felt there were some scale economies in developing customer databases to support gift retailing. The lack of large suppliers meant that vendors' bargaining power wasn't a problem, and competitive rivalry was minimal because the gift business was not a critical part of a department store's overall business. In addition, merchandise carried by the various retailers offered considerable differentiation opportunities.

Environmental Dynamics   Environmental dynamics that can affect market attractiveness include technological, economic, regulatory, and social changes. When a retail market is going through significant changes in technology, existing competitors are vulnerable to new entrants that are skilled at using the new technology. Many traditional store-based retailers were slow to develop their multichannel strategies fully. For instance, even today, many multichannel retailers do not offer customers the ability to purchase over the Internet and return merchandise to a store. Retailing View 5.5 illustrates how changes in the competitive environment forced Hot Topic to reevaluate its entire retail format.

Government regulations can reduce the attractiveness of a retail market. For example, until recently, government regulations made it difficult for retailers to open big-box stores in France and Germany.[52] Also, many local governments within the United States have tried to stop Walmart from entering their markets in an attempt to protect locally owned retailers.

Retailers need to answer three questions about each environmental factor:

1. What new developments or changes might occur, such as new technologies and regulations or different social factors and economic conditions?

2. What is the likelihood that these environmental changes will occur? What key factors affect whether these changes will occur?

3. How will these changes affect each retail market, the firm, and its competitors?

Kelly Bradford's primary concern when she did an environmental analysis was the potential growth of Internet gift retailers such as RedEnvelope. Gifts seem ideal for an electronic channel, because customers can order the item over the Internet and have it shipped directly to the gift recipient. Kelly also recognized that the electronic channel could effectively collect information about customers and then target promotions and suggestions to them when future gift-giving occasions arose.

RETAILING VIEW   Hot Topic Emphasizes Its Strength in Indie Music   5.5

Hot Topic, which started in the late 1980s, differentiated itself from other mall-based retailers targeting the Generation Y segment by offering an edgier alternative. It offered goth merchandise in its stores, which were frequented by customers and sales associates with tattoos, multiple piercings, spiked hair, and all-black clothing. Over time, Hot Topic looked like an also-ran in the crowded teen-retailer market. The tastes of fickle teens had changed. Its sales were stagnant. Mall foot traffic was down.

Hot Topic analyzed its situation and discovered that its basis of advantage among teens wasn't its goth image but its connection to the indie music scene—the small avant-garde bands it promoted with its private-label T-shirts. So it repositioned itself, reducing its emphasis on goth-look apparel and placing more emphasis on merchandise linked to cutting-edge music and entertainment.

Today, its stores feel more like campus student centers with loud music, dark walls, and bulletin boards crammed with concert flyers and staff music picks. Hot Topic began hosting free acoustic shows, called Local Static, featuring bands chosen by salespeople in its local stores. The company stresses its connection with music through its music download site, ShockHound.

It also licensed exclusively *Twilight's* four-book-and-film franchise about teen vampire love. The movie's stars did a national tour of Hot Topic stores, and the retailer supplied hot chocolate and pizza to thousands of fans.

When Hot Topic's market declined, it altered its strategic positioning to target young consumers that prefer local bands.

Sources: Schuyler Velasco, "How 'The Hunger Games' Scored a Marketing Win," *Christain Science Monitor*, March, 2012, p. 10; Nivedita Bhattacharjee, "And Hot Topic Gets Hunger Games Lift but May Not Last," *March*, March 2012: and http://community.hottopic.com/content/about-hot-topics, accessed September 6, 2012.

DISCUSSION QUESTION

Describe Hot Topic's target market. How has this changed over time?

Step 3: Identify Strategic Opportunities

After completing the SWOT analysis, the next step is to identify opportunities for increasing retail sales. Kelly Bradford presently competes in gift retailing using a specialty store format. The strategic alternatives she is considering are defined in terms of the growth opportunities in Exhibit 5–4. Note that some of these growth strategies involve a redefinition of her mission.

Step 4: Evaluate Strategic Opportunities

The fourth step in the strategic planning process is to evaluate opportunities that have been identified in the SWOT analysis. The evaluation determines the retailer's potential to establish a sustainable competitive advantage and reap long-term profits from the opportunities being evaluated. Thus, a retailer must focus on opportunities that utilize its strengths and its competitive advantage.

Both the market attractiveness and the strengths and weaknesses of the retailer need to be considered in evaluating strategic opportunities. The greatest investments should be made in market opportunities for which the retailer has a strong competitive position. Here's Kelly's informal analysis:

Growth Opportunity	Market Attractiveness	Competitive Position
Increase size of present stores and amount of merchandise in stores	Low	High
Open additional gift stores in Chicago area	Medium	Medium
Open gift stores outside the Chicago area (new geographic segment)	Medium	Low
Sell lower-priced gifts in present stores or open new stores selling low-priced gifts (new benefit segment)	Medium	Low
Sell apparel and other nongift merchandise to same customers in same or new stores	High	Medium
Sell similar gift merchandise to same market segment using the Internet	High	Low
Open apparel stores targeted at teenagers	High	Low
Open a category specialist selling low-priced gifts	High	Low

Step 5: Establish Specific Objectives and Allocate Resources

After evaluating the strategic investment opportunities, the next step in the strategic planning process is to establish a specific objective for each opportunity. The retailer's overall objective is included in the mission statement; the specific objectives are goals against which progress toward the overall objective can be measured. Thus, these specific objectives have three components: (1) the performance sought, including a numerical index against which progress may be measured; (2) a time frame within which the goal is to be achieved; and (3) the level of investment needed to achieve the objective. Typically, the performance levels are financial criteria such as return on investment, sales, or profits. Kelly's objective is to increase profits by 20 percent in each of the next five years. She expects she will need to invest an additional $25,000 in her apparel and other nongift merchandise inventory.

Step 6: Develop a Retail Mix to Implement the Strategy

The sixth step in the planning process is to develop a retail mix for each opportunity in which an investment will be made and control and evaluate performance. Decisions related to the elements in the retail mix are discussed in Sections III and IV.

Step 7: Evaluate Performance and Make Adjustments

The final step in the planning process is to evaluate the results of the strategy and implementation program. If the retailer is meeting or exceeding its objectives, changes aren't needed. But if the retailer fails to meet its objectives, reanalysis is required. Typically, this reanalysis starts with reviewing the implementation programs, but it may indicate that the strategy (or even the mission statement) needs to be reconsidered. This conclusion would result in starting a new planning process, including a new SWOT analysis.

Strategic Planning in the Real World

The planning process in Exhibit 5–7 suggests that strategic decisions are made in a sequential manner. After the business mission is defined, the SWOT analysis is performed, strategic opportunities are identified, alternatives are evaluated, objectives are set, resources are allocated, the implementation plan is developed, and, finally, performance is evaluated and adjustments are made. But actual planning processes have interactions among the steps. For example, the SWOT analysis may uncover a logical alternative for the firm to consider, even though this alternative isn't included in the mission statement. Thus, the mission statement may need to be reformulated. The development of the implementation plan might reveal that the resources allocated to a particular opportunity are insufficient to achieve the objective. In that case, the objective would need to be changed, the resources would need to be increased, or the retailer might consider not investing in the opportunity at all.

SUMMARY

LO1 **Define the retail strategy.**

A retail strategy is a statement that identifies (1) the retailer's target market, (2) the format and resources the retailer plans to use to satisfy the target market's needs, and (3) the bases on which the retailer plans to build a sustainable competitive advantage. The target market is the market segment(s) toward which the retailer plans to focus its resources and retail mix. A retail format describes the nature of the retailer's operations—its retail mix. A sustainable competitive advantage is an advantage the retailer has over its competition that is not easily copied by competitors and thus can be maintained over a long period of time.

LO2 **Illustrate how retailers build a sustainable competitive advantage.**

Three approaches for developing a sustainable competitive advantage are (1) building strong relationships with customers, (2) building strong relationships with suppliers, and (3) achieving efficient internal operations. Each of these approaches involves developing an asset—loyal customers, strong vendor relationships, committed effective human resources, efficient systems, and attractive locations—that is not easily duplicated by competitors. Three approaches for developing a sustainable competitive advantage are (1) building strong relationships with customers, (2) building strong relationships with suppliers, and (3) achieving efficient internal operations. To build an advantage that is sustainable for a long period of time, retailers typically cannot rely on a single approach, such as good locations or excellent customer service. Instead, they use multiple approaches to build as high a wall around their position as possible.

LO3 **Classify the different strategic growth opportunities retailers pursue.**

Four types of growth opportunities that retailers may pursue are market penetration, market expansion, retail format development, and diversification. The success in pursuing these growth opportunities is the synergies between the retailer's present markets and the growth opportunity—whether the opportunity involves markets the retailer is presently pursuing or new markets—and the synergies between the retailer's present retail mix and the retail mix of the growth opportunity—whether the opportunity exploits the retailer's skills and knowledge in operating its present format or requires new capabilities to operate a new format.

LO4 **Identify issues that arise as domestic retailers become global retailers.**

By expanding internationally, retailers can increase their sales, leverage their knowledge and systems across a greater sales base, and gain more bargaining power with vendors. But international expansion is risky because retailers must deal with different government regulations, cultural traditions, consumer preferences, supply chains, and languages. The attractiveness of international opportunities is assessed by (1) the potential size of the retail market in the country, (2) the degree to which the country does and can support the entry of foreign retailers engaged in modern retail practices, and (3) the risks or uncertainties in sales and profits. The most attractive international markets are India, China, and Brazil.

LO5 Know the steps retailers go through to develop a strategic plan.

Strategic planning is an ongoing process. Every day, retailers audit their situations, examine consumer trends, study new technologies, and monitor competitive activities. But the retail strategy statement does not change every year or every six months; the strategy statement is reviewed and altered only when major changes in the retailer's environment or capabilities occur.

When a retailer undertakes a major reexamination of its strategy, the process for developing a new strategy statement may take a year or two.

Potential strategic directions are generated by people at all levels of the organization and then evaluated by senior executives and operating personnel to ensure that the eventual strategic direction is profitable in the long run and can be implemented.

The strategic planning process consists of a sequence of steps: (1) define the business mission, (2) conduct a SWOT analysis, (3) identify strategic opportunities, (4) evaluate the alternatives, (5) establish specific objectives and allocate resources, (6) develop a retail mix to implement the strategy, and (7) evaluate performance and make adjustments.

KEY TERMS

GET OUT AND DO IT!

1. **CONTINUING CASE ASSIGNMENT** Prepare an analysis of the company you selected for the continuing assignment. Identify its direct competitors, its target market and positioning, its strategy with respect to its competitors, its retail format (the elements in its retail mix—merchandise variety and assortment, pricing, locations), and its bases for developing a competitive advantage relative to its competitors. Outline the retailer's strengths, weaknesses, opportunities, and threats relative to its competitors. Pick a specific country in which the firm does not operate, and make a recommendation about whether the retailer should enter the country and, if so, how it should do so.

2. **INTERNET EXERCISE** Visit the websites for IKEA (www.ikea.com) and Starbucks (www.starbucks.com). Are the look and feel of these Internet sites consistent with the in-store experience of these retailers?

3. **INTERNET EXERCISE** Go to the websites for Walmart (www.walmartstores.com), Carrefour (www.carrefour.fr), Royal Ahold (www.ahold.com), and Metro AG (www.metro.de). Which chain has the most global strategy? Justify your answer.

4. **GO SHOPPING** Visit two stores that sell similar merchandise categories and cater to the same target segment(s). How are their retail formats (the elements in their retail mixes) similar? Dissimilar? On what bases do they have a sustainable competitive advantage? Explain which you believe has a stronger position.

5. **WEB OLC EXERCISE** Go to the student side of the book's website, and click on "Market Position Matrix."
   Exercise 1: This spreadsheet describes an analysis of international growth opportunities. What numbers in the matrices would have to change to make China and France more attractive opportunities? To make Brazil and Mexico less attractive opportunities? Change the numbers in the matrices, and see what effect this has on the overall position of the opportunity in the grid.

Exercise 2: The market attractiveness/competitive position matrix can also be used by a department store to evaluate its merchandise categories and determine how much it should invest in each category. Fill in the importance weights (10 = very important, 1 = not very important) and the evaluations of the merchandise categories (10 = excellent, 1 = poor), and then see what is recommended by the plot on the opportunity matrix.

Exercise 3: Think of another investment decision that a retailer might make, and analyze it using the strategic analysis matrix. List the alternatives and the characteristics of the alternatives, and then put in the importance weights for the characteristics (10 = very important, 1 = not very important) and the evaluation of each alternative on each characteristic (10 = excellent, 1 = poor).

DISCUSSION QUESTIONS AND PROBLEMS

1. For each of the four retailers discussed at the beginning of the chapter (Chipotle Mexican Grill, Lululemon, Chico's, and Save-A-Lot), describe its strategy and the basis of its competitive advantage.

2. Choose a retailer, and describe how it has developed a competitive strategic advantage.

3. Give an example of a market penetration, a retail format development, a market expansion, and a diversification growth strategy that Best Buy might use.

4. Choose your favorite retailer. Draw and explain a positioning map, like that shown in Exhibit 5–3, that includes your retailer, retailers that sell the same types of merchandise, and the target customer segments (ideal points).

5. Do a SWOT analysis for McDonald's. What is its mission? What are its strengths and weaknesses? What opportunities and environmental threats might it face over the next 10 years? How could it prepare for these threats?

6. What are Neiman Marcus's and PetSmart's bases for sustainable competitive advantage? Are they really sustainable, or are they easily copied?

7. Assume you are interested in opening a restaurant in your town. Go through the steps in the strategic planning process shown in Exhibit 5–7. Focus on conducting a SWOT analysis of the local restaurant market, identifying and evaluating alternatives, and selecting a target market and a retail mix for the restaurant.

8. The Gap owns several chains, including Old Navy, Banana Republic, Piperlime, and Athleta. What type of growth opportunity was The Gap pursuing when it opened each of these retail concepts? Which is most synergistic with the original Gap chain?

9. Identify a store or service provider that you believe has an effective loyalty program. Explain why it is effective.

10. Choose a retailer that you believe could be, but is not yet, successful in other countries. Explain why you think it could be successful.

11. Amazon.com started as an Internet retailer selling books. Then it pursued a variety of growth opportunities, including expanding to groceries, DVDs, apparel, software, and travel services; introducing e-readers (Kindle); operating the Internet channel for other retailers; and hosting virtual stores for small, independent retailers. Evaluate these growth opportunities in terms of the probability that they will be profitable businesses for Amazon.com. What competitive advantages does Amazon.com bring to each of these businesses?

SUGGESTED READINGS

Aaker, David. *Strategic Market Management*, 6th ed. New York: Wiley, 2009.

Cao, Lanlan, and Marc Dupuis. "Strategy and Sustainable Competitive Advantage of International Retailers in China." *Journal of Asia-Pacific Business* 11, no. 1 (2010), pp. 6–27.

Cuthbertson, Christine, and Jonathan Reynolds. *Retail Strategy*. London: Routledge, 2012.

Etgar, M., and D. Rachman-Moore. "The Relationship between National Cultural Dimensions and Retail Format Strategies." *Journal of Retailing and Consumer Services* 18, no. 5 (2011), pp. 397–404.

Fox, Edward J., and Raj Sethuraman. "Retail Competition." In *Retailing in the 21st Century—Current and Future Trends*, 2nd ed., eds. Manfred Kraft and Murali Mantrala. Berlin: Springer, 2010, pp. 239–256.

Gamble, John E., Arthur A Thompson Jr., and Margaret Peteraf. *Essentials of Strategic Management: The Quest for Competitive Advantage*, 3rd ed. New York: McGraw-Hill, 2013.

Grewal, Dhruv, Ram Krishnan, Michael Levy, and Jeanne Mungar. "Retail Success and Key Drivers." In *Retailing in the 21st Century—Current and Future Trends*, 2nd ed., eds. Manfred Kraft and Murali Mantrala. Berlin: Springer, 2010, pp. 15–30.

Lehmann, Donald, and Russell Winer. *Analysis for Marketing Planning*, 8th ed. Burr Ridge, IL: McGraw-Hill/Irwin, 2010.

Ortinau, D. J., B. J. Babin and J. C. Chebat, "Retailing Evolution Research: Introduction to the Special Section on Retailing Research," *Journal of Business Research* 64, no. 6 (2011), pp. 541–542.

Rothaermel, Frank T. *Strategic Management: Concepts*. New York: McGraw-Hill, 2013.

Zentes, Joachim, Dirk Morschett, and Hanna Schramm-Klein. *Strategic Retail Management: Text And International Cases*, 2nd ed. Weisbaden: Springer, 2011.

Financial Strategy

EXECUTIVE BRIEFING

Ken Hicks, Chairman and CEO,
Foot Locker Inc.

After graduating from the U.S. Military Academy and serving six years as an artillery officer, I earned an MBA from Harvard Business School and went to work as a consultant for McKinsey. However, I realized that I wanted to develop and implement strategies, rather than just analyzing situations and making recommendations. Through my consulting experience, I recognized the exciting challenges and opportunities retailing had to offer and took a position in strategic planning for May Department Stores. Prior to becoming the chairman and CEO of Foot Locker, I had senior executive management positions at Home Shopping Network, Payless Shoes, and JCPenney.

My career path is a bit unusual for a retail executive. There aren't many jobs in the private sector for artillery officers. But, in the military, I learned how to motivate people and coordinate their activities to achieve an organization's goals, and I learned the importance of execution. These skills were particularly useful at Foot Locker when I became CEO in 1999. Foot Locker was not meeting the expectations of its customers, employees, and shareholders. Sales, comparable store sales, and earnings per share had declined significantly during the previous four years. To turn around this downward trend, the senior

management team and I developed a four-year plan that set goals and developed strategies for achieving those goals. The goals we set for 2013 were inventory turnover, 3.0; sales per square foot, $400; sales, $6 billion; net profit margin, 5 percent; and EBIT, 8 percent.

The key strategic change we made was clearly differentiating our five retail brands—Foot Locker, Footaction, Lady Foot Locker, Kids Foot Locker, and Champs Sports. The brands were operating as independent businesses, each trying to maximize their own profits and sales. Over time, the five brands lost their identities. They all offered similar assortments and stocked the most popular athletic shoes. Their stores had the same look and feel, and they competed vigorously against each other. We needed to turn the guns outward and develop a unique position for each brand, but still exploit the operational synergies among the five brands.

CHAPTER 6

LEARNING OBJECTIVES

LO1 Review the strategic objectives of a retail firm.

LO2 Contrast the two paths to financial performance using the strategic profit model.

LO3 Illustrate the use of the strategic profit model for analyzing growth opportunities.

LO4 Analyze the financial risks facing a retail firm.

LO5 Review the measures retailers use to assess their performance.

Our brands are like ice cream sundaes. They all have the same vanilla ice cream, but each specializes in different toppings for customers who like hot fudge or banana sundaes. For example, Champs focuses on customers engaged in team sports, Foot Locker on performance-oriented customers, and Footaction for fashionable shoes and apparel.

In 2011, we exceeded all of our goals two years into our four-year plan. So we adopted some more ambitious goals, which you can see at www.footlocker-inc.com/. In retailing, some performance measures are available daily or even hourly. But retailers need to balance their long-term goals with short-term measures. Foot Locker is now the leading global retailer of athletically inspired shoes and apparel. We operate more than 3,400 stores in 23 countries and have a successful Internet channel and social media program. We have more than 6 million Facebook fans and 65,000 Twitter followers.

Financial objectives and goals are an integral part of a retailer's market strategy. In Chapter 5, we examined how retailers develop their strategy and build a sustainable competitive advantage to generate a continuing stream of profits. In this chapter, we look at how financial analysis is used to assess the retailer's market strategy—to monitor the retailer's performance, assess the reasons its performance is above or below expectations, and provide insights into appropriate actions that can be taken if performance falls short of expectations.

For example, Kelly Bradford, the owner of Gifts To Go, whom we described in Chapter 5, needs to know how well she is doing because she wants to stay in business, be successful, increase the profitability of her company, and realize her goal of generating an annual income of $100,000. To assess her performance, she can add up the receipts at the end of each day. But this simple measure, sales, doesn't provide a complete assessment of how she is doing financially, and it may even be misleading. For instance, she might find that sales meet expectations and her accountant confirms that her business is profitable, but she doesn't have the cash to buy new merchandise or pay her employees. When this happens, Kelly needs to analyze her business to determine the cause of the problem and what can be done to overcome it.

In this chapter, we first review the types of objectives that retailers have. Then we introduce the strategic profit model and use it to discuss the two paths for achieving the desired financial performance. To illustrate the use of this model, we examine and compare the factors affecting the financial performance of Costco and Macy's, two very successful retailers with different retail strategies. Then we demonstrate how the model can be used to evaluate one of the growth opportunities Kelly Bradford is considering. In the last part of this chapter, we examine productivity measures that assess the performance of merchandise management and store operations decisions.

OBJECTIVES AND GOALS

LO1

Review the strategic objectives of a retail firm.

As we discussed in Chapter 5, the first step in the strategic planning process involves articulating the retailer's objectives and the scope of activities it plans to undertake. These objectives guide the development of the retailer's strategy and the specific performance goals the retailer plans to achieve. When the goals are not being achieved, the retailer knows that it must take corrective actions. Three types of objectives that a retailer might have are (1) financial, (2) societal, and (3) personal.

Financial Objectives

When assessing the financial performance of a firm, most people focus on profits: What were the retailer's profits or profit as a percentage of sales last year, and what will they be this year and into the future? But the appropriate financial performance measure is not profits but return on assets. **Return on assets (ROA)** is the profit generated by the assets possessed by the firm. A retailer might set a financial objective of making a profit of at least $1,000,000 a year, but the retailer really needs to consider the assets it needs to employ to make the desired $1,000,000. The retailer would be delighted if it made $1,000,000 and only needed $5,000,000 in assets (a 20 percent ROA) but would be disappointed if it had to use $40,000,000 in assets to make $1,000,000 profit (a 2.5 percent ROA).

Societal Objectives

Societal objectives are related to broader issues that make the world a better place to live. For example, retailers might be concerned about providing employment opportunities for people in a particular area or for minorities or for people with disabilities. Other societal objectives might include offering people unique merchandise, such as environmentally friendly products; providing an innovative service to improve personal health, such as weight reduction programs; or sponsoring community events. Retailing View 6.1 describes a retail entrepreneur offering shoes for poor families.

Compared with financial objectives, societal performance objectives are more difficult to measure. But explicit societal goals can be set, such as specific reductions in energy usage and excess packaging, increased use of renewable resources, and support for nonprofit organizations such as the United Way and Habitat for Humanity.

REFACT

In 1946, George Nelson Dayton, the son of Target Corporation's founder, established a standard of contributing 5 percent of the corporation's income to programs that serve the communities in which it has stores.[1]

Personal Objectives

Many retailers, particularly owners of small, independent businesses, have important personal objectives, including self-gratification, status, and respect. For example, the owner/operator of a bookstore may find it rewarding to interact with others who like reading and authors who visit the store for book-signing promotions. By operating a popular store, a retailer might become recognized as a well-respected business leader in the community.

While societal and personal objectives are important to some retailers, all retailers need to be concerned about financial objectives or they will fail. Therefore,

---

RETAILING VIEW   One for One to Achieve TOMS Shoes'
Societal Objectives   6.1

In 2006, after competing on the second season of *The Amazing Race*, Blake Mycoskie visited Argentina, where he was struck by the poverty—including the number of children walking around without shoes. Because the traditional Argentine alpargata shoe offers a simple, revolutionary solution for providing footwear, he set out to provide footwear for poor families by reinventing the alpargata for the U.S. market. To make the connection, Mycoskie committed to providing one new pair of shoes to a child living in poverty for every pair of shoes that consumers purchased from the One for One website. As he recounted, "I was so overwhelmed by the spirit of the South American people, especially those who had so little. And I was instantly struck with the desire—the responsibility—to do more."

The success of the initial idea pushed Mycoskie to move beyond just the Argentinean-styled classic alpargata shoes. Thus, TOMS today sells Cordones, for wear with or without laces; Botas, for both women and men; Stitchouts, which are only for men; Wedges and Wrap Boots for women; and of course, Youth and Tiny TOMS for children and toddlers. The social activist also decided that the company could increase the number of shoes provided to needy children by selling T-shirts, accessories, and hats—all of which spark the same one-to-one exchange.

This socially responsible business model appeals particularly to Millennial consumers in developed economies who want to be able to shop, socialize, and save the world, simultaneously. Wearing TOMS shoes is a

Achieving societal objectives is important to Blake Mycoskie, founder, CEO, and chief giving officer of TOMS shoes.

fashion statement that also provides a public proclamation of their own social responsibility. Through their social media networks, these TOMS afficionados, many of whom belong to the thousands of TOMS university clubs, affirm their love for TOMS and encourage others to join the movement. With annual sales estimated at greater than $100 million, by 2012, TOMS had provided more than 1 million pairs of new shoes to children in more than 25 countries—including the United States.

Sources: www.toms.com; Ricardo Lopez, "It's Doing Well by Doing Good," *Los Angeles Times,* January 25, 2012, p. B.1; and Gregory Ferenstein, "TOMS Shoes Generation Y Strategy," *Fast Company,* June 9, 2010.

DISCUSSION QUESTIONS

Does TOMS's socially responsible business model make you more likely to buy its shoes?

REFACT

Eighty percent of Millennials would be likely to switch to a brand associated with a good cause if product price and quality were comparable; 53 percent had purchased a product or service tied to a cause in the last year.[2]

the remaining sections of this chapter focus on financial objectives and the factors affecting a retailer's ability to achieve financial goals.

STRATEGIC PROFIT MODEL

LO2

Contrast the two paths to financial performance using the strategic profit model.

The **strategic profit model,** illustrated in Exhibit 6–1, is a method for summarizing the factors that affect a firm's financial performance, as measured by return on assets. Return on assets is an important performance measure for a firm and its stockholders because it measures the profits that a firm makes relative to the assets it possesses. Two retailers that each generate profits of $1 million, at first glance, might look like they have comparable performance. But the performance of the retailers looks quite different if one has $10 million in assets and the other has $25 million. The performance of the first would be higher because it needs fewer assets to earn its profit than does the other. Thus, a retailer cannot only concern itself with making a profit. It must make a profit efficiently by balancing both profit and the assets needed to make the profit.

The **operating profit margin,** also called **earnings before interest, taxes, and depreciation (EBITDA),** is a measure of the profitability from continuing operations of a retailer and is a useful predictor of the retailer's profitability in the future. **Asset turnover** is the retailer's net sales divided by its assets. This financial measure assesses the productivity of a firm's investment in its assets. It indicates how many sales dollars are generated for each dollar of assets. Thus, if a retailer's asset turnover is 3.0, it generates $3 in sales for each dollar invested in the firm's assets.

The retailer's ROA is determined by multiplying the two components together:

$$\text{Operating profit margin percent} \times \text{Asset turnover} = \text{Return on assets (ROA)}$$

$$\frac{\text{Operating profit margin percent}}{\text{Net sales}} \times \frac{\text{Net sales}}{\text{Total assets}} = \frac{\text{Operating profit margin}}{\text{Total assets}}$$

The strategic profit model decomposes ROA into two components: (1) operating profit margin percentage and (2) asset turnover. These two components illustrate that ROA is determined by two sets of activities—profit margin management and asset turnover management—and that a high ROA can be achieved by various combinations of operating profit margins and asset turnover levels.

EXHIBIT 6–1
Strategic Profit Model

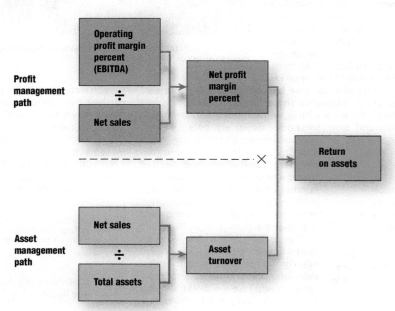

	Net Profit Margin	×	Asset Turnover	=	Return on Assets
La Chatelaine Bakery	1%		10 times		10%
Lehring Jewelry	10%		1 time		10%

EXHIBIT 6–2
Different Approaches for Achieving an Acceptable ROA

To illustrate the different approaches for achieving a high ROA, consider the financial performance of two very different hypothetical retailers, as shown in Exhibit 6–2. La Chatelaine Bakery has a net operating profit margin percentage of only 1 percent and an asset turnover of 10, resulting in an ROA of 10 percent. Its operating profit margin percentage is low because it is in a highly competitive market with little opportunity to differentiate its offering. Consumers can buy basically the same baked goods from a wide variety of retailers, as well as from the other bakeries in the area. However, its asset turnover is relatively high because the firm has a very low level of inventory assets—it sells everything the same day it is baked.

On the other hand, Lehring Jewelry Store has a net operating profit margin percentage of 10 percent—10 times higher than that of the bakery. Even though it has a much higher operating profit margin percentage, the jewelry store has the same ROA because it has a very low asset turnover of 1. Lehring's asset turnover is low compared with the bakery's because Lehring has a high level of inventory and stocks a lot of items that take many months to sell.

In the following sections, we take a closer look at these two components of ROA. We examine the relationship between these ratios and a firm's retail strategy and describe how these financial measures can be used to assess performance with traditional accounting information. To illustrate the financial implications of different retail strategies, we compare the financial performance of Costco and Macy's. The retail strategies of these two retailers are described in Retailing View 6.2.

RETAILING VIEW Macy's and Costco—Successful Retailers Using Different Retail Strategies   6.2

Costco (left) and Macy's (right) have very different retail strategies and financial performance measures. Costco focuses on the asset management path for achieving a high ROA, while Macy's focuses on the profit management path.

Costco

Costco pioneered the membership warehouse club format when it opened its first store in 1983. It is now the largest warehouse club chain, generating annual sales of $89 billion from its 433 locations in 40 states and Puerto Rico, as well as 162 stores in Canada, the United Kingdom, Korea, Taiwan, Japan, Australia, and Mexico. The member-oriented stores promises low prices on a limited range of around 4,000 branded and private-label products, across

(continued)

160   SECTION II   Retailing Strategy

a vast span of merchandise categories. In addition to commodity items, such as dairy products and toilet paper, the stores stock special, unique items that are always a surprise. The "treasure hunt" environment created by opportunistic buying gives the customer a sense of urgency to buy the item immediately. Some of these products with limited availability could be a four-carat diamond ring, a Louis Vuitton handbag, or a Versace china set. Costco is committed to delivering the customer a good value—low prices and high quality.

Costco's unusually high inventory turnover—combined with operating efficiencies achieved by volume purchasing, efficient distribution, and reduced handling of merchandise in no-frills, self-service warehouse facilities—enables it to operate profitably at significantly lower gross margins than traditional wholesalers, mass merchandisers, supermarkets, and supercenters. The small number of SKUs allows Costco's buyers to have a strong grasp on the movement and quality of the goods. In turn, its customers understand and appreciate its assortment better than they would if they were shopping at a supermarket or discount store that would carry many more SKUs.

Its private-labeled merchandise accounts for 20 percent of its sales. Costco is concentrating on growing its private-label, Kirkland Signature, products. It has a diverse selection of Kirkland-branded products ranging from wines and champagnes to bakery items. Its buyers make quality relationships with its vendors and can thus capitalize on a trend to develop products for the store. Many of its items are co-branded with manufacturers such as Hormel bacon, Stonyfield Farm's organic smoothies, Dannon's Activia, and Borghese upscale cosmetics. The co-branded products signal to customers that they are receiving a quality product from a trusted name at a value price.

Costco's target market is not limited to low-income customers who have to shop for the lowest prices. It has a loyal, upscale clientele who also enjoy bargains. The retailer marks products up no more than 14 percent, giving its customers true value, whether the product is a quart of ketchup or an LCD television.

Costco also is committed to carrying healthy products and being environmentally friendly. It ensures that the raw materials that are used in the products that it sells (e.g., cocoa, coffee, seafood, etc.) are all grown and produced in a fair and healthy way. It is also trying to cut down on the packaging used. The company evaluates its suppliers closely so it knows how everything is being processed. For example, Costco inspects a seafood supplier by meeting the boats when they come in to see how the products were being iced, how they are unloaded, and how they maintain the temperature from the dock to the plant. It is protocols such as this allow the company to maintain consistent quality.

Macy's

Macy's, established in 1858, is the Great American Department Store—an iconic retailing brand with more than 800 stores operating coast-to-coast and online at macys.com. It is the largest department store retailer in the United

States with annual sales of more than $26 billion. Its typical store anchors an enclosed mall and includes 180,000 square feet of selling space stocking 50,000 SKUs.

Macy's primary target market is females between 25 and 54 years old who typically work outside the house, have children, and have an average family income of more than $75,000. Macy's has been particularly effective in developing private brands such as I.N.C., Charter Club, Club Room, Ideology, Jenna, Tasso Elba, Style & Co., JM Collection, Epic Threads, and First Impressions. Its store brands presently account for 20 percent of annual sales with exclusive, limited distribution brands accounting for an additional 23 percent of annual sales.

Three key strategic initiatives for Macy's are (1) My Macy's localization, (2) multichannel integration, and (3) MAGIC Selling. First, the localization initiative involves tailoring the merchandise assortment and shopping experience to the needs of the local market. Second, through multichannel integration, Macy's seeks to combine its store, Internet, and mobile operations, mainly to optimize its inventory offerings. An out-of-stock situation in a local store prompts sales associates to seek replacement merchandise from the online fulfillment centers and have the items shipped to the customer's home address; online fulfillment centers also can turn to store inventories to fill orders that originate online or through mobile devices. Third, "MAGIC Selling" refers to an acronym used in sales training that seeks to improve customers' shopping experiences: "Meet and make a connection; Ask questions and listen; Give options, give advice; Inspire to buy . . . and sell more; and Celebrate the purchase."

Together with these strategic initiatives, Macy's is experimenting with various new in-store and online technologies. For example, tablet computers located in departments throughout the store provide customers with additional information, give them the option of obtaining paperless receipts, engage them with QR code technology, link to a smartphone app with which customers can use their phones to "tap, pay, and save," and deliver special offers to them through social media (e.g., Foursquare, Shopkick, Google, Facebook).

Sources: 2012 Macy's Factbook; 2011 Costco Annual Report; Karen Talley, "Three Stores, Three Scenes; Fortunes Diverge for Macy's, Penney and Kohl's," *The Wall Street Journal (Online)*, August 12, 2012; and Annie Gasparro and Timothy Martin, "What's Wrong With America's Supermarkets? Traditional Grocery Stores Are Caught in the Middle," *The Wall Street Journal (Online)*, July 12, 2012.

DISCUSSION QUESTION

What are the differences in the retailing mixes used by Costco and Macy's?

Profit Margin Management Path

The information used to examine the profit margin management path comes from the retailer's **income statement,** also called the **statement of operations.** The income statement summarizes a firm's financial performance over a period of time, typically a quarter (three months) or year. To capture all the sales, gift card purchases, and returns from the holiday season, Macy's, like many retailers, sets its fiscal year as beginning on February 1 and ending on January 31 of the following year. So its 2012 Annual Report actually focuses on 11 months in 2011 and 1 month in 2012. Costco's fiscal year begins on October 1, so most recent annual report includes 9 months in 2012 and 3 months in 2011.

Exhibit 6–3 shows income statements adapted from the annual reports of Macy's and Costco. The components in the profit margin management path portion of the strategic profit model are summarized for both retailers in Exhibit 6–4.

Components in the Profit Management Path   The four components in the profit margin management path are net sales, cost of goods sold (COGS), gross margin, and operating profit margin. **Net sales** are the total revenues received by a retailer that are related to selling merchandise during a given time period minus returns, discounts, and credits for damaged merchandise.

Sources of revenue that are not considered part of net sales are special charges to customers, membership fees, and credit card interest. For example, warehouse clubs generate revenue from annual membership fees, and retailers with frequent shopper programs may charge customers for enrolling in the program. Costco does not consider membership fees as part of its net sales because they reflect business activities unrelated to its primary activity of selling merchandise. Macy's has its own credit card on which it receives revenues from late payments, which are therefore also not part of net sales.

Some retailers have additional revenue sources related to merchandise sales, such as payments from vendors. For example, retailers often charge vendors for space in their stores known as a **slotting fee** or **slotting allowance.** Retailers may also require that vendors pay a fee, known as a **chargeback fee** when the merchandise bought from the vendor does not meet all the terms of the

	Costco Income Statement 2012	Macy's Income Statement 2012
Net sales	97,062	26,405
Membership fees	2,075	
Total revenue	99,137	26,405
Cost of goods sold (COGS)	(86,823)	(15,738)
Gross margin	12,314	10,667
Selling, general, and administrative (SG&A)	9,518	8,281
Operating profit	2,796	2,386
Other income (expenses)	(95)	25
Interest income	103	(447)
Provision for income tax		(712)
Net profit	2,720	1,252
g = + Gross margin percent	10.5%	40.4%
SG&A percent of sales	9.8%	31.4%
Operating profit percent	2.9%	9.0%
Net profit percent	2.8%	4.7%

EXHIBIT 6–3
Income Statements for Macy's and Costco

Sources: 10-K filings with the SEC.

purchase agreement, such as those regarding delivery. Such payments from vendors are typically incorporated into the income statement as a reduction in the COGS.

Cost of goods sold (COGS) is the amount a retailer pays to vendors for the merchandise the retailer sells. **Gross margin,** also called **gross profit,** is the net sales minus the cost of the goods sold. It is an important measure in retailing because it indicates how much profit the retailer is making on merchandise sold, without considering the expenses associated with operating the store and corporate overhead expenses.

Gross margin = Net sales − Cost of goods sold

Operating expenses include **selling, general, and administrative (SG&A) expenses.** SG&A expenses are overhead costs associated with normal business operations, such as salaries for sales associates and managers, advertising, utilities, office supplies, transportation from the retailer's warehouses to its stores, and rent.

Some retailers include other expenses, such as the cost of opening or closing stores and/or the cost of integrating an acquisition in their operations, as a part of their operating expenses. When estimating a retailer's operating expenses, one needs to decide whether these other expenses are related to the normal operations of the retailer or are extraordinary nonrecurring expenses that arise only during the year in which they are incurred. For example, the expenses for store openings might occur each year as a growing retailer opens new stores, while expenses related to an acquisition probably occur only in the specific year of the acquisition and may not reflect the operating income the retailer will realize in the future.

Operating profit margin, also called *earnings before interest, taxes, and depreciation (EBITDA)*, is the gross margin minus operating and extraordinary recurring expenses. Finally, **net profit margin** is the operating profit margin minus interest, taxes, and depreciation. We focus on the operating profit margin (EBITDA) because it reflects the performance of retailers' fundamental operations, not the financial decisions retailers make concerning depreciation of assets, taxes and capital structure (borrowing money versus selling stock to raise capital).

Operating profit margin = Gross margin − Operating expenses − Extraordinary (recurring) operating expenses

Net profit margin = Operating profit margin − Extraordinary nonrecurring expenses − Interest − Taxes − Depreciation

Analyzing Performance on the Profit Margin Management Path The level of sales, gross margin, and operating profit in Exhibit 6–4 provide some useful information about the financial performance of the two retailers. However, it is difficult to compare the performance of the retailers when they differ in size. If Costco was interested in comparing its performance with Walmart, it would expect that Walmart would have a much greater gross margin and operating profit margin because it has five times greater sales than Costco. Thus, some of the differences in the income statement numbers will be due to differences in size, not in the performance of the retailers. Thus, it is useful to consider ratios with net sales in the denominator when evaluating a retailer's performance and comparing it to other retailers. Three useful ratios in the profit management path are gross margin percentage, operating profit margin percentage, and SG&A as a percentage of sales.

Gross margin percentage is gross margin divided by net sales. Retailers use this ratio to compare (1) the performance of various types of merchandise and

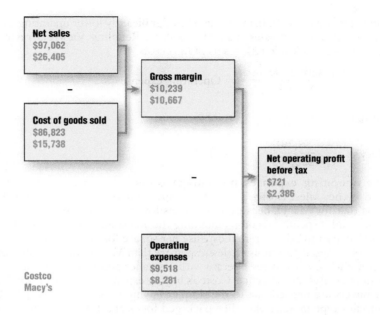

EXHIBIT 6–4
Profit Management
Path of Strategic Profit
Model

(2) their own performance with that of other retailers with higher or lower levels of sales.

$$\frac{\text{Gross margin}}{\text{Net sales}} = \text{Gross margin percent}$$

Costco: $\dfrac{\$12,314}{\$97,062} = 12.7\%$

Macy's: $\dfrac{\$10,667}{\$26,405} = 40.4\%$

Even though Costco has more than double the sales of Macy's, Macy's has a much higher gross margin percentage. This difference in gross margin percentage can be traced back to the retail strategies of the companies. Department stores generally have higher gross margin percentages than warehouse clubs because they target less-price-sensitive customers who are interested in branded fashion merchandise and personal service and are willing to pay for it. Warehouse club stores sell primarily staples, which are not as easy to differentiate as fashion apparel. That is, customers are more willing to pay a premium price for a high-fashion dress by a famous designer than for a 16-pack of kitchen towels or a quart of peanut butter. It is important for department stores to achieve a relatively high gross margin because their operating expenses are typically higher than those of some other retail formats.

Operating expenses are costs, other than the cost of merchandise, incurred in the normal course of doing business, such as salaries for sales associates and managers, advertising, utilities, office supplies, and rent. These costs are typically referred to as selling, general and administrative expenses (SG&A).

Neither Costco nor Macy's indicate other expenses or income besides the normal SG&A expenses, and all their overhead expenses are included in SG&A. However, retailers will often have other expenses. Macy's income statement shows expenses related to the acquisition of the May Company—income and expenses from inventory reevaluation, integration expenses and income from selling its **accounts receivable** (the money it is owed by customers who buy on credit), and expenses for opening new stores.

Like the gross margin, operating expenses are expressed as a percentage of net sales to facilitate comparisons across items, stores, and merchandise categories within firms and between firms. Costco has significantly lower operating expenses as a percentage of net sales than Macy's does. Retailing View 6.3 reviews the creative ways that Costco reduces its SG&A costs.

$$\frac{\text{Operating expenses}}{\text{Net sales}} = \text{Operating expenses \%}$$

$$\text{Costco:} \quad \frac{\$9,518}{\$97,062} = 9.8\%$$

$$\text{Macy's :} \quad \frac{\$8,281}{\$26,405} = 31.4\%$$

The **operating expenses percentage** is operating expenses (i.e., SG&A) divided by net sales. Costco's operating expense percentage is about a third as large as that for Macy's because Costco has lower customer service and selling expenses, and it spends less on maintaining the appearance of its stores. For store spaces that are rented, the rental expense per square foot is lower for Costco because its standalone locations are less expensive than Macy's anchor mall locations. Also, warehouse club stores operate with a smaller administrative staff than do department stores. For instance, Costco's buying expenses are much lower because fewer buyers are needed due to the simpler buying process and fewer SKUs for commodity-type merchandise, like packaged foods and fresh meat and produce,

6.3   RETAILING VIEW   Cutting Costs at Costco

Costco's retail strategy focuses on offering its customer a good value—quality products at a reasonable price—on a wide merchandise assortment ranging from wheels of Parmesan cheese to 60-inch flat-screen TVs. Keeping prices low is challenging in light of increasing commodity prices, so Costco works with its vendors to control costs.

For example, Costco typically buys 70 percent of the large, premium macadamia nuts produced by Mauna Loa, a division of Hershey, leaving Mauna Loa with an inventory of small nuts. Costco buyers have worked with Mauna Loa to use smaller nuts in a new chocolate-nut cluster that will be sold exclusively at Costco. Because Mauna Loa won't have to face the uncertainty of selling those smaller nuts at a steep discount, it can afford to offer Costco better prices for its premium nuts.

Simple packaging changes can result in cost savings. For example, packaging cashews into square containers instead of traditional round ones enables Costco to increase the number of units it can stack on a pallet from 280 to 426. This relatively minor change to a product selling $100 million a year decreases the number of pallets shipped annually by 24,000 and decreases the number of truck trips by 600.

However, Costco does not scrimp on its employees. Eighty-six percent of its employees get health care and other benefits, even though half of its employees are part-timers. The average compensation of store employees is $20 an hour, more than 50 percent higher than the industry average. No Costco employees were laid off as a result of the recent recession. Costco believes that treating its employees well actually reduces labor costs in the long run. Its employee turnover is only 13 percent, among the lowest in the retail industry.

Changing this jar of nuts from a round shape to a square shape made a significant reduction in Costco's SG&A.

Sources: Zeynep Ton, "Why 'Good Jobs' Are Good for Retailers," *Harvard Business Review,* January–February 2012; Christopher Matthews, "Future of Retail: Companies That Profit by Investing in Employees," *Time,* June 18, 2012; and "Costco's Artful Discounts," *Business Week,* October 20, 2008.

DISCUSSION QUESTION

What are advantages and disadvantages of paying employees more than they can earn at comparable firms?

compared with fashion apparel. Finally, its buyers don't have to travel to fashion markets around the world like department store buyers do.

Like the gross margin and operating expenses, operating profit is often expressed as a percentage of net sales to facilitate comparisons across items, merchandise categories, and departments within and between firms. **Operating income percentage** is gross margin minus operating expenses divided by net sales.

$$\frac{\text{Gross margin} - \text{Operating expenses}}{\text{Net sales}} = \text{Operating income \%}$$

Costco: $\dfrac{\$12,314 - \$9,518}{\$97,062} = 2.9\%$

Macy's: $\dfrac{\$10,667 - \$8,281}{\$26,405} = 9.0\%$

Macy's operating profit margin percentage is more than three times greater than Costco's. Thus, this component of the strategic profit model suggests that Macy's is outperforming Costco. But the following discussion of the asset management path tells a different story.

Asset Management Path

The information used to analyze a retailer's asset management path primarily comes from the retailer's balance sheet. While the income statement summarizes financial performance over a period of time (usually a year or quarter), the balance sheet summarizes a retailer's financial position at a given point in time, typically the end of its fiscal year. Costco's and Macy's balance sheets are shown in Exhibit 6–5, and the asset management path components in the strategic profit model are shown in Exhibit 6–6.

Components in the Asset Management Path   **Assets** are economic resources (e.g., inventory, buildings, computers, store fixtures) owned or controlled by a firm. There are two types of assets, current and fixed.

Current assets are assets that can normally be converted to cash within one year. For retailers, current assets are primarily cash, accounts receivable, and merchandise inventory.

Current assets = Cash + Accounts receivable + Merchandise inventory + Other current assets

	Costco	Macy's
Cash and cash equivalents	4,009	2,827
Short-term investments	1,604	
Accounts receivable	965	368
Merchandise inventory	6,638	5,117
Other current assets	490	465
Total current assets	13,706	8,777
Property and equipment (net)	12,432	8,400
Other assets	623	4,918
Total assets	26,761	22,095
Current liabilities	12,050	6,263
Long-term debt	1,253	6,655
Other liabilities	885	2,344
Total liabilities	14,188	15,262
Stockholder equity	12,573	6,833

EXHIBIT 6–5
Balance Sheet for Macy's and Costco

Sources: 10-K reports filed with the SEC.

EXHIBIT 6–6
Asset Management
Path in Strategic
Profit Model

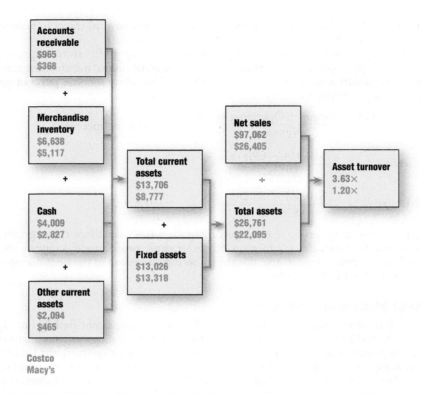

Costco
Macy's

Merchandise inventory is a critical retailer asset that provides benefits to customers. It enables customers to get the right merchandise at the right time and place. Stocking more merchandise increases sales because it increases the chances that customers will find something they want. But increasing the level of inventory also increases the amount that retailers need to invest in this asset.

Inventory turnover, which measures how effectively retailers utilize their investment in inventory, is another important ratio for assessing retail performance. **Inventory turnover** is COGS during a time period, typically a year, divided by the average level of inventory (expressed at cost) during the time period. A surrogate measure for average inventory is the inventory value at the end of the fiscal year reported on the balance sheet. Note that the inventory level reported on the balance sheet is the level on the last day of the fiscal year, not the average level. To measure the average inventory level more accurately, you would have to measure the level on each day of the year and divide by 365 or each month (see Chapter 12).

$$\frac{\text{COGS}}{\text{Average inventory at cost}} = \text{Inventory turnover}$$

Costco: $\dfrac{\$86,823}{6,638} = 13.08$

Macy's: $\dfrac{\$15,738}{5,117} = 3.08$

Inventory turnover is a measure of the productivity of inventory. It shows how many times, on average, inventory cycles through the store during a specific period of time (usually a year). Costco's higher inventory turnover is expected due to the nature of its retail strategy and the merchandise it sells. That is, most items in Costco are commodities and staples such as food, batteries, housewares, and basic apparel items. Unlike apparel fashions that are the mainstay for department stores like Macy's, these staples can be replenished quickly. Costco stores typically have only 4,000 SKUs in total; for example, it may only offer one brand of ketchup in two different sizes, which represents two inventory items. Department stores, on the other hand, usually stock more than 100,000 SKUs. This store format may stock 500 SKUs of just men's dress shirts (different colors, sizes, styles, and brands). Larger assortments, like those in department stores, require relatively higher inventory investments, which slows inventory turnover.

Fixed assets are assets that require more than a year to convert to cash. In retailing, the principal fixed assets are buildings (if store property is owned by the retailer rather than leased), distribution centers, fixtures (e.g., display racks), and equipment (e.g., computers, delivery trucks).

Asset turnover is net sales divided by total assets. It is a measure assessing the performance of the asset management component in the strategic profit model.

$$\frac{\text{Net sales}}{\text{Total assets}} = \text{Asset turnover}$$

Costco: $\dfrac{97,062}{26,761} = 3.63$

Macy's: $\dfrac{26,405}{22,095} = 1.20$

Intangible Assets   Notice that the balance sheet does not include most of the critical assets used by retailers to develop a sustainable competitive advantage (discussed in Chapter 5) such as brand image, customer loyalty, customer service, information and supply chain systems, human resources (committed, knowledgeable employees), and a database of customer buying behaviors and preferences. Due to accounting rules, the balance sheet includes only tangible assets for which there is an objective measure of value. For example, the value of a building is based on the amount the firm paid for the asset, less depreciation, not what it is worth at the end of the fiscal year.

The assets discussed in Chapter 5 are largely intangible. They cannot be objectively measured and thus are not included in the balance sheet assets. However, these intangible assets are important in generating long-term financial performance. As discussed in Retailing View 6.4, private equity firms are making significant investments in retail firms because of these intangible assets and other characteristics of the retail industry.

Analyzing the Performance of the Asset Management Path   Costco's asset turnover is more than two times greater than that of Macy's. The difference in their asset turnovers is largely due to Costco's higher inventory turnover. Typically, retailers like Costco that sell a limited assortment of commodity-type products have a higher inventory turnover than fashion apparel sold by retailers like Macy's. The sales of commodity-type products are easier to forecast accurately and thus makes it easier to control inventory levels.

Combining the Profit and Asset Management Paths

In terms of the profit management path, Macy's has a higher operating profit margin and thus performs better than Costco. But Costco has a higher asset turnover than Macy's and thus performs better on the asset management path. Although this type of performance is expected, given their overall strategy and retail formats, both retailers strive to increase their performance on these key ratios. For example, department stores like Macy's develop supply chains and buying systems that allow less merchandise to be delivered more often—more closely matching supply and demand. This lowers average inventory and, in turn, total assets, while at the same time may actually increase sales, resulting in higher inventory and asset turnovers. Warehouse club stores like Costco attempt to increase their gross margins by carrying more fresh produce, meat, and prepared foods. To further increase its margins, Costco in particular creates a treasure hunt environment by offering branded apparel and jewelry.

6.4 RETAILING VIEW Private Equity Firms Invest in Retailers

Private equity firms make investments in retail chains such as Krispy Kreme and Neiman Marcus because retail firms typically have a high cash flow and intangible assets.

Private equity firms such as Bain Capital, the Blackstone Group, and Texas Pacific have made substantial investments in retail firms. For example, KKR teamed with several other private equity firms to buy Toys "R" Us for $6.6 billion. Some other major retailers owned by private equity firms are Neiman Marcus, Burger King, Container Store, Dollar General, Domino's, Gymboree, Hilton Hotels, Krispy Kreme, Michaels, and Sports Authority.

Rather than buying stock in companies, private equity firms buy the entire company from its stockholders, improve the efficiency of the firm (often by hiring new senior managers), and/or simply restructure the firm's financial structure, and then sell shares in the acquired company several years later. Because shares for the acquired company after the acquisition are not traded on the stock exchange, the company can take a long-term perspective toward improving the firm's operations; that is, it does not have to justify its investments to stockholders or issue the quarterly reports required by the Securities and Exchange Commission (SEC).

Private equity firms find retailers attractive investments because many of them have strong cash flows, little debt, and undervalued assets and respond quickly to efficiency improvements and changes in strategic direction. Undervalued assets include well-known store brands, leases for space in attractive locations, or the land on which their stores are located. A private equity company can sell these assets after it acquires a retailer or use the assets as collateral to get loans to finance the acquisition. For example, a private equity firm might sell the rights to use a well-known store brand like Sears' Kenmore appliances, Craftsman tools, and DieHard batteries to another company that would license the brand to other firms.

Often, private equity owners split the retail chain into an operating company that operates the stores and a property company that owns all of the chain's real estate assets. Proceeds from the sale of the real estate assets are used to repay the private equity owners for their initial investment, guaranteeing that the private equity partners will prosper regardless of whether the retail chain is successful. For example, Cerberus Capital Management LP and a group of private equity investors bought the Mervyn's chain of discount department stores from Target Corp. for $1.25 billion. The investor group structured the buyout as two separate purchases—one for the retail operations and one for the chain's valuable real-estate holdings. It earned more than $250 million in fees for managing the real estate transactions. But the retail operation was liquidated because of poor performance, eventually closing 177 stores, cutting the jobs of 18,000 employees.

Sources: Karen Talley, "Sears to License Names of Kenmore, Craftsman Brands," *The Wall Street Journal,* April 5, 2012; Dan McCrum and Stanley Pignal, "New KKR Funds to Target Retail Investors," *FT.com,* July 19, 2012; Eileen Appelbaum and Rosemary Batt, *A Primer on Private Equity at Work: Management, Employment, and Sustainability* (Washington, DC: Center for Economic and Policy Research, February 2012); Elaine Misonzhnik, "Private Equity Firms Are Hungry for Retailers, But Only the Best of Them," *Retailtraffic.com,* September 27, 2012; and Peg Brickley, "Mervyns Creditors Are Offered a Deal," *The Wall Street Journal,* October 26, 2012.

DISCUSSION QUESTION

What are the benefits to a retailer of being owned by a private equity firm?

Strategic Profit Model Ratio for Selected Retailers   EXHIBIT 6–7

	Sales	Operating Profit	Total Assets	Operating Profit Percentage	Asset Turnover	ROA (Operating Profit)
Department Stores						
JCPenney	17,260	1,109	11,424	6.4%	1.51	9.7%
Kohl's	18,804	2,936	14,094	15.6%	1.33	20.8%
Macy's	26,405	2,386	22,095	9.0%	1.20	10.8%
Discount Stores						
Costco	87,048	2,494	27,261	2.9%	3.19	9.1%
Walmart	443,854	26,558	193,406	6.0%	2.29	13.7%
Target	65,786	6,592	43,705	10.0%	1.51	15.1%
Specialty—Appparel						
The Gap	14,549	1,438	7,422	9.9%	1.96	19.4%
Abercrombie & Fitch	4,158	194	1,489	4.7%	2.79	13.0%
American Eagle Outfitter	3,160	393	3,048	12.4%	1.04	12.9%
Specialty—Category						
Home Depot	70,395	8,234	40,518	11.7%	1.74	20.3%
Lowe's	50,208	4,757	33,559	9.5%	1.50	14.2%
Best Buy	50,705	2,331	16,005	4.6%	3.17	14.6%
Office Depot	11,489	34	4,250	0.3%	2.70	0.8%
Staples	25,022	1,693	13,430	6.8%	1.86	12.6%
Supermarket						
Kroger	90,347	410	23,478	0.5%	3.85	1.7%
Safeway	43,630	1,134	15,074	2.6%	2.89	7.5%

Sources: SEC 10-K filings.

The two retailers' overall performance, as measured by ROA, is determined by considering the effects of both paths, that is, by multiplying the net profit margin by asset turnover:

	Asset turnover	$\times$	Profit operating margin percent	$=$	Return on assets
Costco:	3.63	$\times$	2.9%	$=$	10.5%
Macy's:	1.20	$\times$	9.0%	$=$	10.8%

Exhibit 6–7 shows the strategic profit model ratios for a variety of retailers. The exhibit illustrates that supermarket and discount chains typically have higher asset turnovers and lower operating profit margin percentages. The apparel specialty retailers have lower asset turnovers and higher net profit margin percentages.

These differences in asset turnover and operating profit margin arise because the needs and buying behavior of customers patronizing these retailers differ, and thus, retailers targeting these customers use different approaches. Discount stores and supermarkets target more price-sensitive consumers, and they need to keep prices low. In addition, the products offered by supermarkets and discount stores are more commodity-like and face intense price competition. Thus, their profit margins are lower and they have to have higher asset turnover to provide an adequate ROA. On the other hand, specialty apparel and department stores are patronized by less-price-sensitive consumers who are looking for more customer service and deeper assortments. To satisfy these needs, inventory levels and turnover, administrative expenses, and margins are higher.

Implications for Improving Financial Performance

The profit management and asset management paths in the strategic profit model suggest different approaches for improving financial performance. Focusing on the profit management path, the operating profit margin could be increased by increasing sales or reducing COGS or operating expenses. For example, Costco could increase its sales by increasing advertising to attract more customers. The increase in sales will have a positive effect on Costco's operating profit margin percentage and its ROA as long as the increase in advertising expense generates more gross margin dollars than the advertising costs. In addition, the increase in sales will increase Costco's asset turnover because sales will increase but assets will remain the same. The net effect will have a positive impact on ROA.

Looking at the asset management path, Macy's could increase its asset turnover by decreasing the amount of inventory in its stores. However, decreasing the level of inventory could actually decrease sales because customers might not find the product they want to buy, causing them to shop elsewhere. If they tell their friends, post negative online reviews, or use social media like Twitter to voice their discontent, the lack of salable inventory could have a cascading deleterious impact on sales and profits.

The strategic profit model illustrates two important issues. First, retailers and investors should consider both operating and net profit margin and asset turnover when evaluating their financial performance. Firms can achieve high performance (high ROA) by effectively managing both profit margin and asset turnover. Second, retailers need to consider the implications of their strategic decisions on both components of the strategic profit model. For example, increasing prices might increase the gross margin and operating profit margin in the profit margin management path. However, increasing prices could also result in fewer sales, thereby having a negative impact on both gross margin and net operating profit margin. At the same time, assuming the level of assets stays the same, asset turnover will decrease. Thus, a simple change in one strategic variable, such as pricing, has multiple repercussions on the strategic profit model, all of which need to be considered when determining the impact on ROA.

EVALUATING GROWTH OPPORTUNITIES

LO3

Illustrate the use of the strategic profit model for analyzing growth opportunities.

To illustrate the use of the strategic profit model for evaluating a growth opportunity, let's look at the opportunity that Kelly Bradford, from Chapter 5, is considering. Recall that Kelly Bradford owns Gifts To Go, a two-store chain in the Chicago area. She's considering several growth options, one of which is to open an Internet channel called www.Gifts-To-Go.com. She has determined that the market size for this channel is large but very competitive. Now she needs to conduct a financial analysis for the proposed online channel, compare the projections with Gifts To Go stores, and determine the financial performance of the combined businesses. We'll first look at the profit margin management path, followed by the asset turnover management path. Exhibit 6–8 shows income statement information for Kelly's Gifts To Go stores, her estimates for Gifts-To-Go.com, and the combined businesses.

Profit Margin Management Path

Kelly thinks she can develop Gifts-To-Go.com into a business that will generate annual sales of $440,000. She anticipates some cannibalization of her store sales by the Internet channel; some customers who would have bought merchandise at Gifts To Go will no longer go into her stores to make their purchases. She also thinks the Internet channel will stimulate some store sales; customers who see gift items on her website will visit the stores and make their purchases there. Thus, she decides to perform the analysis with the assumption that her store sales will remain the same after the introduction of the Internet channel.

Gross Margin Percentage   Kelly plans to charge the same prices and sell basically the same merchandise, with an extended assortment, on Gifts-To-Go.com as

	Gifts To Go Stores	Gifts-To-Go.com (Projected)	Businesses Combined
Income Statement			
Net sales	$700,000	$440,000	$1,140,000
Less: Cost of goods sold	350,000	220,000	570,000
Gross margin	350,000	220,000	570,000
Less: Operating expenses (SG&A)	250,000	150,000	400,000
Net operating profit before tax and interest	100,000	70,000	170,000
Less: Taxes	32,200	24,500	56,700
Less: Interest	8,000	0	8,000
Net profit after taxes	24,200	24,500	48,700
Gross margin %	50%	50%	50%
Operating expenses %	36%	34%	35%
Net operating profit %	14%	16%	15%
Net operating income %	3%	6%	4%

EXHIBIT 6–8
Income Statement Information of Analysis of Gifts To Go Growth Opportunities

in her stores. Thus, she expects the gross margin percentage for store sales will be the same as the gross margin percentage for Gifts-To-Go.com sales.

$$\frac{\text{Gross margin}}{\text{Net sales}} = \text{Gross margin \%}$$

$$\text{Stores:} \quad \frac{350,000}{\$700,000} = 50\%$$

$$\text{Gifts-To-Go.com:} \quad \frac{220,000}{\$440,000} = 50\%$$

Operating Expenses   Initially, Kelly thought that her operating expenses as a percentage of sales would be lower for Gifts-To-Go.com because she would not need to pay rent or have highly trained salespeople. But she discovered that her operating expenses as a percentage of sales will be only slightly lower for Gifts-To-Go.com because she needs to hire a firm to maintain the website, process orders, and get orders ready for shipment. Also, Gifts To Go stores have an established clientele and highly trafficked locations with good visibility. Although some of her current customers will learn about the website from her in-store promotions, Kelly will have to invest in advertising and promotions to create awareness for her new channel and inform people who are unfamiliar with her stores.

Net Profit Margin   Because the gross margin and operating expenses as a percentage of sales for the two operations are projected to be about the same, Gifts-To-Go.com is expected to generate a slightly higher net profit margin percentage:

$$\frac{\text{Net profit}}{\text{Net sales}} = \text{Net profit \%}$$

$$\text{Stores:} \quad \frac{\$100,000}{\$700,000} = 14.3\%$$

$$\text{Gifts-To-Go.com:} \quad \frac{70,000}{\$440,000} = 15.9\%$$

Asset Turnover Management Path

Now let's compare the two operations using the asset turnover management path with the balance sheet information in Exhibit 6–9. Because the percentage of credit card sales is higher over the Internet channel than in stores, Kelly expects that the accounts receivable will be higher for the Internet channel than for the store channel.

EXHIBIT 6–9
Balance Sheet
Information of Analysis
of Gifts To Go Growth
Opportunities

	Gifts To Go Stores	Gifts-To-Go.com (Projected)	Businesses Combined
Accounts receivable	$140,000	$120,000	$260,000
Merchandise inventory	175,000	70,000	245,000
Cash	35,000	11,000	46,000
Total current assets	350,000	201,000	551,000
Fixed assets	30,000	10,000	40,000
Total assets	380,000	211,000	591,000
Ratios			
Inventory turnover	2.00	3.1	2.3
Asset turnover	1.84	2.09	1.93
ROA (%)	25.29%	33.25%	28.77%

Kelly estimates that Gifts-To-Go.com will have a higher inventory turnover than Gifts To Go stores because it will consolidate the inventory at one centralized distribution center that serves a large sales volume, as opposed to Gifts to Go, which has inventory sitting in several stores with relatively lower sales volumes. Additionally, Gifts-To-Go.com will have relationships with several of its vendors in which they "drop ship," or send merchandise directly from the vendor to the customer. In these situations, Gifts-to-Go.com has no inventory investment.

$$\frac{\text{Cost of goods}}{\text{Average inventory}} = \text{Inventory turnover}$$

Stores: $\quad \dfrac{350,000}{\$175,000} = 2.0$

Gifts-To-Go.com: $\quad \dfrac{220,000}{\$70,000} = 3.1$

Gifts To Go's store space is rented. Thus, Kelly's fixed assets consist of the fixtures, lighting, and other leasehold improvements for her stores, as well as equipment such as point-of-sale terminals. Kelly also has invested in assets that make her stores aesthetically pleasing. Gifts-To-Go.com is outsourcing the fulfillment of orders placed on its website, so it has no warehouse assets. Thus, its fixed assets are its website and order-processing computer system.

As she expects, Gifts-To-Go.com's projected asset turnover is higher than that of Gifts To Go's stores because Kelly estimates that Gifts-To-Go.com will have a higher inventory turnover, and its other assets are lower.

$$\frac{\text{Net sales}}{\text{Total assets}} = \text{Asset turnover}$$

Stores: $\quad \dfrac{700,000}{\$380,000} = 1.84$

Gifts-To-Go.com: $\quad \dfrac{440,000}{\$211,000} = 2.09$

Because Kelly's estimates for the net profit margin and asset turnover for Gifts-To-Go.com are higher than those for her stores, Gifts-To-Go.com achieves a higher ROA. Thus, this strategic profit model analysis indicates that Gifts-To-Go.com is a financially viable growth opportunity for Kelly.

	Net profit margin	×	Asset turnover	=	Return on assets
Stores:	14.29%	×	1.84	=	26.29%
Gifts-To-Go.com:	15.91%	×	2.09	=	33.25%

Using the Strategic Profit Model to Analyze Other Decisions

Another investment that Kelly might consider is installing a computerized inventory control system that would help her make better decisions about which merchandise to order, when to reorder merchandise, and when to lower prices on merchandise that is not being bought.

If she buys the system, her sales will increase because she will have a greater percentage of merchandise that is selling well and fewer stockouts. Her gross margin percentage will also increase because she won't have to mark down as much slow-selling merchandise.

Looking at the asset turnover management path, the purchase of the computer system will increase her fixed assets by the amount of the system, but her inventory turnover will increase and the level of inventory assets will decrease because she is able to buy more efficiently. Thus, her asset turnover will probably increase because sales will increase at a greater percentage than will total assets. Total assets may actually decrease if the additional cost of the inventory system is less than the reduction in inventory.

ANALYSIS OF FINANCIAL RISK

The previous sections have illustrated how the strategic profit model can be used to analyze the factors affecting some key retail performance ratios—operating profit margin percentage and asset turnover. The model provides insights into how retailers can improve their performance. However, retailing is a highly competitive industry, and thus major bankruptcies are common. Exhibit 6–10 lists some retailers of significant size that have filed for bankruptcy protection since 2000. Retailers, vendors, and investors need to assess the financial strength of a firm. Specifically, what are the chances that the retailer will continue to operate or will go bankrupt? In this section, we discuss measures used to assess the financial risk of retailers—the probability that they will go bankrupt. These measures include cash flow, debt-to-equity ratio, quick ratio, and current ratio.

LO4

Analyze the financial risks facing a retail firm.

Cash Flow Analysis

You might think that a retailer's profits determine its financial strength. If a retailer is profitable, there is little chance it will go bankrupt; but if it incurs losses for an extended period of time, the chances of its going bankrupt are significant. However, retailers can be forced to declare bankruptcy even when they show a profit

	Filing Year	Assets ($ bililons)
Kmart	2002	14.60
Circuit City	2008	3.76
Montgomery Ward	2000	3.49
A&P	2010	2.53
Ames Department Stores	2001	2.00
Spiegel	2003	1.89
U.S. Office Products	2001	1.75
Linens 'n' Things	2008	1.74
Heilig-Meyers	2000	1.46
Borders	2011	1.28
Blockbuster	2010	1.02

EXHIBIT 6–10
Largest U.S. Retail Bankruptcies since 2000

Source: "FACTBOX—Largest U.S. Retailer Bankruptcies since 2000," *Reuters*, February 16, 2011.

on their income statements. Retailers become insolvent and declare bankruptcy when they do not have the cash needed to meet their obligations—when they cannot pay their employees, their landlords (rent), and/or their vendors.

Profits are not the same as cash flow. For example, a retailer might borrow money from a bank. The loan appears as a liability on its balance sheet. The interest on the loan, a relatively small percentage of the loan value, appears as an interest expense on the retailer's income statement and reduces the retailer's profits slightly. However, when the retailer is required to pay back the loan to the bank, the retailer must have a significant amount of cash available to pay for the entire amount of the loan.

Retailers have cash coming in from the sales of merchandise, and they use this cash to pay vendors, employees, developers, utilities, and the like. The amount of cash coming into the business, and when it comes into the business, is crucial because the availability of cash allows retailers to continue operating in the longer term.

The cash receipts and expenditures tend to be fairly stable. Employee salaries, vendor invoices, and rent, for example, are paid monthly or weekly. Sometimes, however, retailers face radical changes in the flow of cash. During the holiday season, for instance, retailers have to buy and pay for more merchandise to support the higher-than-normal level of sales. One measure of financial strength is cash flow. In addition to providing a balance sheet and income statement, firms also provide a **cash flow statement** as another indicator of the financial strength of the firm.

Debt-to-Equity Ratio

The **debt-to-equity ratio** is the retailer's short- and long-term debt divided by the value of the owners' or stockholders' equity in the firm. Owners' equity is the difference after subtracting all liabilities from assets. **Liabilities** are a company's debts, such as its accounts payable, which is the money it owes its vendors for merchandise. Owners' equity is the owners' (or stockholders') investment in the business. The debt-to-equity ratio measures how much money a company can safely borrow over long periods of time. A high ratio means the retailer faces greater risk and more potential for bankruptcy. Generally, when retailers that have a debt-to-equity ratio of more than 40 to 50 percent, they face significant risk of financial problems.

Current Ratio

The current ratio is probably the best-known and most often used measure of financial strength. The **current ratio** is short-term assets divided by short-term liabilities. It evaluates the retailer's ability to pay its short-term debt obligations, such as accounts payable (payments to suppliers) and short-term loans payable to a bank, with short-term assets such as cash, accounts receivable, and inventory.

Quick Ratio

The **quick ratio,** sometimes called the **acid-test ratio,** is short-term assets less inventory divided by short-term liabilities. It is a more stringent test of financial strength than the current ratio because it removes inventory from the short-term assets. Inventory is the short-term asset that takes the longest to convert into cash. Thus, if a retailer needs cash to pay its short-term liabilities, it cannot rely on inventory to provide an immediate source for cash.

The financial strength measures for Costco and Macy's are shown in Exhibit 6–11. These measures of financial strength indicate that Costco and Macy's are in relatively strong financial positions. Both have a significant positive cash flow. Macy's has a higher debt-to-equity ratio but strong current and quick ratios.

	Costco 8/29/2011	Macy's 1/30/2012
Net profit ($ billions)	16.1	1.25
Cash flow ($ billions)	530	1.36
Debt-to-equity	.10	.97
Current ratio	1.51	2.01
Quick ratio	1.14	1.40

EXHIBIT 6–11
Financial Risk
Measures for Costco
and Macy's

Source: Calculations from financial statements in 10-K reports filed with SEC.

SETTING AND MEASURING PERFORMANCE OBJECTIVES

In the previous sections, we discussed the measures used to evaluate the overall financial performance of a retailer—ROA and its components, as well as measures for determining its financial risk. In this section, we review some measures used to assess the performance of specific assets possessed by a retailer—its employees, real estate, and merchandise inventory. Retailers use these measures to evaluate the firm's performance and set objectives.

LO5

Review the measures
retailers use to assess their
performance.

Setting performance objectives is a necessary component of any firm's strategic management process. Performance objectives should include (1) a numerical index of the performance desired against which progress may be measured, (2) a time frame within which the objective is to be achieved, and (3) the resources needed to achieve the objective. For example, "earning reasonable profits" isn't a good objective. It doesn't provide specific goals that can be used to evaluate performance. What's reasonable? When do you want to realize the profits? A better objective would be "earning $100,000 in profit during calendar year 2014 on a $500,000 investment in inventory and building."

Top-Down versus Bottom-Up Process

Setting objectives in large retail organizations entails a combination of the top-down and bottom-up approaches to planning. **Top-down planning** means that goals get set at the top of the organization and are passed down to the lower operating levels. In a retailing organization, top-down planning involves corporate officers developing an overall retail strategy and assessing broad economic, competitive, and consumer trends. With this information, they develop performance objectives for the corporation. These overall objectives are then broken down into specific objectives for each buyer and merchandise category and for each region, store, and even department within stores and the sales associates working in those departments.

The overall strategy determines the merchandise variety, assortment, and product availability, plus the store size, location, and level of customer service. Then the merchandise vice presidents decide which types of merchandise are expected to grow, stay the same, or shrink. Next, performance goals are established for each buyer and merchandise manager. This process is reviewed in Chapter 12.

Similarly, regional store vice presidents translate the company's performance objectives into objectives for each district manager, who then develops objectives with the store managers. The process then trickles down to department managers in the stores and individual sales associates. The process of setting objectives for sales associates in stores is discussed in Chapter 16.

This top-down planning is complemented by a bottom-up planning approach. **Bottom-up planning** involves lower levels in the company developing performance objectives that are aggregated up to develop overall company objectives. Buyers and store managers estimate what they can achieve, and their estimates are transmitted up the organization to the corporate executives.

Frequently there are disagreements between the goals that have trickled down from the top and those set by lower-level employees of the organization. For example, a store manager may not be able to achieve the 10 percent sales growth set for his or her region because a major employer in the area has announced plans to lay off 2,000 employees. The differences between bottom-up and top-down plans are resolved through a negotiation process involving corporate executives and operating managers. If the operating managers aren't involved in the objective-setting process, they won't accept the objectives and thus will be less motivated to achieve them.

Who Is Accountable for Performance?

At each level of the retail organization, the business unit and its manager should be held accountable only for the revenues, expenses, cash flow, and contribution to ROA that they can control. Thus, expenses that affect several levels of the organization (e.g., labor and capital expenses associated with operating a corporate headquarters) shouldn't be arbitrarily assigned to lower levels. In the case of a store, for example, it may be appropriate to set performance objectives based on sales, sales associate productivity, store inventory shrinkage due to employee theft and shoplifting, and energy costs. If the buyer makes poor decisions and has to lower prices to get rid of merchandise and therefore profits suffer, it is not fair to assess a store manager's performance on the basis of the resulting decline in store profit.

Performance objectives and measures can be used to pinpoint problem areas. The reasons that performance may be above or below planned levels must be examined. Perhaps the managers involved in setting the objectives aren't very good at making estimates. If so, they may need to be trained in forecasting. Also, buyers may misrepresent their business unit's ability to contribute to the firm's financial goals to get a larger inventory budget than is warranted and consequently earn a higher bonus. In either case, investment funds would be misallocated.

Actual performance may differ from what the plan predicts due to circumstances beyond the manager's control. For example, there may have been a recession. Assuming the recession wasn't predicted, or was more severe or lasted longer than anticipated, there are several relevant questions: How quickly were plans adjusted? How rapidly and appropriately were pricing and promotional policies modified? In short, did the manager react to salvage an adverse situation, or did the reaction worsen the situation?

Performance Objectives and Measures

Many factors contribute to a retailer's overall performance, and this makes it hard to find a single measure to evaluate performance. For instance, sales are a global measure of a retail store's activity level. However, as illustrated by the strategic profit model, a store manager could easily increase sales by lowering prices, but the profit realized on that merchandise (gross margin) would suffer as a result. An attempt to maximize one measure may lower another. Managers must therefore understand how their actions affect multiple performance measures.

The measures used to evaluate retail operations vary depending on (1) the level of the organization at which the decision is made and (2) the resources the manager controls. For example, the principal resources controlled by store managers are space and money for operating expenses (such as wages for sales associates and utility payments to light and heat the store). Thus, store managers focus on performance measures like sales per square foot, employee costs, and energy cost as a percent of sales.

Types of Measures

Exhibit 6–12 breaks down a variety of retailers' performance measures into three types: input measures, output measures, and productivity measures. **Input measures** are the resources or money allocated by a retailer to achieve outputs, or results. For example, the amount and selection of merchandise inventory, the number of stores, the size of the stores, the employees, advertising, markdowns, store hours, and promotions all require managerial decisions on inputs.

Measure for Assessing the Performance of Retailers   **EXHIBIT 6–12**

Level of Organization	Output	Input	Productivity (Output/Input)
Corporate (measures for entire corporation)	Net sales Net profits Growth in sales, profits, comparable-store sales	Square feet of store space Number of employees Inventory Advertising expenditures	Return on assets Asset turnover Sales per employee Sales per square foot
Merchandise management (measures for a merchandise category)	Net sales Gross margin Growth in sales	Inventory level Markdowns Advertising expenses Cost of merchandise	Gross margin return on investment (GMROI) Inventory turnover Advertising as a percentage of sales* Markdown as a percentage of sales*
Store operations (measures for a store or department within a store)	Net sales Gross margin Growth in sales	Square feet of selling areas Expenses for utilities Number of sales associates	Net sales per square foot Net sales per sales associate or per selling hour Utility expenses as a percentage of sales* Inventory shrinkage*

*These productivity measures are commonly expressed as an input-output ratio.

Output measures assess the results of a retailer's investment decisions. For example, sales revenue, gross margin, and net profit margin are all output measures and ways to evaluate a retailer's input or resource allocation decisions. A **productivity measure** (the ratio of an output to an input) determines how effectively retailers use their resources—what return they get on their investments in inputs.

In general, because productivity measures are ratios of outputs to inputs, they are very useful for comparing the performance of different business units. Suppose Kelly Bradford's two stores are different sizes: One has 5,000 square feet, and the other has 10,000 square feet. It's hard to compare the stores' performances using just output or input measures because the larger store will probably generate more sales and have higher expenses. But if the larger store has lower space productivity because it generates $210 net sales per square foot and the smaller store generates $350 per square foot, Kelly knows that the smaller store is operating more efficiently, even though it's generating lower sales.

Corporate Performance   At a corporate level, retail executives have three critical resources (inputs)—merchandise inventory, store space, and employees—that they can manage to generate sales and profits (outputs). Thus, effective productivity measures of the utilization of these assets include asset and inventory turnover, sales per square foot of selling space, and sales per employee.

As we have discussed, ROA is an overall productivity measure combining the operating profit margin percentage and asset turnover. Another commonly used measure of overall performance is **comparable-store sales growth** (also called **same-store sales growth**), which compares sales growth in stores that have been open for at least one year. Growth in sales can result from increasing the sales generated per store or by increasing the number of stores. Growth in same-store sales assesses the first component in sales growth, and thus indicates how well the retailer is doing with its core business concept. New stores do not represent growth from last year's sales but, rather, new sales created where no other sales existed the year before. Thus, a decrease in same-store sales indicates that the retailer's fundamental business approach is not being well received by its customers, even if overall sales are growing because the retailer is opening more new stores.

Merchandise Management Measures   The critical resource (input) controlled by merchandise managers is merchandise inventory. Merchandise managers also have the authority to set initial prices and lower prices when merchandise is not selling (i.e., take a markdown). Finally, they negotiate with vendors over the price paid for merchandise.

Inventory turnover is a productivity measure of the management of inventory; higher turnover means greater inventory management productivity. Gross margin percentage indicates the performance of merchandise managers in negotiating with vendors and buying merchandise that can generate a profit. Discounts (markdowns) as a percentage of sales are also a measure of the quality of the merchandise buying decisions. If merchandise managers have a high percentage of markdowns, they may not be buying the right merchandise or the right quantities, because they weren't able to sell some of it at its original retail price. Note that gross margin and discount percentages are productivity measures, but they are typically expressed as an input divided by an output as opposed to the typical productivity measures that are outputs divided by inputs.

Store Operations Measures   The critical assets controlled by store managers are the use of the store space and the management of the store's employees. Thus, measures of store operations productivity include sales per square foot of selling space and sales per employee (or sales per employee per working hour, to take into account that some employees work part-time). Store management is also responsible for controlling theft by employees and customers (referred to as inventory shrinkage), store maintenance, and energy costs (lighting, heating, and air conditioning). Thus, some other productivity measures used to assess the performance of store managers are inventory shrinkage and energy costs as a percentage of sales.

Assessing Performance: The Role of Benchmarks

As we have discussed, the financial measures used to assess performance reflect the retailer's market strategy. For example, because Costco has a different business strategy than Macy's, it has a lower profit margin. But it earns an acceptable ROA because it increases its inventory and asset turnovers by stocking a more limited merchandise assortment of less fashionable, staple items. In contrast, Macy's offers a broad and deep merchandise assortment in fashionable apparel and accessories. Thus, it has lower inventory and asset turnover but achieves an acceptable ROA through its higher profit margins. In other words, the performance of a retailer cannot be assessed accurately simply by looking at isolated measures because they are affected by the retailer's strategy. To get a better assessment of a retailer's performance, we need to compare it to a benchmark. Two commonly used benchmarks are (1) the performance of the retailer over time and (2) the performance of the retailer compared with that of its competitors.

Performance over Time   One useful approach for assessing a retailer's performance compares its recent performance with its performance in the preceding months, quarters, or years. Exhibit 6–13 shows the performance measures for Costco and Macy's over a three-year period.

Over the three years, the financial performance of both Costco and Macy's has improved. ROA for both retailers has increased; however, the increases in Macy's ROA are due primarily to improvements in operating profit percentage, while Costco's ROA improvements are due to an increasing asset turnover. Costco's sales increases and comparable-store sales percentages are greater than Macy's. The gross margin percentages for both retailers have remained the same over the three years. Both retailers have reduced their SG&A and improved their labor and space productivity.

Performance Compared to Competitors   A second approach for assessing a retailer's performance involves comparing its performance with that of its competitors. Exhibit 6–14 compares the performance of Macy's with two other national department store chains, Kohl's and Nordstrom. Kohl's has the highest ROA but the lowest growth in sales and SG&A percent of sales. Macy's has the highest gross margin percent but also has the highest administrative costs. Nordstrom has the highest space and labor productivity.

Performance Measures for Costco and Macy's over Time   EXHIBIT 6–13

	COSTCO			MACY'S		
	2012	2011	2010	2012	2011	2010
Sales ($ millions)	97,062	87,048	76,255	26,405	25,003	23,489
Annual sales growth	11.5%	14.2%	9.1%	5.6%	6.4%	−5.6%
Gross margin percentage	11.3%	10.7%	10.8%	40.4%	40.7%	40.5%
SG&A percent of sales	10.5%	10.0%	10.3%	31.4%	33.0%	34.3%
Operating profit percentage	2.8%	2.9%	2.8%	9.0%	7.7%	6.2%
Net profit percentage	1.8%	2.0%	1.8%	4.7%	3.4%	1.4%
Inventory turnover	12.2	11.71	12.06	3.08	3.12	3.03
Asset turnover	3.6	3.32	3.27	1.20	1.21	1.10
ROA	10.2%	9.3%	8.8%	10.8%	9.3%	6.8%
Sales per employee	557,830	540,671	518,741	154,415	150,620	145,894
Sales per store ($ millions)	159	147	141	31	29	28
Sales per square foot	1,117	1,031	986	174	162	152
Current ratio	1.10	1.14	1.04	1.40	1.38	0.81
Debt-to-equity ratio	0.11	0.11	0.12	2.23	2.73	8.62
Quick ratio	0.58	0.59	0.54	0.58	0.43	0.27
Cash flow ($ millions)	3,057	3,198	2,780	1,363	(222)	301
Comparable-store sales	8.1	7.0	10.0	3.5	3.0	4.6

	Kohl's	Macy's	Nordstrom
Sales ($ millions)	10,497	26,405	18,804
Annual sales growth	2.2%	5.6%	12.7%
Gross margin percentage	38.2%	40.4%	37.9%
SG&A percent of sales	22.6%	31.4%	26.7%
Operating profit percentage	15.6%	9.0%	11.2%
Net profit percentage	6.2%	4.7%	6.5%
Inventory turnover	3.63	3.08	5.68
Asset turnover	1.33	1.20	1.24
ROA	20.8%	10.8%	13.8%
Sales per employee ($)	132,423	154,415	185,788
Sales per store ($ millions)	16.7	31.4	41.2
Sales per square foot ($)	229	174	424
Comparable-store sales	0.5	3.5	7.3

EXHIBIT 6–14
Financial Performance of Macy's Compared with Kohl's and Nordstrom

SUMMARY

LO1 **Review the strategic objectives of a retail firm.**

This chapter explains some basic elements of the retailing financial strategy and examines how retailing strategy affects the financial performance of a firm. The strategy undertaken by retailers is designed to achieve financial, societal, and personal objectives. However, the financial objectives are of greatest importance to large, publicly owned retailers.

LO2 **Contrast the two paths to financial performance using the strategic profit model.**

The strategic profit model is used as a vehicle for understanding the complex interrelations between financial ratios and retailing strategy. Different types of retailers have different financial operating characteristics. Specifically, department store chains like Macy's generally have higher profit margins and lower turnover ratios than warehouse club stores like Costco. Yet when margin and turnover are combined into return on assets, it is possible to achieve similar financial performance.

LO3 Illustrate the use of the strategic profit model for analyzing growth opportunities.

In addition to helping retailers understand the financial implications of the tradeoffs they face in developing a retail strategy, this chapter illustrates how the strategic profit model can be used to evaluate growth and investment opportunities.

LO4 Analyze the financial risks facing a retail firm.

In addition to assessing the performance of a retail operation, the chapter also examines measures used to assess the financial strength of a retailer—the

probability of the business declaring bankruptcy. Four measures of financial strength are cash flow, debt-to-equity ratio, current ratio, and quick ratio.

LO5 Review the measures retailers use to assess their performance.

Some financial performance measures are used to evaluate different aspects of a retailing organization. Although the return-on-assets ratio in the strategic profit model is appropriate for evaluating the performance of the retail executives responsible for managing the firm, other measures are more appropriate for more specific activities. For instance, inventory turnover and gross margin are appropriate for buyers, whereas store managers should be concerned with sales or gross margin per square foot or per employee.

KEY TERMS

accounts receivable, *163*
acid-test ratio, *174*
assets, *165*
asset turnover, *158*
bottom-up planning, *175*
cash flow statement, *174*
chargeback fee, *161*
comparable-store sales growth, *177*
cost of goods sold (COGS), *162*
current assets, *165*
current ratio, *174*
debt-to-equity ratio, *174*
earnings before interest, taxes, and depreciation (EBITDA), *158*

fixed assets, *167*
gross margin, *162*
gross margin percentage, *162*
gross profit, *162*
income statement, *161*
input measures, *176*
inventory turnover, *166*
liabilities, *174*
merchandise inventory, *166*
net profit margin, *162*
net sales, *161*
operating expenses, *162*
operating expenses percentage, *164*

operating income percentage, *165*
operating profit margin, *158*
output measures, *177*
productivity measures, *177*
quick ratio, *174*
return on assets (ROA), *156*
same-store sales growth, *177*
selling, general, and administrative (SG&A) expenses, *162*
slotting allowance, *161*
slotting fee, *161*
statement of operations, *161*
strategic profit model, *158*
top-down planning, *175*

GET OUT AND DO IT!

1. **CONTINUING CASE ASSIGNMENT** Evaluate the financial performance of the retailer you have selected for the Continuing Case Assignment and of another store that sells similar merchandise categories but to a very different target market. If yours is a high-margin–low-turnover store, compare it with a low-margin–high-turnover store. You can get this information from your chosen store's latest annual report, available in the "investor relations" area of its website, at Hoovers Online, or in the Edgar files at www.sec.gov. Explain why you would expect the gross margin percentage, expense-to-sales ratio, net profit margin percentage, inventory turnover, asset turnover, and return on assets to differ between the two stores. Which retailer achieves better overall financial performance?

2. **INTERNET EXERCISE** Go to the latest annual reports, and use the financial information to update the numbers in the net profit margin management model and the asset turnover management model for Costco and Macy's. Have there been any significant changes in their financial performance? Why are the key financial ratios for these two retailers so different?

3. **GO SHOPPING** Go to your favorite store, and interview the manager. Determine how the retailer sets its performance objectives. Evaluate its procedures relative to the procedures presented in the text.

4. **WEB OLC EXERCISE** Go to the strategic profit model (SPM) on the student side of the book's website. The SPM tutorial was designed to provide a refresher course on the basic financial ratios leading to

return on assets and walks you through the process step-by-step. A calculation page is also included that will calculate all the ratios. You can type in the numbers from a firm's balance sheet and income statement to see the financial results produced with the current financial figures. You can also access an Excel spreadsheet for SPM calculations. The calculation page or the Excel spreadsheet can be used for Case 11, "Tiffany's and TJX: Comparing Financial Performance," page 563.

DISCUSSION QUESTIONS AND PROBLEMS

1. What are the key productivity ratios for measuring the retailer as a whole, its merchandise management activities, and its store operations activities? Why are these ratios appropriate for one area of the retailer's operation and inappropriate for others?

2. What are examples of the types of objectives that entrepreneurs might have for a retail business they are launching?

3. Buyers' performance is often measured by the gross margin percentage. Why is this measure more appropriate than operating or net profit percentage?

4. A supermarket retailer is considering the installation of self-checkout POS terminals. How would the replacement of cashiers with these self-checkouts affect the elements in the retailer's strategic profit model?

5. Neiman Marcus (a chain of high-service department stores) and Walmart target different customer segments. Which retailer would you expect to have a higher gross margin? Higher expense-to-sales ratio? Higher net profit margin percentage? Higher inventory turnover? Higher asset turnover? Why?

6. Why do investors place more weight on comparable-store sales than growth in sales?

7. What metrics should be used to measure the financial risk of a retailer? How is each metric used?

8. Blue Nile is a jewelry retailer than only uses an Internet channel for interacting with its customers. What differences would you expect in the strategic profit model and key productivity ratios for Blue Nile and Zales, a multichannel jewelry retailer?

9. Using the following information taken from the 2012 balance sheet and income statement for Urban Outfitters, develop a strategic profit model. (Figures are in millions of dollars.) You can access an Excel spreadsheet for SPM calculations on the student portion of the book's website.

Net sales	$2473.8
Cost of goods sold	$1316.2
Operating expenses	$ 575.8
Inventory	$ 250.1
Accounts receivable	$ 36.7
Other current assets	$ 68.9
Fixed assets	$ 690.0

10. A friend of yours is considering buying some stock in retail companies. Your friend knows that you are taking a course in retailing and ask for your opinion about Costco. Your friend is concerned that Costco is not a good firm to invest in because it has such a low net operating profit. What advice would you give your friend? Why?

SUGGESTED READINGS

Anderson, Torben Juul, and Peter Winther Schrøder. *Strategic Risk Management Practice: How to Deal Effectively with Major Corporate Exposures.* Cambridge: Cambridge University Press, 2010.

Appelbaum, E., and R. Batt. *A Primer on Private Equity at Work.* Armonk, NY: ME Sharpe, 2012.

Baud, Celine, and Cedric Durand. "Financialization, Globalization and the Making of Profits by Leading Retailers," *Socio-Economic Review* 10 (2012), pp. 241–266.

Brealey, Richard, Stewart Myers, and Alan Marcus. *Corporate Finance,* 7th ed. New York: McGraw Hill, 2012.

Farris, Paul, Neil Bendle, Phillip Pfeifer, and David Reibstein. *Marketing Metrics: The Definitive Guide to Measuring Marketing Performance,* 2nd ed. New York: Pearson Prentice-Hall, 2010.

Financial Performance Report—Profitable Growth: Driving the Demand Chain. New York: PWC, 2012.

Garrison, Ray H., Eric Noreen, and Peter C. Brewer. *Managerial Accounting,* 14th ed. New York: McGraw-Hill, 2012.

Lichtenstein, Donald, Richard G. Netemeyer, and James G. Maxham III. "The Relationships among Manager-, Employee-, and Customer-Company Identification: Implications for Retail Store Financial Performance," *Journal of Retailing* 86 (March 2010), pp. 85–93.

"Monitoring Operational and Financial Performance." In Joachim Zentes, Dirk Morschett, and Hanna Schramm-Klein, eds. *Strategic Retail Management,* pp. 383–402, New York: Springer, 2012.

Perrini, Francesco, Angelo Russo, Antonio Tencati, and Clodia Vurro. "Deconstructing the Relationship between Corporate Social and Financial Performance," *Journal of Business Ethics* 102, Suppl. 1 (2011), pp. 59–76.

Ross, Stephen, Randolph Westerfield, and Bradford Jordan. *Fundamentals of Corporate Finance,* 10th ed. New York: McGraw Hill, 2013.

Retail Locations

EXECUTIVE BRIEFING

Michael Kercheval, President and CEO
International Council of Shopping Centers

While I was going to college, I became very concerned about the poor quality of life in much of the world and volunteered to work on several economic development projects in Latin America sponsored by the Peace Corps and the Pan American Health Organization. From these experiences, I decided to go to medical school, become a doctor, and then return to Latin America. But pre-med chemistry did not agree with me. I discovered economics and majored in developmental economics.

After graduate school, I went to work for Equitable Life Insurance and eventually became involved in managing real estate investment activities in Latin America. I observed keenly how retail developments are a catalyst for economic development. They create a virtuous cycle: retail developments → more goods, more choices, lower prices, and greater income → more retail development. The shopping centers provided goods to people with higher quality at lower prices and greater convenience. By saving people money on necessities, they can have a higher standard of living and greater disposable income. In addition, the retail developments provided jobs that increased the incomes. Then the increased incomes spurred more retail developments.

I am president of the International Council for Shopping Centers (ICSC), which offers me a chance to serve an industry that is very involved in economic development around the world, as well as in U.S. urban and rural communities.

The retail development industry is at an interesting crossroads now. Demand for retail space across the globe is far greater than supply, and there is considerable capital available to invest in new retail developments. The primary restraint to growth is from government policymakers who are tempering new development out of concern for small retail businesses, the environment, and what they see as suburban sprawl. ICSC and its members are working on ways to meet the retail needs of consumers, stimulate economic growth, and address the concerns of policymakers.

CHAPTER 7

LEARNING OBJECTIVES

LO1 Describe the types of retail locations available to retailers.

LO2 Review the types of unplanned locations.

LO3 Analyze the characteristics of the different types of shopping centers.

LO4 Discuss nontraditional retail locations.

LO5 Match the locations to the retailer's strategy.

LO6 Review the societal and legal considerations in selecting locations.

The oft-referenced response to the question "What are the three most important things in retailing?" is "Location, location, location." Why is store location such an important decision for a retailer? First, location is typically one of the most influential considerations in a customer's store-choice decision. For instance, when choosing where you're going to have your car washed, you usually pick the location closest to your home or work. Most consumers similarly shop at the supermarket closest to them.

Second, location decisions have strategic importance because they can be used to develop a sustainable competitive advantage. If a retailer has the best location, that is, the location that is most attractive to its customers, competitors can't copy this advantage. Competitors are relegated to occupying the second-best location.

Third, location decisions are risky. Typically, when retailers select a location, they either must make a substantial investment to buy and develop the real estate or must commit to a long-term lease with developers. Retailers often commit to leases for 5 to 15 years.

In the first part of this chapter, we discuss the types and relative advantages of three types of locations available to retailers—unplanned, planned, and nontraditional. We then examine how the location decision fits into the retailer's strategy. For example, the best locations for a 7-Eleven convenience store are not the best locations for a category specialist such as a Best Buy. We end this chapter by discussing the societal and legal considerations affecting a retailer's location decisions. In the next chapter, we discuss the issues involved in selecting areas of the country in which to locate stores and how to evaluate specific locations and negotiate leases.

TYPES OF RETAIL LOCATIONS

LO1

Describe the types of retail locations available to retailers.

Many types of locations are available for retail stores, each type with its benefits and limitations. The two basic types of location are unplanned (freestanding and urban sites) and planned (shopping centers). **Unplanned locations** do not have centralized management that determines what stores will be in a development, where the specific stores will be located, and how they will be operated. In **planned locations,** the shopping center developer and/or manager makes and enforces policies that govern store operations, such as the hours that a store must be opened. The shopping center management also maintains the common facilities such as the parking area—an arrangement referred to as **common area maintenance (CAM)**—and is responsible for providing security, parking lot lighting, outdoor signage for the center, advertising, special events to attract consumers, and so on.

In the United States, about 47 percent of the gross leasable square feet of retail space is in planned locations and the remaining in unplanned locations.[1] **Gross leasable area (GLA)** is the real estate industry's term for the total floor area designed for the retailer's occupancy and exclusive use, including any basements, mezzanines, or upper floors.

When choosing a particular location type, retailers evaluate a series of trade-offs involving the size of the trade area, the occupancy cost of the location (rent, maintenance, energy cost, etc.), the pedestrian and vehicle customer traffic associated with the location, the restrictions placed on store operations by the shopping center management, and the convenience of the location for customers. The **trade area** is the geographic area that encompasses most of the customers who would patronize a specific retail site. The following sections describe the characteristics of each type of location, as summarized in Exhibit 7–1.

EXHIBIT 7–1   Characteristics of Different Retail Locations

	Size (000 sq. ft.)	Trading Area (Miles)	Annual Occupancy Cost ($ per sq. ft.)	Shopping Convenience	Pedestrian Traffic	Vehicular Traffic	Restrictions on Operations	Typical Tenants
UNPLANNED AREAS								
Freestanding	Varies	3–7	15–30	High	Low	High	Limited	Convenience, drug stores, category specialists
Urban locations/ central business district	Varies	Varies	8–20	Low	High	Low	Limited to medium	Specialty stores
SHOPPING CENTERS								
Neighborhood and community shopping centers	30–350	3–6	8–20	High	Low	High	Medium	Supermarkets, discount stores
Power centers	250–600	5–10	10–20	Medium	Medium	Medium	Limited	Category specialists
Regional and super-regional enclosed malls	400–1,000	5–25	10–70	Low	High	Low	High	Department and specialty apparel stores
Lifestyle centers	150–800	5–15	15–35	Medium	Medium	Medium	Medium to high	Specialty apparel and home stores, restaurants
Outlet centers	50–400	25–75	8–15	Low	High	High	Limited	Off-price retailers and factory outlets
Theme/festival centers	80–250	N/A	20–70	Low	High	Low	Highest	Specialty stores and restaurants

Sources: Personal communications with industry executives; "North American Retail Highlights 2009," http://www.colliers.com/Content/Repositories/Base/Corporate/English/Market_Report_Corporate/PDFs/RetailNaHighlightsSpring2009.pdf; http://www.icsc.org/srch/lib/2009_S-C_CLASSIFICATION_May09.pdf.

UNPLANNED LOCATIONS

The three types of unplanned retail locations are freestanding sites, urban locations, and mainstreet locations.

Freestanding Sites

Freestanding sites are retail locations for an individual, isolated store unconnected to other stores; however, they might be near other freestanding stores or near a shopping center. The advantages of freestanding locations are their convenience for customers (easy access and parking); high vehicular traffic and visibility to attract customers driving by; modest occupancy costs; and fewer restrictions on signs, hours, or merchandise that might be imposed by management of planned locations.

Drugstore chains use freestanding locations for their stores with drive-through windows to make it easy for customers to pick up prescription pharmaceuticals.

There are several disadvantages to freestanding sites. First, is their limited trade area. Typically, there are no other nearby retailers to attract customers interested in conveniently shopping for multiple categories of merchandise on one trip. In addition, freestanding locations typically have higher occupancy costs than shopping centers because they do not have other retailers to share the common area maintenance costs. Finally, freestanding locations generally have little pedestrian traffic, limiting the number of customers who might drop in because they are walking by.

Some retailers are shifting from planned locations to freestanding locations to offer their customers a better shopping experience. The three major drugstore chains (CVS, Walgreens, and Rite Aid) have shifted their emphasis from strip malls to freestanding locations because they want accessible drive-through windows for pharmacies, more floor space, and better access for receiving merchandise.

Outparcels are freestanding stores that are not connected to other stores in a shopping center, but are located on the premises of a shopping center, typically in a parking area. Some advantages of outparcels compared to other freestanding locations are that they can offer customers the convenience of a drive-through window, extensive parking, and clear visibility from the street. These locations are popular for fast-food restaurants and banks.

Urban Locations

Urban areas in large cities offer three types of locations: the central business district, inner city, and gentrified residential sites.

Central Business District   The **central business district (CBD)** is the traditional downtown financial and business area in a city or town. Due to its daily activity, it draws many people and employees into the area during business hours. There is a high level of pedestrian traffic, but shopping flow in the evening and on weekends is slow in many CBDs. Vehicular traffic is limited due to congestion in urban areas, and parking problems reduce consumer convenience. Many CBDs have a large number of residents living in nearby areas.

Risk-taking entrepreneurial developers working with forward-thinking urban planners and city leaders are slowly attracting more people to the CBD at night and during weekends. For example, coal and steel are no longer the backbone of Cleveland's economy. City leaders and local developers reinvented the CBD using an entertainment-focused strategy to redevelop East Fourth Street. Retail stores occupy about one-third of the 600,000-square-foot, $110 million, historic redevelopment project. The rest is housing. The area is spectacularly designed

Cleveland's East Fourth Street development attracts consumers to the CBD.

with art, flowers, decorative paving, planters, outdoor seating, and special overhead lighting. To increase the foot traffic, two new stadiums for the city's football and baseball teams, a new arena for its basketball team, and the Rock and Roll Hall of Fame were built. Today, city residents and suburbanites flock to East Fourth Street before and after sports and entertainment events, as well as for an interesting afternoon or evening "on the town."[2]

Inner City During the 1970s and 1980s, many U.S. and some European cities experienced urban decay. **Urban decay** is the process of a previously functioning city, or part of a city, falling into disrepair. The **inner city** is a low-income residential area within a large city. Empty lots, buildings, and condemned houses attract criminals and street gangs that make living in the inner city dangerous. One of the major causes of urban decay is when businesses relocate from the inner city to suburbs.

Some U.S. retailers avoid opening stores in the inner city because they think these stores are riskier and produce lower returns than other areas. Although income levels are lower in inner cities than in other neighborhoods, inner-city retailers often achieve a higher sales volume and higher margins, resulting in higher profits.

Inner-city residents and public policy advocates are concerned about the offerings at inner-city grocery stores. Instead of offering fresh meat and produce, they tend to feature lower-priced packaged foods that have longer shelf lives. As a result, inner-city consumers often have to travel to the suburbs using buses to shop for healthy food items. Government programs, in partnership with nonprofit organizations, are working to change the inner-city supermarket landscape. For instance, in an inner-city Philadelphia neighborhood, a new supermarket, stocked with fresh produce, a pharmacy, and various ethnic products, has opened within walking distance of most of the neighborhood. Nonprofit organizations such as Philadelphia's Food Trust lobby for loans and government subsidies to support supermarkets in lower-income areas.[3] Retailing View 7.1 describes how Magic Johnson has brought retailing to the inner city.

Retailing can play an important role in inner-city redevelopment activities by providing needed services and jobs for inner-city residents, as well as property taxes to support the redevelopment. Because of the potential of this untapped market and incentives from local governments, developers are increasing their focus on opportunities in the inner city. However, inner-city redevelopments can be controversial. Often local governments will use the right of eminent domain to buy buildings and land and then sell it to developers at an attractive price. For instance, people are concerned about the residents displaced by the development, increased traffic, and parking.

Gentrified Residential Areas Many inner-city areas are going through a process of **gentrification**—the renewal and rebuilding of offices, housing, and retailers in deteriorating areas—coupled with an influx of more affluent people that displaces the former, lower-income residents. Young professionals and retired empty-nesters are moving into these areas to enjoy the convenience of shopping, restaurants, and entertainment near where they live.

Some retailers are finding urban locations attractive, particularly in cities that are redeveloping their urban areas. Big-box retailers like Target, Walmart, Office Depot, Home Depot, and Costco, which usually locate in the suburbs, are now opening outlets in cities, typically with smaller stores.[4]

While some U.S. cities are still struggling to rekindle their business, social, cultural, and retail vitality, others like New York, Chicago, and many Canadian and European cities have not experienced significant urban decay. These cities offer very attractive markets for retailers. For example, the world's five most famous locations for high-fashion retailers are in these locations—Oxford and Regent Street in London, Fifth Avenue between 49th and 58th Streets in New York City, Rue du Faubourg Saint-Honoré in Paris, Rodeo Drive in Los Angeles, and Passeig de Gràcia in Barcelona.[5]

Retailers need to tailor their offerings to the unique characteristics of urban gentrified consumers and the restrictions associated with these locations. When selecting a store to patronize, these urban consumers, compared with suburban consumers, typically place more importance on reducing their shopping time rather than the

RETAILING VIEW   Magic Johnson Brings Retailing to the Inner City   7.1

They called him "Magic" because of the way he knew where to pass the ball without looking and his ability to make jump shots that seemingly had no hope of going in. But since retiring from the NBA and becoming one of the first public figures to announce his HIV-positive status, Earvin Johnson also has turned his magic touch to urban redevelopment and growth, creating a whole new meaning for his famous nickname.

In the mid-1990s, Magic Johnson announced a partnership with Loews Cineplex, which would seek to open more movie theaters in underserved inner-city markets. Research showed that approximately one-third of movie tickets were being purchased by lower-income, minority audiences. Yet most of these consumers had to travel long distances, often taking up to an hour, to get to a theater, because few theaters were located in urban locations. For Johnson, the natural response was to build more urban movie theaters.

Once the Magic Johnson Theaters group had built a few facilities, Johnson and his partners recognized that their success depended on attracting customers by offering complementary entertainment as well. People love to have dinner before or dessert after catching a movie, but many casual dining franchises avoided urban locations. Instead, their conventional strategies involved targeting middle-class, suburban markets, with little consideration of diverse demographics. Again weaving his magic, Johnson ultimately convinced Starbucks to enter into an exclusive joint partnership with the theater group, after which T.G.I. Fridays came on board as well.

Today, the Johnson Development Corporation (JDC) consists of four separate enterprises. In addition to Magic Johnson Theatres, it includes Urban Coffee Opportunities, Magic Johnson's T.G.I. Friday's, and the Canyon Johnson Urban Fund. Through these entitites, the JDC seeks to establish entertainment complexes, featuring theaters, coffee shops, restaurants, and retailing, in underserved U.S. markets. The 50–50 partnerships thus give JDC connections to some of the most successful names in each

Doris Jackson, 8, left, sits at a computer as Earvin "Magic" Johnson looks over her shoulder at the Mattie Koonce Learning Center in the Overtown section in Miami, Florida. Through his foundation, Johnson has helped donate $200,000 in computer equipment to the learning center.

market, such as Loews Cineplex Entertainment, Starbucks, and T.G.I. Friday's—and they give urban consumers a fun way to spend their Saturday nights.

Sources: Roger Vincent, "Magic Johnson Built Business Empire after Court Glories Ended," *Los Angeles Times,* March 28, 2012; "Meet Magic Johnson, the Media Mogul," *CNN Money,* March 15, 2012; and Danielle Kwateng, "Decoding the Business of Earvin "Magic" Johnson," *Black Enterprise,* March 30, 2012.

DISCUSSION QUESTION

Among all of the potential retailers that could be interested in an inner-city location, why have Loews Cineplex Entertainment, Starbucks, and T.G.I. Friday's been particularly interested in working with Magic Johnson?

Rodeo Drive is an CBD location that is one the most highly regarded locations by retailers of high-fashion merchandise.

breadth and depth of the retailer's assortment. For example, Office Depot's urban stores are 5,000 square feet, about a fifth of a suburban store. The shelves are about 6 feet high, much shorter than in a suburban store, so visitors can navigate quickly. The signs above the aisles are simplified so customers do not waste time interpreting them. A suburban Office Depot store has 9,000 SKUs for sale, while its urban stores have half that number. The merchandise offered focuses on immediate-replacement items (a pen) versus stock-up items (a 25-pack of pens).

Retailers with urban locations also need to recognize the differences in consumer needs within these markets. For example, the Walgreens store in New York City's Union Square attracts commuters and tourists using the subway; the store a few blocks north draws mostly local residents. So the Union Square site carries lots of products such as umbrellas for the unprepared tourists, along with cosmetics and snacks; the other store is more heavily stocked with household-cleaning items and toothpaste.[6]

Finally, to deal with the traffic and parking problems in these gentrified residential areas, many residents use public transportation or walk when they go shopping. As a result, they are reluctant to buy bulky items like a 24-pack of toilet paper and are active users of Internet retail channels.

Main Street

Main Street refers to the traditional downtown shopping area in smaller towns and secondary shopping areas in large cities and their suburbs. Over the past 30 years, many downtowns in small U.S. towns have experienced decay similar to that of inner cities. When Walmart and other big-box retailers opened standalone stores on the outskirts of these towns, local retailers could not compete effectively with these big boxes and went out of business. In response, smaller towns are undertaking redevelopment programs to draw residents back to their downtown areas, and retailers play a major role in these efforts.

To attract consumers and retailers, these Main Street redevelopment efforts focus on providing a better shopping experience than big-box retailers do. Instead of streets, they develop pedestrian walkways. Next to major crosswalks, pedestrian shelters equipped with benches provide shady resting spots for mobile shoppers, helping them extend their visits and prolong their shopping excursions. Property owners can also receive grants if they agree to maintain and enhance their shops' appearance with necessary repairs, new signage, attractive entrances, attention-grabbing windows, and nice awnings. Furthermore, the town administrations work to improve downtown aesthetics with landscaping, which surrounds repaved sidewalks and updated (and functioning) street lights.[7]

Main Street locations share most of the characteristics of locations in gentrified urban areas, but their occupancy costs are generally lower. Main Street locations do not draw as many people as the CBD because fewer people work in the area, and the fewer stores generally mean a smaller overall draw to the area. In addition, Main Streets typically don't offer the range of entertainment and recreational activities available in the more successful primary CBDs. Finally, the planning organization for the town or redevelopment often imposes some restrictions on Main Street store operations.

SHOPPING CENTERS AND PLANNED RETAIL LOCATIONS

In this section, we discuss the different types of shopping centers—planned locations. A **shopping center** is a group of retail and other commercial establishments that are planned, developed, owned, and managed as a single property. After discussing the role of shopping center developers and management, each type of center is discussed.

By combining many stores at one location, developments attract more consumers to the shopping center than would be the case if the stores were at separate locations. The developer and shopping center management carefully select a set of retailers that are complementary to provide consumers with a comprehensive shopping experience at one, convenient location.

Lease agreements typically require that retailers in the center pay a portion of the common area maintenance (CAM) costs for the center according to the size of their store's space and/or sales volume and a retail fee based on sales. As mentioned earlier, the shopping center management group can place restrictions on the operating hours, signage, and even the type of merchandise sold in the stores.

Most shopping centers have at least one or two major retailers, referred to as **anchors,** such as Macy's, Walmart, or Kroger. These retailers are courted by the center's developer because they attract a significant number of consumers and consequently make the center more appealing for other retailers. To get these anchor retailers to locate in a center, developers frequently give them special deals, such as reduced lease costs.

These shopping centers are generally managed by a **shopping center property management firm,** which is a company that specializes in developing, owning, and/or managing shopping centers. Management of these shopping malls entails selecting and negotiating leases with retail tenants, maintaining the common areas, marketing the centers to attract consumers, and providing security. Retailing View 7.2 describes the evolution of Simon Properties—the largest retail management company in the world.

In Exhibit 7–2, the characteristics of the different types of shopping centers are outlined followed by a discussion of each type. As you can see, strip centers account for the vast majority of retail GLA. The growth rate in terms of the number of shopping centers is limited; however, the greatest growth has been lifestyle centers followed by power centers. Regional and super-regional enclosed malls have the highest sales per square foot.

LO3

Analyze the characteristics of the different types of shopping centers.

REFACT

There are 23.1 square feet of retail GLA per person in the United States.[8]

REFACT

Highland Park Shopping Village in Dallas, Texas, developed by Hugh Prather in 1931, was the first planned shopping center. Its stores were built with a unified image and managed under the control of a single owner.[9]

REFACT

There are more than 107,000 shopping centers in the United States and fewer than 7,000 in the European Union.[10]

Number, Sales per Square Foot, and Growth Rate of Shopping Centers   **EXHIBIT 7–2**

	Number	Total GLA (millions of square feet)	Percentage of Overall Shopping Center GLA	Growth in Number of Centers 2008–2011	Anchor GLA Percentage of Total Center GLA	Sales per Square Foot ($)	Growth Rate in Sales per Square Foot 2009–2011
Community, neighborhood, and convenience	101,630	4,981	67.8%	1.3%	30–60%	12.68	5.7%
Regional and super-regional enclosed malls	1,505	1,321	18.0	1.1%	40–70	21.20	1.7
Power centers	2,023	822	11.2	2.8%	N/A	10.85	4.1
Lifestyle center	396	126	1.7	6.9%	0–50	N/A	N/A
Outlet centers	334	71	1.0	1.9%	N/A	N/A	N/A
Theme/festival centers	201	27	0.4	1.2%	N/A	N/A	N/A

Source: eData, International Council of Shopping Centers.

190   SECTION II   Retailing Strategy

REFACT

In 1938, one of the first strip shopping centers, Silver Springs Shopping Center in Maryland, opened with a 1,000-seat movie theater, a grocery store anchor, and 19 additional stores.[11]

Convenience, Neighborhood, and Community Shopping Centers

Convenience, neighborhood, and **community shopping centers** (also called **strip shopping centers**) are attached rows of open-air stores, with onsite parking usually located in front of the stores. The most common layouts are linear, L-shaped, and inverted U-shaped. Historically, the term *strip center* has applied to the linear configuration.

Smaller centers (convenience and neighborhood centers) are 10,000 to 60,000 square feet and are typically anchored by a supermarket. They are designed for convenience shopping. These centers typically have 10 to 15 smaller retailers such as a bakery, dollar store, dry cleaner, florist, laundry center, barber shop, and mail service. The larger centers (community centers) are typically 25,000 to

7.2 RETAILING VIEW Simon Properties: The Largest Shopping Center Management Company in the World

Simon Properties owns, develops, and manages 326 retail real estate properties in the United States, including 151 regional malls, 58 premium outlet malls, and 66 lifestyle centers. This empire got its start in 1960, when Melvin Simon and Associates (MSA; the associates were Melvin's brothers Fred and Herbert) opened a shopping plaza in Bloomington, Indiana, followed quickly thereafter by four similar Indianapolis-area plazas. Melvin had previously established himself as a leasing agent in a local real estate firm, and MSA soon gained a reputation for managing its plazas well. Large tenants flocked to the retail centers; with big-name contracts with retailers such as Sears, Roebuck, MSA had easy access to bank financing for still more construction projects.

One of those projects was MSA's first enclosed mall, opened in the early 1960s. This format dominated its developments for years; then in the 1990s, MSA reinvented the retail real estate development market yet again by combining its malls with entertainment options. These multi-use centers attracted vast numbers of visitors, most of whom remained in the centers for hours. For example, The Forum Shops at Caesars Palace in Las Vegas sit between Caesars Palace and The Mirage, evoking an ancient Roman street. Visitors interact with animatronic statues, stop to rest at bubbling fountains, and enjoy simulated views of the awesome Mediterranean sky. In addition, MSA is responsible for perhaps the best known mall in America, that is, the Mall of America in Minnesota.

Today, the U.S. market allows for fewer new shopping centers, so Simon Properties—now led by Melvin's son David—aggressively pursues international growth and earns approximately 5.4 percent of its new operating income from international operations. In addition to investments in outlet centers in Japan, South Korea,

The Forum Shops at Caesars Palace in Las Vegas, developed and managed by Simon Properties, meld entertainment with shopping.

Malaysia, and Mexico, Simon Properties and its Paris-based Klépierre SA own nearly 300 shopping centers in 13 European countries. The global financial crisis has made Europe less attractive as a market for shopping center development; instead, Asia—particularly Shanghai, Mumbai, Dubai, and Tokyo—represent the most attractive regions with the greatest growth in rental rates.

Sources: "Buy Simon Property Group: Growth to Come from International Expansion," September 18, 2012; www.seekingalpha.com; "David Simon: Most Respected CEOs," and www.simon.com.

DISCUSSION QUESTION

What are the challenges facing Simon Properties as it pursues international growth opportunities?

50,000 square feet and are anchored by at least one big-box store such as a discount department store, an off-price retailer, or a category specialist.

The primary advantages of these centers are that they offer customers convenient locations and easy parking, and they have relatively low occupancy costs. The primary disadvantage is that smaller centers have a limited trade area due to their size, and they lack entertainment and restaurants to keep customers in the center for a longer time. In addition, there is no protection from the weather. As a result, neighborhood and community centers do not attract as many customers as do larger, enclosed malls.

National chains such as The Children's Place, Kohl's, Radio Shack, and Marshalls compete effectively against their rival mall-based retailers by offering the convenience of a neighborhood or community center. In these locations, they can offer lower prices, partly because of the lower occupancy cost, and their customers can drive right up to the door.[12]

Power Centers

Power centers are shopping centers that consist primarily of collections of big-box retail stores, such as full-line discount stores (Target), off-price stores (Marshalls), warehouse clubs (Costco), and category specialists (Lowe's, Staples, Michaels, Barnes & Noble, Best Buy, Sports Authority, and Toys "R" Us). Although these centers are open air, unlike traditional strip centers, power centers often consist of a collection of freestanding (unconnected) "anchor" stores and only a minimum number of smaller specialty store tenants. Many power centers are located near an enclosed shopping mall.

Power centers offer low occupancy costs and modest levels of consumer convenience and vehicular and pedestrian traffic. The growth in power centers reflects the growth of category specialists. Many power centers are now larger than regional malls and have trade areas as large as regional malls.

REFACT

The first power center was the 280 Metro Center in Colma, California, which opened in 1993.[13]

Enclosed Shopping Malls

Shopping malls are enclosed, climate-controlled, lighted shopping centers with retail stores on one or both sides of an enclosed walkway. Parking is usually provided around the perimeter of the mall. Shopping malls are classified as either **regional malls** (less than 800,000 square feet) or **super-regional malls** (more than 800,000 square feet). Super-regional centers are similar to regional centers, but because of their larger size, they have more anchors, specialty stores, and recreational opportunities and draw from a larger geographic area. They often are considered tourist attractions.

Enclosed shopping malls have several advantages over alternative locations. First, shopping malls attract many shoppers and have a large trade area because of the number of stores and the opportunity to combine shopping with an inexpensive form of entertainment. Older citizens get their exercise by walking the malls, and teenagers hang out and meet their friends, though some malls are restricting their admittance in the evenings. Thus, malls generate significant pedestrian traffic inside the mall and have sales per square foot almost twice that of power centers and strip centers. Second, customers don't have to worry about the weather, and thus malls are appealing places to shop during cold winters and hot summers. Third, mall management ensures a level of consistency that benefits all the tenants. For instance, most major malls enforce uniform hours of operation.

However, malls also have disadvantages. First, mall occupancy costs are higher than those of strip centers, freestanding sites, and most central business districts. For example, the occupancy cost (rent, common area maintenance, and taxes) for an enclosed mall is almost 140 percent greater than that for an open-air shopping center ($35.42 compared to $14.55 per square foot).[15] Second, some retailers may not like mall management's control of their operations,

REFACT

The first enclosed mall, called Southdale, opened in Edina, Minnesota (near Minneapolis), in 1956.[14]

REFACT

The two largest enclosed shopping malls in the United States, King of Prussia Mall in Pennsylvania and Mall of America in Bloomington, Minnesota, each have more than 2.7 million square feet of retail space and 400 stores. The largest mall in the world, New South China, has more than 7 million square feet of retail space and can accommodate more than 2,500 stores, but it is 99 percent vacant.[16]

such as strict rules governing window displays and signage. Third, competition within shopping centers can be intense. Several specialty and department stores might sell very similar merchandise and be located in close proximity. Fourth, freestanding locations, strip centers, lifestyle centers, and power centers are more convenient because customers can park in front of a store, go in and buy what they want, and go about their other errands. Fifth, some malls were built more than 40 years ago and have not been subject to any significant remodeling, so they appear run-down and unappealing to shoppers. Furthermore, these older malls are often located in areas with unfavorable demographics because the population has shifted from the near suburbs to outer suburbs. Sixth, the consolidation in the department store sector has decreased the number of potential anchor tenants and diminished the drawing power of enclosed malls. Finally, the growing sales through the Internet channel is cannibalizing sales through the store channel.

For these reasons, mall traffic and sales are declining. The last new mall was opened in 2006, and it is estimated that 10 percent of the 1,500 enclosed malls will close in the next three years (see www.deadmalls.com).[17] Most malls that close are razed; however, mall managers and developers are trying to redevelop failing malls. Some redevelopment projects become mixed-used spaces, incorporating unconventional tenants like government offices, churches, medical clinics, and satellite university campuses. Others seek to turn malls into one-stop sources for various services, not just fashionable apparel. A busy working mother visiting The Westside Pavilion mall in Los Angeles can thus drop off her kids for piano lessons at Music Stars & Masters on the second floor. During their lesson, she also can send an overnight package, get a haircut, have her purse repaired, and check out some books for the kids from the public library. If the kids do well with their lessons, mom might treat them to ice cream, too.[18]

Another approach for dealing with aging malls and the changing demographics in their trade areas is to tailor the offerings to the markets that do exist today. Older shopping centers such as Northridge Mall in northern California (built in 1972) can be repositioned to appeal to immigrant populations. In recent decades, the demographics of Monterey County have changed, producing a rich Latino culture in which approximately 75 percent of the population in the mall's trade area is of Latino heritage. Thus, the courtyard at the entryway to the mall hosts mariachi bands on weekend afternoons, while clowns and dancers provide family-friendly entertainment underneath colorful piñatas that have been suspended from the ceiling. To appeal to the large Roman Catholic population, the mall also offers services with religious themes, such as celebrations on Día de los Santos Reyes and shrines to the Virgen de Guadalupe Las Posadas. The idea is that the mall can be so welcoming that the local community views it more like a weekend home than a retail destination.[19]

While the percentage of mall retail sales has declined over the past 10 years, recently malls have experienced a slight increase in market share. This increase is due to the redevelopment efforts previously described plus an influx of exciting new tenants such as Aeropostale, Forever 21, Sephora, and H&M and the improved performance of anchors such as Macy's and Nordstrom.[20]

An increasing number of malls are using exciting stores like Forever 21 to attract younger customers.

Lifestyle Centers

Lifestyle centers are shopping centers that have an open-air configuration of specialty stores, entertainment, and restaurants, with design ambience and amenities such as fountains and street furniture. Lifestyle centers resemble the main streets in small towns, where people stroll from store to store, have lunch, and sit for a while on a park bench talking to friends. Thus, they cater to the "lifestyles" of consumers in their trade areas. Lifestyle centers are particularly attractive to specialty retailers.

People are attracted to lifestyle centers not only because of their shops and restaurants but also because of their outdoor attractions such as a pop-up fountain, ice cream carts, stilt walkers, balloon artists, magicians, face painters, concerts, and other events. Because lifestyle centers have some limited auto access, customers can be dropped off right in front of a store.

Because lifestyle centers are open air, bad weather can be an impediment to traffic. But some centers, like the Easton Town Center in Columbus, Ohio, thrive despite the climate.[21] When the weather is bad, tough Ohioans simply bundle up and take a stroll.

Due to the ease of parking, lifestyle centers are very convenient for shoppers, and the occupancy costs, like those of all open-air developments, are considerably lower than those for enclosed malls. But they typically have less retail space than enclosed malls and thus may attract fewer customers than enclosed malls. Many lifestyle centers are located near higher-income areas, so the higher purchases per visit compensate for the fewer number of shoppers. Finally, many lifestyle centers are part of larger, mixed-use developments, which are described in the next section.

Mixed-Use Developments

Mixed-use developments (MXDs) combine several different uses into one complex including retail, office, residential, hotel, recreation, or other functions. They are pedestrian-oriented and therefore facilitate a live-work-play environment.[22] They appeal to people who have had enough of long commutes to work and the social fragmentation of their neighborhoods and are looking for a lifestyle that gives them more time for the things they enjoy and an opportunity to live in a genuine community. In addition, MXDs are popular with retailers because they bring additional shoppers to their stores. They are also popular with governments, urban planners, developers, and environmentalists because they provide a pleasant, pedestrian environment and are an efficient use of space. For instance, land costs the

Mizner Park in Boca Raton, Florida, combines retail, residential, and entertainment offerings in one location with unique boutiques, eateries, music, movies, and art galleries conveniently located close to ocean-front apartments and condos.

same whether a developer builds a shopping mall by itself or an office tower on top of the mall or parking structure.

The Boca Mall, a 430,000-square-foot regional shopping mall in Boca Raton, Florida, opened in 1974. Decades later, the mall was plagued by two trends: population growth occurring elsewhere and competing malls that were attracting most of its patrons. The original anchors and many of the specialty stores departed. The Boca Mall was demolished and replaced with a mixed-use development called Mizner Park. Mizner Park has commercial office space located above the ground-floor retail space on one side of the street, and residential units sit above the retail space on the opposite side of the street.[23]

Outlet Centers

Outlet centers are shopping centers that contain mostly manufacturers' and retailers' outlet stores.[24] Some outlet centers have a strong entertainment component, including movie theaters and restaurants to keep customers on the premises longer. For example, the Outlets at Orange, in Orange, California, has a multiplex theater, with an IMAX movie theater; a children's play area; and Thrill It Fun Center.[25]

In the past, outlet stores sold damaged merchandise or excess production overruns. However, retailers have improved their demand forecasting, reducing the availability of production overruns. In addition, the availability of damaged goods has been reduced because these goods are weeded out before being shipped to the United States. Thus, 82 percent of products at outlet centers are made specifically for the outlets. The quality of these made-for-outlet products is not always the same quality as the branded merchandise sold in department or specialty stores.[26]

Typically, outlet centers are in remote locations. These remote locations offer lower costs and reduce the competition between the outlet stores and department and specialty stores offering the branded merchandise at full price.

Tourism represents 50 percent of the traffic generated for many outlet centers. Thus, many are located with convenient interstate access and close to popular tourist attractions. Some center developers actually organize bus tours to bring people hundreds of miles to their malls. As a result, the primary trade area for some outlet centers is 50 miles or more.

Outlet centers are also very popular in Europe, Japan, and China. Retailing View 7.3 describes an upscale outlet center with a unique theme in China.

Theme/Festival Centers

In **theme/festival centers,** a unifying theme generally is reflected in each individual store, both in their architecture and the merchandise they sell. This seemingly simple idea was introduced relatively late in the progression of retail ideas. In the late 1970s, a private developer took Boston's historic Faneuil Hall and reconceived it as a "festival marketplace." The goal was to attract multitudes of tourists and local visitors by being more fun and interesting than a basic suburban mall. The Faneuil Hall Marketplace resonates with a colonial history theme. Subsequent applications of the idea have included Baltimore's Inner Harbor and the Grand Canal Shops at the Venetian Hotel in Las Vegas.

When they first opened, some of these festival locations were successful at drawing visitors and reinvigorating urban centers suffering from crime and an exodus of population. But now, with invented themes, generic stores, and vigorous competition from other nearby retailers, such centers are viewed by many as tourist traps and are avoided by many locals. In 1985, the themed shopping center that opened on Pier 17 in Lower Manhattan promised to reinvigorate the South Street

Seaport, but today, its owners are seeking to tear down the three-story building to replace it with a different, upscale shopping center.[27]

Larger, Multiformat Developments—Omnicenters

New shopping center developments are combining enclosed malls, lifestyle centers, and power centers. Although centers of this type do not have an official name, they may be referred to as **omnicenters.**

Omnicenters represent a response to several trends in retailing, including the desire of tenants to lower CAM charges by spreading the costs among more tenants and to function inside larger developments that generate more pedestrian traffic and longer shopping trips. In addition, they reflect the growing tendency of consumers to **cross-shop,** which is a pattern of buying both premium and low-priced merchandise or patronizing expensive, status-oriented retailers and price-oriented retailers, as occurs when a customer shops at both Walmart and Nordstrom's. Time-scarce customers are also attracted to omnicenters because they can get everything they need in one place. For example, the 1.3 million-square-foot St. John's Town Center in Jacksonville, Florida, is divided into three components: a lifestyle center with a Dillard's department store anchor, a mini-power center anchored by Dick's Sporting Goods and a Barnes & Noble bookstore, and a Main Street with Cheesecake Factory and P.F. Chang's restaurants as anchors.[28]

RETAILING VIEW   For China's High-End Fashion Consumers, "Italy" Is Now Just a Bullet Train Away   7.3

Between Beijing and Tijanjin, you can find an Italian village—or at least a themed outlet mall that seeks to recreate one. With its luxury brand offerings, Florentia Village draws approximately 25,000 visitors daily, most of whom come to check out a sixteenth-century Italian village, with its narrow streets and piazzas. Once they have experienced a trip back in history, they can indulge in the purchase of Italian luxury brands, including Zegna, Armani, Ferragamo, Prada, Fendi, Bulgari, and Moncler. Near the "Colosseum," Tod's, Frette, Piquadro, and Brooks Brothers maintain their storefronts, whereas customers move through the "Grand Canal Promenade" to find Fendi, Gucci, and Prada.

China is both the largest source of counterfeits in the world and one of the biggest markets for luxury goods. The visitors who arrive at Florentia Village in the morning come by train. Wearing Western clothes, they are mostly young, evidently wealthy, and obviously Chinese. Later in the day, wealthy women wearing designer clothing drive their SUVs into the parking lots; they actively avoid the crowds of visitors on the weekends.

Although Chinese-owned outlet malls have existed for more than a decade, their success has been limited by their failure to attract top brands. These top brands worried about the effect of outlet sales on their brand images. The lesson learned is that an outlet mall's quality image is crucial; it must look like a location that sells luxury. Although "re-creating the Italian style has not been easy, with these kinds of projects, details make the difference. Asking Chinese workers to re-create Italian

The Florentia Village outlet center in China draws young and evidently wealthy customers from around the country.

style pink rock, pilasters, frames, and copper eaves was hard. But we did it."

Sources: Christopher Carothers, "A New Outlet for China's Consumerism," *The Wall Street Journal,* March 8, 2012; and Peter Foster, "China Builds Replica of Italian Town Called Florentia Village," *The Telegraph,* June 27, 2011.

DISCUSSION QUESTION

Why is the Florentia Village outlet center successful while Chinese-owned outlet centers have not been?

NONTRADITONAL LOCATIONS

LO4

Discuss nontraditional retail locations.

Pop-up stores, stores within a store, kiosks, and airports are other location alternatives for many retailers. Retailing View 7.4 describes some of Subway's nontraditional locations and the accommodations it needed to make to secure those locations.

Pop-Up Stores and Other Temporary Locations

Pop-up stores are stores in temporary locations that focus on new products or a limited group of products. These "stores" have been around for centuries as individuals sold merchandise on city streets and at festivals or concerts, such as the Newport Jazz Festival, weekend crafts fairs, or farmers' markets. For instance, in New York's Columbus Circle, 100 vendors sell a variety of gifts from yogawear to handmade glass jewelry. Cities around the United States generally welcome these temporary retailers because they bring people and money to areas, creating excitement. Local retailers, who pay high rents, aren't necessarily so enthusiastic because some of the temporary retailers sell competing merchandise.

7.4   RETAILING VIEW   Subway Goes to Church

In 2011, Subway Restaurants passed McDonald's to become the largest restaurant chain in the world, in terms of number of locations. Subway has achieved this rapid growth partly by opening stores in nontraditional locations: an appliance store in Brazil, a California automobile showroom, a Goodwill store in South Carolina, a riverboat in Germany. One of the more remarkable locations is its One World Trade Center construction site in New York City, where the restaurant gets hoisted up to the next level as each floor of the 105-story building is completed. As the chain's chief development officer puts it, "We're continually looking at just about any opportunity for someone to buy a sandwich, wherever that might be. The closer we can get to the customer, the better." Noting the nearly 8,000 Subways in unusual locations, he adds, "The non-traditional is becoming traditional."

With its menu of sandwiches, Subway has an easier time opening in unusual venues because it has a simpler kitchen than traditional fast-food restaurants, which require frying and grilling equipment. Hospitals and religious facilities have a favorable attitude toward Subway because it promotes its sandwiches as a fresher, healthier alternative to traditional fast food.

Subway often has to make special accommodations when opening stores in nontraditional locations, though. For example, the first of many kosher Subway stores opened in the Jewish Community Center of Cleveland in 2006, and Subway is now the largest kosher chain in the United States. The kosher stores still have steak and cheese subs, except the cheese is a soy-based product. In observance of the Jewish Sabbath, these restaurants are closed on Friday afternoon and all day Saturday.

When a Subway opened in the True Bethel Baptist Church of Buffalo, New York, in a low-income area of town, the franchisee worked closely with church leaders. To support the congregation and create jobs, church leaders had approached several fast-food franchisers about

To maintain growth, Subway has opened outlets in nontraditional locations like this one at a Baptist church in Buffalo, New York.

opening a franchise in a corner of the church. Subway was the only chain that was flexible enough toward the space available and the operating hours to accommodate the church. The chain agreed to waive its requirement of a Subway sign on the outside of the building and created a parking pattern to keep restaurant traffic from displacing churchgoers during services.

Sources: Julie Jargon, "Unusual Store Locations Fuel Subway's Growth," *The Wall Street Journal*, March 10, 2011; and Alan J. Liddle, "10 Non-Traditional Subway Restaurants," *Nation's Restaurants*, July 26, 2011.

DISCUSSION QUESTION

What are the advantages and disadvantages to Subway's nontraditional location strategy?

Due to the recession and retail industry consolidation, shopping center vacancies have increased and occupancy costs have decreased. Retailers and manufacturers are opening pop-up stores in these vacant locations. Pop-up stores are particularly attractive to retailers with highly seasonal sales such as Toys "R" Us. Toys "R" Us has been experimenting with pop-ups for several years. In 2009, Toys "R" Us had 90 "Express" pop-up stores, and in 2010 it increased the number dramatically to 600. Opening, managing, and closing that large number of stores strained the management capabilities of the company. So, the company only opened 160 pop-ups in 2011. In 2012, it complemented its own pop-ups with pop-ups inside Macy's stores. The temporary Toys "R" Us units inside 24 Macy's stores were leased from October 15 through January 15. Each pop-up is roughly 1,500 square feet and includes items such as dolls, action figures, and puzzles.[29]

This Kate Spade pop-up store is an attractive temporary location for the high-fashion retailer/designer.

Cities have adopted the pop-up store concept to revitalizing their urban neighborhoods. In Oakland, California, the Pop-Up Hood concept grants six months' worth of rent-free space to independent retailers if they agree to test their innovative retail concepts in designated parts of the city.[30]

Store-within-a-Store

Store-within-a-store locations involve an agreement in which a retailer rents a part of the retail space in a store operated by another independent retailer. The host retailer basically "sublets" the space to the store-within retailer.[31] The store-within retailer manages the assortment, inventory, personnel, and systems and delivers a percentage of the sales or profits to the host. Grocery stores have been experimenting with the store-within-a-store concept for years with service providers such as coffee bars, banks, film processors, and medical clinics. Starbucks operates cafés in many retail stores.

Department stores in the United States have traditionally leased some space to other retailers, such as retailers of beauty salons, fine jewelry, and furs. However, most department stores in Europe, Japan, and China are a collection of store-within-a-store retailers. For example, Modern Plaza, a luxury department store in Beijing, "rents" all of the space in its store to a set of luxury brands, and the brands operate a store within Modern Plaza. Thus, Modern Plaza and European department stores perform the role of mall managers rather than retail stores.

In contrast, JCPenney's relationship with Sephora is more of a partnership. Sephora designs and develops the merchandise, and JCPenney is responsible for managing the sales associates and inventory sold in the Sephora boutique within a JCPenney store. The sales are made through JCPenney's POS system, and customers can use their JCPenney card when shopping in the Sephora boutique. The Sephora stores do not have a separate entrance, so there is some sense of creating a cohesive JCPenney experience.[32]

JCPenney has a partnership with Sephora using a store-within-a-store strategy.

Stores-within-a-store can be mutually beneficial to the store within and the host retailer. The store within gets an excellent location with high pedestrian traffic of customers in its target market. The host retailer generates increased revenue from the space and enhances its brand image. For example, JCPenney's relationship with Sephora enables it to offer a fashionable brand that it would not be able to offer normally through its channels. Similarly, Banfield Veterinarian services within PetSmart stores offers pet owners a true one-stop shop.[33] However, there are risks associated with this arrangement. Over time, the host or store within could have conflicting, rather than synergistic, target markets and/or brand images.

Merchandise Kiosks

Merchandise kiosks are small selling spaces, typically located in the walkways of enclosed malls, airports, college campuses, or office building lobbies. Some are staffed and resemble a miniature store or cart that could be easily moved. Others are twenty-first-century versions of vending machines, such as the Apple kiosks that sell iPods and other high-volume Apple products.

For mall operators, kiosks are an opportunity to generate rental income in otherwise vacant space and offer a broad assortment of merchandise for visitors. They also can generate excitement from retailers like national cell phone provider Sprint to smaller niche products like Israeli Dead Sea cosmetics, leading to additional sales for the entire mall. Moreover, mall kiosks can be changed quickly to match seasonal demand.

When planning the location of kiosks in a mall, operators are sensitive to their regular mall tenants' needs. They are careful to avoid kiosks that block any storefronts, create an incompatible image, or actually compete directly with permanent tenants by selling similar merchandise.

Airports

A high-pedestrian area that has become popular with national retail chains is airports.[34] Passengers arrive earlier for their flights than they did in the past, leaving them more time to shop. In addition, a cutback in airline food service has more people seeking sustenance in the airport. As a result, sales per square foot at airport malls are often much higher than at regular mall stores. However, rents are higher too. Also, costs can be higher—hours are longer, and because the location is often inconvenient for workers, the businesses have to pay higher wages. The best airport locations tend to be ones where there are many connecting flights (Atlanta and Frankfurt) and international flights (New York's Kennedy and London's Heathrow) because customers have downtime to browse through stores. The best-selling products are those that make good gifts, necessities, and easy-to-pack items. However, airport sales of consumer electronics accessories are increasing. The largest retailer of electronics at airports is InMotion Entertainment that rents DVD players and sells a wide variety of electronics and accessories in its 68 stores at 33 airports in the United States.

REFACT

Passengers spend an average of 136 minutes at Kennedy International Airport in New York from arrival to boarding.[35]

LOCATION AND RETAIL STRATEGY

LO5

Match the locations to the retailer's strategy.

The selection of a location type reinforces the retailer's strategy. Thus, the location-type decision is consistent with the shopping behavior and size of the target market and the retailer's positioning in its target market. Each of these factors is discussed next.

Shopping Behavior of Consumers in Retailer's Target Market

A critical factor affecting the type of location that consumers select to visit is the shopping situation in which they are involved. Three types of shopping situations are convenience shopping, comparison shopping, and specialty shopping.

Convenience Shopping   When consumers are engaged in **convenience shopping** situations, they are primarily concerned with minimizing their effort to get the product or service they want. They are relatively insensitive to price and indifferent about which brands to buy. Thus, they don't spend much time evaluating different brands or retailers; they simply want to make the purchase as quickly and easily as possible. Examples of convenience shopping situations are getting a cup of coffee during a work break, buying gas for a car, or buying milk for breakfast in the morning.

Retailers targeting customers involved in convenience shopping, such as quick service restaurants, convenience stores, and gas stations, usually locate their stores close to where their customers are and make it easy for them to access the location, park, and find what they want. Thus, convenience stores, drugstores, fast-food restaurants, supermarkets, and full-line discount stores are generally located in neighborhood strip centers and freestanding locations.

Comparison Shopping   Consumers involved in **comparison shopping** situations are more involved in the purchase decision. They have a general idea about the type of product or service they want, but they do not have a well-developed preference for a brand or model. Because the purchase decisions are more important to them, they seek information and are willing to expend effort to compare alternatives. Consumers typically engage in this type of shopping behavior when buying furniture, appliances, apparel, consumer electronics, and hand tools.

Furniture retailers, for instance, often locate next to one another to create a "furniture row." In New York City, a number of retailers selling houseplants and flowers are all located in Chelsea between 27th and 30th Streets on 6th Avenue, and diamond dealers are located on West 47th Street between 5th and 6th Avenues. These competing retailers locate near one another because doing so facilitates comparison shopping and thus attracts many customers to the locations.

Enclosed malls offer the same benefits to consumers interested in comparison shopping for fashionable apparel. Thus, department stores and specialty apparel retailers locate in enclosed malls for the same reason that houseplant retailers locate together on 6th Avenue in New York City. By co-locating in the same mall, they attract more potential customers interested in comparison shopping for fashionable apparel. Even though the enclosed mall might be inconvenient compared with a freestanding location, comparison shopping is easier after the customers have arrived.

Category specialists offer the same benefit of comparison shopping as a collection of co-located specialty stores like those described previously. Rather than going to a set of small hardware stores when comparison shopping for an electric drill, consumers know they can get almost anything they need to fix or build a house in either Home Depot or Lowe's. Thus, category specialists are **destination stores,** places where consumers will go even if it is inconvenient, just like enclosed malls are destination locations for fashionable-apparel comparison shopping. Category specialists locate in power centers, primarily to reduce their costs and create awareness of their location and secondarily to benefit from multiple retailers that attract more consumers and the resulting potential for cross-shopping. Basically, power centers are a collection of destination stores.

Specialty Shopping   When consumers go **specialty shopping,** they know what they want and will not accept a substitute. They are brand and/or retailer loyal and will pay a premium or expend extra effort, if necessary, to get exactly what they want. Examples of these shopping occasions include buying organic vegetables, a luxury automobile, or a high-end road or mountain bike. The retailers they patronize when specialty shopping also are destination stores. Thus, consumers engaged in specialty shopping are willing to travel to an inconvenient location. Having a convenient location is not as important for retailers selling unique merchandise or services.

Density of Target Market

A second, but closely related, factor that affects the retailer's choice of location type is the density of the retailer's target market in relation to the location. A good location has many people in the target market who are drawn to it. Thus, a convenience store located in a CBD can be sustained by customers living or working in fairly close proximity to the store. Similarly, a comparison shopping store located next to a Walmart is a potentially good location because Walmart draws lots of customers from a very large area. It is not as important to have high customer density near a store that sells specialty merchandise because people are willing to search out this type of merchandise. A Porsche dealer, for instance, need not be near other car dealers or in close proximity to its target market, because those seeking this luxury car will drive to wherever the dealer may be.

Uniqueness of Retail Offering

Finally, the convenience of their locations is less important for retailers with unique, differentiated offerings than for retailers with an offering similar to other retailers. For example, Bass Pro Shops provides a unique merchandise assortment and store atmosphere. Customers will travel to wherever the store is located, and its location will become a destination.

SOCIETAL AND LEGAL CONSIDERATIONS

LO6

Review the societal and legal considerations in selecting locations.

Societal and legal considerations often restrict where retailers can locate and operate their stores. These restrictions reflect the general concern that many communities have with urban sprawl, and more specifically with the opening of big-box retail stores in their communities. These restrictions on store location are often implemented through local zoning ordinances.

While there are relatively few restrictions on where stores can be located in the United States, location decisions are more restricted in other areas of the world. For example, western Europe and Asia have higher population densities and more people living and shopping in urban environments. Thus, less space is available for retailing, and the space that is available is costly. In addition, many western European countries restrict retailing to specific areas and then restrict the sizes of the stores that can be built.

In this section, we discuss the nature of the restrictions, reasons communities impose these restrictions, and the impact of these restrictions on society.

Urban Sprawl

Urban sprawl is the increased expansion of residential and shopping center development in suburban and rural areas outside of their respective urban centers. Before World War II, the downtown urban area was a community's commercial hub. Consumers shopped at local businesses downtown. The presence of offices, banks, and libraries guaranteed traffic in the downtown center. Downtown also was an important part of an area's social life. On weekends, people met to window shop, eat at restaurants, and go to the movies.

The interstate highway system and growth of the suburbs changed the way Americans live and work. With improved transportation, people could travel longer distances to work or shop. As a result, many downtown retailers went out of business. As customers and sales dwindled, property values and tax revenues dropped. Historic buildings were neglected and storefronts boarded up, reinforcing the decline of downtown areas.

In addition to the decline of the downtown, some other negative consequences of urban sprawl are congestion and air pollution due to increased auto-

Main Street locations in the U.K. and in U.S. towns face intense competition from hypermarkets located on the outskirts of the towns.

mobile travel, loss of farmland, concentrated poverty, and racial and economic segregation. On the other hand, some desirable outcomes of this migration to the suburbs are better housing opportunities, public schools, and less crime.[36]

The European Union is very concerned about urban sprawl and the effects of big-box retailers locating outside the city limits. The EU is trying to restrain the growth of big-box retailers, limiting their size and subsidizing the redevelopment of inner city (called the High Street in the United Kingdom) to help local retailers compete. Europe has greater population density and less space than the United States, and stricter planning and greenbelt laws provide a sharp division between town and country. Suburbs are few, thus minimizing urban sprawl. But preserving the environment comes at a cost for Europe. The limits on out-of-town, big-box retailing reduce competition and retailing efficiency, causing higher prices.[37]

Opposition to Big-Box Retailers

Retailers that operate big-box stores like Walmart, Target, Costco, and Home Depot often meet with a great deal of resistance when they plan to build a store in a community. Many people vehemently oppose big-box stores entering their community. The opponents of the store openings argue that these retailers sell merchandise at lower prices that drive local retailers out of business; do not provide a living wage for employees; hire part-time workers to avoid providing health insurance benefits; and achieve their low prices by manufacturing merchandise outside the United States, thus contributing to the decline of U.S. jobs.

Discussions between big-box stores and local communities continue to occur throughout the United States and other countries. Some communities have allowed for the building of such stores when the retailers agree to pay employees a set wage or fund low-cost housing for employees. Zoning, discussed in the following section, is one method used by local communities to restrict big-box retailers.

Zoning

Local governments in the United States use **zoning** to regulate land uses in specific areas to prevent any interference with existing uses by residents or businesses, as well as encourage the preservation of a community's sense of identity. Thus, zoning ordinances might keep McDonald's from opening a franchise in a residential neighborhood. In other nations, such as France and Germany, zoning regulations and planning are enforced at national or state levels instead of locally.

EXHIBIT 7–3   Zoning Map for a Small Town

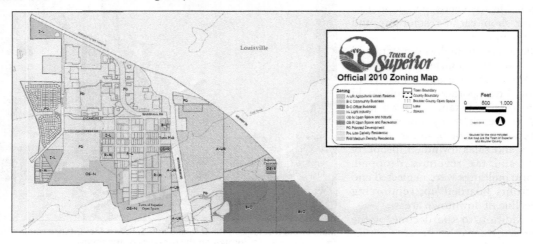

In urban areas, zoning ordinances often specify five categories of activities that are acceptable in a certain region or on a particular site: residential, commercial, mixed residential and commercial, industrial, or special. In addition, most zoning regulations include detailed density limitations, such as those indicating whether an area may host high-density high rises or instead is limited to low-density, single-family housing. Noting that exceptions can exist, most ordinances denote the conditions—usually hardship-related—that must be met for variances to be granted.

Exhibit 7–3 describes the zoning restrictions in Superior, Wisconsin. These zoning maps are typically developed by a planning commission and approved by the city council. Note that the areas dedicated for retailing shown in red are adjacent to the two major highways. Some areas (shown in green) are dedicated open spaces and residential areas are shown in yellow.

Building Codes

Building codes are legal restrictions that specify the type of building, signs, size and type of parking lot, and so forth, that can be used at a particular location. Some building codes require a certain-size parking lot or a particular architectural design. In Santa Fe, New Mexico, for instance, building codes require that buildings keep a traditional mud stucco (adobe) style.

Signs   Restrictions on the use of signs can affect a particular site's desirability. Sign sizes and styles may be restricted by building codes, zoning ordinances, or even the shopping center management group. At the Bal Harbour Shops in North Miami Beach, for example, all signs (even sale signs) must be approved by the shopping center management group before implementation by each individual retailer.

Licensing Requirements   Licensing requirements may vary in different parts of a region. For instance, some Dallas neighborhoods are dry, meaning no alcoholic beverages can be sold; in other areas, only wine and beer can be sold. Such restrictions can affect retailers other than restaurants and bars. For instance, a theme/festival shopping center that restricts the use of alcoholic beverages may find its clientele limited at night.

Legal issues such as those mentioned here can discourage a retailer from pursuing a particular site. These restrictions aren't always permanent, however. Although difficult, time consuming, and possibly expensive, lobbying efforts and court battles can change these legal restrictions.

SUMMARY

LO1 **Describe the types of retail locations available to retailers.**

Store location decisions are important decisions for a retailer because location is typically one of the most influential considerations in a customer's store-choice decision. Location decisions also have strategic implications because they can be used to develop a sustainable competitive advantage and location decisions are risky.

LO2 **Review the types of unplanned locations.**

Two basic types of location are unplanned (freestanding and urban sites) and planned (shopping centers). Unplanned locations do not have centralized management that determines what stores will be in a development, where the specific stores will be located, and how they will be operated. The three types of unplanned retail locations are freestanding sites, urban and Main Street locations. Freestanding locations are convenient for customers and have high vehicular traffic and visibility, modest occupancy costs, and few restrictions. But freestanding sites are higher in cost and have smaller trade areas. In general, urban locations have lower occupancy costs than enclosed malls; vehicular traffic is limited, and parking problems reduce consumer convenience.

LO3 **Analyze the characteristics of the different types of shopping centers.**

By combining many stores at one location, shopping centers attract more consumers to the center than would be the case if the stores were at separate locations. The developer and shopping center management carefully select a set of retailers that are complementary to provide consumers with a comprehensive shopping experience at one, convenient location. Each of the types of shopping centers has its advantages and disadvantages. Many central business

districts, inner-city, and Main Street locations have become more viable options than they were in the past because of gentrification of the areas, tax incentives, and lack of competition. There also are a wide variety of shopping center types for retailers. They can locate in a strip or power center; an enclosed mall; or a lifestyle, theme/festival, or outlet center.

LO4 **Discuss nontraditional retail locations.**

Pop-up stores, stores-within-a-store, kiosks, and airports are other location alternatives for many retailers. Pop-up stores are particularly attractive to retailers with highly seasonal sales. Store-within-a-store locations involve an agreement in which a retailer rents a part of the retail space in a store operated by another independent retailer. These locations are mutually beneficial to the host and store within.

LO5 **Match the locations to the retailer's strategy.**

The selection of a location type reinforces the retailer's strategy. Thus, the location-type decision is consistent with the shopping behavior and size of the target market and the retailer's positioning in its target market. Different shopping locations are more appropriate for consumers engaged in three types of customer shopping situations: convenience shopping, comparison shopping, and specialty shopping.

LO6 **Review the societal and legal considerations in selecting locations.**

Societal and legal considerations often restrict the locations and operations of standalone stores and shopping centers. These restrictions reflect the general concern that many communities have with urban sprawl and, more specifically, with the opening of big-box retail stores in their communities. Shopping center developers and retailers often need to deal with zoning ordinances before they open stores in a community.

KEY TERMS

anchor, *189*
building codes, *202*
central business district (CBD), *185*
common area maintenance (CAM), *184*
community shopping center, *190*
comparison shopping, *199*
convenience shopping center, *190*
convenience shopping, *199*
cross-shop, *195*
destination store, *199*

freestanding site, *185*
gentrification, *186*
gross leasable area (GLA), *184*
inner city, *186*
lifestyle center, *193*
Main Street, *188*
merchandise kiosk, *198*
mixed-use development (MXD), *193*
neighborhood shopping center, *190*
omnicenter, *195*

outlet center, *194*
outparcel, *185*
planned location, *184*
pop-up store, *196*
power center, *191*
regional mall, *191*
shopping center, *189*
shopping center property management firm, *189*
shopping mall, *191*
specialty shopping, *200*

GET OUT AND DO IT!

1. **CONTINUING CASE ASSIGNMENT** Interview the manager of the shopping center that contains the retailer you selected for the Continuing Assignment. Write a report summarizing which retailers the shopping center manager thinks are his or her best tenants and why they are valued. How does the manager rate the retailer you have selected? What criteria does he or she use?

2. **INTERNET EXERCISE** Go to the web page for Faneuil Hall Marketplace at www.faneuilhallmarketplace.com and the online site for CocoWalk at www.cocowalk.net. What kinds of centers are these? List their similarities and differences. Who is the target market for each of these retail locations?

3. **GO SHOPPING** Go to your favorite shopping center, and analyze the tenant mix. Do the tenants appear to complement one another? What changes would you make in the tenant mix to increase the overall performance of the center?

4. **GO SHOPPING** Visit a lifestyle center. What tenants are found in this location? Describe the population characteristics around this center. How far would people drive to shop at this lifestyle center? What other types of retail locations does this lifestyle center compete with?

5. **INTERNET EXERCISE** Go to the home page for Simon Property Group, www.simon.com/about_simon/our_business/default.aspx, and read about the businesses that Simon is in. What is the difference between their businesses?

6. **INTERNET EXERCISE** Go to the home page of your favorite enclosed mall, and describe the mall in terms of the following characteristics: number of anchor stores, number and categories of specialty stores, number of sit-down and quick-service restaurants, and types of entertainment offered. What are the strengths and weaknesses of this assortment of retailers? What are the unique features of this particular mall?

7. **GO SHOPPING** Visit a power center that contains a Target, Staples, Sports Authority, Home Depot, or other category specialists. What other retailers are in the same location? How is this mix of stores beneficial to both shoppers and retailers?

8. **INTERNET EXERCISE** Go to www.pbs.org/itvs/storewars/. This site contains information about the Ashland town council's decision to allow Walmart to open a store in Ashland, Virginia. Summarize the pros and cons of allowing Walmart to open a store in town. Were you surprised by the town council's decision? Why or why not?

DISCUSSION QUESTIONS AND PROBLEMS

1. Why is store location such an important decision for retailers?

2. Pick your favorite store. Describe the advantages and disadvantages of its current location, given its store type and target market.

3. Home Depot typically locates in either a power center or a freestanding site. What are the strengths of each location for this home improvement retailer?

4. As a consultant to 7-Eleven convenience stores, American Eagle Outfitters, and Porsche of America, what would you say is the single most important factor in choosing a site for these three very different types of stores?

5. Retailers are locating in shopping centers and freestanding locations in central business districts that have suffered decay. As a result, these areas are rejuvenating, a process known as gentrification. Some people have questioned the ethical and social ramifications of this process. Discuss the benefits and detriments of gentrification.

6. Staples, Office Max, and Office Depot all have strong multichannel strategies. How do competition and the Internet affect their strategies for locating stores?

7. In many malls, quick-service food retailers are located together in an area known as a food court. What are the advantages and disadvantages of this location for the food retailers? What is the new trend for food retailers in the shopping environment?

8. Why would a Payless ShoeSource store locate in a neighborhood shopping center instead of a regional shopping mall?

9. How does the mall near your home or university combine the shopping and entertainment experiences?

10. Consider a big city that has invested in an urban renaissance. What components of the gentrification project attract both local residents and visiting tourists to spend time shopping, eating, and sightseeing in this location?

SUGGESTED READINGS

Brooks, Charles, Patrick J. Kaufmann, and Donald R. Lichtenstein. "Trip Chaining Behavior in Multi-Destination Shopping Trips: A Field Experiment and Laboratory Replication." *Journal of Retailing* 84, no. 1 (2008), pp. 29–38.

Curtiss, Donald L. *Operation Shopping Centers; Guidebook to Effective Management & Promotion.* Ulan Press, 2011.

Gibbs, Robert J. *Principles of Urban Retail Planning and Development.* New York: Wiley, 2012.

International Council of Shopping Centers. *Winning Shopping Center Designs,* 35th ed. New York: ICSC, 2012.

Kim, Jung-Hwan, and Rodney Runyan. "Where Did All the Benches Go? The Effects of Mall Kiosks on Perceived Retail Crowding." *International Journal of Retail & Distribution Management* 39, no. 2 (2011), pp. 130–143.

Roslin, Rosmimah, and Mohd Herwina Rosnan. "Location as a Strategic Retail Decision: The Case of the Retail Cooperative." *International Journal of Commerce and Management* 22, no. 2 (2012), pp. 152–158.

Ruoh-Nan, Yan, and Molly Eckman. "Are Lifestyle Centres Unique? Consumers' Perceptions across Locations." *International Journal of Retail & Distribution Management* 37, no. 1 (2009), pp. 24–42.

Schewel, Laura B., and Lee J. Schipper. "Shop 'Till We Drop: A Historical and Policy Analysis of Retail Goods Movement in The United States." *Environmental Science and Technology* 46, no. 18 (2012), pp. 9813–9821.

Yiu, C. Y., and Sys Xu. "A Tenant-Mix Model for Shopping Malls," *European Journal of Marketing,* 46, no. 3 (2012), pp. 234–256.

Retail Site Location

EXECUTIVE BRIEFING
Brenden O'Brien, Senior Real Estate Manager
Walgreen Co.

In May 2006, I graduated from Miami University (Oxford, Ohio). I competed on their varsity swimming and diving team while double majoring in marketing and entrepreneurship. During my senior year in college, I was fortunate to receive a job offer from Walgreens in its corporate real estate department. Growing up on the North Shore of Chicago, I never thought I would join corporate America; however, my career continues to be an exceptionally rewarding learning experience.

Our locations are critical strategic assets, and we take a long-term perspective in developing each and every store. A team comprised of market planning and research, a market VP from operations, and a real estate manager evaluate new opportunities. Accessing a vast amount of collected data in a geographic information system, the team identifies ideal target locations for our stores. Walgreens strives to lock down the best real estate deal in each neighborhood, which generally equates to the intersection with the most amount of traffic. Because we target the best locations for future stores, the real estate is not easy to put under contract nor are all locations commercially feasible. Sometimes the real estate prices are so high that the economics become cost prohibitive. To finalize each and every opportunity,

real estate managers must present them for approval to the Walgreens real estate committee. This committee is comprised of a panel of executives at corporate headquarters. Many of the highest-level executives in Walgreens are involved in the final decision, which includes the location, the economics, and a specific plan for each store. I am amazed that after only six years from college graduation, I am interacting with corporate-level executives in one of the 10 largest retail companies in the world.

Walgreens gives me the opportunity to be creative, develop new ideas, and also learn from others in the company. For example, one of my most exciting projects was developing a location directly across from SeaWorld on International Drive in Orlando, Florida. International Drive attracts a massive number of tourists who flock to the area to spend money at stores, restaurants, and attractions. Walgreens already had five successful stores on International Drive; however, I negotiated a deal to include a nontraditional store at an underserved fabulous location. We designed the exterior of the store to include unique architectural elements and designed the interior of the store to include special features

CHAPTER 8

LEARNING OBJECTIVES

LO1 Summarize the factors considered in locating a number of stores.

LO2 Review the characteristics of a particular site.

LO3 Understand how retailers analyze the trade area for a site.

LO4 Determine the forecasted sales for a new store location.

LO5 Illustrate the site selection process.

LO6 Explain the different types and terms of leases.

such as a curved ceiling, in order to enhance the customer experience. The merchandise is uniquely designed for tourists with an emphasis on souvenirs, an expanded food offering, and an assortment of health and beauty aids.

To be successful in any endeavor, you need to stay ahead of the curve by continuing to learn.

Walgreens provides an atmosphere that supports my interest in developing my knowledge in real estate (my job), finance, and business in general. The company was very supportive of my efforts to complete the course work and examinations required to become a certified commercial investment member, or CCIM.

Chapter 5 emphasized the strategic importance of location decisions. Although location decisions can create strategic advantage, like all strategic decisions, they are also risky because they involve a significant commitment of resources. Opening a store at a site often involves committing to a lease of five years or more or purchasing land and building a store. If the store's performance is below expectations, the retailer may not be able to recover its investment easily by having another party move in and assume the lease or buy the building.

Chapter 7 reviewed the different types of locations available to retailers and why certain types of retailers gravitate toward particular locations. This chapter takes a closer look at how retailers choose specific sites to locate their stores.

Selecting retail locations involves the analysis of a large amount of data and the use of sophisticated statistical models. Because most retailers make these decisions infrequently, it is not economical for them to employ full-time real estate analysts with state-of-the-art skills. Thus, small retailers often use firms that provide the geographic and demographic data and consulting services needed to evaluate specific sites. However, there continues to be an element of art in making these location decisions.

This chapter reviews the steps retailers go through in selecting their store locations and negotiating leases. The first part of the chapter examines the factors retailers consider when selecting a general area for locating stores and determining the number of stores to operate in each area. Then this chapter reviews different approaches used to evaluate specific sites and estimate the expected sales if and when a store is located at that site. Finally, the chapter looks at the various terms that are negotiated when a retailer commits to leasing space for its store.

EVALUATING AREAS FOR LOCATIONS AND DETERMINING THE NUMBER OF STORES IN AN AREA

LO1

Summarize the factors considered in locating a number of stores.

The first part of this section discusses the areas retailers typically analyze when making location decisions, and the second section reviews factors retailers consider when evaluating these areas for locating stores and determining the number of stores to put in an area.

Metropolitan Statistical Area

Areas that retailers consider for locating stores might be countries, areas within a country such as a province in France or a state in the United States, particular cities, or areas within cities. In the United States, retailers often focus their analysis on a **metropolitan statistical area (MSA)** because consumers tend to shop within an MSA, and media coverage and demographic data for analyzing location opportunities often are organized by MSA.

An MSA is a core urban area containing a population of more than 50,000 inhabitants, together with adjacent communities that have a high degree of economic and social integration with the core community. For example, many people in an MSA commute to work in the central business district but live in the surrounding areas. An MSA can consist of one or several counties and usually is named after the major urban area in the MSA. For example, the Cincinnati-Middleton MSA consists of 15 counties (3 in Indiana, 7 in Kentucky, and 5 in Ohio) with a population of 2,172,191; the Missoula, Montana, MSA consists of one county with a population of 110,138.

In contrast, a **micropolitan statistical area (μSA)** is somewhat removed from larger U.S. cities, often by up to 100 miles. Although they lack big cities' pull and economic significance, these notable population centers often are responsible for substantial production capabilities and provide reasonable housing accommodations for many residents. The designation refers to the core population of a central town, so regardless of their name, a micropolitan area could be larger than a metropolitan area. The largest μSA is Seaford, Delaware, with a population of 200,330.[3]

REFACT

California has the most shopping centers (6,379) and Wyoming has the fewest (55).[1]

REFACT

There are 366 MSAs and 576 μSAs in the United States.[2]

Considerations in Evaluating Store Locations

The best areas for locating stores are those that generate the highest long-term profits for a retailer. Some factors affecting the long-term profit generated by stores that should be considered when evaluating an area include: (1) the economic conditions, (2) competition, (3) the strategic fit of the area's population with the retailer's target market, and (4) the costs of operating stores (see Exhibit 8–1). Note that these factors are similar to those that retailers consider when evaluating an investment in a new business growth opportunity or entry into a foreign market, as discussed in Chapter 5.

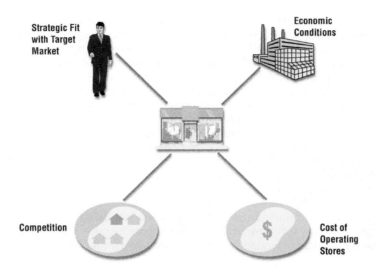

EXHIBIT 8–1
Factors Affecting the Attractiveness of an Area for Locating Stores

Economic Conditions   Because locations involve a commitment of resources over a long time horizon, it is important to examine an area's level and growth of population and employment. A large, fully employed population means high purchasing power and high levels of retail sales.

But population and employment growth alone aren't enough to ensure a strong retail environment in the future. Retail location analysts need to determine how long such growth will continue and how it will affect demand for merchandise sold in the stores. For instance, if growth is not diversified in various industries, the area may be unattractive because of extreme cyclical trends. The economies of some Rust Belt cities like Flint, Michigan, experience greater peaks and valleys because of their dependence on specific industries such as automobiles.

Also, it is useful to determine which areas are growing quickly and why. For instance, the east side of Seattle, Washington, has become a desirable retail location because of its proximity to Microsoft's corporate headquarters. But the performance of these retail locations is linked to the financial performance of Microsoft.

In most cases, areas where the population is large and growing are preferable to those with declining populations. However, some retailers, such as Subway, often go into new strip shopping centers with few nearby households with the anticipation that the surrounding suburban area will eventually be built up enough to support the stores.

Competition   The level of competition in an area affects the demand for a retailer's merchandise. Walmart's early success was based on a location strategy of opening stores in small towns with little competition. It offered consumers in small towns quality merchandise at low prices. Previously, rural consumers either shopped in small stores with limited assortments or drove to larger towns.

Although they once were viewed as undesirable areas, inner-city neighborhoods today host many full-service restaurant chains, including Chili's, Denny's, IHOP, and so forth. For such casual restaurants, underserved urban locations offer some strong attractions, including minimal competition levels; a large, readily accessible labor force; and, in some neighborhoods, a surrounding market of customers with high disposable incomes.

Retailing View 8.1 describes the success realized by Stage Stores targeting small towns with limited competition for fashionable apparel.

Strategic Fit   Economic conditions and competition alone don't tell the whole story. The area needs to have consumers who are in the retailer's target market—who are attracted to the retailer's offerings and interested in patronizing its stores. Thus, the area must have the right demographic and lifestyle profile. The size and composition of households in an area can be an important determinant of success. For instance, electronics, appliance, and home goods store, La Curacao, focuses on Hispanic consumers. Thus it has 11 locations in southern California and Arizona—all locations are areas with at least 250,000 Hispanics.[4] Ethnic composition of the trade area, however, is not a particularly critical issue for Toys "R" Us, which is interested in locations with heavy concentrations of families with young children.

Party City, the world's largest party supply retailer, sells celebratory merchandise for happy occasions—birthdays, holiday parties, anniversaries—through more than 600 company-owned franchised stores. Party City chooses locations that have a high density of middle-income shoppers with children.[5]

Finally, lifestyle characteristics of the population may be relevant, depending on the target market(s) that a particular retailer is pursuing. For example, areas with consumers interested in outdoor activities are attractive for REI and Bass Pro Shops.

Operating Costs   The cost of operating stores can vary across areas. For example, store rental and advertising costs in the Missoula, Montana, MSA are significantly lower than those in the Cincinnati-Middletown MSA. But, of course,

---

8.1   RETAILING VIEW   Big Payoff from Small Towns

Even though Stage Stores is a billion-dollar retail chain operating in more than 800 locations, it is relatively unknown because most of its stores are located in small towns. Being outside the big city has advantages, though. "The beauty of our business model is that we have no natural competitor," said Andy Hall, former president and CEO of Stage Stores: "Most small towns are not big enough for two stores like ours. The first one in wins." Typically, the nearest thing to competition for Stage Stores' small-town locations are regional malls 40 miles away and online sites.

Among the 801 stores, 521 are in small markets (small MSAs and larger μSAs), mostly in strip centers in towns with less than 50,000 people within a 10-mile radius. Stage Stores operates under the names Palais Royal, Bealls, Goody's, Peebles, and Stage. Of the 521 small-town Stage Store locations, 510 are near a Walmart. Customers buy their groceries and hard goods at Walmart and their apparel at Stage stores. Name brands, such as Lee, Levi's, Calvin Klein Jeans, Izod, Nike, Nautica, Dockers, Nine West, Clinique, and Estee Lauder, are 80 percent of sales.

A downside of being small-town-focused is being overlooked by many investors, according to Hall. "Most city dwellers don't understand the vibrancy of small markets. It's an amazing culture in small markets," Hall said.

Bealls, a subsidiary of Stage Stores focus on small towns where it faces little competition for its assortment of designer fashion apparel and accessories.

Sales associates and customers there are more likely to know each other, and their relationships in the stores are often warm.

Sources: David Kaplan, "Stage Stores' Strategy Pays Off Big in Small Towns," *Houston Chronicle*, August 1, 2011; www.stagestores.com.

DISCUSSION QUESTION

What are the opportunities and threats Stage Stores faces?

the potential sales and profits from stores located in the Cincinnati-Middletown MSA are substantially greater due to its larger and denser population.

Operating costs are also affected by the proximity of the area being considered to other areas in which the retailer operates stores. For example, if a store is located near other stores and the retailer's distribution centers, the cost of shipping merchandise to the store is lower, as is the cost and travel time spent by the district manager supervising the stores' operations.

The local and state legal and regulatory environment can have a significant effect on operating costs. Some retailers are reluctant to locate stores in California because they feel that the state and local governments, the political process of voter-initiated referendums, and a legal environment that fosters class-action lawsuits result in higher operating costs.[6]

Number of Stores in an Area

Having selected an area in which to locate its stores, a retailer's next decision is how many stores to operate in the area. At first glance, you might think that a retailer should choose the one best location in each MSA, but clearly, larger MSAs can support more stores than smaller MSAs. It may, therefore, be more advantageous to locate several stores in one MSA and none in others. But there is a limit to how many stores can be operated in even the largest MSAs. When making the decision about how many stores to open in an area, retailers must consider the trade-offs between lower operating costs and potential sales cannibalization from having multiple stores in an area.

Economies of Scale from Multiple Stores   Most retail chains open multiple stores in an area to lower promotion and distribution by realizing economies of scale. A retailer's total promotional costs are the same for newspaper advertising that promotes 20 stores in a MSA or only 1 store. Multiple stores in an MSA can be serviced by the same distribution center. Thus, chains like Walmart expand into areas only where they have a distribution center in place to support the stores.[7] When Kohl's entered the Florida market, it opened 14 stores in Jacksonville and Orlando on the same day. Finally, when stores are located close each other, district store managers visit each of their stores more frequently.

Cannibalization   Although retailers gain scale economies from opening multiple locations in an MSA, they also suffer diminishing returns associated with locating too many additional stores in an area. For example, suppose the first four stores opened in an MSA by a specialty store retailer generate sales of $2 million each. Because they are located far apart from one another, customers consider patronizing only the store nearest to them, and there is no cannibalization. When the retailer opens a fifth store close to one of the existing stores, it hopes for a net sales increase for the area of $2 million; the new store should generate the same sales level as the four existing stores. Instead, the increase in incremental sales might be only $1.5 million because the sales in the nearest existing store's sales drop to $1.7 million and sales from the new store are only $1.8 million because its location is only the fifth best in the area. Thus, because the new store cannibalizes sales from the closest store, it only contributes sales of $1.5 million.

Because a primary retailing objective is to maximize profits for the entire chain, retailers should continue to open stores only as long as profits continue to increase or, in economic terms, as long as the marginal revenues achieved by opening a new store are greater than the marginal costs. Exhibit 8–2 shows the location of customers that are 3 (yellow), 6 (pink), and 9 (blue) minutes from a retailer's four stores in an area. Note how there is very little overlap, thus little cannibalization except for the City East and the South East stores.

For franchise retail operations, the objectives of the franchisor and franchisee differ, and thus, disputes can arise over the number of locations in an area. The

EXHIBIT 8–2
Location of Customers
Patronizing a Retailer's
Store

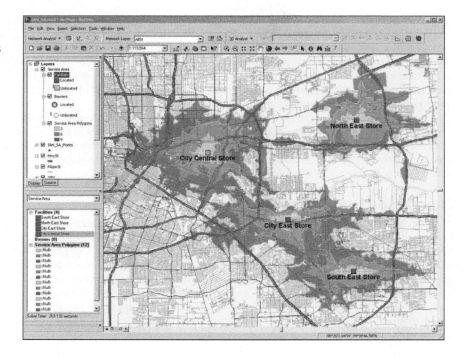

franchisor is interested in maximizing the sales of all stores because it earns a royalty based on total store sales. The franchisee is interested in just the sales and profits from its store(s). Thus, the franchisor is not as concerned about cannibalization as the franchisee is. To reduce the level of conflict, most franchise agreements grant franchisees an exclusive territory to protect them from another franchisee cannibalizing their sales.[8]

CONSIDERATIONS IN EVALUATING STORE LOCATIONS

LO2

Review the characteristics
of a particular site.

Having decided to locate stores in an area, the retailer's next step is to evaluate and select a specific site. In making this decision, retailers consider three factors: (1) the characteristics of the site, (2) the characteristics of the trading area for a store at the site, and (3) the estimated potential sales that can be generated by a store at the site. The first two sets of factors are typically considered in an initial screening of potential sites. The methods used to forecast store sales, the third factor, can involve a more complex analytical approach. Each of these factors is discussed in the following sections.

Site Characteristics

Some characteristics of a site that affect store sales and thus are considered in selecting a site are (1) the traffic flow past the site and accessibility to the site, (2) parking, (3) visibility, (4) adjacent tenants, and (5) restrictions and costs.

Traffic Flow and Accessibility   One of the most important factors affecting store sales is the **traffic flow**—the number of vehicles and pedestrians that pass by the site. When the traffic is greater, more consumers are likely to stop in and shop at the store. Thus, retailers often use traffic count measures to assess a site's attractiveness. Traffic counts are particularly important for retailers offering merchandise and services bought on impulse or on frequent trips such as grocery stores, convenience, and car washes. In contrast, traffic flow is not as important for destination retailers such as The Container Store.

More traffic flow is not always better. Traffic volume counts for surrounding roadways are often used to assess the attractiveness of a retail site. But these measures can be misleading. While these measures can give a reasonable estimate of the level of activity in an area, they do not provide any indication of how much of that volume actually stops and shops at a particular retail location. Most shopping centers are located along heavily traveled roads and highways. As such, these roads are heavily traveled by drivers commuting to and from work or carrying out a number of other daily activities that don't include shopping. As such, daily traffic counts are skewed during rush hours, which creates congestion that impedes access to the stores. Also, traffic volume counts are collected over a 24-hour period, and average rates are reported, whereas retail properties are typically only open for 8 to 12 hours each day.

The **accessibility** of the site, which can be as important as traffic flow, is the ease with which customers can get into and out of the site. Accessibility is greater for sites located near major highways, on uncongested highways, and at streets with traffic lights and lanes that enable turns into the site. Retailing View 8.2 describes the importance of accessibility to a retailer's business.

Natural barriers, such as rivers or mountains, and **artificial barriers**, such as railroad tracks, divided or limited-access highways, or parks, may also affect accessibility. These barriers' impact on a particular site primarily depends on whether the merchandise or services will appeal to customers so strongly that they cross the barrier. For example, a supermarket on one side of a divided highway with no convenient crossover point will appeal only to consumers going in one direction.

A more accurate measure of traffic, which can be obtained from several specialized companies, is the number of consumers entering the shopping center, collected at store entrances within the shopping center. This measure provides a more accurate picture of the number of consumers actually patronizing the shopping center. Additionally, the measure is available for every day of the year individually, rather than the annual averages provided by firms specializing in traffic counts. This allows for more detailed and targeted analyses based on seasonal or week-to-week comparisons.

In the United States, most consumers drive to shopping centers, and thus vehicular traffic is an important consideration when evaluating a site. However, pedestrian traffic flow and access by public transportation are more important for analyzing sites in countries such as China where consumers do not drive to shop or for evaluating urban sites and sites within an enclosed mall.

Parking The amount and quality of parking facilities are critical for evaluating a shopping center. On the one hand, if there aren't enough spaces or the spaces are too far from the store, customers will be discouraged from patronizing the site and the store. On the other hand, if there are too many open spaces, the shopping center may be perceived as having unpopular stores. A standard rule of thumb is 5.5:1,000 (five and one-half spaces per thousand square feet of retail store space) for a shopping center and 10 to 15 spaces per 1,000 square feet for a supermarket.

The parking around this Best Buy store contributes to the quality of this location.

8.2   RETAILING VIEW   It Pays to Locate on the Right Side of the Road

For U.S. drivers, businesses and stores located on the right side of the road, rather than on the left, are the ones they see most readily on their commutes home from work or school. That is, if we were to measure the volume of traffic on a road, we would find that the right-hand side of the yellow lines takes up far more afternoon volume. Accordingly, for many businesses, a location on that right-hand side can be highly desirable because it is easy for customers to make a quick right turn into their properties, then an easier right turn out of the retail parking area, without having to cross many lanes of traffic.

In the morning, a right-side location might be ideal for a coffee shop or newspaper stand. But most commuters have little time to spare in the mornings, so they reserve their stops to fill up on gas, grab a gallon of milk, or perhaps sneak in an afternoon candy bar for their rides home.

For Hess gas stations and convenience stores, locating on the right-hand side for afternoon commuters is a priority. As a vertically integrated energy company, Hess is involved in oil exploration and refining, but its most familiar presence is its approximately 1,400 green-logoed retail stores, running up and down the East Coast of the United States. For its 1.3 million daily customers, "The location of our stores is critical to providing value . . . and is paramount to our success," according to Rick Lawlor, vice president of retail marketing for Hess. To generate its $6 billion in annual sales, Hess maintains

Rick Lawlor at Hess positions Hess's convenience stores on the right side of the road.

a staff that evaluates the location of stores we are considering to build or acquire. When evaluating locations, we look at all the numbers—the size and characteristics of the store's trading area, the demographics and geodemographics of the customers that drive by the location and live in the area. However, the most important factors for us are visibility and access—that is, can customers see the signage for our stores and easily make a right turn into the location on their way home? While the data on a location are useful, we never open a location without looking at it in person to assess its visibility and access.

Right turns into and out of Hess locations are particularly important for its customers, who demand a maximum of convenience from their convenience stores. For many drivers, being required to cross multiple lanes of traffic (and hold up frustrated drivers behind them) to make a left turn simply isn't worth the hassle. If they also need to make a left turn out of the parking lot to continue their commute, their quick pit stop could turn into an extended chore as they wait for gaps in the heavy rush hour traffic to enter the flow of cars.

Locations on the left-hand side of the road, from commuters' perspective, also have grown increasingly problematic with the expansion of "access control" policies by local, county, and state transportation agencies. Such controls include the installation of medians and curbing that limit left turns, as well as prohibitions on U-turns at traffic signals.

As a result of these consumer preferences and governmental policies, being on the "wrong" side of the road can result in a 5 to 20 percent decrease in customer transactions, depending on the road's specific traffic volume patterns.

The bottom line is thus that it is no longer just "location, location, location" that matters for retail sales. Location questions must be evaluated in the context of "access, access, access," especially for customers seeking convenience. Any retailer evaluating locations for stores therefore should think carefully about the traffic patterns whizzing by. Are you on the right side, or the wrong side, of the road?

Sources: "It Pays to Be on the Right Side of the Road," *TSImaster,* 2011; Rick Lawlor, personal communication.

DISCUSSION QUESTIONS

For what types of retailers is being on the right side more important during afternoon commutes? For which types of retailers is it more important during the morning commute? Are there any types of retailers for which a right-hand side location is not particularly important?

Retailers need to observe the shopping center at various times of the day, week, and season. They also must consider the availability of employee parking, the proportion of shoppers using cars, parking by non-shoppers, and the typical length of a shopping trip.

An issue closely related to the amount of available parking facilities but extended into the shopping center itself is the relative congestion of the area. **Congestion** is an excess level of traffic that results in customer delays. There is an optimal level of congestion for customers. Too much congestion can make shopping slow, irritate customers, and generally discourage sales. However, a relatively high level of activity in a shopping center creates excitement and can stimulate sales.

The location of this store is poor because the store and its signage are not visible.

Visibility   **Visibility** refers to customers' ability to see the store from the street. Good visibility is less important for stores with a well-established and loyal customer base, but most retailers still want a direct, unimpeded view of their store. In an area with a highly transient population, such as a tourist center or large city, good visibility from the road is particularly important.

Adjacent Tenants   Locations with complementary, as well as competing, adjacent retailers have the potential to build traffic. Complementary retailers target the same market segment but have a different, noncompeting merchandise offering. For example, Save-A-Lot, a limited-assortment supermarket targeting price-sensitive consumers, prefers to be co-located with other retailers targeting price-sensitive consumers, such as Big Lots, Family Dollar, or even Walmart.

Have you ever noticed that competing fast-food restaurants, automobile dealerships, antique dealers, or even shoe and apparel stores in a mall are located next to one another? Consumers looking for these types of merchandise are involved in convenience or comparison shopping situations, as we described in Chapter 7. They want to be able to make their choice easily in the case of convenience shopping, or they want to have a good assortment so that they can "shop around," in the case of shopping goods. This grouped location approach is based on the principle of **cumulative attraction,** which states that a cluster of similar and complementary retailing activities will generally have greater drawing power than isolated stores that engage in the same retailing activities.[9]

Restrictions and Costs   As we learn later in this chapter, retailers may place restrictions

Save-A-Lot prefers locations next to Big Lots or Family Dollar because the presence of the two retailers will attract additional consumers.

on the type of tenants that are allowed in a shopping center in their lease agreement. Some of these restrictions can make the shopping center more attractive for a retailer. For example, a specialty men's apparel retailer may prefer a lease agreement that precludes other men's specialty apparel retailers from locating in the same center. A florist in a strip center may specify that if the grocery anchor tenant vacates the center, it can be released from its lease. Retailers would look unfavorably on a shopping center with a sign size restriction that prevented easy visibility of the store's name from the street. At the end of the chapter, we discuss some other restrictions and cost issues involved in negotiating a lease.

Locations within a Shopping Center

While the previous discussion focused on factors affecting the attractiveness of a shopping center location, the location within a shopping center has a significant effect on both sales and occupancy costs. The better locations have higher occupancy costs. In a strip shopping center, the locations closest to the supermarket are more expensive because they attract greater foot traffic. So a flower shop or sandwich shop that may attract impulse buyers should be close to the supermarket. But a shoe repair store, which does not cater to customers shopping on impulse, could be in a lower-traffic location farther away from the supermarket because customers in need of this service will seek out the store. In other words, it is a destination store.

The same issues apply to evaluating locations within a multilevel, enclosed shopping mall. Stores that cater to consumers engaging in comparison shopping, such as shoppers buying fashionable apparel, benefit from being in more expensive locations near the department store anchors, which are destinations for comparison apparel shoppers. As apparel shoppers enter and leave the department store, they walk by and may be attracted to neighboring specialty store retailers. In contrast, a retailer such as Foot Locker, another destination store, need not be in the most expensive location, because many of its customers know they're in the market for its type of product before they even go shopping.

Another consideration is how to locate stores that appeal to similar target markets. In essence, customers want to shop where they'll find a good assortment of merchandise. The principle of cumulative attraction applies to both stores that sell complementary merchandise and those that compete directly with one another. Consider the location of retailers in The Mall in Columbia, the centerpiece of the planned community of Columbia, Maryland. The mall's trade area includes about three-quarters of a million people, located in wealthy Howard County, which is positioned halfway between Baltimore, Maryland, and Washington, DC. Many of the tenants are positioned within the mall into category zones to better match their target markets.[10] For example, at the Mall in Columbia, retailers selling jewelry are located near each other. On the lower level are Zales Jewelers, Shaw's Jewelers, Pandora, Littman Jewelers, Monica Jewelers, and Fire and Ice. A short escalator ride to the upper level are Eastern Coral, Edward Arthur, Helzberg Diamond, Michael Kors, Reed's Jewelers, and Icing Ice.

TRADE AREA CHARACTERISTICS

LO3

Understand how retailers analyze the trade area for a site.

After identifying several sites that have acceptable traffic flow, accessibility, and other location characteristics, the next step is to collect information about the trade area that can be used to forecast sales for a store located at the site. The retailer first needs to define the trade area for the site. Once the trade area is defined, the retailer can use several different information sources to develop a detailed understanding of the nature of consumers in the site's trade area.

EXHIBIT 8–3
Zones in a Trade Area

Trade Area Definition

A **trade area** is a contiguous geographic area that accounts for the majority of a store's sales and customers. Trade areas can be divided into three zones, as shown in Exhibit 8–3. The exhibit shows the trade area zones for a shopping center located at the red square: the 5-minute drive-time zone (light brown), the 10-minute zone (blue), and the 15-minute zone (green).

The trade area zones shown in Exhibit 8–3 are not concentric circles based on distance from the store but, rather, are irregular polygons based on the location of roads, highways, and natural barriers, like rivers and valleys, that affect the driving time to the store. The location of competitive stores can also affect the actual trade area configuration.

The **primary trading area** is the geographic area from which the shopping center or store site derives 50 to 70 percent of its customers. The **secondary trading area** is the geographic area of secondary importance in terms of customer sales, generating about 20 to 30 percent of the site's customers. The **tertiary trading area** or **fringe** (the outermost area) includes the remaining customers who shop at the site but come from widely dispersed areas. These customers might travel an unusually long distance because they do not have comparable retail facilities closer to home, or they may drive near the store or center on their way to or from work.

The best way to define the three zones is based on driving time rather than distance. Thus, the primary trading area might be defined as customers within 5 minutes' driving time of the site; the secondary trading area, as customers with a 10-minute drive; and the tertiary zone, as customers more than 15 minutes away from the site by car. In bigger cities where driving times are lengthy, such as Los Angeles, the primary trading area may be 15 minutes; the secondary trading area, 40 minutes; and the tertiary trading area, more than 1 hour. However, it is much easier to collect information about the number of people and their characteristics in the different zones by geographic distance than by driving time. Thus, retailers often define the zones by distance—such as 3, 5, and 10 miles from the site— rather than driving time.

Factors Affecting the Size of the Trade Area

The actual boundaries of a trade area are determined by the store's accessibility, natural and physical barriers, level of competition, nature of the merchandise sold, the assortment offered, and the location of alternative sources for the merchandise.

A Starbucks in a central business district, for example, may have a trade area of only two or three blocks; a category specialist like Michaels may draw customers from 10 miles away; and The Container Store, which is the only store of its kind in a city, might draw customers from 30 miles away. Category specialists offer a large choice of brands and products for which customers are engaged in comparison shopping. Thus, customers generally drive some distance to shop at these stores. In general, destination stores have a large trade area—people are willing to drive farther to shop there.

Measuring the Trade Area for a Retail Site

Retailers can determine the trade area for their existing stores by customer spotting. **Customer spotting** is the process of locating the residences of customers for a store on a map and displaying their positions relative to the store location. The addresses for locating the customers' residences usually are obtained by asking the customers, recording the information from a check or Internet channel purchase, or collecting the information from customer loyalty programs. The data collected from customer spotting can be processed in two ways: manually plotting the location of each customer on a map or using a geographic information system like those described later in this chapter.

Multichannel retailers use their catalog and Internet sales data to spot customers and use that information to identify potential store locations. The number of catalog and Internet channel customers in an area can be used predict the sales of a store placed in the area.

Sources of Information about the Trade Area

To analyze the attractiveness of a potential store site, retailers use information about both the consumers and the competitors in the site's trade area. Two widely used sources of information about the nature of consumers in a trade area are (1) data published by the U.S. Census Bureau, based on the Decennial Census of the United States, and (2) data from geographic information systems, provided by several commercial firms.

REFACT

The United States was the first country to institute a periodic census.[11]

Demographic Data from U.S. Census Bureau   Every 10 years, **census** takers gather demographic information (sex, age, ethnicity, education, marital status, etc.) from every household in the United States. The decennial census is more than just a head count; it provides a snapshot of the country's demographic, social, and economic characteristics. The U.S. Census Bureau prepares periodic reports summarizing the data. There are 8 million **census blocks** in the United States, each containing the residences of about 40 people. The smallest unit of analysis is the **block group**, a collection of adjacent blocks that contain between 300 and 4,000 people.[12]

REFACT

California, Florida, and New York account for one-quarter of the U.S. population.[13]

Although the data from the U.S. Census Bureau can be used to develop a better understanding of the nature of consumers in a region or trade area, these data have several limitations. First, because they are based on information collected every 10 years, they are not very current, although the projections are reasonably accurate. Second, the data are not particularly user-friendly. It is difficult to utilize census data to examine the trade areas for various locations for specific products or services. Thus, most retailers rely on the geographic information system data offered by a number of companies to examine trade areas for potential stores.

Geographic Information System Suppliers   A **geographic information system (GIS)** is a system of hardware and software used to store, retrieve, map, and analyze geographic data; a GIS also includes the operating personnel and the data that go into the system. The key feature of GIS data is that they are identified with a coordinate system (latitude and longitude) that references a particular place on Earth. The data in the systems include spatial features such as rivers and roads,

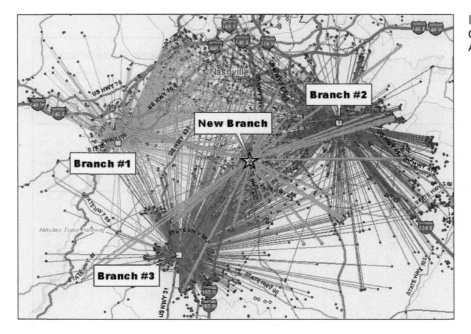

EXHIBIT 8–4
GIS Map for the Trade Area of a Bank

as well as descriptive information associated with the spatial features, such as the street address and the characteristics of the household at the address.

Firms such as ESRI (www.esri.com), Nielsen, which purchased Claritas (www.claritas.com/sitereports/Default.jsp), and Pitney Bowes, which purchased MapInfo (www.pbinsight.com/welcome/mapinfo/) offer services that combine updated demographic census data with data from other sources that describe consumer spending patterns and lifestyles in a geographic area. In addition, they provide a user-friendly interface so that the data can be accessed and analyzed easily. Frequently, the outputs from the system are maps that enable retailers to visualize the implications of the data quickly. For example, the map in Exhibit 8–4 shows the trade areas for three branch banks that a retailer has in an MSA and a fourth branch it is considering, as well as the residences of its customers relative to the branch at which they bank. This map suggests that people bank near their work and, thus, that the new location might cannibalize from the other branches.

Retailers interested in developing a deeper understanding of their trade areas for several sites can provide one of these firms with the street addresses for the sites under consideration. The system then provides the projected data shown in the following table for current year estimates and five-year projections pertaining to people living within a 3-, 5-, and 10-mile radius of the sites. In addition, these GIS firms can provides data on the lifestyles of consumers, consumer spending potential, and the locations of competitive retailers. An example of a report on the retail goods and services purchased by residents in a trade area is shown in Exhibit 8–5.

Gender	Occupation
Income	Travel time to work
Disposable income	Transportation mode to work
Net worth	Household composition
Education	Household expenditures by NAICS categories
Age	Geodemographic market segment
Race/ethnicity	Market potential index
Employment status	Spending potential index

EXHIBIT 8–5   GIS Data for Retail Expenditures in a Trade Area

esri

Retail Goods and Services Expenditures
Sample Report

Proposed Location
100 S Wacker Dr, Chicago, IL 60606-4006
Ring: 1 mile radius

Latitude: 41.8805
Longitude: -87.63715

Top Tapestry Segments:		Demographic Summary	2010	2015
Metro Renters	68.4%	Population	45,534	50,151
Laptops and Lattes	23.4%	Households	24,338	26,808
City Strivers	2.7%	Families	7,223	7,843
Main Street, USA	1.8%	Median Age	35.7	35.8
Metropolitans	1.6%	Median Household Income	$81,441	$100,632

	Spending Potential Index	Average Amount Spent	Total
Apparel and Services	120	$2,873.94	$69,945,928
Men's	112	$512.65	$12,476,953
Women's	104	$861.55	$20,968,522
Children's	121	$485.96	$11,827,277
Footwear	84	$349.13	$8,497,153
Watches & Jewelry	173	$335.43	$8,163,589
Apparel Products and Services[1]	352	$329.21	$8,012,434
Computer			
Computers and Hardware for Home Use	169	$324.62	$7,900,647
Software and Accessories for Home Use	169	$48.15	$1,171,788
Entertainment & Recreation	155	$4,996.06	$121,594,105
Fees and Admissions	155	$960.54	$23,377,534
Membership Fees for Clubs[2]	155	$253.65	$6,173,216
Fees for Participant Sports, excl. Trips	145	$154.42	$3,758,358
Admission to Movie/Theatre/Opera/Ballet	172	$260.56	$6,341,578
Admission to Sporting Events, excl. Trips	149	$88.77	$2,160,410
Fees for Recreational Lessons	147	$201.16	$4,895,736
Dating Services	257	$1.98	$48,236
TV/Video/Audio	161	$2,003.60	$48,763,617
Community Antenna or Cable TV	157	$1,130.81	$27,521,629

Tapestry Segmentation ERSI and other GIS suppliers have developed schemes for classifying geographic areas in the United States by combining census and survey data about people's lifestyles and purchasing behavior with the mapping capabilities of GIS. The analysis is based on the premise that "birds of a feather flock together." Specifically, people who live in the same neighborhoods tend to have similar lifestyles and consumer behavior patterns.

The ESRI Tapestry Segmentation system classifies all U.S. residential neighborhoods into 65 distinctive segments, based on demographic and socioeconomic characteristics. Exhibit 8–5 is a hypothetical report for the area within a 1.5-mile radius of 100 S. Wacker Drive in Chicago. Each segment provides a description of the typical person in that segment. The largest segment in the trade area report in Exhibit 8–5 is Metro Renters.[14] According to ESRI, residents of Metro Renters neighborhoods are young (approximately 30 percent are in their 20s), well-educated singles beginning their professional careers in some of the largest U.S. cities such as New York City, Los Angeles, and Chicago. The median age is 33.6 years; the median household income is $56,311. Most rent apartments in high-rise buildings, living alone or with a roommate. They travel, read two or more daily newspapers, listen to classical music and public radio, and go online. To stay fit, they work out regularly at clubs, play tennis and volleyball, practice yoga, ski, and jog. They go dancing and to the movies, attend rock concerts, visit museums, and

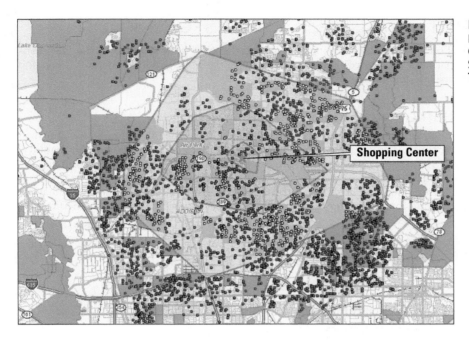

EXHIBIT 8–6
Location of Target
Customers in a
Shopping Center
Trade Area

throw frisbees. Painting and drawing are favorite hobbies. They are politically liberal. Several similar, competing segmentation systems are currently commercially available, including PRIZM (Potential Rating Index for Zip Markets), which was developed by Nielsen Claritas.

Exhibit 8–6 shows the location of customers who have the desired geodemographic profile on a trade area map for a shopping center. Note that most of the retailer's desirable customers are not even in the tertiary trade area; thus, this shopping center would not be a desirable location. (The shopping center is designated by the red star. The primary trade area is green; the secondary trade area is lavender; and the tertiary trade area is turquoise.)

Spending Potential Index   Data in ESRI's consumer spending database is reported by product or service; variables include total expenditures, average amount spent per household, and a **Spending Potential Index (SPI).** The SPI compares the local average expenditure by product to the national average amount spent. An index of 100 is average. For example, an SPI of 120 shows that average spending by local consumers is 20 percent above the national average; an SPI of 80 means that average local spending is 20 percent below the national average. (See Exhibit 8–5.)

Competition in the Trade Area

In addition to needing information about the residents in a trade area, retailers need to know about the amount and type of competition in the trade area. Although GIS vendors provide data on the location of competitive retailers, there are also other sources for this information. For example, most retailer websites list not only all current store locations, but future sites as well. A more traditional method of accessing competitive information is to look through the Yellow Pages of the telephone book. Other sources of competitive information include directories published by trade associations, chambers of commerce, Chain Store Guide (published by CSG Information Services, www.csgis.com), and municipal and county governments.

ESTIMATING POTENTIAL SALES FOR A STORE SITE

LO4

Determine the forecasted sales for a new store location.

Three approaches for using information about the trade area to estimate the potential sales for a store at the location are (1) the Huff gravity model, (2) regression analysis, and (3) the analog method.

Huff Gravity Model

The **Huff gravity model** is used to predict the probability that a consumer will patronize a store.[15] The model specifies two factors that assess the probability: (1) the attractiveness of the store's location (larger stores and shopping centers are more attractive) and (2) the time it takes a consumer to travel to the store (stores that take more time to get to are less attractive). The mathematical formula for predicting the probability of a customer's going to a specific store location is

$$P_{ij} = \frac{S_j/T_{ij}^{\lambda}}{\Sigma S_j/T_{ij}^{\lambda}}$$

where

P_{ij} = probability that customer i shops at location j

S_j = size of the store at location j

T_{ij} = travel time for customer i to get to location j

The formula indicates that the larger the size (S_j) of the store compared with competing stores' sizes, the greater the probability that a customer will shop at the location. A larger size is generally more attractive in consumers' eyes because it means more merchandise assortment and variety. Travel time or distance (T_{ij}) has the opposite effect on the probability that a consumer will shop at a location. The greater the travel time or distance from the consumer, compared with that of competing locations, the lower the probability that the consumer will shop at the location. Generally, customers would rather shop at a close store than a distant one.

The exponent λ reflects the relative effect of travel time versus store size. When λ is equal to 1, store size and travel time have an equal but opposite effect on the probability of a consumer's shopping at a store location. When λ is greater than 1, travel time has a greater effect, and when λ is less than 1, store size has a greater effect. The value of λ is affected by the nature of the shopping trips consumers generally take when visiting the specific type of store. For instance, travel time or distance is generally more important for convenience goods than for shopping goods because people are less willing to travel a great distance for a quart of milk than they are for a new pair of shoes. Thus, a larger value for λ is assigned if the store being studied specializes in convenience shopping trips rather than comparison shopping trips. The value of λ is usually estimated statistically using data that describe shopping patterns at existing stores.

To illustrate the use of the Huff model, consider the situations shown in Exhibit 8–7. A small town has two communities, Rock Creek and Oak Hammock. The town currently has one 5,000-square-foot drugstore with annual sales of $8 million, $3 million of which come from Oak Hammock residents and $5 million from Rock Creek residents. A competitive chain is considering opening a 10,000-square-foot store. As the exhibit illustrates, the driving time for the average Rock Creek resident to the existing store is 10 minutes, but it would be only 5 minutes to the new store. In contrast, the driving time for the typical Oak Hammock resident to the existing drugstore is 5 minutes and would be 15 minutes

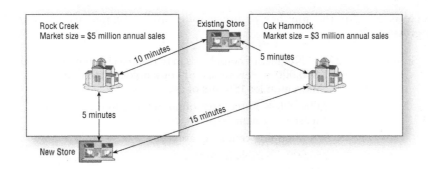

EXHIBIT 8–7
Application of the Huff Gravity Model for Estimating Store Sales

to the new store. Based on its past experience, the drugstore chain has found that λ equals 2 for its store locations. Using the Huff formula, the probability of a Rock Creek resident's shopping at the new location, P_{RC}, is

$$P_{RC} = \frac{10,000/5^2}{10,000/5^2 + 5,000/10^2} = .889$$

The probability of Oak Hammock residents shopping at the new location, P_{OH}, is

$$P_{OH} = \frac{10,000/15^2}{10,000/15^2 + 5,000/5^2} = .182$$

This simple application assumes that the market size for drugstores in the community will remain the same at $8 million with the addition of the new store. We also could have considered that two drugstores would increase the total size of the market. In addition, rather than doing the calculations for the average customer located in the middle of each community, we could have calculated the probabilities that each customer in the two communities would go to the new location.

Even though the Huff gravity model considers only two factors affecting store sales—travel time and store size—its predictions are quite accurate because these two factors typically have the greatest effect on store choice.[16] The regression approach discussed in the next section provides a way to incorporate additional factors into the sales forecast for a store under consideration.

Regression Analysis

The **regression analysis** approach is based on the assumption that factors that affect the sales of existing stores in a chain will have the same impact on stores located at new sites being considered. When using this approach, the retailer employs a technique called multiple regression to estimate a statistical model that predicts sales at existing store locations. The technique can consider the effects of the wide range of factors discussed in this chapter, including site characteristics, such as visibility and access, and characteristics of the trade area, such as demographics and lifestyle segments represented.

Consider the following example: A chain of sporting goods stores has analyzed the factors affecting sales in its existing stores and found that the following model is the best predictor of store sales (the weights for the factors, such as 275 for the number of households, are estimated using multiple regression):

Stores sales = 275 × Number of households in trade area (15-minute drive time)
+ 1,800,000 × Percentage of households in trade area with children under 15 years of age
+ 2,000,000 × Percentage of households in trade area in Tapestry segment "aspiring young"
+ 8 × Shopping center square feet
+ 250,000, if visible from street
+ 300,000, if Walmart in center

The sporting goods retailer is considering the following two locations:

Variable	Estimated Weight	Location A	Location B
Households within a 15-minute drive time of the location	275	11,000	15,000
Percentage of households with children under 15	1,800,000	70%	20%
Percentage of households in the Aspiring Young Tapestry geodemographic segment	2,000,000	60%	10%
Gross leasable square feet of shopping center	8	200,000	250,000
Visibility of store (1 = yes, 0 = no)	250,000	yes	no
Walmart store in shopping center (1 = yes, 0 = no)	300,000	yes	no

Using the regression model, the forecasted sales for location A are:

Stores sales at location A = \$7,635,000 = 275 × 11,000
+ 1,800,000 × 0.7
+ 200,000 × 0.6
+ 8 × 200,000
+ 250,000 × 1
+ 300,000 × 1

and forecasted sales for location B are:

Store sales at location B = \$6,685,000 = 275 × 15,000
+ 1,800,000 × 0.2
+ 2,000,000 × 0.1
+ 8 × 250,000
+ 250,000 × 0
+ 300,000 × 0

Note that location A has greater forecasted sales, even though it has fewer consumers in its trading area and shopping center size, because the profile of its target market fits the retailer's target market (families with children under 15 and in the Aspiring Young Tapestry segment) better.

Analog Approach

To estimate a regression model to predict sales from a site, a retailer needs data about the trade area and site characteristics from a large number of stores. Because small chains cannot use the regression approach, they use the similar but more subjective analog approach. When using the **analog approach,** the retailer simply describes the site and trade area characteristics for its most successful stores and attempts to find a site with similar characteristics. The use of this approach is described in the following illustration.

ILLUSTRATION OF SITE SELECTION: EDWARD BEINER PURVEYOR OF FINE EYEWEAR

Edward Beiner Purveyor of Fine Eyewear is an 11-store Florida retailer specializing in upper-end, high-fashion eyewear. Its store in South Miami lacks the entertainment and recreation found in shopping centers. Other problems with the location are a lack of protection against the heavy rains that characterize the area's subtropical climate, security, and parking. However, some positive features of the location are the low rent, high pedestrian traffic, few restrictions, and no other high-quality and fashion optical stores in the area, although there are other optical stores in the general area.

LO5
Illustrate the site selection process.

Edward Beiner Purveyor of Fine Eyewear wants to open a new location. Because the South Miami site is its best store, it would like to find a location whose trade area has similar characteristics. It has identified several potential locations that it is evaluating.

Using the analog approach, Edward Beiner undertakes the following steps:

1. Conduct a competitive analysis.

2. Define present trade area.

3. Analyze trade area characteristics.

4. Match characteristics of present trade area with potential sites.

Edward Beiner Purveyor of Fine Eyewear specializes in high-fashion eyewear and targets affluent customers.

EXHIBIT 8–8   Competitive Analysis of Potential Locations

(1) Trade Area	(2) Eyeglasses/ Year/ Person	(3) Trade Area Population	(4) Total Eyeglasses Potential	(5) Estimated Eyeglasses Sold	(6) Trade Area Potential Units	(7) Trade Area Potential Percentage	(8) Relative Level of Competition
South Miami	0.2	85,979	17,196	7,550	9,646	56.09%	Low
Site A	0.2	91,683	18,337	15,800	2,537	13.83	Medium
Site B	0.2	101,972	20,394	12,580	7,814	38.32	Low
Site C	0.2	60,200	12,040	11,300	740	6.15	High
Site D	0.2	81,390	16,278	13,300	2,978	18.29	Medium

Step 1: Conduct Competitive Analysis

The competitive analysis of the four potential sites being considered by Edward Beiner is shown in Exhibit 8–8. To perform the analysis, Edward Beiner first estimated the number of eyeglasses sold per year per person (column 2), obtained from industry sources. Then the area population was taken from U.S. Census data (column 3). Column 4 is an estimate of the trade area potential reached by multiplying column 2 by column 3.

The estimates of the number of eyeglasses sold in the trade areas, column 5, are based on visits to competitive stores. Column 6 represents the unit sales potential for eyeglasses in the trade areas, or column 4 minus column 5. Then the trade area potential penetration is calculated by dividing column 6 by column 4. For instance, because the total eyeglass potential for the South Miami store trade area is 17,196 pairs and an additional 9,646 pairs could be sold in that trade area, 56.1 percent of the eyeglass market in this area remains untapped. The bigger the number, the lower the competition.

Column 8, the relative level of competition, is subjectively estimated on the basis of column 7. Unlike other optical stores in the trade area, Edward Beiner carries a very exclusive merchandise selection. In general, however, the higher the trade area potential, the lower the relative competition will be.

On the basis of the information in Exhibit 8–8, Edward Beiner should locate its new store at site B. The trade area potential is high, and competition is relatively low. Of course, relative competition is only one issue to consider. Later in this section, we'll consider competition along with other issues to determine which is the best new location for Edward Beiner.

Step 2: Define Present Trade Area

On the basis of customer spotting data gathered from Beiner's data warehouse of current customers, the trade area map in Exhibit 8–9 was generated using ESRI's GIS software. The zones are based on drive times: 5 minutes for the primary trade area (red), 10 minutes for the secondary trade area (purple), and 20 minutes for the tertiary trade area (green). Note that the trade area boundaries are oblong because the major highways, especially U.S. 1, run north and south. Not only do the north–south highways bring traffic to the area, but heavy traffic often makes them difficult to cross. Biscayne Bay also limits the trade area on the east.

Edward Beiner trade area is smaller than it would be if the store were located in a regional shopping mall. However, Edward Beiner is one of several optical shops in this business district. Having similar shopping goods stores in the same vicinity expands its trade area boundaries; more people are drawn to the area to shop because of its expanded selection. In addition, Edward Beiner's trade area is limited

Trade Area for Edward Beiner Purveyor of Fine Eyewear   EXHIBIT 8–9

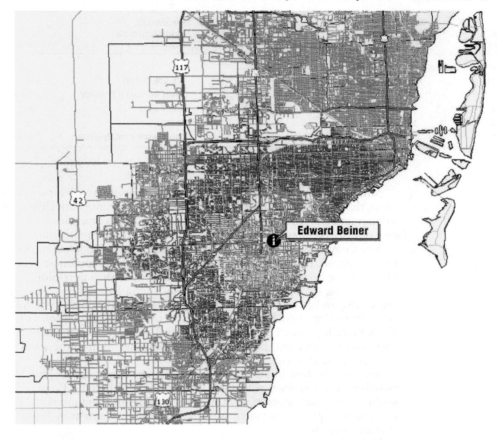

on the south by a large regional shopping center that has several stores carrying similar merchandise.

Step 3: Identify Trade Area Characteristics

Having defined its trade area, Edward Beiner reviewed a number of reports describing the characteristics of its trade area. Some of interesting findings from these reports were:

- The average household income is $92,653. In addition, 27.6 percent of the households have incomes between $75,000 and $149,000, and 13.7 percent have incomes greater than $150,000. The 3-mile ring surrounding Edward Beiner is very affluent.

- The area surrounding Edward Beiner has a population that is more than 50 percent Hispanic.

Step 4: Match Characteristics of Present Trade Area with Potential Sites

Edward Beiner believes that the profile of its current trade area is high income, predominantly white-collar occupations, a relatively large percentage of older residents, upscale geodemographic segments, and relatively low competition for expensive, high-fashion eyewear. Exhibit 8–10 compares Edward Beiner's current location with four potential locations on these five factors.

EXHIBIT 8–10   Four Potential Locations for a New Store

Store Location	Average Household Income	White-Collar Occupations	Percentage Residents Age 45 and Over	Predominant Geodemographic Segments	Level of Competition
Edward Beiner Optical	$100,000	High	37%	Top One Percent	Low
Site A	60,000	High	25	Young Immigrant Families	Medium
Site B	70,000	Low	80	Gray Power	Low
Site C	100,000	High	30	Young Literati	High
Site D	120,000	High	50	Upper-Income Empty-Nesters	Medium

Although the potential customers of site A typically have white-collar occupations, they also have relatively low incomes and are comparatively young. Young Immigrant Families also tend to have young families, so expensive eyewear may not be a priority purchase. Finally, there's a medium level of competition in the area.

The Gray Power residents surrounding site B have moderate incomes and are mostly retired. Even though competition would be low and most residents need glasses, these customers are more interested in value than in fashion.

Site C has strong potential because the Young Literati residents in the area are young and have a strong interest in fashion. Although working, they are busy furnishing their first homes and apartments and paying off college loans. They probably would appreciate Edward Beiner's fashionable assortment, but they won't appreciate the high prices. Also, other high-end optical stores are entrenched in the area.

Site D is the best location for Edward Beiner. The residents are older professionals or early retirees with high incomes. Upper-Income Empty-Nesters are sophisticated consumers of adult luxuries like high-fashion eyewear. Importantly, this geodemographic segment is similar to a large segment in Edward Beiner's current location.

Unfortunately, finding analogous situations isn't always as easy as in this example. The weaker the analogy, the more difficult the location decision will be. When a retailer has a relatively small number of outlets (say, 20 or fewer), the analog approach is often best. As the number of stores increases, it becomes more difficult for the analyst to organize the data in a meaningful way. More analytical approaches, such as regression analysis, then are necessary.

NEGOTIATING A LEASE

LO6

Explain the different types and terms of leases.

Once a particular site is chosen, retailers still face a multitude of decisions, including the types and terms of the lease.

Types of Leases

There are two basic types of leases: percentage and fixed rate.

Percentage Leases   Although there are many combinations within each type of lease, the most common form is a **percentage lease,** in which the rent is based on a percentage of sales. In addition to the percentage of sales, retailers typically pay a common area maintenance (CAM) fee based on a percentage of their gross leasable square footage. Most malls use some form of percentage lease. Because retail leases typically run for 5 to 10 years, they appear equitable to both parties if rents go up (or down) with sales and inflation.

A **percentage lease with a specified maximum** is a lease that pays the shopping center manager a percentage of sales up to a maximum amount. This type of lease rewards good retailer performance by allowing the retailer to hold rent constant above a certain level of sales. A similar variation, the **percentage lease with a specified minimum,** specifies that the retailer must pay a minimum rent, no matter how low sales are.

Another type of percentage lease is a **sliding scale lease,** in which the percentage of sales paid as rent decreases as the sales go up. For instance, a retailer may pay 4 percent on the first $200,000 in sales and then 3 percent on sales greater than $200,000. Similar to the percentage lease with a specified maximum, the sliding scale rewards high-performing retailers.

Fixed-Rate Leases   The second basic type of lease is a **fixed-rate lease,** most commonly used by community and neighborhood centers. A retailer pays a fixed amount per month over the life of the lease. With a fixed-rate lease, the retailer and shopping center management know exactly how much will be paid in rent, but this type of lease is not as popular as the various forms of percentage leases.

A variation of the fixed-rate lease is the **graduated lease,** in which rent increases by a fixed amount over a specified period of time. For instance, rent may be $1,000 per month for the first three years and $1,250 for the next five years.

Terms of the Lease

Although leases are formal contracts, they can be changed to reflect the relative power of the retailer and shopping center management and specific needs of the retailer. In addition to the rent, some other negotiable aspects of the lease are cotenancy, prohibited-use, and exclusive-use clauses.

Cotenancy Clause   Some retail leases contain **cotenancy clauses.** These clauses may require that a certain percentage of a shopping center be leased or that specified stores be in the center. For example, if The Gap goes into a mall, it doesn't want to be by itself. In all likelihood it has a group of retailers that it views as complements. These may include Abercrombie and Fitch, Banana Republic (also owned by The Gap), Aeropostale, American Eagle Outfitters, Ann Taylor, Anthropologie, and bebe, among others. It would not be uncommon to see a lease requirement where The Gap will only sign if at least four of the seven retailers just listed are also in the development.

If these terms are violated, the retailers with the cotenancy clauses may demand rent reductions or leave altogether. Cotenancy clauses have become particularly important in the past few years because many retailers, including several large chains like Circuit City, Borders, and Linens 'N Things, have created vacancies as a result of their bankruptcies.[17]

Prohibited-Use Clause   A **prohibited-use clause** limits the shopping center management from leasing to certain kinds of tenants. Many retailers don't want the shopping center space to be leased to establishments that take up parking spaces but do not bring in shoppers, such as a bowling alley, skating rink, meeting hall, dentist, or real estate office. Retailers may also wish to restrict the use of space from those establishments that could harm the shopping center's image. Prohibited-use clauses often specify that bars, pool halls, game parlors, off-track betting establishments, massage parlors, and pornography retailers are unacceptable.

Suppose, for instance, that Tiffany & Co., the famous jeweler, has a store in a high-end shopping center that is about to sign a lease with H&M. It could envoke its lease's prohibited-use clause in a lawsuit against the shopping center management company. Specifically, the lease forbids retailers "whose merchandise and/or price points are not considered to be luxury, upscale or better by conventional retail industry standards" to use or lease certain spaces within, fronting, or adjacent to the Tiffany store.

Exclusive-Use Clause   An **exclusive-use clause** prohibits the shopping center management from leasing to retailers that sell competing products. For example, a discount store's lease may specify that the landlord cannot lease to other discount stores, variety stores, or limited-assortment value retailers.

Some retailers also are particular about how the storefront appears. For instance, a women's specialty store may specify that the storefront must have floor-to-ceiling glass to maximize window displays and improve customers' ability to see into the store. Other retailers believe it is important that nothing blocks the view of the store from the street, so they specify that the landlord cannot place any outparcels in the parking lot. An **outparcel** is a building (such as a bank or McDonald's) or kiosk (such as an automatic teller machine) that sits in the parking lot of a shopping center but is not physically attached to the center.

Common Area Maintenance Costs   In retail leases, **common area maintenance (CAM) clauses** often require the most extensive negotiations. These clauses traditionally assign responsibilities for taking care of common areas, including sidewalks or parking lots. Modern versions have extended these responsibilities such that tenants might need to agree to contribute to capital improvement projects, pay for new roofing, or participate in the purchase of adjoining land parcels. As a result of this expansion of the meaning of CAM clauses, many leases today call them simply operating costs; in some cases, these costs outpace even rents. This status helps explain why they require such extensive negotiations. Retail tenants seek to limit their responsibilities, and they ask for the right to monitor any common area costs, to confirm their portion is charged legitimately.[18]

SUMMARY

LO1   Summarize the factors considered in locating a number of stores.

Four factors that retailers consider when evaluating an area for store locations are economic conditions, competition, strategic fit, and operating costs. Areas where the population is large and growing, have limited competition, and have a profile that matches the retailer's target market are more attractive. Finally, the cost of servicing an area needs to be considered. When determining the number of stores to locate in an area, retailers need to determine the incremental sales and profits from exploiting scale economies and increasing cannibalization by adding more stores.

LO2   Review the characteristics of a particular site.

Some characteristics of a site that affect store sales and thus are considered in selecting a site are (1) the traffic flow past the site and accessibility to the site, (2) parking, (3) visibility, (4) adjacent tenants, and (5) restrictions and costs.

LO3   Understand how retailers analyze the trade area for a site.

Trade areas are typically divided into primary, secondary, and tertiary zones. The boundaries of a trade area are determined by how accessible it is to customers, the natural and physical barriers that exist in the area, the type of shopping area in which the store is located, the type of store, and the level of competition. Two sources of information to assess the trade areas are census data and GIS.

LO4   Determine the forecasted sales for a new store location.

Once retailers have the data that describe their trade areas, they use several analytical techniques to estimate demand. The Huff gravity model predicts the probability that a customer will choose a particular store in a trade area. The model is based on the premise that customers are more likely to shop at a given store or shopping center if it is conveniently located and offers a large selection. Regression analysis is a statistically based model that estimates the effects of a variety of factors on existing store sales and uses that information to predict sales for a new site. The analog approach—one of the easiest to use—can be particularly useful for smaller retailers. Using the same logic as regression analysis, the retailer can make predictions about sales by a new store on the basis of sales in stores in similar areas.

LO5 **Illustrate the site selection process.**

Edward Beiner Purveyor of Fine Eyewear is used to illustrate the analysis involved in opening a new location using the analog technique. This example

illustrates how to (1) conduct a competitive analysis, (2) define the present trade area, (3) analyze the trade area's characteristics, and (4) match characteristics of the present trade area with potential sites.

LO6 **Explain the different types and terms of leases.**

Retailers need to negotiate the terms of a lease. Although leases are formal contracts, they can be changed to reflect the relative power of the retailer and shopping center management and specific needs of the retailer. These lease terms affect the cost of the location and may restrict retailing activities. There are two basic types of leases: percentage and fixed rate. In addition to the rent, some other negotiable aspects of the lease are cotenancy, prohibited-use, and exclusive-use and common area maintenance clauses.

KEY TERMS

accessibility, *213*
analog approach, *225*
artificial barrier, *213*
block group, *218*
census, *218*
census block, *218*
common area maintenance (CAM) clause, *230*
congestion, *215*
cotenancy clause, *229*
cumulative attraction, *215*
customer spotting, *218*
exclusive-use clause, *230*
fixed-rate lease, *229*

fringe, *217*
geographic information system (GIS), *218*
graduated lease, *229*
Huff gravity model, *222*
metropolitan statistical area (MSA), *208*
micropolitan statistical area (μSA), *208*
natural barrier, *213*
outparcel, *230*
percentage lease, *228*
percentage lease with a specified maximum, *229*

percentage lease with a specified minimum, *229*
primary trading area, *217*
prohibited-use clause, *229*
regression analysis, *223*
secondary trading area, *217*
sliding scale lease, *229*
Spending Potential Index (SPI), *221*
tertiary trading area, *217*
trade area, *217*
traffic flow, *212*
visibility, *215*

GET OUT AND DO IT!

1. **CONTINUING CASE ASSIGNMENT** Evaluate the location of a store operated by the retailer you have selected for the Continuing Case. What is the size and shape of the retailer's trade area? Describe the positive and negative aspects of its location. Compare the store's location with the locations of its competitors.

2. **INTERNET EXERCISE** Go to www.esri.com/library/fliers/pdfs/tapestry_segmentation.pdf and identify five segments that you would expect to find in your zip code. Then go to www.esri.com/data/esri_data/zip-tapestry and type in your zip code. Compare the segments that are found in your zip code with your initial prediction. Are they similar or different?

3. **INTERNET EXERCISE** Go to http://www.esri. com/what-is-gis, the home page for ESRI Geographical Information Systems, and read about GIS. Afterwards, explain how retailers can make better decisions with GIS.

4. **INTERNET EXERCISE** The U.S. Census Bureau tracks key population characteristics, such as age, gender, disability, employment, income, language, poverty, and race. Go to the U.S. Census Bureau home page at http://factfinder2.census.gov/faces/nav/jsf/pages/index.xhtml, and, using the Population Finder, look up key demographic data for your state. Explain which factors would be most important for retailers considering this location to evaluate.

5. **GO SHOPPING** Go to a shopping mall. Get or draw a map of the stores. Analyze whether the stores are clustered in some logical manner. For instance, are all the high-end stores together? Is there a good mix of retailers catering to comparison shoppers near one another?

6. **GO SHOPPING** Visit a jewelry store in an enclosed mall and one in a neighborhood strip shopping center. List the pros and cons for each location. Which location is the most desirable? Why is this the case?

7. **WEB OLC EXERCISE** Go to the student side of the book's website, and click on "Location." You will see an Excel spreadsheet that contains the sales for 45 retail locations of a sporting goods retail chain, plus the characteristics of each location: number of households in trading area, percentage of households with children under 15 years old, percentage of households in appropriate Tapestry segments that the retailer is targeting, distance from a Walmart store, and distance from a Sports Authority store. Estimate a multiple regression model that predicts sales as a function of the site characteristics, and use the estimate weights to evaluate the two sites at the bottom of the spreadsheet.

DISCUSSION QUESTIONS AND PROBLEMS

1. Which factors do retailers consider when evaluating an area of the country to locate stores? How do retailers determine the trade area for a store?

2. True Value Hardware plans to open a new store. Two sites are available, both in middle-income neighborhood centers. One neighborhood is 20 years old and has been well maintained. The other was recently built in a newly planned community. Which site is preferable for True Value? Why?

3. Trade areas are often described as concentric circles emanating from the store or shopping center. Why is this practice used? Suggest an alternative method. Which would you use if you owned a store in need of a trade area analysis?

4. Under what circumstances might a retailer use the analog approach for estimating demand for a new store? What about regression analysis?

5. Retailers have a choice of locating on a mall's main floor or second or third level. Typically, the main floor offers the best, but most expensive, locations. Why would specialty stores such as Radio Shack and Foot Locker choose the second or third floor?

6. What retail locations are best for department stores, consumer electronics category killers, specialty apparel stores, and warehouse stores? Discuss your rationale.

7. If you were considering the ownership of a Taco Bell franchise, what would you want to know about the location in terms of traffic, population, income, employment, and competition? What else would you need to research about a potential location?

8. A drugstore is considering opening a new location at shopping center A, with hopes of capturing sales from a new neighborhood under construction. Two nearby shopping centers, B and C, will provide competition. Using the following information and the Huff gravity model, determine the probability that residents of the new neighborhood will shop at shopping center A:

Shopping center	Size (000's sq. ft.)	Distance from new neighborhood (miles)
A	3,500	4
B	1,500	5
C	300	3

Assume that $\lambda = 2$.

SUGGESTED READINGS

Baumgartner, H., and J. B. E. M. Steenkamp. "Retail Site Selection." In L.A.M. Moutinho and G.D. Hutcheson (Eds), *The SAGE Dictionary of Quantitative Management Research*. Thousands Oak, CA: Sage, 2011.

Can, Cui, Jiechen Wang, Yingxia Pu, Jinsong Ma, and Gang Chen, "GIS Based Method of Delimitating Trade Area for Retail Chains," *International Journal of Geographical Information Science* 26, 19 (2012), pp. 1863–1879.

Cox, Emmett. *Retail Analytics: The Secret Weapon*. Hoboken, NJ: Wiley, 2011.

Duggal, Nini. *Use of GIS in Retail Location Analysis*. Saarbrücken, Germany: VDM Verlag, 2008.

Gibbs, Robert. *Principles of Urban Retail Planning and Development*. Hoboken, NJ: Wiley, 2012.

Joseph, Lawrence, and Michael Kuby. "Gravity Modeling and Its Impacts on Location Analysis." In H. A. Eiselt (Ed), *Foundations of Location Analysis*. New York: Springer, 2011.

Ki, Yingru Li, and Lin Liu. "Assessing the Impact of Retail Location on Store Performance: A Comparison of Wal-Mart and Kmart Stores in Cincinnati." *Applied Geography* 32, no. 2 (March 2012), pp. 591–600.

Suárez-Vega, Rafael, Dolores R. Santos-Peñate, and Pablo Dorta-González. "Location Models and GIS Tools for Retail Site Location." *Applied Geography* 35, no. 1–2 (November 2012), pp. 2, 35.

Teller, Christoph, and Thomas Reutterer. "The Evolving Concept of Retail Attractiveness: What Makes Retail Agglomerations Attractive When Customers Shop at Them?" *Journal of Retailing and Consumer Services* 15, no. 3 (2008), pp. 127–143.

Tyman, Jeff, and Lewis Poi. "Retail Site Selection and Geographic Information Systems." *Journal of Applied Business Research* 11, no. 2 (2011), pp. 46–54.

Wood, Steve, and Sue Browne. "Convenience Store Location Planning and Forecasting—a Practical Research." *International Journal of Retail and Distribution Management* 35, no. 4 (2007), pp. 233–255.

Human Resource Management

Home Depot has a strong, "orange-blooded" organizational culture based on eight core values. The core values are excellent customer service, taking care of our employees, building strong relationships, respect for all people, entrepreneurial spirit, doing the "right" thing, giving back, and creating shareholder value. These values, emblazoned on our orange aprons, guide the actions of our associates as they interact with customers as well as each other. We encourage an "open door" philosophy and associates frequently make suggestions on how we might do a better job of living our core values. Our facility in Atlanta is called a store support center or SSC for short. It is not referred to as the "corporate headquarters" for several reasons. One key reason is our desire to reinforce our role in supporting the activities of our front line associates in servicing customers. We think with a mindset of simplification: Everything we do must make the role of our store-based associates easier so they can provide excellent customer service to our end consumers.

My functional responsibilities are developing and managing Home Depot's compensation, health and welfare benefits, and medical health management programs. In addition to these corporate-wide responsibilities, I am the senior HR business partner responsible for supporting HR activities in the company's merchandising, marketing, and supply chain organizations.

The human resource department plays a critical role in reinforcing these messages and it is how we define HR's strategic value. At The Home Depot, we believe that paying attention to HR, adopting progressive policies, and using these to distinguish ourselves in the marketplace is a source of sustainable competitive advantage. This takes a lot of work and "investment," but pays dividends that competitors can't easily replicate (e.g., by matching prices) and builds real employee connection/commitment. Our founders said it best: "Take care of our associates, they will take care of our customers, and everything else will take care of itself." These efforts help build an employment brand linked to understanding employees' real needs and it is part of the strategic way HR contributes to how we go to market.

CHAPTER 9

LEARNING OBJECTIVES

LO1 Review the objectives of human resource management.

LO2 Discuss the major issues facing human resource managers.

LO3 Summarize the activities retail employees undertake and how they are typically organized.

LO4 Present activities undertaken to win the talent war.

LO5 Identify the legal issues involved with human resource management.

As noted above, "Taking Care of Our People" is one of our core values. One of the ways my team demonstrates this is in the design and execution of what we believe is one of the best total reward packages in the retail industry. In addition to the routinely provided base pay and competitive suite of benefits, we have added a unique component to our rewards program known as "Success Sharing." The program is designed to share the rewards from our associates' efforts for achieving certain benchmark levels of financial performance. Payments in the program are made two times a year and can average between 2% and 6% of the associates' pay. All hourly associates are included in the program. In the last year, virtually every associate received a payment and we paid out almost $200 million! This program helps drive a closer link between the associates' efforts and the financial results they help achieve.

In another example, a survey of our associates revealed that providing daycare for their children was a major challenge. In addition, we noted that providing elder care was an emerging trend. We considered a number of alternatives to solve this problem. Having onsite daycare centers at the approximately 2,000 Home Depot locations across the United States was not a feasible solution. However, we were able to partner with a third party who could provide both child and elder care for our associates as the need arose. Providing this type of support is yet another way to emphasize our core value of supporting our sales associates, while at the same time enabling them to provide excellent customer service.

For our Atlanta-based associates, we were able to take that a step further. We built an onsite daycare facility. It is one of the largest corporate-sponsored daycare facilities in the United States. The facility is open to all Home Depot employees in the Atlanta area, not just those who work at the SSC. In addition, for school-age children, we have summer camps. The daycare center gives our employees an opportunity to check up on their children during the day and even have lunch with them in the company cafeteria. It provides an important advantage in our search for talent in Atlanta's highly competitive labor market.

To bolster our efforts to attract and retain the best merchandising talent available we have developed an integrated recruiting and talent management program. We seek out the most talented prospects to fill critical leadership roles in merchandising. Once we have identified the right people, we individually tailor a program to provide them with the necessary skills and knowledge to be successful in their role. Ongoing formal learning and on-the-job training are key components of the program.

The Home Depot provides a great environment where you can test your skills in the rapidly changing retail environment. It is energizing and a great place to fulfill a person's career ambitions.

Retailers achieve their financial objectives by effectively managing five critical assets: location, merchandise inventory, channels, employees, and customers. This chapter focuses on managing employees—building a human resource competitive advantage. Sam Walton, founder of Walmart, famously warned that if employee support was not the top priority for members of his management team, they would no longer be part of that team. To ensure company success, he believed that the workforce had to be inspired to contribute their ideas actively, as well as engage with their job and the company.[1] Howard Schultz, founder and CEO of Starbucks, supporting this perspective said, "The relationship that we have with our people and the culture of our company are our most sustainable competitive advantages."[2]

Human resource management (HRM) is responsible for aligning the capabilities and behaviors of employees with the short- and long-term goals of the retail firm. Effective management of HRM can build a competitive advantage by lowering costs and/or increasing differentiation. In particular, as the largest controllable expense for most retailers, labor might take up around 10 percent of revenues earned, which means that effective HRM also has an opportunity to produce a cost advantage.[3] In addition, employees can play a major role in differentiating a retailer's offering by enhancing a customer's experience through the information and assistance they provided. The differentiating advantages gained through HRM are difficult for competitors to duplicate. For example, Nordstrom sales associates are known for providing outstanding customer service. However, most retailers are not able to develop Nordstrom's customer-oriented culture in their own firms.

Two chapters in this text are devoted to HRM because it is such an important function. This chapter focuses on the broad strategic issues involving organization structure; the general approaches used for motivating and coordinating employee activities; and the management practices for building an effective, engaged workforce and reducing turnover. The specific activities undertaken to implement the retailer's human resource strategy, including recruiting, selecting, training, supervising, evaluating, and compensating sales associates, are typically undertaken by store management. These more operational issues are discussed in more detail in Chapter 16 in the Store Management section of this textbook.

OBJECTIVES OF HUMAN RESOURCE MANAGEMENT

LO1

Review the objectives of human resource management.

HRM Performance Measures

Three measures that retailers frequently use to assess HRM performance are employee productivity, turnover, and engagement.

Productivity   **Productivity** is the sales generated per employee calculated as follows:

$$\text{Employee productivity} = \frac{\text{Net sales}}{\text{Number of full-time equivalent employees (FTEs)}}$$

A full-time equivalent is the number of hours worked by an employee divided by the number of hours considered to be a full-time workweek for an employee. Thus, a sales associate who worked 12 hours for a retailer with a standard workweek of 36 hours would be considered a one-third FTE. Employee productivity can be improved by increasing the sales generated by employees, reducing the number of employees, or both.

Turnover   Another HRM performance measure is turnover. Employee **turnover** is calculated as follows:

$$\text{Employee turnover} = \frac{\text{Number of employees voluntarily leaving their job during the year}}{\text{Number of positions}}$$

Thus, if a store owner had five sales associate positions but three employees left their jobs and were replaced during the year, the turnover would be $3/5 = 60$ percent. Note that turnover can be greater than 100 percent if a substantial number of people are replaced more than once during the year. In our example, if the replacements for the three employees who left also left during the year, the turnover would be $6/5 = 120$ percent.

Engagement   **Engagement** is an emotional commitment by an employee to the organization and its goals. It goes beyond employee happiness and satisfaction.[5] Employees might be happy at work, but that doesn't necessarily mean they are working hard to make sure the retailer achieves its goals. Similarly satisfied employees might not expend extra effort on their own. Engaged employees care about their work and their company. They don't just work for a paycheck, or just for the next promotion, but they also work to enable the retailer to achieve its goals. They are more motivated to support the retailer in its efforts to improve the satisfaction of customers and build customer loyalty. Engaged employees also are less likely to leave the company. Typically, retailers use employee surveys to measure employee engagement.[6]

The mismanagement of human resources can lead to a downward performance spiral, as shown in Exhibit 9–1. Sometimes, when retailers' sales and profits decline due to increased competition, retailers respond by decreasing labor costs because labor is often a retailer's largest controllable expense. They reduce the number of sales associates in stores, hire more part-timers, and spend less on training. A consequence of these decisions is that sales decline even further to create this downward spiral.

Many retailers view employees as a cost rather than as an investment to improve customer service and increase sales. Therefore, these retailers focus on minimizing labor costs. Retailers often provide their store managers with monthly (or weekly) labor cost budgets and evaluate managers on meeting the target payrolls as a percentage of sales. For some managers, these cost pressures become so intense that they require employees to work without clocking in, such that the employees receive wages for fewer hours than they really work.[8] Although these actions may increase short-term productivity and profits, they have an adverse effect on long-term performance because employees are less engaged, and their reduced morale leads to declines in customer service and sales.[9]

REFACT

Apple's employee productivity is $473,000 per employee. The national average is $206,000 in net sales.[4]

REFACT

Over a five-year period, highly engaged workers provide their employers with better profit margins (6 percent greater) and shareholder returns (five times higher).[7]

EXHIBIT 9–1
Downward
Performance Spiral

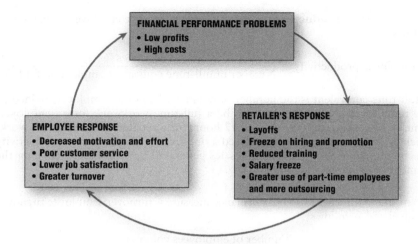

FINANCIAL PERFORMANCE PROBLEMS
• Low profits
• High costs

RETAILER'S RESPONSE
• Layoffs
• Freeze on hiring and promotion
• Reduced training
• Salary freeze
• Greater use of part-time employees
  and more outsourcing

EMPLOYEE RESPONSE
• Decreased motivation and effort
• Poor customer service
• Lower job satisfaction
• Greater turnover

CHALLENGES IN RETAIL HUMAN RESOURCE MANAGEMENT

LO2

Discuss the major issues
facing human resource
managers.

Effective HRM in retailing is very challenging for several reasons. First, it is difficult to achieve a delicate balance between the needs of employees, the development of policies and procedures at the corporate offices, and the implementation of these policies in geographically diverse locations. Second, retailers have increased their proportion of part-time employees in an effort to reduce expenses. Third, as the U.S. population has become more diverse, so has retailers' labor pool, making managing diversity an important objective for HR professionals in retailing. Finally, retailers that have expanded beyond their home country's borders need to modify and adjust their HR perspectives, policies, and procedures.

Balancing the Human Resource Triad

Many retailers feel that human resources are too important to be left only to the human resource department. The full potential of a retailer's human resources is realized when three elements of the HR triad work together—HR professionals, store managers, and employees (see Exhibit 9–2).

Human resource professionals, who typically work out of the corporate office, have specialized knowledge of HR practices and labor laws. They are responsible

EXHIBIT 9–2
Human Resource Triad

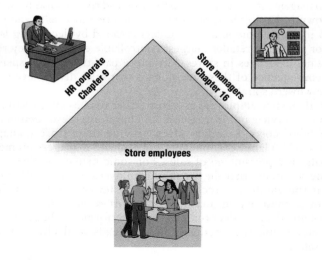

HR corporate
Chapter 9

Store managers
Chapter 16

Store employees

for establishing HR policies that support the retailer's strategy and providing the tools and training used by managers and employees to implement those policies. Store managers are responsible for bringing the policies to life through their daily management of the employees who work for them. The issues confronting HR professionals are discussed in this chapter. Chapter 16, in the Store Management section of this book, reviews the responsibilities of store managers. Finally, the employees also share in the management of human resources. They can play an active role by defining their job functions, providing feedback on the policies, evaluating the performance of managers and coworkers, and managing employee careers.

Expense Control

Retailers must control their expenses if they are to be profitable. Thus, they are cautious about paying high wages to hourly employees who perform low-skill jobs. To control costs, retailers often hire people with little or no experience to work as sales associates, bank tellers, and waiters. High turnover, absenteeism, and poor performance often result from this use of inexperienced, low-wage employees.

The lack of experience and motivation among many retail employees is particularly troublesome because these employees are often in direct contact with customers. Poor appearance, manners, and attitudes can have a negative effect on sales and customer loyalty. Research has shown that in some types of retail operations, a modest investment in hiring more staff will result in a significant increase in sales.[11] If customers can't find a particular product on their own, or if they can't get an explanation of how it works or how it is used, they are not likely to buy the product.

Part-Time Employees

One method of controlling expenses is the use of part-time employees. Retailers' needs for store employees vary depending on the time of day, day of week, time of year, and promotion schedule. With computerized scheduling systems, retailers can control their costs, as well as improve their service provision, because they can match their staffing to customer demand on an hourly basis. The systems account for special events in the surrounding area (e.g., a downtown ice cream shop increases its staffing during the annual town fair), the timing of marketing promotions, and weather and seasonal patterns to make staffing recommendations. To minimize costs, the systems suggest that retailers complement their full-time (40-hours-per-week) store employees with part-time workers. Part-time employees are less expensive than comparable full-time employees. Further, they are usually offered no health or retirement benefits and little job security. However, part-time employees are typically less engaged than full-time employees.[14]

Utilizing Diverse Employee Groups

The changing demographic pattern in the United States will result in a chronic shortage of qualified sales associates. So, besides utilizing less expensive part-time labor, retailers are increasing their efforts to recruit, train, manage, and retain mature, minority, and handicapped workers.

Although young employees have traditionally made up the majority of the retail labor force, retailers have realized that what these employees want out of their jobs and work environments is quite different from what their older supervisors want. Therefore, different approaches need to be used to manage them. Younger employees want more flexibility, meaningful jobs, professional freedom, and a better work–life balance than older employees. They readily switch jobs if their expectations aren't met, making employee turnover high.[16]

To help ease the overall labor shortage and the perceived deficiencies of younger workers, retailers are increasingly turning to older employees because they are more reliable, have lower turnover rates, and often have better work performance.[17] Training costs are also lower for older people because they generally have had strong work experience. These advantages of hiring older employees counterbalance any increased costs in missed days for medical problems.

International Human Resource Issues

The management of employees working for international retailers is especially challenging. Differences in work values, economic systems, and labor laws mean that HR practices that are effective in one country might not be effective in another. For example, U.S. retailers rely heavily on individual performance appraisals and rewards tied to individual performance—a practice consistent with the individualistic U.S. culture. However, in countries with a more collectivist culture, such as China and Japan, many employees downplay individual desires and focus on the needs of the group. Thus, group-based evaluations and incentives are more effective in those countries.[19]

The legal/political system in countries often dictates the human resource management practices that retailers can use. For example, in Spain, a company must pay 20 days of salary for every year worked if it fires an employee. In the Netherlands, employers must get approval from the government to lay off employees. Governments in Colombia, Venezuela, Japan, Korea, and China can also block layoffs. In the EU, McDonald's is required by law to give employees two weeks paid vacation if they work more than 25 hours a week during the year.[20]

The staffing of management positions in foreign countries raises a wide set of issues. Should management be local, or should expatriates be used? How should the local managers or expatriates be selected, trained, and compensated?[21] For example, at the France-based hypermarket chain Carrefour, it is likely for a Brazilian to be managing a store in China. In fact, Carrefour prides itself on grooming managers for global experiences.

The next three sections of this chapter examine three important strategic issues facing retail HR professionals: (1) the design of the organization structure for assigning responsibility and authority for tasks to people and business units, (2) the approaches used to coordinate the activities of the firm's departments and employees and motivate employees to work toward achieving company goals, and (3) the programs used to build employee engagement and retain valuable human resources.

DESIGNING THE ORGANIZATION STRUCTURE FOR A RETAIL FIRM

LO3

Summarize the activities retail employees undertake and how they are typically organized.

The **organization structure** identifies the activities to be performed by specific employees and determines the lines of authority and responsibility in the firm. The first step in developing an organization structure is to determine the tasks that must be performed. Exhibit 9–3 shows tasks that are typically performed in a retail firm.

These tasks are divided into four major categories in retail firms: strategic management, administrative management (operations), merchandise management, and

Tasks Performed by the Typical Multichannel Retail Firm   **EXHIBIT 9–3**

STRATEGIC MANAGEMENT
- Develop overall retail strategy
- Identify the target market
- Determine the retail format
- Design organizational structure
- Develop private-label merchandise
- Develop Internet/catalog strategy
- Develop global strategy
- Coordinate multichannel offering

MERCHANDISE MANAGEMENT
- Buy merchandise
  - Select, negotiate with, and evaluate vendors
  - Select merchandise
  - Place orders
- Control merchandise inventory
  - Develop merchandise budget plans
  - Allocate merchandise to stores
  - Review open-to-buy and stock positions
- Price merchandise
  - Set initial prices
  - Adjust prices

STORE MANAGEMENT
- Recruit, hire, and train store personnel
- Plan labor schedules
- Evaluate store and personnel performance
- Maintain store facilities
- Locate and display merchandise
- Sell merchandise to customers
- Repair and alter merchandise
- Provide services such as gift wrapping and delivery
- Handle customer complaints
- Take physical inventory
- Prevent inventory shrinkage

	Strategic management		Store management
	Merchandise management		Administrative management

ADMINISTRATIVE MANAGEMENT
- Marketing
  - Promote the firm, its merchandise, and its services
  - Plan communication programs including advertising
  - Plan special promotions and events
  - Manage public relations
  - Coordinate social media programs
- Manage human resources
  - Develop policies for managing store personnel
  - Recruit, hire, and train managers
  - Keep employee records
- Manage supply chain
  - Receive merchandise
  - Store merchandise
  - Ship merchandise to stores
  - Return merchandise to vendors
- Manage financial performance
  - Provide timely information on financial performance
  - Forecast sales, cash flow, and profits
  - Raise capital from investors
  - Select and manage locations (real estate)
- Visual merchandising
  - Develop and coordinate displays in stores and windows
- Management information systems
  - Work with all functional areas to develop and operate information systems for merchandising, marketing, accounting, finance, etc.
- General counsel (legal)
  - Work with all functional areas to be in compliance with laws and regulations

store management. The organization of this textbook is based on these tasks and the managers who perform them. Section II of this text focuses on strategic and administrative tasks. Strategic marketing decisions (discussed in Chapters 5 and 6) are undertaken primarily by senior management: the CEO, chief operating officer, vice presidents, and the board of directors that represents shareholders in publicly owned firms. Administrative tasks (discussed in Chapters 7 through 11) are performed by corporate managers who have specialized skills in human resource management, finance, accounting, real estate, supply chain, management information systems, marketing, visual merchandising, and legal issues.

In retail firms, category managers, buyers, and merchandise planners are involved in merchandise management (Section III of this textbook), and store managers and the regional managers above them are involved in the management of the stores (Section IV). These managers are responsible for implementing the strategic plans and making the day-to-day decisions that directly affect the retailer's performance.

To illustrate the connection between the tasks performed in Exhibit 9–2 and the organization structure presented in the following sections, the tasks are color-coded. Green ▢ is used for the strategic tasks, orange ▢ for the administrative tasks, yellow ▢ for the merchandising tasks, and blue ▢ for the store management tasks.

Organization of a Single-Store Retailer

Initially, the owner-manager of a single store may be the entire organization. When he or she goes to lunch or heads home, the store closes. As sales grow, the owner-manager may hire employees. Coordinating and controlling employee activities is easier in a small store than in a large chain of stores. The owner-manager simply assigns tasks to each employee and watches to see that these tasks are performed properly. Because the number of employees is limited, single-store retailers have little **specialization**. Each employee may perform a wide range of activities, while the owner-manager is responsible for all strategic decisions.

As sales continue to increase, specialization in management may occur when the owner-manager hires additional management employees. Exhibit 9–4 illustrates the common division of management responsibilities into merchandise and store management. The owner-manager continues to perform strategic management tasks. The store manager may be responsible for administrative tasks associated with receiving and shipping merchandise and managing the employees. The merchandise manager or **buyer** may handle the advertising and promotion tasks, as well as merchandise selection and inventory management tasks. Often the owner-manager contracts with an accounting firm to perform financial control tasks for a fee.

EXHIBIT 9–4   Organization Structure for a Small Retailer

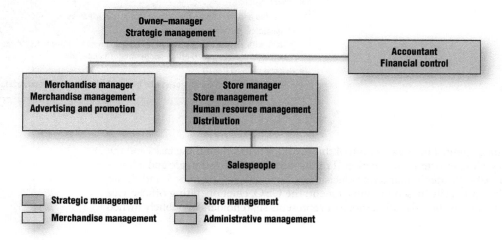

Organization of a National Retail Chain

In contrast to the management of a single store, the management of a retail chain is complex. Managers must supervise units that are geographically diverse. In the following sections, we discuss the organization structure of a typical retail chain.

Exhibit 9–5 shows the organization chart of a typical department store. The **chief executive officer (CEO)** is responsible for overseeing the entire organization. Reporting to the CEO are the presidents of global operations, the Internet channels, and private-label management and the senior vice presidents of merchandising, stores, and administration.

Merchandising   Looking at the merchandising division, the **senior vice president (SVP) of merchandising** works with buyers and planners to develop and coordinate the management of the retailer's merchandise offering and ensure that it is consistent with the firm's strategy. The organization and responsibilities of the merchandising division are detailed in Chapters 12, 13, and 14 of the textbook.

The buyers in the merchandise division are responsible for determining the merchandise assortment, pricing, and managing relationships and negotiating with vendors. Most retail chains have a set of planning positions parallel to the buying positions supervised by a senior vice president of planning. The **merchandising**

Organization of a Typical Department Store Chain   EXHIBIT 9–5

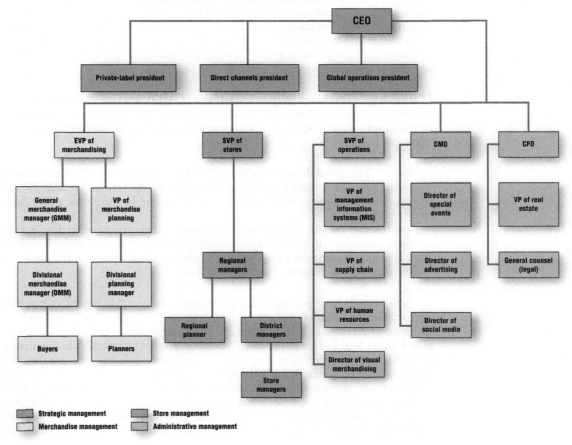

planners are responsible for allocating merchandise and tailoring the assortment of several categories for specific stores in a geographic area.

As shown in Exhibit 9–5, there are several levels of management in the merchandise division—general merchandise managers (GMMs), divisional merchandise managers (DMMs), and buyers. Most large retailers have several GMMs who are responsible for several merchandise classifications. Similarly, several DMMs report to each GMM and a number of buyers report to each DMM.

Stores   The **senior vice president (SVP) of stores** supervises all activities related to stores, including working with the regional managers, who supervise district managers, who supervise the individual store managers.

Store managers in large stores have several assistant store managers who report to them (not depicted in Exhibit 9–5). Typically, one assistant manager is responsible for administration and manages the receiving, restocking, and presentation of the merchandise in the store. Another is responsible for human resources, including selecting, training, and evaluating employees. A third is responsible for operations such as store maintenance and store security.

Each region often has regional planners who work as liaisons between stores in their region and the corporate planners to ensure that the stores have the right merchandise, at the right time, in the right quantities. The stores division also works closely with the real estate division (under the chief financial officer) to plan new stores and with those in charge of visual merchandising, layout, and store design.

Operations   The **executive vice president (EVP) of operations** oversees managers in charge of management information systems (MISs), supply chain, human resources, and visual merchandising. The EVP of operations is also in charge of shrinkage and loss prevention and the operation and maintenance of the physical assets of the firm, such as stores, offices, distribution and fulfillment centers, and trucks (these functions are not reflected in Exhibit 9–5).

Marketing   The **chief marketing officer (CMO)** works with staff to develop advertising, promotion, and social media programs. Managers in charge of public relations, annual events, credit marketing, and cause-related marketing initiatives also report to the CMO.

Finance   The **chief financial officer (CFO)** works with the CEO on financial issues such as equity-debt structure and credit card operations. In addition, the real estate division and general counsel (legal) divisions, headed by vice presidents, report to the CFO.

Retailers vary considerably on how they organize their private-label development activities, international operations, and Internet/catalog channels. Exhibit 9–5 shows these activities as being performed by wholly owned subsidiaries with the presidents of three subsidiaries reporting to the CEO.

Private Label   The **private-label president** is responsible for the conceptualization, design, sourcing, quality control, and marketing of private-label and exclusive merchandise. When the private-label organization is a separate division, as in Exhibit 9–5, buyers in the merchandising division often evaluate the private-label merchandise offering as they would any other vendor, and they are therefore free to accept or reject the private-label merchandise presented. In some retail organizations, decisions on what private-label merchandise is included in the retailer's assortment are strategic decisions made by senior managers. In these cases, the buyers are required to carry private-label merchandise, and the sourcing and quality control are done by a VP of private-label development. In either case, the managers involved with private-label merchandise work closely with buyers and planners to ensure that the merchandise offered in each category is coherent and meets the needs of the retailer's target market. (See Chapter 13 for more on how private labels are purchased.)

Internet, Mobile, and Catalog Channels   The **president of direct channels** is responsible for the selection and pricing of the merchandise assortment offered through the Internet, mobile, and catalog channels, the maintenance and design of the retailer's website, customer call centers, and the fulfillment centers that fill orders for individual customers. However, many multichannel retailers are integrating the operation of the Internet, mobile, and catalog channels with their store channel. At these retailers, the selection and management of the merchandise offered in all four channels (stores, Internet, mobile, and catalog) for a category are handled by the same buying team, rather than by separate buyers for each channel. The buying team might include specialists in direct channels and a financial analyst in addition to associate and assistant buyers.

Global   The **global operations president** oversees retailing operations outside the home country. The size and complexity of this operation are determined by the number of countries served and the number of stores within each country. Regardless of size, many of the functions performed by the home-country operation are duplicated in the global operations. For instance, the global organization typically has merchandising, administration, stores, and operations divisions for each country or region.

Centralization and Coordination

Two important organizational issues are (1) the degree to which decision making is centralized or decentralized and (2) the approaches used to coordinate merchandise and store management. The first issue translates into whether the decisions about activities such as merchandise management, information and distribution systems, and human resource management are made by region, district, or store managers or by managers in the corporate headquarters. The second issue arises because retailers divide merchandise and store management activities into different organizations within the firm. Thus, these interdependent activities must be coordinated.

Centralization   **Centralization** occurs when the authority for retailing decisions is delegated to corporate managers rather than to geographically dispersed managers. **Decentralization** occurs when the authority for decisions is assigned to lower levels in the organization. Retailers reduce costs when decision making is centralized in corporate management. First, overhead falls because fewer managers are required to make the merchandise, human resource, marketing, real estate, information system, and financial decisions.

Second, by coordinating buying across geographically dispersed stores, the company can bargain for lower prices from suppliers. The retailer can negotiate better purchasing terms by placing one large order rather than a number of smaller orders.

Third, centralization provides an opportunity to have the best people make decisions for the entire corporation. For example, in a centralized organization, people with the greatest expertise in areas such as management information systems (MISs), buying, store design, or visual merchandise can offer all stores the benefit of their skills.

Fourth, centralization increases efficiency. Standard operating policies developed at the corporate headquarters are applied to the stores, allowing store managers to focus on their core responsibilities. For example, corporate merchandisers perform considerable research to determine the best method of presenting merchandise. They provide detailed guides for displaying merchandise to each store manager so that all stores have a consistent brand image throughout the country. Because they offer the same core merchandise in all stores, centralized retailers can achieve economies of scale by advertising through national media rather than more costly local media.

For Home Depot, centralization has been particularly effective in its hiring policies. The retailer hires more than half a million salespeople every year. With its previously decentralized screening process, Home Depot relied on store managers—many of whom lacked much hiring experience—to assess applicants and provide them with all the necessary information. The system was inefficient and often ineffective, for both the company and the newly hired employees. In the centralized system, all applications get reviewed by human resource specialists, who first ensure that the candidates meet some minimum requirements. In telephone interviews, these specialists ask carefully designed questions to assess the job seeker's capabilities, such as whether they like to solve problems. In addition, they describe the job in detail, including the need for heavy lifting, the likelihood of weekend and evening shifts, and the exact pay scale. Only after going through this process, which is the same for every applicant, do the store managers get involved to conduct individualized, face-to-face interviews.[24]

Although centralization has advantages in reducing costs, its disadvantage is that it makes it more difficult for a retailer to adapt to local market conditions. For example, Gainesville is located in central Florida, and thus the manager in charge of the fishing category at the Sports Authority corporate office might think that the Gainesville store's customers primarily engage in freshwater fishing. But the local store manager knows that most of his customers drive 90 miles to go saltwater fishing in either the Gulf of Mexico or the Atlantic Ocean.

In addition to problems with tailoring its merchandise to local needs, a centralized retailer may have difficulty responding to local competition and labor markets. When prices and employee wages are established centrally, individual stores may not be able to respond quickly to competition in their market. Finally, centralized personnel policies may make it hard for local managers to pay competitive wages in their area or hire appropriate types of salespeople.

However, centralized retailers are relying more on their information systems to react to local market conditions. For example, many retailers are now using merchandise and pricing optimization techniques. With specialized software packages, buyers can determine optimal pricing, markdowns, and size and quantity allocations on a store-by-store or region-by-region basis. These techniques are discussed in detail in Chapters 12 and 14.

Macy's is an example of a retail corporation that has migrated from a decentralized organization to a more centralized one so that it can offer its geographically dispersed customers customized assortments. See Retailing View 9.1.

Coordinating Merchandise and Store Management   Small, independent retailers have little difficulty coordinating their stores' buying and selling activities. Owner-managers typically buy the merchandise and work with their salespeople to sell it. In close contact with customers, the owner-managers know what their customers want.

In contrast, large retail firms organize the buying and selling functions into separate divisions. Buyers specialize in buying merchandise and have limited contact with the store management responsible for selling it. While this specialization increases buyers' skills and expertise, it makes it harder for them to understand differences in customers' needs in their target markets. Three approaches large retailers use to coordinate buying and selling are (1) improving buyers' appreciation for the store environment, (2) making store visits, and (3) assigning employees to coordinating roles.

Improving Appreciation for the Store Environment　Some retailers have all management trainees work in the stores before they become buyers or managers in other functional areas. Others utilize a mixed career path in which managers are encouraged to float between store and corporate assignments. This store

RETAILING VIEW　My Macy's—Combining the Benefits of Centralization and Decentralization　9.1

Macy's Inc. evolved into a national department store chain with more than 800 stores through the acquisition of regional chains such as Burdines (Florida), Lazarus (Midwest), and Bullock's (California). However, most of the acquired regional chains kept their original identities and operated as independent businesses with their own buying organizations, information and supply chain systems, and human resource management policies. Due to this extreme decentralization, 7 to 10 buyers from the regional chains would negotiate independently with each vendor, and the Macy's corporation was not realizing the benefits from pooling its orders or the scale economies from developing and maintaining one information system.

In 2009, Macy's began the process of centralizing the decision making in the corporation. All of the regional names acquired through acquisitions and mergers were converted to the name "Macy's." The merchandise buying activities were consolidated in New York City, and the systems and policies were standardized across the regions. These changes enabled Macy's to bargain for lower prices from vendors, reduce administrative expenses, undertake national ad campaigns, and create a consistent brand image.

But when Macy's centralized the buying function, buyers had difficulties in tailoring assortments across more than 800 stores. For example, the national buyer responsible for men's casual T-shirts might not realize that in Columbus, Ohio, there is a tremendous demand for golf apparel because people wear it on the golf course, to parties, and even to church. So Columbus stores should carry more golf apparel. In Chicago, the women's shoe buyer should increase the number of size-11 women's shoes because of the unusually high demand in that area. So, to address this shortcoming of centralization, Macy's launched the My Macy's program.

The first step in the program was to create a new position, district planner, responsible for understanding the unique needs of customers in their region. Each district planner is responsible for one category, such as women's dresses, men's accessories, or food processors. The planners spend time in the stores, talking to customers, employees, and store managers and communicating this information to the central buying office.

Now Macy's is also embracing social media to further personalize its offerings. Through its partnership with

Macy's has launched the My Macy's program to better tailor its offering to the needs of regional markets.

Shopkick, it has provided customers with rewards simply for coming into its stores. It also was an early adopter of QR codes in its marketing communications, and its Backstage Pass app allows shoppers to access unique video content tied to the product offerings. Macy's also is an active participant in the Facebook community. Its Facebook page offers its fans the opportunity to find out what's happening at a store near them; check out the latest trends, sales, and exclusive offers; and play interactive games. For example, Macy's launched its exclusive brand, Impulse by Nicole Richie. Its Facebook community could review and order merchandise before it was available through Macy's store and Internet channels.

Sources: Walter Loeb, "Macy's New Focus: Will Transformation Bring Customer Growth?" *Forbes*, May 31, 2012; Alex Palmer, "Macy's Transformation," *Direct Marketing*, April 1, 2012, Margaret Case Little, "Macy's Exec Shares the Do's and Dont's of Localization," *NRF Blog*, January 9, 2012; and "CEO Terry Lundgren: A Focus on Turning 'My Macy's' into Your Macy's," *Knowledge@Wharton*, November 11, 2009.

DISCUSSION QUESTION

Why did Macy's make such a large investment in social media?

Terry Lundgren, CEO of Macy's, gets to know his customers and employees by visiting stores.

experience helps corporate managers and buyers gain an appreciation for the activities performed in the stores, the problems salespeople and department managers encounter, and the needs of customers.

Making Store Visits   Another approach to increasing customer contact and communication is to have buyers and other executives visit the stores. Every week, Terry Lundgren, Macy's CEO, goes into several stores, calls the store managers on their cell phones, and asks them to meet him on the selling floor. These unannounced visits don't give the stores or their managers time to prepare to answer questions or change anything on the selling floor, so he sees the stores just as the customers do.[25]

Assigning Employees to Coordinating Roles   Some retailers maintain people in both the merchandise division (planners and allocators who work with buyers) and stores who are responsible for coordinating buying and selling activities. Many national retail chains have regional and even district personnel to coordinate buying and selling activities. For example, Zara store managers around the globe have biweekly meetings via telephone with the design team at the corporate headquarters in A Coruña, Galicia, Spain, to communicate new fashion trends and coordinate inventory issues.

WINNING THE EMPLOYEE TALENT WAR

LO4

Present activities undertaken to win the talent war.

The pool of potential retail employees is decreasing due to changing demographics. There is, however, a need for managers who can effectively deal with the increased complexities of retail jobs, such as the use of new technologies, increased global competition, and a diverse workforce. Sherry Hollock, former vice president of talent and organization development at Macy's, summarizes the importance and challenges of HRM activities for retailers and their customers:

> One of the biggest challenges facing retailers is hiring and retaining managers to lead their companies in the coming years. Over the next 10 years, a lot of senior retail managers, members of the Baby Boomer generation, will be retiring. So retailers are going to be competing with each other and firms in other industries for a smaller pool of available managers in the generations behind the Boomers. In addition, retailing is becoming a much more sophisticated business. Retail managers need to be comfortable with new technologies, information and supply chain management systems, and international business as well as managing a diverse workforce and buying merchandise.[26]

In the following section, we examine how retailers meet these challenges and engage in a "war" with their competitors for talent. Corporate HR departments are the generals in the war for talent. They are responsible for developing programs that will attract, develop, motivate, and keep talent.

Employment Branding

The HR departments for retailers such as Starbucks and Marriott are developing marketing programs to attract and retain the "best and brightest" employees. These programs, called **employment branding** or **employment marketing,** involve undertaking marketing research to understand what potential and current employees are seeking as well as what they think about the retailer; developing a value proposition and an employment brand image; communicating that brand image to potential employees; and then fulfilling the brand promise by ensuring that the employee experience matches the image created.[27] Retailers often use advertising agencies that specialize in employment marketing to develop creative approaches to attract employees.[28] Retailing View 9.2 describes elements of Starbuck's employment branding program.

Developing Talent: Selection and Training

The first step in building an engaged workforce is to recruit and train the right employees. Engagement increases when retailers are very selective in hiring people and make significant investments in training them.

Selective Hiring   Selective hiring leads to employee engagement. When retailers are selective in hiring employees, the selected candidates feel they are special and they are working for a special company—a company that won't take just anybody. Every year The Container Store, a national chain selling products to organize homes and offices, is ranked as one of *Fortune's* 100 best companies to work for. One of the core principals of The Container Store is that one great person is equal to three good people in terms of business productivity. So it takes a lot more than simply going online and filling out an application to get a job with the

The Container Store is very selective in its hiring. Its best hires come from its customer base.

company. Applicants have a phone interview, a two-hour group interview, and as many as three additional one-on-one meetings. During the group interview, applicants asked how Container Store products would help them organize an area in their home. The whole process can take three weeks or more, and that's just for a sales associate position. Most current employees are former customers. Many were approached by sales associates or managers on the sales floor when they were shopping.[29]

Zappos, the online shoe, apparel, and accessories retailer, takes special care in its hiring process. It wants people who believe in what they are doing and love doing it. Hiring the right people is so important to Zappos that it offers new hires $4,000 to quit—although that might not be enough because only 1 percent of new hires take Zappos up on the offer.[30]

Training   Training is particularly important in retailing because the overwhelming majority of retail employees have direct contact with customers. They are responsible for helping customers satisfy their needs and resolve their problems. Training also increases employee engagement. Employees are more committed to companies they are working for when they feel the company is making an investment in them.[31]

9.2   RETAILING VIEW   Employment Branding at Starbucks

To develop its employment branding program, Starbucks undertook research to better understand the best prospective and existing employees. The research revealed that the top performers are engaged. They like their jobs and are emotionally committed to Starbucks. The rewards they receive or will receive from working at Starbucks go beyond pay and promotion opportunities. So Starbucks developed an employment marketing program based on the theme "Love What You Do and Share It with Others." The employment branding program is designed to create the following associations that current and potential employees have with the Starbucks brand: that Starbucks provides an opportunity for employees to express themselves at work, embrace human connection, provide great customer service, develop their own careers, and work for a growing, global company.

Starbucks uses the "Love What You Do and Share it With Others" theme on its Internet site, in its printed material available to prospective employees in stores, and in videos designed to describe the Starbucks employee experience. In this collateral material, real employees describe why they love what they do. Starbucks encourages all of its partners (employees) to get involved in recruiting potential employees. Employees in its stores are trained to respond to customer inquiries about job opportunities and questions about working in the stores.

Starbucks uses social media to build its employment brand to recruit employees and increase the engagement of current employees. Its job app shows open positions by location, videos about what it's like to work at Starbucks, and links to information about benefits, all within Starbucks' Facebook page.

Employees can share information about open positions with their Facebook friends and reach out to the 32 million people who already "Like" the Starbucks page on Facebook. Starbucks isn't just using Facebook. Starbucks

Starbucks builds its employment branding program around the theme "Love What You Do and Share It With Others."

posts jobs on Twitter and LinkedIn, and even has an Instagram page where it posts photos of employees that showcase what it's like to be a partner at Starbucks.

Sources: Emily Parkhurst, "Starbucks Turns to Social Media to Attract Job Candidates," *Puget Sound Business Journal*, November 12, 2012; Sarah Kessler, "Inside Starbucks's $35 Million Mission to Make Brand Evangelists of Its Front-Line Workers," *Fast Company*, October 22, 2012; Louisa Peacock, "Inside HR: Interview with Sandra Porter, HR director at Starbucks," *The Telegraph*, January 31, 2011; Bobbie Gossage, "Howard Schultz, on How to Lead a Turnaround," *Inc.*, April 2011; and Howard Schultz, *Onward: How Starbucks Fought for Its Life Without Losing Its Soul* (New York: Rodale, 2011).

DISCUSSION QUESTION

If you were considering a job at Starbucks, would its social media campaign influence your decision?

At REI, a category killer of active outdoors apparel and equipment, all new employees participate in an orientation program called Base Camp, in which long-time managers and other employees demonstrate workplace solutions to common situations. But rather than taking place in a break room, the Base Camp orientation gets the staff outdoors, interacting with nature as well as with one another. Thus, the training reflects REI's focus on outdoor adventures and respect for nature. The next step takes place on the job, when new hires get paired with a "buddy" for the first two weeks working in the store. Although such training practices demand substantial time investments by the company, its employees, and its prospective employees, it also grants the new hires confidence in their ability to handle any crisis that might arise, and it encourages all employees to share their experience to ensure better customer service.[32]

At Zappos, a new hire, regardless of position, begins his or her job with five weeks of training, including time taking phone orders. This allows new employees to learn about the merchandise and the importance of satisfying customers. This experience also helps weed out employees who believe they are too important to spend time helping customers.

As a final example, Starbucks runs its Leadership Lab to encourage bonds among the nearly 20,000 managers that run its stores. During the lab, managers receive leadership training and problem-solving skills. Furthermore, the massive, 300,000 square foot lab space provides new product and sales technique demonstrations. Beyond these demonstrations, the lab features high-tech lighting and music designs, making the ambiance dramatic and inspiring, in line with the coffee chain's sense of purpose and preferred image. According to CEO Howard Schultz,

> [Employees] are the true ambassadors of our brand, the real merchants romance and theater, and as such the primary catalysts for delighting customers'. The merchant's success depends on his or her ability to tell a story. . . . What people see or hear or smell or do when they enter a space guides their feelings, enticing them to celebrate whatever the seller has to offer.[34]

Retailing View 9.3 describes how a unique quick-service restaurant (QSR) chain selects and trains its employees to build an engaged workforce.

Motivating Talent: Aligning Goals

The task of aligning the employees' and the firm's goals is often difficult, because employees' goals usually differ from those of the firm. For example, a sales associate might find it more personally rewarding to arrange a display creatively than to help a customer. Retailers generally use three methods to motivate and coordinate their employees' activities: (1) written policies and supervision, (2) compensation-based incentives, and (3) organization culture.

Policies and Supervision   Perhaps the most fundamental method of coordination is to prepare written policies that indicate what employees should do and then to have supervisors enforce these policies. For example, retailers may set policies about when and how merchandise can be returned by customers. If employees use the written policies to make return decisions, their actions will be consistent with the retailer's strategy. But strict reliance on written policies also can reduce employee motivation because employees have little opportunity to use their own initiative to improve performance in their areas of responsibility. As a result, they eventually might find their jobs uninteresting and be less engaged.[35] So retailers empower their employees to make decisions about how they do their jobs and interact with customers. (Empowerment is discussed later in this chapter and in Chapter 18).

Compensation-Based Incentives   The second method of motivating and coordinating employees involves the use of various forms of compensation to

REFACT

A full-time salesperson at The Container Store receives about 241 hours of training, compared to the retail industry average of about 7 to 10 hours—the lowest of all industries. Averaging only 7 hours per employee per year, the retail industry spends less time on training than all other industries.[33]

REFACT

The late Mary Kay Ash, founder of Mary Kay Cosmetics, was fond of saying, "There are two things that people want more than sex and money—recognition and praise."[36]

encourage them to perform activities consistent with the retailer's objectives. A common type of compensation for retail sales associates is a **commission,** which is an incentive based on a percentage of their sales made or margin generated by the employee. Many retailers base at least part of salespeople's compensation on commissions.

Another individual incentive is a **bonus,** which is additional compensation awarded periodically on the basis of an evaluation of the employee's performance.

9.3   RETAILING VIEW   Pret A Manger Is Not Your Typical Fast-Food Restaurant

With headquarters in the United Kingdom, Pret A Manger ("ready to eat" in French) operates more than 300 stores in the United Kingdom, United States, and Hong Kong—but 80 percent of its locations are in London. Its menu includes sushi, salads, soups, wraps, and sandwiches complemented with hot and cold drinks and desserts. What differentiates its offering from most other quick-service restaurants is that all items are fresh, healthy, and made with natural ingredients. All sandwiches are made on the day of purchase in a kitchen at each location. Food unsold at the end of the day is donated to charities. In addition, its employees provide speedy customer service with a smile.

Pret's goal is to serve customers within 60 seconds. The challenge of providing a fast, efficient, and professional service to the customer can be exciting—as long as the employees find the setting motivational instead of stressful. To foster buzz, Pret seeks out prospective hires who are good humored, friendly, fun, and lively, such that they are likely to live up to the company's key values: team working, clear talking, passion. Good prospects undergo a one-day trial run in an actual restaurant; the staff in that branch vote, at the end of the day, whether to hire the candidate. Anyone who is not caught up in the buzz gets paid for their time, thanked politely, and then shown the door.

But for those who make the grade, the training process has just begun. A 10-day program focuses on the Pret way—summarized in the training booklet *Pret Behaviors*—as well as basic hygiene and safety topics. If, throughout their training, the new hires pass tests in "bustling around and being active" rather than "standing around looking bored," for example, they achieve team member status. Then they enter yet another training process, this one lasting for 10 weeks. During this extended training, they learn the practices of both the front and the back of the restaurant. Successful completion of this training qualifies them to be team member stars. With these policies and training, Pret has achieved a remarkably low employee turnover rate of

Pret A Manger feels it can teach employees how to make sandwiches, but it can't teach people to be happy. So it hires happy people.

just 60 percent, whereas its competitors in the fast-food market often suffer 400 percent turnover.

Sources: Julia Werdigier, "Rallying the Team to Cater to the Company's Strengths," *The New York Times*, May 9, 2012; "Smiley Culture: Pret A Manger's Secret Ingredient?" *The Telegraph*, March 2012; and Stephanie Clifford, "Would You Like a Smile with That?" *The New York Times*, August 6, 2011.

DISCUSSION QUESTION

What does Pret A Manger do to build employee engagement?

For example, store managers often receive bonuses at the end of the year based on their store's performance relative to its budgeted sales and profits. In addition to receiving compensation-based incentives based on individual performance, retail managers often receive income based on their firm's performance. Known as **profit sharing,** this type of incentive can be offered as a cash bonus based on the firm's profits or as a grant of stock options that link additional income to the performance of the firm's stock.

Some retailers use stock incentives to motivate and reward all employees, including sales associates. Employees are encouraged to buy shares in their companies at discounted prices through payroll deduction plans. These stock incentives align employees' interests with those of the company and can be very rewarding when the company does well. However, if growth in the company's stock price declines, employee morale declines too, corporate culture is threatened, and demands for higher wages and more benefits develop.

Incentives are very effective at motivating employees to perform the activities on which the incentives are based. But incentives also may cause employees to ignore other activities.[37] For example, salespeople whose compensation is based entirely on their sales may be reluctant to spend time restocking fixtures and shelves. Excessive use of incentives to motivate employees also can reduce employee commitment. Company loyalty falls because employees feel that the firm hasn't made a commitment to them (because it is unwilling to guarantee their compensation). Thus, if a competitor offers to pay a higher commission rate, they'll feel free to leave.

Organization Culture   The final method for motivating and coordinating employees is to develop a strong organization culture. An **organization culture** is the set of values, traditions, and customs of a firm that guides employee behavior. These guidelines aren't written down as a set of policies and procedures; they are traditions passed along by experienced employees to new employees. Organization culture often has a much stronger effect on employees' actions than do rewards offered through compensation plans, directions provided by supervisors, or written company policies.[38]

Many retail firms have strong organization cultures that give employees a sense of what they ought to do on their jobs and how they should behave to be consistent with the firm's strategy.[39] For example, Nordstrom's strong organization culture emphasizes customer service, whereas Walmart's focuses on reducing costs so that it can provide low prices to its customers.

Nordstrom emphasizes the strength of its organization culture in the policy manual given to new employees. The manual has one rule: "Use your best judgment to do anything you can to provide service to our customers." Lack of written rules doesn't mean that Nordstrom employees have no guidelines or restrictions on their behavior; rather, the organization culture guides employees' behavior. New salespeople learn from other employees that they should always wear clothes sold at Nordstrom, that they should park their cars at the outskirts of the parking lot so that customers can park in more convenient locations, that they should approach customers who enter their department, that they should accept any merchandise returned by a customer even if the merchandise wasn't purchased at a Nordstrom store, and that they should offer to carry packages to the customer's car.

Organization cultures are developed and maintained through stories and symbols. Values in an organization culture are often explained to new employees and reinforced to present employees through stories.

Whole Foods strengthens its organization culture by working in teams and using its employees during the hiring process.[40] Each store is organized into approximately 10 teams, each responsible for a different category or aspect of store operations, such as customer service or checkout lines. Store operations are highly decentralized, so many purchasing and operational decisions are made by the teams. When hiring, team leaders screen candidates, but a two-thirds majority of the team must approve each hire. Target also emphasizes teamwork by calling sales associates "team members" and store managers "team leaders."

Using symbols is another technique for managing organization culture and conveying its underlying values. Symbols are an effective means of communicating with employees because the values they represent can be remembered easily. Walmart makes extensive use of symbols and symbolic behavior to reinforce its emphasis on controlling costs and keeping in contact with its customers. Photocopy machines at corporate headquarters have cups on them for employees to use to pay for any personal copying. At the traditional Saturday morning executive meeting, employees present information on the cost-control measures they've recently undertaken. Managers who have been traveling in the field report on what they've seen, unique programs undertaken in the stores, and promising merchandise. Headquarters are spartan. Founder Sam Walton, one of the world's wealthiest people before he died, lived in a modest house and drove a pickup truck to work.

Keeping Talent   Having selected, trained, and aligned the employees' and the retailers' goals, HRM needs to keep the talent—that is, reduce turnover. High turnover reduces sales and increases costs. Sales are lost because inexperienced replacement employees lack the skills and knowledge about company policies and merchandise to interact effectively with customers; costs increase due to the need to recruit and train new employees.

Consider what happens when Bob Roberts, meat department manager in a supermarket chain, leaves the company. His employer promotes a manager from a smaller store to take Bob's position, promotes an assistant department manager to the position in the smaller store, promotes a meat department trainee to the assistant manager's position, and hires a new trainee. Now the supermarket chain needs to train two meat department managers and one assistant manager and hire and train one trainee. The estimated cost for replacing Bob Roberts is almost $10,000.

To reduce turnover and engage employees, retailers need to build an atmosphere of mutual commitment in their firms. When a retailer demonstrates its commitment, employees respond by developing loyalty to the company. Employees improve their skills and work hard for the company when they feel the company is committed to them over the long run, through thick and thin. Some approaches that retailers take to build mutual commitment are (1) empowering employees and (2) creating a partnering relationship with employees.

Empowering Employees   **Empowerment** is a process in which managers share power and decision-making authority with employees. When employees have the authority to make decisions, they are more confident in their abilities, have a greater opportunity to provide service to customers, and are more committed to the firm's success.[42]

Convenience store chain Quik Trip not only empowers its employees to make decisions about routine transactions, such as remaking a sandwich or giving a customer a refund, but also allows them to make decisions about how to help individuals in need. Quik Trip is integrally involved in a youth outreach program called National Safe Place. The goal of this program is to teach potential runaways about the dangers they will face; it also provides suggestions for ways to resolve problems. In addition to hosting "safe locations" at schools and libraries, Safe Place cites Quik Trip stores as havens for kids. When they seek out a Quik Trip sanctuary because they feel threatened or are afraid to go home for whatever reason, Quik Trip employees are trained to do whatever it takes to make them feel safe until a trained counselor arrives.[43]

The first step in empowering employees is reviewing employee activities that require a manager's approval. For example, an upscale department store chain changed its check authorization policy, thereby empowering sales associates to accept personal checks of up to $1,000 without a manager's approval. Under the

REFACT
Sam Walton had flown first-class only once in his life, on a trip to Africa.[41]

old policy, a customer often had to wait more than 10 minutes for the sales associate to locate a manager. Then the busy manager simply signed the check without reviewing the customer's identification. When the sales associates were empowered to make approvals, service improved, and the number of bad checks decreased, because the sales associates felt personally responsible and checked identification carefully.[44]

Empowerment of retail employees transfers authority and responsibility for making decisions to lower levels in the organization. Because these employees are closer to the customers, they are in a good position to know what it takes to satisfy them. For empowerment to work, managers must have an attitude of respect and trust, not control and distrust.

Engaging Employees   There are five HR management activities that build employee engagement: (1) reduce status differences, (2) promote from within, (3) enable employees to balance their careers and families (4) provide benefits, and (5) use social media.

Reduce Status Differences   Many retailers attempt to reduce status differences among employees. With limited status differences, employees feel that they play important roles in the firm's ability to achieve its goals and that their contributions are valued.

Status differences can be reduced symbolically through the use of language and substantively by lowering wage differences and increasing communications among managers at different levels in the company. To build engagement among its employees, JCPenney has dropped many of the traditional pretenses that defined an old-style hierarchical organization.[45] For instance, at the Plano, Texas, corporate headquarters, all employees are on a first-name basis, have a flexible workweek, and may attend leadership workshops intended to build an executive team for the future.

Whole Foods has a policy of limiting executive compensation to 19 times the compensation of the average full-time salaried employee. CEO John Mackey receives a total compensation of $760,000, much less than CEOs at other large retail chains.[46] Sam Walton typically appeared on lists of the most underpaid CEOs.

Promote from Within   This staffing policy involves hiring new employees only for positions at the lowest level in the job hierarchy and then promoting experienced employees to openings at higher levels in the hierarchy. Many retailers, including Kroger, have a policy of promoting from within when possible. Marnette Perry, for instance, is currently Kroger's senior vice president of strategy and operations and has about 40 percent of the company reporting to her. But she has served the organization in many capacities, including as a produce manager, as manager of the floral and natural food centers, and as president of several of Kroger's divisions.[47]

Promotion-from-within policies establish a sense of fairness. When employees do an outstanding job and then outsiders are brought in over them, the employees feel that the company doesn't care about them. Promotion-from-within policies also commit the retailer to developing its own employees.[48]

Balance Careers and Families   The increasing number of two-income and single-parent families makes it difficult for employees to effectively do their jobs and manage their households simultaneously. Further, the difficult economy retailers have experienced for the past few years has caused retailers to lay off some employees and cut some benefits to others. Some retailers recognize that although some perks are expensive, they aren't nearly as expensive as losing good employees. So retailers are building employee engagement by offering services such as child care centers, backup child care, scholarships for employees' kids, concierge services, adoption benefits, onsite health clubs, and even massages.[49]

Flextime is a job scheduling system that enables employees to choose the times they work. With **job sharing,** two employees voluntarily are responsible for a job that was previously held by one person. Both programs let employees accommodate their work schedules to other demands in their lives, such as being home when their children return from school.[50]

Best Buy has gone one step further with its ROWE, or "results-only work environment." In a classic flextime structure, workers arrange their schedules with their supervisors in advance. In the ROWE program, the supervisor has no say in scheduling or in the place where the work is conducted. Employees work as long as it takes to get their assigned tasks completed. They are evaluated only on the tasks successfully completed—even if they did not complete any of them in the office.[51]

Provide Benefits   Benefits provide another opportunity for retailers to signal their concerns for their employees and build engagement. Heath care benefits are an increasingly important benefit for retail employees. A survey of Wegmans employees, for example, revealed that they stay with the company mainly because it offers health benefits (as well as flexible schedules and good job security). The grocer pays approximately 85 percent of its full-time employees' health care costs; part-time employees can receive single-coverage health care benefits, too. Moreover, Wegmans provides access to dental insurance, retirement investments, scholarships, adoption assistance, and medical leave to its happy staffers.

Every three years, Whole Foods lets employees nominate benefits, and if other employees agree, the benefit is added. In addition, the company has a health program whereby employees with high risk of developing Type 2 diabetes, or those already diagnosed with the disease, are encouraged to attend a one-week immersion program that teaches them about the importance of diet and exercise in managing their disease. Employees in the program are transformed and become missionaries for better eating, diet, and exercise, and their productivity goes up.[52]

Use Social Media   A number of retailers are using social media to communicate and engage their employees. For example, to interact with its nearly 200,000 employees, spread across approximately 3,000 locations worldwide, Best Buy hosts Geek Squad forums to let its "geeky" or technologically focused employees get to know one another. On internal blogs, employees can learn about the latest product introductions and updates; on wikis such as the "Loop Marketplace," they can offer suggestions for the corporation.[53] Starbucks has an employee page on its Facebook timeline for brands entitled "Starbucks Partners." It has information about new product releases, awards, and recognition and provides an opportunity for senior managers to communicate with employees.

Some retailers are concerned about using social media internally for two reasons. First, consumers and/or competitors might get access to sensitive company information. Second, social media may encourage the airing of employee complaints and might, therefore, reduce employee engagement. Because of these concerns, some retailers—like 7-Eleven, Darden Restaurants and Supervalu—utilize a private social network such as Yammer, which can only be accessed by people within the company. Another challenge is to create compelling content that motivates employees to frequent the site and participate in the conversations. Retailing View 9.4 reviews REI's experience with a Facebook-like intranet site.

Managing Diversity

A more diverse labor force requires more and different management skills than was the case in the past. **Managing diversity** is a human resource management activity designed to realize the benefits of a diverse workforce, which includes but is not limited to skin color, nationality, gender, sexual orientation, and people with disabilities.

Some legal restrictions promote diversity in the workplace by preventing retailers from practicing discrimination based on non-performance-related employee characteristics. But retailers now recognize that promoting employee diversity also can improve financial performance. Bill Hawthorne, Macy's senior vice president of diversity strategies and legal affairs, emphasizes that diversity makes financial sense. "Diversity is serious business at Macy's. Our stores need to reflect the communities in which they operate. Our top markets include cities like New York, Chicago, Atlanta, Houston, and Los Angeles. The demographic profile of these cities is majority-minority. It makes sense that diversity is included in virtually every aspect of our business: hiring, vendors, marketing, communications, and community involvement."[54]

A diverse workforce enables retailers to better service the diversity in their customers.

By encouraging diversity in their workforce, retailers can better understand and respond to the needs of their customers and deal with the shrinking labor market. For example, because the majority of merchandise sold in department stores and home improvement centers is bought by women, these retailers feel that they must have women in senior management positions—people who really understand their female customers' needs.

In addition to gaining greater insight into customer needs, many retailers have found that emerging groups are more productive than traditional employees. After renovating its national reservation center to accommodate workers with

RETAILING VIEW   REI Employees Meet and Communicate around the Campfire   9.4

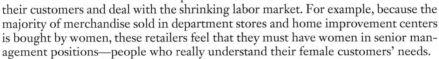

REI has an online, virtual "campfire" where top managers can share ideas with employees and get their comments. Although its main purpose is to serve as a sort of executive blog, the campfire also summarizes relevant news updates in one place. The executives' contributions can focus on any topic of their choosing and are barely edited, such that their authentic typos and misspellings help reveal their true personalities. Most of these posts prompt responses from employees, and approximately 5,000 of these employees have logged into the system. Even when disagreements arise, they tend to be civil, leading REI to consider building up the campfire to include more contributors.

Sources: "Around the Company Campfire," Rules of Engagement, *CFM Marketing blog*, August 23, 2012; and Matt Wilson, "REI's Internal Hub Gives Voiceless Employees a Voice," *Ragan.com*, August 22, 2012.

REI encourages its employees to engage in frank, online "campfire" discussions with executives about the company through an intranet blog.

DISCUSSION QUESTION

What are the advantages and disadvantages of REI's executive blog from the perspectives of the employees and the executives? What features would you change? Why?

disabilities, Days Inn found that turnover among disabled workers was only 1 percent annually, compared with 30 percent for its entire staff. Lowe's, a home improvement center chain, changed floor employees' responsibilities so that the employees wouldn't have to lift heavy merchandise. By assigning the heavy-lifting tasks to the night crew, the firm was able to shift its floor personnel from male teenagers to older employees who provided better customer service and had personal experience with do-it-yourself projects. Effectively managing a diverse workforce isn't just morally correct, it's necessary for business success.[55]

The fundamental principle behind managing diversity is the recognition that employees have different needs and require different approaches to accommodating those needs. Managing diversity goes beyond meeting equal employment opportunity laws. It means accepting and valuing differences. Some programs that retailers use to manage diversity involve offering diversity training, providing support groups and mentoring, and managing career development and promotions.

Diversity Training   Diversity training typically consists of two components: developing cultural awareness and building competencies. The cultural awareness component teaches people about how their own culture differs from the culture of other employees and how the stereotypes they hold influence the way they treat people, often in subtle ways that they might not realize. Then role-playing is used to help employees develop their competencies, such as better interpersonal skills that enable them to show respect and treat people as equals.

Support Groups and Mentoring   Many retailers help form **support groups** of minority employees that exchange information and provide emotional and career support for members who traditionally haven't been included in the majority's networks. **Mentoring programs** assign higher-level managers to help lower-level managers learn the firm's values and meet other senior executives. At Giant Foods, a Maryland-based supermarket chain, the mentoring program has reduced turnover of minorities by making them more aware of the resources available to them and giving them practical advice for solving problems that might arise on their jobs.[56]

REFACT

In 1866, Macy's employed the first female executive in retailing when Margaret Getchell was promoted to the position of store superintendent.[57]

Career Development and Promotions   Although laws provide entry-level opportunities for women and minority groups, these employees often encounter a glass ceiling as they move through the corporation. A **glass ceiling** is an invisible barrier that makes it difficult for minorities and women to be promoted beyond a certain level. To help employees break through this glass ceiling, JCPenney monitors high-potential minority and female employees and makes sure they have opportunities for store and merchandise management positions that are critical for their eventual promotion to senior management. Similarly, women in the supermarket business have traditionally been assigned to peripheral departments like the bakery and deli, while men were assigned to the critical departments in the store like meat and grocery. Even in the supermarket chain corporate office, women traditionally have been in staff-support areas like HR management, finance, and accounting, whereas men have been more involved in store operations and buying. To make sure that more women have an opportunity to break through the glass ceiling in the supermarket industry, more firms are placing them in positions critical to the firm's success.

LEGAL ISSUES IN HUMAN RESOURCE MANAGEMENT

LO5

Identify the legal issues involved with human resource management.

The proliferation of laws and regulations affecting employment practices in the 1960s was a major reason for the emergence of human resource management as an important organization function. Managing in this complex regulatory environment requires expertise in labor laws, as well as skills in helping other managers comply with those laws. The major legal and regulatory issues involving the management of retail employees are (1) equal employment opportunity, (2) compensation, (3) labor relations, (4) employee safety and health, (5) sexual harassment, and (6) employee privacy.

Equal Employment Opportunity

The basic goal of equal employment opportunity regulations is to protect employees from unfair discrimination in the workplace. **Illegal discrimination** refers to the actions of a company or its managers that result in members of a protected class being treated unfairly and differently from others. A **protected class** is a group of individuals who share a common characteristic as defined by the law. Companies cannot treat employees differently simply on the basis of their race, color, religion, sex, national origin, age, or disability status. There is a very limited set of circumstances in which employees can be treated differently. For example, it is illegal for a restaurant to hire young, attractive servers because that is what its customers prefer. Such discrimination must be absolutely necessary, not simply preferred.

In addition, it is illegal to engage in a practice that disproportionately excludes a protected group, even though it might seem nondiscriminatory. For example, suppose that a retailer uses scores on a test to make hiring decisions. If a protected group systematically performs worse on the test, the retailer is illegally discriminating, even if there was no intention to discriminate.

Compensation

Laws relating to compensation define the workweek, the pay rate for working overtime, and the minimum wage, and they protect employee investments in their pensions. In addition, they require that firms provide the same pay for men and women who are doing equal work.

A recent issue related to compensation involves the criteria used to classify employees as managers who are paid a salary and not eligible for overtime pay. A number of lawsuits have been filed by assistant managers, claiming that they do the same job as hourly employees but are classified as managers so that their retail employer can avoid paying them overtime wages. For example, one lawsuit claimed that Walmart's district managers frequently encourage store managers to send hourly workers home before their shift is over to avoid overtime pay and then require the assistant managers to continue working to compensate for the absence of hourly workers.

These lawsuits point out the difficulty in distinguishing the tasks of assistant managers and hourly workers. Federal law requires that managers be paid overtime if more than 40 percent of their time is not spent supervising or if their jobs do not include making decisions. However, many retailers feel that managers perform other activities, such as interviewing job candidates, making schedules, and handling other supervisory duties. Because so many lawsuits regarding overtime pay are filed each year, the Labor Department has developed overtime rules and regulations, such as defining specific jobs as managerial and paying overtime to managers who earn less than $455 per week but denying overtime to employees who earn more than $100,000 annually.[58]

Labor Relations

Labor relations laws describe the process by which unions can be formed and the ways in which companies must deal with the unions. They precisely indicate how negotiations with unions must take place and what the parties can and cannot do. Walmart has vigorously challenged attempts by unions to represent its employees. Supermarket chains, in contrast, are typically unionized and, therefore, believe they have a labor cost disadvantage that makes it difficult for them to compete effectively with Walmart.

REFACT

In the United States, 5.3 percent of the workforce in retailing are represented by a union.[59]

Unwelcome sexual advances, requests for sexual favors, and other inappropriate verbal or physical conduct, whether from a man or from a woman, is sexual harassment.

Employee Safety and Health

The basic premise of **health and safety laws** is that the employer is obligated to provide each employee with an environment that is free of hazards that are likely to cause death or serious injury. Compliance officers from the Occupational Safety and Health Administration (OSHA) conduct inspections to ensure that employers are providing such an environment for their workers. OSHA even gets involved in ensuring the safety of customers in stores.[60] For instance, it provides guidance to retailers on how to control crowds on Black Friday, the busy shopping day after Thanksgiving. The guidelines include using a bullhorn to manage crowds, setting up barricades or rope lines , and clearing the entrances of shopping carts and other potentially dangerous obstacles.

Sexual Harassment

Sexual harassment includes unwelcome sexual advances, requests for sexual favors, and other inappropriate verbal or physical conduct. Harassment is not confined to requests for sexual favors in exchange for job considerations such as a raise or promotion. Simply creating a hostile work environment can be considered sexual harassment. For example, actions considered sexual harassment include lewd comments, joking, and graffiti, as well as showing obscene photographs, staring at a coworker in a sexual manner, alleging that an employee got rewards by engaging in sexual acts, and commenting on an employee's moral reputation.

Customers can engage in sexual harassment as much as supervisors and coworkers. For example, if a male customer is harassing a female server in a restaurant and the restaurant manager knows about it and does nothing to stop the harassment, the employer can be held responsible for that sexual harassment.

Employee Privacy

Employees' privacy protection is very limited. For example, employers can monitor e-mail and telephone communications, search an employee's workspace and handbag, and require drug testing. However, employers cannot discriminate among employees when undertaking these activities unless they have a strong suspicion that specific employees are acting inappropriately.

Developing Policies

The HR department is responsible for developing programs and policies to make sure that managers and employees are aware of the legal restrictions and know how to deal with potential violations. The legal and regulatory requirements are basically designed to treat people fairly. Employees want to be treated fairly, and companies want to be perceived as treating their employees fairly. The perception of fairness encourages people to join a company and leads to the trust and commitment of employees to a firm. When employees believe they are not being treated fairly, they can complain internally, stay and accept the situation, stay but engage in negative behavior, quit, complain to an external authority, or even sue the employer.

Perceptions of fairness are based on two perceptions: (1) distributive justice and (2) procedural justice. **Distributive justice** arises when the outcomes received are viewed as fair with respect to the outcomes received by others. However, the perception of distributive justice can differ across cultures. For example, in the individualistic culture of the United States, merit-based pay is perceived as fair, whereas in collectivist cultures such as China and Japan, equal pay is viewed as fair. **Procedural justice** is based on the fairness of the process used to determine the outcome. American workers consider formal processes as fair, whereas group decisions are considered fairer in collectivist cultures.[61] Some illustrations of policies that pertain to procedural justice are presented in Chapter 16.

SUMMARY

LO1 **Review the objectives of human resource management.**

Retailers achieve their financial objectives by effectively managing their five critical assets: their locations, merchandise inventory, channels, employees, and customers. Three measures that retailers frequently use to assess HRM performance are employee productivity, turnover, and engagement.

LO2 **Discuss the major issues facing human resource managers.**

Human resource management (HRM) is responsible for aligning the capabilities and behaviors of employees with the short- and long-term goals of the retail firm.

Although human resource management plays a vital role in supporting a retailing strategy, HR managers face many challenges. They have to be able to balance the needs of various constituencies. They are constantly forced to control expenses, causing them to increase the proportion of part-time employees and undertake other cost-cutting initiatives. A more diverse U.S. population challenges HR managers to create and maintain a diverse labor force. As retailers go global, HR managers must adapt to new environments.

LO3 **Summarize the activities retail employees undertake and how they are typically organized.**

The organization structure defines supervisory relationships and employees' responsibilities.

The four primary groups of tasks performed by retailers are strategic decisions, administrative tasks by the corporate staff, merchandise management by the buying organization, and store management.

In developing an organization structure, retailers must make trade-offs between the cost savings gained through centralized decision making and the benefits of tailoring the merchandise offering to local markets—benefits that arise when decisions are made in a decentralized manner.

LO4 **Present activities undertaken to win the talent war.**

Retailers are engaged in a war for talent. They develop marketing programs, referred to as employment branding, to attract and retain the "best and brightest" employees. To win the war for talent, retailers develop programs to attract, develop, motivate, and keep talent.

LO5 **Identify the legal issues involved with human resource management.**

The human resource department is also responsible for making sure that its firm complies with the laws and regulations that prevent discriminatory practices against employees and making sure that employees have a safe and harassment-free work environment.

KEY TERMS

bonus, *252*
buyer, *242*
centralization, *245*
chief executive officer (CEO), *243*
chief financial officer (CFO), *244*
chief marketing officer (CMO), *244*
commission, *252*
decentralization, *245*

distributive justice, *260*
employment branding, *249*
employment marketing, *249*
empowerment, *254*
engagement, *237*
executive vice president (EVP) of
    operations, *244*
flextime, *256*

glass ceiling, *258*
global operations president, *245*
health and safety laws, *260*
illegal discrimination, *259*
job sharing, *256*
labor relations laws, *259*
managing diversity, *256*
mentoring program, *258*

GET OUT AND DO IT!

1. **CONTINUING CASE ASSIGNMENT** Meet with the store manager of the retailer you have chosen for this Continuing Case Assignment. Ask the store manager which company HR policies he or she feels are very effective and which are not effective. Why? Also ask the manager about the store's policies concerning the legal and regulatory issues discussed in the chapter. Does the retailer have written policies that enable the manager to deal effectively with any situations that arise? Have situations arisen that were not covered by the policies? How were the situations addressed? To what degree does the manager feel that he or she is empowered to make decisions that affect the performance of the store? Would the manager like more or less decision-making authority? Why?

2. **INTERNET EXERCISE** Go to the Society of Human Resource Management's home page, www.shrm.org. An organization of human resource professionals, SHRM publishes *HR Magazine*, with articles available online at www.workforceonline.com. Find and summarize the conclusions of articles addressing the HR challenges that retailers are facing, such as the management of a diverse workforce, international expansion, and the use of technology to increase productivity.

3. **INTERNET EXERCISE** The Fair Measures Law Consulting Group provides training and legal services for employers. Go to its website, www.fairmeasures. com, and choose one of the legal areas to investigate (sexual harassment, wrongful termination, and so forth). Another source of information about legal issues regarding employees is http://www.law.cornell. edu/wex/employment. Read the most recent court opinions and articles about employment issues, and summarize the implications for human resource management in retailing.

4. **INTERNET EXERCISE** Go to the home page of the National Retail Federation Foundation (NRFF), at http://nrffoundation.com/content/retail-careers-center, and click on "Experience Retail" to read about the different career paths in marketing/advertising, store operations, loss prevention, store management, finance, human resources, IT and e-commerce, sales and sales-related, distribution/logistics/supply chain management, merchandise buying/planning, and entrepreneurship. Which area appeals to you the most? Explain your preference for this career direction.

5. **LIBRARY EXERCISE** Go to one of your college's or university's library business databases, and find a recent newspaper or journal article that discusses human resource management in the retail industry. Briefly tie the concepts in the article back to the chapter or to your Continuing Case Assignment (question 1).

6. **OLC EXERCISE**
   a. Update your résumé, and prepare for an interview for a manager training program with a large lumber and building supply retailer. This full-time position promises rapid advancement upon completion of the training period. A college degree and experience in retail, sales, and marketing are preferred. The base pay is between $35,000 and $59,000 per year. This retailer promotes from within, and a new manager trainee can become a store manager within two to five years, with an earning potential of $100,000 or more. The package is generous, including medical/hospitalization/dental/disability/life insurance, a 401(k) plan, profit sharing, awards and incentives, paid vacations, and holidays. Your résumé should include your contact information, education and training, skills, experience and accomplishments, and honors and awards.

   b. Role-play a practice interview for this position. Pair up with another student, and read each other's résumés; then spend 20 to 30 minutes on each side of the interview. One student should be the human resource manager screening applicants, and the other person should be the candidate for the manager training program. Here are some questions to use in the role-play scenario:

   Why are you applying for this position?

   What are your strengths and weaknesses for this position?

   Why should this organization consider you for this position?

   Why are you interested in working for this company?

   What are your career goals for next 5 to 10 years?

   Describe your skills when working in a team setting.

   What questions do you have about the company?

DISCUSSION QUESTIONS AND PROBLEMS

1. Why is human resource management more important in retailing firms than in manufacturing firms?

2. How can retailers use hiring, selecting, training, and motivating employees in their human resource management practices to gain competitive advantage?

3. Describe the similarities and differences between the organizations of small and large retail companies. Why do these similarities and differences exist?

4. Some retailers have specific employees (merchandise assistants) assigned to restock the shelves and maintain the appearance of the store. Other retailers have sales associates perform these tasks. What are the advantages and disadvantages of each approach?

5. How can national retailers like Best Buy and Victoria's Secret, which both use a centralized buying system, make sure that their buyers are aware of the local differences in consumer needs?

6. Reread Retailing View 9.4 on REI's internal use of social media. What are the positive and negative aspects of this internal use of social media in general and,

more specifically, REI's use of an internal intranet rather than a platform like Facebook?

7. To motivate employees, several major department stores are experimenting with incentive compensation plans, although compensation plans with a lot of incentives often don't promote good customer service. How can retailers motivate employees to sell merchandise energetically and, at the same time, not jeopardize customer service?

8. Assume that you're starting a new restaurant that caters to college students and plans to use college students as servers. What human resource management problems would you expect to have? How could you build a strong organization culture in your restaurant to provide outstanding customer service?

9. Three approaches for motivating and coordinating employee activities are policies and supervision, incentives, and organization culture. What are the advantages and disadvantages of each?

10. What HR trends are helping meet employees' needs, increase job satisfaction, and lower turnover?

SUGGESTED READINGS

Barrow, Simon, and Richard Mowley. *Employer Brand Management: Practical Lessons from the World's Leading Employer Brands.* New York: Wiley, 2010.

Baumgardner, Catherine, and Jennifer L. Myers. "Employee Engagement, and Why it is Important." *The Encyclopedia of Human Resource Management: HR Forms and Job Aids,* 2012, pp. 202–204.

Cui, Xiaomin, and Junchen Hu. "A Literature Review on Organization Culture and Corporate Performance." *International Journal of Business Administration* 3, no. 2 (2012): pp. 28–45.

Kruse, Ken. *Employee Engagement.* Richboro PA: The Kruse Group, 2012.

Lashley, Conrad. *Empowerment: HR Strategies for Service Excellence.* Oxford: Routledge, 2012.

Macey, William H., Benjamin Schneider, Karen M. Barbera, and Scott A. Young. *Employee Engagement: Tools for Analysis, Practice, and Competitive Advantage.* London: Wiley Blackwell, 2009.

Schlager, Tobias, Mareike Bodderas, Peter Maas, and Joël Luc Cachelin. "The Influence of the Employer Brand on Employee Attitudes Relevant for Service Branding: An Empirical Investigation." *Journal of Services Marketing* 25, 7 (2011), pp. 497–508.

"The 100 Best Companies to Work For 2013," *Fortune,* February 2013.

Vance, Charles M., and Yongsun Paik. *Managing a Global Workforce: Challenges and Opportunities in International Human Resource Management.* Amonk, NY: M.E. Sharpe Inc., 2010.

Wilson, John P. *International Human Resource Development: Learning, Education and Training for Individuals and Organizations.* London: Kogan Page, 2012.

Information Systems and Supply Chain Management

EXECUTIVE BRIEFING

Don Ralph, Senior Vice President,
Supply Chain & Logistics, Staples, Inc.

Prior to joining Staples, I worked 27 years in the department store business, for both Federated Department Stores and The May Department Stores Company where I held positions that included vice president of logistics and senior vice president of operations. Then I moved to Staples, the world's largest office products company, as senior vice president of supply chain and logistics. I have been at Staples for the last 14 years. Staples conducts retail and B2B operations in 27 countries in North and South America, Europe, Asia, and Australia.

I am responsible for the development of Staples' supply chain and logistics strategy and the execution of supply chain operations including its fulfillment, delivery, transportation, inventory management, wholesaler, and merchandising operations areas, as well as its planning and engineering, logistics strategy, and project management office. It is a big job! We have over 15,000 associates who work in our supply chain globally and operate over 300 facilities worldwide.

One of my most important responsibilities is to make sure we get our processes right before we make investments in technology. For instance, since inventory is one of the largest components of our

balance sheet, a lot of time and effort is devoted to inventory management.

The new technologies we are developing are particularly fascinating to me personally, and important to Staples. For instance, Staples has developed a portal called StaplesPartners.com through which our partners can see the inventory available in each store and fulfillment center and what is sold every day—in real time! It has been a very effective tool to help us with our collaborative efforts with our partners.

We supply like products for like prices in many cases. I believe that the value chain is a strategic competitive differentiator and it adds shareholder value. The supply chain sits in the middle of the company and integrates the majority of the functions. It is a fun place to be. I view my job being like an orchestra conductor—synchronizing the various functional experts (my direct reports—all very smart folks in their own areas). The fun and challenging

CHAPTER 10

LEARNING OBJECTIVES

LO1 Understand the strategic advantage generated by a supply chain.

LO2 Describe the information and merchandise flows in a supply chain.

LO3 Consider the activities that are undertaken in a distribution center.

LO4 Review the considerations in the design of supply chains.

LO5 Explain how retailers and vendors collaborate to make sure the right merchandise is available when customers are ready to buy it.

LO6 Discuss RFID and its implications for retailers.

part of the job is optimizing all the moving parts (thousands of SKUs and hundreds of distribution and fulfillment centers). Having inquisitive DNA is a real plus in my job.

Supply chain management is a great place to start a career. Supply chain managers have to coordinate with marketing, finance, inventory management, and merchandising, among others. As such, they learn from the ground up how the company really works. As a result, I think that in the future a lot of corporate-level executives will have some tenure in supply chain management.

Joe Jackson wakes up in the morning, takes a shower, dresses, and goes to his kitchen to make a cup of coffee and toast a bagel. He slices the bagel and puts it in his toaster oven, but, to his dismay, the toaster oven is not working. He reviews his e-mails as he is eating his untoasted bagel with his coffee and notices an electronic coupon from Target for home appliances. He reviews the toaster ovens sold by Target on its website, decides he likes a Michael Graves toaster oven best, and sees it available at a store near his apartment. So, on his way home from work, he stops at a Target store. He finds the Michael Graves model his likes on the shelf and buys it.

Joe expected to find the Michael Graves toaster oven, as well as other models, available at Target, but he probably didn't realize that a lot of behind-the-scenes activities were going on to get those toaster ovens to the store. Target uses sophisticated information and supply chain management systems to make sure that the Michael Graves toaster and other brands are available in its stores whenever Joe and other customers want them. When Joe bought the toaster oven, the information about his transaction was automatically forwarded by the information systems to Target's regional distribution center (DC), the home appliance planner at Target's corporate headquarters in Minneapolis, and the toaster oven manufacturer in China. A computer information system monitors all toaster oven sales and inventory levels in every Target store and indicates when to have toaster ovens shipped from the manufacturer in China to the regional distribution centers and then from the centers to the stores. Shipments to the DCs and stores are monitored using a satellite tracking system that locates the ships and trucks transporting the toaster ovens.

Of course, Target could ensure the availability of toaster ovens and other merchandise by simply keeping a large number of units in the stores at all times. But stocking a large number of each model would require much more space to store the items and a significant investment in additional inventory. So the challenge for Target is to limit its inventory and space investment but still make sure products are always available when customers want them.

This chapter begins by outlining how retailers can gain a strategic advantage through supply chain management and information systems. Then the chapter describes information and product flows in the supply chain and the activities undertaken in DCs. Next, it examines a set of decisions that retailers make to determine the structure of the supply chain, such as whether to use DCs or direct store deliveries and whether to outsource some supply chain functions. The chapter continues with a discussion of how vendors and retailers work together to efficiently manage the movement of merchandise from the vendor through the retailer's DCs to its stores and customers. The chapter concludes with a discussion of how radio frequency identification (RFID) is being used to improve supply chain efficiency.

CREATING STRATEGIC ADVANTAGE THROUGH SUPPLY MANAGEMENT AND INFORMATION SYSTEMS

LO1

Understand the strategic advantage generated by a supply chain.

As discussed in Chapter 1, retailers are the connection between customers and manufacturers. It is the retailer's responsibility to gauge customers' wants and needs and work with the other members of the supply chain—distributors, vendors, and transportation companies—to make sure the merchandise that customers want is available when they want it. A simplified supply chain is illustrated in Exhibit 10–1. Vendors ship merchandise either to a **distribution center** (DC) (as is the case for vendors V_1 and V_3) or directly to stores (as is the case for vendor V_2). The factors considered in deciding to ship directly to stores versus to DCs are discussed later in this chapter.

Supply chain management is a set of activities and techniques firms employ to efficiently and effectively manage the flow of merchandise from the vendors to the retailer's customers. These activities ensure that the customers are able to purchase merchandise in the desired quantities at a preferred location and appropriate time.[1]

Retailers are increasingly taking a leadership role in managing their supply chains. When retailers were predominantly small businesses, larger manufacturers and distributors dictated when, where, and how merchandise was delivered. But with the consolidation and emergence of large, international retail chains, retailers often play a dominant role in coordinating supply chain management activities. As we will discuss later in the chapter, retailers are sharing their data on shopping behaviors with suppliers to plan production, promotions, deliveries, assortments, and inventory levels. Efficient supply chain management is important to retailers because it can provide a strategic advantage from increases in product availability and inventory turnover and produces a higher return on assets.

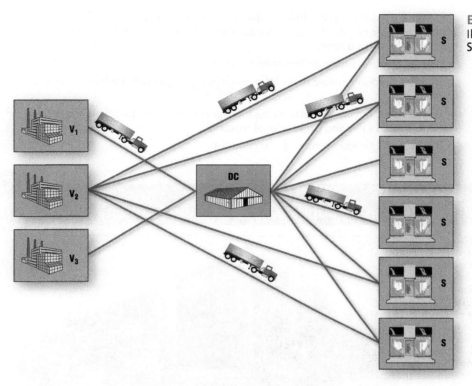

EXHIBIT 10–1
Illustration of a Supply Chain

Improving supply chain efficiency has significant implications with respect to environmental sustainability. Retailing View 10.1 outlines Walmart's efforts toward making its supply chain greener.

Strategic Advantage

As we discussed in Chapter 5, strategic advantages are unique, and sustainable advantages enable retailers to realize a higher-than-average return on their assets. Of course, all retailers strive to develop a competitive advantage, but not all retailers can develop a competitive advantage from their information and supply chain systems.[3] However, if they do develop such an advantage, the advantage is sustainable because it is difficult for competitors to duplicate.

For example, a critical factor in Walmart's success is its information and supply chain management systems. Even though competitors recognize this advantage, they have difficulty achieving the same level of performance as Walmart's systems for four reasons. First, Walmart has made substantial initial and continuing investments in developing its systems over a long time period. Second, it has the size and scale economies to justify these investments. Third, its supply chain activities take place within the firm and are not easily known and copied by competitors. Its systems are not simply software packages that any firm can buy from a software supplier. Through its continuous learning process, Walmart is always refining its systems to improve its performance. Fourth, the coordinated effort of employees and functional areas throughout the company is supported by Walmart's top management and organization culture.

Consider the various activities that retailers undertake to keep merchandise in stock:

- Accurately forecast sales and needed inventory levels for each category and SKU.
- Monitor sales to detect deviations from the forecast.
- Transport the right amount of merchandise from the DCs to each store.

- Make sure that accurate information is available that indicates where the merchandise is—in the vendor's warehouse, the DC, the store, sold to customer, or in transit.
- Place accurate, timely orders with vendors.
- Replenish merchandise from DCs with the right quantities when the stores need it.
- Ensure that buyers and marketing managers coordinate merchandise delivery with special sales and promotional materials.
- Collect and process returned merchandise.

10.1   RETAILING VIEW   Walmart Builds a Greener Supply Chain

Walmart has made significant strides in recent years to become a green company. Some of Walmart's green logistical activities involve improving the efficiency of its truck fleet and reducing transportation miles and packaging material. To improve the efficiency of its U.S. truck fleet, Walmart has sought to include more pallets on each truck, both in initial deliveries and in their return trips to eliminate empty "backhauls," and it closely monitors the routes that its trucks travel. **Backhauls** are trucks returning to the DCs after delivering merchandise to the stores. Typically, these trucks only have some packaging material and returns when making a backhaul. Rather than having these half-empty trucks returning to the DCs, Walmart has them picking up loads from vendors that need to ship their merchandise to Walmart's DCs.

Walmart is greening its supply chain by making its trucks more efficient.

Walmart is also making significant investments in developing and testing a number of advanced technologies to improve truck efficiencies. For example, Walmart is testing various configurations of hybrid trucks and studying improvements that make its trucks more aerodynamic. These and other technologies are helping Walmart achieve its objective of doubling the efficiency of its truck fleet, such that even as it reduced its driving distances by 28 million miles, Walmart achieved the delivery of 65 million more cases. These efficiency gains also led to another benefit: a 41,000-metric-ton reduction in CO_2 emissions.

In addition, Walmart works with its vendors to eliminate a variety of single-use packaging, such as wire ties from most toys, and reduce the weight and materials associated with a number of grocery items. Although plastic is an essential element to packaging, the 5.85 billion pounds of plastic sent annually to U.S. landfills produces 3.8 million tons of greenhouse gas (GHG). One example of Walmart's activities in this area involves thermoform, the plastic clamshell packaging used for berries, mixed salads, toys, and even some electronics. Walmart helped its vendors to identify the types of plastics that were reusable and encourages them to use more of these plastics in the packaging of their products.

Finally, Walmart is encouraging its vendors to propose green supply chain projects. For example, one of Walmart's tier 1 vendors suggested a project to increase the temperature of the vendors' cold supply chain and reduce temperature spikes. The work Walmart is doing with the vendor on this project has the potential to reduce energy consumption, product waste, and associated GHG emissions.

Sources: *2012 Global Responsibility Report,* Walmart, Bentonville, Arkansas; Andrew Winston, "How Walmart's Green Performance Reviews Could Change Retail for Good," *HBR Blog,* October 2, 2012; and Stephanie Rosenbloom, "Wal-Mart Unveils Plan to Make Supply Chain Greener," *The New York Times,* February 25, 2010.

DISCUSSION QUESTION

What are the benefits and costs of Walmart's efforts to make its supply chain greener?

REFACT

More than 80 percent of Walmart's physical waste in the United States is recycled. In the United Kingdom, its ASDA stores send no waste to landfills.[2]

Improved Product Availability

Efficient supply chain management provides two benefits to retailers and their customers: (1) fewer stockouts and (2) tailored assortments. These benefits translate into greater sales, lower costs, higher inventory turnover, and lower prices (markdowns) for retailers.

Fewer Stockouts   A **stockout** occurs when an SKU that a customer wants is not available. What would happen if Joe went to the Target store and the store did not have the Michael Graves toaster oven he wants because the DC did not ship enough to the store? The store would give Joe a **rain check** so that he could come back and still pay the sale price when the store receives a new shipment. But Joe would not be pleased because he would have made a wasted trip to the store. As a result of the stockout, Joe might decide to buy another model, or he might go to a nearby Walmart to buy a toaster oven. While at Walmart, he could buy other items in addition to the toaster oven. He also might be reluctant to shop at Target in the future and might tell his friends about the negative experience he had or post a negative review on Yelp or Twitter. This bad experience could have been avoided if Target had done a better job of managing its supply chain.

In general, stockouts have significant negative short- and long-term effects on sales and profits. Data from apparel shoppers show that when experiencing a stockout, 17 percent of consumers will switch to another brand, 39 percent will go to another store to buy the product, and the remaining 44 percent will just stop shopping. In addition, when experiencing multiple stockouts, customers typically switch to another retailer.[4]

Tailored Assortments   Another benefit provided by information systems that support supply chain systems is making sure that the right merchandise is available at the right store. Most national retail chains adjust assortments in their stores on the basis of climate—stocking more wool sweaters in northern stores and cotton sweaters in southern stores during the winter. Some retailers are now using sophisticated statistical methods to analyze sales transaction data and adjust store assortments for a wide range of merchandise on the basis of the characteristics of customers in each store's local market. (See Chapter 12 for more information on assortment planning.)

Higher Return on Assets

From the retailer's perspective, an efficient supply chain and information system can improve its return on assets (ROA) because the system increases sales and net profit margins, without increasing inventory. Net sales increase because customers are offered more attractive, tailored assortments that are in stock. Consider Joe Jackson's toaster oven purchase. Target, with its information systems, could accurately estimate how many Michael Graves toaster ovens each store would sell during the special promotion. Using its supply chain management system, it would make sure sufficient stock was available at Joe's store so that all the customers who wanted to buy one could.

Net profit margin is improved by increasing the gross margin and lowering expenses. An information system that coordinates buyers and vendors allows retailers to take advantage of special buying opportunities and obtain the merchandise at a lower cost, thus improving their gross margins. Retailers also can lower their operating expenses by coordinating deliveries, thus reducing transportation expenses. With more efficient DCs, merchandise can be received, prepared for sale, and shipped to stores with minimum handling, further reducing expenses.

By efficiently managing their supply chains, retailers can carry less backup inventory, yet still avoid stockouts. Thus, inventory levels are lower, and with a lower inventory investment, total assets are also lower, so the asset and inventory turnovers are both higher. Retailing View 10.2 describes how supply chain management is changing the way fashion comes to market.

10.2   RETAILING VIEW   Zara Delivers Fast Fashion

Fast fashion is a strategy used by fashion apparel retailers that offers customers inexpensive fashionable merchandise early in the fashion life cycle. The approach is particularly effective for specialty apparel retailers that target fashion-conscious consumers who simply must have the latest looks but are also on a very limited budget. These retailers motivate shoppers to buy new fashionable apparel every few weeks instead of purchasing a few higher-priced items every few months. The strategy was pioneered by Zara, a global specialty apparel chain located in La Coruña, Spain, and has been adopted by other retailers, including H&M (headquartered in Sweden), TopShop (United Kingdom), World (Japan), and Forever 21 (United States).

To achieve a short time between design concept and availability in stores, the fast-fashion process starts with the receipt of timely information from store managers. Headquarters staff, using the company's information system, knows what is currently selling. But the store managers interacting directly with customers find out what customers want that is not available in the stores. At Zara, store managers always have their reporting devices literally in hand. These handheld devices, which are linked directly to the company's corporate office in Spain, enable daily reports on what customers are asking for but not finding.

For example, customers might want a purple version of a pink shirt that they see in the store. Managers immediately pass the information on to the designers in Spain. If the firm believes there will be sufficient demand for the purple shirt, the designers communicate electronically with the factory that produces fabric for shirts. Assembler firms have highly automated equipment to dye the fabric purple and sew the shirts. Finally, to ensure timely delivery, the shirts get shipped by truck to stores in Europe and by air express to stores in the rest of the world.

Zara's main advantage over its more traditional competitors is its highly responsive and tightly organized supply chain. Unlike its competitors, Zara uses factories located in close geographic proximity to the company's headquarters in Spain. Although this approach increases labor costs compared with outsourced production in lower-cost countries in Asia, it also improves communication, reduces shipping costs and time, and reduces the time to get new fashions in stores.

Due to its efficient supply chain, Zara can get new fashionable apparel from design to stores in six weeks, compared to the six months that department stores typically take.

Instead of shipping new products every three months like other fashion apparel retailers, Zara's stores have new merchandise delivered several times during a month. The purple shirts would be in stores in six weeks, compared with the several months it would take for most department stores and other specialty apparel stores. Because its fast-fashion system ensures a relatively short time to get merchandise to stores, it is less likely that any Zara store will be out of stock before the next shipment arrives. Limiting the stock in stores can create a sense of scarcity among its customers. If they don't buy now, the item might not be available the next time they visit the store.

Sources: Seth Stevenson, "Polka Dots Are In? Polka Dots It Is! How Zara Gets Fresh Styles to Stores Insanely Fast—Within Weeks," *Slate*, June 21, 2012; Suzy Hansen, "How Zara Grew into the World's Largest Fashion Retailer," *The New York Times*, November 9, 2012; and Greg Petro, "The Future of Fashion Retailing—The Zara Approach," *Forbes.com*, October 25, 2012.

DISCUSSION QUESTION

What are some of the ways that Zara's supply chain management system has helped create value for its customers? Provide specific examples.

THE FLOW OF INFORMATION AND MERCHANDISE IN A SUPPLY CHAIN

LO2

Describe the information and merchandise flows in a supply chain.

The complexities of the merchandise and information flows in a typical multistore chain are illustrated in Exhibit 10–2. Although information and merchandise flows are intertwined, in the following sections we describe first how information about customer demand is captured at the store, which triggers a series of responses from buyers and planners, DCs, and vendors. This information is used to make sure that merchandise is available at the store when the customer wants it. Then we discuss the physical movement of merchandise from vendors through DCs to the stores.

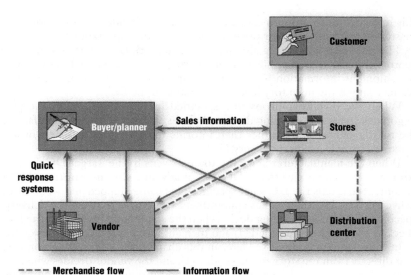

EXHIBIT 10–2
Information and Merchandise Flows

Information Flows

When Joe Jackson bought his toaster oven at Target, he initiated the information flows illustrated in Exhibit 10–3 (the numbers in parentheses refer to the path in the exhibit).

The Target cashier scans the **universal product code (UPC)** tag on the toaster oven box (1), and a sales receipt is generated for Joe. The UPC tag is a black-and-white UPC bar code containing a 13-digit code that indicates the manufacturer of the item, a description of the item, information about special packaging, and special promotions. The codes for all products are issued by GS1 US (gs1us.org), formerly the Uniform Code Council. In the future, RFID tags, discussed later in this chapter, may replace UPC tags.

The information about the transaction is captured at the **point-of-sale (POS) terminal** and sent to Target's information system, where it can be accessed by the merchandise planner for the toaster oven product category (2). The planner uses

REFACT

Shortly after 8 a.m. on June 26, 1974, the first UPC tag was scanned in Troy, Ohio, when Clyde Dawson bought a 10-pack of Wrigley's Juicy Fruit gum for 67 cents in a Marsh supermarket. Now, billions of items are scanned each day.[5]

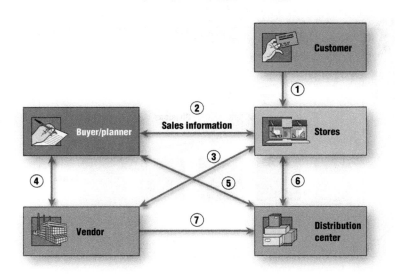

EXHIBIT 10–3
Information Flows

this information to monitor and analyze sales and decide when to reorder more toaster ovens or reduce their prices if sales are below expectations.

The sales transaction data also are sent to Target's DC (6). When the store inventory drops to a specified level, more toaster ovens are shipped to the store, and the shipment information is sent to the Target computer system (5) so that the planner knows the inventory level that remains in the DC.

When the inventory drops to a specified level in the DC (4), the planner negotiates terms and shipping dates and places an order with the manufacturer of the toaster ovens. The planner then informs the DC about the new order and when the store can expect delivery (5).

When the manufacturer ships the toaster ovens to the Target DC, it sends an advanced shipping notice to the DC (7). An **advance shipping notice (ASN)** is a document that tells the DC what specifically is being shipped and when it will be delivered. The DC then makes appointments for trucks to make the delivery at a specific time, date, and loading dock. When the shipment is received at the DC and checked, the planner is notified (5) and then authorizes payment to the vendor.

In some situations, discussed later in this chapter, the sales transaction data are sent directly from the store to the vendor (3), and the vendor decides when to ship more merchandise to the DC and stores. The fulfillment of sales from nonstore channels may involve the vendor shipping merchandise directly to the customer. In other situations, especially when merchandise is reordered frequently, the ordering process is done automatically, bypassing the planners.

Data Warehouse   Purchase data collected at the point of sale goes into a database known as a *data warehouse*. The information stored in the data warehouse is accessible on various dimensions and levels, as depicted in the data cube in Exhibit 10–4.

As shown on the horizontal axis, data can be accessed according to the level of merchandise aggregation—SKU (item), vendor, category (toaster ovens), or all merchandise. Along the vertical axis, data can be accessed by level of the

EXHIBIT 10–4   Retail Data Warehouse

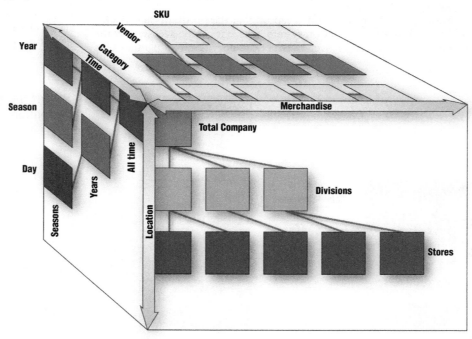

company—store, division, or total company. Finally, along the third dimension, data can be aggregated to day, season, or year.

The CEO might be interested in how the corporation is generally doing and could look at the data aggregated by quarter for a merchandise division, a region of the country, or the total corporation. A buyer may be more interested in a particular vendor in a specific store on a particular day. Analysts from various levels of the retail operation extract information from the data warehouse to make a plethora of retailing decisions about developing and replenishing merchandise assortments.

Data warehouses also contain detailed information about customers, which is used to target promotions and group products together in stores. These applications are discussed in Chapter 11. To economically collect this information, most of the communication between vendors and retailers and within the retailer is done via electronic data interchange (EDI).

Electronic Data Interchange   In the past, retailer–vendor information flows were accomplished by sending handwritten or typed documents through the mail or by fax. Now most communications between vendors and retailers occur via electronic data interchange. **Electronic data interchange (EDI)** is the computer-to-computer exchange of business documents using a standardized format. To facilitate the adoption of EDI, the retail industry agreed to use specific symbols to delineate the purchase order number, the vendor's name, the address the merchandise is being shipped to, and so forth.[7]

Retailers also have developed standards for exchanging information about purchase order changes, order status, transportation routings, advance shipping notices, on-hand inventory status, and vendor promotions, as well as information that enables vendors to put price tags on merchandise. The development and use of these standards is critical to the use of EDI because they enable all retailers to use the same format when transmitting data to their vendors.

EDI transmissions between retailers and vendors occur over the Internet. Because the Internet is a publicly accessible network, its use to communicate internally and externally with vendors and customers raises security issues. Some potential implications of security failures are the loss of business data essential to conducting business, disputes with vendors and customers, loss of public confidence and its effect on brand image, bad publicity, and loss of revenue from customers using an electronic channel.

To help secure information, retailers have incorporated security policies. A **security policy** is the set of rules that apply to activities involving computer and communication resources that belong to an organization. Retailers also train employees and add the necessary software and hardware to enforce the rules. The objectives of a security policy are:

- *Authentication.* The system ensures or verifies that the person or computer at the other end of the communication really is who or what it claims to be.

- *Authorization.* The system ensures that the person or computer at the other end of the communication has permission to carry out the request.

- *Integrity.* The system ensures that the arriving information is the same as that sent, which means that the data have been protected from unauthorized changes or tampering through a data encryption process.

The Physical Flow of Merchandise—Logistics

Exhibit 10–5 illustrates the physical flow of merchandise within the supply chain.

1. Merchandise flows from vendor to DC.

2. Merchandise goes from DC to stores.

3. Alternatively, merchandise can go from vendor directly to stores or even the customer.

EXHIBIT 10–5 Merchandise Flow

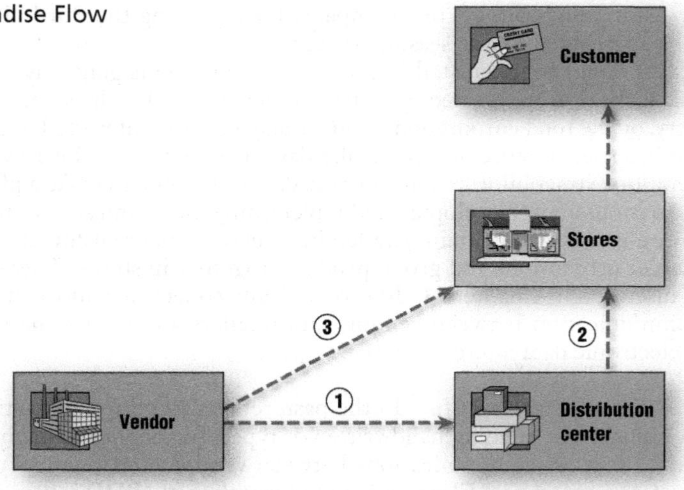

REFACT
Located strategically across the United States, Walmart's disaster DCs are well stocked with supplies that communities affected by a natural disaster are likely to need so that the company can ensure a rapid response.[9]

Logistics is the aspect of supply chain management that refers to "the planning, implementation, and control of the efficient flow and storage of goods, services, and related information from the point of origin to the point of consumption to meet customers' needs."[8] In addition to managing inbound and outbound transportation, logistics involves the activities undertaken in the retailer's DC. For example, sometimes merchandise is temporarily stored at the DC; other times it just passes directly through the center from an inbound to an outbound truck. Merchandise shipments also might be prepared for stores in the center. For example, the center might break down received shipping cartons into smaller quantities that can be more readily utilized by the individual stores and/or apply price tags and the retailer's labels. The next section describes activities undertaken in a DC.

THE DISTRIBUTION CENTER

LO3
Consider the activities that are undertaken in a distribution center.

DCs perform the following activities: coordinating inbound transportation; receiving, checking, storing, and cross-docking merchandise; getting merchandise "floor-ready"; and coordinating outbound transportation. To illustrate these activities, we will follow a shipment of Nintendo's WiiU consoles that arrive at a Best Buy DC.

REFACT
On Cyber Monday, Amazon shipped more than 17 million items, 200 items per second, from its 40 DCs.[10]

Management of Inbound Transportation

Traditionally, buyers focused their efforts, when working with vendors, on developing merchandise assortments, negotiating prices, and arranging joint promotions. Now, buyers and planners are much more involved in coordinating the physical flow of merchandise to the stores. The Best Buy video game buyer has arranged for a truckload of WiiU consoles to be delivered to its Houston, Texas, DC on Monday between 1 and 3 p.m. The buyer has also specified the number of units per carton and the particular way that the merchandise should be placed on pallets for easy unloading.

The truck must arrive within the specified time because the DC has all of its 100 receiving docks allocated throughout the day, and much of the merchandise on this particular inbound truck is going to be cross-docked and loaded into an outbound truck going to a store that evening. Unfortunately, the truck was delayed due to an engine problem. The **dispatcher**—the person who coordinates deliveries to the DC—reassigns the truck delivering the WiiU consoles to a Wednesday morning delivery slot, notifies the planner, and charges the vendor several hundred dollars for missing its delivery time. Although many manufacturers pay transportation expenses, some retailers negotiate with their vendors to absorb this expense.

Receiving and Checking

Receiving is the process of recording the receipt of merchandise as it arrives at a DC. **Checking** is the process of going through and verifying the merchandise listed on the ASN is the same as the merchandise received.

Checking merchandise is a very labor-intensive and time-consuming task. When retailers have developed good relationships with vendors, they often do not check the number of items received on each carton compared to the number sent as indicated on the vendor's ASN. They might randomly check a sample of shipments to monitor the accuracy of the vendor's ASNs. In the future, as discussed later in this chapter, retailers may be able to automatically check the contents of each carton by detecting signals sent from RFID chips placed on each item of merchandise in a carton.

Storing and Cross-Docking

After the WiiU consoles are received and checked, they are either stored or cross-docked. When the WiiU consoles are stored, the cartons are transported by a conveyor system and forklift trucks to racks that go from the DC's floor to its ceiling. Then, when the consoles are needed in the stores, a forklift driver goes to the rack, picks up the carton, and places it on a conveyor system that routes the carton to the loading dock of a truck going to the stores.

Cross-Docking   The cartons with WiiU consoles that are cross-docked are prepackaged by Nintendo for a specific store. The UPC label attached to the carton indicates the store to which it is to be sent. Nintendo may also affix a price tag to each item in the carton. The WiiU cartons are unloaded from the inbound truck and placed on a conveyor system that routes them across the loading dock to the truck going to the specific store—thus, the term **cross-docked.** The cartons are routed on the conveyor system automatically by sensors that read the UPC labels on the cartons. These cross-docked cartons are only in the DC for a few hours before they are shipped to the stores.

REFACT

Cartons on the conveyor belt at Amazon's DC travel at 20 miles per hour.[11]

Not all of the cartons received can be cross-docked. For example, it would be inefficient to cross-dock toothbrush cartons if a received carton contained 600 units but a store only sold 50 units a day. In this situation, the received toothbrush carton would be opened and a smaller number of units along with other merchandise would be put in a carton going to a store. This is done in a **break pack area** in the DC. Finally, when cross-docking cartons, retailers assume that the number and type of merchandise in each carton and the store designations are correctly encoded in the vendor's UPC labels. Thus, retailers are reluctant to cross-dock merchandise from unreliable vendors. These errors are ultimately uncovered when the cross-docked cartons are opened at the store. At this point, it is very costly to send the incorrect merchandise back to the DC or vendor through the retailers' reverse logistics system, as discussed later in the chapter.

No hands are needed to cross-dock merchandise. The automated conveyor systems move merchandise from the unloading area for a vendor's inbound truck to the loading area for a retailer's outbound truck going to its store.

Ticketing and marking are often done in the DC so that the merchandise is floor-ready—that is, ready to put on the sales floor when the carton is opened at the store.

Getting Merchandise Floor-Ready

For some merchandise, additional tasks are undertaken in the DC to make the merchandise floor-ready. **Floor-ready merchandise** is merchandise that is ready to be placed on the selling floor in a store. Getting merchandise floor-ready entails ticketing, marking, and, in the case of some apparel, placing garments on hangers.

Ticketing and marking refer to affixing price and identification labels to the merchandise. It is more efficient for a retailer to perform these activities at a DC than in its stores. In a DC, an area can be set aside and a process implemented to efficiently add labels and put apparel on hangers. Conversely, getting merchandise floor-ready in stores can block aisles and divert sales associates' attention from their customers. An even better approach from the retailer's perspective is to get vendors to ship floor-ready merchandise, thus totally eliminating the expensive, time-consuming, ticketing and marking process.

Preparing to Ship Merchandise to a Store

At the beginning of the day, the computer system in the DC generates a list of items to be shipped to each store on that day. For each item, a pick ticket and shipping label are generated. The **pick ticket** is a document or display on a screen in a forklift truck that indicates how many cartons to get from specific storage areas. The forklift driver goes to the storage area, picks up the number of cartons indicated on the pick ticket, places UPC shipping labels on the cartons that indicate the stores to which the cartons are to be shipped, and puts the cartons on the conveyor system, where they are automatically routed to the loading dock for the truck going to the stores.

Pick tickets and labels are also generated for the break pack area. In the break pack area, open cartons shipped by the vendors are placed on shelves. Employees with pick tickets, or robots, pick the number of items designated for a store and put the items into a new carton designated for the store. When the new carton for the store is full, a label with the UPC code is affixed, and the carton is put on the conveyor system, directing it to the loading dock for the truck going to the store.

When it is not economical to send a carton of a single item to a store, the multiple items are picked from the shelves and put into a carton for shipment to the store.

Thus, the conveyor system feeds cartons from three sources to the loading dock for a truck going to a specific store: (1) cross-docked cartons directly from the vendor's delivery trucks, (2) cartons stored in the DC, and (3) cartons from the break pack area. The cartons are then loaded onto the trucks by employees.

Management of Outbound Transportation

The management of outbound transportation from DC to stores is quite complex. Most DCs run 50 to 100 outbound truck routes each day. To handle this complex transportation problem, the centers use sophisticated routing and scheduling software that considers the locations of the stores, road conditions, and transportation operating constraints for developing the most efficient routes possible. As a result, stores are provided with an accurate estimated time of arrival, and vehicle utilization is maximized.

Retailers also need to determine the mode of transportation—planes, ships, or trucks. Some retailers mix modes of transportation to reduce overall costs and time delays. For example, many Chinese vendors send Europe-bound cargo by ship to the U.S. West Coast. From there, the cargo is flown to its final destination in Europe. By combining the two modes of transport, sea and air, the entire trip takes about two weeks, as opposed to four or five weeks with an all-water route, and the cost is about half that of an all-air route.

Dollar General, an extreme-value retailer, developed an interesting, low-tech approach for dealing with a challenge it faced with outbound transportation to its stores. Controlling cost and distributing merchandise efficiently to its 10,000 stores is key to maintaining its low prices and still making a profit. Each week, more than 2,000 cartons are delivered to a typical store, and 12 person-hours are required to unload a delivery truck—time the employees could have spent helping customers. Labor scheduling is a real problem because store managers have to schedule additional staff on truck delivery days and then, in some cases, the drivers cannot make deliveries at the preplanned time. In addition, many of the stores are located in urban areas that make it difficult to park delivery trucks at a convenient location for an extended time period.

To address these challenges, Dollar General invested $100 million in a delivery system called EZ store. The EZ store system involves packing merchandise for shipment to stores in easy-to-move containers called roll-tainers that serve to protect the merchandise better than regular boxes. Instead of having store staff unload the truck when it arrives, the truck drivers unload these roll-tainers on their own. A usual store receives deliveries of around 25 roll-tainers, which take a driver about 90 minutes to unload. Using the EZ store system, store employees quickly unpack the merchandise from the roll-tainers and place it on shelves. When drivers make their next delivery, they offload the filled roll-tainers and pick up the empty ones. The system has led to significant reductions in labor-hours, injuries, and employee turnover. It has also decreased the turnaround time for the truck drivers.[12]

SYSTEM DESIGN ISSUES

This section reviews the factors affecting the decisions made by retailers concerning their supply chains. These decisions involve determining what activities, if any, should be outsourced to independent firms; what merchandise, if any, should be delivered directly to the store, bypassing the DC; and how shipments directly to customers should be made.

LO4
Review the considerations in the design of supply chains.

Outsourcing Logistics

To streamline their operations and make more productive use of their assets and personnel, some retailers **outsource** supply chain functions. Many independent companies are very efficient at performing individual activities or all the supply chain activities. There are a large number of companies that can transport merchandise from the vendor to DCs or from the centers to the retailer's stores. Rather than owning warehouses to store merchandise, retailers can use **public warehouses** that are owned and operated by an independent company. Rather than outsource specific activities, retailers can use freight forwarders to arrange for the storage and shipping of their merchandise. **Freight forwarders** provide a wide range of services: tracking transportation routes, preparing export and shipping documentation, booking cargo space (or warehousing items until the cargo space is needed), negotiating the charges for and consolidating freight, and insuring the cargo or filing insurance claims as necessary.[13]

Advantages and Disadvantages of Outsourcing Supply Chain Activities
The primary benefit of outsourcing is that the independent firms can perform the activity at a lower cost and/or more efficiently than the retailer. Independent firms typically have a lower cost because they perform the activity for many retailers and thus realize scale economies. For example, independent trucking firms have more opportunities to fill their trucks on the return trip (backhaul) with merchandise for other retailers after delivering merchandise to one retailer's stores. In addition, when there are many independent firms available to undertake the activity, retailers can have the firms bid against each other to undertake the activity and thus drive down the costs.

However, when retailers outsource a supply chain activity they can no longer develop a competitive advantage based on the performance of this activity. If the retailer's competitor discovers that the retailer is significantly reducing its costs or improving its efficiency by using an independent firm, the competitor can match the performance improvement by contracting with the same provider.[14]

Pull and Push Supply Chains

Another supply chain decision retailers make is determining whether merchandise will be pushed from the DCs to the stores or pulled from the DCs to the stores. Information and merchandise flows such as those described in Exhibit 10–2 illustrate a **pull supply chain**—a supply chain in which requests for merchandise are generated at the store level on the basis of sales data captured by POS terminals. Basically, in this type of supply chain, the demand for an item pulls it through the supply chain. An alternative is a **push supply chain,** in which merchandise is allocated to stores on the basis of forecasted demand. Once a forecast is developed, specified quantities of merchandise are shipped (pushed) to DCs and stores at predetermined time intervals.

In a pull supply chain, there is less likelihood of being overstocked or out of stock because the store requests for merchandise are based on customer demand. A pull approach increases inventory turnover and is more responsive to changes in customer demand, and it becomes even more efficient than a push approach when demand is uncertain and difficult to forecast.[15]

Although generally more desirable, a pull approach is not the most effective in all situations. First, a pull approach requires a more costly and sophisticated information system to support it. Second, for some merchandise, retailers do not have the flexibility to adjust inventory levels on the basis of demand. For example, commitments must be made months in advance for fashion and private-label apparel. Because these commitments cannot be easily changed, the merchandise has to be allocated to the stores at the time the orders are formulated.

DCs versus Direct Store Delivery

As indicated in Exhibit 10–5, retailers can have merchandise shipped directly to their stores—direct store delivery (path 3)—or to their DCs (paths 1 and 2). **Direct store delivery (DSD)** is a distribution method that bypasses the retailer's DC and delivers the merchandise directly to the retailer's stores.[16] Typically, vendors offering DSD provide additional services such as assessing the store's stock levels and backroom inventory to determine the right amount needed and then have the store manager approve a replenishment order. The vendor's representative may also restock the shelves or racks, rearrange merchandise, and remove dated products.

In general, using DCs results in overall lower inventory levels because the amount of backup stock needed in a centralized DC is less than the amount of backup stock needed in all the stores served by the center. For example, if a retailer had merchandise directly shipped to its stores, each store might need to stock 10 Michael Graves toasters for a total of 500 units in the 50 stores served by a DC. By delivering products to a DC, the same level of availability could be achieved with 350 toasters (5 in each store and 100 in the DC). Because the stores get frequent deliveries from the DC, they need to carry relatively less extra merchandise as backup stock. Thus, DCs enable the retailer to carry less merchandise in individual stores resulting in lower inventory investments systemwide.

However, DSD is more efficient for the following situations:

- Products such as potato chips and bread that have low value density (cost per cubic inches) and can be easily damaged if handled through multiple checkpoints.

- Products such as milk and eggs that have a short shelf life and where freshness is important to customers.

- Products like bottled water that are costly to transport.

- Products that are supplied by vendors' warehouses that are in close proximity to high-volume retail stores.

- Suppliers, like Hallmark and American Greetings cards, that have a large assortment of low-priced merchandise that can be easily shipped in small packages to retail stores.

- Retailers that have a limited number of outlets, and therefore do not have the scale economies to build and operate DCs.

- Products like video games and fashion apparel for which speed to the market is necessary to satisfy customer demand early in its life cycle (e.g., video games need to be available for sale on their launch date).

- Products such as ice cream requiring special storage or handling that cannot easily be provided by a retailer.

Many larger vendors such as Coca-Cola, Kraft Foods, Frito-Lay, PepsiCo, and Hallmark distribute extensively through DSD. However, the rising transportation costs (e.g., higher gasoline prices) are reducing the amount of DSD merchandise.[18]

Dolly Madison's baked goods are delivered directly to the retailer's store, bypassing the DC, ensuring that customers can get the freshest merchandise.

Reverse Logistics

Reverse logistics is the process of capturing value from and/or properly disposing of merchandise returned by customers and/or stores. A reverse logistics system processes merchandise that is returned because it is damaged, has been recalled, is no longer sold to customers because its selling season has ended, the merchandise was incorrectly sent to a store or directly to a customer, the product has been discontinued, or there is excessive inventory in stores or DCs. The returned merchandise might involve returns from a customer to a retail store, from a retail store to a DC, or from a DC to a vendor.[19]

When customers return items to retail stores, the stores collect the items and send them to DCs or centralized returns centers. Sophisticated retailers enter

REFACT

In supermarkets, more than 20 percent of unit sales and 50 percent of the profits in supermarkets is generated from products distributed by DSD.[17]

REFACT

The return rates from retailers for magazines are 50 percent, books 20 to 30 percent, greeting cards 20 to 30 percent, nonstore retailers 18 to 35 percent, and discount stores 4 to 15 percent.[20]

information about each item into their information systems so that it can be used to evaluate products, vendors, and the returns process. When the product arrives at the center, the retailer needs to examine the product and decide what do with it. Some of the potential dispositions are return it to the vendor for a refund, repair and/or repackage it and sell it as new, sell it to an outlet store or broker, donate it to charity, or recycle it. In general, retailers prefer to return items to the vendor for a refund. Due to the high cost of refurbishing and transporting small quantities, some vendors negotiate with retail buyers to offer a percent of sales discount for returns and have the retailers dispose of the merchandise, either giving it to charity or throwing it away.

Reverse logistics systems are challenging. Some differences between the forward flow of merchandise, shown in Exhibit 10–5, and the reverse flow include the forms of consolidation, product quantities, the distribution patterns, and cost transparency. First, a forward process sends goods from a few DCs to a vast number of stores or customers, whereas with a reverse process, goods come from all over and must be consolidated in one or a few receiving centers. Second, the goal of the forward process is consistent quality; the reverse process exists inherently because of the lack of consistency in the products involved. Third, a distribution plan in a forward process is designed carefully and set in advance. For a reverse process, the ad hoc distribution pattern can take a variety of unpredictable patterns. Fourth, the forward process constantly seeks more cost transparency in its standardized cost structures, but such a goal is not pertinent to the reverse process, for which none of the cost-imposing processes are likely to be standardized.[21]

Two reasons more attention is being directed toward reverse logistics are the growth of sales through Internet channels and the increasing interest in environmental sustainability. First, the percentage of returned merchandise is much greater for purchases made through the Internet channel compared to the store channel. Because the percentage of merchandise returns bought through the Internet channel is as much as four times greater than for merchandise bought through the store channel, the growth in Internet sales is going to significantly increase the number of returns and the cost of processing them through the reverse logistics system.

Second, the efficiency of reverse logistics affects environmental sustainability because packaging and shipping materials are processed through the reverse logistics system. When retailers reduce transportation costs by consolidating shipments to stores and DCs and optimize the disposal of returned merchandise, they reduce harmful emissions, energy usage, and their costs. Green logistics is becoming a standard business practice.

Drop Shipping

Drop shipping, or **consumer direct fulfillment,** is a system in which retailers receive orders from customers and relay these orders to vendors; the vendors then ship the merchandise ordered directly to the customer. Such systems are especially popular among companies that need to ship products made from bulky or heavy materials (e.g., lumber, iron).[23]

From the retailer's perspective, drop shipping reduces the retailer's supply chain costs and investment because the vendor, rather than the retailer, assumes the costs and risks of supplying merchandise to customers. The vendor has to build and operate the DCs, hire and pay for employees to pick and pack individual orders, and manage inventory. Drop shipping is particularly attractive for retailers that do not have DCs capable of fulfilling individual orders from customers. However, drop shipping can lengthen delivery times and increase costs, particularly for customers who order multiple items from different vendors. In addition, retailers do not have control over an aspect of their offering that is of importance to their

REFACT

The cost of processing a return can be up to three times the cost of an outbound shipment of an item.[22]

customer—how and when orders are delivered. Finally, defining the process for handling returns is an issue.

Supply Chain for Fulfilling Catalog and Internet Orders

The DCs and supply chain and information systems for supporting catalog and Internet channels are very different from those supporting the store channel. The typical retail DC supporting a store channel is designed to receive a relatively small number of cartons from vendors and ship about the same number of cartons to its stores. In contrast, DCs supporting nonstore channels are designed to receive about the same number of cartons from vendors but ship a very large number of small packages to customers. Thus, warehouses designed to support nonstore channels are basically one large break pack area. In addition, the information system for supporting a store channel focuses on products—making sure that the right number of products are delivered to each store—while information systems supporting nonstore channels are focused on the customer—making sure that the right customer receives the right product.

Because completely different DC designs are required for supporting the different channels, when a store-based retailer adds nonstore channels, it has to outsource fulfillment of the nonstore sales, designate separate areas within the present DCs for shipments to individual consumers, build different DCs for the new channels, or fulfill orders by picking and packing merchandise in their stores.

Some retailers initially outsourced the fulfillment function when they added an Internet channel. For example, Toys "R" Us turned to Amazon for help after a disastrous holiday season when many of its customers did not receive their orders on time, creating many unhappy children and angry parents on Christmas morning. Toys "R" Us entered into a 10-year agreement with Amazon to outsource the fulfillment of its sales through nonstore channels. Even though Amazon's fulfillment capability is very efficient, over time Toys "R" Us acquired this capability and found that outsourcing its Internet channels was an impediment to creating a unified, multichannel offering. So, Toys "R" Us ultimately terminated its outsourcing contract with Amazon.[24]

Instead of building DCs for nonstore sales fulfillment, Macy's is using the backroom of its stores as impromptu shipping centers, because, as one executive noted, "We've spent the last 153 years building warehouses. We just called them stores."[25] To make use of this existing capacity, Macy's will convert nearly 300 of its more than 800 stores into fulfillment centers. These centers should facilitate inventory management; a store with too much inventory can ship the extra to the fulfillment site, which can then place the items up for sale online. Orders placed online can get filled by the nearest stores, which should reduce shipping costs and time.

Yet because filling orders by hand using inexperienced workers is relatively inefficient, there is some debate about whether retailers should operate separate DCs to deal with store and nonstore channels or use the same DCs for both. Synergies between the channels can be exploited if the same centers are used for all. For example, less inventory is needed to support distribution for all channels from one center. However, these potential synergies might be limited, and the difference between the operations of each area might cause confusion. In addition, if same-day or next-day delivery for orders placed through nonstore channels is very important to customers, retailers might develop a dedicated hub-and-spoke design for nonstore channel fulfillment. The hub-and-spoke design would have many geographically diverse smaller distribution centers supporting a large center. The smaller centers would be located closer to customers allowing for faster and cheaper shipping times for the retailer.[26]

COLLABORATION BETWEEN RETAILERS AND VENDORS IN SUPPLY CHAIN MANAGEMENT

LO5

Explain how retailers and vendors collaborate to make sure the right merchandise is available when customers are ready to buy it.

As we discussed previously, retailers' and vendors' objectives for supply chain management are to minimize investments in inventory and costs and still make sure that merchandise is available when and where customers want it. Retailing View 10.1 at the beginning of this chapter illustrated how fast-fashion specialty retailers, such as Zara, excel at coordinating their stores, designers, and production capability to achieve these objectives.

Benefits of Coordination

Supply chain efficiency dramatically improves when vendors and retailers share information and work together. By collaborating, vendors can plan their purchases of raw materials and their production processes to match the retailer's merchandise needs. Thus, vendors can make sure that the merchandise is available "just in time," when the retailer needs it, without having to stock excessive inventory in the vendor's warehouse or the retailer's DCs or stores.

When retailers and vendors do not coordinate their supply chain management activities, excess inventory builds up in the system, even if the retail sales rate for the merchandise is relatively constant. This buildup of inventory in an uncoordinated channel is called the **bullwhip effect.** The effect was first discovered by Procter & Gamble, which saw that its orders from retailers for Pampers disposable diapers were shaped like a bullwhip, with wide swings in quantity ordered, even though retail sales were relatively constant (see Exhibit 10–6). Its retailers were ordering, on average, more inventory than they really needed.

Research has found that the bullwhip effect in an uncoordinated supply chain is caused by the following factors:

- *Delays in transmitting orders and receiving merchandise.* Even when retailers can forecast sales accurately, there are delays in getting orders to the vendor and receiving those orders from the vendor. In an uncoordinated supply chain, retailers might not know how fast they can get the merchandise, and thus they order more than they need to prevent stockouts.

- *Overreacting to shortages.* When retailers find it difficult to get the merchandise they want, they begin to play the shortage game. They order more than they need to prevent stockouts, hoping they will receive a larger partial shipment. So, on average, the vendor ships more than the retailer really needs.

- *Ordering in batches.* Rather than generating a number of small orders, retailers wait and place larger orders to reduce order processing and transportation costs and take advantage of quantity discounts.[27]

EXHIBIT 10–6
Bullwhip Effect in Uncoordinated Supply Chain

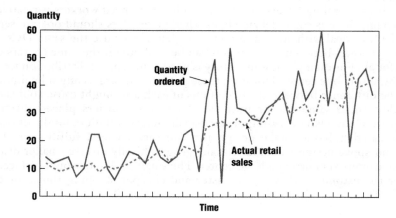

These factors cause the bullwhip effect even when sales are fairly constant. However, for many retailers, sales are not constant. They go up dramatically when retailers put merchandise on sale and during special gift-giving times of the year. These irregularities in sales heighten the bullwhip effect and the buildup of inventory in the supply chain.

Vendors and retailers have found that by working together, they can reduce the level of inventory in the supply chain and the number of stockouts in the stores. Four approaches for coordinating supply chain activities, in order of the level of collaboration, are (1) using EDI; (2) sharing information; (3) using vendor-managed inventory; and (4) employing collaborative planning, forecasting, and replenishment.

Using EDI

The use of EDI to transmit purchase order information reduces the time it takes for retailers to place orders and for vendors to acknowledge the receipt of orders and communicate delivery information about those orders. In addition, EDI facilitates the implementation of other collaborative approaches discussed in the following sections. However, the use of EDI without other collaborative approaches only addresses one factor discussed previously—the delay in transmitting and receiving orders—that causes the buildup of inventory in the supply chain.

Sharing Information

One of the major factors causing excessive inventory in the supply chain is the inability of vendors to know what the actual level of retail sales are. For instance, suppose a consumer packaged goods vendor offered discounts to retailers several times a year, hoping that the price reduction would be passed on to customers. Instead, however, the retailers purchased extra inventory and kept the extra discounts to increase their margins. Just looking at the orders it received, the vendor might think that demand for its products had increased significantly and therefore increase its production, causing an inventory buildup. To reduce this effect, vendors are using the retailer's sales data.

Sharing sales data with vendors is an important first step in improving supply chain efficiency. With the sales data, vendors can improve their sales forecasts, improve production efficiency, and reduce the need for excessive backup inventory. But additional levels of collaboration are needed to use this information effectively. The sales data reflect historical data, not what the retailer's plans are for the future. For example, the retailer might decide to delete a vendor's SKU from its assortment—a decision that clearly affects future sales. The two approaches discussed in the next sections introduce a forward-looking collaborative perspective.

Vendor-Managed Inventory

Vendor-managed inventory (VMI) is an approach for improving supply chain efficiency in which the vendor is responsible for maintaining the retailer's inventory levels. The vendor determines a **reorder point**—a level of inventory at which more merchandise is ordered. The retailer shares sales and inventory data with the vendor via EDI. When inventory drops to the order point, the vendor generates the order and delivers the merchandise.[28]

In ideal conditions, the vendor replenishes inventories in quantities that meet the retailer's immediate demand and reduce stockouts with minimal inventory. In addition to better matching retail demand to supply, VMI can reduce the vendor's and the retailer's costs. Vendor salespeople no longer need to spend time generating orders on items that are already in the stores, and their role shifts to selling new items and maintaining relationships. Retail buyers and planners no longer need to monitor inventory levels and place orders.

The use of VMI is not a new approach. Frito-Lay and other snack food, candy, and beverage vendors have used VMI combined with direct store delivery to manage the inventory of their products on supermarket shelves for a long time.

However, technological advances have increased the sophistication of VMI. The sharing of POS transaction data, for instance, allows vendors to sell merchandise on **consignment:** The vendor owns the merchandise until it is sold by the retailer, at which time the retailer pays for the merchandise. Consignment selling provides an incentive for the vendor to pick SKUs and inventory levels that will minimize inventory and generate sales. Because the vendor is bearing the financial cost of owning the inventory, retailers are more willing to allow the vendor to be responsible for determining the inventory plan and appropriate assortment for each store.

Although it is a more advanced level of collaboration than simply using EDI and sharing information, VMI has its limitations. While the vendor coordinates the supply chain for its specific products, it does not know what other actions the retailer is taking that might affect the sales of its products in the future. For example, Pepsi might not know that a supermarket will be having a big promotion in three weeks for a new beverage introduced by Coca-Cola. Without this knowledge, Pepsi would ship too much merchandise to the supermarket.

Collaborative Planning, Forecasting, and Replenishment

Collaborative planning, forecasting, and replenishment (CPFR) is the sharing of forecasts and related business information and collaborative planning between retailers and vendors to improve supply chain efficiency and product replenishment. Although retailers share sales and inventory data when using a VMI approach, the vendor remains responsible for managing the inventory. In contrast, CPFR is a more advanced form of retailer–vendor collaboration that involves sharing proprietary information such as business strategies, promotion plans, new-product developments and introductions, production schedules, and lead-time information.

A precursor to the Internet-based systems used for CPFR occurred in 1987 when Walmart and Procter & Gamble forged a partnership to control their inventory. The partnership program improves product availability, decreases inventory, and reduces costs, which Walmart passes on as savings to its customers in the form of lower prices. Retailing View 10.3 describes West Marine's CPRF collaborations with its vendors.

RADIO FREQUENCY IDENTIFICATION DEVICES

LO6

Discuss RFID and its implications for retailers.

Radio frequency identification (RFID) is a technology that allows an object or person to be identified at a distance by means of radio waves. Radio frequency identification devices are tags that transmit identifying information and are attached to individual items, shipping cartons, and containers. They then transmit data about the objects in which they are embedded. The RFID technology has two advantages over traditional bar codes. First, the devices can hold more data and update the data stored. For instance, the device can keep track of where an item has been in the supply chain and even where it is stored in a DC. Second, the data on the devices can be acquired without a visual line of sight. Thus, RFID enables the accurate, real-time tracking of every single product, from manufacturer to checkout in the store. It eliminates the manual point-and-read operations needed to get data from UPC bar codes.[29]

In 2003, Walmart announced its plan to require a few hundred suppliers to put RFID tags on full pallets and individual cases of products sent to select DCs. The roll-out started in 2005 but rapidly fizzled for a variety of reasons, including unclear cost savings for Walmart, supplier push-back on absorbing the tagging costs, and Walmart's attention being diverted to other priorities such as sustainability.

Now the RFID gold rush may be on again for two reasons. First, the value proposition and return on investment (ROI) for item-level tagging of apparel and accessories is becoming increasingly clear. Second, it appears that retailers are willing to absorb part of the cost because both retailers and vendors benefit from item-level RFID tagging. Consequently Walmart, Macy's, Marks & Spencer, Dillard's, JCPenney, and others have implemented large-scale, item-level RFID initiatives. Macy's announced that items representing about 30 percent of its total

REFACT

More than 1 million apparel items had RFID tags in 2012, and the number of tagged items is expected to grow substantially in the coming years.[30]

annual sales are being tagged. Marks & Spencer is tagging all apparel and home goods products at all of its stores.[31]

Benefits of RFID

Item-level RFID can be a win–win benefiting both retailers and vendors.

Retailer Benefits   The primary benefit of tagging individual items to retailers is to economically provide an accurate, real-time measure of item inventory levels. With these data, retailers can dramatically reduce inventory levels and stockouts.

RETAILING VIEW   West Marine's Collaboration with Its Vendors   10.3

Apparently, at one time, retailers believed that boaters liked dark, poorly organized stores and staffers who were better at telling stories than locating necessary items. We can guess that because boating supply stores were just like that for many years—at least until West Marine decided to change the rules of the game.

The founder of the company, Randy Repass, envisioned great customer service provided to boaters who could stop by a single source for all their boating needs. The vision was clearly a good one, and West Marine has grown into a chain with more than 400 North American stores. These stores, along with West Marine's catalog and Internet channels, provide everything from ropes to electronics, covering more than 50,000 SKUs.

For most boaters, the time to buy these supplies is during boating season: April through October. Unlike most retailers, which enjoy sales peaks during the holiday season, West Marine looks forward every year to the 4th of July holiday. Promotions offered frequently by suppliers also helped create substantial uncertainty in West Marine's demand predictions, which in turn led to lost sales due to supply chain inefficiencies.

To deal with these inefficiencies and demand challenges, West Marine adopted collaborative planning, forecasting, and replenishment (CPFR) programs, in conjunction with most of its key suppliers. To start, it met with its key suppliers so that together they could develop better forecasts. The result was a system that collects daily SKU-level sales, together with store-level inventory information, then generates a year-long forecast that is specific to the level of demand that day, by store and by SKU. West Marine then sends the forecast to its suppliers to help them schedule their production, and together, they use the information to time their marketing and promotional events.

Because CPFR has become so integral to West Marine's merchandising and planning, it also has revised the retailer's organizational structure. Every category manager (CM) for West Marine works closely with a merchandise

West Marine was a pioneer in the use of CPFR to work with its vendors to coordinate supply their chains.

planner (MP). While the CM takes responsibility for vendor strategies and marketing links, the MP directs supply chain relationships. Together, these MPs and CMs host quarterly meetings with suppliers to update their supply chain planning, keeping the marketing, production, distribution, and transportation departments from both firms closely in the loop. In monthly meetings—to which all team members are invited—the planners also review recent CPFR results to identify any supply chain hindrances, plan new initiatives, and resolve any remaining concerns.

Sources: www.westmarine.com; Joel Wisner, Keah-Choon Tan, and G. Keong Leong, *Principles of Supply Chain Management: A Balanced Approach*, 3rd ed. (Mason, OH: Southwestern, 2011); T. Schoenherr and V. M. R. Tummala, "Best Practices for the Implementation of Supply Chain Management Initiatives," *International Journal of Logistics Systems and Management* 4, no. 4 (2008), pp. 391–410.

DISCUSSION QUESTION

What benefits and risks face West Marine as it engages in CPFR with its vendors?

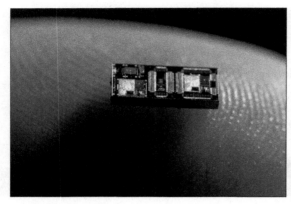

This RFID chip can be embedded in merchandise to determine where the merchandise is in the supply chain.

The following situation illustrates this benefit. Assume one of GameStop's stores has just received a shipment of 10 units of the hottest new video game. The store sold 5 units and 5 units were stolen by an employee. GameStop's inventory control systems thinks there are still 5 units on the shelf at the store and thus does not send more replenishment units of the video game to the store. Customers trying to buy the game are frustrated and may think that GameStop is not a good place to buy the hottest video games. To correct this problem, GameStop needs to frequently have its employees count up the number of units on the shelf for each SKU, compare the physical count with the number of units indicated by the inventory control system, and make a correction when there is a difference. If the video games had RFID tags, each unit on the shelf would be sending out a radio signal. There would be no signals from the stolen items, and the inventory control system would have accurate, real-time data. Stockouts would be reduced, and sales associates would have more time to provide customer service instead of counting inventory.

Another benefit of item-level RFID is to reduce theft. The technology can track products throughout the supply chain and identify their locations at all times. This helps reduce theft in transportation, at DCs, or in stores.

Retailing View 10.4 describes how Lord & Taylor uses RFID tags on shoes to provide a better shopping experience as well as to reduce costs.

10.4   RETAILING VIEW   RFID at Lord & Taylor

Lord & Taylor's shoe department faced a common retail problem: It's hard to sell a product that customers can't see. In its flagship Fifth Avenue store in New York, thousands of different styles and colors of shoes are displayed every day. Sales associates try to restock the samples on the selling floor, but to identify the styles missing from each display, sales associates had to physically touch every shoe to scan its bar code. It took two to four people working about six to eight hours just to do a complete scan. Thus, it was only economically feasible to take the inventory of samples weekly. Ironically, high traffic and sales actually compounded the problem—as more shoes were sold, more display samples went missing. Days might pass with dozens of styles missing from display samples. Useful data for restocking the displays came slowly. After the scan, stores received their missing style list the next day.

To deal with this, Lord & Taylor installed a new system to put RFID chips in each shoe and collect information from the signal coming from the RFID chips. Each day before the department opened, one or two associates walked the department with handheld RFID readers to inventory the sample shoes on the floor. As soon as the inventory was complete, a missing sample report was printed from a local PC. With this report in hand, associates then located and replaced the missing samples. With the RFID system, it only took an hour to complete the scan and get the report.

The company is looking to expand its RFID program to other departments. Regional Operations Manager Rosemary Ryan says, "We are trying to figure out how we can make it work for our jewelry departments. We're also trying to pilot it in luggage this fall—that would be another easy win for us—and men's suits. Wherever we have an inventory with a

By putting RFID chips on its shoes, Lord & Taylor can get an accurate count of its merchandise in an hour, reducing both labor cost and stockouts.

lot of sizes, styles, and colors that must be constantly replenished, RFID has proven to deliver big benefits. We want to reap those benefits across our operations."

Sources: "More Sales: RFID Speeds Accurate Inventory of Display Samples," *Motorola Solutions*, 2012; "Macy's, Lowe's, Lord & Taylor Receive VICS Achievement Awards," *RIS*, May 10, 2012; and "Lord & Taylor Deploys Motorola Solution at Flagship Store in New York," *RFIDNews*, January 4, 2012.

DISCUSSION QUESTION

For what types of merchandise is using RFID systems most appropriate? Why?

Vendor Benefits   RFID is not free for suppliers. Tags are the main cost. They can add 5 to 30 cents per item shipped, depending on volumes, the type of tag, and services provided by a service bureau and/or label convertor. In addition, there are one-time costs for readers and implementation costs such as retraining staff and IT integration (depending on what the supplier is trying to accomplish). Thus per-item cost is a problem for low margin items.

When retailers' sales increase due to fewer stockouts, vendor sales also increase. In addition, there are potential process improvements that vendors can realize. Some of the more immediate and obvious ones involve using RFID for pack verification, ship verification, and ASN generation. **Pack verification** happens after a worker has packed a case or carton, usually just before sealing it. All of the RFID tags in the case are read and compared against the ship order. **Ship verification** is similar, except that it happens as cartons are loaded onto the truck or onto a pallet. This confirms again that the right items are being loaded. Using RFID provides an almost 100 percent guarantee that the ASN will always match exactly what was shipped.

For luxury items, RFID can be used to verify authenticity. However, this requires strict security and control over tags, as well as thinking through the supply chain and where in the chain authentication might best be done. Today, luxury brands are building systems and infrastructure for distributors, retailers, and end-consumers to verify the RFID tags and the authenticity of the item.[32]

SUMMARY

LO1 Understand the strategic advantage generated by a supply chain.

Supply chain management is a set of activities and techniques firms employ to efficiently and effectively manage the flow of merchandise from the vendors to the retailer's customers. These activities ensure that the customers are able to purchase merchandise in the desired quantities at a preferred location and appropriate time. Efficient supply chain management provides two benefits to retailers and their customers: (1) fewer stockouts and (2) tailored assortments. Supply chain management coupled with improving supply chain efficiency also has significant implications with respect to environmental sustainability.

LO2 Describe the information and merchandise flows in a supply chain.

A retailer's information system tracks the flow of merchandise through distribution centers to retail stores and their customers. Most communications between vendors and retailers occur via electronic data interchange over the Internet. Most multistore retailers operate their own distribution centers. Sometimes merchandise is temporarily stored at the DC; other times it just passes directly through the center from an inbound to an outbound truck. Retailers have developed data warehouses that provide them with intimate knowledge of who their customers are and what they like to buy. The data warehouses are being used to strengthen the relationships with their customers and improve the productivity of their marketing and inventory management efforts.

LO3 Consider the activities that are undertaken in a distribution center.

Most large retailers own and operate their own DCs. Some of the activities performed by the center are managing inbound and outbound transportation, receiving and checking merchandise shipments, storing and cross-docking merchandise, and getting merchandise floor-ready.

LO4 Review the considerations in the design of supply chains.

In designing their supply chain management systems, retailers make decisions about what activities to outsource; when to use a push and pull system for replenishing stores; what merchandise to cross-dock; and whether to ship merchandise to stores through a DC, use direct store delivery, or have products drop shipped to customers. The DCs and supply chain and information systems for supporting catalog and Internet channels are very different from those supporting the store channel. The importance of reverse logistics is growing because of the high returns for merchandise bought through the Internet channel and environmental sustainability issues.

LO5 **Explain how retailers and vendors collaborate to make sure the right merchandise is available when customers are ready to buy it.**

Retailers and vendors are collaborating to improve supply chain efficiency. Electronic data interchange enables retailers to communicate electronically with their vendors. Effective collaborative approaches include information sharing, VMI, and CPFR. These approaches represent the nexus of information systems and logistics management. They reduce lead time, increase product availability, lower inventory investments, and reduce overall logistics expenses.

LO6 **Discuss RFID and its implications for retailers.**

RFID has the potential of further streamlining the supply chain. Small RFID devices are affixed to pallets, cartons, and individual items and can be used to track merchandise through the supply chain and store information, such as when an item was shipped to a DC. Most of the recent applications involve tagging individual items and focusing on reducing inventory and stockouts.

KEY TERMS

advance shipping notice (ASN), *272*

backhaul, *268*

break pack area, *275*

bullwhip effect, *282*

checking, *275*

collaborative planning, forecasting, and replenishment (CPFR), *284*

consignment, *284*

consumer direct fulfillment, *280*

cross-docked, *275*

direct store delivery (DSD), *278*

dispatcher, *274*

distribution center (DC), *266*

drop shipping, *280*

electronic data interchange (EDI), *273*

fast fashion, *270*

floor-ready merchandise, *276*

freight forwarders, *277*

logistics, *274*

outsource, *277*

pack verification, *287*

pick ticket, *276*

point-of-sale (POS) terminal, *271*

public warehouse, *277*

pull supply chain, *278*

push supply chain, *278*

radio frequency identification (RFID), *284*

rain check, *269*

receiving, *275*

reorder point, *283*

reverse logistics, *279*

security policy, *273*

ship verification, *287*

stockout, *269*

supply chain management, *266*

ticketing and marking, *276*

universal product code (UPC), *271*

vendor-managed inventory (VMI), *283*

GET OUT AND DO IT!

1. **CONTINUING ASSIGNMENT** Interview the store manager working for the retailer you have selected for the Continuing Case assignment. Write a report that describes and evaluates the retailer's information and supply chain systems. Use this chapter as a basis for developing a set of questions to ask the manager. Some of the questions might be these: Where is the store's DC? Does the retailer use direct store delivery from vendors? How frequently are deliveries made to the store? Does the merchandise come in ready for sale? What is the store's percentage of stockouts? Does the retailer use a push or pull system? Does the store get involved in determining what merchandise is in the store and in what quantities? Does the retailer use VMI, EDI, CPFR, or RFID?

2. **INTERNET EXERCISE** Go to Barcoding Incorporated's web page at www.barcoding.com/, and

search for *retail*, *warehouse management*, and *RFID*. How is this company using technology to support retailers with information systems and supply chain management?

3. **INTERNET EXERCISE** Go to the home page of *RFID Journal* at www.rfidjournal.com/, and search for *supply chain* in the current issue. Summarize one of the recent articles, and explain how the key concept(s) described could make the shopping experience better for consumers and improve efficiency in the supply chain.

4. **INTERNET EXERCISE** Go to the home page of Vendor Managed Inventory at www.vendormanagedinventory.com/index.php, and answer the following questions: What is vendor-managed inventory? What are the benefits and limitations of a vendor-managed inventory approach?

DISCUSSION QUESTIONS AND PROBLEMS

1. Retail system acronyms include DSD, VMI, EDI, CPFR, and RFID. How are these terms related to one another?

2. Explain how an efficient supply chain system can increase a retailer's level of product availability and decrease its inventory investment.

3. This chapter presents some trends in logistics and information systems that benefit retailers. How do vendors benefit from these trends?

4. What type of merchandise is most likely to be cross-docked at retailers' DCs? Why is this often the case?

5. Why haven't more fashion retailers adopted an integrated supply chain system similar to Zara's?

6. Explain the differences between pull and push supply chains.

7. Consumers have five key reactions to stockouts: buy the item at another store, substitute a different brand, substitute the same brand, delay the purchase, or do not purchase the item. Consider your own purchasing behavior, and describe how various categories of merchandise would result in different reactions to a stockout.

8. Abandoned purchases as a result of stockouts can mean millions of dollars a year in lost sales. How are retailers and manufacturers using technology to reduce stockouts and improve sales?

9. What is a universal product code (UPC)? How does this code enable manufacturers, distributors, and retailers to track merchandise throughout the supply chain?

10. For what types of products is item-level RFID most beneficial for retailers?

SUGGESTED READINGS

Bardaki, Cleopatra, Panos Kourouthanassis, and Katerina Pramatari. "Deploying RFID-Enabled Services in the Retail Supply Chain: Lessons Learned toward the Internet of Things." *Information Systems Management* 29, no. 3 (2012), pp. 233–245.

Benton, W. C. *Purchasing and Supply Chain Management*, 3rd ed. New York: McGraw-Hill, 2014.

Dittmann, J. Paul. *Supply Chain Transformation: Building and Executing an Integrated Supply Chain Strategy*. New York: McGraw-Hill, 2011.

Fernie, John, and Leigh Sparks. *Logistics and Retail Management: Emerging Issues and New Challenges in the Retail Supply Chain*, 3rd ed. London: Kogan, 2009.

Finne, Sami, and Hanna Sivonen. *The Retail Value Chain: How to Gain Competitive Advantage through Efficient Consumer Response (ECR) Strategies*. London: Kogan, 2009.

Fisher, Marshall, and Ananth Raman. *The New Science of Retailing: How Analytics Are Transforming the Supply Chain and Improving Performance*. Boston: Harvard Business Press, 2010.

Haag, Stephen, and Maeve Cummings. *Management Information Systems for the Information Age*, 9th ed. New York: McGraw-Hill, 2013.

Hofer, Christian, Henry Jin, R. David Swanson, Matthew A. Waller, and Brent D. Williams. "The Impact of Key Retail Accounts on Supplier Performance: A Collaborative Perspective of Resource Dependency Theory," *Journal of Retailing*, 2012. Vol 83, number 3, September 2012, pp. 412–420.

Kauremaa, Jouni, Johanna Smaros, and Jan Holmstrom. "Patterns of Vendor-Managed Inventory: Findings from a Multiple-Case Study." *International Journal of Operations & Production Management* 29, no. 11 (2009), pp. 1109–1139.

Sari, Kazim. "On the Benefits of CPFR and VMI: A Comparative Simulation Study." *International Journal of Services and Operations Management* 6, no. 1 (2010), pp. 73–88.

Customer Relationship Management

EXECUTIVE BRIEFING
Jim Lewis, Founder and CEO,
Enhanced Retail Solutions

In 2002, after working in store management in South Florida and merchandise management at JCPenney's corporate headquarters in Plano, Texas, I decided to open my own software/consulting firm. At the time, retailers and vendors were collecting massive amounts of sales and inventory data that helped profile their customers' purchase behaviors (now referred to as "big data"), but they were not converting this data into actionable information they could use to make better decisions.

The first software applications we developed were for vendors. A number of retailers give vendors access to the POS data associated with the vendor's sales. But most vendors do not have the capability to crush this massive data describing every transaction or how to make it useful in optimizing sales and inventory at the store level. So we developed software that summarizes the vendor's performance much like the dashboard on a car. It allowed the vendor to communicate more effectively with its retail buyers and make actionable recommendations that the buyers appreciated. Soon after its introduction, many retail buyers recognized its benefits and now use the software.

While our initial activities provided vendors and retailers with a tool to access *how* well they are performing, we now are concentrating on examining

why vendors and retailers are doing well or poorly. For example, one of our apparel clients was concerned when a large, national retail customer was going to drop their line due to low sales. When we analyzed their sales data with the retailer, we found that the client's line was selling very well in some stores and poorly in others. Using the census data we have in our database, we found that the stores that were doing well for the vendor's line were in trading areas dominated by minority consumers. We helped our client make a presentation showing that the retailer would increase its profits if it didn't stock our client's line in about half its stores but increased its assortments in the retailer's stores located in areas with a high concentration of minorities.

We are now finding that the assortment decisions can integrate with supply chain activities. When analyzing a retailer's sales pattern for an imported, private-label product line, we found that the product line sold much better on the East Coast than on the West Coast. When the retailer's supply chain sourcing people learned about this sales pattern, they changed

CHAPTER 11

LEARNING OBJECTIVES

LO1 Describe the customer relationship management process.

LO2 Understand how customer shopping data are collected.

LO3 Explain the methods used to analyze customer data and identify target customers.

LO4 Outline how retailers develop their frequent-shopper programs.

LO5 Explain various ways to implement effective CRM programs.

the sourcing for the product line from East Asia to Mexico and saved $2 million in transportation costs—$2 million on one product line!

Store-level data is also being used to significantly improve forecasting accuracy. Advanced features in our software analyze in-stock patterns by store and update future inventory requirements accordingly. This enabled a client that supplies bed sheets to the major chains to reduce their overhead by 20 percent because they don't have to keep products as long in their warehouse.

Today most retailers collaborate with their vendors to use retail analytics to optimize their business. It certainly has been a competitive advantage for Walmart. While the techniques may be advanced, the basis for use is not—it builds on the fundamentals of retail—getting the right product at the right time to the right place in the right amount.

The business press and retailers are talking a lot about the importance of becoming more customer-centric and managing their customer relationships better. Retailers are spending millions of dollars on computer systems to collect and analyze data about their customers. With all this buzz, you would think that the customer is a popular new kid in the neighborhood. However, the customer is more like an old friend who's been taken for granted—until now.

Consider the following: Shari Ast is on her third business trip this month. She takes a cab from Boston's Logan Airport to the Ritz-Carlton, her favorite hotel in Boston. As the doorman opens the car door for her, he greets her with, "Welcome back to the Ritz-Carlton, Ms. Ast." When she goes to the registration desk, the receptionist gives her a room key. Then she goes to her room and finds just what she likes—a room with a view of the Boston Common, a single king-size bed, an extra pillow and blanket, a printer with a wireless connection for her laptop, and a basket with her favorite fruits and snacks.

The Ritz-Carlton provides personalized service for its preferred customers.

Shari Ast's experience is an example of Ritz-Carlton's customer relationship management program. **Customer relationship management (CRM)** is a business philosophy and set of strategies, programs, and systems that focuses on identifying and building relationships with a retailer's valued customers. CRM enables retailers to develop a base of loyal customers and increase its **share of wallet**—the percentage of the customers' purchases made from the retailer.

Traditionally, retailers have focused their attention on encouraging more customers to visit their stores, look through their catalogs, and visit their websites. To accomplish this objective, they have used mass-media advertising and sales promotions to attract visits from customers. This approach treats all existing and potential customers the same. They all receive the same messages and the same promotions.

Now, retailers are concentrating on developing customer loyalty and increasing share of wallet by providing more value to their best customers by using targeted, personalized merchandise, services, and promotions. Mindy Grossman, CEO of HSN, believes "it would take 10 new customers to replace one 'best' customer."[1] Her perspective is supported by research indicating that retailers are more profitable when they focus on retaining and increasing sales to their best customers rather than attempting to generate sales from new customers or less profitable existing customers.[2] In the following sections of this chapter, we discuss in more depth the objective of CRM programs and the elements of the CRM process.

THE CRM PROCESS

LO1

Describe the customer relationship management process.

The objective of the CRM process is to develop loyalty and repeat-purchase behavior among a retailer's best customers. Customer loyalty is more than having customers satisfied with a retailer and making repeat visits. For example, a customer might exclusively patronize a local supermarket because it is the only supermarket convenient to her house, but not be loyal to the supermarket. If another supermarket opened with a somewhat better offering, the customer might immediately switch to the new supermarket even though she was a repeat customer at her present supermarket.

Customer loyalty means that customers are committed to purchasing merchandise and services from the retailer and will resist the activities of competitors attempting to attract their patronage. Thus, if our preceding consumer was loyal, she would not switch to the new supermarket even though its offering was somewhat better.

Loyal customers have a bond with the retailer based on an emotional connection that is more than a just having a positive feeling about the retailer. This emotional bond is a personal connection. They feel that the retailer is a friend. Their goodwill toward the retailer encourages them to make repeat purchases and recommend it to their friends and family.

All elements in the retail mix contribute to the development of customer loyalty and repeat-purchase behavior.[3] Customer loyalty can be enhanced by creating an appealing brand image, offering exclusive merchandise, providing convenient locations, and providing an engaging shopping experience. However, personal attention and customer service are two of the most effective methods for developing loyalty. For example, many small, independent restaurants build loyalty by functioning as neighborhood cafés, where servers recognize customers by name and know their preferences. Nordstrom invites its best customers to grand-opening celebrations, pampers them during private shopping parties, and provides

EXHIBIT 11–1
The CRM Process Cycle

concierge services and free alterations. Such practices are more effective than discounts because when a retailer develops a personal connection with customers, it is difficult for any competitors to attract them away. The CRM programs and activities discussed in this chapter use information systems and customer data to personalize a retailer's offering and increase the value that its best customers receive. Personalized value also can be provided by employees in face-to-face interactions with customers. These forms of personalization are discussed in more detail in Chapter 18.

Overview of the CRM Process

Exhibit 11–1 illustrates that CRM is an iterative process that turns customer data into customer loyalty and repeat-purchase behavior through four activities: (1) collecting customer data, (2) analyzing customer data and identifying target customers, (3) developing CRM through frequent-shopper programs, and (4) implementing CRM programs.[4] The process begins with the collection and analysis of data about a retailer's customers and the identification of its best customers. The analysis translates the customer data into information and activities that offer value to these targeted customers. Then these activities are executed through personalized communications with customers. Each of the four activities in the CRM process is discussed in the following sections. Retailing View 11.1 describes the how Kroger uses customer data to facilitate its decisions.

COLLECTING CUSTOMER SHOPPING DATA

The first step in the CRM process is to construct a **customer database.** This database is part of the data warehouse described in Chapter 10. It contains all the data the firm has collected about its customers and is the foundation for subsequent CRM activities.

LO2
Understand how customer shopping data are collected.

Customer Database

Ideally, the customer database should contain the following information:

* *Transactions.* A complete history of the purchases made by the customer, including the purchase date, the SKUs purchased, the price paid, the amount of profit, and whether the merchandise was purchased in response to a special promotion or marketing activity.

REFACT

Walmart records 1 million customer transactions each hour in its customer database that contains more than 2.5 petabytes of data, which is equal to nearly 170 times the data in all of the books in the Library of Congress.[5]

- *Customer contacts.* A record of the interactions that the customer has had with the retailer, including visits to the retailer's website, inquiries made through in-store kiosks, comments made on blogs and Facebook pages, merchandise returns, and telephone calls made to the retailer's call center, plus information about contacts initiated by the retailer, such as catalogs and e-mails sent to the customer.

- *Customer preferences.* What the customer likes, such as favorite colors, brands, fabrics, and flavors, as well as apparel sizes.

- *Descriptive information.* Demographic and psychographic data describing the customer that can be used in developing market segments.

11.1   RETAILING VIEW   Using Customer Data at Kroger

Kroger is the largest supermarket retailer in the United States, with more than $70 billion in sales. It is also the sixth largest retailer in the world. Its impressive status is largely the result of a strategic decision it made to build a competitive advantage by collecting and analyzing customer data, then to use such data to manage its customer relationships. It began working with the UK-based consulting firm Dunnhumby in 2001. Since then, the partners have developed a joint venture called Dunnhumby USA that is responsible for converting all the data that Kroger collects from its customers when they swipe loyalty cards or enter their phone numbers at the point-of-sale into viable information that can help Kroger make decisions.

Similar to most supermarkets, Kroger's primary communication tool is a weekly newspaper circular featuring sale products. Category managers nominate products to include in the circular, and space is allocated according to the importance of the product category, any special promotions offered by vendors, and the margin Kroger earns on the advertised item.

REFACT

Dunnhumby USA has grown from 3 employees in 1992 to more than 1,000 today.[6]

By analyzing which items customers purchase in each trip, Dunnhmby USA has been able to improve this method and increase the effectiveness of the weekly circular. In particular, the purchase data identified complementary products, such that they prompted the sale of other items. For example, when customers purchase sliced deli roast beef, they also tend to purchase other deli meats, cheese, mustard, mayonnaise, and a loaf of fresh rye bread. But when they buy deli turkey, they don't buy these additions. Thus, roast beef is a better candidate for the circular, because it will tend to trigger the purchase of other items.

Kroger mails 55 million loyal customer mailings to their frequent-shopper cardholders every quarter. These mailings offer promotions on products that customers normally buy, as well as on products that Kroger predicts they would like, based on its analyses of what similar customers buy. So, for instance, if Kroger can predict that a customer is part of a young family, based on the purchase of hot dogs, Kellogg's Cocoa Krispies, and a lot of animal crackers, it can provide that family with a coupon for milk.

Retailers frequently segment their market using demographic variables, such as age, income, and education,

Dunnhumby USA analyzes the products that customers buy at the same time to make assortment and promotion decisions.

but they are poor predictors of sales (see Chapter 4). Dunnhumby USA's analyses enable Kroger to develop a better segmentation scheme based on actual purchase behavior rather than demographics. With these analyses, Kroger can identify customer segments that have a newborn baby, like to cook, or entertain frequently. Such precise segmentation capabilities not only help Kroger appeal appropriately to customers, encouraging their loyalty, but they also enable better decisions about in-store assortments, merchandise locations, store locations, and promotional designs.

Sources: Dhruv Grewal, Michael Levy, and Britt Hackmann, "Making Loyalty Programs Sing," Working Paper, Babson College, 2013; Josh Pichler, "Firm Remakes Retailers' Knowledge of Shoppers," *The Cincinnati Enquirer*, January 31, 2013; and Josh Pichler, "DunnhumbyUSA Combs through Data to Help Retailers Reward their Most Loyal Customers," *The Cincinnati Enquirer*, January 31, 2013.

DISCUSSION QUESTION

Why is segmentation based on purchase behavior superior for encouraging customer loyalty to segmentation based on demographics?

Customer transactions are collected from a POS terminal and stored in a customer database.

Different members of the same household might also have interactions with a retailer. Thus, to get a complete view of the customer, retailers need to be able to combine individual customer data from each member of a household. For example, Richards is a family-owned apparel chain in Westport and Greenwich, Connecticut. Spouses often buy presents for each other at Richards. The chain's database keeps track of both household-level purchases and individual purchases so that sales associates can help one spouse buy a gift for the other. The database also keeps track of spending changes and habits. Anniversaries, birthdays, and even divorces and second marriages are tracked along with style, brand, size, and color preferences, hobbies, and sometimes pets' names and golf handicaps.[7]

Identifying Information

It is relatively easy for retailers to construct a database for customers using nonstore channels because these customers must provide their contact information, name and address, so that the purchases can be sent to them. It is also easy to keep track of purchases made by customers patronizing warehouse clubs because they need to present their membership cards when they make a purchase. In these cases, the identification of the customer is always linked to the transaction. When retailers issue their own credit cards, they also can collect the contact information for billing when customers apply for the card. However, identifying most customers who are making in-store transactions is more difficult because they often pay for the merchandise with a check, cash, or a third-party credit card such as Visa or MasterCard.

Five approaches that store-based retailers use to overcome this problem are to (1) ask customers for identifying information, (2) connect Internet and store purchasing data, (3) offer frequent-shopper programs, (4) use biometrics to identify customers, and (5) place RFID chips on merchandise.

Ask for Identifying Information   Some retailers have their sales associates ask customers for identifying information, such as their phone number, e-mail address, or name and home address, when they process a sale. This information is then used to link all the transactions to the customer. However, some customers may be reluctant to provide the information because they feel that the sales associates are violating their privacy.

Connect Internet and Store Purchasing Data   When customers use third-party credit cards such as Visa or MasterCard to make a purchase in a store, the retailer cannot identify the purchase by the customer. However, if the customer used the same credit card while shopping at the retailer's website and provided shipping information, the retailer could connect the credit card purchases through its store and electronic channels.

Offer Frequent-Shopper Programs   **Frequent-shopper programs,** also called **loyalty programs,** are programs that identify and provide rewards to customers who patronize a retailer. Some retailers issue customers a frequent-shopper card. In both cases, customer transaction data are automatically captured when the card is scanned at the point-of-sale terminal. Customers are enticed to enroll in these programs and provide some descriptive information about themselves by offering them discounts if they use the cards when making purchases from the retailer. These frequent-shopper programs are discussed in more depth in following section of this chapter.

Use Biometrics   Rather than asking for identifying information or having to present a frequent-shopper card, some retailers use biometrics to identify customers and provide a cardless, cashless method of payment. When retailers use **biometrics,** they are measuring human characteristics such as a person's hand geometry, fingerprints, iris, or voice. When a retailer installs a biometric system, customers can preregister their fingerprints and credit card information and pay for products by simply placing their finger for a second or two on a fingerprint scanner at the checkout POS terminal. The use of biometrics can ensure that key customer data are captured consistently. Using biometrics results in faster checkout and the ability to target promotions. In addition, customers who enroll in the program can have their fingerprint scanned when entering the store and receive a printout of personalized product discounts.

Customers benefit from the convenience of faster checkout and receipt of frequent-shopper coupons and discounts without having to carry a lot of cards in their wallets. The faster checkout also benefits retailers by reducing labor costs. The retailers can accumulate the customer information quickly and accurately. In addition, retailers are using biometric systems to reduce employee fraud and shoplifting. These systems can detect when employees have had a coworker check in or out for them and whether the person returning merchandise for cash is the same as the person who bought it, not someone who stole it from the store.[9]

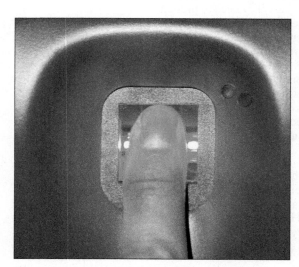

Biometrics are used to link transactions to individuals.

Place RFID Chips on Merchandise   Perhaps RFID provides the most convenient approach, from the customer's perspective, for customers to make purchases. An RFID reader in the store can acquire the customer's personal information from small devices carried by customers and RFID tags on the merchandise they want to purchase. In addition, using a global satellite tracking system, the store reader could also collect information about where the customer has been in the store.

Privacy and CRM Programs

The collection and analysis of data about customer attitudes, preferences, and shopping behaviors enables retailers to target information and promotions and provide greater value to their customers. However, many customers are concerned that retailers violate their privacy when they collect detailed personal information. Even if customers trust a retailer, they are concerned that the data may not be secure and/or may be sold to other businesses.

Privacy Concerns   There is no consensus about the definition of personal information. Some people feel that personal information is all information that is not publicly available; others include both public (e.g., driver's license, mortgage data) and private (e.g. hobbies, income) information. The degree to which consumers feel their privacy has been violated depends on:

- *Their control over their personal information when engaging in marketplace transactions.* Do they feel they can decide the amount and type of information that is collected by the retailer?
- *Their knowledge about the collection and use of personal information.* Do they know what information is being collected and how the retailer will be using it? Will the retailer be sharing the information with other parties?[10]

These concerns are particularly acute for customers using an Internet channel, because many of them do not realize the extensive amount of information that can be collected without their knowledge. This information is easily collected using cookies. **Cookies** are small files stored on a customer's computer that identify customers when they return to a website. Because of the data in cookies, customers do not have to identify themselves or use passwords every time they visit a site. However, cookies also can enable the collection of data about what pages people have viewed, other sites the people have visited, how they spend money online, and their interactions on social networking sites.

Protecting Customer Privacy   In the United States, existing consumer privacy legislation is limited to the protection of information associated with government functions and with practices in credit reporting, video rentals, banking, and health care. Thus, in the United States, the privacy of most consumer data is not protected. However, Congress is considering new legislation on consumer privacy, which is guided by three principles:[11]

- *Privacy by design.* Encourage businesses to treat consumer privacy as their "default setting," thus shifting the responsibility for privacy protection from consumers to retailers. Companies should also delete information about their customers that is no longer needed, provide reasonable security for data, limit collection of data consistent with the context of a particular transaction, and implement guidelines on how and when customer data will be eliminated.
- *Simplified consumer choice.* Develop ways that consumers can track their online activities. Specifically, they should have a simple method of turning off the ability of a firm to install a cookie that permits them to track the web pages consumers have viewed. This Do Not Track (DNT) function is similar in concept to the Do Not Call (DNC) list that consumers can join to opt-out of telemarketing calls.
- *Greater transparency.* Improve consumer understanding of how consumer data are collected through better education and information.

In response to potential government regulations, proactive U.S. retailers are attempting to self-regulate by developing privacy policies. Some retailers have appointed privacy advocates, including the creation of an executive chief privacy officer. Such appointments help ensure that privacy concerns are communicated throughout the organization, that an appropriate organizational privacy-sensitive culture is in place, and that the organization is adhering to its privacy policies.

While there are few consumer privacy regulations affecting retailers in the United States, the European Union (EU), Australia, New Zealand, and Canada have more stringent consumer privacy laws, and they are contemplating an increase in these restrictions. Some of the provisions of the EU directive on consumer privacy are the following:

- Businesses can collect consumer information only if they have clearly defined the purpose, such as completing the transaction.
- The purpose must be disclosed to the consumer from whom the information is being collected.
- The information can be used only for that specific purpose.
- The business can keep the information only for the stated purpose. If the business wants to use the information for another purpose, it must initiate a new collection process.
- Businesses operating in Europe can export information from the 27 EU countries only to importing countries with similar privacy policies. Thus, U.S. retailers, hotel chains, airlines, and banks cannot transfer information from Europe to the United States because the United States does not have similar privacy policies.[12]

Basically, the EU perspective is that consumers own their personal information, so retailers must get consumers to agree explicitly to share this personal information. This agreement is referred to as **opt in.** In contrast, personal information in the United States is generally viewed as being in the public domain, and retailers can use it any way they desire. American consumers must explicitly tell retailers not to use their personal information—they must explicitly **opt out.**[13]

In summary, there is growing consensus that personal information must be fairly collected; that the collection must be purposeful; and that the data should be relevant, accurate, essential to the business, subject to the rights of the owning individual, kept reasonably secure, and transferred only with the permission of the consumer. Many retailers that collect customer information have privacy policies. Retailers need to assure their customers that information about them is held securely and not passed on to other companies without the customer's permission.

REFACT

Eighty percent of U.S. consumers believe that it is important to be able to opt out of the sharing or sale of collected data.[14]

ANALYZING CUSTOMER DATA AND IDENTIFYING TARGET CUSTOMERS

LO3

Explain the methods used to analyze customer data and identify target customers.

The next step in the CRM process (see Exhibit 11–1) is to analyze the customer data and convert them into information that will help retailers develop programs for increasing the value they offer to their best customers, or those customers whose loyalty and repatronage will add significantly to the retailer's bottom line. Two objectives for analyzing the customer database are (1) identifying the retailer's best customers and (2) using analytical methods to improve decisions made by retail managers. These two objectives are discussed in this section.

Identifying the Best Customers

One of the goals of CRM is to identify and cater to the retailer's most valuable customers. Retailers often use information in their customer databases to determine how valuable each customer is to their firm. The value of a customer, called **customer lifetime value (CLV),** is the expected contribution from the customer to the retailer's profits over their entire relationship with the retailer. Retailers typically use past behaviors to forecast their CLV. To illustrate some of the factors considered in developing a measure of CLV, consider the purchase histories of two customers during the last 12 months shown here:

	December	January	February	March	April	May	June	July	August	September	October	November	Total
Shirley	$400	0	0	0	0	0	0	0	0	0	0	0	$400
Marcia	$10	$10	$25	$25	$15	$25	$40	$20	$35	$35	$50	$65	$355

Which woman has the highest CLV—that is, who would be the most valuable customer for the retailer in the future? If the retailer only considered the purchases made by the two women over the past 12 months, the retailer might conclude that Shirley is most valuable because she has bought the most merchandise during the last 12 months ($400 versus $355). But Shirley's purchase history might reflect her visit to the United States from Brazil, making a one-time purchase, and being very unlikely to patronize the retailer again. As the retailer digs deeper into the data, it might decide that Marcia is the most valuable customer because she purchases merchandise both more frequently and more recently. In addition, her monthly purchases are trending up. Even though Shirley might have bought more in the last 12 months, Marcia's purchase pattern suggests she will buy more in the future. Retailing View 11.2 illustrates the use of an **RFM analysis**—a method often used in catalog and Internet channels to determine customer segments that a retailer should target for a promotion or catalog mailing. The method uses three factors to evaluate the potential contribution of each customer segment: how *recently* the customers in the segment made a purchase, how *frequently* they make purchases, and how much *money* they have spent.

In the example, the classification of customers into these segments is based on the profitability of the customers, not sales. The use of sales to identify a retailer's best customers can be misleading. For example, airlines assign rewards in their frequent-flyer programs on the basis of miles flown. These programs provide the same rewards to customers who take low-cost, less profitable flights as to those who make a larger contribution to the airline's profit by flying first class and paying full prices. Sophisticated statistical methods are typically used to estimate the CLV for each customer, like Shirley and Marcia, based on more than their recency, frequency, and amount purchased.[15] These deeper analyses consider the gross margin from the customer's purchases and the costs associated with the purchase, such as the cost of advertising and promotions used to acquire the customers, and the cost of processing merchandise that the customer returned. For example, customers who pay full price and buy the same amount of merchandise have a higher CLV than customers who only buy items on sales. Customers who return 30 percent of the merchandise they purchase have a lower CLV than customers who rarely return merchandise.

Retail Analytics

Retailers can use data they have collected about their customers to measure each customer's CLV. In the remaining portion of this section, we explain how the availability of a customer database provides a resource that retailers can use to develop strategies and make better decisions. Retailing View 11.3 describes how the drugstore chain CVS derives insights by analyzing its extensive customer database.

Retail analytics are applications of statistical techniques and models that seek to improve retail decisions through analyses of customer data.[16] **Data mining** is an information processing method that relies on search techniques to discover new insights into the buying patterns of customers, using large databases.[17] Three of the most popular applications of data mining are market basket analysis, targeting promotions, and assortment planning.

Market Basket Analysis   In a **market basket analysis,** the data mining tools determine which products appear in the market basket that a customer purchases during a single shopping trip. This analysis can suggest where stores should place merchandise and which merchandise to promote together based on merchandise that tends to show up in the same market basket.

To perform a market basket analysis, a computer program counts the number of times two products get purchased at the same time. An often-used example of market basket analysis is the discovery by a supermarket chain that on Friday

11.2   RETAILING VIEW   Illustration of RFM Analysis

The RFM analysis in Exhibit 11–2 was conducted by an apparel retailer that needed to decide to which customer segments to send its catalogs. The retailer divided its catalog channel customers into 32 segments on the basis of how many orders each customer placed during the previous year, how much merchandise the customer purchased during the past 12 months, and the last time the customer placed an order. Each segment is represented by one cell in Exhibit 11–2. For example, the customers in the upper-left cell have made a purchase within the last 2 months (recency), made one or two purchases in the last year (frequency), and spent less than $50 over the last 12 months (money). For each RFM segment, the retailer determined the percentage of customers in the segment who made a purchase from the last catalog sent to them. For example, 5 percent of the customers in the upper-left cell of Exhibit 11–2 placed an order from the last catalog sent to them. With information about the response rate and the average gross margin from orders placed by customers in each cell, the retailer can calculate the expected profit from the last catalog sent to customers in each cell. For example, if the average gross margin from orders placed by customers in the upper-left cell is $20 and the cost of sending a catalog to customers in the cell is $0.75, with a five percent

response rate the catalog would make $0.25 per customer mailed a catalog in that segment:

$20 contribution × 0.05 response rate = $1.00 expected revenue per person

$1.00 − $0.75 cost person = $0.25 expected contribution per person

Using the 32 segments in Exhibit 11–2, the retailer might develop a strategy for each segment, as shown in Exhibit 11–3. For example, the retailer might focus on building its loyalty among customers in the segments in the lower-left area but not send any more catalogs to customers in the upper-right segments, because they are not profitable.

Sources: David Gillman, "Use SPSS Statistics Direct Marketing Analysis to Gain Insight: Analyze Customer History Using RFM," October 26, 2012, ibm.com/developerworks/; Jayanthi Ranjan and Ruchi Agarwal, "Application of Segmentation in Customer Relationship Management: A Data Mining Perspective," *International Journal of Electronic Customer Relationship Management* 3, no. 4 (2009), pp. 402–414; and Ching-Hsue Cheng and You-Shyang Chen, "Classifying the Segmentation of Customer Value Via RFM Model and RS Theory." *Expert Systems with Applications* 36, no. 3 (2009), pp. 4176–4184.

DISCUSSION QUESTION

How and why would a retailer use RFM analysis?

EXHIBIT 11–2
RFM Analysis for a Catalog Retailer

		RECENCY			
Frequency	Monetary	0–2 months	3–4 months	5–6 months	Over 6 months
1–2	<$50	5.0%*	3.5%	1.0%	0.1%
1–2	Over $50	5.0	3.6	1.1	0.1
3–4	<$150	8.0	5.0	1.5	0.6
3–4	Over $150	8.8	5.0	1.7	0.8
5–6	<$300	10.0	6.0	2.5	1.0
5–6	Over $300	12.0	8.0	2.7	1.2
Over 6	<$450	15.0	10.0	3.5	1.8
Over 6	Over $450	16.0	11.0	4.0	2.0

*Percentage of customers in the cell who made a purchase from the last catalog mailed to them.

EXHIBIT 11–3
RFM Target Strategies

		RECENCY			
Frequency	Monetary	0–2 months	3–4 months	5–6 months	Over 6 months
1–2	<$50	First-time customers		Low-value customers	
1–2	Over $50				
3–4	<$150	Early repeat customers		Defectors	
3–4	Over $150				
5–6	<$300	High-value customers		Core defectors	
5–6	Over $300				
Over 6	<$450				
Over 6	Over $450				

evenings between 6 and 7 p.m., many market baskets, particularly those bought by men, contained both beer and baby diapers. This relationship between beer and baby diapers arises because diapers come in large packages, so wives, who do most of the household shopping, leave the diaper purchase to their husbands. When husbands buy diapers at the end of the workweek, they also want to get some beer for the weekend. When the supermarket discovered this shopping pattern, it put a premium beer display next to the diapers. Because the premium beer was so conveniently placed next to the diapers, men tend to be up-sold and buy the premium brands rather than spend time going to the beer aisle for lower-priced brands.

RETAILING VIEW   CVS Caremark Gains Useful Insights from Its Customer Database

11.3

The market intelligence group at CVS Caremark is responsible for building the firm's data warehouse and analyzing the data to develop programs and promotions that increase its share of wallet. Customers in its ExtraCare frequent-shopper program earn a percentage of their purchases back as ExtraBucks that they can use in the store during future shopping trips. The percentages earned as ExtraBucks vary by product type, from 2 percent of all in-store sales to 10 percent on beauty products. Customers also earn double ExtraBucks on more than 100 diabetes-related products and 5 ExtraBucks for every 10 prescriptions they fill. E-mails and direct mail provide them with helpful health and beauty insights, new-product information, and coupons, in addition to free merchandise when CVS Caremark has special vendor promotions. Using each member's buying habits, CVS Caremark personalizes the coupons it gives to ExtraCare program participants. With a "Send to Card" feature, it also eliminates the need for paper coupons: ExtraCare members can assign their ExtraBucks rewards and coupons directly to their loyalty cards, or else they can upload all the information to their smartphones, using the ExtraCare mobile app.

REFACT

ExtraCare, the top frequent-shopper program in the retail industry, attracts approximately 92 million active cardholders. More than 67 percent of all transactions and 82 percent of front-end sales in CVS stores feature the use of ExtraCare loyalty cards.[18]

The use of data to make better decisions at CVS Caremark starts with customers scanning in their ExtraCare card.

By analyzing the buying behavior of ExtraCare customers, CVS has discovered some interesting cross-promotional opportunities. For example, about two-thirds of customers who buy toothpaste did not buy toothbrushes. To encourage them to do so, the retailer targets toothpaste consumers with special toothbrush promotions. It also uses special promotions to increase the overall size of their market baskets. For example, it offers a $4 coupon to customers whose average market basket is $15 if they reach $25 in purchases, whereas customers who normally spend $25 get a $10 coupon if they make a $50 purchase.

Beyond the store, CVS Caremark analyzes its database to tailor its assortment and location decisions to the needs of its loyal, local community. For example, it identified a segment of customers who lived in urban areas with a dearth of grocery store options. So it expanded grocery, fresh, and on-the-go food items available in stores located in the same neighborhoods.

Finally, to ensure that they never question their own loyalty, CVS Caremark is very protective of customers' privacy. Its programs are all opt-in, and it sends mailings only to customers who give it permission to do so. At times, it uses outside processing companies as agents to help print and send mailings, but these agents never receive any personal customer information beyond names and addresses. CVS Caremark commits to never granting or selling any specific information to any manufacturer or direct marketer.

Sources: www.cvs.com/ExtraCare; Greg Jacobson, "CVS Aims to Personalize Retail Experience," *Chain Drug Review*, April 23, 2012.

DISCUSSION QUESTION

How does CVS Caremark use the data it collects from its ExtraCare program?

Some other examples of how market basket analyses have revised product locations are as follows:

- Bananas are the most common item in Americans' grocery carts, so supermarkets often place bananas both in the cereal aisle and in the produce section.
- Tissues are in the paper goods aisle but also mixed in with cold medicine.
- Measuring spoons appear in the housewares section and also hang next to baking supplies, such as flour and shortening.
- Flashlights are placed in the hardware aisle and with a seasonal display of Halloween costumes.
- Snack cakes appear in the bread aisle, but they also are available next to the coffee.
- Bug spray is merchandised with hunting gear and with household cleaning supplies.

Targeting Promotions   Beyond aiding decisions about where to place products in a store, market basket analysis can help provide insights into assortment decisions and promotions. For example, retailers might discover that customers typically buy a specific brand of conditioner and shampoo at the same time (in the same market basket). With this information, the retailer might offer a special promotion on the conditioner, anticipating that customers will also buy the (higher margin) shampoo at its full price.

Assortment Planning   Managers have to make decisions about what merchandise to carry in each category. Customer data also can be mined to help with these assortment decisions. By analyzing which products the retailer's most valued customers purchase, the manager can ensure that they are available in the store at all times. For example, an analysis might discover that customers in its highest CLV segment are very loyal to a brand of gourmet mustard. However, this brand of mustard is only the tenth best seller in the retailer's mustard category across all customers. Due to its relatively low sales, the retailer might consider dropping the mustard brand from its assortment. But based on this analysis, the retailer would decide to continue offering the mustard, fearing that these high CLV customers would defect to another retailer if the gourmet brand was no longer stocked in its stores.

DEVELOPING CRM THROUGH FREQUENT-SHOPPER PROGRAMS

LO4

Outline how retailers develop their frequent-shopper programs.

As mentioned earlier, frequent-shopper programs, or loyalty programs, are marketing efforts that reward repeat buying behavior. Two objectives of these programs are to (1) to build a customer database that links customer data to their transactions and (2) to encourage repeat purchase behavior and loyalty. The implications of the first objective are discussed in a preceding section of this chapter; the implications of the second objective are reviewed in the following section.

Effectiveness of Frequent-Shopper Programs

Although frequent-shopper programs are useful for building customer databases, they are not particularly useful for building long-term customer loyalty.[19] The perceived value of these programs by consumers is low, because consumers perceive little difference among the programs offered by competing retailers. Most programs simply offer customers price discounts that are available to all customers that register for the programs. These discounts are appealing to price-conscious shoppers but not necessarily to the high CLV shoppers. In addition, competitive advantages based on frequent-shopper programs are rarely sustainable. The programs are very visible, so they can be easily duplicated by competitors. They also are very expensive in most cases.[20] A one percent price discount might cost large retailers around $100 million—and that is only after they invest up to $30 million to get the loyalty program up and running. Over time, they must continue to invest, up to $10 million annually, to maintain the program, including IT costs, marketing efforts, and training.

Finally, loyalty programs are difficult to revise or correct. Once they become part of customers' shopping experience, the retailer has to inform customers about even the smallest changes. If those changes imply that customers are losing some of the benefits of the programs, a strong negative reaction is likely, even from customers who exhibit relatively little loyalty in the first place.

Frequent-shopper programs have limited effectiveness because consumers join all of the programs offered by competing retailers.

Making Frequent-Shopper Programs More Effective

Frequent-shopper programs seek to encourage repeated purchases and develop customer loyalty. To build true loyalty, retailers need an emotional connection with consumers, as well as a sense of commitment from them. When a Starwood Hotels representative helped a frequent customer find a car when she was stranded in Chicago, then called the woman's husband to let him know she was fine, that associate ensured the traveler's loyalty.[22] Therefore, to move frequent-shopper programs beyond simple data collection and short-term sales effects, retailers might (1) create tiered rewards, (2) treat frequent shoppers as VIPs, (3) incorporate charitable activities, (4) offer choices, (5) reward all transactions, and (6) make the program transparent and simple.[23]

Offer Tiered Rewards   Many frequent-shopper programs contain cascading tier levels, such as silver, gold, and platinum. The higher the tier, the better the rewards. This reward structure provides an incentive for customers to consolidate their purchases with one retailer to reach the higher tiers. Some programs combine both discounts and points. For example, a retailer might offer a $5 discount on purchases between $100 and $149.99, $10 dollars off purchases from $150 to $249.99, and $15 off purchases of $250 or more. Then beyond $250, customers accumulate points that can be redeemed for special, unique rewards, such as a free shirt or tickets to a local baseball game.

A key requirement for a tiered program is designing tiers that consumers perceive as attainable. Frequent shoppers can calculate the tier level they can achieve with their usual spending pretty easily. They may be less inclined to shop at a retailer or participate in its frequent-shopper program if the tiers are impossibly distant. Although Neiman Marcus has a reward tier for customers who make $600,000 in annual purchases, a similar reward tier would be vastly inappropriate for a grocery store loyalty program.

Treat High CLVs as VIPs   Consumers respond to being treated as if they are someone special. Effective programs, therefore, go beyond discounts on purchases to offer unique rewards. For example, in its PowerUp Rewards program, GameStop encouraged its target customers to spend more on racing and fantasy video games by offering tickets to NASCAR races or backstage access to Comic-Con.[25] The rewards accordingly should match the retailer's target market to make customers feel really special: A private shopping night might be important for a heavy Nordstrom shopper, whereas an exclusive tour of the company's facility might be more interesting for Apple customers. These events also should be promoted in advance to encourage

REFACT

More than 17 percent of customers indicate that loyalty programs are "very influential" in their purchase decisions.[21]

REFACT

American Airlines launched the first frequent-flyer program in 1981. In 1984, Neiman Marcus launched the first frequent-shopper program by a retailer selling products.[24]

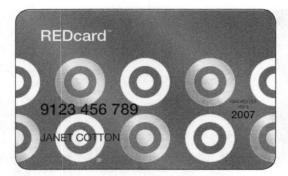

Target enhances the effectiveness of its frequent-shopper program by linking it to donations to local schools.

more customers to enroll and pursue enough points to be invited to attend the events.

Incorporate Charitable Contributions Many programs are linked to charitable causes. For example, Target donates one percent of all purchases made with its REDcard to local schools. Although these altruistic rewards can be an effective element of a frequent-shopper program, they probably should not be the focal point of the program.

Offer Choices Not all customers value the same rewards, so the most effective frequent-shopper programs offer choices. Sainsbury, a UK supermarket chain, allows customers to use their Nectar points for vouchers at a variety of retail partners. Caesars Entertainment has different programs for guests who live close to one of its properties and for customers who must fly to its casinos or resorts. It also introduced Total Rewards Member Pricing, which enables loyalty program members to get better pricing than nonmembers at Caesars property restaurants as well as the opportunity to purchase presale show tickets.[26]

Starwood Hotels (which owns the Westin, W, Sheraton, and Four Points chains, among others) maintains a program within its Starwood Preferred Guest program, called Moments, that gives point-holders chances to bid in an auction for spectacular experiences. Participants use their earned points to bid on the right to attend a variety of exclusive access events: meeting Coldplay backstage before a concert, playing golf with pro Lorena Ochoa, or meeting the chef while having dinner at the famous Per Se restaurant.[27]

Reward All Transactions To ensure that the retailer collects all customer transaction data and encourages repeat purchases, programs need to reward all purchases, not just purchases of selected merchandise or those made through certain channels (e.g., in-store versus online). Customers should gain entry to an introductory tier with nearly their first purchase, to encourage them to join. Accordingly, Sephora designates customers as Beauty Insiders the moment they sign up for a card. Once they spend $100—not much at the cosmetics counter—they qualify to receive a free sample-sized product.[28]

Make the Program Transparent and Simple Effective programs are transparent in that they make it easy for customers to keep track of their spending and available rewards. When they are both transparent and convenient, loyalty programs can quickly become integral to shoppers' consumption choices. Thus, there is an increasing use of smartphone-linked programs that let customers earn and redeem rewards through a mobile app, instead of requiring them to remember their cards or coupons. With a push of a button, shoppers can recall their point totals, how much more they need to spend to reach a desired prize, or whether they can redeem points for something great today.

When loyalty programs also are simple, their effectiveness increases even more. A program with a confusing maze of rules and regulations has little appeal to consumers. Some airlines have suffered from accusations that their confusing blackout dates and redemption rules make their loyalty programs virtually useless. Instead, simple, straightforward programs can succeed just by offering a few options consistently and dependably.

Retailing View 11.4 describes how the Neiman Marcus InCircle program goes beyond offering price discounts to building loyalty with its best customers.

Neiman Marcus targets the top two percent of consumers, in terms of their income, which generally means that people in its stores are well-educated and well-traveled. These sophisticated shoppers are attracted to the retailer's InCircle frequent-shopper program, widely considered a CRM best practice.

The InCircle program is linked to the store credit card and offers six levels of benefits, based on annual purchases at Neiman Marcus. Circle 1 indicates purchases less than $2,500; the Chairman's Level means the customer has spent more than $600,000 that year.

Depending on their tier, customers receive from two to five InCircle points for every dollar charged on their credit cards. For every 10,000 points earned, the members receive a $100 gift card. In addition, they accrue other benefits, depending on their spending level: discounts on in-store dining, free alterations, store delivery, hassle-free parking, fur storage, free repair and cleaning of jewelry, engraving, shoe and handbag repair, monogramming, and discounts at salons, to name a few. Customers at the higher levels also receive some unusual rewards, such as a concierge service that will locate an item that customers have seen on TV or a fashion runway, make a reservation at an exclusive restaurant, and run errands.

InCircle members can quickly look up their point balance on the InCircle website. They receive e-mails announcing special events and notifications when they are approaching a new tier level. They also get *Entrée* magazine, a publication produced by Time Warner exclusively for Neiman Marcus. In turn, Neiman Marcus asks for feedback about how it can help improve its value for InCircle members.

REFACT

More than 35 percent of Neiman Marcus sales are to customers enrolled in the InCircle program.[29]

Neiman Marcus' InCircle frequent-shopper program is a benchmark for other programs.

At the store level, sales associates unobtrusively gather insights about customers, using their prior purchases and behaviors in the store. Once they have struck up a relationship, the sales associates contact customers directly when a new shipment of their favorite brand has arrived, for example. The sales associates also move freely throughout the store to find whatever items their InCircle members want at the time or to encourage them to make use of the services available, such as gift wrap and travel advice.

Sources: www.incircle.com, www.neimanmarcus.com, and 10K 2012 Neiman-Marcus annual report.

DISCUSSION QUESTION

What are the elements of Neiman-Marcus's InCircle program that build customer loyalty?

IMPLEMENTING CRM PROGRAMS

Having developed CRM through frequent-shopper programs, the last step in the CRM process is to implement those programs (see Exhibit 11–1).

LO5

Explain various ways to implement effective CRM programs.

Customer Pyramid

For most retailers, a relatively small number of customers account for the majority of their profits. This condition is often called the **80-20 rule**—80 percent of the sales or profits come from 20 percent of the customers. Thus, retailers could group their customers into two categories on the basis of their CLV scores. One group would be the 20 percent of the customers with the highest CLV scores, and the other group would be the rest. However, this two-segment scheme, "best" and "rest," does not consider important differences among the 80 percent of customers in the "rest" segment. Many of the customers in the "rest" category are potentially "best," or at least, good customers. A commonly used segmentation scheme divides

EXHIBIT 11–4
The Customer Pyramid

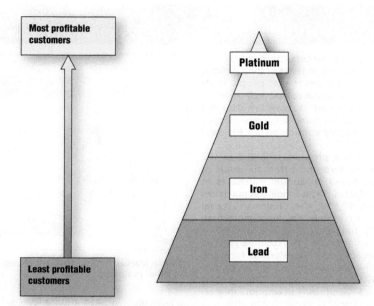

SOURCE: Valarie Zeithaml, Roland Rust, and Katherine Lemon, "The Customer Pyramid: Creating and Serving Profitable Customers," *California Management Review* 43 (Summer 2001), p. 124. Reprinted with permission.

customers into four segments, as illustrated in Exhibit 11–4, or even 10 deciles. This scheme allows retailers to develop more effective strategies for each of the segments. Different CRM programs are directed toward customers in each of the segments. Each of the four segments is described next.[30]

Platinum Segment   This segment is composed of the customers with the top 25 percent CLVs. Typically, these are the most profitable and loyal customers who, because of their loyalty, are typically not overly concerned about prices. Customers in this quartile buy a lot of the merchandise sold by the retailer and often place more value on customer service than price.

Gold Segment   The next quartile of customers, in terms of their CLVs, make up the gold segment. Even though they buy a significant amount of merchandise from the retailer, they are not as loyal as platinum customers and patronize some of the retailer's competitors. The profitability levels of the gold-tier customers are less than those of the platinum-tier customers because price plays a greater role in their decision making. An important objective of any CRM program is to provide incentives to move gold-tier customers to the platinum level.

Iron Segment   The customers in this quartile purchase a modest amount of merchandise, but their spending levels, loyalty, and profitability are not substantial enough for special treatment. Although it could be possible to move these people up to higher tiers in the pyramid, for reasons such as limited income, price sensitivity, or shared loyalties with other retailers, additional expenditures on them may not be worth it.

Lead Segment   Customers with the lowest CLVs can make a negative contribution to the firm's income. They often demand a lot of attention but do not buy much from the retailer. When they do buy from the retailer, they often buy merchandise on sale or abuse return privileges. They may even cause additional problems by complaining about the retailer to others. As a result, retailers do not direct any attention to these customers.

In the following sections, we discuss programs retailers use to retain their best customers, convert good customers into high-CLV customers, and get rid of unprofitable customers.

Customer Retention

Two approaches that retailers use to retain customers and increase the share of wallet are personalization and community.

Personalization An important limitation of CRM strategies developed for market segments, such as a platinum segment in the customer pyramid (Exhibit 11–4), is that each segment is composed of a large number of customers who are not identical. Thus, any offering will be most appealing for only the typical customer and not as appealing to the majority of customers in the segment. For example, customers in the platinum segment with the highest CLVs might include a 25-year-old single woman whose needs are quite different from those of a 49-year-old working mother with two children.

The availability of customer-level data and analysis tools helps retailers overcome this problem and offer unique benefits and targeted messages to individual customers in a cost-effective manner. Some retailers provide unusually high-quality, personalized customer service to build and maintain the loyalty of their best customers. For example, upscale department stores such as Saks Fifth Avenue and Neiman Marcus provide wardrobe consultants for their best customers. These consultants can arrange special presentations and fittings in the store during hours when the store is not open or at the customers' offices or homes. Nordstrom holds complimentary private parties for invitees to view new clothing lines. Saks Fifth Avenue offers free fur storage, complimentary tailoring, and dinner at the captain's table on a luxury cruise line. At Andrisen Morton, a Denver men's apparel specialty retailer, salespeople occasionally contact customers directly; if the store receives a new shipment of Brioni suits, they call customers who have purchased Brioni in the past. If a customer has been relatively inactive, the associates might offer him a $100 certificate for something he has not bought in a while.

Developing retail programs for small groups or individual customers is referred to as **1-to-1 retailing.** Many small, local retailers have always practiced 1-to-1

Amazon personalizes its Internet interactions with customers by analyzing its customer database to present offerings that will be of interest to each of its customers.

retailing. They know each of their customers, greet them by name when they walk into the store, and then recommend merchandise they know the customers will like. These local store owners do not need customer databases and data mining tools because they can keep the information in their heads. But most large retail chains and their employees lack such intimate knowledge of their customers. Thus, CRM enables larger retailers to develop relationships similar to those that many small local retailers have with customers.

Another aspect of personalization is to involve the best customers in the retailer's business decisions. Some retailers ask their best customers to participate in focus groups to evaluate alternatives the retailer is considering. Loyalty increases when customers feel valued for not just the money they have spent, but for their opinions.

The personalized rewards or benefits that customers receive are based on unique information possessed by the retailer and its sales associates. This information, in the retailer's customer database, cannot be accessed or used by competitors. Thus, it provides an opportunity to develop a sustainable competitive advantage.

The effective use of this information creates the positive feedback cycle in the CRM process (see Exhibit 11–1). Increasing repeat purchases from a retailer increases the amount of data collected from the customer, which enables the retailer to provide more personalized benefits, which in turn increases the customer's purchases from the retailer.

Community   A second approach for building customer retention and loyalty is to develop a sense of community among customers. A **retail brand community** is a group of customers who are bound together by their loyalty to a retailer and the activities the retailer sponsors and undertakes. Community members identify themselves with other members and share a common interest and participation in activities related to the retailer. They also feel an obligation to attract new members of the community and help other members of the community by sharing their experiences and product knowledge. By participating in such a community, customers become more reluctant to leave the "family" of other people patronizing the retailer.[31]

The Nike stores create a sense of community by hosting running groups that meet weekly at the store for refreshments. Members who have logged more than 100 miles earn special recognition, and the Nike Plus website communicates with runners' Apple iTouches/iPhones to track their running metrics. More than half of the runners involved in Nike's program use this system, visiting the website more than four times a week.

TAG/Burger and Bar at Madison Street in Denver creates a sense of community by encouraging customers to send in original hamburger combination recipes through e-mail, Facebook, and Twitter. Every month, management chooses the best one and offers it for sale for a month. The winner gets as many as he or she wants for the month that it is featured.

Walmart solicited its community of "Walmart Moms" from among bloggers who already were writing about the challenges of modern motherhood—and the quest for savings and value. The 11 original bloggers offered high-quality content and had strong influences on their readers, leading Walmart to enlist them to share their advice and insights on "living well." Although many of the posts, hosted through Walmart's website, are specific to finding grocery bargains, the community site covers a broad range of topics, from green living to politics to health issues. The retailer does not pay the mothers and even requires them to disclose any forms of compensation they might receive (e.g., travel expenses, free products for trials). Yet, in many cases, the information they post resonates with Walmart's brand image. Furthermore, Walmart gains invaluable feedback from not only the bloggers (who now number more than 20), but also all the other moms who follow their posts. By entering into conversations with the bloggers,

Walmart supports blogs by independent bloggers to encourage a community of value-oriented moms.

posters, and commentators, Walmart builds connections with a critical target market of modern moms.[32]

Customer Conversion: Making Good Customers into Best Customers

In the context of the customer pyramid (Exhibit 11–4), increasing the sales made to good customers can be referred to as customer alchemy—converting iron and gold customers into platinum customers.[33] A way to achieve customer alchemy is through **add-on selling,** which involves offering and selling more products and services to existing customers to increase the retailer's share of wallet with these customers.

A retailer's customer database reveals opportunities for add-on selling. Many retailers use their data on customers' shopping histories to suggest products to them. For example, if a supermarket discovers that customers are buying cat food and not kitty litter, it might distribute coupons for kitty litter to the customers. These coupons could be provided to the customers when they enter the store and swipe their frequent-shopper cards, when they log on to the retailer's website, or through messages sent to the customers' mobile phones.

Amazon.com is a master at generating add-on sales through its recommendations. Personalized recommendations, based on past purchases, are made when consumers first visit the website. If they scroll down to get more information about a book, the site recommends other books that have been bought by customers who purchased the book being examined. Then a bundle of two books, the one being examined and a complementary book, is offered at a discounted price. Retailing View 11.5 describes how American Girl increases its share of wallet.

Dealing with Unprofitable Customers

In many cases, the bottom tier of customers actually has a negative CLV. Retailers lose money on every sale they make to these customers. For example, catalog retailers have customers who repeatedly buy three or four items and return all but one of them. The cost of processing two or three returned items is much greater than the profits coming from the one item that the customer kept. Customers in the bottom tier may also be there because they stopped buying from the retailer for a period of time and then resumed patronizing the retailer. For example, customers may vanish because a competitor is offering a more attractive offer, or they are dissatisfied and then return months or years later as a new customer. The costs of their (re)acquisition make them unprofitable. The process of no longer selling to these unprofitable customers can be referred to as "getting the lead out," in terms of the customer pyramid.[34]

Approaches for getting the lead out are (1) offering less costly services to satisfy the needs of lead customers and (2) charging customers for the services they

11.5   RETAILING VIEW   American Girl Motivates Customers to Purchase Doll Add-Ons

When American Girl first hit the market in 1986, the limited line of dolls represented 9-year-old girls who lived at different times in history, combined with books that told each doll's story. Youthful consumers loved the 18-inch dolls and learned a little bit of history as they read about how a young girl would have lived at different points in the past. The popularity of the line encouraged the retailer to expand the associated items available, creating many opportunities for customers to buy add-on merchandise.

For example, for shoppers less interested in history than in the present, the Just Like You line features contemporary dolls. If a younger sister at home wants her own doll, American Girl offers the Bitty Baby line, with soft dolls more appropriate for 3- to 6-year olds. Across all these lines, consumers can find a wealth of accessories to buy for their dolls, including clothing, accessories, toys, and so forth.

Because the dolls and their accessories promise education and embrace diversity, millions of girls and their parents exhibit significant loyalty to American Girl. To enable them to live an American Girl life, the company released a film, *Kit Kittredge: An American Girl*. The book series also has expanded, to include six texts about each doll; really active readers also can keep up with their monthly *American Girl* magazine.

Perhaps the greatest add-on opportunity is available through the American Girl stores (currently, there are 14 throughout the United States). Families make vacations out of visits to the store. Each trip is likely to include a photo shoot of the girl and her doll; a salon visit to shape and style her doll's hair; a three-course lunch at the café, with a seat provided for her doll; and a new outfit for the doll, with a matching version for the girl. If a doll has had too many adventures and needs repairs, the store has a hospital. Such an outing can cost more than $300, but parents, after getting over the sticker shock, often indicate that they believe the experience is worth it.

American Girl increases its share of wallet with customers by offering special services like hairdressing and dining with dolls.

Community activities also have been developed around American Girl dolls. For example, local libraries host American Girl parties. The events attract dozens of girls and their dolls and feature events and discussions that are specific to the time periods that each doll represents. Service organizations even have developed American Girl fashion shows to support local charities.

Sources: www.americangirl.com; David Rosenberg, "Looking at American Girls with Their American Girls," *Slate*, January 25, 2013; Michelle Wildgen, "The Rise of American Girl Rebecca Rubin," *Forward*, January 2, 2012; and Amy Ziettlow, "Lessons From American Girl Dolls: The Divorce Generation," *The Atlantic*, January 18, 2013.

DISCUSSION QUESTION

How does American Girl help ensure that its existing customers spend more with it?

are abusing. For example, a retailer might get 70,000 daily calls, about three-quarters of which go to automated systems that cost the company less than $1 each. The remaining calls are handled by call center agents that cost $13 per call. The retailer could contact 25,000 lower-tier customers who placed a lot of calls to agents and tell them they must use the website or automated calls for simple account and price information. Each name could be flagged and routed to a special representative who would direct callers back to automated services and tell them how to use it.

Rejecting customers is a delicate business, though. Sierra Trading Post, an on-line retailer of apparel and outdoor equipment, has been criticized by customers who received e-mails, seemingly out of the blue, informing them they can no longer shop with the retailer because they have returned too many items. Yet, the company guarantees satisfaction and offers a full refund to any unhappy customer, regardless of how long the customer has owned a product.

SUMMARY

LO1 Describe the customer relationship management process.

Customer relationship management (CRM) is a business philosophy that includes a set of strategies, programs, and systems that focus on identifying and building repeat purchase behavior and loyalty with a retailer's most valued customers. Loyal customers are committed to patronizing a retailer and are not prone to switch to competitors. In addition to building loyalty by increasing customer value, CRM programs are designed to increase the share of wallet that a retailer earns from its better customers.

Customer relationship management is an iterative process that allows the retailer to encourage increased loyalty through its efforts to (1) collect customer data, (2) analyze the customer data and identify target customers, (3) develop CRM and frequent-shopper programs, and (4) implement CRM programs.

LO2 Understand how customer shopping data are collected.

Retailers collect extensive data about customers, which they store in their databases. To gather these data, retailers might ask for it at the point of sale, obtain it through online channels, or gather it from applications that customers submit to a loyalty program. Although it can be challenging to ensure that all collected data are accurately connected with each customer transaction, the collection and analysis of data about customer attitudes, preferences, and shopping behaviors enables retailers to closely target their promotions and provide more value to their customers.

However, many customers are concerned that retailers might violate their privacy when they collect detailed personal information. There is a growing consensus that personal information must be fairly collected, that the collection must be purposeful, and that the data should be relevant and kept reasonably secure. Anticipating increasing data privacy regulations, many retailers are working proactively to establish secure methods that can guarantee the privacy of their customers' data.

LO3 Explain the methods used to analyze customer data and identify target customers.

Once retailers have collected sufficient data, they must analyze them to derive actionable information. A common measure for describing shoppers is their customer lifetime value (CLV). Another method describes the recency, frequency, and monetary amount (RFM) of their purchases. More sophisticated retail analytics also include market basket analysis, which provides information about the products most commonly purchased together. Such information can inform retail decisions about which assortment to maintain in a store to appeal best to valuable customers, as well as which merchandise items to promote together to increase sales.

LO4 Outline how retailers develop their frequent-shopper programs.

Frequent-shopper programs serve two main purposes: (1) build a customer database that links customers to transactions and (2) encourage repeat purchase behavior and loyalty. Frequent-shopper programs can be effective for building a customer database, but they are not very useful for ensuring long-term customer loyalty. To enhance their loyalty effects, frequent-shopper programs should seek to (1) create tiered rewards, (2) treat frequent shoppers as VIPs, (3) incorporate charitable activities, (4) offer choices, (5) reward all transactions, and (6) make the rewards program transparent and simple.

LO5 Explain various ways to implement effective CRM programs.

Using this information about customers, retailers can develop programs to build loyalty in their best customers, increase their share of wallet with better customers (e.g., convert gold customers into platinum customers), and deal with unprofitable customers (getting the lead out). Four approaches that retailers use to build loyalty and retain their better customers are (1) launch frequent-shopper programs, (2) offer special customer services, (3) personalize the services they provide, and (4) build a sense of community. To deal with unprofitable customers identified by their CRM data, retailers need to develop lower-cost approaches to serve them, or else exclude those customers altogether from the retail offer.

KEY TERMS

add-on selling, *309*

biometrics, *296*

cookies, *297*

customer database, *293*

customer lifetime value (CLV), *298*

customer loyalty, *292*

customer relationship management (CRM), *292*

data mining, *299*

80-20 rule, *305*

frequent-shopper program, *296*

loyalty program, *296*

market basket analysis, *299*

1-to-1 retailing, *307*

opt in, *298*

opt out, *298*

retail analytics, *299*

retail brand community, *308*

RFM analysis, *299*

share of wallet, *292*

GET OUT AND DO IT!

1. **CONTINUING ASSIGNMENT** Interview the store manager working for the retailer you have selected for the continuing assignment. Ask the manager if the store offers a frequent-shopper/loyalty program and how effective it is in terms of increasing the store's sales and profits. Find out why the manager has these views and what could be done to increase the effectiveness of the program. Then talk to some customers in the store. Ask them why they are or are not members. Find out how membership in the program affects their shopping behavior and relationship with the retailer.

2. **INTERNET EXERCISE** Go to the home page of a retailer that you frequent and review its privacy policy. How is this retailer protecting its customers' information? Which policies, or lack of policies, raise your concern? Why? Which policies give you comfort that your private information is being protected? Why?

3. **INTERNET EXERCISE** Go to the website of the Electronic Privacy Information Center (www.epic.org), and review the issues raised by the organization. What does this watchdog organization feel are the most important retailers' consumer privacy issues? How will these issues evolve in the future?

4. **INTERNET EXERCISE** Go to the home page of 1-800-Flowers at www.1800flowers.com, and read about the Fresh Rewards program. How does this company's CRM program help it to track its better customers, grow its business, and increase customer loyalty?

DISCUSSION QUESTIONS AND PROBLEMS

1. What is a customer relationship management (CRM) program? Describe one CRM program that you have participated in as a customer.

2. Why do retailers want to determine the lifetime value of their customers? How does past customer behavior help retailers anticipate future customer retention?

3. Why do some customers have a low or negative CLV value? What approach can retailers take with these customers to minimize their impact on the bottom line?

4. Why do customers have privacy concerns about the frequent-shopper programs that supermarkets offer,

and what can supermarkets do to minimize these concerns?

5. Why are most frequent-shopper programs ineffective in terms of building loyalty? What can be done to make them more effective?

6. Which of the following types of retailers do you think would benefit most from instituting a CRM program: (a) supermarkets, (b) banks, (c) automobile dealers, or (d) consumer electronics retailers? Why?

7. Develop a CRM program for a local store that sells apparel and gifts with your college's or university's logo. What type of information would you collect about your customers, and how would you use this information to increase the sales and profits of the store?

8. What are the different approaches retailers can use to identify customers by their transactions? What are the advantages and disadvantages of each approach?

9. A CRM program focuses on building relationships with a retailer's better customers. Some customers who do not receive the same benefits as the retailer's best customers may be upset because they are treated differently. What can retailers do to minimize this negative reaction?

10. Think of one of your favorite places to shop. How does this retailer create customer loyalty and satisfaction, encourage repeat visits, establish an emotional bond between the customer and the retailer, know the customer's preferences, and provide personal attention and memorable experiences to its best customers?

SUGGESTED READINGS

Blattberg, Robert, Edward Malthouse, and Scott Neslin. "Customer Lifetime Value: Empirical Generalizations and Some Conceptual Questions." *Journal of Interactive Marketing* 23 (May 2009), pp. 157–168.

Cox, Emmett. *Retail Analytics: The Secret Weapon.* Hoboken, NJ: Wiley, 2011.

Christopher, Martin, Adrian Payne, and David Ballantyne. *Relationship Marketing.* New York: Routledge, 2012.

Gandomi, Zolfaghari. "Profitability of Loyalty Reward Programs: An Analytical Investigation," *Omega* 41, 4 (August 2013), pp. 797–807.

Gomez, Blanca, Ana Arranz, and Jesus Cillan. "Drivers of Customer Likelihood to Join Grocery Retail Loyalty Programs. An Analysis of Reward Programs and Loyalty Cards," *Journal of Retailing and Consumer Services* 19, 5 (September 2012), pp. 492–500.

Hochman, Larry. *The Relationship Revolution: Closing the Customer Promise Gap.* Hoboken, NJ: Wiley, 2010.

Kumar, V., and Werner Reinartz. *Customer Relationship Management*, 2nd ed. New York: Springer, 2012.

Linoff, Gordon, and Michael Berry. *Data Mining Techniques: For Marketing, Sales, and Customer Relationship Management*, 3rd ed. Hoboken, NJ: Wiley, 2011.

Nguyen, Bang. "The Dark Side of Customer Relationship Management: Exploring the Underlying Reasons for Pitfalls, Exploitation and Unfairness." *Journal of Database Marketing & Customer Strategy Management* 19 (2012), pp. 56–70.

Peltier, James, Debra Zahay, and Donald Lehmann. "Organizational Learning and CRM Success: A Model for Linking Organizational Practices, Customer Data Quality, and Performance." *Journal of Interactive Marketing*, 27, 1 (2013), pp. 1–13.

Verhoef, Peter, Rajkumar Venkatesan, Leigh McAlister, Edward C. Malthouse, Manfred Krafft, and Shankar Ganesan. "CRM in Data-Rich Multichannel Retailing Environments: A Review and Future Research Directions." *Journal of Interactive Marketing*, 24, no. 2 (2010), pp. 121–137.

Merchandise Management

Merchandise Management

Section II reviewed the strategic decisions made by retailers—the development of their retail market strategy, their financial strategy associated with the market strategy, their store location opportunities and factors affecting the selection of a specific site, their development of human resources, the systems they use to control the flow of information and merchandise, and the approaches they take to manage relationships with their customers. These decisions are more strategic than tactical because they involve committing significant resources to develop long-term advantages over the competition in a target retail market segment.

This section, Section III, examines the more tactical merchandise management decisions undertaken to implement the retail strategy.

Section I
Introduction
to the World
of Retailing

Section II
Retailing
Strategy

Section III
Merchandise
Management

Section IV
Store
Management

Chapter 12 provides an overview of how retailers manage their merchandise inventory—how they organize the merchandise planning process, evaluate their performance, forecast sales, establish an assortment plan, determine the appropriate service levels, allocate merchandise to stores, and monitor the performance of the merchandise inventory control activities.

Chapter 13 explores how retailers buy merchandise from vendors—their branding options, negotiating processes, and vendor relationship-building activities.

Chapter 14 addresses the question of how retailers set and adjust prices for the merchandise and services they offer.

Chapter 15 looks at the approaches that retailers take to build their brand image and communicate with their customers.

The next section, Section IV, focuses on store management decisions.

Managing the Merchandise Planning Process

EXECUTIVE BRIEFING

Moussa Coulibaly, Senior Vice President, Planning and Allocation, DICK'S Sporting Goods, Inc.

I'm a numbers guy; I have always been one. I purchased one of the first IBM PCs while studying finance and accounting at Duquesne University and used it early in my career to analyze margin and inventory turnover. What I was doing back then didn't have a name, but today it's known as retail analytics.

Currently, I serve as the senior vice president of planning and allocation at DICK'S Sporting Goods. However, I began my career in merchandising at Horne's Department Store corporate headquarters in Pittsburgh, PA. This role was unique, as Horne's corporate headquarters was located in the same building as its downtown flagship store. As a result, all merchandising associates were required to work the floor every day during high-traffic lunch hours to interact with customers. Looking back, it was this hands-on experience that was one of the most valuable aspects in my career as it gave me unique insight into providing superior customer service.

On my own time, I analyzed the productivity of jewelry showcases at Horne's for different vendors. Using my IBM PC, I determined the margin and inventory turnover for each vendor's merchandise. When vendors would meet with our buyers to present their new merchandise, our buyers would use my data to show them how the performance of their jewelry compared with other vendors. The vendors with low productivity would work to identify ways to increase their productivity, ensuring they did not lose space in the display cases.

Eventually, Horne's was merged into Lazarus department store (Macy's predecessor), and I accepted a merchandising role at Kaufmann's. During my tenure there, I held a variety of merchandising-related positions working with buyers to track inventory, place re-orders and set discounts. In addition, I also worked to develop reports to identify and address slow-moving items. I spent eight years at Kaufmann's, and served as the director of financial planning

LEARNING OBJECTIVES

LO1 Explain the merchandise management organization and performance measures.

LO2 Contrast the merchandise management processes for staple and fashion merchandise.

LO3 Describe how to predict sales for merchandise categories.

LO4 Summarize the trade-offs for developing merchandise assortments.

LO5 Illustrate how to determine the appropriate inventory levels.

LO6 Analyze merchandise control systems.

LO7 Describe how multistore retailers allocate merchandise to stores.

LO8 Review how retailers evaluate the performance of their merchandise management decisions.

when the headquarters closed in 2002. When this occurred I joined DICK'S Sporting Goods.

Retailing offers many different career paths and opportunities for people with a wide variety of skills and interests. I joined DICK'S in 2002 as the director of planning, and in 2003, I was promoted to vice president, planning and allocation. After several years, I assumed the role of treasurer and vice president of strategic planning where I was involved in a broad spectrum of responsibilities, from analyzing potential acquisitions and mergers to securing a revolving credit facility. In 2012, I was promoted to my current role, senior vice president of planning and allocation, where I am responsible for both hard and soft lines. As my experience illustrates, a successful career can begin with experimenting on your personal computer and eventually lead to a leadership role within a great company.

Merchandise management activities are undertaken primarily by buyers and their superiors, divisional merchandise managers (DMMs), and general merchandise managers (GMMs). Many people view these jobs as very exciting and glamorous. They think that buyers spend most of their time trying to identify the latest fashions and trends, attending designer shows replete with celebrities in Paris and Milan, and going to rock concerts and other glamorous events to see what the trendsetters are wearing. But, in reality, the activities of retail buyers are more like those of Wall Street investment analysts than globe-trotting trend spotters.

Investment analysts manage a portfolio of stocks. They buy stocks in companies they think will increase in value and sell stocks in companies they believe do not have a promising future. They continuously monitor the performance of the stocks they own to see which are increasing in value and which are decreasing.

Retail inventory management is similar to managing an investment portfolio.

Sometimes, they make mistakes and invest in companies that do not perform well. So they sell their stock in these companies and lose money, but they use the money from the sold stocks to buy more attractive stocks. Other times, the stocks they buy increase dramatically in price, and they wish they had bought more shares.

Rather than managing a portfolio of stocks, retail buyers manage a portfolio of merchandise inventory. They buy merchandise they think will be popular with their customers. Like investment analysts, they use an information system to monitor the performance of their merchandise portfolio—to see what is selling and what is not. Retail buyers also make mistakes. When the merchandise they bought is not selling well, they get rid of it by putting it on sale so that they can use the money to buy better-selling merchandise. However, they also might take a chance and buy a lot of a new merchandise item and be rewarded when it sells well, while competitors, who were more conservative, don't have enough of the product.

Chris Manning, a former swimwear buyer at Macy's, draws an analogy between surfing and buying merchandise:

> My job is like surfing. Sometimes you catch a big wave (trend) and it's exhilarating, and sometimes you think you've caught a good wave and brown turns out not to be the color this season. But the real fun is getting the most out of the wave you can. Let me give you an example of how I worked a big wave. Vendors started to show tankinis— women's bathing suits with bikini bottoms and tank tops. My customers were women in their 40s that had a couple of kids. I thought they would really go for this new style because it had the advantages of a two-piece bathing suit, but wasn't much more revealing than a one-piece suit. I bought a wide color assortment—bright reds, yellows, pink, and black—and put them in our fashion-forward stores in January for a test. The initial sales were good, but our customers thought they were a little too skimpy. Then I started to work the wave. I went back to the vendor and got them to recut the top so that the suit was less revealing, and I placed a big order for the colors that were selling best. Sales were so good that the other Macy's divisions picked up on it, but we rode the wave the longest and had the best swimwear sales of all of the divisions.[1]

Merchandise management is the process by which a retailer attempts to offer the appropriate quantity of the right merchandise, in the right place and at the right time, so that it can meet the company's financial goals. Buyers need to be in touch with and anticipate what customers will want to buy, but this ability to sense market trends is just one skill needed to manage merchandise inventory effectively. Perhaps an even more important skill is the ability to analyze sales data continually and make appropriate adjustments in prices and inventory levels.

The first part of this chapter provides the background needed to understand the merchandise management process. In this introduction, we discuss how the process is organized, who makes the merchandise decisions, and how merchandise management performance is evaluated. The last part of the chapter examines the steps in the merchandise management process—forecasting sales, formulating an assortment plan, determining the appropriate inventory level, developing a merchandise management plan, allocating merchandise to stores, and monitoring performance. The appendix to this chapter provides a more detailed discussion of the steps used to develop a merchandise budget plan. The other activities involved in merchandise management reviewed in subsequent chapters are buying merchandise (Chapter 13) and pricing (Chapter 14).

MERCHANDISE MANAGEMENT OVERVIEW

This section provides an overview of the merchandise management process, including the organization of a retailer's merchandise management activities and the objectives and measures used to evaluate merchandise management performance. In the following section, we review the differences in the process for managing fashion and seasonal merchandise versus basic merchandise and each of the steps in the merchandise management process.

LO1

Explain the merchandise management organization and performance measures.

The Buying Organization

Every retailer has its own system for grouping categories of merchandise, but the basic structure of the buying organization is similar for most retailers. Exhibit 12–1 illustrates this basic structure by depicting the organization of the merchandise division for a department store chain such as Macy's, Belk, or Dillard's. Exhibit 12–1 shows the organization of buyers in the merchandise division. A similar structure for planners parallels the structure for buyers.

The highest classification level is the **merchandise group.** The organization chart shown in Exhibit 12–1 has four merchandise groups: (1) women's apparel; (2) men's, children's, and intimate apparel; (3) cosmetics, shoes, jewelry, and accessories; and (4) home and kitchen. Each of the four merchandise groups is managed

Illustration of Merchandise Classifications and Organization   **EXHIBIT 12–1**

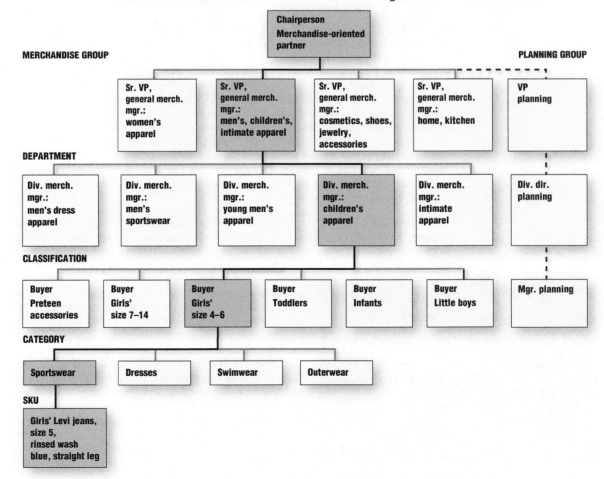

by a general merchandise manager (GMM), who is often a senior vice president in the firm. Each of the GMMs is responsible for several departments. For example, the GMM for men's, children's, and intimate apparel makes decisions about how the merchandise inventory is managed in five departments: men's dress apparel, men's sportswear, young men's apparel, children's apparel, and intimate apparel.

The second level in the merchandise classification scheme is the **department.** Departments are managed by divisional merchandise managers (DMMs). For example, the DMM highlighted in Exhibit 12–1 manages the buyers responsible for six children's apparel merchandise departments.

The **classification** is the third level for categorizing merchandise and organizing merchandise management activities. A classification is a group of items targeting the same customer type, such as girls' sizes 4 to 6. Categories are the next lower level in the classification scheme. Each buyer manages several merchandise categories. For example, the girls' sizes 4 to 6 buyer manages the sportswear, dresses, swimwear, and outerwear categories for girls who wear sizes 4 to 6.

A **stock-keeping unit (SKU)** is the smallest unit available for inventory control. In soft-goods merchandise, for instance, a SKU usually means a particular brand, size, color, and style—for example, a pair of size 5, rinsed wash, blue, straight-legged Levi jeans is a SKU.

Merchandise Category—The Planning Unit

The merchandise category is the basic unit of analysis for making merchandising management decisions. A **merchandise category** is an assortment of items that customers see as substitutes for one another. For example, a department store might offer a wide variety of girls' dresses sizes 4 to 6 in different colors, styles, and brand names. A mother buying a dress for her daughter might consider the entire set of dresses when making her purchase decision. Lowering the price on one dress may increase the sales of that dress but also decrease the sales of other dresses. Thus, the buyers' decisions about pricing and promoting specific SKUs in the category will affect the sales of other SKUs in the same category. Typically, a buyer manages several categories of merchandise.

Some retailers may define categories in terms of brands. For example, Tommy Hilfiger and Polo/Ralph Lauren each might be categories because the retailer feels that the brands are not substitutes for each other. A "Tommy" customer buys Tommy and not Ralph. Also, it is easier for one buyer to purchase merchandise and coordinate distribution and promotions for the merchandise offered by a national-brand vendor.

Category Management   While retailers, in general, manage merchandise at the category level, many supermarkets organize their merchandise management around brands or vendors. For instance, a supermarket chain might have three different buyers for breakfast cereals—one each for Kellogg's, General Mills, and General Foods.

Managing merchandise within a brand category can lead to inefficiencies because it fails to consider the interdependencies among SKUs in the category. For example, the three breakfast cereal buyers for a supermarket chain, one for each major brand, might each decide to stock a new product line of gluten-free breakfast cereals offered by Kellogg, General Mills, and General Foods. However, if the brand-organized buyers had taken a category-level perspective, they would have realized that the market for gluten-free cereals was limited and the supermarket would generate more sales by stocking one brand of gluten-free cereals and using the space set aside for the other gluten-free cereal brands to stock a locally produced cereal that has a strong following among some of its other customers.

The chilled drink department consists of several categories.

The **category management** approach to managing merchandise assigns one buyer or category manager to oversee all merchandising activities for the entire category. Managing by category can help ensure that the store's assortment includes the "best" combination of sizes and vendors—the one that will get the most profit from the allocated space.[2]

Category Captain   Some retailers select a vendor, such as General Mills or Kellogg's, to help them manage a particular category. The vendor, known as the **category captain,** works with the retailer to develop a better understanding of consumer shopping behaviors, create assortments that satisfy consumer needs, and improve the profitability of the merchandise category.

Selecting vendors as category captains has several advantages for retailers. It makes merchandise management tasks easier and can increase profits. Vendors are often in a better position to manage a category than are retailers because they have superior information about a category. The vendor's entire focus is on a specific category, while buyers are typically responsible for several categories. In addition, the insights that vendors acquire from managing the category for other retailers can be applied to a current problem.

A potential problem with establishing a vendor as a category captain is that the vendor could take advantage of its position. It is somewhat like "letting the fox into the henhouse." Suppose, for example, that Frito-Lay chose to maximize its own sales, rather than the retailer's sales, in managing the salty snack category. It could suggest an assortment plan that included most of its SKUs and exclude SKUs that are more profitable to the retailer, such as high-margin, private-label SKUs. Thus, retailers are becoming increasingly reluctant to turn over these important decisions to their vendors. They have found that working with their vendors and carefully evaluating their suggestions is a much more prudent approach. There are also antitrust considerations. The vendor category captain could collude with the retailer to fix prices. It could also block other brands, particularly smaller ones, from access to shelf space.[3]

Evaluating Merchandise Management Performance

As we discussed in Chapter 6, a good performance measure for evaluating a retail firm is ROA. Return on assets is composed of two components, asset turnover and net profit margin percentage. But ROA is not a good measure for evaluating the performance of merchandise managers because they do not have control over all of the retailer's assets or all the expenses that the retailer incurs. Merchandise managers have control only over what merchandise they buy (the retailer's merchandise inventory), the price at which the merchandise is sold, and the cost of the merchandise. Thus, buyers generally have control over the gross margin but not operating expenses, such as store operations, human resources, real estate, and logistics and information systems.

GMROI   A financial ratio that assesses a buyer's contribution to ROA is gross margin return on inventory investment (GMROI, typically pronounced "jim-roy"). It measures how many gross margin dollars are earned on every dollar of inventory investment made by the buyer. GMROI combines gross margin percentage and the sales-to-stock ratio, which is related to inventory turnover.

$$\text{GMROI} = \text{Gross margin percentage} \times \text{Sales-to-stock ratio}$$
$$= \frac{\text{Gross margin}}{\text{Net sales}} \times \frac{\text{Net sales}}{\text{Average inventory at cost}}$$
$$= \frac{\text{Gross margin}}{\text{Average inventory at cost}}$$

The reason we use the sales-to-stock ratio to calculate GMROI (instead of inventory turnover) is that GMROI is a type of return on investment measure, so the investment in inventory is expressed at cost. Inventory turnover and sales-to-stock ratios are very similar in concept, but they are calculated slightly differently.

322   SECTION III   Merchandise Management

EXHIBIT 12–2
Illustration of GMROI

				Fresh Bakery Bread	Gourmet Canned Food
			Sales	$1,000,000	200,000
			Gross margin	200,000	100,000
			Average inventory	100,000	50,000
	GMROI	=	$\frac{\text{Gross margin}}{\text{Net sales}}$ ×	$\frac{\text{Net sales}}{\text{Average inventory}}$ =	$\frac{\text{Gross margin}}{\text{Average inventory}}$
Fresh Bakery Bread	GMROI	=	$\frac{200{,}000}{1{,}000{,}000}$ ×	$\frac{1{,}000{,}000}{100{,}000}$ =	$\frac{200{,}000}{100{,}000}$
		=	20% ×	10 =	200%
Gourmet Canned Food	GMROI	=	$\frac{100{,}000}{200{,}000}$ ×	$\frac{200{,}000}{50{,}000}$ =	$\frac{100{,}000}{50{,}000}$
		=	50% ×	4 =	200%

The difference between the sales-to-stock ratio and inventory turnover is the numerator of the equation. When you are calculating the sales-to-stock ratio, the numerator is net sales. When you are calculating inventory turnover, the numerator is the cost of goods sold. To convert the sales-to-stock ratio to inventory turnover, simply multiply the sales-to-stock ratio by (1 − Gross margin percentage). Thus, if the sales-to-stock ratio is 9.0 and the gross margin percentage is 0.40, the inventory turnover for the category is 5.4:

Inventory turnover = (1 − Gross margin percentage) × Sales-to-stock
5.4 = (1 − 0.4) × 9.0

Buyers have control over both components of GMROI. The gross margin component is affected by the prices they set and the prices they negotiate with vendors when buying merchandise. The sales-to-stock ratio is affected by the popularity of the merchandise they buy. If they buy merchandise that customers want, it sells quickly and the sales-to-stock ratio is high.

Like the profit and asset management paths to assess ROA, there are two paths to achieving high GMROI: gross margin and inventory turnover (sales-to-stock ratio). For instance, within a supermarket, some categories (e.g., wine) are high-margin–low-turnover, while other categories (e.g., milk) are low-margin–high-turnover. If the wine category's performance were compared with that of milk using inventory turnover alone, the contribution of wine to the supermarket's performance would be undervalued. In contrast, if only gross margin were used, wine's contribution would be overvalued.

The bakery department in a supermarket typically has a high sales-to-stock ratio and a low gross margin.

Consider the situation in Exhibit 12–2, in which a supermarket wants to evaluate the performance of two categories: fresh bakery bread and gourmet canned food. If evaluated on gross margin percentage or sales alone, gourmet canned food is certainly the winner, with a 50 percent gross margin and sales of $300,000, compared with fresh bakery bread's gross margin of 1.33 percent and sales of $150,000. Yet gourmet canned food's sales-to-stock ratio is only 4, whereas fresh bakery bread has a sales-to-stock ratio of 150. Using GMROI, both categories achieve a GMROI of 200 percent and so are equal performers from an ROA perspective.

Measuring Sales-to-Stock Ratio   Retailers normally express inventory turnover (sales-to-stock) ratios

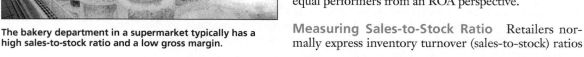

on an annual basis rather than for part of a year. If the sales-to-stock ratio for a three-month season equals 2.3, the annual sales-to-stock ratio will be four times that number (9.2). Thus, to convert a sales-to-stock ratio based on part of a year to an annual figure, multiply it by the number of such time periods in the year.

The most accurate way to measure average inventory is to measure the inventory level at the end of each day and divide the sum by 365. Most retailers can use their information systems to get accurate average inventory estimates by collecting and averaging the inventory in stores and distribution centers at the end of each day. Another method is to take the end-of-month (EOM) inventories for several months and divide by the number of months. For example,

Month	End-of-Month Inventory
January	$22,000
February	35,000
March	38,000
Total	$93,000
Average (Total/3)	$31,000

Improving GMROI

There are two paths that buyers can take to increase GMROI: (1) improve inventory turnover (sales-to-stock ratio) or (2) increase gross margin.

Improve Inventory Turnover (Sales-to-Stock Ratio)   To improve the inventory turnover (sales-to-stock ratio), buyers can either reduce the level of inventory or increase sales. One approach that buyers take to increase inventory turnover is to reduce the number of SKUs within a category. Buyers need to provide backup stock for each SKU so that the products will be available in the sizes and colors that customers are seeking. Fewer SKUs means that less backup stock is needed. However, reducing the number of SKUs could reduce sales because customers will be less likely to find what they want. Even worse, if they continually can't find the brand or product line at all, customers might start shopping at a competitor and also urge their friends to do the same.[4]

A second approach for reducing the level of inventory is to keep the same number of SKUs but reduce the backup stock for each SKU. This approach has the same problem as reducing the number of SKUs. Less backup stock increases the chances that customers will not find the size and color they want when visiting a store or website.

A third approach for increasing inventory turnover is to buy merchandise more often but in smaller quantities because this reduces average inventory without reducing sales. But buying smaller quantities decreases the gross margin because buyers can't take advantage of quantity discounts and transportation economies of scale. It also requires the buying staff to spend more time placing orders and monitoring deliveries.

A fourth approach is to increase sales and not increase inventory proportionally. For example, buyers could increase sales by reducing prices. While inventory turnover would increase in this situation, gross margin would also decrease, which could have a negative impact on GMROI.

Increasing inventory turnover can have positive impacts on sales by attracting more customer visits, improving sales associate morale, and providing more resources to take advantage of new buying opportunities. Higher inventory turnover increases sales because new merchandise is continually available to customers. New merchandise attracts customers to visit the store more frequently because they know they will be seeing different merchandise each time they visit the store. When inventory turnover is low, the merchandise begins to look **shopworn**—slightly damaged from being displayed and handled by customers for a long time.

Salespeople are excited about and more motivated to sell the new merchandise, and thus sales increase, increasing inventory turnover even further. Finally, when inventory turnover increases, more money is available to buy new merchandise. Having money available to buy merchandise late in a fashion season can open up profit opportunities. For instance, buyers can take advantage of special prices offered by vendors that have too much inventory left over at the end of the season.

Increase Gross Margin   Three approaches to increasing the gross margins are increasing prices, reducing the cost of goods sold, or reducing customer discounts. Increasing prices increases gross margin, but it can also decrease sales and inventory turnover, because price-sensitive customers buy less. Buyers usually attempt to lower the cost of goods sold by negotiating for better prices from vendors, though they also might increase the percentage of private-label merchandise in a category's assortment, because private-label merchandise is generally less costly than similar merchandise made by national brand vendors (see Chapter 13). Finally, buyers can increase gross margins by reducing the customer discounts needed to sell unwanted merchandise or merchandise left over at the end of the season. To minimize these discounts, buyers need to do a better job of buying products that customers want and accurately forecasting sales.

In summary, when attempting to increase GMROI, buyers need to strike a balance to determine appropriate levels of inventory turnover and gross margins. Some approaches for improving inventory turnover have secondary effects that can lower GMROI by lowering sales volume or reducing gross margins. As we discussed in Chapter 10, several steps can be taken to improve supply chain efficiency, such as improved vendor relationships, VMI, and CPFR, which increase inventory turnover without negative side effects.

MERCHANDISE PLANNING PROCESSES

LO2

Contrast the merchandise management processes for staple and fashion merchandise.

As shown in Exhibit 12–3, the merchandise management process involves buyers forecasting category sales, developing an assortment plan for merchandise in the category, and determining the amount of inventory needed to support the forecasted sales and resulting assortment plan. Then buyers develop a plan outlining the sales expected for each month, the inventory needed to support the sales, and the money that can be spent on replenishing sold merchandise and buying new merchandise. Along with developing the plan, the buyers or planners decide what type and how much merchandise should be allocated to each store. Having developed the plan, the buyer negotiates with vendors and buys the merchandise. Merchandise buying activities are reviewed in Chapter 13.

Finally, buyers continually monitor the sales of merchandise in the category and make adjustments. For example, if category sales are less than forecasted in the plan and the projected GMROI for the category falls below the buyer's goal, the buyer may decide to dispose of some merchandise by putting it on sale and then use the money generated to buy merchandise with greater sales potential

EXHIBIT 12–3
Merchandise Planning Process

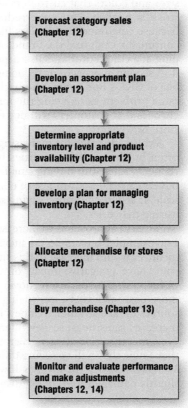

or to reduce the number of SKUs in the assortment to increase inventory turnover.

Although Exhibit 12–3 suggests that these decisions follow each other sequentially, in practice, some decisions may be made at the same time or in a different order. For example, a buyer might first decide on the amount of inventory to invest in the category, and this decision might determine the number of SKUs that can be offered in the category.

Types of Merchandise Management Planning Systems

Retailers use different types of merchandise planning systems for managing (1) staple and (2) fashion merchandise categories. **Staple merchandise** categories, also called **basic merchandise** categories, are those categories that are in continuous demand over an extended time period. While consumer packaged goods companies introduce many "new products" each year, the number of "new to the world" product introductions each year in staple categories is limited. Some examples of staple merchandise categories include most categories sold in supermarkets, white paint, copy paper, and basic casual apparel such as T-shirts and men's underwear.

Because sales of staple merchandise are fairly steady from week to week, it is relatively easy to forecast demand, and the consequences of making mistakes in forecasting are not great. For example, if a buyer overestimates the demand for canned soup and buys too much, the retailer will have excess inventory for a short period of time. Eventually the canned soup will be sold without having to resort to discounts or special marketing efforts.

Because the demand for staple merchandise is very predictable, merchandise planning systems for staple categories often involve **continuous replenishment.** These systems involve continuously monitoring merchandise sales and generating replacement orders, often automatically, when inventory levels drop below predetermined levels.

Fashion merchandise categories are in demand only for a relatively short period of time. New products are continually introduced into these categories, making the existing products obsolete. In some cases, the basic product does not change, but the colors and styles change to reflect what is "hot" that season. Some examples of fashion merchandise categories are athletic shoes, tablets, smartphones, and women's apparel. Retailing View 12.1 describes how Mango creates and manages its fashion merchandise assortments.

Forecasting the sales for fashion merchandise categories is much more challenging than doing so for staple categories. Buyers for fashion merchandise categories have much less flexibility in correcting forecasting errors. For example, if the tablet buyer for Best Buy purchases too many units of a particular model, the excess inventory cannot be easily sold when a new upgraded model is introduced. Due to the short selling season for most fashion merchandise, buyers often do not have a chance to reorder additional merchandise after an initial order is placed. So if buyers initially order too little fashion merchandise, the retailer may not be able to satisfy the demand for the merchandise and will develop a reputation for not having the most popular merchandise in stock. If buyers order too much fashion merchandise, they will have to put it on sale at a discount or dispose of it in some other way at the end of the season. Thus, an important objective of merchandise planning systems for fashion merchandise categories is to be as close to out of stock as possible at the same time that the SKUs move out of fashion.

Seasonal merchandise categories consist of items whose sales fluctuate dramatically depending on the time of year. Some examples of seasonal merchandise are Halloween candy, Christmas ornaments, swimwear, and snow shovels. Both

12.1   RETAILING VIEW   Fast Fashion at Mango

Mango is a specialty apparel fast-fashion retailer headquartered in Barcelona, Spain, though its more than 2,500 stores spread across 107 countries. Mango places more emphasis on the "fashion" rather than the "fast" element in its "fast-fashion" retail concept—as pioneered by Spain's Zara, Sweden's H&M, and the United States' Forever 21.

Mango's Hangar Design Center, the biggest design center in Europe, spreads over more than 100,000 square feet and houses around 550 sharply dressed professionals, creating fashion garments and accessories, predominately for women. The design, purchasing, and quality departments are also located in the Hangar. More than 80 percent of the company's employees are women, with an average age of 32 years. The work environment is very casual, in that suits or ties are rare, but fashion creativity is abundant, with employees expressing themselves through the way they dress. Mango headquarters also includes 2,000 employees representing 37 nationalities, communicating in several languages.

Mango's merchandise planning cycle begins every three months, when designers meet to discuss important new trends for each of its main collections, each of which contain five or six mini-collections. Shops receive a near-constant stream of new merchandise, ranging from clingy short dresses to work wear and sparkly evening gowns. New items get sent to stores once a week, roughly six times as often as typical apparel clothing chains.

To get ideas for each collection, designers attend traditional fashion shows and trade fairs. But they also stay close to the customer. They take photos of stylish young women and note what people are wearing on the streets and in nightclubs. "To see what everyone's going to do for next season is very easy," says David Egea, Mango's merchandising director, "but that doesn't mean this is the thing that is going to catch on." Hoping to stay *au courant,* design teams meet each week to adjust to ever-changing trends.

Mango describes each of its stores and clothing designs according to a set of traits: trendy, dressy, suitable for hot weather, and so on. When collection designs are set, a proprietary computer program then matches the new products' traits with compatible stores.

In addition, Mango stores display only a limited merchandise assortment. On each rack, only one item per size hangs. This policy encourages a sense of urgency by

Mango uses celebrity models such as Miranda Kerr to emphasize its fashion orientation.

playing on customers' worst fear: Maybe your size is going to run out.

Sources: www.mango.com; Jennifer Overstreet, "Mango Executive Shares Global Expansion Insights," *NRF Blog,* January 3, 2013; Kim Bhasin, "There Has Been a Changing of the Guard at Mango," *The Guardian,* November 24, 2012; and Vertica Bhardwaj and Ann Fairhurst, "Fast Fashion: Response to Changes in the Fashion Industry," *International Review of Retail, Distribution and Consumer Research* 20 (February 2010), pp. 165–173.

DISCUSSION QUESTION

What are the benefits of fast-fashion retailing from a retailer's perspective?

fashion and more mundane merchandise can be seasonal categories. For example, swimwear is fashionable and snow shovels are more mundane.

However, from a merchandise planning perspective, retailers buy seasonal merchandise in much the same way that they buy fashion merchandise. Retailers could store unsold snow shovels at the end of the winter season and sell them the next winter, but it is typically more profitable to sell the shovels at a steep discount near the end of the season rather than incur the cost of carrying this excess inventory until the beginning of the next season. Thus, plans for seasonal merchandise, like fashion merchandise, hope to zero out inventory at the end of the season.

These two different merchandise planning systems, staple and fashion, affect the nature of the approaches used to forecast sales and manage inventory. In the following section, each of the steps in the merchandise management process for staple and fashion merchandise is described.

FORECASTING CATEGORY SALES

As indicated in Exhibit 12–3, the first step in merchandise management planning is to develop a forecast for category sales. The methods and information used for forecasting staple and fashion merchandise categories are discussed in this section.

LO3
Describe how to predict sales for merchandise categories.

Forecasting Staple Merchandise

The approach for forecasting sales of staple merchandise is to project past sales trends into the future, while making adjustments for any anticipated factors, such as promotions and weather, that may affect future sales.

Use of Historical Sales   The sales of staple merchandise are relatively constant from year to year. Thus, forecasts are typically based on extrapolating historical sales. Because there are substantial sales data available, sophisticated statistical techniques can be used to forecast future sales for each SKU.[5] However, these statistical forecasts are based on the assumption that the factors affecting item sales in the past will be the same and have the same effect in the future. Thus, even though sales for staple merchandise categories are relatively predictable, controllable and uncontrollable factors can have a significant impact on sales.

Adjustments for Controllable and Uncontrollable Factors   Controllable factors include the opening and closing of stores, the price set for the merchandise in the category, special promotions for the category, the pricing and promotion of complementary categories, and the placement of the merchandise categories in the stores. Some factors beyond the retailer's control are the weather, general economic conditions, special promotions or new product introductions by vendors, and the new product, pricing, and promotional activities by competitors.[7] Thus, buyers need to adjust the forecast on the basis of statistical projections to reflect the effects of these controllable and uncontrollable factors. Retailing View 12.2 illustrates how retailers use long-range weather forecasts to improve their forecasts.

Forecasting Fashion Merchandise Categories

Forecasting sales for fashion merchandise is challenging because buyers typically need to place orders and commit to buying specific quantities between three to

12.2   RETAILING VIEW   Weather's Effects on Retail Sales

Home improvement centers know that when hurricane season comes, they need to be ready with bottled water, batteries, flashlights, plywood, and generators. However, more subtle weather conditions, like a warmer-than-normal holiday season, can have a significant impact on retail sales as well. As the weather becomes warmer in the summer, some obvious categories increase sales, such as ice, bottled water, and sports drinks. A hot summer results in consumers seeking out air-conditioned spaces. Big-box retailers and movie theatres offer a chilly respite from the sweltering heat. A warm winter stimulates sales of lawn tools, barbeques, and garden equipment in February and March rather than April, May, or June. One category that thrives during extended summer seasons is fashion. Retailers typically roll out their summer collections well before consumers can comfortably wear the clothes outside, but if the weather is already warm, it will ignite sales early. If the summer stays warmer longer, retailers can delay sales discounts, thus improving their margins.

To incorporate weather effects into their forecasts, many retailers subscribe to long-range weather forecasting services. Merchandise managers use the information provided by these services to make decisions about the timing of merchandise deliveries, promotions, and price discounts. Thus, when one year Planalytics (one of the companies offering long-range weather forecasts) informed a Canadian men's clothing retailer that the spring would be colder than normal, but the summer temperatures would be higher than normal, it made a few strategic movies. First, it delayed taking markdowns on shorts for sale. Second, it moved nearly 10,000 pairs of shorts to stores along the west coast, which was predicted to be even hotter than the east. Third, it adjusted its sales staff to match the weather-related demands. As a result, it earned an additional $250,000 in revenues, beyond its expectations.

However, clothing retailers that target younger shoppers tend to rely less on weather forecasts, because 18-to-24-year-olds buy clothes well

REFACT

When the temperature increases by 18 degrees, sales of barbecue meat generally triple, while demand for lettuce jumps 50 percent.[8]

REFACT

According to some estimates, approximately one-third of U.S. gross domestic product depends, directly or indirectly, on the climate.[9]

The first cold snap in the fall stimulates the sale of winter apparel.

in advance of the season they need to wear them. In contrast, retirees and older shoppers wait until it feels warm before they load up on summertime gear.

Sources: www.planalytics.com; Catherine Valenti, "More Companies Use Weather to Forecast Sales," *ABC News*, March 12, 2013; "How Does Hot Weather Affect People's Buying Patterns?" *CBC*, July 2012; Cecilia Sze and Paul Walsh, "How Weather Influences the Economy," *ISO Review*, www.iso.com/Research-and-Analyses/ISO-Review/How-Weather-Influences-the-Economy.html.

DISCUSSION QUESTION

Why might Kohl's sales be more affected by the weather than Nordstrom's sales?

six months before the merchandise will be delivered and made available for sale.[10] In addition, for fashion items, there often is no opportunity to increase or decrease the quantity ordered before the selling season has ended. Suppliers of popular merchandise usually have orders for more merchandise than they can produce and excess inventory of unpopular items. Finally, forecasting fashion merchandise sales is particularly difficult because some or all of the items in the category are new and different from units offered in previous seasons or years. Some sources of information that retailers use to develop forecasts for fashion merchandise categories are (1) previous sales data, (2) market research, (3) fashion and trend services, and (4) vendors.

Previous Sales Data   Although items in fashion merchandise categories might be new each season, many items in a fashion category are often similar to items sold in previous years. Thus, accurate forecasts might be generated by simply projecting past sales data. For example, football video games, such as *Madden NFL*, might change from season to season with new editions, but while the SKUs are different each season, the total number of football video games sold each year might be relatively constant and predictable.

Market Research   Buyers for fashion merchandise categories undertake a variety of market research activities to help them forecast sales. These activities range from informal, qualitative research about trends affecting the category to more formal experiments and surveys.

To find out what customers are going to want in the future, buyers immerse themselves in their customers' world. For example, buyers look for information about trends by going to Internet chat rooms and blogs, attending soccer games and rock concerts, and visiting hot spots around town like restaurants and nightclubs to see what people are talking about and wearing. Buyers are information junkies and read voraciously. What movies are hits at the box office, and what are the stars wearing? Who is going to see them? What books and albums are on the top 10 lists? What magazines are consumers purchasing? Are there themes that keep popping up across these sources of information?

Social media sites are important sources of information for buyers. Buyers learn a lot about their customers' likes, dislikes, and preferences by monitoring their past purchases and by monitoring their interactions with social network sites such as Facebook, Pinterest, and Twitter. Customers appear keen to submit their opinions about their friends' purchases, interests, and blogs.

Retailers also use traditional forms of marketing research such as in-depth interviews and focus groups. The **in-depth interview** is an unstructured personal interview in which the interviewer uses extensive probing to get individual respondents to talk in detail about a subject. For example, one grocery store chain goes through the personal checks received each day to identify customers to interview. Representatives from the supermarket chain call these customers and interview them to find out what they like and don't like about the merchandise in the store.

A more informal method of interviewing customers is to require that buyers spend some time on the selling floor waiting on customers. Buying offices for Target and The Gap are in Minnesota and northern California, respectively, yet their stores are located throughout the United States. It has become increasingly hard for buyers in large chains to be attuned to local customer demand. Frequent store visits help resolve the situation. Some retailers require that their buyers spend a specified period of time, like one day a week, in a store. Lululemon, the yoga and athletic gear retailer, is one such company: Its CEO, Christine Day, spends several hours each week in one of the chain's stores, solely to listen to customers' complaints and feedback. Furthermore, the design of the stores turns each

REFACT

The top fashion blog based on an analysis of 20 factors is *CollegeFashion.net*.[11]

employee into a corporate eavesdropper. The tables at which sales clerks fold merchandise are located next to changing rooms, where shoppers tend to critique items openly. A whiteboard in the dressing room also encourages them to leave written feedback, if necessary.[12]

A **focus group** is a small group of respondents interviewed by a moderator using a loosely structured format. Participants are encouraged to express their views and comment on the views of others in the group. To keep abreast of the teen market, for instance, some stores have teen boards consisting of opinion leaders who meet to discuss merchandising and other store issues. Abercrombie & Fitch brings in groups of teenagers and has them rate their preferences for different items.

Asda, a U.K. supercenter owned by Walmart, regularly surveys its customers to forecast sales of new products. It e-mails a group of 25,000 customers, which it has termed its "Pulse of the Nation" group, sets of images and descriptions of new products. The Pulse group is asked to respond, positively or negatively, and indicate whether or not they think the new products should be carried in the stores.[13]

Finally, many retailers have a program for conducting merchandise sales experiments. For example, retailers continually run experiments to determine whether new merchandise concepts will produce adequate sales. They introduce the new merchandise into a representative sample of stores and sees what sales are generated for the items. Multichannel retailers often run similar experiments by offering new items on their websites before making a decision to stock them in their stores.

Fashion Trend Services   There are many services that buyers—particularly buyers of apparel categories—can subscribe to that forecast the latest fashions, colors, and styles. For example, Doneger Creative Services offers various forecasting services, describing the color trends it anticipates for men's, women's, and children's apparel, lifestyle products, and accessories. Its color forecast service provides color direction for each season using dyed-to-specification color standards, plus suggested color combinations and applications for specific categories. Its online clipboard reports present actionable information and style news from the runways to the streets.

Vendors   Vendors have proprietary information about their marketing plans, such as new product launches and special promotions that can have a significant impact on retail sales for their products and the entire merchandise category. In addition, vendors tend to be very knowledgeable about market trends for particular merchandise categories because they typically specialize in fewer merchandise categories than do retailers. Thus, information from vendors about their plans and market research about merchandise categories is very useful to buyers as they develop category sales forecasts.

Sales Forecasting for Service Retailers

Due to the perishable nature of services, service retailers face an even more extreme problem than fashion retailers. Their offering perishes at the end of the day, not at the end of the season. If there are empty seats when a plane takes off or a rock concert ends, the revenue that might have been generated from these seats is lost forever. Likewise, if more people are interested in dining at a restaurant than there are tables available, a revenue opportunity also is lost. So service retailers have devised approaches for managing demand for their offering so that it meets but does not exceed capacity.

Some service retailers attempt to match supply and demand by taking reservations or making appointments. Physicians often overbook their appointments, so many patients have to wait. They do this so that they will always fill their capacity and not have unproductive, non-revenue-generating time. Restaurants take reservations so that customers will not have to wait for a table. In addition, the reservations indicate the staffing levels needed for the shift. Another approach is to sell advance tickets for a service, such as arenas do for concerts.[14]

DEVELOPING AN ASSORTMENT PLAN

After forecasting sales for the category, the next step in the merchandise management planning process is to develop an assortment plan (see Exhibit 12–3). An **assortment plan** is the set of SKUs that a retailer will offer in a merchandise category in each of its stores and from its website.

LO4
Summarize the trade-offs for developing merchandise assortments.

Category Variety and Assortment

The assortment plan reflects the breadth and depth of merchandise that the retailer plans to offer in a merchandise category. In the context of merchandise planning, **variety,** or **breadth,** of a merchandise category is the number of different merchandising subcategories offered, and the **assortment,** or **depth,** of merchandise is the number of SKUs within a subcategory.

Determining Variety and Assortment

The process of determining the variety and assortment for a category is called **editing the assortment.** An example of an assortment plan for girls' jeans shown in Exhibit 12–4 includes 10 types or varieties (skinny or boot-cut, distressed denim or rinsed wash, and three price points reflecting different brands). For each type, there are 81 SKUs (3 colors × 9 sizes × 3 lengths). Thus, this retailer plans to offer 810 SKUs in girls' jeans.

When editing the assortment for a category like jeans, the buyer considers the following factors: (1) the firm's retail strategy, (2) the effect of assortments on

Assortment Plan for Girls' Jeans   **EXHIBIT 12–4**

Styles	Skinny	Skinny	Skinny	Skinny	Skinny	Skinny
Price levels	$20	$20	$35	$35	$45	$45
Fabric composition	Distressed	Rinsed wash	Distressed	Rinsed wash	Distressed	Rinsed wash
Colors	Light blue	Light blue	Light blue	Light blue	Light blue	Light blue
	Indigo	Indigo	Indigo	Indigo	Indigo	Indigo
	Black	Black	Black	Black	Black	Black

Styles	Boot-Cut	Boot-Cut	Boot-Cut	Boot-Cut
Price levels	$25	$25	$45	$45
Fabric composition	Distressed	Rinsed wash	Distressed	Rinsed wash
Colors	Light blue	Light blue	Light blue	Light blue
	Indigo	Indigo	Indigo	Indigo
	Black	Black	Black	Black

GMROI, (3) the complementarities among categories, (4) the effects of assortments on buying behavior, and (5) the physical characteristics of the store.[15]

Retail Strategy The number of SKUs offered in a merchandise category is a strategic decision. For example, ALDI supermarkets focus on customers who are looking for low prices and do not care much about brands, so they offer very few SKUs in a category. With limited SKUs, ALDI can increase its inventory turnover, lower costs, and charge lower prices. In contrast, Best Buy's target customers are interested in comparing many alternatives, so the retailer must offer several SKUs in each consumer electronics category.

The breadth and depth of the assortment in a merchandise category can affect the retailer's brand image too. Retailers might increase the assortment in categories that are closely associated with their image. For example, Staples carries only a few SKUs of candy bars because candy is not part of the core office supply assortment for which it is known. But it carries a much broader and deeper assortment of paper products, because its customers expect to find such options when they visit the office supplier.

Assortments and GMROI In developing the assortment plan, buyers need to be sensitive to the trade-off of increasing sales by offering greater breadth and depth but, at the same time potentially reducing inventory turnover and GMROI because of the increased inventory investment. Increasing assortment breadth and depth also can decrease gross margin. For example, the more SKUs offered, the greater the chance of **breaking sizes**—that is, stocking out of a specific size or color SKU. If a stockout occurs for a popular SKU in a fashion merchandise category and the buyer cannot reorder during the season, the buyer will typically discount the entire merchandise type, thus reducing gross margin. The buyer's objective is to remove the merchandise type from the assortment altogether so that customers will not be disappointed when they don't find the size and color they want.

Complementary Merchandise When buyers develop assortment plans, they need to consider the degree to which categories in a department complement each other. For instance, Blu-Ray players may have a low GMROI, suggesting that the retailer carry a limited assortment. But customers who buy a Blu-Ray player might also buy complementary products and services such as accessories, cables, and warranties that have a high GMROI. Thus, the buyer may decide to carry more Blu-Ray player SKUs to increase the more profitable accessory sales.

Effects of Assortment Size on Buying Behavior Offering large assortments provides a number of benefits to customers. First, increasing the number of SKUs that customers can consider increases the chance they will find the product that best satisfies their needs. Second, large assortments are valued by customers because they provide a more informative and stimulating shopping experience due to the complexity associated with numerous products and the novelty associated with unique items. Third, large assortments are particularly appealing to customers who seek variety—those who want to try new things. However, offering a large assortment can make the purchase decision more complex and time-consuming and potentially overwhelms the consumer, which could reduce sales.

Research indicates that customers' perceptions of assortments are not based simply on the number of SKUs offered in a product category. Instead, assortment perceptions are affected by the similarity of the SKUs in the category, the size of the category's display, and the availability of the customer's favorite SKU. Perceived assortment is greater when the items in the assortment are different, the category occupies more space, and the customer's favorite product is available. In one study, customer perception of the assortment offered by a retailer did not change when a retailer decreased the number of SKUs by 54 percent, but kept the category display size, similarity of the products, and availability of the favorite product the same. In another study, the perceived assortment actually increased by 25 percent when the actual assortment decreased but the display of the most popular brands increased because customers could more easily locate their favorite brand. Other factors affecting how customers perceive assortments are discussed in Chapter 17.[16]

Many retailers have initiated **SKU rationalization programs** in their efforts to analyze the benefits they might gain from deleting, adding, or keeping certain items in their assortments. The objective of such a program is to increase inventory turnover by reducing the number of SKUs without reducing sales. Of the 40,000 SKUs offered by a typical supermarket, the average household annually uses only 350 SKUs. Because typically 20 percent of the SKUs account for 80 percent of sales, eliminating the bottom 15 percent of the SKUs should have limited effect on sales. Retailing View 12.3 illustrates how Costco and Walmart rationalizes their assortment.

Physical Characteristics of the Store   Buyers need to consider how much space to devote to a category. More space is needed to display categories with large assortments. In addition, a lot of space is needed to display individual items in some categories, and this limits the number of SKUs that can be offered in stores. For example, furniture takes up a lot of space, and thus furniture retailers typically display one model of a chair or sofa and then have photographs and cloth swatches or a virtual display on a computer to show how the furniture would look with different upholstery.

Multichannel retailers address space limitations in stores by offering a greater assortment through their Internet and catalog channels than they do in stores. For example, Staples offers more types of laptop computers and printers on its Internet site than it stocks in its stores. If customers do not find the computer or printer they want in the store, sales associates direct them to the company's Internet site and can even order the merchandise for them on the spot from a POS terminal.

SETTING INVENTORY AND PRODUCT AVAILABILITY LEVELS

Model Stock Plan

The **model stock plan,** illustrated in Exhibit 12–5, is the number of each SKU in the assortment plan that the buyer wants to have available for purchase in each store. For example, the model stock plan in Exhibit 12–5 includes nine units of size 1, short, which represent 2 percent of the 429 total units for girls' skinny $20 denim jeans in light blue. Note that there are more units for more popular sizes.

Retailers typically have model stock plans for the different store sizes in a chain. For example, retailers typically classify their stores as A, B, and C stores on the basis of their sales volume. The basic assortment in a category is stocked in C stores. For the larger stores, because more space is available, the number of SKUs increases. The larger A and B stores may have more brands, colors, styles, and sizes.

LO5

Illustrate how to determine the appropriate inventory levels.

12.3 RETAILING VIEW   Costco and Walmart: Two Approaches to SKU Rationalization

Costco's sale items create a sense of a treasure hunt.

Costco is a master of continually editing its assortment. Costco stores feature 3,950 SKUs, compared with 5,250 at Sam's Club and 6,890 at B.J.'s. Although it collaborates with various partners to devise appealing products, new items only qualify for a 13-week run, and if they fail to perform, Costco does not hesitate to yank them from its shelves. As a result, customers constantly find a new assortment of shifting products, even if the overall number of SKUs in the store remains relatively constant. Thus, Costco's approach to SKU rationalization has a positive impact on GMROI. The sales-to-stock ratio (inventory turnover) is strong because its total number of SKUs is relatively low. Customers shop often, looking for new deals and "treasures." Its gross margin and sales are also strong because it carries high-demand items for which there is no need for significant markdowns.

Reducing the number of SKUs is not always a good strategy, however. Walmart, like many retailers, initiated a SKU rationalization program. The initiative was spurred by an industry study showing that shoppers thought Target had a larger assortment than Walmart, even though Walmart stores had more SKUs. So Walmart reduced the number of SKUs in its stores and added some SKUs that appealed to higher-income households. However, sales declined, particularly in rural areas, so Walmart reversed its decision and added back 8,000 SKUs.

Sources: "Costco Keeps It Simple," *Frozen Food and Dairy Buyer*, March 12, 2012; Warren Thayer and Miguel Bustillo, "Wal-Mart Merchandise Goes Back to Basics," *The Wall Street Journal*, April 11, 2011; and "Changes in the Wind at Wal-Mart," *RFF Retailer*, February 17, 2009.

DISCUSSION QUESTION

Why does maintaining a relatively low number of SKUs work at Costco, but not at Walmart?

EXHIBIT 12–5
Model Stock Plan
for Girls' Jeans

LENGTH		SIZE								
		1	2	4	5	6	8	10	12	14
Short	%	2	4	7	6	8	5	7	4	2
	units	9	17	30	26	34	21	30	17	9
Medium	%	2	4	7	6	8	5	7	4	2
	units	9	17	30	26	34	21	30	17	9
Long	%	0	2	2	2	3	2	2	1	0
	units	0	9	9	9	12	9	9	4	0
	Total 100%									
	429 units									

Product Availability

The number of units of **backup stock,** also called **buffer** or **safety stock,** in the model stock plan determines product availability. **Product availability** is defined as the percentage of the demand for a particular SKU that is satisfied. For instance, if 100 people go into a PetSmart store to purchase a small Great Choice portable kennel but only 90 people can make the purchase before the kennel stock is depleted, the product availability for that SKU is 90 percent. Product availability is also referred to as the **level of support** or **service level.**

More backup stock is needed in the model stock plan if a retailer wants to increase product availability—that is, increase the probability that customers will find the product they want when they visit the retailer's store or website. Choosing an appropriate amount of backup stock is critical to successful assortment planning. If the backup stock is too low, the retailer will lose sales and possibly customers as well when they find that the products they want are not available from the retailer. If the level is too high, scarce financial resources will be wasted on needless inventory, which lowers GMROI, rather than being more profitably invested in increasing variety or assortment.

Exhibit 12–6 shows the trade-off between inventory investment and product availability. Although the actual inventory investment varies in different situations, the general relationship shows that extremely high levels of product availability result in a prohibitively high inventory investment.

The trade-off among variety, assortment, and product availability is a crucial issue in determining a retailer's merchandising strategy. Buyers have a limited budget for the inventory investments they can make in a category. Thus, they are forced to sacrifice breadth of merchandise if they opt to increase depth, or they must reduce both depth and breadth to increase product availability.

Retailers often classify merchandise categories or individual SKUs as A, B, or C items, reflecting the product availability the retailer wants to offer. The A items are best-sellers bought by many customers. For example, white paint is an A item for Sherwin Williams, and copy paper is an A item for Office Depot. A retailer rarely wants to risk A-item stockouts because running out of these very popular SKUs would diminish the retailer's brand image and customer loyalty. On the other hand, lower product availability is acceptable for C items, which are purchased by a small number of customers and are not readily available from other retailers. The greater the fluctuations in demand, the lead time for delivery from the vendor, and the fluctuations in vendor lead time, the greater the backup stock

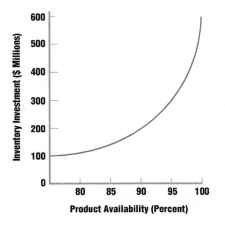

EXHIBIT 12–6
Inventory Investment
and Product
Availability

levels required to maintain a particular product availability level. However, less backup stock is needed to maintain a particular product availability level with more frequent store deliveries.

ESTABLISHING A CONTROL SYSTEM FOR MANAGING INVENTORY

LO6

Analyze merchandise control systems.

The first three steps in the merchandise planning process—forecasting SKU and category sales, determining the assortment plan, and establishing the model stock plan (see Exhibit 12–3)—quantify the buyer's sales expectations and service level. The fourth step in the merchandise management process is to establish a control system for how the orders, deliveries, inventory levels, and merchandise sales will evolve over time. The objective of this control system is to manage the flow of merchandise into the stores so that the amount of inventory in a category is minimized but the merchandise will still be available when customers want to buy it. The differences between the control systems for staple and fashion merchandise are discussed in the following sections.

Control System for Managing Inventory of Staple Merchandise

The SKUs in a staple merchandise category are sold month after month, year after year. Lowe's sales of purple paint this month will be about the same as they were during the same month a year ago. If the sales of purple paint are below forecast this month, the excess inventory of purple paint can be sold during the following month. Thus, an automated continuous replenishment control system is used to manage the flow of staple merchandise SKUs and categories. The continuous replenishment system monitors the inventory level of each SKU in a store and automatically triggers the reorder of an SKU when the inventory falls below a predetermined level.

Flow of Staple Merchandise   Exhibit 12–7 illustrates the merchandise flow in a staple merchandise management system. At the beginning of week 1, the retailer had 150 units of the SKU in inventory and the buyer or merchandise planner placed an order for 96 additional units. During the next two weeks, customers purchased 130 units, and the inventory level decreased to 20 units. At the end of week 2, the 96-unit order from the vendor arrived, and the inventory level jumped up to 116 units. The continuous replenishment system placed another order with the vendor that will arrive in two weeks, before customer sales decrease the inventory level to zero and the retailer stocks out.

Inventory for which the level goes up and down due to the replenishment process is called **cycle stock** or **base stock** (shown in gold in Exhibit 12-7). The retailer hopes to reduce the cycle stock inventory to keep its inventory investment low. One approach for reducing the cycle stock is to reorder smaller quantities more frequently. But more frequent, smaller orders and shipments increase administrative and transportation costs, and reduce quantity discounts.

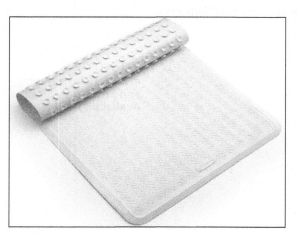

Staple merchandise management systems are used for items like this rubber mat.

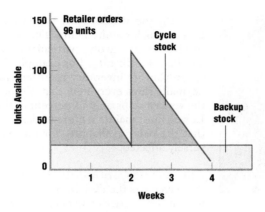

EXHIBIT 12–7
Merchandise Flow of a Staple SKU

Because sales of each SKU and on-time deliveries of orders from vendors cannot be predicted with perfect accuracy, the retailer has to carry backup stock, as a cushion, so that it doesn't stock out before the next order arrives. Backup stock is shown in green in Exhibit 12–7. Backup stock is the level of inventory needed to ensure merchandise is available in light of these uncertainties.

Determining the Level of Backup Stock   Several factors determine the level of backup stock needed for an SKU. First, the level depends on the product availability the retailer wants to provide. As discussed previously, more backup stock is needed when the retailer wants to reduce the chances of a stockout and increase the availability of the SKU. Thus, if Lowe's views white paint as an A item and rarely wants to stock out of it, a higher level of backup stock is needed. However, if melon paint is a C item and 75 percent product availability is acceptable, the level of backup stock can be lowered.

Second, the greater the fluctuation in demand, the more backup stock is needed. Suppose a Lowe's store sells an average of 30 gallons of purple paint in two weeks. Yet in some weeks sales are 50 gallons, and in other weeks they are only 10 gallons. When sales are less than average, the store ends up carrying a little more merchandise than it needs. But when sales are much more than average, there must be more backup stock to ensure that the store does not stock out. Note in Exhibit 12–7 that during week 4, sales were greater than average, so the retailer had to dip into its backup stock to avoid a stockout.

Third, the amount of backup stock needed is affected by the lead time from the vendor. **Lead time** is the amount of time between the recognition that an order needs to be placed and the point at which the merchandise arrives in the store and is ready for sale. If it took two months to receive a shipment of purple paint, the possibility of running out of stock is greater than it would be if the lead time was only two weeks. The shorter lead times inherent in collaborative supply chain management systems like CPFR (described in Chapter 10) result in a lower level of backup stock required to maintain the same level of product availability.

Fourth, fluctuations in lead time also affect the amount of backup stock needed. If Lowe's knows that the lead time for purple paint is always two weeks, plus or minus one day, it can more accurately plan its inventory levels. But if the lead time is one day on one shipment and then ten days on the next shipment, the stores must carry additional backup stock to cover this uncertainty in lead time. Many retailers using collaborative supply chain management systems require that their vendors deliver merchandise within a very narrow window—sometimes two or three hours—to reduce the fluctuations in lead time and thus the amount of required backup stock.

When planning the amount of inventory to order for a staple merchandise category, such as paint, Lowe's buyers must consider current inventory, customer demand, lead time for replenishment, and backup stock needed to avoid stockouts in the department.

Fifth, the vendor's fill rate affects the retailer's backup stock requirements. The percentage of SKUs received complete on a particular order from a vendor is called the **fill rate.** For example, Lowe's can more easily plan its inventory requirements if the vendor normally ships every item that is ordered. If, however, the vendor ships only 75 percent of the ordered items, Lowe's must maintain more backup stock to be certain that the paint availability for its customers isn't adversely affected.

Automated Continuous Replenishment Once the buyer sets the desired product availability and determines the variation in demand and the vendor's lead time and fill rate, the continuous replenishment systems for staple SKUs can operate automatically. The retailer's information system determines the inventory level at each point in time, the **perpetual inventory,** by comparing the sales made through the POS terminals with the shipments received by the store. When the perpetual inventory level falls below the predetermined level, the system sends an EDI reorder to the retailer's distribution center and the vendor. When the reordered merchandise arrives at the store, the level of inventory is adjusted up.

However, it is difficult to achieve fully automated continuous replenishment of staple merchandise because of errors in determining the actual inventory. For example, the retailer's information system might indicate that 10 Gillette Fusion razors are in the store when, in fact, 10 razors were stolen by a shoplifter and there are actually zero razors in the store. Because there are no razors in the store, there are no sales, and the automated continuous replenishment system will never reorder razors for the store. Such inaccuracies also can arise when an incorrect number of units is input into the information system about a shipment from the distribution center to the store when it is delivered. To address these problems, store employees need to periodically check the inventory recorded in the system with an actual inventory of the store by physically counting all inventory.

Inventory Management Report The inventory management report provides information about the inventory management for a staple category. The report indicates the decision variables set by the buyer, such as product availability, the backup stock needed to provide the product availability, the order points and quantities plus performance measures such as planned and actual inventory turnover, the current sales rate or velocity, sales forecasts, inventory availability, and the amount on order. Exhibit 12–8 is an inventory management report for Rubbermaid bath mats.

EXHIBIT 12–8   Inventory Management Report for Rubbermaid SKUs

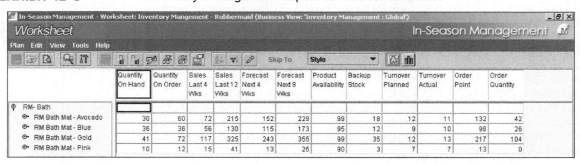

	Quantity On Hand	Quantity On Order	Sales Last 4 Wks	Sales Last 12 Wks	Forecast Next 4 Wks	Forecast Next 8 Wks	Product Availability	Backup Stock	Turnover Planned	Turnover Actual	Order Point	Order Quantity
RM- Bath												
RM Bath Mat - Avocado	30	60	72	215	152	229	99	18	12	11	132	42
RM Bath Mat - Blue	36	36	56	130	115	173	95	12	9	10	98	26
RM Bath Mat - Gold	41	72	117	325	243	355	99	35	12	13	217	104
RM Bath Mat - Pink	10	12	15	41	13	25	90	3	7	7	13	0

The first five columns of Exhibit 12–8 contain the descriptions of each item, how many items are on hand and on order, and sales for the past 4 and 12 weeks. The first-row SKU is a Rubbermaid bath mat in avocado green. There are 30 units on hand and 60 on order. Thus, the quantity available of this SKU is 90. Sales for the past 4 and 12 weeks were 72 and 215 units, respectively.

Sales forecasts for the next 4 and 8 weeks are determined by the system using a statistical model that considers the trends in past sales and the seasonal pattern for the SKU. However, in this case, the buyer made an adjustment in the forecast for the next 4 weeks to reflect an upcoming special promotion on avocado, blue, and gold bath mats.

The product availability is a decision variable that is input by the buyer. For the avocado bath mat SKU, the buyer wants 99 out of every 100 customers to find it in stock (99 percent product availability). But the buyer is less concerned about stocking out of pink bath mats and thus sets its product availability at 90 percent (on average, 90 out of 100 customers will find it in stock). The system then calculates the necessary backup stock for the avocado bath mat based on a predetermined formula—18 units. This number is determined by the system on the basis of the specified product availability, the variability in demand, the vendor delivery lead time, and the variability in the lead time.

The planned inventory turnover for the SKU, 12 times, is a decision variable also set by the buyer on the basis of the retailer's overall financial goals; it drives the inventory management system. For this SKU, the system determined that the actual turnover, based on the cost of goods sold and average inventory, is 11.

Order Point   The **order point** is the amount of inventory below which the quantity available shouldn't go or the item will be out of stock before the next order arrives. This number tells the buyer that when the inventory level drops to this point, additional merchandise should be ordered. For this SKU, the buyer needs to place an order if the quantity in inventory falls to 132 or fewer units to produce the desired product availability.

Order Quantity   When inventory reaches the order point, the buyer, or system, needs to order enough units to ensure product availability before the next order arrives. Using the avocado bath mats in Exhibit 12–8 as an example, the order quantity is 42 units.

Control System for Managing Inventory of Fashion Merchandise

The control systems for managing fashion merchandise categories are the merchandise budget plan and the open-to-buy.

Merchandise Budget Plan   The **merchandise budget plan** specifies the amount of merchandise in dollars (not units) that needs to be delivered during each month, based on the sales forecast, the planned discounts to employees and customers, and the level of inventory needed to support the sales and achieve the desired GMROI objectives.

Exhibit 12–9 shows a six-month merchandise budget plan for men's casual slacks at a national specialty store chain. Appendix 12A describes in detail how the plan is developed. Most retailers use commercially available software packages to develop merchandise budget plans.

Inventory turnover, GMROI, and the sales forecast are used for both planning and control. Buyers negotiate GMROI, inventory turnover, and sales forecast goals with their superiors, the GMMs and DMMs. Then, merchandise budgets are developed to meet these goals. Well before the season, buyers purchase the amount of merchandise specified in the last line of the merchandise budget plan to be delivered in those specific months—the monthly additions to stock.

EXHIBIT 12–9   Six-Month Merchandise Budget Plan for Mens' Casual Slacks

	Spring	April	May	June	July	August	September
1. Sales % Distribution to Season	100.00%	21.00%	12.00%	12.00%	19.00%	21.00%	15.00%
2. Monthly Sales	$130,000	$27,300	$15,600	$15,600	$24,700	$27,300	$19,500
3. Reduc % Distribution to Season	100.00%	40.00%	14.00%	16.00%	12.00%	10.00%	8.00%
4. Monthly Reductions	$16,500	$6,600	$2,310	$2,640	$1,980	$1,650	$1,320
5. BOM Stock to Sales Ratio	4.00	3.60	4.40	4.40	4.00	3.60	4.00
6. BOM Inventory	$98,280	$98,280	$68,640	$68,640	$98,800	$98,280	$78,000
7. EOM Inventory	$65,600	$68,640	$68,640	$98,800	$98,280	$78,000	$65,600
8. Monthly Additions to Stock	$113,820	$4,260	$17,910	$48,400	$26,160	$8,670	$8,420

After the selling season, the buyer must determine how the category actually performed compared with the plan. If the actual GMROI, inventory turnover, and forecast are greater than those in the plan, performance is better than expected. However, performance evaluations should not be based solely on any one of these measures. Several additional questions should be answered to evaluate the buyer's performance: Why did the performance exceed or fall short of the plan? Was the deviation from the plan due to something under the buyer's control? For instance, was too much merchandise purchased? Did the buyer react quickly to changes in demand by either purchasing more or having a sale? Was the deviation instead due to some external factor, such as a change in the competitive level (e.g., new competitors' stores opened in the area) or economic activity (e.g., recession)? Every attempt should be made to discover answers to these questions. Later in this chapter, several additional tools used to evaluate merchandise performance will be examined.

Open-to-Buy System   After the merchandise is purchased on the basis of the merchandise budget plan, the **open-to-buy** system is used to keep track of the actual merchandise flows—what the present inventory level is, when purchased merchandise is scheduled for delivery, and how much has been sold to customers. In the same way that you must keep track of the checks you write, buyers need to keep track of the merchandise they purchase and when it is to be delivered so they don't buy more (over-bought) or less (under-bought) than they have money in their budget to spend each month. Without the open-to-buy system keeping track of merchandise flows, merchandise could be delivered when it isn't needed or be unavailable when it is needed.

The open-to-buy system compares the planned end-of-month inventory to the actual end-of-month inventory. Differences between actual and planned levels may arise because an order was shipped late or sales deviated from the forecast. When sales are greater than planned, the system determines how much merchandise to buy, in terms of dollars the buyer has available, to satisfy the increased customer demand.

ALLOCATING MERCHANDISE TO STORES

LO7

Describe how multistore retailers allocate merchandise to stores.

After developing a plan for managing merchandise inventory in a category, the next step in the merchandise management process is to allocate the merchandise purchased and received to the retailer's stores (see Exhibit 12–3). Research indicates that these allocation decisions have a much bigger impact on profitability than does the decision about the quantity of merchandise to purchase.[17] In other words, buying too little or too much merchandise has less impact on a category's profitability than does making mistakes in allocating the right amount and type of merchandise to stores. Allocating merchandise to stores involves three decisions: (1) how much merchandise to allocate to each store, (2) what type of merchandise to allocate, and (3) when to allocate the merchandise to different stores.

Amount of Merchandise Allocated

Retail chains typically classify each of their stores on the basis of annual sales. Thus, A stores would have the largest sales volume and typically receive the most inventory, while C stores would have the lowest sales volume and receive the least inventory for a category. In addition to the store's sales level, when making allocation decisions for a category, allocators consider the physical characteristics of the merchandise and the depth of assortment and level of product availability that the firm wants to portray for the specific store.

Type of Merchandise Allocated

The geodemographics of a store's trading area (discussed in Chapter 8) are considered in making allocation decisions. Consider the allocation decision of a national supermarket for its ready-to-eat cereal assortment. Some stores are located in areas dominated by segments called "Rustbelt Retirees," and other areas are dominated by the "Laptops and Lattes" segment, as described in Exhibit 12–10.

The ready-to-eat breakfast cereal planner would offer different assortments for stores in these two areas. Stores with a high proportion of Rustbelt Retirees in their trading areas would get an assortment of lower-price, well-known brands and more private-label cereals. Stores in areas dominated by the Laptops and Lattes geodemographic segment would get an assortment with higher-price brands that feature low sugar, organic ingredients, and whole wheat. Private-label cereals would be de-emphasized.

Even the sales of different apparel sizes can vary dramatically from store to store in the same chain. Exhibit 12–11 illustrates this point. Notice that store X sells significantly more large sizes and fewer small sizes than is average for the chain. If the planner allocated the same size distribution of merchandise to all stores in the chain, store X would stock out of large sizes, have an oversupply of small sizes, and be out of some sizes sooner than other stores in the chain. Retailing View 12.4 provides a glimpse of how Saks Fifth Avenue allocates merchandise to stores on the basis of customer characteristics.

REFACT

Southerners prefer white, green, and pink. Women on the East and West Coasts wear smaller sizes than their middle-American counterparts.[18]

EXHIBIT 12–10
Examples of Geodemographic Segments

Laptops and Lattes: The most eligible and unencumbered marketplace	Rustbelt Retirees
Laptops and Lattes are affluent, single, and still renting. They are educated, professional, and partial to city life, favoring major metropolitan areas such as New York, Boston, Chicago, Los Angeles, and San Francisco. Median household income is more than $87,000; median age is 38 years. Technologically savvy, the Laptops and Lattes segment is the top market for notebook PCs and PDAs. They use the Internet on a daily basis to trade stocks and make purchases and travel plans. They are health conscious and physically fit; they take vitamins, use organic products, and exercise in the gym. They embrace liberal philosophies and work for environmental causes.	Rustbelt Retirees can be found in older, industrial cities in the Northeast and Midwest, especially in Pennsylvania and other states surrounding the Great Lakes. Households are mainly occupied by married couples with no children and singles who live alone. The median age is 43.8 years. Although many residents are still working, labor force participation is below average. More than 40 percent of the households receive Social Security benefits. Most residents live in owned, single-family homes, with a median value of $118,500. Unlike many retirees, these residents are not inclined to move. They are proud of their homes and gardens and participate in community activities. Some are members of veterans' clubs. Leisure activities include playing bingo, gambling in Atlantic City, going to the horse races, working crossword puzzles, and playing golf.

EXHIBIT 12–11
Apparel Size
Differences for the
Average and Specific
Store in a Chain

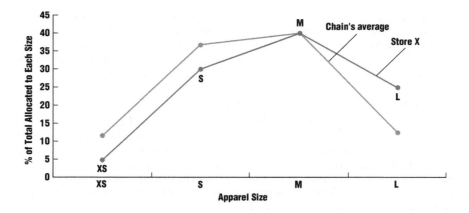

Timing of Merchandise Allocation

In addition to the need to allocate different inventory levels and types of merchandise across stores, differences in the timing of category purchases across stores need to be considered. Exhibit 12–12 illustrates these differences by plotting sales data over time for capri pants in different regions of the United States. Comparing regions shows that capri sales peak in late July in the Midwest and at the beginning of September in the West, due to seasonality

12.4   RETAILING VIEW   Customer-Centric Merchandise Allocation at Saks Fifth Avenue

Having the right merchandise in the right stores at the right time is the key to merchandising success for fashion retailers like Saks Fifth Avenue. For instance, Saks considers its core shopper at its New York flagship store in Manhattan to be a woman, between 46 and 57 years of age, with a largely "classic" style, especially when it comes to work clothes, and a taste for slightly more modern looks when she goes out with friends on weekends. But it also recognizes that the merchandise selections for stores located elsewhere needs to be less New York–centric. Even stores close to New York City attract different types of shoppers. A Greenwich, Connecticut, Saks caters to a slightly older shopper than does the Saks in Stamford, Connecticut, about five miles away. Stamford shoppers tend to be women who work in town, whereas Greenwich attracts a higher proportion of women who are at home full-time. Online Saks shoppers are seven years younger than a regular Saks customer, but they seek out specific items, whereas in-store shoppers are looking to be outfitted from head to toe during a single shopping trip.

To better match its assortments with its stores, Saks has developed a nine-box grid. On one side of the matrix are style categories: "Park Avenue," or classic; "Uptown," or modern; and "Soho," meaning trendy or contemporary. On the other axis are pricing levels, from "good" (brands such as Dana Buchman, Real Clothes [Saks's private label], and Eileen Fisher) to "better" (Piazza Sempione and Armani Collezioni) to "best" (Chanel, Gucci, and Yves

Saint Laurent). By cross-referencing the preferred styles and spending levels for each assortment at each location, the grid charts the best mix of clothes, brands, and accessories to stock at the store.

Such careful assortment planning was not quite sufficient to enable Saks to weather the recent global economic crisis, though. Assortments chosen during boom years led to massive leftover inventory during the bust times, prompting Saks to take more and deeper discounts—of up to 75 percent—than it ever had in its long history. When sales rebounded by about 15 percent with a slightly improved economy, Saks slowly eliminated its discounts and increased its inventory levels. But rather than returning to pre-recession levels, the bump in inventory was less than 3 percent overall to ensure it was never again stuck with massive overstocks.

Sources: Elizabeth Holmes, "At Saks, It's Full Price Ahead as CEO Pares Back Discounts," *The New York Times,* September 12, 2011; Stephanie Rosenbloom, "As Saks Reports a Loss, Its Chief Offers a Plan," *The New York Times,* February 26, 2009; Vanessa O'Connell, "Park Avenue Classic or Soho Trendy?" *The Wall Street Journal,* April 20, 2007, p. B1; and www.saks.com.

DISCUSSION QUESTION

What box on the grid best describes the Saks Fifth Avenue closest to where you live? Do you think it is the most appropriate box for that store's target market?

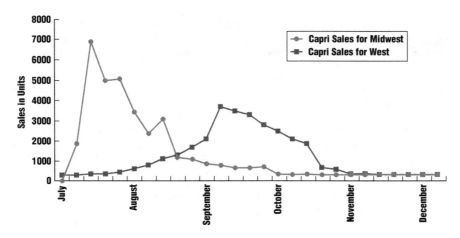

EXHIBIT 12–12
Sales of Capri Pants by
Region

differences and differences in consumer demand. To increase inventory turnover in the category, buyers need to recognize these regional differences and arrange for merchandise to be shipped to the appropriate regions when customers are ready to buy.

Retailers are also considering the "paycheck cycle" when making merchandise allocation and promotion decisions, particularly in difficult economic times. Cash-strapped consumers are showing a tendency to make their largest purchases when they get their paychecks at the beginning of the month and to cut back on purchases as that money runs out toward the end of the month. As a result, some supermarket chains devote more shelf space and promote larger-package sizes at the beginning of the month and smaller sizes at the end of the month.[19]

ANALYZING MERCHANDISE MANAGEMENT PERFORMANCE

The next step in the merchandise planning process (see Exhibit 12–3) is to analyze the performance of the process and make adjustments, such as ordering more or less merchandise, lowering prices to increase sales, allocating different assortments to specific stores, or changing the assortment and model stock plans. Three types of analyses related to the monitoring and adjustment step are (1) sell-through analysis, (2) ABC analysis of assortments, and (3) multiattribute analysis of vendors. The first analysis provides an ongoing evaluation of the merchandise management plan compared with actual sales. The remaining two analyses offer approaches for evaluating and altering the assortment plan using the specific SKUs in the plan and the vendors that provide the merchandise to support the plan.

LO8
Review how retailers evaluate the performance of their merchandise management decisions.

Sell-Through Analysis: Evaluating the Merchandise Plan

A **sell-through analysis** compares actual and planned sales to determine whether more merchandise is needed to satisfy demand or whether price reductions (markdowns) are required. Exhibit 12–13 shows a sell-through analysis for blouses for the first two weeks of the season.

These blouses are high-fashion items that experience significant uncertainty in sales. Thus, after two weeks in the stores, the buyer reviews sales and determines if adjustments are needed. Buyers would use a longer review period for merchandise with an extended fashion cycle. The need to make adjustments depends on a

EXHIBIT 12–13
Example of Sell-
Through Analysis

Stock Number		Description	WEEK 1			WEEK 2		
			Plan	Actual-to-Plan Actual	Percentage	Plan	Actual-to-Plan Actual	Percentage
1011	Small	White silk V-neck	20	15	−25%	20	10	−50%
1011	Medium	White silk V-neck	30	25	−16.6	30	20	−33
1011	Large	White silk V-neck	20	16	−20	20	16	−20
1012	Small	Blue silk V-neck	25	26	4	25	27	8
1012	Medium	Blue silk V-neck	35	45	29	35	40	14
1012	Large	Blue silk V-neck	25	25	0	25	30	20

variety of factors, including experience with the merchandise in the past, plans for featuring the merchandise in advertising, and the availability of **markdown money** from vendors (funds that a vendor gives a retailer to cover lost gross margin dollars that result from markdowns).

In this case, the white blouses are selling significantly less well than planned. Therefore, the buyer makes an early price reduction to ensure that the merchandise isn't left unsold at the end of the season. The decision regarding the blue blouses isn't as clear. The small blue blouses are selling slightly ahead of the plan, and the medium blue blouses are also selling well, but the large blue blouses start selling ahead of plan only in the second week. In this case, the buyer decides to wait another week or two before taking any action. If actual sales stay significantly ahead of planned sales, a reorder might be appropriate.

Evaluating the Assortment Plan and Vendors

ABC Analysis   An **ABC analysis** identifies the performance of individual SKUs in the assortment plan. It is used to determine which SKUs should be in the plan and how much backup stock and resulting product availability are provided for each SKU in the plan. In an ABC analysis, the SKUs in a merchandise category are rank-ordered by several performance measures, such as sales, gross margin, inventory turnover, and GMROI. Typically, this rank order reveals the general 80–20 principle; namely, approximately 80 percent of a retailer's sales or profits come from 20 percent of the products. This principle suggests that retailers should concentrate on the products that provide the biggest returns.

After rank-ordering the SKUs, the next step is to classify the items. On the basis of the classification, the buyer determines whether to maintain the items in the assortment plan and, if so, what level of product availability to offer. For example, a men's dress shirt buyer might identify the A, B, C, and D SKUs by rank-ordering them by sales volume.

The A items account for only 5 percent of the SKUs in the category but represent 70 percent of sales. The buyer decides that these SKUs should never be out of stock and thus plans to maintain more backup stock for A items, such as keeping more units for each SKU of long- and short-sleeved white and blue dress shirts, than of the B and C items.

The B items represent 10 percent of the SKUs and 20 percent of sales. These items include some of the other better-selling colors and patterned shirts and contribute to the retailer's image of having fashionable merchandise. Occasionally, the retailer will run out of some SKUs in the B category because it does not carry the same amount of backup stock for B items as it does for A items.

The C items account for 65 percent of SKUs but contribute to only 10 percent of sales. The planner may plan to carry some C items only in the most popular sizes of the most basic shirts, with special orders used to satisfy customer demand.

Finally, the buyer discovers that the remaining 20 percent of the SKUs, D items, have virtually no sales until they are marked down. Not only are these items excess merchandise and an unproductive investment, but they also distract from the rest of the inventory and clutter the store shelves. The buyer decides to eliminate most of these items from the assortment plan.

Multiattribute Method for Evaluating Vendors   The **multiattribute analysis** method for evaluating vendors uses a weighted-average score for each vendor.[20] The score is based on the importance of various issues and the vendor's performance on those issues. This method is similar to the multiattribute approach that can be used to understand how customers evaluate stores and merchandise, as we discussed in Chapter 4.

To better understand the multiattribute method of evaluating vendors, either current or proposed, consider the example in Exhibit 12–14 for vendors of men's casual slacks.

A buyer can evaluate vendors using the following five steps:

1. Develop a list of issues to consider in the evaluation (column 1).

2. In conjunction with the GMM, determine the importance weights for each issue in column 1 on a 1-to-10 scale (column 2), where 1 equals not important and 10 equals very important. For instance, the buyer and the merchandise manager believe that vendor reputation should receive a 9 because it's very important to the retailer's image. Merchandise quality receives a 5 because it's moderately important. Finally, a vendor's selling history is less important, so it could be rated 3.

3. Make judgments about each individual brand's performance on each issue (remaining columns). Note that some brands have high ratings on some issues but not on others.

4. Develop an overall score by multiplying the importance of each issue by the performance of each brand or its vendor. For instance, vendor reputation importance (9) multiplied by the performance rating for brand A (5) is 45.

EXHIBIT 12–14
Multiattribute Method for Evaluating Vendors

Issues (1)	Importance Evaluation of Issues (I) (2)	PERFORMANCE EVALUATIONS OF INDIVIDUAL BRANDS ACROSS ISSUES			
		Brand A (P_a) (3)	Brand B (P_b) (4)	Brand C (P_c) (5)	Brand D (P_d) (6)
Vendor reputation	9	5	9	4	8
Service	8	6	6	4	6
Meets delivery dates	6	5	7	4	4
Merchandise quality	5	5	4	6	5
Markup opportunity	5	5	4	4	5
Country of origin	6	5	3	3	8
Product fashionability	7	6	6	3	8
Selling history	3	5	5	5	5
Promotional assistance	4	5	3	4	7
Overall evaluation a $\sum_{i=1}^{n} I_i \times P_{ij}$		280	298	212	341

$\sum_{i=1}^{n}$ = Sum of the expression.

I_i = Importance weight assigned to the ith dimension.

P_{ij} = Performance evaluation for jth brand alternative on the ith issue.

I = Not important.

10 = Very important.

Promotional assistance importance (4) multiplied by the performance rating (7) for vendor D is 28. This type of analysis illustrates an important point: It doesn't pay to perform well on issues that retailers don't believe are very important. Although vendor D performed well on promotional assistance, the buyer didn't rate this issue highly in importance, so the resulting score was still low.

5. To determine a vendor's overall rating, add the products for each brand for all issues. In Exhibit 12–14, brand D has the highest overall rating (341), so D is the preferred vendor.

SUMMARY

LO1 Explain the merchandise management organization and performance measures.

Merchandise is broken down into categories for planning purposes. Buyers and planners manage these categories, often with the help of their major vendors. The key performance measures used to assess merchandise management are GMROI and its components; sales-to-stock ratio, which is similar to inventory turnover; and gross margin. High inventory turnover is important for a retailer's financial success. But if the retailer attempts to push inventory turnover to its limit, stockouts and increased costs may result.

LO2 Contrast the merchandise management processes for staple and fashion merchandise.

Retailers use different types of merchandise planning systems for managing (1) staple and (2) fashion merchandise categories. Staple merchandise categories, also called basic merchandise categories, are categories that are in continuous demand over an extended time period. Fashion merchandise categories are in demand only for a relatively short period of time. New products are continually introduced into these categories, making the existing products obsolete. Seasonal merchandise categories consist of items whose sales fluctuate dramatically depending on the time of year.

The steps in the merchandise management planning process are (1) forecast category sales, (2) develop an assortment plan, (3) determine appropriate inventory levels and product availability, (4) develop a plan for managing inventory, (5) allocate merchandise to stores, and (6) monitor and evaluate performance and make adjustments.

LO3 Describe how to predict sales for merchandise categories.

The first step in merchandise management planning is to develop a forecast for category sales. The approach for forecasting sales of staple merchandise is to project past sales trends into the future, making adjustments for anticipated factors affecting future sales.

Forecasting sales for fashion merchandise is challenging because buyers typically need to

place orders and commit to buying specific quantities between three and six months before the merchandise will be delivered and made available for sale. Some sources of information that retailers use to develop forecasts for fashion merchandise categories are (1) previous sales data, (2) market research, (3) fashion and trend services, and (4) vendors.

LO4 Summarize the trade-offs for developing merchandise assortments.

After forecasting sales for the category, the next step in the merchandise management planning process is to develop an assortment plan. An assortment plan is the set of SKUs that a retailer will offer in a merchandise category in each of its stores and from its website. When determining the assortment for a category, buyers consider the following factors: the firm's retail strategy, the effect of assortments on GMROI, the complementarities between categories, the effects of assortments on buying behavior, and the physical characteristics of the store.

LO5 Illustrate how to determine the appropriate inventory levels.

After developing the assortment plan, the third step in the merchandise planning process is to determine the model stock plan for the category. The model stock plan is the number of units of backup stock for each SKU. Retailers typically have different model stock plans for the different store sizes in a chain.

The first three steps in the merchandise planning process—forecast SKU and category sales, determine the assortment plan, and establish the model stock plan—quantify the buyer's sales expectations and service level.

LO6 Analyze merchandise control systems.

The fourth step in the merchandise management process is to establish a control system for how the orders, deliveries, inventory levels, and merchandise sales will evolve over time. The objective of this control system is to manage the flow of merchandise into the stores so that the amount of inventory in a category is minimized but the merchandise will still be available when customers want to buy it.

Buying systems for staple merchandise are very different from those for fashion merchandise. Because staple merchandise is sold month after month and the sales levels are predictable, an automated continuous replenishment system is often used to manage staple merchandise categories. By definition, SKUs within a fashion category change rapidly, so fashion merchandise categories are managed in dollars (i.e., how much money is spent on each category), rather than in units as is staple merchandise.

LO7 Describe how multistore retailers allocate merchandise to stores.

Allocating merchandise to stores involves three decisions: (1) how much merchandise to allocate to each store, (2) what type of merchandise to allocate, and (3) when to allocate the merchandise to different stores. Retail chains typically classify each of their stores on the basis of annual sales. Thus, A stores would have the largest sales volume and typically receive the most inventory, while C stores would have the lowest sales volume and receive the least inventory for a category. In

addition to the store's sales level, when making allocation decisions for a category, allocators consider the physical characteristics of the merchandise and the depth of assortment and level of product availability that the firm wants to portray for the specific store.

LO8 Review how retailers evaluate the performance of their merchandise management decisions.

Three different approaches for evaluating aspects of merchandise management and planning performance are sell-through analysis, ABC analysis, and the multiattribute model. The sell-through analysis is useful for examining the performance of individual SKUs in the merchandise plan. The buyer compares actual with planned sales to determine whether more merchandise needs to be ordered or whether the merchandise should be put on sale. In an ABC analysis, merchandise is rank-ordered from highest to lowest. The merchandising team uses this information to set inventory management policies. The multiattribute analysis method for evaluating vendors uses a weighted-average score for each vendor based on the importance of various issues and the vendor's performance on those issues. Buyers choose the vendor with the highest weighted score.

KEY TERMS

ABC analysis, *344*
assortment, *331*
assortment plan, *331*
backup stock, *335*
base stock, *336*
basic merchandise, *325*
breaking sizes, *332*
breadth, *331*
buffer stock, *335*
category captain, *321*
category management, *321*
classification, *320*
continuous replenishment, *325*
cycle stock, *336*
department, *320*

depth, *331*
editing the assortment, *331*
fashion merchandise, *325*
fill rate, *338*
focus group, *330*
in-depth interview, *329*
lead time, *337*
level of support, *335*
markdown money, *344*
merchandise budget plan, *339*
merchandise category, *320*
merchandise group, *319*
merchandise management, *318*
model stock plan, *333*
multiattribute analysis, *345*

open-to-buy, *340*
order point, *339*
perpetual inventory, *338*
product availability, *335*
safety stock, *335*
seasonal merchandise, *325*
sell-through analysis, *343*
service level, *335*
shopworn, *323*
shrinkage, *351*
SKU rationalization program, *333*
staple merchandise, *325*
stock-keeping unit (SKU), *320*
stock-to-sales ratio, *351*
variety, *331*

GET OUT AND DO IT!

1. **CONTINUING ASSIGNMENT** Go to a store of the retailer you selected for the continuing assignment, and and audit the variety and assortment for a specific merchandise category. Record the breadth and depth of the assortment and the level of support (average number of items for the SKUs in each category). Compare the variety, assortment, and support for the same category in a competing retail store.

Evaluate both stores' assortment on that category. Which is better?

2. **INTERNET EXERCISE** Go to the home page of Merchandise Management Company (MMC) at www.merchmanco.com. Watch the three-minute video, and read the posted information and press releases at this website. How does this service provider support vendors to manage merchandise sold at this discount department store? What is the "Store Vision" system? How is it used to measure merchandise performance?

3. **IN-STORE OR INTERNET EXERCISE** Go to the store location or home page of a craft store such as Michaels Stores, Jo-Ann Fabric and Craft Stores, or A.C. Moore Arts & Crafts (www.michaels.com, www.joann.com, or www.acmoore.com). How does this retailer organize its merchandise in terms of merchandise group, department, category, and stock-keeping unit? Select two categories of merchandise: one that you would expect to have a high inventory turnover and the other, a low inventory turnover. Explain your reasoning for each selection.

4. **GO SHOPPING** Visit a big-box office supply store and then a discount store to shop for school supplies. Contrast the variety and assortment offered at each. What are the advantages and disadvantages of breadth versus depth for each retailer? What are the advantages and disadvantages from the consumer's perspective?

5. **INTERNET EXERCISE** Go to the home page of the following three retail trade publications: *Chain Store Age* at www.chainstoreage.com, and *Retailing Today* at www.retailingtoday.com. Find an article in each that focuses on managing merchandise. How can these articles assist retailers with merchandise planning decisions?

6. **INTERNET EXERCISE** Go to http://www.sas.com/industry/retail/merchandise/index.html, the SAS Merchandise Intelligence website. How does the SAS Merchandise Intelligence product provide retailers with information to support merchandising planning, forecasting, and measurement?

7. **WEB OLC EXERCISE** The merchandise budget plan determines how much merchandise should be purchased in each month of a fashion buying season (in dollars), given the sales and reduction forecast, inventory turnover goals, and seasonal monthly fluctuations in sales. Go to the student side of the Online Learning Center, and click "Merchandise Budget Plan." The merchandise budget plan generally covers one fashion season for one merchandise category. This application presents both one-month and six-month examples. In addition, practice calculations are presented for the one-month example. Have your calculator ready! In the calculation section, you have access to an Excel-based six-month merchandise budget plan that can be used to complete Case 20 in the text.

8. **WEB OLC EXERCISE** The vendor evaluation model utilizes the multiattribute method to evaluate vendors. Go to the student side of the Online Learning Center, and click "Vendor Evaluation Model." There are two spreadsheets. Open the first spreadsheet, vendor evaluation 1.xls. This spreadsheet is the same as Exhibit 12–14. If you were selling brand A to the retailer, which numbers would change? Change the numbers in the matrix, and see the effect of that change on the overall evaluation. Go to the second spreadsheet, evaluation 2.xls. This spreadsheet can be used to evaluate brands or merchandise you might stock in your store. Assume you own a bicycle shop. List the brands you might consider stocking and the issues you would consider in selecting the brands to stock. Fill in the importance of the issues (10 = very important, 1 = not very important) and the evaluation of each brand on each characteristic (10 = excellent, 1 = poor). Determine which is the best brand for your store.

DISCUSSION QUESTIONS AND PROBLEMS

1. How and why would you expect variety and assortment to differ between JCPenney's store and Internet channel?

2. Simply speaking, increasing inventory turnover is an important goal for a retail manager. What are the consequences of turnover that's too low? Too high?

3. Assume you are the grocery buyer for canned fruits and vegetables at a five-store supermarket chain. Del Monte has told you and your boss that it would be responsible for making all inventory decisions for those merchandise categories. Del Monte will now determine how much to order and when shipments should be made. It promises a 10 percent increase in gross margin dollars in the coming year. Would you take Del Monte up on its offer? Justify your answer.

4. A buyer at Old Navy has received a number of customer complaints that he has been out of stock on some sizes of men's T-shirts. The buyer subsequently decides to increase this category's product availability from 80 percent to 90 percent. What will be the impact on backup stock and inventory turnover? Would your answer be the same if the product category were men's fleece sweatshirts?

5. Variety, assortment, and product availability are the cornerstones of the merchandise planning process.

Provide examples of retailers that have done an outstanding job of positioning their stores on the basis of one or more of these issues.

6. The fine jewelry department in a department store has the same GMROI as the small appliances department, even though characteristics of the merchandise are quite different. Explain this situation.

7. Calculate the GMROI and inventory turnover given annual sales of $20,000, average inventory (at cost) of $4,000, and a gross margin of 45 percent.

8. As the athletic shoe buyer for Sports Authority, how would you go about forecasting sales for a new Nike running shoe?

9. Using the 80–20 principle, how can a retailer make certain that it has enough inventory of fast-selling merchandise and a minimal amount of slow-selling merchandise?

10. A buyer at a sporting goods store in Denver receives a shipment of 400 ski parkas on October 1 and expects to sell out by January 31. On November 1, the buyer still has 350 parkas left. What issues should the buyer consider in evaluating the selling season's progress?

11. A buyer is trying to decide from which vendor to buy a certain item. Using the information in the accompanying table, determine from which vendor the buyer should buy.

	VENDOR PERFORMANCE		
	Importance Weight	Vendor A	Vendor B
Reputation for collaboration	8	9	8
Service	7	8	7
Meets delivery dates	9	7	8
Merchandise quality	7	8	4
Gross margin	6	4	8
Brand name recognition	5	7	5
Promotional assistance	3	8	8

SUGGESTED READINGS

Broniarczyk, Susan, and Wayne Hoyer. "Retail Assortment: More ≠ Better." In M. Kraft and M. Mantrala (Eds.), *Retailing in the 21st Century*, 2nd ed. New York: Fairchild Books, 2010, pp. 271–284.

Connell, Dana. *A Buyer's Life: A Concise Guide to Retail Planning and Forecasting*. New York: Fairchild, 2010.

Donnellan, John Do. *Buying and Management*, 4th ed. New York: Fairchild, 2013.

Fowler, Deborah, and Ben Goh. *Retail Category Management*. Englewood Cliffs, NJ: Prentice Hall, 2011.

Heller, Al. *Consumer-Centric Category Management: How to Increase Profits by Managing Categories Based on Consumer Needs*. New York: Wiley, 2012.

Kok, A. Gorhan, Marshall Fisher, and Ramnath Vaidyanathan. "Assortment Planning: Review of Literature and Industry Practice." In Narendra Agrawal and Stephen A. Smith (Eds.),

Retail Supply Chain Management: Quantitative Models and Empirical Studies. New York: Springer, 2009, pp. 99–150.

Murtulus, Mumin, and L. Berl Toktay. "Category Captaincy in the Retail Industry," in Narendra Agrawal and Stephen A. Smith (Eds.), *Retail Supply Chain Management: Quantitative Models and Empirical Studies*. New York: Springer, 2008, pp. 79–99.

Mantrala, Murali, Michael Levy, Barbara Kahn, Edward Fox, Peter Gaidarev, Bill Dankworth, and Denish Shahg. "Why Is Assortment Planning So Difficult for Retailers? A Framework and Research Agenda." *Journal of Retailing* 85, no. 1, pp. 71–83.

Zinn, Walter and Peter Liu. "A Comparison of Actual and Intended Consumer Behavior in Response to Retail Stockouts." *Journal of Business Logistics* 29, no. 2 (2008), pp. 141–159.

APPENDIX 12A   Merchandise Budget Report and Open-to-Buy System for a Fashion Merchandise Category

MERCHANDISE BUDGET PLAN

In this appendix, we describe the steps in developing the merchandise budget plan for a fashion merchandise category. These steps are taken to develop the bottom line—line 8, "Monthly Additions to Stock"—in Exhibit 12–15. The figures on this line tell the buyer how much merchandise in retail dollars he or she needs to have, on average, at the beginning of each month for the retailer's financial goals to be met. Note that Exhibit 12–15 is the same as Exhibit 12–9 in the chapter.

EXHIBIT 12–15   Six-Month Merchandise Budget Plan for Men's Casual Slacks

Worksheet	Spring	April	May	June	July	August	September
1. Sales % Distribution to Season	100.00%	21.00%	12.00%	12.00%	19.00%	21.00%	15.00%
2. Monthly Sales	$130,000	$27,300	$15,600	$15,600	$24,700	$27,300	$19,500
3. Reduc % Distribution to Season	100.00%	40.00%	14.00%	16.00%	12.00%	10.00%	8.00%
4. Monthly Reductions	$16,500	$6,600	$2,310	$2,640	$1,980	$1,650	$1,320
5. BOM Stock to Sales Ratio	4.00	3.60	4.40	4.40	4.00	3.60	4.00
6. BOM Inventory	$98,280	$98,280	$68,640	$68,640	$98,800	$98,280	$78,000
7. EOM Inventory	$65,600	$68,640	$68,640	$98,800	$98,280	$78,000	$65,600
8. Monthly Additions to Stock	$113,820	$4,260	$17,910	$48,400	$26,160	$8,670	$8,420

Monthly Sales Percentage Distribution to Season (Line 1)

Line 1 of the plan projects what percentage of the total sales is expected to be sold in each month. In Exhibit 12–15, 21 percent of the six-month sales are expected to occur in April.

		SPRING			SUMMER		
	Six-Month Data	April	May	June	July	August	September
Sales % distribution to 1 Month	100.00%	21.00%	12.00%	12.00%	19.00%	21.00%	15.00%

Historical sales data provide the starting point for determining the percentage distribution of sales by month. The percentage of total category sales that occurs in a particular month doesn't vary much from year to year. However, the buyer might adjust the historical percentages to reflect changes in buying patterns and special promotions. For instance, the buyer might feel that the autumn selling season for men's casual slacks continues to be pushed further back into summer and thus increase the percentages for July and decrease the percentages for August and September. The buyer might also decide to hold a special Easter sale promotion, increasing the April percentage and decreasing the other percentages.

Monthly Sales (Line 2)

Monthly sales are the forecasted total sales for the six-month period in the first column ($130,000) multiplied by each monthly sales percentage (line 1). In Exhibit 12–15, monthly sales for April = $130,000 × 21 percent = $27,300.

		SPRING			SUMMER		
	Six-Month Data	April	May	June	July	August	September
Sales % distribution to 1 Month	100.00%	21.00%	12.00%	12.00%	19.00%	21.00%	15.00%
2 Monthly sales	$130,000	$27,300	$15,600	$15,600	$24,700	$27,300	$19,500

Monthly Reductions Percentage Distribution to Season (Line 3)

To have enough merchandise every month to support the monthly sales forecast, the buyer needs to consider other factors that reduce the inventory level in addition to sales made to customers. Although sales are the primary reduction, the value of the inventory is also reduced by markdowns (sales discounts), shrinkage, and discounts to employees. The merchandise budget planning process builds these additional reductions into the planned purchases. If these reductions were not considered, the category would always be understocked. Note that in Exhibit 12–15, 40 percent of the season's total reductions occur in April as a result of price discounts (markdowns) during end-of-season sales as well.

Markdowns also can be forecasted from historical records. However, changes in markdown strategies—or changes in the environment, such as competition or general economic activity—must be taken into consideration when forecasting markdowns as well.

Discounts to employees are like markdowns, except that they are given to employees rather than to customers. The level of the employee discount is tied fairly closely to the sales level and number of employees. Thus, employee discounts also can be forecasted from historical records.

Shrinkage refers to inventory losses caused by shoplifting, employee theft, merchandise being misplaced or damaged, and poor bookkeeping. Retailers measure shrinkage by taking the difference between (1) the inventory's recorded value based on merchandise bought and received and (2) the physical inventory actually in stores and distribution centers. Shrinkage varies by department and season, but typically it varies directly with sales as well. So if sales of men's casual pants increase by 10 percent, then the buyer can expect a 10 percent increase in shrinkage.

		SPRING			SUMMER		
	Six-Month Data	April	May	June	July	August	September
3 Reduction % distribution to season	100.00%	40.00%	14.00%	16.00%	12.00%	10.00%	8.00%

Monthly Reductions (Line 4)

Monthly reductions are calculated by multiplying the total reductions by each percentage in line 3. The total reductions for this example are based on historical data. In Exhibit 12–15, April reductions = $16,500 × 40 percent = $6,600.

		SPRING			SUMMER		
	Six-Month Data	April	May	June	July	August	September
3 Reduction % distribution to season	100.00%	40.00%	14.00%	16.00%	12.00%	10.00%	8.00%
4 Monthly reductions	$16,500	$6,600	$2,310	$2,640	$1,980	$1,650	$1,320

BOM (Beginning-of-Month) Stock-to-Sales Ratio (Line 5)

The **stock-to-sales ratio,** listed in line 5, specifies the amount of inventory that should be on hand at the beginning of the month to support the sales forecast and maintain the inventory turnover objective for the category. Thus, a stock-to-sales ratio of 2 means that the retailer plans to have twice as much inventory on hand at the beginning of the month as there are forecasted sales for the month. Both the BOM stock and forecasted sales for the month are expressed in retail sales dollars.

		SPRING			SUMMER		
	Six-Month Data	April	May	June	July	August	September
5 BOM stock-to-sales ratio	4.0	3.6	4.4	4.4	4.0	3.6	4.0

Rather than specifying the stock-to-sales ratio, many retailers specify a related measure, weeks of inventory. A stock-to-sales ratio of 4 means there are 16 weeks of inventory, or approximately 112 days, on hand at the beginning of the month. A stock-to-sales ratio of 1/2 indicates a two-week supply of merchandise, or enough for approximately 14 days. The stock-to-sales ratio is determined so the merchandise category achieves its targeted performance—its planned GMROI and inventory turnover. The steps in determining the stock-to-sales ratio for the category are shown next.

Step 1: Calculate Sales-to-Stock Ratio   The GMROI is equal to the gross margin percentage times the sales-to-stock ratio. The sales-to-stock ratio is conceptually similar to inventory turnover except the denominator in the stock-to-sales ratio is expressed in retail sales dollars, whereas the denominator in inventory turnover is the cost of goods sold (sales at cost). The buyer's target GMROI for the category is 123 percent, and the buyer feels the category will produce a gross margin of 45 percent. Thus,

GMROI = Gross margin percent × Sales-to-stock ratio

Sales-to-stock ratio = GMROI/Gross margin percent = 123/45 = 2.73

Because this illustration of a merchandise budget plan is for a six-month period rather than a year, the sales-to-stock ratio is based on six months rather than annual sales. So for this six-month period, sales must be 2.73 times the inventory cost to meet the targeted GMROI.

Step 2: Convert the Sales-to-Stock Ratio to Inventory Turnover   Inventory turnover is

$$
\begin{aligned}
\text{Inventory turnover} &= \text{Sales-to-stock ratio} \times (1.00 - \text{Gross margin \%}/100) \\
&= 2.73 \times (1.00 - 45/100) \\
1.50 &= 2.73 \times .55
\end{aligned}
$$

This adjustment is necessary because the sales-to-stock ratio defines sales at retail and inventory at cost, whereas inventory turnover defines both sales and inventory at cost. Like the sales-to-stock ratio, this inventory turnover is based on a six-month period.

Step 3: Calculate Average Stock-to-Sales Ratio   The average stock-to-sales ratio is

$$
\begin{aligned}
\text{Average stock-to-sales ratio} &= 6 \text{ months}/\text{Inventory turnover} \\
4 &= 6/1.5
\end{aligned}
$$

If preparing a 12-month plan, the buyer divides 12 by the annual inventory turnover. Because the merchandise budget plan in Exhibit 12–15 is based on retail dollars, it's easiest to think of the numerator as BOM retail inventory and the denominator as sales for that month. Thus, to achieve a six-month inventory turnover of 1.5, on average, the buyer must plan to have a BOM inventory that equals four times the amount of sales for a given month, which is equivalent to four months, or 16 weeks of supply.

One needs to be careful when thinking about the average *stock-to-sales ratio*, which can be easily confused with the *sales-to-stock ratio*. These ratios are not the inverse of each other. Sales are the same in both ratios, but stock in the sales-to-stock ratio is the average inventory at cost over all days in the period, whereas stock in the stock-to-sales ratio is the average BOM inventory at retail. Also, the BOM stock-to-sales ratio is an average for all months. Adjustments are made to this average in line 5 to account for seasonal variation in sales.

Step 4: Calculate Monthly Stock-to-Sales Ratios   The monthly stock-to-sales ratios in line 5 must average the stock-to-sales ratio calculated previously to achieve the planned inventory turnover. Generally, monthly stock-to-sales ratios vary in the opposite direction of sales. That is, in months when sales are larger, stock-to-sales ratios are smaller, and vice versa.

To make this adjustment, the buyer needs to consider the seasonal pattern for men's casual slacks in determining the monthly stock-to-sales ratios. In the ideal situation, men's casual slacks would arrive in the store the same day and in the same quantity that customers demand them. Unfortunately, the real-life retailing world isn't this simple. Note in Exhibit 12–15 (line 8) that men's casual slacks for the spring season start arriving slowly in April ($4,260 for the month), yet demand lags behind these arrivals until the weather starts getting warmer. Monthly sales then jump from 12 percent of annual sales in May and June to 19 percent in July (line 1). But the stock-to-sales ratio (line 5) decreased from 4.4 in May and June to 4.0 in July. Thus, in months when sales increase (e.g., July), the BOM inventory also increases (line 6) but at a slower rate, which causes the stock-to-sales ratios to decrease. Likewise, in months when sales decrease dramatically, like in May (line 2), inventory also decreases (line 6), again at a slower rate, causing the stock-to-sales ratios to increase (line 5).

When creating a merchandise budget plan for a category such as men's casual slacks with a sales history, the buyer also examines previous years' stock-to-sales ratios. To judge how adequate these past ratios were, the buyer determines if inventory levels were exceedingly high or low in any months. Then the buyer makes minor corrections to adjust for a previous imbalance in inventory levels, as well as for changes in the current environment. For instance, assume the buyer is planning a promotion for Memorial Day. This promotion has never been done before, so the stock-to-sales ratio for the month of May should be adjusted downward to allow for the expected increase in sales. Note that monthly stock-to-sales ratios don't change by the same percentage that the percentage distribution of sales by month is changing. In months when sales increase, stock-to-sales ratios decrease but at a slower rate. Because there is no exact method of making these adjustments, the buyer must make some subjective judgments.

BOM Stock (Line 6)

The amount of inventory planned for the beginning-of-the-month (BOM) inventory for April equals

BOM inventory = Monthly sales (line 2) × BOM stock-to-sales ratio (line 5)
$98,280   = $27,300   × 3.6

		SPRING			SUMMER		
	Six-Month Data	April	May	June	July	August	September
6 BOM inventory	$98,280	$98,280	$68,640	$68,640	$98,800	$98,280	$78,000

EOM (End-of-Month) Stock (Line 7)

The BOM stock for the current month is the same as the EOM (end-of-month) stock in the previous month. That is, BOM stock in line 6 is simply EOM inventory in line 7 from the previous month. Thus, in Exhibit 12–15, the EOM stock for April is the same as the BOM stock for May, $68,640. Forecasting the ending inventory for the last month in the plan is the next step in the merchandise budget plan. Note that EOM inventory for June is high, which indicates planning for a substantial sales increase in July.

		SPRING			SUMMER		
	Six-Month Data	April	May	June	July	August	September
7 EOM inventory	$65,600	$68,640	$68,640	$98,800	$98,280	$78,000	$65,600

Monthly Additions to Stock (Line 8)

The monthly additions to stock needed is the amount to be ordered for delivery in each month to meet the inventory turnover and sales objectives.

Additions to stock = Sales (line 2) + Reductions (line 4) + EOM inventory (line 7)
                     − BOM inventory (line 6)
Additions to stock (April) = $27,300 + 6,600 + 68,640 − 98,280 = $4,260

At the beginning of the month, the inventory level equals BOM stock. During the month, merchandise is sold, and various inventory reductions affecting the retail sales level occur, such as markdowns and theft. So the BOM stock minus monthly sales minus reductions equals the EOM stock if nothing is purchased. But something must be purchased to get back up to the forecast EOM stock. The difference between EOM stock if nothing is purchased (BOM stock − sales − reductions) and the forecast EOM stock is the additions to stock.

		SPRING			SUMMER		
	Six-Month Data	April	May	June	July	August	September
8 Monthly additions to stock	$113,820	$4,260	$17,920	$48,400	$26,160	$8,670	$8,420

OPEN-TO-BUY SYSTEM

The open-to-buy system is used after the merchandise is purchased and is based on the merchandise budget plan or staple merchandise management system. The merchandise management systems discussed previously provide buyers with a plan for purchasing merchandise. The **open-to-buy** system keeps track of merchandise flows while they are occurring. It keeps a record of how much is actually spent purchasing merchandise each month and how much is left to spend.

Open-to-buy is like the buyer's checkbook. It keeps track of how much money has been spent and how much money is left to spend.

In the same way that you must keep track of the checks you write, buyers need to keep track of the merchandise they purchase and when it is to be delivered. Without the open-to-buy system keeping track of merchandise flows, buyers might buy too much or too little. Merchandise could be delivered when it isn't needed and be unavailable when it is needed. Thus, sales and inventory turnover would suffer. For consistency, we will continue with our example of an open-to-buy system using the merchandise budget plan previously discussed. The open-to-buy system is also applicable to staple goods merchandise management systems.

To make the merchandise budget plan successful (i.e., meet the sales, inventory turnover, and GMROI goals for a category), the buyer attempts to buy merchandise in quantities with delivery dates such that the actual EOM stock for a month will be the same as the forecasted EOM stock. For example, at the end of September, which is the end of the spring/summer season, the buyer would like to be completely sold out of spring/summer men's casual slacks so there will be room for the fall styles. Thus, the buyer would want the projected EOM stock and the actual EOM stock for this fashion and/or seasonal merchandise to both equal zero.

Calculating Open-to-Buy for the Current Period

Buyers develop plans indicating how much inventory for the merchandise category will be available at the end of the month. However, these plans might be inaccurate. Shipments might not arrive on time, sales might be greater than expected, and/or reductions (price discounts due to sales) might be less than expected.

The open-to-buy is the difference between the planned EOM inventory and the projected EOM. Thus, open-to-buy for a month is:

Open-to-buy = Planned EOM inventory − Projected EOM inventory

If open-to-buy is positive, then the buyer still has money in the budget to purchase merchandise for that month. If the open-to-buy is negative, then the buyer has overbought, meaning he or she has spent more than was in the budget.

The planned EOM inventory is taken from the merchandise budget plan, and the projected EOM inventory is calculated as follows:

Projected EOM inventory = Actual BOM inventory
+ Monthly additions actual (received new merchandise)
+ On order (merchandise to be delivered)
− Sales plan (merchandise sold)
− Monthly reductions plan

Six-Month Open-to-Buy System Report   **EXHIBIT 12–16**

Loc - 10 / Merch - Aged Soft	April	May	June	July	August	September
EOM Stock Plan	$68,640	$68,640	$98,800	$98,280	$78,000	$65,600
EOM Actuals	$69,950					
BOM Stock Plan	$98,280	$68,640	$68,640	$98,800	$98,280	$78,000
BOM Stock Actual	$95,000	$59,500				
Monthly Additions Plan	$4,260	$17,910	$48,400	$26,160	$8,670	$8,420
Monthly Additions Actuals	$3,500	$7,000				
OnOrder	$45,000	$18,000	$48,400			
Sales Plan	$27,300	$15,600	$15,600	$24,700	$27,300	$19,500
Sales Actuals	$26,900					
Monthly Reductions Plan	$6,800	$2,310	$2,640	$1,980	$1,650	$1,320
Monthly Reductions Actuals	$1,650					
Projected EOM Stock Plan	$59,500	$66,590	$96,750	$70,070	$41,120	$20,300
Projected BOM Stock Plan	$24,570	$59,500	$66,500	$96,750	$70,070	$41,120
OTB	$0.00	$2,050	$2,050	$28,210	$36,880	$45,300

Exhibit 12–16 presents the six-month open-to-buy for the same category of men's casual slacks discussed in the fashion merchandise planning section of this chapter. Consider May as the current month. The BOM stock (inventory) actual level is $59,500, but there is no EOM actual inventory yet because the month hasn't finished. When calculating the open-to-buy for the current month, the projected EOM stock plan comes into play. Think of the projected EOM stock plan as a new and improved estimate of the planned EOM stock from the merchandise budget plan. This new and improved version takes information into account that wasn't available when the merchandise budget plan was made. The formula for projected EOM inventory for the category is

$$
\begin{aligned}
\text{Projected EOM inventory} = \text{Actual BOM inventory} & & \$59,500 \\
+ \text{ Monthly additions actual} & & 7,000 \\
+ \text{ On order} & & 18,000 \\
- \text{ Sales plan} & & 15,600 \\
- \text{ Monthly reductions plan} & & \underline{2,310} \\
= & & \$66,590
\end{aligned}
$$

The open-to-buy for the current month is:

$$
\begin{aligned}
\text{Open-to-buy plan} &= \text{EOM inventory planned} - \text{Projected EOM inventory} \\
\$2,050 &= \$68,640 - \$66,590
\end{aligned}
$$

Therefore, the buyer has $2,050 left to spend in May to reach the planned EOM stock of $68,640. This is a relatively small amount, so we can conclude that the buyer's plan is right on target. But if the open-to-buy for May were $20,000, the buyer could then go back into the market and look for some great buys. If one of the vendors had too much stock of men's casual slacks, the buyer might be able to use the $20,000 to pick up some bargains that could be passed on to customers.

If, however, the open-to-buy was a negative $20,000, the buyer would have overspent the budget. Similar to overspending your checkbook, the buyer would have to cut back on spending in future months so the total purchases would be within the merchandise budget. Alternatively, if the buyer believed that the overspending was justified because of changes in the marketplace, a negotiation could take place between the buyer and the divisional merchandise manager to get more open-to-buy.

Buying Merchandise

EXECUTIVE BRIEFING
Audrey Schwarz, Director of Merchandising, Chico's Brand

I have been fortunate to work for Chico's FAS (comprised of four brands: Chico's, White House/Black Market, Soma, and Boston Proper) for five years and be a part of a team that is committed to putting our customers first. What makes the Chico's brand unique is that almost all of the merchandise we sell in our 600+ Chico's boutiques and through our Internet and mobile channels is private label. What that means is our teams collaborate on strategies, design the merchandise, and have it manufactured to our exact specifications—from every detail (thread color, zippers, buttons, etc.) to the type of fabric and the fit. My responsibility within the organization is to help lead our cross-functional team to deliver a merchandise assortment that our customers will love and purchase and achieve our financial objectives. The teams consist of many individuals partnering together with the objective of providing an amazing product that will delight our customers—merchandising, planning, allocation, design, product development, sourcing, technical design, visual merchandising, and marketing.

In today's environment, fast fashion retailers like Forever 21, Zara, and H&M are getting a lot of attention for their "speed to market" ability and being ahead of the trends. Chico's also has the ability to quickly react to fashion trends and respond to our customers' needs based on our strategic initiatives and innovative processes. Our competitive advantage is that we focus on quality as well as fashion to provide great value in our product. Our customers want to be stylish and see the versatility in our pieces to help them create many fabulous looks. They trust us to be the fashion experts and look to us to give them many outfitting options to fit into their busy lifestyles.

To be a successful merchant in the specialty retail sector, you have to (1) be aware of who your target customer is, (2) know what they are looking for, (3) know what they don't have yet, (4) know how to attract a new customer, and (5) know how to emotionally connect with them as you innovate the product. You need to be a student and learn from as many resources as possible, such as fashion magazines and runway shows on the Internet, and study aspirational brands as well as your direct competition. You need to be able to identify the trends and understand how to interpret them for your customer. In addition, many valuable insights come from observing what people are wearing everyday—whether

CHAPTER 13

LEARNING OBJECTIVES

LO1 Identify the branding options available to retailers.

LO2 Describe how retailers buy national brands.

LO3 List the issues retailers consider when developing and sourcing store-branded merchandise internationally.

LO4 Understand how retailers prepare for and conduct negotiations with their vendors.

LO5 Determine why retailers build strategic relationships with their vendors.

LO6 Indicate the legal, ethical, and social responsibility issues involved in buying merchandise.

it's on the streets or on TV/Internet, you can see trends change. My husband claims that when we are out at a restaurant, shopping, or basically anywhere, I spend more time looking at what everyone is wearing than talking with him. I like to think that my anthropology undergraduate degree has paid off as it reflects my interest in observing people, what they wear, and how they behave.

One of the most rewarding aspects of my job is seeing how the apparel we develop and sell can actually change the way our customers look and feel about themselves. You just know when someone feels good about how they look and what they are wearing as they have an undeniable confidence. Clothing has the ability to transform a person, and I love being a little part of making a difference in people's lives.

The preceding chapter outlined the merchandise management process and the steps in the process that buyers go through to determine what and how much merchandise to buy. After creating an assortment plan for the category, forecasting sales, and developing a plan outlining the flow of merchandise (how much merchandise needs to be ordered and when it needs to be delivered), the next step in the merchandise management process is to acquire the merchandise.

Buying merchandise isn't easy. At a grocery chain like Kroger, for instance, the soup category manager must decide on the mix between purchasing well-known national brands like Campbell or Progresso or developing store brands like Wholesome@Home. Whether offering national or store brands, the category manager negotiates many issues, such as prices, delivery dates, payment terms, and financial support for advertising and markdowns. The buying process for store brands is often more complex than for national brands because the store takes an active role in developing the products.

This chapter begins with a description of the different merchandise branding alternatives. Then we review the issues involved in buying national and store brands, including negotiating with vendors. Next, the development of strategic partnering relationships between retailers and their suppliers is discussed. The chapter concludes with an examination of the legal, ethical, and social responsibility issues surrounding the buying of merchandise.

BRAND ALTERNATIVES

LO1

Identify the branding options available to retailers.

REFACT

Private-label sales in grocery stores, drugstores, and discount department stores in the United States have been growing at more than 7 percent each year, such that they now amount to $86 billion annually, including sales by Walmart. In contrast, sales of national brands have been declining by approximately 3 percent each year.[1]

REFACT

The five most valuable world brands are Coca-Cola, Apple, IBM, Google, and Microsoft. The value of each of these brands is more than $50 billion.[2]

REFACT

Macy's was among the first department stores to pioneer the concept of private-label brands for fashion goods. In the 1890s, its "Macy's" and "Red Star" brands were the rage in New York.[3]

REFACT

In Europe, consumers buy store brands just as much as they do national brands; in many countries, they view the store brands as equally good, if not better in quality, as national brands. Store brands have a 30 percent market share on average.[4]

Retailers and their buyers face a strategic decision about the mix of national brands and private-label brands offered in a category. Three types of brands discussed in this section are national, store, and generic brands.

National Brands

National brands, also known as **manufacturer's brands,** are products designed, produced, and marketed by a vendor and sold to many different retailers. The vendor is responsible for developing the merchandise, producing it with consistent quality, and undertaking a marketing program to establish an appealing brand image. Examples of national brands are Tide detergent, Ralph Lauren polo shirts, and Hewlett-Packard printers.

In some cases, vendors use an **umbrella** or **family brand** associated with their company and a **subbrand** associated with the product, such as Kellogg's (family brand) Frosted Flakes (subbrand) or Ford (family brand) F-series trucks (subbrand). In other cases, vendors use individual brand names for different product categories and do not associate the brands with their companies. For example, most consumers probably don't know that Procter & Gamble makes Iams pet food, Crest toothpaste, Ivory soap, Vick's NyQuil, Hugo by Hugo Boss cologne, and Swiffer.

Some retailers organize their buying activities around national-brand vendors that cut across merchandise categories. Thus, buyers in department stores may be responsible for all cosmetic brands offered by Estée Lauder (Estée Lauder, Origins, Clinique, and Prescriptives) rather than for a product category (such as skin care or eye makeup). Managing merchandise by vendor rather than by category gives retailers more clout when dealing with vendors. However, as indicated in Chapter 12, there are inefficiencies associated with managing merchandise at the brand or vendor level rather than the category level.

Store Brands

Store brands, also called **private-label brands**, **house brands**, or **own brands**, are products developed by retailers. In many cases, retailers develop the design and specifications for their store-brand products, then contract with manufacturers to produce those products. In other cases, national-brand vendors work with a retailer to develop a special version of its standard merchandise offering to be sold exclusively by the retailer. In these cases, the national-brand vendor or manufacturer is responsible for the production of the merchandise.

In the past, sales of store brands were limited. National brands had the resources to develop customer loyalty toward their brands through aggressive marketing. It was difficult for smaller local and regional retailers to gain the economies of scale in design, production, and promotion that were needed to develop well-known brands. In recent years, though, as the size of retail firms has increased, more retailers have obtained sufficient scale economies to develop store brands and use this merchandise to establish a distinctive identity. Now, retailers offer a broad spectrum of store brands ranging from lower price/lower quality products, to those with superior quality and performance to national brands. Three examples of store brands are premium store brands, exclusive brands, and copycat brands.

Premium Store Brands   **Premium store brands** offer the consumer a product that is comparable to a manufacturer's brand quality, sometimes with modest price savings. Examples of premium store brands include Kroger's Private Selection, Tesco Finest (UK), "The Men's Collection" at Saks Fifth Avenue, and Bloomingdale's Aqua.[5] Safeway, a leading grocery chain, earns a substantial portion of its $45 billion in sales from its premium store brands. Not only is its main store brand, Safeway Select, recognized for its high quality, but it also stocks various other strong store brands, such as Signature Café (fresh food), Primo Taglio (premium cheese and cold cuts), Eating Right (healthy foods), Snack Artist (nuts and snacks), and Open Nature (natural foods).[6]

Safeway's customers increasingly are drawn to strong store brands.

Exclusive Brands   An **exclusive brand** is a brand that is developed by a national-brand vendor, often in conjunction with a retailer, and sold exclusively by the retailer. The simplest form of an exclusive brand occurs when a national-brand manufacturer assigns different model numbers and has different exterior features for the same basic product sold by different retailers, but the product is still marketed under the manufacturer's brand. For example, a Canon digital camera sold at Best Buy might have a different model number than a Canon digital camera with similar features available at Walmart. These exclusive models make it difficult for consumers to compare prices for virtually the same camera sold by different retailers.

A more sophisticated form of exclusive branding occurs when a manufacturer develops an exclusive product or product category for a retailer and markets it under a brand name that is exclusive to the retailer. For example, cosmetics powerhouse Estée Lauder sells two brands of cosmetics and skin care products—American Beauty and Flirt—exclusively at Kohl's. The products are priced between mass-market brands such as Cover Girl or Maybelline (sold mainly in drugstores, discount stores, and supermarkets) and Lauder's higher-end brands (sold primarily in more fashion-forward department stores such as Macy's and Dillard's). Levi Strauss has also developed its Signature brand jeans for sale at Walmart.

Exclusive branding with manufacturers or designers is effectively applied by HSN. Rather than creating entirely new private-label products, this retailer "invests in partners that help it develop products, such as a jewelry line with R. J. Graziano or Tori Spelling . . . handbags from Chi by Falchi, Serious Skin Care and Beauty from Jennifer Stallone."[8] Some of these designers, such as R. J. Graziano, sell separate lines in other outlets. Others, including Paula Abdul, are totally exclusive to HSN. In differentiating itself, whether in terms of an individual line of products or the entire collection associated with a designer, HSN promises customers that they can find items here that they find nowhere else.

The highest level of differentiation takes place when a retailer develops a store brand with its own unique identity. At Macy's, for example, customers do not often realize that the brands they purchase are its store brands. Thus, its American Rag brand has reached a significant market share in the young men's category, without ever communicating to this brand-conscious customer segment that the brand is produced by Macy's. In this case, it becomes difficult to distinguish Macy's brands, such as American Rag and INC, from national brands such as Levi's—except that consumers can find American Rag and INC only in Macy's stores.

Several well-known examples of exclusive store brands appear in Exhibit 13–1.

REFACT

Exclusive and limited distribution brands from Martha Stewart, Donald Trump, and Tommy Hilfiger account for approximately 43 percent of merchandise and 20 percent of sales at Macy's.[7]

Copycat Brands   **Copycat brands** imitate the manufacturer's brand in appearance and packaging, generally are perceived as lower-quality, and are offered at lower prices. Copycat brands abound in drugstores and grocery stores. For

EXHIBIT 13–1   Exclusive Store Brands

Retailer	Manufacturer/Designer	Product Category	Product Name
Kohl's	Estée Lauder	Cosmetics	American Beauty, Flirt, and Good Skin
Walmart	Mary Kate and Ashley Olsen	Apparel and accessories	Mary Kate and Ashley
HSN	Chris Lu, R. J. Graziano Tory Spelling, Paula Abdul, Iman, Serena Williams (jewelry); Chi by Falchi (handbags); Jennifer Stallone (skin care)	Jewelry, handbags, skin care	
Macy's	Martha Stewart	Soft home (sheets, towels)	Martha Stewart Collection
Macy's	Jones Apparel Group (Rachel Roy)	Apparel and accessories	Rachel by Rachel Roy
Macy's	Karl Lagerfeld	Apparel and accessories	Karl Lagerfeld Capsule Collection
McDonald's	Newman's Own Organic	Coffee	Newman's Own Organic
JCPenney	Ralph Lauren	Home goods, apparel, and accessories	American Living
Target	Gwen Stefani	Children's apparel	Harajuku Mini

instance, CVS or Walgreens brands are placed next to the manufacturer's brands and often look like them.

Generic Brands

In a sense, a generic brand isn't actually a brand at all and, as such, is neither a store nor a national brand. **Generic brands** are labeled with the name of the commodity and thus actually have no brand name distinguishing them. These products target a price-sensitive segment by offering a no-frills product at a discount price. They are used typically for prescription drugs and commodities like milk or eggs. Except for prescription drugs, where the use of generics has increased significantly over the last few decades, the sales of generics have declined significantly.

National Brands or Store Brands?

When determining the mix between national versus store brands, retailers consider the effect on their overall assortment, profitability, and flexibility.

Store Brands Enhance and Expand Assortments   Retailers examine their assortments to make sure they are providing what their customers want. They may introduce an innovative new store-branded product that isn't being offered by their national brand vendors or a product that can be offered at a better value—or both. Staples, for example, carries a large number of shredders, produced by many different manufacturers. But the company's market researchers found that people tend to sort through their mail in their kitchens. Thus, it produces, under its store brand, the MailMate, a small shredder that fits on a kitchen counter and is less expensive than the national-brand options. Thus, Staples filled a key gap in its assortment by producing an innovative, yet value-oriented product for families tired of stacks of junk mail but also worried about their privacy.

Many categories contain a market-leading national brand, such as Tide or All in the laundry detergent category. There may be opportunities for store brands in these categories, but the greatest potential appears in categories where there is no national-brand domination, such as with organic products in grocery stores. Whole Foods largely pioneered the concept in grocery retailing, but competitors such as Supervalu (which owns the Shaw's and Albertsons chains) have rapidly increased the number of products offered under its organic labels, such as Wild Harvest. At the wholesale club retailer BJ's, shoppers choose between the basic Elias store-brand frozen pizza and the premium organic store-brand Earth's Pride.

Many store brands today extend assortments by creating multiple price tiers, often referred to as low cost, value, and premium. The low-cost and value tiers have long been in place; the premium option is relatively newer. Such premium options offer consumers quality that is comparable to that of national brands, sometimes (but not always) at a modest price savings. Retailing View 13.1 examines how Kroger uses price tiers in its store brands to enhance and expand its assortments.

Profitability   Stocking national brands is a double-edged sword for retailers. Many customers have developed loyalty to specific national brands. They only patronize retailers selling these national-brand merchandise. This loyalty toward the national brand develops because customers know what to expect from the products and like them. They trust the brand to deliver consistent quality. Every bottle of Chanel No. 5 will have the same fragrance, and every pair of Levi's 501 jeans will have the same fit. In addition, the availability of national brands can affect customer's image of the retailer. For example, the fashion image of JCPenney increased when it added Liz Claiborne and Sephora to its assortment. If a retailer

REFACT

Store brands sales are worth almost $100 billion and account for more than 17 percent of total retail food and beverage sales.[9]

RETAILING VIEW   Kroger's Store Brands Have It All   13.1

Kroger runs its own store brands as if they were separate vendors, demanding high-quality standards and price competitiveness. The grocer even demands that its store brands earn 50 percent higher rankings than national brands in taste tests. In response, customers express their loyalty to the store brands, which means they are loyal to the store. The retailer can even brag that among the customers it cares most about, "99.5 percent of our loyal and our premium loyal customer segments are buying our corporate brands."

Yet Kroger also takes a broad perspective on its use of store brands. It acknowledges that "our stores would go away if we didn't have national brands. And our stores would go away if we didn't have our own brand. And there is a lot of upside for both of them."

Kroger's vision for its store brands is to build loyalty among customers, with strong store brands that are exclusive to the retailer. It pursues a multiple-tier store brand strategy to provide Kroger products to all customer segments. In the ice cream category, for instance, it offers the "Value" brand for its price-sensitive customers, with "adequate" packaging and quality. In the middle is the "Banner Brand," which is geared to the customer who wants ice cream comparable to Breyers. At the higher end is the "Private Selection" brand, which competes with Dove and Häagen Dazs. Developing products for all these customer segments means that Kroger closes any gaps in the ability of its current assortment to meet customers' needs.

Not all three tiers appear in every product category, though. For commodities with minimal differentiation (sugar is sugar), it limits the assortment to two store brands, Value and Banner—although it recently has added a specialty line of organic sugar, "Private Selection Organic." The flower selection in stores consists of only the "Private Selection" label. Figuring that flowers must

be alive and attractive if they are to sell, Kroger assumes it can target mainly upscale or aspirational customers willing to spend money simply to make their homes more beautiful. Similarly, homemade breads, pies, and cookies are branded by "Private Selection," whereas in the bread aisle, packaged bread carries the Banner and Value brand labels.

Coordinating store brands within and across categories is difficult. At Kroger, in the past, the category managers had control of the store brands within their category. For example, the category manager for canned soup bought national brands like Campbell's and Progresso and managed the store brands. The category manager would control the store brand's packaging, pricing, promotion, and even the brand's name. Because of this relative autonomy, Kroger had more than 40 store-brand names. Because there was little synergy between the brands, each brand had relatively low customer recognition. Through an extensive editing process, Kroger developed a structure that stresses a consistent vision for each brand. Customers have come to recognize and demand these store brands, resulting in synergies across categories. So, if a customer likes Kroger's "Private Selections" ice cream, they will likely be drawn to its "Private Selections" angus beef or artisan breads.

Source: Personal Communication with Linda Severin, Kroger.

DISCUSSION QUESTION

When you buy store brands, what is the primary reason: price, quality, or value?

does not offer the national brands, customers might view its assortment as lower in quality, with a resulting loss of profits.

On the other hand, the consistency of national brands means that it is easy to compare the retailer's prices for national brands. Thus, the same national brands offered by competing retailers can only be differentiated on price, which means retailers often have to offer significant discounts on some national brands to attract customers to their stores, further reducing their profitability.

While store brands offer an opportunity for retailers to differentiate their products and reduce price competition, the retailer incurs additional costs designing and marketing store brands, which reduces its profitability. In addition, the retailers assume the risk associated with uncertain sales. If, for instance, a product doesn't sell, the retailer can negotiate to either send the merchandise back to the vendor, have the vendor pay for the difference in lost gross margin if the merchandise has to be marked down, or sell the inventory to an off-price retailer. Retailers have no such cushions for their store brands. Because private-label products are specific to the store, there are few alternative options for getting rid of excess inventory.

The potential profitability for exclusive store brands is stronger, however. Customers can't compare prices for these products because they are, in fact, exclusive to one retailer. Because the retailers are less likely to compete on price when selling exclusive brands, the profitability potential for exclusive store brands is higher, and they are motivated to devote more resources toward selling them than they would for similar national brands.[11]

Flexibility   National brands can limit a retailer's flexibility. Vendors of strong brands can dictate how their products are displayed, advertised, and priced. Ralph Lauren, for instance, tells retailers exactly when and how its products should be advertised.

REFACT

Although on average, store brands cost 29 percent less than national versions, their prices are rising by 5.3 percent annually, whereas the industry average is only 1.9 percent. In some categories, store brands are the most expensive choices.[10]

BUYING NATIONAL-BRAND MERCHANDISE

LO2

Describe how retailers buy national brands.

In this section, we review how retail buyers of national brands meet with vendors, review the merchandise they have to offer at wholesale markets, and place orders.

Meeting National-Brand Vendors

A **wholesale market** for retail buyers is a concentration of vendors within a specific geographic location, perhaps even under one roof or over the Internet. Wholesale markets may be permanent wholesale market centers, annual trade shows, or trade fairs. Retailers also interact with vendors at their corporate headquarters. News about various tradeshows is readily available on the Trade Show News network (www.tsnn.com). Its database features more than 25,000 tradeshows and 100,000 registered users.[12]

Wholesale Market Centers   For many types of merchandise, particularly fashion apparel and accessories, buyers regularly visit with vendors in established market centers. Wholesale market centers have permanent vendor showrooms that retailers can visit throughout the year. At specific times during the year, these wholesale centers host **market weeks,** during which buyers make appointments to visit the various vendor showrooms. Vendors that do not have permanent showrooms at the market center lease temporary space to participate in market weeks.

Probably the world's most well-known wholesale market center for many merchandise categories is in New York City. The Fashion Center, also known as the Garment District, is located from Fifth to Ninth Avenues and from 34th to 41st Streets. Thousands of apparel buyers visit every year for five market weeks and numerous annual trade shows. The Garment District hosts thousands of show-rooms and factories.[13] There are also major wholesale market centers in London, Milan, Paris, and Tokyo. The United States also has various regional wholesale market centers—like the Dallas Market Center (positioned as the world's most complete wholesaler) or the Atlanta Merchandise Mart—that smaller retailers rely on to view and purchase merchandise.

Trade Shows   **Trade shows** provide another opportunity for buyers to see the latest products and styles and interact with vendors. Vendors display their merchandise in designated areas and have sales representatives, company executives, and sometime seven celebrities available to talk with buyers as they walk through the exhibit area. For example, consumer electronics buyers always make sure that they attend the annual International Consumer Electronics Show (CES) in Las Vegas, the world's largest trade show for consumer technology (www.cesweb.org). The most recent show was attended by 153,000 people (including more than 34,000 international attendees), such as vendors, developers, and suppliers of consumer technology hardware, content, technology delivery systems, and related products and services. Nearly 3,100 vendor exhibits take up 1.861 million net square feet of exhibit space, showcasing the very latest products and services. Vendors often use CES to introduce new products, including the first camcorder (1981), high-definition television (HDTV, 1998), and Internet protocol television (IPTV, 2005). More than 20,000 new products were launched at the 2012 conference alone.[15]

Trade shows are typically staged at convention centers not associated with wholesale market centers. McCormick Place in Chicago (the nation's largest convention complex, with more than 2.7 million square feet) hosts more than 65 meetings and trade shows a year, including the National Hardware Show and National Houseware Manufacturers Association International Exposition.[16]

Vendors from outside the United States and store-brand manufacturers attend trade shows to learn about the market and pick up on trend information. Some store-brand manufacturers attend and display at trade shows, but most participants are national-brand vendors.

REFACT

Wholesale transactions amounting to more than $8 billion are conducted within the Dallas Market Center complex annually.[14]

The International Consumer Electronics Show (CES) in Las Vegas is the world's largest trade show for consumer technology.

National-Brand Buying Process

When attending market weeks or trade shows, buyers and their supervisors typically make a series of appointments with key vendors. During these meetings, the buyers discuss the performance of the vendor's merchandise during the previous season, review the vendor's offerings for the coming season, and possibly place orders for the coming season. These meetings take place in conference rooms in the vendors' showrooms at wholesale market centers. During trade shows, these meetings typically are less formal. The meetings during market weeks offer an opportunity for an in-depth discussion, whereas trade shows provide the opportunity for buyers to see a broader array of merchandise in one location and gauge reactions to the merchandise by observing the level of activity in the vendor's display area.

Often, buyers do not negotiate with vendors or place orders during the market week or trade show. They typically want to see what merchandise and prices are available from all the potential vendors before deciding what items to buy. So, after attending a market week or trade show, buyers return to their offices, review requested samples of merchandise sent to them by vendors, meet with their supervisors to review the available merchandise, make decisions about which items are most attractive, and then negotiate with the vendors before placing an order. The issues involved in negotiating the purchase of national-brand merchandise are discussed later in this chapter.

DEVELOPING AND SOURCING STORE-BRAND MERCHANDISE

LO3

List the issues retailers consider when developing and sourcing store-branded merchandise internationally.

Retailers use a variety of different processes to develop and buy store brands.

Developing Store Brands

Larger retailers that offer a significant amount of store-brand merchandise, such as J.Crew, Macy's, The Gap, and American Eagle Outfitters, have large divisions with people devoted to the development of their store-brand merchandise. Employees in these divisions specialize in identifying trends, designing and specifying products, selecting manufacturers to make the products, maintaining a worldwide staff to monitor the conditions in which the products are made, and managing facilities to test the quality of the manufactured products. For example, MAST Global Fashion lives up to its name by maintaining joint ventures and manufacturing operations in dozens of countries, where it fulfills contracts for manufacturing, importing, and distributing various products. In addition to being the major store-brand supplier of Limited Brands (Victoria's Secret and Bath & Body Works), it provides store-brand merchandise for Express, Chico's, and Betsey Johnson. However, most retailers do not own and operate or have ownership stakes in manufacturing facilities.[17]

Smaller retail chains can offer store brands without making a significant investment in the supporting infrastructure. Smaller retailers often ask national-brand or store-brand suppliers to make minor changes to products they offer and then provide the merchandise with the store's brand name or a special label copyrighted by the national brand. Alternatively, store-brand manufacturers can sell to them from a predetermined stock selection. Hollander thus makes more than 30 million pillows, for companies such as Laura Ashley, Karen Neuberger, and Simmons. It also makes store-brand versions for various retailers (e.g., Walmart, JCPenney).[18] Retailing View 13.2 describes how the Chinese government has helped create specialized apparel cities with economies of scale so great that they dominate apparel manufacturing in the world.

Sourcing Store-Brand Merchandise

Once the decision has been made about which and how much store-brand merchandise will be acquired, the designers develop a complete specification plan and work with the sourcing department to find a manufacturer for the merchandise. For example, JCPenney has sourcing and quality assurance offices in 19 countries. These offices take the specification developed by the designer, negotiate a contract to produce the item with manufacturers, and monitor the production

RETAILING VIEW Chinese Government Creates Specialized Apparel Cities   **13.2**

As a result of government and private investment, China has become the leading manufacturer of apparel.

In the 1970s, the residents of Datang, China, grew rice; for extra income, they also stitched socks to sell to travelers passing through. Noting these tendencies, China's central government designated Datang a sock-production village. Today, it has been informally renamed "Sock City" because it is the source of approximately one-third of the world's supply, making two pairs for every person in the world every year.

Other specialized production sites focus on everything from underwear to neckties to sweaters to children's clothing. As a result, Chinese development zones achieve impressive economies of scale and other competitive benefits that enable them to outperform decentralized manufacturing firms in other countries. Industrial parks planned by the state enjoy tax breaks, as well as partnerships with logistics providers and other firms that provide the necessary input to support their own output. Furthermore, the rapid development of China's infrastructure has helped these firms move their

products into global markets quickly and efficiently. In turn, with the support of the central government, these private companies host massive dormitory complexes for their workers, providing shelter, food, basic necessities, and health care.

Sources: Tania Branigan, "Sock City's Decline May Reveal an Unravelling in China's Economy," *The Observer*, September 8, 2012; "Datang Socks It to the Financial Crisis," *Xie Frang (China Daily)*, March 4, 2009; and Geoffrey Colvin, "Saving America's Socks—but Killing Free Trade," *Fortune*, August 22, 2005, p. 38.

DISCUSSION QUESTION

From a retail buyer's perspective, what are the opportunities and threats associated with buying from vendors located in one of China's specialized production sites?

The rise of the value of the U.S. dollar against the euro and other important world currencies in recent years has made imports to the United States less expensive and exports from the United States more expensive.

process.[19] As barriers to international trade continue to fall, retailers can consider more sources for merchandise, anywhere in the world. In this section, we examine the cost factors and managerial issues that influence global sourcing.

Costs Associated with Global Sourcing Decisions

Retailers use production facilities located in developing economies for much of their private-label merchandise because of the very low labor costs in these countries. To counterbalance the lower acquisition costs, however, there are other expenses that can increase the costs of sourcing private-label merchandise from other countries. These costs include the relative value of foreign currencies, tariffs, longer lead times, and increased transportation costs.[20]

Retailers can hedge against short-term foreign currency fluctuations by buying contracts that lock the retailer into a set price, regardless of how the currency fluctuates. But in the longer term, the relative value of foreign currencies can have a strong influence on the cost of imported merchandise. For example, if the Indian rupee has a sustained a significant increase relative to the U.S. dollar, the cost of store-brand merchandise produced in India and imported for sale into the United States will increase. **Tariffs,** also known as **duties,** are taxes collected by a government on imports. Import tariffs have been used to shield domestic manufacturers from foreign competition. Inventory turnover also is likely to be lower when purchasing from foreign suppliers. Because lead times are longer and more uncertain, retailers using foreign sources must maintain larger inventories to ensure that the merchandise is available when the customer wants it. Larger inventories mean larger inventory carrying costs. Finally, transportation costs are higher when merchandise is produced in foreign countries.

Managerial Issues Associated with Global Sourcing Decisions

Whereas the cost factors associated with global sourcing are easy to quantify, some more subjective issues include quality control, time to market, and social/political risks. When sourcing globally, it is harder to maintain consistent quality standards than it is when sourcing domestically. Quality control problems can cause delays in shipment and adversely affect a retailer's image.

The collaborative supply chain management approaches described in Chapter 10 are more difficult to implement when sourcing globally. Collaborative systems are based on short and consistent lead times. Vendors provide frequent deliveries of smaller quantities. For a collaborative system to work properly, there must be a strong alliance between the vendor and the retailer that is based on trust and shared information. These activities are more difficult to perform globally than domestically.

Another issue related to global sourcing is the problem of policing potential violations of human rights and child labor laws. Many retailers have had to publicly defend themselves against allegations of human rights, child labor, or other abuses involving the factories and countries in which their goods are made. Due to the efforts of U.S. retailers and nonprofit organizations, fewer imported goods are produced in sweatshop conditions today. Some retailers are quite proactive in enforcing the labor practices of their suppliers. Limited Brands, for instance, was one of the first U.S. apparel manufacturers to develop and implement policies requiring that vendors and their subcontractors and suppliers observe core labor standards as a condition of doing business. Among other things, this requirement ensures that each supplier pays minimum wages and benefits; limits overtime to local industry standards; does not use prisoners, forced labor, or child labor; and provides a healthy and safe environment.[21] Other companies that rely on firms in low-wage countries for their production also pursue self-policing to avoid unpleasant surprises and reputational risks. Retailing View 13.3 examines how Walmart is pushing its vendors to be environmentally responsible.

Resident Buying Offices   Many retailers purchasing private-label merchandise use **resident buying offices,** which are organizations located in major market centers that provide services to help retailers buy merchandise. As retailers have become larger and more sophisticated, these third-party, independent resident buying offices have become less important. Now, many large retailers have their own buying offices in other countries.

RETAILING VIEW   It Isn't Easy to Sell to Walmart   13.3

Walmart is known for its low prices—and for driving its vendors to tears to get them. Now it is pressuring its vendors to also supply it with environmentally friendly merchandise, with labels to prove it. In the future, merchandise sold at Walmart will have the environmental equivalent of nutritional labels, providing information on the product's carbon footprint, the amount of water and air pollution used to produce it, and other environmental issues. To measure how a vendor's products are doing, Walmart has developed a sustainability index that simultaneously takes several issues into consideration.

REFACT

Walmart buys from more than 100,000 vendors, from all over the globe.[22]

Walmart has laid out three goals that it aspires to achieve: to use 100 percent renewable energy, to reduce its waste production to zero, and to market products that will sustain both customers and the environment. These are very lofty aspirations that have resulted in multiple, concrete goals.

Walmart is also requiring that its top 200 factories become 20 percent more energy efficient by 2012, a feat that many experts believe may be impossible, even with Walmart's help. Initial results are promising, though. For example, Jiangsu Redbud Dyeing Technology in China has cut its coal consumption by one-tenth and is attempting to cut its toxic emissions to zero.

Walmart hasn't always been touted as such a good corporate citizen, though. In the 1990s, it came to light that workers at some factories producing clothing for Walmart were subjected to inhumane conditions. More recently, two government organizations accused Walmart of buying from 15 factories that engage in abuse and labor violations, including child labor, 19-hour shifts, and below-subsistence wages. Walmart and other companies have also been accused of dumping hazardous waste in Oklahoma City.

Some wonder why Walmart is attempting to position itself as the retail industry's sustainability leader. Certainly, initiatives that show that it is a good corporate citizen enhance its image. But Walmart expects that these initiatives will be good for business as well. Its customers, especially those born between 1980 and 2000, are increasingly concerned about how the products they use affect the environment and the people who produce them. Also, Walmart believes that many of these initiatives will help streamline supply chain processes and, therefore, provide additional financial benefits to its suppliers and customers.

Laura Phillips, Walmart's Senior Vice President for Global Sustainability, attended the 2017 United Nations Climate Change Conference in Bonn, Germany.

Sources: "Beyond 50 Years: Building a Sustainable Future," Walmart 2012 Global Responsibility Report; http://sustainabilitycases.kenexcloud.org/about; http://corporate.walmart.com/global-responsibility/environment-sustainability/sustainability-index; Stephanie Rosenbloom, "At Wal-Mart, Labeling to Reflect Green Intent," *The New York Times,* July 16, 2009; Stephanie Rosenbloom, "Wal-Mart to Toughen Standards," *The New York Times,* October 22, 2008; and Adam Aston, "Wal-Mart: Making Its Suppliers Go Green," *BusinessWeek,* May 18, 2009.

DISCUSSION QUESTION

Is Walmart trying to be a good corporate citizen with its sustainability initiatives, or is it doing these things just because it is good business?

To illustrate how buying offices operate, consider how David Smith of Pockets Men's Store in Dallas uses his when he goes to market in Milan. Smith meets with market representative Alain Bordat of the Doneger Group. Bordat, an English-speaking Italian, knows Smith's store and his upscale customers, so before Smith's visit, he sets up appointments with Italian vendors that he believes will fit Pockets' image.

When Smith is in Italy, Bordat accompanies him to the appointments and acts as a translator, negotiator, and accountant. Bordat informs Smith of the cost of importing the merchandise into the United States, taking into account duty, freight, insurance, processing costs, and so forth.

Once the orders are placed, Bordat writes the contracts and follows up on delivery and quality control. The Doneger Group also acts as a home base for buyers like Smith, providing office space and services, travel advisers, and emergency aid. Bordat and his association continue to keep Smith abreast of what's happening on the Italian fashion scene through reports and constant communication. Without the help of a resident buying office, it would be difficult, if not impossible, for Smith to access the Italian wholesale market.

Reverse Auctions   Rather than negotiating with a specific manufacturer to produce the merchandise, some retailers use reverse auctions to get quality private-label merchandise at low prices.[23] In traditional auctions like those conducted on eBay, there is one seller and many buyers. Auctions conducted by retailer buyers of private-label merchandise are called **reverse auctions** because there is one buyer (the retailer) and many potential sellers (the manufacturing firms). In a reverse auction, the retail buyer provides a specification for what it wants to a group of potential vendors. The competing vendors then bid on the price at which they are willing to sell until the auction is over. However, the retailer is not required to place an order with the lowest bidder. The retailer can choose to place an order at the offered price from whichever vendor the retailer feels will provide the merchandise in a timely manner and with the specified quality.

The most common use of reverse auctions is to buy the products and services used in retail operations rather than merchandise for resale. Some operating materials that are frequently bought through reverse auctions are store carpeting, fixtures, and supplies. However, reverse auctions also are being used by several retailers to procure store-brand merchandise, such as commodities and seasonal merchandise like lawn furniture.

Reverse auctions are not popular with vendors. Few vendors want to be anonymous contestants in bidding wars where price alone, not service or quality, seems to be the sole basis for winning the business. Strategic relationships are also difficult to nurture when the primary interactions with vendors are through electronic auctions.

NEGOTIATING WITH VENDORS

LO4

Understand how retailers prepare for and conduct negotiations with their vendors.

When buying national brands or sourcing private-label merchandise, buyers and firm employees responsible for sourcing typically enter into negotiations with suppliers. To understand how buyers negotiate with vendors, consider a hypothetical situation in which Carolyn Swigler, women's jeans buyer at Bloomingdale's, is preparing to meet with Dario Carvel, the salesperson from Juicy Couture, in his office in New York City. Swigler, after reviewing the merchandise during the women's wear market week in New York, is ready to buy Juicy Couture's spring line, but she has some merchandising problems that have yet to be resolved from last season.

Knowledge Is Power

The more Carolyn Swigler knows about her situation and Juicy Couture's, as well as the trends in the marketplace, the more effective she will be during the negotiations. First, Swigler assesses the relationship she has with the vendor. Although Swigler and Carvel have met only a few times in the past, their companies have had a long, profitable relationship. A sense of trust and mutual respect has been established, which Swigler feels will lead to a productive meeting.

Although Juicy Couture jeans have been profitable for Bloomingdale's in the past, three styles sold poorly last season. Swigler plans to ask Carvel to let her return some merchandise. Swigler knows from past experience that Juicy Couture normally doesn't allow merchandise to be returned but does provide **markdown money**—funds vendors give retailers to cover lost gross margin dollars due to the markdowns needed to sell unpopular merchandise.

Vendors and their representatives are excellent sources of market information. They generally know what is and isn't selling. Providing good, timely information about the market is an indispensable and inexpensive marketing research tool. So Swigler plans to spend at least part of the meeting talking to Carvel about market trends.

Just as Carvel can provide market information to Swigler, she can provide information to him. For example, on one of her buying trips to Japan, she found jeans in a great new wash made by a small Japanese firm on old selvage looms. She bought a pair and gave them to Carvel, who passed it along to Juicy Couture's designers. They used the jeans to develop a new wash that was a big success.

When negotiating with a vendor, the more knowledge that is available about the vendor, the market, and the products, the more successful the negotiation will be.

Swigler also knows that Carvel will want her to buy some of the newest and most avant-garde designs in Juicy Couture's spring product line. Carvel knows that many U.S. buyers go to market in New York and that most stop at Bloomingdale's to see what's new, what's selling, and how it's displayed. Thus, Carvel wants to make sure that Juicy Couture is well represented at Bloomingdale's.

Negotiation Issues

In addition to taking care of last season's leftover merchandise, Swigler is prepared to discuss six issues during the upcoming meeting: (1) prices and gross margin, (2) additional markup opportunities, (3) terms of purchase, (4) exclusivity, (5) advertising allowances, and (6) transportation.

Price and Gross Margin   Of course, Swigler wants to buy the merchandise at a low price so that she will have a high gross margin. In contrast, Carvel wants to sell the jeans at a higher price because he is concerned about Juicy Couture's own margins. Two factors that affect the price and gross margin are margin guarantees and slotting allowances.

Margin Guarantees by Providing Markdown Money   Swigler, like most buyers, has a gross margin goal for each merchandise category that is quantified in her merchandise budget plans (Chapter Appendix 12A). The wholesale price Swigler negotiates for the Juicy Couture merchandise might enable her to achieve her gross margin goal. However, if the merchandise does not sell as expected, Swigler might have to put the items on sale, and she will not make her margin goal. Faced with this uncertainty, Swigler, and other buyers, may seek a commitment from Juicy Couture to "guarantee" that she will realize her gross margin goal on marked-down merchandise by providing Bloomingdale's with markdown money to make up the lost margin due to the markdown.

Carvel, like many vendors, might be willing to provide this gross margin guarantee. However, Carvel is concerned that Swigler might not aggressively promote Juicy Couture's merchandise if she knows that her gross margin is guaranteed. Thus, Carvel will offer the guarantee only in exchange for a commitment from Swigler that she will feature Juicy Couture merchandise in the store and advertise the product line.

Slotting Fees   In addition to negotiating the wholesale price, supermarket buyers often negotiate slotting fees. **Slotting fees,** or **slotting allowances,** are charges imposed by a retailer to stock a new item. When a vendor agrees to pay that fee, the retailer will stock the product for a period of time, assess its sales and margin, and, if it is successful, continue to offer the product after the trial period. For example, when Kraft wants to introduce a new product, supermarket chains might charge between $1 million and $2 million for a national rollout to stock the product. The fee varies, depending on the nature of the product and the relative power of the retailer. Products with low brand loyalty pay the highest slotting allowances. Likewise, large supermarket chains can demand higher slotting allowances than can small, independent retailers.

Vendors may view slotting allowances as extortion, and small vendors believe these fees preclude their access to retail stores. However, retailers and most economists argue that slotting allowances are a useful method for retailers to determine which new products merit inclusion in their assortment. The vendor has more information than the retailer about the quality of its new product. Thus, the slotting fee is a method for getting the vendor to reveal this private information. If the new product is good, the vendor will be willing to pay the fee because the vendor knows that the product will sell and generate adequate margins during the trial period. However, a vendor promoting a poor product will be reluctant to pay the fee.[24]

Additional Markup Opportunities   At times in the past, Juicy Couture has offered Swigler discounted prices to take excess merchandise. The excessive merchandise arises from order cancellations, returned merchandise from other retailers, or simply an overly optimistic sales forecast. Although Swigler can realize higher-than-normal gross margins on this merchandise or put the merchandise on sale and pass the savings on to customers, Bloomingdale's has to preserve its image as a fashion leader, and thus Swigler is not very interested in any excess inventory that Juicy Couture has to offer.

Terms of Purchase   Swigler would like to negotiate for a long period in which to pay for merchandise. A long payment period improves Bloomingdale's cash flow, lowers its liabilities (accounts payable), and can reduce its interest expense if it is borrowing money from financial institutions to pay for its inventory. But Juicy Couture also has its own financial objectives it wants to accomplish and thus would like to be paid soon after it delivers the merchandise.

Exclusivity   Retailers often negotiate with vendors for an exclusive arrangement so that no other retailer can sell the same item or brand. Through an exclusive arrangement, the retailer can differentiate itself from competitors and realize higher margins due to reduced price competition. In some cases, vendors also benefit by making sure that the image of retailers selling their merchandise is consistent with their brand image. For example, Prada might want to give exclusive rights for its apparel to only one store in a major market, such as Neiman Marcus. In addition, an exclusive arrangement offers a monopoly to the retailer and thus a strong incentive to promote the item.

In fashion merchandise categories, being the first retailer in a market to carry certain products helps that retailer hold a fashion-leader image and achieve a differential advantage. Swigler wants her shipment of the new spring line to arrive as early in the season as possible and would like to have some jeans styles and washes that won't be sold to competing retailers. In contrast, Juicy Couture wants to have its products sold by many different retailers to maximize its sales.

Advertising Allowances   Retailers often share the cost of advertising through a cooperative arrangement with vendors known as **co-op (cooperative) advertising**—a program undertaken by a vendor in which the vendor agrees to pay for all or part of a pricing promotion. As a fashion leader, Bloomingdale's advertises heavily. Swigler would like Juicy Couture to support an advertising program with a generous advertising allowance.

Transportation   Transportation costs can be substantial, though this concern is less prominent for Juicy Couture jeans because its merchandise has a high unit price and low weight. Nonetheless, the question of who pays to ship merchandise from the vendor to the retailer remains a significant negotiating point.

Now that some of the issues involved in the negotiation between Juicy Couture and Bloomingdale's are on the table, the next section presents some tips for effective negotiations.

Tips for Effective Negotiating[25]

Have at Least as Many Negotiators as the Vendor   Retailers have a psychological advantage at the negotiating table if the vendor is outnumbered. At the very least, retailers want the negotiating teams to be the same size. Swigler plans to invite her divisional merchandise manager (DMM) to the discussion if Carvel comes with his sales manager.

Choose a Good Place to Negotiate   Swigler may have an advantage in the upcoming meeting because it will be in her office. She'll have ready access to information, plus secretarial and supervisory assistance. From a psychological perspective, people generally feel more comfortable and confident in familiar surroundings. However, Swigler also might get more out of the negotiation if Carvel feels comfortable. In the end, selecting the location for a negotiation is an important decision.

In a negotiation, have at least as many negotiators as the vendor.

Be Aware of Real Deadlines Swigler recognizes that Carvel must go back to his office with an order in hand because he has a quota to meet by the end of the month. She also knows that she must get markdown money or permission to return the unsold jeans by the end of the week or she won't have sufficient open-to-buy funds to cover the orders she wishes to place. Recognizing these deadlines will help Swigler come to closure quickly in the upcoming negotiation.

Separate the People from the Problem Suppose Swigler starts the meeting with, "Dario, you know we've been friends for a long time. I have a personal favor to ask. Would you mind taking back $10,000 in shirts?" This personal plea puts Carvel in an uncomfortable situation. Swigler's personal relationship with Carvel isn't the issue here and shouldn't become part of the negotiation. An equally detrimental scenario would be for Swigler to say, "Dario, your line is terrible. I can hardly give the stuff away. I want you to take back $10,000 in jeans. After all, you're dealing with Bloomingdale's. If you don't take this junk back, you can forget about ever doing business with us again." Threats usually don't work in negotiations. They put the other party on the defensive. Threats may actually cause negotiations to break down, in which case no one wins.

Insist on Objective Information The best way to separate the people from the business issues is to rely on objective information. Swigler must know exactly how many jeans need to be returned to Juicy Couture or how much markdown money is necessary to maintain her gross margin. If Carvel argues from an emotional perspective, Swigler will stick to the numbers. For instance, suppose that after Swigler presents her position, Carvel says that he'll get into trouble if he takes back the merchandise or provides markdown money. With the knowledge that Juicy Couture has provided relief in similar situations in the past, Swigler should ask what Juicy Couture's policy is regarding customer overstock problems. She should also show Carvel a summary of Bloomingdale's buying activity with Juicy Couture over the past few seasons. Using this approach, Swigler forces Carvel to acknowledge that providing assistance in this overstock situation—especially if it has been done in the past—is a small price to pay for a long-term profitable relationship.

Invent Options for Mutual Gain Inventing multiple options is part of the planning process, but knowing when and how much to give, or give up, requires quick thinking at the bargaining table, and, as such, should be decided in advance, whenever possible. Consider Swigler's overstock problem. Her objective is to get the merchandise out of her inventory without significantly hurting her gross margin. Carvel's objective is to maintain a healthy, yet profitable, relationship with Bloomingdale's. Thus, Swigler must invent options that could satisfy both parties, such as offering to buy some of Juicy Couture's most avant-garde jeans in return for markdown money for her excess inventory.

Let Them Do the Talking There's a natural tendency for one person to continue to talk if the other person involved in the conversation doesn't respond. If used properly, this phenomenon can work to the negotiator's advantage. Suppose Swigler asks Carvel for special financial support for Bloomingdale's Christmas catalog. Carvel begins with a qualified no and cites all the reasons he can't cooperate. But Swigler doesn't say a word. Although Carvel appears nervous, he continues to talk. Eventually, he comes around to a yes. In negotiations, those who break the silence first lose.

Know How Far to Go There's a fine line between negotiating too hard and walking away from the table without an agreement. If Swigler negotiates too aggressively for the markdown money, better terms of purchase, and a strong advertising allowance, the management of Juicy Couture may decide that other retailers are more worthy of early deliveries and the best styles. Carvel may not be afraid to say no if Swigler pushes him beyond a legal, ethical, profitable relationship.

Don't Burn Bridges   Even if Swigler gets few additional concessions from Carvel, she shouldn't be abusive or resort to threats. Bloomingdale's may not want to stop doing business with Juicy Couture on the basis of this one encounter. From a personal perspective, the world of retailing is relatively small. Swigler and Carvel may meet at the negotiating table again, possibly both working for different companies. Neither can afford to be known in the trade as unfair, rude, or worse.

Don't Assume   Many issues are raised and resolved in any negotiating session. To be certain there are no misunderstandings, participants should orally review the outcomes at the end of the session. Swigler and Carvel should both summarize the session in writing as soon as possible after the meeting.

STRATEGIC RELATIONSHIPS

Chapter 5 emphasized that maintaining strong vendor relationships is an important way to develop a sustainable competitive advantage. Chapters 10 and 12 discussed some of the ways partnering relationships can improve information exchange, planning, and the management of supply chains. For example, a vendor-managed inventory system cannot operate effectively without the vendor and retailer making a commitment to work together and invest in the relationship.[26] In this section, we examine how retailers develop strategic relationships and the characteristics of successful long-term relationships.

LO5
Determine why retailers build strategic relationships with their vendors.

Defining Strategic Relationships

Traditionally, relationships between retailers and vendors have focused on haggling over how to split up a profit pie.[27] The relationships were basically win–lose encounters because when one party got a larger portion of the pie, the other party got a smaller portion. Both parties were interested exclusively in their own profits and unconcerned about the other party's welfare. These relationships continue to be common, especially when the products being bought are commodities and have limited impact on the retailers' performance. In these situations, there is no benefit to the retailer from entering into a strategic relationship.

A **strategic relationship,** also called a **partnering relationship,** emerges when a retailer and vendor are committed to maintaining the relationship over the long term and investing in opportunities that are mutually beneficial to both parties. In this relationship, it is important for the partners to take risks to expand the profit pie to give the relationship a strategic advantage over other companies. In addition, the parties have a long-term perspective: They are willing to make short-term sacrifices because they know that they will get their fair share in the long run.[28]

Strategic relationships are win–win relationships. Both parties benefit because the size of the profit pie increases. Both the retailer and the vendor increase their sales and profits, because the parties in strategic relationships work together to develop and exploit joint opportunities. They depend on and trust each other heavily. They share goals and agree on how to accomplish those goals, and they thus reduce the risks of investing in the relationship and sharing confidential information. Even as the power in supply chains has shifted from large manufacturers to large retailers such as Walmart and Target, the relationships are generally not adversarial. Instead, these supply chain partners share point-of-sale data and collaborate and cooperate on issues such as which items to buy, how much, and when. As a result of these collaborative efforts, financial performance throughout the supply chain has been enhanced.[29]

For example, when Karl Lagerfeld, designer of brands such as Chanel and Fendi, embarked on an exclusive branding program with Macy's, he worked together with its merchandising team to determine their customers' needs, likes, and dislikes.[30] Then they jointly developed an assortment and pricing strategy that has proved to be much more successful than would have been possible if the two sides had worked separately and just negotiated a quantity and price. To sustain their successful momentum, they share trends in the market and agree to respond quickly when a change occurs or when a product should be produced in a short time.

A strategic relationship is like a marriage. When businesses enter strategic relationships, they're wedded to their partners for better or worse. For example, Spain-based fast-fashion retailer Zara manufactures about 40 percent of its finished garments with the help of about 450 independently owned workshops located near the corporate headquarters that sew pre-cut fabric into finished garments.[31] Most of these relatively small workshops have had long-term relationships with Zara. Zara provides them with technology, logistics, and financial support, as well as other types of assistance. In return, the workshops support Zara's mission of being able to quickly provide women and men in 73 countries with relatively inexpensive fashion apparel. Like any supplier, these small workshops sometimes miss a deadline or make a mistake on a garment. But as in a marriage, Zara doesn't dump them and move on to someone else. It works with them to make things work. Another company that works closely with its vendors, Zappos, is discussed in Retailing View 13.4.

REFACT

Bentonville, Arkansas, the corporate headquarters for Walmart, has a population of 36,000. Hundreds of suppliers have offices in northwest Arkansas. Vast numbers of them have even opened offices in Bentonville, otherwise known as Vendorville, including Microsoft, Oracle, Rubbermaid, Disney, Dreamworks, and Procter & Gamble.[32]

Building Partnering Relationships

Although not all retailer–vendor relationships should or do become strategic partnerships, the development of strategic partnerships tends to go through a series of phases characterized by increasing levels of involvement: (1) awareness, (2) exploration, (3) expansion, and (4) commitment.

Awareness   In the awareness stage, no transactions have taken place. This phase might begin with the buyer seeing some interesting merchandise at a retail market or an ad in a trade magazine. The reputation and image of the vendor can play an important role in determining if the buyer moves to the next stage.

Exploration   During the exploration phase, the buyer and vendor begin to explore the potential benefits and costs of a partnership. At this point, the buyer may make a small purchase and try to test the demand for the merchandise in several stores. In addition, the buyer will get information about how easy it is to work with the vendor.

Expansion   Eventually, the buyer has collected enough information about the vendor to consider developing a longer-term relationship. The buyer and the vendor determine if there is the potential for a win–win relationship. They begin to work on joint promotional programs, and the amount of merchandise sold increases.

Commitment   If both parties continue to find the relationship mutually beneficial, it moves to the commitment stage and becomes a strategic relationship. The buyer and vendor then make significant investments in the relationship and develop a long-term perspective toward it.

It is difficult for retailer–vendor relationships to be as committed as some supplier–manufacturer relationships. Manufacturers can enter into monogamous (sole-source) relationships with other manufacturers. However, an important function of retailers is to provide an assortment of merchandise for

RETAILING VIEW   Zappos Values Relationships with Its Vendors, the Merchandise Experts   **13.4**

High efficiency light-emitting diode (LED) lights are featured at Home Depot. Most screw-in incandescent light bulbs have been phased out because they use too much energy.

Founded in 1999, Zappos is best known as an online shoe retailer. Through its emphasis on customer service, it has grown into the largest shoe retailer in the world. Acquired by Amazon in July 2009, Zappos was recently valued at more than $1.6 billion. It may sell shoes, clothing, and more, but the "secret sauce" that has led to its blockbuster success has less to do with the products Zappos sells and more to do with the relationships it builds—with customers, employees, and every supplier with which it deals. Its customer service and resulting customer satisfaction are legendary. For employees, its emphasis on relationships is evidenced by Zappos' consistent rating as one of the best companies to work for, buoyed by its offerings of benefits such as onsite "laughter yoga" classes and opportunities for every employee to pitch new business ideas.

But with a portfolio of more 50 brands, strong vendor relations may be even more key to the success of Zappos. Vendors feel valued, respected, and appreciated in all aspects of the business relationship. When vendors come to visit, a Zappos representative picks them up at the airport using the corporate shuttle and snacks and drinks await them when they arrive. New vendors receive a tour of the facilities. If a vendor contacts Zappos, the company either calls back the same day or responds to e-mails within a few hours. When they dine out together, Zappos always picks up the bill. Its signals of appreciation don't stop with one-on-one visits; Zappos hosts appreciation events for its vendors year-round. The last Friday of every month, Zappos hosts a golf tournament for vendors, and once a year, it hosts a lavish vendor appreciation party.

Cleary, Zappos is interested in strong vendor relationships. But what exactly does the company get out of it?

What's the return on its investment? Normally, retailers seek to beat vendors in negotiations, to get the lowest prices and best terms. Zappos believes, instead, that strong relationships lead to better partnerships. Instead of adversarial negotiations, it embraces transparency. Vendors gain access to information on Zappos' inventory, sales, and profitability. With these collaborative efforts, it seeks to encourage shared risks and rewards, and thus shared goals. With shared goals also come greater accountability and, at the end of the day, more committed vendors.

In a time when most retailers are trying to reduce their costs by cutting back on employee and vendor benefits, Zappos has taken the opposite strategy. As a top online retailer, its emphasis on building strong relationships with its vendors has resulted in a unique competitive advantage. Instead of buyers needing to wrestle with more than 50 vendors, Zappos has converted them into advocates for the company.

Sources: Tom Ryan, "Zappos Makes Nice with Vendors," *Retail Wire*, March 2, 2011; Tony Hisch, "A Lesson from Zappos: Follow the Golden Rule," *HBR Blog*, June 4, 2010; "About Us," Zappos, about.zappos.com; and Aida Ahmed, "Zappos Ranks No. 11 on List of Best Companies to Work For," *VegasInc*, January 19, 2012.

DISCUSSION QUESTIONS

Why do Zappos' vendors love them? Why are these relationships good for Zappos?

their customers. Thus, they must always deal with multiple, sometimes competing suppliers.

Regardless of which partner-building phase a retailer is in with a supplier, the retailer is constantly involved in the give-and-take process of negotiations. The next section looks at some of the legal and ethical issues that arise when buying merchandise.

Maintaining Strategic Relationships

The four foundations of successful strategic relationships are: (1) mutual trust, (2) common goals, (3) open communication, and (4) credible commitments.

Mutual Trust   The glue in a strategic relationship is trust. **Trust** is a belief that a partner is honest (reliable and stands by its word) and benevolent (concerned about the other party's welfare).[33] When vendors and buyers trust each other, they are more willing to share relevant ideas, clarify goals and problems, and communicate efficiently. Information shared between the parties becomes increasingly comprehensive, accurate, and timely. There is less need for the vendor and buyer to constantly monitor and check up on each other's actions, because each believes the other will not take advantage, even when given the opportunity.[34] If Walmart's sustainability initiatives described previously in Retailing View 13.3 are to be achieved, it is important for Walmart to trust its vendors, and vice versa.

Common Goals   Vendors and buyers must have common goals for a successful relationship to develop.[35] Shared goals give both members of the relationship an incentive to pool their strengths and abilities and exploit potential opportunities between them. They also create an assurance that the other partner will not do anything to hinder goal achievement within the relationship.

For example, Walmart and its vendors have recognized that it was in their common interest to develop and sell products that have a positive impact on the environment. Walmart cannot demand that its vendors take on sustainability programs that are so expensive that they won't make money, and its vendors must try to accommodate the demands of its biggest customer. With a common goal, Walmart and its suppliers have an incentive to cooperate because they know that by doing so, both can achieve their common sustainability goals and still make profits.

Common goals also help sustain the relationship when goals are not realized according to plan. If, for instance, a vendor fails to reach an acceptable score on Walmart's sustainability index but has made significant progress, Walmart won't suddenly call off the whole arrangement. Instead, Walmart is likely to work harder to help the vendor raise its score and remain in the relationship because Walmart knows that it and the vendor are committed to the same goals in the long run.

Open Communication   To share information, develop sales forecasts together, coordinate deliveries, and achieve their sustainability common goals, Walmart and its vendors must have open and honest communication. This requirement may sound easy in principle, but most businesses don't like to share information with their business partners. They believe it is none of the other's business. But open, honest communication is a key to developing successful and profitable relationships.[36] Buyers and vendors in a relationship need to understand what is driving each other's business, their roles in the relationship, each firm's strategies, and any problems that arise over the course of the relationship.

Credible Commitments   Successful relationships develop because both parties make credible commitments. Credible commitments are tangible investments in the relationship. They go beyond just making the hollow statement, "I want to be your partner." Credible commitments involve spending money to improve

Walmart builds strategic relationships with its vendors by fostering mutual trust, having open communications and common goals, and making credible commitments.

products or services and, in the case of Walmart and its vendors, taking mutual steps to improve the sustainability index. For example, the goal of reducing Jiangsu Redbud Dyeing Technology's toxic emissions in China is a joint effort and investment by Walmart and Jiangsu.

LEGAL, ETHICAL, AND SOCIAL RESPONSIBILITY ISSUES FOR BUYING MERCHANDISE

Legal and Ethical Issues

Given the many negotiations and interactions between retail buyers and vendors, ethical and legal issues are bound to arise. This section reviews some practices that arise in buyer–vendor negotiations that may have legal and/or ethical implications, and it looks at some ways that retailers are becoming more socially responsible in their buying practices.

LO6

Indicate the legal, ethical, and social responsibility issues involved in buying merchandise.

Counterfeit Merchandise   Selling counterfeit merchandise can negatively affect a retailer's image and its relationship with the vendor of the legitimate brand. **Counterfeit merchandise** includes goods made and sold without the permission of the owner of a trademark or copyright. Trademarks and copyrights are **intellectual property,** that is, intangible and created by intellectual (mental) effort as opposed to physical effort. A **trademark** is any mark, word, picture, device, or nonfunctional design associated with certain merchandise (e.g., the crown on a Rolex watch, the red Levi's tag on the back pocket of a pair of jeans). A **copyright** protects the original work of authors, painters, sculptors, musicians, and others who produce works of artistic or intellectual merit. This book is copyrighted, so these sentences cannot be used by anyone without the consent of the copyright owners.

The nature of counterfeiting has changed during the past decade. Counterfeit name-brand merchandise, such as women's handbags or dresses, has improved in quality, making these items more expensive and difficult to distinguish from the real merchandise. In response, Chanel made the bold move of filing a cyberpiracy and trademark infringement lawsuit, accusing 399 websites of selling counterfeit items under the Chanel name.[37] Chanel believes that these websites operate in China, the Bahamas, and other overseas areas, where trademark infringement law often is not strictly enforced.

Historically, high-end brands have focused their battle tactics on minimizing the sales of street corner knock-offs. Chanel's lawsuit transforms this fight into a larger war by seeking to seize or permanently disable websites from selling any counterfeit merchandise, from T-shirts to expensive jewelry, bearing the Chanel name. Tiffany filed a similar suit targeting 223 unnamed websites: Louis Vuitton filed a suit against 182 websites. Each of these lawsuits includes several website operators that are also named in the Chanel case.

Also, there is a thriving business in counterfeit information products such as music, software, and Blu-Rays. This type of merchandise is attractive to counterfeiters because it has a relatively high unit value, is easy to duplicate and transport, and prompts high consumer demand. The ease of illegally downloading and distributing music means that neither the record label nor the artist receives any money for their investment, work, or talent, and thus both may be less motivated to develop and produce music.

It is illegal for this "street retailer" to sell counterfeit watches because it violates the watch manufacturers' rights to control the use of their trademarks.

Gray-Market, Diverted, and Black-Market Merchandise   **Gray-market goods,** also known as **parallel imports,** involve the flow of merchandise through distribution channels, usually across international borders, other than those authorized or intended by the manufacturer or producer. For example, to increase its profits, McGraw-Hill, the publisher of this textbook, charges a higher wholesale price for this textbook in the United States than in other countries. An importer could buy textbooks at a low price in other countries, import them into the United States, and sell them at a price lower than that in U.S. bookstores.

Diverted merchandise is similar to gray-market merchandise except there need not be distribution across international borders. Suppose, for instance, that the fragrance manufacturer Givenchy grants an exclusive scent to Saks Fifth Avenue. The Saks buyer has excess inventory and sells it at a low price to a discount retailer in the United States, such as an off-price retailer. In this case, the merchandise has been diverted from its legitimate channel of distribution, and Saks would be referred to as the diverter.

A **black market,** on the other hand, occurs when consumer goods are scarce, such as water or gasoline after a natural disaster; heavily taxed, such as cigarettes or alcohol; or illegal, such as drugs or arms. We rarely see black-market merchandise sold through legitimate channels in the United States.

While Saks may benefit from diverting its excess inventory to an off-price retailer, the fragrance manufacturer is concerned about gray markets and diversions. Making the product available at discount stores at low prices may reduce the vendor's brand image and the service normally provided with the brand. So, though such practices are usually legal, vendors seek to minimize gray-market and diverted merchandise.

In a recent U.S. Supreme Court case, Omega SA, a subsidiary of Swatch Group Ltd., alleged that Costco violated U.S. copyright law by selling watches it had obtained from a third party at a significantly lower price than was suggested by Omega.[38] Costco argued that Omega could not impose limits on how its watches were imported and resold, once the watchmaker made its first sale of the goods abroad. The Court was deadlocked with a 4–4 vote, which means that a lower-court ruling against Costco was upheld, though the decision failed to set any precedent because of the tie vote.

Vendors engage in other activities to avoid gray-market/diversion problems, though. They require that all of their retail and wholesale customers sign a contract stipulating that they will not engage in gray marketing. If a retailer is found in violation of the agreement, the vendor will refuse to deal with it in the future. Another strategy is to produce different versions of products for different markets. For instance, McGraw-Hill sells a different version of this textbook in India than it sells in the United States.

Terms and Conditions of Purchase   The Robinson-Patman Act, passed by the U.S. Congress in 1936, potentially restricts the prices and terms that vendors can offer to retailers. The act makes it illegal for vendors to offer different terms and conditions to different retailers for the same merchandise and quantity. Sometimes called the Anti-Chain-Store Act, it was passed to protect independent retailers from chain-store competition. Thus, if a vendor negotiates a good deal on the issues discussed in the previous section (price, advertising allowance, markdown money, transportation), the Robinson-Patman Act requires that the vendor offer the same terms and conditions to other retailers.

However, vendors can offer different terms to retailers for the same merchandise and quantities if the costs of manufacturing, selling, or delivery are different. The cost of manufacturing is usually the same, but selling and delivery could be more expensive for some retailers. For example, vendors may incur larger transportation expenses due to smaller shipments to independent retailers.

Different prices can also be offered if the retailers are providing different functions. For example, a large retailer can get a lower price if its distribution centers store the merchandise or its stores provide different services valued by customers. In addition, lower prices can be offered to meet competition and dispose of perishable merchandise.[39]

Commercial Bribery   **Commercial bribery** occurs when a vendor or its agent offers or a buyer asks for "something of value" to influence purchase decisions. Say a salesperson for a ski manufacturer takes a sporting goods retail buyer to lunch at a fancy private club and then proposes a ski weekend in Vail. These gifts could be construed as bribes or kickbacks, which are illegal unless the buyer's manager is informed of them. To avoid such problems, many retailers forbid employees to accept any gifts from vendors. Other retailers have a policy that it is fine to accept limited entertainment or token gifts, such as flowers or wine for the holidays. As we discussed in Retailing View 13.4, Zappos stops potential commercial bribery in its tracks by bestowing free lunches and other favors on its vendors, rather than accepting anything from vendors. In any case, retailers want their buyers to decide on purchases solely on the basis of what is best for the retailer.

Chargebacks   A **chargeback** is a practice used by retailers in which they deduct money from the amount they owe a vendor. Retailers often use a chargeback when a vendor did not meet the agreed-on terms, for example, if it improperly applied labels to shipping containers or merchandise or sent shipments that had missing items or were late. Chargebacks are especially difficult for vendors because once the money is deducted from an invoice and the invoice is marked "paid," it is difficult to dispute the claim and get the amount back. Vendors sometimes feel that the chargebacks retailers take are not justifiable and thus are unethical.

Buybacks   Similar to slotting allowances, **buybacks,** also known as **stocklifts** or **lift-outs,** are activities engaged in by vendors and retailers to get old products out of retail stores and new products in their place. Specifically, in a buyback situation, either a retailer allows a vendor to create space for its merchandise by "buying back" a competitor's inventory and removing it from the retailer's system, or the retailer forces a vendor to buy back slow-moving merchandise. A vendor with significant market power can violate federal antitrust laws if it stocklifts from a competitor so often that it shuts the competitor out of a market, but such cases are difficult to prove.

Exclusive Dealing Agreements   **Exclusive dealing agreements** occur when a vendor restricts a retailer to carrying only its products and nothing from competing vendors. For example, Ford may require that its dealers sell only Ford cars and no cars made by General Motors. The effect of such arrangements on competition is determined by the market power of the vendor. For example, it may be illegal for a market leader like Coca-Cola to sell its products to a small supermarket chain only if the chain agrees not to sell a less popular cola product like RC Cola.

Tying Contract   A **tying contract** exists when a vendor requires that a retailer take a product it doesn't necessarily desire (the tied product) to ensure that it can buy a product it does desire (the tying product). Tying contracts are illegal if they substantially lessen competition or tend to create a monopoly. But the complaining party has the burden of proof. Thus, it is typically legal for a vendor to require that a buyer buy all items in its product line. For example, if a gift store sued a postcard manufacturer for requiring that it purchase as many "local view" postcards (the tied product) as it did licensed Disney character postcards (the tying product), the court would probably dismiss the case because the retailer would be unable to prove a substantial lessening of competition.

Refusal to Deal   The practice of refusing to deal (buy or sell to) can be viewed from both vendors' and retailers' perspectives. Generally, both vendors and retailers have the right to deal or refuse to deal with anyone they choose. But there are exceptions to this general rule when there's evidence of anticompetitive conduct by one or more firms that wield market power. A vendor may refuse to sell to a particular retailer, but it cannot do so for the sole purpose of benefiting a competing retailer. For example, Mattel decided not to offer certain popular Barbie packages to wholesale clubs. This action in itself would not have been illegal. However, it was determined that Mattel agreed to do so as part of a conspiracy among 10 toy manufacturers orchestrated by Toys "R" Us to prevent wholesale clubs from underselling the same toy packages that Toys "R" Us sold. The refusal to deal then became an illegal group boycott.[40]

Corporate Social Responsibility

Corporate social responsibility describes the voluntary actions taken by a company to address the ethical, social, and environmental impacts of its business operations. Retailers act socially responsible in many ways, from giving to charity to donating time to philanthropic community activities. Recently, however, retailers have been increasing their efforts to buy merchandise in a socially responsible way.

Whole Foods considers local to be anything produced within seven hours or fewer from one of its stores. It requires that all its stores buy from at least four local farmers. It gives $10 million a year in low-interest loans to help small, local farmers and producers of grass-fed and humanely raised meat, poultry, and dairy animals.[41]

Some retailers are getting involved in **fair trade**, a socially responsible movement that ensures that producers receive fair prices for their products. The coffee retailers Starbucks and Peet's offer some, but not all, blends that use fair trade coffee.[43] Walmart is investing heavily in fair trade coffee, partially in response to a new corporate philosophy that goes beyond "everyday low prices" to "doing well by doing good." Bono, the U2 lead singer and an activist, is selling his high-priced fair trade apparel line, Edun, to stores such as Saks Fifth Avenue and Nordstrom.

Home Depot is encouraging its suppliers to include their products in its Eco Options marketing campaign. Some products are obviously attractive to green customers, such as organic gardening products and high-efficiency light bulbs. But a number of less obvious products are also good for the environment. Home Depot also has introduced some new environmentally sensitive products into its assortment, including solar-powered landscape

REFACT

A *locavore* is a person whose primary source of food is from his or her local foodshed or areas within a relatively modest radius.[42]

How green are these solar-powered landscape lights?

lighting, biodegradable peat pots, and paints that discharge fewer pollutants. Home Depot encourages its vendors to use recyclable plastic or cardboard packaging.[44] While these are examples of what retailers are doing to change their green orientation, Retailing View 13.5 discusses how one retailer seized the opportunity to sell eco-friendly products.

Other retailers are demanding smaller, eco-friendly packages from their suppliers. Smaller packages save not only materials but also energy. Because more packages can be transported on a truck, the transportation cost per unit goes down. Several other manufacturers (Patagonia and Timberland), retailers (e.g., Walmart, JCPenney, H&M), and organizations involved in the supply chain (e.g., Environmental Protection Agency, Environmental Defense Fund) have recently cooperated to create the Sustainable Apparel Coalition. One of the Coalition's key objectives is to create a database that summarizes the environmental issues associated with each manufacturer and its processes, such that ultimately the Coalition can provide a score or ranking for each garment that consumers may consider.[45]

These initiatives and many others suggest a complicated business model. Are socially responsible activities good for business? Some are more expensive than traditional products and initiatives. Are consumers interested in or willing to pay the higher prices? Are firms really interested in improving the environment, or are they **greenwashing** (doing a green whitewash) or practicing **green sheen**, which is the disingenuous practice of marketing products or services as being environmentally friendly with the purpose of gaining public approval and sales rather than actually improving the environment. Consumers should question whether a firm is spending significantly more money or time advertising that it is **green** or that it operates with consideration for the environment rather than spending resources on environmentally sound practices.

13.5   RETAILING VIEW   Buying Green on an Amazon-Owned Site

Over the past decade, consumers have become increasingly environmentally conscious, or "green." For example, for the end-of-year holidays, some consumers are choosing to either forgo purchasing new items and regift or purchase eco-friendly products. Some forward-thinking retailers are cashing in on this trend.

One of these retailers is Amazon. Working with Quidsi, a company that Amazon acquired in 2010, the retailing giant launched Vine.com. Similar to other Amazon-owned companies like Zappos and Woot, Vine does not carry the Amazon brand name. The company sells a great variety of products—everything from household paper products to groceries, to beauty supplies, to pet food. Exercise enthusiast and environmentally conscious? Vine.com has just the thing for you. How about a Kulae Organic Yoga Mat Cleaner ($14.84) or a Mountainsmith Recycled Series Vibe TS R Backpack ($27.99)?

Vine.com appeals to a very specific market segment, the environmentally conscious, and as such, lays out specific guidelines for all of the products it carries. To be sold at Vine, a product must be energy efficient, natural, organic, powered by renewable energy, reusable, designed to remove toxins, made of sustainable materials, or water efficient. Not all of its products have all of these attributes, but each has at least one. Because bamboo is a

sustainable material, bamboo cutting boards are sold. Similarly, low-flow shower heads conserve water, and cloth diapers can be washed and reused. To further ensure they are carrying "green" products, Vine requires vendors to certify that their products meet Vine's standards and do not contain substances banned by Vine. These rigorous standards led Seventh Generation to be the official launch sponsor of Vine.com, further adding to its credibility. By paying attention to emerging trends, retailers such as Vine can offer innovative products that attract segments of consumers that have previously been underserved.

Sources: Justin Gillis, "An Odometer Moment on a Warming Planet," *The New York Times*, December 17, 2012; "Green," *The New York Times Environment Blog*, Claire Cain Miller, "Amazon Starts a Shopping Site for the Environmental Crowd," *The New York Times: Bits*, September 26, 2012; John Cook, "Amazon Unveils Eco-Friendly Products Site Vine.com," *Geek Wire*, September 26, 2012; and "About Us," *Vine.com*.

DISCUSSION QUESTIONS

Would you shop at Vine.com? Does it help or hurt to know it is owned by Amazon.com?

SUMMARY

LO1 **Identify the branding options available to retailers.**

Retailers can purchase either national brands or store (or private-label) brands. Each type has its own relative advantages. Choosing appropriate brands and a branding strategy is an integral component of a firm's merchandise and assortment planning process.

LO2 **Describe how retailers buy national brands.**

Buyers of manufacturer's brands attend trade shows and wholesale market centers to meet with vendors, view new merchandise, and place orders. Virtually every merchandise category has at least one annual trade show at which retailers and vendors meet.

LO3 **List the issues retailers consider when developing and sourcing store-branded merchandise internationally.**

Buying merchandise sometimes is facilitated by resident buying offices. Market representatives of the resident buying offices facilitate merchandising purchases in foreign markets. The process for buying store brands or private-label merchandise can be more complicated than that for buying national brands because the retailer takes on some of the responsibilities that a national-brand manufacturer normally would have, such as designing and specifying products and selecting manufacturers to make the products. A large percentage of private-label merchandise is manufactured outside the United States. The cost, managerial, and ethical issues surrounding global sourcing decisions must be considered.

LO4 **Understand how retailers prepare for and conduct negotiations with their vendors.**

Buyers of both national brands and store brands engage in negotiating a series of issues with their vendors, including markdown money, slotting fees, advertising allowances, terms of purchase, exclusivity, and transportation costs. Successful vendor relationships depend on planning for and being adept at negotiations.

LO5 **Determine why retailers build strategic relationships with their vendors.**

Retailers that can successfully team up with their vendors can achieve a sustainable competitive advantage. There needs to be more than just a promise to buy and sell on a regular basis. Strategic relationships require trust, shared goals, strong communications, and a financial commitment.

LO6 **Indicate the legal, ethical, and social responsibility issues involved in buying merchandise.**

Buyers need to be aware of ethical and legal issues that can guide them in their negotiations and purchase decisions. There are also problems associated with counterfeit and gray-market merchandise and issues that vendors face when selling to retailers, such as exclusive territories and tying contracts. Care should be taken by vendors when placing restrictions on which retailers they will sell to, what merchandise, how much, and at what price. Some retailers are taking giant steps toward being more socially responsible.

KEY TERMS

black market, *379*

buybacks, *380*

chargeback, *380*

commercial bribery, *380*

co-op (cooperative) advertising, *371*

copycat brands, *359*

copyright, *378*

corporate social responsibility, *381*

counterfeit merchandise, *378*

diverted merchandise, *379*

duties, *366*

exclusive brands, *359*

exclusive dealing agreements, *380*

fair trade, *381*

family brand, *358*

generic brands, *360*

gray-market goods, *379*

green, *382*

green sheen, *382*

greenwashing, *382*

house brands, *358*

intellectual property, *378*

lift-outs, *380*

manufacturer's brands, *358*

markdown money, *369*

market weeks, *362*

national brands, *358*

own brands, *358*

parallel imports, *379*

partnering relationship, *373*

premium store brands, *359*

private-label brands, *358*

resident buying offices, *367*

reverse auctions, *368*

slotting allowances, *370*

slotting fees, *370*

stocklifts, *380*

store brands, *358*

strategic relationship, *373*

subbrand, *358*

tariffs, *366*

trademark, *378*

trade shows, *363*

trust, *376*

tying contract, *380*

umbrella brand, *358*

wholesale market, *362*

384   SECTION III   Merchandise Management

GET OUT AND DO IT!

1. **CONTINUING ASSIGNMENT** Go visit the retailer you have selected for the continuing assignment and perform an audit of its manufacturer's and store brands. Ask the manager to comment on the store's philosophy toward manufacturer's versus store brands. Why does it use store brands? Does it offer different store brands to appeal to different customer segments? Select three different merchandise categories. Compare the price of the same item for store versus the manufacturer brand. Has the percentage of store brands increased or decreased during the past five years? On the basis of what you see and hear, assess its branding strategy.

2. Read articles about the NBA warning fans about counterfeit merchandise. Go to the home page for the

Coalition to Advance the Protection of Sports Logos (CAPS) at www.capsinfo.com, and read "About CAPS." What are college and professional sports teams doing to prevent the sale of counterfeit merchandise? Will these measures be effective? Explain why or why not.

3. Go to the home page for the Private Label Manufacturers Association (PLMA), and read the "What are Store Brands?" page, which can be found at http://plma.com/storeBrands/facts13.html. What are store-brand products? Who purchases store brands? Who makes store brands? What store brands are you purchasing on a regular basis?

DISCUSSION QUESTIONS AND PROBLEMS

1. Assume you have been hired to consult with Forever 21 on sourcing decisions for sportswear. What issues would you consider when deciding whether you should buy from Mexico or China or find a source within the United States?

2. What are the differences among counterfeit, gray-market, and black-market merchandise? Is the selling of this type of merchandise legal? Do you believe that selling these types of merchandise should be allowed? Provide a rationale for your position. Would you purchase a counterfeit wallet? What about a counterfeit car part or prescription medication?

3. What are the advantages and disadvantages of manufacturer's brands versus store brands? Consider both the retailer's and customer's perspectives.

4. Does your favorite clothing store have a store-brand strategy? If yes, how does it build store loyalty? If no, how could a store brand create loyalty?

5. Explain why a grocery store, such as Kroger, offers more than one tier of store brands within a particular product category.

6. Why have retailers found exclusive store brands to be an appealing branding option? Choose a department store, a discount store, and a grocery store. What exclusive store brands do they offer? How are they positioned in relation to their national brand counterparts?

7. When you go shopping, in which product categories do you prefer store brands or national brands? Explain your preference.

8. What are retailers doing to be more socially responsible in buying merchandise? Why are they becoming more socially responsible? Do you buy products that you believe were produced in a socially responsible manner, even if they cost more?

9. You have decided that you don't want to take the final in this class. Explain how you would negotiate this request with the instructor. Consider place, deadlines, past relationship, possible objections, options for mutual gain, and how to maintain a professional relationship.

SUGGESTED READINGS

Boyle, Peter J., and E. Scott Lathrop. "The Value of Private Label Brands to U.S. Consumers: An Objective and Subjective Assessment," *Journal of Retailing and Consumer Services* 20 (January 2013), pp. 80–86.

Deepak, Malhotra, and Max Bazerman. *Negotiation Genius: How to Overcome Obstacles and Achieve Brilliant Results at the Bargaining Table and Beyond.* New York: Bantam, 2008.

Diamond, Jay. *Retail Buying*, 9th ed. Upper Saddle River, NJ: Pearson, 2012.

Donaldson, Bill, and Tom O'Toole. *Strategic Market Relationships: From Strategy to Implementation*, 2nd ed. Indianapolis: Wiley, 2007.

Fisher, Roger, William L. Ury, and Bruce Patton. *Getting to Yes: Negotiating Agreement Without Giving In.* New York: Penguin Books, 2011.

Foros, Oystein, Hans Jarle Kind, and Jan Yngve Sand. "Slotting Allowances and Manufacturers' Retail Sales Effort." *Southern Economic Journal* 76, no. 1 (2009), pp. 266–282.

Johnston, Robert, and Roy Staughton. "Establishing and Developing Strategic Relationships: The Role for Operations Managers." *International Journal of Operations & Production Management* 29, no. 6 (2009), pp. 564–590.

Kennedy, Gavin. *Negotiation: An A–Z Guide (Economist A–Z Guide)*. London: Economist Books, 2009.

Kumar, Nirmalya, and Jan-Benedict E. M. Steenkamp. *Private Label Strategy: How to Meet the Store Brand Challenge*. Boston: Harvard Business Press, 2007.

Lamey, L., B. Deleersnyder, Jan-Benedict E. M. Steenkamp, and Marnik G. Dekimpe. "Effect of Business Cycle Fluctuations on Private-Label Share: What Has Marketing Conduct Got to Do with It?" *Journal of Marketing* 76 (January 2012), pp. 1–19.

Lincoln, Keith, and Lars Thomassen. *Private Label: Turning the Retail Brand Threat into Your Biggest Opportunity*. London: Kogan, 2009.

Quelch, John A. "Brands vs. Private Labels: Fighting to Win." *Harvard Business Review*, March 3, 2009.

Sugden, David R. *Gray Markets: Prevention, Detection and Litigation*. New York: Oxford University Press, 2009.

Retail Pricing

EXECUTIVE BRIEFING
Debbie Harvey, President and Chief Operating
Officer, Ron Jon Surf Shop

I am proud to be the president of Ron Jon Surf Shop, one of the most recognized names in surfing. Ron Jon started on the New Jersey Shore in 1959 when the founder, Ron DiMenna, sold his first surfboard. Two years later he opened a tiny oceanside shop in Long Beach Island, New Jersey. A much larger "original" store is still located in Ship Bottom, New Jersey. Our flagship store located in Cocoa Beach, Florida, was opened in 1963 and has grown over the years to be known as the world's largest surf shop. The 52,000-square-foot store is open 24 hours a day, 365 days a year and welcomes about two million visitors annually. Ron Jon has expanded over the last couple of years and now owns and operates 11 stores at coastal locations in Florida, South Carolina, Maryland, and New Jersey. We also have licensees that operate airport locations, Caribbean locations, and a Ron Jon resort.

Ron Jon's targets families with active lifestyles who are looking for entertaining and fun experiences. Our customers typically visit us while on vacation or during a visit to the beach. Our marketing goal is to continue to build the Ron Jon brand and experience rather than focus our customers on price or a particular product. Our extensive billboard program has made us familiar to millions of visitors to our market areas. Every customer in our stores receives a free sticker for his or her car. We promote the surfing lifestyle by sponsoring surf teams and contests. In addition we use the Internet, not only for a shopping site, but also to promote our brand through social media.

In setting our prices, we do not use a specific pricing formula. We price our products at the final price we feel our customers will pay; and we try to keep the prices on our exclusive Ron Jon merchandise at or below the prices of similar brands. We do not run regular sales events, we typically only markdown or promote slow-selling merchandise. We want our customers to feel our prices are price neutral: both fair and that they are getting a good value when they buy our merchandise. Our prices are the same across all of our locations and channels.

CHAPTER 14

LEARNING OBJECTIVES

LO1 Explain the difference between a high/low pricing strategy and an everyday low-pricing strategy.

LO2 Identify the factors retailers consider when pricing their merchandise.

LO3 Describe how retailers set prices.

LO4 Examine how and why retailers take markdowns.

LO5 Identify the pricing techniques retailers use to increase sales and profits.

LO6 Describe how the Internet and social and mobile channels are used to make pricing decisions.

LO7 Indicate the legal and ethical issues retailers should consider when setting prices.

Frequently when families visit our stores, the parents give the children a "budget" they can spend during the visit. For example, the children are told they can spend $10 or $25. Keeping this in mind, we develop merchandise assortments that accommodate different budgets. We have the inexpensive souvenir for the customer on a budget as well as products that would appeal more to the high-end shopper. We strive to have deep assortments in the categories we carry and offer products at a variety of price points.

I graduated from the University of Florida with a BSBA in marketing on a Friday and started working for Maas Brothers (now part of Macy's) on the following Monday. I have been working in the retail industry ever since. My first position was as a manager of the women's department. After about a year of working in the stores, I was promoted to a position in the buying office and eventually held senior merchandising leadership positions at Maas Brothers, Bealls Florida, HSN, and Goody's before joining Ron Jon.

I was attracted to retail because of family friends who were in the retail business. They both had worked for several large retailers, working their way up the ladder before starting their own businesses. After years in the business they still looked forward to the diversity and challenges that each new day presented. This has also been my experience. I truly look forward to coming to work each day. While each company I have worked for had a different culture and customer profile, the basics of retailing are the same: you have to serve your customers' needs.

Retailing is an industry that offers many daily challenges. Our business is not static and is constantly evolving and changing. For me that is what makes it fun and rewarding. We have to figure out what merchandise the customers want, manage the logistics of the merchandise flow, have efficient operations, provide outstanding customer service, and provide an exciting shopping environment for our customers.

The decisions examined in this textbook are directed toward facilitating exchanges between retailers and their customers. As discussed in Chapter 1, retailers offer a number of benefits to their customers, including making merchandise available to customers when they want it, at a convenient location, and in the quantities they want. In addition, retailers provide services, such as the opportunity for customers to see and try out merchandise before buying it. In exchange for these benefits, customers pay money for the merchandise and services provided by retailers.

The importance of pricing decisions is growing because today's customers have more alternatives to choose from and are better informed about the alternatives available in the marketplace. Thus, they are in a better position to seek a good value when they buy merchandise and services. **Value** is the ratio of what customers receive (the perceived benefit of the products and services offered by the retailer) to what they have to pay for it:

$$\text{Value} = \frac{\text{Perceived benefits}}{\text{Price}}$$

Retailers can increase value and stimulate more sales (exchanges) by either increasing the perceived benefits offered or reducing the price. To some customers, a good value means simply paying the lowest price because other benefits offered by retailers are not important to them. Others are willing to pay extra for additional benefits as long as they believe they're getting their money's worth in terms of product quality or service.

If retailers set prices higher than the benefits they provide, sales and profits will decrease. In contrast, if retailers set prices too low, their sales might increase but profits might decrease because of the lower profit margin. In addition to offering an attractive value to customers, retailers need to consider the value proposition offered by their competitors and legal restrictions related to pricing. Thus, setting the right price can be challenging.

The first section of this chapter examines two very different pricing strategies used by retailers. The factors retailers consider in setting retail prices are then reviewed. Then the actual process that retailers use to determine prices is described. The next section examines the reasons retailers reduce their prices when taking markdowns. The pricing techniques retailers use for increasing sales and profits are then examined. How the Internet and social and mobile channels have changed the way retailers price merchandise and communicate price to customers is then described. The chapter concludes with a discussion of the legal and ethical issues retailers should consider when making pricing decisions.

PRICING STRATEGIES

Explain the difference between a high/low pricing strategy and an everyday low-pricing strategy.

Retailers use two basic retail pricing strategies: high/low pricing and everyday low pricing. Each of these strategies and its advantages and disadvantages is discussed in this section.

High/Low Pricing

Retailers using a **high/low pricing strategy** frequently—often weekly—discount the initial prices for merchandise through sales promotions. However, some customers learn to expect frequent sales and simply wait until the merchandise they want goes on sale and then stock up at the low prices.

Everyday Low Pricing

Many retailers, particularly supermarkets, home improvement centers, and discount stores, have adopted an **everyday low-pricing (EDLP) strategy.** This strategy emphasizes the continuity of retail prices at a level somewhere between

The retailer on the left is using a high/low pricing strategy, whereas the one on the right is using an everyday low pricing strategy.

the regular nonsale price and the deep-discount sale price of high/low retailers. Although EDLP retailers embrace their consistent pricing strategy, they occasionally have sales, just not as frequently as their high/low competitors.

The term *everyday low pricing* is somewhat misleading because low doesn't mean "lowest." Although retailers using EDLP strive for low prices, they aren't always the lowest prices in the market. At any given time, a sale price at a high/low retailer may be the lowest price available in a market. Retailing View 14.1 highlights how a number of retailers have experimented with EDLP but have reversed their

RETAILING VIEW   Does Everyone Love an Everyday Low Price?   14.1

In light of the number of retail sales, many consumers are concerned that they are paying too much when they buy merchandise at full price. Thus, they wait for products to go on sale before they buy them. JCPenney's announcement that it would offer "fair and square pricing," issued through an extensive advertising campaign, reflects its attempt to revamp its image among consumers. It also hopes that by issuing straightforward prices, it can prevent or reverse the trend in which shoppers always wait for a sale before they buy. As part of this strategy, JCPenney is trying to eliminate coupons and reduce the number of annual sales from 600 to a more manageable number. By doing so, JCPenney is trying to emulate Walmart's longstanding everyday low-price strategy. However, JCPenney has realized that changing customer behaviors is difficult. As a result of the difficulties inherent in an implementing an EDLP strategy, especially after years of using a high/low strategy, JCPenney found it necessary to bring back sales events and highlight reference prices, such as Penney's everyday price, manufacturer's suggested list price, and prices elsewhere.

Lowe's built its business around EDLP but started offering more sales when the housing market began to sour. Recently, Lowe's has been dramatically cutting prices to compete with Home Depot. Lowe's is struggling to find the right balance between everyday low pricing and temporary promotional discounts. SteinMart similarly is cutting back on the number of coupons it offers, by 50 percent, while also lowering its regular prices. The Mango chain is simply dropping all prices by 20 percent. And both American Eagle Outfitters and Urban Outfitters are overhauling their pricing systems to get away from the glut of promotions they had been running.

Yet these retailers might want to examine their industries' recent history. Several years ago, when Macy's decided to slash the number of coupons it offered, customers revolted. Angered by the disappearance of their coveted clearance promotions, customers demanded their return, and within six months, Macy's relented. The same reaction might be in the works for these current price cutters.

EDLP is a hard sell for many customers. For example, America's Research Group found that almost 75 percent of consumers surveyed said it would take discounts of more than half-off to persuade them to purchase a product. Some retail experts say that retailers have to take responsibility for their customers' reluctance to give up their bargains. After all, the retailers started the vicious sale and promotion cycle, not their customers. Their customers will expect a lot in return—top-notch service or access to exclusive merchandise.

Sources: Anne D'Innocenzio, "Penney Brings Back the Big Discounts It Ditched Last Year in a Bid to Woo Back Shoppers," *Associated Press*, January 28, 2013; Anne D'Innocenzio, "Deal Junkies Hurt Stores' Profits," *Associated Press*, September 2, 2012; and Stephanie Clifford, "Knowing Cost, the Customer Sets the Price," *The New York Times*, March 27, 2012.

DISCUSSION QUESTION
Why might customers prefer EDLP pricing in one situation but like coupons and promotions in another?

strategies because of its implementation difficulties. To reinforce their EDLP strategy, many retailers have adopted a **low-price guarantee policy** that guarantees customers that the retailer will have the lowest price in a market for products it sells. The guarantee usually promises to match or beat any lower price found in the market and might include a provision to refund the difference between the seller's offer price and the lower price.

Advantages of the Pricing Strategies

The high/low pricing strategy has the following advantages:

- *Increases profits.* High/low pricing allows retailers to charge higher prices to customers who are not price-sensitive and will pay the "high" price and to charge lower prices to price-sensitive customers who will wait for the "low" sale price.

- *Creates excitement.* A "get them while they last" atmosphere often occurs during a sale. Sales draw a lot of customers, and a lot of customers create excitement. Some retailers augment low prices and advertising with special in-store activities, such as product demonstrations, giveaways, and celebrity appearances.

- *Sells slow moving merchandise.* Sales allow retailers to get rid of slow-selling merchandise by discounting the price.

The EDLP approach has its own advantages, as follows:

- *Assures customers of low prices.* Many customers are skeptical about initial retail prices. They have become conditioned to buying only on sale—the main characteristic of a high/low pricing strategy. The EDLP strategy lets customers know that they will get the same low prices every time they patronize the EDLP retailer. Customers do not have to read the ads and wait for items they want to go on sale.

- *Reduces advertising and operating expenses.* The stable prices caused by EDLP limit the need for the weekly-sale advertising used in the high/low strategy. In addition, EDLP retailers do not have to incur the labor costs of changing price tags and signs and putting up sale signs.

- *Reduces stockouts and improves inventory management.* The EDLP approach reduces the large variations in demand caused by frequent sales with large markdowns. As a result, retailers can manage their inventories with more certainty. Fewer stockouts mean more satisfied customers, resulting in higher sales. In addition, a more predictable customer demand pattern enables the retailer to improve inventory turnover by reducing the average inventory needed for special promotions and backup stock.

CONSIDERATIONS IN SETTING RETAIL PRICES

LO2

Identify the factors retailers consider when pricing their merchandise.

Four factors retailers consider in setting retail prices are: (1) the price sensitivity of consumers, (2) the cost of the merchandise, (3) competition, and (4) legal constraints. Legal constraints are discussed at the end of the chapter. The other considerations occur when setting prices for services and are discussed in this section.

Customer Price Sensitivity and Cost

Generally, as the price of a product increases, the sales for the product will decrease because fewer and fewer customers feel the product is a good value. The price sensitivity of customers determines how many units will be sold at different price levels. If customers in the target market are very price-sensitive, sales will decrease significantly when prices increase. If customers are not very price-sensitive, sales will not decrease significantly if the prices are increased.

One approach that can be used to measure the price sensitivity of customers is a price experiment. Consider the following situation: A restaurant chain wants to determine the best price for a new item, a riblet basket. It selects restaurants in the chain with very similar trade areas and sets prices at different levels in each of the restaurants for a week. Assume that the variable cost of the riblets is $5 per plate and the fixed cost of operating the restaurant for a week, the cost for rent, labor and energy, is $8,000.

The results of this experiment are shown in Exhibit 14–1. Notice in Exhibit 14–1a that as prices increase, the fixed costs remain the same, sales and variable costs both decrease, but sales decrease at a faster rate than variable costs (Exhibit 14–1b). So the

To determine the most profitable price for a riblet basket, a restaurant chain may set different prices at different locations.

Price Experiment   **EXHIBIT 14–1**

(a) Data from Price Experiment   EXHIBIT 14–1a

(1) Theater	(2) Price	(3) Quantity Sold	(4) Column (2) × Column (3) = Revenue	(5) Column (3) × $5 Variable Cost per Riblet Basket = Variable Cost	(6) Fixed Cost	(7) Column (4) − Column (5) − Column (6) = Contribution to Profit
1	$6.00	9,502	$57,012	$47,510	$8,000	$1,502
2	6.50	6,429	41,789	32,145	8,000	1,644
3	7.00	5,350	37,450	26,750	8,000	2,700
4	7.50	4,051	30,383	20,255	8,000	2,128
5	8.00	2,873	22,984	14,365	8,000	619
6	8.50	2,121	18,029	10,605	8,000	−577

EXHIBIT 14–1b
(b) Quantity Sold at Different Prices

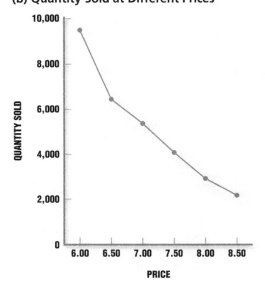

EXHIBIT 14–1c
(c) Profit at Different Prices

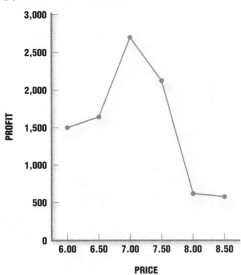

highest profit level occurs at a $7 price (Exhibit 14–1c). If the restaurant considers only customers' price sensitivity and cost in setting prices, it would set the price for the riblet basket with these demand characteristics at $7 to maximize profits. Retailing View 14.2 highlights how showrooming and mobile apps are increasing consumers' price sensitivity.

14.2   RETAILING VIEW   Turning Showrooming on Its Head

The costs of maintaining a well-staffed, effectively inventoried, nicely decorated store are much higher than the costs of hosting a website. Accordingly, many retailers offer lower prices online than in stores, which leaves them at the mercy of a rapidly increasing trend: showrooming. **Showrooming** customers visit stores to touch and feel the available products or receive advice from expert salespeople, then purchase their preferred item from the firm's website, at a price lower than the store would charge, or even worse, from a competitor's website.

Amazon has embraced and encouraged this practice, naturally. Its price check app allows customers to scan bar codes in competing stores, and then provides them with Amazon's price for the same item. Best Buy has grown so frustrated with such efforts that it stopped posting manufacturers' bar codes on its shelf labels. But even without such an app, the ubiquity of smartphones makes it easy for customers to search for lower-priced alternatives for national-brand products online, at the very moment they are holding the product in their hand.

The solutions for retailers operating a store channel are varied. Some commentators suggest that multichannel retailers should embrace the trend and truly turn their stores into showrooms, encouraging buyers to use their websites to purchase. Retailers such as Walmart and The Container Store have expanded their offerings to appeal to potential showroomers, such as providing free shipping for items purchased in store or allowing customers to order online and then pay and pick up the items in stores. The latter option is particularly appealing for customers without credit or debit cards who need to pay cash for their purchases.

For retailers determined to fight the trend, the options focus mainly on branding and pricing choices. Showrooming can be reduced by placing more emphasis on store brands. Store brands are more difficult to compare on price because the exact same brand is not available from a competing retailer.

If the retailer can match prices in stores and online, it is less likely to lose price-sensitive customers. At the very least, stores must make sure their in-store prices are aligned with online competitors' price offerings. Alternatively, some stores seek to stock more unique merchandise that simply is not subject to price comparisons.

Finally, some stores have chosen to exploit the presence of mobile phones in other ways. By requiring customers to check-in at a store before they receive exclusive coupons, retailers draw coupon-loving shoppers into their locations. The same deals are not available

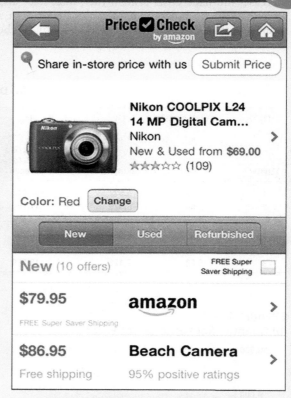

Amazon's price check app allows customers to scan bar codes in stores and then provides them with Amazon's price for the same item.

online, which means the store can circumvent the appeal of showrooming.

Sources: Suzy Sandberg, "4 Ways Retailers Can Fight Showrooming," *Mobile Commerce Daily*, March 15, 2012; Chantal Tode, "How to Leverage Mobile to Combat Showrooming," *Mobile Commerce Daily*, May 31, 2012; and Stephanie Clifford, "Luring Online Shoppers Offline," *The New York Times*, July 4, 2012.

DISCUSSION QUESTION

Which of the activities mentioned would be most effective to prevent you from showrooming?

Price Elasticity   A commonly used measure of price sensitivity is **price elasticity,** or the percentage change in quantity sold divided by the percentage change in price:

$$\text{Elasticity} = \frac{\text{Percentage change in quantity sold}}{\text{Percentage change in price}}$$

Assume that a retailer originally priced a private-label DVD player at $90 and then raised the price to $100. Before raising the price, the retailer was selling 1,500 units a week. When the price increased, sales dropped to 1,100 units per week. The calculation of the price elasticity is as follows:

$$\text{Elasticity} = \frac{\text{Percentage change in quantity sold}}{\text{Percentage change in price}}$$

$$= \frac{(\text{New quantity sold} - \text{Old quantity sold}) \div (\text{Old quantity sold})}{(\text{New price} - \text{Old price}) \div (\text{Old price})}$$

$$= \frac{(1100 - 1500)/1500}{(10 - 9)/9} = \frac{-0.2667}{.1111} = -2.4005$$

Because the quantity sold usually decreases when prices increase, price elasticity is a negative number.

The target market for a product is generally viewed to be price-insensitive (referred to as **inelastic**) when its price elasticity is more positive than −1.0 (e.g., −0.50)—that is, when a 1 percent decrease in price results in a 1/2 percent increase in quantity sold. The target market for a product is price-sensitive (referred to as **elastic**) when the price elasticity is more negative than −1 (e.g., −2.0), that is, when a 1 percent decrease in price produces a 2 percent increase in quantity sold. The price elasticity for a product can be estimated by conducting an experiment as described previously or by using statistical techniques to analyze how sales have changed in the past when prices changed.

Various factors affect the price sensitivity for a product. First, the more substitutes a product or service has, the more likely it is to be price-elastic (sensitive). For example, there are many alternatives for a riblet basket at a restaurant like Applebee's, and thus fast-food prices are typically price-elastic, but branded luxury goods have almost no substitutes and are price-inelastic (insensitive). Second, products and services that are necessities are price-inelastic. Thus, medical care is price-inelastic, whereas airline tickets for a vacation are price-elastic. Third, products that are expensive relative to a consumer's income are price-elastic. Thus, cars are price-elastic, and books and movie tickets tend to be price-inelastic. The estimated elasticities for some commonly purchased items are shown in the following table.[1]

Product Class	PRICE ELASTICITY	
	Short Run	Long Run
Clothing	−0.90	−2.90
Wine	−0.88	−1.17
Jewelry and watches	−0.44	−0.67
Gasoline	−0.20	−0.60

On the basis of these estimates, a 1 percent decrease in the price of clothing would result in only a 0.9 percent increase in the quantity sold in the short run but a 2.9 percent increase in the long run. So, if you must have that new sweater today, you are much less responsive to a low price than you would be if you could wait for the sweater to be on sale three months from now. In contrast, Americans aren't going to change their gasoline purchases much in the short or long run, regardless of slight price decreases or increases. However, these elasticity estimates are based on relatively small changes in prices and might be different for large price changes.

For products with price elasticities less than 1, the price that maximizes profits can be determined by the following formula:

$$\text{Profit-maximizing price} = \frac{\text{Price elasticity} \times \text{Cost}}{\text{Price elasticity} + 1}$$

So, if the private-label DVD player described in the preceding example costs $50, the profit-maximizing price would be:

$$\text{Profit-maximizing price} = \frac{\text{Price elasticity} \times \text{Cost}}{\text{Price elasticity} + 1}$$

$$= \frac{-2.4005 \times \$50}{-2.4005 + 1} = \$85.70$$

Competition

Consumers have lots of choices for goods and services, and they typically search for the best value. Retailers therefore need to consider competitors' prices when setting their own. The previous discussion about setting price on the basis of customer price sensitivity (elasticity) ignores the effects of competitors' prices. For example, assume the restaurant chain that conducted the experiment had a $7.50 price for the riblet basket and, following the results of its experiment, dropped its price to $7 to increase sales and profits. If the increased sales occurred, other restaurant chains would see a decline in their sales and react by dropping their prices to $7, and the experimenting restaurant chain might not realize the sales and profit increases it anticipated. Retailing View 14.3 examines the impact of intense price competition among the big discounters.

Retailers can price above, below, or at parity with the competition. The chosen pricing policy must be consistent with the retailer's overall strategy and its relative market position. Consider, for instance, Walmart and Tiffany and Co. Walmart tries to price the products it sells below its competition. Tiffany, in contrast, offers significant benefits to its customers beyond just the merchandise. Its brand name and customer service assure customers that they will be satisfied with the jewelry they purchase. Due to the unique nature of its offering, Tiffany is able to set its prices higher than those of competitors.

Collecting and Using Competitive Price Data   Most retailers routinely collect price data about their competitors to see if they need to adjust their prices to remain competitive. Competitive price data are typically collected using store personnel, but pricing data also are available from business service providers such as The Nielsen Company and SymphonyIRI.

Pricing Strategies Used by Services Retailers

Additional issues that need to be considered when pricing services are (1) the need to match supply and demand and (2) the difficulties customers have in determining service quality.[2]

Matching Supply and Demand   Services are intangible and thus cannot be inventoried. When retailers are selling products, if the products don't sell one day, they can be stored and sold the next day. However, when a plane departs with empty seats or a play is performed without a full house, the potential revenue from the unused capacity is lost forever. In addition, most services have limited capacity. For example,

Airlines use yield management to adjust prices in response to demand.

Although Target might try to tempt customers with designer-named brands, and Walmart might promise green practices, when it comes down to consumer choice between these two discount store giants, the store that offers the lowest prices will probably win in the long run. In this battle, Walmart has won the price competition battle most of the time. As the self-professed leader of everyday low pricing, Walmart has tended to beat Target's price on a typical basket of 150 similar goods.

But a recent comparison showed that Target was victorious—it was 0.46 percentage point less expensive. That is, had the basket cost $100, Target shoppers would have saved 46 cents over Walmart shoppers. This cost margin also was the widest one found in nearly two years. Considering such incredibly slim margins, does the comparison really matter?

Because of the stores' promises to customers, it does. Discounters struggle to attract price-conscious customers while also protecting their market from increasing competition from online retailers such as Amazon. Both Target and Walmart claim in their well-known slogans that customers can "Expect More. Pay Less" or "Save Money. Live Better." The one that gets to show that it really does live up to this slogan better than the other is likely to be the one customers prefer.

At the same time, another study suggested that for parents seeking back-to-school supplies for their children, the best prices were neither at Walmart nor Target. For that type of merchandise, they would have to visit a store that isn't even a discounter: Office Depot.

Target is reinforcing its low prices by highlighting its price match guarantee.

Sources: Matt Townsend and David Welch, "Target Cheaper Than Wal-Mart as Gap Widest in Two Years," *Bloomberg News*, August 23, 2012; Brad Tuttle, "Target Battles Walmart for Low-Price Supremacy," *Time*, August 27, 2012; and David Welch, "Target Undercuts Wal-Mart on Price," *Star Tribune*, August 23, 2012.

DISCUSSION QUESTIONS

Which retailer do you prefer—Walmart, Target, or Amazon? Do you shop there because you think it has the lowest prices?

restaurants are limited in the number of customers that can be seated. Due to capacity constraints, services retailers might encounter situations in which they cannot realize as many sales as they could make.

To maximize sales and profits, many services retailers engage in yield management.[3] **Yield management** is the practice of adjusting prices up or down in response to demand to control the sales generated. Airlines are masters at yield management. Using sophisticated computer programs, they monitor the reservations and ticket sales for each flight and adjust prices according to capacity utilization. Prices are lowered on flights when sales are below forecasts and there is significant excess capacity. As ticket sales approach capacity, prices are increased.

Other services retailers use less sophisticated approaches to match supply and demand. For example, more people want to go to a restaurant for dinner or see a movie at 7 p.m. than at 5 p.m. Restaurants and movie theaters thus might not be able to satisfy the demand for their services at 7 p.m. but have excess capacity at 5 p.m. Therefore, restaurants and movie theaters often price their services lower for customers who use them at 5 p.m. rather than 7 p.m. in an effort to shift demand from 7 p.m. to 5 p.m.

Theaters use a variety of strategies to try to ensure that the seats are sold and that they are sold at prices equivalent to what customers are willing to pay.

Targeted direct mail coupons are often used when a play opens, and two-for-one tickets are introduced about halfway through the run. In some cities, like New York and Boston, theaters partner with half-price ticket brokers, which sell unsold tickets for 50 percent off the ticket price but only for performances on the same day.

Determining Service Quality   Due to the intangibility of services, it is often difficult for customers to assess service quality, especially when other information is not available.[4] Thus, if consumers are unfamiliar with a service or service provider, they may use price to make quality judgments. For example, most consumers have limited information about lawyers and the quality of legal advice they offer. They may, therefore, base their assessment of the quality of legal services offered on the fees they charge. They may also use other nondiagnostic cues to assess quality, such as the size and décor of the lawyer's office.

Another factor that increases the dependence on price as a quality indicator is the risk associated with a service purchase. Higher-risk situations tend to arise in relation to credence services—legal or medical services, even hair salons—for which the customer may need price to provide a surrogate for quality.

Because customers depend on price as a cue of quality and because price creates expectations of quality, service prices must be determined carefully. In addition to being chosen to manage capacity, prices must be set to convey the appropriate quality signal. Pricing too low can lead to inaccurate inferences about the quality of the service. Pricing too high can set expectations that may be difficult to match in service delivery.

SETTING RETAIL PRICES

LO3

Describe how retailers set prices.

As described in the previous section, theoretically, retailers maximize their profits by setting prices on the basis of the price sensitivity of customers and the cost of merchandise. One limitation of just using price sensitivity and cost for setting prices is that doing so fails to consider the prices being charged by competitors. Another problem is that implementing this approach requires knowledge of the price sensitivity (price elasticity) of each item. Many retailers have to set prices for more than 50,000 SKUs and make thousands of pricing decisions each month. From a practical perspective, they cannot conduct experiments or do statistical analyses to determine the price sensitivity for each item.

Setting Prices Based on Costs

Most retailers set price by marking up the item's cost to yield a profitable gross margin. Then, this initial price is adjusted on the basis of insights about customer price sensitivity and competitive pricing. The following section describes how retailers typically set prices solely on the basis of merchandise cost.

Retail Price and Markup   When setting prices on the basis of merchandise cost, retailers start with the following equation:

Retail price = Cost of merchandise + Markup

The **markup** is the difference between the retail price and the cost of an item. Thus, if a sporting goods retailer buys a tennis racket for $75 and sets the retail price at $125, the markup is $50. The appropriate markup is the amount that covers all of the retailer's operating expenses (labor costs, rent, utilities, advertising, etc.) incurred to sell the merchandise and produces a profit for the retailer.

The **markup percentage** is the markup as a percentage of the retail price:

$$\text{Markup percentage} = \frac{\text{Retail price} - \text{Cost of merchandise}}{\text{Retail price}}$$

Thus, the markup percentage for the tennis racket is:

$$\text{Markup percentage} = \frac{\$125 - \$75}{\$125} = 40\%$$

The retail price based on the cost and markup percentage is:

$$\begin{aligned}\text{Retail price} &= \text{Cost of merchandise} + \text{Markup} \\ &= \text{Cost of merchandise} + \text{Retail price} \times \text{Markup percentage} \\ &= \frac{\text{Cost of merchandise}}{1 - \text{Markup percentage (as a fraction)}}\end{aligned}$$

Thus, if a buyer for an office supply category specialist purchases calculators at $14 and needs a 30 percent markup to meet the financial goals for the category, the retail price needs to be:

$$\text{Retail price} = \frac{\text{Cost}}{1 - \text{Markup percentage}} = \frac{\$14.00}{1 - 0.30} = \$20$$

For instance, if an apparel retailer used a 50 percent markup, an approach referred to as **keystoning,** the retail price would be double the cost.

Initial Markup and Maintained Markup   The previous discussion is based on the assumption that the retailer sells all items at an initially set price. However, retailers rarely sell all items at the initial price. They frequently reduce the price of items for special promotions or to get rid of excess inventory at the end of a season. In addition, discounts are given to employees, and some merchandise is lost to theft and accounting errors (**inventory shrinkage**). These factors that reduce the actual selling price from the initial sales price are called **reductions.** Thus, there is a difference between the initial markup and the maintained markup.

The **initial markup** is the retail selling price initially set for the merchandise minus the cost of the merchandise. The **maintained markup** is the actual sales realized for the merchandise minus its costs. It is the amount of profit realized from merchandising decisions.

Thus, the maintained markup is conceptually similar to the gross margin, but slightly different. Some retailers have workroom costs, such as alterations of a suit or assembly of a bicycle, that would reduce the maintained markup compared with the gross margin. Retailers often receive cash discounts from vendors for paying invoices early, which increase the maintained markup compared with the gross margin. Because workroom costs and cash discounts are not typically under the buyer's control, they are accounted for separately. To summarize:

$$\text{Gross margin percentage} = \frac{\text{Maintained markup} - \text{Workroom costs} + \text{Cash discounts}}{\text{Net sales}}$$

The difference between the initial and maintained markups is illustrated in Exhibit 14–2. The item illustrated costs $0.60, and the initial price for the item is $1.00, so the initial markup is $0.40 and the initial markup percentage is 40 percent. However, the average actual sale price for the item is $0.90. The reductions are $0.10, so the maintained markup is $0.30 and the maintained markup percentage is 33 percent (0.30/0.90).

The relationship between the initial and maintained markup percentages is:

$$\text{Initial markup percentage} = \frac{\begin{array}{c}\text{Maintained markup percentage} \\ \text{(as a percentage of planned} \\ \text{actual sales)}\end{array} + \begin{array}{c}\text{Percent reductions} \\ \text{(as a percentage of planned} \\ \text{actual sales)}\end{array}}{100\% + \begin{array}{c}\text{Percent reductions} \\ \text{(as a percentage of planned} \\ \text{actual sales)}\end{array}}$$

EXHIBIT 14–2
Difference between
Initial Markup and
Maintained Markup

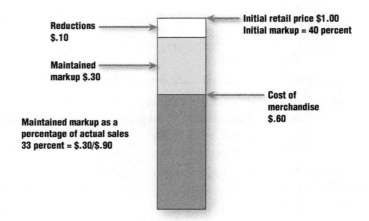

Reductions $.10

Maintained markup $.30

Maintained markup as a percentage of actual sales
33 percent = $.30/$.90

Initial retail price $1.00
Initial markup = 40 percent

Cost of merchandise $.60

Thus, if the buyer setting the price for the item shown in Exhibit 14–2 planned on reductions of 10 percent of actual sales and wanted a maintained markup of 33 percent, the initial markup should be:

$$\text{Initial markup percentage} = \frac{33\% + (\$0.10/\$0.90 = 11.111\%)}{100\% + 11.111\%} = 40\%$$

and the initial retail price should be:

$$\text{Initial retail price} = \frac{\text{Cost}}{1 - \text{Initial markup percentage}} = \frac{\$0.60}{1 - 0.40} = \$1.00$$

Pricing Optimization Software

Setting prices by simply marking up the merchandise cost neglects a number of other factors that retailers need to consider, such as price sensitivities, competition, and the sales of complementary products. Since the early 2000s, many retailers have taken a comprehensive approach to setting prices that uses **pricing optimization software.** The software programs use a set of algorithms that analyze past and current merchandise sales and prices, as well as competitors' prices; estimate the relationship between prices and sales generated; and then determine the optimal (most profitable) initial price for the merchandise and the appropriate size and timing of markdowns. Optimization can be accomplished at the store level and even sometimes at the individual customer level, which is very useful for creating loyalty and behavioral intentions.

To set initial prices, the software uses historical sales data from its own and competitors' stores. It determines the price–sales relationship of complementary items— those that have a similar sales pattern, such as Pepsi and Lays Potato Chips. Thus, not only can the software tell buyers the best price for Pepsi, but it also suggests a price for the chips. Buyers can also determine how much Pepsi they will sell at a given price if they lower the price of Coke or their private-label (or store) brand. The software can incorporate other factors, such as the store's image (e.g., cheap or premium price), where the nearest rival is located, seasonal factors (e.g., soft drinks sell better in the summer than in the winter), or whether an item is featured in coupons.[5] It can set decision rules, such as optimizing the regular price to never be more than a nickel above a competitor's price. Or the software might suggest offering a very competitive price on products for which customers are very sensitive, such as milk or diapers, but take a larger margin on less price-sensitive items, such as baby accessories and store brands.[6] Merchandising optimization software can be expensive, but its use can have an impressive impact on bottom-line profitability. For instance, the Walgreens-owned and New York City–based Duane Reade pharmacy chain used merchandising optimization software to boost its sales of diapers.[7] The chain had tried discounts and coupons, but the category was losing ground to the competition. The software indicated that the markup should be a function of the age of the child for whom parents were buying diapers. For newborn sizes, Duane Reade raised prices, but once the child got to the training pants stage, it offered lower unit prices. A year later, Duane Reade's revenues in the baby care category had jumped 27 percent, with gross margin increases of 2 percent. With a traditional analysis, the chain was unlikely to ever guess that brand-new parents exhibit little price sensitivity, compared with parents who have been at it a while.

Profit Impact of Setting a Retail Price: The Use of Break-Even Analysis

Retailers often want to know the number of units they need sell to begin making a profit. For example, a retailer might want to know:

- Break-even sales to generate a target profit.
- Break-even volume and dollars to justify introducing a new product, product line, or department.
- Break-even sales change needed to cover a price change.

A useful analytical tool for making these assessments is **break-even analysis**, which determines, on the basis of fixed and variable costs, how much merchandise needs to be sold to achieve a break-even (zero) profit.

The **break-even point quantity** is the quantity at which total revenue equals total cost, and then profit occurs for additional sales.

The formula for calculating the sales quantity needed to break even is:

$$\text{Break-even quantity} = \frac{\text{Total fixed costs}}{\text{Actual unit sales price} - \text{Unit variable cost}}$$

The following examples illustrate the use of this formula in determining the break-even volume of a new private-label product and the break-even change in volume needed to cover a price change.

Calculating Break-Even for a New Product   Hypothetically, PetSmart is considering an introduction of a new private-label, dry dog food targeting owners of older dogs. The cost of developing this dog food is $700,000, including salaries for the design team and costs of testing the product. Because these costs do not change with the quantity of product produced and sold, they're known as **fixed costs.** PetSmart plans to sell the dog food for $12 a bag—the unit price. The **variable cost** is the retailer's expenses that vary directly with the quantity of product produced and sold. Variable costs often include direct labor and materials used in producing the product. PetSmart will be purchasing the product from a private-label manufacturer. Thus, the only variable cost is the dog food's cost, $5, from the private-label manufacturer.

$$\text{Break-even quantity} = \frac{\text{Fixed costs}}{\text{Actual unit sales price} - \text{Unit variable cost}}$$
$$= \frac{\$700,000}{\$12 - \$5} = 100,000 \text{ bags}$$

Thus, PetSmart needs to sell 100,000 bags of dog food to break even, or make zero profit, and for every additional bag sold, it will make $7 profit.

Now assume that PetSmart wants to make $100,000 profit from the new product line. The break-even quantity now becomes:

$$\text{Break-even quantity} = \frac{\text{Fixed cost}}{\text{Actual unit sales price} - \text{Unit variable cost}}$$
$$= \frac{\$700,000 + \$100,000}{\$12 - \$5} = 114,286 \text{ bags}$$

Calculating Break-Even Sales   An issue closely related to the calculation of a break-even point is determining how much unit sales would have to increase to make a profit from a price cut or how much sales would have to decline to make a price increase unprofitable. Continuing with the PetSmart example, assume the break-even quantity is 114,286 units, based on the $700,000 fixed cost, the $100,000 profit, a selling price of $12, and a cost of $5. Now PetSmart is considering lowering the price of a bag of dog food to $10. How many units must it sell to break even if it lowers its selling price by 16.67 percent, to $10? Using the formula,

$$\text{Break-even quantity} = \frac{\text{Fixed cost}}{\text{Actual unit sales price} - \text{Unit variable cost}}$$

$$= \frac{\$700,000 + \$100,000}{\$10 - \$5} = 160,000 \text{ bags}$$

So, if PetSmart decreases its price by 16.67 percent, from $12 to $10, unit sales must increase by 40 percent: $(160,000 - 114,286) \div 114,286$.

MARKDOWNS

LO4

Examine how and why retailers take markdowns.

REFACT

During difficult economic times, if a brand lowers its prices, 70 percent of consumers believe "the brand is normally overpriced," and 62 percent think "the product is old, about to expire or about to be updated, and the company is trying to get rid of it to make room for the new stuff." When a brand does not lower its prices during tough times, 64 percent believe "the product is extremely popular," and another 64 percent assume "the product is already a good value."[8]

REFACT

Some vendors, such as Gucci, Cartier, and Christian Louboutin, have become so concerned with protecting their images that they require that some of their retailers exclude their products from certain markdown sales events.[9]

The preceding section reviewed how retailers initially set prices on the basis of the merchandise cost and desired maintained margin. However, retailers also take **markdowns** by reducing the initial retail price. This section examines why retailers take markdowns, how they optimize markdown decisions, how they reduce the amount of markdowns, and how they liquidate markdown merchandise.

Reasons for Taking Markdowns

Retailers' reasons for taking markdowns can be classified as either clearance (to dispose of merchandise) or promotional (to generate sales). Clearance markdowns are examined in this section, while promotional markdowns are discussed later in this chapter as a method of increasing sales and profits.

When merchandise is selling at a slower rate than planned and will become obsolete at the end of its season, or is priced higher than competitors' goods, buyers generally mark it down for clearance purposes. As discussed in Chapter 12, slow-selling merchandise decreases inventory turnover; prevents buyers from acquiring new, better-selling merchandise; and can diminish the retailer's image for selling the most current styles and trends.

Markdowns are part of the cost of doing business, and thus buyers plan for them. They tend to order more fashion merchandise than they forecast actually selling because they are more concerned about under-ordering and stocking out of a popular item before the end of the season than about over-ordering and having to discount excess merchandise at the end of the season. Stocking out of popular merchandise can have a detrimental effect on a fashion retailer's image, whereas discounting merchandise at the end of the season just reduces maintained markup.

Thus, a buyer's objective isn't to minimize markdowns. If markdowns are too low, the buyer is probably pricing the merchandise too low, not purchasing enough merchandise, or not taking enough risks with the merchandise being purchased. Thus, buyers set the initial markup price high enough that even after markdowns and other reductions have been taken, the planned maintained markup is still achieved.

Optimizing Markdown Decisions   Retailers have traditionally created a set of arbitrary rules for taking markdowns to dispose of unwanted merchandise. One retailer, for instance, identifies markdown candidates when its weekly sell-through percentages fall below a certain level. Another retailer cuts prices on the basis of

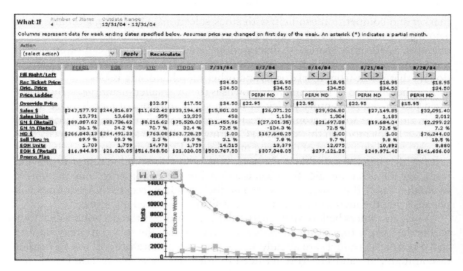

The output from the Oracle Retail markdown model indicates that the model's recommended markdown of $18.95 will result in more than $5,000 greater profit than the buyer's planned markdown of $22.95.

how long the merchandise has been in the store—marking products down by 20 percent after 8 weeks, then by 30 percent after 12 weeks, and finally by 50 percent after 16 weeks. Such a rule-based approach, however, is limiting because it does not consider the demand for the merchandise at different price points or in different locations and thus produces less-than-optimal profits.

The optimization software described previously in this chapter, used to set initial retail prices, can also indicate when to take markdowns and how much they should be in different locations.[10] It works by continually updating its pricing forecasts on the basis of actual sales throughout the season and factoring in differences in price sensitivities. For example, the software recognizes that in early November, a winter item's sales are better than expected in Colorado, so it delays taking a markdown that had been planned but takes the markdown in New England. Each week, as new sales data become available, it readjusts the forecasts to include the latest information. It computes literally thousands of scenarios for each item—a process that is too complicated and time-consuming for buyers to do on their own. It then evaluates the outcomes on the basis of expected profits and other factors and selects the action that produces the best results across all regions.

Reducing the Amount of Markdowns   Retailers have several options for reducing the amount of markdowns. They can work closely with vendors to choose merchandise and coordinate deliveries to help reduce the financial burden of taking markdowns. They can also buy smaller quantities to make it easier to forecast demand for a shorter time period and create a feeling of scarcity. Finally, retailers can strive to offer a good value.

Vendors have a partnering relationship with their retailers and thus a vested interest in their success. Vendors that are knowledgeable about the

Pricing optimization software recognizes when sales for winter coats are slower than expected and suggests both the timing and amount of markdowns.

market and competition can help with stock selections. Of course, a retailer must also trust its own taste and intuition; otherwise, its store will have the same merchandise as all other stores. As discussed in Chapter 13, buyers can often obtain markdown money—funds a vendor gives the retailer to cover lost gross margin dollars that result from markdowns and other merchandising issues.

Another method of reducing markdowns is to buy smaller quantities.[11] By adopting a just-in-time inventory policy, in which small amounts of merchandise arrive just in time to be sold, customers perceive a scarcity and purchase at full price. (See Chapter 13 for more on this strategy.) Creating a feeling of scarcity among customers is an excellent method of reducing markdowns. Even if there are adequate quantities of merchandise available in the stockroom or in a distribution center, displaying just a few items on the sales floor sends a signal to the customer to "buy them now, while they last!" If retailers simply change their displays frequently, customers will perceive that the merchandise is new and available in limited quantities.

When customers believe that a particular retailer offers them a good value, they will be less likely to wait for markdowns. An everyday low-price strategy implies that a retailer's products are already at low prices and therefore will not be further discounted. Zara and H&M don't need to advertise their low prices. Loyal customers return time after time to look for low-priced treasures. A few retailers, like Apple, focus on quality and image and therefore simply don't have sales! It is an enviable position, to which most retailers can only aspire.

Liquidating Markdown Merchandise   Even with the best planning, some merchandise may remain unsold at the end of a season. Retailers use one of six strategies to liquidate this unsold merchandise.

Sell to Another Retailer   Selling the unsold merchandise to another retailer is a very popular strategy among retailers. For instance, off-price retailers such as TJX Corporation (owners of TJ Maxx and Marshalls) and Bluefly.com purchase end-of-season merchandise from other retailers and sell it at deep discounts. However, this approach for liquidating unsold merchandise only enables retailers to recoup a small percentage of the merchandise's cost—often a mere 10 percent.

Consolidate Unsold Merchandise   Markdown merchandise can be consolidated in a number of ways. First, the consolidation can be made into one or a few of the retailer's regular locations. Second, markdown merchandise can be consolidated into another retail chain or an outlet store under the same ownership. Saks Fifth Avenue OFF Fifth, Nordstrom Rack, and Neiman Marcus Last Call Clearance Center each use this approach. Third, unsold merchandise can be shipped to a distribution center or a rented space such as a convention center for final sale. However, consolidation sales can be complex and expensive due to the extra transportation and record keeping involved.

Sell at Internet Auction   The Internet is increasingly useful for liquidating unsold merchandise. For example, an electronics store might utilize eBay to sell goods it has received from trade-ins. Many retailers have separate areas of their websites for clearance merchandise.

Return to Vendor   Some large retailers have enough clout to negotiate an agreement that some merchandise be returned to vendors. Although an outstanding option, it is not generally viable unless the balance of power rests solidly with the retailer.

Donate to Charity   Donating clearance merchandise to charities is a common practice. Charitable giving is always a good corporate practice. It is a way of giving back to the community and has strong public relations benefits. Also, the cost value of the merchandise can be deducted from income, thus reducing the firm's tax liability.

Carry the Merchandise Over to the Next Season   The final liquidation approach—to carry merchandise over to the next season—is used with relatively high-priced nonfashion merchandise, such as traditional men's clothing and furniture. Generally, however, it is not profitable to carry over merchandise because of excessive inventory carrying costs and the potential of having the merchandise look "shopworn" or outdated.

PRICING TECHNIQUES FOR INCREASING SALES AND PROFITS

This section reviews several techniques used by retailers to increase sales and profits. The first is variable pricing, in which retailers charge different prices to different customers. The other techniques—dealing with perceptions of fairness, leader pricing, price lining, and odd pricing—take advantage of the way customers process information. The section concludes with a discussion of how the Internet has changed the way retailers and their customers make pricing decisions.

> **LO5**
> Identify the pricing techniques retailers use to increase sales and profits.

Variable Pricing and Price Discrimination

Retailers use a variety of techniques to maximize profits by charging different prices to different customers.

Individualized Variable Pricing   Ideally, retailers could maximize their profits if they charged each customer as much as the customer was willing to pay. For instance, if a wealthy, price-insensitive customer wants to buy a new car battery, AutoZone would like to price the battery at $200 but then price the same battery at $125 to make a sale to a more price-sensitive, lower-income customer. Charging each individual customer a different price based on their willingness to pay is called **first-degree price discrimination**.[12]

> REFACT
> The most expensive charity auction ever on eBay was for a lunch with Warren Buffett, the CEO of investment company Berkshire Hathaway. The anonymous winner paid $2.6 million.[13]

Pricing merchandise through auction bidding is an example of first-degree price discrimination. A retailer offering a Rolls Royce on eBay Motors maximizes its profits because the customer with the highest willingness to pay bids and pays the highest price.

Although individualized variable pricing is legal and widely used in some retail sectors, such as automobile and antique dealers, it is not very practical in most retail stores. First, it is difficult to assess each customer's willingness to pay; second, retailers cannot change the posted prices in stores as customers with different willingness to pay enter the store. In addition, customers might feel they are being

By selling on eBay Motors' online auction, this seller is using first-degree price discrimination to get the highest price for this Rolls Royce.

treated unfairly if they realize that they are being charged a higher price than other customers. Staples, however, uses individualized variable pricing at the point-of-sale as a strategic differentiator. The best loyalty program customers receive different (lower) prices than "regular" customers. When these loyal customers swipe their cards, the point-of-sale system automatically re-prices the items in that shopper's basket. No one other than Staples and the customer knows—certainly not the next person in line or the competition.[14]

Now, more and more retailers have started to use sophisticated models that allow them to increase the frequency of updating their prices and the ability to implement the price changes throughout the chain. The prices are driven by changes in demand and supply and price elasticities and takes into account localized market issues. A limitation of these models tends to be the fact that the input is historical data, which may reduce their predictive ability.[15]

Retailers have increased their use of dynamic pricing techniques due to the information that is available from point-of-sale data collected on Internet purchases and in stores. **Dynamic pricing**, also known as **individualized pricing**, refers to the process of charging different prices for goods or services based on the type of customer, time of the day, week, or even season, and level of demand. Retailers may also charge customers different prices based on their loyalty status derived from their CRM systems—that is, platinum customers receive lower prices than silver ones. Early adopters of dynamic pricing techniques were service retailers, such as airlines, hotels, and cruises lines. It is quite common for passengers on the same plane to have paid different fares depending on when they bought their ticket. The ease of using dynamic pricing when selling merchandise on the Internet is much greater than in a store because only one person sees the price. Retailing View 14.4 highlights how some retailers are using dynamic pricing.

14.4   RETAILING VIEW   Just What Makes Dynamic Pricing So Appealing?

Today, it is easier for retailers using an Internet channel to change their online prices than the prices in their physical stores. These retailers are using software that allows them to adjust prices the moment it finds a competitor selling the same item for a lower (or higher) price. As an example, in one day Amazon changed the price of a single microwave oven nine times. If buyers happened to be shopping at the right time or had the right characteristics, they might have gotten a lower price. Those shopping an hour later or having different characteristics probably paid a higher price.

Such price shifts are familiar to travelers: Buying an airline ticket on a Tuesday is often cheaper than buying the exact same flight on a Saturday. Consumers' sense that such tactics are unfair led to the unique selling proposition of Orbitz, which promises that if another customer books the same flight for less, it will refund a higher-price-point customer the difference.

In some cases, online retailers are less interested in the actual price than in what the lowest price does for them. By ensuring they have a lower price than any other competitor—even if just by a cent or two—a retailer earns the top rank in a price comparison search engine. Also, if they find that all their competitors are charging higher prices, retailers learn that they can bump up their own

price and margins, without losing customers. Thus the increasing use of dynamic prices appears largely driven by the upside profit potential—being higher in the online search ranking enables them to sell more and charge higher prices.

Customers may not embrace retailers that use dynamic pricing. Charging different prices according to the time of day or the identity of the shopper is not illegal, but a survey showed that 87 percent of people thought it should be. If consumers find these changing rules, prices, and methods irritating, tiresome, or unfair, they may choose to avoid retailers that engage in dynamic pricing.

Sources: Julia Angwin and Dana Mattioli, "Coming Soon: Toilet Paper Priced Like Airline Tickets," *The Wall Street Journal*, September 5, 2012; Gilon Miller, "How Online Dynamic Pricing Can Hurt Retailers and Consumers," *UpsteamCommerce.com*, September 11, 2012; Laura Gunderson, "Amazon's 'Dynamic' Prices Get Some Static," *The Oregonian*, May 5, 2012; and Susan Reda, "Pricing Transparency," *Stores*, February 2012.

DISCUSSION QUESTION

Would you patronize a retailer that used dynamic pricing?

Self-Selected Variable Pricing   An alternative approach for dynamic pricing is to offer the same multiple-price schedule to all customers, which encourages price-sensitive customers to take advantage of the lower price. This approach is referred to as **second-degree price discrimination.** Retailers use second-degree price discrimination when they offer promotional and clearance markdowns, coupons, price bundling, and multi-unit pricing.

Promotional Markdowns   Retailers employ promotional markdowns to promote merchandise and increase sales. Markdowns can increase customer traffic flow. Retailers plan promotions in which they take markdowns for holidays, for special events, and as part of their overall promotional program. Retailers hope that customers will purchase other products at regular prices while they're in the store. Another opportunity created by promotional markdowns is to increase the sale of complementary products. For example, a supermarket's markdown on hot-dog buns may be offset by increased demand for hotdogs, mustard, and relish—all sold at regular prices.

Clearance Markdowns for Fashion Merchandise   While the discussion of clearance markdowns earlier in the chapter focused primarily on how retailers get rid of unwanted merchandise, this merchandise can also be used to attract different market segments based on their degree of price sensitivity. Fashion-conscious customers who have a high willingness to pay because they want to be the first to wear the latest fashions self-select to pay higher prices. More price-sensitive customers wait to buy the merchandise at the end of the season when prices are lower.

Coupons   **Coupons** offer a discount on the price of specific items when they're purchased. Coupons are issued by manufacturers and retailers in newspapers, on products, on the shelf, at the cash register, over the Internet and mobile devices, and through the mail. Retailers use coupons because they are thought to induce customers to try products for the first time, convert first-time users to regular users, encourage large purchases, increase usage, instill loyalty, and protect market share against the competition. Coupons are an attractive way to target price-sensitive customers because they will likely expend the extra effort to collect and redeem coupons, whereas price-insensitive customers will not. Retailers are increasingly concerned about the growth of extreme couponing (see Retailing View 14.5).

Price Bundling   **Price bundling** is the practice of offering two or more different products or services for sale at one price.[17] For instance, McDonald's offers a bundle of a sandwich, French fries, and a soft drink in a Value Meal at a discount compared with buying the items individually. Price bundling increases both unit and dollar sales by increasing the amount of merchandise bought during a store visit. The practice is an example of second-degree price discrimination because it offers more price-sensitive customers a lower-priced alternative.

Multiple-Unit Pricing   The term **multiple-unit pricing,** or **quantity discounts,** refers to the practice of offering two or more similar products or services for sale at one lower total price. For example, a convenience store may sell three one-liter bottles of soda for $2.39 when the price for a single one-liter bottle is 99 cents—a saving of 58 cents. Like price bundling, this variable-pricing approach is used to increase sales

McDonald's uses price bundling when it combines a sandwich, side, and a soft drink in an Extra Value Meal.

14.5   RETAILING VIEW   Moving Beyond Extreme Couponing

Initially presented as a somewhat odd and possibly compulsive behavior on TV shows such as *Extreme Couponing*, the practice of relying heavily on coupons for a household's grocery purchases has gone mainstream. Increasing rates of heavy use of coupons by customers challenges retailers, especially in their supply chains. If a single extreme couponer buys out all of the store's stock on a particular SKU, other customers are bound to be frustrated.

In response, several grocers and drugstore chains have implemented limits on coupon redemptions. Rite Aid limits the number of coupons any one customer may use in one trip. Kroger has banned stacking, which is when a customer combines paper and online coupons for a given item. Walmart rings up multiple coupon purchases separately, creating more inconvenience for extreme couponers.

Yet as these brick-and-mortar stores work to mitigate the impacts of coupon use, online merchants are ramping up their offers. Foursquare introduced a targeted couponing extension to its service. With it, businesses can offer impressive coupons, but only to those Foursquare users who check in to their location. As Amazon continues its efforts to provide virtually everything a household might need, it has added manufacturers' coupons to its site. Thus, if a shopper is willing to buy diapers from Amazon, he or she can "clip" a coupon by simply clicking on it through the site. Amazon promises that by using its electronic coupons, shoppers can stop worrying, because they will "never leave the coupon book at home or walk out of the store without redeeming your discounts again."

For traditional retailers, extreme couponers disrupt their long-standing tactics to attract shoppers to their stores. For online retailers, this situation may be just the thing to encourage more consumers to buy their products online, where no one will tell them how to coupon.

Extreme couponing causes havock on a retailer's supply chain when one customer buys all of a store's stock of a single SKU.

Sources: E. J. Schultz, "Retailers Start to Suffer Super-Couponer Fatigue," *Advertising Age*, July 11, 2011; Martha C. White, "Stores Confront Extreme Couponers' Tactics with Policy Changes," *Time*, February 29, 2012; Amanda Fortini, "Honey, I Got a Year's Worth of Tuna Fish: Coupon Clipping as the Key to Economic Rebirth," *The New York Times*, May 3, 2012; Spencer E. Ante, "Foursquare Joins the Coupon Craze," *The Wall Street Journal*, May 8, 2012; and "Amazon Coupons," *Amazon.com*, www.amazon.com/Coupons/b?ie=UTF8&node=2231352011.

DISCUSSION QUESTION

Is extreme couponing worth the trouble to you? What about your parents?

volume. Depending on the type of product, however, customers may stockpile the items for use at a later time, thus having no impact on sales over time. Multi-unit pricing is an example of second-degree price discrimination because customers who buy and consume more of a product are presumably more price-sensitive and thus attracted by the lower prices if they buy more units.

Offering two or more similar products or services for sale at one lower price is called multiple-unit pricing.

Variable Pricing by Market Segment   Retailers often charge different prices to different demographic market segments, a practice referred to as **third-degree price discrimination.** For example, movie theaters have lower ticket prices for seniors and college students, presumably because these segments are more price-sensitive than other customers. This practice is generally legal, although gender-based pricing, in which men and women are charged different prices for the same service, has come into question, and it is not always clear whether this type of pricing is legal. For instance, New York salons were issued numerous gender-pricing violations. Salons routinely charge men and women different prices for things such as haircuts and waxing. Salon owners argue that men should get lower prices for haircuts because they are generally less work and they come in more often, sometimes as much as twice a month; they also argue that men should be charged more for waxing as a man's back is generally much more labor-intensive. The city views these pricing policies as discrimination.[18]

Another example is women have always paid more to have their shirts laundered, and that tradition continues to endure. Dry cleaners argue that women's shirts don't fit properly on the industrial presses, so they have to be done by hand. Some dry cleaners have taken a rational and presumably fairer approach. Shirts that can be pressed on the shirt-pressing machines get one price, while hand-pressed shirts get another, higher price. All dry-cleaned shirts are charged the same price.[19]

Another example of third-degree price discrimination is zone pricing. **Zone pricing** is the practice of charging different prices in different stores, markets, regions, or zones. Retailers generally use zone pricing to address different competitive situations in their various markets. For example, some multichannel retailers implement zone pricing by asking customers to enter their zip code if they want a price quote. A single city might comprise five or so pricing zones, categorized by their proximity to a Walmart versus a less economical regional grocery chain, for example. Although widely considered unethical, many retailers have charged higher prices in stores located in lower-income or urban areas because these customers, including elderly retirees, have less access to alternatives. Furthermore, the cost of operating businesses in those areas can be more expensive than in others. Thus, such third-degree price discrimination, when used in this manner to discriminate on the basis of income and age, is considered an unethical practice by many.

Dealing with Perceptions of Fairness   Setting different prices for similar products or services, such as a shirt sold at the manufacturer's suggested retail price versus discounted at the end of the season, or a seat on an airplane discounted on the day of the flight, may seem unfair to customers. To lessen this feeling, retailers can offer additional benefits, such as an unlimited return policy or customization, with the higher-priced products or services, whereas they place more restrictions on the less-expensive items.[20]

Beyond encouraging consumers to recognize the greater value of a higher-priced option, stores can engage in tactics to reduce the sense of unfairness overall. By providing more information, such as where a product was made or what sorts of tools a service provider needs, the customer can more effectively decide whether the price is fair. That is, a consumer who regards the prices for a bunch of carrots unfairly high might revise his or her perception upon learning that the carrots were grown in organic soil by a local farmer who uses no chemical pesticides. These attributes imply the higher quality of the product and the high costs of production, which should help the buyer recognize the justification for the higher price.

To lessen the impacts of a perceived unfair price, retailers also can draw the customer's attention to particular attributes that add perceived value to the product or service, such as handwork on apparel or friendly cancellation policies at a hotel.

Leader Pricing

Leader pricing is the practice of pricing certain items lower than normal to increase customers' traffic flow or boost sales of complementary products. Some retailers call these products **loss leaders.** In a strict sense, loss leaders are sold below cost and would therefore be considered predatory pricing, which is discussed in the next section. But a product doesn't have to be sold below cost for the retailer to use a leader-pricing strategy.

The best items for leader pricing are frequently purchased products like white bread, milk, and eggs or well-known brand names like Coca-Cola and Kellogg's Corn Flakes. Customers take note of ads for these products because they're purchased weekly. The retailer hopes consumers will also purchase their entire weekly grocery list while buying the loss leaders.

When retailers like Kroger offer three SKUs for ice cream that reflect good, better, and best quality at three different price points, they are using a price lining technique.

One problem with leader pricing is that it might attract shoppers referred to as **cherry pickers,** who go from one store to another, buying only items that are on special. These shoppers are clearly unprofitable for retailers.[21]

Price Lining

Retailers frequently offer a limited number of predetermined price points within a merchandise category, a practice known as **price lining.** For instance, because Kroger's vision for its store brands is to build loyalty among customers, with strong store brands that are exclusive to the retailer, it pursues a price lining store brand strategy to provide Kroger products to all customer segments. As discussed in Chapter 13, in the ice cream category, for instance, it offers the "Value" brand for its price-sensitive customers, with "adequate" packaging and quality. In the middle is the "Banner Brand," which is geared to the customer that wants ice cream comparable to Breyers. At the higher end is the "Private Selection" brand, which competes with Dove and Häagen Dazs. Developing products for all these customer segments means that Kroger closes any gaps in the ability of its current assortment to meet customers' needs. Other reasons customers and retailers benefit from price lining are:

- Confusion that often arises from multiple-price choices is essentially eliminated. The customer can choose the ice cream with the low, medium, or high price.
- From the retailer's perspective, the merchandising task is simplified. That is, all products within a certain price line are merchandised together. Furthermore, when going to market, the firm's buyers can select their purchases with the predetermined price lines in mind.
- Price lining can also give buyers greater flexibility. If a strict formula is used to establish the initial retail price (initial markup), there could be numerous price points. But with a price-lining strategy, some merchandise may be bought a little below or above the expected cost for a price line. Of course, price lining can also limit retail buyers' flexibility. They may be forced to pass up potentially profitable merchandise because it doesn't fit into a price line.

Although many manufacturers and retailers are simplifying their product offerings to save distribution and inventory costs and make the choice simpler for consumers, price lining can be used to get customers to "trade up" to a more expensive model.

Odd Pricing

Odd pricing refers to the practice of using a price that ends in an odd number, typically a 9. Odd pricing has a long history in retailing. In the nineteenth and early twentieth centuries, odd pricing was used to reduce losses due to employee theft. Because merchandise had an odd price, salespeople typically had to go to the cash register to give the customer change and record the sale, making it more difficult for salespeople to keep the customer's money. Odd pricing was also used to keep track of how many times an item had been marked down. After an initial price of $20, the first markdown would be $17.99, the second markdown $15.98, and so on.

The results of empirical studies in this area are mixed;[23] however, many retailers believe that odd pricing can increase profits. The theory behind odd pricing is the

REFACT

Apple Computer may have saved the music industry from oblivion by pricing songs on iTunes at 99 cents in 2003. At the time, no one was sure that anyone would pay for online music when people could steal it from several peer-to-peer networks.[22]

The practice of offering odd prices—a price that ends in an odd number, typically a 9—is more than 100 years old. Although empirical studies have mixed results, many retailers believe that the practice can increase profits.

assumption that shoppers don't notice the last digit or digits of a price, so that a price of $2.99 is perceived as $2. An alternative theory is that "9" endings signal low prices. Thus, for products that are believed to be sensitive to price, many retailers will round the price down to the nearest 9 to create a positive price image. If, for example, the price would normally be $3.09, many retailers will lower the price to $2.99.

Research results suggest the following guidelines for making price-ending decisions:

- When the price sensitivity of the market is high, it is likely to be advantageous to raise or lower prices so that they end in high numbers such as 9.

- When the price sensitivity of the market is not especially high, the risks to the retailer's image of using "9" endings are likely to outweigh the benefits. In such cases, the use of even dollar prices and round-number endings would be more appropriate.

- Many upscale retailers appeal to price-sensitive segments of the market through periodic discounting, which suggests the value of a combination strategy: Only break from a standard policy of round-number endings to use "9" endings when communicating discounts and special offers.

Using the Internet and Social and Mobile Channels to Make Pricing Decisions

The growth of the electronic channel, the popularity of social media and the adoption of smartphones has greatly changed the way consumers get and use information to make purchasing decisions based on price. Traditionally, price competition between store-based retailers offering the same merchandise was reduced by geography because consumers typically shop at the stores and malls closest to where they live and work. However, Internet sites such as Shopzilla, RedLaser, TheFind, ShopStyle, and PriceGrabber allow customers to compare prices across a range of retailers. As discussed earlier in this chapter, showrooming enables customers with mobile devices to check prices in stores and purchase online, ostensibly at a lower price.

Today, growing numbers of consumers are opting into services provided by various mobile firms and their applications (e.g., Foursquare, LocalResponse) to receive mobile offers (see Exhibit 14–3). The latest generation of price promotional offers takes into account the consumers' geographical location that is

LO6
Describe how the Internet and social and mobile channels are used to make pricing decisions.

REFACT

In 2011, consumers redeemed more than 3 billion coupons using their mobile devices.[24]

EXHIBIT 14–3
How Consumers Get
Mobile Coupons

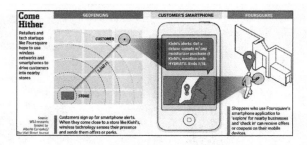

accessed from their phone location or locational coding via certain sites and offers them localized promotions for retailers who are in close proximity. This concept is called **geofencing.** As a consequence, these coupons and offers are increasingly relevant, and the redemption of online coupons is growing at an astronomical rate.

These mobile offers can be delivered by a host of different methods. For example, Meijer supermarkets has created an application for its consumers called Meijer Find-it.[25] This application has a host of interesting features from providing customers the ability to create shopping lists, access Meijer perks (Mperks coupons and sale items), and find the merchandise in a given store. Sensors in the store allow the app to offer appropriate coupons and to constantly organize the list by the user's location in the store.[26]

Although consumers shopping electronically can collect price information with little effort, they also can get a lot of other information about the quality and performance of products, thus making them less sensitive to price. For instance, an Internet site that offers custom-made Oriental rugs can clearly show real differences in the patterns and materials used for construction. Electronic grocery services offered by Safeway allow customers to sort cereals by nutritional content, thus making it easier to use that attribute in their decision making. If a customer wants to make an egg dish for breakfast, the site can also recommend numerous recipes that include eggs, as well as providing the nutritional information. The additional information about product quality might lead customers to pay more for high-quality products, thus decreasing the importance of price.

The classic response to the question "What are the three most important things in retailing?" used to be "location, location, location." In the new world of social, mobile, and online, the answer will be "information, information, information."

LEGAL AND ETHICAL PRICING ISSUES

LO7

Indicate the legal and ethical issues retailers should consider when setting prices.

Retailers consider certain legal and ethical issues when setting prices. Some of the legal and ethical pricing issues are predatory pricing, resale price maintenance, horizontal price fixing, bait-and-switch tactics, scanned versus posted prices, and deceptive reference prices.

Predatory Pricing

Predatory pricing arises when a dominant retailer sets prices below its costs to drive competitive retailers out of business. Eventually, the predator hopes to raise prices when the competition is eliminated and earn back enough profits to compensate for its losses. For instance, independent booksellers accuse Walmart, Target, and Amazon of pricing best-selling books below their cost, such as Walter

Isaacson's biography of Steve Jobs, for as low as $8.95 when the cover price is $35. The American Booksellers Association has complained to the Department of Justice, claiming that these retailers are engaging in illegal predatory pricing, which is damaging to the book industry and harmful to consumers.[27] They have also complained about Amazon's e-book low-pricing strategy. The latest court ruling allows Amazon to continue to offer low prices on its Kindle books based on how difficult it is to prove whether e-book retailers will really drive the competition out of business and then raise the prices.[28] It appears that lower prices for e-books are here to stay. Some states have old statutes that declare it illegal to sell goods at unreasonably low prices, usually below their cost. However, a retailer generally may sell merchandise at any price as long as the motive isn't to eliminate competition.

Independent booksellers accuse Walmart, Target, and Amazon of predatory pricing when they sell best-selling books below their cost, such as Walter Isaacson's biography of Steve Jobs.

Resale Price Maintenance

As discussed in Chapter 13, vendors often encourage retailers to sell their merchandise at a specific price, known as the manufacturer's suggested retail price (MSRP). Vendors set MSRPs to reduce retail price competition among retailers and stimulate retailers to provide complementary services. Vendors enforce MSRPs by withholding benefits such as cooperative advertising or even refusing to deliver merchandise to noncomplying retailers. The latest U.S. Supreme Court ruling suggests that the ability of a vendor to require that retailers sell merchandise at MSRPs would be decided on a case-by-case basis, depending on the individual circumstances.[29]

Horizontal Price Fixing

Horizontal price fixing involves agreements between retailers that are in direct competition with each other to set the same prices. This practice clearly reduces competition and is illegal. As a general rule of thumb, retailers should refrain from discussing prices or terms and conditions of sale with competitors. If buyers or store managers want to know competitors' prices, they can look at a competitor's advertisements, its websites, or check out its stores.

Bait-and-Switch Tactics

A **bait and switch** is an unlawful, deceptive practice that lures customers into a store by advertising a product at a lower-than-normal price (the bait) and then, once they are in the store, induces them to purchase a higher-priced model (the switch). Bait and switch usually involves the store either having inadequate inventory for the advertised product or pushing salespeople to disparage the quality of the advertised model and emphasize the superior performance of a higher-priced model. To avoid disappointing customers and risking problems with the Federal Trade Commission (FTC), the retailer should have sufficient inventory of advertised items and offer customers rain checks if stockouts occur. A **rain check** is a promise to customers to sell currently out-of-stock merchandise at the advertised price when it arrives.

Scanned versus Posted Prices

Although customers and regulators are concerned about price-scanning accuracy, studies usually find a high level of accuracy. In general, retailers lose money from scanning errors because the scanned price is below the posted price.[30] However, consumer groups and states' attorneys general do find and pursue price discrepancies in retailers' favor. Periodic price audits are an essential component of good pricing practices. Price audits of a random sample of items should be done periodically to identify the extent and cause of scanning errors and develop procedures to minimize errors.

Deceptive Reference Prices

A **reference price** is the price against which buyers compare the actual selling price of the product, and thus it facilitates their evaluation process. Typically, the retailer labels the reference price as the "regular price" or "original price." When consumers view the "sale price" and compare it with the provided reference price, their perceptions of the value of the product or service will likely increase.[31]

If the reference price is bona fide, the advertisement is informative. If the reference price has been inflated or is just plain fictitious, however, the advertisement is deceptive and may cause harm to consumers. But it is not easy to determine whether a reference price is bona fide. What standard should be used? If an advertisement specifies a "regular price," just what qualifies as regular? How many units must the store sell at this price for it to be a bona fide regular price—half the stock? A few? Just one? Finally, what if the store offers the item for sale at the regular price but customers do not buy any? Can it still be considered a regular price? In general, if a seller is going to label a price as a regular price, the Better Business Bureau suggests that at least 50 percent of the sales should have occurred at that price.[32] Retailing View 14.6 highlights the ethical issues associated with advertised discounts.

14.6   RETAILING VIEW   Is It Really 45 Percent Off?

For the truly fashionable—or at least those who consider themselves as members of that group—the trade-off between luxury and affordability can be a tricky one. You want the newest, hottest fashion, but trying to keep up can be exhausting on your wallet. What's a maven to do?

Private-sale online sites such as Gilt, RueLaLa, and HauteLook promise a solution. They host limited-time sales of products from high-end fashion brands. A sale starts at a specified time and lasts for 48 hours, or until the sale is sold out. So, if you must have the Nova Armored Baby Beaton handbag from Burberry, you can have it for 45 percent off the list price, or $877 instead of $1,595, as long as you are on HauteLook.com when the sale starts. Brick-and-mortar retailers are following suit with "flash sales," such as when Banana Republic offers 40 percent off its full-priced sweaters but only between 11:00 a.m. and 2:00 p.m. on specific days.

But is it really 40 or 45 percent off—and 45 percent off what? A reference price like $1,595 gives consumers a clue as to what that specific handbag should be worth. Research shows that the greater the difference between a suggested retail and a sale price, the greater the perceived value. When customers see Sears offering a refrigerator for $1,300 off its original price, that huge number is nearly impossible to ignore. The better the deal, the more consumers will be attracted to buy. But if the retailer inflates the suggested or original price, the percentage discount and dollars off seem much better than they actually are.

When the private sale sites have been caught inflating the suggested retail prices to show a greater percentage

discount, they generally claim that the original prices they list are accurate and come from the manufacturer. Any errors, they argue, are because the manufacturer gave them the wrong price, or else it might be due to employee error. For example, if the suggested retail price of the Burberry bag was actually only $1,100 instead of $1,595, then the bag was only discounted 20 percent. A customer in the heat of the moment may buy the bag because it is reported to be 45 percent off; were it only 20 percent off, she might not have purchased.

In some cases, the complicated coupon, discount, and flash pricing offers make it nearly impossible to determine the extent of the deal without a calculator. Because consumers rarely have the time or energy to calculate exactly what kind of discount they are getting, retailers can play on their excitement when it seems like a great deal.

Sources: Carl Bialik, Elizabeth Holmes, and Ray A. Smith, "Many Discounts, Few Deals," *The Wall Street Journal*, December 15, 2010; Vanessa O'Connell, "It's 50% Off . . . Well, Maybe 35%. How Good Are Deals on Members'-Only Web Sites?" *The Wall Street Journal*, January 16, 2010; www.hautelook.com; and www.gilt.com.

DISCUSSION QUESTIONS

Should private-sale sites and in-store retailers be required to substantiate their reference prices? Which price should they use as the reference price?

SUMMARY

LO1 Explain the difference between a high/low pricing strategy and an everyday low-pricing strategy.

Setting prices is a critical decision in implementing a retail strategy because price is a critical component in customers' perceived value. Retailers use two basic retail pricing strategies: everyday low pricing (EDLP) and high/low pricing. Each of these strategies has its advantages and disadvantages. The high/low strategy increases profits through price discrimination, creates excitement, and provides an opportunity to sell slow-moving merchandise. The EDLP approach assures customers of low prices, reduces advertising and operating expenses, reduces stockouts, and improves supply chain management.

LO2 Identify the factors retailers consider when pricing their merchandise.

In setting prices, retailers consider the price sensitivity of customers in their target market, the cost of the merchandise and services offered, competitive prices, and legal and ethical restrictions. Theoretically, retailers maximize their profits by setting prices on the basis of the price sensitivity of customers and the cost of merchandise. However, this approach does not consider the prices being charged by competitors. Another problem with attempting to set prices on the basis of customer price sensitivity is the implementation challenges associated with the large number of pricing decisions a retailer must make. Additional challenges arise when pricing services, due to the need to match supply and demand and the difficulties customers have in determining service quality. Retailers use yield management techniques to match supply and demand for services.

LO3 Describe how retailers set prices.

Most retailers set price by marking up the item's cost to yield a profitable gross margin. Then this initial price is adjusted on the basis of insights about customer price sensitivity and competitive pricing. To determine the initial retail price, retailers apply a markup as a percentage of the retail price. Retailers often do not sell merchandise at the initial retail price. The average initial price is reduced by markdowns, discounts given to employees, and theft.

Planning for these so-called reductions is important when determining the initial retail price so that the planned profit for the merchandise is obtained. Pricing optimization software can be used to determine the most profitable initial retail price and the appropriate size and timing of markdowns. Break-even analysis is also useful for determining how much a retailer needs to sell to begin making a profit.

LO4 Examine how and why retailers take markdowns.

Initial prices are adjusted over time using markdowns and for different market segments using variable-pricing strategies. Retailers take markdowns to either dispose of merchandise or generate sales. Markdowns are part of the cost of doing business, and thus buyers plan for them.

LO5 Identify the pricing techniques retailers use to increase sales and profits.

Retailers use a variety of techniques to maximize sales and profits by charging different prices to different customers. These techniques include setting different prices for individual customers, providing an offering that enables customers to self-select the price they are willing to pay, and setting different prices according to customer demographics. Retailers also use price lining, leader pricing, and odd pricing to stimulate sales.

LO6 Describe how the Internet and social and mobile channels are used to make pricing decisions.

The increased access to the Internet and the use of social media and smartphones has resulted in consumers having greater access to product and price information as they go about making purchasing decisions. It has also resulted in a growth in dynamic price promotions.

LO7 Indicate the legal and ethical issues retailers should consider when setting prices.

There are several legal and ethical issues retailers consider when setting prices. These include predatory pricing, resale price maintenance, horizontal price fixing, bait-and-switch tactics, scanned versus posted prices, and deceptive reference prices.

KEY TERMS

bait and switch, *411*

break-even analysis, *399*

break-even point quantity, *399*

cherry picker, *408*

coupons, *405*

dynamic pricing, *404*

elastic, *393*

everyday low pricing (EDLP) strategy, *388*

first-degree price discrimination, *403*

fixed cost, *399*

geofencing, *410*

high/low pricing strategy, *388*

horizontal price fixing, *411*

individualized pricing, *404*

inelastic, *393*

initial markup, *397*

inventory shrinkage, *397*

keystoning, *397*

leader pricing, *407*

GET OUT AND DO IT!

1. **CONTINUING ASSIGNMENT** Go shopping at the retailer you have selected for the continuing assignment. Does the retailer use high/low pricing or an EDLP strategy? Ask the store manager how markdown decisions are made and how the store decides how much a markdown should be. What rule-based approaches are used to make markdowns, or does the retailer use markdown optimization software? Does the retailer use techniques for stimulating sales such as price lining, leader pricing, bundling, or multi-unit and odd pricing? Are the prices on its website the same as those in the store? Evaluate your findings. Do you believe the retailer is using the best pricing strategies and tactics for its type of store? What, if anything, could it do to improve?

2. Go to the web page of Overstock.com, and look at its top-selling merchandise. Select a few key items, and compare the price of each product at other online retail sites, such as Target.com, Amazon.com, Sears.com, and Macys.com. How do the prices at this Internet outlet compare to those at a discount store, online retailer, and department store? Are the results what you expected, or were you surprised? Explain your reaction.

3. Go to the website of Sandals (www.sandals.com), and see what you can get for an all-inclusive price. Describe how bundling services and products provides vacationers with value. Find an example of price bundling outside the travel industry. Which method, bundling or nonbundling, do you believe provides the customer with the best value? Which makes the retailer or service provider more profits?

4. Go to your favorite food store and your local Walmart to find their prices for the market basket of goods listed in the accompanying table. What was the total cost of the market basket at each store? How did the prices compare? Did Walmart live up to its slogan of "Always lower prices"?

Competitive Pricing: Grocery Store vs. Walmart

Item	Size	Brand	Grocery	Walmart	Price Difference	Percent Savings
Grocery						
Ground coffee	11.5 oz can	Folgers				
Raisin Bran	25.5 oz box	Kellogg's				
Pet Supplies						
Puppy Chow	4.4 lb bag	Purina				
Cleaning						
Liquid laundry detergent	100 oz bottle	All				
Dryer sheets	80 count	Bounce				
Liquid dish detergent	25 oz bottle	Palmolive				
Health and beauty						
Shampoo	12 oz bottle	Dove				
Toothpaste	4.2 oz tube	Colgate Total				
Total cost of the market basket of goods						

DISCUSSION QUESTIONS AND PROBLEMS

1. What types of retailers often use a high/low pricing strategy? What types of retailers generally use an everyday low-pricing strategy? How would customers likely react if a retailer switched its pricing strategy from one to the other? Explain your response.

2. Why would sewing pattern manufacturers such as Simplicity, Butterick, and McCall's print a price of $12.95 (or more) on each pattern and then two times a year offer patterns for sale at $1.99 each? How could this markdown influence demand, sales, and profits?

3. Reread Retailing View 14.1. Will an EDLP strategy work for JCPenney? Explain your answer.

4. Reread Retailing View 14.5. What are your thoughts about extreme couponing? Should retailers take steps to restrict it?

5. What is the difference between bundled pricing and multiunit pricing?

Note: **For questions 6–10, you may use the Online Learning Center. Click on "pricing."**

6. A department store's maintained markup is 38 percent, reductions are $560, and net sales are $28,000. What's the initial markup percentage?

7. Maintained markup is 39 percent, net sales are $52,000, and reductions are $2,500. What are the gross margin in dollars and the initial markup as a percentage? Explain why initial markup is greater than maintained markup.

8. The cost of a product is $150, markup is 50 percent, and markdown is 30 percent. What's the final selling price?

9. Men's Wearhouse purchased black leather belts for $15.99 each and priced them to sell for $29.99 each. What was the markup on the belts?

10. Answer the following questions:
    (a) The Limited is planning a new line of jackets for fall. It plans to sell the jackets for $100. It is having the jackets produced in the Dominican Republic. Although The Limited does not own the factory, its product development and design costs are $400,000. The total cost of the jacket, including transportation to the stores, is $45. For this line to be successful, The Limited needs to make $900,000 profit. What is its break-even point in units and dollars?
    (b) The buyer has just found out that The Gap, one of The Limited's major competitors, is bringing out a similar jacket that will retail for $90. If The Limited wants to match The Gap's price, how many units will it have to sell?

SUGGESTED READINGS

Ashworth, Lawrence, and Lindsay McShane. "Why Do We Care What Others Pay? The Role of Other Consumers' Prices in Inferences of Seller Respect." *Journal of Retailing* 88, no. 1 (2012), pp. 145–155.

Bambauer-Sachse, Silke, and Dhruv Grewal, "Temporal Price Reframing: When Is It Beneficial?" *Journal of Retailing* 87, no. 2 (2011), pp. 156–165.

Dutta, Sujay, Abhijit Biswas, and Dhruv Grewal. "Regret from Post-Purchase Discovery of Lower Market Prices: Do Price Refunds Help?" *Journal of Marketing* 75 (November 2011), pp. 124–138.

Grewal, Dhruv, Kusum Ailawadi, Dinesh Gauri, Kevin Hall, Praveen Kopalle, and Jane Robertson, "Innovation in Pricing and Promotion Strategies," *Journal of Retailing* 87S, no. 1 (2011), pp. S43–S52.

Ho, Hillbun (Dixon), Shankar Ganesan, and Hermann Oppewal. "The Impact of Store-Price Signals on Consumer Search and Store Evaluation." *Journal of Retailing* 87, no. 2 (2011), pp. 127–141.

Kopalle, Praveen, P. K. Kannan, Lin Bao Boldt, and Neeraj Arora. "The Impact of Household Level Heterogeneity in Reference Price Effects on Optimal Retailer Pricing Policies." *Journal of Retailing* 88, no. 1 (2012), pp. 102–114.

Maxwell, Sarah. *The Price Is Wrong: Understanding What Makes a Price Seem Fair and the True Cost of Unfair Pricing.* New York: Wiley, 2008.

Nagle, Thomas T., John E. Hogan, and Joseph Zale. *The Strategy and Tactics of Pricing: A Guide to Growing More Profitably*, 5th ed. Upper Saddle River, NJ: Prentice Hall, 2010.

Spann, Martin, Gerald Haubl, Bernd Skiera, and Martin Bernhardt. "Bid-Elicitation Interfaces and Bidding Behavior in Retail Interactive Pricing." *Journal of Retailing* 88, no. 1 (2012), pp. 131–144.

Suri, Rajneesh, Jane Zen Cai, Kent Monroe, and Mrugank V. Thakor. "Retailers' Merchandise Organization and Price Perceptions," *Journal of Retailing* 88, no. 1 (2012), pp. 168–179.

Theotokis, Aris, Katerina Pramatari, and Michael Tsiros. "Effects of Expiration Date-Based Pricing on Brand Image Perceptions." *Journal of Retailing* 88, no. 1 (2012), pp. 72–87.

Retail Communication Mix

EXECUTIVE BRIEFING

Katrina Davis, Social Media and
Communications Coordinator, Body Central

Body Central is a multichannel specialty apparel retailer with more than 250 stores located in enclosed malls and lifestyle centers in the South, mid-Atlantic, and Midwest United States. Our target market is women from diverse cultural backgrounds interested in wearing the latest fashions at value prices. The presentation of our merchandise emphasizes coordinated outfits of tops, dresses, bottoms, jewelry, accessories, and shoes fits the many lifestyles of our customers—casual, club, dressy, and active. The majority of our products are priced under $30.

When I came to work at Body Central four years ago, I realized that I really enjoyed marketing communications and branding.

I was an early adopter of Facebook, and social media was an attractive communication vehicle, particularly for our target market. The company created a position for me to see what returns we could get communicating with our customers using social media. Now we have 150,000 organic likes on Facebook, and we have a presence on all other major social media channels, including Twitter, Pinterest, Instagram, YouTube, and a corporate blog with new posts five days a week.

Our goal for using social media is to develop a close relationship and loyalty with customers in our target market and the bloggers they follow. You can stir up a lot of activity by running contests, but people who visit us just to participate in a contest don't

LEARNING OBJECTIVES

LO1 Identify the traditional media elements.

LO2 Identify the new media elements.

LO3 Understand how retailers use communication programs to develop

brand images and build customer loyalty.

LO4 List the steps involved in developing a communication program.

always become loyal customers or followers. The loyalty comes when we get the customers to engage in a dialogue with us and other members of our community. In 2012, I launched Fan of the Month on our Facebook page. It encouraged Body Central shoppers to share pictures of themselves in their Body Central outfits on our Facebook wall. Each month, a new fan is chosen to have her picture posted on Facebook by Body Central and is sent a prize pack full of accessories and other merchandise. Not only does it give customers a monthly incentive to follow us, but the relationships made along the way are invaluable. It's truly rewarding to Like and comment on photos of mother/daughter shopping trips, birthdays, personal weight loss success stories, and engagements. A customer was even proposed to in one of our store locations and shared it with us on Facebook. Our store associates kept her busy in the dressing room while the fiancé-to-be picked up the ring from a jeweler in the mall.

Building relationships with bloggers and encouraging them to be part of our community really pays off. There are thousands of fashion apparel bloggers. We are contacted almost every day by a blogger looking to make a connection. I spend time building relationships with the ones that appeal to our target market. The relationship can be beneficial on both ends. We reap the benefits of having our merchandise promoted by a trusted fashion voice outside of the brand. If a blogger has a big enough following, a collaborative project can drive traffic and revenue for the brand. The bloggers can increase their reach with exposure to new potential readers on our social media platforms and benefit from the exclusivity of having a personal relationship with a brand they genuinely enjoy.

To build this dialogue and sense of community, you need to communicate regularly and address problems that might arise quickly. I check our various social media platforms at the beginning of every day and address any issues. Most of these issues can be handled with a quick send of a link or a reference to customer service.

The preceding chapters in this section on merchandise management described how retailers develop an assortment and merchandise budget plan, then buy and price the merchandise. The next step is to develop and implement a communication program that will attract customers to retail locations (whether in stores or online) and encourage them to buy the merchandise available. The communication program informs customers about the retailer, describes the merchandise and services offered, helps develop the retailer's brand, and plays a critical role in encouraging repeat visits and customer loyalty.

At the end of the twentieth century, most retail communication programs were fairly simple. Local newspaper advertising was the primary medium, and the message was typically oriented toward providing incentives—usually a special price—to motivate customers to visit the store. Today, successful retailers utilize an **integrated marketing communication program** in which they integrate a variety of communication elements to deliver a comprehensive, consistent message to all customers over time, across all elements of their retail mix and across all delivery channels. For example, Chili's Grill and Bar Restaurants uses traditional media—television, radio, and billboards. But its customers can also go to Chilis.com to find restaurant locations and place an order. It also communicates with its customers on Facebook and Twitter, but believes its most effective Internet-based communication tool is through the Chili's opt-in e-mail list.[1]

Coordination among the communication elements is critical to its success. For example, if Chili's televised advertising campaign tries to build an exciting image, based on its innovative food options and friendly customer service, while its sales promotions focus on low prices, its communication methods are not consistent. Accordingly, its customers may become confused about its image and therefore not patronize Chili's.

For any communications campaign to succeed, the retailer must deliver the right message to the right audience through the right media at the right time, with the ultimate goal of profiting from long-term customer relationships, as well as short-term sales. Reaching the right audience is becoming more difficult as the media environment grows more complicated. No single type of media is necessarily better than another. The goal of a retail communication strategy is to plan all of the elements to work together so the sum exceeds the total of the individual media parts.

We now examine the individual elements of a retail communication strategy and the way each contributes to a successful communication campaign (see Exhibit 15–1). These elements are divided into traditional and new media. Traditional media elements include mass advertising, promotions, in-store marketing, direct mail, personal selling, and public relations. The new media elements include online (e-mail, mobile, websites) and social media (YouTube, Facebook, blogs, and Twitter). These media elements vary on five dimensions: personalization, interactivity, message control, extent of information provided, and the cost per exposure.

EXHIBIT 15–1   Elements of an Integrated Marketing Communication Strategy

Media/Characteristics	Personalization	Interactivity	Message Control	Information	Cost per Exposure
Traditional Media					
• Mass advertising	None	None	High	Low	Very low
• Sales promotions	Depends	Depends	High	Low	Low
• In-store marketing/ design elements	Depends	Depends	High	Depends	Low
• Personal selling	High	High	Medium	High	Very high
• Public relations	None	None	Depends	Medium	Low
New Media					
• Online	Depends	Depends	High	High	Depends
• Social media	High	High	Depends	Depends	Low

TRADITIONAL MEDIA ELEMENTS

Retailers use various traditional media elements: mass media advertising, promotions, in-store marketing, personal selling, and public relations. Each of these five media elements and their subcategories is discussed next.

LO1

Identify the traditional media elements.

Mass Media Advertising

Advertising entails the placement of announcements and persuasive messages purchased by retailers and other organizations that seek to inform and/or persuade members of a particular target market or audience about their products, services, organizations, or ideas.[2] After automobile manufacturers, retailers are the second-largest group of national advertisers, spending more than $20 billion annually. Amazon, Apple, Best Buy, Walt Disney, McDonald's, Sears Holding, Macy's, Target, and Home Depot are among the largest advertisers.[3]

Mass advertising is typically used to generate awareness in the need recognition stage of the buying process (see Chapter 4) because of its low cost per exposure and the control retailers have over content and the timing of the communication. But it is not as effective for helping consumers search for information because the amount of information that can be transmitted is limited. By its very nature, it is impossible to personalize messages or interact directly with customers. But it is a cost-effective method for announcing sales or new-store openings. Traditionally, mass advertising has been limited to newspapers, magazines, direct mail, TV, radio, and billboards.

REFACT

On a list of the top U.S. advertisers, Amazon ranks fourth among the various retailers that appear on the list. In 2011, it spent $1.4 billion worldwide ($778 million in the United States) on advertising in various formats—largely to promote its Kindle devices.[4]

Newspapers   Retailing and newspaper advertising grew up together over the past century. But the growth in newspaper advertising by retailers has slowed recently as retailers have begun using other media. Still, 57 percent of newspapers' advertising dollars are generated by retailers.[5] In addition to displaying ads with their editorial content, newspapers distribute freestanding inserts. A **freestanding insert (FSI),** also called a **preprint,** is an advertisement printed at the retailer's expense and distributed as an insert in the newspaper. Although popular with advertisers, there are so many FSIs in some newspapers that readers can become overwhelmed. As a result, some retailers have reduced the number of FSIs they use because of the clutter and because younger readers, who may be their primary target market, don't regularly read newspapers.

Newspapers are distributed in well-defined local market areas, so they are effective for targeting specific retail markets. Newspapers also offer a quick response. There's only a short time between the deadline for receiving the advertisement and the time that the advertisement will appear. Thus, newspapers are useful for delivering messages on short notice.

Newspaper readers can go through an advertisement at their own pace and refer to the part of the advertisement when they want. But newspaper ads

When customers see this ad, it highlights the deals that are being offered at Target.

aren't effective for showing merchandise, particularly when it is important to illustrate colors, because of the poor reproduction quality.

The life of a newspaper advertisement is short because the newspaper is usually discarded after it gets read. In contrast, magazine advertising has a longer life because consumers tend to save magazines and read them several times during a week or month.

Finally, the cost of developing newspaper ads is relatively low. However, the cost of delivering the message may be high if the newspaper's circulation is much broader than the retailer's target market, requiring the retailer to pay for exposure that won't generate sales.

Magazines   Advertising in national magazines is mostly done by national retailers such as Target and The Gap. With the growth of local magazines, regional editions of national magazines, and specialized magazines, local retailers can take advantage of this medium. Many magazines either offer both a print and an online version, or have transitioned to online only. This change in the business model for some magazines from print to online (or both) enables retailers to reach potential customers at a lower cost per exposure. Retailers tend to use it for image advertising because the reproduction quality is high. Due to the lead time—the time between submitting the advertisement and publication—a major disadvantage of magazine advertising is that the timing is difficult to coordinate with special events and sales.

Direct Mail   **Direct mail** includes any brochure, catalog, advertisement, or other printed marketing material delivered directly to the consumer through the mail or a private delivery company.[6] Retailers have communicated with their customers through the mail for as long as the mail has existed. The vast majority of direct mail goes to customers or the current resident of the household on a nonpersonalized basis. With the advent of loyalty and CRM programs, retailers are now able to personalize their direct mail to all customers, to a subset of the customers according to their previous purchases, or even on a personalized basis to individual customers. Although relatively expensive on a per-customer basis (because of printing, mail costs, and a relatively low response rate), direct mail is still extensively used by many retailers because people respond favorably to personal messages.

Television   Television commercials can be placed on a national network or local station. Retailers typically use TV for image advertising, to take advantage of the high production quality and the opportunity to communicate through both visual images and sound. Television ads can also demonstrate product usage. For example, TV is an excellent medium for car, furniture, and consumer electronics dealers.

In addition to its high production costs, broadcast time for national TV advertising is expensive. **Spots,** which are ads in local markets as opposed to national ads, have relatively small audiences, but they may be economical for local retailers. To offset the high production costs, many vendors provide modular commercials in which the retailer can insert its name or a "tag" after information about the vendor's merchandise.

Radio   Many retailers use radio advertising because messages can be easily targeted to a specific segment of the market.[7] Some radio stations' audiences are highly loyal to their announcers, especially in a "talk radio" format. When these announcers promote a retailer, listeners are impressed. The cost of developing and broadcasting radio commercials is relatively low.

One disadvantage of radio advertising, however, is that listeners generally treat the radio broadcast as background, which limits the attention they give the message. Consumers must get the information from a radio commercial when it is broadcast; they cannot refer back to the advertisement for information they didn't hear or don't remember.

Sales Promotions

Sales promotions are special incentives or excitement-building programs that encourage consumers to purchase a particular product or service. Some sales promotions have become integral components of retailers' long-term customer relationship management programs, which they use to build customer loyalty. The ability to personalize messages and interact directly with customers depends on the type of sales promotion retailers use. Generally, however, sales promotions provide relatively little information. But on the positive side, the ability to control the message is high and the cost per exposure is low. The tools used in sales promotions, such as coupons, rebates, and premiums, are discussed next.

REFACT

The Christmas story about Rudolph the Red-Nosed Reindeer was developed by a Montgomery Ward copywriter in 1939 for a store promotion.[8]

Coupons   **Coupons** offer a discount on the price of specific items when they are purchased. Coupons are issued by manufacturers and retailers in newspapers, on products, on the shelf, at the cash register, over the Internet, on mobile devices, and through the mail. Retailers use coupons because they are thought to induce customers to try products for the first time, convert first-time buyers into regular users, encourage large purchases, increase usage, and protect market share against competition. Some retailers have linked coupons directly to their loyalty programs. Using detailed consumer behavior data collected through its loyalty cards, Safeway offers very personalized bargains. If one consumer buys several of the store's private-label products, such as paper towels and glass cleaner for example, she will receive an enticing coupon for the store's private-label dishwashing detergent too. Another customer might receive a coupon for the same item, but if his behavior indicates he is less likely to buy the store brand (because he has purchased name brand paper towels in the past), that coupon will be worth much less.[9]

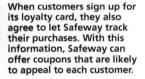

REFACT

The first coupons were handwritten notes given out by Asa Chandler, offering customers a free glass of the new soft drink, Coca-Cola, in 1887. In the period between 1894 and 1913, 8,500,000 free drinks were given out; put another way, one in nine Americans redeemed a Coca-Cola coupon during this 17-year span.[10]

When customers sign up for its loyalty card, they also agree to let Safeway track their purchases. With this information, Safeway can offer coupons that are likely to appeal to each customer.

Rebates   **Rebates** provide another form of discounts for consumers. In this case, however, the manufacturer, instead of the retailer, issues the refund as a portion of the purchase price returned to the buyer in the form of cash. Retailers generally welcome rebates from vendors because they generate sales in the same way that coupons do, but the retailers incur no handling costs. Vendors can offer generous rebates because the likelihood that consumers will actually apply for the rebate is low because of the hassle involved in doing so. But some retailers offer "instant rebates" that can be redeemed at the point-of-purchase. Staples and Apple have simplified the rebate redemption process with "Easy Rebates" and Apple.com/promo.[11]

Premiums   A **premium** offers an item for free or at a bargain price to reward some type of behavior, such as buying, sampling, or testing. Such rewards build goodwill among consumers, who often perceive high value in them. Premiums can be distributed in a variety of ways: They can be included by the manufacturer in the product packaging, such as the toys inside cereal boxes; placed visibly on the package, such as a coupon for free milk on a box of Cheerios; handed out in the store; or delivered in the mail, such as the free perfume offers that Victoria's Secret mails to customers.

In-Store Marketing/Design Elements

Retailers and their vendors are focusing considerable attention on in-store marketing design elements and activities. As we discussed in Chapter 4, customers often make purchase decisions while in the store. So store environmental elements, such as eye-catching point-of-purchase displays, and in-store activities, such as providing merchandise samples and special events, can increase customers' time in the store and their propensity to purchase. These in-store marketing/design elements are discussed next. Chapter 17 examines other store design and visual merchandising techniques that influence customers' purchase behavior.

Point-of-Purchase Displays   **Point-of-purchase (POP) displays** are merchandise displays located at the point of purchase, such as at the checkout counter in a supermarket. Retailers have long recognized that the most valuable real estate in the store is at the POP. Customers see products like a magazine or a candy bar while they are waiting to pay for their items and impulsively purchase them. POP displays can't be personalized to each customer because the message is the same to everyone. Interactivity is low. Information content can range from minimal to high. Finally, the cost per exposure is low.

Samples   **Samples** offer potential customers the opportunity to try a product or service before they make a buying decision. Distributing samples is one of the most costly sales promotion tools, but it is also one of the most effective. Retailers of cosmetics and fragrances, as well as grocery stores, frequently employ sampling. For instance, Whole Foods provides samples of products to customers. Costco uses so many samples that customers can have an entire meal during their shopping trip. In the case of cosmetics and fragrances, sampling can be highly personal because the sales associate can easily switch to a sample a customer might want or need; but this is generally not the case for food stores because everyone typically receives the same sample. Sampling can also be highly interactive, the message can be controlled, and the information provided can be high because the sales associate

Point-of-purchase displays stimulate impulse purchases while customers are waiting to pay for their purchases.

can adapt based on the situation and the customer. Cost per exposure, however, is relatively high.

Special Events   A **special event** is a sales promotion program comprising a number of sales promotion techniques built around a seasonal, cultural, sporting, musical, or some other type of activity.[12] Special events can generate excitement and traffic to the store. Apparel and department stores do trunk shows, made-to-measure events, and fashion shows. Sporting goods stores offer demonstrations of equipment, while grocery stores might have cooking classes. Bookstores hold readings and book signings. Car dealerships can have rallies or shows of new or vintage models. Even if the sales registered during the event aren't significant, the long-term effect can be quite beneficial.

Home Depot is a proud sponsor of NASCAR.

Although it does not always take place in stores, **event sponsorship** occurs when retailers support various activities (financially or otherwise), usually in the cultural or sports and entertainment sectors. Some retailers sponsor sporting events such as the Little Caesar's Pizza Bowl in Detroit. Others buy naming rights to a sporting venue, such as Target Field, which is home to MLB's Minnesota Twins, and HSBC Arena, home to the NHL's Buffalo Sabres, or to a NASCAR car, as Home Depot has done.[13]

Special events can't be personalized, but they are highly interactive. The message and information can be controlled, and the cost per exposure is low.

Personal Selling

Personal selling is a communication process in which sales associates help customers satisfy their needs through face-to-face exchanges of information. Salespeople can personalize every message to fit the customers' needs and provide as much information as needed. It is highly interactive, and to the extent that the salespeople are well trained, the message can be controlled. Yet, the cost of communicating directly with a potential customer is quite high compared with other forms of promotion. Customers can buy many products and services without the help of a salesperson, but salespeople simplify the buying process by providing information and services that save customers time and effort. The impact of personal selling on customer service is examined further in Chapter 18.

Public Relations

Public relations (PR) involves managing communications and relationships to achieve various objectives, such as building and maintaining a positive image of the retailer, handling or heading off unfavorable stories or events, and maintaining positive relationships with the media. In many cases, public relations activities support other promotional efforts by generating "free" media attention and general goodwill. PR activities cannot be personalized and are not interactive. To the extent that the media interprets the message the way the retailer has intended and disseminates it, the message can be somewhat controlled, and the information content is modest. The cost per exposure is relatively low. The types of PR campaigns retailers use are as varied as the retailers themselves. We examine several different ways in which retailers employ public relations in their communications strategy.

Neiman Marcus and Its Christmas Catalog   The Neiman Marcus Christmas book is perhaps the nation's best-known retail catalog. Its reputation is largely due to its annual tradition of ultra-extravagant his-and-hers gifts. The unique

A recent Neiman Marcus Christmas catalog features a McLaren 12C Spider for $354,000, and his-and-hers watches, featuring scenes of Paris and Geneva, and trips to each location for $1.1 million.

merchandise generates free publicity as journalists and style watchers are astonished at what the retailer came up with each year.

The Christmas book was first distributed in 1915 as a Christmas card, inviting Neiman Marcus customers to visit the store during the holiday season. In the late 1950s, customers were asking Neiman Marcus about unique gifts and merchandise not available in the store or from other catalogs. In the 2012 Christmas book, readers came across "the most technologically advanced supercar ever," the 2013 McLaren 12C Spider, for $354,000. That price might seem like a bargain compared with the gift listed a few pages later: a set of $1.1 million, his-and-hers watches, by Van Cleef & Arpels, that featured scenes of Paris and Geneva—and came complete with trips to each location.[14] The Neiman Marcus Christmas book is mailed to 1.8 million customers and is also available on its website.

Macy's and Cause-Related Marketing   Starting in 2011, Macy's partnered with many charities in a successful **cause-related marketing campaign** (i.e., commercial activity in which businesses and charities form a partnership to market an image, product, or service for their mutual benefit). In addition to providing a benefit for society, its Shop for a Cause campaign generates a lot of publicity. The program allowed partnering charities to sell coupons, at $5 each, that gave the purchaser a 25 percent discount at Macy's on a specific day. As long as they were nonprofit organizations, charities were eligible to participate, leading to a wide range of partnerships, from Autism Speaks to The Greater Boston Food Bank to YMCAs to animal rescues to the Alliance for Lupus Research. Meanwhile, Macy's sold coupons in its stores to benefit the March of Dimes. Each charity retained all proceeds from the coupon sales, and Macy's benefited from increased sales. In 2011, the campaign raised $38 million for charity, and Macy's earned approximately $600 million in sales.[15]

This scene from the 2006 movie, *Talladega Nights: The Ballad Of Ricky Bobby,* is packed with product placements from apparel to food and beverages.

Retailers and Product Placement   When retailers and vendors use **product placement**, they pay to have their product included in nontraditional situations, such as in a scene in a movie or television program.[16] The characters played by Salma Hayak and Alec Baldwin discuss, during an episode of *30 Rock*, whether McDonald's McFlurry is the best dessert in the world. On *The Big Bang Theory*, the characters frequently appear eating at Penny's workplace, The Cheesecake Factory, and Sheldon once demanded "access to The Cheesecake Factory walk-in freezer." Even in reality shows such as *The Biggest Loser*, contestants run from one Subway restaurant to the next.

NEW MEDIA ELEMENTS

Over the past decade or so, the use of newer forms of media, such as online (e.g., websites, e-mail, and mobile), and social media (e.g., YouTube, Facebook, blogs, and Twitter) has exploded. Each of these new media elements is discussed next.

LO2
Identify the new media elements.

Online Media

Websites   Retailers are increasing their emphasis on communicating with customers through their websites, which are used to build their brand images; inform customers of store locations, special events, and the availability of merchandise in local stores; and sell merchandise and services. Many retailers also devote areas of their websites to community building. These sites offer an opportunity for customers with similar interests to learn about products and services that support their hobbies and to share information with others. Visitors can also post questions seeking information and/or comments about issues, products, and services. For example, REI, an outdoor apparel and equipment retailer, offers adventure travel planning resources for hiking trips, bike tours, paddling, adventure cruises, and other trips. By doing so, REI creates a community of customers who engage in activities using the merchandise that REI sells. The community thus reinforces REI's brand image.

Many retailers encourage customers to post reviews of products they have bought or used on their websites. Research has shown that these online product reviews increase customer loyalty and provide a competitive advantage for sites that offer them.[18]

Depending on how customers use retailers' websites, they can experience a very personalized and interactive experience. The message can contain lots of information and is easily controlled. The cost per exposure is comparatively moderate because the cost of maintaining and operating a website can be expensive.

Retailers are actively using **search engine marketing (SEM)** to improve the visibility of their websites in searches. One SEM method is to use **search engine optimization (SEO)**, which is creating and adjusting website content to show up closer to the top of a **search engine results page (SERP).** These SERPs list the results that a search engine provides, in response to a user's keyword query. Thus, SEO is used to enhance unpaid or organic searches. Another SEM method is using paid search through Google's sponsored link advertising program. These results are placed above and to the right of natural or organic search results.[19]

REFACT

Despite the promise of communicating with customers and integrating promotions across various channels, only about 12 percent of retailers can access customers' online orders from within their stores. Furthermore, less than half of all retailers actually provide tailored recommendations to their customers.[17]

E-mail   **E-mail** involves sending messages over the Internet to specific individuals. Retailers use e-mail to inform customers of new merchandise and special promotions, confirm the receipt of an order, and indicate when an order has been shipped. The increased use of customer databases has enabled retailers to identify and track consumers over time and across purchase situations (see Chapter 11). As a result, e-mail can be highly personal and the message very controlled. However, when the same message is delivered electronically to all recipients, e-mails more closely resemble the more impersonal medium, mass advertising. Because e-mail recipients can respond back to the retailer, it is considered an interactive medium. Finally, the cost per exposure is low.

REFACT

According to a recent online poll, 93 percent of people would use a "Do Not Track" function if it were available on web browsers to limit intrusions on their privacy by marketers.[20]

Mobile Communications   **Mobile communications** are delivered through wireless handheld devices, such as cellular telephones, and **m-commerce** or **mobile commerce** can involve completing a transaction via the cell phone.[21] Smartphones have become far more than tools for placing calls; they offer a kind

Once Foursquare users check in at participating Walgreen's stores, they can download special deals to their phone, along with a scannable barcode.

of mobile computer with the ability to obtain sports scores, weather, music, videos, and text messages, as well as purchase merchandise. Retailers' success with mobile communications rests on apps that enable effective communications through a device with a small screen.

Retailers use applications such as Foursquare to communicate with mobile phone users and send them messages on the basis of their location, as determined by GPS technology.[22] Foursquare awards points to consumers who try out local retailers. With the GPS-based application, users also can recommend nearby retailers to friends in the area. Furthermore, the app's data analytic capabilities allow retailers to track the impact of mobile marketing campaigns.

Target uses the Shopkick app to award points to customers who walk around a store and scan products; they can redeem these points for various rewards. Other retailers use mobile channels to deliver coupons or other promotional offers, such as free shipping to customers who purchase online from the retailer while in its brick-and-mortar store. Finally, retailers might use the related location-based technology to deliver tailored, local messages to customers to drive them into their stores.

Despite the promise of mobile communications, it continues to have its drawbacks. One study found that 90 percent of U.S. survey respondents had absolutely no interest in receiving mobile ads.[23] Combining geographic location services with social media could increase crime rates;[24] for example, burglars would know how far away homeowners are from their homes.

Numerous retailers have developed applications that their consumers can use on their smartphones to access a host of services. Retailing View 15.1 highlights Staples' efforts to make things easy for their customers.

15.1   RETAILING VIEW   Staples' Mobile Strategy: Reaching Customers through Smartphones

The world's largest office products company, Staples, with annual sales of approximately $25 billion, is taking an aggressive stance toward entering the mobile world. Sensing an opportunity, it is making its customers' lives easier through its mobile site and application. In 2010, the company initiated its mobile strategy by launching a mobile-optimized website to allow customers easier access on smartphones. In June 2011, it relaunched the mobile site, m.staples.com, to include product ratings and reviews, a store locator, and a store inventory search.

Also in 2011, Staples introduced a mobile application for both iPhone and Android smartphones. The app provides a streamlined version of the website, but it also supports coupon and promotion downloads. Furthermore, the app is geo-aware, such that as soon as a customer comes within a mile of a Staples store, a coupon is automatically offered.

Finally, the app allows users to build smart lists that track their supply needs and links to their Staples Rewards status (the retailer's loyalty program). By combining the smart list capability of the app with a customer's purchase history, Staples builds "virtual supply closets" for customers. The virtual supply closets combine not just customers' purchase history but also their scanned SKUs that they saved in their phones while in a store.

Sources: Christopher Hosford, "Staples' Mobile Strategy Based on Customer Convenience, Loyalty," *B to B Magazine*, March 12, 2012; Staples.com, "About Us," and "Staples Helps Small Business Owners Get Ahead in the New Year"; and Ben Stillitoe, "Staples Plans New Social Media Strategy," *Retail Gazette*, December 13, 2011.

DISCUSSION QUESTIONS

Have you used mobile apps developed by retailers? If yes, do you find them useful?

Social Media

Social media include various forms of electronic communication, which users can employ to create online communities in which they share ideas, information, their interpersonal messages, and other content (e.g., videos). Three major online facilitators of social media are YouTube, Facebook, and Twitter. As another online vehicle that encourages word-of-mouth communications, online forums enable consumers to review, communicate about, and aggregate information about products, prices, and promotions. These forums also allow users to interact among themselves (e.g., form a community).[25] Such online communities enable users to provide other like-minded consumers and retailers with their thoughts about and evaluations of a retailer's products or services.

Retailers use social media to engage their customers in proactive dialogue. When a retailer provides content in a social media website, people often begin sharing and commenting on it. The retailer then must monitor the feedback and respond if necessary—especially if the commentary is negative. For example, **sentiment mining** is a process whereby retailers can tap into a variety of online chat formats to collect consumer comments and then analyze these data to identify customers' overall attitudes and preferences for products and advertising campaigns. Scouring millions of sites by combining automated online search tools with text analysis techniques, sentiment mining yields qualitative data that provide new insights into what consumers really think. Retailers plugged into this real-time information can become more nimble, allowing for quick changes in a product rollout or a new advertising campaign. Retailing View 15.2 highlights how Dell uses the various social media analysis tools to better serve its customers.

RETAILING VIEW   Harnessing the Power of Social Media to Make Customers Happy   **15.2**

Social media has revolutionized how companies communicate with, listen to, and learn from their customers. The volume of information generated can be a powerful tool for improving all business operations, including product design, technical support, and customer service, but it is also a very daunting task simply to make sense of it all! Consistent with its image as a global leader in computing, Dell is recognized as one of the top social media brands worldwide.

The company has always valued consumer input, according to founder and CEO Michael Dell: "One of Dell's founding principles was really about listening and learning from our customers, and being able to take that feedback to improve." Dell still offers traditional online support forums, which post questions and answers for different user groups and by topic. Now, however, social media channels like Facebook and Twitter have vastly accelerated that learning curve. Dell's mobile phone app also helps users stay connected on the road.

Each of Dell's multiple, highly developed social media channels differs qualitatively. They give the company and its customers the immediacy of instant chat and conversations through Facebook, LinkedIn, Twitter, and Google+, as well as Dell's flagship blog Direct2Dell.com and a host of other blogs.

Listening and analysis—or social media monitoring—is key. It enables Dell to identify salient customer input and trends. By teaming with social media monitor partner Salesforce Radian6, for example, Dell couples text analysis and high-volume, digital content-gathering technology methods to monitor approximately 25,000 conversations a day. In addition to customer support, the new media provide company and product news, as well as food for thought to its customers about digital business and digital life.

Dell gathers and monitors these online chats, posts responses or ideas, and engages in other discussions from its new social media listening command center. The staff includes 70 trained employees who follow and respond to social media conversations in 11 languages. All tweets, Facebook posts, and other comments that warrant a Dell response are answered within 24 hours.

Sources: Andrea Edwards, "Dell—a Top Five Social Media Brand—Looking for Fresh Ideas," *SAJE Communication*, October 12, 2011; "Introducing Dell's Social Media Command Center," Dell.com; Ed Twittel, "How Dell Really Listens to Its Customers," *ReadWriteEnterprise*, July 22, 2011; and "Social Media," Dell.com.

DISCUSSION QUESTION

Have you interacted with a retailer using one of its social media tools? If yes, was the response satisfactory?

Social media not only allow retailers to respond to unhappy customers but also to monitor trends and respond to consumer demand. Walmart uses social media to develop services and select products, such as a Christmas layaway option, by engaging with them on Facebook and Twitter.[26] Not all social media invokes positive results, though.[27] For a high-end Australian fashion boutique called Gasp, social media's power to eliminate boundaries led one of its managers to make things worse after a customer complained online of treatment she received in the store. Rather than apologizing, the manager dismissed her as unlikely to have purchased anyway, because she was "acclimated to buying from 'clothing for the masses' type retailers."[28]

As these various examples of social media indicate, they can be very personal and interactive. When the message is produced by the retailer, it can be controlled, but when customers are involved, as is the case with reviews, there is little control over the message whatsoever. Likewise, the level of information content is dependent on who is doing the communications. The cost per exposure for social media is relatively low compared to traditional media. The largest facilitators of online social media today are YouTube, Facebook, blogs, and the microblog, Twitter.

Home Depot fosters its identity with instructional do-it-yourself videos on YouTube.

YouTube   On this video-sharing social media platform, users upload, share, view, and comment on videos. This medium gives retailers a chance to express themselves in a different way than they have before. A retailer such as the television home shopping company HSN, discussed in Retailing View 15.3, can broadcast its own channel, that is, a YouTube site that contains content relevant only to the company's own products.[29]

YouTube also provides an effective medium for hosting contests and posting instructional videos. Home Depot has attracted more than 18,000 subscribers and racked up more than 41 million views with an array of videos detailing new products available in stores, as well as instructional do-it-yourself videos, like "How-to Tips for Mowing Your Lawn" or "How to Repair a Toilet."[30] These videos maintain the core identity of the Home Depot brand, while also adding value for consumers, who learn useful ways to improve their homes.

Facebook   This social media platform with more than 1 billion active users[31] gives companies a forum to interact with fans. Retailers have access to the same features that regular users do, including a "wall" where they can post company updates, photos, and videos or participate in a discussion board.

For Macy's, Facebook has long been a promising communication outlet, so it also became one of the first retailers to adopt the Facebook Page format. Furthermore, the Facebook timeline format has worked well in highlighting its events. Macy's has started to advertise more on Facebook, using more targeted ads to communicate with current and potential fans. Adapting along with the social media site represents just one facet in its broader plan to revamp its social media initiatives to attract more 25- to 54-year-old female consumers, along with some Gen Y fashionistas. It believes that Facebook is a great way to get the right message in front of the right people.[32]

It also provides an appealing means to target local groups of consumers for smaller retailers. For example, PCC Natural Markets in Seattle engages customers

RETAILING VIEW   YouTube and HSN   15.3

Begun as a local cable channel in 1982, Home Shopping Network (HSN) offered consumers a central location from which to buy through their televisions. As competition in this field increased, HSN tailored its communication strategy to reach more shoppers. For example, HSN.com is one of the most visited e-commerce sites. But perhaps the most powerful tool HSN has added to its communication strategy is YouTube.

By reaching 40 to 50 percent of the company's target market, YouTube gives HSN a way to interact differently with customers and further increase its share of wallet with its current customers. The video format humanizes the connection and provides additional information about products.

For consumers, YouTube offers a seamless experience. Products promoted on HSN, such as Tori Spelling's jewelry line, are available on YouTube almost immediately after they appear on television. Then, HSN marketers can use the information gathered from YouTube to target its direct mail campaigns. For example, it could send jewelry promotions to households that viewed the YouTube video clip for a necklace from the Tori Spelling Collection. Consumer responses get monitored 24/7 and measured against hourly sales goals. There's never a dull moment—it's like the CNN of shopping.

Sources: www.gstatic.com/youtube/engagement/platform/autoplay/advertise/downloads/YouTube_InTheKnow.pdf; www.gstatic.com/youtube/engagement/

YouTube allows customers to view Tori Spelling's jewelry line almost immediately after it appears on HSN.

platform/autoplay/advertise/downloads/YouTube_BrandChannels.pdf; www.gstatic.com/youtube/engagement/platform/autoplay/advertise/downloads/YouTube_Insight.pdf; and http://mediacommons.futureofthebook.org/imr/2010/03/24/re-branding-dynasty-tori-spellings-hsn-clips-youtube.

DISCUSSION QUESTION

Do you think accessing HSN merchandise via YouTube is useful?

---

in social media dialogue on Facebook about local products. To encourage participation in local events, such as its "Taste PCC: A Local Food Celebration" or "Deli Throw Down" contest, it spread vast word-of-mouth communication with minimal investment by relying on postings and tweets through Facebook and Twitter.[33]

 Blogs   On a **blog (weblog)**, an individual blogger or a group of users regularly post their opinions and various topical information on a web page. The administrator of the blog can either be a retailer, an independent person or a firm. A well-received blog can communicate trends, announce special events, and create **word of mouth**, which is communication among people about an entity such as a retailer or a product or service.[34] Blogs connect customers by forming a community, allowing the company to respond directly to customers' comments, and facilitate long-term relationships between customers and the company. By their very nature, blogs are supposed to be transparent and contain authors' honest observations, which can help customers determine their trust and loyalty levels. If, however, the blog is created or sponsored by a retailer, the information may be positively biased. Also, retailers have limited control over the content posted on blog; thus the information

Retailers like PCC Natural Markets use Facebook to communicate with customers and create a sense of community.

posted can be negative or incorrect. Many retailers use blogs as part of the communication strategy. A top-ranked retailer blog is Omnivoracious, Amazon's blog, which is, naturally, about books. Dell, Apple, Sears, Best Buy, and QVC also have highly rated blogs.[35]

Twitter   In discussions of social media, Facebook and Twitter often get mentioned in the same breath, but they differ in some critical ways. Twitter is a **microblog**—a short version of a blog—in which users are limited to 140-character messages. The use of 140-character messages forces retailers to post short, timely and relevant posts. Where a retailer may use Facebook to encourage discussions of their brand, promotions, or even ask their "friends" to post videos, they are more likely to use Twitter to announce up-to-date or fast changing information to excite consumers. Twitter is actively used by both small and large retailers. Smaller retailers with limited marketing budgets love the response they can induce by sending a promotional message immediately. Before the 2013 blizzard Nemo, a local food truck tweeted at the beginning of the day, "Headed to @dumbofoodtrucks Front St & Main St! Come get Korilla before Nemo does!" allowing its customers to know both where to find them and create a sense of urgency before the storm—a huge captive audience for a local entity.[36]

Large retailers may have enough funds to mass-market through national campaigns, but Twitter provides them with a way to stay in personal touch with customers. The well-reputed Wegmans grocery store chain posts the dates and times on which it receives its produce deliveries, so customers who prize the very freshest produce can show up just as the vegetables are getting unloaded. Along with these delivery details, Wegmans tweets grower and farmer information, as well as available stock. Wegmans also uses social media to answer customer questions.

Twitter has also changed the way customers get product or service information and register praise and complaints. Whereas once customers with questions about a product or service had to call up the retailer's customer service line and sit through prerecorded voice prompts, today they can turn to Twitter to get immediate feedback. Retailers measure Twitter customer service success by the quality, accuracy, and timeliness of their response to customers' service issues.

Penske and other retailers use Twitter to address customer questions.

For example, the Penske car rental agency implemented its Twitter customer service program after spending an entire year observing how customers were using Twitter for customer service issues. In line with its findings, it trained its call-center employees to use the new technology and monitor the Twitter feed from 7:00 a.m. to 11:00 p.m. daily. Customers who tweet their car rental questions receive nearly instantaneous responses.[37]

COMMUNICATION PROGRAMS BUILD BRAND IMAGES AND CUSTOMER LOYALTY

Communication programs using the old and new media discussed in the previous sections can have both long-term and short-term effects on a retailer's business. From a long-term perspective, communications programs can be used to create and maintain a strong, differentiated image of the retailer and its store brands. This image develops customer loyalty and therefore creates a strategic advantage. Thus, brand image-building communication programs complement the objective of a retailer's CRM program discussed in Chapter 11.

LO3
Understand how retailers use communication programs to develop brand images and build customer loyalty.

On the other hand, retailers frequently use communication programs to realize the short-term objective of increasing sales during a specified time period. For example, retailers often have sales during which some or all of its merchandise is priced at a discount for a short time. Grocery stores usually place weekly ads with coupons that can be used to save money on purchases made during the week.

In this section, we discuss the role of communications programs in building **brand images**—a strategic objective. The following sections focus on the operational issues involved in developing and implementing communication programs.

Brands

A **brand** is "a name, term, design, symbol or any other feature that identifies one seller's good or service as distinct from those of other sellers."[38] In a retailing context, the name of the retailer usually serves as the brand. This type of brand informs consumers of the type of merchandise and services provided by this particular named retailer. As we discussed in Chapter 13, some retailers develop private-label brands that are exclusively sold through their channels. In some cases, private-label merchandise bears the retailer's name, such as Walgreens aspirin and Victoria's Secret lingerie. In other cases, special brand names are used, such as Walmart's Ol' Roy dog food and Sears' Die Hard batteries.

Value of Brand Image

Brands provide value to both customers and retailers. For customers, they provide information in advance about the shopping experience that they are likely to face when they patronize this retailer. They also affect customers' confidence in their decisions to buy merchandise from a retailer. Finally, brands can enhance customers' satisfaction with merchandise and services. Consumers feel different when wearing jewelry bought from Tiffany & Co. rather than Zales or when staying at a Ritz-Carlton hotel rather than a Fairfield Inn.

The value a brand image provides retailers is referred to as **brand equity**. A brand with good equity, also known as a strong brand name, influences customers'

The Ace Hardware ad on the left focuses on a short-term objective—building sales during Mother's Day. The Abt ad on the right is directed toward building Abt's brand image—a long-term objective.

decision processes, often by encouraging their repeat visits, which in turn leads to greater loyalty. In addition, strong brand names enable retailers to increase their margins because customers will tolerate higher prices. When retailers have high customer loyalty, they can engage in premium pricing and reduce their reliance on price promotions to attract customers. Brands with weaker images instead must offer lower prices and have frequent sales to maintain their market share.

Customer loyalty to brands arises from heightened awareness of the brand and beliefs and emotional ties to it. As noted in Chapter 4, retailers need to appear in a customer's consideration set, and awareness can help guarantee this presence. Retail brands such as Walmart and Target are so well known by consumers that they nearly always appear in their consideration sets. Customers also identify with specific brands. They have beliefs about the retailer's offering and have strong emotional ties to its brands. Going to Target has become a cool experience because people consider it trendy to save money and buy fashionable merchandise—including a limited collection by the haute couture designer Missoni—all at the same time and in the same store in which they grab laundry detergent.[39] These customers affectionately use the faux French pronunciation "Tar-zhay" to refer to Target. High brand awareness and strong emotional connections reduce their incentives or motivation to switch to competing retailers.

Finally, retailers with strong brand names can leverage their brands to introduce new retail concepts with only a limited amount of marketing effort. For example, The Gap has efficiently extended its brand to GapKids, gapbody, GapMaternity, and babyGap. Retailing View 15.4 outlines how J.Crew has managed to develop its own brand identity, distinct from those of its closest competitors.

Building Brand Equity

The activities that a retailer needs to undertake to build brand equity for its firm or its private-label merchandise are to create a high level of brand awareness, develop favorable associations with the brand name, and consistently reinforce the image of the brand.

Brand Awareness   **Brand awareness** refers to a potential customer's ability to recognize or recall that the brand name is a particular type of retailer or product/service. Thus, brand awareness is the strength of the link between the brand name and the type of merchandise or service in the minds of customers.

There is a range of awareness, from aided recall to top-of-mind awareness. **Aided recall** occurs when consumers indicate they know the brand when the

---

RETAILING VIEW   Building the J.Crew Brand   15.4

The brand has strong name recognition: Lots of shoppers have heard of J.Crew. But in the mid-2000s, many of those shoppers heard the name and thought only "boring and preppy." When CEO Millard "Mickey" Drexler took the reins in 2003, he decided that to change J.Crew's image, he needed to appeal to customers' hearts through their fingers—that is, with the feel and look of quality clothing. By providing high-quality versions of classic clothing pieces at what it considers reasonable prices, J.Crew has been able to increase its profits, lower its debt, and expand the number of stores.

As the company promises on its website, it "partners with the finest global fabric mills and craftsmen—as well as with iconic brands such as Jack Purcell, Timex, Thomas Mason and Red Wing (to name just a few)." Customers, therefore, come to associate the J.Crew name with high-end suppliers. But such

J.Crew's CEO Mickey Drexler helped change the retailer's image by providing high-quality versions of classic clothing at what it considers to be reasonable prices.

quality comes at a price. Customers of J.Crew pay more for these brands for the promise of higher quality.

Other mall-based retailers operate at much lower price points. No one is likely to find leather shoes made by Alden at The Gap, as customers can at J.Crew. Even for seemingly similar offerings, J.Crew sets itself apart in discernible ways, such as adding hand-stitched sequins to a basic T-shirt.

Mickey Drexler also believes in allowing customers to dictate the brand image, which has resulted in the launch of uniquely female- and male-oriented lines and stores. When he received feedback indicating that women were purchasing multiple J.Crew sundresses in different colors to use as bridesmaids' gowns, he launched J. Crew bridal. The line opened its first dedicated bridal store in May 2010. Spurred by the success of its Ludlow line of men's suits, sports coats, and slacks, J.Crew opened several standalone Ludlow shops, as well as its men's-only Liquor Store in the Tribeca neighborhood of Manhattan, named after its former tenant, a liquor store. These shops carry not only Ludlow clothing, but also famous name-brand accessories. When European customers complained about

their inability to have J.Crew merchandise shipped overseas, he entered a partnership with an online retailer to make items available nearly worldwide.

Such positioning is part of what has earned Drexler the nickname "the merchant prince." Although J.Crew holds tight to its hard-earned preppy reputation, it has gained a position in customers' minds as a source of quality at reasonable prices. It also has revealed its ongoing willingness to shift as needed to meet customers' changing, demanding expectations.

Sources: Matthew Sebra, "Store Spotlight: J.Crew Opens Inaugural Ludlow Shop," *GQ*, March 1, 2012; "J.'s Crew," *The Wall Street Journal*, November 26, 2011; Tina Gaudoin, "Mickey Drexler: Retail Therapist," *The Wall Street Journal*, June 10, 2010; Meryl Gordon, "Mickey Drexler's Redemption," *New York Magazine*, May 21, 2005; and www.jcrew.com/AST/FooterNavigation/aboutus.jsp.

DISCUSSION QUESTIONS

How has your perception of J.Crew changed in recent years? Do you like the changes?

name is presented to them. **Top-of-mind awareness**, the highest level of awareness, occurs when consumers mention a specific brand name first when they are asked about the type of retailer, a merchandise category, or a type of service. For example, Container Store has a high top-of-mind awareness if most consumers respond "Container Store" when asked about retailers that sell merchandise for storing and organizing things. High top-of-mind awareness means that a retailer probably will be in the consideration set when customers decide to shop for a type of product or service.

Retailers build top-of-mind awareness by having memorable names; repeatedly exposing their names to customers through advertising, locations, and sponsorships; and using memorable symbols. Some brand names are easy to remember, such as the name Home Depot; because "Home" is in its brand name, it probably is more memorable and closely associated with home improvements than the name Lowe's.

Zara does very little advertising but has high awareness because of the large number of stores it has in great locations. Customers walk and drive by the stores, look at their artfully designed windows, and are drawn in to check out the offerings. They also know that if they don't purchase the fashionable, reasonably priced apparel when they see it in the store, it probably won't be there the next time.

Symbols involve visual images that typically are more easily recalled than words or phrases and thus are useful for building brand awareness. For example, the images of an apple with an artful "bite" missing and the golden arches enhance the ability of customers to recall the names Apple and McDonald's, respectively.

Sponsorships of well-publicized events also can provide considerable exposure to a retailer's name and increase awareness. For example, watching the Macy's

Macy's annual Thanksgiving Day parade and the accompanying publicity have built top-of-mind awareness for the retailer since 1924.

Thanksgiving parade in New York City has become a holiday tradition for many families. The Macy's brand name is exposed to tens of millions of television viewers for three hours. In addition, newspaper articles are devoted to previewing the parade and describing it afterward.

REFACT

The first Macy's Thanksgiving Day parade, held in 1924, was organized by a handful of volunteer, immigrant employees.[41]

Associations   Building awareness is only one step in developing brand equity, but the value of the brand is largely based on the associations that customers make with the brand name. **Brand associations** are anything linked to or connected with the brand name in a consumer's memory. For example, some of the associations that consumers might have with Apple are its innovative products, easy-to-use interface, Genius Bar, and unique store design, as well as specific products like the iPhone, iPad, and Mac computers. These associations can be negative as well as positive. For example, the brand Apple might also be associated with high prices. These strong associations influence consumer buying behavior. Some common associations that retailers seek to develop with their brand names are as follows:

1. *Merchandise category*. The most common association is to link the retailer to a category of merchandise. For example, Office Depot would like to have consumers associate its name with office supplies. Then, when a need for office supplies arises, consumers immediately think of Office Depot.

2. *Price/quality*. Some retailers, such as Saks Fifth Avenue, want to be associated with offering unique, high-fashion merchandise. Other retailers, such as Walmart, want associations with low prices and good value.

3. *Specific attribute or benefit*. A retailer can link its stores to attributes, such as 7-Eleven's association with providing convenience or Nordstrom's connection with offering a high level of customer service.

4. *Lifestyle or activity*. Some retailers associate their name with a specific lifestyle or activity. For example, Patagonia, a retailer offering outdoor sports equipment, is linked to an active, environmentally friendly lifestyle. Pottery Barn is associated with comfortable living in the home.

When people think of Patagonia, they think about an active, environmentally friendly lifestyle.

436   SECTION III   Merchandise Management

PLANNING THE RETAIL COMMUNICATION PROGRAM

LO4

List the steps involved in developing a communication program.

Exhibit 15–2 illustrates the four steps involved in developing and implementing a retail communication program: establish objectives, determine a budget, allocate the budget, and implement and evaluate the program. The following sections detail each of these steps.

EXHIBIT 15–2   Steps in Developing a Retail Communication Program

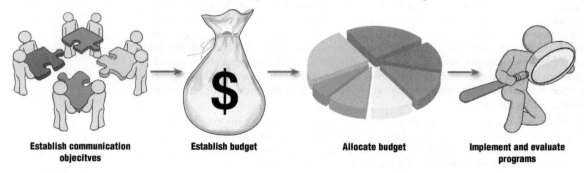

Establish communication objecitves   Establish budget   Allocate budget   Implement and evaluate programs

Establish Objectives

Retailers establish objectives for their communication programs to provide direction for people implementing the program, and a basis for evaluating its effectiveness. As discussed at the beginning of this chapter, some communication programs can have a long-term objective, such as creating or altering a retailer's brand image. Other communication programs focus on improving short-term performance, such as increasing store traffic on a specific weekend.

Although retailers' overall objective is to generate long- and short-term sales and profits, they often use communication objectives rather than sales objectives to plan and evaluate their communication programs. **Communication objectives** are specific goals related to the retail communication mix's effect on the customer's decision-making process.

Exhibit 15–3 shows some hypothetical information about customers in the target market for a Safeway supermarket. This information illustrates the goals

EXHIBIT 15–3
Communication Objectives and Stages in Consumer's Decision-Making Process

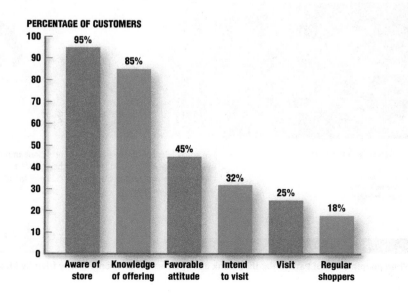

PERCENTAGE OF CUSTOMERS

Aware of store	Knowledge of offering	Favorable attitude	Intend to visit	Visit	Regular shoppers
95%	85%	45%	32%	25%	18%

related to the stages in the consumer decision-making process outlined in Chapter 4. Note that 95 percent of the customers are aware of the store (the first stage in the decision-making process) and 85 percent know the type of merchandise it sells. But only 45 percent of the customers in the target market have a favorable attitude toward the store. Thirty-two percent intend to visit the store during the next few weeks, 25 percent actually visit the store during the next two weeks, and 18 percent regularly shop at the store.

In this hypothetical example, most people know about the store and its offering. The major problem confronting Safeway is the big drop between knowledge and favorable attitudes. Thus, the store should develop a communication program with the objective of increasing the percentage of customers with a favorable attitude toward it.

To effectively implement and evaluate a communication program, its objectives must be clearly stated in quantitative terms. The target audience for the communication mix needs to be defined, along with the degree of change expected and the time period during which the change will be realized.

For example, a communication objective for a Safeway program might be to increase the percentage of customers within a five-mile radius of the store who have a favorable attitude toward the store from 45 to 55 percent within three months. This objective is clear and measurable. It indicates the task that the program should address. The people who implement the program thus know what they're supposed to accomplish.

The communication objectives and approaches used by vendors and retailers differ, and the differences can lead to conflicts. Some of these points of conflict are as follows:

- *Long-term versus short-term goals.* Most communications by vendors are directed toward building a long-term image of their products. In contrast, retailer communications typically are used to announce promotions and special sales that generate short-term revenues.

- *Product versus location.* When vendors advertise their branded products, they aren't concerned about where customers buy them as long as they buy their brands. In contrast, retailers aren't concerned about what brands customers buy as long as they buy them in their stores.

Safeway's communications objective should be to increase the number of people with a favorable attitude toward it.

- *Breadth of merchandise.* Typically, because vendors have a relatively small number of products to promote, they can devote a lot of attention to developing consistent communication programs for each brand they make. Retailers have to develop communication programs that promote a much wider range of products.

Determine the Communication Budget

The second step in developing a retail communication program is to determine a budget (see Exhibit 15–3). The economically correct method for setting the communication budget is marginal analysis (discussed shortly). Even though retailers usually don't have enough information to perform a complete marginal analysis, the method shows managers how they should approach budget-setting programs. The marginal analysis method for setting a communication budget is the approach that retailers should use when making all of their resource allocation decisions, including the number of locations in a geographic area (Chapter 8), the allocation of merchandise to stores (Chapter 13), the staffing of stores (Chapter 16), and the floor and shelf space devoted to merchandise categories (Chapter 17).

An important source of the communication budget is co-op advertising programs. A **co-op (cooperative) program** is a promotional program undertaken by a vendor and a retailer working together. The vendor pays for part of the retailer's promotion but dictates some conditions. For example, Best Buy might pay half of the expenses for ads that feature Sony digital TVs. In addition to lowering costs, co-op advertising enables a retailer to associate its name with well-known national brands and use attractive artwork created by the national brands.

A co-op advertising program with Sony provides funds for Best Buy's promotions.

Marginal Analysis Method   Marginal analysis is based on the economic principle that firms should increase communication expenditures as long as each additional dollar spent generates more than a dollar of additional contribution. To illustrate marginal analysis, consider Diane West, the owner and manager of a specialty store selling women's business clothing. Exhibit 15–4 shows her analysis to determine how much she should spend next year on her communication program.

For 21 different communication expense levels (column 1), West estimates her store sales (column 2), gross margin (column 3), and other expenses (columns 4 and 5). Then she calculates the contribution, excluding expenses on communications (column 6), and the profit when the communication expenses are considered (column 7). To estimate the sales generated by different levels of communications, West can simply rely on her judgment and experience, or she might analyze past

Marginal Analysis for Setting Diane West's Communication Budget   EXHIBIT 15–4

Level	Communication Expenses (1)	Sales (2)	Gross Margin Realized (3)	Rental Expense (4)	Personnel Expense (5)	Contribution before Communication Expenses (6) = (3) − (4) − (5)	Profit after Communication Expenses (7) = (6) − (1)	
1	$ 0	$240,000	$ 96,000	$44,000	$52,200	$ (200)	$ (200)	
2	5,000	280,000	112,000	48,000	53,400	10,600	5,600	
3	10,000	330,000	132,000	53,000	54,900	24,100	14,100	
4	15,000	380,000	152,000	58,000	56,400	37,600	22,600	
5	20,000	420,000	168,000	62,000	57,600	48,400	28,400	
6	25,000	460,000	184,000	66,000	58,800	59,200	34,200	
7	30,000	500,000	200,000	70,000	60,000	70,000	40,000	Last year
8	35,000	540,000	216,000	74,000	61,200	80,800	45,800	
9	40,000	570,000	228,000	77,000	62,100	88,900	48,900	
10	45,000	600,000	240,000	80,000	63,000	97,000	52,000	
11	50,000	625,000	250,000	82,500	63,750	103,750	53,750	
12	55,000	650,000	260,000	85,000	64,500	110,500	55,500	Chosen budget
13	60,000	670,000	268,000	87,000	65,100	115,900	55,900	
14	65,000	690,000	276,000	89,000	65,700	121,300	56,300	Best profit
15	70,000	705,000	282,000	90,500	66,150	125,350	55,350	
16	75,000	715,000	286,000	91,500	66,450	128,050	53,050	
17	80,000	725,000	290,000	92,500	66,750	130,750	50,750	
18	85,000	735,000	294,000	93,500	67,050	133,450	48,450	
19	90,000	745,000	298,000	94,500	67,350	136,150	46,150	
20	95,000	750,000	300,000	95,000	67,500	137,500	42,500	
21	100,000	750,000	300,000	95,000	67,500	137,500	37,500	

data to determine the relationship between communication expenses and sales. Historical data also provide information about the gross margin and other expenses as a percentage of sales.

Notice that at low levels of communication expenses, an additional $5,000 in communication expenses generates more than a $5,000 incremental contribution. For example, increasing the communication expense from $15,000 to $20,000 increases the contribution by $10,800 (or $48,400 − $37,600). When the communication expense reaches $65,000, further increases of $5,000 generate less than $5,000 in additional contributions. For example, increasing the budget from $65,000 to $70,000 generates only an additional $4,050 in contribution ($125,350 − $121,300).

In this example, West determines that the maximum profit would be generated with a communication expense budget of $65,000. But she notices that expense levels between $55,000 and $70,000 all result in about the same level of profit. Thus, West makes a conservative decision and establishes a $55,000 budget for her communication expenses.

In most cases, it's very hard to perform a marginal analysis because managers don't know the relationship between communication expenses and sales. Note that the numbers in Exhibit 15–4 are simply West's estimates, and they may not be accurate.

Sometimes retailers perform experiments to get a better idea of the relationship between communication expenses and sales. Say, for example, a catalog retailer selects several geographic areas in the United States with the same sales potential. The retailer then distributes 100,000 catalogs in the first area, 200,000 in the second area, and 300,000 in the third. Using the sales and costs for each distribution level, it could conduct an analysis like the one in Exhibit 15–4 to determine the most profitable distribution level. (Chapter 14 described the use of experiments to determine the relationship between price and sales.)

EXHIBIT 15–5
Illustration of Objective-and-Task Method for Setting a Communication Budget

Objective: Increase the percentage of target market (working women) who know of our store's location and who purchase business attire from 25 percent to 50 percent over the next 12 months.	
Task: 480, 30–second radio spots during peak commuting hours	$12,000
Task: Sign with store name near entrance to mall	4,500
Task: Display ad in the Yellow Pages	500
Objective: Increase the percentage of target market who indicate that our store is their preferred store for buying their business wardrobe from 5 percent to 15 percent in 12 months.	
Task: Develop TV campaign to improve image and run 50, 30–second commercials	$24,000
Task: Hold four "Dress for Success" seminars followed by a wine-and-cheese party	8,000
Objective: Sell merchandise remaining at end of season.	
Task: Special event	$6,000
Total budget	$55,000

Some other methods that retailers use to set communication budgets are the objective-and-task and rules-of-thumb methods, which include the affordable, percentage-of-sales, and competitive parity methods. These methods are easy to use but do not result in the optimal level of communication expenditures.

Objective-and-Task Method   The **objective-and-task method** determines the budget required to undertake specific tasks to accomplish communication objectives. To use this method, the retailer first establishes a set of communication objectives and then determines the necessary tasks and their costs. The total of all costs incurred to undertake the tasks is the communication budget.

Exhibit 15–5 illustrates how Diane West could use the objective-and-task method to complement her marginal analysis. West establishes three objectives: to increase awareness of her store, to create a greater preference for her store among customers in her target market, and to promote the sale of merchandise remaining at the end of each season. The estimated communication budget she requires to achieve these objectives is $55,000.

In addition to defining her objectives and tasks, West rechecks the financial implications of the communication mix by projecting the income statement for next year using the communication budget (see Exhibit 15–6). This income statement includes an increase of $25,000 in communication expenses compared with last year. But West believes this increase in the communication budget will boost annual sales from $500,000 to $650,000. According to West's projections, the increase in communication expenses will raise store profits. The results of both the marginal analysis and the objective-and-task methods suggest a communication budget between $55,000 and $65,000.

Rule-of-Thumb Methods   The previous two methods set the communication budget by estimating communication activities' effects on the firm's future sales or communication objectives. The **rule-of-thumb methods** discussed in this section use the opposite logic. They use past sales and communication activities to determine the present communication budget.[42]

EXHIBIT 15–6
Financial Implications of Increasing the Communication Budget

	Last Year	Next Year
Sales	$500,000	$ 650,000
Gross margin (realized)	200,000	260,000
Rental, maintenance, etc.	−70,000	−85,000
Personnel	−60,000	−64,500
Communications	−30,000	−55,000
Profit	$ 40,000	$ 55,500

Affordable Budgeting Method   When using the **affordable budgeting method,** retailers first forecast their sales and expenses, excluding communication expenses, during the budgeting period. The difference between the forecast sales and expenses plus the desired profit is then budgeted for the communication mix. In other words, the affordable method sets the communication budget by determining what money is available after operating costs and profits are subtracted.

The major problem with the affordable method is that it assumes that communication expenses don't stimulate sales and profit. Communication expenses are just a cost of business, like the cost of merchandise. When retailers use the affordable method, they typically cut "unnecessary" communication expenses if sales fall below the forecast rather than increasing communication expenses to increase sales.

Percentage-of-Sales Method   The **percentage-of-sales method** sets the communication budget as a fixed percentage of forecast sales. Retailers use this method to determine the communication budget by forecasting sales during the budget period and then applying a predetermined percentage to set the budget. The percentage may be the retailer's historical percentage or the average percentage used by similar retailers.

The problem with the percentage-of-sales method is that it assumes that the same percentage used in the past, or used by competitors, is appropriate for the future. Also, like the affordable method, it assumes that communication expenses don't stimulate sales and profit. Consider a retailer that hasn't opened new stores in the past but plans to open many new stores in the current year. It must create customer awareness for each of these new stores, so the communication budget should be much larger in the current year than in the past.

Using the same percentage as competitors also may be inappropriate. For example, a retailer might have better locations or brand image than its competitors. As a result, customers may already have a high awareness of the retailer's stores. Thus, the retailer may not need to spend as much on communication as competitors with poorer locations or brands.

One advantage of both the percentage-of-sales method and the affordable method for determining a communication budget is that the retailer won't spend beyond its means. Because the level of spending is determined by sales, the budget will go up only when sales go up and as the retailer generates more sales to pay for the additional communication expenses. When times are good, these methods work well because they allow the retailer to communicate more aggressively with customers. But when sales fall, communication expenses are cut, which may accelerate the sales decline.

Competitive Parity Method   Under the **competitive parity method**, the communication budget is set so that the retailer's share of its communication expenses equals its share of the market. For example, consider a sporting goods store in a small town. To use the competitive parity method, the owner-manager would first estimate the total amount spent on communication by all sporting goods retailers in town. Then the owner-manager would estimate his or her store's market share for sporting goods and multiply that market share percentage by the sporting goods stores' total advertising expenses to set the budget. Assume that the owner-manager's estimate of advertising for sporting goods by all stores is $5,000 and the estimate of his or her store's market share is 45 percent. On the basis of these estimates, the owner-manager would set the store's communication budget at $2,250 to maintain competitive parity.

Similar to the other rule-of-thumb methods, the competitive parity method doesn't allow retailers to exploit the unique opportunities or problems they confront in a market. If all competitors used this method to set communication budgets, their market shares would stay about the same over time (assuming that the retailers develop equally effective campaigns and other retail mix activities).

Allocate the Promotional Budget

After determining the size of the communication budget, the third step in the communication planning process is to allocate the budget (see Exhibit 15–2). In this step, the retailer decides how much of its budget to allocate to specific communication elements, merchandise categories, geographic regions, or long- and short-term objectives. For example, Dillard's must decide how much of its communication budget to spend in each area it has stores: Southeast, Mid-Atlantic, Southwest, Midwest, and West Coast. Michaels decides how much to allocate to merchandise associated with different crafts. The sporting goods store owner-manager must decide how much of the store's $2,250 communication budget to spend on promoting the store's image versus generating sales during the year and how much to spend on advertising and special promotions.

Research indicates that allocation decisions are more important than the decision about the amount to spend on communications.[43] In other words, retailers often can realize the same objectives by reducing the size of the communication budget but allocating it more effectively.

An easy way to make such allocation decisions is to spend about the same in each geographic region or for each merchandise category. But this allocation rule probably won't maximize profits, because it ignores the possibility that communication programs might be more effective for some merchandise categories or for some regions than for others. Another approach is to use rules of thumb, such as basing allocations on the sales level or contributions for the merchandise category.

Allocation decisions, like budget-setting decisions, should use the principles of marginal analysis. The retailer should allocate the budget to areas that will yield the greatest return. This approach for allocating a budget is sometimes referred to as the **high-assay principle.** Consider a miner who can spend his time digging on two claims. The value of the gold on one claim is assayed at $20,000 per ton, whereas the assay value on the other claim is $10,000 per ton. Should the miner spend two-thirds of his time at the first mine and one-third of his time at the other mine? Of course not! The miner should spend all of his time mining the first claim until the assay value of the ore mined drops to $10,000 a ton, at which time he can divide his time equally between the claims.

Similarly, a retailer may find that its customers have a high awareness and very favorable attitude toward its women's clothing but do not know much about its men's clothing. In this situation, a dollar spent on advertising men's clothing might generate more sales than a dollar spent on women's clothing, even though the sales of women's clothing are greater than the sales of men's clothing.

Plan, Implement, and Evaluate Communication Programs—Three Illustrations

The final stage in developing a retail communication program is its implementation and evaluation (see Exhibit 15–2). This final section of the chapter illustrates the planning and evaluation process for three communication programs: a traditional advertising campaign, a Facebook campaign, and a Google AdWords campaign by a small specialty retailer.

Advertising Campaign Hypothetically, imagine Fabulous Fromage is a specialty import cheese shop, located just outside New York City. The store's appearance

Communicating great products and knowledgeable employees help specialty import cheese stores thrive.

combines the ambiance of a French café with the conveniences of a modern retailer; most of its merchandise is imported from France and a few other renowned cheese-making regions around the world.

Harry Owens, the owner, realizes that his communication budget is considerably less than the budget of the local Whole Foods store, which also sells gourmet cheeses. He, therefore, decides to concentrate his limited budget on a specific segment and use very creative copy and distinctive artwork in his advertising. His target market is knowledgeable, sophisticated consumers of gourmet foods and kitchenwares. His experience indicates the importance of personal selling for these seasoned shoppers because they (1) make expensive purchases but (2) seek considerable information before making their decisions. Thus, Owens spends part of his communication budget on training his sales associates.

The advertising program Owens develops emphasizes his store's distinctive image. He uses the newspaper as his major vehicle. Whereas the ads issued by Whole Foods tend to highlight price promotions on specialty cheeses, the advertising for Fabulous Fromage emphasizes French country imagery, including off-the-beaten-path scenes of French pastures and unusual art objects. This theme is also reflected in the store's atmosphere.

To evaluate his communication program, Owens needs to compare the results of his program with the objectives he has developed during the first part of the planning process. To measure his campaign's effectiveness, he conducts an inexpensive tracking study. Telephone interviews are performed periodically with a representative sample of customers in his store's trading area. Communication objectives are assessed using the following questions:

Communication Objectives	Questions
Awareness	What stores sell imported cheese?
Knowledge	Which stores would you rate outstanding on the following characteristics . . . (e.g., sales assistance)?
Attitude	On your next shopping trip for imported cheese, which store would you visit first?
Visit	Which of the following stores have you been to?

Here are the survey results for one year:

Communication Objective	Before Campaign	6 Months After	One Year After
Awareness (% mentioning store)	38%	46%	52%
Knowledge (% giving outstanding rating for sales assistance)	9	17	24
Attitude (% first choice)	13	15	19
Visit (% visited store)	8	15	19

The results show a steady increase in awareness, knowledge of the store, and choice of the store as a primary source of fine imported cheeses. This research thus provides evidence that the advertising is conveying the intended message to the target audience.

Facebook Marketing Campaign   Owens is developing a Facebook marketing campaign for a new product line he plans to import from Italy using the steps outlined in Exhibit 15–2.[44]

1. *Establish objectives.* Owens must determine the objectives he hopes to achieve through his campaign. Is it designed to increase awareness of the product line? Is he hoping more potential customers might visit and Like his Facebook page? Is his focus mainly on increasing sales of the product line? Depending on what he aims to achieve, he might focus on developing a Facebook Page, creating a Facebook App, or hosting a Facebook Event.

   As part of his objectives, he also needs to determine whom Fabulous Fromage is targeting. Facebook enables Owens to perform targeting based on location, language, education, gender, profession, age, relationship status, likes/dislikes, and friends or connections. Owens' aim is to find a big enough audience to reach those who might buy the new product line without being so big that he ends up trying to appeal to someone way outside of his target audience. A Facebook targeting example is depicted in Exhibit 15–7.

2. *Develop the budget.* Budgeting is key. Facebook allows advertisers to set a daily budget: Once the costs (usually per click) reach a certain level, the ad disappears for the rest of the day. Of course, this option can be risky if the retailer is getting great feedback, and all of a sudden, a compelling ad disappears. Therefore, similar to the campaign content, budgets demand nearly constant review. For example, if a competitor lowers its price significantly, it might be necessary to follow suit to avoid being excluded from customers' consideration sets.

3. *Allocate budget (develop the campaign).* Now that Owens knows who he is targeting and what his budget is for the campaign, the next step is to develop the communication, including the copy and images. Here again, the process is not very different from any other marketing communications campaign. There should be a call to action that is clear and compelling. Strong, eye-catching images and designs are important. And the campaign must appeal to the right customers. However, an aspect that is more critical with social media than other forms of marketing communications is that the images and messages need to be updated almost constantly. Because people expect changing content online, it would be inappropriate to run the same campaign for several months, as the shop might if it were advertising on television, for example.

2. Targeting

Location

Country: (?)   [New York]
    ○ Everywhere
    ○ By State/Province (?)
    ◉ By City (?)

Demographics

Age: (?)   [24 ⇕] – [35 ⇕]

Demographics

Age: (?)   [24 ⇕] – [35 ⇕]
    ☐ Require exact age match
Sex: (?)   ◉ All   ○ Men   ○

Interests

Precise interests: (?)   [Cooking]

Switch to Broad Category Targeting (?)

Estimated Reach (?)

266,920 people
- **who live in the** United States
- **who live within 50 miles of** New York, NY
- **between the ages of** 24 **and** 35 **inclusive**
- **who are in the category** Cooking

EXHIBIT 15–7
Example Facebook Targeting Choices

4. *Implement and evaluate the program.* The final step is to implement and review the success of the campaign and make changes as necessary. Facebook's Ad Manager offers various metrics and reports, such as number of clicks on ads, audience demographics, and ad performance for specific time periods.

Google AdWords Campaign   Fabulous Fromage's target market is young, well-educated, men and women aged 30 to 40 years interested in food and wine. The owner's experience indicates the importance of personal selling for his so-phisticated target market because the marketed customers (1) make large pur-chases and (2) seek information about gourmet products before making a decision. Owens has, therefore, decided to concentrate his limited budget on a specific seg-ment and use electronic media in his IMC program to generate business through his new website.

To reach new customers, Owens is actively using search engine marketing. In particular, he is using Google AdWords, a search engine marketing tool offered by Google that allows advertisers to show up in the ad section of the search results page based on the keywords potential customers use (see the ad section in the right-hand column of the Google screen grab on the next page). Owens is also using what he has learned from his interactions with Google consultants and is rewriting content on his website to achieve search engine optimization (as we dis-cussed earlier in the chapter). Thus, Owens is experimenting with both paid search through Google's advertising program and organic search through his revised website content.

Owens must determine the best keywords to use for his sponsored-link advertising program. Some potential customers might search using the key words, "New York Gourmet Cheese," "Imported Cheese," or other such ver-sions. Using Google AdWords, Owens can assess the effectiveness of his

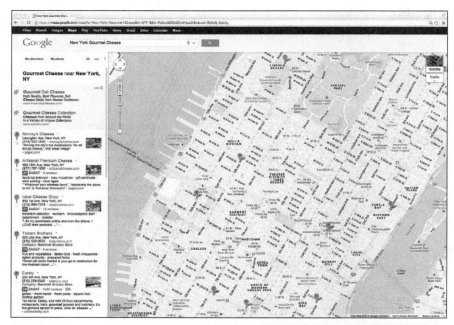

Advertisers pay Google to show up in the ad section in the right-hand column of this screen grab based on the keywords customers use in their searches.

advertising expenditures by measuring the reach, relevance, and return on advertising investment for each of the keywords that potential customers used during their Internet searches.

To estimate reach, Owens uses the number of **impressions** (the number of times the ad appears in front of the user) and the **click-through rate (CTR)**. To calculate CTR, he takes the number of times a user clicks on an ad and divides it by the number of impressions.[45] For example, if a sponsored link was delivered 100 times and 10 people clicked on it, then the number of impressions is 100, the number of clicks is 10, and the CTR would be 10 percent. The **relevance** of the ad describes how useful an ad message is to the consumer doing the search. Google provides a measure of relevance through its AdWords system using a proprietary metric known as a Quality Score.[46] The Quality Score uses multiple factors to measure the keyword's relevance to the ad text or a user's search. A high Quality Score generally implies that the keyword will result in ads that appear higher on the page, with a lower cost per click.[47] In a search for "gourmet cheese," the Fabulous Fromage ad showed up fourth, suggesting high relevance.

Using the following formula, Owens also can determine an ad's **return on advertising investment (ROAI)**:

$$ROAI = \frac{\text{Net sales} - \text{Advertising cost}}{\text{Advertising cost}}$$

For the two keyword searches in Exhibit 15–8, Owens finds how much the advertising cost him (column 3), the sales produced as a result (column 4), and the ROAI (column 6). For "New York Gourmet Cheese," the website had a lot more clicks (110) than the clicks received from "Imported Cheese" (40) (see column 2, Exhibit 15–8). Even though the sales were lower for the keywords "New York Gourmet Cheese" at $35 per day, versus $40 per day for the keywords "Imported

(1) Keyword	(2) Clicks	(3) Cost	(4) Sales	(5) Revenue − Cost (Col. 4 − Col. 3)	(6) ROAI (Col. 5/Col. 3) × 100)
New York Gourmet Cheese	110	$10/day	$35/day	$25	250%
Imported Cheese	40	$25/day	$40/day	$15	60%

EXHIBIT 15–8
ROAI Assessment for Two Google AdWords

Cheese," the ROAI was much greater for the "New York Gourmet Cheese" keyword. In the future, Owens should continue using this keyword, in addition to producing others that are similar to it, in the hope that he will attain an even greater return on investment.

SUMMARY

LO1 Identify the traditional media elements.

Retailers communicate with customers using a variety of traditional media elements. These include mass media advertising, sales promotions, in-store marketing, personal selling, and public relations.

LO2 Identify the new media elements.

In the past decade or so, retailers have embraced several new media elements. The online elements include websites, e-mail, and mobile. Examples of the social media elements embraced by retailers are YouTube, Facebook, blogs, and Twitter.

LO3 Understand how retailers use communication programs to develop brand images and build customer loyalty.

An important use of communication programs is to develop strong brand images that enhance customer loyalty. Brands are very valuable to both customers and retailers because they provide information that helps enhance the shopping experience and create loyalty toward the retailer and its products and services. To enhance customers' brand image, retailers undertake communications activities that create a high level of brand awareness, develop favorable associations with the brand name, and reinforce the image of the brand.

LO4 List the steps involved in developing a communication program.

Retailers go through four steps to develop and implement their communication program: establish objectives, determine a budget, allocate the budget, and implement and evaluate the program. Marginal analysis is the most appropriate method for determining how much should be spent to accomplish the retailer's objectives because it maximizes the profits that could be generated by the communication mix. Because marginal analysis is difficult to implement, however, many retailers use rule-of-thumb methods to determine the size of the promotion budget.

KEY TERMS

advertising, *419*
affordable budgeting method, *441*
aided recall, *433*
blog (weblog), *429*
brand, *431*
brand associations, *435*
brand awareness, *433*
brand equity, *431*
brand image, *431*
cause-related marketing campaign, *424*
click through rates, *446*
communication objectives, *436*

competitive parity method, *441*
cooperative (co-op) advertising, *438*
coupons, *421*
direct mail, *420*
e-mail, *425*
event sponsorship, *423*
freestanding insert (FSI), *419*
high-assay principle, *442*
impressions, *446*
integrated marketing communication program, *418*
marginal analysis, *438*

m-commerce, *425*
microblog, *430*
mobile commerce, *425*
mobile communication, *425*
objective-and-task method, *440*
percentage-of-sales method, *441*
personal selling, *423*
point-of-purchase (POP) display, *422*
premium, *421*
preprint, *419*
product placement, *424*
public relations (PR), *423*

GET OUT AND DO IT!

1. **CONTINUING ASSIGNMENT** Evaluate the communication activities undertaken by the retailer you have selected for the continuing assignment. Describe your retailer's brand image. Briefly explain how your retailer uses each of the following elements of its communication program: direct marketing, online marketing, personal selling, sales promotions, direct mail and e-mail, mobile marketing, advertising (media used?), social media, public relations, website, and events. Do all of these elements send a consistent brand-image message to customers? Why, or why not?

2. Go to the home page for BrandZ at www.brandz.com, and click on "BrandZ Reports," then select the Top 100 Global Brands Report. On the basis of this report, list the top 20 global retail brands. In two or three paragraphs, describe what makes a strong retail brand. How were brand equity and financial performance used to measure brand value for these retailers?

3. Retailers and manufacturers deliver coupons through the Internet in addition to delivering them by mail or as inserts. Go to retailmenot.com for coupons offered over the Internet. How does this coupon distribution system compare with the other two distribution systems?

4. Trader Joe's is a gourmet grocery store offering items such as health foods, organic produce, and nutritional supplements. The company has nearly 400 stores in 37 states at which it offers more than 2,000 private-label products. Go to www.traderjoes.com, and see how the firm uses its Internet site to promote its retail stores and merchandise. Why does this retailer include recipes and a seasonal guide on its website? Does the information provided on the web page reinforce the store's upscale grocery image? Explain why or why not.

5. Go to the social media site for a retailer that you have shopped at during the last few weeks. How was social media used as an element in the retailer's communication program? What audience is being reached with social media? Is the social media message consistent or inconsistent with other communication elements? Is this a strong or weak strategy? Please explain.

6. Go to the home page for Target's Pressroom at pressroom.target.com. How does this retailer use public relations to communicate with investors and customers? Is this an effective communication tool for this retailer? Provide support for your response.

7. Go to www.facebook.com/business to see how to build pages, ads, and sponsored stories, as well as how to take advantage of mobile applications. What are some of the steps that Facebook suggests a person consider when marketing using ads?

DISCUSSION QUESTIONS AND PROBLEMS

1. How do brands benefit consumers? Retailers?

2. What are the positive and negative aspects of direct marketing from the customer's perspective?

3. What types of sales promotions have been successful with you as a consumer? Which ones have not been successful? Explain your responses.

4. What factors should be considered in dividing up the advertising budget among a store's different merchandise areas? Which of the following should receive the highest advertising budget: staple, fashion, or seasonal merchandise? Why?

5. Outline some elements in a communication program that can be used to achieve the following objectives: (a) Increase store loyalty by 20 percent. (b) Build awareness of the store by 10 percent. (c) Develop an image as a low-price retailer. How would you determine whether the communication program met each of these objectives?

6. A retailer plans to open a new store near a university. It will specialize in collegiate merchandise such as apparel, accessories, and school supplies. Consider the pros and cons of each of the following media: TV, radio, city newspaper, university newspaper, local

magazine, website, blog, and event sponsorship for this retailer to capture the university market.

7. Why do some online retailers include editorials and customer reviews along with product information on their websites? Explain how this may influence the consumer's buying behavior.

8. Assume you work for a large consumer-packaged goods firm that has learned its latest line of snack foods is moving very slowly off store shelves. Recommend a strategy for listening to what consumers are saying on blogs, review sites, and the firm's website. Describe how your strategy might provide insights into consumers' sentiments about the new product line.

9. As an intern for Dunkin' Donuts, you have been asked to develop a social media campaign for a new glazed muffin. The objective of the campaign is to increase awareness and trial of the new line of muffins. How would you go about putting such a campaign together?

SUGGESTED READINGS

Aaker, David, and Erich Joachimsthaler. *Brand Leadership: Building Assets in an Information Economy*. New York: Free Press, 2009.

Belch, George, and Michael Belch. *Advertising and Promotion: An Integrated Marketing Communications Perspective*, 9th ed. New York: McGraw-Hill, 2012.

Scott Lerman, *Building Better Brands: A Comprehensive Guide to Brand Strategy and Identity Development*, HOW Books, 2013.

Ludwig Stephan, Ko de Ruyter, Mike Friedman, Elisabeth C. Brüggen, Martin Wetzels, and Gerard Pfann. "More Than Words: The Influence of Affective Content and Linguistic Style Matches in Online Reviews on Conversion Rates." *Journal of Marketing*, 77 (January 2013), pp. 87–103.

Rapp, Adam, Lauren Bietelspacher, Dhruv Grewal, and Doug Hughes. "Understanding Social Media Effects Across Seller, Retailer, and Consumer Interactions," *Journal of the Academy of Marketing Science*, 41 (September 2013), pp. 547–66.

Sernovitz, Andy. *Word of Mouth Marketing: How Smart Companies Get People Talking*. Austin, TX: Greenleaf Press, 2012.

Smith, Ron, *Public Relations: The Basics*. New York: Routledge, 2012.

Sponder, Marshall. *Social Media Analytics: Effective Tools for Building, Interpreting, and Using Metrics*. New York: McGraw Hill, 2011.

Weaver, Jason. *Manager's Guide to Online Marketing*. New York: McGraw-Hill, 2013.

Store Management

Store Management

Section IV focuses on the implementation issues associated with store management, including managing store employees and controlling costs (Chapter 16), presenting merchandise (Chapter 17), and providing customer service (Chapter 18).

Traditionally, the issues pertaining to merchandise management were considered the most important retail decisions, and buying merchandise was considered the best career path for achieving senior retail management positions. Today, developing a strategic advantage through merchandise management is becoming more difficult because competing firms often have similar assortments of national brand merchandise.

Because customers can find the same assortments in a number of conveniently located retail stores and through the Internet, effective store management has become a critical basis for developing strategic advantages. Retailers are increasing their emphasis on differentiating their offering from those of competitors on the basis of the customer's experiences in the retailer's stores and websites, including the service they get from store employees and the quality of the shopping environment.

Managing the Store

When I was attending the University of Florida, I really didn't know what I wanted to do when I graduated. As a classics major, I hoped to work in a museum or take the graduate school route, but I was ready to stop taking classes. Upon graduation and a brief hiatus overseas, I began my career with Kohl's as an assistant store manager. As is often the case in retail, mobility facilitates promotions; unfortunately for me, my mobility was somewhat limited due to my husband's job, so after only five years and two moves I was happily promoted to store manager.

I love my job, and I love working for Kohl's. My store near Amelia Island, Florida, is only one year old and is in a smaller building than your typical Kohl's. Our sales neared $8 million last year, and I have about 75 associates on my team. To me, those 75 associates are the heartbeat of the building, and it's my job as a store manager to make them feel valued and appreciated. I truly believe a happy associate makes for a happy customer. Although managing goals and workload can be challenging and stressful, I've instituted "Thank you Thursdays" in the building, which can be anything from Oreos and milk to popcorn and a movie. These events are meant to show my appreciation and, I hope, to make what might seem to some a boring, minimum-wage job

into a fun and motivating career. From Good Fortune Fridays with Chinese food and fortune cookies to cupcake bake-off wars, my main roles in the building are cheerleader, coach, and party planner.

Kohl's values the manager-on-duty program highly and refers to it as "E3," for "Every Customer, Every Time, Every Store." With this mantra in mind, I go about my day with a strong customer focus and model the behavior I expect from my team. I have created games and contests to help them meet and exceed store-specific goals and have been known to use crowns, scepters, hats, and bling to keep the fun and positive atmosphere new and exciting. This type of atmosphere not only makes our customers laugh, it piques their interest, and they often want to know what we are celebrating. This results in consistently high customer service scores, which we are always proud to boast about!

CHAPTER 16

LEARNING OBJECTIVES

LO1 Describe how to improve the ability of workers through efficient recruiting, socializing, and training.

LO2 Examine how to improve the effort of workers through proper motivation, evaluation, rewards, and compensation.

LO3 Illustrate effective leadership strategies of a store manager.

LO4 Explore the various strategies a store manager can undertake to control costs.

Finding a job that pays six figures and is wholly fulfilling right out of college is an improbability. I recommend that you find a career that allows you to use your skills in a way that positively affects those around you; when you do, you'll find not only success, but happiness as well.

Store managers play an important role in formulating and executing retail strategies. Due to their frequent contacts with customers, they have the best knowledge of local customer needs and competitive activity. They also provide the shopping experience that plays a major role in building customer loyalty. Buyers can develop exciting merchandise assortments and procure them at low cost, but retailers realize the benefits of the buyers' efforts only when the merchandise is sold. Good merchandise doesn't sell itself. Store managers make sure that the merchandise is presented effectively, and sales associates offer services that stimulate and facilitate customer buying decisions.

Some store managers are responsible for $150 million in annual sales and manage more than 1,000 employees. Even in national chains, store managers are treated as relatively independent managers of a business within the corporation. For example, James Nordstrom, former CEO of Nordstrom, told his store managers, "This is your business. Do your own thing. Don't listen to us in Seattle, listen to your customers. We give you permission to take care of your customers."

Store managers are responsible for the productivity of two of the retailer's most important assets: the firm's investments in its employees and its real estate. Most of this chapter is devoted to increasing labor productivity—the sales generated by each store employee. Three critical drivers of labor productivity and performance

EXHIBIT 16–1
Drivers of Employee
Performance

of store employees, and employees in general, are ability, effort, and leadership. *Ability* is the skills that employees possess to do their job; *effort* is how hard they work; and *leadership* is the degree to which store managers influence employees to engage in behaviors consistent with firms' objectives.[1] In the next three sections, we examine management practices that affect each of these performance drivers as shown in Exhibit 16–1.

In addition to increasing labor productivity, store managers affect their stores' profits by controlling costs. The major costs are employee compensation and benefits. Efficiently scheduling labor offers another opportunity for store managers to control labor costs. In addition, they are responsible for costs associated with operating and maintaining their buildings and reducing inventory shrinkage resulting from shoplifting and employee theft. These cost-control issues are discussed at the end of the chapter.

The first portion of this chapter focuses on the management of store employees and complements the strategic human resource management issues discussed in Chapter 9. Chapter 9 examined the organization of the tasks performed by retail managers and the general approaches for motivating retail employees and building their engagement with the firm. This chapter discusses how store managers implement the retailer's human resource strategy.

RECRUITING, SOCIALIZATION, AND TRAINING OF STORE EMPLOYEES

LO1

Describe how to improve the ability of workers through efficient recruiting, socializing, and training.

This section examines how store managers can improve the abilities of their employees through effective recruiting, socializing, and training.

Recruiting Employees

To recruit skillful, or potentially skillful, employees, store managers prepare a job description, find potential applicants with the desired capabilities, and screen the best candidates to interview.[2] These steps in the recruiting process are described in this section. (Appendix 1A of Chapter 1 describes the recruiting and selection process from the perspective of people interested in pursuing retail careers and applying for management trainee positions.)

Developing the Job Description   The **job description** identifies essential activities to be undertaken and is used to determine the qualifications of potential employees. It includes specific activities the employee needs to perform and the

- How many salespeople will be working in the department at the same time?
- Do the salespeople have to work together in dealing with customers?
- How many customers will the salesperson have to work with at one time?
- Will the salesperson be selling on an open floor or working behind the counter?
- How much and what type of product knowledge does the salesperson need?
- Does the salesperson need to sell the merchandise or just ring up the orders and provide information?
- Is the salesperson required to make appointments with customers and develop a loyal customer base?
- Does the salesperson have the authority to negotiate price or terms of the sale?
- Does the salesperson need to demonstrate the merchandise?
- Will the salesperson be expected to make add-on sales?
- Is the salesperson's appearance important? How should an effective salesperson look?
- Will the salesperson be required to perform merchandising activities such as stocking shelves and setting up displays?
- Whom will the salesperson report to?
- What compensation plan will the salesperson be working under?

EXHIBIT 16–2
Questions for Undertaking a Job Description

performance expectations expressed in quantitative terms. The job description is a guideline for recruiting, selecting, training, and eventually evaluating employees. Retail salespeople's responsibilities vary from company to company and department to department within a store. Retail employees in self-service stores such as supermarkets and full-line discount stores typically help customers find merchandise, bring out and display merchandise, and ring up sales. In contrast, employees who work in jewelry stores, high-end apparel department stores, or furniture stores typically get involved in a more extensive selling process that begins with determining the customer's needs, then proposing solutions, overcoming objections, closing the sale, and providing after-sale support.[3] The skill level required for employees engaged in selling high-involvement merchandise such as jewelry or home entertainment systems are much greater than the skills needed for employees who have limited interactions with customers. Exhibit 16–2 lists some questions that managers use when undertaking a job description of store employees.

Locating Prospective Employees   Some creative approaches being used by retailers to recruit applicants, in addition to placing ads on Craigslist and posting job openings on websites such as LinkedIn and TweetMyJobs, are working with

Many retailers find that the productivity and engagement of older employees is greater than younger employees.

the American Association of Retired Persons (AARP) to match seniors with job openings at their companies. Other options include partnering with government agencies to recruit the unemployed, veterans, and former welfare recipients, or using employees as talent scouts. That is, retailers often ask their own employees if they know someone the company could hire.[4] When Starbucks store managers receive exceptional service from other providers, they give the associate a business card, inviting him or her to drop into Starbucks, have a free latte, and discuss employment opportunities. Some employers provide employees rewards, such as $500 for every full-time hire and $200 for every part-timer.

Screening Applicants to Interview   The screening process matches applicants' qualifications with the job description. Many retailers use automated pre-screening programs as a low-cost method of identifying qualified candidates. Applicants initially apply in the store using a traditional paper application or through a web-enabled store kiosk. They can also apply online or call a toll-free telephone number.

Application Forms   **Job application forms** contain information about the applicant's employment history, previous compensation, reasons for leaving his or her previous employment, education and training, and references. This information enables the manager to determine whether the applicant has the minimum qualifications, and it also provides information that is useful when the manager interviews the applicant. Today, many large retailers have found that having a nationwide centralized recruiting process reduces costs considerably and improves the quality of candidates that are eventually hired. Retailing View 16.1 describes the benefits Home Depot realizes by centralizing its recruitment processes.

References and Online Checks   Most retailers verify the information given on an application form by contacting the applicant's references and doing an online search. Because people are more likely to be honest in conversations, managers often talk to the references, rather than relying on written opinions. Due to potential legal problems, however, many companies have a policy of not commenting on prior employees. A Google search can also be useful for finding out information that may not appear on the job application or emerge through contacts with references.

Store managers generally expect to hear favorable comments from an applicant's references or previous supervisors, even if they may not have thought highly of the applicant. One approach to reduce this positive bias is to ask the reference to rank the applicant relative to others in the same position. For example, the manager might ask, "How would you rate Pat's customer service skills in relation to other retail sales associates you have worked with?"

Social Media   Social media such as Twitter, Facebook, and LinkedIn are excellent sources of information on prospective employees. These sites often reveal more about the person than a face-to-face interview. While social media platforms can provide employers with a wealth of information about job candidates, there is a risk of relying too heavily on this information for selecting employees. Much of the information on social media sites—such as ethnicity, age, religion, marital status, and sexual orientation, is sensitive and protected by law. The use of sensitive, protected information could expose an employer to discrimination claims, especially if it is not relevant for the employee's eventual job performance.[6]

Testing   Some retailers use intelligence, ability, personality, and interest tests to gain insights about candidates. Tests also can be used to match applicants with job openings and to develop training programs. However, tests must be scientifically and legally valid. They can be used only when the scores have been shown to be

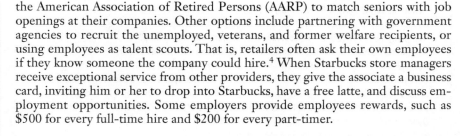

related to job performance. It is illegal to use tests that assess factors that are not job-related or discriminate against specific groups.

Due to potential losses from theft, many retailers require that applicants take drug tests. Some retailers also use tests to assess applicants' honesty and ethics. Paper-and-pencil honesty tests include questions designed to find out if an applicant has ever thought about stealing and if he or she believes other people steal ("What percentage of people take more than $1 from their employer?").

Realistic Job Preview   Turnover declines when applicants understand both the attractive and unattractive aspects of the job.[9] For example, PetSmart, a pet supply category specialist, shows each applicant a 10-minute video that begins with the advantages of being a company employee and continues with scenes of employees dealing with irate customers and cleaning up animal droppings. Using job previews like this typically screens out many applicants who would most likely have quit due to the job requirements within three months if hired.

Selecting Applicants   After screening applicants, the selection process typically involves a personal interview. Because the interview is usually the critical factor in the hiring decision, the store manager needs to be well prepared and have complete control over the interview.

Preparation for the Interview   The objective of the interview is to gather relevant information, not simply to ask a lot of questions. The most widely used

REFACT

Of retailers, 71 percent check references as part of the selection process, 54 percent do drug screening, and 43 percent use paper-and-pencil honesty tests.[8]

RETAILING VIEW   Home Depot Centralizes Its Recruitment Processes   16.1

Before Home Depot centralized its recruitment process, the management in its 2,200 U.S. stores wasted a lot of time interviewing applicants who were not qualified or interested when they found out what the job entailed. So Home Depot decided to centralize its recruitment process—a decision that reduced costs and increased the quality of the more than 200,000 sales associates hired each year. Today, most of the recruitment process is done by 450 people in Home Depot's human resource department at its corporate headquarters in Atlanta.

The process begins with a candidate submitting an application using a kiosk located in every store. When a store has an opening, the HR department goes to its applicant pool and identifies 10 or more potential candidates. Then each candidate is interviewed by telephone twice. During the interviews, candidates are told about the job, the responsibilities, and the pay. If speaking Spanish is required for the position, interviewers fluent in Spanish talk with the candidates to assess their language skills. The phone interviews enable the screeners to assess the enthusiasm and energy level of

Home Depot attracts and does an initial screening of prospective employees using web-enabled kiosks in their stores.

the candidates—characteristics that are important to Home Depot but not easily assessed from an application form. Then the store managers interview the four or five best candidates and select one.

Due to the centralized process, the number of candidates store managers need to interview is dramatically reduced, leaving the store managers with more time to spend on improving the customer's shopping experience. Because the corporate screeners have more experience in screening candidates than the store managers, the quality of the new hires has increased, and the legal violations have decreased.

Sources: www.homedepot.com; and Arielle Kass, "Home Depot Centralizes In-store Hiring Process," *The Atlanta Journal-Constitution*, March 13, 2011.

DISCUSSION QUESTION

How has centralized recruiting improved the candidate pool at Home Depot?

interview technique, called the **behavioral interview,** asks candidates how they have handled actual situations they have encountered in the past, especially situations requiring the skills outlined in the job description. For example, applicants applying for a job requiring that they handle customer complaints would be asked to describe a situation in which they were confronted by someone who was angry about something they had done. Candidates might be asked to describe the situation, what they did, and the outcomes of their actions. These situations also can be used to interview references for the applicants. Exhibit 16–3 lists some questions that manager might ask. Here are some suggestions for questioning the applicant during the interview:

- Encourage long responses by asking questions like "What do you know about our company?" rather than "How familiar are you with our company?"
- Avoid asking questions that have multiple parts.
- Avoid asking leading questions like "Are you prepared to provide good customer service?"
- Be an active listener. Evaluate the information being presented and sort out the important comments from the unimportant ones. Some techniques for active listening include repeating or rephrasing information, summarizing the conversation, and tolerating silences.

EXHIBIT 16–3   Interviewing Questions

EDUCATION	**PREVIOUS EXPERIENCE**	**QUESTIONS THAT SHOULD NOT BE ASKED PER EQUAL EMPLOYMENT OPPORTUNITY GUIDELINES**
What were your most and least favorite subjects in college? Why?	What's your description of the ideal manager? Subordinate? Coworker?	Do you have plans for having children/a family?
What types of extracurricular activities did you participate in? Why did you select those activities?	What did you like most/least about your last job?	What are your marriage plans?
	What kind of people do you find it difficult/easy to work with? Why?	What does your husband/wife do?
If you had the opportunity to attend school all over again, what, if anything, would you do differently? Why?	What has been your greatest accomplishment during your career to date?	What happens if your husband/wife gets transferred or needs to relocate?
How did you spend the summers during college?	Describe a situation at your last job involving pressure. How did you handle it?	Who will take care of your children while you're at work?
Did you have any part-time jobs? Which of your part-time jobs did you find most interesting? What did you find most difficult about working and attending college at the same time? What advice would you give to someone who wanted to work and attend college at the same time?	What were some duties on your last job that you found difficult?	(Asked of men) How would you feel about working for a woman?
	Of all the jobs you've had, which did you find the most/least rewarding?	How old are you?
		What is your date of birth?
	What is the most frustrating situation you've encountered in your career?	How would you feel working for a person younger than you?
What accomplishments are you most proud of?	Why do you want to leave your present job?	Where were you born?
	What would you do if . . . ?	Where were your parents born?
	How would you handle . . . ?	Do you have any handicaps?
	What would you like to avoid in future jobs?	As a handicapped person, what help are you going to need to do your work?
	What do you consider your greatest strength/weakness?	How severe is your handicap?
	What are your responsibilities in your present job?	What's your religion?
		What church do you attend?
	Tell me about the people you hired on your last job. How did they work out? What about the people you fired?	Do you hold religious beliefs that would prevent you from working on certain days of the week?
	What risks did you take in your last job, and what were the results of those risks?	Do you feel that your race/color will be a problem in your performing the job?
	Where do you see yourself in three years?	Are you of _____ heritage/race?
	What kind of references will your previous employer give?	
	What do you do when you have trouble solving a problem?	

Legal Considerations in Selecting and Hiring Store Employees   Heightened social awareness and government regulations emphasize the need to avoid discriminating against hiring people with disabilities, women, minorities, and older workers.[10] Title VII of the Civil Rights Act prohibits discrimination on the basis of race, national origin, gender, or religion in company personnel practices. Discrimination is specifically prohibited in the following human resource decisions: recruitment, hiring, firing, layoffs, discipline, promotion, compensation, and access to training. The expansion of this Act in 1972 led to the creation of the **Equal Employment Opportunity Commission (EEOC),** which allows employees to sue employers that violate the law. Several major retailers have been successfully sued because they discriminated in hiring and promoting minorities and women.

Discrimination arises when a member of a **protected class** (women, minorities, etc.) is treated differently from nonmembers of that class (**disparate treatment**) or when an apparently neutral rule has an unjustified discriminatory effect **(disparate impact).** An example of disparate treatment occurs when a qualified woman does not receive a promotion, which instead goes to a less qualified man. Disparate impact occurs, for instance, when a retailer requires a college degree for all its employees, thereby excluding a larger proportion of disadvantaged minorities, when at least some of the jobs (e.g., store maintenance) could be performed just as well by people who did not graduate from high school. In such cases, the retailer is required to prove that the imposed qualification is actually needed to be able to perform the job. The **Age Discrimination in Employment Act** makes it illegal to discriminate in hiring and terminating people over the age of 40 years.

Finally, the **Americans with Disabilities Act (ADA)** opens up job opportunities for disabled individuals by requiring that employers provide accommodating work environments. A **disability** is any physical or mental impairment that substantially limits a person's major life activities or any condition that is regarded as being such an impairment. Although being HIV-positive does not limit any life activities, it may be perceived as doing so and is therefore protected as a disability under the ADA.

Socialization of New Store Employees

Having hired employees with the required skills or potential to develop these skills, retailers need to introduce the new employees to the firm and its policies, values, and strategies. This **socialization process** affects the degree to which newcomers become involved, engaged contributors to the firm's successful performance. In addition, socialization helps newly hired employees learn about their job responsibilities and the company they've decided to join.

Orientation Programs   Orientation programs are critical in socializing new employees.[11] For example, overcoming the shock of starting a new job can be a problem for even the most knowledgeable and mature new employees. College students who accept management trainee positions often find significant differences between their role as students and employees. Retailing View 16.2 describes some of these differences.

The orientation and training program for new store employees might be limited to several hours during which the new employee learns the retailer's policies and procedures and how to use the point-of-sale (POS) terminal. Other retailers, like The Container Store, have a much more intensive training program. Selected by *Fortune* magazine as one of the best places to work, new The Container Store employees go through a program called Foundation Week.[12] Before employment really begins, they receive a handbook and assignments to complete. The first day of Foundation Week begins with the company philosophy and a visit from store managers. Employees immediately see this introduction as different from the traditional first day, which typically entails completing forms and learning where to park. Days 2 through 5 continue with hands-on, on-the-floor training, including

460   SECTION IV   Store Management

RETAILING VIEW Transition from Student to
Management Trainee

Many students have some difficulty adjusting to the demands of their first full-time job because student life and professional life are very different. Students typically "report" to three or four supervisors (professors) and they select new "supervisors" every three or four months. In contrast, management trainees have limited involvement, if any, in selecting the one supervisor they'll report to, and they often report to the supervisor for several years.

Student life has fixed time cycles—one- to two-hour classes with a well-defined beginning and end. Retail managers, however, are involved in a variety of activities with varied time horizons, ranging from having a five-minute interaction with a customer to implementing a six-month plan to develop a sales associate into an assistant manager.

The decisions students encounter differ dramatically from the decisions retailers make as well. For example, business students might make several major decisions in a day when they discuss cases in class. These decisions are made and implemented in one class period, and then a

new set of decisions is made and implemented in the next class. In a retail environment, however, strategic decisions evolve over a longer time period. Most decisions, such as those regarding merchandise buying and pricing, are made with incomplete information. Store managers in real life often lack the extensive information provided in many business cases studied in class. Finally, there are long periods of time when store managers undertake mundane tasks associated with implementing decisions and no major issues are being considered. Students typically don't have these mundane tasks to perform in their classes.

Source: Professor Daniel Feldman, University of Georgia.

DISCUSSION QUESTION

How can universities improve the socialization process for college students entering their first jobs?

interaction with and instruction about various positions in the store. The culmination of Foundation Week is a ceremony during which the new employees finally receive their aprons, signifying their membership in this elite organization. The orientation process also continues past Foundation Week. Customer service is the company's core competency, so every first-year, full-time salesperson receives about 263 hours of training, compared with 8 hours in the retail industry, on average. Training continues throughout an employee's career.[13]

The orientation program is just one element in the overall training program. It needs to be accompanied by a systematic follow-up to ensure that any problems and concerns arising after the initial period also are considered.

In this structured training program, newly hired Men's Wearhouse sales associates learn about the merchandise they will be selling.

Training Store Employees

To be effective, new employee training should feature both structured and more informal, on-the-job lessons.[14]

Structured Program A **structured training program** helps new employees acquire basic skills and knowledge, which they need to be able to do their jobs. For example, sales associates learn what the company policies are, how to use the POS terminal, and basic selling skills. Stockroom employees learn procedures for receiving merchandise.

Some retailers find that providing structured training over the

Internet offers benefits compared to the on-the-job training. There is greater consistency, because the same material is presented rather than having material presented by different trainers or supervisors. Costs are lower; once the system is set up, there is no need for instructors or travel, and employees can undertake the training whenever they want.

JCPenney has used an e-training system that combines one-way video with two-way audio and data exchange capability, which allows instructors to chat on-line with students during training programs. Along with the presentations from the instructors, the training includes pre-class and post-class testing to measure comprehension levels. Instructors also break students into groups in which they are given case studies and asked to make recommendations.

On-the-Job Training   Structured training programs also need to be combined with **on-the-job training** in which new employees work in specific jobs under the direct supervision of their managers. New employees can learn about company policies and skills needed to perform their jobs through structured programs, but they must be able to apply the information they have learned from training programs on the job. The best way to learn is to practice what is being taught. New employees learn by engaging in activities, making mistakes, and then learning how not to make those mistakes again.

The outdoor equipment retailer Recreational Equipment Inc. (REI), for instance, spends hours helping new salespeople spot the difference between trans-actional customers, who want a specific product, and consultative customers, who want to chat about choices.[15] This knowledge helps salespeople engage in productive selling interactions and provides a pleasant experience for customers. It would be difficult to teach this type of skill using a structured program.

Blended Approach   Because of the relative advantages of structured and on-the-job training, many firms use a blended approach. Teams of Best Buy associates attend monthly, nearly three-hour long training sessions led by qualified instructors. As a result, Best Buy often is ranked among the top 30 firms for employee training.[16] The after-hours training sessions focus on new products, service up-dates, or concerns related to their departments. Furthermore, the employees role-play to practice customer interactions. In online training sessions, available through the retailer's proprietary learning management system, associates complete courses that enable them to use virtual versions of the products they sell or play interactive video games to practice challenging interactions with virtual customers.

Analyzing Successes and Failures
Every new employee makes mistakes. Effective store managers provide an atmosphere in which sales associates can try out different approaches for providing customer service and selling merchandise. Store managers need to recognize that some of these new approaches are going to fail, and when they do, effective managers do not criticize the individual sales associate. Instead, they talk about the situation, analyze why the approach didn't work,

Best Buy employees receive a lot of training about the latest products and services.

and discuss how the sales associate could avoid the problem in the future. Managers also work with employees to help them understand and learn from their successes. For example, salespeople shouldn't consider a large, multiple-item sale to occur simply due to luck. They should be encouraged to reflect on the sale, identify their key behaviors that facilitated the sale, and then remember these sales behaviors for future use.

It's important to help sales associates assign the right kinds of reasons for their performance. For example, some sales associates take credit for successes and blame the company, the buyers, or the merchandise for their failures. This tendency to avoid taking responsibility for failures doesn't encourage learning. When sales associates adopt this reasoning pattern, they aren't motivated to change their sales behavior because they don't take personal responsibility for losing a sale.

Managers can help sales associates constructively analyze their successes and failures by asking "why" questions that force them to analyze the reasons for effective and ineffective performance. To encourage learning, managers get salespeople to recognize that they could have satisfied the customer if they had used a different approach or been more persistent. When sales associates accept such responsibility, they'll be motivated to search for ways to improve their sales skills.[17]

MOTIVATING, EVALUATING, REWARDING, AND COMPENSATING STORE EMPLOYEES

LO2

Examine how to improve the effort of workers through proper motivation, evaluation, rewards, and compensation.

The second performance driver is effort (see Exhibit 16–1). High-performance store employees work hard, and the activities they work on should be consistent with the retailer's strategy and goals. Motivating employees to perform up to their potential may be store managers' most important and challenging task. The implementation of the retailer's evaluation, rewards, and compensation schemes, discussed in this section, together affect the motivation of store employees and the effort they expend. We use the following hypothetical situation to illustrate some issues pertaining to employee motivation.

After getting an associate's degree at a local community college, Jim Taylor was hired for a sales position at a department store in San Jose's Eastridge Mall. The position offered firsthand knowledge of the firm's customers, managers, and policies. Taylor was told that if he did well in this assignment, he could become a management trainee.

After observing Taylor on the sales floor, his manager, Jennifer Chen, evaluated Taylor's performance as average. She felt he was only effective when interacting with customers like himself: young, career-oriented men and women. To encourage Taylor to sell to other types of customers, Chen reviewed Taylor's performance goals with him. She reduced the portion of his compensation composed of a fixed salary and increased his commission rate. Taylor now feels a lot of pressure to increase his sales level. He's beginning to dread coming to work in the morning and is thinking about getting out of retailing and working for a bank.

In this hypothetical situation, Chen focused on increasing Taylor's motivation by providing some feedback and more incentive-based compensation. In discussing this illustration, we'll examine the appropriateness of this approach versus other approaches for improving Taylor's performance.

Setting Goals to Motivate Employees

To effectively motivate employees, store managers need to set goals for their employees and provide feedback on the employees' performance relative to those goals.

Employee performance improves when employees feel that (1) their efforts will enable them to achieve the goals set for them by their managers and (2) they'll receive rewards they value if they achieve their goals. Thus, managers can motivate employees by setting realistic goals and offering rewards that employees want.[18]

For example, Jennifer Chen set specific selling goals for Jim Taylor when he started to work in her department. Taylor, like other store sales associates, has goals in five selling areas: sales per hour, average amount per transaction (size of average sale), percentage multiple transactions (percentage of sales with add-on items), number of preferred customers, and number of preferred customer appointments made. This retailer defines preferred clients as customers who have a high CLV (see Chapter 11). In addition to being evaluated on their selling goals, sales associates like Taylor are often evaluated on the overall department inventory loss due to stolen merchandise (departmental shrinkage), the errors they make in using the POS terminal (system errors), and their contribution to maintaining the department's appearance (merchandise presentation). In addition to the evaluation, Chen also designed a program for Taylor's development as a sales associate. The activities she outlined over the next six months required Taylor to attend in-house classes to improve his selling skills.

Chen needs to be careful in setting goals for Taylor. If she sets the goals too high, he might become discouraged, feel the goals are unattainable, and thus not be motivated to work harder. However, if she sets the goals too low, Taylor can achieve them easily and won't be motivated to work to his full potential.

Goals are most effective at motivating employees when they're based on the employee's experience and confidence. Experienced salespeople have confidence in their abilities and should have "stretch" goals (high goals that will make them work harder). New salespeople need lower goals that they have a good chance of achieving. The initial good experience of achieving and surpassing goals builds new salespeople's confidence and motivates them to improve their skills. The use of rewards to motivate employees is discussed later in this chapter.

Evaluating Store Employees and Providing Feedback

The objective of the evaluation process is to identify the employees who are performing well and those who aren't. On the basis of the evaluation, high-performing employees should be rewarded and considered for positions with greater responsibility. Plans need to be developed to increase the productivity of employees performing below expectations. Should poor performers be terminated? Do they need additional training? If yes, what kind of training do they need?[19]

Who Should Do the Evaluation?   In large retail firms, the evaluation system is usually designed by the human resource department. But the evaluation itself is done by the employee's immediate supervisor—the manager who works most closely with the employee. For example, in a discount store, the department manager is in the best position to observe a sales associate in action and understand the reasons for the sales associate's performance. The department manager also oversees the recommendations that come out of the evaluation process. Inexperienced supervisors are often assisted by a senior manager in evaluating employees.

How Often Should Evaluations Be Made?   Most retailers evaluate employees annually or semiannually. Feedback from evaluations is the most effective method for improving employee skills. Thus, evaluations should be done more frequently when managers are developing inexperienced employees. However, frequent formal evaluations are time-consuming for managers and may not give employees enough time to respond to suggestions before the next evaluation. Effective managers supplement formal evaluations with frequent informal ones. For example, Jennifer Chen should work with Jim Taylor informally and not wait for the formal six-month evaluation. The best time for Chen to provide this informal feedback is immediately after she has obtained, through observations or reports, positive or negative information about Taylor's performance.

464   SECTION IV   Store Management

EXHIBIT 16–4   Factors Used to Evaluate Sales Associates at a Specialty Store

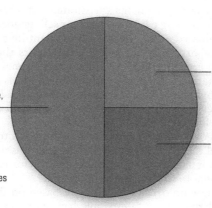

50%
SALES/CUSTOMER RELATIONS

1. Greeting. Approaches customers within 1 to 2 minutes with a smile and friendly manner. Uses open-ended questions.

2. Product knowledge. Demonstrates knowledge of product, fit, shrinkage, and price and can relay this information to the customer.

3. Suggests additional merchandise. Approaches customers at fitting room and cash/wrap areas.

4. Asks customers to buy and reinforces decisions. Lets customers know they've made a wise choice and thanks them.

25%
OPERATIONS

1. Store appearance. Demonstrates an eye for detail (color and finesse) in the areas of display, coordination of merchandise on tables, floor fixtures, and wall faceouts. Takes initiative in maintaining store presentation standards.

2. Loss prevention. Actively follows all loss prevention procedures.

3. Merchandise control and handling. Consistently achieves established requirements in price change activity, shipment processing, and inventory control.

4. Cash/wrap procedures. Accurately and efficiently follows all register policies and cash/wrap procedures.

25%
COMPLIANCE

1. Dress code and appearance. Complies with dress code. Appears neat and well groomed. Projects current fashionable store image.

2. Flexibility. Able to switch from one assignment to another, open to schedule adjustments. Shows initiative, awareness of store priorities and needs.

3. Working relations. Cooperates with other employees, willingly accepts direction and guidance from management. Communicates to management.

Format for Evaluations   Evaluations are only meaningful if employees know what they're required to do, the expected level of performance, and how they'll be evaluated. Exhibit 16–4 shows a specialty retailer's criteria for evaluating sales associates.

In this case, the employee's overall evaluation is based on subjective evaluations made by the store manager and assistant managers. It places equal weight on individual sales/customer relations activities and activities associated with overall store performance. By emphasizing overall store operations and performance, the assessment criteria motivate sales associates to work together as a team.

The criteria used at the department store to evaluate Jim Taylor are objective sales measures based on point-of-sale data, not subjective measures like those used by the specialty store. Exhibit 16–5 summarizes Taylor's formal six-month evaluation. The evaluation form lists results for various factors in terms of both what's considered average performance for company salespeople and Taylor's actual

EXHIBIT 16–5
Summary of Jim Taylor's Six-Month Evaluation

	Average Performance for Sales Associates in Department	Actual Performance for Jim Taylor
Sales per hour	$75	$65
Average amount per transaction	$45	$35
Percentage multiple transactions	55%	55%
Number of preferred customers	115	125
Number of preferred customer appointments	95	120
Departmental shrinkage	2.00%	1.80%
Systems errors	10	2
Merchandise presentation (10-point scale)	5	8

performance. His department has done better than average on shrinkage control, and he has done well on system errors and merchandise presentation. However, his sales performance is below average even though he made more than the average number of presentations to preferred customers. These results suggest that Taylor's effort is good but his selling skills may need improvement.

Evaluation Errors   Managers can make evaluation errors when they first form an overall opinion of the employee's performance and then allow this opinion to influence their ratings of each performance factor. For example, a store manager might feel that a salesperson's overall performance is below average and then rate the salesperson as below average on selling skills, punctuality, appearance, and stocking. When an overall evaluation casts such a negative halo on multiple aspects of a salesperson's performance, the evaluation is no longer useful for identifying specific areas that need improvement.

In making evaluations, managers are often unduly influenced by recent events and their evaluations of other salespeople. For example, a manager might remember a salesperson's poor performance with a customer the day before and forget the salesperson's outstanding performance over the past three months. Similarly, a manager might be unduly harsh in evaluating an average salesperson just after completing an evaluation of an outstanding salesperson. Finally, managers have a natural tendency to attribute performance (particularly poor performance) to the salesperson and not to the environment in which the salesperson is working. When making evaluations, managers tend to underemphasize effects of external factors on the department, such as merchandise and competitors' actions.

The department store's approach for evaluating sales associates avoids many of these potential biases because most of the ratings are based on objective data. In contrast, the specialty store's evaluation approach (Exhibit 16–4) considers a wider range of activities but uses more subjective performance measures. Because subjective information about specific skills, attitudes about the store and customers, interactions with coworkers, enthusiasm, and appearance aren't used in the department store's evaluation, performance on these factors might not have been explicitly communicated to Jim Taylor. The subjective characteristics in the specialty store evaluation are more prone to bias, but they also might be more helpful to salespeople as they try to improve their performance. To avoid bias when making subjective ratings, managers need to observe performance regularly, record their observations, avoid evaluating many salespeople at one time, and remain conscious of the various potential biases.

Rewarding Store Employees

Store employees receive two types of rewards from their job: extrinsic and intrinsic.

Extrinsic Rewards   **Extrinsic rewards** are rewards provided by either the employee's manager or the firm, such as compensation, promotion, and recognition.[20] Managers can offer a variety of extrinsic rewards, such as compensation, as discussed in the next section, to motivate employees.[21] However, store employees don't all seek the same rewards. For example, some salespeople want more compensation; others strive for a promotion in the company or public recognition of their performance. Jim Taylor wants a favorable evaluation from his manager so that he can enter the management training program.

Because of these different employee needs, managers may not be able to use the same rewards to motivate all employees. However, it is hard to develop unique reward programs for each individual, as some (especially part-time employees) are more motivated by nonmonetary compensations such as time off and store discounts. One response is to offer **à la carte plans** that give effective employees a choice of rewards for their good performance. For example, salespeople who achieve their goals could choose a cash bonus, extra days off, or a better discount on merchandise sold in the store. This type of compensation plan enables employees to select the rewards they want and thus will be the strongest individual motivators.

Recognition is another important nonmonetary extrinsic reward for many employees. Although telling employees they've done a job well is appreciated, it's typically more rewarding for them when their good performance is recognized publicly. In addition, public recognition can motivate all store employees, not just the star performers, because it demonstrates management's interest in rewarding employees.

Benefits, another extrinsic reward, are often more important to employees than financial compensation. For example, an employee survey conducted by a quick-service restaurant chain revealed that the top concern of the chain's employees was affordable health care. The chain invested approximately $1.5 million to offer an affordable health care plan, such that any employee who worked at least 20 hours a week and had been there for at least six months could pay a $30 monthly fee ($150 for family coverage) and receive health coverage. Before the restaurant implemented the plan, turnover rates hovered around 125 percent. One year after the new initiative went into effect, turnover dropped to 54 percent and stayed there. The reduced turnover rates allowed the company to save approximately $500,000 in training and recruitment costs annually. In addition, both productivity and employee confidence jumped, while absenteeism fell drastically.

Intrinsic Rewards   **Intrinsic rewards** are rewards employees get personally from doing their job well. For example, salespeople often like to sell because they think it's challenging and fun. Of course, they want to be paid, but they also find it rewarding to help customers and make sales.[22] Most managers focus on extrinsic rewards to motivate employees.[23] However, an emphasis on extrinsic rewards can make employees lose sight of their job's intrinsic rewards. Employees can begin to feel that their only reason for working is to earn money and that the job isn't fun. Note that Jennifer Chen tried to motivate Jim Taylor by using extrinsic rewards when she linked more of his compensation to how much he sold. This increased emphasis on extrinsic financial rewards may be one reason Taylor now dreads coming to work in the morning. He might not think his job is fun anymore.

When employees find their jobs intrinsically rewarding, they're motivated to learn how to do their job better. This is similar to a person who runs a marathon or climbs a mountain simply for the pride and joy they get from accomplishing it. Some managerial actions that affect intrinsic rewards are contests and job enrichment.[24]

Contests   An approach to making work fun is to hold contests with relatively small prizes. Contests are most effective when everyone has a chance to win. Contests in which the best salespeople always win aren't exciting and may even be demoralizing. For example, consider a contest in which a playing card is given to salespeople for each men's suit they sell during a two-week period. At the end of two weeks, the best poker hand wins. This contest motivates all salespeople during the entire period of the contest. A salesperson who sells only four suits can win with four aces on cards they got on the last day of the contest. Contests should be used to create excitement and make selling challenging for everyone, not to pay the best salespeople more money.[25]

Job Enrichment   Experienced employees often lose interest in their jobs. Extrinsic rewards, such as pay or promotion, may not be particularly motivating because the employees might be satisfied with their present income and job responsibilities. But these employees can be motivated by intrinsic rewards presented as job enrichment. **Job enrichment** is the redesign of a job to include a greater range of tasks and responsibilities, including skill variety, task significance, autonomy, and job feedback.[26] For example, an experienced sales associate who has lost some interest in his or her job could be given responsibility for merchandising a particular area, training new salespeople, or planning and managing a special event.

Compensation Programs

The objectives of a compensation program are to attract and keep good employees, motivate them to undertake activities consistent with the retailer's strategy, and strike a balance between controlling labor costs and providing enough compensation to keep high-quality employees.

A compensation plan is most effective for motivating and retaining employees when the employees feel that the plan is fair and that their compensation is related to their efforts. In general, simple plans are preferred to complex plans because they are easier to administer and employees have no trouble understanding them.

Types of Compensation Plans   Retail firms typically use one or more of the following compensation plans: straight salary, straight commission, salary plus commission, and quota-bonus.

With **straight salary compensation,** salespeople receive a fixed amount of compensation for each hour or week they work. For example, a salesperson might be paid $12 an hour or a department manager $1,000 a week. This plan is easy for the employee to understand and for the store to administer. Under a straight salary plan, the retailer has flexibility in assigning salespeople to different activities and sales areas. For example, salaried salespeople will undertake nonselling activities, such as stocking shelves, and won't be upset if they're transferred from a high-sales-volume department to a low-sales-volume department.

The major disadvantage of the straight salary plan is employees' lack of immediate incentives to improve their productivity. They know their compensation won't change in the short run, regardless of whether they work hard or slack off. Another disadvantage for the retailer is that a straight salary becomes a fixed cost that the firm incurs even if sales decline, which means a greater loss of profits during hard economic times.

Incentive compensation plans reward employees on the basis of their productivity. Many retailers use monetary incentives to motivate greater sales productivity by their employees.[27] With some incentive plans, a salesperson's income is based entirely on commission—called a **straight commission.** For example, a salesperson might be paid a commission based on a percentage of sales made minus merchandise returned. Normally, the percentage is the same for all merchandise sold (such as 7 percent of sales). But some retailers use different percentages for different categories of merchandise (such as 4 percent for low-margin items and 10 percent for high-margin items). Different percentages provide additional incentives for salespeople to sell specific items. Typically, the compensation of salespeople selling high-priced items such as men's suits, cars, furniture, and appliances is based largely on their commissions.

Incentive plans also may include a fixed salary plus a commission on total sales or a commission on sales over quota. For example, a salesperson might receive a salary of $200 per week plus a commission of 2 percent on all sales over a quota of $50 per hour.

Incentive compensation plans are a powerful motivator for salespeople to sell merchandise, but they have a number of disadvantages. For example, it's hard to get salespeople who are compensated totally by commission to perform nonselling activities. They're reluctant to spend time stocking shelves when they could be making money by selling. Also, salespeople will concentrate on the more expensive, fast-moving merchandise and neglect other merchandise. Sales incentives can also discourage salespeople from providing good customer service. Finally, salespeople compensated primarily by incentives don't develop loyalty to their employer. The employer doesn't guarantee them an income, so they feel no obligation to the firm.

Under a straight commission plan, salespeople's incomes can fluctuate from week to week, depending on their sales. Because retail sales are seasonal, salespeople might earn most of their incentive income during the Christmas season but much less during the summer months. To provide a more steady income for salespeople who are paid by high-incentive plans, some retailers offer a drawing account. With a **drawing account,** salespeople receive a weekly check based on their estimated annual income, and commissions earned are credited against the weekly payments. Periodically, the weekly draw is compared with the commissions earned. If the draw exceeds the earned commissions, the salespeople return the excess money they've been paid, and their weekly draw is reduced. If the earned commissions exceed the draw, salespeople are paid the difference.

Quotas are often used with compensation plans. A **quota** is a target level used to motivate and evaluate performance. Examples might include sales per hour for salespeople or maintained margin and inventory turnover for buyers. For department store salespeople, selling quotas vary across departments due to differences in sales productivity levels.

A **quota-bonus plan** provides sales associates with a bonus when their performance exceeds their quota. A quota-bonus plan's effectiveness depends on setting reasonable, fair quotas, but this can be hard to do. Usually, quotas are set at the same level for everyone in a department, yet salespeople in the same department may have different abilities or face different selling environments. For example, in the men's department, salespeople in the suit area have much greater sales potential than salespeople in the accessories area. Newly hired salespeople might have a harder time achieving a quota than more experienced salespeople. Thus, a quota based on average productivity may be too high to motivate the new salesperson and too low to motivate experienced salespeople. Thus quotas should be developed for each salesperson based on their experience and abilities.

To encourage employees in a department or store to work together, some retailers provide additional **team incentives** based on the performance of the department or store as a whole. For example, salespeople might be paid a commission based on their individual sales and then receive additional compensation according to the amount of sales generated by all salespeople in the department. The group incentive encourages salespeople to work together in their nonselling activities and while handling customers so that the department sales target will be achieved.[28]

Designing the Compensation Program A compensation program's two elements are the total amount of compensation and the percentage of compensation based on incentives. Typically, market conditions determine the amount of compensation. When economic conditions are good and labor is scarce, retailers pay higher wages. Retailers that hire inexperienced salespeople pay lower wages than those that recruit experienced salespeople who are motivated and have good skills and abilities.

Incentive compensation is most effective when a salesperson's performance can be measured easily and precisely. It's difficult to measure individual performance when salespeople work in teams or must perform a lot of nonselling activities. Retailers can easily measure a salesperson's actual sales, but it's hard to measure her or his customer service or merchandising performance.

When the salesperson's activities have a great impact on sales, incentives can provide additional motivation. For example, salespeople who are simply cashiers have little effect on sales and thus are not typically compensated with incentives. However, incentives are appropriate for salespeople who provide a lot of information and assistance to customers about complex products, such as designer dresses or automobiles. Incentives are less effective with inexperienced salespeople, who are less confident in their skills, because they inhibit learning and thereby can cause excessive stress.

Finally, compensation plans in which too much of the incentive is based on sales may not promote good customer service. Salespeople on commission become interested in selling anything they can to customers, and they aren't willing to spend time helping customers buy the merchandise they need. They tend to stay close to the cash register or the dressing room exits so that they can ring up a sale for customers who are ready to buy.

Setting the Commission Percentage   Assume that a specialty store manager wants to hire experienced salespeople. To get the type of people she wants, she feels she must pay $12 an hour, and her selling costs are budgeted at 8 percent of sales. With compensation of $12 an hour, salespeople each need to sell $150 worth of merchandise every hour ($12 divided by 8 percent) for the store to keep within its sales cost budget. The manager believes the best compensation would be two-thirds salary and one-third commission, so she decides to offer a compensation plan consisting of an $8-an-hour salary (66 percent of $12) and a 2.66 percent commission on sales. If salespeople sell $150 worth of merchandise an hour, they'll earn $12 an hour ($8 an hour in salary plus $150 multiplied by 2.66 percent, which equals $4 an hour in commission).

Legal Compensation Issues

The **Fair Labor Standards Act** of 1938 set minimum wages, maximum hours, child labor standards, and overtime-pay provisions. Enforcement of this law is particularly important to retailers because they hire many low-wage employees and teenagers and ask their employees to work long hours.

The **Equal Pay Act,** now enforced by the EEOC (Equal Employment Opportunity Commission), prohibits unequal pay for men and women who perform equal work or work of comparable worth. Equal work means that the jobs require the same skills, effort, and responsibility and are performed in the same working environment. Comparable worth implies that men and women who perform different jobs of equal worth should be compensated the same. Differences in compensation are legal when compensation is determined by a seniority system, an incentive compensation plan, or market demand.

LEADERSHIP

LO3

Illustrate effective leadership strategies of a store manager.

The third driver of employee performance is leadership (see Exhibit 16–1). **Leadership** is the process by which a person attempts to influence others to accomplish a common goal or task. Store managers are leaders of their group of employees. They use a variety of motivational techniques to increase productivity by helping employees achieve professional goals consistent with their firm's objectives.[29]

Types of Leader Behavior

Leaders engage in task performance and group maintenance behaviors. **Task performance behaviors** are the store manager's efforts to plan, organize, motivate, evaluate, and coordinate store employees' activities. **Group maintenance behaviors** are the activities store managers undertake to make sure that employees are satisfied and work well together. These activities include considering employees' needs, showing concern for their well-being, and creating a pleasant work environment.

Leader Decision Making Style

Store managers vary in how much they involve employees in making decisions. **Autocratic leaders** make all decisions on their own and then announce them to employees. They use the authority of their position to tell employees what to do.

Great leaders know when to use democratic and autocratic styles to produce happy, motivated employees.

For example, an autocratic store manager determines who will work in each area of the store, when they'll take breaks, and what days they'll have off.

In contrast, **democratic leaders** seek information and opinions from employees and base their decisions on this information. Democratic store managers share their power and information with their employees. They ask employees where and when they want to work and make schedules to accommodate those employee desires as much as possible.

There is no one best leadership style. Effective store managers use all styles, selecting the style most appropriate for each situation. For example, a store manager might be autocratic with an insecure new trainee but democratic with an effective, experienced employee.

The best store managers (leaders) go beyond influencing employee behaviors. **Transformational leaders** get people to transcend their personal needs for the sake of the group or organization. They are engaged and generate excitement. They revitalize organizations. Transformational store managers create this enthusiasm in their employees through their personal charisma. They are self-confident and have a clear vision that grabs employees' attention. They communicate this vision through words and symbols. Finally, transformational leaders delegate challenging work to subordinates, have free and open communication with them, and provide personal mentoring to develop subordinates.

Maintaining Morale

Store managers play an important role in improving the work atmosphere and its effect on the performance of store employees. Typically, morale goes up when things are going well and employees are highly motivated. But when sales aren't

Apple Store managers build morale and motivate their sales associates by holding "morning meetings" before the store opens.

going well, morale tends to decrease and employee motivation declines. Effective managers build morale by doing small but meaningful things for employees like throwing a party when goals are met or dividing the charity budget by the number of employees and inviting them to suggest how their "share" should be used. One store manager used real-time sales data collected in her firm's information system (see Chapter 10) to build excitement among her employees. On the first day of the Christmas season, she wrote $4,159 on a white board in the store. That was the store's sales during the first day of the Christmas season last year. She told her sales associates that beating that number was not enough; she wanted to see a 25 percent increase, the same sales increase the store achieved over the previous Christmas season. By setting financial objectives and keeping sales associates informed of up-to-the-minute results, managers can convert an eight-hour shift of clock watchers into an excited team of racers. All day, as customers come and go, sales associates take turns consulting the backroom computer that records sales from the store's POS terminals.

Sexual Harassment

Sexual harassment is an important issue affecting the productivity of the work environment. Managers must avoid, and make sure that store employees avoid, any actions that are, or can be interpreted as, sexual harassment. Otherwise, the retailer and the manager may be held liable for the harassment. The EEOC guidelines define **sexual harassment** as a form of gender discrimination, as follows:

> Unwelcome sexual advances, requests for sexual favors, and other verbal or physical conduct of a sexual nature constitutes sexual harassment when . . . submission to or rejection of such conduct by an individual is used as a basis for employment decisions affecting such individual, or . . . such conduct has the purpose or effect of unreasonably interfering with an individual's work performance or creating an intimidating, hostile, or offensive working environment.

An appropriate procedure for dealing with a sexual harassment allegation involves establishing and posting an anti-sexual harassment policy including a complaint procedure, treating complaints seriously, creating a safe environment for individuals to make complaints without retaliation, getting information from the alleged victim, document the meeting with the alleged victim, and informing the human resource department or the next-higher level of company management of the complaint and of the meeting with the alleged victim.[30]

CONTROLLING COSTS

Labor scheduling, store maintenance, and inventory shrinkage offer three opportunities to reduce store operating expenses. Retailing View 16.3 describes how a convenience store chain reengineered its operations to reduce costs and increase customer service.

LO4
Explore the various strategies a store manager can undertake to control costs.

Labor Scheduling

Using store employees efficiently is an important and challenging problem. Although store employees provide important customer service and merchandising functions that can increase sales, they also are the store's largest operating expense. **Labor scheduling** (determining the employees assigned to each area of the store

16.3   RETAILING VIEW   Sheetz Increases Operating Efficiency

Sheetz, a Pennsylvania-based convenience store chain, reengineered its operations to reduce costs and increase customer service.

Sheetz, a convenience store chain with 441 stores based in Altoona, Pennsylvania, started a series of detailed studies to determine how store-level tasks could be performed more efficiently. The research considered everything, from how employees emptied trash to how managers closed out at the end of each day. In the latter case, it found that managers were required to complete information sheets that took up 40 different computer screens. Such demands meant that they needed up to four hours to close out an eight-hour workday.

Furthermore, the time spent to close stores was affecting customer service. Managers would do the paperwork during the morning of the following day, the busiest traffic time, when they should have been out in the stores managing. When Sheetz reexamined these practices, it eliminated more than 160,000 hours annually of time the store managers were spending on nonproductive administrative tasks.

Sheetz also found that a lot of the information being sent to store managers was of questionable value. There were too many redundant reports. Thus, the 204 reports that had been available on the store managers' computers were reduced to 23.

Then, Sheetz saved 55 employee-hours per week per store by reexamining its labor scheduling. Before the study, staffing for stores was based on sales. But this universal approach ignored differences among stores. For example, some stores generated most of their sales through food service, which demanded substantial labor. Others earned most of their revenue from gasoline sales, which required minimal employee effort (i.e., *outside sales* in convenience store lingo).

As the company has added distribution centers and its own bakery, managers have gained greater control over product delivery timing and levels as well. The distribution center and Sheetz Bros. Kitchen provide personalized deliveries to approximately 350 stores. By coordinating these deliveries with their staffing levels, store managers also ensure they have enough staff to restock shelves, usually during customer downtimes.

In addition, some in-store tasks were eliminated. In particular, noting that it made minimal margins on newspaper sales, Sheetz stopped tracking its newspaper sales at the individual level. By eliminating this task for store employees, it made sure it continued to earn at least some money on each paper it sells.

As a result of these changes and implemented recommendations, within two years, Sheetz had saved $5.1 million, just in payroll costs. These savings, together with increased efficiency achieved through a chainwide switch to more efficient LED lighting in stores, suggest great promise for the future of the convenient store chain.

Sources: Walt Frank, "From Dairy Store to Convenience Restaurants, Sheetz Empire Now Spans Six States," *Altoona Mirror*, November 18, 2012; "LED Lighting Improves Sheetz Convenience Restaurants," *Restaurant Facilities Business*, November 28, 2012; "Sheetz Hits the Mark," *Retail Merchandiser*, September–October 2007, pp. 28–31; and Neil Stern, "Convenience Reborn," *Chain Store Age*, May 2007, pp. 34–39.

DISCUSSION QUESTION

What types of data would Sheetz need to have collected to implement all of these changes?

Labor scheduling software assures that there are enough associates to take care of customers when it is busy (left), but not so many that the associates have little to do when business is slow (right).

during each hour) is difficult because customer traffic varies greatly during the day and the week. In addition, multiple shifts are required to staff stores up to 24 hours a day, seven days a week. Poor labor scheduling can result in long checkout lines, sales associates with nothing to do, and lower labor productivity. For example, if 6 percent of a store's sales volume and 9 percent of the total labor-hours occur between 2 and 3 p.m., the store might be overstaffed during this time period and understaffed in others.

Many retailers utilize computer software to deal with the complexities of labor scheduling. By analyzing sales, transactions, and customer traffic for each time period, the software determines the appropriate number of employees to have in each area of the store during each time period and develops a work schedule for each employee.[31]

Although these scheduling systems benefit both retailers and customers, they can have an adverse impact on employees. The schedules suggested by this software often recommend the use of part-time workers and irregular work hours. Sales associates can be burdened with unpredictable schedules, including requirements that they remain "on call" on their days off. While some employees prefer part-time work because it fits in with their lifestyle, many others prefer to work full-time.[32]

Store Maintenance

Store maintenance entails the activities involved with managing the exterior and interior physical facilities associated with the store. The exterior facilities include the parking lot, entrances to the store, and signs on the outside of the store. The interior facilities include the walls, flooring, ceiling, bathrooms, HVAC systems, and displays and signs. Store maintenance affects both the sales generated in the store and the cost of running the store. A store's cleanliness and neatness affect consumer perceptions of the quality of its merchandise, but this maintenance is costly. For instance, floor maintenance for a 40,000-square-foot home center runs about $10,000 a year. Poor maintenance shortens the useful life of air-conditioning units, floors, and fixtures.

Inventory Shrinkage

Shrinkage is the inventory loss due to employee theft, shoplifting, mistakes, inaccurate records, and vendor errors. It is the difference between the recorded value of inventory (at retail prices) based on merchandise bought and received and the value of the actual inventory (at retail prices) in stores and distribution centers, divided by retail sales during the period. For example, if accounting records indicate that inventory should be $1,500,000, the actual count of the inventory reveals $1,236,000, and sales were $4,225,000, the shrinkage is 6.2 percent [($1,500,000 − $1,236,000) ÷ $4,225,000].

Reducing shrinkage is an important store management issue because retailers' annual loss from shrinkage averages about 1.5 percent of total sales.[33] Worldwide, retail theft costs retailers more than $107 billion annually. In the United States alone, retailers lost nearly $3 billion to theft, which is equivalent to costing each U.S. family $422.68 each year.[34]

Although shoplifting receives the most publicity, employee theft accounts for more inventory loss. A recent survey attributes 44 percent of inventory shrinkage to employee theft, 36 percent to shoplifting, 15 percent to mistakes and inaccurate records, and 3 percent to vendor fraud, with an unaccounted for 2 percent.[35] Examples of employee mistakes are failing to ring up an item when it's sold and miscounting merchandise when it's received or during physical inventories. Inventory shrinkage due to vendor mistakes arises when vendor shipments contain less than the amount indicated on the packing slip and the retailer fails to recognize this error. The remainder of this section focuses on losses due to shoplifting and employee theft.

Shoplifting

To develop a loss prevention program to reduce shoplifting, retailers confront a trade-off between providing shopping convenience on the one hand, and preventing losses due to shoplifting on the other. The key to an effective loss prevention program is determining the most effective way to protect merchandise while preserving an open, attractive store atmosphere and a feeling among employees that they are trusted. Loss prevention requires coordination among store management, visual merchandising, and store design.

In response to the high rates of theft, retailers spent $28.3 billion on security measures in 2011.[37] Losses due to shoplifting can be reduced by store design, security measures, and personnel policies.

Store Design   The following store design choices may help deter shoplifting:

- Do not place expensive or small merchandise near an entrance.
- Put easily stolen merchandise near POS terminals because there typically is an employee near the terminal.
- Keep the height of fixtures low so employees can see customers in the store and have an open line-of-sight to the dressing rooms and exits.
- Use mirrors.
- Alternate clothing hanger directions so professional shoplifters cannot easily grab a lot of apparel at once.
- Lock up all items that are easily stolen.

Security Measures   The following security measures may help deter shoplifting:

- Use closed-circuit TV cameras.
- Include some nonoperating equipment that looks like a TV camera to provide a psychological deterrent to shoplifters and save costs.
- Use **electronic article surveillance (EAS)** and **radio-frequency identification (RFID) systems.** These special tags are placed on merchandise. When the merchandise is purchased, the tags are deactivated by the point-of-sale (POS) scanner.
- Have an employee stationed at the door to check receipts.

Personnel Policies   The following personnel policies may help deter shoplifting:

- Use mystery and honesty shoppers to watch for employee and customer theft.
- Have store employees monitor fitting rooms.
- Store employees should be trained to be aware, visible, and alert to potential shoplifting situations.
- Provide attentive customer service.

Exhibit 16–6 outlines some rules for spotting shoplifters. Perhaps the best deterrent to shoplifting is an alert employee who is very visible.

Prosecution   Many retailers have a policy of prosecuting all shoplifters. They feel a strictly enforced prosecution policy deters shoplifters. Some retailers also sue shoplifters in civil proceedings for restitution of the stolen merchandise and the time spent in the prosecution.

Retailers use EAS tags to reduce shoplifting. The tags contain a device that is deactivated when the merchandise is purchased. If a customer has not purchased the merchandise, an alarm is triggered when the stolen merchandise passes through sensor gates at the store's exit.

Although many of these measures reduce shoplifting, they can also make the shopping experience more unpleasant for honest customers. The atmosphere of an apparel store, for example, is diminished when guards, mirrors, and TV cameras are highly visible. Customers may find it hard to try on clothing secured with a lock and chain or an electronic tag. They can also be uncomfortable trying on clothing if they think they're secretly being watched via a surveillance monitor. Thus, when evaluating security measures, retailers need to balance the benefits of reducing shoplifting with the potential losses in sales.

Using Technology   Retailers are turning to technology to help stop shoplifting. Some stores have installed systems that use computer software to analyze

DON'T ASSUME THAT ALL SHOPLIFTERS ARE POORLY DRESSED
To avoid detection, professional shoplifters dress in the same manner as customers patronizing the store. Over 90 percent of all amateur shoplifters arrested have the cash, checks, or credit to purchase the merchandise they stole.

SPOT LOITERERS
Amateur shoplifters frequently loiter in areas as they build up the nerve to steal something. Professionals also spend time waiting for the right opportunity but less conspicuously than amateurs.

LOOK FOR GROUPS
Teenagers planning to shoplift often travel in groups. Some members of the group divert employees' attention while others take the merchandise. Professional shoplifters often work in pairs. One person takes the merchandise and passes it to a partner in the store's restroom, phone booths, or restaurant.

LOOK FOR PEOPLE WITH LOOSE CLOTHING
Shoplifters frequently hide stolen merchandise under loose-fitting clothing or in large shopping bags. People wearing a winter coat in the summer or a raincoat on a sunny day may be potential shoplifters.

WATCH THE EYES, HANDS, AND BODY
Professional shoplifters avoid looking at merchandise and concentrate on searching for store employees who might observe their activities. Shoplifters' movements might be unusual as they try to conceal merchandise.

EXHIBIT 16–6
Spotting Shoplifters

shoppers' movements captured by TV cameras. When the system recognizes unusual activity, such as when dozens of items get moved off the shelf or a locked case is opened, it sets off an alarm for security guards. If someone enters the store at an unauthorized time, the system takes a picture of the entrant, as well as of the people who entered before and after.[38]

Because some shoplifters are less subtle—they simply load a lot of stuff into a cart and run—stores have started adding RFID chips to the carts themselves. If a cart with unpaid for merchandise approaches the sensor-equipped doors, its wheels simply lock, such that it stops moving easily. In addition, new cameras mounted to the bottom of checkout stations check to make sure thieves have not stuck stolen items underneath their carts, in the hope that no one will notice that they never paid for them. Such technologies enable immediate, unobtrusive identification of theft, using signals that can be sent to security guards' handheld devices.[39]

Customers continue to steal merchandise using conventional methods that haven't changed for thousands of years. They hide it under their clothing or at the bottom of their shopping carts, attempt to divert store employees, or simply walk out of the store quickly in the hope that they won't be noticed. Like retailing itself, shoplifting has become sophisticated, as described in Retailing View 16.4.

Reducing Employee Theft   Like shoplifting, employee theft has become a more sophisticated, high-tech activity. The increasing use of gift cards has created new opportunities for employee theft. In collaboration with criminal accomplices, retail employees accept fake merchandise returns and put the "refund" onto gift cards. The employee might use the card him- or herself or hand it to the accomplice. Later, they redeem the card at another store or sell it online. The Internet makes it easy to convert such gift cards into cash. In response, many retailers have hired loss prevention specialists who spend most of their time searching auction sites for suspicious gift card offerings, such as those for much below face value or sales of dozens of cards from the same retailer.[40] Similarly, a great deal of credit card sales information is entered manually. Multiple returns, or multiple returns of the same item, suggest that the employee at that register is acting illegally, whether stealing from the store or from the customer. Retailers are utilizing software that monitors abnormal sales at the POS. Video technology complements this software, allowing managers to see exactly what cashiers are doing when the irregular patterns of activity occur.[41]

The most effective approach for reducing employee theft and shoplifting is to create a trusting, supportive work environment. When employees feel they're respected members of a team, they identify their goals with the retailer's goals. Stealing from their employer thus becomes equivalent to stealing from themselves or their family, and they go out of their way to prevent others from stealing from the "family." Thus, retailers with a highly committed workforce and low turnover typically have low inventory shrinkage. Additional approaches for reducing employee theft are carefully screening employees, creating an atmosphere that encourages honesty and integrity, and establishing security policies and control systems.

Other approaches for reducing employee theft are discussed in the following sections.

Screening Prospective Employees   As mentioned previously, many retailers use paper-and-pencil honesty tests and undertake extensive reference checks to screen out potential employees with theft problems. A major problem related to employee theft is drug use. Some retailers now require that prospective employees submit to drug tests as a condition of employment. Employees

RETAILING VIEW   Using Technology to Steal Merchandise   16.4

Although shoplifting, in which customers steal merchandise from retailers, is an age-old problem, thieves have become more high tech and often work in gangs. One popular scam used by thieves is to create counterfeit bar codes at lower prices. For example, a thief created $19 bar codes for $100 Lego sets and got away with sets worth approximately $600,000. Bar-code thieves are hard to catch, because when an alert cashier notices the mispriced item, the thief can either pay the difference or just walk out the door. A similar technique is to create fake receipts. A thief in New Mexico simply created Sam's Club receipts for electronic products, which he used to walk out of the store with merchandise that he never paid for, even though his fake receipt indicated that he had. This criminal stole more than $25,000 in electronics from his local warehouse club before being caught and arrested.

Another technology-based scam is tampering with gift cards by professional and amateur shoplifters and employees. The thieves may create duplicate gift cards that can be used by the thief or resold online, or they may use active gift card account information to create duplicate cards or make web purchases. Thieves also have been known to steal merchandise and then return it to the store for credit in the form of gift cards, which they can then sell online, often at less than face value.

Furthermore, 96 percent of retailers recently surveyed indicated that they had been victims of organized retail theft. Gangs of professional thieves concentrate in over-the-counter medications, infant formula, health and beauty aids, electronics, and specialty clothing. Internet sales, especially through auctions, have provided a ready outlet to sell this merchandise. Some gangs of thieves are using store credits to steal. In one case, a gang took a valid $500 store credit receipt, digitally altered it to read $1,200, printed multiple copies that it distributed to gang members across the country, and then sent the members out to 16 stores in 12 states to get their refunds—all within the same hour.

Another gang-related high-tech method of shoplifting known as **flash robs,** is when groups plot via social media and text messages to arrive suddenly at retail stores and wreak havoc, usually by stealing large amounts of merchandise. A Sears store in Philadelphia experienced a flash rob when about 40 boys flooded the store and stole thousands of dollars in merchandise. Chicago's Magnificent Mile was less than magnificent when teens ran into Armani Exchange and The North Face stores screaming,

Professional shoplifters are developing new approaches to stealing that include flash robs.

knocking over displays and merchandise, and fleeing with expensive jeans and other merchandise. A survey by National Retail Federation (NRF) found that 10 percent of the retailers surveyed had experienced a flash rob.

Sources: Liz Parks, "Allied Against ORC," *Stores Magazine*, August 2012; Chris Morran, "Man Scores 100% Discount on Electronics by Making Fake Receipts at Home," *Consumerist*, January 25, 2011; Michael Hartnett, "Remaining Vigilant," *Stores Magazine*, December 2011; Ann Zimmerman and Miguel Bustillo, "'Flash Robs' Vex Retailers," *The Wall Street Journal*, October 21, 2011; and Ann Zimmerman, "As Shoplifters Use High-Tech Scams, Retail Losses Rise," *The Wall Street Journal*, October 25, 2006, p. A1.

DISCUSSION QUESTION

What should retailers do to address new forms of high-tech shoplifting?

with documented performance problems, an unusual number of accidents, or erratic time and attendance records are also tested. Unless involved in selling drugs, employees who test positive are often offered an opportunity to complete a company-paid drug program, submit to random testing in the future, and remain with the firm.

Establishing Security Policies and Control Systems   To control employee theft, retailers need to adopt policies related to certain activities that may facilitate theft. Some of the most prevalent policies are:

- Randomly search containers, such as trash bins, where stolen merchandise can be stored.
- Require that store employees enter and leave the store through designated entrances.
- Assign salespeople to specific POS terminals, and require that all transactions be handled through those terminals.
- Restrict employee purchases to working hours.
- Provide customer receipts for all transactions.
- Have all refunds, returns, and discounts cosigned by a department or store manager.
- Change locks periodically, and issue keys to authorized personnel only.
- Provide a locker room where all employees' handbags, purses, packages, and coats must be checked before the employees leave.
- Maintain rotating employee assignments. Team different employees together.

In the end, it is important that employees do not feel that management is overly suspicious of their actions or that they are treated with disrespect, as this sense will erode morale.

SUMMARY

LO1 Describe how to improve the ability of workers through efficient recruiting, socializing, and training.

Store managers can improve the abilities of their employees through effective recruiting, socializing, and training. To recruit skillful, or potentially skillful, employees, store managers prepare a job description, find potential applicants with the desired capabilities, and screen the best candidates to interview. Having hired employees with the required skills or potential to develop these skills, retailers need to introduce the new employees to the firm and its policies, values, and strategies. This socialization process affects the degree to which newcomers become involved, engaged contributors to the firm's successful performance. In addition, socialization helps newly hired employees learn about their job responsibilities and the company they've decided to join. Effective training for new store employees includes both structured and on-the-job learning experiences.

LO2 Examine how to improve the effort of workers through proper motivation, evaluation, rewards, and compensation.

High-performance store employees work hard, and the activities they work on are consistent with the retailer's strategy and goals. Motivating employees to perform up to their potential may be store managers' most important and challenging task. To effectively motivate employees, store managers need to set goals for the employees and provide feedback on the employee's performance relative to these goals. Store employees receive two types of rewards from their job: extrinsic and intrinsic. Extrinsic rewards are rewards provided by either the employee's manager or the firm, such as compensation, promotion, and recognition. Intrinsic rewards are rewards employees get personally from doing their job well. For example, salespeople often like to sell because they think it's challenging and fun. The compensation program is the strongest motivator. It attracts and keeps good employees, motivates them to undertake activities consistent with the retailer's strategy, and strikes a balance between controlling labor costs and providing enough compensation to keep high-quality employees.

LO3 Illustrate effective leadership strategies of a store manager.

Leadership is the process by which a person attempts to influence others to accomplish a common goal or task. Store managers are leaders. The best store managers (leaders) go beyond influencing employee behaviors. There is no one best leadership style. Effective store managers use all styles, selecting the style most appropriate for each situation. Transformational leaders get people to transcend their personal needs for the sake of the group or organization so they are engaged and excited about their job.

LO4 Explore the various strategies a store manager can undertake to control costs.

Labor scheduling, store maintenance, and inventory shrinkage offer three opportunities to reduce store operating expenses. Using store employees efficiently is an important and challenging problem. Although store employees provide important customer service and merchandising functions that can increase sales, they also are the store's largest operating expense. An important issue facing store management is reducing inventory losses due to employee theft, shoplifting, mistakes, inaccurate records, and vendor errors. In developing a loss prevention program, retailers confront a trade-off between providing shopping convenience and a pleasant work environment on the one hand, and preventing losses due to shoplifting and employee theft on the other. The key to an effective loss prevention program is determining the most effective way to protect merchandise while preserving an open, attractive store atmosphere and a feeling among employees that they are trusted. Loss prevention requires coordination among store management, visual merchandising, and store design.

KEY TERMS

GET OUT AND DO IT!

1. **CONTINUING CASE ASSIGNMENT** Go to the store you have selected for the continuing case assignment, and meet with the person responsible for personnel scheduling. Report on the following:

   - Who is responsible for employee scheduling?
   - How far in advance is the schedule made?
   - How are breaks and lunch periods planned?
   - How are overtime hours determined?
   - On what is the total number of budgeted employee hours for each department based?

   - How is flexibility introduced into the schedule?
   - How are special requests for days off handled?
   - How are peak periods (hours, days, or seasons) planned for?
   - What happens when an employee calls in sick at the last minute?
   - What are the strengths and weaknesses of the personnel scheduling system from the manager's and employees' perspectives?

2. **CONTINUING CASE ASSIGNMENT** Go to the store you have selected for the continuing case assignment, and talk to the person responsible for human resource management to find out how sales associates are compensated and evaluated for job performance.

- How are sales associates trained? What are the criteria for evaluation?
- How often are they evaluated?
- Do salespeople have quotas? If they do, how are they set? What are the rewards of exceeding quotas? What are the consequences of not meeting these objectives?
- Can sales associates make a commission? If yes, how does the commission system work? What are the advantages of a commission system? What are the disadvantages?
- If there is no commission system, are any incentive programs offered? Give an example of a specific program or project used by the store to boost employee morale and productivity.

Evaluate each of the answers to these questions, and make recommendations for improvement where appropriate.

3. **GO SHOPPING** Go to a store, observe the security measures in the store, and talk with a manager about the store's loss prevention program.

- Are there surveillance cameras? Where are they located? Are the cameras monitored, or are they just there to thwart shoplifting?
- What is the store's policy against shoplifters?
- What are the procedures for approaching a suspected shoplifter?

- What roles do sales associates and executives play in the security programs?
- Is employee theft a problem? Elaborate.
- How is employee theft prevented in the store?
- How is customer service related to loss prevention in the store?
- What is this retailer doing well in terms of security and loss prevention, and in which areas should it improve its policies and procedures?

4. **INTERNET EXERCISE** Go online and research the shoplifting laws implemented by the state where you live or attend school. What are the fines, jail time, community service, or punishments for perpetrators in your local jurisdiction? What factors are weighed and evaluated in shoplifting cases? Are the laws in your state a deterrent to shoplifting? Please explain.

5. **LIBRARY EXERCISE** Go to one of your library's business databases and find an article that describes a case of a retailer violating Title VII in either its hiring or promotion practices. Summarize the case and court decision. What should this retailer do differently in the future to improve its employment policies?

6. **INTERNET EXERCISE** Go to the home page for Greening Retail (www.greeningretail.ca), and examine the company's research and programs that help retailers implement environmental best practices. Select a company in the "Featured Retailer Archive" (www.greeningretail.ca/featured/archive.dot) as a case example, and briefly descibe what this retailer is doing to be a more sustainable company.

DISCUSSION QUESTIONS AND PROBLEMS

1. How do on-the-job training, Internet training, and classroom training differ? What are the benefits and limitations of each approach?

2. Give examples of a situation in which a manager of a McDonald's fast-food restaurant should utilize different leadership styles.

3. Using the interview questions in Exhibit 16–3, role-play with another student in the class as both the interviewer and the applicant for an assistant store manager position at a store of your choice.

4. Name some laws and regulations that affect the employee management process. Which do you believe are the easiest for retailers to adhere to? Which are violated the most often?

5. What's the difference between extrinsic and intrinsic rewards? What are the effects of these rewards on the behavior of retail employees? Under what conditions would you recommend that a retailer emphasize intrinsic rewards over extrinsic rewards?

6. Many large department and specialty stores are changing their salespeople's reward system from a

salary to a commission-based system. What problems can commission-based systems cause? How can department managers avoid these problems?

7. When evaluating retail employees, some stores use a quantitative approach that relies on checklists and numerical scores similar to the form in Exhibit 16–5. Other stores use a more qualitative approach, whereby less time is spent checking and adding and more time is devoted to discussing strengths and weaknesses in written form. What are the advantages and disadvantages of quantitative versus qualitative evaluation systems?

8. Some staff pharmacists working for retail chains refuse to dispense the Plan B "morning after" contraceptive pill because of their religious beliefs. In another situation, Muslims and Jewish checkout clerks working for supermarket chains refused to touch, scan, or bag products that contained any pork because of their religious beliefs. Do managers have the right to force employees to take actions that are contrary to their beliefs? Should customers be unable to buy products they want because of an employee's beliefs?

Should employee be required to ignore their religious beliefs? What would you do if you were faced with these or similar ethically sensitive situations?

9. Discuss how retailers can reduce shrinkage from shoplifting and employee theft.

10. Drugstore retailers such as CVS place diabetic test strips and perfume behind locked glass cabinets and nearly all over-the-counter medicines behind Plexiglas panels. What are the pros and cons of these locked glass cabinets from the retailer's perspective? From the customer's perspective?

SUGGESTED READINGS

Arthur, Diane. *Recruiting, Interviewing, Selecting & Orienting New Employees*, 5th ed. New York: AMACOM, 2012.

Bell, Simon, Bülent Mengüç, and Robert E. Widing II. "Salesperson Learning, Organizational Learning, and Retail Store Performance." *Journal of the Academy of Marketing Science* 38, no. 2 (2010), pp. 187–201.

Bernardin, H. John. *Human Resource Management: An Experiential Approach*, 5th ed. Burr Ridge, IL: McGraw-Hill, 2010.

Carmel-Gilfilen, Candy. "Advancing Retail Security Design: Uncovering Shoplifter Perceptions of the Physical Environment." *Journal of Interior Design* 36, no. 2 (2011), pp. 21–38.

Hollinger, Richard, and Amanda Adams. *2011 Annual Retail Security Survey*. Gainesville, FL: Security Research Project, University of Florida, 2012.

Ng, Eddy, Sean Lyons, and Linda Schweitzer. *Managing the New Workforce: International Perspectives on the Millennial Generation*. Northampton, MA: Edward Elgar Publishing, 2012.

Purpura, Philip. *Security and Loss Prevention*, 6th ed. New York: Butterworth-Heinemann, 2013.

Phillips, Jack J. *Handbook of Training Evaluation and Measurement Methods*. New York: Routledge, 2012.

Rothstein, Mark, and Lance Leibman. *Employment Law*, 7th ed. St. Paul, MN: Thomson/West, 2012.

U.S. Equal Employment Opportunity Commission. "Sexual Harassment." Washington, DC: 2011.

Store Layout, Design, and Visual Merchandising

EXECUTIVE BRIEFING
Fredrik Holmvik, Head of Media, ICA Sweden

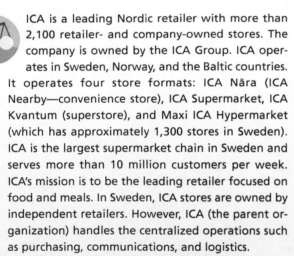

ICA is a leading Nordic retailer with more than 2,100 retailer- and company-owned stores. The company is owned by the ICA Group. ICA operates in Sweden, Norway, and the Baltic countries. It operates four store formats: ICA Nära (ICA Nearby—convenience store), ICA Supermarket, ICA Kvantum (superstore), and Maxi ICA Hypermarket (which has approximately 1,300 stores in Sweden). ICA is the largest supermarket chain in Sweden and serves more than 10 million customers per week. ICA's mission is to be the leading retailer focused on food and meals. In Sweden, ICA stores are owned by independent retailers. However, ICA (the parent organization) handles the centralized operations such as purchasing, communications, and logistics.

I am currently the head of ICA media. I have been actively working with ICA for many years, first as a consultant and now as an employee. Prior to this, I was the CEO of QB Food Tech Ltd. I have also worked as a consultant for Accenture and at Unilever in a variety of roles.

ICA has historically used a variety of traditional media (e.g., TV commercials, home flyers) and in-store paper signage to provide our customers relevant information, ranging from prices to campaigns to cooking tips. Some years ago, we introduced

digital screens and signage (what we call ICA's in-store media channel) to augment the traditional media. These screens allow us to provide relevant content, such as ICA campaigns, cooking tips, as well as vendor commercials and point-of-purchase promotions.

Our goals for these digital displays include increasing sales, improving campaign reach and effectiveness, and creating a more up-to-date image and feel for our stores. In a short time frame, we have introduced digital signage in 350 stores, covering a reach of more than 55 percent of our weekly customers. Price deals that have been advertised using our digital screens have seen sales go up by almost 100 percent. Traditional vendor advertisements drive sales as well as brand awareness. These digital displays attract consumer attention and increase their likelihood of purchasing the products being displayed. Our research shows that digital displays with moving images or films, compared to ordinary displays, double customer attention.

CHAPTER 17

These insights have important implications for the design of stores, such as where to locate digital displays, what type of displays to use, and most importantly, what to communicate in certain departments/areas of the store. For instance, displays in the fruit and vegetable section focus on relevant communication in that area, just as displays in the bread section focus within its relevant communication range. The effectiveness of these displays varies as a function of their location in the store and the type of store. For instance, our research has shown that these digital signs can increase sales by as much as 5 percent in hypermarkets. In smaller stores, sales are also affected, and the most interesting finding here is the actual effect on being more up-to-date. The customer actually experiences a more "modern" store environment, which contributes to the overall perception of the store in a favorable way.

These digital screens also provide cost efficiencies through lower costs associated with production, printing, and getting the traditional printed material to the stores, as well as better coordination of promotions between our vendors and stores.

The environment in a store, the design of the store, and the presentation and location of merchandise in the store have significant impacts on shopping behavior. The design of a store or website attracts customers to visit the location, increases the time they spend in the store or on the site, and increases the amount of merchandise they purchase. Store design also has long-term effects on building customer loyalty toward the retailer by enhancing the retailer's brand image and providing rewarding shopping experiences that encourage repeat visits.

This chapter is part of the Store Management section because store managers are responsible for implementing the design and visual merchandising developed by specialists at the retailer's corporate headquarters. They adapt the prototype plans to the unique characteristics of their stores, then make sure the image and experience provided by the design are consistent over time. However, as discussed in this chapter, store design and visual merchandising are also elements of a retailer's communication mix and play an important role in creating and reinforcing a retailer's brand image.

The chapter begins with a discussion of store design objectives. Next, the elements of store design are discussed. The decisions about how much space to allocate to different merchandise categories and departments and where they should be located in the store are reviewed. The chapter concludes with an examination of how retailers use store design elements, such as color, lighting, and music, to enhance the customer's shopping experience.

STORE DESIGN OBJECTIVES

LO1

Identify the critical issues retailers need to consider while designing a store.

Some store design objectives are to (1) implement the retailer's strategy, (2) build loyalty by providing a rewarding shopping experience, (3) increase sales on a visit, (4) control costs, and (5) meet legal requirements.

Implement the Retail Strategy

The primary objective for store design is to implement the retailer's strategy. The design must be consistent with and reinforce the retailer's strategy by meeting the needs of the target market and building a sustainable competitive advantage. Starbucks' store designs are inspired by the Italian coffee bars that not only have great coffee, but also serve as a place to meet friends, socialize, and relax. Soft lighting, wood tables, comfortable seating, free wi-fi, and clean bathrooms make Starbucks a place where people just want to hang out and have a good cup of coffee. Retailing View 17.1 details how another innovative retailer, Apple, makes store design decisions to reinforce its overall strategy.

Build Loyalty

When customers consistently have rewarding experiences when patronizing a retailer's store and/or website, they are motivated to visit repeatedly and develop loyalty toward the retailer. Store design plays an important role in making shopping experiences rewarding. Customers seek two types of benefits when shopping—utilitarian and hedonic benefits.[1]

Store design provides **utilitarian benefits** when it enables customers to locate and purchase products in an efficient and timely manner with minimum hassle. Such utilitarian benefits are becoming increasingly important in today's time-poor society. Therefore, drugstore retailers such as CVS and Walgreens have designed their stores to include drive-through pharmacies and have invested in various technologies to augment customer convenience associated with these store design elements. They have developed mobile apps to help people refill their prescriptions; they then pick them up through the drive-through. These design elements and connected apps are further speeding up customers' shopping trips.[2]

Store design provides **hedonic benefits** by offering customers an entertaining and enjoyable shopping experience. They then want to spend more time in the store or on the website because the visit itself is rewarding. For example, Cabela's, a chain of stores catering to outdoor enthusiasts, provides an educational and entertaining experience that mixes museum-quality dioramas of wildlife on display, massive huge aquariums featuring native fish, a restaurant where diners can order wild-game sandwiches, and a shooting gallery that teaches basic shooting and

RETAILING VIEW The Innovator Designs a Space, By and For the Geniuses

17.1

The glass cube that sits on Fifth Avenue has become nearly legendary at this point—just one more example of how Apple continually seeks new ideas to appeal to people's aesthetic and tactile senses. The cube and other visually remarkable glass entryways tell consumers that they have arrived at an Apple destination. Once they enter the light-filled spaces, Apple applies its design genius to keep them shopping happily.

Consider, for example, the Shanghai store. A glass cylinder (Apple had already done the cube in New York) rises up, seemingly from the ground. In the Hamburg, Germany, stores, the stairs to move between floors are all glass and are attached only at the top and bottom, creating a sense as if they are hanging in the air. As the architect hired to conceive of these ideas noted, "Steve [Jobs] wanted us to push the edge of technology, but it had to be comfortable for people. . . . It's an interesting challenge, how to marry the two."

Not all stores can afford a glass entryway, though. For more traditional retail spaces, such as in malls, Apple instead focuses on drawing people in by creating high ceilings, using bright but soft lighting, and placing its offerings on warm wood tables. The physical retail atmosphere helps build the communal sense initiated by its products. It also encourages and enables consumers to interact with Apple's technologically sophisticated products in a safe, inviting setting.

The layout of the stores and the products they feature also draw people further into the stores. To get to the Genius bar, they have to traverse all the way to the back of the store, walking past appealingly designed products as they do so. Even the displays of the computers are tilted at just the right angle to draw their eye.

Overall though, Apple stores reinforce the image of Apple as an innovation master. By adding unique and

The unique design of the Apple store in New York City reinforces the company's image of developing and retailing products with innovative design features.

unseen architectural elements to its flagship stores and ensuring all its stores are appealing, Apple shows just how cutting edge it remains. As the architect for the stores further noted, in lamenting Jobs's death, "Steve was a great client. . . . He would not discourage innovation that was within his vision of what Apple is or he is."

Sources: James B. Stewart, "A Genius of the Storefront, Too," *The New York Times,* October 15, 2011; Matthew Carroll, "How Retailers Can Replicate the Magic of the Apple Store . . . Online," *Forbes,* June 26, 2010; and Apple Store, www.apple.com.cn/retail/pudong/.

DISCUSSION QUESTION

How has Apple's innovative store design reinforced its innovative image?

safety lessons while also providing a fun experience. These shopping and tourism destinations draw customers from the local area certainly, but they also can attract travelers from hundreds of miles away.

Of course, few retailers can offer only utilitarian or hedonic benefits. Most need to use both routes to ensure customer loyalty. Thus, in the face of the global economic downturn, Wegmans has applied a more utilitarian look and feel in some sections, to welcome price-sensitive customers and reassure its existing shoppers that it recognizes their economic constraints.[3] The Wegmans supermarket chain explicitly designs its stores to make the chore of grocery shopping more fun: Instead of linoleum floors, harsh fluorescent lights, and narrow aisles, shoppers experience the feel of an open air market. Wegmans also offers various eat-in options, an exotic tea bar, a trail mix bar, and gourmet chef-prepared meals to take

To enhance the shopping experience, Wegmans offers gourmet chef-prepared meals to take home.

home. This unique experience for customers has helped Wegmans' 77 stores earn nearly $6 billion in sales annually.[4]

Increase Sales on Visits

A third design objective is to increase the sales made to customers on any particular visit. Store design has a substantial effect on which products customers buy, how long they stay in the store, and how much they spend during a visit. Because most consumers spend very little time and thought on shopping and selecting items in supermarkets, these purchase decisions are greatly influenced by what products customers see during their visit. What they see in turn is affected by the store layout and how the merchandise is presented. Thus, retailers attempt to design their stores in a manner that motivates unplanned purchases. As discussed later in this chapter, retailers use the cash wrap area, where people pay for merchandise, to display and therefore stimulate the sale of impulse items such as candy at a supermarket check-out terminal or jewelry at a women's apparel store.

Control Costs to Increase Profits

The fourth design objective is to control the cost of implementing the store design and maintaining the store's appearance. Although the types of lighting that Neiman Marcus shines on its expensive jewelry and crystal use more electricity and are less ecologically friendly than rows of bare fluorescent bulbs, the retailer considers such costs necessary to highlight these high-ticket items. In contrast, other retailers have embraced the notion of gaining efficiency in their energy use, as Retailing View 17.2 details.

Store designs can also affect labor costs and inventory shrinkage. Some stores are organized into isolated departments, which provides an intimate, comfortable shopping experience that can result in more sales. However, the design prevents sales associates from observing and covering adjacent departments, which makes it necessary to have at least one sales associate permanently stationed in each department to provide customer service and prevent shoplifting.

Another design consideration related to controlling cost is flexibility. Retailing is a very dynamic business. Competitors enter a market and cause existing retailers to change the mix of merchandise offered. As the merchandise mix changes, so

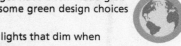

RETAILING VIEW   Walmart Goes Green and Lowers Its Energy Costs   17.2

In an initiative begun several years ago, Walmart continues to design new stores and retrofit older stores to ensure their energy efficiency. These stores are among the "greenest" in the world. The three main design objectives for these stores are reducing the amount of energy and other natural resources required for store operations, minimizing the raw materials used to construct each facility, and using renewable materials whenever possible.

These design elements reflect Walmart's three broad environmental goals: (1) to be supplied 100 percent by renewable energy, (2) to create zero waste, and (3) to sell products that sustain the world's resources and environment. Although such design features reduce the stores' impact on the environment, they also are expensive to build. Initial projections call for the energy used at these new stores to be 25 to 30 percent less than older stores that have not been retrofitted, reducing a store's energy costs by $500,000 annually. Such savings could increase if energy costs continue to climb.

Some of the sustainable features that have passed these steps or are currently being tested are as follows:

- A wind turbine on top of a store that produces sufficient energy to offset 5 percent of each store's electricity consumption.

- A system to collect and treat rainwater, which in turn can provide nearly all of the water required for irrigation and thus will reduce demands placed on local stormwater systems.

- The use of grass for landscaping that does not need irrigation or mowing.

- LEDs, instead of fluorescent lighting, in refrigerated cases. In cold temperatures, fluorescent lights lose life expectancy every time they are switched on and off; LEDs do not suffer from this limitation. The lights stay off until the customer opens the case. In addition to saving energy, the lights add a theatrical appeal for customers.

- A system that captures the heat generated by each building's refrigeration system, then redirects that

heat to warm the water in restroom sinks or support new radiant, floor-heating systems located beneath the entries and other areas.

Although many of these changes have been made globally, Walmart also customizes some green design choices by region:

- Brazil: Stores employ smart lights that dim when natural sunlight is available.

- Mexico: Walmart invested 640 million pesos (US$57 million) to convert a 25-acre, 50-foot deep dump into a green mall, which created 1,500 jobs. The trash produced energy through a bio-gas burning process. The green mall is now home to a Walmart supercenter, Sam's Club, Vips, and El Porton restaurants.

- Central America: 70 percent of stores have installed skylights to reduce lighting costs, covering approximately 15 percent of the roof space of each store.

- China: Walmart has begun to switch over to LED lighting throughout stores and integrated lighting controls to reduce energy usage by a target amount of 30 percent in existing stores and 40 percent in prototype stores.

- Japan: Prototype stores use a desiccant temperature and humidity system to reduce energy costs and CO_2 emissions.

Sources: "Taking Sustainability to New Heights," www.walmartgreeenroom/com, October 15, 2012; "No Matter the Season, Our Energy Commitment Is Always On," www.walmartgreenroonm.com, September 28, 2012; Michelle Moran, "Seeing Green," *Progressive Grocer*, March 2010, pp. 16–31; Cathy Jett, "New Design's Goal: To Cut the Clutter," *McClatchy-Tribune Business News*, October 14, 2009; and Aaron Besecker, "Walmart Store Gets Green Light," *McClatchy-Tribune Business News*, August 31, 2009.

DISCUSSION QUESTION

Are green store designs worth their cost? Why or why not?

---

must the space allocated to merchandise categories and the layout of the store. Thus, store designers attempt to design stores with maximum flexibility.

Flexibility is an important design consideration for college bookstores because they need to expand and contract their spaces to accommodate the large seasonal fluctuations inherent in the college-bookstore business. At the beginning of a semester, considerable space needs to be allocated to textbooks. But after the first week of the semester, the demand for textbooks decreases quickly, and space allocated to textbooks needs to be reallocated to apparel and consumer electronics. The key to providing this flexibility often lies in innovative fixture and wall systems that portion off the textbook area. **Fixtures** refer to the equipment used to display merchandise.

Legal Considerations—Americans with Disabilities Act

All store design and redesign decisions must comply with the 1990 Americans with Disabilities Act (ADA) and its 2008 amendments.[5] This law protects people with disabilities from discrimination in employment, transportation, public

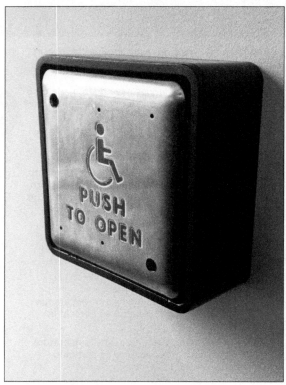

The ADA has made stores more accessible for disabled consumers.

accommodations, telecommunications, and activities of state and local governments. It affects store design because the act calls for "reasonable access" to merchandise and services in retail stores built before 1993; stores built after 1993 must be fully accessible.

The act also states that retailers should not have to incur "undue burdens" to comply with ADA requirements. Although retailers are concerned about the needs of their disabled customers, they are also worried that making merchandise completely accessible to people in a wheelchair or a motorized cart will result in less space available to display merchandise and thus will reduce sales. However, providing for wider aisles and more space around fixtures can result in a more pleasant shopping experience for able-bodied as well as disabled customers.

The ADA does not clearly define critical terms such as "reasonable access," "fully accessible," or "undue burden." So the actual ADA requirements are being defined through a series of court cases in which disabled plaintiffs have filed class-action suits against retailers.[6] On the basis of these court cases, retailers are typically required to (1) provide 32-inch-wide pathways in the main aisle, to bathrooms, dressing rooms, and elevators, and around most fixtures; (2) lower most cash wraps (checkout stations) and fixtures so that they can be reached by a person in a wheelchair; (3) create disability-accessible checkout aisles; (4) provide bathrooms with handrails or grab bars; and (5) make dressing rooms fully accessible. Nor does the ADA stop at the store exit. Very clear guidelines establish the number of handicapped accessible parking spaces that stores must provide.[7] Some of these accessibility requirements are somewhat relaxed for retailers in very small spaces and during peak sales periods such as the Christmas holidays.

Design Trade-Offs

Few store designs can achieve all of these objectives, so any store design involves trade-offs among the objectives. Home Depot's traditional warehouse design can efficiently store and display a lot of merchandise with long rows of floor-to-ceiling racks, but this design is not conducive for a pleasant shopping experience.

Retailers often make trade-offs between stimulating impulse purchases and making it easy to buy products. For example, supermarkets place milk, a commonly purchased item, at the back of the store to make customers walk through the entire store, thus stimulating more impulse purchases. Realizing that some customers may want to buy only milk, Walgreens places its milk at the front of the store, enabling it to compete head-to-head with convenience stores.

The trade-off between making it easy to find merchandise and providing an interesting shopping experience is determined by the customer's shopping needs. For example, supermarket and drugstore shoppers typically focus on utilitarian benefits and want to minimize the time they spend shopping, so the design of supermarkets emphasizes the ease of locating merchandise (there are exceptions, such as Wegmans). In contrast, customers shopping for specialty goods like a computer, a home entertainment center, or furniture are more likely to spend time in the store browsing, comparing, and talking with the salesperson. Thus, specialty store retailers that offer this type of merchandise place more emphasis on providing hedonic benefits and encouraging exploration than on making it easy to find merchandise.

Another trade-off is the balance between giving customers adequate space in which to shop and productively using this scarce resource for merchandise. Customers are attracted to stores with wide aisles and fixtures whose primary purpose is to display rather than hold the merchandise. Also, shoppers do not like it when a store is so cramped that they touch one another, a phenomenon known as the "butt-brush effect."[8] However, a spacious design reduces the amount of merchandise that can be available to buy and thus may also reduce impulse purchases and the customers' chances of finding what they are looking for. But too many racks and displays in a store can cause customers to feel uncomfortable and even confused. There must be a compromise between been having a store that is too spacious and one that is overcrowded.

This section examined the various objectives retailers seek to satisfy when designing their stores. In the next section, important elements of design are explored.

STORE DESIGN ELEMENTS

Three elements in the design of stores are the (1) layout, (2) signage, and (3) feature areas. Each of these elements is discussed in this section.

LO2

List the advantages and disadvantages of alternative store layouts.

Layouts

Retailers use three general types of store layout design: grid, racetrack, and free form. Each of these layouts has advantages and disadvantages.

Grid Layout   The **grid layout**, illustrated in Exhibit 17–1, has parallel aisles with merchandise on shelves on both sides of the aisles. Cash registers are located at the entrances/exits of the stores.

The grid layout is well suited for customers who are primarily interested in the utilitarian benefits offered by the store. They are not interested in the hedonic

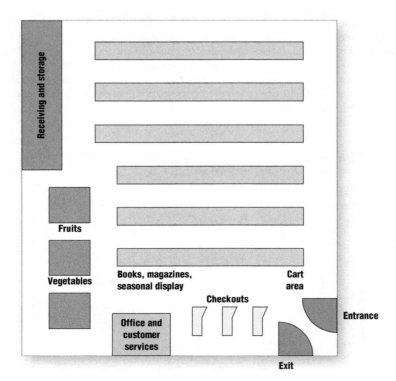

EXHIBIT 17–1
Grid Store Layout

benefits provided by a visually exciting design. They want to easily locate products they want to buy, and they make their purchases as quickly as possible. Most supermarkets and full-line discount stores use the grid layout, because this design enables their customers to easily find the product they are looking for and minimize the time spent on a shopping task that most don't enjoy.

The grid layout is also cost-efficient. There's less wasted space with the grid layout than with other layouts because the aisles are all the same width and designed to be just wide enough to accommodate shoppers and their carts. The use of high shelves for merchandise enables more merchandise to be on the sales floor compared with other layouts. Finally, because the fixtures are generally standardized, the cost of the fixtures is low.

One limitation of the grid layout, from the retailer's perspective, is that customers typically aren't exposed to all the merchandise in the store because, due to the height of the shelves, they see only products displayed in the aisle they are in. Thus the layout does not encourage unplanned purchases. Supermarket retailers overcome this limitation, to some extent, by complementing the packaged goods in the center-store grid with a racetrack of fresh, perishable merchandise categories (meat, seafood, dairy, poultry, baked goods, and produce) around the periphery of the store. Unplanned purchases are also stimulated by special displays, which are discussed later in the chapter.

In the past, supermarket retailers and consumer packaged goods manufacturers did not feel this limitation was very important. They believed that customers would be exposed to all the merchandise in the store because they would walk up and down each aisle, pushing their shopping carts. However, researchers have equipped carts with GPS locators and found that most supermarket customers enter a supermarket, turn right, go along the periphery of the store looking down the aisles, and occasionally walk down an aisle with their carts or leave the cart at the end of the aisle and walk down the aisle to select a specific item and return to the cart. A path taken by a typical customer is shown in Exhibit 17–2.[9]

Supermarket retailers and consumer packaged goods companies now recognize this problem of decreased traffic in the center core of supermarkets. Whereas the outer circumference of the store has seen some exciting improvements, such that "store perimeters have become warm, inviting, exciting, genuine and diverse," according to David Milka, director of consumer insight for S.C. Johnson, the center of the store has remained "cold, obscure, boring and non-differentiated."[10]

The answer is to get customers to spend more time in the center store. Recent research shows that the more time customers spend in stores in general, the more unplanned purchases they make.[11] One way to extend their shopping time is to make their shopping path less efficient. Thus, to expose customers to more

EXHIBIT 17–2
Example of a Traffic Pattern in a Grid Layout Supermarket

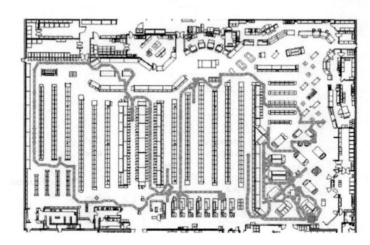

merchandise and increase their unplanned purchases in the core, supermarket retailers need to get customers to walk down more aisles. One potential approach for increasing traffic in the core would alter the straight aisles to form a zig-zag pattern. As discussed in Retailing View 17.3, IKEA uses a similar method. Another approach locates power brands—those with high awareness and market share such as Coca-Cola and Tide—and eye-attracting displays in the middle of the aisle rather than at the ends. The power brands appear from the top to the bottom, creating a swath of color that captures the attention of customers as they peek down the aisle.

RETAILING VIEW   A Hedonic Maze Filled with Utilitarian Products   17.3

IKEA stores are designed to inspire customers to weave their way through the store.

At its largest North American store in Montreal, IKEA offers 464,694 feet of functional, reasonably priced furniture, décor, and housewares. It contains various settings that showcase its products, including three full homes and approximately 50 "inspirational room settings," as well as a market hall and a restaurant that can seat 600. If you walked the entire store, you'd have completed a nearly one-mile hike.

Of course, few shoppers want to cover all that ground. Visitors looking for a new ottoman for their living room have little reason to swing through the bedroom sets. And yet, somehow, most of them wind up doing just that.

The reason is likely IKEA's distinctive, maze-like layout for its stores. Once customers enter the maze, it is difficult for them to find a specific department, or even the exit, unless they follow the path laid out for them. According to IKEA, this layout benefits customers by giving them inspiration and decorating ideas. But still the notion seems contradictory. Shouldn't a retailer make it easier for customers to find what they want?

Instead, IKEA's store flows create disorientation and directional confusion to push customers through each department. That means they spend more time in the stores and may consider more purchases. They might have stopped for an ottoman, but the bedside lamp they see in

an inspirational bedroom setting might be just the thing. In addition, customers are more likely to place appealing items in their carts for fear that they will be unable to find it again if they leave it behind. Finally, the length of time customers spend in the store makes them feel committed to the visit. If they don't pick up a few items, all that expenditure of time might seem wasted.

According to various observers, the effect is either brilliant or underhanded—or both. No one seems to leave IKEA without buying more than he or she had planned. This near-inability to stick to a shopping list seems a direct result of the carefully designed layout that causes customers to buy a number of uplanned items.

Sources: Elizabeth Tyler, "How IKEA Seduces Its Customers: By Trapping Them," *Time*, January 28, 2011; and Kathryn Blaze Carlson, "Enter the Maze: IKEA, Costco, Other Retailers Know How to Get You to Buy More," *National Post*, June 1, 2012.

DISCUSSION QUESTION

What features of IKEA and its strategy make its unique store layout appropriate for it, but not for other types of retailers?

Retailers are experimenting with creative promotional approaches to keep people shopping. For example, LocalResponse allows retailers to know what merchandise customers are talking about using social media (e.g., a tweet, Facebook update, photo on Instagram, or check-in using Foursquare) while in the store. Consequently, retailers can use the latest advances in technology to offer customers instant coupons on their mobile phones for merchandise adjacent to where they are physically located, which might entice them to find the product and buy it. Additionally, giving them an electronic coupon for merchandise located at another, potentially distant, location in the store, along with a map of where it is located, may lure them to meander through the store with the possibility that they will purchase other items along the way.

Racetrack Layout   The **racetrack layout,** also known as a **loop,** is a store layout that provides a major aisle that loops around the store to guide customer traffic around different departments within the store. Point-of-sale terminals are typically located in each department bordering the racetrack.

The racetrack layout facilitates the goal of getting customers to see the merchandise available in multiple departments and thus encourages unplanned purchasing. As customers go around the racetrack, their eyes are forced to take different viewing angles rather than looking down one aisle, as in the grid design. Low fixtures are used so that customers can see merchandise beyond the products displayed on the racetrack.

Exhibit 17–3 shows the layout of a department store. Because the store has multiple entrances, the racetrack layout places all departments on the main aisle by drawing customers through the store in a series of major and minor loops. To entice customers through the various departments, the design places some of the more

EXHIBIT 17–3   Racetrack Layout

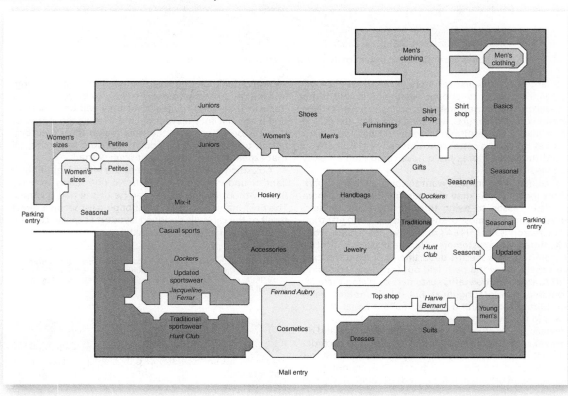

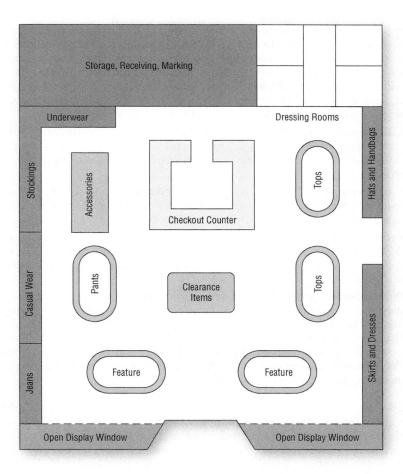

EXHIBIT 17–4
Free-Form Store
Layout

popular departments, like juniors, toward the rear of the store. The newest items also are featured on the aisles to draw customers into departments and around the loop.

The racetrack usually is wider than other aisles and defined by a change in flooring surface or color. For instance, the aisle flooring might be marblelike tile, whereas the department floors vary in material, texture, and color, depending on the desired ambience.

Free-Form Layout   A **free-form layout**, also known as **boutique layout**, arranges fixtures and aisles in an asymmetric pattern (Exhibit 17–4). It provides an intimate, relaxing environment that facilitates shopping and browsing. It appears most commonly in specialty stores or as departments within department stores. However, creating this pleasing shopping environment is costly. Because there is no well-defined traffic pattern, as there is in the racetrack and grid layouts, customers aren't naturally drawn around the store or department, and personal selling becomes more important to encourage customers to explore merchandise offered in the store. In addition, the layout reduces the amount of merchandise that can be displayed.

Signage and Graphics

Signage and graphics help customers locate specific products and departments, provide product information, and suggest items or special purchases. Graphics, such as photo panels, can reinforce a store's image. Signage is used to identify the location of merchandise categories within a store and the types of products offered in the category. The signs are hung typically from the ceiling to enhance their visibility. Frequently, icons rather than words are used to facilitate communication with customers speaking different languages. For example, a red and yellow circus tent icon identifies the area for children's toys more effectively than a black and white, worded rectangular sign. Smaller signs are used to identify sale items and provide more information about specific products. Finally, retailers may use images, such as pictures of people and places, to create moods that encourage customers to buy products. Some different types of signs are:

- **Call-to-action signage.** Placed in strategic locations in the store can convey how, where, and why to engage with the retailer via QR codes on customers' cellphones, via e-mail, short-message services, Facebook, or other digital channels.

- **Category signage.** Used within a particular department or sector of the store to identify types of products offered. They are usually located near the goods to which they refer.

- **Promotional signage.** Describes special offers and found within the store or displayed in windows to entice the customer into the store. For instance, value apparel stores for young women often display large posters in their windows of models wearing new or sale items.

- **Point-of-sale signage.** Point-of-sale signs are placed near the merchandise they refer to so that customers know its price and other detailed information. Some of this information may already be on product labels or packaging. However, point-of-sale signage can quickly identify for the customer those aspects likely to be of greater interest, such as whether the product is on sale. Walmart uses this sort of signage effectively to show customers when the price of an item has been "rolled back."

Digital Signage   Many retailers are replacing traditional signage with digital signage systems.[12] **Digital signage** includes signs whose visual content is delivered electronically through a centrally managed and controlled network, distributed to servers in stores, and displayed on flat-panel screens. The content delivered can range from entertaining video clips to simple price displays.

Digital signage provides a number of benefits over traditional static-print signage. Due to their dynamic nature, digital signs are more effective in attracting the attention of customers and helping them recall the messages displayed. Digital signage also offers the opportunity to enhance a store's environment by displaying complex graphics and videos to provide an atmosphere that customers find appealing.[13] Because the content is delivered digitally, it can easily be tailored to a store's market and remain consistent in every store, displayed at the right time and right place. Furthermore, by overcoming the time-to-message hurdle associated with traditional print signage, digital signage enables the content to be varied within and across stores at different times of the day or days of the week—without incurring the expense of printing, distributing, and installing new static signs or hiring labor to post them. If the temperatures rise, digital in-store signage might automatically advertise cold drinks; if the forecast continues to be warm and sunny, it might promote sunscreen. Of course, there is a drawback too. The initial

In-store digital displays highlight key product features and experiential elements at the point of purchase.

cost of the display devices and the system that supports the delivery of signage can be quite high.

Recent research shows customers spend $1.52 more, per trip, at grocery stores when digital displays are used. Less than $2 might not seem like that much, but the overall effect is huge in the grocery sector, with its tight margins and high volume of shoppers.[14] The effect of digital signage on sales is not limited to grocers. Lord & Taylor has added digital signage to its flagship store in Manhattan and plans to expand its use. The store reports the addition of digital signage in its fragrance department paid for itself in less than a year, and digital technology in the men's suit department led to double-digit sales increases.[15]

Feature Areas

In addition to using layout and signage, retailers can guide customers through stores and influence buying behavior through the placement of feature areas. **Feature areas** are the areas within a store that are designed to get customers' attention. They include windows, entrances, freestanding displays, mannequins, end caps, promotional aisles or areas, walls, dressing rooms, and cash wraps.

Windows   Window displays draw customers into the store and provide a visual message about the type of merchandise offered in the store and the type of image the store wants to portray. Research suggests that storefront window displays are an effective tool for building the store image, particularly with new customers who are unfamiliar with the store.[17]

Effective window displays are not easy to achieve, however, and they often demand the collaboration of a large team of designers. At The Limited, an extensive design team, led by the senior vice president of visual merchandising and store design and construction, takes several weeks, or even months, to find just the right combination of women's fashions that will attract mall shoppers strolling by the stores. Only after extensive analysis does the design team introduce their display to the stores throughout the nation.[18]

Entrances   The first impression caused by the entry area affects the customer's image of the store. Department stores typically have the cosmetics and fragrance categories at the main entrance, while grocery stores have fresh produce because these categories are visually appealing and create a sense of excitement. Whole Foods places cut flowers near the entrance to connote freshness.[19]

While the entry area plays a prominent role in creating an image, the first 10 feet of the store are often referred to as the "decompression zone," because customers are making an adjustment to the new environment: escaping from the noisy street or mall, taking off their sunglasses, closing their umbrellas, and developing a visual impression of the entire store. Customers are not prepared to evaluate merchandise or make purchase decisions in the decompression zone, so retailers try to keep this area free of merchandise, displays, and signage.[20]

Freestanding Displays   **Freestanding displays** are fixtures that are located on aisles and designed primarily to attract customers' attention and bring them into a department. These fixtures often display and store the newest, most exciting merchandise in the particular department.

REFACT
Whereas 85 percent of shoppers walking through mall concourses approach the various stores from the side, nearly all signs that appear in store windows offer a head-on appeal.[16]

Window displays need to catch the attention of the shopper and draw them into the store.

Whimsical mannequins attract the attention of children in Disney stores.

Mannequins A **mannequin** is a life-size representation of the human body, used for displaying apparel. In the past, mannequins were often plain and boring. Twenty-first-century retailers have begun to realize that mannequins don't need to be hairless, featureless, blindingly white, skinny space holders. They can help personify a brand, push customers to enter their stores, and perhaps even offer an ideal image that encourages shoppers to buy a little something extra that looks great on display. At the Disney Store, children are enchanted as whimsical mannequins swoop down from the ceiling or execute a perfect princess curtsy. The stylish customers moving through Ralph Lauren stores instead perceive a sense of style and sophistication, conveyed through the mannequin with a recreated face of British model Yasmin Le Bon.[21]

End Caps **End caps** are displays located at the end of an aisle in stores using a grid layout. Due to the high visibility of end caps, sales of a product increase dramatically when that merchandise is featured on an end cap. Thus, retailers use end caps for higher-margin, impulse, and sale merchandise. In the supermarket industry, vendors often negotiate for their products to be on end-cap displays when they are offering special promotional prices.

REFACT

An international survey of supermarket shoppers found that end caps are noticed by more than three-quarters of shoppers and could influence 60 percent to make a purchase.[22]

Promotional Aisle or Area A **promotional aisle** or **promotional area** is a space used to display merchandise that is being promoted. Drugstores, for instance, use promotional aisles to sell seasonal merchandise, such as lawn and garden products in the summer and Christmas decorations in the fall. Specialty stores and department stores tend to locate a promotional area at the back of the store or department. To get to the items on sale, customers must pass through all the full-price merchandise, which makes it more likely that something will catch their eye.

The arrangement of merchandise helps tells the story.

Walls Because retail floor space is often limited, many retailers increase their ability to store extra stock, display merchandise, and creatively present a message by utilizing wall space. Merchandise can be stored on shelving and racks and coordinated with displays, photographs, or graphics featuring the merchandise. At the French clothier Lacoste, for instance, merchandise is displayed in bold color swaths relatively high on the wall. Not only does this allow the merchandise to "tell a story," but it also helps customers feel more comfortable because they aren't crowded by racks or by other people, and they can get a perspective on the merchandise by viewing it from a distance.

Dressing Rooms Dressing rooms are critical spaces, where customers often decide whether to purchase an item. Large, clean, and comfortable dressing rooms put customers in the mood to buy. In recent years, retailers have even begun to compete aggressively on the basis of the quality of their dressing rooms. Old Navy has moved dressing rooms to the front of stores, so they no longer feel like "dungeons." To achieve a more refined, upscale feel, Ann Taylor stores feature chandeliers and attractive color accents in fitting rooms. Recognizing that many shoppers make trying on clothes a social event, Anthropologie has expanded the size of dressing rooms to make it easier for women to bring friends in with them. And to make the experience of waiting for a spouse trying on clothes more enjoyable, Macy's has added couches and flat-screen televisions outside dressing rooms.[23]

Virtual dressing rooms are becoming more important and interesting to online shoppers. People cannot try on clothes displayed on a website, but the spread of webcams embedded in laptops, tablets, and desktop computers is making it possible for programmers to create "virtual dressing rooms" that could permit Internet customers to "try on" clothing and accessories, simply by standing in front of their webcams.[24]

Although technology and decor can enhance the experience of trying on clothing, some retailers are cautious about the extent to which they will use technology. The personal attention provided by sales associates remains the most effective agent for providing customer service.

Cash Wraps **Cash wraps**, also known as **point-of-purchase (POP) counters** or **checkout areas**, are places in the store where customers can purchase merchandise. Because many customers go to these areas and wait in line to make a purchase, retailers often use them to display impulse purchase items. For example, in supermarkets, batteries, candy, gum, and magazines are often shelved at the checkout counter.

SPACE MANAGEMENT

The space within stores and on the stores' shelves and fixtures is a scarce resource. Space management involves key resource decisions: (1) the allocation of store space to merchandise categories and brands,[26] (2) the location of departments or merchandise categories in the store, and (3) the size of the store.

LO3
Describe how to assign store floor space to merchandise departments and categories.

Space Allocated to Merchandise Categories

Some factors that retailers consider when deciding how much floor or shelf space to allocate to merchandise categories and brands are (1) the productivity of the allocated space, (2) the merchandise's inventory turnover, (3) the impact on overall store sales, and (4) the display needs for the merchandise.

Space Productivity A simple rule of thumb for allocating space is to allocate on the basis of the merchandise's sales. For example, if artificial plants represent 15 percent of the total expected sales for a hobby and craft retailer such as Michaels, then 15 percent of the store's space is allocated to artificial plants.

But as the discussion of marginal analysis for advertising allocations in Chapter 15 indicated, retailers really should allocate space to a merchandise category on the basis of its effect on the profitability of the entire store. In practice, this recommendation means that Michaels should add more space to the artificial plant section as long as the profitability of the additional space is greater that the profitability of the category from which space was taken away. In this condition, the additional space for artificial plants will increase the profitability of the entire store. However, at some point, it will be more profitable to not take away space from other categories.

Two commonly used measures of space productivity are **sales per square foot** and **sales per linear foot.** Apparel retailers that display most of their merchandise on freestanding fixtures typically measure space productivity as sales per square foot. In supermarkets, most merchandise is displayed on shelves. Because the shelves have approximately the same width, only the length, or the linear dimension sales per linear foot, is used to assess space productivity.

A more appropriate productivity measure, such as gross margin per square foot, would consider the contribution generated by the merchandise, not just the sales. Thus, if salty snacks generate $400 in gross margin per linear foot and canned soup generates only $300 per linear foot, more space should be allocated to salty snacks. However, factors other than marginal productivity need to be considered when making space allocation decisions. These factors are discussed in the next section.

In addition, retailers need to allocate space to maximize the profitability of the store, not just a particular merchandise category or department. Supermarkets often "overallocate" space to some low-profitability categories such as milk because an extensive assortment in these categories attracts customers to the store and positively affects the sales of other categories. Retailers might also overallocate space to categories purchased by their platinum customers—that is, those customers with the highest lifetime value.

Inventory Turnover   Inventory turnover affects space allocations in two ways. First, as discussed in Chapter 12, both inventory turnover and gross margin contribute to GMROI—a measure of the retailer's return on its merchandise inventory investment. Thus, merchandise categories with higher inventory turnover merit more space than merchandise categories with lower inventory turnover. Second, merchandise displayed on the shelf is depleted more quickly for items with high inventory turnover. Thus, more space needs to be allocated to this fast-selling merchandise to minimize the need to restock the shelf frequently and reduce stockouts. Many retailers, however, compensate for high inventory turnover items by assigning them more frequent deliveries so they don't take up so much space.

Display Considerations   The physical limitations of the store and its fixtures affect space allocation. Of course, store planners must provide enough merchandise to fill an entire fixture dedicated to a particular item. But in addition, a retailer might decide it wants to use a merchandise display to enhance its image. For Target to set itself apart as a source of high-quality home goods, it makes its display of private-label organic cotton sheets attractive and expansive. To really emphasize this offering, it even might overallocate space for the sheets and present a wide range of colors.

Location of Merchandise Categories and Design Elements

As discussed previously, the store layout, signage, and feature areas can guide customers through the store. The location of merchandise categories also plays a role in how customers navigate the store. By strategically placing impulse and demand/destination merchandise throughout the store, retailers increase the chances that customers will shop the entire store and that their attention will be focused on the merchandise that the retailer is most interested in selling—merchandise with a high GMROI. **Demand/destination merchandise** refers to products that customers have decided to buy before entering the store.

As customers enter the store and pass through the decompression zone, they are welcomed with introductory displays, including graphics. Once through the decompression zone, they often turn right (in Western cultures) and observe the prices and quality of the first items they encounter. This area, referred to as the "strike zone," is critical, because it creates the customer's first impression of the store's offering. Thus, retailers display some of their most compelling merchandise in the strike zone.

After passing through the strike zone, the most heavily trafficked and viewed area is the right-hand side of the store because most people turn right when come into a store. By this point in their journey through the store, customers have become accustomed to the environment, have developed a first impression, and are ready to make purchase decisions. Thus the right-hand side is a prime area for displaying high GMROI merchandise. For example, supermarkets typically locate the produce section in this area because produce appeals to the shoppers' senses. The visual/color appeal of all the different produce—bright oranges, deep reds of tomatoes and peppers, rich greens of zucchini and kale—gets a shopper's mouth watering, and the best grocery store customer is a hungry one.

Impulse Merchandise   The prime store locations for selling merchandise are heavily trafficked areas such as 10 feet beyond the entrance on the right side of the store and areas near escalators and cash wraps. In multilevel stores, a space's value decreases the farther it is from the entry-level floor. Thus, **impulse products,** or products that are purchased without planning, such as fragrances and cosmetics in department stores and magazines in supermarkets, are almost always located near the front of the store, where they're seen by everyone and may actually draw people into the store.

The checkout counter at a supermarket is an ideal place to display merchandise typically bought on impulse.

Demand and Promotional Merchandise Demand merchandise and promotional merchandise are often placed in the back left-hand corner of the store. Placing high-demand merchandise in this location pulls customers through the store, increasing the visibility of other products along the way. So supermarkets typically put items almost everyone buys— milk, eggs, butter, and bread—in the back left-hand corner. In department stores, children's merchandise and furniture, as well as customer service areas like beauty salons, credit offices, and photography studios, are demand or destination areas and thus located in lightly trafficked areas of the store.

Special Merchandise   Some merchandise categories involve a buying process that is best accomplished in a lightly trafficked area. For example, women's lingerie is typically located in a remote area to offer a more private shopping experience. Categories that require large amounts of floor space, like furniture, are often located in less desirable locations. Some categories, like curtains, need significant wall space, whereas others, like shoes, require easily accessible storage rooms.

Category Adjacencies   Retailers often put complementary categories next to each other to encourage unplanned purchases. Thus at the end of the cereal aisle, grocery shoppers often find an end cap filled with fresh bananas, and audio cables tend to hang on a display near the section featuring sound systems in an electronics store. Such displays help encourage cross-selling, as discussed in Chapter 5.

Another option is to contradict traditional placement schemes to surprise and excite shoppers. A well-known example places beer next to diapers, based on the observation that fathers making an emergency diaper run often late at night buy themselves a treat during the same trip. Consumer goods companies also hope to exploit a "halo effect" created by the fresh produce aisle in supermarkets.[27] If their

Retailers often place complementary products, such as chips and salsa, next to each other to increase unplanned purchases.

packaged goods appear next to healthy, fresh vegetables and fruit, consumers are more likely to associate those appealing traits with the manufacturers' products. But supermarkets are cautious about such moves, because the quality of the fresh produce section is a real competitive advantage. These critical trade-offs remain a constant challenge for grocers.

Location of Merchandise within a Category   As discussed in Chapter 4, most purchases in food, discount, drug, and many category specialists are either based on limited problem solving or habitual decision making. As such, retailers have a very short time, often a matter of a few seconds, to get their attention and induce them to grab an item for purchase. Retailers use a variety of rules to locate specific SKUs within a category.[29] For instance, supermarkets and drugstores typically place private-label brands to the right of national brands. Because Western consumers read from left to right, they will see the higher-priced national brand first and then see and possibly purchase the lower-priced, higher-margin private-label item on the right that looks similar to the national brand. Produce departments in grocery stores are arranged so that apples are the first item most customers see because apples are a very popular produce item and thus can best initiate a buying pattern.

Supermarkets typically display merchandise on four shelves, with the most profitable merchandise on the third shelf from the floor. The third shelf attracts the most attention because it is at eye level for adults. Merchandise that appeals to a smaller group of customers is often displayed on the top shelf because reaching for the items requires significant effort. Heavy, bulky items are stocked on the bottom shelf for safety reasons.

However, when purchase decisions are influenced by shorter consumers, positioning merchandise on the lower shelves might be more effective. For example, children may influence breakfast cereal purchases when accompanying their parents to the supermarket. Thus, the second shelf from the floor might be a prime location for the most profitable cereal brands.

Exhibit 17–5 illustrates some innovative merchandise placement options with which some grocery stores are experimenting. Specifically,

1. Place the dairy section near the front of the store so it is associated with fresh produce.

2. Place other premium products in the produce section since it makes them sell better.

3. Redesign carts to have a second shelf for fragile items and have holders for flowers and coffee.

4. Have a small milk refrigerator near the front door to better compete with convenience stores.

5. Use wood and other natural materials to induce a "farm-fresh" image.

6. Group ingredients necessary for a particular recipe, such as tomatoes, basil, and mozzarella cheese.

7. Place some organic products together and others throughout the produce section to experiment with how they sell best.

8. Bananas should go at the back of the produce department to get customers to walk through the entire department.

9. To simulate farmers' markets, add some low shelves so customers can see through the department and locate various-colored items adjacent to each other for visual appeal.

Some tools that retailers use to make decisions on the positioning of items in a category are planograms, virtual-store software, and videotapes of consumers as they move through the store.

Planograms   A **planogram** is a diagram that shows how and where specific SKUs should be placed on retail shelves or displays to increase customer purchases. The locations can be illustrated using photographs, computer output, or artists' renderings. In developing the planogram, the retailer needs to make the category visually appealing, consider the manner in which customers shop (or the manner in which it would like customers to shop), and work to achieve its strategic and financial objectives. Planograms are also useful for merchandise that doesn't fit nicely on shelves in supermarkets or discount stores. Most specialty apparel retailers provide their managers with photographs and diagrams of how merchandise should be displayed. Retailing View 17.4 describes how the SAS planogramming system automated Marks & Spencer's food business.

Virtual-Store Simulation   Virtual-store simulations are another tool used to determine the effects of placing merchandise in different areas of a store and evaluating the profit potential for new items.[30] In these simulations, customers sit in front of computer screens that depict a store aisle. Retina-tracking devices record the eye movements of the customers. When the customers push forward on a handle, similar to the handle on a shopping cart, they progress down the simulated aisle. Customers can virtually reach forward, pick an item off the shelf, look at the packaging, and then place the item in the virtual cart. These virtual shopping trips allow retailers and their suppliers to develop a better understanding of how customers will respond to different planograms.

Videotaping Consumers Another research method used to assess customer reactions to planograms involves tracking customers in actual store environments. Traditionally, retailers would videotape customers' movements, but Microsoft's Kinect sensors are providing a less intrusive option. Discretely embedded in aisles, the sensors provide three-dimensional spatial recognition.

17.4 RETAILING VIEW   Marks & Spencer Automates with Planograms

Marks & Spencer is a large retailer of clothing, home goods, and high-quality food products in the United Kingdom. Its food business, specializing in high-quality convenience and fresh foods, such as sandwiches and take-home dinners, occupies a prominent position in the U.K. food retailing sector.

The retailer is continuously updating its product range with new products. That process was incredibly labor-intensive: Adjusting 50 displays in 50 stores required 2,500 new, individual planograms. It took 80 to 100 full-time planogrammers to implement weekly changes in its approximately 300 stores. So, the $8.6 billion retailer worked with SAS to develop an automated planogramming system that could optimize weekly fresh-food assortments to individual stores, as well as improve product layout and customer satisfaction.

The Marks & Spencer SAS system calculates an optimal layout by determining how many shelf facings are needed for each SKU in each store. At the same time, the system maintains a consistent look but considers specific fixtures and store layouts.

By implementing automated space planning, Marks & Spencer has greatly increased the productivity of its space-planning team and gained control over store layout and product presentation. It can now do weekly plans with 20 planogrammers—and it does a much better job than before. Product placement is more efficient and uniform throughout the chain, and customers can more easily find specific products.

Such successes have driven other grocers to follow this lead. In Finland, the SOK supermarket chain is using SAS analytics to shift from 1,500 cut-and-paste planograms to store-specific versions, or around 100,000 plans to meet the needs of its 800 stores. As a further step, SOK integrates customer data gathered through its loyalty card program into the planograms. It also shares the resulting information with its suppliers to improve efficiency and supply chain planning.

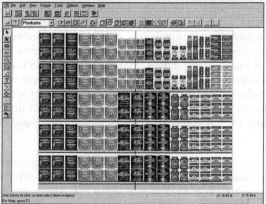

Marks & Spencer in the United Kingdom uses a planogram system developed by SAS to develop a layout that maximizes space productivity.

DISCUSSION QUESTION

Why are planograms particularly helpful for grocery retailers?

Sources: Communication with SAS; and Joanna Perry, "SOK: Using Store-Specific Plans," *RetailWeek*, November 20, 2009.

Thus, retailers can unobtrusively track the amount of time people spend in front of a shelf, which products they touch or pick up, the products they return to shelves, and finally what they add to their carts to purchase.[31] The data gathered can be used to improve layouts and planograms because they can identify causes of slow-selling merchandise, such as poor shelf placement. By studying customers' movements, retailers can also learn where customers pause or move quickly or where there is congestion. This information can help them decide if the layout and merchandise placement is operating as expected, such as whether new or promoted merchandise is getting the attention it deserves.

Determining Store Size

A key space management decision is deciding how big the store should be. With the rise of online shopping and the recent recession, retailers are coming to find that bigger is not always better. Improvements in supply chain management enable stores to decrease their size but still provide sufficient inventory levels. Thus, some big-box stores are reducing their inventory on hand while also looking for other creative ways to increase their revenue. However, some of these tactics appear contradictory with the recommendations for creating an inviting atmosphere.

Stores such as Walmart and Anchor Blue simply reduced their inventory; Anchor Blue actually erected temporary walls to reduce available floor space and stopped carrying unpopular styles and sizes. Other chains, including Kmart and Home Depot, leased their unused space to other retailers, such as related small business owners and fast-food restaurants. In the longer term, most large retailers also are looking for ways to reduce store footprints. Smaller stores mean fewer SKUs available, but they also can be erected in new markets that could never support a supercenter. Small-format "Walmart Express" stores target urban markets with shops that are approximately one-third the square footage of a regular Walmart location. Staples and Office Depot similarly are opening smaller formats, between 5,000 and 8,000 square feet, to service smaller and urban trade areas.[32]

Such changes do not come easy, nor without cost. There are potentially significant benefits to retailers, though. With their smaller spaces, they likely pay less rent, can hire fewer employees and thus reduce their payroll costs, minimize inventory costs by reducing the number of SKUs, and gain access to new

504   SECTION IV   Store Management

Small-format "Walmart Express" stores (left) target urban markets with shops that are approximately one-third the square footage of a regular Walmart location (right).

markets. There are also negative effects of the change, and most of those focus on the customer. Customers face reduced selection, decreased comfort, and little entertainment. Smaller formats mean there is no room for communal dressing rooms, entertaining digital displays, or wide aisles that facilitate browsing. The potential outcomes suggest a broader question: Are modern consumers—time-pressured, price-sensitive, and computer-savvy—likely to embrace these new, smaller-format stores that cannot offer one-stop shopping or a seemingly unlimited selection? The promise is great for retailers that hope to entice new segments of customers, but their offer might not be enough for the average consumer.

While this section explored how retailers manage the precious and scarce resource of space in their stores, the next section looks at the "softer side" of managing a store's interior—visual merchandising.

VISUAL MERCHANDISING

LO4

Illustrate the best techniques for merchandise presentation.

Visual merchandising is the presentation of a store and its merchandise in ways that will attract the attention of potential customers. This section examines issues related to the presentation of merchandise, and the following section explores more sensory aspects of the store's environment. This section begins with a review of the fixtures used to display merchandise and then discusses some merchandise presentation techniques.

Fixtures

The primary purposes of fixtures are to efficiently hold and display merchandise. At the same time, they define areas of a store and direct traffic flow. Fixtures work in concert with other design elements, such as floor coverings and lighting, as well as the overall image of the store. For instance, in stores designed to convey a sense of tradition or history, customers automatically expect to see lots of wood rather than plastic or metal fixtures. Wood mixed with metal, acrylic, or stone changes the traditional orientation. Apparel retailers utilize the straight-rack, rounder, and four-way fixtures, while the principle fixture for most other retailers is the gondola.

The **straight rack** consists of a long pipe balanced between supports in the floor or attached to a wall (Exhibit 17–6A). Although the straight rack can hold a lot of apparel, it cannot effectively feature specific styles or colors. All the customer can see is a sleeve or a pant leg. As a result, straight racks are often found in discount and off-price apparel stores.

(A) Straight rack

EXHIBIT 17–6
Types of Fixtures

(B) Rounder

(C) Four-way

(D) Gondola

A **rounder,** also known as a **bulk fixture** or **capacity fixture,** is a round fixture that sits on a pedestal (Exhibit 17–6B). Although smaller than the straight rack, it's designed to hold a maximum amount of merchandise. Because they are easy to move and efficiently store apparel, rounders are found in most types of apparel stores. But, as with the straight rack, customers can't get a frontal view of the merchandise.

A **four-way fixture,** also known as a **feature fixture,** has two crossbars that sit perpendicularly on a pedestal (Exhibit 17–6C). This fixture holds a large amount of merchandise and allows the customer to view the entire garment. The four-way is harder to maintain properly than is the rounder or straight rack, however. All merchandise on an arm must be of a similar style and color, or the customer may become confused. Due to their superior display properties, four-way fixtures are commonly utilized by fashion-oriented apparel retailers.

A **gondola** is an island type of self-service counter with tiers of shelves, bins, or pegs. (Exhibit 17–6D). Because they are extremely versatile, they are used extensively, but not exclusively, in grocery and discount stores to display everything from canned foods to baseball gloves. Gondolas are also found displaying towels, sheets, and housewares in department stores. Folded apparel can be efficiently displayed on gondolas as well, but because the items are folded, it's even harder for customers to view apparel on gondolas than it is on straight racks.

Presentation Techniques

Some presentation techniques are idea-oriented, item and size, color, price lining, vertical merchandising, tonnage merchandising, and frontage presentation.

Idea-Oriented Presentation   Some retailers use an **idea-oriented presentation**—a method of presenting merchandise based on a specific idea or the image of the store. Individual items are grouped to show customers how the items could be used and combined. Women's blouses are often displayed with skirts and accessories to present an overall image or idea. Also, furniture stores display a combination of furniture in room settings to give customers an idea of how it would look in their homes. This approach encourages the customer to make multiple complementary purchases.

Item and Size Presentation   Probably the most common technique of organizing stock is by style or item. Discount stores, grocery stores, hardware stores, and drugstores employ this method for nearly every category of merchandise, as do many apparel retailers. When customers look for a particular type of merchandise, such as breakfast cereals, they expect to find all items in the same location. Arranging items by size is a common method of organizing many types of merchandise, from nuts and bolts to apparel. Because the customer usually knows the desired size, it's easy to locate items organized in this manner.

Color Presentation   A bold merchandising technique is organizing by color. For instance, Ralph Lauren stores often have entire collections in one color hue, all merchandised together. White House/Black Market women's apparel stores take color presentation to an extreme—most of its merchandise is black, white, or a combination of the two.

Price Lining   **Price lining** occurs when retailers offer a limited number of predetermined price points and/or price categories within another classification that are merchandised together. This approach helps customers easily find merchandise at the price they wish to pay. For instance, men's dress shirts may be organized into three groups selling for $49, $69, and $99 (see Chapter 14).

Vertical Merchandising   Another common way of organizing merchandise is **vertical merchandising.** In this approach, merchandise is presented vertically using walls and high gondolas. Customers shop much as they read a newspaper— from left to right, going down each column, top to bottom. Stores can effectively organize merchandise to follow the eye's natural movement. Retailers take advantage of this tendency in several ways. Many grocery stores put national brands at eye level and store brands on lower shelves because customers scan from eye level down. In addition, retailers often display merchandise in bold vertical bands of an item. For instance, you might see vertical columns of towels of the same color displayed in a department store or a vertical band of yellow and orange boxes of Tide detergent followed by a band of blue Cheer boxes in a supermarket.

Tonnage Merchandising   As the name implies, **tonnage merchandising** is a display technique in which large quantities of merchandise are displayed together. Customers have come to equate tonnage with low price, following the retail adage "Stock it high and let it fly." Tonnage merchandising is therefore used to enhance and reinforce a store's price image. Using this display concept, the merchandise itself is the display. The retailer hopes customers will notice the merchandise and be drawn to it. For instance, grocery stores often use an entire end of a gondola (i.e., an end cap) to display six-packs of Pepsi.

Frontal Presentation   Often, it's not possible to create effective displays and efficiently store items at the same time. But it's important to show as much of the merchandise as possible. One solution to this dilemma is the **frontal presentation,** a method of displaying merchandise in which the retailer exposes as much of the product as possible to catch the customer's eye. Book manufacturers, for instance, make great efforts to create eye-catching covers. But bookstores usually display books exposing only the spine. To create an effective display and break the monotony, book retailers often face an occasional cover out like a billboard to catch the customer's attention. A similar frontal presentation can be achieved on a rack of apparel by simply turning one item out to show the merchandise.

CREATING AN APPEALING STORE ATMOSPHERE

To provide a rewarding shopping experience, retailers go beyond presenting appealing merchandise. **Atmospherics** refers to the design of an environment by stimulation of the five senses.[33] Many retailers have discovered the subtle benefits of developing atmospherics that complement other aspects of the store design and the merchandise. Therefore, they use lighting, colors, music, scent, and even flavors to stimulate customers' perceptual and emotional responses and ultimately affect their purchase behavior. Research has shown that it is important for the atmospheric elements to work together—for example, the right music with the right scent.[34]

LO5

Understand how retailers can create a more appealing shopping experience.

Lighting

Good lighting in a store involves more than simply illuminating space. Lighting can highlight merchandise and capture a mood or feeling that enhances the store's image. Retailers also are exploring ways to save energy with technologically advanced lighting. Having the appropriate lighting positively influences customer shopping behavior.[35]

Highlighting Merchandise   A good lighting system helps create a sense of excitement in the store. At the same time, lighting must provide an accurate color rendition of the merchandise. It also allows the retailer to focus spotlights on special featured areas and items. The key determinant appears to be achieving an appropriate level of contrast, which helps attract visual attention.[36] Using lighting to focus on strategic pockets of merchandise trains shoppers' eyes on the merchandise and draws customers strategically through the store. Nike, for example, uses a lot of contrast and shadows, highlighting the merchandise but not necessarily the architecture.

Mood Creation   Retailers use lighting to set the mood for their customers. Ralph Lauren stores and boutiques in department stores use low levels of light to coordinate with their overall ambience of resembling a townhouse. Abercrombie & Fitch keeps stores purposefully dark, discouraging too many parents from entering. With their lesser concern about atmospherics, full-line discount stores, food retailers, and category specialists tend to brighter and less-expensive fluorescent lighting.

Energy-Efficient Lighting   As the price of energy soars and retailers and their customers become more energy-conscious, retailers are looking for ways to cut their energy costs and be more ecologically friendly. One obvious source of energy consumption is the lighting in a store, which makes up approximately one-third of a large store's energy costs. Light-emitting diode (LED) lighting is replacing fluorescent lighting in many stores because it reduce these costs by up to 75 percent, and they last 10 times longer than standard bulbs. Yet LEDs are more expensive initially than traditional lighting.[37]

Color

The creative use of color can enhance a retailer's image and help create a mood. Warm colors (red, gold, and yellow) produce emotional, vibrant, hot, and active responses. Thus, for sellers using online auction sites like eBay, it may be a good

Abercrombie & Fitch creates a dark environment targeted at the younger consumer.

idea to use red tones, because bidders instinctively respond with higher bids in the online auction, compared with a sale page dominated by blue hues.[38] Cool colors (white, blue, and green) have a peaceful, gentle, calming effect and appear to induce abstract thinking, leading customers to view products more favorably. Thus brick-and-mortar stores may want to use these more relaxing colors of the spectrum.[39] Although these trends are common, colors can have differential impacts, depending on various consumer traits, such as their culture (e.g., in the East, white is a color of mourning, whereas in the West, it often implies purity), their age, and their gender.

Music

Music can either add to or detract from a retailer's total atmospheric package. Most shoppers notice music playing in stores, and nearly half of them say they will leave if they do not like the selections being played.[40]

Fortunately, unlike other atmospheric elements though, music can be easily changed. For example, one retailer has a system that allows different types of music to be played at certain times of the day. It can play jazzy music in the morning when its customer base is older and adult contemporary in the afternoon for a 35-to-40-year age range customer. For its West Coast stores, it wants modern rock in the morning and Caribbean beats in the afternoon. And in Texas, it's country music all day, every day. The retailer also can "zone" music by demographics, playing more Latin music in stores that attract a higher Hispanic population.

Retailers also can use music to affect customers' behavior. Music can control the pace of store traffic, create an image, and attract or direct consumers' attention. For instance, one U.K. toy store switched from children's songs like "Baa Baa Black Sheep" to relaxed classical music and watched sales jump by 10 percent.[41] Managers realized that though children are the consumers of their products, adults are the customers. In general, slow is good. A mix of classical or otherwise soothing music encourages shoppers to slow down, relax, and take a good look at the merchandise.

Scent

Smell has a large impact on a customer's mood and emotions. In conjunction with music, it can increase customers' excitement and satisfaction with the shopping experience.[42] Customers in scented stores think they spent less time in the store than do those in unscented stores. Scents thus can improve customers' subjective shopping experience by making them feel that they are spending less time examining merchandise, waiting for sales help, or checking out.

Retailers also use different essences in different departments: baby powder in the baby store; suntan lotion in the bathing suit area; lilacs in lingerie; and cinnamon and pine scents during the holiday season.[43] Some high-end retailers, such as Saks Fifth Avenue, utilize their own unique scents, and mall shoppers can sniff out an Abercrombie & Fitch store yards away. Yet these apparel retailers are not the only ones to use this atmospheric tool. Goodwill Stores now disperse the scent of honeysuckle and sweet orange in an attempt to make its retail sites more appealing. According to a Goodwill spokesperson, "Even if the recession weren't happening, we'd be doing everything we can to create a great shopping experience. We've already taken the approach of trying to have better lighting, [a] great layout . . . this is just one more thing that we hope will help enhance the shopping environment."[44]

When New Balance spread into China, it aimed for a (Western) nostalgic sensory experience to introduce the U.S. brand. Thus, not only did the stores feature wooden floors and 1950s pop music, but they also smelled like wood and leather. Even pop singers get in on this scent action. During her California Dreaming tour, Katy Perry appealed to young fans by spreading the scent of cotton candy throughout the stadiums she played.[45]

Taste

It is a little more difficult to appeal subtly to consumers' taste buds. However, many department stores are reintroducing an old-fashioned offering to appeal to shoppers: the store restaurant. The option to grab a bite without leaving the store encourages customers to linger longer and enjoy their shopping experience more. Café SFA at Saks Fifth Avenue offers a stellar view of Rockefeller Center, while Bergdorf Goodman's BG Restaurant shows off Central Park. And for those shoppers who must have a $36 lobster club sandwich to complete their shopping expedition, Fred's at Barney's New York is the place to go.[46]

Just How Exciting Should a Store Be?

Retailers such as Cabela's, REI, Bass Pro Shops, and Barnes & Noble attempt to create an entertaining shopping environment by viewing their stores as theatrical scenes: The floor and walls constitute the stage and scenery; the lighting, fixtures, and displays are the props; and the merchandise represents the performance. This

Customers enjoying a bite between their purchases stimulates longer stays and more purchases.

creation of a theatrical experience in stores has resulted in the combination of re-tailing and entertainment. In contrast, retail chains such as Costco and Home Depot successfully use minimalist, warehouse-style shopping environments, but create excitement in other ways, such as giving away food samples and hosting do-it-yourself classes.

Does providing an exciting, entertaining store environment lead customers to patronize a store more frequently and spend more time and money during each visit? The answer to this question is: It depends.[47]

The impact of the store's environment depends on the customer's shopping goals. The two basic shopping goals are task completion (utilitarian), such as buy-ing a new suit for a job interview, and recreation (hedonic), such as spending a Saturday afternoon with a friend wandering through a mall. When customers are shopping to complete a task that they view as inherently unrewarding, they prefer to be in a soothing, calming environment—a simple atmosphere with slow music, dimmer lighting, calming scents, and blue-green colors. However, when custom-ers go shopping for fun, an inherently rewarding activity, they want to be in an exciting atmosphere—a complex environment with invigorating smells, fast tempo music, bright lighting, and red-yellow colors.

What does this mean for retailers? They must consider the typical shopping goals for their customers when designing their store environments. Grocery shop-ping is typically viewed as an unpleasant task, and thus supermarkets should be designed in soothing colors and use slow background music. In contrast, shopping for fashion apparel is typically viewed as fun, so an arousing environment in ap-parel retail outlets will have a positive impact on the shopping behavior of their customers.

The level of excitement caused by the environment might vary across the store. A consumer electronics retailer might create a low-arousal environment in the accessories area to accommodate customers who typically are task oriented when shopping for print cartridges and batteries, and it might create a high-arousal environment in the home-entertainment centers that are typically visited by more pleasure-seeking shopping customers.

Finally, retailers might vary the nature of their websites for customers depend-ing on their shopping goals. For example, research suggests that Amazon should serve up complex, high-arousal websites with rich media to customers who indi-cate they are browsing but provide simpler, low-arousal sites to customers looking for a specific book.[48]

SUMMARY

LO1 Identify the critical issues retailers need to consider when designing a store.

To design a store, retailers must consider their main objectives: (1) implement their strategy, (2) influence customer buying behavior, (3) provide flexibility, (4) control design and maintenance costs, and (5) meet legal requirements. Because few store designs can achieve all of these objectives, managers make trade-offs among objectives, such as providing convenience rather than encouraging exploration or vice versa.

LO2 List the advantages and disadvantages of alternative store layouts.

Regardless of the type used, a good store layout helps customers find and purchase merchandise.

The grid design is best for stores in which custom-ers are likely to explore the entire store, such as grocery stores and drugstores. Racetrack designs are more common in large upscale stores, such as department stores. Free-form designs are usually found in small specialty stores and within the de-partments at department stores.

LO3 Describe how to assign store floor space to merchandise departments and categories.

Space management involves three decisions: (1) allo-cating store space to merchandise categories and brands, (2) locating departments or merchandise categories in the store, and (3) determining the appropriate store size. To determine how much floor or shelf space to allocate to merchandise categories, retailers might consider the productivity of the allocated space (e.g., using sales per square foot or sales per linear foot), the merchandise's inventory turnover, its impact on store sales, and display needs. In addition, by strategically placing impulse and demand/destination merchandise throughout the store, retailers can encourage customers to shop the entire store and focus their attention on merchandise that the retailer wants to sell most.

LO4 **Illustrate the best techniques for merchandise presentation.**

Signage and graphics help customers locate specific products and departments, provide product information, and suggest items or special purchases. Digital signage has several advantages over traditional printed signage, but the initial fixed costs have made its adoption slow. Feature areas are designed to get customers' attention. They include windows, entrances, freestanding displays, mannequins, end caps, promotional aisles or areas, walls, dressing rooms, and cash wraps. Finally, various types of display racks and shelving are more or less appropriate for different types of merchandise.

LO5 **Understand how retailers can create a more appealing shopping experience.**

Retailers employ various forms of atmospherics—lighting, colors, music, scent, and even taste—to influence shopping behaviors. The use of these atmospherics can create a calming environment for task-oriented shoppers or an exciting environment for recreational shoppers.

KEY TERMS

atmospherics, *507*
boutique layout, *493*
bulk fixture, *505*
call-to-action signage, *494*
capacity fixture, *505*
cash wrap, *497*
category signage, *494*
checkout area, *497*
demand/destination
  merchandise, *498*
digital signage, *494*
end cap, *496*
feature area, *495*
feature fixture, *505*
fixture, *487*

four-way fixture, *505*
free-form layout, *493*
freestanding display, *495*
frontal presentation, *506*
gondola, *505*
grid layout, *489*
hedonic benefit, *484*
idea-oriented presentation, *506*
impulse product, *499*
loop, *492*
mannequin, *496*
planogram, *501*
point-of-purchase (POP)
  counter, *497*
point-of-sale signage, *494*

price lining, *506*
promotional aisle, *496*
promotional area, *496*
promotional signage, *494*
racetrack layout, *492*
rounder, *505*
sales per linear foot, *497*
sales per square foot, *497*
straight rack, *504*
tonnage merchandising, *506*
utilitarian benefit, *484*
vertical merchandising, *506*
visual merchandising, *504*

GET OUT AND DO IT!

1. **CONTINUING ASSIGNMENT** Go into the physical store location of the retailer you have chosen for the continuing assignment, and evaluate the store layout, design, and visual merchandising techniques employed. Explain your answers to the following questions:
   (a) In general, are the store layout, design, and visual merchandising techniques consistent with the exterior of the store and its location?
   (b) Is the store's ambience consistent with the merchandise presented and the customer's expectations?
   (c) How do the store's layout, design, and visual merchandising support the following objectives: (1) implements the retailer's strategy, (2) builds

   loyalty, (3) increases sales, (4) controls costs, and (5) meets legal requirements?
   (d) To what extent are the store's layout, design, and merchandising techniques flexible?
   (e) How does the store utilize atmospheric elements such as color, lighting, music, and scent? Are these uses appropriate given the store's merchandise and target market?
   (f) Is the store's design environmentally friendly? If yes, please describe. If no, how could it become more "green"?
   (g) Are the fixtures consistent with the merchandise and the overall ambience of the store? Are they flexible?

(h) Evaluate the store's signage. Does it do an effective job of selling merchandise?

(i) Has the retailer used any theatrical effects to help sell merchandise?

(j) Does the store layout help draw people through the store?

(k) Has the retailer taken advantage of the opportunity to sell merchandise in feature areas?

(l) Does the store make creative use of wall space?

(m) What type of layout does the store use? Is it appropriate for the type of store? Would another type of layout be better?

(n) Ask the store manager how the profitability of space is evaluated (e.g., profit per square foot). Is there a better approach?

(o) Ask the store manager how space is assigned to merchandise. Critically evaluate the answer.

(p) Ask the store manager if planograms are used. If so, try to determine what factors are considered when putting together a planogram.

(q) Are departments in the most appropriate locations? Would you move any departments?

(r) What method(s) has the retailer used to organize merchandise? Is this the best way? Suggest any appropriate changes.

2. **INTERNET EXERCISE** Go to the home page of CoolHunters (www.thecoolhunter.net). Look at examples posted in their retail subpage. How can this information of latest trends assist with store layout, design, and visual merchandising?

3. **INTERNET EXERCISE** VMSD is the leading resource for retail designers and store display professionals, serving the retail industry since 1869 (then called Display World). Go to its web page at http://vmsd.com, and develop a list of three or four items that describe the latest trends in visual merchandising.

4. **INTERNET EXERCISE** Go to the home page of Envirosell (www.envirosell.com). How does this marketing research consulting firm support retailers by collecting consumer information to assist with store layout, design, and visual merchandising?

DISCUSSION QUESTIONS AND PROBLEMS

1. One of the fastest-growing sectors of the population is the over-60 age group. Customers in this group may have limitations in their vision, hearing, and movement. How can retailers develop store designs with this population's needs in mind?

2. Assume you have been hired as a consultant to assess a local discount store's floor plan and space productivity. Look back at Chapter 6 and decide which analytical tools and ratios you would use to assess the situation.

3. What are the different types of design that can be used in a store layout? How does the layout impact the types of fixtures used to display merchandise? Describe why some stores are more suited for a particular type of layout than others.

4. A department store is building an addition. The merchandise manager for furniture is trying to convince the vice president to allot this new space to the furniture department. The merchandise manager for men's clothing is also trying to gain the space. What points should each manager use when presenting his or her rationale?

5. As an architect for retail space, you are responsible for Americans with Disabilities Act compliance. How would you make sure that a store's retail layout both meets accessibility requirements and enables the company to reach profitability objectives?

6. What are the advantages and disadvantages of offering virtual dressing rooms from the retailers' perspective?

7. Complete the following table by briefly describing how the different retail formats could use each of the areas listed to enhance the store's image and atmosphere.

Area	Drugstore	Clothing Store	Music Store	Restaurant
Entrance				
Walls				
Windows				
Merchandise displays				
Cash wrap				

8. Reread Retailing View 17.2, "Walmart Goes Green and Lowers Its Energy Costs." Which of the environmental practices discussed do you think will be implemented by other retailers? Explain your response.

9. Reread Retailing View 17.3, "A Hedonic Maze Filled with Utilitarian Products." What do you think about IKEA's layout? Does it provide them with a competitive edge? Explain your response.

10. How can signage and graphics help both customers and retailers? Consider the following types of retail formats that you likely have visited in the past: discount store, department store, office superstore, and card and gift store. Describe which retail formats have implemented the best practices for coordinating signs and graphics with each store's image and which formats should improve this aspect of their store layout, design, and visual merchandising.

SUGGESTED READINGS

Krishna, Aradhna (Ed.). *Sensory Marketing: Research on the Sensuality of Consumers*. New York: Routledge, 2009.

Bell, Judy, and Kate Ternus. *Silent Selling: Best Practices and Effective Strategies In Visual Merchandising*, 4th ed. New York: Fairchild Publication, 2011.

Law, Derry, Christina Wong, and Joanne Yip, "How Does Visual Merchandising Affect Consumer Affective Response?: An Intimate Apparel Experience." *European Journal of Marketing*, 46 no. 1/2 (2012), pp. 112–133.

Manganari, Emmanouela E., George J. Siomkos, and Adam P. Vrechopoulos. "Store Atmosphere in Web Retailing." *European Journal of Marketing* 43 (September 2010), pp. 1140–1153.

Nordfalt, Jens. *In-Store Marketing*, 2nd ed. Sweden: Forma Magazine, 2011.

Ortinau, David J., Barry J. Babin, and Jean-Charles Chebat. "Development of New Empirical Insights in Consumer–Retailer Relationships within Online and Offline Retail Environments: Introduction to the Special Issue." *Journal of Business Research*, available electronically 2011.

Pegler, Martin. *Store Presentation and Design*, 3rd ed. New York: RSD, 2010.

Pegler, Martin. *Visual Merchandising and Display*, 6th ed. New York: Fairchild Publication, 2012.

Sorensen, Herb. *Inside the Mind of the Shopper*. Upper Saddle River, NJ: Pearson Education, 2009.

Underhill, Paco. *Why We Buy: The Science of Shopping*, 3rd ed. New York: Simon and Schuster, 2009.

Valenzuela, Ana, Priya Raghubir, and Chrissy Mitakaki. "A Shelf Space Schemas: Myth or Reality?" *Journal of Business Research*, available online, 11 January 11, 2012.

Wang, Yong Jian, Michael S. Minor, and Jie Wei. "Aesthetics and the Online Shopping Environment: Understanding Consumer Responses." *Journal of Retailing*, 87 (March 2011), pp. 46–58.

Customer Service

EXECUTIVE BRIEFING
Elizabeth Hebeler, ROLE Manager,
Wyndham Worldwide

At Wyndham Worldwide, we don't serve customers, we serve guests. As a Resort Operations Leadership Experience (ROLE) manager, I focus on serving our guests with excellent customer service and creating vacation memories that will last a lifetime. Wyndham Worldwide is the world's largest hospitality company consisting of vacation ownership, hotels, and an international exchange network. Wyndham's customer service philosophy can be summed up in our motto, "Count on Me." At Wyndham, "Count on Me" means that our guests can count on us to be responsive to their needs, to be respectful in every way and to deliver a great experience.

Currently, I am a ROLE manager with Wyndham, which involves rotating through every single position the company offers on both the Wyndham Vacation Ownership and Worldmark sides of the company. After the program is complete, I will be serving as an assistant resort manager at one of our properties. Most recently, I served as the guest services supervisor for the team responsible for customer service in the presidential tower at Wyndham Bonnet Creek in Orlando, Florida. While completing my MS degree in management and BS degree in public relations at the University of Florida, I was able to have internships in guest services and housekeeping departments. As a

team manager, I have to extend the "Count on Me" philosophy to my teammates at work, as well as to our guests. Excellent guest service comes from having a knowledgeable, supportive, and content associate team. The resort world doesn't provide a 9-to-5 Monday through Friday job; but I look forward to every day because I know I will be facing new challenges and opportunities.

The presidential tower in Orlando consists of 300 units of various sizes and becomes home throughout the year to different VIP guests in the Wyndham family, including our presidential reserve owners, which is a new concept for Wyndham. Presidential reserve owners have access to special inventory reserved just for them. Additionally, there are special perks, including unit set up, unit inventory, special check-in, grocery services, chef services, and many others that can vary from resort to resort. To establish the high service level expected by these

CHAPTER 18

LEARNING OBJECTIVES

LO1 Identify how retailers can build a competitive advantage through customer service.

LO2 Explain how customers evaluate a retailer's customer service.

LO3 Indicate the activities a retailer can undertake to provide high-quality customer service.

LO4 Articulate retailers' service failure strategies.

guests, I worked for months putting together a team of seven associates and creating a guide on developing strong relationships with our guests.

We had one particular guest stay with us during the peak time of summer who I will never forget. He came alone, had just lost his wife, and had various health problems. The entire team made sure he ate regularly and had his medical supplies delivered. One of our bellmen, Tim, and I gave him a property tour and brought him to the pool for 15 minutes one day. We could see instantly how much meaning this gave to his experience with us at Wyndham. Wyndham was more than just a place to stay for him, it was a second home where he could recover and be taken care of—a place where associates were more like family and really cared about him as a person, where they would go above and beyond to do anything they could to take care of him. At Wyndham, we truly believe that hospitality starts when you put someone else's needs before you own.

S uppose you are surfing the Internet for a digital camera. You start at Amazon.com, where you type in the name of the specific brand and model number you want. The website provides you a list of different retailers that sell the product, including Amazon, and their quoted prices. You can also read other consumers' reviews, as well as excerpts of reviews by critics. If you have already signed in to your Amazon account, you can simply choose a retailer and have the purchase charged to your saved credit card number and sent to your preset shipping address with a single click.

But perhaps instead of starting at Amazon, you visit Best Buy's website, www. bestbuy.com. You can go through similar steps to find prices and place an order for a digital camera, but you find specifications for different cameras as well. You can

REFACT

To better understand customer service and customer needs, every Amazon employee, including the CEO Jeff Bezos, spends two days every two years answering service calls.[1]

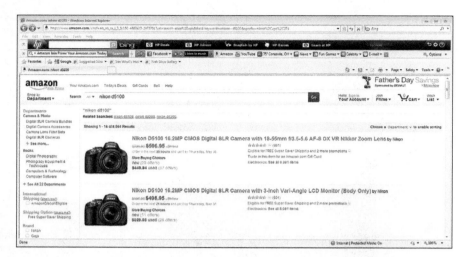

Shopping at Amazon is very easy.

then go to a store to see the other cameras, get additional information about them from a sales associate, and look at accessories, such as a carrying case and additional memory units. Thus, Best Buy's multichannel offering is providing some valuable services to you—services that you cannot get from Amazon. However, Amazon's prices might be better, and it enables you to receive your purchase without ever leaving your home. If you're a Prime customer, you would obtain the service benefit of free two-day shipping.

Customer service is the set of activities and programs undertaken by retailers to make the shopping experience more rewarding. These activities increase the value customers receive from the merchandise and services they purchase. Some of these services are provided by store and call-center employees interacting directly with customers, while others are provided by the design of the retailer's store and/or website.

The next sections discuss retailers' opportunities to develop strategic advantages through customer service, the nature and types of customer service provided, and how customers evaluate a retailer's customer service. Then we outline how retailers exploit these opportunities to build a competitive advantage by providing high-quality customer service.

STRATEGIC ADVANTAGE THROUGH CUSTOMER SERVICE

LO1

Identify how retailers can build a competitive advantage through customer service.

Many stores differentiate their retail offerings, build customer loyalty, and develop sustainable competitive advantages by providing excellent customer service. Customer service provides a strategic advantage because good service can be important to customers, difficult for competitors to duplicate, keeps customers returning to a retailer, and generates positive word-of-mouth communication, which attracts new customers.[2] Unfortunately, the flip side is also true: Poor service by retailers increases negative word of mouth in addition to reducing future visits. Customers are turned off by rude and ill-informed retail service personnel, frustrated by a lack of available personnel to answer their queries, and irritated by website inadequacies such as poor navigation or the lack of human interaction.[3]

Perceptions of customer service are often developed through interactions with frontline employees. Managing these employees to provide consistent good service is challenging. Every department store retailer envies the customer service provided by Nordstrom, but Nordstrom spent years developing a strong customer service culture—and it will take a competitor even longer to duplicate that culture.

EXHIBIT 18.1
Services Offered by Retailers

Acceptance of credit cards	Free shipping
Alterations of merchandise	Gift wrapping and notes
Assembly of merchandise	Information on product availability in a specific store
ATM terminals	Layaway plans
Blogs	Online chat
Bridal registry	Online customization
Check cashing	Parking
Child care facilities	Personal assistance in selecting merchandise
Coat checks	Personal shoppers
Credit	Repair services
Customer reviews	Restrooms
Delivery to home or work	Return privileges
Demonstrations of merchandise	Shipping to store or home address
Display of merchandise	Shopping carts
Dressing rooms	Signage to locate and identify merchandise
Easy returns to bricks-and-mortar location or online	Special orders
Extended store hours	Valet parking
Facilities for shoppers with special needs (physically handicapped)	Warranties

Exhibit 18–1 lists some of the services provided by retailers. Most of these services furnish information about the retailer's offering and make it easier for customers to locate and buy its products and services. Services such as alterations and assembly of merchandise actually adapt the merchandise to fit the needs of specific customers.

All employees of a retail firm and all elements of the retailing mix can provide services that increase the value of merchandise to customers. For example, employees in the distribution center contribute to customer service by making sure the merchandise is in stock at the retailer's stores. The employees who choose store locations and design their interiors contribute by increasing customer convenience, both in terms of getting to the store and finding merchandise once they are in the store.

Providing high-quality service is difficult for retailers. Automated manufacturing makes the quality of most merchandise consistent from item to item. For example, all Nikon CoolPix cameras typically perform alike. But the quality of retail service can vary dramatically from store to store and from sales associate to sales associate within a store. For retailers, it becomes difficult to control the performance of employees who provide service because they are not machines that can be programmed. Sales associates have good days and bad days and, thus, may provide great service to one customer and poor service to the next.

In addition, most services provided by retailers are intangible. Customers cannot see or feel services. Apparel can be held and examined, unlike the assistance provided by a sales associate or an electronic agent. Intangibility makes it hard to provide and maintain high-quality service because retailers cannot easily measure or check the service before it gets delivered to customers.

The challenge of providing consistent, high-quality service offers an opportunity for retailers to develop a sustainable competitive advantage. For example, L.L. Bean has devoted considerable time and effort to developing an organizational culture that stimulates and supports excellent customer service. Competing sporting goods stores would love to offer the same level of service but find it hard to match L.L. Bean's performance—an asset that L.L. Bean has built over the past 75 years. Exhibit 18–2 lists several retailers, ranked according to their level of customer service.

REFACT

Shopping carts, a basic form of customer service, were first introduced in 1937 in a Humpty Dumpty store in Oklahoma City.[4]

One of the services offered by most brick-and-mortar retailers is the opportunity to try out the merchandise.

EXHIBIT 18–2
Top 10 Retailers for Customer Service

Ranking	2010	2011
1.	Zappos	Amazon.com
2.	Amazon.com	L.L. Bean
3.	L.L. Bean	Zappos
4.	Overstock.com	Overstock.com
5.	Lands' End	QVC
6.	JCPenney	Kohl's
7.	Kohl's	Lands' End
8.	QVC	JCPenney
9.	Nordstrom	Newegg
10.	Newegg	Nordstrom

Source: NRF Foundation/American Express, "Consumer Choice Awards," www.nrffoundation.com/content/customers-choice-awards.

Customer Service Approaches

To develop a sustainable customer service advantage, retailers offer a combination of personalized and standardized services. **Personalized service** requires that service providers tailor their services to meet each customer's personal needs.[5] Successful implementation of the personalized service relies on sales associates or the "personalization" offered by the retailer's electronic channel.[6] **Standardized service** is based on establishing a set of rules and procedures for providing high-quality service and ensuring that they get implemented consistently. The effectiveness of standardized services relies mainly on the quality of the retailer's policy, procedures, and store, as well as its website design and layout.

Personalized Service   Personalized customer service is less consistent than standardized service. The delivery of personalized service depends on the judgment and capabilities of each service provider. Some service providers are better than others, and even the best service providers can have a bad day. In addition, providing consistent, high-quality personalized service is costly because well-trained service providers or sophisticated computer software generally are needed to implement the service.[7]

Fifty years ago, managers and employees in local stores knew their customers personally and offered recommendations of products that they thought their customers would like. This personal touch has all but disappeared with the growth of national chains that emphasize self-service and lower costs. However, recommendation engines coupled with a database of customer transactions are providing automated personalization.

The Internet has made vast amounts of information on products and retailers available to consumers, and recommendation engines are a response to this information overload. At the appropriate moment—generally when you're about to make a retail purchase—the engine subtly makes a product suggestion. Amazon was the pioneer of automated recommendations, but the service has now been adopted by other retailers. For example, the Wine.com site offers customized pages for customers. Once they log into the site, customers receive recommendations based on their past purchases and their interests.[8]

Standardized Service   Retailers standardize the service they offer to increase the consistency of the service quality and avoid the costs of paying the more skilled service providers required to effectively personalize customer services. For example, McDonald's and other quick-service restaurants develop and strictly enforce a set of policies and procedures to provide an acceptable, consistent service quality. The food may not be considered gourmet, but it is consistently served in a timely manner at a relatively low cost throughout the world.

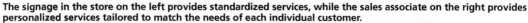

The signage in the store on the left provides standardized services, while the sales associate on the right provides personalized services tailored to match the needs of each individual customer.

IKEA effectively uses standardized services through its signage, information on displays, and merchandise.

REFACT

IKEA stores contain more than 9,500 home furnishing items.[9]

Store or website designs and layout also play important roles in the delivery of standardized service. In some situations, customers do not want to use the services employees provide. They know what they want to buy, and their objective is to find it in the store or on the website and buy it quickly. In these situations, retailers offer good service by simply providing a layout and signs that enable customers to locate merchandise easily, having relevant information on display, and minimizing the time required to make a purchase.

IKEA uses a standardized, self-service approach with some unique elements to attract customers who expect the traditional personalized approach commonly used in furniture retailing. Every product available is displayed in more than 70 roomlike settings throughout the 150,000-square-foot warehouse stores. Customers don't need a decorator to help them picture how the furniture will go together. Although IKEA uses a "customers do it themselves" approach, it also offers some services that traditional furniture stores do not, such as in-store child care centers, restaurants serving fast food, and extensive information and displays about the quality of the furniture. In many stores, sales associates use tablets with specially designed applications to enhance their interactions with customers. Yet, IKEA still maintains its self-service focus: A new app enables users to browse through IKEA products on their smartphones, download a store map, and locate items on their shopping list in the store.[10]

Use of Service Approaches   As we discussed in Chapter 4, the buying process that consumers go through depends on the consumers' past experiences and the risk associated with the purchase decision. Thus, the level of customer service and personalized information desired from sales associates varies for different buying situations. Most consumers have significant knowledge and experience shopping for most products sold by supermarkets, convenience stores, and general merchandise retailers. Thus, these retailers tend to emphasize standardized service rather than the more costly and informative personalized service. For example, more than two-thirds of grocery retailers in the United States now use self-checkout lines.[11]

In the two decades since the first self-scanner made an appearance in a grocery store, such do-it-yourself technology has proliferated not only in supermarket checkout aisles but also throughout libraries and pharmacies and at airports. Before long, self-checkout will go mobile, with smartphone apps that allow customers to scan the bar code on their purchases and enter credit card information, without standing in line. To leave the store, customers need only show the itemized receipt displayed on their phone to an employee.[12]

Another checkout option uses a store-issued, handheld scanning unit while shopping. The customers pay at either a staffed or a self-checkout register. Such technology is attractive to retailers because it reduces the need for employees to staff registers, and it improves customer satisfaction by reducing checkout times.[13]

The buying process might differ even for the same customer patronizing the same retailer. For example, a Best Buy customer may seek personalized service when buying a home entertainment system and standardized service when buying CDs. Thus, many retailers provide different types of service for different types of merchandise sold in different areas of a store. Retailing View 18.1 describes how retailers are learning when to provide customer service and when to let their customers experiment and experience the products with minimal interference.

RETAILING VIEW   Self-Service Cosmetics Counters for Those Who
Want to Do It Themselves   18.1

Sephora employees and customers can use an in-store iPad to look up cosmetic recommendations as well as a customer's prior purchases.

The high-end cosmetics market is both large—worth approximately $8.7 billion according to recent estimates—and growing. To capture more share from this lucrative segment, department store cosmetic counters are following the lead of Sephora, a firm that has changed the way many people purchase cosmetics.

Sephora stocks approximately 15,000 SKUs and more than 200 brands, including its own, private-label brand. Merchandise is grouped by product category, with the brands displayed alphabetically so customers can locate them easily. Customers are free to shop and experiment on their own, and sampling is encouraged. An iPad on the counter also allows them to search for new options and ideas. These in-store iPads automatically launch a customized Sephora application. Thus, a visitor to the cosmetics stores can immediately look up the last lipstick she bought, even if she can't recall the name of the color. She also can read about whether a lotion she is considering buying has any allergy warnings or negative reviews from other customers. This low-key, self-service environment has prompted many customers to spend a lot more time shopping in its stores. Also, these recommendation services provide an effective competitive advantage because the customer database used to develop the recommendations is proprietary in nature.

In contrast, the cosmetics counters in most department stores are staffed by salespeople who immediately swoop down on any customers passing by, offering a makeover, skin analysis, or in-depth discussion on cosmetic trends. When Clinique realized that more than one-quarter of shoppers stopped by its counters to grab a refill of a product they already used, it also recognized that it might

be alienating its most loyal return customers. Thus, it has embraced the notion of self-service for its white-coated sales associates.

The change in Clinique's strategy includes a large display of "Grab and Go" products—moisturizers, soaps, and clarifying lotions that many buyers buy repeatedly and without any need for searching other options. Other products, such as foundation, eye shadow, mascara, and lipstick, are stocked in shelves on the front side of the counter so that customers can sample them on their own. Prices are displayed prominently, not kept behind the counter. There are large jars of cotton swabs and tissues at hand, in case a new color just doesn't work. And of course, an iPad is available for people to list their skincare or makeup concerns and get recommendations.

Not to be outdone, Macy's is testing the idea of eliminating the intrusion of salespeople altogether. The retailer currently is testing a cosmetics kiosk, Beauty Spot, that provides all the necessary details about any makeup, cleanser, beauty tool, or cosmetic accessory a customer might want. The only time the sales associate shows up is when it is time to check out.

Sources: Meghan Kelly, "Makeup Retailer Sephora Launches iPad Program," *Venture Beat*, March 13, 2012; Lev Grossman, "If You Liked This . . . ," *Time*, June 7, 2010, p. 44; Elizabeth Holmes, "Leave Me Alone, I'm Shopping," *The Wall Street Journal*, June 28, 2012; "Macy's Adopts New Technologies in Stores and Online," *Los Angeles Times*, September 13, 2011; and Taffy Brodesser-Akner "'Can I Help You?' Irks the Web-Savvy Customer," *The New York Times*, January 12, 2012.

DISCUSSION QUESTION

Is the low-key self-service cosmetic approach likely to result in greater time being spent trying out cosmetics and ultimately more sales?

REFACT

The name *Sephora* is derived from the Greek word for beauty, "sephos," and the name of Moses' beautiful wife, Zipporah, described in the Book of Exodus.[14]

In the following section, we discuss how customers evaluate the quality of customer service and what retailers can do to alter the actual and perceived levels of customer service.

CUSTOMER EVALUATIONS OF SERVICE QUALITY

LO2

Explain how customers evaluate a retailer's customer service.

When customers evaluate customer service, they compare their perceptions of the service they receive with their expectations. Customers are satisfied when the perceived service meets or exceeds their expectations. They are dissatisfied when they feel that the service falls below their expectations.

So, when retailers attempt to differentiate their offerings by developing a reputation for outstanding customer service, they need to consider both the perception of the actual service offered and the expectations of their customers.

Perceived Service

Customers' perceptions of a retailer's customer service depend on the actual service delivered. However, because services are intangible, it is difficult for customers to evaluate the service offered by retailers accurately. Customers are often influenced by the manner in which employees provide the service, not just the outcome.[15] Consider the following situation: A customer goes to return an electric toothbrush that is not working properly to a retailer with a no-questions-asked, money-back return policy. In one case, the employee asks the customer for a receipt, checks to see if the receipt shows that the toothbrush was bought from the retailer, examines the toothbrush to see if it really doesn't work properly, completes some paperwork while the customer is waiting, and finally gives the customer the amount paid for the toothbrush in cash. In a second case, the store employee simply asks the customer how much he paid and gives him a cash refund. The two cases have the same outcome: The customer gets a cash refund. But the customer might be dissatisfied in the first case because the employee appeared not to trust the customer and took too much time providing the refund. In most situations, employees have an important impact on the process of providing services and thus on the customer's eventual satisfaction with the services.

Five customer service characteristics that affect perceptions of service quality are reliability, assurance, tangibility, empathy, and responsiveness.[16] Nordstrom, a fashion specialty retailer, is renowned for its customer service. Let's look at how it addresses each of these five service characteristics.[17]

Reliability   **Reliability** is the ability to perform the service dependably and accurately, such as performing the service as promised or contracted or meeting promised delivery dates. To assure service reliability, new Nordstrom salespeople go through training and extensive mentoring by managers and seasoned salespeople. Employees are trained to give their customer the best service possible every time based on the cardinal rule: "Use good judgment in all situations."[18] Good judgment at Nordstrom involves such issues as the following: Always check with the alteration department before promising a pick-up date. Don't answer any questions you don't know the answer to. Check with someone if you don't know the answer. Inaccurate information only frustrates customers.

Assurance   **Assurance** is the knowledge and courtesy of employees and their ability to convey trust and confidence. Trust and confidence are particularly important at Nordstrom, where merchandise can be relatively expensive and customers rely on the good taste and fashion judgment of its sales associates. When a customer asks, "How do I look in this dress?" she doesn't always want to hear, "Great!" She wants a truthful answer that shows knowledge of the products and fashions, as well as an eye toward what is best for her. If the customer is sold something that, upon reflection, does not meet her needs or look good on her, Nordstrom may lose her as a customer forever. Thus, looking out for what is best for the customer is the best strategy for long-term customer retention.

Great customer service is always a priority at Nordstrom.

Tangibility   **Tangibility** is associated with the appearances of physical facilities, equipment, personnel, and communication materials. Nordstrom has always prided itself in providing a modern, but classic ambiance with wide unobstructed aisles. It maintains a consistent image throughout all the touch points with its customers including Nordsrom Rack, its catalogs, and other media like Facebook, Twitter, YouTube, and an array of fashion and photo-sharing sites.[19]

Empathy   **Empathy** refers to the caring, individualized attention provided to customers. Nordstrom attempts to hire people that are knowledgeable about fashion. But equally important, they must love helping others. Salespeople use a CRM software that tracks customer information such as preferences for brands and sizes and describes what was purchased in the past. Sales representatives often proactively call customers to alert them to new shipments of their favorite brands. If a customer's favored salesperson is unavailable when she comes in, another salesperson can access her record to better provide that famous individualized attention.

Responsiveness   **Responsiveness** means to provide customer service personnel and sales associates that really want to help customers and provide prompt service. Unlike so many retailers during recessionary times, Nordstrom has not cut back on customer service and sales personnel. Customers don't have to go looking for salespeople to ring up a sale. Nor do salespeople disappear when a customer appears with a bag full of returns. Personnel are always eager to help at Nordstrom.

One way to promptly solve service issues is to empower its employees. For example, a Nordstrom shoe sales associate decided to break up two pairs of shoes, one a size 10 and the other a size 10½, to sell a hard-to-fit customer. Although the other two shoes were unsalable and therefore made for an unprofitable sale, the customer purchased five other pairs that day and became a loyal Nordstrom customer as a result. Empowering service providers with a rule like "Use your best judgment" might cause chaos at some stores. At Nordstrom, however, department managers avoid abuses by coaching and training salespeople to understand what "Use your best judgment" means.

Role of Expectations

In addition to the perceptions of the actual service delivered, expectations affect the judgment of service quality. Customer expectations are based on a customer's knowledge and experiences. For example, on the basis of past experiences, customers

REFACT

Organizations that effectively meet customers' expectations spend only 10 percent of their operating budget fixing issues related to poor customer service, whereas ineffective organizations can spend up to 40 percent of their operating budget doing so.[21]

have different expectations for the quality of service offered by different types of retailers. Customers expect a traditional supermarket to provide convenient parking, be open from early morning to late evening, have an intuitive layout, position and display products so they can be easily found, and offer a fast and pleasant checkout experience. They do not expect the supermarket to have store employees stationed in the aisle to offer information about groceries or show them how to prepare meals. When these unexpected services are offered, and the services are important to them, then customers are delighted—the retailer has significantly exceeded their expectations.[20] However, when the same customers shop in a specialty food store like Whole Foods Market, they expect the store to have knowledgeable employees who can provide expert information and courteous assistance.

Some examples of unexpected positive service experiences are:

- A restaurant that sends customers who have had too much to drink home in a taxi and then delivers their cars in the morning.
- A jewelry store that cleans customers' jewelry and replaces batteries in watches for free.
- A men's store that sews numbered tags on each garment so that the customer will know what goes together.

Customer service expectations also vary around the world.[22] Although Germany's manufacturing capability is world-renowned, its poor customer service is also well known. People wait years to have telephone service installed. Many restaurants do not accept credit cards, and customers who walk into stores near closing time

Retailers are enhancing their service levels in Germany.

often receive rude stares. Customers typically have to bag merchandise they buy themselves. Because Germans are unaccustomed to good service, they do not demand it. But as retailing becomes global and new foreign competitors enter, German retailers are becoming more concerned about how they serve their customers.

In contrast, the Japanese expect excellent customer service from their higher-end stores. In the United States, it's said that "the customer is always right." In Japan, the equivalent expression is *okyakusama wa kamisama desu,* "the customer is God." When customers come back to a store to return merchandise, they are dealt with even more cordially than when their original purchases were made. Customer satisfaction simply is not negotiable, and customers are never wrong. Even if a customer misused the product, the retailer generally acts as if it was responsible for not telling the customer how to use it properly. The first employee in the store who hears about the problem must take full responsibility for dealing with the customer, even if the problem involved another department.[23]

Another trend that spans cultures is the way technology is dramatically changing customer expectations. Customers expect to be able to interact with companies through automated voice response systems and place orders and check on delivery status through the Internet. Retailers that do not offer these multichannel services are not favorably viewed. Customers still expect good service, which is defined by companies' responsiveness, flexibility, dependability, ease of access, apologies, or compensation when necessary. But now they expect this level of service even when people are not involved.[24] The activities that retailers take to close the gap between customer expectations and perceptions of the actual service delivered are discussed in the following sections.

THE GAPS MODEL FOR IMPROVING RETAIL CUSTOMER SERVICE QUALITY

When the customer's perception of the service delivered by a retailer fails to meet the customer's expectations, a **service gap** results. Exhibit 18–3 illustrates four gaps that contribute to the service gap:

LO3

Indicate the activities a retailer can undertake to provide high-quality customer service.

1. The **knowledge gap** reflects the difference between customers' expectations and the retailer's perception of those customer expectations. Retailers can close this gap by developing a better understanding of customer expectations and perceptions.

2. The **standards gap** pertains to the difference between the retailer's knowledge of customers' perceptions and expectations and the service standards it sets. By setting appropriate service standards and measuring service performance, retailers can close this gap.

3. The **delivery gap** is the difference between the retailer's service standards and the actual service it provides to customers. This gap can be reduced by getting employees to meet or exceed service standards through training and/or appropriate incentives.

4. The **communication gap** is the difference between the actual service provided to customers and the service that the retailer's promotion program promises. When retailers are more realistic about the services they can provide, customer expectations can be managed effectively to close this gap.[25]

Knowing What Customers Want: The Knowledge Gap

The first step in providing good service is knowing what customers want, need, and expect and then using this information to improve customer service.[26]

EXHIBIT 18.3   Gaps Model for Improving Retail Service Quality

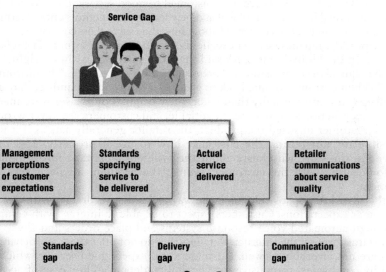

When retailers lack this information, they can make poor decisions. For example, a supermarket might hire extra people to make sure the shelves are stocked and organized so that customers will find what they want. But the supermarket's service perceptions may not improve because the supermarket did not realize that its customers were most concerned about waiting in the checkout line. From the customer's perspective, the supermarket's service would improve if the extra employees were used to open more checkout lines rather than to stock shelves.

Retailers can reduce the knowledge gap and develop a better understanding of customer expectations by undertaking customer research, increasing interactions between retail managers and customers, and improving communication between managers and the employees who provide customer service.[27] Retailers use a variety of approaches for assessing customer perceptions and expectations of customer service.

Social Media   Retailers can learn a lot about their customer expectations and perceptions of their service quality by monitoring what they say about the retailer's offering and the offerings of competitors on their social networks, blogs, review sites, and what they are posting on sites like YouTube and Flickr. Numerous retailers have started to use a technique known as **sentiment analysis** to assess the favorableness (or lack of favorableness) in their customers' sentiments by monitoring these social media. Scouring millions of sites with sentiment analysis techniques provides new insights into what consumers really think. Retailers plugged into this real-time information can become more nimble, allowing for quick changes, such as product rollouts, new advertising campaigns, or responses to customer complaints. For instance, retailers like GNC and Crocs use the latest tools to listen for customers'

REFACT

Three million *new* blogs are created each month.[28]

questions or concerns. They identify negative consumer sentiment and then offer customers a chance to try a related product or even receive store credit to encourage customer retention. Reacting to attitudes uncovered in sentiment analysis allows companies to counteract negative opinions, maybe influence those perceptions, and perhaps win customer loyalty.[29]

Surveys, Panels, and Contests Many retailers survey customers immediately after a retail transaction has occurred. For example, airlines, automobile dealers, hotels, and restaurants give customers surveys, encourage them to take an online survey, or call them on the phone to ask them questions about their service experience, such as how helpful, friendly, and professional the employees were.

Although some retailers use surveys as just described, others interview panels of 10 to 15 customers to gain insights into expectations and perceptions. For example, some store managers meet once a month for an hour with a select group of customers who are asked to provide information about their experiences in the store and offer suggestions for improving service.

When Domino's undertook a massive revamp of its image, it focused largely on customer feedback. Pizza connoisseurs had long complained about its cardboard crust and use of canned tomatoes. The delivery chain improved its quality, but to enhance people's expectations, it needed to find out if customers really thought its food was better. Rather than traditional surveys, Domino's sponsored a photo contest: Take a picture of your pizza right after it arrives and upload it to a website. Great-looking food shots helped convince others that Domino's was providing a quality product. Problematic shots helped Domino's identify service concerns. And if customers' pictures ultimately appeared in ads, they earned cash prizes.[30]

Interact with Customers, Either Directly or through Observation Owner-managers of small retail firms typically have daily contact with their customers and get accurate, firsthand information about them. Some managers go through the receipts from each day and

Sentiment analysis is allowing Crocs to better serve its customers.

Domino's has revamped its image—both the food and its service.

select customers who have made particularly large or small purchases. They call these customers and ask them what they liked or did not like about the store. These customer contacts not only provide information but also indicate the retailer's interest in providing good service. Because the responses can be linked to a specific encounter, they also provide a method for rewarding employees who provide good service and correcting those who exhibit poor performance.

In large retail firms, managers often learn about customers through reports, so they may miss the rich information provided by direct contact with customers. Disney offers a stellar example of a large firm that constantly interacts with customers to learn about them and their preferences. For example, through careful observation, Disney learned that visitors to its parks will carry a piece of trash approximately 27 paces before dropping it on the ground. So the entertainment conglomerate made sure to place trash receptacles every 27 paces throughout its parks. In its consulting with other service providers, Disney has suggested ways they can interact better, too.[31]

Customer Complaints   Complaints allow retailers to interact with their customers and acquire detailed information about their service and merchandise. Handling complaints is an inexpensive means to isolate and correct service problems.[32] Catalog and Internet retailer L.L. Bean keeps track of all complaints and reasons for returned merchandise. These complaints and returns are summarized daily and given to customer service representatives so that they can improve their service. The information is also used by buyers to improve vendor merchandise.

REFACT

Dissatisfied customers tell 9 to 15 people they know in person.[33]

Although customer complaints can provide useful information, retailers cannot rely solely on this source of market information. Dissatisfied customers typically did not complain, though this tendency is changing as customers turn to blogs, review sites (e.g., Yelp), retailers' own online review systems, and customer service messaging systems more frequently.[34] These methods of interacting with retailers can be useful, because they tend to feature very frank comments, compared with information gathered through more traditional research methods.[35]

Feedback from Store Employees   Salespeople and other employees in regular contact with customers often have a good understanding of customer service expectations and problems. This information can improve service quality only if the employees are encouraged to communicate their experiences to high-level managers who can act on it.[36]

Using Customer Research   Collecting information about customer expectations and perceptions is not enough. The knowledge gap diminishes only when retailers use this information to improve service. For example, store managers need to review the suggestions and comments made by customers daily, summarize the information, and distribute it to service providers and managers.

Feedback on service performance needs to be provided to employees in a timely manner. Reporting the July service performance in December makes it hard for employees to reflect on the reason for the reported performance. Finally, feedback must be prominently presented so that service providers are aware of their performance. For example, at Marriott, front-desk personnel's performance feedback is displayed behind the front desk, while restaurant personnel's performance feedback is displayed behind the door to the kitchen. The next section reviews several approaches for reducing the service standards gap.

Setting Service Standards: The Standards Gap

After retailers gather information about customer service expectations and perceptions, the next step is to use this information to set standards and develop systems for delivering high-quality service. Service standards should be based on

The Ritz-Carlton clearly outlines its service standards to its employees.

customers' perceptions rather than internal operations. For example, a supermarket chain might set an operations standard of a warehouse delivery every day to each store. But frequent warehouse deliveries may not result in more merchandise on the shelves and therefore may not improve customers' impressions of their shopping experience. To close the standards gap, retailers need to (1) commit their firms to providing high-quality service, (2) define the role of service providers, (3) set service goals, and (4) measure service performance.

Commitment to Service Quality   Service excellence is achieved only when top management provides leadership and demonstrates commitment. Top management must be willing to accept the temporary difficulties and even the increased costs associated with improving service quality. This commitment needs to be demonstrated to the employees charged with providing the service.

Top management's commitment sets service quality standards, but store managers are the key to achieving those standards. Store managers must see that their efforts to provide service quality are noticed and rewarded. Providing incentives based on service quality makes service an important personal goal, so rather than bonuses based only on store sales and profit, part of store managers' bonuses should be determined by the level of service provided.[37] For example, some retailers use the results of customer satisfaction studies to help determine bonuses.

Defining the Role of Service Providers   Managers can tell service providers that they need to provide excellent service but not clearly indicate what excellent service means. Without a clear definition of the retailer's expectations, service providers are directionless.

The Ritz-Carlton Hotel Company, winner of multiple Malcolm Baldrige National Quality Awards, has its "Gold Standards" printed on a wallet-size card carried by all employees. The card contains the hotel's motto ("We Are Ladies and Gentlemen Serving Ladies and Gentlemen"), the three steps for high-quality service (warm and sincere greeting, anticipation of and compliance with guests' needs, and fond farewell), and 12 basic rules for Ritz-Carlton employees, including "I build strong relationships and create Ritz-Carlton guests for life" (No. 1) and "I am proud of my professional appearance, language, and behavior" (No. 10).[38]

The golden rules for Zappos are a little different, though the goal of excellent customer service is the same, as Retailing View 18.2 reveals.

18.2   RETAILING VIEW   Zappos Speaks with One Voice

How can a service firm ensure that employee–customer interactions consistently meet, or exceed, the company's service standards? It's a simple question, but only a few companies have the answer. Zappos, the Las Vegas–based online clothing and shoe retailer owned by Amazon, is one of them. Zappos may sell apparel, but it really has built its business on its superb service. The company's core values stress that customer satisfaction is more important than cost cutting; that message permeates every single aspect of its operations. The goal is to "wow" each customer in every interaction.

Instilling such values in every worker begins with the interview process. Applicants undergo separate interviews for experience and fit within the company culture. During training, which lasts up to five weeks, all new employees are required to work in the call center. Anyone who thinks the assignment is beneath them is paid for his or her time and shown the door. Trainees are not given a script or a time limit for calls. Instead, during training and once on the job, workers are urged to creatively solve problems, even if customer satisfaction means doing something a little "weird," like buying shoes from a competing retailer for a customer in distress—and even footing the bill for their delivery. That approach was totally consistent with Zappos' core values, which suggest that a little "weird-ness" may be just the right approach if it helps solve a customer problem. And of course, the company doesn't mind the "wow" stories that such efforts generate for customers to share with all their friends.

Zappos' shopping procedures are also designed to please. Customers are encouraged to order multiple sizes and colors of an item, so they can touch, feel, and try on prospective purchases. Returned goods ship free for up to a year. And Zappos likes to impress customers with speedy delivery, so it ships items faster than its website indicates. Good customers often get upgraded to next- or second-day air shipping at no extra cost. Employees who meet Zappos' unconventional customer service standards are rewarded. Its most common salaried job, fulfillment center process manager, pays more than $47,500 a year, and the company is ranked 11th among the country's best places to work.

Sources: Armando Roggio, "The Zappos Effect: 5 Great Customer Service Ideas for Smaller Businesses," *Practical Ecommerce*, www.practicalecommerce.com/articles/2662-The-Zappos-Effect-5-Great-Customer-Service-Ideas-for-Smaller-Businesses; Janine Popick, "Zappos: A Great Example of Exceeding Expectations," *Vertical Response*, http://blog.verticalresponse.com/vertical response_blog/2011/08/zappos-email.html; and Aida Ahmed, "Zappos Ranks No. 11 on List of Best Companies to Work For," *VegasInc*, January 19, 2012.

DISCUSSION QUESTION

Why is Zappos one of the top 10 retailers for customer service?

Setting Service Goals   To deliver consistent, high-quality service, retailers need to establish goals or standards to guide employees. These goals should be based on their beliefs about the proper operation of the business rather than the customers' needs and expectations. For example, a retailer might set a goal that all monthly bills are to be mailed five days before the end of the month. This goal reduces the retailer's accounts receivable but offers no benefit to customers. Research undertaken by American Express showed that customer evaluations of its service were based on perceptions of timeliness, accuracy, and responsiveness. Management then established goals (e.g., responding to all questions about bills within 24 hours) related to these customer-based criteria.

Employees are motivated to achieve service goals when the goals are specific, measurable, and participatory in the sense that the employees participated in setting them. Vague goals—such as "Approach customers when they enter the selling area" or "Respond to e-mails as soon as possible"—don't fully specify what employees should do, nor do they offer an opportunity to assess employee performance. Better goals would be "All customers should be approached by a salesperson within 30 seconds after entering a selling area" or "All e-mails should be responded to within three hours." These goals are both specific and measurable. Retailing View 18.3 considers the problems in setting standards for the time customers wait to be served.

Employee participation in setting service standards leads to better understanding and greater acceptance of the goals. Store employees resent and resist goals arbitrarily imposed on them by management. See Chapter 16 for more about goal setting.

Measuring Service Performance   Retailers need to assess service quality continuously to ensure that goals will be achieved.[39] Many retailers conduct periodic customer surveys to assess service quality. Retailers also use **mystery shoppers** to assess their service quality. These professional shoppers visit stores to assess the

RETAILING VIEW   The Waiting Game

Many retailers with multiple checkout lanes in their stores set standards to reduce the time that customer have to wait in line. For example, a retailer might have a policy that a new checkout lane should be opened when more than three people are waiting at each of the open lanes.

While Americans spend relatively little time in queues, they will often leave a store and not patronize the retailer in the future if they feel the wait to check out or talk to a sales associate is too long or unjust. The simplest way to reduce wait time is also the most costly: adding more employees and making them more efficient. But many retailers question the benefit of adding employees to reduce wait times because customer perceptions of wait times are inaccurate and are affected by the waiting context. Research has found that customers overestimate the time they wait in line by as much as 50 percent and that the estimates are affected by store atmospherics such as a pleasant aroma.

From an operational perspective, the fastest way to process customers is to create a single line of customers and have the person in front go to the next open cash register—the system used at airports and occasionally in fast-food restaurants and banks. In addition to reducing the overall wait time, this approach increases perceived fairness and customer satisfaction because it ensures that customers are served in the order of their arrival.

Customers' satisfaction decreases if they have to wait in checkout lines too long or if they feel others who arrived later are checked out before them.

Supermarkets have been one of the last major service industry holdouts in the United States that do not offer single, serpentine lines feeding multiple checkout clerks. That status is changing slowly though, as chains such as Whole Foods and Kroger have experimented such a layout. Kroger also has installed a new system that counts customers entering the store, estimates how many will finish their shopping in, say, a half-hour, and then opens an appropriate number of checkout lines at that time.

Other supermarkets establish express lanes for shoppers with few items so that they don't have to wait behind customers checking out with large baskets of items. However, this practice has the perverse effect of treating the best customers the worst. The Stop & Shop grocery chain's Scan It! app lets shoppers use their smartphones to scan price codes and bag their own groceries as they move through stores. But as one industry observer warned, "At the end of the day, nothing beats having plenty of registers and staffing them right."

Sources: Maria Halkias, "Supermarket Checkout Still Stuck in the Past," *Los Angeles Times*, March 28, 2012; Carl Bialik, "Justice—Wait for It—On the Checkout Line," *The Wall Street Journal*, August 19, 2009; H. A. Eiselt and C. L. Sandblom, "Waiting Line Models," in *Operations Research* (Berlin: Springer, 2010), pp. 379–394; Piyush Kumar, "The Competitive Impact of Service Process Improvement: Examining Customers' Waiting Experiences in Retail Markets," *Journal of Retailing* 81, no. 3 (2005), pp. 171–189.

REFACT

The place Americans most hate to wait is the Department of Motor Vehicles; the second-, third-, and fourth-worst places are those for registering at clinics or hospitals, checking in for flights at airports, and ordering at fast-food restaurants or delis.[40]

DISCUSSION QUESTION

What are different ways to reduce the wait time at checkouts?

service provided by store employees and the presentation of merchandise. Some retailers use their own employees as mystery shoppers, but most contract with an outside firm to provide the assessment.

The retailer typically informs salespeople that they have "been shopped" and provides feedback from the mystery shopper's report. Some retailers offer rewards to sales associates who receive high marks and schedule follow-up visits to sales associates who prompt low evaluations.

Meeting and Exceeding Service Standards: The Delivery Gap

To reduce the delivery gap and provide service that exceeds standards, retailers must give service providers the necessary information and training, empower employees to act in the customers' and firm's best interests, provide instrumental and emotional support, provide appropriate incentives, improve internal communications, and use technology.[41]

Give Information and Training Service providers need to know about the retailer's service standards and the merchandise it offers, as well as the customers' needs. With this information, employees can answer customers' questions and suggest products. This knowledge also instills confidence and a sense of competence, which is needed to overcome service problems.

Because Steve Jobs believed "Good artists copy; great artists steal," Apple stores have used the Ritz model to train its employees. Staffers in Apple stores are encouraged to greet and say farewell to customers warmly. They are taught to "own" each customer interaction, even if it is not their specific job. In addition, Apple personnel are encouraged to anticipate needs, even if the customer doesn't express them. A PC user who keeps stopping by the store might need some encouragement about how easily Apple will help him convert his files, for example.[42]

Service providers also need specific training in interpersonal skills. Dealing with customers is hard—particularly when they are upset or angry. All service providers, even those who work for retailers that provide excellent service, encounter dissatisfied customers. Through training, employees can learn to provide better service and cope with the stress caused by disgruntled customers. Specific service providers typically get designated to interact with and provide service to customers. However, all retail employees should be prepared to deal with customers.[43]

Empower Service Employees **Empowerment** means allowing employees at the firm's lowest levels to make important decisions regarding how service will be provided to customers. When the employees responsible for providing service are authorized to make important decisions, service quality improves.[45] When they are not, even the best employee winds up being stymied in his or her efforts to please the customer. In call centers, this problem seems particularly acute. A customer who calls in with a product complaint and encounters a polite, respectful,

REFACT

Ritz-Carlton personnel at the front desks of its hotels are empowered to issue unhappy customers up to $2,000 credit without asking a supervisor's approval.[44]

Apple personnel are trained to anticipate needs and be very well versed with the products.

professional service employee who lacks the authority to issue a refund or mail out a replacement is not a satisfied customer. In this case though, the fault is the company's, not the employee's.[46]

Nordstrom is well known for its employee empowerment. It provides an overall objective—satisfy customer needs—and then encourages employees to do whatever is necessary to achieve the objective. For example, a Nordstrom department manager bought 12 dozen pairs of hosiery from a competitor in the mall when her stock was depleted because the new shipment was delayed. Even though Nordstrom lost money on this hosiery, management applauded her actions to make sure customers found hosiery when they came to the store looking for it.

However, empowering service providers can be difficult.[47] Some employees prefer to have the appropriate behaviors clearly defined for them. They do not want to spend the time learning how to make decisions or assume the risks of making mistakes. For example, a bank found that when it empowered its tellers, the tellers were afraid to make decisions about large sums of money. The bank had to develop decision guideposts and rules until tellers felt more comfortable.

In some cases, the benefits of empowering service providers may not justify the costs. If a retailer uses a standardized service delivery approach like McDonald's, the cost of hiring, training, and supporting empowerment may not lead to consistent and superior service delivery. Also, studies have found that empowerment is not embraced by employees in different cultures. For example, employees in Latin America expect their managers to possess all the information needed to make good business decisions. The role of employees is not to make business decisions; their job is to carry out the decisions of managers.[48]

Provide Instrumental and Emotional Support   Service providers need to have **instrumental support** (appropriate systems and equipment) to deliver the service desired by customers. Customers in need of an oil change expect and get a quick turnaround at Jiffy Lube because the entire operation, including the service personnel, equipment, and layout of the building, is designed to get customer's vehicles in and out in a "jiffy."

In addition to needing instrumental support, service providers need emotional support from their coworkers and supervisors. **Emotional support** involves demonstrating a concern for the well-being of others. Dealing with customer problems and maintaining a smile in difficult and stressful situations can be psychologically demanding. Service providers need to maintain a supportive, understanding atmosphere and attitude to deal with these demands effectively.[49] When "The customer is always right" is a business mantra, service employees also tend to feel as if they have to accept the cliché that their job is to "grin and bear it." Instead, retail employers should recognize just how stressful customer interactions can be, as well as assess the resulting effects on their employees' morale and performance.[50] Companies use various methods to reduce the stress that their service employees experience. Physical activity often helps relieve stress, so many employers offer fitness clinics or yoga classes. To tend to emotional stressors more directly, other retailers install entertainment/media rooms or provide massages in stores. Companies also can offer coaching on how to deal with the abuse meted out by angry customers. For example, call-center employees are encouraged not to take insults personally, fix problems, avoid engaging in arguments, and try to find the root issues of callers' complaints.[51]

Provide Incentives   As discussed in Chapter 16, many retailers use incentives, like paying commissions on sales, to motivate employees.[52] If service personnel feel incentivized and satisfied with their rewards, they likely offer improved productivity. But commissions on sales also can decrease customer service and job satisfaction while motivating high-pressure selling, which leads to customer dissatisfaction. Therefore, incentives should aim to improve customer service more effectively. When American Express started training and incentivizing its sales staff to engage customers, it empowered them by eliminating sales scripts or time limits on calls. It also radically changed the compensation system. Incentive pay is now based on customer satisfaction feedback. The result was a 10 percent increase in customer spending on American Express products, as well as a 5 percent bump in revenue.[53]

Improve Internal Communications   When providing customer service, frontline service providers often must manage a conflict between customers' and their employer's needs.[54] For example, retailers expect their sales associates to encourage customers to make multiple purchases and buy more expensive items;[55] customers are looking for the best value choices that fit their needs. Sales associates, therefore, may be conflicted between meeting corporate and customer goals.

Retailers can reduce such conflicts by issuing clear guidelines and policies concerning service and explaining the rationale for these policies. For example, training should teach employees to apologize for a service failure, even if the failure was caused by someone else in the organization or was a result of something the customer did. It is difficult for many people to apologize for something that is not their fault. But if employees realize that an apology for a service failure can help retain the customer, they should also recognize that it is necessary and therefore apologize for any service failure.

Conflicts can also arise when retailers set goals that are inconsistent with the other behaviors expected from store employees. For example, as we discussed in Chapter 16, if salespeople are expected to provide customer service, they should be evaluated and compensated on the service they provide, not just the sales they make.

Finally, conflicts can arise between different areas of the firm. A men's specialty store known for its high levels of customer service has salespeople who promise rapid alterations and deliveries to please their customers. Unfortunately, the alterations department includes two elderly tailors who work at their own speed, regardless of the workload. From time to time, management must step in to temper the salespeople's promises and reallocate priorities for the tailors.

Use Technology   Retailers have been actively engaged in implementing a vast variety of technology tools in their stores and websites to help their customers.[56] These technologies include self-scan checkout stations, web-linked kiosks, service personnel equipped with iPads, various types of apps, digital displays, online agents,

QR codes on store shelves enable customers to learn about products before they buy.

and QR codes. These technologies help customers find and learn more about products and services offered. They also enable faster and more efficient payment. For the service personnel, these technologies improve their ability to offer good service to customers, including up-to-date product information and access to merchandise available from an online channel if it is not in stock at the store.[57]

For example, Massachusetts-based Zoots dry cleaners does not want to mimic its competitors, which are open from 8:00 a.m. to 6:00 p.m.—right when most customers are at work. So it supports 24/7 pickup and drop-off with an automated system that allows customers to swipe their credit cards. With this information, the system brings up their account, whether to accept a new order or to find their clean garments and bring them to the front for customers to retrieve and take home.[58]

Communicating the Service Promise: The Communications Gap

The fourth factor leading to a customer service gap is the difference between the service promised by the retailer and the service actually delivered. Overstating the service offered raises customer expectations. Then, if the retailer fails to follow through by improving actual customer service, expectations exceed perceived service, and customers are dissatisfied. For example, if an apparel store advertises free alterations, and then informs customers that it is free only on full-priced items, customers shopping the sales racks may be disappointed. Raising expectations beyond what can be delivered might bring in more customers initially, but it can also create dissatisfaction and reduce repeat business. Disgruntled customers may then write negative online reviews or use social media such as Twitter to express their dissatisfaction. The communications gap can be reduced by making realistic commitments and managing customer expectations.

Realistic Commitments   Promotion programs are typically developed by the marketing department, whereas the store operations division delivers the service. Poor communication between these areas can result in a mismatch between a promotional campaign's promises and the service the store can actually offer. This problem is well illustrated by Best Buy's 2011 holiday season. After very successfully promoting its Black Friday sales online, Best Buy attracted far more sales than it was expecting but allowed back-ordering of many products promising they would arrive in time for Christmas. Two days before Christmas, customers received notifications that products they had purchased online as far back as November would not be delivered in time for the holiday. Consumer backlash was immediate and intense, including designations of the retailer as "The Grinch That Stole Christmas." Although it apologized through select media outlets, it failed to communicate through Twitter or Facebook—two vehicles the chain had used to create the initial demand.[60]

Managing Customer Expectations   How can a retailer communicate realistic service expectations without losing business to a competitor that makes inflated service claims? One common problem is not having clear expectations of how long a customer has to wait at the deli counter. Retailers have addressed this problem by providing electronic signs representing the customer number that is being served. A more sophisticated solution to managing customers' expectations about their wait time is being used at more than 200 Stop & Shop stores. Customers place their orders at a touchscreen computer, receive a ticket, and then continue their shopping trip. When their ticket number is announced over the store's loudspeaker, their order is ready.[61] This technology, along with its Scan It! devices to help customers scan and tally the cost of the items in their cart, made Stop & Shop one of the 10 most innovative food companies for 2012.[62]

Information presented at the point of sale can be used to manage expectations. For example, theme parks and restaurants indicate the waiting time for an attraction or a table. Online retailers tell their customers whether merchandise is in stock and when customers can expect to receive it. Providing accurate information can increase customer satisfaction, even when customers must wait longer than desired.

Sometimes service problems are caused by customers. Customers may use an invalid credit card to pay for merchandise, not take time to try on a suit and have it altered properly, or use a product incorrectly because they fail to read the instructions. Communication programs can inform customers about their role and responsibility in getting good service and give tips on how to get better service, such as the best times of the day to shop and the retailer's policies and procedures for handling problems.

SERVICE RECOVERY

LO4

Articulate retailers' service failure strategies.

The delivery of customer service is inherently inconsistent, so service failures are bound to arise. Rather than dwelling on negative aspects of customer problems, retailers should focus on the positive opportunities the problems generate. Service problems and complaints are an excellent source of information about the retailer's offering (its merchandise and service). Armed with this information, retailers can make changes to increase their customers' satisfaction.[63]

Service problems also enable a retailer to demonstrate its commitment to providing high-quality customer service. By encouraging complaints and handling problems, a retailer has an opportunity to strengthen its relationship with its customers. Effective service recovery efforts significantly increase customer satisfaction, purchase intentions, and positive word of mouth. However, post-recovery satisfaction generally is less than the satisfaction level before the service failure.[64]

Most retailers have standard policies for handling problems. If a correctable problem is identified, such as defective merchandise, many retailers will make restitution on the spot and apologize for inconveniencing the customer. The retailer will offer replacement merchandise, a credit toward future purchases, or a cash refund.

In many cases, the cause of the problem may be hard to identify (did the salesperson really insult the customer?), uncorrectable (the store had to close due to bad weather), or a result of the customer's unusual expectations (the customer didn't like his haircut). In these cases, service recovery might be more difficult. The steps in effective service recovery are (1) listen to the customer, (2) provide a fair solution, and (3) resolve the problem quickly.[65]

When resolving customers' problems, service representatives should listen to customers, provide a fair solution, and resolve the problems quickly.

Listening to Customers

Customers can become very emotional about their real or imaginary problems with a retailer. Often, this emotional reaction can be reduced by simply giving customers a chance to get their complaints off their chests. Store employees should allow customers to air their complaints without interruption. Interruptions can further irritate customers who may already be emotionally upset. It becomes very hard to reason with or satisfy an angry customer. Customers want a sympathetic response to their complaints. Thus, store employees need to make it clear that they are happy that any problem has been brought to their attention. Satisfactory solutions rarely arise when store employees have an antagonistic attitude or assume that the customer is trying to cheat the store. Store employees should never assume they know what the customer is complaining about or what solution the customer is seeking.[66] As we mentioned previously, more customers are posting their concerns and complaints on blogs and microblogs. In response, Best Buy has hired a host of employees to manage its Twitter accounts (e.g., @Best Buy, @BestBuy_Deals, @GeekSquad, and @BestBuyNews). The specialists who work Best Buy's help desk also answer questions through Twitter, at @Twelpforce. Manning the social network airways is an excellent way to listen to customer problems and attempt to fix them.[67]

REFACT

Approximately a dozen new Twitter accounts open every second; more than 175 million tweets are posted daily.[68]

Providing a Fair Solution

Customers like to feel that they are being treated fairly. They base their perceptions of fairness on how they think others were treated in similar situations and with other retailers. Customers' evaluations of complaint resolutions thus are based on distributive fairness and procedural fairness.[69] **Distributive fairness** is a customer's perception of the benefits received compared with his or her costs in terms of inconvenience or monetary loss. What seems to be fair compensation for a service failure for one customer may not be adequate for another. So, service providers probe customers to determine what would help resolve their issue.

Procedural fairness is the perceived fairness of the process used to resolve complaints. Customers typically feel they have been dealt with fairly when store employees follow company guidelines. Guidelines reduce variability in handling complaints and lead customers to believe that they are being treated like everyone else. But rigid adherence to guidelines can have negative effects. Store employees need some flexibility and empowerment capabilities to resolve complaints, or customers may feel they had no influence on the resolution.

Resolving Problems Quickly

Customer satisfaction is affected by the time it takes to get an issue resolved. So, empowering the first contact employee to move quickly to solve a problem increases customer satisfaction. When customers get referred to several different employees, they waste a lot of time repeating their story. Also, the chance of conflicting responses by store employees increases.

Although resolving customer complaints promptly generally increases satisfaction, if the complaints are resolved too abruptly, customers might feel dissatisfied because of the lack of personal attention they received. Retailers must recognize the trade-off between resolving the problem quickly and taking the time to listen to and show concern for the customer.[70]

SUMMARY

LO1 Identify how retailers can build a competitive advantage through customer service.

Customer service provides an opportunity for retailers to develop a strategic advantage through two basic strategies: personalized or standardized customer service. The personalized approach relies primarily on sales associates. The standardized approach places more emphasis on developing appropriate rules, consistent procedures, and optimum store designs.

LO2 Explain how customers evaluate a retailer's customer service.

Customers evaluate customer service by comparing their perceptions of the service delivered with their expectations. If their perceptions are lower than their expectations, customers are dissatisfied. If their perceptions are better than their expectations, they might be satisfied or even delighted.

LO3 Indicate the activities a retailer can undertake to provide high-quality customer service.

To ensure excellent service, retailers need to close the gaps between the service they deliver and the service that customers expect. To reduce the gap, they need to know what customers expect, set standards to provide the expected service, provide support so that store employees can meet the standards, and realistically communicate the service offered to customers.

LO4 Articulate retailers' service failure strategies.

An effective service recovery requires (1) listening to the customer, (2) providing a fair solution, and (3) resolving the problem quickly. Then retailers must use the information gained from customer complaints and learn from their recovery efforts to prevent service failures in the future.

KEY TERMS

assurance, *522*

communication gap, *525*

customer service, *516*

delivery gap, *525*

distributive fairness, *537*

emotional support, *533*

empathy, *523*

empowerment, *532*

instrumental support, *533*

knowledge gap, *525*

mystery shopper, *530*

personalized service, *519*

procedural fairness, *537*

reliability, *522*

responsiveness, *523*

sentiment analysis, *526*

service gap, *525*

standardized service, *519*

standards gap, *525*

tangibility, *523*

GET OUT AND DO IT!

1. **CONTINUING ASSIGNMENT** Go to a local store outlet of the retailer you selected for the continuing assignment and describe and evaluate the service it offers. What service is being offered? Is the service personalized or standardized? Ask the store manager if you may talk to some customers and employees. Choose customers who have made a purchase, customers who have not made a purchase, and customers with a problem (refund, exchange, or complaint). Talk with them about their experiences. Also ask employees what the retailer does to assist and motivate them to provide good service. Then, write a report describing your conversations in which you make suggestions for improving the store's customer service.

2. **INTERNET EXERCISE** Qthru (www.Qthru.com) is a company that has created a mobile application to increase the speed of the checkout process by enabling customers to scan the products they want to purchase and pay for them on their smartphones.

Visit the company's website and review both the application and the provided checkout process. How useful is this application for retailers? What sorts of retailers seem most likely to adopt it?

3. **INTERNET EXERCISE** Visit Amazon.com and shop for a best-selling book. How does the website help you locate best sellers? How does the customer service offered by this website compare with the service you would get at another book retailer's website or in a brick-and-mortar bookstore?

4. **GO SHOPPING** Go to a discount store such as Walmart, a department store, and a specialty store to buy a pair of jeans. After visiting all three, compare and contrast the level of customer service you received in each of the stores. Which store made it easiest to find the pair of jeans you would be interested in buying? Evaluate the perceived service experience in terms of reliability, assurance, tangibility, empathy, and responsiveness. Does the service quality match the store format? Explain your response.

DISCUSSION QUESTIONS AND PROBLEMS

1. For each of the following services, give an example of a retailer for which providing the service is critical to its success and an example of a retailer for which providing the service is not critical: (a) personal shoppers, (b) home delivery, (c) money-back guarantees, and (d) credit.

2. Both Nordstrom and McDonald's are noted for their high-quality customer service, but their approaches to providing quality service are different. Describe this difference. Why has each of these retailers elected to use its particular approach?

3. Have you ever worked in a job that required you to provide customer service? If yes, describe the skills you needed and tasks you performed on this job. If no, what skills and abilities would you highlight to a potential employer that was interviewing you for a position that included customer service in the job description?

4. Consider customer service at IKEA. How does this retailer utilize a self-service model to gain a competitive advantage over traditional furniture stores?

5. Review Retailing View 18.2 about customer service at Zappos. How does Zappos create such a positive culture among its service personnel?

6. Assume you're the department manager for menswear in a local department store that emphasizes empowering its managers. A customer returns a dress shirt that's no longer in the package in which it was sold. The customer has no receipt, says that when he opened the package he found that the shirt was torn, and wants cash for the price at which the shirt is now being sold. The shirt was on sale last week when the customer claims to have bought it. What would you do?

7. Consider a situation in which you received poor customer service in a retail store or from a service provider. Did you make the store's management aware of

your experience? To whom did you relay this experience? Have you returned to this retailer or provider? For each of these questions, explain your reasons.

8. Gaps analysis provides a systematic method for examining a customer service program's effectiveness. Top management has told an information systems manager that customers are complaining about the long wait to pay for merchandise at the checkout station. Taking the role of the systems manager, use the following gap analysis table to evaluate this problem and suggest possible strategies for reducing the wait time.

	Problem Encountered	Strategies to Close this Gap
Knowledge gap		
Standards gap		
Delivery gap		
Communication gap		

9. How can retailers provide high-quality personalized service? Use an ophthalmologist's office that also sells eyeglass frames and fills prescriptions for contact lenses as your example. How does this retailer's service compare with the service provided by 1-800 CONTACTS online or in-store at its bricks-and-mortar partner, Walmart?

10. Consider a recent retail service experience you have had, such as a haircut, doctor's appointment, dinner in a restaurant, bank transaction, or product repair (not an exhaustive list), and answer the following questions:
    (a) Describe an excellent service delivery experience.
    (b) What made this quality experience possible?
    (c) Describe a service delivery experience in which you did not receive the performance that you expected.
    (d) What were the problems encountered, and how could they have been resolved?

SUGGESTED READINGS

Berry, Leonard L. *Management Lessons from Mayo Clinic: Inside One of the World's Most Admired Service Organizations.* New York: McGraw-Hill, 2010.

Berry, Leonard L., Ruth N. Bolton, C. H. Bridges, J. Meyer, A. Parasuraman, and Kathleen Seiders. "Opportunities for Innovation in the Delivery of Interactive Retail Services." *Journal of Interactive Marketing* 24, no. 2 (2010), pp. 155–167.

Bettencourt, Lance. *Service Innovation: How to Go from Customer Needs to Breakthrough Services.* New York: McGraw-Hill, 2010.

Bolton, Ruth N., Dhruv Grewal, and Michael Levy. "Six Strategies for Competing through Service: An Agenda for Future Research." *Journal of Retailing* 83, no. 1 (2007), pp. 1–4.

Gallo, Carmine. *The Apple Experience: Secrets to Building Insanely Great Customer Loyalty.* New York: McGraw-Hill, 2012.

Gerson, Richard F. *Beyond Customer Service: Keep Your Customers and Keep Them Satisfied,* 3rd ed. Mississauga, Ontario, Canada: Crisp Learning, 2010.

Gremler, Dwayne D., Mary Jo Bitner, and Valarie Zeithaml. *Services Marketing,* 6th ed. New York: McGraw-Hill, 2012.

Köhler, Clemens F., Andrew Rohm, Ko de Ruyter, and Martin Wetzels. "Return on Interactivity: The Impact of Online Agents on Newcomer Adjustment." *Journal of Marketing* 75, no. 2 (2011), pp. 93–108.

Spector, Robert, and Patrick McCarthy. *The Nordstrom Way to Customer Service Excellence: The Handbook for Becoming the "Nordstrom" of Your Industry.* Hoboken, NJ: John Wiley & Sons, 2012.

Zeithaml, Valarie. *Delivering Quality Service.* New York: The Free Press, 2010.

APPENDIX
Starting Your Own Retail Business

Starting a retail business can be an enticing and daunting prospect. On the one hand, you can be your own boss, enjoy complete creative control, and reap the full rewards of your hard work. On the other hand, retail business owners must assume large amounts of responsibility, bear the consequences of poor decisions, and ultimately shoulder the blame for the success or failure of the business. Owning your own business involves a great deal of effort, sacrifice, and patience. It is inherently risky, and consequently, fewer than 20 percent of new retail businesses survive to the five-year mark. Yet the rewards of successfully navigating the unpredictable landscape of business ownership can be enormous, both personally and financially. You might grow your business and become the next Sam Walton (Walmart), Maxine Clark (Build-A-Bear Workshop), or John Mackey (Whole Food Markets).

The sense of accomplishment garnered from creating and sustaining a thriving enterprise of one's own is immense. Retail owners have the uniquely satisfying opportunity to craft a tangible expression of their own professional visions, talents, and hard work. In addition, they can contribute value to their communities by creating jobs, strengthening the economy, and providing excellent service to customers. Those who join the successful 20 percent of retail entrepreneurs often earn sufficient financial rewards to live securely and comfortably according to their own standards.

The purpose of this appendix is to demonstrate broadly how to achieve these goals by starting a retail business. A wealth of information discusses entrepreneurship, retailing, and business start-ups—and all of it could not possibly be contained within the confines of an appendix. Instead, this appendix provides an overview of the process and offers some further resources that anyone with serious aspirations for starting his or her own retail business can use to take the first step.

DO YOU HAVE WHAT IT TAKES TO BE A SUCCESSFUL ENTREPRENEUR?

Before starting a business, it is important to take an inventory of skills. Debate continues about the inherent nature of entrepreneurial success. Can someone acquire entrepreneurial skills, or are successful entrepreneurs just people with an innate ability to see and seize an opportunity? It seems that the answer lies somewhere in between.

The skills needed to be a successful entrepreneur can by divided into two broad skill categories: technical training and personal characteristics. To start a retail business, it is very important that the owner possess business skills. Do you understand how to read a financial statement and evaluate your performance and viability? Can you make an effective presentation to potential investors? Do you have an understanding of what customers want? Can you manage the people who work for you? Do you have an understanding of how to launch an electronic channel for your retail business?

For those lacking these business skills, many major universities offer online degrees in a wide variety of disciplines, including business, as well as the option of full-time enrollment. It may be difficult to balance family, work, and school, but owning a business will be just as time consuming. This process can be a litmus test for a person's entrepreneurial work ethic.

A work ethic is a quality that cannot be taught, and for entrepreneurs it is vital. Passion for a chosen business is another quality that cannot be taught. No one will be looking over a retail business owner's shoulder to ensure he or she is doing everything possible to guarantee

*This appendix was prepared by Christian Tassin MSE 2008, University of Florida, under the supervision of Professor Barton Weitz.

the success of the venture. Can you maintain the level of energy required to sustain a business? Can you handle rejection from investors and still have the confidence to keep going? Seeing opportunity is another skill that is difficult to acquire, but it can be learned through practice. A person can train his or her mind to look for ways to improve the things that need improvement. Visit a retail store to evaluate its practices. What works? What does not? Where is the opportunity to improve on the qualities that do not work? How can value be created from improving on the shortcomings of current business practices?

DEVELOPING A CONCEPT FOR THE RETAIL VENTURE

The genesis of any business venture starts with an idea. A retail store concept should satisfy three objectives. First, the pursuit should be something that the retailer is passionate about. With the intense effort required for successful entrepreneurship, why would a person want to be involved in something that he or she does not enjoy? Sustainability in a retail business becomes virtually impossible if the owner does not have a burning desire to see it succeed. Second, the concept must provide sufficient value to its customers. The purpose of a business is to make a profit, and if people are not willing to pay for the products or services offered, then failure is ensured. Third, the concept must provide an offering that is differentiated—not available from competitors and not something that competitors can easily copy.

An important issue to consider is the application of intellectual property to the retail concept. Do you have a patentable concept? Do you have a trademark for your brand name and logo? If an entrepreneur crafts a business venture on company time at his or her day job, it is considered that company's property. Working in an industry related to the retail concept can make this ownership even easier to prove. Will the concept compete with an existing employer? Many companies require that employees sign noncompete clauses. If an idea violates one of those agreements, the business could be over before it even gets started. If you believe your concept or business process is unique, or are not sure if you can legally execute your retail concept, an attorney who deals in intellectual property can be a great resource.

THE "QUICK SCREEN"

The first step in deciding whether to start a retail business is to examine the retail concept in detail. Essentially, the prospective retailer wants to determine whether he or she merely has an interesting idea or a viable opportunity. Four questions that help determine the viability of an opportunity are as follows:

1. Does it create or add significant value for customers?
2. Does it solve a significant problem or meet a significant demand or need in the marketplace for which someone is willing to pay a premium?
3. Is there a large enough market and sufficient margins to generate profits?
4. Is there a good fit between the skills of the management team and the skills required to operate the business?

If an idea does not fulfill these four requirements, the potential retailer needs to revise it, or else create a new one. For example, if you love the beach and want to start a retail store that sells bathing suits and beach accessories, but you also live in Colorado, the concept lacks the key elements of success. The market for beach goods will not be significant enough, no financially realizable value is being created for the people in the community, and even with a competent team, the idea would be unattractive. Answers to these questions may not be as readily apparent for different concepts, but this simplified example illustrates the effectiveness that the "Quick Screen" can have in testing an idea for true value. Revising an idea is much more efficient in the planning stages than it would be midexecution.

A potential revision of the beachwear retail concept in Colorado would be to open a sporting goods store named, say, "Mountain Sporting Goods," that caters to people who participate in mountain sports such as skiing, hiking, climbing, and rafting. This concept passes the "Quick Screen," in that it creates value for customers, fulfills a need, has good market potential, and has a suitable risk/reward balance. If a potential venture passes this quick test, it is time to become immersed in the details of its potential by preparing a business plan.

542   APPENDIX   Starting Your Own Retail Business

PREPARING A BUSINESS PLAN

The preparation of a business plan is an excellent way to take a hard look at the concept in a structured, practical way. A well-done business plan can help mitigate or address the potential risks involved in starting a business before they actually occur. By thoroughly considering both the merit and the execution strategy of a vision, a prospective retailer can significantly improve its chances of success. A good business plan should concisely and effectively demonstrate the value of the concept to others—especially potential investors. The more prepared the retailer is to demonstrate and execute the value of the proposition, the less risk it poses, and the better investment opportunity the retail concept presents.

Business plans are dynamic and should evolve with the business. There is no set formula for a business plan, but there are some elements that every good business plan should include. First and foremost, a business plan should be well written, concise, and professional. No one will ever invest in a new venture if the business plan is verbose, boring, sloppy, or unprofessional. Nowhere is this more important than in the executive summary. Investors often see hundreds of business plans, and many of them read no further than the executive summary. If a plan does not grab their attention, or inadvertently casts a negative light, the venture proposal will not make it past a cursory reading at best. Structurally, a business plan should include at least the following content:

1. Executive summary.
2. Environmental analysis (trends, customers, competitors, economy).
3. Description of the retail concept and strategy (target market, retail format, competitive advantage).
4. Implementation plan, including the approach for attracting customers.
5. Team, or the other people involved in business.
6. Funding request.
7. Financial plan.

The key points of writing a retail business plan are illustrated in this section with the creation of a fictitious retail business. The examples include less detail than an actual business plan would require, but they are designed as a starting point from which the entrepreneur can initiate further research. The overarching themes also can be applied to a wide variety of retail businesses.

Environmental Analysis

The scope of the environmental analysis depends on the long-term objective. If the retailer's objective is simply to operate one or two outlets, the environmental analysis should focus on the local environment, such as the trade area of the store, as discussed in Chapter 8. However, if the long-term objective is to open and operate multiple retail outlets, the retailer needs to examine all the elements in the macroenvironment, such as industry size and trends and the competition and profitability of the industry, as discussed in Chapter 5. The elements in the environmental analysis detailed next apply to supporting a venture that starts in Colorado Springs, with ambitions to expand regionally and potentially nationally.

Industry Size and Trends   Various databases can provide detailed information about industrywide figures. For example, Hoover's Online and IBISWorld US Industry reports both provide detailed industry data, analyses of publicly traded companies, and customer demographics. Many libraries subscribe to these types of services, and a local librarian can be helpful in providing guidance on accessing them. Many publicly traded companies offer information on their websites, and they are required to publish financial data with the Securities and Exchange Commission. Trade organizations and publications such as the Sporting Goods Manufacturers Association (sgma.com), the National Sporting Goods Association (nsga.com), and *Sporting Goods Dealer* often provide detailed information about specific retail sectors. Census data, available at census.gov, give great insight into the population of the focal community in terms of companies and people. For example, there are 625 specialty-line sporting goods establishments in Colorado, according to the Census Bureau.

For smaller local businesses, it can more difficult to find information. Knowledge of the local area therefore can be a great asset. Also, gathering information from the customers and suppliers of competitors in the industry can provide valuable information. Resourcefulness and persistence are keys to discovering certain information, and it can be very beneficial to take the time to do so. Visit similar retailers and look at what they have to offer. Where is the unmet need? How can a new retailer rise to meet it?

Market size also is critical. How much money is being generated in the specific retail area? How is the money distributed within the industry? For example, the sporting goods industry in the United States generates about $55 billion in sales annually. This number is a significant starting point, in that it illustrates the overall monetary potential of the industry, but more focused data also are necessary.

Research shows that the sporting goods industry is highly fragmented, with many small retailers rather than dominant control by larger players. Therefore, opportunity appears to exist for the growth and expansion of a smaller retailer. Information like this is important to investors, because it can be used to illustrate that the industry is ready for a new retail business concept. For example, the implementation plan for the new store could demonstrate the growth potential that would enable it to consolidate smaller businesses and gain a significant market share in the sporting goods industry. The correlation of industry data to real opportunity makes for a compelling narrative that entices financiers to invest in the company. In other words, an implementation plan should demonstrate how an interesting opportunity can provide a high return on investment.

To find where the specific opportunity lies, you must whittle industry data down to the niche level. In the United States, sporting goods sales derive from retailers such as Sports Authority, Walmart, and a multitude of smaller retailers. These stores sell equipment, apparel, and shoes for every sporting need imaginable all across the country. For simplicity, Mountain Sporting Goods might focus only on sporting equipment, which makes up 46 percent of the sporting goods industry. It can further narrow its focus by defining what mountain sports mean for Mountain Sporting Goods. What mountain sports segments will be targeted?

Examination of the sports equipment data makes it apparent that camping, fishing tackle, hunting, and firearms account for 6.9, 9.0, and 12.1 percent (hunting and firearms combined) of the sports equipment market, respectively. Should the concept therefore be expanded to include these segments, in addition to skiing, hiking, rafting, and climbing? A moral disagreement with hunting might be a factor to consider as well. Does the significant financial opportunity outweigh the ethical uncertainty that selling hunting equipment might cause? What are the federal and local licenses required to sell firearms? Will the store sell tags for hunting certain animals? The reconciliation of these types of conflicting issues will help refine the concept.

Target Customers   Another critical element is defining the target market. What age demographic is the typical customer? What is his or her socioeconomic status and gender? Where do customers live in relation to the proposed store location? Where do they work? Will the store provide goods for the whole family or focus on individuals? How will the retail concept provide them with value? Will it compete on the basis of low prices or differentiated, higher-quality products? Finding the right balance of these factors is key. An overly narrow focus can be problematic, because it implies insufficient demand for the offering. A focus that is too broad also can hinder the retailer's ability to forge its own identity. Research findings might narrow these options. For example, if Mountain Sporting Goods opened in Aspen, Colorado, it would be reasonable for it to deal in specialty, high-quality, high-price goods because of the affluent customer base that resides there.

Competitors   The final step in analyzing the retail environment is to study potential competitors. How does the retail concept compare with those of others that offer similar merchandise? How do these competitors reach their customers? What kind of advertising strategy do they use? How long have they been in business? Do they have an e-commerce component to their business? How similar are the products they sell? How high are their goods priced? How well do their employees know their product? What is their store layout like?

Many larger sporting goods retailers carry a broad array of sporting products, so naturally there will be some overlap in what Walmart sells and what Mountain Sporting Goods offers. How important is this overlap? Walmart may take a small portion of customers, but it offers only a general sampling of what Mountain Sporting Goods specializes in providing. Sports Authority would be a bigger threat though, because it offers only sporting goods, spanning the spectrum of equipment, shoes, apparel, camping equipment, and more. Walmart and Sports Authority also can leverage their sizes to compete on price more easily than can a small retail business. Factors such as these must be considered when establishing the new retailer's strategic position. Initially, Mountain Sporting Goods would have to compete on the basis of its ability to offer more differentiated specialty products than some of the bigger chains, and create an environment that draws customers to the store. After a good deal of growth, it might achieve economies of scale by purchasing high volumes of products, as this lowers costs and increases its ability to compete on price.

The other segment of sporting goods retailers, which makes up the majority of the industry, is local businesses. Local research will be very important in determining local competitors' strengths and weaknesses. Do some reconnaissance work to see how competitors operate, and put yourself in the role of the customer to browse their shops. How big is the store? Does it feel cramped? Were you treated well by employees? How knowledgeable were they about the products they sell? Did they have the range of goods that you desire? Were the hours of operation adequate to meet local needs? How can a new store create a more pleasurable shopping experience?

Other issues to consider are the location of competitors, their proximity to the desired demographic, parking lot layout, building condition, and so forth. If Mountain Sporting Goods sells almost the same goods for the same price as a competitor but customers do not have to drive as far, can park more easily, and can enjoy a nicer facility, Mountain Sporting Goods gains a distinct competitive advantage.

Retail Concept

After completing the industry analysis, it is time to combine the original conceptual idea with the data uncovered through industry research in the form of a company description. Who is Mountain Sporting Goods? To whom will it sell its products? How does it do so better than others? How can it exploit competitive advantages to make the company grow?

Mountain Sporting Goods has decided to include the following information in its company description: It will locate in Colorado Springs, Colorado, to exploit the rapid growth of the community and the prevalence of a young, ecocentric population. Colorado Springs has an unmet need for ecofriendly stores and a large enough population of people who are willing to pay a premium for that attribute. Therefore, the store will sell the best-quality, most environmentally friendly skiing, hiking, whitewater rafting, mountain climbing, and camping equipment available. Customers will range in age from 23 to 35 years, and they will place environmental friendliness at the top of their priority list. These young single or coupled professionals without children have a fair amount of disposable income.

In turn, the management for the company must have an extensive background in sustainability and a passion for outdoor activities. As Mountain Sporting Goods gains customers and increases sales revenue, it might begin to acquire other, similarly sized firms to gain market share. These firms must be geographically accessible so that the company can pool resources and increase its purchasing power, as well as reduce costs through the consolidation of tasks such as distribution, purchasing, and accounting. In this way, the firm will be able to achieve the benefits of size and develop economies of scale.

A business plan must present these facets of the business in such a way that they draw the reader into the concept. The company description segment therefore should illustrate the founder's passion for the concept. It should also emphasize the opportunities that it creates and explain the competitive advantages that enable those opportunities to reach fruition.

The research and brainstorming accomplished thus far are detailed in the remainder of the business plan, so the following portions are the most finely detailed. The potential investor should have been able to recognize the value of the potential business already; the remainder of the plan provides proof of that value. The marketing, operations, management, and financial segments of the business plan thus tell the investor how the concept will be executed, what the retailer intends to sell, who will execute the process, how much money will be required to make it happen, and the money that can be earned as a result.

THE IMPLEMENTATION PLAN

The main goal of an implementation plan is to determine how the retail business will attract consumers in the target market and convert them into loyal customers. This essential portion of a retail business plan not only describes how the company will position itself in the market but also outlines the components required to make it a reality. The plan should describe the following elements in detail:

1. *Merchandise offered.* Number and breadth of lines to be carried, styles of merchandise and accessories, names of suppliers, supplier credit terms, quality of merchandise, opening stock, inventory levels, and expected turnover rate (see Chapters 12 and 13).
2. *Customer services offered.* Customer service levels and contact provided, credit policies, exchange and return policies, alterations, and gift wrapping (Chapter 18).
3. *Facilities.* Store appearance, any renovation required, interior decor, storefront, layout, lighting, window displays, wall displays, and overall atmosphere (Chapter 17).
4. *Location.* Buy, lease, or rent; terms of contract; local ordinances; zoning regulations; parking; accessibility; local demographics; and conditions for remodeling (Chapters 7 and 8).
5. *Pricing.* Price ranges to offer, competitive pricing, profitable pricing, margins, markdowns, and discount prices (Chapter 14).
6. *Promotion.* One-year promotional plan, advertising budgets, selection of media, cost of local media options, promotional displays, cooperative advertising efforts, and public relations (Chapter 15).
7. *Employees.* Compensational plan and wage scale to be offered, job specifications, employee training program, career and promotion schedule, employee benefits, social security taxes, sources and types of employees to hire (e.g., age, gender, appearance, education level), and policy on family employees (Chapters 9 and 16).
8. *Security.* Security guards, fire and theft alarms, computer security system, windows, locks, merchandise protection services, liability insurance, and other insurance (Chapter 16).
9. *Equipment.* Cash registers, sales desk, computer systems, display racks, office equipment, office supplies, telephone systems, management information system, software, security, and personal computer requirements (Chapter 10).
10. *Controls.* Inventory control and replenishment methods and financial performance analysis. (Chapters 6 and 12).

Team

Who will help to execute the vision? One of the most important factors in starting a business is finding a group of people whose skill sets complement those of the founder. It is virtually impossible for one person to possess all of the requisite skills for creating and growing a business. For example, if Mountain Sporting Goods intends to follow through with its plans to acquire other businesses, it would be beneficial to bring someone into the group with experience in the area of mergers and acquisitions. Also, the owner-manager of Mountain Sporting Goods has a background in sustainability, which represents a great asset in setting up a business whose cornerstone is environmental awareness.

The team section showcases the talent of the people who will run the retail start-up. It is both a "who's who" of the business venture and a way to assure investors that their money will be handled by people of quality. This assurance is especially effective if someone with experience in starting retail stores joins the team. Such a person lends significant credibility to the business endeavor, as well as a great deal of sage advice. Experienced people do not necessarily have to be paid employees or managers but instead could serve on a board of advisors or board of directors. Each person should be listed, with his or her credentials outlined and role within the company clarified.

Funding Request

One of the objectives of a business plan is to seek financing and show how the firm might use investors' money, whether debt or equity financing. For a small retailer, a loan request (debt financing) is more common. If Mountain Sporting Goods' aspiration is to be a local lifestyle business, it still needs to show where the money is going and how the lender will receive a return on its investment through the company's ability to generate enough revenue to repay the loan, as well as the timing of the repayments.

A company with higher aims might seek venture capital support for its major growth. The owner-manager of this company would negotiate with venture capitalists about what portion of their equity should be provided for the desired financial support. Investors would receive shares (equity) in the company in exchange for the financing that they provide.

At a certain point, probably within a few years, venture capitalists typically can monetize those shares after the company is bought by another company, has its initial public offering (IPO), or buys the investors' share of the company back. For example, Mountain Sporting Goods might explain how it will execute its growth plans and generate a return on investment for its financiers. At a specified time, Mountain Sporting Goods will have enough revenue growth and profits to go public, represent a significant enough threat to larger competitors that they buy it out, or pay back the investors at the desired rate of return. Investors base their evaluation of the venture on how much they predict the company will be worth at the designated time of sale, IPO, or buyback. If they believe the company can generate the intended value that they seek, they will invest.

Financial Plan

The financial plan can be one of the more intimidating aspects of business plan writing, but it also is essential to determine the value of the retail business. The financial plan provides investors with information that enables them to decide whether the business concept is worth their risk. Taking the time to learn how to create the financial plan therefore has great value. Moreover, the financial plan offers the prospective retailer a detailed understanding of the major contributing factors that might result in success or failure. With this knowledge, the retailer can safeguard the business and deal with accomplished businesspeople and investors with greater confidence. Financial projections vary depending on the degree of complexity sought for the financing, but the following discussion provides a simple overview of the process. The only way to learn, though, is to roll up your sleeves and do it.

Financial projections for a completely new business are especially difficult, in that they must be based solely on assumptions because there are no historical data. No one has uncovered the secret to predicting the future, but it is possible to make educated estimates. The key is finding where to start. What are the initial elements that an entrepreneur requires to build a financial model of a potential venture?

The income statement, cash flow, balance sheet, financing, and break-even analysis constitute the basics that must be included. The purpose of these projections is to tell investors when the business will actually become profitable and how fast it will grow. The groundwork laid by the implementation plan is a good place to start.

The elements required to reach target customers indicate both start-up and fixed costs, which represent the basis of the financial projections. For example, if Mountain Sporting Goods has done enough research, it will have narrowed down how much the location lease or mortgage will cost and, from merchandise sources, learned how much the inventory will cost. These and many other factors will be "known" entities, from which the fixed start-up and operating costs can be established. Other miscellaneous start-up elements, such as legal fees, also should be included.

After the costs have been established, sales figures must be projected. There are two methods for estimating financial statements: the comparable method and the build-up method. The retailer should employ both methods and compare their results to come up with the final projection. The comparable method uses financial data from a similar company or ratios from the industry and then compares them to the projected data for the concept company. The build-up method examines sales and builds expected revenues and expenses by determining what they might be on an average day, such as the products sold on an average day, the types of products, the buyers and how many people buy, and the amount each would spend. By establishing an average day's sales, the retailer can extrapolate these data to months, years, and so on. The data also can be adjusted for seasonal variances, which are important for any retail business. After reconciling any differences between the estimates produced by the two different methods, all that remains is to construct the financial statements for inclusion in the business plan.

The business plan requires perpetual refining and updating as new information, such as opportunities and threats in the environment that prompt a change in the retail concept, becomes available. The business plan also should be referred to and used at all stages of growth. Just as in a business's infancy, it remains important to evaluate who it is, what it does, and how it will do so on a continuing basis.

GETTING STARTED

Now that the business plan has been completed, there are a few other miscellaneous costs and issues that must be considered. With a strong retail concept, the business must address certain procedural processes. One of the most important is to set up its legal structure. Will the company be a sole proprietorship, a partnership, or an incorporated firm? These structures all incur unique costs although the least expensive is a sole proprietorship. A sole proprietorship, however, does not remove any personal assets from the responsibility owed to creditors for the failure or success of the business. If an entrepreneur elects to sell shares of the company to investors, he or she will need to have the appropriate structure in place, and this often requires the assistance of an attorney, who can help file for the appropriate business structure that shields personal assets from certain risks and that has the most advantageous tax implications. Another necessary regulatory step is to file for an employer identification number (EIN) or federal tax identification number, which is required by law to operate a business.

Assuming that the company finds the financing required to launch the retail concept, the entrepreneur is now staring at the precipice of opportunity. The groundwork laid by the business plan now can be put to excellent use. It is a time of mixed emotions. The plan that the retailer has toiled so long and hard to craft will soon be battle tested. Theory will be put into practice, and the owner will determine its true value according to the response of the market. Will you achieve the fulfilling personal and financial success to which you aspire? The only way to know is to take that first step off the edge.

ADDITIONAL SOURCES OF INFORMATION

Bond, Ronald L. *Retail in Detail: How to Start and Manage a Small Retail Business*. Irvine, CA: Entrepreneur Press, 2005.

Davis, Charlene. *Start Your Own Clothing Store and More*. Irvine, CA: Entrepreneur Press, 2007.

Dion, Jim, and Ted Topping. *Start & Run a Retail Business*, 2nd ed. Bellingham, WA: Self-Counsel Press, 2007.

Mikaelsen, Debbra, and Pamela Skillings. *FabJob Guide to Become a Boutique Owner*. Calgary, Alberta, Canada: FabJob Guides, 2007.

Schroeder, Carol L. *Specialty Shop Retailing: Everything You Need to Know to Run Your Own Store*, 3rd ed. Indianapolis, IN: Wiley, 2007.

Kingaard, Jan. *Start Your Own Successful Retail Business*. Irvine, CA: Entrepreneur Press, 2003.

Cases

SECTION V

Cases

Cases	1	2	3	4	5	6	7	8	9	10	11	12	13	14	15	16	17	18
																		CHAPTER
1 Tractor Supply Company Targets the Part-Time Rancher	P	P			P		S											S
2 Build-A-Bear Workshop—Where Best Friends are Made	P	P			S													
3 Blue Tomato			P															
4 Staples Inc.			P															P
5 The Decision Making Process for Buying a Bicycle				P														
6 Parisian Patisserie "Maison Ladurée": The Conquest of the US Market		S	S		P		S											
7 Retailing in India—The Impact of Hypermarkets	P	S		S	P													
8 Diamonds from Mine to Market				S	P						P		P					
9 Starbucks' Expansion into China					P													
10 Walmart: Pioneer in Supply Chain Management										P								
11 Tiffany & Co. and TJX: Comparing Financial Performance						P												
12 Choosing a Store Location for a Boutique								P										
13 Hutch: Locating a New Store									P									
14 Avon Embraces Diversity			S		S				P									
15 Sephora Loyalty Programs: A Comparison between France and the US											P							
16 Attracting Generation Y to a Retail Career									P						S			
17 Active Endeavors Analyzes Its Customer Database											P							
18 Mel's Department Store Under New Management												P						
19 Developing an Assortment Plan for Hughes												P						
20 Preparing a Merchandise Budget Plan												P						
21 Kroger and Fred Meyer: Sourcing Products in a Global Marketplace													P					
22 Target and Its New Generation of Partnerships													P					
23 American Furniture Warehouse Sources Globally													P					
23 Merchandise Exclusively for JCPenney													P					
24 JCPenney: Are Customers Addicted to Sales?														P				
25 How Much for a Good Smell?														S	P			

continued

550   SECTION V   Cases

	CHAPTER																	
Cases	1	2	3	4	5	6	7	8	9	10	11	12	13	14	15	16	17	18
26 Promoting a Sale														S	P			
27 Target Marketing with Google Adwords			S												P			
28 Enterprise Rent-A-Car Focuses on Its People					S											P		S
29 Diamond in the Rough																P		
30 A Stockout at Discmart																S		P
31 Customer Service and Relationship Management at Nordstrom						S			S									P
32 Zipcar: Delivering Only as Much Driving as You Want																		P
33 Building the Apple Store																	P	S
34 Generating Advertising Revenue from a Digital Screen Network at Harrods of London					S											S	P	
34 Starbucks' Retail Strategy																S		
35 Yankee Candle: New Product Innovation													S		S			
36 Petsmart: Where Pets Are Family						S			S									
37 Lindy's Bridal Shop						S	S					S				S		
38 Interviewing for a Management Trainee Position	P								S							S		

Ⓟ **Primary Use**

Ⓢ **Secondary Use**

CASE 1   Tractor Supply Company Targets the Part-Time Rancher

Tractor Supply Company (TSC), a large and fast-growing retailer with more than $4 billion in annual sales and more than 100 stores in 44 states, was the inventor of the "do-it-yourself" (DIY) trend. Its origins date to 1938, when Charles E. Schmidt Sr. established a mail-order tractor parts business. After the success of his first retail store in Minot, North Dakota, he opened additional stores to serve the needs of local farmers. But eventually TSC's sales stagnated because small farms and ranches were being acquired by large farming and ranching corporations. These large agricultural firms buy supplies and equipment directly from manufacturers rather than through local farm supply stores like TSC.

TARGET MARKET

Since the early 1990s, TSC has targeted a growing group of people interested in recreational farming and ranching. Called "sundowners," "U-turners," "hobby farmers," "ruralpolitans," "micropolitans," "gentlemen farmers," and "ex-urbanites," these people have turned to farming to escape the hubbub of urban and suburban life. They are drawn to what they believe is a more private, simple, and stress-free lifestyle. They typically live on 5 to 20 acres in a rural community outside a metropolitan area, where they work at a full-time profession, and use some of their earnings to keep their farms in operation. Many of them are the sons and daughters of traditional production farmers and inherited the family farm and decided to keep it running. Today less than 10 percent of TSC's customers classify themselves as full-time farmers or ranchers, and many of its customers do not farm at all.

RETAIL OFFERING

The typical TSC store has 15,000 to 24,000 square feet of inside selling space and a similar amount of outside space used to display agricultural fencing, livestock equipment, and horse stalls. The company tries to locate stores in the prime retail corridor of rural communities, two or three counties away from major metropolitan areas. Fifty percent of its stores are in previously occupied buildings.

The typical store stocks about 15,000 SKUs, using a combination of national and private-label brands. TSC constantly tests new merchandise programs in its stores. For instance, based on a successful test of expanded clothing and footwear categories, TSC doubled the size of these areas of the store and added more lifestyle clothes and workwear for both men and women.

TSC stores are designed to make shopping an enjoyable experience and, at the same time, maximize sales and

CASE 1   Tractor Supply Company Targets the Part-Time Rancher

Tractor Supply Company (TSC), a large and fast-growing retailer with more than $4 billion in annual sales and more than 100 stores in 44 states, was the inventor of the "do-it-yourself" (DIY) trend. Its origins date to 1938, when Charles E. Schmidt Sr. established a mail-order tractor parts business. After the success of his first retail store in Minot, North Dakota, he opened additional stores to serve the needs of local farmers. But eventually TSC's sales stagnated because small farms and ranches were being acquired by large farming and ranching corporations. These large agricultural firms buy supplies and equipment directly from manufacturers rather than through local farm supply stores like TSC.

TARGET MARKET

Since the early 1990s, TSC has targeted a growing group of people interested in recreational farming and ranching. Called "sundowners," "U-turners," "hobby farmers," "ruralpolitans," "micropolitans," "gentlemen farmers," and "ex-urbanites," these people have turned to farming to escape the hubbub of urban and suburban life. They are drawn to what they believe is a more private, simple, and stress-free lifestyle. They typically live on 5 to 20 acres in a rural community outside a metropolitan area, where they work at a full-time profession, and use some of their earnings to keep their farms in operation. Many of them are the sons and daughters of traditional production farmers and inherited the family farm and decided to keep it running. Today less than 10 percent of TSC's customers classify themselves as full-time farmers or ranchers, and many of its customers do not farm at all.

RETAIL OFFERING

The typical TSC store has 15,000 to 24,000 square feet of inside selling space and a similar amount of outside space used to display agricultural fencing, livestock equipment, and horse stalls. The company tries to locate stores in the prime retail corridor of rural communities, two or three counties away from major metropolitan areas. Fifty percent of its stores are in previously occupied buildings.

The typical store stocks about 15,000 SKUs, using a combination of national and private-label brands. TSC constantly tests new merchandise programs in its stores. For instance, based on a successful test of expanded clothing and footwear categories, TSC doubled the size of these areas of the store and added more lifestyle clothes and workwear for both men and women.

TSC stores are designed to make shopping an enjoyable experience and, at the same time, maximize sales and

EXHIBIT 1
TSC's Mission and
Value Statements

operating efficiencies. Their environment allows plenty of space for individual departments and visual displays. Informative signs assist customers with purchasing decisions by delineating "good, better, best" qualities, pointing out their "everyday low-pricing" policy, and providing useful information regarding product benefits and suggestions for appropriate accessories.

TSC emphasizes customer service. The company tries to hire store employees who have farming and ranching backgrounds. Its training programs include (1) a full management training program, which covers all aspects of its operations; (2) product knowledge modules produced in conjunction with key vendors; (3) frequent management skills training classes; (4) semiannual store managers' meetings, with vendor product presentations; (5) vendor-sponsored in-store training programs; and (6) ongoing product information updates at its management headquarters. This extensive training, coupled with a management philosophy that stresses empowerment, enables store employees to assist customers in making their purchase decisions and solve customer problems as they arise. Store employees wear highly visible red vests, aprons, or smocks and nametags. TSC uses a variety of incentive programs that provide the opportunity for store employees to receive additional compensation based on their team, store, and/or company performance.

While TSC creates a "hometown farmer" shopping experience for customers, there is nothing "small-town" or "laid back" about its operations and use of technology. Its management information and control systems include a point-of-sale system, a supply chain management and replenishment system, a radio-frequency picking system in the distribution centers, a vendor purchase order control system, and a merchandise presentation system. These systems work together to track merchandise from the initial order through to the ultimate sale.

TSC has a centralized supply chain management team that focuses on replenishment and forecasting and a buying team that selects merchandise, develops assortments, and evaluates new products and programs. Almost all purchase orders and vendor invoices are transmitted through an electronic data interchange (EDI) system.

MISSION AND VALUES

Despite changes to TSC's retail strategy in the past 70 years, its mission and values have remained constant. The company's mission and value statements appear on its website (Exhibit 1), on cards handed out to all employees, and on the walls of every store. According to TSC management, the first discussion with new employees centers on the firm's values and mission because the firm steadfastly maintains that "being a great place to work enables the company to be a great place to shop and invest."

Sources: Tractor Supply Co., Annual Report 2011; www.tractorsupply.com.

This case was written by Barton Weitz, University of Florida.

DISCUSSION QUESTIONS

1. What is Tractor Supply Company's growth strategy? What retail mix does TSC provide?

2. Why and how has TSC's target customer changed over time?

3. How does TSC's retail mix provide the benefits sought by its target market?

4. How vulnerable is TSC to competition? Why is this the case?

5. Why does TSC place so much emphasis on training employees?

CASE 2   Build-A-Bear Workshop: Where Best Friends Are Made

Modern consumers want good value, low prices, and convenience, but they also appreciate a great shopping experience. Build-A-Bear Workshop usually locates its more than 425 stores in malls worldwide. It generates more than $390 million in annual sales by offering customers the opportunity to make their own stuffed animals, complete with clothing and accessories.

In 1997, Maxine Clark came up with the idea for Build-A-Bear Workshop and opened a storefront in St. Louis. She had plenty of experience in the corporate side of retailing, having worked for Payless ShoeSource and May Department Stores. Clark left corporate America on a mission to bring the fun back to retailing. Currently, the company has sold more than 70 million furry friends.

The bear-making process consists of eight steps, Choose Me, Hear Me, Stuff Me, Stitch Me, Fluff Me, Dress Me, Name Me, and Take Me Home. The stores mirror the chain's name: Customers, or builders, choose an unstuffed animal and, working with the retailer's staff, move through eight "creation stations" to build their own bear (or other animal). At the first station, the Stuffiteria, children can pick fluff from bins marked "Love," "Hugs and Kisses," "Friendship," and "Kindness." The stuffing is sent through a long, clear tube and into a stuffing machine. A sales associate holds the bear to a small tube while the builder pumps a foot peddle. In seconds, the bear takes its form. Before the stitching, builders must insert a heart. The builders follow the sales associates' instructions and rub the heart between their hands to make it warm. They then close their eyes, make a wish, and kiss the heart before putting it inside the bear. After selecting a name and having it stitched on their animal, builders take their bears to the Fluff Me station, where they brush their bears on a "bathtub" that features spigots blowing air. Finally, they move to a computer station to create a birth certificate.

Bears go home in Cub Condo carrying cases, which act as mini-houses complete with windows and doors. In addition to serving as playhouses, the boxes advertise Build-A-Bear Workshop to the child's friends. "[You] could buy a bear anywhere," says Clark, Chief Executive Bear. "It's the experience that customers are looking for." The experience isn't limited to the stores themselves. The retailer's website, buildabear.com, embraces the same theme. Build-A-Bearville (buildabearville.com) is its online virtual world where users can play with each other and play games. The bears that they bought at the store have a unique code that allows the user to redeem gifts while playing games in Build-A-Bearville.

Customers pay about $25 for the basic bear, but they can also buy music, clothing, and accessories. To keep the experience fresh, Build-A-Bear Workshop regularly introduces new and limited-edition animals. Clothes and accessories are also updated to reflect current fashion trends. Outfits for the bears complement the owner's interests and personalities with themes such as sports, colleges, hobbies, and careers. Some children and their parents hold in-store birthday parties, with music playing from the store's official CD. To ensure customers enjoy a great experience every time they visit, all sales associates attend a three-week training program at "Bear University," and the firm offers incentive programs and bonuses. The inventory in the stores changes frequently, with different bear styles arriving weekly. Build-A-Bear Workshops also feature limited-edition and seasonal merchandise, such as a Beary Businesslike Curly Teddy for Father's Day; mummy, wizard, and witch bears for Halloween; and a Sweet Hugs & Kisses Teddy for Valentine's Day.

In 2013, responding to the changing interests of children, Build-A-Bear announced a sweeping upgrade to its retail stores. Clark noted that developments in digital technology have changed how kids play: "[In 1997] children were playing board games. Now they're playing games online . . . Kids are being bombarded with the next new shiny objects. But they've always loved teddy bears and that's not going to change."[1]

Because the stores are a mix between the product (the teddy bear) and the experience of creating the teddy bear, the new design incorporates several digital upgrades. To help determine appropriate changes, the company enlisted several children, termed "Cub Advisors," and their moms for advice on the changes they would like to see in the stores.

Based on this research and advice, the stores are undergoing a massive redesign. Starting at the storefront, signage has been incorporated with Microsoft Kinect technology that enables kids to play with the signage before entering. The use of digital signage allows stores to highlight sales and new products, as well as several holiday themes. The revamped "Love Me" station allows kids to give their stuffed animals personalities at an interactive table using emoticons, which are pictorial representations of a facial expression like a happy face. The "Hear Me" station has a touchscreen that allows customers to choose and load prerecorded music and animal noises, or record their own voice. The "Stuff Me" station offers the option to add custom scents such as bubble gum, cotton candy, and chocolate chip. Finally, kids can wash their bears in a digital bathtub at the "Fluff Me" station. In an effort at contingency planning, "low-tech" options are being designed that can be put over the digital stations if computers act up.

REFACT

The teddy bear came into being in 1903, when President Teddy Roosevelt refused to shoot a cub while bear hunting. The spared animal was thereafter referred to as the Teddy Bear.

[1]Sandy Smith, "Integration Specialists," *Stores*, January 2013.

Sources: www.buildabear.com; www.buildabearville.com; Sandy Smith, "Integration Specialists," *Stores*, January 2013; Tom Ryan, "Build-A-Bear Workshop Goes High-Tech," *Retail Wire*, October 8, 2012.

This case was written by Barton Weitz, University of Florida; and Scott Motyka, Babson College.

DISCUSSION QUESTIONS

1. **Is the Build-A-Bear Workshop concept a fad, or does it have staying power?**

2. **Describe the target customer for this retailer.**

3. **What can Build-A-Bear Workshop do to generate repeat visits to the store?**

CASE 3   Blue Tomato: Internationalization of a Multichannel Retailer

I. THE HISTORY OF BLUE TOMATO: A BRICK-AND-MORTAR RETAILER

When Blue Tomato started, it was at the initiative of Gerfried Schuller, a former European snowboard champion who opened a snowboarding school in 1988 and then launched a small store for snowboarders in Schladming, an Austrian ski resort, in 1994. Since that time, Blue Tomato has opened eight brick-and-mortar stores throughout Austria and Germany. Three shops are located in ski areas, and five of them function in more urban locations. To expand its business activities, Blue Tomato has expanded the variety of merchandise its sells, including products for not just snowboarders but also surfers, skaters, and freeskiers.

II. EVOLUTION OF BLUE TOMATO INTO A MULTICHANNEL RETAILER

The number of brick-and-mortar stores that a small company like Blue Tomato could open easily was relatively limited, which meant its potential customer contacts were limited, too. Therefore, it expanded into the online realm in 1997, allowing Austrian customers to place orders 24 hours a day, seven days a week. By 1999, its first large-scale web store was online; in 2008, it relaunched its website (www.blue-tomato.com) to facilitate the product-ordering process and introduced a product finder, designed to help customers locate just the right snowboards, boot bindings, snow gear, and street wear (see Exhibit 1). Using predetermined characteristics (e.g., preferred brands, size, price), this sophisticated product finder helps consumers identify their ideal product alternatives. For the company, the website relaunch was a great success, leading to sales increases of 35 percent in the first year. In general, Blue Tomato's web store has enabled it to attract new customers without investing in finding, building, or stocking new stores. In addition, it has been able to offer far more products online than it could stock in any single brick-and-mortar outlet.

In 2002, Blue Tomato expanded its multichannel strategy even further by publishing a new, printed snowboard catalog (with a print run of 130,000 in the first year), targeting convenience-oriented customers who avoided online shopping. This catalog has expanded to a print run of 500,000; in addition, the company offers not just the snowboard catalog but also a freeski catalog (with a print run of 170,000 in 2013), a skate and streetstyles catalog (print run of 80,000 in 2013), and a surf/summer catalog (print run of 350,000 in summer 2013). To distribute these catalogs, Blue Tomato uses direct mailings to selected customers, hands them out at events, and promoted them with flyers in snowboard, freeski, and surf magazines. Interested consumers also can request catalogs on the company's website, download them from its website, or view the pages online.

Although many of the company's sales come through its online orders, it relies on its brick-and-mortar stores to maintain close, direct contacts with its (potential) customers, in line with its overall corporate philosophy. To ensure direct customer contact and attract new customers, Blue Tomato also opened two test centers in ski resorts, which allow (potential) customers to try out new snowboards, boots, and bindings. The company hosts four snowboard schools in local ski areas, together with special events, such as its "Kids Days," during which children can attend its snowboard courses for free.

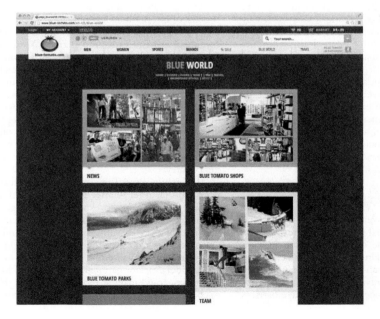

EXHIBIT 1
Blue Tomato's
Product Finder

III. SYNERGIES ACROSS DISTRIBUTION CHANNELS

In addition to its individual strengths, Blue Tomato relies on the synergies it has created across its different distribution channels. Since 2011, it has installed media boxes, or kiosks, in its brick-and-mortar stores that allow consumers to look up personalized information about special offers in particular stores. They also can log on to their Facebook (or other social media) page, connect with their friends, and ask about how well the latest snowgear or streetwear suits them. Furthermore, customers can search for products in the printed or online catalogs and order them online, or vice versa. According to Blue Tomato, the printed catalogs have contributed to and extended its online business; the opportunity to view catalogs online might further boost its online sales. For the future, the company plans to add pickup and return services to its brick-and-mortar stores, enabling customers to order a product online and pick it up in their local store.

IV. CHALLENGES COORDINATING DIFFERENT DISTRIBUTION CHANNELS

The main challenge of operating multiple distribution channels is for Blue Tomato to provide a consistent face to customers across all contact points. For example, it seeks to reinforce its commitment to customer service throughout its web store. To meet this challenge, it also standardizes all prices and communication. With regard to price, the company simply guarantees to offer the best price. If a consumer orders a product on the telephone, after receiving a catalog, but the product is listed at a cheaper price on the website because the price dropped since the catalog was published, Blue Tomato charges the customer the lower price. Its return policy—customers can return products within 21 days—also is consistent in each channel. In terms of communication, Blue Tomato's devotion to snowboarding, skating, and freeskiing is manifested by employees in the brick-and-mortar stores, as well as through the events the company hosts. Beyond this content-oriented integration, the company's communication is formally integrated.

However, the product overlap across the different distribution channels is relatively minimal. Whereas the brick-and-mortar stores and catalogs offer limited merchandise variety and assortment, its website posts more than 450,000 products, from approximately 400 brands, available for purchase. This poor overlap might be a challenge for Blue Tomato in terms of reinforcing its retail brand image among customers.

V. INTERNATIONALIZATION

To initiate its internationalization moves, in 1997, Blue Tomato installed international purchasing facilities on its website. The focus of these early internationalization efforts was on German-speaking countries (i.e., Germany and Switzerland) and German-speaking customers. The website thus was available only in German. This strategy represented an easy choice, because the language barriers between different German-speaking countries are negligible, nor did Blue Tomato face many barriers in terms of export or customs regulations. Austria and Switzerland participate in stable exchange rates, and Austria and Germany already relied on a common currency (the euro).

But this internationalization process also has expanded, particularly in the catalog channel, in which catalogs are available in different languages (e.g., the snowboard catalog is issued in five languages, and the surf/summer catalog is offered in four). The relaunch of the company's website in 2008 also sparked advances in the internationalization process, because the web store was no longer restricted to German-speaking customers; today, it has been translated into 14 languages. Thus, customers from countries throughout the world can place an order with Blue Tomato. Its most important foreign markets remain geographically nearby, including Germany, Switzerland, Scandinavia, the Benelux countries, Great Britain, and Spain, but it also has received orders from exotic destinations such as Hawaii, Hong Kong, and Argentina. Furthermore, Blue Tomato has earned the distinction of offering the largest selection of snowboards in the world on its website. As a result, 70 percent of its online orders come from foreign markets. In 2011, its products were delivered to 65 countries.

By the end of 2012, Blue Tomato's internationalization remained focused solely on its web store and printed catalogs. In these channels, it relies on direct exports. Furthermore, regardless of the channel used to support the internationalization, it has maintained its standardization strategy with respect to prices charged and communication. That is, the prices are the same for all customers in all countries, without any international price differentiation. The catalog layout also remains standardized, though the specific products included in each catalog issue vary slightly to reflect the varying appeal of certain brands in some international markets.

These eventual outcomes are not to suggest that the process of internationalization was easy. Blue Tomato has confronted several challenges, stemming largely from the complexity of the European market. Most countries in Europe are members of the European Union, but different legal conditions and tax rates arise in each member-state, and their cultural differences remain pertinent. Logistics costs and economic power also differ from country to country, with notable effects on the level of income of (potential) customers. Against this background, Blue Tomato decided to undertake some foreign direct investment in Germany: As of the end of 2012, the company had opened three brick-and-mortar stores in its neighboring country.

Meanwhile, Blue Tomato ranks as the leading European multichannel retailer for board sports and related apparel. If it decides to expand its internationalization further, by opening stores in other countries, it clearly will need to invest additional financial and personnel resources. Regardless of the strategy it might choose for such a foreign market entry, tackling more markets, with more widely variant national, legal, tax, and logistic characteristics, could make it more difficult for the company to continue with its strategy of standardization.

In 2012, Blue Tomato was acquired by Zumiez Inc., a leading North American specialty retailer of action sports–related apparel, footwear, equipment, and accessories. Zumiez already operates more than 450 stores in the United States and Canada and maintains a web store (www.zumiez.com). Despite this acquisition, Blue Tomato plans to continue to keep its headquarters in Austria, even as it seeks to meet its latest objective: to become the world leader in action sports retailing.

This case was written by Professor Thomas Foscht and Assistant Professor Marion Brandstaetter, both of Karl-Franzens-University, Graz, Austria.

DISCUSSION QUESTIONS

1. What strengths do the different distribution channels have from the company's perspective?

2. Which synergies has Blue Tomato created across different channels? What additional actions might it take to become an omnichannel retailer?

3. What key challenges remain for Blue Tomato in its efforts to coordinate these different channels?

4. Which challenges might Blue Tomato face as it expands its business activities internationally?

CASE 4 Staples Inc.

Staples operates in the highly competitive office products market. The office supply category specialists, including Staples, Office Depot, and Office Max (the big three), dramatically changed the landscape of the office supply industry. First, they greatly expanded the use of retail stores and Internet channels as means of distributing office supply products, capitalizing in part on the significant increase in the number of home offices. Prior to the mid-1980s, office supply customers primarily placed their orders through commissioned salespeople or catalogs.

Warehouse clubs, supermarkets, and full-line discount retailers also have begun taking market share away from the big three office supply retailers because of their ability to sell the bulk items at lower prices. Retailers such as Walmart and Costco offer low prices on office supplies, which forces the major office supply retailers to offer more than just products, such as extra services and greater customer service. The big three office supply stores have also expanded their business-to-business (B2B) efforts to sell to other companies, such as Wells Fargo or IBM. Staples Advantage, for example, offers a range of products and services to its B2B customers.

COMPANY BACKGROUND

Originally opened in 1986 by executive-turned-entrepreneur Tom Stemberg, Staples has reached sales of more than $25 billion. Staples also has been credited with pioneering the high-volume office products superstore concept. By evolving its original mission of slashing the costs and eliminating the hassles of running an office to one of making it easy to buy office products, Staples has become the world's largest office products company.

To distinguish itself in this competitive industry, Staples strives to provide a unique shopping experience to customers in all its market segments. Central to maintaining customer satisfaction is developing strong customer relationship skills and broad knowledge about office products among all associates hired by the company. Therefore, Staples includes formal training as an integral part of the development of its associates.

Another truly important aspect of customer service is the availability of merchandise. In the office supply industry, customers have very specific needs, such as finding an ink cartridge for a particular printer, and if the store is out of stock of a needed item, the customer may never come back.

Staples uses various marketing channels to address the needs of its different segments. Smaller businesses are generally served by a combination of retail stores, the catalog, and the Internet. Retail operations focus on serving the needs of consumers and small businesses, especially through an in-store kiosk that enables customers to order a product that may not be available in the store and receive the product via overnight delivery. In-store kiosks allow them to choose to have the product delivered to their home, business, or local store. If a customer does not want to shop in the store, he or she can visit Staples.com to order required products and select from a much larger assortment. The typical Staples retail store maintains approximately 8,000 stockkeeping units (SKUs), but Staples.com offers more than 45,000 SKUs. This multichannel approach allows Staples to increase its productivity by stocking only more popular items in stores but not sacrificing product availability.

MULTICHANNEL INTEGRATION

Staples' overall goal has been to become the leading office products and services provider by combining its existing experience, extensive distribution infrastructure, and customer service expertise with web-based information technology. As a result, the integration of different channels of distribution into one seamless customer experience has been of particular interest to the company. Staples, like many other multichannel retailers, has found that many customers use multiple channels to make their Staples purchases and that sales increase when customers use more than one channel (e.g., customers who shop two channels spend twice as much as a single-channel shopper; a tri-channel shopper spends about three times as much as a single-channel shopper). Therefore, the greater the number of channels a particular customer shops, the greater the overall expenditures he or she is likely to make.

Staples faces several challenges in integrating its channels of distribution, though, most of which are related to its Internet channel. First, it must consider the extent to which the Internet may cannibalize its retail store sales. The most attractive aspect of the Internet is its potential to attract new customers and sell more to existing customers.

But if overall sales are flat—that is, if online retailing only converts retail store sales to Internet sales—Staples suffers increased overhead costs and poorer overall productivity. Second, Staples must be concerned about the merchandise position of its retail stores compared with that of alternative channels. Because a retail store cannot carry as much merchandise as the Internet channel, the challenge is to keep an appropriate balance between minimizing stockouts and avoiding the proliferation of too many SKUs in retail stores. Finally, Staples has to contend with price competition, both within its own multichannel organization and from competitors.

STAPLES' ADDED SERVICES

Such competition means that Staples must continue to differentiate itself from other office supply retailers by adding extra value to office supplies, which themselves represent commoditized products. For example, its Copy and Print centers within its big-box stores enable customers to order print jobs and receive the help of an in-store print specialist. To increase this business line further, Staples also has opened standalone Staples Copy and Print centers, which are approximately 2,000 square feet, compared with its typical 30,000-square-foot, big-box stores. The small size of these stores allows them to be located in metropolitan areas or places where there would not be sufficient space for a large, big-box store. Customers can order their copies through the Staples website, then pick them up in the store or have them delivered. The Copy and Print stores also sell basic office supply products that customers may need to pick up at the last minute when they come to collect their print orders.

Sources: Office Supply Stores in the US—Industry Report," *IBIS World*, March 23, 2010; 2012 Staples Annual Report; interview with Max Ward, vice president of technology at Staples; W. Caleb McCann, J. P. Jeannet, Dhruv Grewal, and Martha Lanning, "Staples," in *Fulfillment in E-Business*, eds. Petra Schuber, Ralf Wolfle, and Walter Dettling (Germany: Hanser, 2001) pp. 239–252 (in German); interview with Staples' Vice President of Stores Demos Parneros and Executive Vice President of Merchandising and Marketing Jevin Eagle.

This case was written by Jeanne L. Munger, University of Southern Maine; Britt Hackmann, Nubry.com; and Dhruv Grewal and Michael Levy, Babson College.

DISCUSSION QUESTIONS

1. Assess the extent to which Staples has developed a successful multichannel strategy. What factors have contributed to its success?

2. What are the advantages and disadvantages of using kiosks as a part of its approach?

3. How should Staples assess which SKUs to keep in its stores versus on the Internet?

4. How do the Staples Copy and Print centers differentiate it from the competition?

CASE 5   The Decision-Making Process for Buying a Bicycle

The Sanchez family lives in Corona, California, west of Los Angeles. Jorge is a physics professor at the University of California–Riverside. His wife Anna is a volunteer, working 10 hours a week at the Crisis Center. They have two children: Nadia, age 10, and Miguel, age 8.

In February, Anna's parents sent her $100 to buy a bicycle for Nadia's birthday. They bought Nadia her first bike when she was 5. Now they wanted to buy her a full-size bike for her 11th birthday. Even though Anna's parents felt every child should have a bike, Anna didn't think Nadia really wanted one. Nadia and most of her friends didn't ride their bikes often, and she was afraid to ride to school because of the traffic. So Anna decided to buy her the cheapest full-size bicycle she could find.

Because most of Nadia's friends didn't have full-size bikes, she didn't know much about them and had no preferences for a brand or type. To learn more about the types available and their prices, Anna and Nadia checked the catalog for Performance Bicycle, a large mail-order bicycling equipment retailer. The catalog was given to them by a friend of Anna's, who was an avid biker. After looking through the catalog, Nadia said the only thing she cared about was the color. She wanted a blue bike, blue being her favorite color.

Using the Internet, Anna located and called several local retail outlets selling bikes. To her surprise, she found that the local Kmart store actually had the best price for a 26-inch bicycle—even lower than Toys "R" Us and Walmart.

Anna drove to Kmart, went straight to the sporting goods department, and selected a blue bicycle before a salesperson approached her. She took the bike to the cash register and paid for it. After making the purchase, the Sanchezes found out that the bike was cheap in all senses. The chrome plating on the wheels was very thin and rusted away in six months. Both tires split and had to be replaced.

A year later, Anna's grandparents sent $200 for a bike for Miguel. From their experience with Nadia's bike, the Anna and Jorge realized that the lowest-priced bike might not be the least expensive option in the long run. Miguel is very active and somewhat careless, so they want to buy a sturdy bike. Miguel said he wanted a red, 21-speed, lightweight mountain bike with a full-suspension aluminum frame and cross-country tires.

Anna and Jorge were concerned that Miguel wouldn't maintain an expensive bike with full suspension. When they saw an ad for a bicycle sale at Target, they went to the store with Miguel. A salesperson approached them at an outdoor display of bikes and directed them to the sporting goods department inside the store. There they found row after row of red, single-speed BMX bikes with no suspension and minimal accessories to maintain—just the type of bike Anna and Jorge felt was ideal for Miguel.

Another salesperson approached them and tried to interest them in a more expensive bike. Jorge dislikes salespeople trying to push something on him and interrupted her in mid-sentence. He said he wanted to look at the bikes on his own. With a little suggestion, Miguel decided he wanted one of these bikes. His desire for accessories was satisfied when they bought a multifunction cyclocomputer for the bike. After buying a bike for Miguel, Jorge decided he'd like a bike for himself to ride on weekends. Jorge had ridden bikes since he was 5. In graduate school, before he was married, he'd owned a 10-speed road bike. He frequently took 50-mile rides with friends, but he hadn't owned a bike since moving to Riverside 15 years ago.

Jorge didn't know much about current types of bicycles. He bought a copy of *Bicycling* at a newsstand to see what was available. He also went online to read *Consumer Reports*' evaluation of road, mountain, and hybrid bikes. On the basis of this information, he decided he wanted a Cannondale. It had all the features he wanted: a lightweight frame, durable construction, and a comfort sports saddle. When Jorge called the discount stores and bicycle shops, he found they didn't carry the Cannondale brand. He thought about buying the bicycle from an Internet site but was concerned about making such a large purchase without a test ride. He then decided he might not really need a bike. After all, he'd been without one for 15 years.

One day, after lunch, he was walking back to his office and saw a small bicycle shop. The shop was run down, with bicycle parts scattered across the floor. The owner, a young man in grease-covered shorts, was fixing a bike. As Jorge was looking around, the owner approached him and asked him if he liked to bicycle. Jorge said he used to but had given it up when he moved to Riverside. The owner said that was a shame because there were a lot of nice places to tour around Riverside.

As their conversation continued, Jorge mentioned his interest in a Cannondale and his disappointment in not finding a store in Riverside that sold them. The owner said that he could order a Cannondale for Jorge but that they weren't in inventory and delivery took between six and eight weeks. He suggested a Trek and showed Jorge one he currently had in stock. Jorge thought the $700 price was too high, but the owner convinced him to try it next weekend. They would ride together in the country. The owner and some of his friends took a 60-mile tour with Jorge. Jorge enjoyed the experience, recalling his college days. After the tour, Jorge bought the Trek.

This case was written by Dan Rice and Barton Weitz, University of Florida.

DISCUSSION QUESTIONS

1. Outline the decision-making process for each of the Sanchez family's bicycle purchases.

2. Compare the different purchase processes for the three bikes. What stimulated each of them? What factors were considered in making the store choice decisions and purchase decisions?

3. Go to the student site of the Online Learning Center (OLC), and click on the multiattribute model. Construct a multiattribute model for each purchase decision. How do the attributes considered and importance weights vary for each decision?

CASE 6   Parisian Patisserie "Maison Ladurée" Goes Global

Ladurée, a famous French pastry company and known worldwide for it macarons, has recently entered the U.S. market, which produces opportunities—but also challenges—for this company.

It all began in 1862, when Louis Ernest Ladurée created a bakery at 16 rue Royale in Paris, where the most prestigious names in French luxury goods were already located. Ernest Ladurée's wife had the idea of mixing the Parisian café and pastry shop, which gave birth to one of the first tea salons in the city. At the beginning of the twentieth century, Pierre Desfontaines, second cousin of Louis Ernest Ladurée, first thought of taking two macaron shells (almond meringue cakes) and joining them with ganache, a creamy smooth filling that gave birth to Ladurée's macarons.

This tea salon imbued with a refined atmosphere and charged with history seduced David Holder and his father, Francis Holder, founder of the Holder Group. The family would have lunch at the original Ladurée every Saturday. When they found out that the company was for sale by descendents of the Ladurée family, they bought it, having convinced the owners that they would preserve its heritage. David Holder likes to tell people that he woke up a sleeping beauty with their macarons. Indeed, macarons in

general were not very popular at the time they bought the company in 1997.

Since then, Holder has run Ladurée more as a *maison de mode* rather than a pastry brand and wants to keep a sense of exclusiveness and luxury. Macarons are his most profitable pastry, which accounts for 40 percent of the sales revenues and comprises 70 percent of the take-away sales. They boast 17 subtle flavors, which change according to the season. In addition to its core range of macarons packed in pale mauve and pistachio boxes, Ladurée also retails its own pastries, coffee, chocolates, ice cream macarons, candies, perfumed candles, bath and body products, and fragrances.

Ladurée has successfully understood the challenge of satisfying the needs of a hip and global clientele and to position itself as *haute couture* of the food market. Since 1997, Ladurée has been expanding, first in several locations within Paris, where it sells 55,000 macarons a day (four boutiques in Paris and one at Chateau de Versailles, boutiques and "coaches" in Orly and Roissy airports, and a boutique in Saint-Tropez), then to other cities, starting with London in 2005. There are currently 39 Ladurée stores in 14 countries. Around the world, each boutique sticks to the Parisian Ladurée signature style. The shops are done in pastel green with traditional decorative accents, mirrors, and dark wood, meant to showcase chocolates and tabletop items—and to respect the French tea salon tradition. Macarons and chocolates are made exclusively in Paris for all the Ladurée shops to protect the secret recipes. Different types of retail formats exist, from standalone retail locations featuring a small footprint, few seats, and excluding pastries and alcohol in Australia, for example, to larger tea salon sites, which are essentially stores with a store in department stores, such as in Printemps in France and Harrod's in the United Kingdom, or within malls such as in the Centria Mall in Riyadh, the Saudi capital.

Ladurée opened its first Australian store in Sydney in July 2012 with its traditional French fit-out. While the company has eight baking facilities around the world, Australian products are frozen and shipped from Switzerland, where a production plant is located. David Holder was looking for production plant locations in the Middle East, in eastern Europe and in Africa. The company chose Switzerland because of social peace, raw materials quality, and fresh air. Holder is not afraid to mention the Swiss-made origin of its macarons.

Ladurée entered the U.S. market in August 2011 by opening a shop on Madison Avenue in New York. After the Japanese, Americans are Ladurée's best customers in the Parisian boutiques. Macarons are all flown in from Paris. The other pastries, shipped from France are stored in refrigerators. If they are successful in the U.S., the Holder family will open a pastry lab in New York. With a $2.70 per unit selling price, all 17 Ladurée flavors will be available, plus a cinnamon-raisin flavor macaron especially created for and only available in the Big Apple boutique. Ladurée expanded to Soho, on West Broadway at Broome Street, in the fall of 2012. The new location boasts a retail shop and a tearoom plus a full-service restaurant with about 200 seats, private dining rooms, and a garden terrace. The new location hosts two chefs from France to prepare everything except the macarons and chocolates.

After New York, Ladurée plans to expand to other American cities, such as Los Angeles and San Francisco. The retailer also plans to open stores in Hong Kong,

Brazil, South Korea, Morocco, and Qatar in 2012 and in well-known jet-set places such as Cannes, Megève, and Courchevel, either by investing directly or working in partnership with local companies. The Holder family never invests directly in countries where political, economical, or religious risk is possible. They own and operate their stores in France, the United States, Japan, and the United Kingdom; for all other locations, boutiques are owned by local franchisees.

Sources: www.laduree.com/; Carla Bridge, "Ladurée," *Inside Retailing*, May 25, 2012; Axel Tardieu "Ladurée arrive à New York Par," September 7, 2011, http://frenchmorning.com/ny/2011/09/07/ouverture-de-la-premiere-boutique-laduree-a-new-york/; Anne-Laure Pham, "Ladurée ouvre boutique à New York," August 31, 2011, http://weekend.levif.be/tendance/culinaire/actualite-culinaire/laduree-ouvre-boutique-a-new-york/article-1195094843984.htm (accessed July 23, 2012); Catherine Dubouloz, "Nous avons d'importants projets de développement à l'international" and "À partir de l'automne 2011, les macarons de Ladurée seront produits en Gruyère," *Le Temps*, November 19, 2010; Mathilde Visseyrias, "Ladurée, l'autre pépite familiale," *Le Figaro*, December 17, 2010; Florence Fabricant "Macarons and Ice Cream, Direct from Paris to the Upper East Side," New York Times, August, 30, 2011; Hannah Leighton, "Maison Ladurée to Open Soho Location this Fall," June 27, 2012, http://ny.eater.com/archives/2012/06/maison_ladure_opening_soho_location_by_fall.php; "Laduree: A Clean Affair with Macarons!" *Arab News*, June12, 2012.

This case was written by Sandrine Heitz-Spahn, Universite De Lorraine and Michael Levy, Babson College.

DISCUSSION QUESTIONS

1. What is Ladurée's target market and retail strategy in the United States?

2. What are the key steps Ladurée has to go through when entering the American market?

3. Explain the reasons Ladurée owns its store in some countries and uses franchising with local licensees in others.

4. Which type(s) of retailing format(s) and location(s) are best suited to match Ladurée's marketing strategy in the United States?

5. Could Ladurée sell its products online? Why or why not? Explain.

CASE 7   Retailing in India: The Impact of Hypermarkets

The history of India contains a wealth of change and alteration, and the modern era is no different as the country blossoms into a major player in the global economy. Sizable economic growth during the past decade, particularly in the retail sector, has changed the way Indian consumers behave. Although the size of the current Indian retail sector is impressive, its potential really speaks to what retailing will mean in the future. The retail market in India was approximately $353 billion in 2010, and by 2014 it will reach $543 billion in total sales, of which modern retailing (described shortly) accounts for 27 percent.

Before 2000, Indian consumers generally purchased many of their retail goods from local mom-and-pop stores called *kiranas*, which sold mainly provisions and groceries. Shopping at *kiranas* is easy and convenient because the small stores serve specific neighborhoods and establish personal relationships with their customers.

International retailers are slowly making their way into India. To enter the country, they have two options: They can either set up a wholly owned subsidiary (WOS) in India, or they can enter a joint venture with an existing Indian firm. Until recently, India's government allowed foreign companies to open only single-brand stores, such as IKEA and Apple, in which the foreign company entered a joint venture with an Indian firm in which they owned no more than 51 percent of the Indian company they were partnering with. In 2012, India made dramatic changes to its laws regarding international retailers doing business in the country. Single-brand retailers are now allowed to retain 100 percent ownership of the subsidiary company (making them into wholly-owned subsidiaries). India also eased its laws for multibrand retailers, though not as much as they did for single-brand retailers. Specifically, multibrand retailers are now allowed to open stores in India's 53 cities with populations greater than 1 million, provided that they retain no more than 51 percent ownership of the Indian firm they are entering the joint venture with, spend at least 50 percent of their investment capital on building supply chain infrastructure, and source a minimum of 30 percent of the manufactured goods they sell from small- to medium-sized local Indian companies.

Walmart, Tesco, and Carrefour have opened hypermarkets in India, but doing so was not an easy process. Carrefour waited 10 years to open its first store as a result of the previous restrictions. The large store layouts and variety of merchandise force customers to spend more time in the stores, which in turn leads to more sales. The potential for hypermarkets in India sheds light on the country's changing retail landscape and the shopping habits of its consumers. The infusion of hypermarkets threatens to rob local store owners of their customer base—approximately a 23 percent decrease in sales in one year.

Although this is good news for hypermarket and supermarket retailers, the changes in the laws are proving difficult to navigate. Although Walmart announced in September 2012 that it would open several retail stores in the next 12 to 18 months with partner Bharti Walmart, Indian regulators quickly brought scrutiny to the partnership. In October 2012, it was announced that Walmart was being investigated for possible violations of the foreign investment laws, and by late November of the same year Walmart had suspended several of its employees, including its Indian CFO, until its own investigation was concluded. Clearly, although India is an excellent business opportunity, the road is rocky.

Currently, there are more than 300 hypermarkets and 3,000 supermarkets in India. India has been experiencing a 20 percent annual growth in retail markets. Each new store opening may draw customers from 20 to 25 *kiranas* and fruit and vegetable stands, affecting more than 100,000 vendors. Most *kiranas* cannot compete with hypermarkets, because these larger retail outlets create more efficiency within the supply chain. Much local produce in India currently is wasted because the country lacks sufficient infrastructure. Even as it progresses through rapid development, India still lacks some amenities that Westerners take for granted, such as refrigeration in retail operations. If a large retailer wants to open a hypermarket in India, it will have to invest capital to ensure freshness throughout the supply chain and help reduce waste. The Indian government is expected to spend $500 billion (U.S.) over the next few years to develop a world-class infrastructure, which should spur growth in the retail sector.

The lack of infrastructure underlies a related issue facing hypermarkets. Unlike in Western nations, India's rather poor roads and transportation systems do not allow retailers to locate on large plots of land on the outskirts of town because few consumers can reach them. Therefore, hypermarkets must look for retail space in more urban areas, which provide little available real estate. Buying up space from existing stores means displacing local corner shops already inhabiting that space, and this may prompt protests from Indian consumers and store owners who value the Indian tradition that the *kiranas* represent. Yet, larger retail outlets in India could have a dramatic impact on the economy, possibly creating millions of jobs in the next 10 years. Although many Indians may not appreciate the notion of hypermarkets immediately, their presence is likely inevitable.

Much of the impetus for the emergence of hypermarkets in India also comes from changes among Indian consumers. The country's younger generations are exposed to a host of innovative products that were unknown to their parents. They are far more receptive to new products and ideas. In addition, this segment of the population reflects the shifting age demographics; more than half of India's current population is younger than 25 years of age. With such a large percentage of younger consumers, it seems inevitable that India's cultural tastes will change. The strength and abundance of local *kiranas* have been a cultural mainstay, but they cannot efficiently offer Indians access to new and technologically advanced products. Because hypermarkets combine department stores and supermarkets, they carry product lines that local vendors cannot. They sell brand-name products at affordable prices, thereby enabling Indians to purchase a wide assortment of goods that they otherwise could not have.

This shift, from local mom-and-pop stores to more organized retail outlets, is happening very quickly in India. It is embraced by many consumers despite the cultural and legal considerations associated with hypermarkets. Furthermore, because hypermarkets offer potential benefits for both the economy and the national infrastructure, local governments generally support the arrival of a hypermarket. The ultimate target market, however, is not the government but the consumers, and just as in any country at any time, the challenge lies in understanding what those consumers want and how to get it to them.

Sources: "Infra Red—India's Ambitious Development Plans Hinge on Attracting Private Capital," *The Economist*, July 8, 2010; "A Wholesale Invasion—a French Supermarket Chain Takes a Bet on India," *The Economist*, May 20, 2010; Armina Ligaya, "India Puts Squeeze on Hypermarkets," *The National*, September 16, 2009; "India—Tier I & II Cities May Have 300 Hypermarkets by 2011," *RNCOS*, August 13, 2009; www.ibef.org/industry/retail.aspx; "Coming to Market—Retailing in India," *The Economist*, April 15, 2006, p. 69; "Despite Growing Debt, the Indian Consumer Banks on Tomorrow," *India Knowledge@Wharton*, October 31, 2006; Ranjan Biswas, "India's Changing Consumers," *Chain Store Age*, May 2006; John Elliott, "Retail Revolution," *Fortune*, August 9, 2007, pp. 14–16; Amelia Gentleman, "Indians Protest Wal-Mart's Wholesale Entry," *The New York Times*, August 10, 2007; "Wal-Mart Enters India's

560   SECTION V   Cases

Retail Market Amid New Rules," *CBCNews*, September 21, 2012; Vikas Bajaj, "India Puts Wal-Mart Deal With Retailer Under Scrutiny," *The New York Times*, October 18, 2012; Vikas Bajaj, "India Unit of Wal-Mart Suspends Employees," *The New York Times*, November 23, 2012; Angelo Young, "FDI In India Retail: Parliament Backs Delhi's Move to Let States Decide on Foreign Retail Competition," *International Business Times*, December 7, 2012; Rachit Vats, "Lure of the Hypermarket," *Hindustan Times*, April 22, 2012; "India: FDI in Single Brand Retail Increased to 100%," *International Law*, November 12, 2012.

This case was written by Todd Nicolini, while an MBA student at Loyola College in Maryland, under the supervision of Professor Hope Corrigan; Britt Hackmann, Nubry.com; and Scott Motyka, Babson College.

DISCUSSION QUESTIONS

1. How might a hypermarket located in India appeal to consumers and orient them to shopping in larger stores?

2. Is the Indian government's willingness to spend $500 billion to improve the nation's infrastructure good news for international retailers? Why or why not?

3. Identify the main changes that mark Indian consumers. How can international retailers learn more about India's youthful demographic?

CASE 8 Diamonds from Mine to Market

According to the American Museum of Natural History, a diamond is carbon in its most concentrated form. Because of their chemical makeup and crystalline structure, diamonds possess unique characteristics. They are the hardest known natural substance. These traits determine their status as the "king of gems," a reference to their vast popularity as jewelry and decoration.

The diamond supply chain consists of six steps: exploration, mining, sorting, cutting and polishing, jewelry design and production, and retail display. According to the website for De Beers, the producer of approximately 40 percent of the world's supply of rough or uncut diamonds, members of this extensive supply chain include geologists, engineers, environmentalists, miners, sorters, distributors,

cutters, polishers, traders, manufacturers, exporters, and salespeople, who in turn employ vast technology, artistic, and skill-related resources to discover, produce, and distribute jewelry-quality diamonds.

The jewelry-quality designation refers to a particular rating according to four key elements of a diamond, better known as the 4Cs: cut, carat, color, and clarity. The De Beers Corporation introduced these criteria in 1939 to provide consumers with a reference for evaluating diamonds, as Exhibit 1 summarizes.

Before they reach showrooms to be evaluated on these criteria, diamonds have endured approximately 3 billion years of hot temperatures and intense pressures under the Earth's surface. Production estimates from the World

EXHIBIT 1
De Beers' Description of the Four Cs for Diamond Quality

Cut	Cut refers to the angles and proportions a skilled craftsperson creates in transforming a rough diamond into a polished diamond.
	A well-cut diamond will reflect light internally from one mirrorlike facet to another, dispersing it through the top of the stone.
	To cut a diamond perfectly, a craftsperson will often need to cut away more than 50 percent of the rough diamond.
	Cut also refers to the shape of a diamond: round, emerald, heart, marquise, or pear.
Carat weight	Carat is often confused with size, even though it is actually a measure of weight. The cut of a diamond can make it appear much larger or smaller than its actual weight.
	One carat is the equivalent of 200 milligrams. One carat can also be divided into 100 "points." A .75-carat diamond is the same as a 75-point- or a three-quarter-carat diamond.
Color	Most diamonds appear icy white, but many have tiny hints of color. Diamonds are graded on a color scale established by the Gemological Institute of America (GIA), ranging from D (colorless) to Z.
	Colorless diamonds are extremely rare and therefore very valuable.
	Diamonds are also sometimes found in "fancy" colors: pink, blue, green, yellow, brown, orange, and, very rarely, red. These diamonds, called "fancies," are incredibly rare and valuable. These colors extend beyond the GIA color grading system.
Clarity	Diamonds, like people, have natural blemishes in their makeup. Minerals or fractures form these tiny faults, or inclusions, while the diamond is forming in the earth.
	When light enters a diamond, it is reflected and refracted. If anything disrupts the flow of light in the diamond, such as an inclusion, a proportion of the light reflected will be lost.
	Most inclusions are not visible to the naked eye unless magnified.
	To view inclusions, trained gemologists use a magnifying loupe. This tool allows experts to see a diamond at 10 times its actual size. Even with a loupe, the birthmarks in the VVS (Very, Very Slightly Included) to VS (Very Slightly Included) range can be extremely difficult to find. It is only when a diamond is graded "I" that it is possible to see the birthmarks with the naked eye.

Diamond Council indicate diamond mining operations are in more than 20 countries, including Russia, Botswana, the Democratic Republic of the Congo, Australia, South Africa, Canada, Angola, Namibia, Ghana, Brazil, and Sierra Leone.

The world diamond supply is dominated by African countries, which generate between 60 and 65 percent (by weight) of current diamond production. Other key sources for diamonds span the globe, for example, the remote northern regions of Western Australia, which produce roughly 30 million carats (20 percent of global production) each year from both open pit and underground operations. These diamonds are known for the range of colors, especially pink stones.

Diamonds prompt significant competition, as depicted in the movie *Blood Diamond*, which portrays the gruesome conflict and violence in Sierra Leone over diamonds. In many countries, profits from diamonds go to fund civil wars that take millions of lives. To prevent such abuses, the Kimberly Process, an international diamond certification scheme, was established to abolish trade in diamonds that fund conflict. Since its launch in 2003, the Kimberly Process has become law in 75 countries and received backing from the United Nations. It requires that governments of diamond-producing nations certify that shipments of rough diamonds are not funding violence.

Even with a certification process though, some diamonds continue to be smuggled out of African countries. Violent groups find ways to exploit the Kimberley Process to traffic in illicit diamonds. "Conflict diamonds continue to be certified in countries that are members of the Kimberley Process, legitimized by the very scheme which was designed to eradicate them." A contrasting report from the World Diamond Council claims that "because of the Kimberly Process, more than 99% of the world's diamond supply is from sources free from conflict."

When the international diamond industry agreed to implement a voluntary system of warranties, it promised consumers it could track diamond jewelry up to the point of sale. Invoices for the sale of conflict-free diamond jewelry must include a written guarantee of that status. To ensure the diamonds they purchase for their spouses, fiancées, or themselves are indeed sourced appropriately, consumers are expected to take some responsibility, such as asking a series of questions of the jeweler from which they are purchasing:

- What is the country of origin for the diamonds in your jewelry?
- Can I see a copy of your company's policy on conflict-free diamonds?
- Can you show me a copy of the written warranty from your diamond supplier stating that your diamonds are conflict-free?

Sources: "Blood Diamonds Are Still a Reality," Amnesty International, http://web.amnesty.org/pages/ec-230107-feature-eng; "Combating Conflict Diamonds," Global Witness, www.globalwitness.org/pages/en/conflict_diamonds.html; "Conflict Free Diamond Jewelry," Brilliant Earth, www.brilliantearth.com/conflict-free-diamond-definition; "Diamond Pipe," Antwerp Diamond Centre, www.awdc.be/diamond-pipeline; "Forever Diamonds," Gemnation, www.gemnation.com/base?processor=getPage'pageName=forever_diamonds_1; "Kimberley Process," www.kimberleyprocess.com/home/index_en.html; "The Argyle Diamond Mine," Argyle Diamonds, www.argylediamonds.com.au/index_whoweare.html; "The Four Cs," DeBeers, www.debeers.com/page/guidance&layout=popups#author2.

This case was written by Hope Bober Corrigan, Loyola University, Maryland.

DISCUSSION QUESTIONS

1. How important is it for consumers to buy conflict-free diamonds? Why?

2. What should the jewelry industry do to inform diamond customers about buying conflict-free gems and about the Kimberley Process?

3. Select a retail jewelry store in your area to visit. Is its policy on conflict diamonds posted anywhere, such as in the store or on the company's website? Ask store personnel the three questions posed at the end of the case. What did you learn from the web page and store visit?

CASE 9   Starbucks' Expansion into China

BRAND HISTORY/GROWTH

Starbucks, an American-based coffee company, opened its first store in Seattle, Washington, in 1971. The mission for this coffee shop was to not only have high-quality coffee, but to create a more relaxed environment where customers could meet and converse with friends. In 1987, Starbucks consisted of 11 stores and 100 employees, with a dream of becoming a national brand. Starbucks coffee shops were opening throughout the United States with 1,015 stores by 1996. The Starbucks Corporation then set its sights on international expansion beginning in 1997, when the number of total stores was 1,412. In 2012, the company operated 17,003 locations, with 37 percent outside of the United States in 40 countries. Starbucks' financial performance showed an accelerated increase in revenue in the early 2000s because of the focus on international expansion.

Starbucks made the decision to concentrate in China in 1998, along with many other businesses. China is an emerging market because the middle class is in a state of constant growth, and companies want to capitalize on the opportunity the China market offers.

Starbucks quickly recognized that there were different cultures within China. Starbucks joined forces with three regional partners as a strategy to enter the emerging market and provide Chinese consumers with more localized products. In 1999, Starbucks launched a joint venture with Mei Da Coffee Company Limited in North China to open locations in Beijing. In this joint venture, both parties are equally invested in the project in terms of money and time. This was followed in 2000 with a joint venture in South China with Maxim's Caterers Limited. Starbucks also partnered with Uni-President in East China to further advance interests in Shanghai, Taipei, and Hong Kong.

Joining forces with Chinese business partners helped Starbucks gain insights into the tastes and preferences of local consumers. Entering a new market with established local partners enabled Starbucks to quickly learn about the different cultures in each individual region in China. It was not necessarily easy for coffee-centric Starbucks to grow its presence in a country that primarily drinks tea. Starbucks was faced with the challenge of creating a new marketing campaign that would revolutionize how the Chinese viewed and drank coffee. Total coffee consumption in China grew from 35.33 thousand metric tons in 2006 to 59.62 thousand metric tons in 2010 (see Exhibit 1).

COMPETITIVE ADVANTAGE

Product

Starbucks is known for selling premium coffee products. However, in China, Starbucks realized that the global brand needed to appeal to local tastes. Starbucks elected to tailor the menu to match the preferences of the local culture. Starbucks began introducing beverages that included regional ingredients, such as green tea. Additional products created specifically for the Chinese market included white tea, black sesame green tea, Frappuccino blended crème, iced rice dumplings, and Starbucks moon cakes. In China, this allowed for customers to select from a wide variety of products to meet their needs.

Promotion

Starbucks used a smart market entry strategy to grow in China. The first step was to select high-visibility and high-traffic locations to project its brand image and attract loyal consumers. Starbucks maintained a strong brand identity and marketed it as a lifestyle "symbol" rather than just a logo. Starbucks wanted consumers to see the green circle Siren logo and to think of sophistication and the ability to afford "personal luxury." One reason this strategy is working is that Starbucks didn't seem to be a threat to the "tea drinking" culture. The company used innovative marketing to create new demand for coffee and the experience that Starbucks stores offer customers.

Price

Starbucks kept its corporate pricing strategy that utilized premium pricing to ensure the desired profit margin. Starbucks believes in the quality of its products. Many competitors cut prices in order to compete in the Chinese market. Starbucks believes this is a losing strategy because companies cannot afford to "out-cut" the local Chinese competitors.

Placement

Starbucks brought the "Western coffee experience" to the Chinese market. This experience was the ability to go somewhere with friends and acquaintances, relax, and drink some favorite beverages. This proved to be a successful strategy when Starbucks first opened in China in January 1999. Many competitors did not offer air conditioning or the atmosphere of Starbucks, which provides a meeting place for business executives and friends. Starbucks' very comfortable environment allows for dine-in service instead of taking a coffee or tea on the go. This is quite different from the experience in the United States, where the majority of sales come from take-out orders. The experience that Starbucks strives to give is not just the comfortable chairs, upbeat music, and chic interior, but the feeling of a more modern lifestyle.

Human Resources

Starbucks has been incredibly successful at recruiting and training employees. The company sends baristas (brand ambassadors) to all new stores and trains employees to preserve its brand integrity. This ensures that, globally, employees stay true to the Starbucks brand. Because the overall experience is what differentiates Starbucks from competitors, this is a critical component. Annual employee turnover rates of 30 percent or higher are common in China, but Starbucks' turnover rate is much lower due to its attractive compensation packages, career paths, and working environment. Starbucks' exceptional service contributes to its success in China. In interviews with people in Shanghai, the majority of the population stated that they preferred the taste of products from competitors, but that they continue to choose Starbucks due to a high level of service.

CHINA TODAY/FUTURE

Starbucks believes that there is still an opportunity to expand in China. As of 2012, Starbucks had more than 570 stores in 48 cities with numerous additional cities for future growth. Starbucks has been in China for 13 years and has laid a foundation for continued development. Belinda Wong was appointed Starbucks' China president in July 2011. Wong's mission is to fulfill the target opening of 1,500 outlets on mainland China by 2015. She believes this will continue to provide jobs and further demonstrate Starbucks' commitment to China.

Starbucks is not the only coffee company looking for continued growth in China. The market has attracted other businesses, such as British brands Costa Coffee and Pacific Coffee Company. Costa Coffee plans to expand to 2,500 stores by 2018 with hopes of taking a third of the market share in China. Starbucks also faces competition from McDonald's, Caribou Coffee, and Dunkin' Brands. Dunkin' Brands anticipates increasing its investment in China and recently named the basketball player LeBron James as the brand ambassador for Asia. Dunkin' Brands added pork donuts to further customize the local menu.

In addition to increased competition, Starbucks also needs to pay careful attention to the average Chinese customer's income and discretionary spending. Chinese customers love the experience that Starbucks offers but may purchase only a coffee and spend all day in the store. However, a customer in the United States normally purchases coffee with a baked good. The Chinese consumer is more price sensitive and therefore tends to spend less.

THOUSAND METRIC TONS

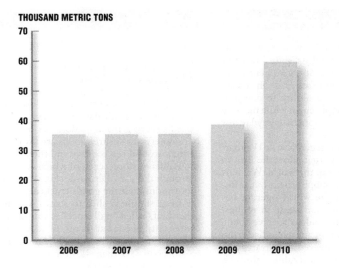

EXHIBIT 1
China's Total Coffee Consumption

Source: "Agriculture Consumption and Production." *China Country Review*, 2012, pp. 159–161.

Finally, Starbucks must ensure not to offend the Chinese population. In September 2012, Starbucks opened a store near the famed Buddhist temple in East China. Some people have expressed concerns over this store's location because it is seen as being disrespectful to the Chinese culture. This is also not the first time that a Starbucks location has created debate. In 2007, Starbucks was forced to close a store in Beijing's Forbidden City as a result of public outcries.

Wong is not concerned with these factors and stated, "We have never felt more confident about accelerating our growth momentum" after opening Starbucks' 500th store in Beijing. Chief Executive Officer Howard Schultz is also confident and believes that Starbucks will continue to be successful in China. Critics are not as confident that Starbucks will continue to be a success in China. In 2008, Starbucks closed 600 underperforming stores in the United States that had opened less than 18 months earlier. Time will tell if rapid expansion in China is a winning strategy for Starbucks.

Sources: "Agriculture Consumption and Production." *China Country Review*, 2012, pp. 159–161; "China: Brewing Up a Success Story," *Thai Press Reports*, March 5, 2012 "China Focus: Starbucks Outlet near Buddhist Temple Triggers Debate," *Xinhua News Agency*, September 24, 2012; "Don't Get Excited About Starbucks' Chinese Expansion Just Yet," *Forbes.com*, May 4, 2012; "Greater China," *News.starbucks.com*, 2012, http://news.starbucks.com/about+starbucks/starbucks+coffee+international/greater+china; "Localization Fuels Starbucks' Success in China," *Business Daily Update*, February 14, 2012; Shaun Rein, "Why Starbucks Succeeds in China and Others Haven't," *USA Today online*, February 10, 2012; Chris Sorensen, "Serving a Billion Latte Sippers," *Maclean's* 125, no. 17 (May 7, 2012), p. 41; "Starbucks Annual Report 1999–2011," *Starbucks Investor Relations*, http://investor.starbucks.com/phoenix.zhtml?c599518&p5irol-reportsannual; "Starbucks Believes That China Will Be Second Largest Market by 2014." *News.starbucks.com*, April 1, 2012; "Starbucks: Company Profile," www.starbucks.com/about-us/company; "Starbucks' Quest for Healthy Growth: An Interview with Howard Schultz," *McKinsey Quarterly* 2

(2011), pp. 34–43; Helen H. Wang, "Five Things Starbucks Did to Get China Right," *Forbes.com*, August 10, 2012.

This case was written by Bethany Wise and Samantha Leib, MBA students at Loyola University, Maryland, under the supervision of Professor Hope Corrigan.

DISCUSSION QUESTIONS

1. Prepare a SWOT analysis based on the case to support Starbucks' expansion plans in China. Based on your SWOT analysis, what recommendations would you make to Starbucks' CEO with regard to the market development growth strategy for this country?

2. Give examples of how Starbucks was successful upon entering the China market. Please use the following videos to frame your response.
   • Starbucks grows coffee in China, *Reuters Video*, available at: www.youtube.com/watch?v=BYSiGomkGdg
   • Starbucks in China, available at: www.youtube.com/watch?v=0A3rnWiEJY8
   • Starbucks wakes up to China, *Reuters Video*, available at: www.youtube.com/watch?v=CgWJAouxorg

3. Compare Starbucks' U.S. and Chinese strategies. What are the similarities and differences? What generalities can you glean from this analysis to help the company expand into other global marketplaces? Please use the case and the following article to frame your response.
   • "Starbucks' Quest for Healthy Growth: An Interview with Howard Schultz," *McKinsey Quarterly* 2 (2011), pp. 34–43, www.mckinseyquarterly.com/Strategy/Growth/Starbucks_quest_for_healthy_growth_An_interview_with_Howard_Schultz_2777.

CASE 10 Walmart: Pioneer in Supply Chain Management

Walmart dominates the retailing industry in terms of its sales revenue, its customer base, and its ability to drive down costs and deliver good value to its customers. After all, the world's largest corporation takes pride in having received numerous accolades for its ability to continuously improve efficiency in the supply chain while meeting its corporate mandate of offering customers everyday low prices.

Tight inventory management is legendary at Walmart through its just-in-time techniques that allow the firm to boast one of the best supply chains in the world. Walmart has not only transformed its own supply chain but influenced how vendors throughout the world operate because the company has the economic clout to request changes from its vendor partners and to receive them. Recognized for its ability to obtain merchandise from global sources, Walmart also pioneered the strategy of achieving high levels of growth and profitability through its precision control of manufacturing, inventory, and distribution. Although the company is not unique in this regard, it is by far the most successful and most influential corporation of its kind and has put into practice various innovative techniques.

And when Walmart does something, it does it on a massive scale. Walmart's computer system, for example, is second only to that of the Pentagon in storage capacity. Its information systems analyze more than 10 million daily transactions from point-of-sale data and distribute their analysis in real time both internally to its managers and externally via a satellite network to Walmart's many suppliers, who use the information for their production planning and order shipment.

Much of the popularity of supply chain management has been attributed to the success of Walmart's partnership with Procter & Gamble. During the 1980s, the two collaborated in building one of the first collaborative planning, forecasting, and replenishment (CPFR) systems, a software system that linked P&G to Walmart's distribution centers, taking advantage of advances in the world's telecommunications infrastructure. When a Walmart store sold a particular P&G item, the information flowed directly to P&G's planning and control systems. When the inventory level of P&G's products at Walmart's distribution center got to the point where it needed to reorder, the system automatically alerted P&G to ship more products. This information helped P&G plan its production. Walmart was also able to track when a P&G shipment arrived at one of its distribution warehouses, which enabled it to coordinate its own outbound shipments to stores. Both Walmart and P&G realized savings from the better inventory management and order processing, savings that in turn were passed on to Walmart's consumers through its everyday low prices.

A history of success doesn't mean Walmart executives can rest. Changes in social values, economic fluctuations, technology advances, and other marketplace factors demand that Walmart continue its search for innovative ways to keep consumer prices down.

WALMART'S INNOVATIONS

Walmart has pioneered many innovations in the purchase and distribution processes of the products it sells. More than 20 years ago, Walmart drove the adoption of UPC bar codes throughout the retail industry; it also pioneered the use of electronic data interchange (EDI) for computerized ordering from vendors. Its hub-and-spoke distribution network ensures goods are brought to distribution centers around the country and then directed outward to thousands of stores, each of which is within a day's travel. Through the use of cross-docking, one of its best-known innovations, half the goods trucked to a distribution center from suppliers ship to stores within 24 hours. The other half, called "pull stock" is stored at the distribution center until needed at stores. In addition, Walmart uses a dedicated fleet of trucks to ship goods from warehouses to stores in less than 48 hours, as well as to replenish store inventories about twice a week. Thus, with flow-through logistics, the company speeds the movement of goods from its distribution centers to its retail stores around the world.

Today, the retail giant continues to push the supply chain toward greater and greater efficiency, prioritizing customer needs while employing new technologies and greener practices. One of the early adopters of RFID technology to increase efficiency in its supply chain, Walmart discovered the value of balancing vision with technology maturity levels after mandating that its suppliers apply RFID tags to crates and pallets bound for its stores. Some companies thrived using the new technology. Others, including Walmart itself, ran into trouble. At the time of the mandate, RFID technology was in its infancy, and costs for planning, hardware, software, and training were prohibitive for many suppliers. Additionally the technology was new enough that the industry lacked best practices for implementation. Indeed, it lacked any examples that might help newcomers avoid pitfalls. Walmart repealed its edict, but continues to probe the usefulness of the technology. Today, Walmart is slowly testing the usefulness of RFID tags with apparel.

In response to criticism from consumer groups, Walmart tackled environmental sustainability in its supply chain and, as is frequently the case because of the company's size, became a trendsetter for other retailers. After vowing to reduce its greenhouse gas emissions by the equivalent of taking nearly 4 million cars off the roads for a year, Walmart directed its suppliers to think green throughout the full product lifecycle. Suppliers are required to pay for sustainability efforts—a price most accept willingly to retain their relationship with Walmart. Many also recognize that reducing energy use will benefit them as energy costs rise. Harnessing energy, increasing recycling, reducing waste, and minimizing packaging and transportation all reduce cost in the supply chain in addition to appealing to today's eco-conscious consumers and preserving global resources.

In a third innovation, Walmart is consolidating its global sourcing. The new model focuses on increasing the percentage of products purchased directly from suppliers and buying from global merchandising centers rather than through individual countries. Third-party procurement providers, who previously enjoyed a substantial business from the retail giant, will find themselves increasingly bypassed in the supply chain. In addition to eliminating the cost of a middle party, this effort may give Walmart increased control over inbound freight. Better control, in turn, can lower inventory costs. Thus, Walmart's continuous use of innovations leads to lower inventory and operating costs, which enables Walmart to keep its lean costs.

Following the fire in a Bangladesh factory that supplied clothing to Walmart in November of 2012 that killed 112 workers, Walmart has further tightened its control over its supply chain. The clothing being made and supplied to Walmart in this factory was done without Walmart's knowledge; it was an unapproved subcontract by one of its vendors. As a result, Walmart has moved to a "zero tolerance" policy on suppliers subcontracting without Walmart's knowledge and approval.

Finally, responding to growing criticism that Walmart purchases too many products from foreign countries and does not do enough to support the American economy, it has announced a new initiative to hire 100,000 veterans and source more products from the United States. As of March 1, 2013, any honorably discharged veteran who applies for a job with Walmart will be given one. The plan is to reach its goal of 100,000 veteran hires in five years. Additionally, over the next 10 years, Walmart plans to purchase an additional $50 billion in U.S.-made goods, increasing its already large share of U.S.-made products. Currently, approximately 55 percent of Walmart's U.S. sales come from items such as groceries, health and beauty products, household goods, and pet supplies, most of which are sourced in the United States.

Walmart continues to hone its management of the flow of products and information among its suppliers, distribution centers, and individual stores through technology to increase its control of logistics and inventory. Thoughtful use of innovation has put Walmart at the top of the retailing game. Not all organizations can pull this approach off as

well. Walmart is a unique case in which a single, very powerful firm took primary responsibility for improving performance across its own supply chain. By developing a superior supply chain management system, it has reaped the rewards of higher levels of customer service and satisfaction, lower production and transportation costs, and more productive use of its retail store space. Fundamentally, it boils down to Walmart's ability to link together suppliers, distribution centers, retail outlets, and, ultimately, customers, regardless of their location. Although operational innovation isn't the only ingredient in Walmart's success, it has been a crucial building block for its strong competitive position.

Sources: Mike Troy, "Wal-Mart's Inventory Equation," *Retailing Today*, September 11, 2006; "Financial Outlook: Restoring the Productivity Loop," *Retailing Today*, June 26, 2006; Sharon Gaudin, "Some Suppliers Gain From Failed Wal-Mart RFID Edict," *Computer World*, April 28, 2008; "RFID News: JC Penney CEO Says Retailer Going All in on RFID, Perhaps with Significant Impact on the Industry," *Supply Chain Digest*, August 15, 2012: William B. Cassidy, "Wal-Mart Tightens the Chain," *Journal of Commerce*, January 18, 2010; "Wal-Mart Tightens Rules for Suppliers," *CBC News*, January 22, 2013; "Walmart Announces $50 Billion Buy American Campaign," *Huffington Post*, January 15, 2013.

This case was written by Jeanne L. Munger, University of Southern Maine; Kate Woodworth; and Dhruv Grewal, Michael Levy, and Scott Motyka, all of Babson College.

DISCUSSION QUESTIONS

1. **How does an individual firm like Walmart manage a supply chain, particularly considering that supply chains include multiple firms with potentially conflicting objectives? Describe some of the conflicts that could arise in such a circumstance.**

2. **What are some of the ways that Walmart's supply chain management system has provided it the benefits of higher levels of product availability and lower merchandise acquisition and transportation costs? Provide specific examples of each benefit.**

CASE 11   Tiffany & Co. and TJX: Comparing Financial Performance

The year 2012 marked the 175th anniversary of Charles Lewis Tiffany's opening of his store in downtown Manhattan in 1837. Tiffany & Co. is mostly known for its exquisite jewelry, but it also has additional luxury items in its product assortment. The Tiffany robin's egg "blue boxes" have become a ubiquitous status symbol, representing the company's brand quality and craftsmanship. Tiffany & Co. has a different strategy and marketing approach than other national retailers. Throughout its history, the company's mission has been to enrich the lives of its customers by creating enduring objects of extraordinary beauty that will be cherished for generations. Tiffany & Co. has accomplished this by crafting beautiful designs, using fine-quality materials and expert workmanship, and presenting those products to its customers at luxurious stores in high-end locations.

TJX Corporation on the other hand, consists of a mix of stores under the names of TJ Maxx, HomeGoods and Marshalls in the United States (with additional stores under different names in Canada and Europe). TJX strives to offer exceptional value through its four pillars of great fashion, brand, quality, and price. It works with a variety of national brands so that its merchandise assortments at these stores are ever-changing. It is willing to purchase less-than-full assortments of items, styles, sizes, and quantities from vendors and pass on the cost savings to its customers. So that it doesn't have to completely rely on merchandise from national-brand vendors for its assortment offerings, TJX offers some private-label merchandise, which is produced specifically for TJX only. TJX does not own any factories, but rather sources its private-label

EXHIBIT 1
2011 Financial Data
for Tiffany and TJX
(in thousands)

	TIFFANY (YEAR ENDING 1/31/2012)	TJX (YEAR ENDING 1/28/2012)
	Income Statement	**Income Statement**
Net sales	$3,642,937	$23,191,455
Less: Cost of goods sold	$1,491,783	$16,854,249
Gross margin	$2,151,154	$ 6,337,206
Less: SG&A expenses	$1,442,728	$ 3,890,144
Operating profit margin	$ 708,426	$ 2,447,062
Less: Interest expense	$ 48,574	$ 35,648
Other income	$ 5,099	$ 0
Net income before taxes	$ 664,951	$ 2,411,414
Less: Taxes	$ 225,761	$ 915,324
Net income after taxes	$ 439,190	$ 1,496,090
	Balance Sheet	**Balance Sheet**
Cash	$ 433,954	$1,507,112
Accounts receivable	$ 184,085	$ 204,304
Inventory	$2,073,212	$2,950,523
Other current assets	$ 198,424	$ 470,693
Total current assets	$2,889,675	$5,132,632
Fixed assets	$ 767,174	$2,706,377
Long term assets	$ 502,143	$ 442,596
Current liabilities	$ 626,677	$3,063,423
Long-term liabilities	$ 186,802	$2,008,892
Stockholders' equity	$2,348,905	$3,209,290

products with manufacturers. It keeps relatively low inventory levels, which has helped it produce relatively fast inventory turns while maintaining strong gross margins.

Sources: Walmart Annual Report, 2012, Tiffany & Co. Annual Report, 2012.

This case was prepared by Nancy J. Murray, University of Wisconsin–Stout, and Michael Levy, Babson College.

DISCUSSION QUESTIONS

1. Calculate the following for both Tiffany and TJX using data from the abbreviated income statements and balance sheets in Exhibit 1.

   a. Gross margin percentage

   b. SG&A expense percentage

   c. Operating profit margin percentage

   d. Net profit margin (after taxes) percentage

   e. Inventory turnover

   f. Asset turnover

   g. Return on assets percentage

2. Compare and contrast the calculated financial figures for Tiffany and TJX. Analyze and discuss why the percentages and ratios differ for the two retailers.

3. Analyze which retailer has the better overall financial performance.

4. Why is ROA a good measure of a retailers' financial performance?

CASE 12 Choosing a Store Location for a Boutique

Stephanie Wilson must decide where to open a ready-to-wear boutique she's been contemplating for several years. Now in her late 30s, she's been working in municipal government ever since leaving college, where she majored in fine arts. She's divorced with two children (ages 5 and 8) and wants her own business, at least partly to be able to spend more time with her children. She loves fashion, feels she has a flair for it, and has taken evening courses in fashion design and retail management. Recently, she heard about a plan to rehabilitate an old arcade building in the downtown section of her midwestern city. This news crystallized her resolve to move now. She's considering three locations.

THE DOWNTOWN ARCADE

The city's central business district has been ailing for some time. The proposed arcade renovation is part of a master redevelopment plan, with a new department store and several office buildings already operating. Completion of the entire master plan is expected to take another six years.

Dating from 1912, the arcade building was once the center of downtown trade, but it's been vacant for the past 15 years. The proposed renovation includes a three-level shopping facility, low-rate garage with validated parking, and convention center complex. Forty shops are planned for the first (ground) floor, 28 more on the second, and a series of restaurants on the third.

The location Stephanie is considering is 900 square feet and situated near the main ground-floor entrance. Rent is $20 per square foot, for an annual total of $18,000. If sales exceed $225,000, rent will be calculated at 8 percent of sales. She'll have to sign a three-year lease.

TENDERLOIN VILLAGE

The gentrified urban area of the city where Stephanie lives is called Tenderloin Village because of its lurid past. Today, however, the neat, well-kept brownstones and comfortable neighborhood make it feel like a trendy enclave. Many residents have done the remodeling work themselves and take great pride in their neighborhood.

About 20 small retailers are now in an area of the village adjacent to the convention center complex, along with some vegetarian and nouveau cuisine restaurants. There are also three small women's specialty clothing stores.

The site available to Stephanie is on the village's main street on the ground floor of an old house. Its space is also about 900 square feet. Rent is $15,000 annually, with no extra charge based on the level of sales. The landlord knows Stephanie and will require a two-year lease.

APPLETREE MALL

This suburban mall has been open for eight years. A successful regional center, it has three department stores and 100 smaller shops just off a major interstate highway about 8 miles from downtown. Of its nine women's clothing retailers, three are in a price category considerably higher than what Stephanie has in mind.

Appletree has captured the retail business in the city's southwest quadrant, although growth in that sector has slowed in the past year. Nevertheless, mall sales are still running 12 percent ahead of the previous year. Stephanie learned of plans to develop a second shopping center east of town, which would be about the same size and character as Appletree Mall. But groundbreaking is still 18 months away, and no renting agent has begun to enlist tenants.

The location available to Stephanie in Appletree is two doors from the local department store chain. At 1,200 square feet, it's slightly larger than the other two possibilities. But it's long and narrow—24 feet in front by 50 feet deep. Rent is $24 per square foot ($28,800 annually). In addition, on sales that exceed $411,500, rent is 8 percent of sales. There's an additional charge of 1 percent of sales to cover common-area maintenance and mall promotions. The mall's five-year lease includes an escape clause if sales don't reach $411,500 after two years.

This case was prepared by Professor David Ehrlich, Marymount University.

DISCUSSION QUESTIONS

1. List the pluses and minuses of each location.

2. What type of store would be most appropriate for each location?

3. If you were Stephanie, which location would you choose? Why?

CASE 13   Hutch: Locating a New Store

In June, after returning from a trip to the Bahamas, Dale Abell, vice president of new business development for the Hutch Corporation, began a search for a good location to open a new store. After a preliminary search, Abell narrowed the choice to two locations, both in Georgia. He now faces the difficult task of thoroughly analyzing each location and determining which will be the site of the next store.

COMPANY BACKGROUND

The Hutch store chain was founded in 1952 by John Henry Hutchison, a musician and extremely successful insurance salesman. Hutchison established the headquarters in Richmond, Virginia, where both the executive offices and one of two warehouse distribution centers are located. Hutch currently operates 350 popularly priced women's clothing stores throughout the Southeast and Midwest. Manufacturers ship all goods to these distribution centers. They are delivered floor-ready, in that the vendor has attached price labels, UPC identifying codes, and source tags for security purposes and placed appropriate merchandise on hangers. Once at the distribution centers, the merchandise is con-

solidated for reshipment to the stores. Some staple merchandise, such as hosiery, is stored at these distribution centers. All Hutch stores are located within 400 miles of a distribution center. This way, as Abell explains, "A truck driver can deliver to every location in two days."

HUTCH FASHIONS

Hutch Fashions is considered one of the leading popularly priced women's fashion apparel chains in the Southeast. The stores carry trendy apparel selections in juniors', misses', and women's sizes, all at popular prices. The chain offers a complementary array of accessories in addition to its main features of dresses, coats, and sportswear. Located mainly in strip centers and malls, these shops typically require 4,000 to 5,000 square feet.

HUTCH EXTRA

Hutch Extra stores are primarily located in strip centers and malls. They bear a strong resemblance to Hutch Fashions. The difference is that Hutch Extra stores require less space (2,000 to 3,000 square feet) and cater to women requiring

EXHIBIT 1
Layout of Hutch Fashions* Hutch Extra Store

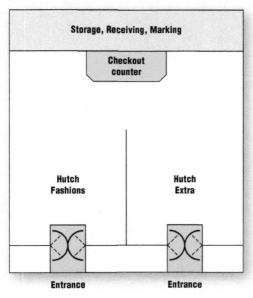

large and half-size apparel. (Women who wear half-sizes require a larger size but are not tall enough to wear a standard large size. In other words, a size 18½ is the same as size 18 except that it is cut for a shorter woman.)

HUTCH FASHIONS*HUTCH EXTRA

Although Hutch Fashions and Hutch Extra stores selectively appear as separate entries, the corporate goal is to position both as a single entity. The combination store emerged in 1986 and is now used for all new stores. The Hutch Fashions*Hutch Extra combination occupies a combined space of 6,000 to 7,000 square feet, with separate entrances for each entity. A partial wall separates the two frontal areas of the store but allows for a combined checkout/customer service area in the rear. These stores are primarily located in strip centers and can occasionally be found in malls. (Exhibit 1 shows a typical layout.)

MARKETING STRATEGY

Customers
Hutch's target market is women between the ages of 18 and 40 years who are in the lower-middle- to middle-income range. Abell explains, "We don't cater to any specific ethnic group, only to women who like to wear the latest fashions."

Product/Price
Hutch positions merchandise and price levels between the mass merchandisers and the department stores. You won't find any bluelight specials or designer boutiques in a Hutch store. By avoiding direct competition for customers with the large discounters (Target, Walmart) and the high-fashion department stores and specialty shops, Hutch has secured a comfortable niche for itself. "Our products must be priced at a level where our customers

perceive our products to be elegant and fashionable but not too expensive," notes Abell.

Location
Hutch stores are located throughout the Southeast and Midwest and must be within a 400-mile radius of a Hutch distribution center. Within this geographic area, Hutch stores are located in communities with a population range of 10,000 to 50,000 and a trade area of 50,000 to 150,000. These locations are characterized by a large concentration of people in the low- to middle-income brackets who work in agriculture and industry.

Hutch stores are primarily located in strip malls or strip centers—generally ones anchored by either a regional or national discount store (Walmart or Target). In addition, these centers contain a mix of several nationally recognized and popular local tenants. Hutch stores are primarily located adjacent to the center's anchor. Mall locations must be on the main corridor, as close to "center court," as economics (rent) will allow. Abell remarked, "We don't care if it's the only center in the region. If the only space available is at the end of the mall, we won't go in there. Our plan is to be a complement to the anchor and to feed off the traffic coming to it. We may have a reputation for being picky and having one of the toughest lease agreements in the business, but it's one of the main reasons for our continued success."

DATA SOURCES

Abell is using several reports generated by Claritas to help him decide which location to choose for the next Hutch store. He has chosen reports that describe the 10-mile ring around each of the proposed locations. Exhibits 2 and 3 summarize these reports. They contain detailed population, household, race, income, education, and employment data, plus figures on retail sales and number of establishments. The reports also provide information about women's apparel sales and give a market index that estimates the annual per-person spending potential for the trade area divided by the national average (see Exhibit 3). Dalton's 99 index means that the spending potential for women's clothing is slightly lower than the national average of 100. Finally, Abell is using Claritas/UDS's PRIZM lifestyle reports. These reports contain numeric figures and percentages on the population, households, families, sex, age, household size, and ownership of housing. An excerpt from the report is given in Exhibit 4. Some of the cluster group names are described in Exhibit 5.

THE POTENTIAL LOCATIONS

Dalton
Dalton produces most of the carpeting in the United States. Consequently, carpet mills are the major employers in Dalton. Stain Master carpeting has been putting a strain on the city's water supply. Stain Master is said to require seven times the amount of water as regular carpeting and is rapidly becoming the largest proportion of carpeting produced. Expressing concern over market viability, Abell said, "If the Dalton area were ever to experience a severe drought, the carpet mills would be forced to drastically reduce production. The ensuing layoffs could put half the population on unemployment."

		Dalton	Hinesville
Population	2015 projection	93,182	64,195
	2010 estimate	87,293	57,945
	1999 Census	79,420	49,853
	1990 Census	71,373	34,125
	% change, 1999–2008	9.9%	16.2%
	% change, 1990–1999	11.3%	46.1%
	In group quarters (military base) 2008	.9%	11.2%
Household	2015 projection	35,570	20,010
	2010 estimate	33,140	17,541
	1999 Census	29,340	14,061
	1990 Census	24,302	8,557
	% change, 1999–2008	12.9%	24.7%
	% change, 1990–1999	20.7%	64.3%
Families	2010 estimate	24,347	14,277
Race	White	92.0%	54.1%
	Black	4.9%	38.3%
	American Indian	0.2%	0.5%
	Asian or Pacific Islander	0.6%	3.1%
	Other	2.3%	4.0%
Age	0–20	31.2%	40.2%
	21–44	37.1%	47.0%
	45–64	21.7%	9.2%
	65+	9.9%	3.4%
	Median age	33.7	23.9
	Male	32.5	23.6
	Female	35.0	24.6
Household size	1 person	21.0%	15.2%
	2 persons	32.3%	26.6%
	3–4 persons	38.1%	45.7%
	5+ persons	8.7%	12.6%
Income	Median household income	$30,516	$23,686
	Average household income	$40,397	$28,677
Sex (% male)		49.1%	55.8%
Education	Population age 25+	49,298	22,455
	No high school diploma	41.0%	15.5%
	High school only	28.6%	41.2%
	College, 1–3 years	19.1%	29.7%
	College, 4+ years	11.3%	13.5%
Industry	Manufacturing: nondurable goods	42.3%	7.2%
	Retail trade	12.6%	23.3%
	Professional and related services	13.3%	21.4%
	Public administration	2.2%	20.0%
Retail sales ($ thousands)	Total	$706,209	$172,802
	General merchandise stores Apparel stores	$26,634	$9,339
Retail establishments	General merchandise stores	12	3
	Women's apparel stores	21	8

EXHIBIT 2
Population and Competitive Profile, 10-Mile Ring from Centers of Dalton and Hinesville, Georgia

	Area Sales ($ mil.)	Area Sales per Capita	U.S. Sales per Capita	Index (area sales ÷ U.S. sales)
Dalton	$18.01	$206.26	$207.65	99
Hinesville	$8.97	$154.74	$207.65	75

EXHIBIT 3
Sales Potential Index for Women's Apparel

570   SECTION V   Cases

EXHIBIT 4   PRIZM Neighborhood Clusters

Prizm Cluster	Population, 2008	Percentage of Population	Prizm Cluster	Population, 2008	Percentage of Population
Dalton			**Mines & mills**	7,694	8.8
Big fish, small pond	4,727	5.4%	Back country folks	4,293	4.9
New homesteaders	6,030	6.9			
Red, white, & blues	31,123	35.7	**Hinesville**		
Shotguns & pickups	8,881	10.2	Military quarters	45,127	77.9
Rural industrial	12,757	14.6	Scrub pine flats	3,476	6.0

EXHIBIT 5   PRIZM Lifestyle Clusters

Big Fish, Small Pond

Small-town executive families; upper-middle incomes; age groups 35–44, 45–54; predominantly white. This group is married, family-oriented, and conservative. Their neighborhoods are older. Best described as captains of local industry, they invest in their homes and clubs and vacation by car in the United States.

Rural Industrial

Low-income, blue-collar families; lower-middle incomes; age groups <24, 25–34; predominantly white, high Hispanic. Nonunion labor found in this cluster, which is comprised of hundreds of blue-collar mill towns on American's rural backroads.

Mines & Mills

Older families; mine and mill towns; poor; age groups 55–64, 65+; predominantly white. Down the Appalachians, across the Ozarks to Arizona, and up the Missouri, this cluster is exactly as its name implies. This older, mostly single population with a few children lives in the midst of scenic splendor.

Shotguns & Pickups

Rural blue-collar workers and families; middle income; age groups 35–44, 45–54; predominantly white. This cluster is found in the Northeast, the Southeast, and the Great Lakes and Piedmont industrial regions. They are in blue-collar jobs; most are married with school-age kids. They are churchgoers who also enjoy bowling, hunting, sewing, and attending car races.

Back Country Folks

Older farm families; lower-middle income; age groups 55–64, 65+; predominantly white. This cluster is centered in the eastern uplands along a wide path from the Pennsylvania Poconos to the Arkansas Ozarks. Anyone who visits their playgrounds in Branson, Missouri, or Gatlinburg, Tennessee, can attest that these are the most blue-

collar neighborhoods in America. Centered in the Bible Belt, many back country folks are hooked on Christianity and country music.

Scrub Pine Flats

Older African American farm families; poor; age groups 55–64, 65+; predominantly black. This cluster is found mainly in the coastal flatlands of the Atlantic and Gulf states from the James to the Mississippi Rivers. These humid, sleepy rural communities, with a mix of blacks and whites, live in a seemingly timeless, agrarian rhythm.

New Homesteaders

Young middle-class families; middle income; age groups 35–44, 45–54; predominantly white. This cluster is above-average for college education. Executives and professionals work in local service fields such as administration, communications, health, and retail. Most are married; the young have children, the elders do not. Life is homespun with a focus on crafts, camping, and sports.

Red, White, & Blues

Small-town blue-collar families; middle income; age groups 35–54, 55–64; predominantly white, with skilled workers primarily employed in mining, milling, manufacturing, and construction. Geocentered in the Appalachians, Great Lakes industrial region, and western highlands, these folks love the outdoors.

Military Quarters

GIs and surrounding off-base families; lower-middle income; age groups under 24, 25–34; ethnically diverse. Because this cluster depicts military life with personnel living in group quarters, its demographics are wholly atypical because they are located on or near military bases. Racially integrated and with the highest index for adults under 35, "Military Quarters" like fast cars, bars, and action sports.

The proposed site for the new store is the Whitfield Square shopping center located off the main highway, approximately two miles from the center of town (see Exhibit 6). After meeting with the developer, Abell was pleased with several aspects of the strip center. He learned that the center has good visibility from the highway, will be anchored by both Walmart and Kroger (a large grocery chain), and has ample parking. Abell is also reasonably pleased with the available location within the center, which is one spot away from Walmart. However, he is concerned about the presence of two large outparcels in front of the center that would reduce the number of parking spaces and direct visibility of the center. (An outparcel is a free-standing structure at the front of a mall, commonly a fast-food outlet, a bank, or a gas station.) Other tenants in the center include a nationally recognized shoe store, a beauty

salon, two popular restaurants (Chinese and Mexican), and McSpeedy's Pizza at the end of the center, as well as a Century 21 real estate training school in the middle.

Hinesville

Like Dalton, Hinesville has one major employer, the Fort Stuart army base. Abell recalls that popularly priced stores generally do very well in military towns. In addition, Fort Stuart is a rapid-deployment force base. Because the United States currently is involved in a number of international activities, Abell is concerned with a comment by a Hinesville native: "If these guys have to ship out, this place will be a ghost town." The location under consideration is the Target Plaza at the junction of State Route 119 and U.S. Highway 82 (see Exhibit 7). The center is anchored by Target and a grocery store that is part of a popular

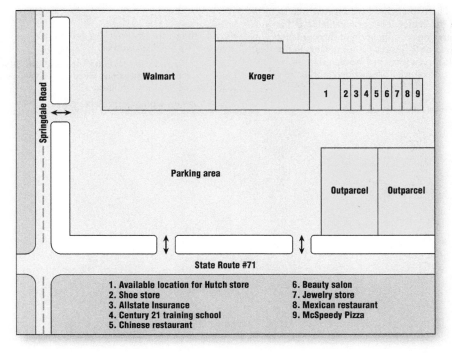

EXHIBIT 6
Whitfield Square
Shopping Center,
Dalton, Georgia

Springdale Road

Walmart   Kroger   1 2 3 4 5 6 7 8 9

Parking area   Outparcel   Outparcel

State Route #71

1. Available location for Hutch store
2. Shoe store
3. Allstate Insurance
4. Century 21 training school
5. Chinese restaurant
6. Beauty salon
7. Jewelry store
8. Mexican restaurant
9. McSpeedy Pizza

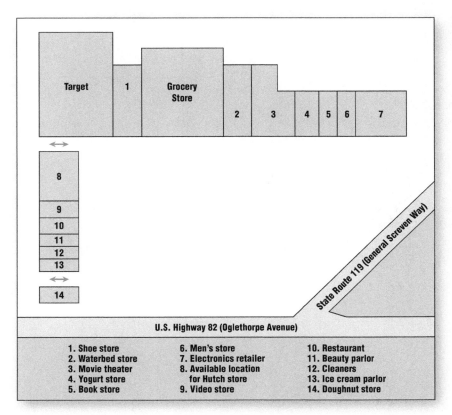

EXHIBIT 7
Target Plaza,
Hinesville, Georgia

Target   1   Grocery Store   2   3   4   5   6   7

8

9
10
11
12
13

14

State Route 119 (General Screven Way)

U.S. Highway 82 (Oglethorpe Avenue)

1. Shoe store
2. Waterbed store
3. Movie theater
4. Yogurt store
5. Book store
6. Men's store
7. Electronics retailer
8. Available location
   for Hutch store
9. Video store
10. Restaurant
11. Beauty parlor
12. Cleaners
13. Ice cream parlor
14. Doughnut store

Eastern U.S. chain. The two anchors are located side by side in the middle of the center. The spot available in the center is a 6,800-square-foot combination of three smaller units immediately adjacent to Target. Other tenants in the center include a bookstore, a waterbed store, a shoe store, an electronics retailer, a yogurt store, a video store, and a movie theater.

This case was written by Michael Levy, Babson College.

DISCUSSION QUESTIONS

1. How do the people living in the trade areas compare with Hutch's target customer?

2. How do the proposed locations, including the cities, tenant mix, and the locations within the malls, fit with Hutch's location requirements?

3. Which location would you select? Why?

CASE 14   Avon Embraces Diversity

Women have always played an important role at Avon, a leading global beauty firm that has $10 billion in annual revenue and is 125 years old. Mrs. P. F. Albee of Winchester, New Hampshire, pioneered the company's now-famous direct-selling method. Women have been selling Avon products since 1886—34 years before women in the United States won the right to vote! As the world's largest direct seller, Avon markets to women in more than 100 countries through the efforts of more than 6 million independent Avon sales representatives. Avon's merchandise includes beauty products, fashion jewelry, and apparel.

Although most of Avon's employees and customers are women, until recently the company was run by men. However, a series of poor strategic decisions in the 1980s led the company to increase aggressively the number of women and minorities in its executive ranks. This decision to increase diversity among its managers was a major factor in Avon's improved financial performance.

Today, Avon is recognized as a leader in management diversity. Fifty-five percent of Avon's management positions are filled by women, and half of the members of its board of directors are women. The company also has undertaken various programs to ensure that women and minorities have opportunities for development and advancement. In the United States and elsewhere, Avon has internal networks of associates, including a parents' network, a Hispanic network, a black professional association, an Asian network, and a gay and lesbian network. The networks act as liaisons between associates and management to bring their voices to bear on critical issues that affect both the workplace and the marketplace. Avon is committed to social responsibility. The Avon Foundation, founded in 1955, is the largest corporate philanthropic organization dedicated to women's causes globally and focuses on breast cancer and domestic violence.

In the 1970s, Avon's top management team was composed solely of men. Avon essentially ignored its own marketing research that indicated more women were entering the workforce and seeking professional careers. It also failed to realize that cosmetic needs were changing and new approaches for selling products to its customers were needed. Sales growth slowed, and the company reacted by seeking growth through unrelated diversifications. Finally, as the firm was on the brink of bankruptcy, a new top management team entered. Led by CEO Jim Preston, Avon refocused itself on its roots and developed strategies to reach women in a changing marketplace.

Preston realized that Avon's customers needed to be represented in the senior management team. He enacted policies to promote more women into higher-level positions. In addition, Preston shifted the firm's organizational culture to being more accommodating of all its employees.

The current management team launched several growth initiatives to build on Avon's strong brand name and distribution channel through its customer representative network. Avon product lines include private-label brands such as Avon Color, Anew, Skin-So-Soft, Advance Techniques Hair Care, Avon Naturals, and Mark. Avon also markets an extensive line of fashion jewelry and apparel.

Avon sells more than 125 million lipsticks per year, or 4 lipsticks every second of the day, making Avon the top seller of lipstick in the mass market. Its Anew brand is the number-one line of anti-aging skin care products in the world. The Advance Techniques hair care line offers high-performance hair products for every hair type, age group, and ethnic background to accommodate a diverse, worldwide consumer base.

Avon Wellness promotes a balanced, healthy lifestyle for women and their families and includes nutritional supplements, a weight management line, and therapeutic products. Avon partnered with the fitness phenomenon Curves, an international fitness franchise, to help women look and feel their best. Through this partnership, Avon Wellness offers an array of Curves-branded exercise videos and DVDs, fitness apparel, accessories, and comfortable footwear that support an active lifestyle.

Finally, Avon is using technology to support the efforts of its 6 million independent sales representatives. An electronic ordering system allows the representatives to run their businesses more efficiently and improve order-processing accuracy. Avon representatives use the Internet to manage their business electronically. In the United States, Avon representatives use an online marketing tool called youravon.com, which helps them build their own Avon business by selling through personalized web pages developed in partnership with Avon. Avon e-representatives can promote special products, target specific groups of customers, place and track orders online, and capitalize on e-mail to share product information, selling tips, and marketing incentives.

Sources: www.avoncompany.com; Avon Annual Report, 2009; www.avonfoundation.org.
This case was written by Barton Weitz, University of Florida, and Hope Bober Corrigan, Loyola College, Maryland.

DISCUSSION QUESTIONS

1. Why is Avon so committed to diversity?

2. Select another retailer that also values diversity. How does this commitment affect its financial results?

3. What values have helped Avon to be a successful company even after 125 years?

CASE 15 Sephora Loyalty Programs: A Comparison between France and the United States

Sephora is a beauty products retail chain founded in France by Dominique Mandonnaud in 1970 and owned today by Louis Vuitton Moet Hennessy (LVMH), the world's leading luxury goods group. Sephora's self-service environment carries classic and emerging brands as well as Sephora's own private label across a broad range of product categories, including skin care, color, fragrance, body, and hair care.

Sephora has a strong presence in several countries around the world. It operates approximately 1,300 stores in 27 countries worldwide, with more than 300 stores in North America. It opened its first U.S. store in New York in 1998. Since 2006, Sephora stores are also found inside some JCPenney stores. These stores, smaller than normal with approximately 1,500 square feet, feature the signature Sephora look and an edited assortment. The company launched its Internet retail store in the United States in 1999 and Canada in 2003, which is Sephora's largest North American store in terms of sales and selection of products and brands.

U.S. LOYALTY PROGRAM: SEPHORA BEAUTY INSIDER

In 2007, Sephora launched a customer loyalty program in the United Stated called "Sephora Beauty Insider." When customers sign up for the program, they become a Beauty Insider and receive a loyalty card. Beauty Insiders earn Perk points for purchases, both in-store and online. For every one dollar spent, one Point is added to the customer's Beauty Insider balance. The rewards for these points are given at two levels: 100 and 500. Insiders don't have to use their points once they hit 100. Instead, they can choose to accumulate points for the 500-point Perk. At the 100-point level, the reward is a sample-sized product. The 500-point level reward is a limited-edition, full-sized product offered exclusively to Beauty Insiders. Sephora typically displays three frequently changing rewards at the point of sale. These rewards are not available at Sephora inside JCPenney stores, even if customers accumulate their points there. Beauty Insiders also receive invitations to Beauty Insider-only events. On Sephora's Insiders account on the Internet, customers also receive special offers on products not available to the general public. Finally, every Insider receives a free birthday gift each year. Last year's gift was a bottle of Philosophy's shampoo,

custom-designed to wish customers a happy birthday. Insiders can get the birthday gift either by visiting a store or by ordering online within 14 days of their birth date.

In 2009, Sephora launched V.I.B. [Very Important Beauty Insider], a premium level for its U.S. Beauty Insiders. V.I.B. status is conferred on customers who spend at least $350 per year at U.S. and Canadian Sephora stores (including Sephora.com and Sephora inside JCPenney locations). The benefits for V.I.B.s, in addition to the regular Beauty Insider benefits, include deluxe samples, exclusive monthly perks and gifts, access to prereleased products, event invitations, a 10 percent savings welcome offer, and special discounts (They recently offered a weeklong 15 percent discount.). V.I.B.s are required to requalify each year by purchasing at least $350 worth of products.

FRENCH LOYALTY PROGRAM

Sephora is the leading perfume and cosmetic chain in France, despite fierce competition. Sephora's French loyalty program, launched in 2003, offers special products, exclusive information, and an all-access pass to personalized beauty products available in Sephora stores nationwide and on its website. It consists of three levels—White, Black, and Gold—and has 8 million members in Europe.

In an attempt to start a relationship with its customers, the White card is offered to anyone who asks for it in the store or applies on the Internet website. It is the first level of the customer relationship. After four purchases on the Internet website or in a store, a 10 percent discount coupon is given for the customer's next purchase.

When customers have at least four purchases during a year, or spend a minimum of 150€ a year, they automatically receive the Sephora Black card, which is the middle-level program. Sephora Black customers get a 10 percent discount coupon either after four purchases or with every 150 points earned (1point earned for 1 euro spent). They also have access to specific and personalized rewards, such as invitations to special Sephora events, a sample-sized birthday surprise, private sales with a 20 percent discount, special discounts on customers' favorite brands, special gifts, updated information on the latest in beauty innovation, and personalized offers based on customers' skin type or makeup style.

574   SECTION V   Cases

The Gold Card, which is the premium-level program, is dedicated to customers who purchase a minimum of 1500€ a year. In addition to the Black Card benefits, Sephora Gold customers get access to exclusive private sales, a full-sized birthday gift of the customer's choice either in-store or online, free shipping on Sephora's website, free access to the Sephora's in-store Beauty Bar once a month (customers get made-up and advised by Sephora's specially trained salespeople), an e-newsletter with exclusive beauty news, a special telephone line, a dedicated in-store salesperson or personal shopper, and access to the Sephora Gold boutique, where they can choose among several limited-edition Sephora Gold gifts in exchange for 1000 points. Since 2012, Gold Card holders must purchase a minimum of 700€ to re-qualify. If they drop below 700€, they receive the Black Card instead.

Sources: http://hittingpan.tumblr.com/post/4962507405/7-reasons-for-joining-sephoras-beauty-insider; http://savingslifestyle.com/2010/08/sephora-beauty-insider-rewards/; www.sephora.fr; www.sephora.com; Astrid de Montbeillard, "Sephora," *Relation Customer Magazine* 86 (April 1, 2010), www.relationcustomermag.fr/Relation-Customer-Magazine/Article/SEPHORA-37070-1.htm.

This case was written by Sandrine Heitz-Spahn, ICN Business School, and Nancy France and Michael Levy, Babson College.

DISCUSSION QUESTIONS

1. Identify the benefits for a company to implement a loyalty program.

2. What are the design characteristics of an effective loyalty program?

3. What are the benefits of having a tiered loyalty program such as Sephora's?

4. Describe Sephora's loyalty program design characteristics in both countries. What are the main differences? Which loyalty program is most effective at developing customer loyalty? Why?

5. Are both Sephora's French and American premium programs worth what they spend to reward customers? Why do both programs have a limited time validity and a specific requirement regarding the amount spent per year?

6. Could the premium loyalty program implemented in France be adapted to the U.S. market? Explain.

CASE 16   Attracting Generation Y to a Retail Career

THE DIVA BRAND

Diva is a specialty retail store focused on fast-fashion jew-elry and accessories. The brand's origins are in Australia, but recent years have seen rapid international expansion, and the brand now has stores in America, Russia, and Europe. Diva is predominantly located in shopping centers, with some stores in high-street locations, and is always positioned in/around apparel fashion clusters. The stores are clean, simplistic, and brightly lit, reflecting their fast-moving, funky, and vibrant product range targeted at the youth market (predominantly 15- to 25-year-old females). Diva's positioning sees it as the only fashion jewelry/hair accessory specialist retailer in Australia.

Due to Diva's recent expansion, staff numbers have grown significantly. However, Diva is confronted with the problem of attracting and retaining experienced and tal-ented people, particularly from Generation Y. In an attempt to counteract this problem, Diva has implemented several internal talent policies to provide a point of difference and be an employer of choice, including:

- Training plans/workshops to fill skill gaps.
- Career development program for top store managers.
- Leadership development program for top regional managers.
- Increased salary package offers for certain roles to attract talent/skill.
- Global expansion, with new offers of career progression.

GENERATIONAL DIFFERENCES IN THE WORKFORCE

As a result of key demographic and lifestyle issues such as aging populations, declining fertility, delayed retirements, rising labor participation rates, and higher life expectan-cies, there is a demographic trough in the Asia Pacific workforce, in which there are soon to be smaller propor-tions of younger-aged members and larger cohorts of mature-aged workers. This is further compounded by a shrinking talent pool and the fact that retail is not per-ceived as a career of choice by the adult population, who have limited sight of career path opportunities "beyond the shop floor."

Although research acknowledges the pertinence of this issue in retailing today, it remains unclear how to effec-tively manage generational diversity in the workplace. This is not a new issue; however, wider age groups are culminating in less segregated work arrangements. In the past, older staff undertook senior managerial positions, while younger workers assumed front-desk or field posi-tions. However, today it is common to see staff members from all age groups working together on projects, with senior employees managing across several generations or younger employees managing older generations. It is im-portant to note that, if managed poorly, intergenerational impacts can cause conflict for employers and among em-ployees, hampering workplace productivity and morale.

Retailers, as well as organizations from many other industries, therefore need to identify and adopt the best approaches in attracting and retaining staff across all retail functions, optimizing the experiences of mature-aged workers while capitalizing on the potential of young employees. This involves understanding each generation and its unique perspectives, communication styles, and working styles in order to provide tailored support. Each generation holds different perspectives of work, including the definition of an attractive working environment, leadership qualities, and preferred team playing approaches, and has an individual information processing style. For example, Generation Y believes in having fluid work patterns and influencing job terms and conditions. Conversely, the baby-boomer generation regards work as a primary security in life, while Generation X values a balance between work and life.

GENERATION Y

Born between 1981 and 2000, members of Generation Y were one of the key segments of focus for Diva given their sheer numbers and prospective employment in retail as recent or upcoming workforce entrants. While organizations have had time to understand baby boomers and Generation X-ers, determining the needs of Generation Y-ers has been challenging, especially given their vastly different values. This is particularly important given the significant career opportunities that exist for Generation Y in retailing. In better understanding the unique career motivations, perceptions, and aspirations of Generation Y, a number of focus groups were conducted with university students who were studying a business major and currently working in retail and high school students who were studying retail-related subjects and currently working in retail or interested in doing so.

In terms of perceptions of working in retail, our research found that retail is simply not viewed as a career of choice by Generation Y. This is primarily due to the feeling that retail involves "just being a checkout chick," has limited or no career paths "beyond the shop floor" and is therefore a short-term employment solution, and has difficult conditions at times (e.g., long hours, repetitive tasks, low salaries). A related concern was that the retail industry is not generally perceived as prestigious in the eyes of the general public.

Despite such issues, there were a number of motivators (other than financial) for working in retail for Generation Y, such as improving one's social life and extending friendship circles, gaining work experience while studying, and following a particular passion (i.e., fashion). Generation Y-ers also reported a variety of career aspirations that were generally consistent with the courses or subjects they were studying. Despite the fact that few listed retail as their number-one career option, a strong desire was found for a career that could be facilitated by the retail industry, such as marketing, human resources, or buying.

Focused on self-improvement, Generation Y-ers also expressed enjoyment in working for organizations that provide constant learning environments; they want to be involved in the organization's vision and mission, desire mobility and flexibility in the workplace, and seek instant gratification. Members of Generation Y also thrive on systematic feedback and value positive reinforcement at accelerated rates, as compared to previous generations. This is the primary reason that Generation Y questions starting at the bottom of the organizational ladder, having developed a strong desire for rapid career progression from years of high-level education.

This case was written by Sean Sands and Carla Ferraro, Monash University, Australia.

DISCUSSION QUESTIONS

1. How can Diva demystify what happens behind the scenes and make potential Generation Y employees aware of the opportunities available to them beyond the shop floor?

2. Diva has implemented a learning organizational culture in an attempt to attract and retain staff. Discuss the possible pros and cons of this strategy for Generation Y.

3. Give examples of how other organizations (perhaps even nonretailers) attract a Generation Y workforce. What could Diva learn from other organizations?

CASE 17   Active Endeavors Analyzes Its Customer Database

Active Endeavors is an outdoor apparel and accessory retailer located in Iowa City, Iowa. The store is locally owned and has been in business for 13 years, and it has a reputation for high quality and product innovation. Its target market is high-income individuals with an interest in outdoor activities and travel.

Ken Stuart, the founder of the store, has felt pressure on profit margins and increased competition, especially due to the emergence of the Internet. He tries to remain on top of competition by offering new products and a wide and deep assortment, but he thinks there might be an opportunity to increase the store's market position by utilizing a transactional database of its customers. The store has the customers' transaction records, which include customer name and address, transaction date, products and quantity purchased, and purchase price. He is thinking of using the transactional database to design and target a direct mail campaign designed to increase traffic.

Ken analyzed the customers' past purchase behavior using the RFM analysis and classified the customers into

576   SECTION V   Cases

EXHIBIT 1   Customer Classification Based on Purchase History

Customer Group	Recency	Frequency	Monetary
1	Purchased within the last 3 months	Purchased 4 or more times	Purchased $337.63 or more
2	Purchased within the last 3 months	Purchased once	Purchased $18.90 or less
3	Purchased between the last 3 months and a year	Purchased 4 or more times	Purchased $338.63 or more
4	Purchased between the last 3 months and a year	Purchased once	Purchased $18.90 or less
5	Purchased more than a year ago	Purchased 4 or more times	Purchased $337.63 or more
6	Purchased more than a year ago	Purchased once	Purchased $18.90 or less

six groups (Exhibit 1). The cutoff figures for the classifications were unique to the store. He is now contemplating the customer profile and what to do with it.

This case was written by Edward Rhee, Stonehill College.

DISCUSSION QUESTIONS

1. Describe the type of customers in each group.
2. What would you recommend Active Endeavors do to get more business from each group?

CASE 18 Mel's Department Store under New Management

Working for Mel's, a mid-sized department store chain, Elise Wickstrom recently was promoted to department manager of the Children's Department. Elise was excited about the opportunity but knew it would be a challenge because this department was not just apparel, but included toys and shoes, each having very different sales plans and margins. She was eager to show management that she was the right person for the job!

HISTORY

Mel's Department Stores had struggled under previous management as the proliferation of larger chains continued. This really hurt Mel's business because these larger conglomerates had increased buying power with vendors, allowing them to constantly underprice Mel's. The Internet also played a role in Mel's deteriorating business. The ability for the consumer to easily compare prices as well as the convenience of shopping 24/7 were hard for Mel's to match. Mel's then began to also cut prices to stay competitive. Margins eroded, and business sales did not increase.

New management recently took over, giving Mel's a makeover. The lighting and layout for each store was improved. The outer façade of locations was painted and updated. With these improvements and fresh thinking, the chain also changed its assortment, including fresher looks and more unique goods. In addition, they re-trained the entire workforce and now not only encourage a high level of customer service, but also give bonuses for such behavior. Mel's hope is that these changes will decrease price pressures and allow it to increase its maintained markup percentages.

CHILDREN'S DEPARTMENT

Under this new plan, Elise has been asked to adhere to the following initial and maintained markup percentages described in the following table:

	Initial Markup %	Maintained Markup %
Soft goods/apparel	60%	34%
Shoes	54%	33%
Toys	45%	25%

Elise just received her first shipment from FUNWEAR, her largest girls' vendor of unique jeans for kids. Its hand-painted designs and jeweled enhancements were adorable and were a real traffic driver in the department. This vendor pre-marks all items for Mel's, allowing Elise to get them from receipt to selling floor quickly. At first glance, Elise wanted to ensure that the tags were correct. Here is how the invoice read:

	Item Description	Retail (on tag)	Cost
200 units	prewashed jeans	$30.50	$16.00
100 units	jeans jeweled	$43.75	$17.50

This case was written by Beth Gallant, Lehigh University.

DISCUSSION QUESTIONS

1. Given the soft-goods targets, are these marked correctly? If not, what should the initial retail price be to obtain her 60 precent minimum initial markup percentage?

2. By noon another shipment arrives. This time it is from SNEAK HERS, delivering her pre-holiday sneakers. Elise notices that the high tops do not have tags and need to be priced for the floor. She has her associate calculate the retail price. The invoice indicates the cost is $8.75. What should the initial retail price be, given her markup target?

3. Elise has been analyzing her sell through and saw that the "hot" T-shirts from back to school have not been moving, and she has sweater shipments due in the next two weeks. She decides to mark the T's down to make room for the anticipated shipment. The cost of the T's was $2.25, and they were on the floor at a 62 percent markup If Elise takes a 33 percent markdown, what is the new selling price?

4. After six weeks passed, Elise analyzes her sales of the FUNWEAR prewashed jeans. Of her original 200 units this is what she found:

   - 50 units sold at the original retail
   - 34 units sold at a 38% markdown
   - 116 units sold at a 44% markdown

   What was her average maintained markup percentage? Did it meet her goals? Explain how this was possible.

5. Using the information in question 4, explain to management the possible reasons multiple markdowns could have been taken and why we compare to plan.

6. FUNWEAR is a long time vendor of Mel's. It provides markdown dollars to help defray the lost gross margin dollars. Why would it provide this money to Elise?

7. Seventy-five toy trains were bought for the toy area at $3.50 each and were then priced at $10.00 each. Elise is running a department promotion and wants to reduce the price of the trains. To what can she reduce the retail price in order to meet her maintained markup goals?

8. Mel's wanted to create unique assortments and increase customer service. How does this strategy allow for better markup percentages? How are these related to perceived value?

CASE 19 Developing an Assortment Plan for Hughes

A well-established, medium-size department store in the Midwest, Hughes satisfies consumers' needs by featuring popular names in fashion for the individual consumer, family, and home. It tries to offer a distinctive, wide assortment of quality merchandise with personalized customer service. The customer services include personal shoppers; credit through in-house charge, American Express, and Visa; and an interior design studio. Hughes' pricing policy permits it to draw customers from several income brackets. Moderate-income consumers seeking value and fashion-predictable soft goods are target customers, as are upscale customers with a special interest in fashion.

The department store is implementing new marketing strategies to prepare for continuing growth and expansion. Hughes' merchandising philosophy is to attract the discerning middle-market customers, who make up 70 percent of the population, as well as sophisticated, fashion-conscious consumers who expect to buy high-quality, brand-name merchandise at competitive prices.

One portion of Hughes' buying staff is responsible for the Oriental rug department within home furnishings. The open-to-buy figure for this classification within the

home furnishings division will be based on last year's sales history (Exhibit 1).

It has been projected that a 15 percent increase over last year's sales volume can be attained due to Oriental rugs' continued popularity. This year's open-to-buy for fall/winter will be $66,200.

The buying staff will be making its purchases for fall/winter in Amritsar, India, a city known for top-quality carpets. Ghuman Export Private Ltd. of Amritsar, Punjab, India, is the manufacturer the buyers will contact. Exhibit 2 shows information about Ghuman to use in the decision-making process.

This case was prepared by Ann Fairhurst, Indiana University.

EXHIBIT 1
Previous Year's Fall/Winter Sales Results for Oriental Rugs

Sales Volume	$120,000			
Markup	51.5%			
	Size	Percentage of Sales	Fabrication	Percentage of Sales
	3' × 5'	20%	Silk	15%
	4' × 6'	40	Cotton	25
	6' × 9'	15	Wool	60
	8' × 10'	10		
	9' × 12'	15		

EXHIBIT 2
Ghuman's Wholesale Price List

Size	FABRICATION		
	Silk	Wool	Cotton
3 × 5'	$ 400	$ 250	—
4 × 6'	700	500	$200
6 × 9'	850	700	275
8 × 10'	1,200	1,000	350
9 × 12'	1,400	1,300	500

Colors: Background colors available are navy, burgundy, black, and cream.

Quantities required for purchase: No minimum orders required.

Payment plan: Payment can be made in American dollars or Indian rupees. Letter of credit needs to be established prior to market trip.

Delivery: Air freight—10 to 14 days delivery time; cost is usually 25 percent of total order.

Ocean freight—39 days plus inland time is necessary; cost is usually 8–10 percent of total order.

Customer loyalty: Loyalty to customers is exceptional. Damaged shipments can be returned. Ghuman's philosophy is to help the retailers obtain a profit on their product lines.

DISCUSSION QUESTIONS

1. Work up a buying plan to use when purchasing merchandise from Ghuman's.

2. How should Hughes distribute the allotted open-to-buy dollars among the available sizes, colors, and fabrics?

3. Because it is dealing with an overseas manufacturer, how should Hughes address additional costs, such as duties and shipping, that need to be covered by the allocated open-to-buy dollars?

CASE 20   Preparing a Merchandise Budget Plan

B-G is a specialty department store chain headquartered in Dallas. The stores are upscale and generally cater to upper-middle-class and well-to-do customers. They are generally located in the more affluent suburbs and downtown central business districts throughout the United States. By offering high-quality merchandise and a high level of service, they are able to promote and maintain customer loyalty. In addition, B-G has its own charge card and a very liberal return policy. Jim Morris is a buyer for men's sportswear. His merchandise manager has asked him to prepare a six-month merchandise budget plan for his department covering the months March through August.

Last year, sales for sportswear during the same six-month period were $1 million. Due to increased advertising, inflation, and a general increase in demand for sportswear, a 19 percent increase in sales is expected for this year. Also, Jim anticipates an additional 10 percent increase in the percentage of sales in March due to an increase in demand. The demand increase, due to forecasted unseasonably warm weather in March, will be offset by decreases in April and May of equal amounts, so total sales will be unchanged. Sportswear has traditionally maintained a high level of profitability, with a gross margin of 48 percent.

The following are the monthly sales percentages for the last three years:

	March	April	May	June	July	August
2009	10%	22%	26%	20%	13%	9%
2010	10%	19%	25%	22%	14%	10%
2011	10%	20%	24%	18%	18%	10%

The expected GMROI is 350 percent, and the forecasted ending stock level is 100,000. Total annual reductions average about 14 percent of total net sales. The breakdown of this figure is 60 percent for markdowns, 35 percent for employee discounts, and 5 percent for shortages. The distribution of reductions is as follows:

	March	April	May	June	July	August
Reductions	15%	20%	20%	15%	15%	15%

Unfortunately, the historical record of stock/sales ratios was temporarily misplaced during a recent office move. However, Jim has access to the National Retail Federation's (NRF's) guidelines on this type of store and department. B-G has a slightly higher than average inventory turnover; therefore the NRF figures must be adjusted.

	March	April	May	June	July	August
NRF	2.50	1.80	1.55	1.70	1.90	2.55

This case was written by Michael Levy, Babson College, and Britt Hackmann, Nubry.com.

STUDENT INSTRUCTIONS

Your assignment is to assist Jim in the preparation of a merchandise budget plan. First, fill out the merchandise budget form for six months. You can use either the form accompanying this case or the spreadsheet at the Online Learning Center. Then, on a separate sheet of paper, type and double space a brief but specific explanation of how you derived the following:

1. Adjustments to percentage distribution of sales by month.

2. Adjustments to stock/sales ratios.

Planning Data															

SALES FORECAST $ _____

Planned GMROI $=\dfrac{\text{Gross Margin}}{\text{Net Sales}} \times \dfrac{\text{Net Sales}}{\text{Inventory Costs}}$

$\square = \dfrac{\$\quad}{\$\quad} \times \dfrac{\$\quad}{\$\quad}$

$\dfrac{\text{Sales}}{\text{Inventory Costs}} \times (100\% - \text{GM}\%) = \text{Inventory Turnover}$

[X   ] × [%   ] = [X   ]

12 ÷ Inventory Turnover = B.O.M. Stock/Sales

÷ [X   ] = [X   ]

Forecasted Ending Inventory [$]

Markdowns [%] [$]
Discounts + [%] [$]
Shortages + [%] [$]
Total Reductions [%] [$]

The Plan

		Jan	Feb	Mar	Apr	May	Jun	Jul	Aug	Sept	Oct	Nov	Dec	Total (Average)	Remarks
% Distribution of Sales by Month	1													100.0%	History/Projection
Monthly Sales	2														Step (1) × Net Sales
% Distribution of Reductions/Mo	3													100.0%	History/Projection
Monthly Reductions	4														Step (3) × Total Reductions
B.O.M. Stock/Sales Ratios	5														Adjusted by Mo. Sales Fluctuations
B.O.M. Stock ($000)	6													(Forecasted End Inventory)	Step (2) × Step (5)
E.O.M. Stock ($000)	7														EOM Jan = BOM Feb
Monthly Additions to Stock ($000)	8														Steps 2 + 4 + 7–6 Sales + Reductions + EOM–BOM

CASE 21   Kroger and Fred Meyer: Sourcing Products in a Global Marketplace

The Kroger Company is among the largest food retailers in the United States, and operates more than 2400 stores under nearly two dozen store brand names. These stores include conventional grocery stores, convenience stores, and approximately 200 supercenters. One of these store brand names is Fred Meyer Inc., a chain of more than 130 supercenters located in Oregon, Washington, Alaska, and Idaho. Fred Meyer has been sourcing products overseas for more than 30 years, and Kroger recognized this expertise early on when it acquired Fred Meyer in 1999. Fred Meyer's Portland, Oregon, headquarters also houses the Kroger Logistics group, and virtually all of the products imported for Kroger's stores are handled in some way by this office.

The cost savings realized by retailers who source products in other countries, especially Asia, have made the logistics function essential to competing in today's cost-conscious marketplace. The investment in the infrastructure to support the complex processes involved in importing products is more than offset by the savings in the cost of the products. This infrastructure is very complex and uses the services and talents of a many specialized personnel. But the costs are not only present in staff salaries, office space, and other tangible investments; the costs also include the lengthy time importing merchandise can take due to the complexity of the processes. This case study follows the steps involved in sourcing products from Asia and bringing them to market. Your challenge will be to estimate the time that is necessary to do this successfully.

The process begins with the Fred Meyer buyer and the Kroger category manager who decide to buy a specific product. Imagine that the objective is to find a small collection of lamps for the back-to-school season next year. The Fred Meyer buyers and the Kroger category managers for general merchandise now go to market together because of the economies of scale that can be achieved when they buy for both chains. This enables them to coordinate buys and make decisions that create the greatest amount of synergy. They have shopped the domestic markets; have paid attention to catalog, newspaper, and online advertising; and have been presented with ideas from various lamp importers. They have settled on three styles: two desk lamps and a floor lamp, with price points of $9.99 and $19.99, and they have made commitments for substantial quantities of these lamps to supply the anticipated demand for the stores.

The buyer and category manager have been in partnership with their product merchandiser in the product development group throughout this initial stage of this process. It is at this point that they hand off the sourcing of the lamps to the product merchandiser, who takes the next step of finding a source to manufacture them. Fred Meyer and Kroger work very closely with Li and Fung, a "global consumer products sourcing company managing the supply chain for high-volume time-sensitive consumer goods." They also rely on U.S. importers for identifying factories in Asia. The product merchandiser uses these contacts to solicit quotations for the lamps. Each potential supplier is sent specifications for the products: visuals, dimensions, colors, packaging, target delivery dates, approximate quantities, required testing, and any other available details. The suppliers are given approximately two weeks to create and submit samples and fill out the detailed paperwork known as quotation sheets. These documents specify to all parties involved what, when, and how all actions are done.

Once the quotation sheets and samples are received, the product merchandiser, Fred Meyer buyer, and Kroger category manager meet to assess and review the various submissions. The factors that influence their decision include product quality, vendor reliability, and product cost. All three of these must be seriously evaluated; if one of them is lacking, the whole program is at risk. In fact, decisions are often made to commit to a vendor with higher prices if there is a high degree of confidence in that vendor's quality and reliability.

When the supplier is chosen, the next step is the creation of purchase orders (POs). Factories do not generally start the acquisition of raw materials and other supplies for manufacturing a product until they have a firm financial commitment from the retailer. This is a very complex process that involves a number of behind-the-scenes support personnel. The Fred Meyer and Kroger buying teams both write purchase orders for their respective stores that are reviewed by the Kroger Logistics group and given to the Bank of America, which processes the payment to the manufacturer.

The creation of the PO sets the actual production and shipping process in motion. During this process, the Kroger Logistics group monitors the purchase order at every step in the supply chain. The Geo. S. Bush Company, a customs broker and provider of international trade services, provides several employees on site to ensure that all U.S. government regulations are complied with. This involves four main agencies: U.S. Customs and Border Protection, the Food and Drug Administration, the Department of Agriculture, and the Consumer Products Safety Commission. Failure to comply with the requirements of these agencies can cause lengthy slow-downs in delivery and possible fines, so Bush ensures that all paperwork is complete five days before the arrival date of the products.

Concurrent with the creation of the purchase orders, the packaging design process begins. These lamps will be packaged in full-color boxes. The vendor will provide the package templates known as die lines for the boxes that will be needed for these lamps. The graphic designs are generally done in-house by Fred Meyer, using predesigned brand templates to ensure consistency of graphic elements with other Kroger/Fred Meyer products and color execution. When color proofs of the designs are created, they are circulated to the buyer and category managers, as well as the merchandise managers to whom the buyer and category manager report. As soon as the necessary approvals are secured, the package designs are sent electronically to the supplier. Closer to the delivery date, the supplier will be required to provide samples of the packages printed overseas to ensure the design has been executed properly by the printer. Because of the complexity of this process, finalizing packaging can sometimes take as much time as manufacturing the product.

Another step in this process that has become increasingly important is product testing. Products that pose a danger to consumers and are distributed by a retailer can result in physical harm and lawsuits and/or legal penalties that total in the millions of dollars. To avoid any such situation, importers must understand the possible ways in which different materials and manufacturing designs can cause harm, as well as the many laws in all 50 states that regulate the safety of products.

When the chosen supplier has received the purchase order and the payment arranged by the bank, the actual manufacturing of the product can begin. This entails acquiring the necessary raw materials, packaging, and scheduling the production. The factory has committed to the lead time specified on the purchase order—usually a minimum of 90 days—and it must coordinate with many different suppliers in order to fulfill this commitment. Any number of obstacles can be encountered at this stage of the process, so strong communication among all involved parties is essential to ensure that shipping deadlines are met. One of the services that an agent such as Li and Fung provides is inspection of the factory at different intervals. Domestic importers often offer these inspections as well. The inspection will not only ensure timely delivery and product quality; it will also ensure that compliance standards (safety, child labor, environmental impacts, etc.) are not violated.

The next step is to arrange for transporting the merchandise. Because lamps are a fairly bulky product, it is not difficult to reach quantities that fill entire containers. Fully loaded containers ensure that handling will move seamlessly from the factory door, to the freight forwarders who load vessels in the Asian port, into the port of entry in the United States, on through customs inspections, and finally to a distribution center. Also, the per-unit transportation cost is significantly lower when full, rather than partial, containers are used. When every connection in the supply chain is functioning properly, shipments from the Pacific Rim to the West Coast can reach port in less than three weeks.

A lamp program such as this is very likely planned to be featured in one or more advertised events in both Fred Meyer and the other Kroger banners. Print advertising for the entire Kroger chain requires significant lead times for photography, production, and printing. The printed copies should be complete and awaiting distribution around four weeks in advance of the planned advertising date. Any delay in the supply chain that might cause the product not to be received early enough could result in advertising without having the advertised product—an unfortunate outcome that disappoints customers.

When these lamp orders from Asia arrive in the Port of Portland, they are separated into Fred Meyer and Kroger orders. The Kroger merchandise is "trans-loaded" and three 40-foot containers are loaded into two 53-foot rail cars and sent east to Kroger distribution centers. This step adds approximately two weeks to the Kroger stores' lead time but reduces the shipping costs substantially. The Fred Meyer portion of the order is directed from the port to the Fred Meyer cross-docking distribution center in Chehalis, Washington. The bar codes on the lamps enable them to be placed on a conveyor belt, received by laser scanners, and then mechanically routed to the correct loading point at the ends of the conveyor system. Several merchandise containers can be received and ready to load on trucks within a matter of several hours. From that point, the lamps will be headed for the stores in the Pacific Northwest, Alaska, and California.

This case study describes the best-case scenario for the importing process at Kroger and Fred Meyer. There are many possible complications that might arise at these stages: production, shipping, customs, port-of-entry, distribution center processing, and domestic transportation arrangements. These complications might add from two weeks to two months to the lead time. Only with the intense focus by the teams at Fred Meyer/Kroger, Bank of America, Li and Fung or other importer, Geo. S. Bush Co., the manufacturer, the manufacturer's suppliers, the freight forwarders, and customs agents will enable this time to be as short and cost-effective as possible.

Sources: D. Gallacher, assistant vice president, Kroger Logistics Imports, and G. Parsons, vice president, product development, Fred Meyer, interviewed August 2, 2012. Geo. S. Bush Co. Inc., www.geosbush.com/, retrieved August 2, 2012; Li and Fung, Ltd., www.lifung.com/eng/global/home.php; The Kroger Co., *Import Shipping Manual for Fred Meyer dba Kroger* (n.d.), www.thekrogerco.com/b2b/documents/Import%20Shipping%20Manual.pdf; The Kroger Co., *Kroger/Fred Meyer Quote Sheet*. (n.d.), www.google.com/url?sa=t&rct=j&q=&esrc=s&source=web&cd=1&ved=0CFIQFjAA&url=http%3A%2F%2Fwww.thekrogerco.com%2Fb2b%2Fdocuments%2FImport%2520Quote%2520Sheet%2520For%2520All%2520Container%2520Sizes.xls&ei=9w8PUNqpBuejiAK95YD4CQ&usg=AFQjCNEhOmCZKVPweSTh.

This case was written by Mary Manning, Portland State University.

DISCUSSION QUESTIONS

1. What factors would you list that need to be evaluated in making a decision to source products overseas? Make a list of pros and cons, and explain what the pressures are that impel manufacturers and retailers to not source products domestically.

2. Based on the information given, how long do you estimate it will take to import these lamps? Create a set of target dates for each step in this process that will enable these products to arrive in time for the planned advertising date and selling period.

3. What areas of expertise do the various members of the product development team have? What are the possible communication issues that might arise between them?

4. There are several opportunities for questionable ethical situations to arise in the importing of products. What do you think the weak points might be? Where in the process is there the potential for unethical actions to occur?

CASE 22   Target and Its New Generation of Partnerships

The country's second-largest retailer, Minneapolis-based Target, has been an innovator in structuring retail partnerships that offer customers something special: fashion-forward housewares and apparel at prices they can afford. In addition to its Target.com website, the company operates nearly 1,800 stores in 49 states, along with 37 distribution centers nationally and a separate headquarters location in India. Apparel and accessories account for approximately 20 percent of Target's annual sales.

Similar to its more standardized rivals Walmart and Kmart, Target offers the vast breadth of a full-line discount store, featuring everything from cosmetics to baby clothes, housewares to electronics. But Target also has uniquely positioned itself through a series of exclusive partnerships with top designers, such as Michael Graves and Isaac Mizrahi, who have collaborated with the retailer to offer limited-edition, distinctive products. Although other retailers also have developed relationships with designers to create exclusive brands—such as

Kohl's Simply Vera line from designer Vera Wang, which accounted for 50 percent of its apparel sales in 2010—those competitors have struggled to maintain their lower prices.

Thus, though it is not alone in partnering with designers, Target appears to be the best practitioner of this strategy. The company launched its first retail partnership in 1999 with renowned architect Michael Graves, whose teakettles and toasters were hailed for having brought the word "design" back to the housewares category. Since then, the company has worked with more than 80 design partners who have generally welcomed the chance to reach a mass market with their exclusive labels.

Most of the partnerships have been limited to a specific time, which also has built a sense of urgency and exclusivity around the offers. Target's 2011 holiday offerings featured a number of designer labels: Harajuku Mini kids' clothing from designer Gwen Stefani, hats from Albertuse Swanepoel, and a jewelry line featuring designs by Dana Kellin. Whether time-limited or longer term, such partnerships have consistently offered high-profile labels at moderate prices, helping the retailer boost its bottom line.

Target's collaboration with Missoni made a splash. The fashion world was stunned when the Italian fashion house agreed to create a collection for Target. The big American retail store is the diametric opposite of the high-end shops that have typically carried Missoni's expensive knitwear and apparel. Target's announcement through Facebook, other social media sites, and a Manhattan pop-up shop for fashion editors, celebrities, and other Missoni clientele helped stoke public excitement.

Of course, such excitement can cause problems as well. Target's website crashed just moments after the Missoni launch, as customers clicked in droves to buy up the designer duds. Although the site remained up when Jason Wu (the designer of Michelle Obama's famous 2010 inaugural gown) released his line, many stores reported nearly immediate stockouts. Customers in a Miami store watched in shock and dismay as one couple swooped in and purchased the entire selection that was on the retail floor.

Although Target learned from its Missoni mistakes, it encountered a new set of problems in 2012. Collaborating with Neiman Marcus, both stores simultaneously introduced several lines of products for the 2012 holiday season. The collection included items from designers such as Marc Jacobs, Oscar de la Renta, and Diane Von Furstenberg. Although it expected popularity similar to its Missoni products, the opposite actually occurred, with prices needing to be marked down as much as 70 percent to get rid of the merchandise. What were the problems? The designers, perhaps trying to protect the image of their brand, released products that were not what they were known for; Tory Burch made thermoses and Diane von Furstenberg made yoga mats. Also, Target may have overpriced its market, offering scarves for as much as $70. Taken together, Target lost sight of its mass-market appeal.

Now, Target has created a new model for retail partnerships as a way to offer its shoppers something different. Through a store-inside-a-store initiative that it has dubbed The Shops at Target, the retailer is partnering directly with small specialty shops and boutiques to offer their limited-edition merchandise, from dog biscuits to vintage furniture, at prices ranging from $1.99 to $159.99.

The store-within-a-store, with dedicated space branded by the designer, has already proven a successful strategy elsewhere. Macy's has Ralph Lauren boutiques; Bloomingdale's has Chanel boutiques; JCPenney, a close Target competitor, also hosts Sephora boutiques and other designer brands.

The Shops at Target collaboration is being rolled out as a series of six-week partnerships. For its first round, which was launched in 2012, the retailer chose five independently owned specialty shops—The Candy Store; the Cos Bar cosmetic shop; Polka Dog Bakery; the Privet House home accessories shop; and The Webster, a high-end Miami clothing store—all getting their first crack at a national market through Target's nearly 1,800 locations, not to mention its website. Target plans to repeat the program subsequently with new sets of boutiques, but the initial group alone will add nearly 400 new and exclusive products to Target's online and store inventories.

Target shoppers thus have come to expect a steady stream of exclusive new designer brands, along with the constant possibility of finding something unique, even unpredictable, in the next aisle over. Now the big merchandiser is hoping to keep that excitement going with its new specialty-shop partnerships. The question going forward will be whether Target—the store loyal customers have dubbed "Tarzhay" for its supply of "cheap chic"—can keep its steady customers coming back, while attracting more shoppers with new rounds of boutique surprises.

This case was written by Laurie Covens, Michael Levy, Dhruv Grewal, and Scott Motyka, all of Babson College.

Sources: Target.com, "Corporate Overview," http://pressroom.target.com/pr/news/corporate-overview.aspx; Jessica Wohl, "Target Hopes Exclusive Designer Deals Boost Sales," *Reuters*, August 2, 2011; Mary Catherine O'Connor, "Target Shoppers: Say Goodbye to Michael Graves' Budget-Friendly Design," *smartplanet*, February 16, 2012; Target.com, "Target Unveils New Design Partnership Program," January 13, 2012; Emanualla Grinberg, "'Missoni for Target' Line Crashes Site," *CNN.com*, September 13, 2011; "Jason Wu for Target Apparel Sells Out in Hours," *ABCNews.com*, February 6, 2012; Ashley Lutz, "Why Target's Neiman Marcus Collaboration was a Horrible Flop," *Business Insider*, January 3, 2013.

DISCUSSION QUESTIONS

1. Assess the role of consumer expectations in Target's success as a major discount retailer.

2. What differentiates Target's new retail partnership model from its longstanding partnerships with top designers? What are the relative strengths of each?

3. What explains Target's ability to attract top designers and high-end specialty shops as retail partners?

CASE 23 American Furniture Warehouse Sources Globally

The year 1975 saw the tail end of a recession that came on the heels of the 1973 Arab oil embargo, the fall of Saigon, and the resignation of Richard Nixon. That same year, Jake Jabs took over the American Furniture Company in Denver, Colorado, renamed it American Furniture Warehouse (AFW), and started turning it into a high-volume discount home furnishings retailer. Jabs responded to concerns that resonated with consumers in a tough economy: tighter pocketbooks, job insecurity, rising energy costs, a growing number of households as baby boomers branched out, and greater receptivity to generic products. Jabs was an experienced furniture retailer and had operated his own furniture manufacturing concern. Unbeknownst to Jabs at the time, global sourcing would become a more prominent way for his company to stock its showrooms.

Fast-forward to the present. Consumers' tastes change at a faster clip. They have higher standards than ever, and they demand bargains. As an inherently frugal man, Jake Jabs loves to give the public good value while keeping overhead low.

Jabs is the CEO, but he employs no executives. No titles of vice president or executive vice president are anywhere in sight. The company is family-owned and is not beholden to stockholders demanding that high profit margins or quarterly objectives be met. Without pressure from such entities, AFW has continued to grow and thrive. Jake Jabs obsessively trolls for ideas on how to keep prices low, quality high, and merchandise current.

People from all over the western United States visit AFW's megastores. They are intrigued with the values and constantly ask that AFW open a showroom near them. To date, AFW has preferred to remain a regional player. Its buys are based on the preferences and trends of Colorado customers.

Some of the many tenets to which AFW subscribes include striving to offer the lowest prices and the best guarantee, employing a no-pressure sales staff, having the best displays and selection, employing a careful delivery staff that works seven days a week, providing outstanding product information and customer service, and repairing merchandise on site rather than shipping anything back to the manufacturer.

In the 38 years AFW has been operating, it has forged strong vendor relationships worldwide. In fact, AFW sources goods from 30 different countries. Its major trading partners include Malaysia, Indonesia, China, Vietnam, and Mexico. It has a buying office in Asia. Its reputation has matured to the point where vendors travel up to 250 miles to bring samples to a foreign AFW buying office. AFW's small buying staff maximizes its time by having vendors come to buyers at specified dates and times; buyers no longer have to make arduous trips through countries such as China. Instead, they spend their time efficiently visiting stateside wholesale market centers and trade shows and working out of the AFW buying offices the majority of the time.

One of the dilemmas AFW has been grappling with centers around setting guidelines under which it will make time to see a new vendor. AFW's reputation is well known, and vendors clamor to get appointments with Jabs and his team on their limited market and trade show visits.

Many factories in developing countries have lower cost structures than those closer to home, often due to less stringent government regulations, lower pay, and fewer benefits for workers. Foreign factories often specialize in manufacturing one or two items well rather than constantly changing what product is on the assembly line, as is often the case in the United States. The one- or two-line process is less flexible but more cost-effective.

Because AFW sells so much, it is able to buy in volume. It directly imports full containers of merchandise. Its buying staff travel the world looking for the best deals. As a result, buyers are often able to negotiate prices 30 to 60 percent less than competitors' prices for comparable merchandise. This is due in part to the size of the order and the manner in which it is shipped. AFW sometimes pays in advance to get a better price, and it has a policy of always paying on time—a value factories respect and reward. Jake Jabs is exploring other ways in which AFW can differentiate itself in the buying process.

An example of how AFW has applied creative problem solving to reduce cost unfolds through its decision to build its own chairs, saving dramatically on freight costs. A garden-variety hardwood dinette chair can be manufactured abroad and the pieces assembled at AFW for much less than the cost if it were shipped already assembled. Typically, 1000 assembled dinette chairs fit in a standard-size container. AFW buys 4000 identical chairs in pieces and fits them in that same container. It pays its domestic workers roughly $2 per chair to assemble them and can sell each chair at retail for less than what other retailers pay for the same chair at wholesale.

Yet another manifestation of its creative solutions to cost-reduction: AFW takes delivery on blanket-wrapped merchandise rather than carton-wrapped. Not only are the blankets reusable, but not putting the merchandise in cartons in the first place can save as much as 5 percent on the total purchase price. Once merchandise arrives at one of two distribution centers, it is placed into storage and samples are immediately shipped to the showrooms.

AFW makes it a policy not to return merchandise to a factory. If something is broken, its staff of 120 trained service technicians can repair just about any furniture problem they may encounter, often for pennies. Because of its no-return policy, if it makes a buying error, AFW will mark down the item and not repurchase it. With no returns to process, vendors sell to AFW for up to 15 percent less than to other retailers for that reason alone.

Artisans in Mexico make and sell accessories to AFW by the truckload. Recently, the accessories buyer was in Mexico at the invitation of the Mexican government. She was advising a group of artisans on what to create to appeal to the Colorado market. Because AFW buys items in bulk, it saves up to 50 percent over what competitors pay for similar items. Jake Jabs would like to replicate this sort of activity in other product categories in other countries. He is pondering the best way to do this.

AFW takes chances on new, upstart vendors that other retailers may not have discovered. There are risks and rewards to this strategy, but AFW has found the rewards outweigh the risks, on balance.

Sources: Jake Jabs, *An American Tiger: An Autobiography* (Denver, CO: 2000); conversation with Jake Jabs, October 9, 2009, in Parker, CO.

This case was written by Lexi Hutto, The Metropolitan State College of Denver.

DISCUSSION QUESTIONS

1. Factories in many developing nations have lower cost structures, but that is often attributable to fewer benefits and lower wages for workers. What are the ethical trade-offs for retailers and shoppers when merchandise is sourced from countries where

labor practices fall short of standards Americans deem acceptable? Do shoppers really care about workers halfway across the globe, or are they more concerned about how many dollars are flowing out of their own pockets?

2. The world is our marketplace. AFW employs global sourcing, uses many negotiating tactics and shifts channel tasks to keep its costs as low as possible.

Enumerate the tactics AFW uses to keep its prices low. What other strategies and tactics could a furniture retailer use to hold the line on retail prices?

3. What criteria should AFW use when deciding whether to see a new vendor? How might it apply some of its best practices with its biggest vendors to new, smaller vendors? What strategies or innovations could it employ to stretch the productivity of its buying staff?

CASE 24   Are Customers Addicted to Sales at JCPenney?

BRIEF HISTORY OF JCPENNEY

JCPenney (JCP), is a mid-market department store that sells men's, women's, and children's clothing along with home furnishings. Founded by James Cash Penney in the early 1900s in Kemmerer, Wyoming, JCPenney was originally called the Golden Rule store. The bedrock of Mr. Penney's business philosophy was to treat customers fairly and honestly by following the Golden Rule: Do unto others as you would have them do unto you.

Penney's philosophy and innovative merchandising practices quickly led to success. By 1971, JCPenney operated more than 2,000 stores throughout the United States and had annual revenues in excess of $5 billion. JCPenney was a pioneer in developing store-branded merchandise. Store brands grew to include Towncraft, a men's sportswear line; St. John's Bay, a line of casual men's and women's clothing; as well as Worthington, a line of women's dress shoes.

CHANGING RETAIL LANDSCAPE

By the 1990s, however, several competitors had encroached on JCPenney's mid-market position, including Macy's, Kohl's, Target, and Walmart. Target had successfully pursued the young adult market with its cheap but chic positioning, and Kohl's had positioned itself as the affordable alternative to upscale department stores by offering name-brand merchandise at reasonable prices. Competitors' success took a heavy toll on JCPenney's sales, and by 2012, the number of JCPenney stores had been pared to 1100.

The Great Recession that began in 2007 also bruised JCPenney. Annual revenue dropped from $19.9 billion in 2007 to $17.3 billion in 2011. During the same four-year span, earnings dropped from $1.1 billion to a net loss of $152 million. These losses caused JCPenney's stock to slide and facilitated the shuttering of its catalog channel.

NEW MANAGEMENT, DRASTIC CHANGES

In June 2011, because of lackluster sales, JCPenney's board of directors fired CEO Myron Ullman III and replaced him with Ron Johnson, a former Apple executive, who had also served as the head of merchandising for Target. Johnson assumed office in November 2011.

Upon analyzing JCPenney's operations, Johnson uncovered some very sobering facts: Close to three-quarters of JCPenney's merchandise was sold at a discount of 50 percent or more. Johnson's team also discovered that JCPenney had run more than 590 sales in 2011, significantly driving up operating expenses and eroding maintain markup. Yet, these deep discounts and heavy promotions were not yielding strong customer loyalty. Johnson analyzed the data, which revealed that the average JCPenney customer made only four purchases a year, which clearly indicated Penney's hi-low pricing was not delivering a high frequency yield among its customers. The second quarter 2011 sales and margins numbers were showing tepid growth at best, or trending negatively. Second quarter 2011 comparable stores sales increased a mere 1.5 percent over second quarter 2010 sales. Penney's gross margin trend painted a very distressing picture, decreasing from 32.4 percent in second quarter 2010 to 31.8 percent in 2011. In contrast, during the same second quarter 2011, Kohl's comparable store sales rose 1.9 percent. More importantly, Kohl's second quarter 2011 gross margin rose to 40.7 percent. In a nutshell, Penney's business model was failing because customers were purchasing relatively infrequently; and when they did purchase, the merchandise was heavily discounted.

To assist him in turning JCPenney's operations around, Johnson hired Michael Francis, the chief marketing officer for Target, to be JCPenney's president. Francis was viewed as one of the architects of Target's popular, hip image.

On January 5, 2012, Johnson and Frances announced their blueprint for turning JCPenney's operations around. At the core of their new strategy was a radical departure from JCPenney's previous practice of heavy discounting and special event pricing. Instead, sales would be replaced with "Fair and Square" pricing that revolved around three core tactics: one "fair" price that would reflect a minimum 40 percent discount from the previous, nondiscounted price; a month-long "value" price, where selected merchandise would be discounted up to 30 percent for an entire month; and lastly, a final "best" price that would be available on the first and third Friday of every month that reflected a discount of up to 40 percent on the "fair" price.

In addition to the radical change in JCPenney's pricing strategy, Johnson and Francis unveiled new merchandising and store layout plans to be implemented in JCPenney stores over the next four years. Basically, the stores would be redesigned around the "Town Square" theme, where each store would have a centralized Town Square

Courtesy of JCPenney.

reminiscent of the Apple Stores' "Genius" bars where customers learn about new products. Also, stores would be remodeled into the store-in-store layout, where different brand shops, like Liz Claiborne, would have dedicated space within the store. A new red-square logo with the letters JCP in the upper-left-hand corner was unveiled to emphasize the "fair and square" pricing theme. Johnson saw JCPenney's new positioning as a return to Mr. Penney's original emphasis on treating customers fairly and following the Golden Rule.

FALL OUT AND BACKPEDALING

Despite an initial jump in JCPenney stock upon hearing the shift in pricing strategy, the numbers quickly told another story: The new strategy did not resonate with consumers. Not only did the "Fair and Square Deal" approach appear to be failing, but it seemed to be driving JCPenney's customers into the competition's stores (see Exhibit 1).

EXHIBIT 1
Q1 Performance for JCPenney and Its Major Competitors (February to April 2012)

	Net Sales (in billions)	Percentage Change versus Q1 2011	Comparable Sales Percentage versus Q1 2011
JCPenney	$3.15	−20.1%	−18.9%
Kohl's	$4.2	1.9	0.2
Target	$16.87	5.9	5.3
Macy's	$6.14	4.3	4.4
TJ Maxx	$5.8	11	8

Data Source: "J.C Penney: Reinventing Fair and Square Deals," Darden Business Publishing.

EXHIBIT 2
Q2 Performance for JCPenney and Its Major Competitors (May to July 2012)

	Net Sales (in billions)	Percentage Change versus Q2 2011	Comparable Sales Percentage versus Q2 2011
JCPenney	$3.02	−22.6%	−21.7%
Kohl's	$4.2	−1	−2.7
Target	$16.45	3.5	3.1
Macy's	$6.11	3	3

Data Sources: Company profile data and SEC filings.

JCPenney's second quarter 2012 financial performance was even poorer with weaker overall and comparable store sales, while its competitors, with the exception of Kohl's, seem to be faring much better (see Exhibit 2).

One casualty of the initially weak performance of the "Fair and Square" concept was Michael Francis, who abruptly resigned from his position in June 2012. Despite the rocky start of "Fair and Square," Johnson sent an e-mail to JCPenney customers in August 2012 that basically reiterated the positives of the "Fair and Square" model and indicated that there would be no shift in strategy.

As 2012 progressed, it became apparent that "Fair and Square" in its original version was no longer a viable pricing strategy. Third quarter 2012 sales results resulted in even more losses for JCPenney, falling an alarming $1.1 billion versus third quarter 2011, from $4.0 billion to $2.9 billion. This resulted in a net loss of $203 million for third quarter 2012 versus net earnings of $38 million in third quarter 2011. Analysts were not optimistic about fourth quarter 2012 sales either, predicting that for 2012, annual sales would have dropped a total of $4 billion, or nearly 23 percent.

In August, 2012, six months after the initial "Fair and Square" launch, the month-long price reduction initiative was terminated with Johnson claiming it was too confusing for shoppers. However, the real reversal of "Fair and Square" began in earnest in January 2013, when JCPenney announced that it was going to commence running sales again. Although claiming sales would be far less frequent than prior to the launch of "Fair and Square," Johnson, citing competitive reasons, did not reveal how many sales would be run. Johnson refused to label this shift in strategy as a retreat from "Fair and Square" but described it as an "evolution." At the same time, Johnson restated that JCPenney would not resume the practice of distributing coupons.

Concurrent with the decision to reinstate sales, JCPenney management decided to implement reference pricing by adding new MSRP price tags to more than half its merchandise. Designed to reinforce savings and perceived value to the customer, reference pricing has long been a staple in deep discount chains, such as TJ Maxx and Marshall's.

So are customers addicted to sales? JCPenney would say that they definitely are. In an unfortunate conclusion to the "fair and square" pricing experiment, JCPenney's stock price dropped 44% in 2012, and as a result, Johnson stepped down as CEO in April 2013. His replacement? Former CEO Mike Ullman.

586   SECTION V   Cases

Sources: Paul Farris and Sylvie Thompson, "J.C. Penney: Reinventing Fair and Square Deals", Case Study, Darden Business Publishing, July 20, 2012; http://xfinity.comcast.net/slideshow/finance-companiesneverrecover/10/; Oliver St. John, "Ron Johnson Steps Down as CEO of Troubled J.C. Penney," *USA Today*, April 10, 2013; Meredith Galante, "How Ron Johnson Plans to Transform JC Penney into 'America's Favorite Store,'" *Businessindsider.com*, January 26, 2012; http://biz.yahoo.com/e/11097/jcp10-q.html; http://finance.yahoo.com/news/Kohls-Earnings-Cheat-Sheet-wscheats-1451845985.html; Farris and Thompson, "J.C. Penney: Reinventing Fair and Square Deals"; Ibid; JCPenney, "A Letter from our CEO" (e-mail), August 6, 2012; Loeb, Walter, "J.C, Penney—Ugly Results Leave More Doubt for 2013", www.forbes.com/sites/walterloeb/2012/11/09 (accessed February 11, 2013); "J.C. Penney Sales Are Back," www.cbsnews.com, January 28, 2013 (accessed February 11, 2013); Ibid.

This case was written by Virginia Weiler, University of Southern Indiana.

DISCUSSION QUESTIONS

1. What environmental factors contributed to JCPenney's "Fair and Square" launch?

2. What were some alternative pricing strategies that Johnson might have considered besides "Fair and Square"?

3. Why did "Fair and Square" fail to connect with JCPenney's existing customers? Why have many retailers retreated from EDLP?

4. Was JCPenney attempting to attract a new customer? If so, describe.

5. What steps could JCPenney have taken, if any, to have increased the chances of success for "Fair and Square"?

CASE 25   How Much for a Good Smell?

For the past two Christmas seasons, Courtney's, an upscale gift store, has carried a sweet-smelling potpourri in a plastic bag with an attractive ribbon. Heavily scented with cloves, the mixture gives a pleasant holiday aroma to any room, including the store.

Two years ago, the mixture cost $4.50 a bag. Courtney's (the only store in town that carried it) sold 300 pieces for $9.50. Courtney's supply ran out 10 days before Christmas, and it was too late to get any more.

Last year, the manufacturer raised the price to $5.00, so Courtney's raised its retail price to $9.95. Even though the markup was lower than that in the previous year, the store owner felt there was "magic" in the $10 ($9.95) price. As before, the store had a complete sellout, this time five days before Christmas. Sales last year were 600 units.

This year, the wholesale price has gone up to $5.50, and store personnel are trying to determine the correct retail price. The owner once again wants to hold the price at $10 ($9.95), but the buyer disagrees: "It's my job to push for the highest possible markup wherever I can. This item is a sure seller, as we're still the only store around with it, and we had some unsatisfied demand last year. I think we should mark it $12.50, which will improve the markup to 56 percent. Staying at $10 will penalize us unnecessarily, especially

considering the markup would be even lower than last year. Even if we run into price resistance, we'll only have to sell 480 to maintain the same dollar volume."

The owner demurs, saying, "This scent is part of our store's ambience. It acts as a draw to get people into the store, and its pleasant smell keeps them in a free-spending state of mind. I think we should keep the price at $9.95, despite the poorer markup. And if we can sell many more at this price, we'll realize the same dollar gross margin as last year. I think we should buy 1000. Furthermore, if people see us raising a familiar item's price 25 percent, they might wonder whether our other prices are fair."

This case was prepared by David Ehrlich, Marymount University.

DISCUSSION QUESTIONS

1. What prices caused Courtney's new charges?
2. Which price would result in the highest profit?
3. What other factors should Courtney's consider?
4. What price would you charge, and how many units would you order?

CASE 26   Promoting a Sale

A consumer electronics chain in the Washington, DC, area is planning a big sale in its suburban Virginia warehouse over the three-day President's Day weekend (Saturday through Monday). On sale will be nearly $2 million worth of consumer electronics products—50 percent of the merchandise sold in the store. The company hopes to realize at least $900,000 in sales during the three days. In the retailer's past experience, the first day's sales were 50 percent of the total. The second day's were 35 percent, and the last day's, 15 percent. One of every two customers who came made a purchase.

Furthermore, the retailer knows that large numbers of people always flock to such sales, some driving as far as 50 miles. They come from all economic levels, but all are confirmed bargain hunters. You're the assistant to the general merchandise manager, who has asked you to plan the event's marketing campaign. You have the following information:

1. A full-page *Washington Post* ad costs $10,000, a half-page ad costs $6,000, and a quarter-page ad costs $3,500. To get the maximum value from a newspaper campaign, it is company policy to run two ads (not necessarily the same size) for such events.

2. The local northern Virginia paper is printed weekly and distributed free to some 15,000 households. Ads cost $700 for a full page and $400 for a half page.

3. To get adequate TV coverage, at least three channels must be used, with a minimum of eight 30-second spots on each at $500 per spot, spread over three or more days. Producing a television advertisement costs $3,000.

4. The store has contracts with three radio stations. One appeals to a broad, general audience aged 25 to 34 years. One is popular with the 18-to-25 age group. The third, a classical music station, has a small but wealthy audience. Minimum costs for a saturation radio campaign, including production, on all three stations are $8,000, $5,000, and $3,000, respectively.

5. Producing and mailing a full-color flyer to the store's 80,000 charge customers cost $10,000. When the company used such a mailing piece before, about 3 percent of recipients responded.

This case was written by Professor David Ehrlich, Marymount University.

DISCUSSION QUESTIONS

1. Knowing that the company wants a mixed-media ad campaign to support this event, prepare an ad plan for the general merchandise manager that costs no more than $40,000.

2. Work out the daily scheduling of all advertising.

3. Work out the dollars to be devoted to each medium.

4. Justify your plan.

CASE 27   Target Marketing with Google AdWords

Australia's oldest retailer evolved from Appleton and Jones in 1835 to David Jones in 1838. Today, David Jones, or simply DJs, has dozens of department stores, predominantly in Australia's capital cities. Similar to many retailers, and despite having a mail-order business since the late 1800s, DJs suffered a few missteps with its online presence in the early 2000s. Now however, the David Jones website, davidjones.com.au, is integral to DJs' daily operations.

Chris Taylor, a recent university graduate, manages DJs' online presence. Thanks to its successful website and changing media habits, David Jones is considering online advertising to drive targeted traffic to the website. Given the prominence of Google and sponsored search, Chris would like to test Google AdWords.

Starting late last century, search engines began to develop interactive advertising models based on user interests, such as keywords typed into a search engine. The concept—sponsored search—aligns online advertisements with search engine queries. In sponsored search—also known as paid search, keyword advertising, pay-per-click (PPC) advertising, and search advertising—advertisers pay for search engine traffic to their websites via link-based ads that search engines display in response to user queries. Thus, if a user searches Google using the keyword *retailers*, AdWords ads that mention retailing would appear. If the user clicks on an ad, the user then goes to a specific web page—the landing page—on the advertiser's website.

As the leading search engine, Google has driven developments in sponsored search beyond search engine results. In addition to placing advertisements on Google and affiliated search engine results, such as AOL.com and Ask.com, advertisers can place AdWords on other websites. Via its content network, Google dynamically matches ads to a web page's content and pays the website owner if a visitor clicks on the ad. Google's content network includes millions of websites in more than 100 countries and 20 languages, such as the British travel site Lonely Planet and the French television channel M6. In the United States, for example, the *New York Times* earns revenue by placing AdWords on its web pages. Thus, advertisers can place AdWords on search engine results and on the millions of websites in Google's content network.

AdWords are simple text-based ads with four lines of copy predominantly in the right-hand column and at the top of Google search results. The first line, or headline, has a maximum of 25 characters. The next two lines and the final line with the website address have a maximum of 35 characters each. Two sample AdWords advertisements for David Jones are shown in Exhibit 1. The copy is identical except for the first half of the third line, "Great holiday specials" versus "Expanded holiday hours." The ad on the left should interest value-conscious market segments, while the one on the right should attract consumers seeking after-hours shopping.

In addition to its simple and nonintrusive nature, AdWords' advantages over traditional advertising such as print or television include better segmentation and more direct targeting. Advertisers select the keywords and the geographic location of the person doing the search. For geographic segmentation, David Jones might want its ads

EXHIBIT 1
Sample AdWords

Christmas at David Jones	**Christmas at David Jones**
Convenient major city locations	**Convenient major city locations**
Great holiday specials; visit now	**Expanded holiday hours; visit now**
DavidJones.com.au	**DavidJones.com.au**

to appear only for people in a key source market such as Sydney or Melbourne.

To target consumer interests, David Jones could use keywords such as *Christmas, holidays, shopping,* and *retailers.* But these keywords could be too expensive because they are so generic. Although generic terms may attract clicks on an AdWords advertisement, many of these clicks may be from random rather than targeted David Jones web shoppers. Unlike a cost-per-thousand model based on impressions, this contextual advertising based on keywords charges advertisers on a cost-per-click basis. Chris and her team want to pay for targeted clicks.

To minimize paying for unwanted clicks, online advertisers also include negative keywords such as *cheap* or *free.* Including the negative keyword *cheap* alongside the keywords *Christmas* and *shopping* means that no AdWords ads will show on search results for users keying in the three keywords *cheap, Christmas,* and *shopping.*

Furthermore, advertisers bid on the cost per click in a dynamic auction. When many advertisers bid on generic terms such as *Christmas* and *shopping,* this drives the cost up for these keywords. Thus, clever advertisers bid on specific phrases such as *Christmas shopping* rather than on *Christmas* and *shopping.*

Chris and her team use four Google websites to understand and determine applicable content network websites, keywords, and estimated keyword costs:

- Google AdWords Glossary (https://adwords.google.com/support/bin/topic.py?topic=29)
- Google Content Network (www.google.com/adwords/contentnetwork/)
- Google Keyword Tool (https://adwords.google.com/select/KeywordToolExternal)
- Google Traffic Estimator (https://adwords.google.com/select/TrafficEstimatorSandbox)

Because AdWords accounts are easy to set up and manage, the testing possibilities are many. Major considerations that Chris and her team would like to test include:

- Appropriate keywords, keyword phrases, and negative keywords
- Geographic segmentation
- Advertising copy and appeals
- Keyword pricing
- Google's content network
- Aligning the landing page with the AdWords copy

The final point—the landing page—leads to a key aspect of David Jones' online presence, its website. As davidjones.com.au illustrates, the website serves many target markets and offers many products. For example, online visitors may find information on store events, employment, publicly traded stock shares, and registration for e-mail alerts and bridal registries, as well as traditional department store products such as clothing. Effective AdWords align the advertising copy with the landing page. That is, the advertisement directs consumers to a relevant web page rather than to the David Jones home page at davidjones.com.au. The left-column ad in Exhibit 1, which focuses on holiday specials, would take visitors to a landing page with holiday specials. Similarly, the right-column ad in Exhibit 1 would take visitors to a landing page featuring expanded holiday hours.

This case was written by Jamie Murphy, Murdoch Business School, Australia; Meghan O'Farrell, Google; and Alex Gibelalde, Google.

DISCUSSION QUESTIONS

1. On the basis of your review of the David Jones website davidjones.com.au, use examples to explain how different sections of the home page serve different audiences. What other audiences would you suggest David Jones serve via its website? Why?

2. On the basis of your review of the David Jones website, davidjones.com.au, design three separate AdWords advertisements.

CASE 28 Enterprise Rent-A-Car Focuses on Its People

Enterprise Rent-A-Car, with annual sales of more than $13 billion, is the largest and most profitable car-rental business in North America. The company runs more than 6000 locations that fall within 15 miles of 90 percent of the U.S. population. Enterprise also operates in Canada, Germany, Ireland, and the United Kingdom.

When Jack Taylor started Enterprise in 1957, he adopted a unique strategy. Most car-rental firms targeted business and leisure travel customers who arrived at an airport and needed to rent a car for local transportation. Taylor decided to target a different segment—drivers whose own cars were being repaired or who were driving on vacation, hauling home improvement materials, or in need of an extra vehicle for an out-of-town guest, or who, for some other reason, simply needed an extra car for a few days.

Traditional car rental companies must charge relatively high daily rates because their locations in or near airports are expensive. In addition, their business customers are price-insensitive because their companies pay for the rental expenses. While the airport locations are convenient for business customers, these locations are inconvenient for people seeking a replacement car while their car is in the shop. Although Enterprise has airport locations, it also maintains rental offices in downtown and suburban areas, near where its target market lives and works. The firm provides local pickup and delivery service in most areas.

Enterprise also rewards entrepreneurship at a local level. The company fosters a sense of ownership among its employees. For example, its management training program starts by defining a clear career path for each management trainee. Then it teaches employees how to build their own business. Their compensation is tied directly to the financial results of the local operation. Employees from the rental branch offices often advance to the highest levels of operating management.

The firm hires college graduates—8000 each year from 1000 campuses—for its management trainee positions because it believes a college degree demonstrates intelligence and motivation. Rather than recruiting students with the highest GPA, it focuses on hiring people who were athletes or officers of social organizations, such as fraternities, sororities, and clubs, because they typically have the good interpersonal skills needed to deal effectively with Enterprise's varied customers.

Jack Taylor's growth strategy is based on providing high-quality, personalized service so that customers will return to Enterprise when they need to rent a car again. One of his often-quoted sayings summarizes his philosophy: "If you take care of your customers and employees, the bottom line will take care of itself." But because operating managers initially were compensated on the basis of sales growth, not customer satisfaction, service quality declined.

The first step Enterprise took to improve customer service was to develop a customer satisfaction measure, called the Enterprise Service Quality Index. The questionnaire that customers complete to assess ESQI was developed on the basis of input from operating managers, which in turn gave those managers a sense of ownership of the measurement tool. As ESQI gained legitimacy, Enterprise made a bigger deal of it. It posted the scores for each location prominently in its monthly operating reports—right next to the net profit numbers that determined managers' pay. The operating managers were able to track how they were doing and how all their peers were doing because all of the locations were ranked.

Feedback is also provided to service providers. If a customer mentions in the questionnaire that "I really liked Jill behind the counter; she just was terrific," that comment gets sent the very next morning to the local branch so that Jill knows that she did a great job and that a customer said something nice about her. Likewise, if somebody said that a car was dirty, the next day the local manager knows it and can determine why it happened.

To increase motivation among managers and improve service at their locations, Enterprise also announced that managers could be promoted only if their customer satisfaction scores were above the company average. Then it demonstrated that it would abide by this policy by failing to promote some star performers who had achieved good growth and profit numbers but had below-average satisfaction scores.

To provide a high level of service, new employees generally work long, grueling hours for what many see as relatively low pay. Before they are put in a branch and learn how to rent a car, Enterprise tells new hires about what the company means, what is important to customers, and what it deems important in terms of being a good team member. The company operates like a confederation of small businesses. New employees, like all Enterprise managers, are expected to jump in and help wash or vacuum cars when the location gets backed up. But all this hard work can pay off. The firm does not hire outsiders for other than entry-level jobs. At Enterprise, every position is filled by promoting someone already inside the company. Thus, Enterprise employees know that if they work hard and do their best, they may very well succeed in moving up the corporate ladder and earning a significant income.

Sources: Fay Hansen, "Enterprise's Recruiting Model Transforms Interns into Managers," *Workforce Management Online*, May 2009; www.erac.com; www.enterprise.com; http://images.businessweek.com/ss/10/02/0218_customer_service_champs/1.htm.

This case was written by Barton Weitz, University of Florida.

DISCUSSION QUESTIONS

1. What are the pros and cons of Enterprise's human resource management strategy?

2. Would you want to work for Enterprise? Why or why not?

3. How does its human resource strategy complement the quality of customer service delivered by its representatives?

CASE 29   Diamond in the Rough

Ruth Diamond, president of Diamond Furriers, was concerned that sales in her store appeared to have flattened out. She was considering establishing a different method for compensating her salespeople.

Diamond was located in an affluent suburb of Nashville, Tennessee. Ruth's father had founded the company 40 years earlier, and she had grown up working in the business. After his retirement in 1980, she moved the store into an upscale shopping mall not far from its previous location, and sales boomed almost immediately, rising to just over $1 million in five years. However, once it reached that sales volume, it remained there for the next three years, making Ruth wonder whether her salespeople had sufficient incentive to sell more aggressively.

Diamond's staff was all women, ranging in age from 27 to 58 years. There were four full-timers and four part-timers (20 hours a week), all of whom had at least three years of experience in the store. All of them were paid at the same hourly rate, $10, with liberal health benefits. Employee morale was excellent, and the entire staff displayed strong personal loyalty to Diamond.

The store was open 78 hours a week, which meant that there was nearly always a minimum staff of three on the floor, rising to six at peak periods. Diamond's merchandise consisted exclusively of fur coats and jackets, ranging in price from $750 to more than $5,000. The average unit sale was about $2,000. Full-timers' annual sales averaged about $160,000, and the part-timers' were a little over half of that.

Diamond's concern about sales transcended her appreciation for her loyalty toward her employees. She asked them, for example, to maintain customer files and call their customers when new styles came in. Although some of them were more diligent about this than others, none of them appeared to want to be especially aggressive about promoting sales.

She began to investigate commission systems and discussed them with some of her contacts in the trade. All suggested lowering the salespeople's base pay and installing either a fixed or a variable commission rate system.

One idea was to lower the base hourly rate from $10 to $7 and let them make up the difference through a 4 percent commission on all sales, to be paid monthly. Such an arrangement would allow them all to earn the same as they currently do.

However, she also realized that such a system would provide no incentive to sell the higher-priced furs, which she recognized might be a way to improve overall sales. So she also considered offering to pay 3 percent on items priced below $2,000 and 5 percent on all those above.

Either of these systems would require considerable extra bookkeeping. Returns would have to be deducted from commissions. And she was also concerned that disputes might arise among her people from time to time over who had actually made the sale. So she conceived of a third alternative, which was to leave the hourly rates the same but pay a flat bonus of 4 percent of all sales over $1 million and then divide it among the salespeople on the basis of the proportion of hours each had actually worked. This "commission" would be paid annually, in the form of a Christmas bonus.

This case was prepared by Professor David Ehrlich, Marymount University.

DISCUSSION QUESTIONS

1. What are the advantages and disadvantages of the various alternatives Ruth Diamond is considering?

2. Do you have any other suggestions for improving the store's sales?

3. What would you recommend? Why?

CASE 30   A Stockout at Discmart

Robert Honda, the manager of a Discmart store (a discount retailer similar to Target and Walmart) in Cupertino, California, was surveying the Sunday morning activity at his store. Shoppers were bustling around with carts; some had children in tow. On the front side of the store, a steady stream of shoppers was heading through the checkout counters. Almost all the cash registers that he could see from his vantage point were open and active. The line in front of register 7 was longer than the other lines, but other than that, things seemed to be going quite smoothly.

The intercom beeped and interrupted his thoughts. A delivery truck had just arrived at the rear of the store. The driver wanted to know which loading dock to use to unload merchandise. Honda decided to inspect the available space before directing the driver to a specific loading dock. As he passed the cash registers on his way to the rear of the store, he noticed that the line at register 7 had gotten a little bit longer. The light over the register was flashing, indicating that the customer service associate (CSA) requested assistance. (At Discmart, all frontline personnel who interact with customers are called CSAs.) As he passed by the register, he could not help overhearing the exchange between what seemed to be a somewhat irate customer and the CSA. The customer was demanding that another item should be substituted for an item that was on sale but currently out of stock, and the CSA was explaining the store policy to the customer. Normally, during a busy time like this, Honda would have tried to help the CSA resolve the situation, but he knew that the truck driver was waiting to unload merchandise that was needed right away on the floor. Hence, he quickly walked to the rear of the store.

After assigning the truck to a docking bay for unloading, Honda headed back toward the front of the store. On the way back, he ducked into the break room to get a Coke and noticed that Sally Johnson, the CSA who had been at register 7, was on a break. Sally had been on the Discmart team for about a year and was considered a very capable employee who always kept the store's interests at heart.

Robert: Hi Sally, I noticed that you had quite a line in front of your register earlier today.

Sally: Hi Robert. Yes, I had a very irate customer, and it took us a while to resolve the issue.

Robert: Oh really! What was he irate about?

Sally: We are out of stock on the 100-ounce Tide Liquid Detergent that was advertised in our flyer and was on sale at 20 percent off. I offered the customer a rain check or the same discount on the same size of another brand, but he kept insisting that he wanted us to substitute a 200-ounce container of Tide Liquid Detergent at the same discount. Apparently, Joe Chang [the assistant manager] had told the customer that we would substitute the 200-ounce size.

Robert: Did you point out to the customer that our sale prices are valid only while supplies last?

Sally: I did mention this to him, but he thought it was strange that we ran out of stock on the morning of the first day of the sale.

Robert: Well, I guess you should have gone ahead and given him what he wanted.

Sally: As you know, our point-of-sale systems allow me to make adjustments only on designated items.

Since the 200-ounce sizes were not designated as substitutes, I had to request a supervisor to help me.

Robert: I am glad that you got it resolved.

Sally: Well, the customer got tired of waiting for the supervisor, who was busy helping another customer, so he decided to take a rain check instead. He seemed quite dissatisfied with the whole episode and mentioned that we should stop running these TV ads claiming that we are always in stock and that we guarantee satisfaction.

Robert: I do hate it when they run these ad campaigns and we have to take the heat on the floor, trying to figure out what those cowboys in marketing promised the customer.

Sally: Well, my break is nearly over. I have to get back.

Honda pondered the encounter that Johnson had with the customer. He wondered whether to discuss this issue with Joe Chang. He remembered talking to him about inventory policies a couple of days ago. Chang had indicated that their current inventory levels were fairly high and that any further increases would be hard to justify from a financial perspective. He mentioned some market research that had surveyed a random sample of customers who had redeemed rain checks. The results of the survey indicated that customers by and large were satisfied with Discmart's rain check procedures. On the basis of this finding, Chang had argued that current inventory levels, supplemented with a rain check policy, would keep customers satisfied.

This case was prepared by Kirthi Kalyanam, Retail Management Institute, Santa Clara University.

DISCUSSION QUESTIONS

1. Why did this service breakdown occur?

2. How was this service gap related to the other gaps (standards, knowledge, delivery, and communications) described in the Gaps model in Chapter 18?

CASE 31   Customer Service and Relationship Management at Nordstrom

Nordstrom's unwavering customer-focused philosophy traces its roots to founder Johan Nordstrom's values. Johan Nordstrom believed in people and realized that consistently exceeding their expectations would lead to success and a good conscience. He built his organization around a customer-oriented philosophy. The organization focuses on people, and its policies and selections are designed to satisfy people. As simple as this philosophy sounds, few of Nordstrom's competitors have truly been able to grasp it.

A FOCUS ON PEOPLE

Nordstrom employees treat customers like royalty. Employees are instructed to do whatever is in the customer's best interest. Customer delight drives the values of the company. Customers are taken seriously and are at the heart of the business. Customers are even at the top of Nordstrom's so-called organization chart, which is an inverted pyramid. Moving down from the customers at the top of the inverted pyramid are the salespeople, department managers, and general managers. Finally, at the bottom is the board of directors. All lower levels work toward supporting the salespeople, who in turn work to serve the customers.

Employee incentives are tied to customer service. Salespeople are given personalized business cards to help them build relationships with customers. Uniquely, salespeople are not tied to their respective departments but to the customer. Salespeople can travel from department to department within the store to assist their customer, if that is needed. For example, a Nordstrom salesperson assisting a woman shopping for business apparel helps her shop for suits, blouses, shoes, hosiery, and accessories. The salesperson becomes the "personal shopper" of the customer to show her merchandise and provide fashion expertise. This approach is also conducive to building long-term relationships with customers, because over time, the salesperson comes to understand each customer's fashion sense and personality.

The opportunity to sell across departments enables salespeople to maximize sales and commissions while providing superior customer service. As noted on a *60 Minutes* segment, "[Nordstrom's service is] not service like it used to be, but service that never was."

Despite the obsession with customer service at Nordstrom, ironically, the customer actually comes second. Nordstrom understands that customers will be treated well by its employees only if the employees themselves are treated well by the company. Nordstrom employees are treated almost like the extended Nordstrom family, and employee satisfaction is a closely watched business variable.

Nordstrom is known for promoting employees from within its ranks. The fundamental traits of a successful Nordstrom salesperson (e.g., commitment to excellence, customer service) are the same traits emphasized in successful Nordstrom executives.

Nordstrom hires people with a positive attitude, a sense of ownership, initiative, heroism, and the ability to handle high expectations. This sense of ownership is reflected in Nordstrom's low rate of shrinkage. Shrinkage, or loss due to theft and record-keeping errors, at Nordstrom is under 1.5 percent of sales, roughly half the industry average. The low shrinkage can be attributed in large part to the diligence of salespeople caring for the merchandise as if it were their own.

Employees at all levels are treated like businesspeople and empowered to make independent decisions. They are

592   SECTION V   Cases

given the latitude to do whatever they believe is the right thing, with the customers' best interests at heart. All employees are given the tools and authority to do whatever is necessary to satisfy customers, and management almost always backs subordinates' decisions.

In summary, Nordstrom's product is its people. The loyal Nordstrom shopper goes to Nordstrom for the service received—not necessarily the products. Of course, Nordstrom does offer quality merchandise, but that is secondary for many customers.

CUSTOMER-FOCUSED POLICIES

One of the most famous examples of Nordstrom's customer service occurred in 1975 when a Nordstrom salesperson gladly took back a set of used automobile tires and gave the customer a refund, even though Nordstrom had never sold tires! The customer had purchased the tires from a Northern Commercial Company store, whose retail space Nordstrom had since acquired. Not wanting the customer to leave the Nordstrom store unhappy, the salesperson refunded the price of the tires.

Nordstrom's policies focus on the concept of the "Lifetime Value of the Customer." Although little money is made on the first sale, when the lifetime value of a customer is calculated, the positive dollar amount of a loyal customer is staggering. The lifetime value of a customer is the sum of all sales and profits generated from that customer, directly or indirectly. To keep its customers for a "lifetime," Nordstrom employees go to incredible lengths. In a Nordstrom store in Seattle, a customer wanted to buy a pair of brand-name slacks that had gone on sale. The store was out of her size, and the salesperson was unable to locate a pair at other Nordstrom stores. Knowing that the same slacks were available at a competitor nearby, the sales clerk went to the rival, purchased the slacks at full price using petty cash from her department, and sold the slacks to the customer at Nordstrom's sale price. Although this sale resulted in an immediate loss for the store, the investment in promoting the loyalty of the happy customer went a long way.

Nordstrom's employees try to "Never Say No" to the customer. Nordstrom has an unconditional return policy. If a customer is not completely satisfied, he or she can return the new and generally even heavily used merchandise at any time for a full refund. Ironically, this is not a company policy; rather, it is implemented at the discretion of the salesperson to maximize customer satisfaction.

Nordstrom's advice to its employees is simply, "Use good judgment in all situations." Employees are given the freedom, support, and resources to make the best decisions to enhance customer satisfaction. The cost of Nordstrom's high service, such as its return policy, coupled with its competitive pricing would, on the surface, seem to cut into profit margins. This cost, however, is recouped through increased sales from repeat customers, limited markdowns, and, if necessary, the "squeezing" of suppliers.

Nordstrom's vendor relationships also focus on maximizing customer satisfaction. According to former CEO Bruce Nordstrom, "[Vendors] know that we are liberal with our customers. And if you're going to do business with us, then there should be a liberal influence on their return policies. If somebody has worn a shoe and it doesn't wear satisfactorily for them, and we think that person is being honest about it, then we will send it back." Nordstrom realizes some customers will abuse the unconditional return policy, but it refuses to impose that abuse back onto the vendors. Here again, the rule of "doing what is right" comes into play.

Nordstrom's merchandising and purchasing policies are also extremely customer-focused. A full selection of merchandise in a wide variety of sizes is seen as a measure of customer service. An average Nordstrom store carries roughly 150,000 pairs of shoes with a variety of sizes, widths, colors, and models. Typical shoe sizes for women range from 2½ to 14, in widths of A to EEE. Nordstrom is fanatical about stocking only high-quality merchandise. Once when the upper parts of some women's shoes were separating from the soles, every shoe from that delivery was shipped back to the manufacturer.

This case was written by Alicia Lueddemann, the Management Mind Group, and Sunil Erevelles, University of North Carolina, Charlotte.

DISCUSSION QUESTIONS

1. What steps does Nordstrom take to implement its strategy of providing outstanding customer service?

2. How do these activities enable Nordstrom to reduce the gaps between perceived service and customer expectations, as described in Chapter 18?

3. What are the pros and cons of Nordstrom's approach to developing a competitive advantage through customer service?

592   SECTION V   Cases

CASE 32   Zipcar: Delivering Only as Much Driving as You Want

The expectation that your car will be waiting at the curb every morning got hard-wired into many Americans, with the growth of the auto industry. But that expectation has gone haywire for many city dwellers, who have been frustrated by the soaring costs and parking pressures that confront modern drivers. For them, Zipcar, the world's leading car-sharing company, offers the pleasure of driving without the hassles of ownership.

The Cambridge, Massachusetts–based company rents self-service vehicles by the hour or day to urban residents who prefer to pay for just as much driving as they abso-

lutely need. Car sharing eliminates issues related to parking shortages; overnight parking restrictions; or soaring gas, insurance, and tax bills. That promise resonates well with consumer expectations on many fronts, especially among Zipcar's primary urban customers, the large segments of college students who also enjoy the service, and even suburbanites who just work in the city.

Still the company's biggest growth obstacle may be Americans' inability to envision life without a car. To push an attitude shift, Zipcar makes the car-sharing experience as easy as possible, with just four simple steps:

1. Join the network.
2. Reserve your car online or from your smartphone.
3. Unlock the car with your Zipcard.
4. Drive away.

Today the car-sharing network offers more than 30 makes and models of cars, and has more than 767,000 members and 10,000 vehicles in major metropolitan areas and college campuses throughout the United States, Canada, United Kingdom, Spain, and Austria. With so many locations, the company could bring convenient car sharing to a far larger market; it estimates that 10 million residents, business commuters, and university students now live or work just a short walk away from an available Zipcar.

Zipcar also is banking on more than shifting attitudes. Emerging trends due to the economic downturn and changing buying habits have helped spur growth. On average, automobiles consume 19 percent of household incomes, yet many cars stand idle for 90 percent of each day. Drivers seeking a less expensive and less wasteful alternative thus might save up to 70 percent on their transportation costs, because an annual Zipcar membership costs just $60, and the average member spends $428 a year.

Zipcar's service model also fits in with the emergence of on-demand, pay-per-use options, such as Netflix for movies, iTunes for music, and e-readers for books. Moreover, the popularity of mobile shopping and the growing expectation that they can order anything, anywhere, anytime from their smartphone have made urban young adults and college students two of Zipcar's most fervent member groups. For these "Zipsters," ordering up a set of wheels on the go is far more appealing than being saddled with car payments.

A strong urban public transportation system also helps make car sharing more attractive. That's why Zipcar started off in high-density urban areas such as Boston, New York, and Washington, DC, with their great public transportation systems already in place. Wherever subways and buses work, car sharing can extend the transit system's reach. By locating cars near transit route endpoints, travelers gain an easy extension on subway or bus schedules to their final destinations.

Finally, the logic of car sharing works well in settings marked by increased urbanization. According to the United Nations, cities will contain 59 percent of the world's population by 2030. Many of these areas already face congestion, space demands, and environmental threats from crowding too many gas-driven vehicles into a small, population-dense space. Zipcar CEO Scott Griffith estimates that every Zipcar would replace 15 to 20 personal cars. Thus, some cities even work with Zipcar to identify and secure parking spaces close to subway stops and rail stations. New York and Chicago also rent Zipcars for municipal workers so they can shuttle more efficiently across city locations during their workday. Zipcar also provides fleet management services to local, state, and federal agencies.

Car sharing could translate into a $10 billion market globally. Cities in Europe and Asia are well primed for car sharing by virtue of their strong rail systems, heavy reliance on public transit, and widespread adoption of mobile and wireless technologies. A deal with Spain's largest car-sharing company, Avancar, is a first venture in Zipcar's planned global expansion.

Such growth requires strong logistics, and Zipcar is backed by a corps of fleet managers and vehicle coordinators who track, schedule, and oversee vehicle maintenance; proprietary hardware and software technology that helps it communicate with drivers and track vehicles; and a large fleet that includes hybrid vehicles for fuel efficiency, as well as minivans to appeal to families who want to take a trip to the beach. Zipcar estimates that it processes 2.6 million reservations per year, and its reservation system has almost never failed.

These behind-the-scenes moves aim to make Zipcar's service simple, convenient, and reliable. But failures are inevitable, as one customer's experience showed. The customer went to pick up his designated vehicle at the time and place reserved for him, but he discovered no car there. The Zipcar representative told him that it might be out, being serviced or cleaned, or it could have been delayed by another driver running late. But such excuses did little to alleviate the frustration of being stuck with no transportation.

Learning of his predicament, Zipcar tried but was unable to find another car in close proximity. Therefore, it quickly authorized the customer to take a taxi and promised to reimburse him up to $100. Although the "free ride" did not altogether mitigate the stress and inconvenience of the service failure, Zipcar's response showed him that the company was committed to doing right by him, even if that meant sending business to a competitor, the taxi company.

The considerable dimensions of a global car-sharing market are already emerging. Zipcar's 10-year experience and first-mover position in the market positions it well to compete. But the race to dominate is sure to intensify, especially as traditional car rental companies with great name recognition, such as Hertz and Enterprise, move into the marketplace. Whether Zipcar can maintain its space in this market depends mostly on its ability to meet its own standards for customer service—simplicity, convenience, and reliability—consistently and effectively.

This case was written by Laurie Covens, Dhruv Grewal and Michael Levy, both at Babson College.

Sources: www.zipcar.com; April Kilcrease, "A Conversation with Zipcar's CEO Scott Griffith," *GigaOM*, December 5, 2011; U.S. Securities and Exchange Commission, "Zipcar S-1 Filing," June 1, 2010; JP Morgan SMid Cap Conference, December 11, 2011; Courtney Rubin, "How Will the IPO Market Treat Zipcar?" *Inc.com*, June 2, 2010.

DISCUSSION QUESTIONS

1. Using the five dimensions of service quality (reliability, assurance, tangibility, empathy, and responsiveness), evaluate Zipcar.

2. Compare Zipcar's service quality performance with that of the most recent car rental service (e.g., Avis, Hertz) that you may have used.

3. How well has Zipcar handled service failure situations? What could it do to improve recovery efforts?

CASE 33 Building the Apple Store

Founded in 1976 by the late Steve Jobs and Steve Wozniak, Apple has become an innovative leader in the consumer electronics industry. In addition to offering traditional desktop and laptop computers, Apple essentially founded the digital music player when it introduced the iPod and online music store markets with iTunes; launched easy-to-use iPhones and iPads with increasingly more features; and introduced online movie/TV services through AppleTV and publishing and multimedia software.

BEFORE APPLE RETAIL STORES

During the early 1990s, Apple struggled as computer sales began shifting from specialized computer stores to mainstream retail stores. Big-box retailers such as Best Buy and Circuit City could offer a wider selection of computers at lower prices, although they lacked adequate customer service and support. These big-box retailers and specialized stores faced even more competition in the form of mail-order outlets, including CompuAdd, Gateway, and Dell.

Beginning in 1990, Dell shifted from selling its computers in warehouse and specialized computer stores to operating as an online direct mail-order company. Dell facilitated its online operations with an efficient online store that could handle high-volume sales. The online Dell store (dell.com) represented a new strategy for manufacturing: Computers were built as they were ordered. In turn, Dell could reduce inventory because it no longer produced computers in mass quantities and then pushed inventory through the channel to resellers.

While establishing its online store, Apple needed to balance its direct orders with the sales initiated by its channel partners, mail-order resellers, independent dealers, and CompUSA, with which it initiated a "stores within stores" strategy to focus on Apple's products. Apple's partnership with CompUSA paid off. When the San Francisco CompUSA store was equipped with Macs, Apple's sales jumped from 15 to 35 percent of overall store sales.

Apple also put its own employees to work in various retail outlets to help inform and educate customers, as well as ensure its products were being displayed in working order. The company estimated it spent between $25,000 and $75,000 per month on this initiative. Apple executives soon realized they could not compete with PC brands by selling just laptops and desktops in big-box retail stores because retailers could earn greater profits by selling lower-quality PC models. They had little to no incentive to sell Macs. Without its own retail store, Apple would always be at the mercy of the independent dealers and partners that operated with different strategic goals.

DESIGNING THE APPLE STORE

To compete with the PCs sold by big-box retailers, Apple needed to shift from selling its electronics through intermediaries to offering products directly through Apple stores. This shift would not come easily. Steve Jobs, Apple's dynamic founder, first looked to bring in new executives. Mickey Drexler, former CEO of The Gap and now CEO of J.Crew, was hired in 1999 as part of Apple's board of directors. Next, Jobs brought in Ron Johnson, who had been a merchandising executive with Target, to run Apple's retail division as vice president of retail operations.

Instead of launching stores from the start, Drexler suggested that Jobs rent a warehouse and build a prototype store, coined Apple Store Version 0.0. Apple executives then continuously redesigned the store until they achieved a layout that would entice shoppers to not only enter, but make purchases. The first store prototype was configured by product category, with hardware laid out according to the internal organization of the company rather than by how customers logically shop. Executives quickly decided to redesign the store to match customer interests better. Although the redesign cost Apple more than six months, the executives believed this time investment was necessary to achieve a successful store that could compete with well-established electronics retailers and remain consistent with the Apple brand. Its first store opened in Tyson's Corner, Virginia, in May 2001.

THE APPLE STORE LAYOUT

When considering a site for a retail store, Apple uses its customer base to forecast visitor volume and revenues. Most Apple stores locate within existing shopping malls or lifestyle centers, where retail traffic is already present. There are two types of full-size stores: a street-facing building or an in-mall store. The stores range from 3,600 to 20,000 square feet, although most fall in the 3,000- to 6,000-square-feet range. Storefronts are typically all glass with a backlit Apple logo, and the front display windows change occasionally to focus on the newest marketing campaign. Apple's internal team designs the window displays, often using slot and cable systems to suspend design elements within the window. In some cases, the swinging entrance doors are in the middle, but in other stores, a logo wall appears in the middle with two doors located on either side. Store interiors feature only three materials: glass, stainless steel, and wood.

In addition to the retail floor, Apple stores have backroom areas that sometimes include a public restroom, offices, and the inventory area. At some sites that lack sufficient space, inventory storage is located at a separate facility, always within walking distance.

The store layout changes multiple times throughout the year. Apple executives organize planograms to coincide with the introduction of new products or heavily marketed merchandise. The layouts depend on the size of the store. A typical in-mall store locates merchandise in the front half of the store and customer service and support areas in the rear. Apple stores carry fewer than 20 products, and every display piece is available for hands-on use so that customers can get an accurate feel for the available hardware and software.

On tables along the right wall, iPhones and iPods take up the front half of the store. Along the left wall, tables hold various models of general and high-end desktop and laptop computers. These displays give way to The Studio, a newer section hosted by experts who will answer application-oriented, creative questions. Two to three island tables in the front center display software on Apple computers; additional island tables exhibit peripherals such as iPod docking stations and printers. A small children's area houses Apple computers running children's software. The Genius Bar takes up the back wall, with stools before a counter staffed with Apple experts for repairs and consultations. Larger stores also have a theater area in the back, featuring a rear-projection screen with an audience area of either U-shaped wooden benches or full theater seats in rows. This store layout is typical for a store located in a super-regional mall.

Apple stores thus follow a free-form layout, which allows customers to browse the store according to their own interests. Signage hanging from the ceiling, for greater visibility, directs customers to specific areas within the store. Bright lighting draws attention to merchandise and creates a sense of excitement. Highlighted merchandise also helps draw customers strategically through the store. As customers browse the products, employees wearing Apple T-shirts and lanyards make themselves available to answer any questions.

Through its intensive development efforts, Apple has created a unique, customer service–oriented shopping experience. Customers can schedule face-to-face appointments at an Apple store to test-drive products. One-to-one personal training sessions help customers become familiar with the array of Apple products. The company also offers free one-hour instructional or informational workshops every day for iPod, iPhone, and Mac owners. It also offers support for business customers by providing insight and advice about how to create a presentation from start to finish using Apple products.

Sources: Philip Elmer-Dewitt, "Apple Ranks No. 4 in E-Retailing Survey," *Fortune*, May 5, 2010; Daniel Eran, "Apple's Retail Challenge," *RDM*, November 8, 2006; "The Stores," *IfoAppleStore.com*; Jerry Useem, "Apple: America's Best Retailer," *Fortune*, March 8, 2007.

This case was written by Brienne Curley, while an MBA student at Loyola College in Maryland, under the supervision of Hope Corrigan.

DISCUSSION QUESTIONS

1. Have you ever visited an Apple store? If yes, did you make a purchase? Why or why not?

2. Why are Apple's store layout and atmosphere important?

3. Is Apple America's best retailer?

4. Visit your local Apple store. Does the layout of the store help to provide you with an excellent customer experience? Explain.

CASE 34   Generating Advertising Revenue from a Digital Screen Network at Harrods of London

Retailers have slowly been implementing digital screen networks. In most instances, the messages are focused on branding and affecting the customer shopping experience. Very few networks, like Walmart's SMART Network and, to a lesser extent, Target's Channel Red, have also been able to generate a stream of advertising revenue. In the department store category, Harrods is the only high-end luxury store to successfully sell advertising on its in-store digital signage network. Factors such as a solid and consistent customer base and the store's unique environment have contributed to the success of the signage.

It is difficult to imagine any retail environment as unique as Harrods. It is a key destination for millions of visitors who come to the United Kingdom every year (it is the UK's third-largest tourist attraction). It houses the world's finest luxury brands across a million square feet of retail space. It has a history dating back to 1849 and can count the rich and famous from all corners of the globe as its customers. The brand is synonymous with luxury, the "finer things in life," and a range of merchandise unequaled under one roof. Average daily traffic is 45,000 customers (occasionally rising to 100,000 on special days). Many of them are high-net-worth individuals, including royalty from around the world, as well as celebrities and billionaires.

Advertisements on the network are sold to premium brands, such as Armani and Cartier. The medium is often sold as part of an integrated marketing campaign, which often includes other media such as posters, lift-wraps (signage on elevator doors), windows, and even pages in the Harrods magazine. Combined with other in-store media, screens are an integral part of the campaign providing impact, awareness, and, often, directional signage leading customers to the "heart of the promotion"—the place where the product and the customer meet.

The specific location of each screen was carefully considered so that each customer would have a multiscreen sight line. In most cases, customers see more than one screen within their view. The same content appears simultaneously on each screen in the network, so the advertisers have high impact with their ads appearing several times at once.

In most cases, screens are positioned on the sides of escalators in the store. Unlike the case at many transport hubs, most customers in Harrods stand still on the moving steps. As they glide up to the next floor, they take in the view, which includes the digital screens. Each advertiser has a 15-second slot.

Harrods' digital screen network is managed all in-house. There is a dedicated ad sales team, an operations team, and a technical and creative team—all of whom are committed Harrods employees who live and breathe the brand. These employees believe in and are included in how and what is being marketed. They sit in the building and pass by the media that they are selling and marketing 20 times a day. They also see with their own eyes the audience that they are selling to the advertisers. They see the clothes they are wearing, the limos that deliver them to the store, and the number of Harrods' famous green bags they are carrying. They can see the impact that the screens can have on a consumer purchasing decision, or even simply see customers watching content through their Dior sunglasses as they glide up an escalator.

Network staff also have relationships with the brands and the advertisers. They have a relationship that has been nurtured and developed so that they are working "alongside" a brand to find marketing solutions to drive brand sales and awareness, which in turn benefits not only the brand, but also Harrods as a store.

The store is continuously changing, and as part of that development, additional digital screens are introduced as part of new departments and remodels. When Harrods first introduced its digital signage network, it realized that it had to do something special to integrate the screens into the environment. It didn't want screens hanging from ceilings above walkways that looked tacky, amateur, and cheap. It invested heavily in each screen installation, with customized reinforced glass, polished steel bezels, additional cooling fans, and color schemes that are consistent with the store's decor. This gave the screens a look of luxury. A lot of care, thought, and attention have been invested in each location to give the advertiser the optimum in presentation.

Harrods monitors the effectiveness of a campaign via sales data. It has some impressive results from advertisers that have enjoyed double-digit sales increases during and following a digital campaign in the store. So, the natural question is, "Well, why isn't everyone advertising on the screens?" The answer to this question involves many factors including, among other things, the following:

- The medium is new and many vendors are unfamiliar with its benefits.
- Vendors are not always sure about where the funding of digital screen ads should come from. That is, is it a marketing/advertising expenditure or an in-store promotional expenditure?

- There are creative challenges associated with messages. For instance, is the message capturing the attention of the customers? Does it have a call to action or an offer?

If there is one way to deter advertisers, then it's to have blank, malfunctioning screens. It seems obvious, but so many networks in retail lumber on with as many as 25 percent of the screens nonoperational. No wonder they find selling ads a struggle! Harrods has a "zero tolerance" strategy within the operations team, resulting in the team's touring the store every morning before the store opens checking that all is as it should be. As well, it has invested heavily in preventive maintenance contracts and has a backup stock of spare screens available should a screen die and require replacement.

Digital networks can make money for a retailer. Harrods has realized both ad sales revenue and increased sales of advertised products. However, such results take significant investments in time, resources, and money. The future success for generating advertising sales is dependent on improvements in technical reliability of the hardware and software, combined with more investment in content and creativity. Interactivity via mobile/cell phones is clearly part of the future. Harrods is investing in the latest technology, implementing new and unique content that captures people's imagination, and working alongside brands that are prepared to invest to realize the benefits.

This case was written by Steven Keith Platt, Platt Retail Institute, and Guy Cheston, Director of Advertising Sales and Sponsorship, Harrods.

DISCUSSION QUESTIONS

1. What are the reasons that Harrods has been successful at selling advertising on its digital signage network and other retailers have not? Why would consumer product manufacturers be interested in advertising on Harrods' network?

2. What are the pluses and minuses for a retailer offering a digital network in its stores?

CASE 35   Yankee Candle: New Product Innovation

Yankee Candle Company (YCC) is a leading designer, manufacturer, wholesaler, and retailer of premium scented candles in the giftware industry. The core product lines for YCC are scented candles and candle accessories. The premium-quality scented candles are offered in more than 150 fragrances. Almost all candles are produced onsite at the advanced manufacturing facility in Whately, Massachusetts. Candles are made by master chandlers (candlemaking experts) who oversee a complex manufacturing process with strict quality control standards. As well as creating the candles themselves, YCC builds competitive advantage through expertise in formulating the scents that make up "the fragrance experience." According to information on the YCC website, master perfumers develop

the fragrances, which are then rigorously screened, reviewed, and tested. The scents are unique compared to competitive products in that they maintain intensity through the life of the candle. In short, quality control of the candles and fragrances ensures premium products that provide high value to customers in the form of a true scent, long burn time, and consistency of fragrance over the life of the candle.

Candles are available in clear or frosted glass Housewarmer jars, Sampler votive candles, wax potpourri Tarts, pillars, tapers, and tea lights. Related products are air fragrance products (sprays, electric air fresheners), car fresheners, odor control and insect repellant items, and candle accessories (decorative lids for the jar candles);

taper holders; pillar and jar bases; matching jar shades, plates, and sleeves; votive holders; and tea light holders.

INNOVATION AT YANKEE CANDLE

Success at YCC over time is due, in large part, to the ability of the management team to implement innovative strategies at two levels—in product development (new fragrances and extensions to the product line) and in selling/distribution strategies.

First, innovation in product development is an ongoing cross-functional effort to keep merchandise offerings new and fresh for consumers. For example, in January 2013, company officials announced the launch of a two new lines—the spring limited-edition collection, Full Bloom, and the Paradise Collection. The Full Bloom line represents simple, quiet beauty of singular blossoms and comes in Perfect Pillar glass holders. The Paradise Collection is themed around exotic vacation destinations and includes fresh beach scents and exotic fruits.

Comments of Yankee Candle executive vice president for branding and innovation, Hope Margala Klein, were included in recent press releases about the new products: "Our goal when developing new products is to take our customers to that special place or evoke a special memory through fragrance and the new Paradise Collection for spring delivers on that." She added, "We also share in our customers' desire to create distinctive experiences in their home and the on-trend colors and fragrance inspiration of this collection add warmth to any decor."

As well as developing new fragrances and product lines in-house, YCC parent Yankee Holding Company acquires small firms whose products fit within the brand portfolio. Aroma Naturals is one such company, founded in California by a noted aromatherapist with a commitment to using natural ingredients. Aroma Naturals, bought in 2005, appeals to consumers interested in wellness and environmentally authentic products. Similarly, the purchase of the Illuminations Company in 2006 gave the Yankee Candle organization a new set of candle and accessory products that appeal to a more upscale demographic. Both of these acquisitions kept their original brand identities in the marketplace to preserve existing brand equity and to avoid consumer confusion with YCC-branded goods.

A second source of success through innovation is the strategy of multichannel distribution. To date, YCC operates more than 500 company-owned retail (bricks-and-mortar) stores nationwide. YCC sells direct to consumers via its online store (yankeecandle.com) and by direct mail catalog orders. In 2001, top management at YCC began cultivating partnerships with mass retailers to carry limited product selections. Past partners include Bed Bath & Beyond and TJ Maxx, to name a few. The wholesale distribution channel is equally important in the multichannel mix. This is a network of approximately 19,100 independent stores that sell YCC products across the United States. Many of these stores are small businesses with Hallmark and other gift-related franchises. For all of these retail and wholesale channels, products are YCC-branded goods.

Again, through the acquisition of Aroma Naturals, Yankee Holding Company was able to generate revenue in new outlets such as mass grocery store chains (e.g., Whole Foods) and others with natural/wellness product areas (e.g., Shaw's, Wegmans). The revenues from the additional channels (supermarkets) and new target markets (health/wellness-conscious consumers) are beneficial for growth. Also, they do not cannibalize the existing YCC lines in traditional distribution channels. The same strategy was used for the Illuminations candle products sold in 28 stores, mostly located on the West Coast of the United States, and direct to consumers via catalog and Internet.

HISTORICAL SUMMARY AND PRESENT-DAY SITUATION

During its 40-year history, the company grew from an entrepreneurial family business started by Mike Kittredge to a publicly traded company in 1999. Craig Rydin joined YCC in 2001 as CEO. Under his leadership, the company flourished; sales climbed higher than ever in company-owned stores and through the wholesale channel. Rydin was instrumental in establishing the partnerships with mass retailers, including Bed Bath & Beyond and Linens 'n Things.

In 2006, YCC purchased Illuminations, the California-based multichannel retailer of high-quality candles and home accessories. The logic behind this decision was sound; acquisition of a similar product in the giftware industry allowed YCC to leverage its position and to target a new, more upscale demographic. In February 2007, YCC went from a publicly traded firm to a private corporation. Madison Dearborn Partners LLC acquired YCC for $1.6 billion, and it was delisted from the New York Stock Exchange.

The major financial crisis in September 2007 caused a dramatic decrease in demand across all consumer sectors of the economy. The giftware industry was hit hard; items such as premium candles are nonessentials for most consumers. YCC and all of its partners were affected. Some partners, such as Linens 'n Things, went completely out of business. Others managed to survive while enduring significant financial losses. YCC was restructured in 2009; this resulted in closure of all 28 Illuminations retail stores, shutting the Aroma Naturals operation, closing one company-owned store, and laying off 330 employees (*Retailer Daily*, 2009).

In 2010, the financial statements and investor information indicated the company was relatively stable while riding some challenging waves due to the lingering effects of the financial crisis. Illuminations-branded products were continuing to be sold through the wholesale network. As of early 2010, 498 company-owned stores in 43 states were in operation. Other channels include the direct mail catalog and website (yankeecandle.com). Aroma Naturals is reported as owned by parent company YCC and a subsidiary of Madison Dearborn Partners. It operates primary as an online retailer at present. Internationally, YCC sells products through a subsidiary, Yankee Candle Company (Europe) Ltd. This subsidiary has an international wholesale customer network of approximately 4,000 stores and distributors across 46 countries.

Since 2010, revenues trended upward but net profits have declined. According to the latest annual report, through the third quarter of 2012, sales revenue is reported to be $502,055,000. Gross profit is $247,567,000, and bottom line net loss is $4,793,000. While revenues and gross profits in 2012 are up compared to the same time in 2011, the net loss in 2012 exceeds the loss incurred in 2011 ($272,000). (*Morningstar*, November 29, 2012, YCC Holdings LLC, pp. 15–20).

Sources: Faye Brookman, "Natural Products Rekindle Candle Sales," *Women's Wear Daily* 193, no. 117 (June 2007), p. 9; Morningstar Document Research, Yankee Holding Corporation, Form 10-K, April 1, 2010; "Yankee Candle to Restructure—Lay Off 330, Close 29 Stores," *Retailer Daily*, January 21, 2009; "Yankee Candle Brings Paradise Home with New Spring 2013 Fragrances," Yankee Candle Company, Press Release, January 22, 2013.

This case was written by Elizabeth J. Wilson, Suffolk University.

DISCUSSION QUESTIONS

1. **What is next for Yankee Holding Company, in general? Consider the three distinct brands under the ownership of Yankee Holding Company—YCC, Illuminations, and Aroma Naturals. Examine the websites of each (yankeecandle.com, illuminations.com, and aromanaturals.com). For this set of offerings, develop a SWOT analysis for Yankee Holding Company.**

2. **It is helpful for a company to periodically assess its core target market in terms of demographics and lifestyles. The investor-owners of YCC, Madison Dearborn Partners LLC, don't want to do an expensive market research study. Using the business and management databases in your university library, research this question: Who is the scented-candle customer?**

   a. **On the basis of secondary data findings, describe the target market that buys premium scented candles.**

   b. **What are the advantages and disadvantages of using secondary data to answer this research question?**

CASE 36   PetSmart: Where Pets Are Family

PetSmart Inc. is the largest specialty pet retailer with more than 1160 brick-and-mortar pet stores in the United States and Canada. This retailer also sells products through its PetSmart website. Each store offers 10,000 products, which are sold under national brands and PetSmart's own private labels. While 89 percent of PetSmart's sales come from pet food and supplies, the service side (grooming, obedience training, boarding, etc.) of its business has been growing. Veterinary services are available in more than 750 locations. PetSmart's key competitors include Petco, Target, and Walmart.

RECENT TRENDS

In the animal-loving society of the United States, 62 percent of households, or 71.4 million homes, own pets. The resulting pet retail industry has benefited from pet owners' tendency to humanize and treat their pets like family members, which has increased industry revenues rapidly. Pet industry expenditures have almost tripled since 1994, making pet care the second fastest growing retail category, with an average annual growth rate of 9 percent. Today, U.S. pet industry expenditures are expected to exceed $47 billion.

An industry once dominated by bland pet food and basic supplies has transformed into a highly differentiated market with diverse and creative offerings, including pet fashions and accessories, gourmet pet cuisine, and even pet massages. The ever-expanding composition of the pet industry spending includes the sale of pet food, supplies, veterinary care, medicine, animal purchases, and pet services such as grooming and boarding.

PETSMART CAPITALIZES ON INDUSTRY TRENDS

A survey conducted by the Washington-based Pew Research Center found that 85 percent of pet owners called their dogs members of the family, as do 78 percent of those with cats. The study also noted that 80 percent of the owners buy holiday and birthday gifts for their pets, and nearly half of the female respondents said that they relied more on their pet's affection than on their spouse's or children's. Pet owners have become emotionally tied to their pets and, in turn, treat their pets like humans by dressing them in the latest fashions, prolonging their lives through expensive medical treatments, and buckling them into specially designed car seats.

PetSmart has taken advantage of pet humanization trends and increased revenues and profitability. Three key features mark the expanded pet retail industry: (1) increased merchandise offerings, (2) more licensing agreements for pet products, and (3) innovative pet services.

Pet ownership drives demand, and retailer profitability depends on the ability to generate store traffic. PetSmart has expanded its store offerings to include a wider range of merchandise and services to meet growing demand. A typical PetSmart store stocks 10,000 in-store products and offers an even larger variety of products online. In addition, this retailer has increased its assortment within each product category. PetSmart presently stocks a deep selection of pet foods from a large array of suppliers, including low-cost, all natural, breed-specific, preservative-free, diet, organic, and premium foods with real meats and vegetables. The company introduced a wide range of private-label brands, positioned as low-cost alternatives to national brands to provide total solutions to its customers. According to the Private Label Manufacturers Association, store brands account for 11 percent of cat food, 12 percent of dog food, 13 percent of pet supplies, and 21 percent of cat litter sales.

Consumers interested in spoiling their pet often walk into a pet store to buy and coordinate outfits for their cat or dog, with choices ranging from personalized T-shirts to dresses to water-activated cooling bandanas. Through partnerships with PetSmart, renowned companies are leveraging their own brands within the pet sector. Store aisles are lined with toys, clothing, accessories, bedding, and aquariums displaying popular cartoon characters such as SpongeBob SquarePants, Clifford the Big Red Dog, Barbie, Blues Clues, Disney, and Peanuts. In an exclusive manufacturing and marketing deal with Martha Stewart Pets, PetSmart is now offering a new line of pet apparel, bedding, grooming, and bath supplies. In addition, companies from a diverse collection of industries—such as Paul Mitchell, Polo Ralph Lauren, Harley Davidson, and Old Navy—have developed their own pet product lines. Even Jeep has released its own line of branded strollers and pet ramps for cars and trucks to attempt to profit from the endless licensing opportunities within the pet retailing industry.

In the past, pet retailers provided just the most basic products. Today, they aim to create lasting relationships with customers. The service sector of the pet retail industry has higher profit margins, so PetSmart is incorporating various service offerings into its business model, including in-store grooming, six- to eight-week obedience training sessions, and doggie day care and "Pet Hotel" boarding facilities with cozy beds and televisions airing Animal Planet programming. As a result, PetSmart's business services represents about 11 percent of its annual sales revenue. Pet service industry competitors similarly attempt to position themselves to reach a portion of the market. Doggie spas, for example, offer high-end services such as massage therapy and pedicures, while pet walking and waste pick-up services enjoy greater success within the industry.

HUMAN RESOURCES AS A BRAND STRATEGY

Through various employee development programs, PetSmart trains its employees to reinforce the firm's brand image. It hires people who love pets and thus helps provide customers with value, quality, and service. PetSmart administers a 120-hour educational program for its trainers, a six-month instructional program for its groomers, and 16 hours of role-play training before any store opens to the public. As a result, the cheerful demeanor of PetSmart employees remains consistent across the country. PetSmart's staff passionately converses with customers, asks pet-related questions, and gives recommendations. This sense of helpfulness and friendliness aligns the service staff with the company's overall brand strategy and creates an emotional connection to the brand. Well-behaved pets are allowed to shop with their owners, which creates a pleasant, comfortable, animal-loving store atmosphere that further supports brand equity.

PetSmart regularly displays highly visible corporate charity and donation-related signs for animal-related causes (spay/neuter initiatives, pet adoption programs, food for pet shelters, etc.) at its checkout counters to reinforce the company's animal-loving culture. The business made a conscious decision to encourage adoption from shelters instead of selling cats and dogs, even though sales of cats and dogs would generate higher annual revenues. The decision to encourage and facilitate adoptions is decreasing euthanization of abandoned animals. PetSmart CEO Philip Francis notes, "by the time you factor in the bed, food, a collar, a leash, a training program, a bath, and a vet appointment, this adopted dog or cat could be a $300 to $400 event for us, and could be the opportunity for a lifetime relationship with that pet and that pet parent."

This case was written by James Pope, while an MBA student at Loyola University, Maryland, and Hope Corrigan, Loyola University, Maryland.

DISCUSSION QUESTIONS

1. Using Excel, create a column graph for U.S. pet industry expenditures over time. The *y*-axis will be sales in billions of dollars and the *x*-axis will be years. Go to the American Pet Products Association Inc. for the industry statistics and trends at: http://americanpetproducts.org/press_industrytrends.asp.

2. Using Excel, create a pie graph for the most recent year of estimated U.S. pet expenditures by category. Be sure to label each pie wedge with the category name and percent value. Go to the American Pet Products Association Inc. for the industry statistics and trends at http://americanpetproducts.org/press_industrytrends.asp.

3. How can PetSmart recruit, hire, and retain the best employees to support its brand strategy, meet customer expectations, and reach sales objectives?

4. What else could PetSmart do to increase store traffic, revenues, and profitability?

5. Consider other retailers that might begin to sell a larger assortment of pet products and services. How will this competition affect PetSmart?

CASE 37   Lindy's Bridal Shop

Located in Lake City (population 80,000), Lindy's Bridal Shop, a small bridal store, sells bridal gowns, prom gowns, accessories, and silk flowers. It also rents men's formal wear and performs various alteration services.

Lindy Armstrong, age 33, has owned the store since its founding in March 2007. She is married to a high school teacher and is the mother of three young children. A former nurse, she found the demands of hospital schedules left too little time for her young family. An energetic, active woman with many interests, she wanted to continue to work but also have time with her children.

The silk flowers market initially enabled Lindy to combine an in-home career with child rearing. She started Lindy's Silk Flowers with $75 of flower inventory in Vernon, a small town of about 10,000 people 10 miles from Lake City. Working out of her home, she depended on word-of-mouth communication among her customers, mainly brides, to bring in business. As Lindy's Silk Flowers prospered, a room was added onto the house to provide more space for the business. Lindy was still making all the flowers herself. Her flower-making schedule kept her extremely busy. Long hours were the norm.

Lindy was approached by a young photographer named Dan Morgan, who proposed establishing a one-stop bridal shop. In this new business, Dan would provide photography, Lindy would provide silk flowers, and another partner, Karen Ross (who had expertise in the bridal market), would provide gowns and accessories. The new store would be located in Vernon in a rented structure. Shortly before the store was to open, Dan and Karen decided not to become partners, and Lindy became the sole owner. She knew nothing about the bridal business. Having no merchandise or equipment, Lindy was drawn to an ad announcing that a bridal store in a major city was going out of business. She immediately called and arranged to meet the owner. Subsequently, she bought all his stock (mannequins, racks, and carpet) for $10,000. The owner also gave her a crash course in the bridal business.

The location in Vernon was chosen primarily because it was close to her home. While Vernon is a very small town, Lindy felt that location was not a critical factor in her store's success. She maintained that people would travel some distance to make a purchase as important as a bridal gown. Rent was $1500 per month plus utilities. Parking was a problem.

Lindy's Bridal Shop has continued to grow. Bridal gowns and accessories as well as prom dresses have sold well. As the time approached for Lindy to renew her lease, she wondered about the importance of location. She decided to move to a much larger town, Lake City, which is the site of a state university.

RETAIL FORMAT

Certain times of the year see more formal events than others. Many school proms are held during late April and May, and June, July, and August are big months for weddings. Because traditional dates for weddings are followed less and less closely, Lindy believes that the business is becoming less seasonal, although January and February are quite slow. Lindy's Bridal Shop's major product lines are new wedding, prom, and party gowns. No used gowns are sold. Discontinued styles or gowns that have been on the rack for a year are sold at reduced prices, primarily because discoloration is a major problem. Gowns tend to yellow after hanging on the racks for a year. A wide variety of accessories are provided. Lindy believes it's important that her customers do not have to go anywhere else for them. These accessories include shoes, veils, headpieces, jewelry, and foundations. Slips may be rented instead of purchased. One room of Lindy's Bridal Shop is used only to prepare silk flowers.

Lindy's Bridal Shop's major service offering is fitting and alteration. Most gowns must be altered, for which there's a nominal charge. Lindy feels that personal attention and personal service set her apart from her competitors. Emphasizing customer satisfaction, she works hard to please each customer. This isn't always easy. Customers can be picky, and it takes time to deal with unhappy people.

Lindy's Bridal Shop engages in various promotional activities but is constrained by limited finances. The firm has no formal operating budget and thus no formal appropriation for advertising expenses. Newspaper ads constitute the primary promotional medium, although radio is occasionally used. Ads for prom dresses are run only during prom season. These ads usually feature a photograph of a local high school student in a Lindy's Bridal Shop gown plus a brief description of the student's activities. Other promotional activities include bridal shows at a local mall. Lindy feels they have been very successful, although such activities are a lot of work. A recent prom show in a local high school used students as models, which proved to be an excellent way to stimulate sales. Lindy hopes to go into several other area high schools during the next prom season, although this expansion will demand much planning.

Lindy's Bridal Shop is located at the end of Lake City's main through-street. Initially, Lindy didn't think location was important to her bridal store's success, but she's changed her mind. Whereas business was good in Vernon, it's booming in Lake City. Vehicular traffic is high, and there's adequate, if not excess, parking.

Lindy's Bridal Shop has a 12-year lease. Rent ($2000 per month) includes heat and water, but Lindy's Bridal Shop must pay for interior decoration. The physical facility is generally attractive, with open and inviting interior display areas. But some areas both inside and outside the store have an unfinished look.

Some storage areas require doors or screens to enhance the interior's appearance. The fitting room ceilings are unfinished, and the carpeting inside the front door needs replacing. One other interior problem is insufficient space; there seems to be inadequate space for supporting activities such as flower preparation, customer fittings, and merchandise storage, which gives the store a cluttered look.

Several external problems exist. The signs are ineffective, and there's a strong glare on the front windows, which detracts from the effectiveness of the overall appearance and interior window displays. The parking lot needs minor maintenance: Parking lines should be painted, and curbs must be repaired. Much should be done to add color and atmosphere through basic landscaping.

STORE OPERATIONS

The majority of Lindy's Bridal Shop's current sales are made to individuals who order bridal gowns from the rack or from the catalogs of three major suppliers. At the time of the order, the customer pays a deposit, usually half of the purchase price. The balance is due in 30 days. Lindy would like payment in full at the time of ordering, regardless of the delivery date, but payment is often delayed until delivery. Once ordered, a gown must be taken and the bill paid when delivered. No tuxedos are carried in the store, so customers must order from catalogs. Fitting jackets and shoes are provided to help patrons size their purchases. Lindy's Bridal Shop rents its men's formal wear from suppliers. Payment from the customer is due on delivery.

Lindy, the sole owner and also the manager of the firm, finds it hard to maintain a capable workforce. A small company, Lindy's Bridal Shop can't offer premium salaries for its few positions. There's one full-time salesperson. The part-time staff includes a salesperson, alterations person, bookkeeper, and custodian. Lindy handles all the paperwork. Her responsibilities include paying bills, ordering merchandise and supplies, hiring and firing personnel, fitting customers, and selling various items. She makes all the major decisions that directly affect the firm's operations. She also makes all the silk flowers herself. This is time-consuming, but she isn't satisfied with how anyone else makes them.

COMPETITION

Lindy's Bridal Shop is the only bridal shop in Lake City. Lindy believes she has four main competitors. Whitney's Bridal Shop is 30 miles from Lake City; Ender's Brides, a new shop with a good operation, is in Spartan City, 50 miles away; Carole's is a large, established bridal shop in Smithtown, 70 miles distant; and Gowns-n-Such is in Andersonville, 75 miles away. A new store in Yorktown (15 miles away) is selling used gowns and discontinued styles at very reduced prices. Lindy watches this new- and used-gown store closely.

Some of her potential customers are buying wedding gowns from electronic retailers such as The Knot (theknot. com) and the Wedding Channel (weddingchannel.com). Lindy is concerned that some of the services offered by these electronic retailers (such as gift registries, e-mail notices, wedding planning, and wedding picture displays) will attract more of her customers.

THE FUTURE

Lindy Armstrong is uncertain about the future. She enjoys the business but feels that she's working very hard and not making much money. During all the years of Lindy's Bridal Shop's operation, she hasn't taken a salary. She works 60 hours or more a week. Business is excellent and growing, but she's tired. She has even discussed selling the business and returning to nursing.

This case was prepared by Linda F. Felicetti and Joseph P. Grunewald, Clarion University of Pennsylvania.

DISCUSSION QUESTIONS

1. Should Lindy change the emphasis of her merchandise mix to increase her sales?

2. Which products should have more emphasis? Which should have less?

3. What personnel decisions must Lindy face to improve her business?

4. How could someone like Lindy Armstrong balance the demands of her family and her business?

CASE 38 Interviewing for a Management Trainee Position

1. Assume the role of the college recruiter for a national retail chain that is reviewing résumés to select candidates to interview for a management trainee position. Which of the three résumés on the following pages do you find effective? Ineffective? Why? Which applicant would you select to interview? Why?

2. Update your résumé and prepare for an interview for a manager training program with a large lumber and building supply retailer. This full-time position promises rapid advancement on completion of the training period. A college degree and experience in retail, sales, and marketing are preferred. The base pay is between $35,000 and $45,000 per year, plus a bonus of up to $7,000. This retailer promotes from within, and a new manager trainee can become a store manager within two to three years, with earnings potential of $100,000 or more. The benefits package is generous, including medical, hospitalization, dental, disability, and life insurance; a 401(k) plan; profit sharing; awards and incentives; and paid vacations and holidays. Your résumé should include your contact information, education and training, skills, experience and accomplishments, and honors and awards.

3. Role-play a practice interview for this position. In pairs, read each other's résumés, and then spend 20 to 30 minutes representing each side of the interview. One student should be the human resource manager screening applicants, and the other should be the candidate for the manager training program. As the human resource manager, ask appropriate questions of the applicant, such as the following:

- Why are you applying for this position?
- What are your strengths and weaknesses for this position?
- Why should this organization consider you for this position?
- Why are you interested in working for this company?
- What are your career goals for the next 5 to 10 years?
- Describe your skills when working in a team setting.
- What questions do you have about the company?

This case was written by Cecelia Schulz, University of Florida.

Marti L. Cox

xxxx@ufl.edu, (xxx) 3xx-xxxx
123 Your Street, Apt. 301
Gainesville, Florida 32605

OBJECTIVE
Seeking a marketing internship utilizing leadership experience, strong work ethic, and interpersonal skills with a focus in product planning.

EDUCATION
Bachelor of Science in Business Administration   May 2009
University of Florida, Gainesville, Florida   GPA 3.69
Major in Marketing

LEADERSHIP
Student Government

Theatre Nights Chair	Jan. 2008-Present
Emerging Leaders Conference Executive Assistant	Sept. 2007-Present
Student Integrity Court Justice	May 2007-Present
Banquet Cabinet Assistant Director	May 2007-Present
Innovate Party House Representative	Jan. 2007-April 2007
Homecoming Supper Staff	Oct. 2006, 2007 Pan-Hellenic Council
Assistant Director of Jr. Pan-Hellenic	Dec. 2006-Present
Jr. Pan-Hellenic Executive VP Int. Relations	Sept. 2006-Jan. 2007 Tri-Delta

Philanthropy   Triple Play

Intramural Soccer-Captain	Oct. 2006, 2007
Intramural Basketball-Captain	Sept. 2007-Present
Member since Aug. 2003	Jan. 2007-Present

HONORS
Savant UF Leadership Honorary	Oct. 2007-Present
Sandra Day O'Connor Pre-Law Society	Sept. 2007-Present
Alpha Lambda Delta Honor Society	Inducted March 2007
Phi Eta Sigma Honor Society	Inducted March 2007

COMMUNITY SERVICE
Mentor to Freshmen Students for SG Mentor/Mentee	Sept. 2007-Present
Basketball On Wheels Volunteer	Sept. 2007-Present
Dance Marathon Dancer	Jan. 2007-March 2007
After School Gators Volunteer	Jan. 2007-April 2007
Pillows for Patriots Service Project Volunteer	Sept. 2006-Dec. 2006

WORK EXPERIENCE
Senior Customer Service Associate, Videos-R-Us, Tampa, FL	Jan. 2005-Aug. 2006
Secretarial Assistant, Law Firm, Mount Dora, FL	June-Aug. 2005

References available upon request.

Tina Acosta
123 Your Street #335
Gainesville, FL 32608
(727) xxx-xxxx
lxxx@ufl.edu

OBJECTIVE
To integrate my financial and business background with my creative and artistic skills in a fast-paced industry

EDUCATION

University of Florida	International Baccalaureate Program
Warrington College of Business	St. Petersburg High School
Bachelor of Science in Finance	Focus in Theatre, English, and History
Minor in Spanish	Graduation 2005
Graduation: May 2009	GPA: 4.0
GPA: 3.73	

RELEVANT CLASSES
Retail Management, Study Abroad in Spain, Business Finance, Managerial Accounting, Problem Solving Using Computer Software, Debt and Money Markets

EXPERIENCE

Abercrombie & Fitch—Gainesville, FL   Brand Representative (October 2007-Present)
- Oversaw customer service on the sales floor
- Maintained and updated the sales floor design
- Handled purchases and returns at the register
- Prepared shipments and the floor for an internal audit
- Promoted the brand name for the women's fashion line

Olive Garden—St. Petersburg, FL   Server (April 2006-August 2006)
- Used a computerized food and beverage ordering system
- Maintained the management's expectations through customer service
- Interacted with customers
- Memorized an extensive menu and recommended foods satisfying customers' needs while maximizing the restaurant's profits

Sacino's Formalwear—St. Petersburg, FL   Sales Representative (August 2004-August 2005)
- Managed incoming and outgoing shipment responsibilities
- Organized financial paperwork
- Oversaw customer service on the sales floor
- Headed the formal wear department for young women

SKILLS
Proficient in Spanish
Office XP: Word-Document Formatting, Letters, Tables, Flyers, and Macros
          Excel-Spreadsheets, Formulas, and Graph Database Analysis, Functions, and Simples Macros
          PowerPoint-Professional Presentations

HONORS
Third place in the preliminary competition for the University of Florida's Center for
     Entrepreneurship and Innovation
Florida's Bright Futures Scholar
University of Florida Dean's List Student 2006

Richard Kates
xxxxxx@ufl.edu

123 Your Street. #164	123 8th Ave N
Gainesville, Florida 32608	Tampa, Florida 33713
(352) xxx-xxxx	(813) xxx-xxxx

Objective	Seeking a position utilizing marketing, management, and organizational abilities, as well as interpersonal skills.

Education	**Marketing Major**	May 2009
	University of Florida	Gainesville, Florida
	Minor in Mass Communications and Minor in	
	Entrepreneurship GPA 3.7	

Experience	**Entrepreneur/CEO,** Long River PC, LLC	August 2005 to
	Tampa, FL	Present
	-Helped create and manage a new software company based in South Florida.	
	-Helped develop revolutionary program that will aid the visually impaired.	
	-Researched and developed multiple original non-disclosure as well as non-compete agreements.	
	-Responsible for hiring, funding, managing, and controlling progress of almost a dozen private software engineers. Reported to and allocated funds of angel investors.	
	Server, Carraba's	April 2007 to
	Gainesville, Florida	Present
	-Help train new employees through shadowing and demonstration.	
	-Serve over 70 guests per day, and ensure customer satisfaction and attentiveness.	
	-Multiple top sales, as well as winner of "Perfect Check" contest.	
	Usher/Security/Technician, Ben Hill Griffin Stadium	August 2005 to
	Gainesville, Florida	August 2007
	Pool/Health Club Attendant, Don Cesar Resort	May 2004 to
	St. Petersburg, Florida	August 2006

Leadership	**Executive Board Member, Varsity Tennis Team. Social Chair**
	University of Florida August 2006 to Present
	Organized, planned, and financed all tennis team social events. In charge of planning large events, gatherings at home and away meets, coordinating the activities of over 60 members.
	Executive Board Member, Fisher School of Accounting
	University of Florida January 2007 to May 2007
	Aided in revision and draft of new official Fisher School of Accounting Council's by-laws. Drafted a new 5-year program for the expansion and direction of the new Fisher School including member growth, activities, graduate prerequisites, and facility uses.
	CHAMPS Mentoring Volunteer Program
	Gainesville Florida January 2007 to Present
	Met with an "at risk" elementary school student 2 hours per week each semester to spend quality time encouraging the child's healthy growth and development.

Affiliations	**Phi Eta Sigma Honor Society,** Member active 2005 to present
	Florida Tennis Team, Fall 2005 to Spring 2007. Varsity Fall 2006 to Spring 2007
	Team Florida Cycling, Spring 2007 to present
	Student Alumni Association Member, Fall 2006 to present
	American Marketing Association, Member Fall 2007
	International Business Society, Fall 2007
	Business Administration College Council, Fall 2007 Member-at-Large
	The Entrepreneurs Club, Fall 2007

Skills	Computer-Fluent in Microsoft Word, Excel, PowerPoint, Explorer, and Media Player, Fluent-Spanish

References	Available upon request.

COMPANY INDEX

648

650   Company Index

652   Company Index

GLOSSARY

ABC analysis An analysis that rank orders SKUs by a profitability measure to determine which items should never be out of stock, which should be allowed to be out of stock occasionally, and which should be deleted from the stock selection.

accessibility (1) The degree to which customers can easily get into and out of a shopping center; (2) ability of the retailer to deliver the appropriate retail mix to customers in the segment.

acid-test ratio Short-term assets less inventory, divided by short-term liabilities. Also known as the *quick ratio*.

actionability Criteria for evaluating a market segment scheme indicating what the retailer should do to satisfy its needs.

add-on selling Selling additional new products and services to existing customers, such as a bank encouraging a customer with a checking account to apply for a home improvement loan from the bank.

advance shipping notice (ASN) An electronic document received by the retailer's computer from a supplier in advance of a shipment.

advertising Paid communications delivered to customers through nonpersonal mass media such as newspapers, television, radio, direct mail, and the Internet.

affinity marketing Marketing activities that enable consumers to express their identification with an organization. An example is offering credit cards tied to reference groups like the consumer's university or an NFL team.

affordable budgeting method A budgeting method in which a retailer first sets a budget for every element of the retail mix except promotion and then allocates the leftover funds to a promotional budget.

aided recall When consumers indicate they know the brand when the name is presented to them.

à la carte plans An employee reward program giving employees a choice of rewards and thus tailoring the rewards to the desires of individual employees.

Americans with Disabilities Act (ADA) A federal civil rights law that protects people with disabilities from discrimination in employment, transportation, public accommodations, telecommunications, and the activities of state and local government.

analog approach A method of trade area analysis also known as the similar store or mapping approach. The analysis is divided into four steps: (1) describing the current trade areas through the technique of customer spotting; (2) plotting the customers on a map; (3) defining the primary, secondary, and tertiary area zones; and (4) matching the characteristics of stores in the trade areas with the potential new store to estimate its sales potential.

anchor A large, well-known retail operation located in a shopping center or Internet mall and serving as an attracting force for consumers to the center.

application form A form used to collect information on a job applicant's education, employment experience, hobbies, and references.

apps Software applications. In a retailing setting, they improve customers' shopping experiences through tablets and smartphones.

artificial barriers In site evaluations for accessibility, barriers such as railroad tracks, major highways, or parks.

assets Economic resources, such as inventory or store fixtures, owned or controlled by an enterprise as a result of past transactions or events.

asset turnover Net sales divided by total assets.

assortment The number of SKUs within a merchandise category. Also called *depth of merchandise*.

assortment plan A list of merchandise that indicates in very general terms what should be carried in a particular merchandise category.

assurance A customer service characteristic that customers use to evaluate service quality; the knowledge and courtesy of the employees performing the service and their ability to convey trust and confidence.

atmospherics The design of an environment through visual communications, lighting, colors, music, and scent to stimulate customers' perceptual and emotional responses and ultimately to affect their purchase behavior.

autocratic leader A manager who makes all decisions on his or her own and then announces them to employees.

automated retailing A retail channel that stores merchandise or services in a machine, then dispenses them to customers who provide cash or a credit card.

backhaul Trips that trucks make to return to distribution centers after delivering merchandise to stores.

backup stock The inventory used to guard against going out of stock when demand exceeds forecasts or merchandise is delayed. Also called *safety stock* or *buffer stock*.

backward integration A form of vertical integration in which a retailer owns some or all of its suppliers.

bait and switch An unlawful deceptive practice that lures customers into a store by advertising a product at lower than usual prices (the bait), then induces the customers to switch to a higher-price model (the switch).

bargaining power of vendors A characteristic of a market in which retailers are so dependent on large, important vendors that their profits are adversely affected.

barriers to entry Conditions in a retail market that make it difficult for firms to enter the market.

base of the pyramid The 25 percent of the world's population at the lowest end of the global income distribution, with combined spending power of approximately US$5 trillion. Also known as the *bottom of the pyramid*.

base stock See *cycle stock*.

basic merchandise See *staple merchandise*.

behavioral interview An interview technique used for selecting employees in which candidates describe how they have handled actual work situations in the past.

benefit segmentation A method of segmenting a retail market on the basis of similar benefits sought in merchandise or services.

big-box stores Large, limited service retailers.

biometrics Measures of human characteristics such as a person's hand geometry, fingerprints, iris, or voice.

black market The availability of merchandise at a high price when it is difficult or impossible to purchase under normal market circumstances; commonly involves illegal transactions.

block group A collection of adjacent census blocks that contain between 300 and 3,000 people that is the smallest unit for the sample data.

blog (weblog) A public website where users post informal journals of their thoughts, comments, and philosophies.

bonus Additional compensation awarded periodically, based on a subjective evaluation of the employee's performance.

bottom of the pyramid (BoP) The 25 percent of the world's population at the lowest end of the global income distribution, with combined spending power of approximately US$5 trillion. Also known as the *base of the pyramid*.

bottom-up planning When goals are set at the bottom of the organization and filter up through the operating levels.

boutique (1) Departments in a store designed to resemble small, self-contained stores; (2) a relatively small specialty store.

boutique layout See *free-form layout*.

brand A distinguishing name or symbol (such as a logo, design, symbol, or trademark) that identifies the products or services offered by a seller and differentiates those products and services from the offerings of competitors.

brand association Anything linked to or connected with the brand name in a consumer's memory.

brand awareness The ability of a potential customer to recognize or recall that a particular brand name belongs to a retailer or product/service.

brand equity The value that brand image offers retailers.

brand image Set of associations consumers have about a brand that are usually organized around some meaningful themes.

brand loyalty Indicates customers like and consistently buy a specific brand in a product category. They are reluctant to switch to other brands if their favorite brand isn't available.

breadth In merchandise planning, the variety in the number of subcategories carried within any particular merchandise category.

breadth of merchandise See *variety*.

break pack area The area in a distribution center where employees open large cartons and distribute their contents into smaller packages for delivery to stores.

break-even analysis A technique that evaluates the relationship between total revenue and total cost to determine profitability at various sales levels.

break-even point quantity The quantity at which total revenue equals total cost and beyond which profit occurs.

breaking bulk A function performed by retailers or wholesalers in which they receive large quantities of merchandise and sell them in smaller quantities.

breaking sizes Running out of stock on particular sizes.

buffer stock Merchandise inventory used as a safety cushion for cycle stock so the retailer won't run out of stock if demand exceeds the sales forecast. Also called *safety stock*.

building codes Legal restrictions describing the size and type of building, signs, type of parking lot, and so on that can be used at a particular location.

bulk fixture See *rounder*.

bullwhip effect The buildup of inventory in an uncoordinated channel.

buyback A strategy vendors and retailers use to get products into retail stores, either when a retailer allows a vendor to create space for goods by "buying back" a competitor's inventory and removing it from a retailer's system or when the retailer forces a vendor to buy back slow-moving merchandise.

buyer Person in a retailing organization responsible for the purchase and profitability of a merchandise category. Similar to *category manager*.

buying process The stages customers go through to purchase merchandise or services.

buying situation A method of segmenting a retail market based on customer needs in a specific buying situation, such as a fill-in shopping trip versus a weekly shopping trip.

call-to-action signage In-store displays placed strategically to encourage customers to engage with the retailer through quick response codes.

capacity fixture See *rounder*.

career path The set of positions to which management employees are promoted within a particular organization as their careers progress.

cash Money on hand.

cash discounts Reductions in the invoice cost that the vendor allows the retailer for paying the invoice prior to the end of the discount period.

cash flow statement A statement highlighting the inflow and outflow of cash during a given accounting time period.

cash wraps The places in a store where customers can purchase merchandise and have it "wrapped"—placed in a bag.

catalog channel A nonstore retailer that communicates directly with customers using catalogs sent through the mail.

category captain A supplier that forms an alliance with a retailer to help gain consumer insight, satisfy consumer needs, and improve the performance and profit potential across the entire category.

category killer A discount retailer that offers a narrow but deep assortment of merchandise in a category and thus dominates the category from the customers' perspective. Also called a *category specialist*.

category management The process of managing a retail business with the objective of maximizing the sales and profits of a category.

category signage Signage within a particular department or sector of the store, category signs are usually smaller than directional signs. Their purpose is to identify types of products offered; they are usually located near the goods to which they refer.

category specialist See *category killer.*

cause-related marketing campaign Commercial activity in which businesses collaborate with a charitable organization to market a product or service for their mutual benefit.

census A count of the population of a country as of a specified date.

census block An area bounded on all sides by visible (roads, rivers, etc.) and/or invisible (county, state boundaries) features that is the smallest geographic entity for which census data are available.

central business district (CBD) The traditional downtown business area of a city or town.

centralization The degree to which authority for making retail decisions is delegated to corporate managers rather than to geographically dispersed regional, district, and store management.

channel migration A customer practice in which customers search for information from a retailer's channel, then purchase in a different channel maintained by a competitor.

chargeback A practice used by retailers in which they deduct money from the amount they owe a vendor.

chargeback fee The fee that retailers require vendors to pay when the provided merchandise does not meet the terms of the purchase agreement.

checking The process of going through goods upon receipt to make sure that they arrived undamaged and that the merchandise received matches the merchandise ordered.

checkout areas See *cash wraps.*

cherry picking Customers visiting a store and buying only merchandise sold at big discounts or buying only the best styles or colors.

chief executive officer (CEO) The executive responsible for overseeing the operations of the entire firm.

chief financial officer (CFO) An executive that works with the CEO on financial issues such as equity-debt structure and credit card operations.

chief marketing officer (CMO) An executive that works with staff to develop marketing, advertising and other promotional programs.

classification A group of items or SKUs for the same type of merchandise, such as pants (as opposed to jackets or suits), supplied by different vendors.

click-through rate The number of times a customer clicks on an online ad, divided by the number of impressions.

closeout (1) An offer at a reduced price to sell a group of slow-moving or incomplete stock; (2) an incomplete assortment, the remainder of a line of merchandise that is to be discontinued and so is offered at a low price to ensure immediate sale.

collaborative planning, forecasting, and replenishment (CPFR) A collaborative inventory management system in which a retailer shares information with vendors. CPFR software uses data to construct a computer-generated replenishment forecast that is shared by the retailer and vendor before it's executed.

commercial bribery A vendor's offer of money or gifts to a retailer's employee for the purpose of influencing purchasing decisions.

commission Compensation based on a fixed formula, such as percentage of sales.

common area maintenance (CAM) The common facilities maintenance that shopping center management is responsible for, such as the parking area, providing security, parking lot lighting, outdoor signage for the center, advertising, and special events to attract consumers.

common area maintenance (CAM) clause Shopping center real estate contract clauses that assign responsibility for maintaining common areas, such as parking lots and sidewalks.

communication gap The difference between the actual service provided to customers and the service promised in the retailer's promotion program. This factor is one of the four factors identified by the Gaps model for improving service quality.

communication objectives Specific goals for a communication program related to the effects of the communication program on the customer's decision-making process.

community strip shopping centers See *neighborhood shopping centers.*

comparable store sales growth See *same-store sales growth.*

comparison shopping situation A type of shopping situation whereby consumers have a general idea about the type of product or service they want, but they do not have a well-developed preference for a brand or model.

compatibility The degree to which the fashion is consistent with existing norms, values, and behaviors.

competitive parity method An approach for setting a promotion budget so that the retailer's share of promotion expenses is equal to its market share.

competitive rivalry The frequency and intensity of reactions to actions undertaken by competitors.

complexity The ease with which consumers can understand and use a new fashion.

composite segmentation A method of segmenting a retail market using multiple variables, including benefits sought, lifestyles, and demographics.

congestion The amount of crowding of either cars or people.

consideration set The set of alternatives the customer evaluates when making a merchandise selection.

consignment Items not paid for by the retailer until they are sold. The retailer can return unsold merchandise; however, the retailer does not take title until final sale is made.

consignment shop A store that sells used merchandise and reimburses the individual customers who provide the items only after they sell.

consumer direct fulfillment See *drop shipping.*

continuous replenishment A system that involves continuously monitoring merchandise sales and generating replacement orders, often automatically, when inventory levels drop below predetermined levels.

convenience shopping When consumers are primarily concerned with minimizing their effort to get the product or service they want.

convenience shopping center An attached row of stores, usually with on-site parking in front of the stores. Also known as *strip*, *neighborhood*, or *community shopping centers*.

convenience store A store that provides a limited variety and assortment of merchandise at a convenient location in a 2,000- to 3,000-square-foot store with speedy checkout.

conventional supermarket A self-service food store that offers groceries, meat, and produce with limited sales of nonfood items, such as health and beauty aids and general merchandise.

conversion rates Percentage of consumers who buy the product after viewing it.

cookies Computer text files that identify visitors when they return to a website.

co-op (cooperative) advertising A program undertaken by a vendor in which the vendor agrees to pay all or part of a promotion for its products.

copy The text in an advertisement.

copycat branding A branding strategy that imitates the manufacturer brand in appearance and trade dress but generally is perceived as lower quality and is offered at a lower price.

copyright A regulation that protects original works of authors, painters, sculptors, musicians, and others who produce works of artistic or intellectual merit.

corporate social responsibility (CSR) Voluntary actions taken by a company to address the ethical, social, and environmental impacts of its business operations and the concerns of its stakeholders.

cost of goods sold (COGS) The fee the retailer pays a vendor for merchandise that the retailer sells.

cotenancy clause A clause in a leasing contract that requires a certain percentage of a shopping center be leased, while others name specific retailers or types of retailers that are to remain open.

counterfeit merchandise Goods that are made and sold without permission of the owner of a trademark, a copyright, or a patented invention that is legally protected in the country where it is marketed.

coupons Documents that entitle the holder to a reduced price or X cents off the actual price of a product or service.

cross-docked Items that are unloaded from the shippers' truck and within a few hours reloaded onto trucks going to stores. These items are prepackaged by the vendor for a specific store, such that the UPC labels on a carton indicate the store to which it is to be sent.

cross-selling When sales associates in one department attempt to sell complementary merchandise from other departments to their customers.

cross-shopping A pattern of buying both premium and low-priced merchandise or patronizing expensive, status-oriented retailers and price-oriented retailers.

culture The meaning and values shared by most members of a society.

cumulative attraction The principle that a cluster of similar and complementary retailing activities will generally have greater drawing power than isolated stores that engage in the same retailing activities.

current assets Cash or any assets that can normally be converted into cash within one year.

current ratio Short-term assets divided by short-term liabilities.

customer database The coordinated and periodic copying of data from various sources, both inside and outside the enterprise, into an environment ready for analytical and informational processing. It contains all of the data the firm has collected about its customers and is the foundation for subsequent CRM activities.

customer delight A high level of customer satisfaction created by retailers providing greatly unexpected services.

customer lifetime value (CLV) The expected contribution from the customer to the retailer's profits over his or her entire relationship with the retailer.

customer loyalty Customers' commitment to shopping at a store.

customer relationship management (CRM) A business philosophy and set of strategies, programs, and systems that focuses on identifying and building loyalty with a retailer's most valued customers.

customer relationship management (CRM) program The set of activities designed to identify and build the loyalty of the retailer's most valuable customers.

customer service The set of retail activities that increase the value customers receive when they shop and purchase merchandise.

customer spotting A technique used in trade area analysis that "spots" (locates) residences of customers for a store or shopping center.

customization approach An approach used by retailers to provide customer service that is tailored to meet each customer's personal needs.

cycle stock The inventory that goes up and down due to the replenishment process. Also known as *base stock*.

data mining Technique used to identify patterns in data found in data warehouses, typically patterns that the analyst is unaware of prior to searching through the data.

debt-to-equity ratio Short- and long-term debt, divided by the value of stockholders' equity in the firm.

decentralization When authority for retail decisions is made at lower levels in the organization.

delivery gap The difference between the retailer's service standards and the actual service provided to customers. This factor is one of the four factors identified by the Gaps model for improving service quality.

demand/destination merchandise Products that customers have decided to buy before entering the store.

democratic leader A store manager who seeks information and opinions from employees and bases decisions on this information.

demographic segmentation A method of segmenting a retail market that groups consumers on the basis of easily measured, objective characteristics such as age, gender, income, and education.

department A segment of a store with merchandise that represents a group of classifications the consumer views as being complementary.

department store A retailer that carries a wide variety and deep assortment, offers considerable customer services, and is organized into separate departments for displaying merchandise.

depth In a merchandise planning context, the assortment of SKUs in a particular merchandise subcategory.

depth of merchandise See *assortment*.

destination store A retail store in which the merchandise, selection, presentation, pricing, or other unique feature acts as a magnet for customers.

digital signage Signs whose visual content is delivered digitally through a centrally managed and controlled network and displayed on a television monitor or flat panel screen.

direct investment The investment and ownership by a retail firm of a division or subsidiary that builds and operates stores in a foreign country.

direct mail Any brochure, catalog, advertisement, or other printed marketing material delivered directly to the consumer through the mail or a private delivery company.

direct selling A retail format in which a salesperson, frequently an independent distributor, contacts a customer directly in a convenient location (either at a customer's home or at work), demonstrates merchandise benefits, takes an order, and delivers the merchandise to the customer.

direct store delivery (DSD) A method of delivering merchandise to stores in which vendors distribute merchandise directly to the stores rather than going through distribution centers.

direct-response TV (DRTV) channel Retail channel in which customers watch televised advertisements that demonstrate the merchandise, then place orders via telephone or through the company's website.

disability Any physical or mental impairment that substantially limits one or more of an individual's major life activities or any condition that is regarded as being such an impairment.

discrimination An illegal action of a company or its managers when a member of a protected class (women, minorities, etc.) is treated differently from nonmembers of that class (see *disparate treatment*) or when an apparently neutral rule has an unjustified discriminatory effect (see *disparate impact*).

disparate impact The case of discrimination when an apparently neutral rule has an unjustified discriminatory effect, such as if a retailer requires high school graduation for all its employees, thereby excluding a larger proportion of disadvantaged minorities, when at least some of the jobs (e.g., custodian) could be performed just as well by people who did not graduate from high school.

disparate treatment The case of discrimination when members of a protected class are treated differently from nonmembers of that class—if a qualified woman (protected class), for example, does not receive a promotion given to a lesser qualified man.

dispatcher A person who coordinates deliveries from the vendor to the distribution center or stores or from the distribution center to stores.

distribution center (DC) A warehouse that receives merchandise from multiple vendors and distributes it to multiple stores.

distributive fairness A customer's perception of the benefits received compared to their costs (inconvenience or loss) when resolving a complaint.

distributive justice Arises when outcomes received are viewed as fair with respect to outcomes received by others.

diversification growth opportunity A strategic investment opportunity that involves an entirely new retail format directed toward a market segment not presently being served.

diverted merchandise Merchandise that is diverted from its legitimate channel of distribution; similar to *gray-market goods* except there need not be distribution across international boundaries.

dollar store Small, extreme value retailers that sell a wide variety but shallow assortment of foods, household goods, and health and beauty care products.

drawing account A method of sales compensation in which salespeople receive a weekly check based on their estimated annual income.

drop shipping A supply chain system in which retailers receive orders from customers and relay these orders to a vendor and then the vendor ships the merchandise ordered directly to the customer.

drugstore Specialty retail store that concentrates on pharmaceuticals and health and personal grooming merchandise.

durable goods Merchandise expected to last for several years, such as appliances and furniture. Also known as *hard goods*.

duty See *tariff*.

dynamic pricing Charging different prices for the same offerings, depending on the time, season, customer, or level of demand. Also known as *individualized pricing*.

earnings before interest, taxes, and depreciation (EBITDA) This profitability measure is the gross margin minus operating and extraordinary recurring expenses. Also known as *operating profit margin*.

editing the assortment Selecting the right assortment of merchandise.

80–20 rule A general management principle where 80 percent of the sales or profits come from 20 percent of the customers.

elastic In a pricing context, when a 1 percent decrease in price produces more than a 1 percent increase in the quantity sold.

electronic article surveillance (EAS) system A loss prevention system in which special tags placed on merchandise in retail stores are deactivated when the merchandise is purchased. The tags are used to discourage shoplifting.

electronic data interchange (EDI) The computer-to-computer exchange of business documents from retailer to vendor and back.

electronic retailing A retail format in which the retailers communicate with customers and offer products and services for sale over the Internet.

e-mail A paid personal communication vehicle that involves sending messages over the Internet.

emotional support Supporting retail service providers with the understanding and positive regard to enable them to deal with the emotional stress created by disgruntled customers.

empathy A customer service characteristic that customers use to evaluate service quality; refers to the caring, individualized attention provided to customers, such as personalized service, sending of notes and e-mails, or recognition by name.

employment branding Programs undertaken by employers to understand what potential employees are seeking, as well as what they think about the retailer; developing a value proposition and an employment brand image; communicating that brand image to potential employees; and then fulfilling the brand promise by ensuring the employee experience matches that which was advertised.

empowerment The process of managers sharing power and decision-making authority with employees.

end cap Display fixture located at the end of an aisle.

engagement An employee's emotional commitment to the organization.

Equal Employment Opportunity Commission (EEOC) A federal commission that was established for the purpose of taking legal action against employers that violate Title VII of the Civil Rights Act. Title VII prohibits discrimination in company personnel practices.

Equal Pay Act A federal act enforced by the Equal Employment Opportunity Commission that prohibits unequal pay for men and women who perform equal work or work of comparable worth.

e-tailing See *electronic retailing*.

ethics A system or code of conduct based on universal moral duties and obligations that indicate how one should behave.

event sponsorship A type of marketing communication for which corporations support various activities usually in the cultural or sports and entertainment sectors.

everyday low pricing (EDLP) strategy A pricing strategy that stresses continuity of retail prices at a level somewhere between the regular nonsale price and the deep-discount sale price of the retailer's competitors.

exclusive brand A brand developed by a national brand vendor, often in conjunction with a retailer, and sold exclusively by the retailer.

exclusive dealing agreement Restriction a manufacturer or wholesaler places on a retailer to carry only its products and no competing vendors' products.

exclusive-use clause A clause in a lease that prohibits the landlord from leasing to retailers selling competing products.

executive vice president (EVP) of operations The executive responsible for overseeing management information systems, human resources, the supply chain, and visual merchandising.

extended problem solving A buying process in which customers spend considerable time at each stage of the decision-making process because the decision is important and they have limited knowledge of alternatives.

external sources (of information) Information provided by the media and other people.

extreme-value food retailers See *limited assortment supermarkets*.

extreme-value retailers Small, full-line discount stores that offer a limited merchandise assortment at very low prices.

extrinsic reward Reward (such as money, promotion, or recognition) given to employees by their manager or the firm.

factory outlet Outlet store owned by a manufacturer.

Fair Labor Standards Act A federal law, enacted in 1938, that sets minimum wages, maximum hours, child labor standards, and overtime pay provisions.

fair trade Purchasing practices that require producers to pay workers a living wage, well more than the prevailing minimum wage, and offer other benefits, like onsite medical treatment.

family brand A product's brand name associated with the company's name.

fashion A type of product or a way of behaving that is temporarily adopted by a large number of consumers because the product, service, or behavior is considered to be socially appropriate for the time and place.

fashion leader Initial customer adopters of a new fashion. Also known as an *innovator* or *trendsetter*.

fashion merchandise Category of merchandise that typically lasts several seasons, and sales can vary dramatically from one season to the next.

fast fashion A fashion retail strategy by which retailers repeatedly offer customers inexpensive, fashionable merchandise early in its lifecycle by implementing a short time between design concept and availability in stores.

feature area Area designed to get the customer's attention that includes end caps, promotional aisles or areas, freestanding fixtures and mannequins that introduce a soft goods department, windows, and point-of-sale areas.

feature fixture See *four-way fixture*.

fill rate The percentage of an order that is shipped by the vendor.

financial risk The risks customers face when purchasing an expensive product or service.

first-degree price discrimination Charging customers different prices on the basis of their willingness to pay.

fixed assets Assets that require more than a year to convert to cash.

fixed costs Costs that are stable and don't change with the quantity of product produced and sold.

fixed-rate lease A lease that requires the retailer to pay a fixed amount per month over the life of the lease.

fixtures The equipment used to display merchandise.

flash rob A gang-related high-tech method of shoplifting where groups plot via social media and text messages to arrive suddenly at retail stores to steal large amounts of merchandise.

flash sale Temporary online sales, announced each day at about the same time, that last for a specified time and are first-come, first-served.

flextime A job scheduling system that enables employees to choose the times they work.

floor-ready merchandise Merchandise received at the store ready to be sold, without the need for any additional preparation by retail employees.

focus group A marketing research technique in which a small group of respondents is interviewed by a moderator using a loosely structured format.

forward integration A form of vertical integration in which a manufacturer owns wholesalers or retailers.

four-way fixture A fixture with two cross-bars that sit perpendicular to each other on a pedestal.

franchising A contractual agreement between a franchisor and a franchisee that allows the franchisee to operate a retail outlet using a name and format developed and supported by the franchisor.

free-form layout A store design, used primarily in small specialty stores or within the boutiques of large stores, that arranges fixtures and aisles asymmetrically. Also called *boutique layout*.

freestanding display Fixtures or mannequins that are located on aisles and designed primarily to attract customers' attention and bring customers into a department in stores using a racetrack or free-form layout.

freestanding insert (FSI) An ad printed at a retailer's expense and distributed as a freestanding insert in the newspaper. Also called a *preprint*.

freestanding site A retail location that is not connected to other retailers.

freight forwarders Companies that purchase transport services. They then consolidate small shipments from a number of shippers into large shipments that move at a lower freight rate.

frequent-shopper program A reward and communication program used by a retailer to encourage continued purchases from the retailer's best customers. See *loyalty program*.

fringe The tertiary trading area of a store.

fringe trade area See *tertiary trade area*.

frontal presentation A method of displaying merchandise in which the retailer exposes as much of the product as possible to catch the customer's eye.

full-line discount store Retailers that offer a broad variety of merchandise, limited service, and low prices.

generic brand Unbranded, unadvertised merchandise found mainly in drug, grocery, and discount stores.

gentrification A process in which old buildings are torn down or restored to create new offices, housing developments, and retailers.

geodemographic segmentation A market segmentation system that uses both geographic and demographic characteristics to classify consumers.

geofencing Offering localized promotions for retailers in close proximity to the customer, as determined by phone location technology.

geographic information system (GIS) A computerized system that enables analysts to visualize information about their customers' demographics, buying behavior, and other data in a map format.

geographic segmentation Segmentation of potential customers by where they live. A retail market can be segmented by countries, states, cities, and neighborhoods.

glass ceiling An invisible barrier that makes it difficult for minorities and women to be promoted beyond a certain level.

global operations president An executive that oversees retailing operations outside the home country.

gondola An island type of self-service counter with tiers of shelves, bins, or pegs.

graduated lease A lease that requires rent to increase by a fixed amount over a specified period of time.

gray-market goods Merchandise that possesses a valid U.S. registered trademark and is made by a foreign manufacturer but is imported into the United States without permission of the U.S. trademark owner.

green A marketing strategy that promotes environmentally safe or beneficial products or services.

green sheen The disingenuous practice of marketing products or services as being environmentally friendly with the purpose of gaining public approval and sales rather than actually improving the environment.

greenwashing See *green sheen*.

grid layout A store design, typically used by grocery stores, in which merchandise is displayed on long gondolas in aisles with a repetitive pattern.

gross leasable area (GLA) Total floor area designated for the retailer's exclusive use, including basements, upper floors, and mezzanines.

gross margin percentage Gross margin divided by net sales.

gross margin The difference between the price the customer pays for merchandise and the cost of the merchandise (the price the retailer paid the supplier of the merchandise). More specifically, gross margin is net sales minus cost of goods sold.

gross profit See *gross margin*.

group maintenance behaviors Activities store managers undertake to make sure that employees are satisfied and work well together.

habitual decision making A purchase decision involving little or no conscious effort.

hard goods Merchandise expected to last for several years, such as appliances and furniture. Also known as *durable goods*.

health and safety laws Regulations that hold that employers must provide every employee with an environment free of hazards that are likely to cause death or serious injury.

hedonic benefit Shopping for pleasure, entertainment, and/or to achieve an emotional or recreational experience.

hedonic needs Needs motivating consumers to go shopping for pleasure.

612   Glossary

high-assay principle A resource allocation principle emphasizing allocating marketing expenditures on the basis of marginal return.

high/low pricing strategy A strategy in which retailers offer prices that are sometimes above their competition's everyday low price, but they use advertising to promote frequent sales.

holding inventory A major value-providing activity performed by retailers whereby products will be available when consumers want them.

horizontal price fixing An agreement between retailers in direct competition with each other to charge the same prices.

house brand See *generic brand*.

Huff gravity model A trade area analysis model used to determine the probability that a customer residing in a particular area will shop at a particular store or shopping center.

hypermarket Large (100,000–300,000 square feet) combination food (60–70 percent) and general merchandise (30–40 percent) retailer.

idea-oriented presentation A method of presenting merchandise based on a specific idea or the image of the store.

identifiability A criteria for evaluating market segments in which retailers must be able to identify the customers in a target segment for the segmentation scheme to be effective. By identifying the segment, it allows retailers to determine (1) the segment's size and (2) with whom the retailer should communicate when promoting its retail offering.

illegal discrimination The actions of a company or its managers that result in a number of a protected class being treated unfairly and differently than others.

impressions The number of times an advertisement appears before a customer.

impulse buying A buying decision made by customers on the spot after seeing the merchandise.

impulse products Products that are purchased by customers without prior plans. These products are almost always located near the front of the store, where they're seen by everyone and may actually draw people into the store.

incentive compensation plan A compensation plan that rewards employees on the basis of their productivity.

income statement A summary of the financial performance of a firm for a certain period of time.

in-depth interview An unstructured personal interview in which the interviewer uses extensive probing to get individual respondents to talk in detail about a subject.

individualized pricing Charging different prices for the same offerings, depending on the time, season, customer, or level of demand. Also known as *dynamic pricing*.

inelastic In a pricing context, when a 1 percent decrease in price produces less than a 1 percent increase in the quantity sold.

infomercials TV programs, typically 30 minutes long, that mix entertainment with product demonstrations and solicit orders placed by telephone from consumers.

information search The stage in the buying process in which a customer seeks additional information to satisfy a need.

infringement Unauthorized use of a registered trademark.

initial markup The retail selling price initially placed on the merchandise less the cost of goods sold.

inner city Typically a high-density urban area consisting of apartment buildings populated primarily by ethnic groups.

innovator In fashion contexts, the initial customer adopters of a new fashion. Also known as *fashion leaders* or *trendsetters*.

input measure A performance measure used to assess the amount of resources or money used by the retailer to achieve outputs.

in-store marketing Features in stores designed to encourage customers to spend more time in the store and purchase more, such as point-of-purchase displays or special events.

instrumental support Support for retail service providers such as appropriate systems and equipment to deliver the service desired by customers.

integrated marketing communication (IMC) program The strategic integration of multiple communication methods to form a comprehensive, consistent message.

intellectual property Property that is intangible and created by intellectual (mental) effort as opposed to physical effort.

internal sources of information Information in a customer's memory such as names, images, and past experiences with different stores.

Internet retailing See *electronic retailing*.

intertype competition Competition between retailers that sell similar merchandise using different formats, such as discount and department stores.

intratype competition Competition between the same type of retailers (e.g., Kroger versus Safeway).

intrinsic rewards Nonmonetary rewards employees get from doing their jobs.

inventory shrinkage See *shrinkage*.

inventory turnover Net sales divided by average retail inventory; used to evaluate how effectively managers utilize their investment in inventory.

irregulars Merchandise that has minor mistakes in construction.

job analysis Identifying essential activities and determining the qualifications employees need to perform them effectively.

job application form A form a job applicant completes that contains information about the applicant's employment history, previous compensation, reasons for leaving previous employment, education and training, personal health, and references.

job description A description of the activities the employee needs to perform and the firm's performance expectations.

job enrichment The redesign of a job to include a greater range of tasks and responsibilities.

job sharing When two or more employees voluntarily are responsible for a job that was previously held by one person.

joint venture In the case of global expansion, an entity formed when the entering retailer pools its resources with a local retailer to form a new company in which ownership, control, and profits are shared. More generally, any business venture in which two or more firms pool resources to form a new business entity.

keystoning A method of setting retail prices in which retailers simply double the cost of the merchandise to obtain the original retail selling price.

knockoff A copy of the latest styles displayed at designer fashion shows and sold in exclusive specialty stores. These copies are sold at lower prices through retailers targeting a broader market.

knowledge gap The difference between customer expectations and the retailer's perception of customer expectations. This factor is one of four identified by the Gaps model for improving service quality.

labor relations laws Regulations that describe how unions can form and how companies must respond to them.

labor scheduling The process of determining the number of employees assigned to each area of the store at each hour the store is open.

leader pricing A pricing strategy in which certain items are priced lower than normal to increase the traffic flow of customers or to increase the sale of complementary products.

leadership The process by which a person attempts to influence another to accomplish some goal or goals.

lead time The amount of time between recognition that an order needs to be placed and the point at which the merchandise arrives in the store and is ready for sale.

level of support See *service level*.

liabilities Obligations of a retail enterprise to pay cash or other economic resources in return for past, present, or future benefits.

lifestyle Refers to how people live, how they spend their time and money, what activities they pursue, and their attitudes and opinions about the world they live in.

lifestyle center A shopping center with an outdoor traditional streetscape layout with sit-down restaurants and a conglomeration of specialty retailers.

lifestyle segmentation A method of segmenting a retail market based on how consumers live, how they spend their time and money, what activities they pursue, and their attitudes and opinions about the world they live in.

lift-out See *buyback*.

limited-assortment supermarkets A supermarket offering a limited number of SKUs.

limited problem solving A purchase decision process involving a moderate amount of effort and time. Customers engage in this type of buying process when they have some prior experience with the product or service and their risk is moderate.

live chat Technology that enables online customers to access an instant messaging or voice conversation with a sales representative in real time.

locavore movement A movement focusing on reducing the carbon footprint caused by the transportation of food throughout the world.

logistics Part of the supply chain process that plans, implements, and controls the efficient, effective flow and storage of goods, services, and related information from the point of origin to the point of consumption to meet customers' requirements.

loop layout See *racetrack layout*.

loss leader An item priced near or below cost to attract customer traffic into the store.

low-price guarantee policy A policy that guarantees that the retailer will have the lowest possible price for a product or group of products and usually promises to match or better any lower price found in the local market.

loyalty program A program set up to reward customers with incentives such as discounts on purchases, free food, gifts, or even cruises or trips in return for their repeated business.

Main Street The central business district located in the traditional shopping area of smaller towns, or a secondary business district in a suburb or within a larger city.

maintained markup The amount of markup the retailer wishes to maintain on a particular category of merchandise; net sales minus cost of goods sold.

managing diversity A set of human resource management programs designed to realize the benefits of a diverse workforce.

mannequin Life-size representation of human bodies, used to display apparel.

manufacturer's brand A line of products designed, produced, and marketed by a vendor. Also called a *national brand*.

marginal analysis A method of analysis used in setting a promotional budget or allocating retail space, based on the economic principle that firms should increase expenditures as long as each additional dollar spent generates more than a dollar of additional contribution.

markdown The percentage reduction in the initial retail price.

markdown money Funds provided by a vendor to a retailer to cover decreased gross margin from markdowns and other merchandising issues.

market basket analysis Specific type of data analysis that focuses on the composition of the basket (or bundle) of products purchased by a household during a single shopping occasion.

market expansion growth opportunity A strategic investment opportunity that employs the existing retailing format in new market segments.

market penetration growth opportunity An investment opportunity strategy that focuses on increasing sales to present customers using the present retailing format.

market week See *trade show*.

markup The increase in the retail price of an item after the initial markup percentage has been applied but before the item is placed on the selling floor.

markup percentage The markup as a percent of retail price.

mass media Channels that reach a broad and varied audience, including television, magazines, and newspapers.

mass-market theory A theory of how fashion spreads that suggests that each social class has its own fashion leaders who play a key role in their own social networks. Fashion information trickles across social classes rather than down from the upper classes to the lower classes.

m-commerce (mobile commerce) Communicating with and even selling to customers through wireless handheld devices, such as cellular telephones and personal digital assistants.

mentoring program The assigning of higher-level managers to help lower-level managers learn the firm's values and meet other senior executives.

merchandise budget plan A plan used by buyers to determine how much money to spend in each month on a particular fashion merchandise category, given the firm's sales forecast, inventory turnover, and profit goals.

merchandise category An assortment of items (SKUs) the customer sees as reasonable substitutes for one another.

merchandise group A group within an organization managed by the senior vice presidents of merchandise and responsible for several departments.

merchandise inventory The goods the retailer invests in and holds in stock, to enable customers to find what they want in the right place at the right time.

merchandise kiosks Small, temporary selling spaces typically located in the walkways of enclosed malls, airports, train stations, or office building lobbies.

merchandise management The process by which a retailer attempts to offer the right quantity of the right merchandise in the right place at the right time while meeting the company's financial goal.

merchandising planner A retail employee responsible for allocating merchandise and tailoring the assortment in several categories for specific stores in a geographic area.

metropolitan statistical area (MSA) A city with 50,000 or more inhabitants or an urbanized area of at least 50,000 inhabitants and a total MSA population of at least 100,000 (75,000 in New England).

microblog A short version of a blog, such as Twitter.

micropolitan statistical area (µSA) A city with only 10,000 inhabitants in its core urban area.

mission statement A broad description of the scope of activities a business plans to undertake.

mixed-use development (MXD) Development that combines several uses in one complex—for example, shopping center, office tower, hotel, residential complex, civic center, and convention center.

mobile commerce See *m-commerce*.

mobile communication Messages delivered through handheld, wireless devices, such as cellular telephones.

mobile retailing Internet channels accessed through tablets, smartphones, or other handheld devices. Also known as *m-commerce*.

model stock list A list of fashion merchandise that indicates in very general terms (product lines, colors, and size distributions) what should be carried in a particular merchandise category; also known as a model stock plan.

multiattribute analysis A method for evaluating vendors that uses a weighted average score for each vendor, which is based on the importance of various issues and the vendor's performance on those issues.

multiattribute attitude model A model of customer decision making based on the notion that customers see a retailer or a product as a collection of attributes or characteristics. The model can also be used for evaluating a retailer, product, or vendor. The model uses a weighted average score based on the importance of various issues and performance on those issues.

multichannel retailing Selling merchandise or services through more than one channel.

multilevel system A retail format in which people serve as master distributors, recruiting other people to become distributors in their network.

multiple-unit pricing Practice of offering two or more similar products or services for sale at one price. Also known as *quantity discounts*.

mystery shopper Professional shopper who "shops" a store to assess the service provided by store employees.

national brand See *manufacturer's brand*.

natural barrier A barrier, such as a river or mountain, that impacts accessibility to a site.

neighborhood shopping center A shopping center that includes a supermarket, drugstore, home improvement center, or variety store. Neighborhood centers often include small stores, such as apparel, shoe, camera, and other shopping goods stores.

net profit margin Profit a firm makes divided by its net sales.

net sales The total number of dollars received by a retailer after all refunds have been paid to customers for returned merchandise.

North American Industry Classification System (NAICS) Classification of retail firms into a hierarchical set of six-digit codes based on the types of products and services they produce and sell.

objective-and-task method A method for setting a promotion budget in which the retailer first establishes a set of communication objectives and then determines the necessary tasks and their costs.

observability The degree to which a new fashion is visible and easily communicated to others in a social group.

odd pricing The practice of ending prices with an odd number (such as 69 cents) or just under a round number (such as $98 instead of $100).

off-price retailer A retailer that offers an inconsistent assortment of brand-name, fashion-oriented soft goods at low prices.

omnicenter A combination of mall, lifestyle, and power center components in a unified, open-air layout.

omniretailing Coordinated multichannel retail offering that ensures a seamless customer experience across all the retailer's channels.

one-price retailer A store that offers all merchandise at a single fixed price.

1-to-1 retailing Developing retail programs for small groups or individual customers.

online retailing See *electronic retailing*.

on-the-job training A decentralized approach in which job training occurs in the work environment where employees perform their jobs.

open-to-buy The plan that keeps track of how much is spent in each month and how much is left to spend.

operating expenses Costs, other than the cost of merchandise, incurred in the normal course of doing business, such as salaries for sales associates and managers, advertising, utilities, office supplies, and rent.

operating expenses percentage Operating expenses divided by net sales.

operating income percentage Gross margin, minus operating expenses, divided by net sales.

operating profit margin This profitability measure is the gross margin minus operating and extraordinary recurring expenses. Also known as earnings before interest, taxes, and depreciation *(EBITDA)*.

opportunities and threats analysis Assessments of features of the environment that might positively or negatively affect the retailer's performance.

opt in A customer privacy issue prevalent in the European Union. Takes the perspective that consumers "own" their personal information. Retailers must get consumers to explicitly agree to share this personal information.

opt out A customer privacy issue prevalent in the United States. Takes the perspective that personal information is generally viewed as being in the public domain and retailers can use it in any way they desire. Consumers must explicitly tell retailers not to use their personal information.

order point The amount of inventory below which the quantity available shouldn't go or the item will be out of stock before the next order arrives.

organization culture A firm's set of values, traditions, and customs that guide employee behavior.

organization structure A plan that identifies the activities to be performed by specific employees and determines the lines of authority and responsibility in the firm.

outlet center Typically stores owned by retail chains or manufacturers that sell excess and out-of-season merchandise at reduced prices.

outlet store Off-price retailer owned by a manufacturer or a department or specialty store chain.

outparcel A building or kiosk that is in the parking lot of a shopping center but isn't physically attached to a shopping center.

output measure Measure that assesses the results of retailers' investment decisions.

outshopping Customers shopping in other areas because their needs are not being met locally.

outsourcing Obtaining a service from outside the company that had previously been done by the firm itself.

own brand See *private-label brand*.

pack verification A check of the contents of a carton, usually just before sealing it.

parallel import See *gray-market goods*.

partnering relationship See *strategic relationship*.

party plan system Salespeople encourage people to act as hosts and invite friends or coworkers to a "party" at which the merchandise is demonstrated. The host or hostess receives a gift or commission for arranging the meeting.

percentage lease A lease in which rent is based on a percentage of sales.

percentage lease with specified maximum A lease that pays the lessor, or landlord, a percentage of sales up to a maximum amount.

percentage lease with specified minimum The retailer must pay a minimum rent no matter how low sales are.

percentage-of-sales method A method for setting a promotion budget based on a fixed percentage of forecast sales.

perceptual map A graphic depiction of customers' images of and preferences for retailers.

perpetual inventory An accounting procedure whose objectives are to maintain a perpetual or book inventory in retail dollar amounts and to maintain records that make it possible to determine the cost value of the inventory at any time without taking a physical inventory.

perpetual ordering system The stock level is monitored perpetually and a fixed quantity is purchased when the inventory available reaches a prescribed level.

personalized service A customer service strategy that requires service providers to tailor their services to meet each customer's personal needs.

personal selling A communication process in which salespeople assist customers in satisfying their needs through face-to-face exchange of information.

physical inventory A method of gathering stock information by using an actual physical count and inspection of the merchandise items.

physical risks The risks customers encounter when they believe using a product or service could impair their health or safety.

pick ticket A document that tells the order filler how much of each item to get from the storage area.

pilferage The stealing of a store's merchandise. See also *shoplifting*.

planned location Shopping centers for which management enforces policies governing store operations, such as operating hours. The shopping center management also maintains the common facilities such as the parking area and is responsible for providing security, parking lot lighting, outdoor signage for the center, advertising and special events to attract consumers, and so on.

planners Employees in merchandise management responsible for the financial planning and analysis of the merchandise category and, in some cases, the allocation of merchandise to stores.

planogram A diagram created from photographs, computer output, or artists' renderings that illustrates exactly where every SKU should be placed.

point-of-purchase (POP) counter Places in the store where customers can purchase merchandise. Also known as *checkout areas*.

point-of-purchase (POP) display A display that is positioned where the customer waits at checkout. This area can be the most valuable piece of real estate in the store, because the customer is almost held captive in that spot.

point-of-sale signage Signs placed near the merchandise they refer to so that customers know the price and other detailed information.

point-of-sale (POS) terminal A cash register that can electronically scan a UPC code with a laser and electronically record a sale.

pop-up store Stores in temporary locations that focus on new products or a limited group of products.

positioning The design and implementation of a retail mix to create in the customer's mind an image of the retailer relative to its competitors.

postpurchase evaluation The evaluation of merchandise or services after the customer has purchased and consumed them.

power center Shopping center that is dominated by several large anchors, including discount stores (Target), off-price stores (Marshalls), warehouse clubs (Costco), or category specialists such as Home Depot, Office Depot, Sports Authority, Best Buy, and Toys "R" Us.

power perimeter The areas around the outside walls of a supermarket that have fresh merchandise categories.

predatory pricing A method for establishing merchandise prices for the purpose of driving competition from the marketplace.

premium A type of sales promotion whereby an item is offered free of charge or at a bargain price to reward some type of behavior, such as buying, sampling, or testing.

premium store brand A branding strategy that offers the consumer a private label at a comparable manufacturer-brand quality, usually with a modest price savings.

preprint An advertisement printed at the retailer's expense and distributed as a freestanding insert in a newspaper. Also called a *freestanding insert (FSI)*.

president of direct channels An executive responsible for the selection and pricing of the merchandise assortment offered through the catalog and Internet channels, the maintenance and design of the retailer's website, customer call centers, and the fulfillment centers that fill orders for individual customers.

price bundling The practice of offering two or more different products or services for sale at one price.

price elasticity of demand A measure of the effect a price change has on consumer demand; percentage change in demand divided by percentage change in price.

price lining A pricing policy in which a retailer offers a limited number of predetermined price points within a classification.

pricing optimization software A type of software program that uses a set of algorithms that analyzes past and current merchandise sales and prices, estimates the relationship between prices and sales generated, and then determines the optimal (most profitable) initial price for the merchandise and the appropriate size and timing of markdowns.

primary trading area The geographic area from which a store or shopping center derives 50 to 70 percent of its customers.

private-label brands Products developed and marketed by a retailer and only available for sale by that retailer. Also called *store brands*.

private-label president An executive responsible for the conceptualization, design, sourcing, quality control, and marketing of private-label and exclusive merchandise.

procedural fairness The perceived fairness of the process used to resolve customer complaints.

procedural justice An employee's perception of fairness (how he or she is treated) that is based on the process used to determine the outcome.

product availability A measurement of the percentage of demand for a particular SKU that is satisfied.

productivity measure The ratio of an output to an input determining how effectively a firm uses a resource.

product line A group of related products.

product placement A type of retail communication whereby retailers and vendors pay to have their product included in nontraditional situations, such as in a scene in a movie or television program.

productivity In a human resources context, it is sales generated per employee.

profit sharing A type of compensation incentive offered to a retail manager as a cash bonus based on the firm's profits or as a grant of stock options that link additional income to the performance of the firm's stock.

prohibited-use clause A clause in a lease that keeps a landlord from leasing to certain kinds of tenants.

promotion Activities undertaken by a retailer to provide consumers with information about a retailer's store, its image, and its retail mix.

promotional aisle Area aisle or area of a store designed to get the customer's attention. An example might be a special "trim-the-tree" department that seems to magically appear right after Thanksgiving every year for the Christmas holidays.

promotional area A feature area in a store in which merchandise on sale is displayed.

promotional signage This signage describes special offers and may be displayed in windows to entice the customer into the store.

protected class A group of people, such as women or minorities, that are treated differently or discriminated against, such as when a qualified woman does not receive a promotion given to a less qualified man.

psychographics Refers to how people live, how they spend their time and money, what activities they pursue, and their attitudes and opinions about the world they live in.

public relations (PR) A retail communication tool for managing communications and relationships to achieve various objectives, such as building and maintaining a positive image of the retailer, handling or heading off unfavorable stories or events, and maintaining positive relationships with the media.

public warehouse Warehouse that is owned and operated by a third party.

pull supply chain Strategy in which orders for merchandise are generated at the store level on the basis of demand data captured by point-of-sale terminals.

push supply chain Strategy in which merchandise is allocated to stores on the basis of historical demand, the inventory position at the distribution center, and the stores' needs.

pyramid scheme When the firm and its program are designed to sell merchandise and services to other distributors rather than to end users.

quantity discount The policy of granting lower prices for higher quantities. Also known as *multiple-unit pricing*.

quick ratio Short-term assets less inventory, divided by short-term liabilities. Also known as the *acid-test ratio*.

quota Target level used to motivate and evaluate performance.

quota–bonus plan Compensation plan that has a performance goal or objective established to evaluate employee performance, such as sales per hour for salespeople and maintained margin and turnover for buyers.

racetrack layout A type of store layout that provides a major aisle to facilitate customer traffic that has access to the store's multiple entrances. Also known as a *loop layout*.

radio frequency identification (RFID) A technology that allows an object or person to be identified at a distance using radio waves.

radio frequency identification (RFID) system Tags that transmit identifying information about the merchandise to which they are attached, whether an individual item, a carton, or a container.

rain check When sale merchandise is out of stock, a written promise to customers to sell them that merchandise at the sale price when it arrives.

reachable A requirement of a viable market segment that the retailer can target promotions and other elements of the retail mix to the consumers in that segment.

rebate Money returned to the buyer in the form of cash based on a portion of the purchase price.

receiving The process of filling out paperwork to record the receipt of merchandise that arrives at a store or distribution center.

reductions Includes three things: markdowns; discounts to employees and customers; and inventory shrinkage due to shoplifting, breakage, or loss.

reference group One or more people whom a person uses as a basis of comparison for his or her beliefs, feelings, and behaviors.

reference price A price point in the consumer's memory for a good or service that can consist of the price last paid, the price most frequently paid, or the average of all prices customers have paid for similar offerings. A benchmark for what consumers believe the "real" price of the merchandise should be.

regional mall Shopping malls less than 1 million square feet.

regression analysis A statistical approach for evaluating retail locations based on the assumption that factors that affect the sales of existing stores in a chain will have the same impact on stores located at new sites being considered.

related diversification growth opportunity A diversification opportunity strategy in which the retailer's present offering and market share something in common with the market and format being considered.

relevance In an advertising context, how helpful the ad message is for a customer searching for information.

reliability A customer service characteristic that customers use to evaluate service quality; the ability to perform the service dependably and accurately, such as performing the service as promised or contracted or meeting promised delivery dates.

reorder point The stock level at which a new order is placed.

resident buying office An organization located in a major buying center that provides services to help retailers buy merchandise.

responsiveness A customer service characteristic that customers use to evaluate service quality; the willingness to help customers and provide prompt service, such as returning calls and e-mails immediately.

retail analytics The application of statistical data analysis techniques to improve retail decision making.

retail brand community A group of customers who are bound together by their loyalty to a retailer and the activities in which the retailer engages.

retail chain A firm that consists of multiple retail units under common ownership and usually has some centralization of decision making in defining and implementing its strategy.

retailer A business that sells products and services to consumers for their personal or family use.

retail channel The means by which a retailer sells and delivers merchandise to customers.

retail community A group of consumers who have a shared involvement with the retailer.

retail format The retailers' type of retail mix (nature of merchandise and services offered, pricing policy, advertising and promotion program, approach to store design and visual merchandising, and typical location).

retail format development growth opportunity An investment opportunity strategy in which a retailer offers a new retail format—a format involving a different retail mix—to the same target market.

retail market A group of consumers with similar needs (a market segment) and a group of retailers using a similar retail format to satisfy those consumer needs.

retail market segment A group of customers whose needs will be satisfied by the same retail offering because they have similar needs and go through similar buying processes.

retail mix The combination of factors used by a retailer to satisfy customer needs and influence their purchase decisions; includes merchandise and services offered, pricing, advertising and promotions, store design and location, and visual merchandising.

retail strategy A statement that indicates (1) the target market toward which a retailer plans to commit its resources, (2) the nature of the retail offering that the retailer plans to use to satisfy the needs of the target market, and (3) the bases upon which the retailer will attempt to build a sustainable competitive advantage over competitors.

retailer loyalty Customers like and habitually visit the same retailer to purchase a type of merchandise.

retailing A set of business activities that adds value to the products and services sold to consumers for their personal or family use.

return on advertising investment (ROAI) Sales revenue minus advertising costs, divided by advertising costs.

return on assets (ROA) Net profit after taxes divided by total assets.

reverse auction Auction conducted by retailer buyers. Known as a *reverse auction* because there is one buyer and many potential sellers. In reverse auctions, retail buyers provide a specification for what they want to a group of potential vendors. The competing vendors then bid down the price at which they are willing to sell until the buyer accepts a bid.

reverse logistics The process of moving returned goods back through the supply chain from the customer, to the stores, distribution centers, and vendors.

RFM (recency, frequency, monetary) analysis Often used by catalog retailers and direct marketers, a scheme for segmenting customers on the basis of how recently they have made a purchase, how frequently they make purchases, and how much they have bought.

rounder A round fixture that sits on a pedestal. Smaller than the straight rack, it is designed to hold a maximum amount of merchandise. Also known as a *bulk* or *capacity fixture*.

rule-of-thumb method A type of approach for setting a promotion budget that uses past sales and communication activity to determine the present communications budget.

safety stock See *buffer stock*.

sales per linear foot A measure of space productivity used when most merchandise is displayed on multiple shelves of long gondolas, such as in grocery stores.

sales per square foot A measure of space productivity used by most retailers since rent and land purchases are assessed on a per-square-foot basis.

sales promotions Paid impersonal communication activities that offer extra value and incentives to customers to visit a store or purchase merchandise during a specific period of time.

same-store sales growth The sales growth in stores that have been open for over one year.

samples A type of sales promotion; a small amount or size of a product given to potential customers as an inducement to purchase.

satisfaction A postconsumption evaluation of the degree to which a store or product meets or exceeds customer expectations.

scale economies Cost advantages due to the size of a retailer.

scrambled merchandising An offering of merchandise not typically associated with the store type, such as clothing in a drugstore.

search engine marketing (SEM) Methods that marketers use to improve the visibility of their websites.

search engine optimization (SEO) Designing website content to improve the positioning of the site on search engine results pages.

search engine results page (SERP) The results a search engine lists in response to a user query.

seasonal merchandise Inventory whose sales fluctuate dramatically according to the time of the year.

secondary trading area The geographic area of secondary importance in terms of customer sales, generating about 20 percent of a store's sales.

second-degree price discrimination Charging different prices to different people on the basis of the nature of the offering.

security policy Set of rules that apply to activities in the computer and communications resources that belong to an organization.

selling, general, and administrative expenses (SG&A) Operating expenses, plus the depreciation and amortization of assets.

sell-through analysis A comparison of actual and planned sales to determine whether early markdowns are required or more merchandise is needed to satisfy demand.

senior vice president (SVP) of merchandising An executive who works with buyers and planners to develop and coordinate the management of the retailer's merchandise offering and ensures that it is consistent with the firm's strategy.

senior vice president (SVP) of stores An executive who supervises all activities related to stores, including working with the regional managers, who supervise district managers, who supervise the individual store managers.

sentiment analysis Assessments that monitor social media to determine how customers view the firm.

sentiment mining The process retailers use to monitor online chat formats, collect customer comments, and analyze the data to learn customers' attitudes and preferences.

service gap The difference between customers' expectations and perceptions of customer service to improve customers' satisfaction with their service.

service level A measure used in inventory management to define the level of support or level of product availability; the number of items sold divided by the number of items demanded. Service level should not be confused with customer service. Compare *customer service*.

services retailer Organization that offers consumers services rather than merchandise. Examples include banks, hospitals, health spas, doctors, legal clinics, entertainment firms, and universities.

sexual harassment Unwelcome sexual advances, requests for sexual favors, or other verbal or physical conduct with sexual elements.

share of wallet The percentage of total purchases made by a customer in a store.

ship verification A check of the contents of a carton, usually as cartons are being loaded on a pallet or truck.

shoplifting The act of stealing merchandise from a store by employees, customers, or people posing as customers.

shopping center A group of retail and other commercial establishments that is planned, developed, owned, and managed as a single property.

shopping center property management firm Company that specializes in developing, owning, and maintaining shopping centers.

shopping mall Enclosed, climate-controlled, lighted shopping centers with retail stores on one or both sides of an enclosed walkway.

shopworn Merchandise that looks damaged because it has been on display for a long time and customers have been handling it.

showrooming A practice in which customers visit stores to interact with a physical product and receive sales assistance, then purchase it through a less expensive channel, such as online.

shrinkage An inventory reduction that is caused by shoplifting by employees or customers, by merchandise being misplaced or damaged, or by poor bookkeeping.

SKU rationalization process An analysis of the potential benefits a retailer could achieve by adding or deleting specific items from their assortments.

SKU See *stockkeeping unit.*

sliding scale lease A part of some leases that stipulates how much the percentage of sales paid as rent will decrease as sales go up.

slotting allowance Fee paid by a vendor for space in a retail store. Also called *slotting fee.*

slotting fee See *slotting allowance.*

social media Media content distributed through social interactions. Three major online facilitators of social media are YouTube, Facebook, and Twitter.

social risk The risk customers perceive when they believe purchasing a product or service will affect how others regard them.

socialization process The steps taken to transform new employees into effective, committed members of the firm.

soft goods Merchandise with a relatively short lifespan, such as clothing or cosmetics.

special event Sales promotion program comprising a number of sales promotion techniques built around a seasonal, cultural, sporting, musical, or other event.

specialization The organizational structure in which employees are typically responsible for only one or two tasks rather than performing all tasks. This approach enables employees to develop expertise and increase productivity.

specialty shopping Shopping experiences when consumers know what they want and will not accept a substitute.

specialty store A type of store concentrating on a limited number of complementary merchandise categories and providing a high level of service.

Spending Potential Index (SPI) Compares the average expenditure in a particular area for a product to the amount spent on that product nationally.

spot A local television commercial.

standardized service A customer service strategy that is based on establishing a set of rules and procedures for providing high-quality service and ensuring that they get implemented consistently by service providers.

standards gap The difference between the retailer's perceptions of customers' expectations and the customer service standards it sets. This factor is one of four factors identified by the Gaps model for improving service quality.

staple merchandise Inventory that has continuous demand by customers over an extended period of time. Also known as *basic merchandise.*

statement of operations A summary of the firm's performance over a period of time (usually one quarter). Also known as the *income statement.*

stock-keeping unit (SKU) The smallest unit available for keeping inventory control. In soft goods merchandise, an SKU usually means a size, color, and style.

stocklift See *buyback.*

stockout A situation occurring when an SKU that a customer wants is not available.

stock-to-sales ratio Specifies the amount of inventory that should be on hand at the beginning of the month to support the sales forecast and maintain the inventory turnover objective. The beginning-of-month (BOM) inventory divided by sales for the month. The average stock-to-sales ratio is 12 divided by planned inventory turnover. This ratio is an integral component of the merchandise budget plan.

store advocates Customers who like a store so much that they actively share their positive experiences with friends and family.

store brand See *private-label brand.*

store maintenance The activities involved with managing the exterior and interior physical facilities associated with the store.

store within a store An agreement in which a retailer rents a portion of retail space in a store operated by a different, independent retailer.

straight commission A form of salesperson's compensation in which the amount paid is based on a percentage of sales made minus merchandise returned.

straight rack A type of fixture that consists of a long pipe suspended with supports going to the floor or attached to a wall.

straight salary compensation A compensation plan in which salespeople or managers receive a fixed amount of compensation for each hour or week they work.

strategic alliance Collaborative relationship between independent firms. For example, a foreign retailer might enter an international market through direct investment but develop an alliance with a local firm to perform logistical and warehousing activities.

strategic profit model (SPM) A tool used for planning a retailer's financial strategy based on both margin management (net profit margin) and asset management (asset turnover). Using the SPM, a retailer's objective is to achieve a target return on assets.

strategic relationship Long-term relationship in which partners make significant investments to improve both parties' profitability.

strategic retail planning process The steps a retailer goes through to develop a strategic retail plan. It describes how retailers select target market segments, determine the appropriate retail format, and build sustainable competitive advantages.

strengths and weaknesses analysis A critical aspect of the situation audit in which a retailer determines its unique capabilities—its strengths and weaknesses relative to its competition.

strip shopping center A shopping center that usually has parking directly in front of the stores and does not have enclosed walkways linking the stores.

structured training program Training that teaches new employees the basic skills and knowledge they will need to do their job.

subbrand Part of a branding strategy in which a product's brand name is associated with the description of the product, such as Frosted Flakes, where the family brand is Kellogg's.

620   Glossary

subculture theory A theory of how fashion spreads that suggests that subcultures of mostly young and less affluent consumers, such as motorcycle riders and urban rappers, have started fashions for such things as colorful fabrics, t-shirts, sneakers, jeans, black leather jackets, and surplus military clothing.

substantial In relation to a market, one that offers enough profits to support retailing mix activities.

supercenter Large store (150,000 to 220,000 square feet) combining a discount store with a supermarket.

superregional mall Shopping center that is similar to a regional center, but because of its larger size, it has more anchors and a deeper selection of merchandise, and it draws from a larger population base.

supply chain A set of firms that make and deliver a given set of goods and services to the ultimate consumer.

supply chain management The set of approaches and techniques firms employ to efficiently and effectively integrate their suppliers, manufacturers, warehouses, stores, and transportation intermediaries to efficiently have the right quantities at the right locations, and at the right time.

support groups A group of employees with common interests, goals or characteristics, such as minority or female executives, that are put together by a retailer to exchange information and provide emotional and career support for members who traditionally haven't been included in the majority's networks.

sustainable competitive advantage A distinct competency of a retailer relative to its competitors that can be maintained over a considerable time period.

SWOT analysis An assessment of the retailer's internal and external environment, as represented by strengths, weaknesses, opportunities, and threats.

tangibility A customer service characteristic that customers use to evaluate service quality; it is associated with the appearance of physical facilities, equipment, personnel, and communication materials when a service is being performed.

target market The market segment(s) toward which the retailer plans to focus its resources and retail mix.

tariff A tax placed by a government upon imports. Also known as *duty*.

task performance behaviors Planning, organizing, motivating, evaluating, and coordinating store employees' activities.

team incentive Sales incentives based on the performance of a group, department, or the store as a whole.

television home shopping A retail format in which customers watch a TV program demonstrating merchandise and then place orders for the merchandise by phone.

tertiary trading area The outermost ring of a trade area; includes customers who occasionally shop at the store or shopping center.

theme/festival center A shopping center that typically employs a unifying theme that is carried out by the individual shops in their architectural design and, to an extent, their merchandise.

third-degree price discrimination Charging different prices to different demographic market segments.

thrift store A retail format offering used merchandise.

ticketing and marking Procedures for making price labels and placing them on the merchandise.

tonnage merchandising A display technique in which large quantities of merchandise are displayed together.

top-down planning One side of the process of developing an overall retail strategy where goals are set at the top of the organization and filter down through the operating levels.

top-of-mind awareness The highest level of brand awareness; arises when consumers mention a brand name first when they are asked about a type of retailer, a merchandise category, or a type of service.

trade area A geographic sector that contains potential customers for a particular retailer or shopping center.

trademark Any mark, work, picture, or design associated with a particular line of merchandise or product.

trade show A temporary concentration of vendors that provides retailers opportunities to place orders and view what is available in the marketplace; also known as a *market week*.

traffic flow The balance between a substantial number of cars and not so many that congestion impedes access to the store.

transformational leader A leader who gets people to transcend their personal needs for the sake of realizing the group goal.

trend setter Initial customer adopters of a new fashion. Also known as an *innovator* or *fashion leader*.

trialability The costs and commitment required to initially adopt a fashion.

trickle-down theory A theory of how fashion spreads that suggests that the fashion leaders are consumers with the highest social status—wealthy, well-educated consumers. After they adopt a fashion, the fashion trickles down to consumers in lower social classes. When the fashion is accepted in the lowest social class, it is no longer acceptable to the fashion leaders in the highest social class.

trust A belief that a partner is honest (reliable, stands by its word, sincere, fulfills obligations) and benevolent (concerned about the other party's welfare).

turnover In a human resources context, the number of employees who voluntarily leave their job, divided by the number of positions in the firm.

tying contract An agreement between a vendor and a retailer requiring the retailer to take a product it does not necessarily desire (the tied product) to ensure that it can buy a product it does desire (the tying product).

umbrella brand See *family brand*.

universal product code (UPC) The black-and-white bar code found on most merchandise; used to collect sales information at the point of sale using computer terminals that read the code. This information is transmitted computer to computer to buyers, distribution centers, and then to vendors, who in turn quickly ship replenishment merchandise.

unorganized retailing Collections of small, independent retailers, especially common in emerging economies.

unplanned location Freestanding and urban retail locations that lack any centralized management to determine which stores locate in them or how they operate.

unplanned purchasing An impulsive purchase that customers make on the spot, after seeing the merchandise briefly.

unrelated diversification growth opportunity Diversification in which there is no commonality between the present business and the new business.

unsatisfied need The condition that arises when a customer's desired level of satisfaction differs from his or her current level of satisfaction.

UPC See *universal product code.*

urban decay The process by which a previously well-functioning area falls into disrepair.

urban sprawl Expansions of residential and shopping center developments into suburban or rural areas, beyond urban centers.

utilitarian benefit A motivation for shopping in which consumers accomplish a specific task, such as buying a suit for a job interview.

utilitarian needs Needs motivating consumers to go shopping to accomplish a specific task.

value Relationship of what a customer gets (goods/services) to what he or she has to pay for it.

values of lifestyle survey (VALS2) A tool used to categorize customers into eight lifestyle segments. Based on responses to surveys conducted by SRI Consulting Business Intelligence.

variable costs Costs that vary with the level of sales and can be applied directly to the decision in question.

variety The number of different merchandise categories within a store or department.

vending machine A nonstore format in which merchandise or services are stored in a machine and dispensed to customers when they deposit cash or use a credit card.

vendor-managed inventory (VMI) An approach for improving supply chain efficiency in which the vendor is responsible for maintaining the retailer's inventory levels in each of its stores.

vertical integration An example of diversification by retailers involving investments by retailers in wholesaling or manufacturing merchandise.

vertical merchandising A method whereby merchandise is organized to follow the eye's natural up-and-down movement.

visibility Customers' ability to see the store and enter the parking lot safely.

visual merchandising The presentation of a store and its merchandise in ways that will attract the attention of potential customers.

warehouse club A retailer that offers a limited assortment of food and general merchandise with little service and low prices to ultimate consumers and small businesses.

wholesale market A concentration of vendors within a specific geographic location, perhaps even under one roof or over the Internet.

wholesaler A merchant establishment operated by a concern that is primarily engaged in buying, taking title to, usually storing, and physically handling goods in large quantities, and reselling the goods (usually in smaller quantities) to retailers or industrial or business users.

wholesale-sponsored voluntary cooperative group An organization operated by a wholesaler offering a merchandising program to small, independent retailers on a voluntary basis.

word of mouth Communications among people about a retailer.

yield management The practice of adjusting prices up or down in response to demand to control sales generated.

zone pricing Charging different prices for the same merchandise in different geographic locations to be competitive in local markets.

zoning The regulation of the construction and use of buildings in certain areas of a municipality.

ENDNOTES

Chapter 1

1. Macy's Inc 10-K Form, filed March 12, 2012.
2. www.thefreedictionary.com/retailer.
3. Chitra Srivastava Dabas, Brenda Sternquist, and Humaira Mahi, "Organized Retailing in India: Upstream Channel Structure and Management," *Journal of Business & Industrial Marketing* 27, no. 3 (2012), pp.176–195; and Rajesh K. Aithal, "Marketing Channel Length in Rural India: Influence of the External Environment and Rural Retailer Buyer Behavior," *International Journal of Retail & Distribution Management* 40, no. 3 (2012), pp. 200–217.
4. Walmart China Fact Sheet, Alex Lawson, "Analysis: Retailing in China," *Retail Week*, April 20, 2012; and Sheng Lu, "Understanding China's Retail Market," *China Business Review*, May–June 2010.
5. John Dawson, "Global Trends: Retail Trends in Europe," in M. Krafft and M. K. Mantrala (Eds.), *Retailing in the 21st Century: Current and Future Trends* (Berlin Heidelberg: Springer-Verlag, 2010); and Grzegorz Karasiewicz and Jan Nowak, "Looking Back at the 20 Years of Retailing Change in Poland," *International Review of Retail, Distribution and Consumer Research* 20, no. 1 (2010), pp. 103–107; and Matthew Shay, "Future of Retail Depends on Today's Policy Decisions," *The Future of Retail*.
6. Martin Baily and Diana Farrell, "How Europe's Regulations Hold It Back," *Financial Times* (UK), October 18, 2005, p. 13.
7. http://about-france.com/shopping-in-france.htm; Marcus Walker, "Longer Store Hours in Germany; Scrapping of Restrictions Is Designed to Boost a Laggard Economy," *The Wall Street Journal*, January 8, 2007, p. A5.
8. "Overview of BLS Statistics on Employment," Bureau of Labor Statistics www.bls.gov/bls/employment.htm; and *Retail Powers the U.S. Economy* (Washington, DC: National Retail Federation, 2012).
9. Ibid.
10. Timothy Creel, "Corporate Social Responsibility: An Examination of Practices in the Retail Industry," *Management Accounting Quarterly* 12, no. 4 (Summer 2011), pp. 23–28.
11. https://corporate.target.com/corporate-responsibility.
12. Marcus Leroux, "Recession Fails to Dent Shoppers' Ethical Beliefs," *The Times*, October 13, 2009.
13. Tiffany Hsu, "For Wal-Mart, Going Green Saves Money," *Los Angeles Times*, June 4, 2011, p. B.1.
14. Cristina Binkley, "Which Outfit Is Greenest? A New Rating Tool," *The Wall Street Journal*, July 26, 2012, p. B1; and Tom Zeller, "Clothes Makers Join To Set 'Green Score,'" *The New York Times*, March 1, 2011, p. B.1.
15. Caroline D. Ditlev Simonsen and Petter Gottschalk, "Stages of Growth Model for Corporate Social Responsibility," *International Journal of Corporate Governance* 2, no. 3–4 (2011), pp. 268–287; and Andreas Georg Scherer and Guido Palazzo, "The New Political Role of Business in a Globalized World: A Review of a New Perspective on CSR and Its Implications for the Firm, Governance, and Democracy," *Journal of Management Studies* 48, no. 4 (2011), pp. 899–931.
16. C. K. Prahalad, *The Fortune at the Bottom of the Pyramid: Eradicating Poverty Through Profits*, revised and updated 5th anniversary edition (Philadelphia: Wharton School Publishing, 2009); Anee Karnani, "The Mirage of Marketing to the Bottom of the Pyramid: How the Private Sector Can Help Alleviate Poverty," *California Management Review* 49 (Summer 2007), pp. 90–111; C. K. Prahalad and A. Hammond, "Serving the World's Poor, Profitability," *Harvard Business Review*, September, 2002, pp. 4–14; and C. K. Prahalad and S. L. Hart, "The Fortune at the Bottom of the Pyramid, *Strategy+Business* 26, pp. 54–67.
17. C. K. Prahalad, "Bottom of the Pyramid as a Source of Breakthrough Innovations," *Journal of Product Innovation Management* 29 (January 2012), pp. 6–12; and A Karamchandani and M Kubzansky, "Is the Bottom of the Pyramid Really for You?" *Harvard Business Review*, March 2011, pp. 2–10.
18. Dan Scheraga, "Penney's Net Advantage," *Chain Store Age*, September 2000, pp. 114–118.
19. National Retail Federation, "Large Retailers Sales and Profitability," based on 2007 Census Bureau Data.
20. Procter & Gamble, 10-K Form, filed August 8, 2012; Walmart 10-K Form, filed March 27, 2012.
21. "Data, Data Everywhere," *The Economist*, February 25, 2010.
22. Ibid.
23. Target, 10-K Form, filed March 11, 2011.
24. Personal conversation with author.
25. *Fortune* 500, 2012.
26. Tom Robinson, *Jeff Bezos: Amazon.com Architect (Publishing Pioneers)* (Edina, MN: Abdo Publishing, 2009); and www.forbes.com/profile/jeff-bezos/.
27. Andrea Chang, "To Forever 21, Big Stores Are a Good Fit," *Los Angeles Times*, May 25, 2011, p. B.1.
28. Robert LaFranco, "Ikea's Kamprad Is Europe's Richest in Billionaire Index," *Bloomberg.com*, March 4, 2012.
29. "The World's Billionaires 2007," *Forbes*, March 8, 2003.
30. www.businessinsider.com/15-facts-about-starbucks-that-will-blow-your-mind-2011-3?op=1#ixzz22368Bd8Q.
31. Howard Schultz and Joanne Gordon, *Onward: How Starbucks Fought for Its Life without Losing Its Soul* (Emmaus, PA: Rodale Books, 2012); and Howard Behar, Janet Goldstein, and Howard Schultz. *It's Not About the Coffee: Lessons on Putting People First from a Life at Starbucks* (New York: Portfolio Trade, 2009).
32. Leslie Kwoh, "Firms Resist New Pay-Equity Rules," *The Wall Street Journal (Online)*, June 26, 2012.
33. "Whole Foods Launches iPhone App," *Austin Business Journal*, June 18, 2009.
34. Kylie Jane Wakefield, "How Whole Foods Maintains a Healthy Twitter Strategy," March 14, 2012, and "Tweeting Without Fear: How Three Companies Have Built Their Twitter Strategies," *The Wall Street Journal*, December 9, 2011.
35. Whole Foods, http://media.wholefoodsmarket.com/news/whole-foods-market-team-members-once-again-place-company-on-fortunes-100-be.
36. www.wholefoodsmarket.com/company; Nick Paumgarten, "Food Fighter," *New Yorker*, January 14, 2010, pp. 36–47; and Angela Cortez, "Whole Foods Holds On to Its Roots," *Natural Foods Merchandise*, October 2009, p. 46.
37. Ibid.

Chapter 2

1. U.S. Census Bureau, "2009 Business Patterns," June 30, 2011.

2. U.S. Census Bureau News.

3. "Sales of Food at Home by Type of Outlet Table," *USDA Economic Research Service*, 2010.

4. "Top 25 Global Food Retailers 2012," *Supermarket News*, 2012.

5. "Top 75 Retailers & Wholesalers 2012," *Supermarket News*, 2012.

6. "A Quick History of the Supermarket," *Groceteria.com*.

7. "Conventional Supermarket," *TermWiki*.

8. "The Fresh Perspective Industry Newsletter," *Perishables Group*, December 2011.

9. John Karolefski, "New Opportunities for Sales Growth in Grocery Center Store," *PG Matters*, June 6, 2012.

10. "Low-End Grocery Stores Carve Out Niche," *Contact Center Solutions Industry News*, October 13, 2007.

11. Ibid.

12. "No Limits on Small Grocers' Growth," *Retail Wire*, February 2, 2011.

13. Emily Bryson York, "Stuck in the Middle, Big Grocers Make Changes," *Chicago Tribune*, January 6, 2011.

14. Tom Ryan, "Family Dollar Antes Up on Food and More," *Retail Wire*, May 1, 2012; and Lynn Celmer, "Family Dollar Goes Gourmet," *Private Label Buyer*, October 24, 2011.

15. George Anderson, "Why People Hate to Grocery Shop," *Retail Wire*, April 4, 2012; and Sarah Mahoney, "Consumers: Plenty to Hate About Supermarkets," *AM Marketing Daily*, February 17, 2011.

16. www.packagedfacts.com/Prepared-Foods-Ready-2694891/.

17. Daniel Smith, "The Ultimate Food Fight," *QSR Magazine*, October 2010.

18. Julie Schmit, "Organic Food Sales Feel the Bite from Sluggish Economy," *USA Today*, August 19, 2008.

19. Industry Intelligence Inc., "Percentage of Consumers in U.S. Stating They Purchased Organic Food Products at 41.8% in January, Up from 39.8% in Year-Ago Period, Survey Says," February 16, 2010.

20. "Hispanic Americans by the Numbers—From the U.S. Census Bureau," *Infoplease.com*.

21. Northgate Markets website, www.northgatemarkets.com; Northgate Markets Newsletter.

22. Nick Wingfield, "Thinking Outside the Redbox," *The New York Times*, February 17, 2012; George Anderson, "Kiosk Krazy," *Retail Wire*, June 7, 2012.

23. Christina Passariello, "Carrefour Tries a Booster for Tiring Hypermarkets," *The Wall Street Journal*, August 25, 2010.

24. "Convenience Store Foodservice Trends in the U.S.," *Packaged Facts*, September 1, 2011.

25. "Giant Eagle FAQ," *Giant Eagle.com*.

26. Renee M. Covino, "C-Stores Go Fresh," *Convenience Store News*, March 22, 2010.

27. "Convenience Store Sales Topped $680 Billion in 2011," *Convenience Store Decisions*, April 4, 2012.

28. Tom Ryan, "C-Stores Morphing into QSRs," *Retail Wire*, April 16, 2012.

29. "Fun Facts," 7-Eleven; and "McDonald's 2011 Annual Report," McDonald's, 2011.

30. "2011 World's Largest Retailers—The Biggest and Best U.S. Retail Chains," *About.com*, July 18, 2012.

31. David Schulz, "2011 Top 100 Power Players: Department Stores," *Stores*, June 2011.

32. Ibid.; Sandra M. Jones, "Department Stores: Mad Rush for Market Share," *Chicago Tribune*, September 16, 2010; and Sarah Mahoney, "Department-Store Decline: It's *Not* the Economy," *AM Marketing Daily*, January 2, 2009.

33. Stephanie Clifford, "To Stand Out, Retailers Flock to Exclusive Lines," *The New York Times*, February 14, 2011; and Amy Verner, "How Department Stores Can Stay Relevant (and Chic)," *Globe and Mail (Toronto)*, April 21, 2012.

34. Ibid.

35. "Private Brands and Exclusive Merchandise," Macy's Inc.

36. "Our Stores," Walmart; *Industry Outlook: Mass Channel*.

37. Sandra M. Jones, "Walmart Making Little Plans," *Chicago Tribune*, May 14, 2011.

38. "Target Hopes Exclusive Designer Deals Boost Sales," *Reuters*, August 2, 2011; "Goodnight Walmart," *Giving Up On Fashion*, February 24, 2012.

39. "About HBTC," *Hudson's Bay Trading Company*.

40. Karen Talley, "Sears to Push to Lease Space to Outside Retailers," *The Wall Street Journal*, September 23, 2011.

41. Joseph Pereira and Ann Zimmerman, "Newcomers Challenge Office-Supply Stalwarts," *The Wall Street Journal*, April 29, 2009.

42. Ibid.

43. Ann Zimmerman, "A General-Store Race is On," *The Wall Street Journal*, April 30, 2012.

44. Stephanie Clifford, "Revamping, Home Depot Woos Women," *The New York Times*, January 28, 2011.

45. "Limited Brands (TD) Nears 52 Week High," *Stock Masters*, September 23, 2009.

46. Brian Zajac, "The Most Profitable Stores in America," *Bloomberg Businessweek*, February 23, 2012.

47. Tanya Rutledge, "Charming Charlie: A Jewel of a Chain," *Houston Chronicle*, December 2, 2011.

48. www.narts.org/i4a/pages/index.cfm?pageid=3285.

49. Kim Williams, "Rise of the Thrift Store Shopper Provides Steady Growth in Resale Industry," April 14, 2011.

50. Patrice J. Williams, "V.I.P. Perks, Secondhand Stores," *The New York Times*, December 29, 2011.

51. Sandra M. Jones, "Resale Shops Remake Empty Retail Spaces as Consumers Reshape Buying Habits," *Chicago Tribune*, April 7, 2011.

52. www.goodwill.org/about-us/newsroom/press-kit/.

53. Walgreen's 2011 10-K Report, Part I.

54. Michael Winerip, "For a Drugstore, 'Nice' Isn't a Panacea," *The New York Times*, February 25, 2010.

55. Katherine Rosman, "Aspirin, Q-Tips and a New You," *The Wall Street Journal*, March 25, 2010; and Sandra M. Jones, "Walgreens Plans Makeover in More Stores," *Chicago Tribune*, March 24, 2010.

56. Susan Berfield, "Duane Reade's Miracle Makeover," *Bloomberg Businessweek*, September 29, 2011.

57. Lydia Dishman, "Why Walgreens' Gamble on Glamming Up Drugstores Is a Winner," *Forbes*, January 20, 2012.

58. George Anderson, "Are Drugstores Priced Too High to Compete in Grocery?" *Retail Wire*, October 7, 2011.

59. George Anderson, "Walgreens on Global Path, Buys Stake in Alliance Boots," *Retail Wire*, June 19, 2012.

624   Endnotes

60. "Helping Shoppers Stretch Food Budgets," *Stores*, July 2008.

61. Ryan, "Family Dollar Antes Up"; Celmer, "Family Dollar Goes Gourmet."

62. Stephanie Clifford, "Stores Scramble to Accommodate Budget Shoppers," *The New York Times*, September 21, 2010.

63. Carol Spieckerman, "Rethinking Retail Scale," *Retail Wire*, October 25, 2011.

64. Ibid.

65. Jesse McKinley, "Bang for the Buck," *The New York Times*, January 11, 2012; Dollar General website; Family Dollar website.

66. Jayne O'Donnell, "Behind the Bargains at T.J. Maxx, Marshalls," *USA Today*, October 25, 2011.

67. Pallavi Gogoi, "Bargain Hunting: Luxury Retailers Find an Outlet," *BusinessWeek*, September 24, 2008.

68. Drew DeSilver, "Nordstrom Expanding through Rack Stores, Online," *Seattle Times*, June 13, 2012.

69. Vanessa O'Connell, "Luxury Retailers Pin Hopes on Outlets," *The Wall Street Journal*, April 30, 2008, p. B1.

70. www.zoots.com

71. Robert Spector. *The Mom & Pop Store: True Stories from the Heart of America* (New York: Walker & Company, 2009).

72. "The Dressing Room—Successful Independent Retailer," July 28, 2011; The Dressing Room website.

73. This section was prepared by Professor Tracy Meyer, University of North Carolina–Wilmington.

74. U.S. Census Bureau, "Census Bureau's First Release of Comprehensive Franchise Data Shows Franchises Make Up More Than 10 Percent of Employer Business," September 14, 2010.

75. Dhruv Grewal, Gopalkrishnan Iyer, Rajshekhar G. Javalgi, and Lori Radulovich, "Franchise Partnership and International Expansion: A Conceptual Framework and Research Propositions," *Entrepreneurial Theory & Practice*, May 2011, pp. 533–557.

Chapter 3

1. Jie Zhang, Paul Farris, John Irvin, Tarun Kushwaha, Thomas J. Steenburgh, and Barton Weitz, "Crafting Integrated Multichannel Retailing Strategies," *Journal of Interactive Marketing* 24, no. 2 (May 2010), pp. 168–80.

2. "Multi-Channel Retail: A Strategic Overview for US and Canadian Retailers," a CDC eCommerce White Paper, January 20, 2011.

3. Nikki Baird and Brian Kilcourse, *Omni-Channel 2012: Cross-Channel Comes of Age, 2012 Benchmark Report* (Miami: Retail Systems Research, 2008), June 2012.

4. Tom Stieghorst, "Miami-Dade's Capt. Harry's Reels in Overseas Sales," *Miami Herald*, June 3, 2012, p. B1.

5. Susan Kuchinskas, "A Decade of E-Commerce," *Internetnews. com*, October 18, 2004.

6. Forrester Research, February 2011.

7. "Understanding How U.S. Online Shoppers Are Reshaping the Retail Experience," PricewaterhouseCoopers LLP, March 2012.

8. Aaron Smith, "The Rise of In-Store Mobile Commerce," Pew Research Center's Internet & American Life Project, Washington, DC, January 30, 2012.

9. www.catalogs.com/info/b2b/catalog-merchandise.html; data from U.S. Census Bureau.

10. Ibid.

11. Michelle Fox, "Why Retail Catalogs Survive, Even Thrive, in Internet Age," *CNBC.com*, 2012; and Paula Rosenblum, "What Is Catalog's Place in a Omnichannel World?" *RSR*, April 3, 2012.

12. Kyle Parks, "Bob Circosta Receives First 'HSN Legend' Award," *PRNewswire*, March 27, 2012.

13. Barbara Thau, "QVC's Mike George on the Shopping Channel's Big Plans," *Daily Finance*, October 5, 2011.

14. Personal communication, Mindy Grossman, CEO of HSN.

15. *Fact Sheet: U.S. Direct Selling in 2011*, Washington, DC: Direct Selling Association, 2011.

16. http://www.dsa.org/about/faq/.

17. Elliot Maras, "2011 State of the Industry: Vending Sales Reflect a Slow Economic Recovery," *Automated Merchandiser*, July 2012.

18. http://inventors.about.com/library/inventors/blvending-machine.htm.

19. Emily Maltby, "Restocking the Old Vending Machine with Live Bait and Prescription Pills," *The Wall Street Journal*, March 22, 2012.

20. http://www.redbox.com/; David Lieberman, "DVD Kiosks Like Redbox Have Rivals Seeing Red," *USA Today*, August 13, 2009.

21. Tom Banks, "Ikea Catalogue Gets an Interactive Overhaul," *Design Week* (Online), July 23, 2012; and Victoria Thompson, "Ikea's Augmented Reality Catalogue Is a Step in the Right Direction," *Retail Week*, August 8, 2012.

22. Bob Tedeschi, "'Live Chat' Gives Push to Buying," *The New York Times*, August 6, 2006.

23. "Sponsored Supplement: Expanding the Reach of Personalization," *Internet Retailer*, March 2010.

24. Scott A. Neslin, Dhruv Grewal, Robert Leghorn, Venkatesh Shankar, Marije L. Teerling, Jacquelyn S. Thomas, and Peter C. Verhoef, "Challenges and Opportunities in Multichannel Customer Management," *Journal of Service Research* 9, no. 2 (2006), pp. 95–112.

25. Randolph E. Bucklin and Catarina Sismeiro, "Click Here for Internet Insight: Advances in Clickstream Data Analysis in Marketing," *Journal of Interactive Marketing*, February 2009, pp. 35–48.

26. Riccardo Mangiaracina and Alessandro Perego, "Payment Systems in the B2C eCommerce: Are They a Barrier for the Online Customer?" *Journal of Internet Banking and Commerce* 14 (December 2009), pp. 1–17.

27. James W. Peltier, George R. Milne, and Joseph E. Phelps, "Information Privacy Research: Framework for Integrating Multiple Publics, Information Channels, and Responses," *Journal of Interactive Marketing*, May 2009, pp. 191–205; Yue Payn, and George M. Zinkhan, "Exploring the Impact of Online Privacy Disclosures on Consumer Trust," *Journal of Retailing* 82, no. 4 (2006), pp. 331–338; and Nam Changi, Chanhoo Song, Euehun Lee, and Chan Ik Park, "Consumers' Privacy Concerns and Willingness to Provide Marketing-Related Personal Information Online," *Advances in Consumer Research* 33 (2006), pp. 213–17.

28. "Why Consumers Don't Pay: Opportunities for Digital Commerce" PaymentOne survey, conducted by Javelin Strategy & Research, December 2011.

29. A. Ant Ozok and June Wei, "An Empirical Comparison of Consumer Usability Preferences in Online Shopping Using Stationary and Mobile Devices: Results from a College Student Population," *Electronic Commerce Research* 10 (2010), pp. P111–37; and Hsi-Peng Lu and Philip Yu-Jen Su, "Factors Affecting Purchase Intention on Mobile Shopping Web Sites," *Internet Research* 19, no. 4 (2009), pp. 442–58.

30. *2012 Adobe 2012 Mobile Consumer Survey Results*, July 2012.

31. Claire Cain Miller, "Retailers Enliven Catalog Offerings Through Apps," *The New York Times*, November 20, 2011.

32. Ibid.

33. Greg Bensinger, "Amazon's Latest Delivery Stop: the Corner Store: Online Retailer Expands Use of Lockers for Package Deliveries," *The Wall Street Journal (Online)*, August 6, 2012; and Barbara Thau, "Is an Amazon Store in the Real World a Good Idea?" *Daily Finance*, August 2, 2012.

34. *Omni-Channel 2012: Cross-Channel Comes of Age, 2012 Benchmark*, RSR, June 2012.

35. Jie Zhang, Paul Farris, John Irvin, Tarun Kushwaha, Thomas Steenburgh, and Barton Weitz, "Crafting Integrated Multichannel Retailing Strategies," *Journal of Interactive Marketing*, Spring 2010, pp. 168–180.

36. "Understanding How US Online Shoppers Are Reshaping the Retail Experience," *pwc* March 2012.

37. Sebastian Van Ball and Christian Dach, "Free Riding and Customer Retention across Retailers' Channels," *Journal of Interactive Marketing* 19 (Spring 2005), pp. 75–85.

38. Stephanie Clifford, "Luring Online Shoppers Offline," *The New York Times*, July 4, 2012; Stephanie Clifford, "Electronics Retailers Scramble to Adapt to Changing Market," *The New York Times*, June 18, 2012; Suzy Sandberg, "4 Ways Retailers Can Fight Showrooming," *Mobile Commerce Daily*, March 15, 2012; and Sarah Mahoney, "Shoppers Mastering Art of Showrooming," *Marketing Daily*, March 2, 2012.

Chapter 4

1. For a detailed discussion of customer behavior, see J. Paul Peter and Jerry C. Olson, *Consumer Behavior*, 9th ed. (New York: McGraw-Hill, 2009); and Michael R. Solomon, *Consumer Behavior: Buying, Having, and Being*, 10th ed. (Upper Saddle River, NJ: Prentice Hall, 2012).

2. Mark J. Arnold and Kristy E. Reynolds (2012), "Approach and Avoidance Motivation: Investigating Hedonic Consumption in a Retail Setting," *Journal of Retailing* 88, no. 3 (September 2012), pp. 399–411; and Jason M. Carpenter and Marguerite Moore, "Utilitarian and Hedonic Shopping Value in the US Discount Sector," *Journal of Retailing and Consumer Services* 16 (January 2009), pp. 68–74.

3. Arnold and Reynolds, "Approach and Avoidance Motivation: Investigating Hedonic Consumption in a Retail Setting."

4. Jason M. Carpenter and Vikranth Balija, "Retail Format Choice in the US Consumer Electronics Market," *International Journal of Retail & Distribution Management* 38 (2010), pp. 258–74; and Kåre Skallerud, Tor Korneliussen, and Svein Ottar Olsen, "An Examination of Consumers' Cross-Shopping Behaviour," *Journal of Retailing and Consumer Services* 16 (May 2009), pp. 181–89.

5. M. P. Mueller, "Small Businesses That Understand Social Media," *The New York Times*, July 11, 2011.

6. Gauri Kulkarni, Brian Ratchford, and P. K. Kannan, "The Impact of Online and Offline Information Sources on Automobile Choice Behavior," *Journal of Interactive Marketing* 26, no. 3 (2012), pp. 167–75; Gauri Kulkarni, P. K. Kannan, and Wendy Moe, "Using Online Search Data to Forecast New Product Sales," *Decision Support Systems* 52, no. 3 (2012), pp. 604–11; and Dhruv Grewal, Anne L. Roggeveen, Larry D. Compeau, and Michael Levy, "Retail Value–Based Pricing Strategies: New Times, New Technologies, New Consumers," *Journal of Retailing*, 88, no. 1 (2012), pp. 1–6.

7. Ruth La Ferla, "The Campus as Runway," *The New York Times*, October 12, 2011; www.signature9.com/fashion/the-20-million-dollar-fashion-blog-refinery29-projects-400-revenue-growth; www.collegefashion.net; and "Quiz: Which Celebrity Is Your Style Icon?" www.collegefashion.net/inspiration/quiz-which-celebrity-is-your-style-icon/.

8. Darren W. Dahl, Jennifer J. Argo, and Andrea C. Morales. "Social Environment: The Importance of Consumption Alignment, Referent Identity, and Self-Esteem," *Journal of Consumer Research* February 2012, pp. 860–71; and Julie Nicholson, "Retail Shopping Communities Attract Shoppers, Influence Purchasing, and Retain Consumers," *ProQuest: PR Newswire*, September 9, 2009.

9. Ying Zhang, Jing Xu, Zixi Jiang, and Szu-chi Huang. "Been There, Done That: The Impact of Effort Investment on Goal Value and Consumer Motivation," *Journal of Consumer Research* 38, no. 1 (June 2011), pp. 78–93.

10. Sungha Jang, Ashutosh Prasad, and Brian T. Ratchford, "How Customers Use Product Reviews in the Purchase Decision Process," *Marketing Letters* 23, no. 3 (2012), pp. 825–38.

11. Tilottama G. Chowdhury, S. Ratneshwar, and Praggyan Mohanty, "The Time-Harried Shopper: Exploring the Differences between Maximizers and Satisficers," *Marketing Letters* 20, no. 2 (2009), pp. 155–167; Peng Huang, Nicholas H. Lurie, and Sabyasachi Mitra, "Searching for Experience on the Web: An Empirical Examination of Consumer Behavior for Search and Experience Goods," *Journal of Marketing* 73, no. 2 (2009), pp. 55–69; and Anna Lund Jepsen, "Factors Affecting Consumer Use of the Internet for Information Search," *Journal of Interactive Marketing* 21, no. 3 (2008), pp. 21–34.

12. Matt Townsend, "Retailers Woo the 'Mission Shoppers'," *Bloomberg Business Week*, November 10, 2011.

13. Think Insights with Google, "The Role of the Internet in New Car Purchases," *NetPop Research*, October 2011; and Thomas Pack, "Kicking the Virtual Tires: Car Research on the Web," *Information Today*, January 2009, p. 44.

14. Matt Townsend, "Retailers Woo the 'Mission Shoppers'," *Bloomberg Business Week*, November 10, 2011.

15. Josh Chasin, "The Impact of Digital on Path to Purchase," Measurable Marketing in the Path-To-Purchase Conference, New York University, September 28, 2012.

16. Ibid.; "Consumers Rely on Online Reviews and Price Comparisons to Make Purchase Decisions," *Lightspeed Research*, April 13, 2011; Spencer E. Ante, "How Amazon Is Turning Opinions into Gold," *BusinessWeek*, October 26, 2009, p. 47; and Tim Sander, "Business Venues Find User Reviews Have a Growing Impact on Guests," *New Media Age*, October 22, 2009, p. 9.

17. Chasin, "The Impact of Digital on Path to Purchase."

18. Jennifer Bergen, "The 10 Best Shopping Apps to Compare Prices," *PCMag.com*, November 25, 2011; Geoffrey A. Fowler and Yukari Iwatani Kane, "Price Check: Finding Deals with a Phone," *The Wall Street Journal*, December 16, 2009; and Philipp Broeckelmann and Andrea Groeppel-Klein, "Usage of Mobile Price Comparison Sites at the Point of Sale and Its Influence on Consumers' Shopping Behaviour," *International Review of Retail, Distribution and Consumer Research* 18 (May 2008), pp. 149–158.

19. Chasin, "The Impact of Digital on Path to Purchase."

20. John Lynch and Dan Ariely, "Wine Online: Search Costs Affect Competition on Price, Quality, and Distribution," *Marketing Science* 19 (Winter 2008), pp. 83–104.

626   Endnotes

21. Tammo H.A. Bijmolt and Michel van de Velden, "Multiattribute Perceptual Mapping with Idiosyncratic Brand and Attribute Sets," *Marketing Letters* 23, no. 3 (2012), pp. 585–601; and William L. Wilkie and Edgar D. Pessimier, "Issues in Marketing's Use of Multi-Attribute Attitude Models," *Journal of Marketing Research*, November 1973, pp. 428–41.

22. Tyler Mathisen, "In Geek Squad City, Dead PCs Come to Life," *CNBC*, January 19, 2012.

23. "The Power of Women and Getting Your Business Noticed," *Chicks Magazine*, June 1, 2012; and Donna Myers, "Cater to Women Shoppers, Ask What They Want," *Casual Living*, August 2009.

24. Leonardo Becchetti, Stefano Castriota, and Melania Michetti, "The Effect of Fair Trade Affiliation on Child Schooling: Evidence from a Sample of Chilean Honey Producers," *Applied Economics* 45 (September 2013), pp. 3552–63; Veronika A. Andorfer and Ulf Liebe, "Research on Fair Trade Consumption—A Review," *Journal of Business Ethics* 106 (April 2012), pp. 415–35; Iain A. Davies, Bob Doherty, and Simon Knox, "The Rise and Stall of a Fair Trade Pioneer: The Cafédirect Story," *Journal of Business Ethics* 92 (March 2010), pp. 127–147; Sandro Castaldo, Francesco Perrini, Nicola Misani, and Antonio Tencati, "The Missing Link between Corporate Social Responsibility and Consumer Trust: The Case of Fair Trade Products," *Journal of Business Ethics* 84 (January 2009), pp. 1–15; and Shih-Mei Chen and Patricia Huddleston, "A Comparison of Four Strategies to Promote Fair Trade Products," *International Journal of Retail & Distribution Management* 37, no. 4 (2009), pp. 336–345.

25. Ruby Roy Dholakia and Miao Zhao, "Retail Web Site Interactivity: How Does It Influence Customer Satisfaction and Behavioral Intentions?" *International Journal of Retail & Distribution Management* 37 (2009), pp. 821–38.

26. Brad Tuttle, "The Passive-Aggressive Way to Haggle Online: Abandon Your Shopping Cart," *Time Moneyland*, September 27, 2012; Claire Cain Miller, "Closing the Deal at the Virtual Checkout Counter," *New York Times*, October 12, 2009.

27. Josh Chasin, "The Impact of Digital on Path to Purchase," Measurable Marketing in the Path-To-Purchase Conference, New York University, September 28, 2012.

28. Deborah J. C. Brosdahl and Jason M. Carpenter, "U.S. Male Generational Cohorts: Retail Format Preferences, Desired Retail Attributes, Satisfaction and Loyalty," *Journal of Retailing and Consumer Services* 19, no. 6 (2012), pp 545–52; Jason M. Carpenter, "Consumer Shopping Value, Satisfaction and Loyalty in Discount Retailing," *Journal of Retailing and Consumer Services* 15 (September 2008), pp. 358–363; Dhruv Grewal, Ram Krishnan, and Joan Lindsey-Mullikin, "Building Store Loyalty through Service Strategies," *Journal of Relationship Marketing* 7, no. 4 (2008), pp. 341–58.

29. Charles Duhigg, "How Companies Learn Your Secrets," *The New York Times*, February 16, 2012.

30. Piyush Sharma, Bharadhwaj Sivakumaran, and Roger Marshall, "Impulse Buying and Variety Seeking: A Trait-Correlates Perspective," *Journal of Business Research* 63 (March 2010), pp. 276–83; David H. Silvera, Anne M. Lavack, and Fredric Kropp, "Impulse Buying: The Role of Affect, Social Influence, and Subjective Wellbeing," *Journal of Consumer Marketing* 25, no. 1 (2008), pp. 23–33; and Ronan De Kervenoael, D. Selcen, O. Aykac, and Mark Palmer, "Online Social Capital: Understanding E-Impulse Buying in Practice," *Journal of Retailing and Consumer Services* 16 (July 2009), pp. 320–28.

31. Dhruv Grewal, Michael Levy, and Britt Hackmann, "Making Loyalty Programs Sing," working paper, Babson College, 2012; and Yuping Liu, "The Long-Term Impact of Loyalty Programs on Consumer Purchase Behavior and Loyalty," *Journal of Marketing* 71, no. 4 (October 2007), pp. 19–35.

32. Yu Ma, Kusum L. Ailawadi, Dinesh Gauri, and Dhruv Grewal, "An Empirical Investigation of the Impact of Gasoline Prices on Grocery Shopping Behavior," *Journal of Marketing* 75 (March 2011), pp. 18–35; and Lisa Bannon and Bob Davis, "Spendthrift to Penny Pincher: A Vision of the New Consumer," *The Wall Street Journal*, December 17, 2009.

33. Anne D'Innocenzio and Rachel Beck, "In a Tough Economy, Old Stigmas Fall Away," *ABC News*, November 8, 2010.

34. Rachel Dodes, "Neiman Marcus Opens Customer Doors Wide," *The Wall Street Journal*, February 15, 2011.

35. Ma, Ailawadi, Gauri, and Grewal, "An Empirical Investigation of the Impact of Gasoline Prices on Grocery Shopping Behavior"; Christina C. Berk, "Gas Crunch Slams Brands—But Not the Ones You Think," *CNBC.com*, March 10, 2011; Stephanie Clifford and Andrew Martin, "In Time of Scrimping, Fun Stuff Is Still Selling," *The New York Times*, September 23, 2011; and Brad Tuttle. "Smart Spending: Consumer Phrase of the Day: 'Lipstick Effect,'" *Time*, April 19, 2011.

36. Pierre Chandon and Brian Wansink, "Is Food Marketing Making Us Fat? A Multi-disciplinary Review," *Foundations and Trends in Marketing* 5, no. 3 (2011), pp. 113–96; Melissa G. Bublitz, Laura A. Peracchio, and Lauren G. Block, "Why Did I Eat That? Perspectives on Food Decision Making and Dietary Restraint," *Journal of Consumer Psychology*, 20 (2012), pp. 239–58; Juliano Laran, "Goal Management in Sequential Choices: Consumer Choices for Others Are More Indulgent than Personal Choices," *Journal of Consumer Research* 37, no. 2 (August 2010), pp. 304–14; and R. K. Srivastava and Beverlee B. Anderson, "Gender Roles and Family Decision Making: A Study of Indian Automobile Purchases," *International Journal of Services, Economics and Management* 2, no. 2 (2010), pp. 109–20.

37. "Hyatt Announces Groundbreaking Children's Menu 'For Kids by Kids' and Three-Course Organic Menu Developed by Alice Waters," press release, July 16, 2012; and "Hyatt Hotels & Resorts and Babies Travel Lite Help Families Lighten Their Load by Offering Convenient Alternatives to Packing and Traveling with Baby Supplies," press release, September 22, 2008.

38. Elizabeth Holmes and Ray A. Smith, "Why Are Fitting Rooms So Awful?" *The Wall Street Journal*, April 6, 2011.

39. Kim Bhasin, "Top 20 Brands with the Most Loyal Customers," *Business Insider*, September 19, 2011.

40. Barbara Farfan (2012), "Retail Stores Brands and Chains Using Pinterest Social Media Network Pinboards: Complete List of Major Retail Pinboards on Pinterest.com Driving Traffic & Sales," *About.com Guide*.

41. JungKun Park, Frances Gunn, and Sang-Lin Han, "Multidimensional Trust Building in e-Retailing: Cross-Cultural Differences in Trust Formation and Implication for Perceived Risk," *Journal of Retailing and Consumer Services* 19 (May 2012), pp. 304–12; Vishag Badrinarayanan, Enrique Beceerra, Chung-Hyun Kim, and Sreedhar Madhavaram, "Transference and Congruence Effects on Purchase Intentions in Online Stores of Multi-Channel Retailers: Initial Evidence from the U.S. and South Korea," *Journal of Academy of Marketing Science* 40 (August 2012); Yoo-Kyoung Seock and Lauren Bailey, "Fashion Promotions in the Hispanic Market: Hispanic Consumers' Use of Information Sources in Apparel Shopping," *International Journal of Retail & Distribution Management* 37, no. 2 (2009), pp. 161–81; and Yoo-Kyoung Seock, "Influence of Retail Store Environmental Cues on Consumer Patronage

Behavior across Different Retail Store Formats: An Empirical Analysis of US Hispanic Consumers," *Journal of Retailing and Consumer Services* 16 (September 2009), pp. 329–39.

42. Hang Nguyen, "Hispanic Retailer Starts Reaching its Customers in English," *The Orange County Register*, August 22, 2012; and Julie Jargon, "Pizza Chain Seeks Slice of Bicultural Pie," *WSJ.com*, December 30, 2010.

43. Sandra M. Jones, "Wal-Mart Making Little Plans," *Chicago Tribune*, May 14, 2011; Shelly Banjo, "Can Wal-Mart Think Small?" *The Wall Street Journal*, May 17, 2012; and Ann Zimmerman, "To Boost Sales, Wal-Mart Drops One-Size-Fits-All Approach," *The Wall Street Journal*, September 7, 2006, p. A1.

44. AI Jarrah and JF Bard, "Pickup and Delivery Network Segmentation Using Contiguous Geographic Clustering," *Journal of the Operational Research Society* 62 (October 2011), pp. 1827–43; James Agarwal, Naresh K. Malhotra, and Ruth N. Bolton, "A Cross-National and Cross-Cultural Approach to Global Market Segmentation: An Application Using Consumers' Perceived Service Quality," *Journal of International Marketing* 18, no. 3 (September 2010), pp. 18–40.

45. Andrea Wilson, "Digital Anatomy of the Affluent Male," *iProspect.com*, May 2, 2012.

46. Jakob Peterson, Maurizio Gibin, Paul Longley, Pablo Mateos, Philip Atkinson, and David Ashby, "Geodemographics as a Tool for Targeting Neighbourhoods in Public Health Campaigns," *Journal of Geographical Systems* 13 (June 2011), pp. 173–92; "Óscar González-Benito, César A. Bustos-Reyes, and Pablo A. Muñoz-Gallego, "Isolating the Geodemographic Characterisation of Retail Format Choice from the Effects of Spatial Convenience," *Marketing Letters* 18, no. 1–2 (2007), pp. 45–59; Richard Harris, Peter Sleight, and Richard Webber, *Geodemographics, GIS and Neighbourhood Targeting* (Hoboken, NJ: Wiley, 2005); and Michael J. Weiss, *The Clustered World* (Boston: Little, Brown, 2000).

47. Esri, "Tapestry Segmentation Reference Guide" and "Tapestry Segmentation: The Fabric of America's Neighborhood," www.esri.com.

48. Esri, "Lifestyles-Esri Tapestry Segmentation."

49. George Anderson, "Zero Waste Grocery Store Readies for Debut," *Retail Wire*, June 30, 2011.

50. John Luciew, "Hershey Learns at Retail Stores How to Get Its Candy into Your Head," February 16, 2010.

51. Personal interviews with Helena Faulkes and Robert Price of CVS.

52. Patrik Asper, *Orderly Fashion* (Princeton, NJ: Princeton University Press, 2010); Grace I. Kunz, *Merchandising: Theory, Principles, and Practice* (New York: Fairchild, 2010); Roman Espejo, *The Fashion Industry* (Farmington Hills, MI: Greenhaven Press, 2010); and Jennifer Craik, *Fashion: The Key Concepts* (Gordonsville, VA: Berg, 2009).

53. Jenna Sauers, "How Forever 21 Keeps Getting Away with Designer Knockoffs," *Jezebel*, July 20, 2011.

54. Adam Sage, "Happy Birthday: The 'Shocking and Immoral' Bikini Hits 60," *The Times*, April 16, 2006.

55. Andrea Chang, "Virtual Fitting Rooms Changing the Clothes Shopping Experience," *Los Angeles Times*, July 13, 2012.

Chapter 5

1. See Robert M. Grant, *Contemporary Strategy Analysis*, 7th ed., (Hoboken, NJ: Wiley, 2010); Arthur Thompson, *Crafting and Executing Strategy: The Quest for Competitive Advantage: Concepts and Cases*, 17th ed. (New York: McGraw-Hill, 2010);

and David Aaker, *Strategic Market Management*, 6th ed. (New York: Wiley, 2009).

2. Roger Evered, "So What Is Strategy?" *Long Range Planning* 16 (Fall 1983), p. 120.

3. Michael E. Porter and Mark R. Kramer, "Strategy and Society: The Link between Competitive Advantage and Corporate Responsibility," *Harvard Business Review*, December 2006; Michael Porter, *On Competition* (Boston: Harvard Business School Press, 1998); and Michael Porter, "What Is Strategy?" *Harvard Business Review*, November–December 1996, pp. 61–78.

4. www.chipotle.com; Matthew Yglesias, "Chipotle Is Apple: The Burrito Chain Is Revolutionizing Food: Why Doesn't It Get More Respect?" *Slate*, February 9, 2012; and Jonathan Gold, "The Fast Food Revolutionary," *WSJ: The Magazine from the Wall Street Journal*, November 2011.

5. Gold, "The Fast Food Revolutionary."

6. www.lululemon.com; Dana Mattioli, "Lululemon's Secret Sauce," *The Wall Street Journal*, March 22, 2012; and Bryant Urstadt, "Lust for Lulu: How the Yoga Brand Lululemon Turned Fitness into a Spectator Sport," *The New York Times*, July 26, 2009.

7. Charles Blankson and John C. Crawford, "Impact of Positioning Strategies on Service Firm Performance," *Journal of Business Research* 65, no. 3 (March 2012), pp. 311–316; and 2011 Chico FAS Inc Annual Report.

8. www.savealot.com.

9. Jorge A. Vasconcellos e Sá, Fátima Olão, and Magda Pereira, "From Levitt to the Global Age: One More Time, How Do We Define Our Business?" *Management Decision* 49, no. 1 (2011), pp. 99–115; and Anthony Boardman and Aidan Vining, "Defining Your Business Using Product-Customer Matrices," *Long Range Planning* 29 (February 1996), pp. 38–48.

10. Jay Barney, David J. Ketchen Jr., and Mike Wright, "The Future of Resource-Based Theory Revitalization or Decline?" *Journal of Management*, 37 (September 2011), pp. 1299–1315; Ingrid Bonn and Josie Fisher, "Sustainability: The Missing Ingredient in Strategy," *Journal of Business Strategy*, 32 (2011), pp. 5–14; Jeffrey H. Dyer and Harbir Singh, "The Relational View: Cooperative Strategy and Sources of Interorganizational Competitive Advantage," *Academy of Management Review* 23 (October 1998), pp. 660–679; and Shelby Hunt and Robert Morgan, "The Comparative Advantage Theory of Competition," *Journal of Marketing* 59 (April 1995), pp. 1–15.

11. Karlene Lukovitz, "GMA Study: Shopper Marketing Still Siloed," *Marketing Daily*, November 3, 2009.

12. Winfrey, Oprah. Oct. 2002: Oprah. Web. 12 Dec. 2012.

13. Best Retail Brands 2011 (Intrabrand, 2011).

14. Michael S. Pepe, Russell Abratt, Paul Dion, "The Impact of Private Label Brands on Customer Loyalty and Product Category Profitability," *Journal of Product & Brand Management*, 20, 1, 2011, pp.27–36 and Nawel Amrouche and Georges Zaccour, "Shelf-Space Allocation of National and Private Brands," *European Journal of Operational Research* 180, no. 2 (2007), pp. 648–663.

15. Simon Clatworthy, "Bridging the Gap between Brand Strategy and Customer Experience," *Managing Service Quality* 22, no. 2 (2012), pp. 108–127; and Bo Edvardsson, Bård Tronvoll, and Thorsten Gruber, "Expanding Understanding of Service Exchange and Value Co-Creation: A Social Construction Approach," *Journal of the Academy of Marketing Science* 39 (2011), pp. 327–339.

16. http://www.nist.gov/baldrige/profiles.cfm.

628 Endnotes

17. William Langley, "Ikea: An Empire Built on Self-assembly," *London Telegraph*, October 9, 2010.

18. Carmine Gallo, "How the Ritz-Carlton Inspired the Apple Store," *Forbes*, April 10, 2012; and Carmine Gallo, "Employee Motivation the Ritz-Carlton Way," *Business-Week*, February 29, 2008.

19. Kyung Hoon Kima, Byung Joo Jeon, Hong Seob Jung, Wei Lu, and Joseph Jones, "Effective Employment Brand Equity Through Sustainable Competitive Advantage, Marketing Strategy, and Corporate Image," *Journal of Business Research*, November 2011, pp. 1207–1211; Lars Meyer-Waarden and Christophe Benavent, "Grocery Retail Loyalty Program Effects: Self-Selection or Purchase Behavior Change?" *Journal of the Academy of Marketing Science* 37 (September 2009), pp. 345–335; and Russell Lacey, "Limited Influence of Loyalty Program Membership on Relational Outcomes," *Journal of Consumer Marketing*, 26, no. 6 (2009), pp. 392–402.

20. Melanie E. Zaglia, "Brand Communities Embedded in Social Networks," *Journal of Business Research*, August 2012; Lisa Harris and Charles Dennis, "Engaging Customers on Facebook: Challenges for E-Retailers," *Journal of Consumer Behaviour* 10, no. 6 (2011), pp. 338–346; and Constance Elise Porter, Naveen Donthu, William H. Macelroy, and Donna Wydra, "How to Foster and Sustain Engagement in Virtual Communities," *California Management Review*, 53, no. 4 (2011), pp. 80–110.

21. Nehal Hesham, "My Starbucks Idea [Case Study]," March 18, 2012.

22. http://mystarbucksidea.force.com/; and Hesham, "My Starbucks Idea [Case Study]."

23. G. N. Nyaga and J. M. Whipple, "Relationship Quality and Performance Outcomes: Achieving a Sustainable Competitive Advantage," *Journal of Business Logistics*, 32 (2011), pp. 345–360.

24. Christie Swanson, "Walmart's Unique Relationships," *101 Ventures*, May 27, 2012.

25. Nyaga and Whipple, "Relationship Quality and Performance Outcomes"; and Murali Mantrala, Suman Basuroy, and Shailendra Gajanan, "Do Style-Goods Retailer's Demands for Guaranteed Profit Margins Unfairly Exploit Vendors?" *Marketing Letters* 16, no. 1 (2005), pp. 53–66.

26. David Lei and John Slocum Jr., "Strategic and Organizational Requirements for Competitive Advantage," *Academy of Management Executive*, February 2005, pp. 31–46.

27. Zeynep Ton, "Why 'Good Jobs' Are Good for Retailers," *Harvard Business Review*, January–February 2012; and T. Russell Crook, Samuel Y. Todd, James G. Woehr; and David J. Ketchen Jr., "Does Human Capital Matter? A Meta-Analysis of the Relationship between Human Capital and Firm Performance," *Journal of Applied Psychology* 96, no. 3 (2011), pp. 443–456.

28. Petra Schubert, Susan P. Williams, and Ralf Woelfle, "Sustainable Competitive Advantage in E-Commerce and the Role of the Enterprise System," *International Journal of Enterprise Information Systems*, 7 (April–June 2011), pp. 1–17; Richard Cuthbertson, Gerd Islei, Peter Franke, and Balkan Cetinkaya, "What Will the Best Retail Supply Chains Look Like in the Future?" *European Retail Digest*, Summer 2006, pp. 7–15; and "Competitive Advantage through Supply-Chain Innovation," *Logistics & Transport Focus*, December 2004, pp. 56–59.

29. *The Great Indian Bazaar* (New York: McKinsey, 2008).

30. Vaidyanathan Jayaraman and Luo Yadong, "Creating Competitive Advantages through New Value Creation:

A Reverse Logistics Perspective," *Academy of Management Perspectives* 21, no. 2 (2007), pp. 56–73; and David Bryce and Jeffrey H. Dyer, "Strategies to Crack: Well-Guarded Markets," *Harvard Business Review* 85, no. 5 (2007), pp. 84–92.

31. Julie Jargon, "How McDonald's Hit the Spot," *The Wall Street Journal*, December 13, 2011.

32. Igor Ansoff, "Strategies for Diversification," *Harvard Business Review*, 35 (September–October 1957), pp. 113–124.

33. Janet Adamy, "Dunkin' Donuts Whips Up a Recipe for Expansion," *The Wall Street Journal*, May 3, 2007, p. B1.

34. www.tescocorporate.com/.

35. Andrew Sorkin and Michael De La Merced, "Home Depot Sells a Unit That Never Fit," *The New York Times*, June 20, 2007, p. C1; Andrew Sorkin and Michael De La Merced, "Home Depot Supply Unit May Be Sold," *The New York Times*, February 13, 2007, p. C1.

36. "2012 Global Powers of Retailing," *Stores*, January 2012, pp. G17–G21.

37. Frank Badillo, "Global Retail Outlook," *Retail Forward*, May 2009; and *2009 Global Retail Development Index* (New York: Kearney, 2009).

38. Hana Ben-Shabat, Helen Rhim, Mike Moriarity, and Fabiola Salman, *Global Retail Expansion Keeps Moving—2012* (New York: ATKearney, 2012).

39. Deepika Jhamb and Ravi Kiran, "Emerging Trends of Organized Retailing in India: A Shared Vision of Consumers and Retailers Perspective," *Middle-East Journal of Scientific Research*, 11, no. 4, (2012), pp. 481–490.

40. Malavika Sharma, "With Wal-Mart Locked Out, India's Billionaires Rush In," *Bloomberg Businessweek*, July 5, 2012; "The Supermarket's Last Frontier," *The Economist*, December 3, 2011; and Egha Bahree, "India Unlocks Door for Global Retailers," *The Wall Street Journal*, November 25, 2011.

41. Alex Lawson, "Analysis: Retailing in China," *Retail Week*, April 20, 2012; and Robert A. Rogowsky, "China Retail Market Booming and Evolving," *China Daily*, August 3, 2012, pp. 2–12.

42. www.transparency.org/country#RUS.

43. Don Lee, "A Chinese Lesson for Big Retailers," *Los Angeles Times*, July 2, 2006; Peter N. Child, "Lessons from a Global Retailer: An Interview with the President of Carrefour China," *McKinsey Quarterly*, 2006; and "Company Spotlight: Carrefour," *MarketWatch: Global Round-Up* 6, no. 4 (2007), pp. 67–72.

44. "India Retail: Foreign Chains Eye the Potential, But Will They Succeed?" *Knowledge at INSTEAD*, May 28, 2007, quotation from Paddy Padmanabhan.

45. www.carrefour.com.

46. Michael R. Czinkota and Ilkka A. Ronkainen, *International Marketing*, 9th ed. (Mason, OH: Thomson South-Western, 2009).

47. www.marksandspencer.com.

48. Donald Lehman and Russell Winer, *Analysis for Marketing Planning*, 7th ed. (Burr Ridge, IL: McGraw-Hill/Irwin, 2007).

49. Linda Stallworth Williams, "The Mission Statement," *Journal of Business Communication* 45, no. 2 (2008), pp. 94–119.

50. Personal communications.

51. Tony Grundy, "Rethinking and Reinventing Michael Porter's Five Forces Model," *Strategic Change* 15, no. 5 (2006), pp. 213–229; Michael Porter, "Strategy and the Internet," *Harvard Business Review*, March 2001, pp. 63–78;

and Michael Porter, *Competitive Strategy* (New York: The Free Press, 1980).

52. Susan Reda, "Sights Set on the Subcontinent," *Stores*, September 2006.

Chapter 6

1. www.Target.com.
2. Ricardo Lopez, "It's Doing Well by Doing Good," *Los Angeles Times*, January 25, 2012, p. B.1.
3. www.macysinc.com/about-us/macysinc-history/macys-a-history/default.aspx.

Chapter 7

1. eData, International Council of Shopping Centers.
2. Keith Schneider, "Cleveland Turns Uptown into New Downtown," *The New York Times*, November 2011, p. B.7; and Sue Halpern, "Mayor of Rust," *The New York Times Magazine*, February 13, 2011, pp. 30–35.
3. David Bornstein, "Conquering Food Deserts with Green Carts," *The New York Times*, April 18, 2012; and Terry Pristin, "With a Little Help, Greens Come to Low-Income Neighborhoods," *The New York Times*, June 17, 2009, p. B6.
4. Stephanie Clifford, "Retailers' Idea: Think Smaller in Urban Push," *The New York Times*, July 25, 2012; and Shan Li, "Target Plans Another Urban-Format Store for Los Angeles," *Los Angeles Times*, May 1, 2012.
5. "The Five Most Famous Shopping Streets in the World," *Partyearth.com*, June 24, 2012.
6. Clifford, "Retailers' Idea: Think Smaller in Urban Push"; and Li, "Target Plans Another Urban-Format Store for Los Angeles."
7. Matthew E. Kures and William F. Ryan, "Challenges of an Organizational Approach to Downtown Market Analysis," *Applied Geography* 32, no. 1 (January 2012), pp. 80–87; and Kent A. Robertson, "The Main Street Approach to Downtown Development: An Examination of the Four-Point Program," *Journal of Architectural and Planning Research* 21, no. 1 (Spring 2004), pp. 55–78.
8. eData at www.icsc.org.
9. "A Brief History of Shopping Centers," International Council of Shopping Centers, June 2000.
10. eData at www.icsc.org.
11. http://history.sandiego.edu/gen/soc/shoppingcenter.html; and www.icsc.org/srch/sct/sct0707/center_stage_art_deco.php.
12. A.D. Pruitt, "A Strip-Mall Revival," *The Wall Street Journal*, September 26, 2012, p. C.11.
13. "A Brief History of Shopping Center," ICSC, June 2000.
14. "Retail Innovations," *About.com*.
15. Brandon Rogoff, "The Performance of U.S. Shopping Centers," *ICSC Research Review* 16, no. 1 (2009), pp. 8–10.
16. "Largest Shopping Malls in the United States," American Studies at Eastern Connecticut State University, April 25, 2009, http://nutmeg.easternct.edu/~pocock/MallsLarge.htm.
17. Kate Murphy, "Revitalizing a Dead Mall (Don't Expect Shoppers)," *The Wall Street Journal*, October 30, 2012; and Kris Hudson, "The Malaise Afflicting America's Malls," *The Wall Street Journal*, March 1, 2012.
18. Kris Hudson, "Malls Make Way for Grocers," *The Wall Street Journal*, August 5, 2012; and Andrea Chang, "Malls Are Morphing into One-Stop Shops," *Los Angeles Times*, November 12, 2011.
19. Jeff Mitchell, "Northridge Mall in Salinas Aims to Capture Latino Customers," *The Californian*, March 9, 2012; and

David Ferry, "Land Battle Stirs Richmond," *The Wall Street Journal*, June 16, 2011.
20. Shelley DuBois, "The American Mall: Back from the Dead," *Fortune*, February 15, 2011.
21. Maria Matzer Rose, "Easton Shuffle," *Columbus Dispatch*, January 31, 2010; and Tim Feran, "Easton Town Center Has Become Such a Popular Fixture, It's Hard to Remember That Its Concept Was a Risky Decision," *Columbus Dispatch*, July 5, 2009.
22. www.icsc.org/srch/lib/Mixed-use_Definition.pdf.
23. www.miznerpark.com/.
24. Sascha M. Pardy, "Outlet Centers Rise to the Top during Recession," *COStar Group News*, September 30, 2009.
25. Jane L. Levere, "Come for the Prices. Stay for the Movie," *The New York Times*, October 22, 2008.
26. Janie Makan, "10 Things Outlet Malls Won't Tell You," *Smart Money*, November 1, 2010.
27. Eliot Brown, "As Urban Centers Rebound, Some Themed Marketplaces Appear Generic and Dated," *The Wall Street Journal*, March 9, 2012.
28. www.simon.com/mall/default.aspx?id=857.
29. Stephanie Clifford and Peter Lattman, "Toys 'R' Us, in a Box," *The New York Times*, April 7, 2012, p. B.1; Peter Evans, "Pop-Up Shops Go Mainstream," *The Wall Street Journal*, September 3, 2012; Tiffany Hsu, "Toys R Us to Open Holiday Pop-Up Shops in Macy's," *Los Angeles Times*, October 10, 2012; and David Kaplan, "A Permanent Trend Of Pop-Up Shops," *McClatchy-Tribune Business News*, December 3, 2011.
30. Doug Stephens, "Temporary Retailing in a Pop-Up World," *Retail Prophet*, February 27, 2012.
31. "The Economic Incentives of the 'Store-within-a-Store' Retail Model," *Knowledge@Wharton*, September 2, 2009.
32. "Stores within Stores: Retail's Savior?" *Fortune*, January 24, 2011; Mercedes Cardona, "Ten Retailers Turning Department Stores into Mini-Malls," *AOL*, November 10, 2010.
33. "Store-Within-A-Store Operating Models," www.floradelaney.com/2011, May 26, 2011; and Karen Talle, "Sears Seeks Trendier 'Vibe' with Forever 21," *The Wall Street Journal*, September 22, 2010.
34. Emily Glazer, "Retail Shopping Is Taking Off at the Airport," *Wall Street Journal*, June 30, 2012; Michael Luongo, "Holiday Shopping on the Fly," *New York Times*, December 10, 2012.
35. Jane L. Levere, "At Kennedy, Shopping and Dining, Followed by a Takeoff," *The New York Times*, July 30, 2008.
36. PBS, "Store Wars: When Wal-Mart Comes to Town," www.pbs.org/itvs/storewars/.
37. "Nation of Shop Critics," *The Economist*, January 21, 2012.
38. Matt Rosenberg, "Zoning: Residential, Commercial, or Industrial?" *Ask.com*, Geography.

Chapter 8

1. Industry Fun Facts, International Council of Shopping Centers.
2. "Annual Estimates of the Population of Metropolitan and Micropolitan Statistical Areas: April 1, 2010 to July 1, 2011," U.S. Census Bureau.
3. Ibid.
4. www.icuracao.com.
5. www.partycity.com.
6. Wendell Cox and Steven Malanga, "California—Toxic for Business," *Los Angeles Times*, November 14, 2011.

7. Thomas J. Holmes, "The Diffusion of Wal-Mart and Economies of Density," *Econometrica* 79, no. 1 (January 2011, pp, 253–302.

8. Patricia Schaefer, "Your Franchise Territory: Cause for Comfort or Conflict?" *FranchiseKnowHow*, October 2010.

9. Christopher Teller and Jonathan R. Elms, "Urban Place Marketing and Retail Agglomeration Customers," *Journal of Marketing Management* 28, no. 5-6 (2012), pp. 546–567; and Ellen Sewell, "Competition and Dealership Agglomeration in New Car Markets," *Applied Economics Letters* 18, no. 13 (2011), pp. 1279–1283.

10. www.themallincolumbia.com/.

11. www.census.gov/mso/www/c2000basics/chapter1.htm.

12. http://www.census.gov/geo/reference/pdfs/GARM/Ch11GARM.pdf.

13. http://www.census.gov/popest/index.html.

14. http://www.esri.com/library/fliers/pdfs/tapestry_segmentation.pdf.

15. David L. Huff, "Defining and Estimating a Trade Area," *Journal of Marketing* 28 (1964), pp. 34–38; and David L. Huff and William Black, "The Huff Model in Retrospect," *Applied Geographic Studies* 1, no. 2 (1997), pp. 22–34.

16. Giuseppe Bruno and Gennaro Improta, "Using Gravity Models for the Evaluation of New University Site Locations: A Case Study," *Computers & Operations Research* 35, no. 2 (2008), pp. 436–444; and Tammy Drezner and Zvi Drezner, "Validating the Gravity-Based Competitive Location Model Using Inferred Attractiveness," *Annals of Operations Research* 111 (March 2002), pp. 227–241.

17. "Top Ten Issues in Co-Tenancy Provisions In Retail Lease," www.coxcastle.com/publications/article.cfm?id=44.

18. Marc Betesh and Nancy Davids, "Negotiating Common Area Maintenance Costs," *Probate and Property*, May/June 2009, pp. 40–45.

Chapter 9

1. Kevin Ready, "What Sam Walton And China's Lao Tzu Can Teach You About Team Building," *Forbes*, June 11, 2012.

2. Susan Jackson and Randall Schuler, *Managing Human Resources through Strategic Relationships*, 10th ed. (Mason, OH: Southwestern, 2008), p. 12.

3. Zeynep Toy, "Why Good Jobs are Good for Retailers," *Harvard Business Review*, January–February 2012.

4. David Segal, "Apple's Retail Army, Long on Loyalty but Short on Pay," *The New York Times*, June 23, 2012.

5. Kevin Kruse, "What is Employee Engagement?" *Forbes*, June 26, 2012; Scott Sonenshein and Utpal Dholakia, "Explaining Employee Engagement with Strategic Change Implementation: A Meaning-Making Approach," *Organization Science* 23, 1 (2012), pp. 1–23; Catherine Baumgardner and Jennifer L. Myers, "Employee Engagement, and Why It Is Important," *The Encyclopedia of Human Resource Management: HR Forms and Job Aids*, 2012, pp. 202–204; Amanda Shantz, Kerstin Alfes, Catherine Truss, and Emma C. Soane, "The Role of Employee Engagement in the Relationship between Job Design and Task Performance, Citizenship and Deviant Behaviours," *International Journal of Human Resource Management*, 2012; and Timothy D. Ludwig and Christopher B. Frazier, "Employee Engagement and Organizational Behavior Management," *Journal of Organizational Behavior Management* 32, 1 (2012), pp. 75–82.

6. Emma Soane, Katie Truss, and Alfes Kerstin, "Development and Application of a New Measure of Employee Engagement: The ISA Engagement Scale," *Human Resource Development International*, 2012; and Emma Soane, K. Alfes, K. Truss, C. Rees, and M. Gatenby. "Employee Engagement: Measure Validation and Associations with Individual Level Outcomes," *Human Resource Development International*, 2013.

7. Kruse, "What is Employee Engagement."

8. Alexandra Marks, "Cracking Down on Employers who Ignore Wage Laws," *The Christian Science Monitor*, June 2, 2005.

9. Ton, "Why 'Good Jobs' Are Good for Retailers"; and Jeffrey Pfeffer, *What Were They Thinking? Unconventional Wisdom about Management* (Boston: Harvard Business School Press, 2007).

10. "Retail Employees by Occupation, Age, and Education," National Retail Federation, http://www.nrf.com/modules.php?name=Pages&sp_id=1245.

11. Marshall L. Fisher and Ananth Raman, *The New Science of Retailing: How Analytics Are Transforming the Supply Chain and Performance.* (Cambridge, MA: Harvard Business School Press, 2010).

12. Ibid.

13. Ibid.

14. Steven Greenhouse, "A Part-Time Life, as Hours Shrink and Shift," *The New York Times*, October 27, 2012.

15. "Retail Employees by Occupation, Age, and Education," In Retail Insights Center. National Retail Federation: New York, 2012.

16. Samuel Bacharach, "Gen-Y Employees: How to Motivate Them," *Inc*, August 14, 2012; Leslie Kwoh, "More Firms Bow to Generation Y's Demands," *The Wall Street Journal*, August 22, 2012; and David Solnet, Anna Kralj, and Jay Kandampully, "Generation Y Employees: An Examination of Work Attitude Differences," *Journal of Applied Management and Entrepreneurship* 17, no. 3 (2012), pp. 36–45.

17. Boris B. Baltes and Lisa M. Finkelstein, "Special Issue: Contemporary Empirical Advancements in the Study of Aging in the Workplace," *Journal of Organizational Behavior* 32, no. 2 (2011), pp. 151–369; and Glen Llopis, "5 Ways Young Professionals Want To Be Led," *Forbes*, March 12, 2012.

18. "Retail Employees by Occupation, Age, and Education," National Retail Federation.

19. Rhokeun Park, "Attitudes of Group Incentive Participants: The Moderating Role of Human Capital Level," *Group & Organization Management*, August 30, 2012; Claudio Feser, "The Limits of Monetary Incentives," *CEO Magazine*, February 3, 2012; and Bruce J. Avolio, "Leadership, Individual Differences, and Work-Related Attitudes: A Cross-Culture Investigation," *Applied Psychology: An International Review* 56, no. 2 (2007), pp. 212–230.

20. Peter J Dowling, and Noelle Donnelly, "Managing People in Global Markets—The Asia Pacific Perspective." *Journal of World Business*, 2012; Evangeline O'Regan, "Spain Hampered by Rigid Labor Laws," *USA Today*, June 11, 2012; and Les Leopold, "Europe's Amazing Vacation Laws," *Salon*, July 5, 2012.

21. David G. Collings, "International Human Resource Management: Policies and Practices for Multinational Enterprises," *International Journal of Human Resource Management* 23, 7 (2012), pp. 1509–1511; and Susan Schneider and Rosalie Tung, "Introduction to International Human Resource Management Special Issue," *Journal of World Business* 36, no. 4 (2011), pp. 341–345.

22. www.mellerio.fr; and "Business Antiquities," *The Wall Street Journal*, November 17, 1999.

23. "Retail Employees by Occupation, Age, and Education," In Retail Insights Center. National Retail Federation: New York, 2012.

24. Arielle Kas, "Home Depot Centralizes In-Store Hiring Process," *Atlanta Journal-Constitution*, March 11, 2011.

25. Adam Bryant, "Knock-Knock: It's the C.E.O.," *The New York Times*, April 12, 2009.

26. Personal communication.

27. Wim Elving, Jorinde Westhoff, Kelta Meeusen, and Jan-Willem Schoonderbeek, "The War for Talent & Quest; The Relevance of Employer Branding in Job Advertisements for Becoming an Employer of Choice," *Journal of Brand Management*, Apr/May 2013, Vol. 20 Issue 5, pp. 355–373; Tobias Schlager, Mareike Bodderas, Peter Maas, and Joël Luc Cachelin. "The Influence of the Employer Brand on Employee Attitudes Relevant for Service Branding: An Empirical Investigation," *Journal of Services Marketing* 25, no. 7 (2011), pp. 497–508; Bernard Kunerth and Richard Mosley, "Applying Employer Brand Management to Employee Engagement," *Strategic HR Review* 10, no. 3 (2011), pp. 19–26; and Carley Foster, Khanyapuss Punjaisri, and Ranis Cheng, "Exploring the Relationship between Corporate, Internal and Employer Branding," *Journal of Product & Brand Management* 19, no. 6 (2010), pp. 401–409.

28. Susan E Myrden and E. Kevin Kelloway, "Employer Branding: Winning the War for Talent." *Marketing Theory and Applications*, 2012, Volume 9, issue 1, pp. 40–51; Simone Hochegger and Ralf Terlutter, "Why Organizations Systematically Engage in Employer Branding: A Conceptual Framework," *Advances in Advertising Research* (Vol. III), 2012, pp. 403–419; and Timothy M. Gardner, Niclas L. Erhardt, and Carlos Martin-Rios, "Rebranding Employment Branding: Establishing a New Research Agenda to Explore the Attributes, Antecedents, and Consequences of Workers' Employment Brand Knowledge," in Joshi Aparna, Hui Liao, and Joseph J. Martocchio (Eds.), *Research in Personnel and Human Resources Management, Volume 30* (Bingley, UK: Emerald Group Publishing Limited, 2012), pp. 253–304.

29. Sue Stock, "Jumping through Hoops for a Retail Sales Job," *Los Angeles Times*, September 8, 2010, p. B.4.

30. "The Happy Wackiness of Zappos.com," *ABC News*, October 26, 2011.

31. Sonia Wadhwa, "Employee Engagement through Collaborative Learning," *Training & Development* 39, no. 4 (2012), pp. 12–22; Guy Millar, "Employee Engagement–A New Paradigm," *Human Resource Management International Digest* 20, no. 2 (2012): pp. 3–5; and Alexander Ellinger, Carolyn Casey Findley Musgrove, Andrea D. Ellinger, Daniel G. Bachrach, and Yu-Lin Wang, "Influences of Organizational Investments in Social Capital on Service Employee Commitment and Performance," *Journal of Business Research*, April, 2012.

32. www.rei.com.

33. www.containerstore.com.

34. Sarah Kessler, "Inside Starbucks's $35 Million Mission to Make Brand Evangelists of Its Front-Line Workers," *Fast Company*, October 22, 2012.

35. Rebecca Johnson, Ramona Houmanfar, and Gregory Smith, "The Effect of Implicit and Explicit Rules on Customer Greeting and Productivity in a Retail Organization," *Journal of Organizational Behavior Management* 30, no. 1 (2010). pp. 38–48.

36. www.searcquotes.com.

37. Angela Chen, "Culture and Compensation—Unpicking the Intricate Relationship between Reward and Organizational Culture," *Thunderbird School of International Management*, 52, no. 3 (2010), pp. 189–202.

38. Xiaomin Cui and Junchen Hu, "A Literature Review on Organization Culture and Corporate Performance," *International Journal of Business Administration* 3, no. 2 (2012), pp. 28–45; Ashly Pinnington, "Chapter13: Organizational Culture." In *Key Issues in Organizational Communication*. 2012, pp. 205–230; Mats Alvesson, "Organizational Culture." In *The Handbook of Organizational Culture and Climate*, 2010, pp. 11–38; and Edgar H. Schein, "What Is Culture?" *Sociology of Organizations: Structures and Relationships*, 2011, pp. 311–342.

39. Lauren Skinner Beitelspacher, Glenn Richey, and Kristy Reynolds. "Exploring a New Perspective on Service Efficiency: Service Culture in Retail Organizations," *Journal of Services Marketing*, 25, no. 3 (2011), pp. 215–228; John Meyer, Tracy Hecht, Harjinder Gill, and Laryssa Toplonytsky, "Person–Organization Culture Fit and Employee Commitment under Conditions of Organizational Change: A Longitudinal Study," *Journal of Vocational Behavior* 76, no. 3 (2010), pp. 458–447; Cynthia Webster and Allyn White, "Exploring the National and Organizational Culture Mix and Service Firms," *Journal of the Academy of Marketing Science* 38, no. 6 (2010), pp. 691–703; and Wei Zheng, Baiyin Yang, and Gary Mclean, "Linking Organizational Culture, Structure, Strategy, and Organizational Effectiveness: Mediating Role of Knowledge Management," *Journal of Business Research* 63, no. 7 (2010), pp. 763–771.

40. www.wholefoodsmarket.com.

41. Sam Walton and John Huey. *Sam Walton: Made in America*. Bantam: New York, 2012.

42. Seyyed Ebrahim Sadati, "A Survey Relation of Organizational Culture and Organizational Citizenship Behavior with Employees' Empowerment," *Management Science* 2 (2012); Antonis Simintiras, Alan Watkins, Kemefasu Ifie, and Konstantinos Georgakas, "Individual and Contextual Influences on the Affective Commitment of Retail Salespeople," *Journal of Marketing Management* 28, no. 11–12 (2012), pp. 1377–1398; M. Travis Maynard, Lucy Gilson, and John Mathieu, "Empowerment—Fad or Fab? A Multilevel Review of the Past Two Decades of Research," *Journal of Management* 38, no. 4 (2012), pp. 1231–1281; and Beom Kim, Gyumin Lee, Suzanne Murrmann, and Thomas R. George, "Motivational Effects of Empowerment on Employees' Organizational Commitment," *Cornell Hospitality Quarterly* 53, no. 1 (2012), pp. 10–19.

43. Personal communication with Chet Cadieux, president and CEO of Quik Trip; John Lofstock, "Applauding the QT Culture," *Convenience Store Decisions*, April 2007, pp. 20–24.

44. Personal communication with authors.

45. Maria Halkias, "Penney Remakes Culture to Remake Image," *Dallas Morning News*, February 12, 2007.

46. Leslie Kwoh, "Firms Resist New Pay-Equity Roles," *The Wall Street Journal*, June 26, 2012; and Forbes CEO Compensation, April 4, 2012.

47. Personal communication.

48. Anne Schwartz, "Leadership Development in a Global Environment: Lessons Learned from One of the World's Largest Employers," *Industrial And Commercial Training*, 43, no. 1 (2011), pp. 13–16; and William Siebert Stanley and J. T. Addison, "Internal Labour Markets: Causes and

632   Endnotes

Consequences," *Oxford Review of Economic Policy* 7, no. 1 (2011), pp. 76–92.

49. Sue Shellenbarger, "Perking Up: Some Companies Offer Surprising New Benefits," *The Wall Street Journal*, March 18, 2009.

50. James Breaugh and Angela Farabee, "Telecommuting and Flexible Work Hours: Alternative Work Arrangements That Can Improve the Quality of Work Life," *Work and Quality of Life*, 2012, pp. 251–274.

51. Erin L. Kelly, Phyllis Moen, and Eric Tranby, "Changing Workplaces to Reduce Work-Family Conflict: Schedule Control in a White-Collar Organization," *American Sociological Review*, 76, no. 2 (2011), pp. 265–290.

52. Andrea Davis, "Whole Foods Take Benefits to a Vote," *Retail Wire*, March 29, 2012.

53. Jeff Bullas, "How Best Buy Energized 170,000 Employees With Social Media."

54. Sandy Smith, "All for One," *Stores*, November 2010; Jie Shen, Ashok Chanda, Brian D'Netto, and Manjit Monga, "Managing Diversity through Human Resource Management: An International Perspective and Conceptual Framework," *International Journal of Human Resource Management* 20, no. 2 (2009), pp. 235–251.

55. Gill Kirton and Anne-Marie Greene, *The Dynamics of Managing Diversity*. Oxford: Routledge, 2012.

56. "2012 Top Women in Grocery," *Progressive Grocer*, June 2012.

57. "80 Most Influential People in Sales and Marketing," *Sales & Marketing Management*, October 1998, p. 78.

58. Paul Davidson, "More American Workers Sue Employers for Overtime Pay," *USA Today*, April 19, 2012, pp. 2–12.

59. "Union Membership News Release," Bureau of Labor Statistics, January 23, 2013.

60. "Crowd Management Safety Guidelines for Retailers," OSHA Fact Sheet, 2012.

61. Paul Dolan, Richard Edlin, Aki Tsuchiya, and Allan Wailoo, "It Ain't What You Do, It's the Way That You Do It: Characteristics of Procedural Justice and Their Importance in Social Decision-Making," *Journal of Economic Behavior and Organization* 64, no. 1 (2007), pp. 157–170.

Chapter 10

1. Paige Baltzan, *Information Systems*, 2nd ed. (New York: McGraw-Hill, 2013); and Donald Bowersox, David Closs, and M. Bixby Cooper, *Supply Chain Logistics Management*, 4th ed. (New York: McGraw-Hill, 2013).

2. *Global Responsibility Report*, Walmart, 2012; http://corporate. walmart.com/global-responsibility/environment-sustainability/ global-responsibility-report.

3. Bob Trebilcock, "Creating Competitive Advantage," *Supply Chain Management Review* 16, no. 6 (November 2012), pp. S61–S62, S62–S67.

4. Zinn Walter and Peter C. Liu, "A Comparison of Actual and Intended Consumer Behavior in Response to Retail Stockouts," *Journal of Business Logistics* 29, no. 2 (2011), pp. 141–159; and Sanjay Puligadda, William T. Ross, Jinje Chen, and Elizabeth Howlett, "When Loyalties Clash Purchase Behavior When a Preferred Brand Is Stocked Out: The Tradeoff between Brand and Store Loyalty," *Journal of Retailing and Consumer Services*, 2012.

5. "Bar Codes Change the Way Retailers Stocked, Priced Products," *Boston Globe*, June 29, 2004, p. C1.

6. Constance Hays, "What Walmart Knows about Customers' Habits," *The New York Times*, November 14, 2004, p. C1.

7. Sriram Narayanan, Ann S. Marucheck, and Robert B. Handfield, "Electronic Data Interchange: Research Review and Future Directions," *Decision Sciences* 40, no. 1 (2009), pp. 121–163.

8. Council of Supply Chain Management Professionals, http://cscmp.org/.

9. Walmart, "U.S. Logistics," http://corporate.walmart.com/ our-story/our-stores/logistics.

10. Megan Rose, "Mind-Blowing Facts about Amazon's Giant Shipping Operations," *Business Insider*, November 26, 2012.

11. Ibid.

12. Kathleen Guion, "Operational Improvements Benefit Employees, Customers," *MMR*, May 17, 2010, p. 10.

13. www.businessdictionary.com/definition/freight-forwarder. html.

14. Oliver E. Williamson, "Outsourcing: Transaction Cost Economics and Supply Chain Management," *Journal of Supply Chain Management* 44, no. 2 (1972), pp. 5–16; Salla Lutza and Thomas Ritter, "Outsourcing, Supply Chain Upgrading and Connectedness of a Firm's Competencies," *Industrial Marketing Management* 38 (May 2009), pp. 387–393; and Erin Anderson and Barton Weitz, "Make or Buy Decisions: Vertical Integration and Marketing Productivity," *Sloan Management Review* 27 (Spring 1986), pp. 3–19.

15. John Hagel III and John Brown, "From Push to Pull: Emerging Models for Mobilizing Resources," *Journal of Service Science*, 2011, pp. 93–110; and Huaqin Zhang and Guojie Zhao, "Strategic Selection of Push-Pull Supply," *Modern Applied Science* 2, no. 1 (2008).

16. John Dawson and Susan Shaw, "Horizontal Competition in Retailing and the Structure of Manufacturer-Retailer Relationships," in Luca Pellegrini and Srinvas Reddy (Eds), *Retail and Marketing Channels* (Routledge, 2012, pp. 4–7; 2 and Andreas Otto, Franz Josef Schoppengerd, and Ramin Shariatmadari, *Direct Store Delivery: Concepts, Applications and Instruments* (New York: Springer, 2009).

17. "Direct Store Delivery versus Centralized Distribution," MWLPV International, 2013.

18. Ibid.

19. Hing Kai Chan, Shizhao Yin, and Felix Chan, "Implementing Just-in-Time Philosophy to Reverse Logistics Systems: A Review," *International Journal of Production Research* 48, no. 21 (2010), pp. 6293–6313; Eric Jack, Thomas Powers, and Lauren Skinner, "Reverse Logistics Capabilities: Antecedents and Cost Savings," *International Journal of Physical Distribution & Logistics Management*, 40, no. 3 (2010), pp. 228–246; and Michael Bernon, Silvia Rossi, and John Cullen, "Retail Reverse Logistics: A Call and Grounding Framework for Research," *International Journal of Physical Distribution & Logistics Management* 41, no. 5 (2011), pp. 484–510.

20. Jack, Powers, and Skinner, "Reverse Logistics Capabilities: Antecedents and Cost Savings."

21. V. G. Venkatesh, "Reverse Logistics: An Imperative Area of Research for Fashion Supply Chain," *IUP Journal of Supply Chain Management*, March 2010, pp. 77–89.

22. Jack, Powers, and Skinner, "Reverse Logistics Capabilities: Antecedents and Cost Savings."

23. W. K. Chiang and Y. Feng, "Retailer or E-tailer? Strategic Pricing and Economic-lot-size Decisions in a Competitive Supply Chain with Drop-Shipping," *Operations Research Management Science* 52, no. 4 (2012); "Top 12 Drop-Shipping Best Practices," *Multichannel Merchant*, October 27, 2009;

Karen E. Klein, "How Drop-Shipping Works for Retailers and Manufacturers," *BusinessWeek*, September 23, 2009; and Elliot Rabinovich, Manus Rungtusanatham, and Timothy M. Laseter, "Physical Distribution Service Performance and Internet Retailer Margins: The Drop-Shipping Context," *Journal of Operations Management* 26 (November 2008), pp. 767–781.

24. Keith Regan, "Toys 'R' Us Wins Right to End Amazon Partnership," *E-Commerce Times*, March 3, 2006.

25. Phil Mahba, "Macy's CEO Sees Stores Borrowing Ideas from Online," *Bloomberg Business Week*, April 12, 2012.

26. "Should E-Commerce Fulfillment and Regular Distribution Be Housed in the Same DC?" *SCDigest*, November 14, 2012.

27. Amit Kumar Gupta, O. P. Singh, and R. K. Garg, "Evolution and Development of Bullwhip Effect and its Contribution towards Supply Chain Management: A Literature Review," *International Journal of Management & Information Technology* 1, no. 3 (2012), pp. 89–98; Giulio Zotteri, "An Empirical Investigation on Causes and Effects of the Bullwhip Effect: Evidence from the Personal Care Sector," *International Journal of Production Economics*, 2012; and Robert Bray and Haim Mendelson, "Information Transmission and the Bullwhip Effect: An Empirical Investigation," *Management Science* 58, no. 5 (2012), pp. 860–875.

28. Yano Dong and Martin Dresner, "Supply Chain Learning And Spillovers In Vendor Managed Inventory," *Decision Sciences* 43, no. 6 (2012), pp. 979–1001; Tarikere Niranjan, Stephan Wagner, and Stephanie M. Nguyen, "Prerequisites to Vendor-Managed Inventory," *International Journal of Production Research* 50, no. 4 (2012), pp. 939–951; Michael Fry, "Vendor-Managed Inventory," in *Wiley Encyclopedia of Operations Research and Management Science* (New York: Wiley, 2011); and Jouni Kauremaa, Johanna Småros, and Jan Holmström, "Patterns of Vendor-Managed Inventory: Findings from a Multiple-Case Study," *International Journal of Operations & Production Management* 29, no. 11 (2009), pp. 1109–1139.

29. Cleopatra Bardaki, Panos Kourouthanassis, and Katerina Pramatari, "Deploying RFID-Enabled Services in the Retail Supply Chain: Lessons Learned toward the Internet of Things," *Information Systems Management* 29, no. 3 (2012), pp. 233–245; Massimo Bertolini, Eleonora Bottani, Gino Ferretti, Antonio Rizzi, and Andrea Volpi, "Experimental Evaluation of Business Impacts of RFID in Apparel and Retail Supply Chain," *International Journal of RF Technologies: Research and Applications* 3, no. 4 (2012), pp. 257–282; and Philip Trocchia and Thomas Ainscough, "Consumer Attitudes toward RFID Tracking in the Retail Environment," *Review of Business Information Systems* 16, no. 2 (2012), pp. 67–72.

30. Bill McBeath, "What Retailer Mandates Mean for Suppliers," *ChainLink Research*, February 6, 2013.

31. "Retailers' RFID Programs Have Major Implications for Relationships with Suppliers," *ChainLink Research*, February 8, 2013; and McBeath, "What Retailer Mandates Mean for Suppliers."

32. McBeath, "What Retail RFID Mandates Mean for Suppliers."

Chapter 11

1. Dhruv Grewal, Michael Levy, and Britt Hackmann, "Making Loyalty Programs Sing," Working Paper, Babson College.

2. V. Kumar and Werner Reinartz, *Close Customer Relationship Management: Concept, Strategy and Tools* (New York: Springer, 2012); Francis Buttle, *Customer Relationship Management* (Hungary: Routledge, 2012); Martin Christopher, Adrian Payne, and David Ballantyne, *Relationship Marketing* (Great Britain: Routledge, 2012); Parul Bajaj, "Role of Customer Relationship Management (CRM) in Retail Industry—An Overview," *International Journal of Business Economics and Management Research* 2, no. 6 (2011), pp. 120–132; Tim Coltman, Timothy M. Devinney, and David F. Midgley, "Customer Relationship Management and Firm Performance." *Journal of Information Technology* 26, no. 3 (2011), pp. 205–219; Martin Reimann, Oliver Schilke, and Jacquelyn S. Thomas, "Customer Relationship Management and Firm Performance: The Mediating Role of Business Strategy," *Journal of the Academy of Marketing Science* 38 (June 2010).

3. Bernhard Swoboda, Bettina Berg, Hanna Schramm-Klein, and Thomas Foscht, "The Importance of Retail Brand Equity and Store Accessibility for Store Loyalty in Local Competition," *Journal of Retailing and Consumer Services*, 2013; Mercedes Martos-Partal and Óscar González-Benit, "Store Brand and Store and Store Loyalty: The Moderating Role of Store Brand Positioning," *Marketing Letters* 22, no. 3 (2011), pp. 297–313; Ipshita Ray and Larry Chiagouris, "Customer Retention: Examining the Roles of Store Affect and Store Loyalty as Mediators in the Management of Retail Strategies," *Journal of Strategic Marketing* 17, no. 1 (2009), pp. 1–20; Wan-I Lee, Chih-Yuan Chang, and Yu-Lun Liu, "Exploring Customers' Store Loyalty Using Means-End Chain Approach," *Journal of Retailing and Consumer Services* 17, no. 5 (2010), pp. 395–405; and Ugar Yavas and Emin Babakus, "Retail Store Loyalty: A Comparison of Two Customer Segments," *International Journal of Retail & Distribution Management* 37, no. 6 (2009), pp. 477–492.

4. Khalid Rababah, Haslina Mohd, and Huda Ibrahim, "Customer Relationship Management (CRM) Processes from Theory to Practice: The Pre-implementation Plan of CRM System," *International Journal of e-Education, e-Business, e-Management and e-Learning*, 2011, pp. 22–27.

5. "Big Data, Bigger Myths," Accenture, 2012.

6. Josh Pichler, "Firm Remakes Retailers' Knowledge of Shoppers," *The Cincinnati Enquirer*, January 31, 2013.

7. Jack Mitchell, *Hug Your Customers: The Proven Way to Personalize Sales and Achieve Astounding Results* (New York: Hyperion, 2003).

8. Eysle Dupre, "Top Five Privacy Issues Revealed," *Direct Marketing News*, February 1, 2013.

9. Cédric Hozanne, "The Future of Biometrics in Retailing," *Biometrics Technology Today*, June 2012, pp. 15–17; Mark Bridge, "Biometrics is the Future of Shopping," *The Times*, December 4, 2012.

10. Jeff Chester, "Cookie Wars: How New Data Profiling and Targeting Techniques Threaten Citizens and Consumers in the 'Big Data' Era." In *European Data Protection*, Serge Gutwirth, Ronald Leenes, Paul De Hert, and Yves Poullet Eds., New York: Springer, 2012, pp. 53–77; Jodie Ferguson, "Consumer Attitudes toward Sharing Personal Health and Shopping Information: A Hierarchical Model to Understanding Privacy Concerns," *Marketing Theory and Applications*, 2012, pp. 140–149; Christy Ashley, Stephanie Noble, Naveen Donthu, and Katherine Lemon, "Why Customers Won't Relate: Obstacles to Relationship Marketing Engagement," *Journal of Business Research* 64, no. 7 (2011), pp. 749–756; France Bélanger and Robert Crossler, "Privacy in the Digital Age: A Review of Information Privacy Research in Information Systems," *MIS Quarterly* 35, no. 4 (2011), pp. 1017–1042; and H. Jeff, Tamara Dinev, and

634 Endnotes

Heng Xu, "Information Privacy Research: An Interdisciplinary Review," *MIS Quarterly* 35, no. 4 (2011), pp. 989–1016.

11. *Protecting Consumer Privacy an Era of Rapid Change* (Washington DC: Federal Trade Commission, March 26, 2012).

12. Kevin O'Brien, "Silicon Valley Companies Lobbying Against Europe Privacy Proposals," *The New York Times*, January 25, 2013; Somini Sengupta, "Europe Weighs Tough Law on Online Privacy," *The New York Times*, January 23, 2012, Omar Tene, "Privacy in United States and Europe: I'll Know It When I See It," *CDNET*, June 27; 2011; and Don Reisinger, "EU Overhauling Data-Privacy Policies to Protect Consumers," *CDNET*, January 25, 2012.

13. www.ftc.gov/bcp/conline/pubs/alerts/privprotalrt.shtm.

14. Eysle Dupre, "Top Five Privacy Issues Revealed," *Direct Marketing News*, February 1, 2013.

15. V. Kumar, Lerzan Aksoy, Bas Donkers, Thorsten Wiesel, Rajkumar Venkatesan, and Sebastian Tillmanns, "Undervalued Customers: Capturing Total Customer Engagement Value," *Journal of Service Research* 13 (2010), pp. 297–310; V. Kumar, "Customer Lifetime Value-Based Approach to Managing Marketing in the Multichannel, Multimedia Purchasing Environment, *Journal of Interactive Marketing* 25, no. 2 (2010), pp. 71–81; V. Kumar, Morten Holm, and Carsten Rohde, "Measuring Customer Profitability in Complex Environments: An Interdisciplinary Contingency Framework," *Journal of the Academy of Marketing Science*, June 2011, pp. 1–15; Chen Zhiyong, Hu Hongshu, and Huang Manyu, "The Application of Customer Lifetime Value in Supermarket Marketing," *Strategic Management* 16, no. 3 (2011), pp. 3–8; Sharad Borle, Siddharth S. Singh, and Dipak C. Jain, "Customer Lifetime Value Measurement," *Management Science* 54 (January 2008), pp. 100–112; and Robert C. Blattberg, Edward C. Malthouse, and Scott A. Neslin, "Customer Lifetime Value: Empirical Generalizations and Some Conceptual Questions," *Journal of Interactive Marketing* 23 (May 2009), pp. 157–168.

16. Emmitt Cox, *Retail Analytics: The Secret Weapon* (Hoboken, NJ: Wiley, 2011).

17. Gordon S. Linoff and Michael J. Berry, *Data Mining Techniques: For Marketing, Sales, and Customer Relationship Management*, 3rd ed. (Hoboken, NJ: Wiley, April 2011); Alexander Tuzhilin, "Customer Relationship Management and Web Mining: the Next Frontier," *Data Mining and Knowledge Discovery*, 2012, pp. 1–29; and Erik Ngaic, Li Xiu, and D. C. K. Chau, "Application of Data Mining Techniques in Customer Relationship Management: A Literature Review and Classification," *Expert Systems with Applications* 36, no. 2 (2009), pp. 2592–2602.

18. Greg Jacobson, "CVS Aims to Personalize Retail Experience," *Chain Drug Review*, April 23, 2012.

19. Matilda Dorotic, Tammo HA Bijmolt, and Peter C. Verhoef. "Loyalty Programmes: Current Knowledge and Research Directions," *International Journal of Management Reviews* 14, No. 3 (2012): pp. 217–237; Myron Gable, Susan S. Fiorito, and Martin T. Topol. "An Empirical Analysis of the Components of Retailer Customer Loyalty Programs." *International Journal of Retail & Distribution Management* 36, No. 1 (2008): pp. 32–49; Lars Meyer-Waarden and Christophe Benavent. "Grocery Retail Loyalty Program Effects: Self-Selection or Purchase Behavior Change?" *Journal of the Academy of Marketing Science* 37, No. 3 (2009): pp. 345–358; Hean Tat Keh and Yih Hwai Lee. "Do Reward Programs Build Loyalty for Services?: The Moderating Effect of Satisfaction on Type and Timing of Rewards." *Journal of Retailing* 82,

No. 2 (2006): pp. 127–136; and M. D. Uncles, G. Dowling, and K. Hammond, "Customer Loyalty and Customer Loyalty Programs." *Journal of Consumer Marketing*, 20, pp. 294–316.

20. Don Peppers, "When Loyalty Programs Are a Waste of Money," *Fast Company*, March 2, 2012.

21. "The Billion Member March: The 2011 COLLOQUY Loyalty Census," *COLLOQUY*, April 2011; and "The Rules of Engagement: Loyalty in the U.S. and Canada," *COLLOQUY*, December 2011.

22. Alexandra Berzon, "Starwood Perks Up Loyalty Program," *The Wall Street Journal*, February 1, 2012.

23. Bryan Pearson, "How to Create Loyalty Programs Consumers Will Actually Get Excited About," *Fast Company*, January 11, 2013; Erdener Ortan, "How to Implement a Customer Loyalty Program?" *Erdener Ortan's blog*, October 20, 2012; and Don Peppers, "5 Best Practices for Loyalty Programs," *Fast Company*, July 8, 2012.

24. "History of Loyalty Program," www.frequentflier.com.

25. Pearson, "How to Create Loyalty Programs Customers Will Actually Get Excited About."

26. Ibid.

27. http://auction.starwoodhotels.com/cgi-bin/ncommerce3/CategoryDisplay?cgmenbr=67280009&cgrfnbr=67772620&ctype=top.

28. www.sephora.com/profile/MyAccount/beautyInsider/beautyInsider.jsp.

29. 2012 Neiman Marcus Group Annual Report.

30. Dennis Pitta, Frank Franzak, and Danielle Fowler, "A Strategic Approach to Building Online Customer Loyalty: Integrating Customer Profitability Tiers," *Journal of Consumer Marketing* 23, no. 7 (2006), pp. 421–429; Werner Reinartz and V. Kumar, "The Mismanagement of Customer Loyalty," *Harvard Business Review*, July 2002; Valarie Zeithaml, Roland Rust, and Katherine Lemon, "The Customer Pyramid: Creating and Serving Profitable Customers," *California Management Review* 43 (Summer 2001), p. 124.

31. Gianluca Marzocchi, Gabriele Morandin, and Massimo Bergami, "Brand Communities: Loyal to the Community or the Brand?" *European Journal of Marketing* 47, no. 1 (2013), pp. 93–114; Zhimin Zhou, Qiyuan Zhang, Chenting Su, and Nan Zhou, "How Do Brand Communities Generate Brand Relationships? Intermediate Mechanisms," *Journal of Business Research* 65, no. 7 (2012), pp. 890–895; Susan Fournier and Lara Lee, "Getting Brand Communities Right," *Harvard Business Review*, July 2009, pp. 106–113; and Hope Jensen Schau, Albert M. Muñiz Jr., and Eric Arnould, "How Brand Community Practices Create Value," *Journal of Marketing* 73 (September 2009), pp. 30–51.

32. http://wm5.walmart.com/walmart-moms/

33. Roland Rust, Valerie Zeithaml, and Katherine Lemon, *Driving Customer Equity* (New York: Free Press, 2002), chap. 13; Zeithaml, Rust, and Lemon, "The Customer Pyramid."

34. Michael Haenlein and Andreas Kaplan, "The Impact of Unprofitable Customer Abandonment on Current Customers' Exit, Voice, and Loyalty Intentions: An Empirical Analysis," *Journal of Services Marketing* 26, no. 6 (2012), pp. 458–470; Kerstin Helmes, *Relationship U-Turn: Approaches to Increase the Value of an Unprofitable Customer* (Berlin : Germany, Bachelor+ Master Publishing, 2011); Vikas Mittal, Matthew Sarkees, and Feisal Murshed, "The Right Way to Manage Unprofitable Customers," *Harvard Business Review*, April 2008; and Rust, Zeithaml, and Lemon, *Driving Customer Equity*, chap. 13.

Chapter 12

1. Personal communication.

2. Deborah Fowler and Ben Goh, *Retail Category Management* (Englewood Cliffs, NJ: Prentice Hall, 2011); and Subir Bandyopadhyay, Anna Rominger, and Savitri Basaviah, "Developing a Framework to Improve Retail Category Management through Category Captain Arrangements," *Journal of Retailing and Consumer Service*, May 7, 2009, pp. 315–319.

3. Richard Gooner, Neil Morgan, and William Perreault Jr., "Is Retail Category Management Worth the Effort (and Does a Category Captain Help or Hinder)?" *Journal of Marketing* 75, no. 5 (2011), pp. 18–33; Joseph Hall, Praveen Kopalle, and Aradhna Krishna. "Retailer Dynamic Pricing and Ordering Decisions: Category Management Versus Brand-by-Brand Approaches," *Journal of Retailing* 86, no. 2 (2010), pp. 172–183; Mümin Kurtuluş and Beril Toktay, "Category Captainship Vs. Retailer Category Management Under Limited Retail Shelf Space," *Production and Operations Management* 20, no. 1 (2011), pp. 47–56; and Joshua D. Wright, "Antitrust Analysis of Category Management: Conwood v United Tobacco," *Supreme Court Economic Review* 17, no. 1 (2009), pp. 27–35.

4. Justin Beneke, Alice Cumming, and Lindsey Jolly, "The Effect of Item Reduction on Assortment Satisfaction—A Consideration of the Category of Red Wine in a Controlled Retail Setting," *Journal of Retailing and Consumer Services* 20, no. 3 (2013), pp. 282–291, Walter Zinn and Peter Liu, "A Comparison of Actual and Intended Consumer Behavior in Response to Retail Stockouts," *Journal of Business Logistics* 29, no. 2 (2011), pp. 141–159; Xiaoqing Jing and Michael Lewis, "Stockouts in Online Retailing," *Journal of Marketing Research* 48, no. 2 (2011), pp. 342–354; Minjeong Kim and Sharron Lennon, "Consumer Response to Online Apparel Stockouts," *Psychology and Marketing* 28, no. 2 (2011), pp. 115–144; and Stephen Castleberry and Brian Davis, "Effects of Stockouts on Purchase Behavior and Retail Patronage: An Experimental Investigation," *Journal of Applied Business Research* 4, no. 3 (2011), pp. 90–97.

5. George Box, Gwilym Jenkins, and Gregory Reinsel, *Time Series Analysis: Forecasting and Control* (New York: Wiley, 2011).

6. Elisa Anniss, "Innovative Retail Ideas Go on the Net," *Financial Times*, June 15, 2009, p. 5.

7. W. J. Maunder, "Weekly Weather and Economic Activities on a National Scale: An Example Using United States Retail Trade Data," *Weather* 28, no. 1 (2012), pp. 2–19; Kyle Murray, Fabrizio Di Muro, Adam Finn, and Peter Popkowski Leszczyc, "The Effect of Weather on Consumer Spending," *Journal of Retailing and Consumer Services* 17, no. 6 (2010), pp. 512–520; and Youngjin Bahng and Doris Kincade, "The Relationship between Temperature and Sales: Sales Data Analysis of a Retailer of Branded Women's Business Wear," *International Journal of Retail & Distribution Management* 40, no. 6 (2012), pp. 410–426.

8. Julia Werdiger, "Tesco, British Grocer, Uses Weather to Predict Sales," *The New York Times*, September 2, 2009.

9. Cecilia Sze and Paul Walsh, "How Weather Influences the Economy," *ISO Review*, www.iso.com/Research-and-Analyses/ISO-Review/How-Weather-Influences-the-Economy.html4.

10. Mijeong Noh and Pamela Ulrich, "Querying Fashion Professionals' Forecasting Practices: The Delphi Method," *International Journal of Fashion Design, Technology and Education* 6, no. 1 (2013), pp. 1–8; and Yong Yu, Tsan-Ming Choi, and Chi-Leung Hui, "An Intelligent Fast Sales Forecasting Model for Fashion Products," *Expert Systems with Applications* 38, no. 6 (2011), pp. 7373–7379.

11. www.invesp.com/blog-rank/fashion#ultimate.

12. Dana Mattiolo, "Lululemon's Secret Sauce," *The Wall Street Journal*, March 22, 2012.

13. http://greenroom.asda.com/2013/3/11/sign-up-to-our-pulse-of-the-nation-colleague-panel.

14. Jinhong Xie and Steven Shugan, "Advance Selling," in V. Rao (Ed.), *Handbook of Pricing Research in Marketing* (North Hampton, MA: Edward Elgar, 2009), pp. 451–477.

15. Murali Mantrala, Michael Levy, Barbara Kahn, Edward Fox, Peter Gaidarev, Bill Dankworth, and Denish Shah, "Why Is Assortment Planning So Difficult for Retailers? A Framework and Research Agenda," *Journal of Retailing* 85, no. 1 (2009), pp. 71–83; and A. Gürhan Kök, Marshall Fisher, and Ramnath Vaidyanathan, "Assortment Planning: Review of Literature and Industry Practice," *Retail Supply Chain Management*, 2009, pp. 99–153.

16. Susan Broniarczyk and Wayne Hoyer, "Retail Assortment: More ≠ Better," in M. Kraft and M. Mantrala (Eds.), *Retailing in the 21st Century*, 2nd ed. (China: Fairchild Books, 2010), pp. 271–284; Christopher Miller, Stephen Smith, Shelby McIntyre, and Dale Achabal, "Optimizing and Evaluating Retail Assortments for Infrequently Purchased Products," *Journal of Retailing* 86, no. 2 (2010), pp. 159–171; Mümin Kurtuluş and Alper Nakkas, "Retail Assortment Planning Under Category Captainship," *Manufacturing & Service Operations Management* 13, no. 1 (2011), pp. 124–142; and Alexander Hübner and Heinrich Kuhn, "Retail Category Management: State-of-the-art Review of Quantitative Research and Software Applications in Assortment and Shelf Space Management," *Omega* 40, no. 2 (2012), pp. 199–209.

17. Murali Mantrala, P. Sinha, and A. Zoltners, "Impact of Resource Allocation Rules on Marketing Investment-Level Decisions and Profitability," *Journal of Marketing Research* 29, no. 2 (May 1992), pp. 162–175.

18. Christina Binkley, "Fashion Nation: What Retailers Know About Us," *The Wall Street Journal*, July 28, 2010.

19. Anjali Cordeiro, "Consumer-Goods Makers Heed 'Paycheck Cycle,'" *The Wall Street Journal*, February 23, 2009.

20. William Ho, Xiaowei Xu, and Prasanta Dey, "Multi-Criteria Decision Making Approaches for Supplier Evaluation and Selection: A Literature Review," *European Journal of Operational Research* 202, no. 1 (2010), pp. 16–24.

Chapter 13

1. Stacy Straczynski, "Nielsen: Private Label Sales Up 7.4%," *Adweek*, August 13, 2009.

2. Best Global Brands 2012, Interbrand.

3. "About Us," Macy's Inc., www.federated-fds.com/AboutUs/.

4. "Symphony IRI: Soaring PL Growth Threatens National Brands in Europe," *Store Brands Decisions*, www.storebrands-decisions.com/news/2011/12/20/symphonyiri-soaring-pl-growth-threatens-national-brands-in-europe.

5. Christina Binkley, "House-Brand Menswear That Aims to Be a Cut Above," *The Wall Street Journal*, July 30, 2009; www.privatelabelmag.com/pdf/pli_fall2004/13.cfm; and Nirmalya Kumar and Jan-Benedict E. M. Steenkamp, *Private Label Strategy: How to Meet the Store Brand Challenge* (Boston: Harvard Business Press, 2007).

6. www.plstorebrands.com/plmag-article-safeway_selective-3689.html.

636   Endnotes

7. "Growth On All Fronts Fact Book 2012," Macy's, www.
   macysinc.com/Assets/docs/for-investors/annual-report/
   2012_fact_book.pdf.

8. Interview with Bryan Bradley, HSN.

9. Hank Schultz, "Private Label Sales Hit $98 Billion on 6%
   Growth, Report Says," *Food Navigator*, October 30, 2012.

10. Christina Cheddar Berk, "Private-Label Brands Gaining
    Clout—And Pricing Power," *CNBC*, January 31, 2012.

11. Mark Bergen, Shantanu Dutta, and Steven Shugan,
    "Branded Variants: A Retail Perspective," *Journal of Market-
    ing Research*, February 1996, pp. 9–20.

12. "About Us," Trade Show News Network (TSNN), www.
    tsnn.com/about-us.

13. The Fashion Center, www.fashioncenter.com

14. "Season's Direct Debuts Season's Garden Showroom in
    Dallas," *Dallas Market Center*, December 3, 2012, www.
    dallasmarketcenter.com/press/seasons-direct-debuts-
    seasons-garden-showroom-in-dallas.

15. "2012 CES Grows, Excites, and Catalyzes," January 13, 2012,
    www.cesweb.org/news/releaseDetail.asp?id=12284.

16. McCormick Place, www.mccormickplace.com.

17. Leonie Barrie, "US: Limited Brands Spins Off Mast Apparel
    Sourcing Unit," *Just-Style*, November 3, 2011.

18. "Hollander Home Fashions, LLC," Answers, www.answers.
    com/topic/hollander-home-fashions-corp.

19. JCPenney, 2011 10-K Report, filed with the Securities and
    Exchange Commission.

20. Bernice Hurst, "Turning Points 2008: Global Sourcing Not
    Always a Sure Winner," *Retail Wire*, December 16, 2008.

21. "Annual Highlights—2011: A Year of Giving Back," Limited-
    Brands, www.limitedbrands.com/responsibility/community/
    annual_highlights.aspx.

22. "Beyond 50 Years: Building a Sustainable Future," Walmart
    2012 Global Responsibility Report.

23. Len Kaplan, "Is e-Sourcing for You," *InShare3*, November
    2012; Marjolein C. J. Caniëls and Erik M. van Raaij, "Do All
    Suppliers Dislike Electronic Reverse Auctions?" *Journal of
    Purchasing and Supply Management* 15, no. 1 (March 2009),
    pp. 12–23; Alberto A. Gaggero, "Retailers Curtail Rising
    Costs through Private Label Procurement." *Internet Wire*,
    August 16, 2011; and Cigdem A. Gumussoy and Fethi
    Calisir, "Understanding Factors Affecting E-Reverse Auc-
    tion Use: An Integrative Approach," *Computers in Human
    Behavior* 25, no. 4 (2009), pp. 975–988.

24. Ravi S. Achrol, "Slotting Allowances: A Time Series Analysis
    of Aggregate Effects over Three Decades," *Journal of the Acad-
    emy of Marketing Science* 40 (September 2012), pp. 673–694;
    Oystein Foros, Hans Jarle Kind, and Jan Yngve Sand, "Slot-
    ting Allowances and Manufacturers Retail Sales Effort,"
    Southern Economic Journal (Southern Economic Association)
    76, no. 1 (2009), pp. 266–282; and David Hoffman, "Vendor
    Allowances in Retail Industry, Not Cut and Dry," *Chain
    Store Age*, July 29, 2009.

25 These guidelines are based on Roger Fisher, William Ury,
    and Bruce Patton, *Getting to Yes: Negotiating Agreements
    Without Giving In* (New York: Penguin, 2011); and Gavin
    Kennedy, *Negotiation: An A–Z Guide (Economist A–Z Guide)*
    (London: Economist Books, May 2009).

26. A. Parmigiani and M. Rivera-Santos, "Clearing a Path through
    the Forest: A Meta-Review of Interorganizational Relation-
    ships," *Journal of Management* 37 (2011), pp. 1108–1136;
    Stephen Samaha, Robert W. Palmatier, and Rajiv P. Dant,
    "Poisoning Relationships: Perceived Unfairness in Channels

    of Distribution," *Journal of Marketing* 75 (May 2011),
    pp. 99–117; Todd Arnold, Eric Fang, and Robert W. Palmatier,
    "The Effects of Customer Acquisition and Retention
    Orientations on Radical and Incremental Innovation Per-
    formance," *Journal of the Academy of Marketing Science* 39
    (April 2011), pp. 234–251.

27. Robert Johnston and Roy Staughton, "Establishing and De-
    veloping Strategic Relationships: The Role for Operations
    Managers," *International Journal of Operations & Production
    Management* 29, no. 6 (2009), pp. 564–590; Thomas Powers
    and William Reagan, "Factors Influencing Successful
    Buyer–Seller Relationships," *Journal of Business Research* 60
    (December 2007), pp. 1234–1242.

28. Frazier, Gary L., Elliot Maltz, Kersi D. Antia, and Aric
    Rindfleisch, "Distributor Sharing of Strategic Information
    with Suppliers," *Journal of Marketing* 73, no. 4 (2009),
    pp. 31–43; G. T. M. Hult, J. A. Mena, O. C. Ferrell, and L. K.
    Ferrell, "Stakeholder Marketing: A Definition and Concep-
    tual Framework," *AMS Review* 1, no. 1 (2011), doi:10.1007/
    s13162-011-0002-5; and Bill Donaldson and Tom O'Toole,
    *Strategic Market Relationships: From Strategy to Implementa-
    tion*, 2nd ed. (Indianapolis: Wiley, 2007).

29. Christian Hofer, Yao Jin, Rodger Swanson, Matthew Waller,
    and Brent Williams, "The Impact of Key Retail Accounts
    on Supplier Performance: A Collaborative Perspective of
    Resource Dependency Theory," *Journal of Retailing* 88, no. 3
    (2012), pp. 412–420.

30. Lydia Dishman, *Style Inc.*, July 21, 2011.

31. Suzy Hansen, "How Zara Grew into the World's Larg-
    est Fashion Retailer," *The New York Times*, November 9,
    2012; Vertica Bhardwaj and Ann Fairhurst, "Fast Fashion:
    Response to Changes in the Fashion Industry," *International
    Review of Retail, Distribution and Consumer Research* 20
    (February 2010), pp. 165–173; Felipe Caro, Jérémie Gallien,
    Miguel Díaz Miranda, Javier García Torralbo, Jose Manuel
    Corrediora Corras, Marcos Montes Vazques, José Antonio
    Ramos Calamonte, and Juan Correa, "Zara Uses Operations
    Research to Reengineer Its Global Distribution Process,"
    Interfaces 40 (2010), pp. 71–84; and Personal communica-
    tion with Jose Martinez, Chief Merchandising and Supply
    Chain Officer, Zara, July 2009.

32. Christie Swanson, "Walmart's Unique Relationships," *101 Ven-
    tures*, May 27, 2012; Bentonville, Arkansas, www.bentonville-
    ar-relocation.com/; "Best Places to Live: Bentonville, AR,"
    CNN Money, http://money.cnn.com/magazines/moneymag/
    bplive/2009/snapshots/PL0505320.html.

33. Robert W. Palmatier, Mark Houston, Rajiv P. Dant, and
    Dhruv Grewal, "Relationship Velocity: Towards Developing
    a Theory of Relationship Dynamics," *Journal of Marketing* 77,
    no. 1 (2013) pp. 13–30; and Robert W. Palmatier, *Relationship
    Marketing* (Cambridge, MA: Marketing Science Institute,
    2008).

34. Plexus Consulting Group, *The Power of Partnership: Principles
    and Practices for Creating Strategic Relationships among Non-
    profit Groups, For-Profit Organizations, and Government Entities*
    (Washington, DC: ASAE & The Center for Association
    Leadership and U.S. Chamber of Commerce, June 25, 2008).

35. Palmatier et al. "Relationship Velocity."

36. Hofer et al., "The Impact of Key Retail Accounts on Sup-
    plier Performance."

37. Ken Ritter, "Chanel Files Internet Trademark Lawsuit in
    Vegas," *Las Vegas Sun*, September 21, 2011.

38. Brent Kentdall, "High Court Splits Evenly in Costco Case,"
    The Wall Street Journal, December 14, 2010.

39. Jane P. Mallor, A. James Barnes, Thomas Bowers, and Arlen W. Langvardt, *Business Law: The Ethical, Global, and E-Commerce Environment*, 15th ed. (New York: McGraw-Hill/Irwin, 2013).

40. *In re Toys R Us AntiTrust Litigation*, 191 F.R.D. 347 (E.D.N.Y. 2000).

41. "Locally Grown: List of Vendor Profiles," Whole Foods, http://wholefoodsmarket.com/locally-grown; "Local Producer Loan Program," Whole Foods, http://wholefoods-market.com/mission-values/caring-communities/local-producer-loan-program. Laura Vozzella, "Grocers Jump on 'Local' Produce Bandwagon," *Baltimore Sun Reporter*, July 9, 2009; Len Lewis, "Eating Locally," *Stores*, April 2008; Len Lewis, "Growing Trend Has Consumers—and Retailers—Seeking Products Sourced Closer to Home, *Stores*, April 2008; Remi Trudeland and June Cotte, "Does Being Ethical Pay?" *The Wall Street Journal*, May 12, 2008, p. R1; Julie Schmit, "'Locally Grown' Food Sounds Great, but What Does It Mean?" *USA Today*, October 27, 2008; Carol Ness, "Whole Foods, Taking Flak, Thinks Local," *San Francisco Chronicle*, July 26, 2006; and "Retailers Push Packagers to Think 'Green,'" *Reuters*, September 4, 2007.

42. Molly Watson, "What Is a Locavore?" *About.com*, http://localfoods.about.com/od/localfoodsglossary/g/locavore.htm. The term was coined by four San Francisco women in proposing that people eat foods grown within 100 miles of their homes. In 2007, it was named "Word of the Year" by the *New Oxford American Dictionary*.

43. Starbucks Campaign," Global Exchange, www.globalexchange.org/campaigns/fairtrade/coffee/starbucks.html.

44. www.ecooptions.homedepot.com/; and www6.homedepot.com/earthday/L105066_GreenGuide_Book.pdf.

45. Tom Zeller, "Clothes Makers Join to Set 'Green Score,'" *The New York Times*, March 1, 2011.

Chapter 14

1. Roger Kerin, Steven Hartley, Eric Berkowitz, and William Rudelius, *Marketing*, 10th ed. (New York: McGraw-Hill, 2010).

2. Valarie A. Zeithaml, Mary Jo Bitner, and Dwayne Gremler, *Service Marketing: Integrating Customer Focus across the Firm*, 6th ed. (New York: McGraw-Hill, 2012).

3. William G. Brunger, "The Impact of the Internet on Airline Fares: The 'Internet Price Effect,'" *Journal of Revenue & Pricing Management* 9, no. 1–2 (2010), pp. 66–93; and Leo MacDonald and Henning Rasmussen, "Revenue Management with Dynamic Pricing and Advertising," *Journal of Revenue & Pricing Management* 9, no. 1–2 (2010), pp. 126–136.

4. Zeithaml, Bitner, and Gremler, *Service Marketing*.

5. John D. Quillinan, "Introduction to Normalization of Demand Data—The First Step in Isolating the Effects of Price on Demand," *Journal of Revenue & Pricing Management* 9, no. 1–2 (2010), pp. 4–22; and Brian Bergstein, "Pricing Software Could Reshape Retail," *Associated Press*, April 27, 2007.

6. Susan Reda, "Pricing Transparency," *Stores*, February 2012.

7. Bergstein, "Pricing Software Could Reshape Retail."

8. Tom Ryan, "The High Cost of Discounting," *Retail Wire*, March 20, 2009, based on a Yankelovich survey.

9. Christina Binkley, "Death to Discounts? The Designers Rebel," *The Wall Street Journal*, April 16, 2009.

10. Praveen K, Kopalle, "Editorial: Modeling Retail Phenomena," *Journal of Retailing* 86, no. 2 (2010), pp. 117–124; and Michael Levy, Dhruv Grewal, Praveen K. Kopalle, and James D. Hess, "Emerging Trends in Retail Pricing Practice: Implications for Research," *Journal of Retailing* 80, no. 3 (2004), pp. xiii–xxi.

11. Steve McKee, "How to Discount (If You Insist)," *Business-Week*, August 14, 2009; and Teri Evans, "An Expert's Guide to Discounting," *BusinessWeek Online*, April 3, 2009.

12. Dimitris Bertsimas, Jeffrey Hawkins, and Georgia Perakis, "Optimal Bidding in Online Auctions," *Journal of Revenue and Pricing Management* 8 (2009), pp. 21–41.

13. Jason Henry McCormick, "10 Most Expensive Items Ever Listed on eBay," *Moneywatch*, May 1, 2012.

14. Personal communication with Don LeBlanc, senior vice president of retail marketing at Staples.

15. Dhruv Grewal, Kusum Ailawadi, Dinesh Gauri, Kevin Hall, Praveen Kopalle, and Jane Robertson, "Innovation in Pricing and Promotion Strategies," *Journal of Retailing* 87S, no. 1 (2011), pp. S43–S52.

16. "80 Most Influential People in Sales and Marketing," *Sales & Marketing Management*, October 1998, p. 78.

17. Raj Arora, "Price Bundling and Framing Strategies for Complementary Products," *Journal of Product & Brand Management* 17, no. 7 (2008), pp. 475–484.

18. Sumathi Reddy and Danny Gold, "City Nails Sex-Based Pricing," *The Wall Street Journal*, May 23, 2012.

19. "Frugal Dilemmas: Women's Drycleaning Costs More than Men's, but Why?" *Baltimore Sun*, June 4, 2009.

20. Sarah Maxwell, The *Price Is Wrong: Understanding What Makes a Price Seem Fair and the True Cost of Unfair Pricing* (New York: Wiley, 2008).

21. Leigh McAlister, Edward I. George, and Yung-Hsin Chien, "A Basket-Mix Model to Identify Cherry-Picked Brands," *Journal of Retailing* 85, no. 4 (2009), pp. 425–436.

22. Tim Arango, "Bet Your Bottom Dollar on 99 Cents," *The New York Times*, February 8, 2009.

23. Sandrine Mace, "The Determinants of Nine-Ending Effects: An Empirical Analysis Using Store-Level Scanner Data," *Journal of Retailing* 88, no. 1 (2012), pp. 115–130; Traci H. Freling, Leslie H. Vincent, Robert Schindler, David M. Hardesty, and Jason Rowe, "A Meta-Analysis of Just-Below Pricing Effects: Separating Reality from the "Magic," Working paper, 2012; R. M. Schindler, "Patterns of Price Endings Used in U.S. and Japanese Price Advertising," *International Marketing Review* 26, no. 1 (2009), pp. 17–29; and R. M. Schindler, "The 99-Price Ending as a Signal of a Low-Price Appeal," *Journal of Retailing* 82, no. 1 (2006), pp. 71–77.

24. Dan Mattioli and Miguel Bustillo, "Can Texting Save Stores?" *The Wall Street Journal*, May 8, 2012.

25. "Meijer Mobile," *Meijer.com*, www.meijer.com/content/content.jsp?pageName=mobile_app#findit.

26. Ibid; Dan Mattioli and Miguel Bustillo, "Can Texting Save Stores?" *The Wall Street Journal*, May 8, 2012.

27. Steven W. Beattie, "Stephen King's New Face of Evil: Predatory Pricing," *Quill & Quire*, October 26, 2009.

28. Jim Milliott, "Authors Guild Sees Return of Predatory Pricing if DoJ Deal Stands," *Publishers Weekly*, June 26, 2012.

29. Gregory T. Gundlach, Joseph P. Cannon, and Kenneth C. Manning, "Free Riding and Resale Price Maintenance: Insights from Marketing Research and Practice," The *Antitrust Bulletin*: 55, no. 2 (Summer 2010), p. 381. Gregory T. Gundlach, Joseph P. Cannon, and Kenneth Manning, "Free Riding and Resale Price Maintenance: Insights from Marketing Research and Practice," *Antitrust Bulletin* 55, no.

638 Endnotes

2 (2010), pp. 381–422; Gregory T. Gundlach, "Overview of the Special Issues: Antitrust Analysis of Resale Price Maintenance After *Leegin,*" *Special Issue (Part II) of the* Antitrust Bulletin 55, no. 2 (2010), pp. 271–276; Gregory T. Gundlach, "Overview and Contents of the Special Issues: Antitrust Analysis of Resale Price Maintenance After *Leegin,*" *Special Issue (Part I) of the* Antitrust Bulletin 55, no. 1 (2010), pp. 1–24.

30. Jenn Abelson, "CVS Called a Leader in Pricing Violations," *Boston Globe,* May 7, 2009; "Making Sure the Scanned Price Is Right," Federal Trade Commission, www.ftc.gov/bcp/edu/pubs/consumer/products/pro01.shtm.

31. Kevin M. Lemley, "Resolving the Circuit Split on Standing in False Advertising Claims and Incorporation of Prudential Standing in State Deceptive Trade Practices Law: The Quest for Optimal Levels of Accurate Information in the Marketplace," *University of Arkansas, Little Rock Law Review* 29 (2007), pp. 283, 285.

32. Martin Eichenbaum, Nir Jaimovich, and Sergio Rebelo, "Reference Prices and Nominal Rigidities," *NBER,* March 5, 2008.

Chapter 15

1. Personal communication, Krista Gibson, vice president of marketing, Chili's Grill and Bar Restaurants.

2. American Marketing Association, *Dictionary of Marketing Terms* (Chicago: American Marketing Association).

3. "Database of 100 Leading Advertisers," *AdAge,* June 2012.

4. "100 Leading National Advertisers," *AdAge,* June 25, 2012.

5. "Advertising Expenditures," *Newspaper Association of America,* March 14, 2012.

6. Sebastian Feld, Heiko Frenzen, Manfred Krafft, Kay Peters, and Peter C. Verhoef, "The Effects of Mailing Design Characteristics on Direct Mail Campaign Performance," *International Journal of Research in Marketing* (2012), doi: 10.1016/j.ijresmar.2012.07.003.

7. "Why Radio," *RadioAdvertising,* http://radioadvertising.co.nz/Site/Why/Default.aspx.

8. "The Man Who Created Rudolph from an Idea that Almost Didn't Fly," *Chicago Tribune,* December 13, 1990, p. 1C.

9. Stephanie Clifford, "Shopper Alert: Price May Drop for You Alone," *The New York Times,* August 9, 2012.

10. "A Brief History of Coupons," *Coupon Sherpa,* April 6, 2010, http://blog.couponsherpa.com/a-brief-history-of-coupons/.

11. www.stapleseasyrebates.com/img/staples/paperless/pages/Landing.html.

12. www.marketingpower.com/_layouts/Dictionary.aspx?dLetter=S.

13. "McDonald's–Olympic Sponsor, Retail Food Services," *Olympic.org,* www.olympic.org/sponsors/mcdonalds.

14. Jaime Stengel, "Neiman Marcus Offers Extravagant Gift Guide Featuring Hen House, Spider for Holiday," *The Huffington Post,* October 9, 2012; and www.neimanmarcus.com.

15. "Shop For a Cause: About," *Macysinc.com,* http://shopforacause.macysinc.com/About.aspx; and Fatima Lora, "Cause-Related Marketing: Building Good Will and Business Growth," *Retailtouchpoints.com,* September 8, 2011, www.retailtouchpoints.com/in-store-insights/1064-cause-related-marketing-building-good-will-and-business-growth.

16. S. Chin and B. Wilson, "Product Placement in the Digital World: A Conceptual Framework," *Proceedings of The Changing Roles of Advertising Conference,* Charles R. Taylor, Patrick De Pelsmacker, Scott Koslow, and Peter Neijens (Eds.), Stockholm, Sweden, June 29–30, 2012; Eva A. van Reijmersdal, Peter C. Neijens, and Edith G. Smit, "A New Branch of Advertising: Reviewing Factors That Influence Reactions to Product Placement," *Journal of Advertising Research* 49, no. 4 (December 2009), pp. 429–449; Pamela Mills Homer, "Product Placement: The Impact of Placement Type and Repetition on Attitude," *Journal of Advertising,* Fall 2009. 38, no. 3.

17. Sara Mahoney, "Best Buy, Sears, Target Lead in Cross-Channel," *MarketingDaily,* August 29, 2011.

18. Peter De Maeyer, "Impact of Online Consumer Reviews on Sales and Price Strategies: A Review and Directions for Future Research," *Journal of Product & Brand Management* 21, no. 2 (2012), pp.132–139; Yue Pan and Jason Q. Zhang, "Born Unequal: A Study of the Helpfulness of User-Generated Product Reviews," *Journal of Retailing* 87, no. 4 (December 2011), pp. 598–612.

19. www.wordstream.com/sponsored-links-google

20. George Anderson, "White House, Web Giants Address Consumer Privacy Online," *Retail Wire,* February 24, 2012.

21. Panos E. Kourouthanassis and George M. Giaglis, "Introduction to the Special Issue Mobile Commerce: The Past Present, and Future of Mobile Commerce Research," *International Journal of Electronic Commerce* 16, no. 4 (Summer 2012), pp. 5–18.

22. Foursquare website, http://foursquare.com/.

23. "New Trend in Social Networking Could Be Open Invitation to Criminals," *PRNewswire,* May 26, 2010.

24. "Number of Cell Phones Worldwide Hits 4.6 Billion," *CBS News,* February 15, 2010.

25. Colin Campbell, Leyland F. Pitt, Michael Parent, and Pierre R. Berthon, "Understanding Consumer Conversations Around Ads in a Web 2.0 World," *Journal of Advertising,* 40, no. 1 (Spring 2011), pp. 87–102.

26. Dinah Wisenberg Brin, "Retailers Use Social Media to Fine-Tune Operations," *CNBC.com,* October 28, 2011.

27. Chrysanthos Dellarocas, "Strategic Manipulation of Internet Opinion Forums: Implications for Consumers and Firms," *Management Science* 52 (October 2006), pp. 1577–1593; and Liyun Jin, "Business Using Twitter, Facebook to Market Goods," *Pittsburgh Post-Gazette,* June 21, 2009.

28. Tom Ryan, "The Customer Is Always Wrong," *Retail Wire,* October 7, 2011.

29. "Brand Channels," *YouTube,* www.gstatic.com/youtube/engagement/platform/autoplay/advertise/downloads/YouTube_BrandChannels.pdf.

30. The Home Depot Branded Channel, www.youtube.com/user/homedepot?blend=2&ob=4#p/a.

31. "Number of Active Users at Facebook Over the Years," *Associated Press,* October 23, 2012.

32. Sarah Mahoney, "Macy's Gets Face(book) Lift; Expands 'Ecosystem,'" *Marketing Daily,* February 29, 2012.

33. Jenna Telesca, "Retailers Flex Creative Marketing Muscles," *Supermarket News,* September 19, 2011.

34. Bin Gu, Jaehong Park, and Prabhudev Konana, "The Impact of External Word-of-Mouth Sources on Retailer Sales of High-Involvement Products," *Information Systems Research* 23, no. 1 (March 2012), pp. 182–96; Jillian C. Sweeney, Geoffrey N. Soutar, and Tim Mazzarol, "Word of Mouth: Measuring the Power of Individual Messages," *European Journal of Marketing* 46, no. 1/2 (2012), pp. 237–257; and

Robert East, Kathy Hammond, and Malcolm Wright, "The Relative Incidence of Positive and Negative Word of Mouth: A Multi-Category Study," *International Journal of Research in Marketing* 24, no. 2 (2007), pp. 175–184.

35. Erin Jo Richey, "15 Top Internet Retailers Who Blog," *flatfrogblog.com*, January 7, 2010.

36. https://twitter.com/DUMBOFoodTrucks

37. Alex Schmidt, "Twitter Lets Customers Skip Recordings, and Make Choices," *NPR*, August 15, 2012.

38. www.marketingpower.com/_layouts/Dictionary.aspx?dLetter=B.

39. Jayne O'Donnell, "Missoni Was Just the Latest Target of 'Retail Scalpers,'" *USA Today*, September 23, 2011.

40. *Best Global Brands 2012* (Interbrand: New York, 2012).

41. "Macy's Thanksgiving Day Parade History," *NYC Tourist*, www.nyctourist.com/macys_history1.htm; and http://social.macys.com/parade2012_kaws/?cm_mmc=VanityUrl-_-parade-_-n-_-n#/home.

42. Murali Mantrala, "Allocating Marketing Resources," in *Handbook of Marketing*, eds. Barton Weitz and Robin Wensley (London: Sage, 2002), pp. 409–435.

43. V. Shankar and Gregory S. Carpenter, *Handbook of Marketing Strategy* (Northhampton, MA: Edward Elgar 2012). See Chapter 9, "Marketing Resource Allocation Strategy."

44. Andy Shaw, "How to Create a Facebook Ad Campaign," *Social Media Tips*, September 23, 2011.

45. "Marketing and Advertising Using Google," Google, 2007.

46. http://support.google.com/adwords/answer/2454010?hl=en.

47. http://publishing2.com/2008/05/27/google-adwords-a-brief-history-of-online-advertising-innovation/.

Chapter 16

1. Raymond Andrew Noe, John R. Hollenbeck, Barry Gerhart, and M. Wright. *Fundamentals of Human Resource Management*, 5th ed. (New York: McGraw Hill, 2013); H. John Bernardin, *Human Resource Management*, 6th ed. (New York: McGraw Hill, 2013); and Scott Carbonara, *Manager's Guide to Employee Engagement* (New York: McGraw Hill, 2013).

2. James Breaugh, "Employee Recruitment: Current Knowledge and Suggestions for Future Research," *The Oxford Handbook of Personnel Assessment and Selection* (New York: Oxford University Press, 2012), pp. 68–87.

3. Stephan Castleberry and John Tanner, *Personal Selling: Building Relationships*, 8th ed. (New York: McGraw-Hill, 2011).

4. Kathleen Keeling, Peter McGoldrick, and Henna Sadhu, "Staff Word-of-Mouth (SWOM) and Retail Employee Recruitment," *Journal of Retailing*, 2013, in press.

5. James Thornton, "All Ages Welcome," *Human Resources*, March 2010, p. 23.

6. "TMI? The Risks of Recruiting Using Social Media Profiles," *HRNews Daily*, December 16, 2012.

7. "A New Era in Recruiting," *HRNews Daily*, November 5, 2012.

8. Richard Hollinger, *National Retail Security Study* (Gainesville, FL: University of Florida, Department of Sociology, 2013).

9. W. Stanley Siebert and Nikolay Zubanov, "Searching for the Optimal Level of Employee Turnover: A Study of a Large U.K. Retail Organization," *Academy of Management Journal* 52 (April 2009), pp. 94–10; and Shari L. Peterson, "Managerial Turnover in US Retail Organizations," *Journal of Management Development* 26, no. 7/8 (2007), pp. 770–789.

10. "Is Pre-Employment Screening (Slowly?) Being 'Outlawed'?" *HR.com blog*, February 2013.

11. Connie Wanberg, "Facilitating Organizational Socialization: An Introduction," in *The Oxford Handbook of Organizational Socialization* (New York: Oxford University Press, 2012), pp. 3–17; and Robert J. Taormina, "Organizational Socialization: The Missing Link between Employee Needs and Organizational Culture," *Journal of Managerial Psychology* 24 (2009), pp. 650–665.

12. Elly Valas, "Training Doesn't Cost, It Pays," *Dealerscope*, April 2008, p. 24; and M. V. Greene, "Train and Retain," *Stores*, November 2007, p. 89.

13. www.containerstore.com/careers/faqs.html#question14

14. Jared Hansen and Michael A. Levin, "Retail E-Learning Assessment: Motivation, Location, and Prior Experience," *International Journal of Retail & Distribution Management* 38, no. 10 (2010), pp. 789–805.

15. George Anders, "Companies Find Online Training Has Its Limits," *The Wall Street Journal*, March 26, 2007, p. B3; and "Recreation Equipment Inc." *NY Job Source*, October 17, 2011.

16. Ed Stych, "Best Buy's Employe e Training Ranked Among Best in Nation," *Minneapolis St. Paul Business Journal*, February 14, 2012; and Lorri Freifeld, "Focus on Retail: Best Buy Connects with Customers," *Sales and Marketing Management*, August 1, 2007.

17. Robert Porter and Gary Latham, "The Effect of Employee Learning Goals and Goal Commitment on Departmental Performance," *Journal of Leadership & Organizational Studies* 20, no. 1 (2013), pp. 62–68; Jean-Francois Coget, "Performance Orientation or Learning Orientation: Which Helps Salespeople Better Adapt to Organizational Change?" *The Academy of Management Perspectives* 24, no. 3 (2010), pp. 106–108; and Simon Bell, Bülent Mengüç, and Robert E. Widing II, "Salesperson Learning, Organizational Learning, and Retail Store Performance," *Journal of the Academy of Marketing Science* 38, no. 2 (2010), pp. 187–201.

18. Marc Bishop, "How Can I Boost Employee Performance?" *Strategic HR Review* 12, no. 2 (2013), p. 8; Frank Q. Fu, Keith A. Richards, and Eli Jones, "The Motivation Hub: Effects of Goal Setting and Self-Efficacy on Effort and New Product Sales," *Journal of Personal Selling and Sales Management*, 29 (Summer 2009), pp. 277–292; and C. Fred Miao and Kenneth R. Evans, "The Impact of Salesperson Motivation on Role Perceptions and Job Performance—A Cognitive and Affective Perspective," *Journal of Personal Selling & Sales Management* 27, no. 1 (2007), pp. 89–101.

19. Vincent Onyemah, "The Effects of Coaching on Salespeople's Attitudes and Behaviors," *European Journal of Marketing* 43 (2009), pp. 938–960.

20. Jo En Yap, Liliana L. Bove, and Michael B. Beverland, "Exploring the Effects of Different Reward Programs on In-Role and Extra-Role Performance of Retail Sales Associates," *Qualitative Market Research* 12, no. 3 (2009), pp. 279–296; Arthur C. Brooks, "I Love My Work," *American: A Magazine of Ideas* 1, no. 6 (2007), pp. 20–28; and John H. Fleming and Jim Asplund, *Human Sigma: Managing the Employee–Customer Encounter* (New York: Gallup Press, 2007).

21. Tará Burnthorne Lopez, Christopher D. Hopkins, and Mary Anne Raymond, "Reward Preferences of Salespeople: How Do Commissions Rate?" *Journal of Personal Selling & Sales Management* 26, no. 4 (2006), pp. 381–390; and Richard G. McFarland and Blair Kidwell, "An Examination of Instrumental and Expressive Traits on Performance: The Mediating Role of Learning, Prove, and Avoid Goal

640   Endnotes

Orientations," *Journal of Personal Selling & Sales Management* 26, no. 2 (2006), pp. 143–159.

22. Yap, Bove, and Beverland, "Exploring the Effects of Different Reward Programs on In-Role and Extra-Role Performance of Retail Sales Associates"; Brooks, "I Love My Work"; *and* Fleming and Asplund, *Human Sigma: Managing the Employee–Customer Encounter.*

23. Walter Tymon, Stephen Stumpf, and Jonathan Doh, "Exploring Talent Management in India: The Neglected Role of Intrinsic Rewards," *Journal of World Business* 45, no. 2 (2010), pp 109–121.

24. Brooks, "I Love My Work"; Fleming and Asplund, *Human Sigma: Managing the Employee–Customer Encounter*; Tará Burnthorne Lopez, Christopher D. Hopkins, and Mary Anne Raymond, "Reward Preferences of Salespeople: How Do Commissions Rate?" *Journal of Personal Selling & Sales Management* 26, no. 4 (2006), pp. 381–390; and Richard G. McFarland and Blair Kidwell, "An Examination of Instrumental and Expressive Traits on Performance: The Mediating Role of Learning, Prove, and Avoid Goal Orientations," *Journal of Personal Selling & Sales Management.* 2006, Vol. 26, No. 2 (Spring), pp. 143–159.

25. William Murphy and Peter A. Dacin, "Sales Contest Research: Business and Individual Difference Factors Affecting Intentions to Pursue Contest Goals," *Industrial Marketing Management* 38, no. 1 (2009), pp. 109–118.

26. Fred C. Lunenburg, "Motivating by Enriching Jobs to Make Them More Interesting and Challenging," *International Journal of Management, Business, and Administration* 15, no. 1 (2011), pp. 1–11.

27. Rachel Dodes and Dana Mattioli, "Theory & Practice: Retailers Try on New Sales Tactics," *The Wall Street Journal,* April 19, 2010.

28. Christopher Barnes, John Hollenbeck, Dustin Jundt, D. Scott DeRue, and Stephen Harmon, "Mixing Individual Incentives and Group Incentives: Best of Both Worlds or Social Dilemma?" *Journal of Management* 37, no. 6 (2011), pp. 1611–1635; and James P. Guthrie and Elaine C. Hollensbe, "Group Incentives and Performance: A Study of Spontaneous Goal Setting, Goal Choice and Commitment," *Journal of Management* 30, no. 2 (2004), pp. 263–285.

29. Annie McKee, Richard Boyatzis, and Fran Johnston, *Becoming a Resonant Leader: Develop Your Emotional Intelligence, Renew Your Relationships, Sustain Your Effectiveness* (Boston: Harvard Business School Press, 2008); and James B. Deconinck, "The Effect of Leader-Member Exchange on Turnover among Retail Buyers," *Journal of Business Research,* 62 (November 2009), pp. 1081–1095.

30. Paula McDonald, "Workplace Sexual Harassment 30 Years On: A Review of the Literature," *International Journal of Management Reviews* 14, no. 1 (2012), pp. 1–17; Heather McLaughlin, Christopher Uggen, and Amy Blackstone, "Sexual Harassment, Workplace Authority and the Paradox of Power," *American Sociological Review* 77, no. 4 (2012), pp. 625–647; Elissa L. Perry, Carol T. Kulik, and Marina P. Field, "Sexual Harassment Training: Recommendations to Address Gaps between the Practitioner and Research Literatures," *Human Resource Management,* 48 (September–October 2009), pp. 817–834; and "What Constitutes 'Harassment,' and What HR Can Do about It," *HR Focus,* December 2008, pp. 4–6.

31. Steven Greenhouse, "A Part-Time Life, as Hours Shrink and Shift," *The New York Times,* October 27, 2012.

32. Dave Jamieson, "Walmart-Contracted Workers Strike Ahead of Black Friday," *The Huffington Post,* November 14, 2012.

33. David P. Schultz, "Global Retail Theft Barometer," *Stores Magazine,* January 2012.

34. David P. Schultz, "The Global Cost of Theft," *Stores Magazine,* January 2011.

35. Richard Hollinger and Amanda Adams, *2011 National Retail Security Survey* (Gainesville, FL: University of Florida, 2011).

36. Rachel Shteir, "Five Myths about Shoplifting," *The Washington Post,* August 2, 2011.

37. Schultz, "Global Retail Theft Barometer."

38. "Shoplifters Beware!" *BusinessWeek,* October 3, 2006.

39. Liz Parks, "The Gold Standard: High-End Jeweler Goes High-Tech for Inventory Control," *Stores Magazine,* April 2013.

40. Ibid.

41. Fred Minnick, "Reality TV: Improving Loss Prevention Starts with Better Surveillance Video," *Stores Magazine,* March 2013.

Chapter 17

1. Simona Botti and Ann L. McGill, "The Locus of Choice: Personal Causality and Satisfaction with Hedonic and Utilitarian Decisions," *Journal of Consumer Research* 37 (April 2011), pp. 1065–1078, Uzma Khan and Ravi Dhar, "Price-Framing Effects on the Purchase of Hedonic and Utilitarian Bundles," *Journal of Marketing Research* 47, no. 6 (2010), pp. 1090–1099; Eileen Bridges and Renée Florsheim, "Hedonic and Utilitarian Shopping Goals: The Online Experience," *Journal of Business Research* 61 (April 2008), pp. 309–314.

2. See www.cvs.com/promo/promoLandingTemplate.jsp?promoLandingId=mobile-apps.

3. George Anderson, "Shopping at Wegmans on a Sunday Afternoon," *RetailWire,* June 27, 2012.

4. Michael Hess, "Could This Be the Best Company in the World?" *CBSNews.com,* September 13, 2011; and "America's Largest Private Companies," *Forbes,* November 16, 2011.

5. Kendall Goodrich and Rosemary Ramsey, "Are Consumers with Disabilities Receiving the Services They Need?" *Journal of Retailing and Consumer Services* 19 (January 2012), pp. 88–97; Cynthia R. Jasper and Paul Waldhart, "Retailer Perceptions on Hiring Prospective Employees with Disabilities," *Journal of Retailing and Consumer Services* 19 (January 2012), pp. 116–123; Stacey Menzel Baker, Jonna Holland, and Carol Kaufman-Scarborough, "How Consumers with Disabilities Perceive 'Welcome' in Retail Servicescapes: A Critical Incident Study," *Journal of Services Marketing* 21, no. 3 (2007), pp. 160–173; Robert Pear, "Plan Seeks More Access for Disabled," *The New York Times,* July 16, 2008, p. 11: Rosemary D. F. Bromley and David L. Matthew, "Reducing Consumer Disadvantage: Reassessing Access in the Retail Environment," *International Review of Retail, Distribution & Consumer Research* 17, no. 5 (2007), pp. 483–501; and Marianne Wilson, "Accessible Fixtures," *Chain Store Age* 83, no. 2 (February 2007).

6. See, for example, *EEOC v. Cottonwood Financial, Ltd.,* No. CV-09-5073-EFS (E. D. Wash.), 2012; *Disabled in Action of Metropolitan New York, Inc. et al. v. Duane Reade, Inc.,* U.S. District Court, Southern District of New York, Civil Action No. 01 Civ. 4692 (WHP), 2004; *Californians for Disability Rights v. Mervyn's,* Superior Court of California, No. 2002-051738 (RMS), 2003; *Shimozono, et al. v. May Department Stores Co. d/b/a Robinsons-May,* Federal Court, Central District of California, Case No. 00-04261 (WJR),

2001; and *Access Now, et al., v. Burdines, Inc.*, Federal Court, Southern District of Florida, Case No. 99-3214 (CIV), 2000.

7. Roger Thorne, "Handicap Requirements for Retail Stores," *eHow*, www.ehow.com/list_6110547_handicap-requirements-retail-stores.html; ADA Accessibility Guidelines for Buildings and Facilities, www.access-board.gov/adaag/html/adaag.htm; and Michael Barbaro, "Department Stores Settle Disability Lawsuit," *Washington Post*, February 9, 2005, p. E02.

8. Paco Underhill, *Why We Buy: The Science of Shopping* (New York: Simon and Schuster, 2000).

9. Herb Sorensen, *Inside the Mind of the Shopper* (Upper Saddle River, NJ: Pearson Education, 2009).

10. Dale Buss, "S. C. Johnson Promotes 'Reinventing' Center Store of Supermarkets," *CPG Matters*, January 5, 2009.

11. Yanliu Huang, Sam K. Hui, J. Jeffrey Inman, and Jacob A. Suher, "Capturing the 'First Moment of Truth': Understanding Point-of-Purchase Drivers of Unplanned Consideration and Purchase," working paper.

12. Fiona Soltes, "It's the Message, Not the Medium," *Stores*, October 2007, p. 26; Michael Curran, "Now Playing: Interactive Retail Marketing 2.0," *Stores*, August 2007, p. 92; Katherine Field, "Digital Signage: A Powerful New Medium," *Chain Store Age*, May 2006, p. 204; and Steven Keith Platt, Kingshuck Sinha, and Barton Weitz, *Implications for Retail Adoption of Digital Signage Systems* (Chicago, IL: Platt Retail Institute, 2004).

13. Raymond R. Burke, "Behavioral Effects of Digital Signage," *Journal of Advertising Research* 49 (June 2009), pp, 180–186.

14. Anne L. Roggeveen, Jens Nordfält, and Dhruv Grewal, "The Effectiveness of Digital Signs: The Impact of Store Type," working paper, 2012.

15. Len Lewis, "Making Signage a Cinch," *Stores*, May 2012; Sandy Smith, "The Big Picture," *Stores*, August 2011; and Len Lewis, "Dynamic Displays," *Stores*, February 2011.

16. Craig Childress, "Sign Language: The Most Ubiquitous Form of Communication in the Store Is Often the Least Effective," *Progressive Grocer*, April 15, 2005.

17. Britta Cornelius, Martin Natter, and Corinne Faure, "How Storefront Displays Influence Retail Store Image," *Journal of Retailing and Consumer Services* 17, no. 2 (March 2010), pp. 143–151; Shuo-Fang Liu, Wen-Cheng Wang, and Ying-Hsiu Chen, "Applying Store Image and Consumer Behavior to Window Display Analysis," *Journal of American Academy of Business*, 3 (2009), pp. 70–75; and Hyunjoo Oh and Jenny Petrie, "How Do Storefront Window Displays Influence Entering Decisions of Clothing Stores?" *Journal of Retailing and Consumer Services* 19 (January 2002), pp. 27–35.

18. JoAnne Klimovich Harrop, "Window Displays Create Interest, Merchants Say," *TribLive*, May 19, 2011.

19. Tom Ryan, "Brandwashed at Whole Foods," *RetailWire*, October 14, 2011.

20. Paco Underhill, *Why We Buy: The Science of Shopping*, 3rd ed. (New York: Simon and Schuster, 2009); and Mindy Fetterman and Jayne O'Donnell, "Just Browsing at the Mall? That's What You Think," *USA Today*, September 1, 2006.

21. Stephanie Clifford, "Stores Demand Mannequins with Personality (Heads Optional)," *The New York Times*, June 15, 2011.

22. Michael Applebaum, "More Eyeballs at Checkout," *Brandweek*, June 27–July 4, 2005, p. 54.

23. Elizabeth Holmes and Ray A. Smith, "Why Are Fitting Rooms So Awful?" *The Wall Street Journal*, April 6, 2011.

24. Daniel Terdiman, "At Demo, Virtual Dressing Rooms Promise Big Sales," *CNet*, February 28, 2011.

25. Holmes and Smith, "Why Are Fitting Rooms So Awful?"

26. Chase C. Murray, Debabrata Talukdar, and Abhijit Gosavi, "Joint Optimization of Product Price, Display Orientation and Shelf-Space Allocation in Retail Category Management," *Journal of Retailing* 86 (June 2010), pp. 125–136; Jared M. Hansen, Sumit Raut, and Sanjeev Swami, "Retail Shelf Allocation: A Comparative Analysis of Heuristic and Meta-Heuristic Approaches," *Journal of Retailing* 86, no. 1 (March 2010), pp. 94–105; and B. Ramaseshan, N. R. Achuthan, and R. Collinson, "Decision Support Tool for Retail Shelf Space Optimization," *International Journal of Information Technology & Decision Making* 7, no. 3 (2008), pp. 547–565.

27. Sarah Nassauer, "A Food Fight in the Produce Aisle," *The Wall Street Journal*, October 20, 2011.

28. Tom Ryan, "'His' and 'Her' Grocery Aisles," *RetailWire*, June 6, 2011.

29. Pierre Chandon, J. Wesley Hutchinson, Eric T Bradlow, and Scott H Young, "Does In-Store Marketing Work? Effects of the Number and Position of Shelf Facings on Brand Attention and Evaluation at the Point of Purchase," *Journal of Marketing* 73 (November 2009), pp. 1–17.

30. Edward Franczek, "Virtual Stores Drive Real Sales," www.greeebbookblog.org, December 13, 2011.

31. "In Retail Stores, Research Tool Uses Kinect to Track Shoppers' Behavior," *Retail*, December 29, 2011.

32. Debra Hazel, "Small Formats, Big Opportunities," *Chain Store Age*, February 2011; Miguel Bustillo, "As Big Boxes Shrink, They Also Rethink," *The Wall Street Journal*, March 3, 2011; Stephanie Clifford, "Stuff Piled in the Aisle? It's There to Get You to Spend More," *The New York Times*, April 7, 2011; Stephanie Clifford, "In These Lean Days, Even Stores Shrink," *The New York Times*, November 9, 2010; and Sarah Mahoney, "Target Keeps Smaller Formats in Spotlight," *PM Marketing Daily*, October 18, 2010.

33. The concept of atmospherics was introduced by Philip Kotler, "Atmosphere as a Marketing Tool," *Journal of Retailing* 49 (Winter 1973), pp. 48–64.

34. Aradhna Krishna, "An Integrative Review of Sensory Marketing: Engaging the Senses to Affect Perception, Judgment and Behavior," *Journal of Consumer Psychology* 22 (2012), pp. 332–351; and May Lwin, Maureen Morrin, and Aradhna Krishna, "Exploring the Superadditive Effects of Scent and Pictures on Verbal Recall: An Extension of Dual Coding Theory," *Journal of Consumer Psychology* 20, no. 3 (2010), pp. 317–326.

35. Jens Nordfalt, *In-Store Marketing*, 2nd ed. (Sweden: Forma Magazine, 2011); and Aradhna Krishna, *Sensory Marketing: Research on the Sensuality of Consumers* (New York: Routledge, 2009).

36. "Latest Findings on Ideal Lighting for Retail Stores," http://lighting.com/ideal-retail-lighting-for-stores/.

37. Kate Linebaugh, "The Math Changes on Bulbs: Modern LEDs, While Expensive, Save Companies on Labor," *The Wall Street Journal*, November 30, 2011.

38. Rajesh Bagchi and Amar Cheema, "The Effect of Red Background Color on Willingness-to-Pay: The Moderating Role of Selling Mechanism," *Journal of Consumer Research* (forthcoming); and Christopher Shea, "Wave a Red Flag in Front of eBay Bidders," *The Wall Street Journal*, June 19, 2012.

39. Tom Ryan, "The Purchasing Power of Om," *Retail Wire*, November 7, 2011.

642 Endnotes

40. "Retail Customer Experience: Consumers Tune Out Stores Playing Annoying Music," *RetailWire*, November 14, 2011.

41. Theunis Bates, "Volume Control," *Time*, August 10, 2007.

42. Krishna, "An Integrative Review of Sensory Marketing"; Lwin, Morrin, and Krishna, "Exploring the Supperadditive Effects"; Renaud Lunardo, "Negative Effects of Ambient Scents on Consumers' Skepticism about Retailer's Motives," *Journal of Retailing and Consumer Services* 19, no. 2 (March 2012), pp. 179–185; Maureen Morrin, Aradhna Krishna, and May Lwin, "Is Scent-Enhanced Memory Immune to Retroactive Interference?" *Journal of Consumer Psychology* 21, no. 3 (July 2011), pp. 354–361; Aradhna Krishna, May Lwin, and Maureen Morrin, "Product Scent and Memory," *Journal of Consumer Research* 37 (June 2010), pp. 57–67; and Ryan Elder and Aradhna Krishna, "The Effect of Advertising Copy on Sensory Thoughts and Perceived Taste", *Journal of Consumer Research* 36, no. 5 (February 2010), pp. 748–756.

43. Eric Markowitz, "How Cinnamon Smells Will Save Holiday Sales," *Inc.*, November 3, 2011.

44. Lauren Covello, "Reaching Out to Customers, through Their Noses," *FOXBusiness*, October 13, 2011.

45. Jane Sutton, "Scent Makers Sweeten the Smell of Commerce," *Reuters*, December 19, 2011.

46. Dick Scanlon, "Lingerie on 6; Lobster on 9," *The New York Times*, December 29, 2011.

47. Velitchka Kalchteva and Barton Weitz, "How Exciting Should a Store Be?" *Journal of Marketing*, Winter 2006, pp. 34–62; and Benjamin Yen and P. C. Yen, "The Design and Evaluation of Accessibility on Web Navigation," *Decision Support Systems* 42, no. 4 (2007), pp. 2219–2235.

48. "Tips on Improving the Checkout Process," www.e-consultancy.com, July 1, 2010.

Chapter 18

1. Amy-Mae Elliott, "Amazon.com Facts: 10 Things You Didn't Know About the Web's Biggest Retailer," *Mashable*, July 22, 2011.

2. Roland Rust and Ming-Hui Huang, "Optimizing Service Productivity," *Journal of Marketing* 76, no. 2 (2012), pp. 47–66; Robert Cooperman, "Value over Profit," *T+D*, May 2010, pp. 58–62; Dhruv Grewal, Ram Krishnan, and Joan Lindsey-Mullikin, Building Store Loyalty through Service Strategies," *Journal of Relationship Marketing* 7, no. 4 (2008), pp. 341–358; and Valarie Zeithaml, Leonard Berry, and A. Parasuraman, "The Behavioral Consequences of Service Quality," *Journal of Marketing* 60 (April 1996), pp. 31–46.

3. Susan Reda, "Driving Shoppers Crazy," *Stores* (June 2012).

4. "Retailers Join the War Effort," *Chain Store Age*, June 1994, p. 15.

5. Dwayne Ball, Pedro S. Coelho, and Manuel J. Vilares, "Service Personalization and Loyalty," *Journal of Services Marketing* 20 (September 2006), pp. 391–403.

6. Kwiseok Kwon, Jinhyung Cho, and Yongtae Park, "How to Best Characterize the Personalization Construct for E-Services," *Expert Systems with Applications* 37 (March 2010), pp. 2232–2240.

7. R. Di Mascio, "The Service Models of Frontline Employees," *Journal of Marketing* 74, no. 4 (2010), pp. 63–80.

8. "Wine.com Launches Advanced Personalized Recommendations to Enhance Shopping Experience," *MarketWire.com*, May 15, 2012.

9. Audrey van Petegem, "Fun Facts About IKEA," *BlogHer*, October 1, 2010, www.blogher.com/fun-facts-about-ikea.

10. "IKEA Canada Just Made Shopping Easier," *MarketWatch*, May 1, 2012; "The Secrets of a Successful Store," *Retail Week*, January 13, 2012; "At IKEA, Kids Play in Free Day Care as Parents Shop in Peace," *Orlando Sentinel*, July 15, 2009; and Bo Edvardsson and Bo Enquist, *Values-Based Service for Sustainable Business: Lessons from IKEA* (Oxford, UK: Routledge, 2008).

11. Raymond D. Jones, "Self-Checkout—What Should Drive the Retailer Decision?" *Retail Wire*, April 25, 2012.

12. See www.qthru.com.

13. Beth Teitell, "A Self-Checkout Way of Life," *Boston Globe*, January 4, 2011.

14. Jessica Anderson, "Sephora 101," *Sephora Blog*, October 9, 2007.

15. J. van Beuningen, Ko de Ruyter, and Martin Wetzels, "The Power of Self-Efficacy Change during Service Provision: Making Your Customers Feel Better about Themselves Pays Off," *Journal of Service Research* 14, no. 1 (2011), pp. 108–125.

16. A. Parasuraman and Valarie Zeithaml, "Understanding and Improving Service Quality: A Literature Review and Research Agenda," in *Handbook of Marketing*, eds. B. Weitz and R. Wensley (London: Sage, 2002); and Michael A. Wiles, "The Effect of Customer Service on Retailers' Shareholder Wealth: The Role of Availability and Reputation Cues," *Journal of Retailing* 83, no. 1 (2007), pp. 19–31.

17. Am Lyman, "Nordstrom—Great Service for Over 100 Years Best Company for 25 Years," Great Place to Work Institute, 2009; www.nordstrom.com.

18. http://about.nordstrom.com/careers/culture.asp.

19. David Hatch, "Nordstrom in Fashion with Social Media, Mobile Tech," *U.S. News Money, Business, & Economy*, May 15, 2012.

20. Adrian Palmer, "Customer Experience Management: A Critical Review of an Emerging Idea," *Journal of Services Marketing* 24, no. 3 (2010), pp, 196–208; and Tomas Falk, Maik Hammerschmidt, and Jeroen J. L. Schepers, "The Service Quality-Satisfaction Link Revisited: Exploring Asymmetries and Dynamics," *Journal of the Academy of Marketing Science* 38 (June, 2010), pp. 288–302.

21. Todd Beck, "Want Loyal Customers? Don't Stop at Satisfaction," *Customer Interaction Solutions*, February 2005, pp. 36–49.

22. C. Webster and A. White, "Exploring the National and Organizational Culture Mix in Service Firms," *Journal of the Academy of Marketing Science* 38, no. 6 (2010), pp. 681–703.

23. M. Sajid Khan, Earl Naumann, Rob Bateman, and Matti Haverila, "Cross-Cultural Comparison of Customer Satisfaction Research: USA vs Japan," *Asia Pacific Journal of Marketing and Logistics* 21, no. 3 (2009), pp. 376–396; and Jingyun Zhanga, Sharon E. Beatty, and Gianfranco Walsh, "Review and Future Directions of Cross-Cultural Consumer Services Research," *Journal of Business Research* 61 (March 2008), pp. 211–224.

24. Jackie L. M. Tam, "Managing Customer Expectations in Financial Services: Opportunities and Challenges," *Journal of Financial Services Marketing* 11 (May 2007), pp. 281–289; Mary Jo Bitner, "Self-Service Technologies: What Do Customers Expect? In This High-Tech World, Customers Haven't Changed—They Still Want Good Service," *Marketing Management*, Spring 2001, pp. 10–15.

25. The discussion of the gaps model and its implications is based on Valerie Zeithaml, Leonard Berry, and A. Parasuraman, "Communication and Control Processes in the Delivery of Service Quality," *Journal of Marketing* 52 (April 1988),

pp. 35–48; Valerie Zeithaml, A. Parasuraman, and Leonard Berry, *Delivering Quality Customer Service* (New York: Free Press, 1990); and Doen Nel and Leyland Pitt, "Service Quality in a Retail Environment: Closing the Gaps," *Journal of General Management* 18 (Spring 1993), pp. 37–57.

26. Ann Thomas and Jill Applegate, *Pay Attention! How to Listen, Respond, and Profit from Customer Feedback* (Hoboken, NJ: Wiley, 2010).

27. C. R. Lages and Nigel F. Piercy, "Key Drivers of Frontline Employee Generation of Ideas for Customer Service Improvement," *Journal of Service Research* 15, no. 2 (2012), pp. 215–230.

28. Danny Brown, "52 Cool Facts about Social Media (2012 Edition)," *PR Daily*, June 8, 2012.

29. www.radian6.com/2011; www.radian6.com/about-us/customers/retail/; Radian6 GNC Case Study, www.radian6.com/wp-content/uploads/2012/03/CaseStudy_GNC_SalesforceRadian6.pdf.

30. Ira Teinowitz, "Naked Pizza: Domino's Launches Ad Campaign Using 'Real' Photos," *Daily Finance*, July 7, 2010.

31. Brooks Barnes, "In Customer Service Consulting, Disney's Small World Is Growing," *The New York Times*, April 21, 2012.

32. Anne L. Roggeveen, Michael Tsiros, and Dhruv Grewal, "Understanding the Co-Creation Effect: When Does Collaborating with Customers Provide a Lift to Service Recovery?" *Journal of the Academy of Marketing Science* 40, issue 6 (November 2012), pp. 771–790. and James C. Ward and Amy L. Ostrom, "Complaining to the Masses: The Role of Protest Framing in Customer-Created Complaint Web Sites," *Journal of Consumer Research* 33 (September 2006), pp. 220–230.

33. James Digby, "50 Facts about Customer Experience" *Return on Behavior Magazine*, 2010.

34. Spencer E. Ante, "Amazon: Turning Consumer Opinions into Gold," *BusinessWeek*, October 15, 2009.

35. Ryan Schuster, "Frustrated with Poor Service?" *Bakersfield Californian*, April 14, 2007.

36. Lages and Piercy, "Key Drivers of Frontline Employee Generation of Ideas for Customer Service Improvement."

37. Z. Ma and L. Dub, "Process and Outcome Interdependency in Frontline Service Encounters," *Journal of Marketing* 75, no. 3 (2011), pp. 83–98.

38. Carmine Gallo, "How Ritz-Carlton Maintains Its Mystique," *BusinessWeek*, February 13, 2007; and Peter Sanders, "Takin' Off the Ritz—a Tad," *The Wall Street Journal*, June 23, 2006, p. B1.

39. Evangelos Grigoroudis and Yannis Siskos, *Customer Satisfaction Evaluation: Methods for Measuring and Implementing Service Quality* (New York: Springer, 2009); Samar I. Swaid and Rolf T. Wigand, "Measuring the Quality of E-Service: Scale Development and Initial Validation," *Journal of Electronic Commerce Research* 10, no. 1 (2009), pp. 13–24; A. Parasuraman, Valarie A. Zeithaml, and Leonard L. Berry, "Alternative Scales for Measuring Service Quality: A Comparative Assessment Based on Psychometric and Diagnostic Criteria," *Journal of Retailing* 70 (Autumn 1994), pp. 201–230.

40. "Customers Seek Self-Service Alternatives," *nacsonline.com*, January 25, 2007.

41. James R. Detert and Ethan R. Burris, "Leadership Behavior and Employee Voice: Is the Door Really Open?" *Academy of Management Journal* 50 (August 2007), pp. 869–884; Gilad Chen, Bradley L. Kirkman, Ruth Kanfer, Don Allen, and Benson Rosen, "A Multilevel Study of Leadership, Empowerment, and Performance in Teams," *Journal of Applied*

Psychology 92 (March 2007), p. 331; and Adam Rapp, Michael Ahearne, John Mathieu, and Niels Schillewaert, "The Impact of Knowledge and Empowerment on Working Smart and Working Hard: The Moderating Role of Experience," *International Journal of Research in Marketing* 23 (September 2006), pp. 279–293.

42. Carmine Gallo, "How the Ritz-Carlton Inspired the Apple Store," *Forbes*, April 10, 2012.

43. Valarie Zeithaml, *Delivering Quality Service* (New York: The Free Press, 2010).

44. Stefan Michel, David Bowen, and Robert Johnston, "Making the Most of Customer Complaints," *Wall Street Journal*, September 22, 2008.

45. Josh Bernoff and Ted Schadler, *Empowered: Unleash Your Employees, Energize Your Customers, and Transform Your Business* (Boston: Harvard Business Press, 2010).

46. Anthony Leaper, "How to Fail Your Call Centers," *Forbes.com*, May 13, 2012.

47. Kimmy Wa Chan and Wing Lam, "The Trade-Off of Servicing Empowerment on Employees' Service Performance: Examining the Underlying Motivation and Workload Mechanisms," *Journal of the Academy of Marketing Science* 39, no. 4 (2011), pp. 609–628.

48. Jyh-Shen Chiou and Tung-Zong Chang, "The Effect of Management Leadership Style on Marketing Orientation, Service Quality, and Financial Results: A Cross-Cultural Study," *Journal of Global Marketing* 22 (April 2009), pp. 95–107.

49. Jason Colquitt, Jeffery LePine, and Michael Wesson, *Organizational Behavior: Improving Performance and Commitment in the Workplace*, 2nd ed. (Burr Ridge, IL: McGraw-Hill, 2010); Felicitas M. Morhart, Walter Herzog, and Torsten Tomczak, "Brand-Specific Leadership: Turning Employees into Brand Champions," *Journal of Marketing* 73 (September 2009), pp. 122–142; Mark S. Rosenbaum, "Exploring Commercial Friendships from Employees' Perspectives," *Journal of Services Marketing* 23, no. 1 (2009), pp. 57–66; and J. Craig Wallace, Bryan D. Edwards, Todd Arnold, M. Lance Frazier, and David M. Finch, "Work Stressors, Role-Based Performance, and the Moderating Influence of Organizational Support," *Journal of Applied Psychology* 94 (January 2009), pp. 254–262.

50. Guy Winch, "The Last Bullying Frontier," *Psychology Today*, March 31, 2011.

51. Roberto L. Bacasong, "Overcoming Call Center Stress," *Article Base*, March 21, 2008.

52. Alicia A. Grandey, Lori S. Goldberg, and S. Douglas Pugh, "Why and When Do Stores with Satisfied Employees Have Satisfied Customers?: The Roles of Responsiveness and Store Busyness," *Journal of Service Research* 14, no. 4 (2011), pp. 397–409.

53 "Want to Improve Customer Service? Treat Your Employees Better," *Knowledge@Wharton*, March 14, 2012.

54. Todd Arnold, Karen E. Flaherty, Kevin E. Voss, and John C. Mowen, "Role of Stressors and Retail Performance: The Role of Perceived Competitive Climate," *Journal of Retailing* 85 (June 2009), pp. 194–205.

55. S. Li, Baohong Sung, and A. Montgomery, "Cross-Selling the Right Product to the Right Customer at the Right Time," *Journal of Marketing Research* 48, no. 4 (2011), pp. 683–700.

56. Leonard L. Berry, Ruth N. Bolton, C. H. Bridges, J. Meyer, A. Parasuraman, and Kathleen Seiders, "Opportunities for Innovation in the Delivery of Interactive Retail Services,"

644   Endnotes

Journal of Interactive Marketing 24, no. 2 (2010), pp. 155–167; Zhen Zhu, Cheryl Nakata, K. Sivakumar, and Dhruv Grewal, "Fix It or Leave it? Customer Recovery from Self-Service Technology Failures," working paper, 2012, Babson College; Peter C. Verhoef, Katherine N. Lemon, A. Parasuraman, Anne Roggeveen, Michael Tsiros, and Leonard A. Schlesinger, "Customer Experience Creation: Determinants, Dynamics and Management Strategies," *Journal of Retailing* 85, no. 1 (2009), pp. 31–41.

57. Clemens F. Köhler, Andrew J. Rohm, Ko de Ruyter, and Martin Wetzels, "Return on Interactivity: The Impact of Online Agents on Newcomer Adjustment," *Journal of Marketing* 75, no. 2 (2011), pp. 93–108.

58. Jenn Abelson, "Bar-Code Tags, ATM-Style Machines Drive High-Tech Laundry Business," *Boston Globe*, July 3, 2006; www.zoots.com.

59. Tammy Joyner, "More Businesses Telling Customers: Do It Yourself," *Atlanta Journal-Constitution*, August 10, 2003, p. B2.

60. "Consumers Calling Best Buy the Grinch That Stole Christmas," *Ad Age*, December 22, 2011.

61. Michael Garry, "Deli Devices: Stop & Shop Launches Deli Management System," *Supermarket News*, March 10, 2008.

62. "Stop & Shop Named Food Innovator," *Supermarket News*, March 13, 2012.

63. Stefan Michel, David Bowen, and Robert Johnston, "Making the Most of Customer Complaints," *The Wall Street Journal*, September 22, 2008.

64. Roggeveen, Tsiros, and Grewal, "Understanding the Co-Creation Effect: When Does Collaborating with Customers Provide a Lift to Service Recovery?"; M. Gabbott, Y. Tsarenko, and M. Wai Hoe, "Emotional Intelligence as a Moderator of Coping Strategies and Service Outcomes in Circumstances of Service Failure," *Journal of Service Research* 14, no. 2 (2011), pp. 234–248.

65. Heiner Evanschitzky, Christian Brock, and Markus Blut, "Will You Tolerate This? The Impact of Affective Commitment on Complaint Intention and Postrecovery Behavior," *Journal of Service Research* 14, no. 4 (2011), pp. 410–425. Chihyung Ok, Ki-Joon Back, and Carol W Shanklin, "Mixed Findings on the Service Recovery Paradox," *Service Industries Journal* 27 (September 2007), p. 671; and Celso Augusto de Matos, Jorge Luiz Henrique, and Carlos Alberto Vargas Rossi, "Service Recovery Paradox: A Meta-Analysis," *Journal of Service Research* 10 (August 2007), pp. 60–77.

66. Hui Liao, "Do It Right This Time: The Role of Employee Service Recovery Performance in Customer-Perceived Justice and Customer Loyalty after Service Failures," *Journal of Applied Psychology* 92 (March 2007), p. 475.

67. Elizabeth Holmes, "Tweeting without Fear," *The Wall Street Journal*, December 9, 2011.

68. Shea Bennet, "Just How Big is Twitter in 2012?" *All Twitter*, February 23, 2012.

69. Anthony W. Ulwick and Lance A. Bettencourt, "Giving Customers a Fair Hearing," *Sloan Management Review*, Spring 2008, pp. 14–22; Betsy Bugg Holloway, Sijun Wang, and Janet Turner Parish, "The Role of Cumulative Online Purchasing Experience in Service Recovery Management," *Journal of Interactive Marketing* 19 (July 2005), pp. 54–66; and Anna S. Mattila and Paul G. Patterson, "Service Recovery and Fairness Perceptions in Collectivist and Individualist Contexts," *Journal of Service Research* 6 (May 2004), pp. 336–346.

70. Kimmy W. Chan, Chi K. Yim, and Simon S. K. Lam, (2010). "Is Customer Participation in Value Creation a Double-Edged Sword? Evidence from Professional Financial Services Across Cultures," *Journal of Marketing* 74, no. 3 (2010), pp. 48–64.

PHOTO CREDITS

Section I
Page 2: © Imaginechina

Chapter 1
Page 4: Courtesy of Mindy Grossman; **p. 8:** © B2MProductions/Photodisc/Getty Images RF; **p. 10:** © Spencer Platt/Getty Images; **p. 11:** Courtesy of Dhruv Grewal; **p. 13** (t) © ZUMA Press, Inc./Alamy, (b) Courtesy of Nike, Inc.; **p. 15:** © Keith Dannemiller/Alamy; **p. 17:** © 2007 Getty Images, Inc. RF; **p. 18:** © Danny Johnston/AP Images; **p. 19:** © Jamie McCarthy/Getty Images for Forever 21; **p. 22:** © Toby Talbot/AP Images; **p. 23:** © Chris Ratcliffe/Bloomberg via Getty Images; **p. 26:** © DailyMail/Rex/Alamy; **p. 27:** © ZUMA Wire Service/Alamy.

Chapter 2
Page 34: Courtesy of Debbie Ferree; **p. 38:** © Holger Burmeister/Alamy; **p. 39:** © Cultura RM/Alamy; **p. 40:** © franky242/Alamy; **p. 41:** © Daniel Acker/Bloomberg via Getty Images; **p. 43:** © Cate Gillon/Getty Images; **p. 44:** © Jay Laprete/Bloomberg/Getty Images; **p. 45:** Courtesy of Costco; **p. 46:** © buzbuzzer/E+/Getty Images; **p. 49:** © STAN HONDA/AFP/Getty Images; **p. 51:** © Seth Perlman/AP Images; **p. 53:** Courtesy of SEPHORA; **p. 55:** © Sze Lung Ng/EyeEm/Getty Images; **p. 56:** © 2013 HauteLook | A Nordstrom Company; **p. 57:** Courtesy of Zoots; **p. 60:** Courtesy of The Dressing Room/www.the-dressingroom.com; **p. 61:** © Stephen & Donna O'Meara/Photo Researchers/Getty Images; **p. 62:** Courtesy of Red Mango, Inc.

Chapter 3
Page 66: Courtesy of Luiza Helena Trajano; **p. 68:** © f8 archive/Alamy Stock Photo; **p. 70:** © HSN, Inc.; **p. 71:** © H. John Maier Jr./Time Life Pictures/Getty Images; **p. 74:** © John Bohn/The Boston Globe/Getty Images; **p. 76:** © XO Group, Inc./www.theknot.com; **p. 77:** © Amazon.com, Inc. or its affiliates; **p. 80:** Copyright © 2013 Apple Inc. All rights reserved; **p. 81:** © David Paul Morris/Bloomberg via Getty Images; **p. 83:** Photographs reproduced courtesy of Build-A-Bear Workshop, Inc. © 2010 Build-A-Bear Workshop, Inc. All Rights Reserved.

Chapter 4
Page 88: Courtesy of Don Unser; **p. 90:** Courtesy of www.nubry.com; **p. 92:** © Punchstock/Creatas RF; **p. 93:** © Mary Altaffer/AP Images; **p. 95:** (t) © John Lund/Blend Images LLC RF, (b) © Edmunds.com, Inc.; **p. 96:** © RUTH FREMSON/The New York Times/Redux; **p. 100:** Courtesy of Lowe's; **p. 105:** © Jeff Frank/ZUMAPRESS.com/Alamy Live News; **p. 107:** Courtesy of Costco.

Section II
Page 120: © redbrickstock.com/Alamy

Chapter 5
Page 122: Courtesy of David Berg; **p. 124:** © Benjamin Norman/Bloomberg/Getty Images; **p. 128:** Courtesy of McDonald's Corporation; **p. 130:** Courtesy of IKEA; **p. 131:** © Oliver Strewe/Lonely Planet Images/Getty Images; **p. 132:** © The McGraw-Hill Companies/Mark Dierker, Photographer; **p. 134:** © Rob Crandall/The Image Works; **p. 135:** Courtesy of The Container Store; **p. 139:** © Mike Kemp/In Pictures Ltd./Corbis/Getty Images; **p. 140:** © Erica Simone Leeds 2007 RF; **p. 142:** © Rony Zakaria/International Herald Tribune/Redux; **p. 149:** © Lance Aram Rothstein/Tampa Bay Times/ZUMAPRESS.com.

Chapter 6
Page 154: Courtesy of Ken Hicks; **p. 157:** Courtesy of TOMS Shoes; **p. 159:** (l) © Steve Proehl/Corbis Documentary/Getty Images, (r) © Alex Segre/Alamy; **p. 164:** Courtesy of Costco; **p. 168:** (l) © Mitch Dumke/Reuters, (r) © Rachel Murray/Neiman Marcus Beverly Hills/Getty Images.

Chapter 7
Page 182: Courtesy of Michael Kercheval; **p. 185:** © Ben Torres/Bloomberg/Getty Images; **p. 186:** © Barney Taxel/The New York Times/Redux; **p. 187:** © William Torres/AP Images; **p. 188:** © Peter Horree/Alamy; **p. 190:** © Robert Mora/Getty Images; **p. 192:** © Per Andersen/Alamy; **p. 193:** Courtesy of General Growth Properties, Inc.; **p. 195:** © WU HL/Newscom; **p. 196:** © David Duprey/AP Images; **p. 197:** (t) © Gary Burke/Moment/Getty Images, (b) Courtesy of JC Penney; **p. 201:** © incamerastock/Alamy.

Chapter 8
Page 206: Courtesy of Brenden O'Brien; **p. 210:** © ZUMA Press, Inc./Alamy; **p. 213:** © Michael Neelon/Alamy; **p. 214:** Courtesy of Rick Lawlor; **p. 215:** (t) © Gary Crabbe/Alamy, (b) Courtesy of Real Estate Southeast, LLC; **p. 225:** Courtesy of The Ed Beiner Group.

Chapter 9
Page 234: Courtesy of Tim Hourigan; **p. 247:** © Francis Dean/123RF; **p. 248:** © Jason DeCrow/AP Images for Macy's Inc.; **p. 249:** Courtesy of The Container Store; **p. 250:** © Ramin Talaie/Corbis/Getty Images; **p. 252:** Courtesy of Pret a Manger; **p. 257:** (b) © Don Farrall/Photodisc/Getty Images RF, (t) © Digital Vision/Punchstock RF; **p. 260:** © Peter M. Fisher/Corbis/Getty Images.

Chapter 10
Page 264: Courtesy of Don Ralph; **p. 268:** © Andrew Francis Wallace/Toronto Star/Getty Images; **p. 270:** © Miguel Vidal/Reuters; **p. 275:** © Rick Wilking/Reuters; **p. 276:** (t) © Arno Masse/Cultura Creative/Alamy Stock Photo, (b) © Peter Essick/Aurora Photos; **p. 279:** © Spencer Grant/PhotoEdit; **p. 285:** Courtesy of West Marine; **p. 286:** (t) © Carlinhos Rodrigues/Agência RBS/AE (Agencia Estado via AP Images, (b) © Brian Harkin.

Chapter 11
Page 290: Courtesy of Jim Lewis; **p. 292:** © Jim Cummins/The Image Bank/Getty Images; **p. 294:** © Brand X Pictures/PunchStock RF; **p. 295:** © Ingram Publishing/The McGraw-Hill Companies RF; **p. 296:** © Peter Macdiarmid/Getty Images; **p. 301:** © Marmaduke St. John/Alamy Stock Photo; **p. 303:** © David De Lossy/Getty Images RF; **p. 304:** Courtesy of the Target Corporation; **p. 305:** Courtesy of Neiman Marcus; **p. 307:** Courtesy of Amazon.com; **p. 309:** © Wal-Mart Stores, Inc.; **p. 310:** Courtesy of American Girl.

Section III
Page 314: © Sandra Baker/Alamy

Chapter 12
Page 316: Courtesy of Moussa Coulibaly; **p. 318:** © Jin Lee/Bloomberg/Getty Images; **p. 320:** © Aardvark/Alamy RF; **p. 322:** © Losevsky Pavel/Alamy RF; **p. 326:** © Eduardo Parra/WireImage/Getty Images; **p. 328:** © Jamie Grill/Iconica/Getty Images RF; **p. 334:** © Ted S. Warren/AP Images; **p. 336:** Courtesy of Rubbermaid; **p. 338:** Courtesy of Lowe's; **p. 354:** © Antony Nagelmann/The Image Bank/Getty Images.

Chapter 13
Page 356: Courtesy of Audrey Schwarz; **p. 359:** © ZUMA Press, Inc./Alamy; **p. 363:** Courtesy of the Consumer Electronics Association; **p. 365:** © STR/AFP/Getty Images; **p. 366:** © Stephen Alvarez/National Geographic/Getty Images; **p. 367:** © Patrik Stollarz/AFP/Getty Images; **p. 369:** © Comstock/PictureQuest RF; **p. 371:** © Royalty-free/Corbis RF; 377: © Kristoffer Tripplaar/Alamy Stock Photo; **p. 378:** © Spencer Platt/Getty Images; **p. 381:** © David Paul Morris/Bloomberg via Getty Images.

646   Photo Credits

Chapter 14

Page 386: Courtesy of Debbie Harvey; **p. 389:** (l) © Mark Lennihan/ AP Images, (r) © Jin Lee/Bloomberg via Getty Images; **p. 391:** © Greg Blomberg/Alamy RF; **p. 392:** Courtesy of Google; **p. 394:** © siriwat sriphojaroen/Shutterstock.com; **p. 395:** © ZUMA Press Inc/ Alamy Stock Photo; **p. 401:** (t) Courtesy of Oracle Retail, (b) © Mark Lennihan/AP Images; **p. 403:** Courtesy of ebay; **p. 405:** © Jamie Rector/Getty Images; **p. 406:** (t) © Tony Avelar/AP Images for LG Electronics USA, (b) © Tim Boyle/Getty Images; **p. 408:** © The Mc-Graw-Hill Companies/Allison Grimes, Photographer; **p. 409:** © Bettmann/Getty Images; **p. 410:** © Alberto Cervantes/Wall Street Journal; **p. 411:** © Scott Eells/Bloomberg via Getty Images.

Chapter 15

Page 416: Courtesy of Katrina Davis; **p. 419:** Courtesy of Target Corporation; **p. 421:** Courtesy of Safeway; **p. 422:** © Charles Stirling/ Alamy Stock Photo; **p. 423:** © Jeff Zelevansky/Getty Images; **p. 424:** (t) Courtesy of Neiman Marcus, (b) © Suzanne Hanover/Columbia/ Kobal/REX/Shutterstock.com; **p. 426:** © CAMERA PRESS/Rob Welham/Redux; **p. 428:** Courtesy of The Home Depot, Inc.; **p. 429:** (t) Courtesy of HSN, Inc., (b) Courtesy of PCC Natural Markets; **p. 430:** Courtesy of Penske; **p. 432:** (l) Courtesy of Ace Hardware, (r) Courtesy of Abt Electronics; **p. 433:** © Vincent Yu/AP Images; **p. 434:** © ASSOCIATED PRESS; **p. 435:** Courtesy of Patagonia, Inc.; **p. 437:** © Tom Williams/CQ Roll Call; **p. 438:** Courtesy of Best Buy; **p. 443:** © Chuck Place/Alamy; **p. 446:** Courtesy of Google.

Section IV

Page 450: © John Gress/Corbis/Getty Images

Chapter 16

Page 452: Courtesy of Tara Carroll; **p. 455:** © Andersen Ross/ Blend Images LLC RF; **p. 457:** © Lars A. Niki RF; **p. 460:** © Jay Freis/The Image Bank/Getty Images; **p. 461:** © Luke Sharrett/ Bloomberg/Getty Images; **p. 470:** (t) © Ariel Skelley/ Blend Images LLC RF, (b) © Ted Soqui/Corbis/Getty Images; **p. 471:** © Jonnyboyca/Wikipedia; **p. 472:** © Gary M. Baranec/AP Images; **p. 473:** (l) © B.O'Kane/Alamy, (r) © Chesnot/Getty Images;

p. 475: Courtesy of Checkpoint Systems, Inc.; **p. 477:** © Chuck Savage/Getty Images.

Chapter 17

Page 482: Courtesy of Fredrik Holmvik; **p. 485:** © Mark Lennihan/ AP Images; **p. 486:** © Jacquelyn Martin/AP Images; **p. 488:** © Fotosearch/SuperStock; **p. 491:** © Archimage/Alamy; **p. 494:** © Dhruv Grewal and Anne Roggeveen; **p. 495:** Courtesy of The Limited; **p. 496:** (t) © Gustavo Caballero/Getty Images for Disney, (b) © Islandstock/Alamy Stock Photo; **p. 499:** © Ed Zurga/ Bloomberg/Getty Images; **p. 500:** © Vicki Beaver/Alamy; **p. 502:** (t) Virtual Baby Aisle, © 2005 Kimberly-Clark Worldwide, Inc. Used with permission, (b) : Courtesy of SAS Institute, Inc.; **p. 504:** © (l) © Marc F. Henning/Alamy Stock Photo; (r) © Radharc Images/ Alamy Stock Photo; **p. 508:** © FRED PROUSER/Reuters; **p. 509:** © Librado Romero/Redux.

Chapter 18

Page 514: Courtesy of Elizabeth Hebeler; **p. 516:** Courtesy of Amazon.com; **p. 518:** © PIXTAL/AGE Fotostock RF; **p. 519:** (l) © Charles Krupa/AP Images, (r) © Gilles Mingasson/Getty Images; **p. 520:** © Stephen Chernin/Getty Images; **p. 521:** © Dado Galdieri/Bloomberg/Getty Images; **p. 523:** © Matthew Simmons/Getty Images; **p. 524:** © Caro/Alamy; **p. 527:** (t) © Lourens Smak/Alamy, (b) Courtesy of Dominos; **p. 529:** © Helen H. Richardson/The Denver Post/Getty Images; **p. 531:** © Rubberball/ Getty Images RF; **p. 532:** © THOMAS SAMSON/AFP/Getty Images; **p. 534:** © Dhruv Grewal and Anne Roggeveen; **p. 536:** © Bruce Forster/The Image Bank/Getty Images.

Section V

Page 546: © Splash News/Corbis

Cases

Page 548: © James D. Morgan/Getty Images News/Getty Images; **Page 549:** © 2013 Tractor Supply Company; **p. 551:** © www.blue-tomato.com; **p. 583:** © 2013 J.C. Penney Corporation, Inc. All rights reserved.

NAME INDEX

654   Name Index

656   Name Index

SUBJECT INDEX

664

Levy/Weitz/Grewal: *Retailing Management* offers a seamless content and technology solution to improve student engagement and comprehension, automation of assignments and grading, and easy reporting to ensure that learning objectives are being met.

Connect® Marketing provides a wide array of tools and content to improve instructor productivity and student performance. In fact, the aggregated results of 34 Connect adoptions showed an 11% improvement in pass rates, a 16% improvement in retention, two times as many students receiving an A, and a 77% reduction in instructor grading time.

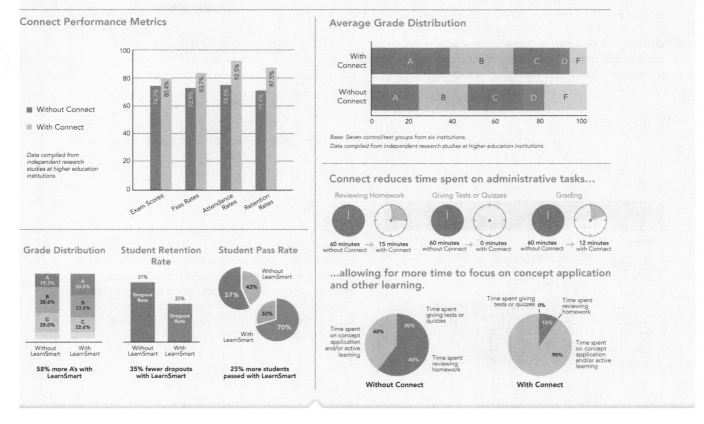

Connect Performance Metrics

■ Without Connect
▨ With Connect

Data compiled from independent research studies at higher education institutions.

Exam Scores: 74.7%, 80.4%
Pass Rates: 72.9%, 83.7%
Attendance Rates: 74.5%, 92.5%
Retention Rates: 71.1%, 87.5%

Average Grade Distribution

With Connect: A B C D F
Without Connect: A B C D F

Base: Seven control/test groups from six institutions.
Data compiled from independent research studies at higher education institutions.

Connect reduces time spent on administrative tasks...

Reviewing Homework: 60 minutes without Connect → 15 minutes with Connect
Giving Tests or Quizzes: 60 minutes without Connect → 0 minutes with Connect
Grading: 60 minutes without Connect → 12 minutes with Connect

...allowing for more time to focus on concept application and other learning.

Without Connect
Time spent giving tests or quizzes: 20%
Time spent reviewing homework: 40%
Time spent on concept application and/or active learning: 40%

With Connect
Time spent giving tests or quizzes: 0%
Time spent reviewing homework: 10%
Time spent on concept application and/or active learning: 90%

Grade Distribution

Without LearnSmart: A 19.3%, B 38.6%, C 28.0%
With LearnSmart: A 30.5%, B 33.5%, C 22.6%

58% more A's with LearnSmart

Student Retention Rate

Without LearnSmart: Dropout Rate 31%
With LearnSmart: Dropout Rate 20%

35% fewer dropouts with LearnSmart

Student Pass Rate

Without LearnSmart: 57% / 43%
With LearnSmart: 30% / 70%

25% more students passed with LearnSmart

LEARNSMART ADVANTAGE

LearnSmart®   Smartbook™

CONNECT FEATURES

Interactive Applications

Interactive Applications offer a variety of automatically graded exercises that require students to **apply** key concepts. Whether the assignment includes a *click and drag*, *video case*, or *decision generator*, these applications provide instant feedback and progress tracking for students and detailed results for the instructor.

eBook

Connect Plus includes a media-rich eBook that allows you to share your notes with your students. Your students can insert and review their own notes, highlight the text, search for specific information, and interact with media resources. Using an eBook with Connect Plus gives your students a complete digital solution that allows them to access their materials from any computer.

Tegrity

Make your classes available anytime, anywhere. With simple, one-click recording, students can search for a word or phrase and be taken to the exact place in your lecture that they need to review.

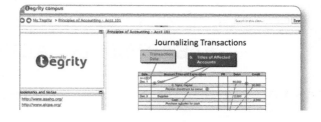

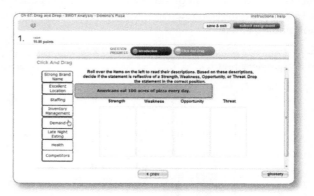

EASY TO USE

Learning Management System Integration

McGraw-Hill Campus is a one-stop teaching and learning experience available to use with any learning management system. McGraw-Hill Campus provides single sign-on to faculty and students for all McGraw-Hill material and technology from within the school website. McGraw-Hill Campus also allows instructors instant access to all supplements and teaching materials for all McGraw-Hill products.

Blackboard users also benefit from McGraw-Hill's industry-leading integration, providing single sign-on to access all Connect assignments and automatic feeding of assignment results to the Blackboard grade book.

POWERFUL REPORTING

Connect generates comprehensive reports and graphs that provide instructors with an instant view of the performance of individual students, a specific section, or multiple sections. Since all content is mapped to learning objectives, Connect reporting is ideal for accreditation or other administrative documentation.

758

Credits